ELECTIONS 2011

By

SEÁN DONNELLY

Published by Seán Donnelly
24 Milltown Avenue
Mount Saint Annes
Milltown
Dublin 6

Tel: 087 2549090

ISBN 978-0-9520197-8-7

First Published: January 2012

Date: 23rd March 2012

CONTENTS

Seán Donnelly was educated at St. Eunan's College, Letterkenny, Co. Donegal and UCD and is a retired Civil Engineer. His first book *Poll Position*, an analysis of the 1991 Local Elections was published in September 1992. His second book *Partnership* the story of the 1992 General Election was published in September 1993. *Elections '97* was published in February 1998. *Elections '99* was published in November 1999. *Elections 2002* was published in December 2002.

AUTHOR'S NOTE

This book is a detailed analysis of the General Election held on 25th February 2011. It also contains details of the Senate Elections and of all by-elections and Referenda held subsequent to the 2007 General Election.

The results of the election to the 31st Dail are contained in Part 1 and cover all 43 constituencies including profiles of all 166 TDs. The layout of this analysis is explained on page 5.

Part 2 details the various summaries of the 2011 election, including party performance, vote management, transfer analysis, women elected and leading votegetters. It also contains details of the Government, the Opposition and the Oireachtas Committees.

Part 3 contains an analysis of all 31 elections since 1918. It also contains details of all governments since the foundation of the state.

Part 4 covers the 127 by-elections held to date

Part 5 covers the Senate Election including profiles of all 60 Senators.

Part 6 contains the results of the 2009 European elections, including profiles of all 13 MEP's.

Part 7 details all Presidential elections to date.

Part 8 contains details of the 2011 referenda. It also contains the results and wordings of all referenda to date.

The Index appears in Part 9 at the end of the book and it contains four separate indices, all in alphabetical order: -

1. All 567 Dail candidates
2. All 177 Seanad candidates
3. All 1,236 TDs elected 1918-2011
4. All 760 Senators elected 1922-2011

An Oireachtas Directory appears at the back of the book containing details of the political parties and TDs and Senators phone numbers and Email addresses.

Layout of Tables

Each Constituency

1. *Analysis*

   A detailed analysis appears at the start of each constituency, including the various boundary changes.

2. *Biographies*

   Details of each TD are listed near the start of each constituency.

3. *First Count Details*

3.1 Valid Poll; Number of Seats; Quota; Total Candidates. Votes required to reclaim expenses.
3.2 Names of Candidates:
Successful candidates are listed in order of election.
Unsuccessful are listed in order of elimination.
Bold denotes those elected.
* denotes outgoing. # denotes former TD.
3.3 Party - see Abbreviations page 7.
3.4 First preference votes
3.5 % of total first preferences (valid poll).
3.6 Fraction of a quota.
3.7 Count elected. Count eliminated. No Expenses.

4. *Party Votes*

4.1 The 2011 Party Vote is compared with the 2007 Party Vote.
4.2 Each party has listed their number of candidates, first preferences, % of first preferences, fraction of a quota and number of seats won.
4.3 The change (2011- 2007) is calculated for change in % first preferences and change in number of seats won. In other words it is the difference between the % first preference vote received in 2011 and that received in 2007. It is not the % increase or decrease. Minus indicates drop in support or seats since 2007. Absence of minus indicates increase in support or seats.
4.4 The total number of candidates is listed at the bottom along with the total first preferences (valid poll) and total seats.
4.5 The electorate, valid poll (votes and %) quota and change in valid poll appear at the bottom of the table.

5. *Count Details*

5.1 Candidates are listed as per item 3.2.
5.2 Candidates whose votes are being distributed are listed above count number. Minus sign indicates whose votes are being distributed.
5.3 Number of votes received by each candidate is listed along with the cumulative total of votes received to date.
5.4 Non-Transferable votes (NT) are listed at the bottom with the cumulative NT.
5.5 The total number of votes (valid poll) is listed at the bottom of each count column and this is the sum of all the cumulative totals including the non-transferable.

6. *Transfer Analysis*

6.1 The parties from whom the votes were transferred are listed in the first column. The total votes transferred from each party are listed in the second column.
6.2 The number of transfers received by each party is listed in the various columns with the % of the total transfers listed under the number of transfers.
6.3 The number and % of non-transferable votes (NT) are listed in the final column.
6.4 The total number of transfers along with the total received by each party and the total NT is detailed at the bottom.
6.5 Where multiple party eliminations occur, the transfers are calculated on a pro-rata basis.

7. *Results 1918 - 2011*

   The results for each election are listed stating the number of seats and % first preference votes won by each party (to two decimal places). At the bottom of the table is the total number of seats won to date along with the total first preference vote. Also listed are the national totals to date.

8. *List of TDs 1918 - 2011*

   All the TDs elected to date are listed in descending order of number of elections won. The years elected and total elections won to date are also listed as well as any by-elections. The party affiliation is in general the final party that the TD was elected for e.g. former Fianna Fáil TDs who joined the Progressive Democrats are listed as PD.

ABBREVIATIONS OF POLITICAL AFFILIATIONS

MAIN PARTIES

FG	Fine Gael (CT: Coalition Treaty 1922; CG : Cumann Na nGael to 1937)
LB	Labour (founded 1912)
FF	Fianna Fail (CR: Coalition Republic 1922; R : Republican to 1927)
SF	Sinn Fein (Hblk: H Block 1981)
SP	Socialist Party (founded 1997)
PBPA	People Before Profit Alliance (replaced SW 2007)
ULA	United Left Alliance (founded 2010)
GP	Green Party (Green Alliance to 1988)
WP	Workers Party (SFWP : Sinn Fein The Workers Party to 1982)
CS	Christian Solidarity Party (founded 1995)
SKIA	South Kerry Independent Alliance (Kerry South)
WUAG	Workers Unemployed Action Group (Tipperary South)
NP	Non Party / Independent / Others

FORMER PARTIES

AE	Aontacht Eireann
BP	Businessmens Party 1923
CnaP	Clann na Poblachta 1946-1965
CP	Centre Party 1932-1933; later merged with Fine Gael
CnaT	Clann na Talmhan 1938-1965
DL	Democratic Left (split from WP in 1992, merged with Labour 1999)
DSP	Democratic Socialist Party 1982-1991 (merged with Labour)
F	Farmers Party 1922-1932
FRR	Fathers Rights-Responsibility Party (2006-2007)
IFF	Independent Fianna Fail (Donegal 1970-2006)
Ind F	Independent Farmer
Ind LB	Independent Labour
Ind R	Independent Republican 1957
Ind UW	Independent Unemployed Worker 1957
IWL	Irish Workers League 1927
MR	Monetary Reform 1943-1944
NLB	National Labour 1943-1950
NL	National League 1926-1931
NL / Nlaw	Natural Law Party 1996-2000
NPD	National Progressive Democrat 1958-1963
NT	National Party 1996-1998
PA	Progressive Association 1923
PD	Progressive Democrats (21/12/85-8/11/08)
SLP	Socialist Labour Party 1981
SW	Socialist Workers Party (1997-2007)

PART 1

GENERAL ELECTION

FOR

31st DAIL

POLLING DATE: THURSDAY 25th February 2011

CONSTITUENCIES

CARLOW-KILKENNY 2011

"A reversal of fortune as Fine Gael win three out of five for the first time and Fianna Fail are reduced to just a single seat"

There were no Constituency Commission boundary changes here since 2007 and it remained a five-seat constituency.

This was another example of Fine Gael's good vote management in this election as they managed to convert 2.4 quotas into three seats. Their vote was up 10 points on 2007 and John Paul Phelan topped the poll, just ahead of outgoing deputy Phil Hogan. This constituency like many others came down to a battle for the final seat, this time between Carlow-based Pat Deering of Fine Gael and Bobby Aylward of Fianna Fáil. Deering was in the frame in fifth place on the first count and about 700 votes ahead of Aylward. He maintained his advantage throughout the count and went on to take the final seat by a comfortable margin.

Former Ceann Comhairle Seamus Pattison had held a seat here for Labour from 1961 until his retirement in 2007 when the party failed to retain his seat. They increased their vote in this election by 7 points on the party's 2007 performance and with one quota between the party's two candidates they were well placed to regain their seat. Kilkenny-based Ann Phelan was well ahead of running mate, Carlow-based Des Hurley on the first count and she went on to take the first seat on the 12th count.

This was another very poor result for Fianna Fáil as the party went from three seats in 2007 to just one in 2011, despite getting their best first preference vote of this election, 28.10% in this five seater. M.J. Nolan retired and Jennifer Murnane O'Connor replaced him on the ticket. The Fianna Fáil vote was down by 20 points but with 1.7 quotas they should have been in contention for a second seat. But their vote was spread over three candidates and this left Aylward outside the frame on the first count and Fianna Fáil ended up with just a single seat as Aylward lost the battle for the final seat.

Sinn Fein increased its vote by six points but with just 0.6 quotas spread over two candidates, the party's leading candidate Kathleen Funchion was too far off the pace and was outside the frame on the first count with less than half a quota. She thus had little chance of a seat and so it proved.

Outgoing Green party TD and Minister of State, Mary White lost her seat as she got just 2.8% of the first preference vote and she, like many of her party colleagues, lost the right to reclaim her expenses.

Conor MacLiam of the Socialist party, the widower of the late Susie Long, did poorly and got just 2% of the vote. He lost his right to reclaim his expenses, as did all seven independent candidates who all polled poorly.

CARLOW–KILKENNY TDs 2011

ANN PHELAN (LB)

Brandondale, Graiguenamanagh, Co. Kilkenny; Tel: 059 9724310; Mobile: 086 3294420
Constituency Office: 18 Patrick Street, Kilkenny;
Leinster House: Tel 01 6183216; Email: ann.phelan@oireachtas.ie
Website: www.labour.ie/annphelan; Twitter: twitter.com/annphelan1

Born Graiguenamanagh 16th September 1961. Married to Kieran Phelan, one son, two daughters. Educated Brigidin College, Goresbridge; Waterford IT. Formerly Accounts Secretary. Elected at her first attempt in 2011.

Member Joint Administration Committee. Elected to Kilkenny County Council in 2004 and 2009. Suffered a stroke in April 2008 while out horse riding but has made a remarkable recovery through rehabilitation.

JOHN McGUINNESS (FF)

Windsmoor, Brooklawn, Ballyfoyle Road, Kilkenny; Mobile: 087 2855834
Constituency Office: 11 O'Loughlin Road, Kilkenny; Tel: 056 7770672;
Leinster House: 01 6183137; Email: john.mcguinness@oireachtas.ie
Website: www. johnmcguinness.com; Facebook: facebook/johnmcguinness

Born Kilkenny 15th March 1955. Married to Margaret Redmond, three sons, Andrew, M.J., John, one daughter Alva. Educated CBS, Kilkenny. Former Managing Director of Fastmac Express Delivery Services Ltd. First elected 1997 and at each subsequent election.

Appointed party spokesperson on Small Business Regulatory Framework April 2011. Appointed Chairman of the Public Accounts Committee June 2011. Minister of State at the Department of Enterprise, Trade and Employment with responsibility for Trade and Commerce, 2007-2009. Vice-Chairman Public Accounts Committee in 30th Dail. Member Kilkenny County Council 1991-2003. Member Kilkenny Corporation 1979-2003. Elected Mayor of Kilkenny in 1996, becoming the third generation of his family to hold the office. His grand uncle John was Mayor eight times and his father Michael was Mayor seven times. Voluntary Directorships: Young Irish Film-Makers, Kilkenny Industrial Development Company, Chairman Kilkenny Information Age Ltd.

JOHN PAUL PHELAN (FG)

Smithstown, Tullogher, via Mullinavat, Co. Kilkenny; Tel: 056 7793210;
Constituency Office: 75A High Street, Kilkenny; Tel: 056 7795608;
Leinster House: 01 6184202; Email: johnpaul.phelan@oireachtas.ie
Website: www.johnpaulphelan.ie Twitter: twitter.com/jpphelan

Born Waterford, 27th September 1978. Single. Educated Good Counsel College, New Ross; Waterford IT (Business Studies). Holds a Diploma in Law and currently studying Legal Studies at the Kings Inn. Contested 2007 general election in Carlow-Kilkenny. First elected 2011.

Member Joint Administration Committee. Member Committee on Investigations, Oversight and Petitions. Senator 2002-2011. Seanad Spokesperson on Enterprise, Trade and Employment 2007-2011. Liaison officer between the Parliamentary Party and Young Fine Gael. Was youngest ever councillor at 20 years old when elected to Kilkenny County Council in 1999. Member Kilkenny County Council 1999-2003.

PHIL HOGAN (FG)

Grovine, Kilkenny, Co. Kilkenny
Constituency Office: New Street, Kilkenny; Tel: 056 7771490;
Email: philip.hogan@oireachtas.ie Website: www.philhogan.ie

Born Tullaroan, Kilkenny 4th July 1960. Separated, one son. Educated St. Joseph's College, Freshford; St. Kieran's College, Kilkenny and UCC (BA, HDipEd). Minister for the Environment, Community and Local Government. Former Insurance Broker and Auctioneer. First elected 1989 and at each subsequent election.

Appointed Minister for the Environment, Community and Local Government 9th March 2011. Led defence of party leader Enda Kenny following challenge by Richard Bruton in June 2010 and retained his front bench position and was also appointed Director of Elections for the 2011 general election. Front Bench Spokesperson on Environment, Heritage and Local Government 2007-March 2011. Front Bench Spokesperson on Enterprise, Trade and Employment 2002-2007. Contested Fine Gael Leadership election in June 2002. Fine Gael National Director of Organisation 2002-2007. Chairman of Parliamentary Party 1995–2001. Minister of State at Department of Finance December 1994 - February 1995 when he resigned due to inadvertent leaking of budget details. Fine Gael front bench spokesperson on Regional Affairs and European Development 1993–1994; Consumer Affairs 1991–1993; Food Industry 1989–1991. Senator 1987-1989. Member Kilkenny County Council 1982-2003 (Chairman 1985/1986 and 1998-1999). Member GAA, Kilkenny Archaeological Society and Castlecomer Golf Club.

PAT DEERING (FG)

Ballyoliver, Rathvilly, Co. Carlow; Mobile: 087 6674024;
Leinster House: 01 6184235; Email: pat.deering@oireachtas.ie
Website: www.patdeering.ie

Born Carlow 2nd February 1967. Married to Paula Byrne, one son, one daughter. Educated Ballyfin College, Co. Laois; Tullow Community School, Co. Carlow; Piltown Agricultural College, Co. Kilkenny. Farmer. Elected at his first attempt in 2011.

Member Committee on Communications, Natural Resources and Agriculture. Elected to Carlow County Council in 2009 succeeding his father who had served for 42 years. GAA activist and member of Rathvilly GAA Club. Former Chairman of Carlow GAA County Board.

	CARLOW-KILKENNY 2011						
	FIRST PREFERENCE VOTES						
	Seats	5			12,291		
	Candidate	Party	1st	%	Quota	Count	Status
1	**Phelan, Ann**	**LB**	**8,072**	**10.95%**	**0.66**	**12**	**Made Quota**
2	**McGuinness, John***	**FF**	**9,531**	**12.92%**	**0.78**	**12**	**Made Quota**
3	**Phelan, John Paul**	**FG**	**10,929**	**14.82%**	**0.89**	**12**	**Made Quota**
4	**Hogan, Phil***	**FG**	**10,525**	**14.27%**	**0.86**	**13**	**Elected**
5	**Deering, Pat**	**FG**	**7,470**	**10.13%**	**0.61**	**13**	**Elected**
6	Aylward, Bobby*	FF	6,762	9.17%	0.55	13	Not Elected
7	Funchion, Kathleen	SF	4,075	5.53%	0.33	11	Eliminated
8	Murnane O'Connor, Jennifer	FF	4,428	6.00%	0.36	10	Eliminated
9	Hurley, Des	LB	3,908	5.30%	0.32	9	Eliminated
10	Cassin, John	SF	2,958	4.01%	0.24	8	Eliminated
11	White, Mary*	GP	2,072	2.81%	0.17	7	No Expenses
12	MacLiam, Conor	SP	1,135	1.54%	0.09	6	No Expenses
13	Kelly, Stephen	NP	601	0.81%	0.05	6	No Expenses
14	Couchman, Johnny	NP	384	0.52%	0.03	5	No Expenses
15	O'Hara, John	NP	253	0.34%	0.02	4	No Expenses
16	Leahy, Ramie	NP	256	0.35%	0.02	3	No Expenses
17	Murphy, David	NP	195	0.26%	0.02	2	No Expenses
18	Walsh, Noel G.	NP	119	0.16%	0.01	1	No Expenses
19	Dalton, John	NP	70	0.09%	0.01	1	No Expenses
19	***Outgoing**		**73,743**	**100.00%**	**12,291**	**3,073**	**No Expenses**

CARLOW-KILKENNY 2011												
PARTY VOTE												
	2011					2007					Change	
Party	Cand	1st	%	Quota	Seats	Cand	1st	%	Quota	Seats	%	Seats
FG	3	28,924	39.22%	2.35	3	3	20,031	29.61%	1.78	1	+9.61%	+2
LB	2	11,980	16.25%	0.97	1	2	6,324	9.35%	0.56		+6.90%	+1
FF	3	20,721	28.10%	1.69	1	3	32,272	47.70%	2.86	3	-19.60%	-2
SF	2	7,033	9.54%	0.57		1	2,568	3.80%	0.23		+5.74%	
SP	1	1,135	1.54%	0.09							+1.54%	
GP	1	2,072	2.81%	0.17		1	5,386	7.96%	0.48	1	-5.15%	-1
PD						1	1,073	1.59%	0.10		-1.59%	
Others	7	1,878	2.55%	0.15							+2.55%	
Total	**19**	**73,743**	**100.0%**	**12,291**	**5**	**11**	**67,654**	**100.0%**	**11,276**	**5**	**0.00%**	**0**
Electorate		**105,449**	**69.93%**				**102,016**	**66.32%**			**+3.62%**	
Spoiled		**821**	**1.10%**				**705**	**1.03%**			**+0.07%**	
Turnout		**74,564**	**70.71%**				**68,359**	**67.01%**			**+3.70%**	

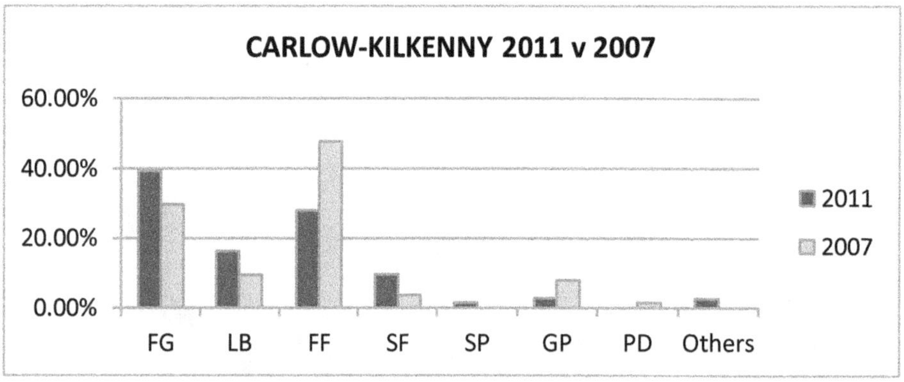

CARLOW-KILKENNY 2011 COUNT DETAILS														
Seats	5												Quota	12,291
Candidate	**Party**	**1st**	**2nd** Walsh Dalton	**3rd** Murphy Votes	**4th** Leahy Votes	**5th** O'Hara Votes	**6th** Couchman Votes	**7th** MacLiam Kelly	**8th** White Votes	**9th** Cassin Votes	**10th** Hurley Votes	**11th** Murnane Votes	**12th** Funchion Votes	**13th** Phelan A Surplus
			+13	+13	+27	+28	+18	+355	+536	+124	+2,447	+433	+2,094	-1,869
Phelan, Ann	LB	8,072	8,085	8,098	8,125	8,153	8,171	8,526	9,062	9,186	11,633	12,066	14,160	12,291
			+12	+5	+35	+12	+17	+155	+172	+60	+109	+1,697	+825	
McGuinness, John*	FF	9,531	9,543	9,548	9,583	9,595	9,612	9,767	9,939	9,999	10,108	11,805	12,630	12,630
			+10	+10	+26	+18	+24	+166	+233	+51	+112	+132	+506	+357
Phelan, John Paul	FG	10,929	10,939	10,949	10,975	10,993	11,017	11,183	11,416	11,467	11,579	11,711	12,217	12,574
			+12	+3	+18	+7	+22	+185	+162	+34	+152	+87	+563	+227
Hogan, Phil*	FG	10,525	10,537	10,540	10,558	10,565	10,587	10,772	10,934	10,968	11,120	11,207	11,770	11,997
			+4	+9	+8	+11	+95	+57	+310	+274	+670	+1,059	+368	+151
Deering, Pat	FG	7,470	7,474	7,483	7,491	7,502	7,597	7,654	7,964	8,238	8,908	9,967	10,335	10,486
			+10	+3	+11	+10	+1	+70	+61	+33	+44	+1,063	+401	+141
Aylward, Bobby	FF	6,762	6,772	6,775	6,786	6,796	6,797	6,867	6,928	6,961	7,005	8,068	8,469	8,610
			+14	+12	+20	+23	+18	+300	+111	+1,885	+301	+332	-7,091	
Funchion, Kathleen	SF	4,075	4,089	4,101	4,121	4,144	4,162	4,462	4,573	6,458	6,759	7,091	Eliminated	
			+3	+3	+1	+18	+40	+40	+225	+307	+571	-5,636		
Murnane O'Connor, J.	FF	4,428	4,431	4,434	4,435	4,453	4,493	4,533	4,758	5,065	5,636	Eliminated		
			+2	+9	+9	+24	+26	+113	+207	+385	-4,683			
Hurley, Des	LB	3,908	3,910	3,919	3,928	3,952	3,978	4,091	4,298	4,683	Eliminated			
			+1	+7	+4	+33	+31	+182	+98	-3,314				
Cassin, John	SF	2,958	2,959	2,966	2,970	3,003	3,034	3,216	3,314	Eliminated				
			+5	+5	+16	+8	+29	+143	-2,278					
White, Mary	GP	2,072	2,077	2,082	2,098	2,106	2,135	2,278	Eliminated					
			+9	+13	+22	+21	+17	-1,217						
MacLiam, Conor	SP	1,135	1,144	1,157	1,179	1,200	1,217	Eliminated						
			+24	+21	+35	+53	+86	-820						
Kelly, Stephen	NP	601	625	646	681	734	820	Eliminated						
			+6	+20	+13	+48	-471							
Couchman, Johnny	NP	384	390	410	423	471	Eliminated							
			+17	+57	+18	-345								
O'Hara, John	NP	253	270	327	345	Eliminated								
			+16	+5	-277									
Leahy, Ramie	NP	256	272	277	Eliminated									
			+12	-207										
Murphy, David	NP	195	207	Eliminated										
			-119											
Walsh, Noel G	NP	119	Eliminated											
			-70											
Dalton, John	NP	70	Eliminated											
Non-transferable			+19	+12	+14	+31	+47	+271	+163	+161	+277	+833	+2,334	+993
Cumulative			19	31	45	76	123	394	557	718	995	1,828	4,162	5,155
Total		**73,743**	**73,743**	**73,743**	**73,743**	**73,743**	**73,743**	**73,743**	**73,743**	**73,743**	**73,743**	**73,743**	**73,743**	**73,743**

CARLOW-KILKENNY 2011 TRANSFER ANALYSIS									
From	**To**	**FG**	**LB**	**FF**	**SF**	**SP**	**GP**	**Others**	**Non Trans**
LB	6,552	1,669	2,447	865	301				1,270
		25.47%	*37.35%*	*13.20%*	*4.59%*				*19.38%*
FF	5,636	1278	433	2,760	332				833
		22.68%	*7.68%*	*48.97%*	*5.89%*				*14.78%*
SF	10,405	1,796	2,603	1,626	1,885				2,495
		17.26%	*25.02%*	*15.63%*	*18.12%*				*23.98%*
SP	1,217	244	280	158	288		85		162
		20.05%	*23.01%*	*12.98%*	*23.66%*		*6.98%*		*13.31%*
GP	2,278	705	743	458	209				163
		30.95%	*32.62%*	*20.11%*	*9.17%*				*7.16%*
Others	2,309	441	357	288	357	82	121	431	232
		19.10%	*15.46%*	*12.47%*	*15.46%*	*3.55%*	*5.24%*	*18.67%*	*10.05%*
Total	**28,397**	**6,133**	**6,863**	**6,155**	**3,372**	**82**	**206**	**431**	**5,155**
		21.60%	***24.17%***	***21.67%***	***11.87%***	***0.29%***	***0.73%***	***1.52%***	***18.15%***

CARLOW-KILKENNY 2011		
MAIN BOUNDARY CHANGES		
Dail	**Constituency**	**Seats**
1 (1918)	Carlow	1
	Kilkenny North	1
	Kilkenny South	1
2 (1921) - 3 (1922)	Carlow-Kilkenny	4
4 (1923) - 8 (1933)	Carlow-Kilkenny	5
9 (1937) - 12 (1944)	Kilkenny	3
13 (1948) - 31 (2011)	Carlow-Kilkenny	5

CARLOW-KILKENNY 2011																	
ALL TDs 1918-2011																	
	Surname	**First Name**	**Party**	**Elected**													**Total**
1	Pattison	Seamus	LB	61	65	69	73	77	81	82	82	87	89	92	97	02	13
2	Derrig**	Thomas	FF	27	27	32	33	37	38	43	44	48	51	54			11
3	Aylward	Liam	FF	77	81	82	82	87	89	92	97	02					9
4	Gorey	Denis	FG	22	23	27J	27*	32	37	38							7
5	Pattison	James	LB	33	37	38	43	44	48	54							7
6	Gibbons	James	FF	57	61	65	69	73	77	82F							7
7	Crotty	Kieran	FG	69	73	77	81	82	82	87							7
8	Cosgrave**	William T.	CG	18	21	22	23	27	27								6
9	Crotty	Patrick	FG	48	51	54	57	61	65								6
10	Governey	Desmond	FG	61	65	69	73	81	82F								6
11	Nolan	M.J.	FF	82N	87	89	92	02	07								6
12	Hogan	Philip	FG	89	92	97	02	07	11								6
13	Nolan	Thomas	FF	65	69	73	77	81									5
14	Hughes	Joseph	FG	48	51	54	57										4
15	McGuinness	John	FF	97	02	07	11										4
16	Doyle	Edward	LB	23	27	27											3
17	Gibbons	Sean	FF	23	32	33											3
18	Holohan	Richard	F	27	27	33											3
19	Humphreys**	Francis	FF	32	51	57											3
20	Walsh	Thomas	FF	48	51	54											3
21	Medlar	Martin	FF	56*	57	61											3
22	Browne	John	FG	89	92	97											3
23	Lennon	James	SF	18	21												2
24	O'Sullivan**	Gearoid	CT	21	22												2
25	Fitzgerald**	Desmond	CG	32	33												2
26	O'Mara	James	SF	18													1
27	Aylward	Edward	SF	21													1
28	Gaffney	Patrick	LB	22													1
29	Skelly	Michael	R	23													1
30	Bolger	Thomas	CG	25*													1
31	De Loughry	Peter	CG	27S													1
32	Mahony	Philip	F	43													1
33	Coogan	Eamonn	FG	44													1
34	Teehan	Patrick	FF	60*													1
35	Dowling	Dick	FG	82N													1
36	Gibbons	Martin	PD	87													1
37	Aylward	Bobby	FF	07													1
38	White	Mary	GP	07													1
39	Phelan	Ann	LB	11													1
40	Phelan	John Paul	FG	11													1
41	Deering	Pat	FG	11													1
41	**Total**									***Includes 4 By-Elections**						*	**147**
	**** Also elected in another constituency**																
	Cosgrave**	William T.	FG	Cork Borough					27	32	33	37	38	43			6
	Fitzgerald**	Desmond	CG	Dublin					18	21	22	23	27	27			6
	Humphreys**	Francis	FF	Kildare					37	38	43	44					4
	O'Sullivan**	Gearoid	CG	Dublin County					27*	27S	32	33					4
CK	Derrig**	Thomas	FF	Mayo North & West					21	22							2
CK	**Included in Carlow-Kilkenny Total**									***Includes 1 By-Election**						*	**22**
	Cosgrave elected in both Carlow-Kilkenny and Cork Borough in September 1927 but chose to sit for Cork																

CARLOW-KILKENNY PARTY VOTE 1918-2011

*No Contest		FG		LB		FF		SF		SP		GP		WP		PD		CnaP		Nat Labour		Farmers		Centre P		Others	
Dail	Seats	S	% Vote	S	% Vote	S	% Vote	S	% Vote	S	% Vote	S	% Vote	S	% Vote	S	% Vote	S	% Vote	S	% Vote	S	% Vote	S	% Vote	S	% Vote
1 1918	3							3																			
2 1921*	4							4																			
3 1922	4	2	31.23%	1	34.83%		14.34%															1	19.60%				
4 1923	5	2	47.43%	1	11.91%	1	24.89%															1	13.77%				2.00%
5 1927	5	2	35.49%	1	19.31%	1	23.73%															1	16.51%				4.96%
6 1927	5	2	44.17%	1	11.52%	1	30.49%															1	10.69%				3.13%
7 1932	5	2	33.48%		8.73%	3	45.14%																				12.65%
8 1933	5	1	31.53%	1	13.32%	2	42.51%																	1	12.64%		
9 1937	3	1	35.37%	1	23.26%	1	41.38%																				
10 1938	3	1	32.53%	1	20.18%	1	47.29%																				
11 1943	3		18.96%	1	26.00%	1	37.68%																			1	17.36%
12 1944	3	1	21.07%			1	46.32%													1	21.65%						10.96%
13 1948	5	2	28.56%		7.73%	2	41.76%												10.50%	1	11.46%						
14 1951	5	2	31.98%		16.51%	3	48.50%												3.00%								
15 1954	5	2	34.57%	1	14.36%	2	46.20%																				4.87%
16 1957	5	2	28.28%		13.17%	3	56.12%												2.43%								
17 1961	5	2	34.00%	1	13.42%	2	43.69%																				8.89%
18 1965	5	2	30.25%	1	20.26%	2	49.10%																				0.39%
19 1969	5	2	34.62%	1	17.34%	2	48.04%																				
20 1973	5	2	38.27%	1	14.53%	2	47.20%																				
21 1977	5	1	28.56%	1	13.90%	3	53.46%								3.01%												1.06%
22 1981	5	2	36.89%	1	12.88%	2	46.90%								3.33%												
23 1982	5	2	35.48%	1	13.10%	2	47.94%								3.23%												0.25%
24 1982	5	2	36.09%	1	13.46%	2	44.58%								3.92%												1.95%
25 1987	5	1	25.87%	1	12.80%	2	44.41%								2.89%	1	14.03%										
26 1989	5	2	30.80%	1	17.60%	2	43.84%								2.13%		5.63%										
27 1992	5	2	27.62%	1	24.59%	2	43.13%																				4.66%
28 1997	5	2	29.19%	1	15.19%	2	42.19%						5.52%				5.64%										2.28%
29 2002	5	1	21.87%	1	13.15%	3	50.20%		3.42%				8.15%														3.20%
30 2007	5	1	29.61%		9.35%	3	47.70%		3.80%			1	7.96%				1.59%										
31 2011	5	3	39.22%	1	16.25%	1	28.10%		9.54%		1.54%		2.81%														2.55%
1918-2011	**143**	**49**	**32.27%**	**23**	**15.12%**	**54**	**42.75%**	**7**	**0.84%**		**0.08%**	**1**	**1.12%**		**0.74%**	**1**	**1.11%**		**0.52%**	**2**	**0.82%**	**4**	**1.67%**	**1**	**0.47%**	**1**	**2.48%**
National	**4,618**	**1,453**	**30.77%**	**482**	**11.53%**	**1,985**	**41.86%**	**232**	**1.99%**	**4**	**0.16%**	**16**	**0.75%**	**17**	**0.78%**	**44**	**1.42%**	**18**	**0.77%**	**9**	**0.16%**	**42**	**0.90%**	**11**	**0.30%**	**305**	**8.59%**

CAVAN-MONAGHAN 2011

"Another major Fine Gael performance as they take three out of five seats for the first time "

There were no boundary changes here since 2007 and it remained a five-seat constituency.

This was another big performance in a five-seater from Fine Gael as they managed to convert 2.4 quotas into three seats. Their three leading candidates were grouped closely together on the first count with their fourth candidate Peter McVitty well off the pace in ninth place. Outgoing Senator Joe O'Reilly was the party's leading vote getter and he was just ahead of newcomers Heather Humphreys and Sean Conlan. They went on to take the final three seats with Humphreys holding off Kathryn Reilly of Sinn Fein for the final seat. Their performance was enhanced by the fact that Fine Gael ran three new Dáil candidates, two of whom got elected, as long serving deputy Seymour Crawford had retired ahead of the election.

The Sinn Fein vote was up 6 points and with 1.6 quotas they were in contention for a second seat. Caoimhghín Ó Caoláin topped the poll and was just over the quota on the first count. His running mate Kathryn Reilly was outside the frame in sixth place on the first count and was eventually beaten by Fine Gael for the final seat by a margin of just 521 votes.

This was another poor performance by Fianna Fáil with their vote down 18 points on 2007 to just 20.15% and they lost two seats, leaving outgoing Minister Brendan Smith as their sole representative after this election. Margaret Conlon was outside the frame in seventh place on the first count with just 0.4 of a quota and was virtually out of contention. Outgoing veteran Fianna Fáil TD and former Cabinet minister Rory O'Hanlon retired ahead of the election.

Labour failed to perform here as they got just 6% and newcomer Liam Hogan was never in contention. Four non party candidates contested including New Vision's John McGuirk but all failed to get enough votes to allow them reclaim their expenses, as well as the Green's Darcy Lonergan.

Caoimhghín Ó Caoláin TD with Sinn Fein Leadership

CAVAN – MONAGHAN TDs 2011

CAOIMHGHÍN Ó CAOLÁIN (SF)

14 Mullaghdun, Monaghan, Co. Monaghan
Constituency Office: 21 Dublin Street, Monaghan; Tel: 047 82917;
Leinster House: 01 6183005; Email: caoimhghin.ocaolain@oireachtas.ie

Born Monaghan 18th September 1953. Married to Briege McGinn, one son, four daughters. Educated St. Mary's CBS, Monaghan. Former Bank Official. Contested 1987, 1989 and 1992 general elections. First elected 1997 making him the first Sinn Fein TD elected since 1957 and the first to take his seat in Leinster House, following the party's abandonment of their abstentionist policy. He has been re-elected at each subsequent election.

Appointed Party spokesperson on the Peace Process and Northern Ireland and Health & Children March 2011. Member Committee on Health and Children. Sinn Fein's Parliamentary Group Leader and spokesperson on the Peace Process and Northern Ireland 2007-2011. He also had responsibility for Finance and Health and Children. Member British Irish Inter-Parliamentary Body. Represented Sinn Fein at the Forum for Peace and Reconciliation and was a member of the Sinn Fein negotiating team during the talks which led eventually to the Good Friday Agreement. Member Monaghan County Council 1985-2003, also a Member of Monaghan UDC 1974-2003. Director of Elections in H-Block campaign 1981 when Kieran Doherty was elected TD for Cavan-Monaghan. General Manager of republican newspaper An Phoblacht 1982-1985. Member of Sinn Fein Ard Chomhairle since 1983.

BRENDAN SMITH (FF)

3 Carrickfern, Keadue, Co. Cavan; Tel: 049 4362366;
Constituency Office: 75 Church Street, Cavan;
Leinster House: Tel 01 6183376; Email: brendan.smith@oireachtas.ie

Born Cavan 1st June 1956. Married to Anne McGarry. Educated St. Camillus College, Killucan, Co. Westmeath and UCD (BA in Politics and Economics). Former Political Adviser. First elected 1992 and at each subsequent election.

Spokesperson on Education and Skills. Member Committee on Jobs, Social Protection and Education. Member Committee on Implementation of Good Friday Agreement. Minister for Agriculture, Fisheries & Food May 2008-2011. Minister of State at the Department of Health and Children with special responsibility for Children June 2007-May 2008 and attended Cabinet meetings. Minister of State at the Department of Agriculture and Food with special responsibility for Food and Horticulture 2004-2007. Co-Chairman British-Irish Inter-Parliamentary Body 2002-2007. He served as advisor to the former Tánaiste John P. Wilson for 15 years. Member Co. Cavan Vocational Education Committee and Chairman Board of Management Virginia Vocational School; member Templeport Gaelic Football Club; Cavan GAA Supporters Club; Cavan Drama Festival. Member Comhaltas Ceoltoiri Eireann and Cumann Seanchais Bhreifne.

JOE O'REILLY (FG)

2 The Willows, Chapel Road, Bailieboro, Co. Cavan; Tel: 042 9666580;
Mobile: 086 2444321; Constituency Office: 11 Rossa Place, Cavan; Tel: 049 4365853
Leinster House: 01 6183721; Email: joe.oreilly@oireachtas.ie
Website: www.joeoreilly.ie

Born Cavan 14th April 1955. Married to Mary Tully, three sons, Alexis, Eoghan and Daire. Educated St. Aidan's Comprehensive School, Cootehill; UCD; St. Patrick's Teachers' Training College; TCD. Former Primary Teacher. Contested 1989, 1992 and 2007 general elections in Cavan-Monaghan. First elected 2011.

Appointed Vice-Chair Committee on Implementation of Good Friday Agreement June 2011. Member Committee on European Union Affairs. Senator 1989-1992 and 2007-2011. Fine Gael Seanad spokesperson on Communications, Energy and Natural Resources, 2007-2011. Former Member Joint Committee on Communications, Energy and Natural Resources. Former Member Joint Committee on the Implementation of the Good Friday Agreement. Member Cavan County Council 1985-1991 and 1999-2007. Champion Irish debater in secondary school.

SEAN CONLAN (FG)

Constituency Office: Ballybay, Co. Monaghan; Tel: 042 9755500; Mobile: 087 6679306
Leinster House: 01 6183154; Email: sean.conlan@oireachtas.ie
Website: sean.conlan@oireachtas.ie

Born Dublin 1975. Single. Educated St. Macartan's College, Monaghan; UCD (BA Honours degree in Economics; The Law Society Primary. Solicitor and Bar Owner. Elected at his first attempt in 2011.

Member Committee on Implementation of Good Friday Agreement. Elected to Ballybay Town Council in 2009. Member of Ballybay Economic Forum and its representative on the County Development Board. Chairman of Young Fine Gael during his time in UCD. Son of John F. Conlan TD for Monaghan 1969-1987.

HEATHER HUMPHREYS (FG)

Dernaroy, Newbliss, Co. Monaghan; Mobile: 086 2380765;
Constituency Office: Unit 2, Mall Road, Monaghan; Tel: 047 71911
Leinster House: 01 6183408; Email: heather.humphreys@oireachtas.ie

Born Drum, Co. Monaghan. Married to Eric Humphreys with two daughters. Educated St. Aidan's Comprehensive School, Cootehill, Co. Cavan; Manager of Cootehill Credit Union. Elected at her first attempt in 2011.

Member Joint Administration Committee. Member Committee on Finance, Public Expenditure and Reform. Co-opted onto Monaghan County Council in 2003 as replacement for Seymour Crawford TD. Retained her seat in 2009. Mayor of County Monaghan 2009-2010.

	CAVAN-MONAGHAN 2011 FIRST PREFERENCE VOTES						
	Seats	5			11,880		
	Candidate	**Party**	**1st**	**%**	**Quota**	**Count**	**Status**
1	**Ó Caoláin, Caoimhghín***	**SF**	**11,913**	**16.71%**	**1.00**	**1**	**Made Quota**
2	**Smith, Brendan***	**FF**	**9,702**	**13.61%**	**0.82**	**8**	**Made Quota**
3	**O'Reilly, Joe**	**FG**	**8,333**	**11.69%**	**0.70**	**9**	**Elected**
4	**Conlan, Sean**	**FG**	**7,864**	**11.03%**	**0.66**	**9**	**Elected**
5	**Humphreys, Heather**	**FG**	**8,144**	**11.43%**	**0.69**	**9**	**Elected**
6	Reilly, Kathryn	SF	6,539	9.17%	0.55	9	Not Elected
7	Conlon, Margaret*	FF	4,658	6.54%	0.39	7	Eliminated
8	Hogan, Liam	LB	4,011	5.63%	0.34	6	Eliminated
9	McVitty, Peter	FG	3,858	5.41%	0.32	5	Eliminated
10	Treanor, Seamus	NP	1,974	2.77%	0.17	4	No Expenses
11	Forde, Caroline	NP	1,912	2.68%	0.16	3	No Expenses
12	McGuirk, John	NV	1,708	2.40%	0.14	2	No Expenses
13	Lonergan, Darcy	GP	530	0.74%	0.04	1	No Expenses
14	Duffy, Joseph	NP	129	0.18%	0.01	1	No Expenses
14	***Outgoing**		**71,275**	**100.00%**	**11,880**	**2,971**	**No Expenses**

CAVAN-MONAGHAN 2011 PARTY VOTE												
	2011					2007					Change	
Party	**Cand**	**1st**	**%**	**Quota**	**Seats**	**Cand**	**1st**	**%**	**Quota**	**Seats**	**%**	**Seats**
FG	4	28,199	39.56%	2.37	3	2	20,528	31.20%	1.56	1	+8.36%	+2
LB	1	4,011	5.63%	0.34		1	796	1.21%	0.06		+4.42%	
FF	2	14,360	20.15%	1.21	1	3	24,851	37.77%	1.89	3	-17.63%	-2
SF	2	18,452	25.89%	1.55	1	1	13,162	20.01%	1.00	1	+5.88%	
GP	1	530	0.74%	0.04		1	2,382	3.62%	0.18		-2.88%	
Others	4	5,723	8.03%	0.48		2	4,068	6.18%	0.31		+1.85%	
Total	**14**	**71,275**	**100.0%**	**11,880**	**5**	**10**	**65,787**	**100.0%**	**13,158**	**5**	**0.00%**	**0**
Electorate		**99,178**	**71.87%**				**92,248**	**71.32%**			**+0.55%**	
Spoiled		**867**	**1.20%**				**760**	**1.14%**			**+0.06%**	
Turnout		**72,142**	**72.74%**				**66,547**	**72.14%**			**+0.60%**	

CAVAN-MONAGHAN 2011 TRANSFER ANALYSIS							
From	**To**	**FG**	**LB**	**FF**	**SF**	**Others**	**Non Trans**
FG	4,246	2,926	205	539	438		138
		68.91%	*4.83%*	*12.69%*	*10.32%*		*3.25%*
LB	4,998	2,054		676	1,303		965
		41.10%		*13.53%*	*26.07%*		*19.31%*
FF	8,066	2,200		3,430	713		1,723
		27.27%		*42.52%*	*8.84%*		*21.36%*
GP	530	135	107	62	68	134	24
		25.47%	*20.19%*	*11.70%*	*12.83%*	*25.28%*	*4.53%*
Others	6,714	2,205	675	879	1,279	857	819
		32.84%	*10.05%*	*13.09%*	*19.05%*	*12.76%*	*12.20%*
Total	**24,554**	**9,520**	**987**	**5,586**	**3,801**	**991**	**3,669**
		38.77%	***4.02%***	***22.75%***	***15.48%***	***4.04%***	***14.94%***

CAVAN-MONAGHAN 2011
COUNT DETAILS

Seats 5 | **Quota 11,880**

Candidate	Party	1st	2nd Lonergan Duffy	3rd McGuirk Votes	4th Forde Votes	5th Treanor Votes	6th McVitty Votes	7th Hogan Votes	8th Conlon Votes	9th Smith Surplus
Ó Caoláin, Caoimhghín*	SF	11,913	11,913	11,913	11,913	11,913	11,913	11,913	11,913	11,913
			+32	*+83*	*+275*	*+157*	*+521*	*+467*	*+3,430*	*-2,787*
Smith, Brendan*	FF	9,702	9,734	9,817	10,092	10,249	10,770	11,237	14,667	11,880
			+28	*+51*	*+187*	*+80*	*+1,813*	*+709*	*+104*	*+129*
O'Reilly, Joe	FG	8,333	8,361	8,412	8,599	8,679	10,492	11,201	11,305	11,434
			+60	*+301*	*+94*	*+409*	*+434*	*+733*	*+728*	*+555*
Conlan, Sean	FG	7,864	7,924	8,225	8,319	8,728	9,162	9,895	10,623	11,178
			+57	*+173*	*+147*	*+365*	*+679*	*+612*	*+348*	*+336*
Humphreys, Heather	FG	8,144	8,201	8,374	8,521	8,886	9,565	10,177	10,525	10,861
			+85	*+234*	*+431*	*+597*	*+438*	*+1,303*	*+257*	*+456*
Reilly, Kathryn	SF	6,539	6,624	6,858	7,289	7,886	8,324	9,627	9,884	10,340
			+45	*+114*	*+62*	*+173*	*+18*	*+209*	*-5,279*	
Conlon, Margaret*	FF	4,658	4,703	4,817	4,879	5,052	5,070	5,279	Eliminated	
			+133	*+129*	*+254*	*+266*	*+205*	*-4,998*		
Hogan, Liam	LB	4,011	4,144	4,273	4,527	4,793	4,998	Eliminated		
			+23	*+31*	*+295*	*+39*	*-4,246*			
McVitty, Peter	FG	3,858	3,881	3,912	4,207	4,246	Eliminated			
			+33	*+372*	*+279*	*-2,658*				
Treanor, Seamus	NP	1,974	2,007	2,379	2,658	Eliminated				
			+81	*+174*	*-2,167*					
Forde, Caroline	NP	1,912	1,993	2,167	Eliminated					
			+52	*-1,760*						
McGuirk, John	NV	1,708	1,760	Eliminated						
			-530							
Lonergan, Darcy	GP	530	Eliminated							
			-129							
Duffy, Joseph	NP	129	Eliminated							
Non-transferable			*+30*	*+98*	*+143*	*+572*	*+138*	*+965*	*+412*	*+1,311*
Cumulative			30	128	271	843	981	1,946	2,358	3,669
Total		**71,275**	**71,275**	**71,275**	**71,275**	**71,275**	**71,275**	**71,275**	**71,275**	**71,275**

CAVAN-MONAGHAN
MAIN BOUNDARY CHANGES

Dail	Constituency	Seats
1 (1918)	Cavan East	1
	Cavan West	1
	Monaghan North	1
	Monaghan South	1
2 (1921) - 3 (1922)	Cavan	3
	Monaghan	3
4 (1923) - 16 (1957)	Cavan	4
	Monaghan	3
17 (1961) - 20 (1973)	Cavan	3
	Monaghan	3
21 (1977) - 31 (2011)	Cavan-Monaghan	5

CAVAN-MONAGHAN																				
ALL TDs 1918-2011																				
	Surname	**First Name**	**Party**	**Elected**																**Total**
1	Smith	Patrick	FF	23	27	27	32	33	37	38	43	44	48	51	54	57	61	65	69	73	17
2	Sheridan	Michael	FF	32	33	37	38	43	44	48	51	54	57								10
3	Dillon**	James	FG	37	38	43	44	48	51	54	57	61	65								10
4	O'Hanlon	Rory	FF	77	81	82	82	87	89	92	97	02	07								10
5	Fitzpatrick	Thomas	FG	65	69	73	77	81	82	82	87										8
6	Blythe	Ernest	CG	18	21	22	23	27	27	32											7
7	Ward	Conn F.	FF	27S	32	33	37	38	43	44											7
8	O'Reilly(Murmod)	Patrick	FG	43	44	51	54	57	61	69											7
9	Wilson	John	FF	73	77	81	82	82	87	89											7
10	Leonard	James	FF	73	77	82	82	87	89	92											7
11	Conlon	John F.	FG	69	73	77	81	82	82												6
12	O'Reilly	John J.	CG	25*	27	27	32	33													5
13	Cole	John J.	NP	23	27S	37	38	43													5
14	Rice	Bridget Mary	FF	38	43	44	48	51													5
15	Tully	John	CnaP	48	51	54	57	65													5
20	Smith	Brendan	FF	92	97	02	07	11													5
28	O Caolain	Caoimhghin	SF	97	02	07	11														4
16	Mooney	Patrick	FF	54	57	61	65														4
17	Childers**	Erskine	FF	61	65	69	73														4
18	Boylan	Andrew	FG	87	89	92	97														4
19	Crawford	Seymour	FG	92	97	02	07														4
21	Griffith**	Arthur	CT	18	21	22															3
22	Milroy	Sean	CG	21	22	23															3
23	McCarvill	Patrick	FF	22	23	27J															3
24	Haslett	Alexander	NP	27	27	33															3
25	O'Hanlon	John F.	NP	27	27	32															3
26	Rice	Eamonn	FF	32	33	37															3
27	McGovern	Patrick	FG	33	37	38															3
29	Galligan	Peter	SF	18	21																2
30	MacEntee**	Sean	SF	18	21																2
31	O'Duffy	Gen Eoin	CT	21	22																2
32	Baxter	Patrick	F	23	27J																2
33	Maguire	Patrick J.	FF	48	51																2
34	Cole	Walter	CT	22																	1
35	Duffy	Patrick	CG	23																	1
36	O'Reilly	Thomas P.	NP	44																	1
37	O'Reilly	Patrick	NP	48																	1
38	Kelly	Edward	FF	54																	1
39	O hAnnluain	Eineachan	SF	57																	1
40	Dolan	Seamus	FF	61																	1
41	Fox	Billy	FG	69																	1
42	Toal	Brendan	FG	73*																	1
43	Doherty	Kieran	HBlk	81																	1
44	Cotter	Bill	FG	89																	1
45	Connolly	Paudge	NP	02																	1
46	Conlon	Margaret	FF	07																	1
47	O'Reilly	Joe	FG	11																	1
48	Conlan	Sean	FG	11																	1
49	Hymphreys	Heather	FG	11																	1
49	**Total**														***Includes 2 By-Elections**					*	**188**
	**** Also elected in another constituency**																				
	MacEntee**	Sean	SF	Dublin		27	27	32	33	37	38	43	44	48	51	54	57	61	65		14
	Childers**	Erskine	FF	Longford-Westmeath					38	43	44	48	51	54	57						7
CM	Dillon**	James	FG	Donegal					32	33											2
CM	Griffith**	Arthur	CT	Tyrone					18												1
CM	**Included in Cavan-Monaghan Total**																				**24**

CAVAN-MONAGHAN 1918-2011

* No Contest		FG		LB		FF		SF		GP		WP		C na P		C na T		Farmers		Nat League		Centre P		Others	
Dail	Seats	S	% Vote	S	% Vote	S	% Vote	S	% Vote	S	% Vote	S	% Vote	S	% Vote	S	% Vote	S	% Vote	S	% Vote	S	% Vote	S	% Vote
1 1918	4							4																	
2 1921*	6							6																	
3 1922	6	5	67.84%			1	11.31%												12.60%						8.25%
4 1923	7	3	37.66%		6.37%	2	20.14%											1	17.81%					1	18.01%
5 1927	7	2	21.01%			2	27.21%											1	5.10%		6.67%			2	40.01%
6 1927	7	2	25.82%			2	37.30%												7.00%					3	29.88%
7 1932	7	2	24.53%			4	45.78%																	1	29.69%
8 1933	7	1	17.46%			4	50.28%															1	12.38%	1	19.88%
9 1937	7	2	27.72%			4	46.89%																	1	25.39%
10 1938	7	2	27.36%		4.57%	4	49.80%																	1	18.26%
11 1943	7		8.93%		7.24%	4	41.01%										4.86%							3	37.96%
12 1944	7					4	53.62%										4.86%							3	41.51%
13 1948	7		3.29%		2.69%	4	44.07%							1	13.93%		2.96%							2	33.06%
14 1951	7	1	7.89%			4	44.36%							1	10.30%									1	37.46%
15 1954	7	2	22.59%			4	41.95%							1	14.13%										21.33%
16 1957	7	2	22.45%			3	41.46%	1	14.48%					1	7.74%										13.87%
17 1961	6	2	31.98%			4	46.87%		7.37%						8.76%										5.01%
18 1965	6	2	43.27%		1.87%	3	46.34%							1	8.52%										
19 1969	6	4	45.91%		5.49%	2	43.25%																		5.35%
20 1973	6	2	44.48%		0.81%	4	44.10%																		10.61%
21 1977	5	2	43.52%			3	51.44%						1.27%												3.77%
22 1981	5	2	41.03%			2	43.87%	1	15.10%																
23 1982	5	2	42.60%			3	48.87%		6.84%				0.91%												0.78%
24 1982	5	2	44.90%			3	54.85%																		0.25%
25 1987	5	2	32.74%			3	54.91%		7.30%				1.00%												4.05%
26 1989	5	2	36.73%			3	50.51%		9.13%																3.63%
27 1992	5	2	34.96%		8.28%	3	44.26%		7.65%				0.29%												4.57%
28 1997	5	2	34.67%		3.96%	2	38.44%	1	19.37%																3.57%
29 2002	5	1	25.18%		0.89%	2	34.95%	1	17.51%		1.78%													1	19.69%
30 2007	5	1	31.20%		1.21%	3	37.77%	1	20.01%		3.62%														6.18%
31 2011	5	3	39.56%		5.63%	1	20.15%	1	25.89%		0.74%														8.03%
1918-2011	**186**	**55**	**29.82%**		**1.73%**	**87**	**41.97%**	**16**	**5.28%**		**0.23%**		**0.11%**	**5**	**2.13%**		**0.46%**	**2**	**1.37%**		**0.25%**	**1**	**0.50%**	**20**	**16.17%**
National	**4,618**	**1,453**	**30.77%**	**482**	**11.53%**	**1,985**	**41.86%**	**232**	**1.99%**	**16**	**0.75%**	**17**	**0.78%**	**18**	**0.77%**	**43**	**1.08%**	**42**	**0.90%**	**10**	**0.24%**	**11**	**0.30%**	**309**	**9.00%**

CLARE 2011

"Fine Gael becomes the biggest party in Clare for the first time"

There were no changes to the boundaries here since 2007.

With more than twice as many votes as anyone else Fine Gael became the biggest party in Clare. Its incumbents Pat Breen and Joe Carey were re-elected without a bother, though Carey may be a little concerned by the strong vote of the third Fine Gael candidate, Tony Mulcahy.

Since the foundation of the state this had been a Fianna Fail stronghold, represented by Éamon de Valera for over forty years. With the retirement of former minister Tony Killeen, Timmy Dooley seemed to have a clear run, but when Dr John Hillery, son of former president (and Clare TD) Patrick Hillery, emerged as the second Fianna Fail candidate, it became apparent that while Fianna Fail seemed certain of one seat, it might not be Dooley. The battle between the two of them was intense, but Dooley had a 600-vote lead on the ninth count, after which Hillery was eliminated.

Favourite for the remaining seat was independent James Breen, who had been a TD here between 2002 and 2007. While he increased his vote slightly over 2007, it was obvious from the first count that he would not be returning to Leinster House.

Instead, this seat was taken by new Labour candidate, farmer and barrister, Michael McNamara. Since Patrick Hogan, who subsequently became Ceann Comhairle, won a seat here in 1951, Labour had only once taken a seat, through Dr Moosajee Bhamjee in 1992, and having won 1.6 per cent of the votes in 2007 it could hardly have had Clare high on its target list. However, McNamara had gained valuable exposure through his 2009 European Parliament campaign, when he had won over 12,000 votes, many in Clare, as an Independent, and he increased the Labour vote share more than nine-fold to sail into the second seat.

Enda Kenny with Pat Breen & Joe Carey

CLARE TDs 2011

PAT BREEN (FG)

Lisduff, Ballynacally, Co. Clare; Tel: 065 6838229; Mobile: 087 2422136;
Constituency Office: Park View House, Lower Market Street Car Park, Ennis, Co. Clare;
Tel: 065 6868466; Email: pat.breen@oireachtas.ie
Leinster House: 01 6184224; Website: www.patbreen.ie

Born Ennis, Co. Clare 21st March 1957. Married to Anne McInerney, two sons, Kenneth and Patrick. Educated St. Flannan's College, Ennis and Limerick IT. Farmer. Former architectural technician. First elected 2002 and at each subsequent election.

Appointed Chairman Committee on Foreign Affairs and Trade June 2011. Deputy Fine Gael spokesperson on Foreign Affairs with special responsibility for Human Rights 2007-2011. Member Joint Committee on European Affairs 2007-2011. Deputy Spokesperson on Transport 2002-2007. Member Joint Committee on Transport; Committee on Procedure and Privileges 2002-2007. Member Clare County Council 1999-2003.

MICHAEL McNAMARA (LB)

Scariff, Co. Clare, Mobile: 087 1384561; Leinster House: 01 6183879
Email: Michael.mcnamara@oireachtas.ie; Website: www.labour.ie/michaelmcnamara

Born Scariff, Co. Clare, 1st March 1974. Single. Educated Scariff Community College, St. Flannan's College, Ennis; UCC, the University of Louvain and the King's Inns. Farmer and Barrister. Elected at his first attempt in 2011.

Member Committee on Communications, Natural resources and Agriculture. Member Committee on Foreign Affairs and Trade. Contested the 2009 European elections in the Ireland North West constituency, winning 3% of the first preference vote. He worked as a human rights lawyer with the OSCE in Eastern Europe and with the United Nations in Afghanistan before returning to Ireland in 2005 to run his family farm and practice at the Bar. He has continued to work as a consultant for the EU and UN. Member of Scarriff GAA Club and the IFA.

JOE CAREY (FG)

3 Thomand Villas, Clarecastle, Co. Clare; Tel: 065 6829191
Constituency Office: 12 Park Row, Francis Street, Ennis, Co. Clare; Tel: 065 6891199;
Leinster House: 01 6183337; Email: joe.carey@oireachtas.ie
Website: www.joecarey.finegael.ie

Born Clarecastle, Co. Clare, 24th June 1975. Married to Grace Fitzell, one daughter Alma. Educated St. Flannan's College, Ennis and Limerick IT and Athlone IT. Accountant. First elected 2007. Retained his seat in 2011.

Member Committee on Procedure and Privileges. Deputy spokesperson on Justice with special responsibility for Juvenile Justice 2007-2011. Member Joint Committee on Social and Family Affairs 2007-2011. Member Clare County Council 1999-2007. Treasurer Ennis General Hospital Development Committee. Son of Donal Carey TD for Clare 1982-2002, Senator 1981-1982 and Minister for State 1995-1997.

TIMMY DOOLEY (FF)

8 The Old Forge, Tulla, Co. Clare; Tel: 065 6831732,
Constituency Office: 8 Mill Road, Ennis, Tel: 065 6891115;
Leinster House: 01 6183514; Email: timmy.dooley@oireachtas.ie
Website: www.timmydooley.ie

Born East Clare, 13th Feb 1969. Married to Emer McMahon, two daughters. Educated Scarriff Community College. UCD. Worked in sales and marketing and business development prior to election to Seanad Eireann in 2002. First elected 2007. Retained his seat in 2011.

Appointed Party Spokesperson on Transport, Tourism and Sport 12th April 2011. Member Committee on Environment, Transport, Culture and the Gaeltacht. Member Committee on European Affairs. Vice-Chairman Joint Committee on European Affairs 2007-2011. Member Joint Committee on European Scrutiny 2007-2011. Member Seanad Eireann 2002-2007. Party spokesperson on Transport in the Seanad. Former Member National Forum on Europe. Former Member Fianna Fail National Executive. Active Member Fianna Fail since 1987.

CLARE 2011							
FIRST PREFERENCE VOTES							
	Seats	**4**			**11,584**		
	Candidate	**Party**	**1st**	**%**	**Quota**	**Count**	**Status**
1	**Breen, Pat***	**FG**	**9,855**	**17.02%**	**0.85**	**11**	**Made Quota**
2	**McNamara, Michael**	**LB**	**8,572**	**14.80%**	**0.74**	**11**	**Made Quota**
3	**Carey, Joe***	**FG**	**7,840**	**13.54%**	**0.68**	**12**	**Made Quota**
4	**Dooley, Timmy***	**FF**	**6,789**	**11.72%**	**0.59**	**12**	**Elected**
5	Breen, James #	NP	6,491	11.21%	0.56	12	Not Elected
6	Mulcahy, Tony	FG	6,829	11.79%	0.59	10	Eliminated
7	Hillery, Dr. John	FF	6,015	10.39%	0.52	9	Eliminated
8	Markham, Brian	NP	1,543	2.66%	0.13	8	No Expenses
9	Meaney, Brian	GP	1,154	1.99%	0.10	7	No Expenses
10	Connolly, Jim	NP	978	1.69%	0.08	6	No Expenses
11	McAleer, Madeline	NP	428	0.74%	0.04	5	No Expenses
12	Cronin, Ann	NP	419	0.72%	0.04	5	No Expenses
13	Walshe, Gerry	NP	328	0.57%	0.03	4	No Expenses
14	Ferrigan, Sarah	NP	252	0.44%	0.02	3	No Expenses
15	McCabe, J.J.	NP	248	0.43%	0.02	2	No Expenses
16	Brassil, Patrick	NP	175	0.30%	0.02	1	No Expenses
16	***Outgoing # Former TD**		**57,916**	**100.00%**	**11,584**	**2,897**	**No Expenses**

CLARE 2011												
PARTY VOTE												
	2011					**2007**					**Change**	
Party	**Cand**	**1st**	**%**	**Quota**	**Seats**	**Cand**	**1st**	**%**	**Quota**	**Seats**	**%**	**Seats**
FG	3	24,524	42.34%	2.12	2	4	19,854	35.21%	1.76	2	+7.13%	
LB	1	8,572	14.80%	0.74	1	1	892	1.58%	0.08		+13.22%	+1
FF	2	12,804	22.11%	1.11	1	3	24,824	44.03%	2.20	2	-21.92%	-1
SF						1	1,929	3.42%	0.17		-3.42%	
GP	1	1,154	1.99%	0.10		1	2,858	5.07%	0.25		-3.08%	
PD						1	810	1.44%	0.07		-1.44%	
Others	9	10,862	18.75%	0.94		1	5,218	9.25%	0.46		+9.50%	
Total	**16**	**57,916**	**100.0%**	**11,584**	**4**	**12**	**56,385**	**100.0%**	**11,278**	**4**	**0.00%**	**0**
Electorate		**82,745**	**69.99%**				**79,555**	**70.88%**			**-0.88%**	
Spoiled		**579**	**0.99%**				**385**	**0.68%**			**+0.31%**	
Turnout		**58,495**	**70.69%**				**56,770**	**71.36%**			**-0.67%**	

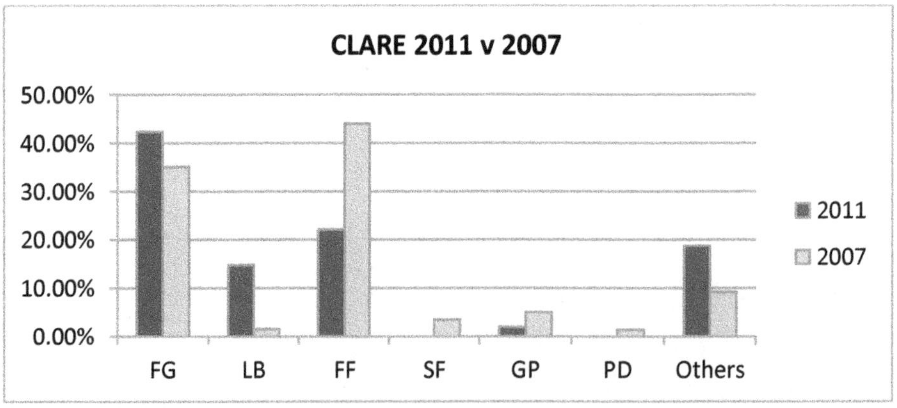

CLARE 2011 COUNT DETAILS													
Seats	4											Quota	11,584
Candidate	**Party**	**1st**	**2nd** Brassil Votes	**3rd** McCabe Votes	**4th** Ferrigan Votes	**5th** Walshe Votes	**6th** McAleer Cronin	**7th** Connolly Kelly	**8th** Meaney Votes	**9th** Markham Votes	**10th** Hillery Votes	**11th** Mulcahy Votes	**12th** Breen Surplus
			+10	*+14*	*+17*	*+21*	*+32*	*+135*	*+123*	*+272*	*+509*	*+2,346*	*-1,750*
Breen, Pat*	FG	9,855	9,865	9,879	9,896	9,917	9,949	10,084	10,207	10,479	10,988	13,334	11,584
			+9	*+34*	*+44*	*+38*	*+174*	*+200*	*+513*	*+401*	*+567*	*+1,331*	
McNamara, Michael	LB	8,572	8,581	8,615	8,659	8,697	8,871	9,071	9,584	9,985	10,552	11,883	11,883
			+19	*+17*	*+12*	*+18*	*+47*	*+75*	*+132*	*+174*	*+283*	*+2,344*	*+1,528*
Carey, Joe*	FG	7,840	7,859	7,876	7,888	7,906	7,953	8,028	8,160	8,334	8,617	10,961	12,489
			+6	*+11*	*+7*	*+10*	*+35*	*+48*	*+57*	*+108*	*+3,526*	*+368*	*+56*
Dooley, Timmy*	FF	6,789	6,795	6,806	6,813	6,823	6,858	6,906	6,963	7,071	10,597	10,965	11,021
			+55	*+37*	*+16*	*+63*	*+133*	*+234*	*+107*	*+542*	*+1,054*	*+622*	*+166*
Breen, James #	NP	6,491	6,546	6,583	6,599	6,662	6,795	7,029	7,136	7,678	8,732	9,354	9,520
			+3	*+29*	*+5*	*+15*	*+51*	*+48*	*+126*	*+122*	*+210*	*-7,438*	
Mulcahy, Tony	FG	6,829	6,832	6,861	6,866	6,881	6,932	6,980	7,106	7,228	7,438	Eliminated	
			+5	*+24*	*+9*	*+13*	*+27*	*+68*	*+81*	*+226*	*-6,468*		
Hillery, Dr. John	FF	6,015	6,020	6,044	6,053	6,066	6,093	6,161	6,242	6,468	Eliminated		
			+4	*+18*	*+20*	*+52*	*+188*	*+239*	*+93*	*-2,157*			
Markham, Brian	NP	1,543	1,547	1,565	1,585	1,637	1,825	2,064	2,157	Eliminated			
			+4	*+5*	*+9*	*+15*	*+79*	*+73*	*-1,339*				
Meaney, Brian	GP	1,154	1,158	1,163	1,172	1,187	1,266	1,339	Eliminated				
			+24	*+13*	*+16*	*+44*	*+141*	*-1,216*					
Connolly, Jim	NP	978	1,002	1,015	1,031	1,075	1,216	Eliminated					
			+1	*+21*	*+37*	*+22*	*-509*						
McAleer, Madeline	NP	428	429	450	487	509	Eliminated						
			+10	*+11*	*+57*	*+24*	*-521*						
Cronin, Ann	NP	419	429	440	497	521	Eliminated						
			+4	*+8*	*+12*	*-352*							
Walshe, Gerry	NP	328	332	340	352	Eliminated							
			+8	*+5*	*-265*								
Ferrigan, Sarah	NP	252	260	265	Eliminated								
			+4	*-252*									
McCabe, J.J.	NP	248	252	Eliminated									
			-175										
Brassil, Patrick	NP	175	Eliminated										
Non-transferable			*+9*	*+5*	*+4*	*+17*	*+123*	*+96*	*+107*	*+312*	*+319*	*+427*	
Cumulative			9	14	18	35	158	254	361	673	992	1,419	1,419
Total		**57,916**	**57,916**	**57,916**	**57,916**	**57,916**	**57,916**	**57,916**	**57,916**	**57,916**	**57,916**	**57,916**	**57,916**

CLARE 2011 TRANSFER ANALYSIS							
From	**To**	**FG**	**LB**	**FF**	**GP**	**Others**	**Non Trans**
FG	9,188	6,218	1,331	424		788	427
		67.68%	*14.49%*	*4.61%*		*8.58%*	*4.65%*
FF	6,468	1,002	567	3,526		1,054	319
		15.49%	*8.77%*	*54.51%*		*16.30%*	*4.93%*
GP	1,339	381	513	138		200	107
		28.45%	*38.31%*	*10.31%*		*14.94%*	*7.99%*
Others	5,447	1,136	900	597	185	2,063	566
		20.86%	*16.52%*	*10.96%*	*3.40%*	*37.87%*	*10.39%*
Total	**22,442**	**8,737**	**3,311**	**4,685**	**185**	**4,105**	**1,419**
		38.93%	***14.75%***	***20.88%***	***0.82%***	***18.29%***	***6.32%***

CLARE		
MAIN BOUNDARY CHANGES		
Dail	**Constituency**	**Seats**
1 (1918)	Clare East	1
	Clare West	1
2 (1921) - 3 (1922)	Clare	4
4 (1923) -12 (1944)	Clare	5
13 (1948) - 18 (1965)	Clare	4
19 (1969) - 21 (1977)	Clare	3
22 (1981) - 31 (2011)	Clare	4

CLARE																				
ALL TDs 1918-2011																				
	Surname	**First Name**	**Party**	**Elected**																**Total**
1	De Valera**	Eamon	FF	18	21	22	23	27	27	32	33	37	38	43	44	48	51	54	57	16
2	Hogan	Patrick	LB	23	27	27	32	33	37	43	48	51	54	57	61	65				13
3	Daly	Brendan	FF	73	77	81	82	82	87	89	97									8
4	O'Grady	Sean	FF	32	33	37	38	43	44	48										7
5	Barrett	Sylvester	FF	68*	69	73	77	81	82	82										7
6	Burke	Patrick	FG	32	33	37	38	43	44											6
7	Hillery	Patrick	FF	51	54	57	61	65	69											6
8	Carey	Donal	FG	82	82	87	89	92	97											6
9	Burke	Thomas	F	37	38	43	44	48												5
10	Murphy	William	FG	51	54	57	61	65												5
11	De Valera**	Sile	FF	87	89	92	97	02												5
12	O'Higgins	Brian	R	18	21	22	23													4
13	Taylor-Quinn	Madeleine	FG	81	82N	87	89													4
14	Killeen	Tony	FF	92	97	02	07													4
15	Houlihan	Patrick	FF	27	27	33														3
16	O Ceallaigh	Sean	FF	59*	61	65														3
17	Taylor	Francis	FG	69	73	77														3
18	Breen	Pat	FG	02	07	11														3
19	Brennan	Patrick	CT	21	22															2
20	Liddy	Sean	CT	21	22															2
21	Kelly	Patrick	CG	27	27															2
22	Sexton	Martin	FF	27S	32															2
23	O'Loghlen	Peter	FF	38	44															2
24	Loughnane**	Bill	FF	81	82F															2
25	Carey	Joe	FG	07	11															2
26	Dooley	Timmy	FF	07	11															2
27	Hogan	Conor	F	23																1
28	MacNeill**	Prof. Eoin	CG	23																1
29	Falvey	Thomas	F	27J																1
30	Shanahan	Patrick	FF	45*																1
31	Bhamjee	Moosajee	LB	92																1
32	Breen	James	NP	02																1
33	McNamara	Michael	LB	11																1
33	**Total**													***Includes 3 By-Elections**					*	**131**
	**** Also elected in another constituency**																			
	MacNeill**	Prof. Eoin	CG	NUI				18	21	22	23									4
	Loughnane**	Bill	FF	Galway				69	73	77										3
C	De Valera**	Eamon	FF	Mayo East				18												1
C	De Valera**	Sile	FF	Dublin Co. Mid				77												1
C	**Included in Clare Total**																			**9**

CLARE PARTY VOTE 1918-2011

*No Contest		FG		LB		FF		SF		GP		CS		PD		C na P		C na T		Farmers		Nat League		Centre P		Others	
Dail	**Seats**	**S**	**% Vote**	**S**	**% Vote**	**S**	**% Vote**	**S**	**% Vote**	**S**	**% Vote**	**S**	**% Vote**	**S**	**% Vote**	**S**	**% Vote**	**S**	**% Vote**	**S**	**% Vote**	**S**	**% Vote**	**S**	**% Vote**	**S**	**% Vote**
1 1918*	2							2																			
2 1921*	4							4																			
3 1922*	4	2				2																					
4 1923	5	1	29.78%	1	10.71%	2	47.38%													1	12.13%						
5 1927	5	1	18.99%	1	10.76%	2	39.77%		3.66%											1	13.33%		7.34%				6.14%
6 1927	5	1	29.56%	1	11.55%	3	52.76%														6.12%						
7 1932	5	1	27.39%	1	13.77%	3	58.84%																				
8 1933	5	1	16.41%	1	9.75%	3	64.68%																		9.15%		
9 1937	5	1	24.23%	1	10.73%	2	46.37%																			1	18.67%
10 1938	5	1	16.07%		11.52%	3	59.25%																			1	13.16%
11 1943	5	1	15.20%	1	11.82%	2	48.32%												10.78%							1	13.87%
12 1944	5	1	13.48%		12.05%	3	56.58%												6.69%							1	11.20%
13 1948	4		11.05%	1	11.05%	2	51.85%										10.11%		4.92%							1	11.02%
14 1951	4	1	23.30%	1	12.57%	2	54.42%																				9.72%
15 1954	4	1	24.66%	1	11.64%	2	57.89%		2.42%								3.40%										
16 1957	4	1	33.50%	1		2	66.50%																				
17 1961	4	1	36.48%	1		2	54.08%		9.44%																		
18 1965	4	1	34.44%	1	6.87%	2	58.70%																				
19 1969	3	1	30.22%		7.67%	2	62.11%																				
20 1973	3	1	32.16%		6.30%	2	61.55%																				
21 1977	3	1	26.32%		4.37%	2	68.87%																				0.45%
22 1981	4	1	30.67%		5.45%	3	58.66%		4.68%																		0.54%
23 1982	4	1	32.53%		4.49%	3	59.39%		2.83%																		0.76%
24 1982	4	2	32.76%		5.18%	2	56.15%																				5.91%
25 1987	4	2	28.02%		1.27%	2	52.82%								11.83%												6.07%
26 1989	4	2	36.37%			2	55.18%								8.45%												
27 1992	4	1	25.65%	1	11.46%	2	51.76%		1.03%						6.98%												3.13%
28 1997	4	1	30.08%		3.59%	3	50.36%				3.59%		1.06%		6.93%												4.38%
29 2002	4	1	25.46%		3.45%	2	45.38%				5.83%		0.35%													1	19.52%
30 2007	4	2	35.21%		1.58%	2	44.03%		3.42%		5.07%				1.44%												9.25%
31 2011	4	2	42.34%	1	14.80%	1	22.11%				1.99%																18.75%
1918-2011	**128**	**34**	**27.17%**	**15**	**7.76%**	**65**	**52.84%**	**6**	**0.95%**		**0.72%**		**0.06%**		**1.38%**		**0.47%**		**0.86%**	**2**	**1.04%**		**0.24%**		**0.34%**	**6**	**6.18%**
National	**4,618**	**1,453**	**30.77%**	**482**	**11.53%**	**1,985**	**41.86%**	**232**	**1.99%**	**16**	**0.75%**		**0.04%**	**44**	**1.42%**	**18**	**0.77%**	**43**	**1.08%**	**42**	**0.90%**	**10**	**0.24%**	**11**	**0.30%**	**282**	**8.33%**

Patrick Hogan (LB) : Ceann Comhairle - automatically returned in 1954,1957, 1961 & 1965

CORK EAST 2011

"Historic win for Sinn Féin as Fianna Fail fails to take a seat"

There was a significant boundary change in this constituency since the last election. It lost the areas of: Ballynaglogh, Glenville, Carrig, Watergrasshill, Kildinan, Ballynamona and Rahan. This meant that a population of 4,255 was transferred to Cork North Central.

Since Ned O'Keeffe joined the Fianna Fail ticket here in November 1982 this had been a bastion for the party, with O'Keeffe and Michael Ahern taking two of the four seats at every election up to 2007, albeit with just the occasional hint of a certain creative tension between the two of them. In 2011 this was yet another of the constituencies where Fianna Fail plunged from 2 seats to none. O'Keeffe senior retired and was succeeded on the ticket by his son Kevin, but many observers felt that Fianna Fail's only hope of retaining one seat would have been to run just one candidate, and so it proved; Ahern was eliminated on the fourth count, and O'Keeffe finished 600 votes short of a seat.

Fine Gael was always going to win two seats; the only question was which of David Stanton's two running mates would accompany him to Leinster House. This race was won by Mallow-based councillor Tom Barry, who had a lead of almost 1,000 votes over Pa O'Driscoll at the decisive stage.

That left two seats for the taking for Labour, if the party managed its votes properly. However, it spectacularly failed to do this, Seán Sherlock running over 6,000 ahead of his running mate, former TD John Mulvihill. If just 500 of Sherlock's voters had switched to Cobh-based Mulvihill, Labour would have taken two seats here. Instead, Mulvihill was eliminated on the 7th count, and his transfers enabled Sinn Féin's Sandra McLellan from Youghal to overhaul Kevin O'Keeffe and win Sinn Féin's first seat in this constituency, becoming the only opposition TD in Cork East.

Minister of State Sean Sherlock TD with EU Commissioner Maire Geoghegan Quinn

CORK EAST TDs 2011

SEÁN SHERLOCK (LB)

Blackwater Drive, Mallow, Co. Cork; Mobile: 087 7402057
Constituency Office: Davis Lane, Mallow, Co. Cork; Tel: 022 53523;
Leinster House: 01 6184049; Email: sean.sherlock@oireachtas.ie

Born Cork 6th December 1972. Single. Educated Patrician Academy, Mallow; College of Commerce, Cork; UCG (BA Economics and Politics). Minister of State. Former Assistant to Proinsias De Rossa MEP. First elected 2007. Retained his seat in 2011.

Appointed Minister of State at the Department of Enterprise, Jobs and Innovation and at Department of Education and Skills with special responsibility for Research and Innovation 10th March 2011. Front bench spokesperson on Agriculture and Food Safety 2007-2011. Member Joint Committee on Agriculture, Fisheries and Food and Member Joint Committee on Economic and Regulatory Affairs 2007-2011. Co-opted to Cork County Council and Mallow Town Council in Sept 2003 as replacement for his father, Joe Sherlock TD, following the introduction of the dual mandate ban. He retained both seats in 2004. Mayor of Mallow Town Council in 2004. Member Blackwater Kayaking Club; Mallow Rugby Club; County Cork VEC; Mountaineering Club of Ireland. Son of the late Joe Sherlock, Dail Deputy for Cork East 1981-Nov 1982, 1987-1992, 2002-2007 and Senator 1993-1997.

DAVID STANTON (FG)

Gearagh Cross, Coppingerstown, Midleton, Co. Cork; Mobile: 087 2349662
Constituency Office: 29 St. Mary's Road, Midleton; Tel: 021 4632867;
Leinster House: 01 6183181; Email: david.stanton@oireachtas.ie
Website: www.stanton.ie; Twitter: twitter.com/davidstantontd;
Facebook: facebook/davidstanton

Born Cork 15th February 1957. Married to Mary Lehane, four sons. Educated St. Colman's Community College, Midleton; Crawford Technical Institute, Cork; UCC (BA, MEd,). Former Teacher and Career Guidance Counsellor. First elected 1997 and at each subsequent election.

Appointed Chairman Select Committee on Justice, defence and Equality June 2011. Member Committee on Members' Interests. Fine Gael front bench spokesperson on Defence 2010-2011. Assistant Whip with special responsibility for Dail Reform and Disability Issues, 2007-2011. Member Joint Administration Committee and Member Dail Committee on Procedure and Privileges 2007-2011. Fine Gael front bench spokesperson on Social & Family Affairs & Equality 2004-2007. Deputy spokesperson on Education and Science with special responsibility for Information Society 2002-2004. Member Joint Committee on Education and Science and Committee on Procedure and Privileges and Joint House Services Committee 2002-2007. Fine Gael Junior spokesperson on Agriculture, Food, Biotechnology and Safety Issues 2000-2001. Junior spokesperson on Labour Affairs, Consumer Rights and Trade 1997-2000. PRO and Director of Midleton and District Day Care Centre. Patron and Member of the Irish Red Cross, Midleton and Carrigtwohill Branch. Formerly a commissioned Officer of An Forsa Cosanta Aitiuil and a past member of Macra na Feirme.

TOM BARRY (FG)

Monanimy Upper, Killavullen, Mallow, Co. Cork; Tel: 022 26800; Mobile: 087 7540438
Constituency Office: 156 Main Street, Mallow, Co. Cork; Tel: 022 58001;
Leinster House: 01 6183328; Email: tom.barry@oireachtas.ie
Website: www.tombarry.ie Twitter: twitter.com/tbarry

Born Cork 10th October 1968. Married to Dr. Kathy Quane, two sons, one daughter. Educated De La Salle College, Waterford; UCC (Bio-Chemistry). Agri-businessman who owns and runs TB Warehousing. Elected at his first attempt in 2011.

Member Committee on Communications, Natural Resources and Agriculture. Member Committee on Foreign Affairs and Trade. Elected to Cork County Council at his first attempt in 2009 in the Mallow electoral area.

SANDRA McLELLAN (SF)

Ardrath, Youghal, Co. Cork, Tel: 024 93042; Mobile: 086 3752944
Leinster House: 01 6183122; Email: Sandra.mclellan@oireachtas.ie

Born Youghal, Co. Cork May 1961. Married to Liam McLellan, 3 children. Educated Loreto Convent, Youghal. Former Shop Steward. Contested the 2007 Dail election in Cork East. First elected 2011.

Appointed Party Spokesperson on Arts, Heritage, Tourism and Sport 22nd March 2011. Member Committee on Environment, Transport, Culture and the Gaeltacht. Elected to Cork County Council in the Midleton electoral area in 2009. Elected to Youghal Town Council in 2004 and retained her seat in 2009.

	CORK EAST 2011						
	FIRST PREFERENCE VOTES						
	Seats	4			11,387		
	Candidate	Party	1st	%	Quota	Count	Status
1	**Sherlock, Sean***	**LB**	**11,862**	**20.84%**	**1.04**	**1**	**Made Quota**
2	**Stanton, David***	**FG**	**10,019**	**17.60%**	**0.88**	**5**	**Made Quota**
3	**Barry, Tom**	**FG**	**5,798**	**10.18%**	**0.51**	**7**	**Made Quota**
4	**McLellan, Sandra**	**SF**	**6,292**	**11.05%**	**0.55**	**7**	**Elected**
5	O'Keeffe, Kevin	FF	5,024	8.82%	0.44	7	Not Elected
6	Mulvihill, John #	LB	5,701	10.01%	0.50	6	Eliminated
7	O'Driscoll, Pa	FG	5,030	8.83%	0.44	4	Eliminated
8	Ahern, Michael*	FF	4,618	8.11%	0.41	3	Eliminated
9	O'Neill, Paul	NV	1,056	1.85%	0.09	2	No Expenses
10	Harty, Malachy	GP	635	1.12%	0.06	2	No Expenses
11	Cullinane, Claire	CPPC	510	0.90%	0.04	2	No Expenses
12	Bulman, Patrick	CPPC	212	0.37%	0.02	2	No Expenses
13	Burke, Paul	NP	176	0.31%	0.02	2	No Expenses
13	***Outgoing # Former TD**		**56,933**	**100.00%**	**11,387**	**2,847**	**No Expenses**

CORK EAST 2011												
PARTY VOTE												
	2011					2007					Change	
Party	**Cand**	**1st**	**%**	**Quota**	**Seats**	**Cand**	**1st**	**%**	**Quota**	**Seats**	**%**	**Seats**
FG	3	20,847	36.62%	1.83	2	2	16,602	30.85%	1.54	1	+5.76%	+1
LB	2	17,563	30.85%	1.54	1	2	11,249	20.91%	1.05	1	+9.94%	
FF	2	9,642	16.94%	0.85		2	20,431	37.97%	1.90	2	-21.03%	-2
SF	1	6,292	11.05%	0.55	1	1	3,672	6.82%	0.34		+4.23%	+1
GP	1	635	1.12%	0.06		1	1,572	2.92%	0.15		-1.81%	
Others	4	1,954	3.43%	0.17		2	282	0.52%	0.03		+2.91%	
Total	**13**	**56,933**	**100.0%**	**11,387**	**4**	**10**	**53,808**	**100.0%**	**10,762**	**4**	**0.00%**	**0**
Electorate		**83,651**	**68.06%**				**84,354**	**63.79%**			**+4.27%**	
Spoiled		**526**	**0.92%**				**477**	**0.88%**			**+0.04%**	
Turnout		**57,459**	**68.69%**				**54,285**	**64.35%**			**+4.34%**	

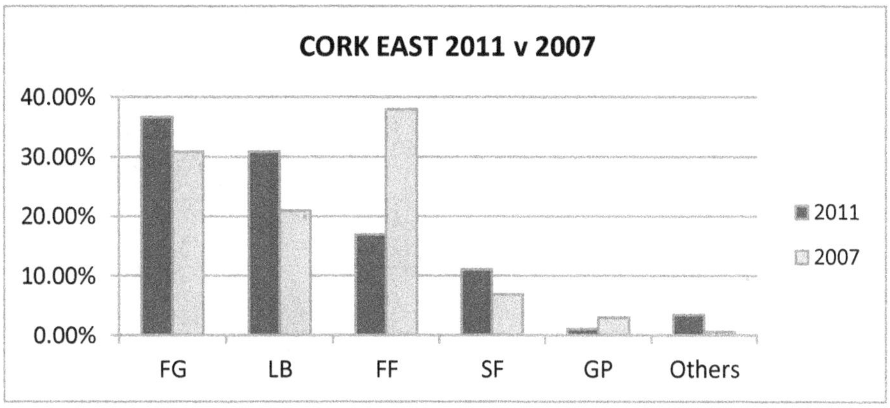

CORK EAST 2011 COUNT DETAILS								
Seats	4						Quota	11,387
Candidate	Party	1st	2nd Sherlock Surplus	3rd O'Neill, Harty Cullinane Bulman Burke Lonergan Duffy	4th Ahern Votes	5th O'Driscoll Votes	6th Stanton Surplus	7th Mulvihill Votes
			-475					
Sherlock, Sean*	LB	11,862	11,387	11,387	11,387	11,387	11,387	11,387
			+28	*+571*	*+463*	*+1,390*	*-1,084*	
Stanton, David*	FG	10,019	10,047	10,618	11,081	12,471	11,387	11,387
			+90	*+209*	*+300*	*+2,501*	*+828*	*+1,724*
Barry, Tom	FG	5,798	5,888	6,097	6,397	8,898	9,726	11,450
			+53	*+532*	*+326*	*+325*	*+58*	*+2,199*
McLellan, Sandra	SF	6,292	6,345	6,877	7,203	7,528	7,586	9,785
			+42	*+79*	*+2,666*	*+590*	*+77*	*+658*
O'Keeffe, Kevin	FF	5,024	5,066	5,145	7,811	8,401	8,478	9,136
			+172	*+515*	*+402*	*+186*	*+121*	*-7,097*
Mulvihill, John #	LB	5,701	5,873	6,388	6,790	6,976	7,097	Eliminated
			+56	*+150*	*+208*	*-5,444*		
O'Driscoll, Pa	FG	5,030	5,086	5,236	5,444	Eliminated		
			+16	*+164*	*-4,798*			
Ahern, Michael*	FF	4,618	4,634	4,798	Eliminated			
			+8	*-1,064*				
O'Neill, Paul	NV	1,056	1,064	Eliminated				
			+5	*-640*				
Harty, Malachy	GP	635	640	Eliminated				
			+3	*-513*				
Cullinane, Claire	CPPC	510	513	Eliminated				
			+1	*-213*				
Bulman, Patrick	CPPC	212	213	Eliminated				
			+1	*-177*				
Burke, Paul	NP	176	177	Eliminated				
Non-transferable				*+387*	*+433*	*+452*		*+2,516*
Cumulative			0	387	820	1,272	1,272	3,788
Total		**56,933**	**56,933**	**56,933**	**56,933**	**56,933**	**56,933**	**56,933**

CORK EAST 2011 TRANSFER ANALYSIS								
From	**To**	**FG**	**LB**	**FF**	**SF**	**GP**	**Others**	**Non Trans**
FG	6,528	4,719	307	667	383			452
		72.29%	*4.70%*	*10.22%*	*5.87%*			*6.92%*
LB	7,572	1,898	172	716	2,252	5	13	2,516
		25.07%	*2.27%*	*9.46%*	*29.74%*	*0.07%*	*0.17%*	*33.23%*
FF	4,798	971	402	2,666	326			433
		20.24%	*8.38%*	*55.56%*	*6.79%*			*9.02%*
GP	640	228	126	60	131			95
		35.63%	*19.69%*	*9.38%*	*20.47%*			*14.84%*
Others	1,967	702	389	183	401			292
		35.69%	*19.78%*	*9.30%*	*20.39%*			*14.84%*
Total	**21,505**	**8,518**	**1,396**	**4,292**	**3,493**	**5**	**13**	**3,788**
		39.61%	***6.49%***	***19.96%***	***16.24%***	***0.02%***	***0.06%***	***17.61%***

CORK EAST		
MAIN BOUNDARY CHANGES		
Dail	**Constituency**	**Seats**
1 (1918)	Cork East	1
	Cork North-East	1
2 (1921) - 3 (1922)	Cork East & North-East	3
4 (1923) - 8 (1933)	Cork East	5
9 (1937) - 12 (1944)	Cork South-East	3
13 (1948) - 16 (1957)	Cork East	3
17 (1961) - 18 (1965)	Cork North-East	5
19 (1969) - 20 (1973)	Cork North-East	4
21 (1977)	Cork North-East	4
22 (1981) - 31 (2011)	Cork East	4

CORK EAST																		
ALL TDs 1918-2011																		
	Surname	**Forename**	**Party**	**Elected**														**Total**
1	Corry	Martin J.	FF	27	27	32	33	37	38	43	44	48	51	54	57	61	65	14
2	Barry	Richard	FG	53*	54	57	61	65	69	73	77							8
3	Ahern	Michael	FF	82	82	87	89	92	97	02	07							8
4	O'Keeffe	Ned	FF	82N	87	89	92	97	02	07								7
5	Hegarty	Patrick	FG	73	77	81	82	82	87									6
6	Kent	David	SF	18	21	22	23	27J										5
7	Sherlock	Joe	LB	81	82F	87	89	02										5
8	Hennessy	Michael	CG	22	23	27	27											4
9	Daly	John	CG	23	27	27	32											4
10	Broderick**	William	FG	32	33	43	44											4
11	Cronin	Jeremiah	FF	65	69	73	77											4
12	Barry	Myra	FG	79*	81	82	82											4
13	Stanton	David	FG	97	02	07	11											4
14	Brasier	Brook	FG	32	37	38												3
15	Moher	John	FF	54	57	61												3
16	Brosnan	Sean	FF	69	74*	77												3
17	Bradford	Paul	FG	89	92	97												3
18	Hunter	Thomas	SF	18	21													2
19	Dineen	John	F	22	23													2
20	Kent	William	CP	27S	33													2
21	Murphy	Patrick	FF	32	33													2
22	Hurley	Jeremiah	LB	37	38													2
23	Keane	Sean	LB	48	51													2
24	O'Gorman	Patrick J.	FG	48	51													2
25	Burton**	Philip	FG	61	65													2
26	McAuliffe**	Patrick	LB	61	65													2
27	Sherlock	Sean	LB	07	11													2
28	Fitzgerald	Seamus	SF	21														1
29	O'Mahony	Thomas	CG	23														1
30	Noonan	Michael K.	CG	24*														1
31	O'Gorman	David	F	27J														1
32	Carey	Edmond	CG	27S														1
33	Daly**	Patrick	FG	33														1
34	Looney	Thomas	LB	43														1
35	MacCarthy**	Sean	FF	44														1
36	Cott	Gerard	FG	69														1
37	Ahern	Liam	FF	73														1
38	Joyce	Carey	FF	81														1
39	Mulvihill	John	LB	92														1
40	Barry	Tom	FG	11														1
41	McLellan	Sandra	SF	11														1
41	**Total**										*** Includes 4 By-Elections**						*	**123**
	**** Also elected in another constituency**																	
1	McAuliffe**	Patrick	LB	Cork North					44	48	51	54	57					5
2	MacCarthy**	Sean	FF	Cork Boro, South, Mid					51	54	57	61						4
3	Daly**	Patrick	FG	Cork North					37	38								2
4	Broderick**	William	FG	Waterford					38									1
5	Burton**	Philip	FG	Cork Mid					69									1
5	**Total**																	**13**

CORK EAST PARTY VOTE 1918-2011

*No Contest		FG		LB		FF		SF		GP		WP		PD		DL		C na T		Nat Labour		Farmers		Centre P		Others	
Dail	Seats	S	% Vote	S	% Vote	S	% Vote	S	% Vote	S	% Vote	S	% Vote	S	% Vote	S	% Vote	S	% Vote	S	% Vote	S	% Vote	S	% Vote	S	% Vote
1 1918*	2							2																			
2 1921*	3							3																			
3 1922	3					1	49.53%															1	29.35%			1	21.12%
4 1923	5	2	31.93%			1	23.50%															1	23.52%			1	21.06%
5 1927	5	1	20.52%		5.29%	1	17.35%	1	11.42%													1	17.20%			1	28.21%
6 1927	5	3	39.64%		8.20%	2	33.19%																13.88%				5.09%
7 1932	5	2	40.76%		5.44%	2	38.68%																4.41%			1	10.71%
8 1933	5	2	26.05%			2	46.29%																	1	17.62%		10.03%
9 1937	3	1	43.24%	1	21.67%	1	35.09%																				
10 1938	3	1	41.19%	1	18.42%	1	40.39%																				
11 1943	3	1	26.65%	1	15.21%	1	36.91%												13.68%								7.54%
12 1944	3	1	17.63%		10.67%	2	43.47%												18.07%		10.17%						
13 1948	3	1	21.30%	1	13.87%	1	38.17%												11.44%		2.81%						12.41%
14 1951	3	1	29.92%	1	17.56%	1	42.07%																				10.45%
15 1954	3	1	38.74%		13.73%	2	42.52%																				5.02%
16 1957	3	1	35.92%		6.37%	2	49.11%		8.60%																		
17 1961	5	2	38.80%	1	17.04%	2	39.80%		4.36%																		
18 1965	5	2	36.09%	1	15.27%	2	48.15%																				0.49%
19 1969	4	2	37.01%		13.07%	2	49.92%																				
20 1973	4	2	35.63%		4.72%	2	50.11%		6.22%																		3.32%
21 1977	4	2	33.24%		2.31%	2	48.18%						9.47%														6.80%
22 1981	4	2	45.31%		1.69%	1	38.09%					1	14.56%														0.35%
23 1982	4	2	41.68%		2.30%	1	39.82%		0.00%			1	16.20%														
24 1982	4	2	42.55%		2.87%	2	39.42%						14.88%														0.28%
25 1987	4	1	30.50%		2.13%	2	39.14%		1.28%			1	16.72%		10.24%												
26 1989	4	1	35.93%		3.36%	2	39.63%					1	18.08%		2.68%												0.32%
27 1992	4	1	33.52%	1	13.75%	2	38.08%		0.88%				0.37%				12.90%										0.51%
28 1997	4	2	30.12%		8.13%	2	36.44%		3.56%						4.25%		10.73%										6.77%
29 2002	4	1	29.09%	1	20.98%	2	41.31%		5.73%		2.48%																0.41%
30 2007	4	1	30.85%	1	20.91%	2	37.97%		6.82%		2.92%																0.52%
31 2011	4	2	36.62%	1	30.85%		16.94%	1	11.05%		1.12%																3.43%
1918-2011	**119**	**43**	**33.44%**	**11**	**10.60%**	**46**	**39.03%**	**7**	**2.30%**		**0.30%**	**4**	**3.42%**		**0.65%**		**0.89%**		**1.20%**		**0.35%**	**3**	**2.39%**	**1**	**0.69%**	**4**	**4.74%**
National	**4,618**	**1,453**	**30.77%**	**482**	**11.53%**	**1,985**	**41.86%**	**232**	**1.99%**	**16**	**0.75%**	**17**	**0.78%**	**44**	**1.42%**	**8**	**0.22%**	**43**	**1.08%**	**9**	**0.16%**	**42**	**0.90%**	**11**	**0.30%**	**276**	**8.22%**

CORK NORTH-CENTRAL 2011

"Massive swing to the left in Cork North-Central"

The redrawing of the boundaries here saw a population of 8,559 transferred from Cork East and Cork North West into this constituency. It meant that Cork North Central was extended further northwards and westwards into the rural areas and the commuter towns north of Cork City.

Another success for Sinn Féin, as Jonathan O'Brien headed the poll and reached the quota seven counts later. He received two and a half thousand transfers when the Socialist Party's Mick Barry was eliminated on the eighth count. Barry significantly improved his own vote over 2007, though without coming close to taking the seat that one opinion poll had seemed to promise.

Fianna Fail was very satisfied with its performance. Noel O'Flynn had stood down at the behest of party leader Micheál Martin, so as to maximise the chances that Billy Kelleher, as Fianna Fail's sole candidate, would be re-elected. Given how well this strategy worked here, Martin may wish he had been firmer with some other recalcitrant incumbents. The Fianna Fail vote dropped from 36% to 15%, but Kelleher just managed to keep his nose ahead of the two Fine Gael candidates to take the third seat. Kelleher was aided by the expansion of the constituency to include some rural areas from Cork East and Cork North West into this predominantly urban constituency.

Both government parties had entertained hopes of taking two seats but had to settle for one. Labour became the strongest party, with 26 per cent of the votes. Its votes were shared fairly evenly between incumbent Kathleen Lynch and running mate John Gilroy. Given that Gilroy was only 63 votes behind Fine Gael's Dara Murphy when he was eliminated, it is possible that a more even distribution would have enabled Gilroy to reap sufficient Fine Gael transfers to take him above Billy Kelleher and into a seat.

The major increase in support for the left (Labour, Sinn Fein and the Socialist Party all making significant advances) meant that this was one of the very few constituencies in the country where Fine Gael's support actually fell compared with 2007. No doubt the retirement of 30-year veteran Bernard Allen was a factor in this. There was a major battle between the two first-time Fine Gael candidates as to which would win the seat. Dara Murphy trailed Glanmire-based Pat Burton throughout the count, until the elimination of Labour's Gilroy on the tenth count took him ahead of his running mate, and in the end he had a margin of nearly 300 votes to spare over Burton.

CORK NORTH-CENTRAL TDs 2011

JONATHAN O'BRIEN (SF)

11 Fairfield Green, Farranree, Cork; Tel: 021 4302530; Mobile: 085 2133907
Leinster House: 01 6184040; Email: jonathan.obrien@oireachtas.ie

Born Cork City, December 1971. Married to Gillian with two sons and two daughters. Educated North Monastery Secondary School, Cork. Contested Dail elections in Cork North Central in 2002 and 2007. First elected 2011.

Appointed Sinn Fein spokesperson on Justice, Equality and Defence 22nd March 2011. Member Committee on Finance, Public Expenditure and Reform. Member Committee on Justice, Defence and Equality. Contested 1999 local election in Cork North West. Co-opted as replacement for Don O'Leary in 2000. Retained his seat in 2004 and 2009. A keen follower of sports, he is a former player with Na Piarsaigh GAA Club and is currently a director of Cork City FC.

KATHLEEN LYNCH (LB)

Farrancleary House, 5 Assumption Road, Blackpool, Cork; Tel: 021 4399930;
Department of Health & Children: Tel: 01 6354426; Email: kathleen.lynch@oireachtas.ie
Website: www.labour.ie/kathleenlynch

Born Cork City, 7th June 1953. Married to Bernard Lynch, three daughters, one son. Educated Blackpool NS, Cork. Minister of State. Contested 1992 general election in Cork South Central for The Workers Party. First elected to the Dail in a by-election in 1994 for Democratic Left in Cork North Central. Lost her seat in 1997 but following merger between DL and Labour, successfully contested 2002 election as a Labour candidate. Retained her seat in 2007 and 2011.

Appointed Minister of State at the Department of Health and at Department of Justice, Equality and Defence with special responsibility for Disability, Older People, Equality and Mental Health, 10th March 2011. Labour spokesperson on Disability Issues and Equality 2007-2011. Member Joint Committee on Health and Children 2007-2011. Spokesperson Consumer Affairs 2002-2007. Member Joint Committee on Justice, Equality, Defence and Women's Rights 2002-2007. Member Joint Committee on Enterprise and Small Business 2002-2006. Former member Constitutional Review Committee. Member Cork City Council 1985-2003. Board member Southern Health Board. Member Cork City Development Board. Board Member Cork Opera House. Sister-in-law of Ciaran Lynch TD for Cork South Central since 2007.

BILLY KELLEHER (FF)

Tower View, Ballyphilip, White's Cross, Glanmire, Co. Cork; Tel: 021 4821045
Constituency Office: 28A Ballyhooley Road, Dillon's Cross, Cork; Tel: 021 4502289,
Mobile; 087 2580521; Leinster House: 01 6183219; Email: billy.kelleher@oireachtas.ie
Website: www.billykelleher.com

Born Cork 20th January 1968. Married to Liza Davis, three children. Educated Sacred Heart College, Carrignavar, Co. Cork, Agricultural College, Pallaskenry, Co. Limerick. Farmer. Contested 1992 general election and November 1994 by-election. First elected 1997 and at each subsequent election.

Appointed Fianna Fail Spokesperson on Health 12th April 2011. Member Committee on Health and Children. Minister of State at the Department of Enterprise and Employment with special responsibility for Trade and Commerce 2009-2011. Minister of State at the Department of Enterprise and Employment with special responsibility for Labour Affairs, 2007-2011. Deputy Government Whip, 2002-2007. Former Member Joint Committee on Environment and Local Government. Senator 1993-1997 (Taoiseach's nominee). Fianna Fail Seanad spokesperson on Social Welfare 1993-1997. Was the youngest Fianna Fail candidate in the 1992 general election. Member Cork City Council 1999-2003. Member IFA, GAA.

DARA MURPHY (FG)

Gardener's Hill, St. Luke's Cross, Cork; Mobile: 086 2533729;
Leinster House: 01 6183862; Email: dara.murphy@oireachtas.ie

Born Cork 2nd December 1969. Married to Tanya, three daughters. Educated. Christian Brothers College, Cork; UCC (Economics). Formerly self-employed in catering industry. Elected at his first attempt in 2011.

Member Committee on Foreign Affairs and Trade. Contested 1999 local election in Cork North East. First elected 2004. Retained his seat in 2009. Lord Mayor of Cork 2009/2010.

	CORK NORTH-CENTRAL 2011 FIRST PREFERENCE VOTES						
	Seats	4			10,428		
	Candidate	Party	1st	%	Quota	Count	Status
1	**O'Brien, Jonathan**	**SF**	**7,923**	**15.20%**	**0.76**	**8**	**Made Quota**
2	**Lynch, Kathleen***	**LB**	**7,676**	**14.72%**	**0.74**	**10**	**Made Quota**
3	**Kelleher, Billy***	**FF**	**7,896**	**15.14%**	**0.76**	**11**	**Elected**
4	**Murphy, Dara**	**FG**	**6,597**	**12.65%**	**0.63**	**11**	**Elected**
5	Burton, Pat	FG	7,072	13.56%	0.68	11	Not Elected
6	Gilroy, John	LB	6,125	11.75%	0.59	9	Eliminated
7	Barry, Mick	SP	4,803	9.21%	0.46	8	Eliminated
8	O'Sullivan, Pádraig	NV	1,020	1.96%	0.10	7	No Expenses
9	Conway, Kevin	NP	958	1.84%	0.09	6	No Expenses
10	Tynan, Ted	WP	681	1.31%	0.07	5	No Expenses
11	Walsh, Ken	GP	524	1.01%	0.05	4	No Expenses
12	Rea, Harry	CS	324	0.62%	0.03	3	No Expenses
13	Adams, John	CPPC	282	0.54%	0.03	2	No Expenses
14	Ashu-Arrah, Benjamin	NP	161	0.31%	0.02	1	No Expenses
15	O'Rourke, Fergus	NP	95	0.18%	0.01	1	No Expenses
15	***Outgoing**		**52,137**	**100.00%**	**10,428**	**2,608**	**No Expenses**

CORK NORTH-CENTRAL 2011 PARTY VOTE												
	2011					2007					Change	
Party	Cand	1st	%	Quota	Seats	Cand	1st	%	Quota	Seats	%	Seats
FG	2	13,669	26.22%	1.31	1	2	11,674	27.57%	1.38	1	-1.35%	
LB	2	13,801	26.47%	1.32	1	1	5,221	12.33%	0.62	1	+14.14%	
FF	1	7,896	15.14%	0.76	1	2	15,136	35.74%	1.79	2	-20.60%	-1
SF	1	7,923	15.20%	0.76	1	1	3,456	8.16%	0.41		+7.04%	+1
SP	1	4,803	9.21%	0.46		1	1,700	4.01%	0.20		+5.20%	
GP	1	524	1.01%	0.05		1	1,503	3.55%	0.18		-2.54%	
WP	1	681	1.31%	0.07		1	263	0.62%	0.03		+0.69%	
CS	1	324	0.62%	0.03							+0.62%	
Others	5	2,516	4.83%	0.24		4	3,394	8.01%	0.40		-3.19%	
Total	**15**	**52,137**	**100.0%**	**10,428**	**4**	**13**	**42,347**	**100.0%**	**8,470**	**4**	**0.00%**	
Electorate		**75,302**	**69.24%**				**67,777**	**62.48%**			**+6.76%**	
Spoiled		**572**	**1.09%**				**471**	**1.10%**			**-0.01%**	
Turnout		**52,709**	**70.00%**				**42,818**	**63.17%**			**+6.82%**	

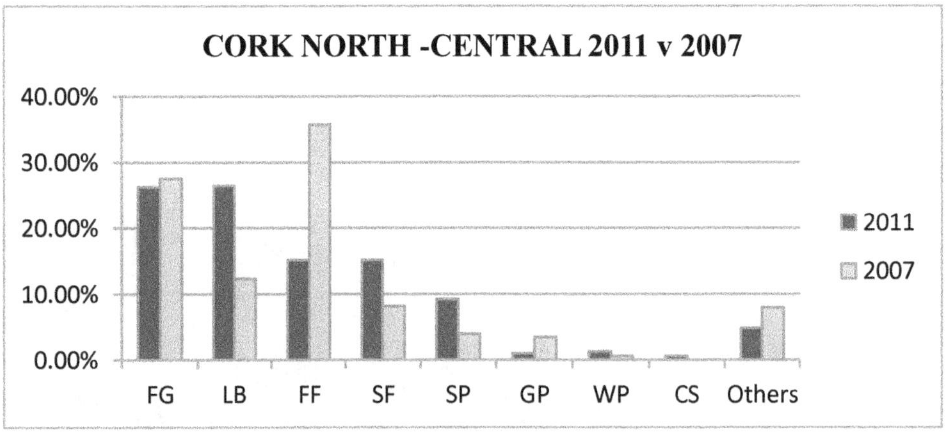

CORK NORTH-CENTRAL 2011 COUNT DETAILS												
Seats 4											Quota	10,428
Candidate	Party	1st	2nd Ashu O'Rourke	3rd Adams Votes	4th Rea Votes	5th Walsh Votes	6th Tynan Votes	7th O'Sullivan Conway	8th Barry Votes	9th O'Brien Surplus	10th Gilroy Votes	11th Lynch Surplus
			+19	+36	+44	+31	+201	+313	+2,564	-703		
O'Brien, Jonathan	SF	7,923	7,942	7,978	8,022	8,053	8,254	8,567	11,131	10,428	10,428	10,428
			+20	+38	+15	+98	+106	+283	+1,268	+411	+4,173	-3,660
Lynch, Kathleen*	LB	7,676	7,696	7,734	7,749	7,847	7,953	8,236	9,504	9,915	14,088	10,428
			+37	+8	+40	+42	+34	+327	+158	+32	+609	+412
Kelleher, Billy*	FF	7,896	7,933	7,941	7,981	8,023	8,057	8,384	8,542	8,574	9,183	9,595
			+18	+27	+40	+86	+41	+229	+233	+85	+1,011	+1,148
Murphy, Dara	FG	6,597	6,615	6,642	6,682	6,768	6,809	7,038	7,271	7,356	8,367	9,515
			+32	+13	+38	+85	+23	+322	+193	+38	+637	+780
Burton, Pat	FG	7,072	7,104	7,117	7,155	7,240	7,263	7,585	7,778	7,816	8,453	9,233
			+9	+20	+4	+87	+58	+356	+497	+137	-7,293	
Gilroy, John	LB	6,125	6,134	6,154	6,158	6,245	6,303	6,659	7,156	7,293	Eliminated	
			+23	+50	+27	+37	+191	+188	-5,319			
Barry, Mick	SP	4,803	4,826	4,876	4,903	4,940	5,131	5,319	Eliminated			
			+30	+35	+51	+47	+47	-1,230				
O'Sullivan, Pádraig	NV	1,020	1,050	1,085	1,136	1,183	1,230	Eliminated				
			+11	+27	+24	+9	+4	-1,033				
Conway, Kevin	NP	958	969	996	1,020	1,029	1,033	Eliminated				
			+7	+19	+17	+17	-741					
Tynan, Ted	WP	681	688	707	724	741	Eliminated					
			+6	+19	+9	-558						
Walsh, Ken	GP	524	530	549	558	Eliminated						
			+2	+5	-331							
Rea, Harry	CS	324	326	331	Eliminated							
			+31	-313								
Adams, John	CPPC	282	313	Eliminated								
			-161									
Ashu-Arrah, Benjamin	NP	161	Eliminated									
			-95									
O'Rourke, Fergus	NP	95	Eliminated									
Non-transferable			+11	+16	+22	+19	+36	+245	+406		+863	+1,320
Cumulative			11	27	49	68	104	349	755	755	1,618	2,938
Total		**52,137**	**52,137**	**52,137**	**52,137**	**52,137**	**52,137**	**52,137**	**52,137**	**52,137**	**52,137**	**52,137**

CORK NORTH-CENTRAL 2011 TRANSFER ANALYSIS										
From	**To**	**FG**	**LB**	**FF**	**SF**	**SP**	**GP**	**WP**	**Others**	**Non Trans**
LB	10,953	3,576	4,173	1,021						2,183
		32.65%	*38.10%*	*9.32%*						*19.93%*
SF	703	123	548	32						
		17.50%	*77.95%*	*4.55%*						
SP	5,319	426	1,765	158	2,564					406
		8.01%	*33.18%*	*2.97%*	*48.20%*					*7.63%*
GP	558	171	185	42	31	37		17	56	19
		30.65%	*33.15%*	*7.53%*	*5.56%*	*6.63%*		*3.05%*	*10.04%*	*3.41%*
WP	741	64	164	34	201	191			51	36
		8.64%	*22.13%*	*4.59%*	*27.13%*	*25.78%*			*6.88%*	*4.86%*
Others	3,163	719	745	412	412	288	34	43	216	294
		22.73%	*23.55%*	*13.03%*	*13.03%*	*9.11%*	*1.07%*	*1.36%*	*6.83%*	*9.29%*
Total	**21,437**	**5,079**	**7,580**	**1,699**	**3,208**	**516**	**34**	**60**	**323**	**2,938**
		23.69%	***35.36%***	***7.93%***	***14.96%***	***2.41%***	***0.16%***	***0.28%***	***1.51%***	***13.71%***

CORK NORTH-CENTRAL		
MAIN BOUNDARY CHANGES		
Dail	**Constituency**	**Seats**
22 (1981) - 29 (2002)	Cork North-Central	5
30 (2007) - 31 (2011)	Cork North-Central	4

CORK NORTH-CENTRAL													
ALL TDs 1981-2011													
	Surname	**Forename**	**Party**	**Elected**									**Total**
1	Allen	Bernard	FG	81	82	82	87	89	92	97	02	07	9
2	Burke**	Liam	FG	81	82	82	87	92	97				6
3	Wallace	Dan	FF	82N	87	89	92	97	02				6
4	Lyons	Denis	FF	81	82	82	87	89					5
5	Lynch**	Kathleen	LB	94*	02	07	11						4
6	Kelleher	Billy	FF	97	02	07	11						4
7	O'Sullivan**	Toddy	LB	81	82	82							3
8	Quill	Mairin	PD	87	89	92							3
9	O'Flynn	Noel	FF	97	02	07							3
10	French**	Sean	FF	81	82								2
11	O'Sullivan	Gerry	LB	89	92								2
12	O'Brien	Jonathan	SF	11									1
13	Murphy	Dara	FG	11									1
13	**Total**					*** Includes 1 By-Election**							**49**
	**** Also elected in another constituency**												
1	French**	Sean	FF	Cork City			67*	69	73	77			4
2	Burke**	Liam	FG	Cork City			69	73	79*				3
3	O'Sullivan**	Toddy	LB	Cork SC			87	89	92				3
3	**Total**					*** Includes 2 By-Elections**							**10**

Minister of State Kathleen Lynch TD with Fr. Peter McVerry

CORK NORTH-CENTRAL 1981-2011

		FG		LB		FF		SF		SP		GP		WP		CS		PD		DL		Others	
Dail	Seats	S	% Vote	S	% Vote	S	% Vote	S	% Vote	S	% Vote	S	% Vote	S	% Vote	S	% Vote	S	% Vote	S	% Vote	S	% Vote
22 1981	5	2	34.02%	1	15.76%	2	37.95%		6.05%						3.30%								2.91%
23 1982	5	2	35.71%	1	13.22%	2	**43.12%**								2.26%								5.69%
24 1982	5	2	**36.01%**	1	13.15%	2	42.51%								4.29%								4.03%
25 1987	5	2	26.24%		8.58%	2	37.21%		1.57%						6.06%			1	**16.72%**				3.62%
26 1989	5	1	26.16%	1	17.11%	2	32.94%		1.86%						**8.23%**			1	10.19%				3.51%
27 1992	5	2	22.74%	1	22.29%	1	28.26%		1.38%				1.82%		2.64%			1	11.56%		4.00%		5.31%
28 1997	5	2	30.16%		5.27%	3	35.53%		3.76%				3.04%		1.24%		**1.77%**		7.51%		**7.15%**		4.57%
29 2002	5	1	20.38%	1	11.77%	3	41.48%		6.34%		2.07%		2.56%		1.01%		0.48%		6.92%				6.99%
30 2007	4	1	27.57%	1	12.33%	2	35.74%		8.16%		4.01%		**3.55%**		0.62%								**8.01%**
31 2011	4	1	26.22%	1	**26.47%**	1	15.14%	1	**15.20%**		**9.21%**		1.01%		1.31%		0.62%						4.83%
1981-2011	**48**	**16**	**28.44%**	**8**	**14.84%**	**20**	**34.60%**	**1**	**4.67%**		**1.68%**		**1.20%**		**3.03%**		**0.30%**	**3**	**5.20%**		**1.11%**		**4.95%**
National	**1,660**	**561**	**30.73%**	**201**	**11.63%**	**716**	**39.85%**	**26**	**3.69%**	**4**	**0.37%**	**16**	**1.73%**	**17**	**1.66%**		**0.09%**	**44**	**3.28%**	**8**	**0.51%**	**67**	**6.45%**

CORK NORTH-WEST 2011

"First ever woman elected in Cork North-West"

A population of 4,334 from the areas of Kilcullen, Dromore, Mountrivers and Kilshannig were moved to Cork North Central in a change to this constituency's boundaries since 2007.

This used to be solid Fine Gael territory, with the party taking two of the three seats at each of the six elections of the 1981–1992 period. In 1997 Fianna Fail moved into the majority position and had remained there ever since, but the nationwide swing away from Fianna Fail and towards Fine Gael made it a virtual certainty that Fine Gael would pick up a second seat, and so it did.

Michael Creed was sure to head the poll – though his decision to oppose Enda Kenny in the failed heave of June 2010 may have cost him a junior ministerial position – and the main interest within Fine Gael lay in the race between the other two candidates. In the event Áine Collins won almost twice as many votes as Derry Canty, whose base in the south of the constituency meant that the odds were always against him. Collins, centrally located near Millstreet, became the first woman ever elected for the constituency.

Labour's Martin Coughlan performed creditably but he needed to do a little better than this to pick up a seat in an area where Labour has had no representation since Paddy McAuliffe lost his seat in 1969.

Fianna Fail's performance was disastrous by the standards of previous elections but not bad in the context of 2011. Batt O'Keeffe's arrival in the constituency in 2007, following a redrawing of the boundaries, had caused some upheaval, and he departed in even more turbulent circumstances. During the fateful 18 hours that spelled the end of the government on 19–20 January, he both resigned from government and stated that he would not be contesting the election, leaving the party's fortunes in Cork North-West in the hands of Michael Moynihan, a TD since 1997. With the aid of nearly 1,700 transfers from his running mate Daithí Ó Donnabháin, Moynihan, well ensconced locally though with no national profile, took the second seat fairly comfortably.

Fine Gael team in Cork North-West
Derry Canty, Áine Collins, Michael Creed

CORK NORTH-WEST TDs 2011

MICHAEL CREED (FG)

1 Sullane Weirs, Killarney Road, Macroom, Co. Cork; Tel: 026 42944; Mobile 087 2424631
Constituency Office: Main Street, Macroom; Tel: 026 41835; Leinster House: 01 6183525;
Email: michael.creed@oireachtas.ie; Website: www.michaelcreed.finegael.ie

Born Cork 29th June 1963. Married to Sinead, two sons, one daughter. Educated St. Colman's College, Fermoy, Co. Cork; De La Salle, Macroom; UCC (BA, HDipEd); College of Commerce, Rathmines. Businessman and Farmer. First elected 1989. Re-elected 1992 and 1997. Lost his seat in 2002 and re-elected 2007. Retained his seat in 2011.

Member Committee on Finance, Public Expenditure and Reform. Member Committee on Justice, Defence and Equality Supported Richard Bruton in his failed attempt to oust Enda Kenny as party leader in June 2010. Fine Gael Spokesperson on Agriculture, Fisheries and Food, 2007-2010. Member Joint Committee on Agriculture, Fisheries and Food 2007-2011. Front bench spokesperson on Youth and Sport 1993-1993; on Health 1989-1993. Member Cork County Council 1985-2007 (Chairman 2005-2006). Son of Donal Creed, Dail deputy for Mid-Cork 1965-1981 and for Cork North West 1981-1989. Minister of State at Department of Education 1982-1986, at the Department of Health June-November 1981 and at the Department of the Environment 1981-1982.

MICHAEL MOYNIHAN (FF)

Meens, Kiskeam, Mallow, Co. Cork; Tel: 029 76200; Mobile: 087 2745810
Constituency Office: Percival Street, Kanturk, Co. Cork; Tel: 029 51299;
Leinster House: 01 6183595; Email: michael.moynihan@oireachtas.ie
Website: www.michaelmoynihantd.ie

Born Cork, 12th January 1968. Married to Brid O'Sullivan, one daughter. Educated Boherbue Comprehensive School, Mallow. Dairy Farmer. First elected 1997 and at each subsequent election.

Appointed Fianna Fail Spokesperson on Agriculture and Food 12th April 2011. Member Committee on Communications, Natural Resources and Agriculture. Chairman Committee on Economic and Regulatory Affairs 2007-2011. Member Joint Committee on Communications, Energy and Natural Resources and Member Joint Committee on Education and Science 2007-2011. Chairman Committee on Education and Science 2004-2007. Former Vice-chairman Joint Committee on Agriculture and Food. Former Member Joint Committees on Heritage & Irish Language; Agriculture, Food & the Marine; Environment & Local Government. Former National Chairman Ogra Fianna Fail. Member ICMSA. Life member Kiskeam GAA Club. Vice-Chairman Kiskeam Sean Moylan Commemoration Committee.

ÁINE COLLINS (FG)

Laught, Rathcoole, Mallow, Co. Cork; Mobile: 087 2326945;
Constituency Office: 2 The Square, Millstreet; Tel: 029 71845;
Leinster House: 01 6183873; Email: aine.collins@oireachtas.ie

Born Banteer, Co. Cork. 9th September 1969. Married to Paul with three children, Ciara, Thomas and Lily. Educated Millstreet Secondary School, North East London Polytechnic. Accountant and Business Consultant. First elected 2011.

Member Joint Administration Committee. Member Committee on Jobs, Social Protection and Education. Elected to Dail Eireann in 2011 at her first attempt and she had never contested any election prior to this.

CORK NORTH-WEST 2011							
FIRST PREFERENCE VOTES							
	Seats	3			11,436		
	Candidate	Party	1st	%	Quota	Count	Status
1	**Creed, Michael***	**FG**	**10,112**	**22.11%**	**0.88**	**5**	**Made Quota**
2	**Moynihan, Michael***	**FF**	**8,845**	**19.34%**	**0.77**	**6**	**Elected**
3	**Collins, Áine**	**FG**	**7,884**	**17.24%**	**0.69**	**6**	**Elected**
4	Coughlan, Martin	LB	6,421	14.04%	0.56	6	Not Elected
5	Canty, Derry	FG	4,325	9.46%	0.38	4	Eliminated
6	O'Grady, Des	SF	3,405	7.44%	0.30	3	Eliminated
7	Ó Donnabháin, Daithí	FF	2,545	5.56%	0.22	2	No Expenses
8	Foley, Ann	PBPA	1,552	3.39%	0.14	1	No Expenses
9	Collins, Mark	GP	651	1.42%	0.06	1	No Expenses
9	***Outgoing**		**45,740**	**100.00%**	**11,436**	**2,860**	**No Expenses**

CORK NORTH-WEST 2011												
PARTY VOTE												
	2011					2007					Change	
Party	Cand	1st	%	Quota	Seats	Cand	1st	%	Quota	Seats	%	Seats
FG	3	22,321	48.80%	1.95	2	2	17,913	38.42%	1.54	1	+10.38%	+1
LB	1	6,421	14.04%	0.56		1	2,288	4.91%	0.20		+9.13%	
FF	2	11,390	24.90%	1.00	1	3	24,732	53.05%	2.12	2	-28.15%	-1
SF	1	3,405	7.44%	0.30							+7.44%	
PBPA	1	1,552	3.39%	0.14							+3.39%	
GP	1	651	1.42%	0.06		1	1,687	3.62%	0.14		-2.20%	
Total	**9**	**45,740**	**100.0%**	**11,436**	**3**	**7**	**46,620**	**100.0%**	**11,656**	**3**	**0.00%**	**0**
Electorate		**62,870**	**72.75%**				**64,085**	**72.75%**			**+0.01%**	
Spoiled		**454**	**0.98%**				**401**	**0.85%**			**+0.13%**	
Turnout		**46,194**	**73.48%**				**47,021**	**73.37%**			**+0.10%**	

CORK NORTH-WEST 2011						
TRANSFER ANALYSIS						
From	To	FG	LB	FF	SF	Non Trans
FG	6,071	4,122	1,176	315		458
		67.90%	*19.37%*	*5.19%*		*7.54%*
FF	2,633	518	189	1,690	136	100
		19.67%	*7.18%*	*64.19%*	*5.17%*	*3.80%*
SF	4,052	1,152	1,697	409		794
		28.43%	*41.88%*	*10.09%*		*19.60%*
PBPA	1,552	448	454	178	360	112
		28.87%	*29.25%*	*11.47%*	*23.20%*	*7.22%*
GP	651	188	191	74	151	47
		28.88%	*29.34%*	*11.37%*	*23.20%*	*7.22%*
Total	**14,959**	**6,428**	**3,707**	**2,666**	**647**	**1,511**
		42.97%	***24.78%***	***17.82%***	***4.33%***	***10.10%***

CORK NORTH-WEST 2011 COUNT DETAILS							
Seats	3					Quota	11,436
Candidate	**Party**	**1st**	**2nd** Foley Collins	**3rd** O Donnabhain Votes	**4th** O'Grady Votes	**5th** Canty Votes	**6th** Creed Surplus
Creed, Michael*	FG	10,112	*+152* 10,264	*+162* 10,426	*+371* 10,797	*+1,618* 12,415	*-979* 11,436
Moynihan, Michael*	FF	8,845	*+164* 9,009	*+1,690* 10,699	*+409* 11,108	*+254* 11,362	*+61* 11,423
Collins, Áine	FG	7,884	*+339* 8,223	*+122* 8,345	*+393* 8,738	*+1,796* 10,534	*+708* 11,242
Coughlan, Martin	LB	6,421	*+645* 7,066	*+189* 7,255	*+1,697* 8,952	*+966* 9,918	*+210* 10,128
Canty, Derry	FG	4,325	*+145* 4,470	*+234* 4,704	*+388* 5,092	*-5,092* Eliminated	
O'Grady, Des	SF	3,405	*+511* 3,916	*+136* 4,052	*-4,052* Eliminated		
Ó Donnabháin, Daithí	FF	2,545	*+88* 2,633	*-2,633* Eliminated			
Foley, Ann	PBPA	1,552	*-1,552* Eliminated				
Collins, Mark	GP	651	*-651* Eliminated				
Non-transferable Cumulative			*+159* 159	*+100* 259	*+794* 1,053	*+458* 1,511	 1,511
Total		**45,740**	**45,740**	**45,740**	**45,740**	**45,740**	**45,740**

CORK NORTH-WEST ALL TDs 1981-2011											
	Surname	**Forename**	**Party**	**Elected**							**Total**
1	Crowley	Frank	FG	81	82	82	87	89	92		6
2	Moynihan	Donal	FF	82	87	92	97	02			5
3	Creed**	Michael	FG	89	92	97	07	11			5
4	Creed**	Donal	FG	81	82	82	87				4
5	Moynihan	Michael	FF	97	02	07	11				4
6	Meaney**	Thomas	FF	81	82						2
7	Kelly	Larry	FF	89							1
8	Murphy	Gerard	FG	02							1
9	O'Keeffe**	Batt	FF	07							1
10	Collins	Aine	FG	11							1
10	**Total**										**30**
	**** Also elected in another constituency**										
1	Creed**	Donal	FG	Cork Mid			65	69	73	77	4
2	Meaney**	Thomas	FF	Cork Mid			65	69	73	77	4
3	O'Keeffe**	Batt	FF	Cork SC			87	92	97	02	4
3	**Total**										**12**

CORK NORTH-WEST		
MAIN BOUNDARY CHANGES		
Dail	Constituency	Seats
22 (1981) - 31 (2011)	Cork North West	3

CORK NORTH-WEST 1981-2011																				
		FG		LB		FF		SF		PBPA		GP		CS		PD		Others		
Dail		Seats	S	% Vote	S	% Vote	S	% Vote	S	% Vote	S	% Vote	S	% Vote	S	% Vote	S	% Vote	S	% Vote
22	1981	3	2	42.06%		11.92%	1	46.02%												
23	1982	3	2	43.43%		9.14%	1	47.44%												
24	1982	3	2	48.93%		6.62%	1	44.45%												
25	1987	3	2	43.37%			1	45.26%										11.36%		
26	1989	3	2	54.56%			1	44.64%												0.80%
27	1992	3	2	44.02%		14.19%	1	41.25%												0.54%
28	1997	3	1	41.12%		7.40%	2	46.50%												4.97%
29	2002	3	1	42.08%		6.87%	2	50.06%								0.99%				
30	2007	3	1	38.42%		4.91%	2	53.05%						3.62%						
31	2011	3	2	48.80%		14.04%	1	24.90%		7.44%		3.39%		1.42%						
1981-2011		**30**	**17**	**44.51%**		**7.65%**	**13**	**44.11%**		**0.93%**		**0.42%**		**0.64%**		**0.10%**		**1.04%**		**0.59%**
National		**1,660**	**561**	**30.73%**	**201**	**11.63%**	**716**	**39.85%**	**26**	**3.69%**	**2**	**0.15%**	**16**	**1.73%**		**0.09%**	**44**	**3.28%**	**94**	**8.84%**

CORK SOUTH-CENTRAL 2011

"Fianna Fáil hold two seats in party leader's constituency"

There were no changes to this urban constituency's boundaries since 2007.

In an election of such upheaval, the big story here was 'hardly any change'. Four of the five incumbents were re-elected, and there was no change of seats between parties. Moreover, it was possibly Fianna Fail's best result in the entire country, showing that Micheál Martin's accession to the party leadership certainly had some impact. The party's vote dropped by a mere 16 per cent on 2007 – the second smallest in the country – and it managed to hold both of the seats it won in 2007, one of only two constituencies where it did not lose a seat. Martin himself headed the poll – one of only two Fianna Fail candidates nationwide to do this – but the real test was whether the other Fianna Fail incumbent Michael McGrath, sometimes tipped as a future party leader himself, would join him in the Dáil. He did so with surprising ease, finishing over 2,000 votes ahead of the runner-up.

This runner-up was Sinn Fein's Chris O'Leary, who had switched both party and constituency since 2007, when he won a mere 1,503 votes as a Green candidate in Cork North-Central. Now he won more than three times as many votes as Green Senator Dan Boyle, whose defeat in 2007 had been one of the shocks of that election but whose support now plunged to a meagre 1,640 votes, only 500 more than he had received when he first stood way back in 1992.

The two parties of the incoming government had unspectacular results. The third seat that Fine Gael had targeted never came into view. Jerry Buttimer increased his own vote impressively and took the fourth seat, but his victim was Fine Gael incumbent Deirdre Clune, who has now been elected twice (1997 and 2007) but has never been re-elected. The Fine Gael vote management here was poor, in contrast to the machine-like efficacy achieved in most other constituencies, but even perfect vote management probably would not have delivered three seats on this occasion.

Labour doubled its vote, but the effect was only to turn a rather marginal seat into a safe one. Ciarán Lynch added over 3,000 votes to his 2007 tally, but it was to be his sister-in-law from Cork North-Central who got the call when the junior ministries were allocated.

Fianna Fail Leader Micheál Martin

CORK SOUTH-CENTRAL TDs 2011

MICHEÁL MARTIN (FF)

"Lios Laoi", 16 Silver Manor, Ballinlough, Cork;
Constituency Office: 137 Evergreen Road, Turners Cross, Cork; Tel: 021 4320088
Leinster House: 01 6184350; Email: michealmartin@eircom.net;
Website: www.michealmartin.ie

Born Cork 1st August 1960. Married to Mary O'Shea, two sons, one daughter. Educated Coláiste Chriost Rí, Cork and UCC (BA, HDip ED, MA). Leader of Fianna Fail and former Secondary School Teacher. First elected 1989 and at each subsequent election.

Elected eighth leader of Fianna Fail 26th January 2011. Party spokesperson on Northern Ireland. Resigned as Minister for Foreign Affairs on 19th January 2011 after challenging Taoiseach Brian Cowen's leadership. Minister for Foreign Affairs 7th May 2008-19th January 2011. Minister for Enterprise, Trade and Employment June 2007–May 2008. Minister for Enterprise, Trade and Employment 2004-2007. Minister for Health & Children 2000-2004. Minister for Education 1997-2000. Fianna Fail front bench spokesperson on Education and the Gaeltacht 1995-1997. Former Chairman of the Oireachtas All Party Committee on the Irish Language. Member Cork Corporation 1985-1997 (Lord Mayor of Cork 1992-1993). Former member of the Governing Body, UCC and of the Governing Body RTC. Former member of the ASTI. Member of Fianna Fail National Executive since 1988. Former National Chairman of Ogra Fianna Fail and was a member of the Commission on the Aims and Structures of Fianna Fail. Winner of the Cork Examiner Political Speaker of the Year Award 1987.

CIARÁN LYNCH (LB)

31 Yewlands, Maryborough Woods, Douglas, Co. Cork; Mobile: 086 6033923
Constituency Office: 29 St. Patrick's Mills, Douglas, Cork; Tel: 021 4366200;
Leinster House: 01 6183666; Email: ciaran.lynch@oireachtas.ie.
Website: www.ciaranlynch.ie

Born 13th June 1964. Married to Bernadette, one daughter, one son. Educated UCC (Social Studies); Waterford IT (Humanities). Formerly Adult Literacy Organiser, City of Cork VEC. First elected 2007. Retained his seat in 2011.

Appointed Chairman Committee on Environment, Transport, Culture and the Gaeltacht June 2011. Front Bench Spokesperson on Housing and Local Government 2007- 2011. Member Joint Committee on the Environment, Heritage and Local Government 2007-2011. Member Cork City Council 2004-2007. Member Teachers Union of Ireland; Adult Literacy Organisers Association National Executive; National Adult Literacy Agency; City of Cork VEC Adult Education Board; Cork City Community Education Network; Cork City Library Committee; Cork Community Research Co-operative; Cork Probation Hostel Management Committee; Kinsale Road Dump Action group; Carr's Hill Famine Cemetery Commemorative Committee; Gillabbey Anglers Association. Brother-in-law of Kathleen Lynch, TD for Cork North-Central 1994-1997 and 2002 to date.

SIMON COVENEY (FG)

The Rock, Carrigaline, Co. Cork; Mobile: 087 8321755
Constituency Office: 6a Anglesea Street, Cork; Tel: 021 4374200
Leinster House: 01 6183666; Email: simon.coveney@oireachtas.ie
Website: www.simoncoveney.ie

Born Cork, 16th June 1972. Married to Ruth Ferney, two daughters. Educated Clongowes Wood College, Co. Kildare; UCC; Gurteen Agricultural College, Royal Agriculture College, Gloucestershire (B.Sc in Agriculture and Land Management). Minister for Agriculture. Former farmer and sailing instructor. First elected at by-election October 1998 and at each subsequent general election.

Appointed Minister for Agriculture and Marine 9th March 2011. Front bench spokesperson on Transport 1st July 2010-March 2011. Supported Richard Bruton in his failed attempt to oust Enda Kenny as party leader in June 2010. Party spokesperson on Communications, Energy and Natural Resources, 2007-2010. Member Joint Committee on Communications, Energy and Natural Resources and Member Joint Committee on Climate Change and Energy Security 2007-2011. MEP 2004-2007. Spokesperson on Communications, Marine and Natural Resources 2002-2004. Member Joint Committee on Communications, Marine and Natural Resources 2002-2007. Spokesperson on Drugs and Youth Issues, Deputy Chief Whip and Secretary Fine Gael Parliamentary Party 1998-2002. Member Cork County Council 1999-2003. Member Southern Health Board 1999-2003. Played rugby for Garryowen, Cork Constitution and Crosshaven. Led the Sail Chernobyl Project which raised £500,000 for charity by sailing a boat around the world along with his sister and brothers. A fully qualified sailing instructor and lifeguard. Won 1998 by-election caused by the death of his father Hugh Coveney TD for Cork South Central 1982-February 82, November 1982–1987, 1994 (by-election) –1998.

JERRY BUTTIMER (FG)

25 Benvoirlich Estate, Bishopstown, Cork; Tel: 021 4541923; Mobile: 086 2356892
Constituency Office: 4A Glasheen Road, Cork; Tel: 021 4840652
Leinster House: 01 6183380; E-mail: jerry.buttimer@oireachtas.ie
Website: www. jerrybuttimer.finegael.ie; Twitter: twitter.com/jerrybuttimer@jerrybuttimer

Born Cork 18th March 1967. Single. Educated St. Finbarr's College, Farranferris; UCC and Maynooth. Secondary School Teacher and Director of Adult Education at Ballincollig Community School. Contested 2007 general election in Cork South-Central. First elected 2011.

Appointed Chairman Committee on Health and Children and Vice-Chairman Joint Administration Committee June 2011. Elected to Senate in 2007. Seanad spokesperson on Community, Rural and Gaeltacht Affairs 2007-2011. Member Joint Committee on Arts, Sport, Tourism, Community, Rural and Gaeltacht Affairs 2007-2011. Member Cork City Council 2004-2007. Former Youth Development Officer of Cork County GAA Board. Member Croke Park's Marketing Committee. Chairman Bishopstown GAA Club.

MICHAEL MCGRATH (FF)

4 North Lawn, Carrig na Curra, Carrigaline, Co. Cork; Tel: 021 4919689
Constituency Office: Kilmoney Road, Carrigaline, Co. Cork; Tel: 021 4376699,
Leinster House: Tel: 01 6183801; Mobile: 086 8393304;
Email: michael.mcgrath@oireachtas.ie; Website: www.michaelmcgrath.ie

Born Cork 23rd August 1976. Married to Sarah O'Brien, five children. Educated St. Peter's Community College, Passage West and UCC (BComm). Chartered Accountant. First elected 2007. Retained his seat in 2011.

Appointed Fianna Fail Spokesperson on Finance 4th August 2011. Member Committee on Finance, Public Expenditure and Reform. Spokesperson on Public Expenditure and Financial Sector Reform April–August 2011. Convenor Joint Committee on European Affairs October 2007-2011. Member Joint Committee on European Scrutiny and Member Joint Committee on Transport 2007-2011. Member Cork County Council 2004-2007. Member Passage West Town Council 1999-2007 (Chairman 2000-2001). Contested 2002 Seanad Election.

CORK SOUTH-CENTRAL 2011							
FIRST PREFERENCE VOTES							
	Seats	5			10,674		
	Candidate	Party	1st	%	Quota	Count	Status
1	**Martin, Micheál***	**FF**	**10,715**	**16.73%**	**1.00**	**1**	**Made Quota**
2	**Lynch, Ciarán***	**LB**	**8,481**	**13.24%**	**0.79**	**9**	**Made Quota**
3	**Coveney, Simon***	**FG**	**9,447**	**14.75%**	**0.89**	**10**	**Made Quota**
4	**Buttimer, Jerry**	**FG**	**7,128**	**11.13%**	**0.67**	**11**	**Made Quota**
5	**McGrath, Michael***	**FF**	**7,221**	**11.28%**	**0.68**	**12**	**Elected**
6	O'Leary, Chris	SF	5,250	8.20%	0.49	12	Not Elected
7	Clune, Deirdre*	FG	5,650	8.82%	0.53	10	Eliminated
8	Desmond, Paula	LB	3,388	5.29%	0.32	8	Eliminated
9	Finn, Mick	NP	2,386	3.73%	0.22	7	Eliminated
10	Boyle, Dan #	GP	1,640	2.56%	0.15	6	No Expenses
11	McCarthy, David	NV	880	1.37%	0.08	5	No Expenses
12	Neville, Ted	NP	523	0.82%	0.05	5	No Expenses
13	Ó Cadhla, Diarmaid	CPPC	508	0.79%	0.05	4	No Expenses
14	Dunphy, Sean	NP	448	0.70%	0.04	3	No Expenses
15	Isherwood, Eric	NP	193	0.30%	0.02	2	No Expenses
16	O'Driscoll, Finbar	NP	92	0.14%	0.01	2	No Expenses
17	Linehan, Gerard	NP	90	0.14%	0.01	2	No Expenses
17	***Outgoing # Former TD**		**64,040**	**100.00%**	**10,674**	**2,670**	**No Expenses**

CORK SOUTH-CENTRAL 2011												
PARTY VOTE												
	2011					2007					Change	
Party	Cand	1st	%	Quota	Seats	Cand	1st	%	Quota	Seats	%	Seats
FG	3	22,225	34.70%	2.08	2	3	16,782	28.41%	1.70	2	+6.29%	
LB	2	11,869	18.53%	1.11	1	1	5,466	9.25%	0.56	1	+9.28%	
FF	2	17,936	28.01%	1.68	2	3	26,154	44.28%	2.66	2	-16.27%	
SF	1	5,250	8.20%	0.49		1	3,020	5.11%	0.31		+3.09%	
GP	1	1,640	2.56%	0.15		1	4,945	8.37%	0.50		-5.81%	
PD						1	1,596	2.70%	0.16		-2.70%	
Others	8	5,120	8.00%	0.48		4	1,105	1.87%	0.11		+6.12%	
Total	**17**	**64,040**	**100.0%**	**10,674**	**5**	**14**	**59,068**	**100.0%**	**9,845**	**5**	**0.00%**	**0**
Electorate		**91,619**	**69.90%**				**91,090**	**64.85%**			**+5.05%**	
Spoiled		**624**	**0.96%**				**592**	**0.99%**			**-0.03%**	
Turnout		**64,664**	**70.58%**				**59,660**	**65.50%**			**+5.08%**	

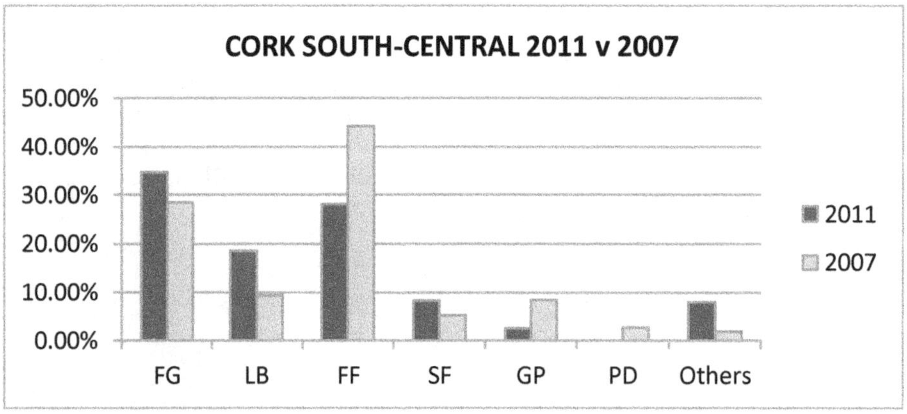

CORK SOUTH-CENTRAL 2011 COUNT DETAILS													
Seats	5											Quota	10,674
Candidate	Party	1st	2nd Martin Surplus	3rd Isherwood O'Driscoll Linehan	4th Dunphy Votes	5th O Cadhla Votes	6th McCarthy Neville Votes	7th Boyle Votes	8th Finn Votes	9th Desmond Votes	10th Lynch Surplus	11th Clune Votes	12th Buttimer Surplus
Martin, Micheál*	FF	10,715	-41 10,674	10,674	10,674	10,674	10,674	10,674	10,674	10,674	10,674	10,674	10,674
Lynch, Ciarán*	LB	8,481	+3 8,484	+32 8,516	+27 8,543	+50 8,593	+217 8,810	+408 9,218	+703 9,921	+2,644 12,565	-1,891 10,674	10,674	10,674
Coveney, Simon*	FG	9,447	+3 9,450	+21 9,471	+50 9,521	+37 9,558	+154 9,712	+264 9,976	+193 10,169	+362 10,531	+341 10,872	10,872	10,872
Buttimer, Jerry	FG	7,128	+2 7,130	+20 7,150	+23 7,173	+21 7,194	+133 7,327	+226 7,553	+269 7,822	+210 8,032	+378 8,410	+4,686 13,096	-2,422 10,674
McGrath, Michael*	FF	7,221	+27 7,248	+26 7,274	+53 7,327	+23 7,350	+134 7,484	+151 7,635	+276 7,911	+209 8,120	+273 8,393	+632 9,025	+998 10,023
O'Leary, Chris	SF	5,250	+1 5,251	+40 5,291	+28 5,319	+95 5,414	+274 5,688	+108 5,796	+667 6,463	+256 6,719	+549 7,268	+372 7,640	+547 8,187
Clune, Deirdre*	FG	5,650	+2 5,652	+20 5,672	+17 5,689	+20 5,709	+94 5,803	+179 5,982	+142 6,124	+240 6,364	+326 6,690	-6,690 Eliminated	
Desmond, Paula	LB	3,388	+1 3,389	+23 3,412	+43 3,455	+44 3,499	+110 3,609	+268 3,877	+250 4,127	-4,127 Eliminated			
Finn, Mick	NP	2,386	+1 2,387	+53 2,440	+100 2,540	+57 2,597	+285 2,882	+78 2,960	-2,960 Eliminated				
Boyle, Dan #	GP	1,640	+1 1,641	+9 1,650	+22 1,672	+36 1,708	+92 1,800	-1,800 Eliminated					
McCarthy, David	NV	880	880	+37 917	+35 952	+85 1,037	-1,037 Eliminated						
Neville, Ted	NP	523	523	+24 547	+34 581	+58 639	-639 Eliminated						
Ó Cadhla, Diarmaid	CPPC	508	508	+23 531	+32 563	-563 Eliminated							
Dunphy, Sean	NP	448	448	+33 481	-481 Eliminated								
Isherwood, Eric	NP	193	193	-193 Eliminated									
O'Driscoll, Finbar	NP	92	92	-92 Eliminated									
Linehan, Gerard	NP	90	90	-90 Eliminated									
Non-transferable Cumulative			0	+14 14	+17 31	+37 68	+183 251	+118 369	+460 829	+206 1,035	+24 1,059	+1,000 2,059	+877 2,936
Total		**64,040**	**64,040**	**64,040**	**64,040**	**64,040**	**64,040**	**64,040**	**64,040**	**64,040**	**64,040**	**64,040**	**64,040**

CORK SOUTH-CENTRAL 2011 TRANSFER ANALYSIS								
From	**To**	**FG**	**LB**	**FF**	**SF**	**GP**	**Others**	**Non Trans**
FG	9,112	4,686 *51.43%*		1,630 *17.89%*	919 *10.09%*			1,877 *20.60%*
LB	6,018	1,857 *30.86%*	2,644 *43.93%*	482 *8.01%*	805 *13.38%*			230 *3.82%*
FF	41	7 *17.07%*	4 *9.76%*	27 *65.85%*	1 *2.44%*	1 *2.44%*	1 *2.44%*	*0.00%*
GP	1,800	669 *37.17%*	676 *37.56%*	151 *8.39%*	108 *6.00%*		78 *4.33%*	118 *6.56%*
Others	6,055	1,214 *20.05%*	1,499 *24.76%*	512 *8.46%*	1,104 *18.23%*	159 *2.63%*	856 *14.14%*	711 *11.74%*
Total	**23,026**	**8,433** ***36.62%***	**4,823** ***20.95%***	**2,802** ***12.17%***	**2,937** ***12.76%***	**160** ***0.69%***	**935** ***4.06%***	**2,936** ***12.75%***

CORK SOUTH-CENTRAL MAIN BOUNDARY CHANGES		
Dail	Constituency	Seats
22 (1981) - 31 (2011)	Cork South-Central	5

CORK SOUTH-CENTRAL 1981-2011																			
		FG		LB		FF		SF		GP		WP		PD		DL		Others	
Dail	Seats	S	% Vote	S	% Vote	S	% Vote	S	% Vote	S	% Vote	S	% Vote	S	% Vote	S	% Vote	S	% Vote
22 1981	5	2	42.25%	1	13.94%	2	43.09%												0.72%
23 1982	5	2	39.63%	1	13.40%	2	41.84%												5.14%
24 1982	5	2	39.97%	1	13.14%	2	39.70%						3.00%						4.19%
25 1987	5	1	21.78%	1	8.64%	2	32.81%						4.18%	1	24.97%				7.62%
26 1989	5	1	25.53%	1	11.75%	2	40.68%						8.31%	1	13.44%				0.28%
27 1992	5	1	18.23%	1	18.03%	2	36.08%		1.10%		2.18%		0.32%	1	12.54%		4.74%		6.78%
28 1997	5	2	30.57%		8.92%	3	42.62%				6.58%				4.19%				7.13%
29 2002	5	1	19.40%		5.94%	3	48.57%		3.73%	1	8.96%								13.39%
30 2007	5	2	28.41%	1	9.25%	2	44.28%		5.11%		8.37%				2.70%				1.87%
31 2011	5	2	34.70%	1	18.53%	2	28.01%		8.20%		2.56%								8.00%
1981-2011	**50**	**16**	**29.80%**	**8**	**12.17%**	**22**	**39.55%**		**2.01%**	**1**	**3.00%**		**1.55%**	**3**	**5.85%**		**0.47%**		**5.61%**
National	**1,660**	**561**	**30.73%**	**201**	**11.63%**	**716**	**39.85%**	**26**	**3.69%**	**16**	**1.73%**	**17**	**1.66%**	**44**	**3.28%**	**8**	**0.51%**	**71**	**6.91%**

CORK SOUTH-CENTRAL ALL TDs 1981-2011											
	Surname	Forename	Party	Elected							Total
1	Barry**	Peter	FG	81	82	82	87	89	92		6
2	Martin	Micheal	FF	89	92	97	02	07	11		6
3	Wyse**	Pierse	PD	81	82	82	87	89			5
4	Coveney	Hugh	FG	81	82N	94*	97				4
5	Dennehy	John	FF	87	89	97	02				4
6	O'Keeffe**	Batt	FF	87	92	97	02				4
7	Coveney	Simon	FG	98*	02	07	11				4
8	Desmond**	Eileen	LB	81	82	82					3
9	Fitzgerald**	Gene	FF	81	82	82					3
10	O'Sullivan**	Toddy	LB	87	89	92					3
11	Clune	Deirdre	FG	97	07						2
12	Lynch	Ciaran	LB	07	11						2
13	McGrath	Michael	FF	07	11						2
14	Corr	James	FG	82F							1
15	Cox	Pat	PD	92							1
16	Boyle	Dan	GP	02							1
17	Buttimer	Jerry	FG	11							1
17	**Total**			*** Includes 2 By-Elections**						*	**52**
	**** Also elected in another constituency**										
1	Desmond**	Eileen	LB	Cork Mid		65*	65	73	77		4
2	Wyse**	Pierse	FF	Cork City		65	69	73	77		4
3	Barry**	Peter	FG	Cork City		69	73	77			3
4	Fitzgerald**	Gene	FF	Cork Mid		72*	73	77			3
5	O'Sullivan**	Toddy	LB	Cork NC		81	82	82			3
6	O'Keeffe**	Batt	FF	Cork NW		07					1
6	**Total**			*** Includes 2 By-Elections**						*	**18**

CORK SOUTH-WEST 2011

"Red back on the map of the country's most south-westerly constituency"

There were no changes to the boundaries of this constituency since 2007.

A constituency ever since 1923, Cork South West was represented by a Labour TD from then until 1981. Timothy J. Murphy carried the torch for over 25 years, was succeeded in 1949 by his son William (at 21 years and 29 days on polling day still the youngest TD ever), and in 1951 Michael Pat Murphy (no relation) won the seat that he held comfortably until he retired in 1981. Since then there had been a consistent pattern of 2 Fine Gael seats and 1 for Fianna Fail, broken only when Fianna Fail, gained a seat in 2002.

With both Fine Gael veterans Jim O'Keeffe (first elected 1977) and P. J. Sheehan (first elected 1981) standing down, and Labour having its best opportunity for 30 years to put some red back on the map of the country's most south-westerly constituency, there was a good chance that Cork South West would return three brand new TDs. Labour candidate Senator Michael McCarthy duly ensured this. Despite a fairly modest increase in his first preference vote, he did well on transfers (nearly 2,200 from the elimination of the bottom seven candidates) and held off the Fianna Fail challenge by 600 votes.

Fine Gael was certain to hold its two seats, and nominated three candidates, who all polled well. Jim Daly from Skibbereen, more or less in the centre of the constituency, comfortably headed the poll, and it was Noel Harrington from Castletownbere who took the other seat, with 456 votes to spare over the third Fine Gael candidate, Kevin Murphy, when it mattered.

Fianna Fail was left to contemplate the wreckage of its campaign. Its two candidates won nearly 10,800 votes between them – over 4,000 more than Labour – yet neither was elected. When incumbent Christy O'Sullivan – a surprise winner in 2007, and still regarded by some in Fianna Fail as a blow-in as he had previously stood as an independent – was eliminated on the fourth count, only 57 per cent of his transfers went to his running mate Denis O'Donovan, who has contested every election since 1987 but was elected only once, in 2002.

Minister Jimmy Deenihan, Maureen O'Hara, Noel Harrington TD

CORK SOUTH-WEST TDs 2011

JIM DALY (FG)

5 Millgrove, Clonakilty, Co. Cork; Tel: 023 35444; Mobile: 087 7465397
Constituency Office: Fernhill Road, Clonakilty; Tel: 023 8843868
Leinster House: 01 6183886; Email: jim.daly@oireachtas.ie
Website: www.jindalytd.ie; Twitter; @jimdalytd; Facebook: www.facebook.com/jimdaly

Born Cork, 20th December 1972. Married to Verge, four sons Daniel, Denis, Conor and Ciaran. Educated Coláiste Mhuire Cobh, NUI Maynooth and Mary Immaculate College, Limerick. Former Primary School Teacher. Elected at his first attempt in 2011.

Member Committee on Finance, Public Expenditure and Reform. Contested 2007 Seanad election on Labour Panel. First elected to Cork County Council in the Skibbereen electoral area in 2004. Retained his seat in 2009. Mayor of Cork 2010.

NOEL HARRINGTON (FG)

Bank Place, Castletownbere, Co. Cork; Mobile: 086 8567178
Constituency Office: High Street, Bantry; Tel027 56222
Leinster House: 01 6183956; Email: noel.harrington@oireachtas.ie
Website: www.noelharrington.com; Twitter: twitter.com/nharrington2;
Facebook: facebook.com/noelharrington

Born Castletownbere 24th December 1970. Married to Catherine, two sons, one daughter. Educated Beara Community School, Castletownbere, Co. Cork. Postmaster in Castletownbere since 1992. Elected at his first attempt in 2011.

Member Committee on Communications, Natural Resources and Agriculture. Contested 2007 Seanad election on Industrial and Commercial Panel. First elected to Cork County Council in the Bantry electoral area in 1999. Retained his seat in 2004 and 2009. Mayor of County Cork in 2008. His father Donie was a member of the council until 1982.

MICHAEL McCARTHY (LB)

Milleenananig, Clonakilty Road, Dunmanway, Co. Cork; Tel: 023 45011,
Mobile: 087 6481004; Constituency Office: Market Square, Dunmanway, Co. Cork;
Tel: 023 8855705; Leinster House: Tel: 01 6183844; Email: michael.mccarthy@oireachtas.ie
Website: www.michaelmccarthy.ie; Twitter: twitter.com/senmccarthy

Born Bantry, Co. Cork, 15th November 1976. Married to Nollagh Patterson, two sons. Educated Coláiste Chairbe, Dunmanway, Co. Cork. Former Schering Plough Employee. Contested 2002 and 2007 general elections in Cork South West. First elected 2011.

Appointed Vice Chairman Dail Committee on Investigations, Oversights and Petitions June 2011 and Member Public Accounts Committee. Senator 2002-2011. Labour Party spokesperson on the Marine and Seanad spokesperson on Communications, Energy and Natural Resources, Marine, Agriculture and Food, 2007-2011. Member Joint Committee on Agriculture, Fisheries and Food and Member Joint Administration Committee 2007-2011. Member Joint Committee on Agriculture and Food and Member Joint Committee on Environment and Local Government 2002-2007. Member Cork County Council 1999-2003.

CORK SOUTH-WEST 2011							
FIRST PREFERENCE VOTES							
	Seats	3			11,415		
	Candidate	Party	1st	%	Quota	Count	Status
1	**Daly, Jim**	**FG**	**8,878**	**19.44%**	**0.78**	**5**	**Made Quota**
2	**Harrington, Noel**	**FG**	**6,898**	**15.11%**	**0.60**	**6**	**Elected**
3	**McCarthy, Michael**	**LB**	**6,533**	**14.31%**	**0.57**	**6**	**Elected**
4	O'Donovan, Denis #	FF	5,984	13.11%	0.52	6	Not Elected
5	Murphy, Kevin	FG	6,386	13.99%	0.56	4	Eliminated
6	O'Sullivan, Christy*	FF	4,803	10.52%	0.42	3	Eliminated
7	Hayes, Paul	SF	3,346	7.33%	0.29	2	Eliminated
8	Kearney, John	NP	772	1.69%	0.07	1	No Expenses
9	McCaughey, Kevin	GP	765	1.68%	0.07	1	No Expenses
10	McInerney, Dave	NV	493	1.08%	0.04	1	No Expenses
11	Butler, Edmund	NP	330	0.72%	0.03	1	No Expenses
12	Doonan, Paul	NV	239	0.52%	0.02	1	No Expenses
13	O'Sullivan, Michael	NP	231	0.51%	0.02	1	No Expenses
13	***Outgoing # Former TD**		**45,658**	**100.00%**	**11,415**	**2,854**	**No Expenses**

CORK SOUTH-WEST 2011													
PARTY VOTE													
	2011					2007					Change	
Party	Cand	1st	%	Quota	Seats	Cand	1st	%	Quota	Seats	%	Seats
FG	3	22,162	48.54%	1.94	2	2	15,299	36.00%	1.44	2	+12.54%	
LB	1	6,533	14.31%	0.57	1	1	4,095	9.64%	0.39		+4.67%	+1
FF	2	10,787	23.63%	0.95		2	18,093	42.57%	1.70	1	-18.95%	-1
SF	1	3,346	7.33%	0.29		1	2,150	5.06%	0.20		+2.27%	
GP	1	765	1.68%	0.07		1	2,860	6.73%	0.27		-5.05%	
Others	5	2,065	4.52%	0.18							+4.52%	
Total	**13**	**45,658**	**100.0%**	**11,415**	**3**	**7**	**42,497**	**100.0%**	**10,625**	**3**	**0.00%**	**0**
Electorate		**62,967**	**72.51%**				**61,577**	**69.01%**			**+3.50%**	
Spoiled		**390**	**0.85%**				**410**	**0.96%**			**-0.11%**	
Turnout		**46,048**	**73.13%**				**42,907**	**69.68%**			**+3.45%**	

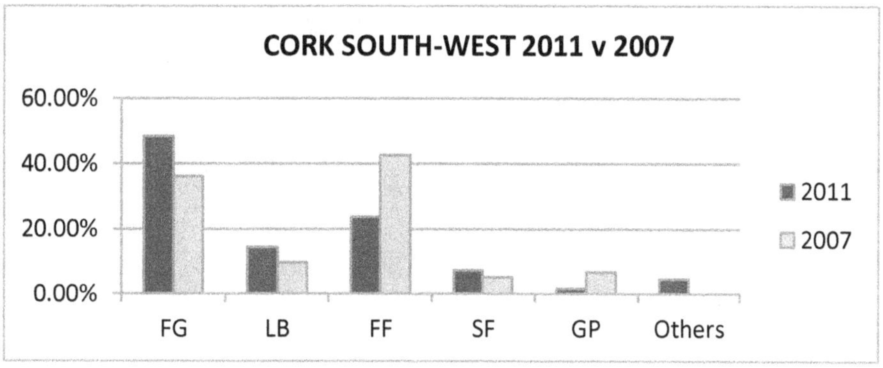

CORK SOUTH-WEST 2011 COUNT DETAILS							
Seats	3					Quota	11,415
Candidate	Party	1st	2nd Kearney McCaughey McInerney Butler Doonan O'Sullivan	3rd Hayes Votes	4th O'Sullivan Votes	5th Murphy Votes	6th Daly Surplus
Daly, Jim	FG	8,878	+377 9,255	+441 9,696	+812 10,508	+2,734 13,242	-1,827 11,415
Harrington, Noel	FG	6,898	+314 7,212	+267 7,479	+189 7,668	+1,900 9,568	+1,536 11,104
McCarthy, Michael	LB	6,533	+724 7,257	+1,452 8,709	+503 9,212	+1,327 10,539	+215 10,754
O'Donovan, Denis #	FF	5,984	+224 6,208	+273 6,481	+2,972 9,453	+626 10,079	+76 10,155
Murphy, Kevin	FG	6,386	+279 6,665	+252 6,917	+295 7,212	-7,212 Eliminated	
O'Sullivan, Christy*	FF	4,803	+155 4,958	+257 5,215	-5,215 Eliminated		
Hayes, Paul	SF	3,346	+397 3,743	-3,743 Eliminated			
Kearney, John	NP	772	-772 Eliminated				
McCaughey, Kevin	GP	765	-765 Eliminated				
McInerney, Dave	NV	493	-493 Eliminated				
Butler, Edmund	NP	330	-330 Eliminated				
Doonan, Paul	NV	239	-239 Eliminated				
O'Sullivan, Michael	NP	231	-231 Eliminated				
Non-transferable Cumulative			+360 360	+801 1,161	+444 1,605	+625 2,230	 2,230
Total		**45,658**	**45,658**	**45,658**	**45,658**	**45,658**	**45,658**

CORK SOUTH-WEST 2011 TRANSFER ANALYSIS						
From	To	FG	LB	FF	SF	Non Trans
FG	9,039	6,170 *68.26%*	1,542 *17.06%*	702 *7.77%*		625 *6.91%*
FF	5,215	1,296 *24.85%*	503 *9.65%*	2,972 *56.99%*		444 *8.51%*
SF	3,743	960 *25.65%*	1,452 *38.79%*	530 *14.16%*		801 *21.40%*
GP	765	262 *34.25%*	196 *25.62%*	103 *13.46%*	107 *13.99%*	97 *12.68%*
Others	2,065	708 *34.29%*	528 *25.57%*	276 *13.37%*	290 *14.04%*	263 *12.74%*
Total	**20,827**	**9,396** ***45.11%***	**4,221** ***20.27%***	**4,583** ***22.01%***	**397** ***1.91%***	**2,230** ***10.71%***

CORK SOUTH-WEST MAIN BOUNDARY CHANGES		
Dail	**Constituency**	**Seats**
4 (1923) - 12 (1944)	Cork West	5
13 (1948) - 16 (1957)	Cork West	3
17 (1961) - 31 (2011)	Cork South-West	3

CORK WEST & SOUTH-WEST ALL TDs 1923-2011															
	Surname	**Forename**	**Party**	**Elected**											**Total**
1	Murphy	Timothy	LB	23	27	27	32	33	37	38	43	44	48		10
2	O'Keeffe	Jim	FG	77	81	82	82	87	89	92	97	02	07		10
3	O'Donovan	Timothy	FG	23	27	27	32	33	37	38	43				8
4	Murphy	Michael Pat	LB	51	54	57	61	65	69	73	77				8
5	Walsh	Joe	FF	77	82	82	87	89	92	97	02				8
6	Sheehan	P.J.	FG	81	82	82	87	89	92	97	07				8
7	O'Sullivan	Ted	FF	37	38	43	44	48	51						6
8	O'Neill	Eamonn	FG	32	33	37	38	44							5
9	Collins	Sean	FG	48	51	54	61	65							5
10	Buckley**	Sean	FF	23	38	43	44								4
11	Cotter	Edward	FF	54	57	61	65								4
12	Wolfe	Jasper	NP	27	27	32									3
13	Crowley**	Flor	FF	69	73	81									3
14	Mullins	Thomas	FF	27	27										2
15	Sheehy	Timothy	CG	27	27										2
16	O'Driscoll	Patrick	CnaT	43	44										2
17	O'Sullivan	John L.	FG	69	73										2
18	Connolly	Cornelius	CG	23											1
19	Prior	John	CG	23											1
20	Keyes	Raphael	FF	32											1
21	Burke	James M.	CG	33											1
22	Hales	Thomas	FF	33											1
23	O'Leary**	Daniel	FG	37											1
24	Murphy	William J.	LB	49*											1
25	Wycherley	Florence	NP	57											1
26	O'Donovan	Denis	FF	02											1
27	O'Sullivan	Christy	FF	07											1
28	Daly	Jim	FG	11											1
29	Harrington	Noel	FG	11											1
30	McCarthy	Michael	LB	11											1
30	**Total**							*** Includes 1 By-Election**						*	**103**
	**** Also elected in another constituency**														
1	O'Leary**	Daniel	FG	Cork North			27	32	33						3
2	Buckley**	Sean	FF	Cork South			48	51							2
3	Crowley**	Flor	FF	Cork Mid			65								1
3	**Total**														**6**

CORK WEST/SOUTH-WEST PARTY VOTE 1923-2011																							
*No Contest		FG		LB		FF		SF		GP		PD		C na P		C na T		Farmers		Centre P		Others	
Dail	Seats	S	% Vote	S	% Vote	S	% Vote	S	% Vote	S	% Vote	S	% Vote	S	% Vote	S	% Vote	S	% Vote	S	% Vote	S	% Vote
4 1923	5	2	38.70%	1	11.83%	1	20.92%											1	16.85%				11.70%
5 1927	5	1	20.45%	1	18.72%	1	19.02%		3.78%									1	22.99%			1	15.05%
6 1927	5	1	25.91%	1	15.34%	1	25.88%											1	16.25%			1	16.62%
7 1932	5	1	24.87%	1	17.71%	1	30.41%											1	12.96%			1	14.05%
8 1933	5	2	34.95%	1	14.51%	1	30.14%													1	20.40%		0.00%
9 1937	5	3	48.33%	1	22.73%	1	24.81%																4.12%
10 1938	5	2	42.07%	1	19.27%	2	38.66%																
11 1943	5	1	28.57%	1	26.40%	2	28.29%									1	16.74%						
12 1944	5	1	21.02%	1	19.86%	2	29.55%									1	26.66%						2.91%
13 1948	3	1	21.58%	1	20.40%	1	32.39%								9.90%		15.72%						
14 1951	3	1	25.65%	1	20.83%	1	37.36%																16.15%
15 1954	3	1	26.52%	1	25.40%	1	33.36%																14.72%
16 1957	3		22.26%	1	24.48%	1	35.57%															1	17.70%
17 1961	3	1	30.42%	1	25.41%	1	30.84%																13.33%
18 1965	3	1	33.10%	1	28.92%	1	37.98%																
19 1969	3	1	40.93%	1	21.89%	1	37.18%																
20 1973	3	1	34.88%	1	21.66%	1	43.47%																
21 1977	3	1	31.50%	1	20.33%	1	48.17%																
22 1981	3	2	45.26%		9.61%	1	41.89%																3.25%
23 1982	3	2	48.39%		6.75%	1	44.86%																
24 1982	3	2	49.85%			1	41.71%																8.44%
25 1987	3	2	43.61%			1	45.30%						10.69%										0.40%
26 1989	3	2	50.57%			1	44.32%						3.89%										1.23%
27 1992	3	2	40.42%		11.28%	1	40.97%		0.99%		4.28%												2.06%
28 1997	3	2	44.18%		6.75%	1	39.05%				3.49%												6.53%
29 2002	3	1	32.33%		9.13%	2	39.48%		5.85%														13.20%
30 2007	3	2	36.00%		9.64%	1	42.57%		5.06%		6.73%												
31 2011	3	2	48.54%	1	14.31%		23.63%		7.33%		1.68%												4.52%
1918-2011	**102**	**41**	**35.65%**	**19**	**15.93%**	**31**	**34.74%**		**0.92%**		**0.61%**		**0.47%**		**0.29%**	**2**	**2.61%**	**4**	**2.39%**	**1**	**0.89%**	**4**	**5.51%**
National	**4,618**	**1,453**	**30.77%**	**482**	**11.53%**	**1,985**	**41.86%**	**232**	**1.99%**	**16**	**0.75%**	**44**	**1.42%**	**18**	**0.77%**	**43**	**1.08%**	**42**	**0.90%**	**11**	**0.30%**	**292**	**8.61%**

CORK REGION		
MAIN BOUNDARY CHANGES		
Dail	**Constituency**	**Seats**
1 (1918)	Cork City	2
	Cork East	1
	Cork Mid	1
	Cork North	1
	Cork North-East	1
	Cork South	1
	Cork South-East	1
	Cork West	1
Total	**8**	**9**
2 (1921) - 3 (1922)	Cork Borough	4
	Cork East & North-East	3
	Cork Mid,North,South,	
	South East & West	8
Total	**3**	**15**
4 (1923) - 8 (1933)	Cork Borough	5
	Cork East	5
	Cork North	3
	Cork West	5
Total	**4**	**18**
9 (1937) - 12 (1944)	Cork Borough	4
	Cork South-East	3
	Cork North	4
	Cork West	5
Total	**4**	**16**
13 (1948) - 16 (1957)	Cork Borough	5
	Cork East	3
	Cork North	3
	Cork South	3
	Cork West	3
Total	**5**	**17**
17 (1961) - 18 (1965)	Cork Borough	5
	Mid-Cork	4
	Cork North-East	5
	Cork South-West	3
Total	**4**	**17**
19 (1969) - 20 (1973)	Cork City North-West	3
	Cork City South-East	3
	Mid-Cork	4
	Cork North-East	4
	Cork South-West	3
Total	**5**	**17**
21 (1977)	Cork City	5
	Mid-Cork	5
	Cork North-East	4
	Cork South-West	3
Total	**4**	**17**
22 (1981) - 29 (2002)	Cork East	4
	Cork North-Central	5
	Cork North-West	3
	Cork South-Central	5
	Cork South-West	3
Total	**5**	**20**
30 (2007) - 31 (2011)	Cork East	4
	Cork North-Central	4
	Cork North-West	3
	Cork South-Central	5
	Cork South-West	3
Total	**5**	**19**

CORK REGION																		
ALL TDs 1918-2011																		
	Surname	Forename	Party	Elected														Total
1	Corry	Martin J.	FF	27	27	32	33	37	38	43	44	48	51	54	57	61	65	14
2	Moylan	Sean	FF	21	22	32	33	37	38	43	44	48	51	54				11
3	Murphy	Timothy	LB	23	27	27	32	33	37	38	43	44	48					10
4	O'Keeffe	Jim	FG	77	81	82	82	87	89	92	97	02	07					10
5	Lynch	Jack	FF	48	51	54	57	61	65	69	73	77						9
6	Wyse	Pierse	PD	65	69	73	77	81	82	82	87	89						9
7	Barry	Peter	FG	69	73	77	81	82	82	87	89	92						9
8	Burke	Liam	FG	69	73	79*	81	82	82	87	92	97						9
9	Allen	Bernard	FG	81	82	82	87	89	92	97	02	07						9
10	O'Donovan	Timothy	FG	23	27	27	32	33	37	38	43							8
11	Murphy	Michael Pat	LB	51	54	57	61	65	69	73	77							8
12	Barry	Richard	FG	53*	54	57	61	65	69	73	77							8
13	Creed	Donal	FG	65	69	73	77	81	82	82	87							8
14	Walsh	Joe	FF	77	82	82	87	89	92	97	02							8
15	Sheehan	P.J.	FG	81	82	82	87	89	92	97	07							8
16	Ahern	Michael	FF	82	82	87	89	92	97	02	07							8
17	Anthony	Richard	LB	27	27	32	33	37	43	44								7
18	McAuliffe	Patrick	LB	44	48	51	54	57	61	65								7
19	Desmond	Eileen	LB	65*	65	73	77	81	82	82								7
20	O'Keeffe	Ned	FF	82N	87	89	92	97	02	07								7
21	Corkery	Daniel	FF	21	22	23	27	27	33									6
22	Buckley	Sean	FF	23	38	43	44	48	51									6
23	Cosgrave**	William T.	FG	27	32	33	37	38	43									6
24	O'Sullivan	Ted	FF	37	38	43	44	48	51									6
25	Meaney	Thomas	FF	65	69	73	77	81	82									6
26	French	Sean	FF	67*	69	73	77	81	82									6
27	Fitzgerald	Gene	FF	72*	73	77	81	82	82									6
28	Hegarty	Patrick	FG	73	77	81	82	82	87									6
29	Crowley	Frank	FG	81	82	82	87	89	92									6
30	O'Sullivan	Toddy	LB	81	82	82	87	89	92									6
31	Wallace	Dan	FF	82N	87	89	92	97	02									6
32	Martin	Micheal	FF	89	92	97	02	07	11									6
33	Kent	David	SF	18	21	22	23	27J										5
34	Walsh	James J.	CG	18	21	22	23	27J										5
35	Vaughan	Daniel	F	22	23	27	27	32										5
36	Flinn	Hugo	FF	27	32	33	37	38										5
37	O'Neill	Eamonn	FG	32	33	37	38	44										5
38	MacCarthy	Sean	FF	44	51	54	57	61										5
39	Collins	Sean	FG	48	51	54	61	65										5
40	Desmond	Daniel	LB	48	51	54	57	61										5
41	Barrett	Stephen	FG	54*	54	57	61	65										5
42	Lyons	Denis	FF	81	82	82	87	89										5
43	Sherlock	Joe	LB	81	82F	87	89	02										5
44	Moynihan	Donal	FF	82	87	92	97	02										5
45	O'Keeffe	Batt	FF	87	92	97	02	07										5
46	Creed	Michael	FG	89	92	97	07	11										5
47	Hennessy	Michael	CG	22	23	27	27											4
48	Daly	John	CG	23	27	27	32											4
49	O'Leary	Daniel	FG	27	32	33	37											4
50	Broderick**	William	FG	32	33	43	44											4
51	Dowdall	Thomas P.	FF	32	33	37	38											4
52	McGrath	Pa	FF	46*	48	51	54											4
53	O'Sullivan	Denis	FG	51	54	57	61											4
54	Casey	Sean	LB	54	57	61	65											4
55	Cotter	Edward	FF	54	57	61	65											4
56	Healy	Gus	FF	57	65	69	73											4

	Surname	Forename	Party	Elected														Total
57	Cronin	Jeremiah	FF	65	69	73	77											4
58	Crowley	Flor	FF	65	69	73	81											4
59	Barry	Myra	FG	79*	81	82	82											4
60	Coveney	Hugh	FG	81	82N	94*	97											4
61	Dennehy	John	FF	87	89	97	02											4
62	Lynch	Kathleen	LB	94*	02	07	11											4
63	Kelleher	Billy	FF	97	02	07	11											4
64	Moynihan	Michael	FF	97	02	07	11											4
65	Stanton	David	FG	97	02	07	11											4
66	Coveney	Simon	FG	98*	02	07	11											4
67	Collins	Michael	CT	18	21	22												3
68	De Roiste	Liam	CT	18	21	22												3
69	Hayes	Sean	CT	18	21	22												3
70	MacSwiney	Mary	R	21	22	23												3
71	Wolfe	Jasper	NP	27	27	32												3
72	Brasier	Brook	FG	32	37	38												3
73	Daly	Patrick	FG	33	37	38												3
74	Linehan	Timothy	FG	37	38	43												3
75	Meaney	Con	FF	37	38	61												3
76	Hickey	James	LB	38	48	51												3
77	Halliden	Patrick J.	CnaT	43	44	48												3
78	Moher	John	FF	54	57	61												3
79	Galvin	John	FF	56*	57	61												3
80	Burton	Philip	FG	61	65	69												3
81	Brosnan	Sean	FF	69	74*	77												3
82	Quill	Mairin	PD	87	89	92												3
83	Bradford	Paul	FG	89	92	97												3
84	O'Flynn	Noel	FF	97	02	07												3
85	Hunter	Thomas	SF	18	21													2
86	O'Keeffe	Patrick	SF	18	21													2
87	Hales	Sean	CT	21	22													2
88	Dineen	John	F	22	23													2
89	Nagle	Thomas	LB	22	23													2
90	Egan	Barry	CG	27	27													2
91	French	Sean	FF	27	27													2
92	Mullins	Thomas	FF	27	27													2
93	Sheehy	Timothy	CG	27	27													2
94	Kent	William	CP	27S	33													2
95	Desmond	William	CG	32	33													2
96	Murphy	Patrick	FF	32	33													2
97	Hurley	Jeremiah	LB	37	38													2
98	Daly	Francis	FF	43	44													2
99	O'Driscoll	Patrick	CnaT	43	44													2
100	Skinner	Leo	FF	43	44													2
101	Keane	Sean	LB	48	51													2
102	Lehane	Patrick	CnaT	48	51													2
103	O'Gorman	Patrick J.	FG	48	51													2
104	O'Higgins(sen)*	Thomas F.	FG	48	51													2
105	Barry	Anthony	FG	54	61													2
106	Manley	Tadhg	FG	54	57													2
107	O'Sullivan	John L.	FG	69	73													2
108	O'Sullivan	Gerry	LB	89	92													2
109	Clune	Deirdre	FG	97	07													2
110	Lynch	Ciaran	LB	07	11													2
111	McGrath	Michael	FF	07	11													2
112	Sherlock	Sean	LB	07	11													2

	Surname	Forename	Party	Elected														Total
113	Lynch	Diarmuid	SF	18														1
114	MacSwiney	Terence	SF	18														1
115	Fitzgerald	Seamus	SF	21														1
116	MacSwiney	Sean	SF	21														1
117	Nolan	Sean	SF	21														1
118	O'Callaghan	Donal	SF	21														1
119	Bradley	Michael	LB	22														1
120	Day	Robert	LB	22														1
121	Beamish	Richard	PA	23														1
122	Connolly	Cornelius	CG	23														1
123	O'Mahony	Thomas	CG	23														1
124	O'Rahilly	Alfred	CG	23														1
125	O'Shaughnessy	Andrew	PA	23														1
126	Prior	John	CG	23														1
127	Egan	Michael	CG	24*														1
128	Noonan	Michael K.	CG	24*														1
129	Horgan	John	NL	27J														1
130	O'Gorman	David	F	27J														1
131	Quill	Timothy	LB	27J														1
132	Carey	Edmond	CG	27S														1
133	Keyes	Raphael	FF	32														1
134	Burke	James M.	CG	33														1
135	Hales	Thomas	FF	33														1
136	Fitzgerald	Seamus	FF	43														1
137	Looney	Thomas	LB	43														1
138	Dwyer	William	NP	44														1
139	Furlong	Walter	FF	44														1
140	Sheehan	Michael	NP	48														1
141	Murphy	William J.	LB	49*														1
142	Donegan	Batt	FF	57														1
143	Wycherley	Florence	NP	57														1
144	Galvin	Sheila	FF	64*														1
145	Cott	Gerard	FG	69														1
146	Forde	Patrick	FF	69														1
147	Ahern	Liam	FF	73														1
148	Cogan	Barry	FF	77														1
149	Kerrigan	Patrick	LB	77														1
150	Joyce	Carey	FF	81														1
151	Corr	James	FG	82F														1
152	Kelly	Larry	FF	89														1
153	Cox	Pat	PD	92														1
154	Mulvihill	John	LB	92														1
155	Boyle	Dan	GP	02														1
156	Murphy	Gerard	FG	02														1
157	O'Donovan	Denis	FF	02														1
158	O'Sullivan	Christy	FF	07														1
159	Barry	Tom	FG	11														1
160	McLellan	Sandra	SF	11														1
161	O'Brien	Jonathan	SF	11														1
162	Murphy	Dara	FG	11														1
163	Collins	Áine	FG	11														1
164	Buttimer	Jerry	FG	11														1
165	Daly	Jim	FG	11														1
166	Harrington	Noel	FG	11														1
167	McCarthy	Michael	LB	11														1
167	**Total**										*** Includes 17 By-Elections**						*	**561**
	**** Also elected in another constituency**																	
	O'Higgins(sen)**	Thomas F.	FG	Laois-Offaly				32	33	37	38	43	44					
				Dublin North				29*										7
C	Cosgrave**	William T.	FG	Carlow-Kilkenny				18	21	22	23	27	27					6
C	Broderick**	William	FG	Waterford				38										1
C	**Included in Cork Total**										*** Includes 1 By-Election**						*	14

CORK REGION PARTY VOTE 1918-2011																									
*No Contest		FG		LB		FF		SF		SP		PBPA		GP		WP		CS		PD		DL		Others	
Dail	Seats	S	% Vote	S	% Vote	S	% Vote	S	% Vote	S	% Vote	S	% Vote	S	% Vote	S	% Vote	S	% Vote	S	% Vote	S	% Vote	S	% Vote
1 1918*	9							9																	
2 1921*	15							15																	
3 1922	15	5	33.46%	3	16.13%	4	27.74%																	3	22.67%
4 1923	18	6	35.43%	2	10.16%	4	22.80%																	6	31.61%
5 1927	18	4	21.14%	3	15.28%	3	14.07%	1	6.33%															7	43.18%
6 1927	18	7	36.03%	2	13.15%	6	30.26%																	3	20.56%
7 1932	18	6	34.33%	1	11.61%	6	36.12%																	5	17.94%
8 1933	18	7	31.71%	1	7.68%	7	40.06%																	3	20.55%
9 1937	16	7	40.02%	2	19.53%	6	33.72%																	1	6.74%
10 1938	16	6	37.45%	3	17.24%	7	42.22%																		3.08%
11 1943	16	4	26.66%	2	18.81%	7	35.68%																	3	18.84%
12 1944	16	2	17.55%	2	13.62%	8	39.51%																	4	29.32%
13 1948	17	3	20.38%	4	17.04%	6	35.72%																	4	26.86%
14 1951	17	4	26.43%	5	20.30%	7	44.02%																	1	9.25%
15 1954	17	6	32.31%	4	19.68%	7	39.13%																		8.88%
16 1957	17	4	26.16%	4	18.06%	8	44.85%		4.73%															1	6.20%
17 1961	17	6	33.52%	4	20.74%	7	39.94%		2.64%																3.16%
18 1965	17	5	31.26%	4	20.65%	8	45.55%																		2.54%
19 1969	17	7	34.28%	1	17.16%	9	46.66%																		1.91%
20 1973	17	6	33.24%	2	11.61%	9	50.14%		1.49%																3.52%
21 1977	17	5	29.11%	3	11.39%	9	53.87%										3.18%								2.46%
22 1981	20	10	41.53%	2	10.75%	7	41.20%		1.34%							1	3.76%								1.42%
23 1982	20	10	41.30%	2	9.24%	7	43.14%									1	3.85%								2.48%
24 1982	20	10	42.78%	2	7.75%	8	41.36%										4.75%								3.35%
25 1987	20	8	31.42%	1	4.55%	8	39.00%		0.58%							1	5.75%			2	15.82%				2.88%
26 1989	20	7	36.52%	2	7.34%	8	40.10%		0.38%							1	7.61%			2	6.86%				1.19%
27 1992	20	8	30.02%	3	16.39%	7	36.40%		0.92%						1.65%		0.73%			2	5.77%		4.69%		3.44%
28 1997	20	9	34.37%		7.39%	11	39.94%		1.50%						2.92%		0.26%				3.51%		3.67%		6.44%
29 2002	20	5	27.74%	2	10.92%	12	44.36%		4.38%		0.42%		0.10%	1	3.25%		0.21%		0.26%		1.40%				6.97%
30 2007	19	7	32.03%	3	11.59%	9	42.79%		5.03%		0.70%				5.14%		0.11%				0.65%				1.96%
31 2011	19	9	38.27%	4	21.24%	4	21.80%	2	9.91%		1.82%		0.59%		1.59%		0.26%		0.12%						4.41%
1918-2011	**544**	**183**	**32.60%**	**73**	**13.76%**	**209**	**38.72%**	**27**	**1.57%**		**0.15%**		**0.03%**	**1**	**0.66%**	**4**	**1.20%**		**0.02%**	**6**	**1.38%**		**0.34%**	**41**	**9.56%**
National	**4,618**	**1,453**	**30.77%**	**482**	**11.53%**	**1,985**	**41.86%**	**232**	**1.95%**	**4**	**0.16%**	**2**	**0.06%**	**16**	**0.75%**	**17**	**0.82%**		**0.04%**	**44**	**1.42%**	**8**	**0.22%**	**375**	**10.40%**

DONEGAL NORTH-EAST 2011

"Sinn Fein make breakthrough as Fianna Fáil hold onto a single seat"

There was a Constituency Commission boundary revision here since 2007, with a transfer of a population of 2,351 out of this constituency into Donegal South West. All divisions of the old Stranorlar Rural District are now within this constituency. However, the constituency did retain its three seats.

This contest was as good as over after the first count as the three leading candidates were well clear of the rest of the field. Fine Gael surprisingly added a second candidate, John Ryan from Inishowen, and their vote was up nine points on 2007 but with just 1.3 quotas the party was never in contention for a second seat. Joe McHugh was in second place on the first count and went on to take the second seat with the help of 65% of his running mate's transfers.

Former Fine Gael candidate Jimmy Harte, whose father Paddy was a long-time Fine Gael TD, joined the Labour party in 2010. He managed to increase the party's vote by 9 points on their poor 2007 result, but with just 4,090 first preferences, he was outside the frame on the first count with just 0.4 of a quota and was too far off the pace.

It was all change in Fianna Fail as Dr Jim McDaid resigned his seat in November 2010 and outgoing deputy Niall Blaney announced his retirement just prior to the party's selection convention. This left Fianna Fáil with just a single candidate, newcomer Charlie McConalogue from Inishowen. There was pressure from former deputy McDaid's supporters to add a Letterkenny-based candidate but the party refused and this proved a prudent decision. The Fianna Fáil vote was down a massive 33 points, their fourth largest loss of support in this election and McConalogue was in third place on the first count with 0.7 of a quota and was nearly 2,000 votes ahead of his nearest rival John Ryan. He was unlikely to be overtaken and so it proved as the single candidate strategy delivered for Fianna Fail. This was in sharp contrast to the neighbouring constituency of Donegal South West where the party ran two candidates and ended up without a seat for the first time.

Sinn Fein went close to winning a seat here at the last election in 2007 and Padraig MacLochlainn made no mistake in 2011 as he topped the poll and was just short of the quota on the first count. He went on to take the first seat on the third count for an impressive performance and another seat gain by Sinn Fein in this election.

Letterkenny based Dessie Shiels failed to take advantage of McDaid's absence, winning just 5%. Dara Blaney, son of former long serving deputy Neil Blaney contested his father's old constituency as a "New Vision" candidate but did poorly and lost the right to reclaim his expenses as did three other non-party candidates along with the Green representative.

DONEGAL NORTH-EAST TDs 2011

PADRAIG Mac LOCHLAINN (SF)

13 The Meadows, Buncrana, Co. Donegal; Tel: 074 9322697; Mobile: 087 2771958
Leinster House: 6184061; Email: padraig.maclochlainn@oireachtas.ie;
Website: www.sinnfein.ie

Born Leeds, England, 12th June 1973. Partner Sinéad, one son, one stepson. Educated: Early school leaver who returned to part time education while working. Diploma in Social Studies. Contested 2002 and 2007 Dail elections in Donegal North-East. First elected 2011.

Appointed Party Spokesperson on Foreign Affairs and Trade March 2011. Member Committee on European Union Affairs. Member Committee on Foreign Affairs and Trade. National Director of Elections for the Lisbon Treaty Referendum in 2008. Contested 2009 Euro election in North West. First elected to Donegal County Council in the Inishowen electoral area in 2004. Retained his seat in 2009. Elected to Buncrana TC in 2004 and 2009.

JOE McHUGH (FG)

Claggan, Carrigart, Co. Donegal, Tel: 074 9155968; Mobile: 087 6241525
Constituency Office: Grier House, Lower Main Street, Letterkenny, Tel: 074 9164787;
Leinster House: 01 6184242; Email: joe.mchugh@oireachtas.ie;
Website: www.donegalmatters.com; Facebook: /joemchughtd

Born Letterkenny 16th July 1971. Married to former TD Olwyn Enright, one son, one daughter. Educated Loreto Convent, Milford, Co. Donegal; NUI, Maynooth (BA, HDipEd). Former Teacher and Community Youth Worker. First elected 2007. Retained his seat in 2011.

Member Committee on the Implementation of the Good Friday Agreement. Fine Gael deputy spokesperson on Foreign Affairs and the Department of an Taoiseach with special responsibility for North-South Co-operation 2007-2011. Member Joint Committee on Communications, Energy and Natural Resources and Member Joint Committee on the Implementation of the Good Friday Agreement 2007-2011. Senator 2002-2007. Member Donegal County Council 1999-2003. Married to Olwyn Enright Fine Gael TD for Laois-Offaly 2002-2011. They were the first married couple in the same Dail since Alexis Fitzgerald (1982) and Mary Flaherty (1981-1997).

CHARLIE McCONALOGUE (FF)

Carrowmore, Gleneely, Cardonagh, Co. Donegal; Mobile: 086 8161078
Leinster House: 01 61843199; Email: charlie.mcconalogue@oireachtas.ie
Website: www.fiannafail.ie/people/charlie-ncconalogue; Facebook: /CharlieMcConalogue

Born Letterkenny 29th October 1977. Single. Educated UCD (Economics, Politics and History).Farmer. Elected at his first attempt in 2011.

Appointed Party Spokesperson on Children April 2011. Member Committee on Health and Children. Member Committee on Investigations, Oversight and Petitions. Worked in Fianna Fail Headquarters prior to his entry into electoral politics in 2009. First elected to Donegal County Council in the Inishowen electoral area in 2009. Deputy Mayor 2009-2010.

DONEGAL NORTH-EAST 2011							
FIRST PREFERENCE VOTES							
	Seats	3			9,480		
	Candidate	Party	1st	%	Quota	Count	Status
1	**MacLochlainn, Padraig**	**SF**	**9,278**	**24.47%**	**0.98**	**3**	**Made Quota**
2	**McHugh, Joe***	**FG**	**7,330**	**19.33%**	**0.77**	**8**	**Made Quota**
3	**McConalogue, Charlie**	**FF**	**6,613**	**17.44%**	**0.70**	**9**	**Elected**
4	Harte, Jimmy	LB	4,090	10.79%	0.43	9	Not Elected
5	Ryan, John	FG	4,657	12.28%	0.49	7	Eliminated
6	Shiels, Dessie	NP	1,876	4.95%	0.20	6	Eliminated
7	McGarvey, Ian	NP	1,287	3.39%	0.14	5	No Expenses
8	Blaney, Dara	NV	1,228	3.24%	0.13	4	No Expenses
9	Holmes, Betty	NP	1,150	3.03%	0.12	2	No Expenses
10	Murphy, Humphrey	GP	206	0.54%	0.02	1	No Expenses
11	Stewart, Ryan	NV	203	0.54%	0.02	1	No Expenses
11	***Outgoing**		**37,918**	**100.00%**	**9,480**	**2,370**	**No Expenses**

DONEGAL NORTH-EAST 2011												
PARTY VOTE												
	2011					2007					Change	
Party	Cand	1st	%	Quota	Seats	Cand	1st	%	Quota	Seats	%	Seats
FG	2	11,987	31.61%	1.26	1	1	8,711	22.60%	0.90	1	+9.01%	
LB	1	4,090	10.79%	0.43		1	703	1.82%	0.07		+8.96%	
FF	1	6,613	17.44%	0.70	1	3	19,374	50.26%	2.01	2	-32.82%	-1
SF	1	9,278	24.47%	0.98	1	1	6,733	17.47%	0.70		+7.00%	+1
GP	1	206	0.54%	0.02		1	520	1.35%	0.05		-0.81%	
Others	5	5,744	15.15%	0.61		4	2,504	6.50%	0.26		+8.65%	
Total	**11**	**37,918**	**100.0%**	**9,480**	**3**	**11**	**38,545**	**100.0%**	**9,637**	**3**	**0.00%**	**0**
Electorate		**59,084**	**64.18%**				**57,244**	**67.33%**			**-3.16%**	
Spoiled		**406**	**1.06%**				**386**	**0.99%**			**+0.07%**	
Turnout		**38,324**	**64.86%**				**38,931**	**68.01%**			**-3.15%**	

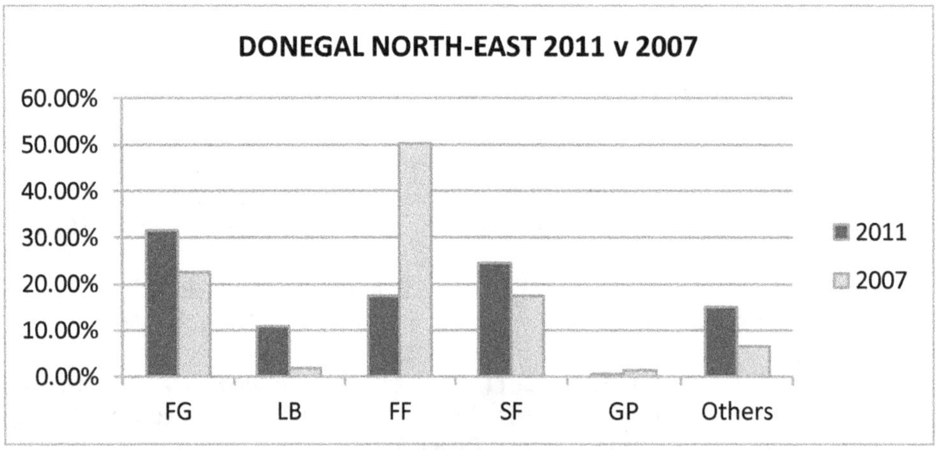

DONEGAL NORTH-EAST 2011
COUNT DETAILS

Seats 3 | **Quota 9,480**

Candidate	Party	1st	2nd Murphy Stewart	3rd Holmes Votes	4th MacLochlainn Surplus	5th Blaney Votes	6th McGarvey Votes	7th Shiels Votes	8th Ryan Votes	9th McHugh Surplus
			+72	+235	-105					
Mac Lochlainn, Padraig	SF	9,278	9,350	9,585	9,480	9,480	9,480	9,480	9,480	9,480
			+38	+145	+11	+138	+485	+584	+3,318	-2,569
McHugh, Joe*	FG	7,330	7,368	7,513	7,524	7,662	8,147	8,731	12,049	9,480
			+48	+134	+21	+248	+191	+256	+734	+731
McConalogue, Charlie	FF	6,613	6,661	6,795	6,816	7,064	7,255	7,511	8,245	8,976
			+72	+139	+18	+216	+266	+845	+485	+1,088
Harte, Jimmy	LB	4,090	4,162	4,301	4,319	4,535	4,801	5,646	6,131	7,219
			+53	+161	+13	+66	+26	+105	-5,081	
Ryan, John	FG	4,657	4,710	4,871	4,884	4,950	4,976	5,081	Eliminated	
			+27	+160	+22	+214	+306	-2,605		
Shiels, Dessie	NP	1,876	1,903	2,063	2,085	2,299	2,605	Eliminated		
			+9	+103	+10	+244	-1,653			
McGarvey, Ian	NP	1,287	1,296	1,399	1,409	1,653	Eliminated			
			+21	+68	+10	-1,327				
Blaney, Dara	NV	1,228	1,249	1,317	1,327	Eliminated				
			+47	-1,197						
Holmes, Betty	NP	1,150	1,197	Eliminated						
			-206							
Murphy, Humphrey	GP	206	Eliminated							
			-203							
Stewart, Ryan	NV	203	Eliminated							
Non-transferable			+22	+52		+201	+379	+815	+544	+750
Cumulative			22	74	74	275	654	1,469	2,013	2,763
Total		**37,918**	**37,918**	**37,918**	**37,918**	**37,918**	**37,918**	**37,918**	**37,918**	**37,918**

DONEGAL NORTH-EAST 2011
TRANSFER ANALYSIS

From	To	FG	LB	FF	SF	Others	Non Trans
FG	7,650	3,318	1,573	1,465			1,294
		43.37%	*20.56%*	*19.15%*			*16.92%*
SF	105	24	18	21		42	
		22.86%	*17.14%*	*20.00%*		*40.00%*	
GP	206	46	36	24	36	53	11
		22.33%	*17.48%*	*11.65%*	*17.48%*	*25.73%*	*5.34%*
Others	6,985	1,755	1,502	853	271	1,146	1,458
		25.13%	*21.50%*	*12.21%*	*3.88%*	*16.41%*	*20.87%*
Total	**14,946**	**5,143**	**3,129**	**2,363**	**307**	**1,241**	**2,763**
		34.41%	***20.94%***	***15.81%***	***2.05%***	***8.30%***	***18.49%***

DONEGAL NORTH-EAST		
MAIN BOUNDARY CHANGES		
Dail	**Constituency**	**Seats**
9 (1937) - 16 (1957)	Donegal East	4
17 (1961) - 20 (1973)	Donegal North-East	3
22 (1981) - 31 (2011)	Donegal North-East	3

DONEGAL NORTH-EAST																			
ALL TDs 1937-2011																			
	Surname	**Forename**	**Party**	**Elected**															**Total**
1	Blaney	Neil T.	IFF	48*	51	54	57	61	65	69	73	77	81	82	82	87	89	92	15
2	Harte	Paddy	FG	61	65	69	73	77	81	82	82	87	89	92					11
3	McMenamin**	Daniel	FG	37	38	43	44	48	51	54	57								8
4	Cunningham	Liam	FF	51	54	57	61	65	69	73									7
5	Sheldon	William	NP	43	44	48	51	54	57										6
6	Friel	John	FF	37	38	43	44	48											5
7	Conaghan	Hugh	FF	77	81	82	82	87											5
8	McDaid	James	FF	89	92	97	02	07											5
9	Blaney**	Neil	FF	37	43	44	48												4
10	Keaveney	Cecilia	FF	96*	97	02													3
11	Myles**	Major James	NP	37	38														2
12	Blaney	Niall	IFF	02	07														2
13	McHugh	Joe	FG	07	11														2
14	McDevitt	Henry	FF	38															1
15	Keaveney	Paddy	IFF	76*															1
16	Blaney	Harry	IFF	97															1
17	MacLochlainn	Padraig	SF	11															1
18	McConalogue	Charlie	FF	11															1
18	**Total**						***Includes 3 By-Elections & 1977 (Donegal)**											*	**80**
	**** Also elected in another constituency**																		
1	Myles**	Major James	NP	Donegal			23	27	27	32	33								5
2	Blaney**	Neil	FF	Donegal			27	27	32	33									4
3	McMenamin**	Daniel	FG	Donegal			27J	32	33										3
	Total																		**12**

Sinn Fein TDs Caoimhghin O Caolain, Padraig Mac Lochlainn, Pearse Doherty

DONEGAL NORTH-EAST PARTY VOTE 1937-2011																				
* No Contest			FG		LB		FF		SF		GP		CS		C na P		C na T		Others	
Dail		Seats	S	% Vote	S	% Vote	S	% Vote	S	% Vote	S	% Vote	S	% Vote	S	% Vote	S	% Vote	S	% Vote
9	1937	4	1	25.60%			2	51.98%											1	22.42%
10	1938	4	1	20.81%		4.38%	2	53.87%											1	20.94%
11	1943	4	1	17.32%		5.53%	2	46.79%									1	9.78%		20.58%
12	1944	4	1	24.24%			2	55.19%											1	20.57%
13	1948	4	1	22.02%			2	49.55%								11.67%			1	16.77%
14	1951	4	1	27.45%		2.52%	2	52.56%											1	17.47%
15	1954	4	1	30.59%			2	49.81%											1	19.60%
16	1957	4	1	22.53%			2	47.82%											1	29.65%
17	1961	3	1	38.62%			2	61.38%												
18	1965	3	1	36.20%		4.52%	2	59.28%												
19	1969	3	1	41.93%		3.62%	2	54.45%												
20	1973	3	1	33.41%			1	36.55%											1	30.04%
22	1981	3	1	35.63%		1.46%	1	38.39%											1	24.53%
23	1982	3	1	38.37%		1.65%	1	33.69%											1	26.30%
24	1982	3	1	36.99%		1.86%	1	34.69%											1	26.45%
25	1987	3	1	29.69%		1.34%	1	32.33%		8.04%									1	28.61%
26	1989	3	1	30.22%			1	39.28%		3.93%									1	26.58%
27	1992	3		22.30%		11.34%	2	36.74%		2.62%		1.96%							1	25.05%
28	1997	3		18.87%		5.48%	2	41.81%		8.11%									1	25.73%
29	2002	3		21.01%		2.81%	2	49.40%		9.93%									1	16.85%
30	2007	3	1	22.60%		1.82%	2	50.26%		17.47%		1.35%		0.88%						5.62%
31	2011	3	1	31.61%		10.79%	1	17.44%	1	24.47%		0.54%								15.15%
1937-2011		**74**	**19**	**27.95%**		**2.79%**	**37**	**44.97%**	**1**	**3.77%**		**0.19%**		**0.05%**		**0.57%**	**1**	**0.48%**	**16**	**19.24%**
National		**4,618**	**1,453**	**30.77%**	**482**	**11.53%**	**1,985**	**41.86%**	**232**	**1.99%**	**16**	**0.75%**		**0.04%**	**18**	**0.77%**	**43**	**1.08%**	**389**	**11.20%**

DONEGAL SOUTH-WEST 2011

"Tánaiste Mary Coughlan loses her seat"

There was a Constituency Commission boundary revision here since 2007, with a transfer of a population of 2,351 into this constituency from Donegal North-East. This means that all of the divisions in the old Stranorlar Rural District are now within this constituency. However, the constituency did retain its three seats.

This was one of the few constituencies where Fine Gael experienced a drop in support in this election as their vote was down three points on 2007. Dinny McGinley was in second place on the first count with 0.8 of a quota and he went on to retain his seat comfortably.

The Fianna Fail performance in this constituency was in sharp contrast to their showing in the neighbouring constituency of Donegal North-East where their single candidate strategy delivered them a seat. It was all so different in South-West as the party went from two seats in 2007 to drawing a blank for the first time since this constituency was set up in 1937. The Fianna Fáil vote was down 28 points but with 0.9 of a quota they should have been in contention for a single seat. However their vote was spread fairly evenly between its two candidates, outgoing Tánaiste Mary Coughlan and outgoing Senator Brían Ó Domhnaill. Both candidates were outside the frame on the first count and with less than half a quota each. O Domhnaill's run-out in the November 2010 by-election gave him a good platform for the general election contest and he overtook Coughlan on the fourth count. But he was still too far off the pace and a relatively poor 55% share of Coughlan's transfers sealed his and his party's fate.

Fianna Fáil's poor candidate strategy presented independent candidate Thomas Pringle with an opportunity for a surprise seat gain. The former Sinn Fein and now independent councillor was in third place on the first count, 889 votes ahead of Coughlan. He did well on transfers and went on to comfortably take the final seat ahead of Ó Domhnaill and extended his winning margin to 1,341. Pringle had performed well in November's by-election and like many a losing by-election candidate before him, went on to win a seat at the following Dail election.

Pat 'The Cope' Gallagher resigned his Dail seat on his election to the European Parliament in 2009. Sinn Féin's Pearse Doherty comfortably won the subsequent by-election in November 2010. He made the most of his by-election win and his Dáil performances as Sinn Fein's finance spokesman enhanced his reputation. Doherty repeated his by-election winning performance in the general election and topped the poll. He was well over the quota on the first count and took the first seat with another impressive performance.

This was a poor performance by the Labour party with Frank McBrearty winning just 5% of the first preference vote to leave him out of contention. He had done poorly in the by-election and it was all downhill after that.

DONEGAL SOUTH-WEST TDs 2011

PEARSE DOHERTY (SF)

Magheraclogher, Derrybeg, Co. Donegal; Tel: 074 9560637; Mobile: 086 3817747
Constituency Office, Tel: 074 9532832; Leinster House: 01 6183960;
Email: pearse.doherty@oireachtas.ie; Website: www.pearsedoherty.ie
Twitter: www.twitter.com/pearsedoherty

Born Glasgow, Scotland 6th July 1977. Married to Róisín, three sons. Educated Pobal Scoil Gaoth Dobhair; Bolton Street DIT (Civil Engineering). Contested 2002 and 2007 general elections in Donegal South-West. Won By-election in November 2010. Retained his seat in 2011.

Appointed Party Spokesperson on Finance March 2011. Member Committee on Finance, Public Expenditure and Reform. Sinn Fein's first elected Senator in 2007. Member Joint Committee on Arts, Sport, Tourism, Community, Rural and Gaeltacht Affairs 2007-2011. Contested European election in 2004 in Ireland North-West. Member Donegal County Council 2004-2007. Member Sinn Fein since 1994 and has served on the National Executive of Ogra Shinn Fein.

DINNY McGINLEY (FG)

Magheralosk, Bunbeg, Co. Donegal; Tel: 074 9531719; Mobile: 087 2414809
Constituency Office, Tel: 074 9531025; Leinster House: Tel: 01 6183452;
Email: dinny.mcginley@oireachtas.ie

Born Gweedore, Co. Donegal 27th April 1945. Single. Educated Coláiste Iosagain, Ballyvourney, Co. Cork; St. Patrick's Teacher Training College, Drumcondra, Dublin and UCD (BA, HDipEd). Minister of State, Former Principal National School Teacher. First elected February 1982 and at each subsequent election.

Appointed Minister of State at the Department of Arts, Heritage and Gaeltacht Affairs with special responsibility for Gaeltacht Affairs 10th March 2011. Deputy spokesperson on Community, Rural and Gaeltacht Affairs with special responsibility for Gaeltacht Affairs, 2007-2011. Vice-Chairman Joint Committee on Justice, Equality, Defence and Women's Rights 2007-2011. Member Joint Committee on Arts, Sport, Tourism, Community, Rural and Gaeltacht Affairs 2007-2011. Front bench spokesperson on Community, Rural and Gaeltacht Affairs, 2004-2007. Front bench spokesperson on Defence, 2002-2004. Spokesperson on Arts, Heritage, Gaeltacht and the Islands 2001-2002. Junior spokesperson on the Islands, Gaeltacht and Western Development 2000-2001. Spokesperson on Gaeltacht and Emigrants Welfare 1991-1994. Front Bench spokesperson on the Gaeltacht 1988-1991. Spokesperson on Youth Affairs and Sport 1987-1988. Member British-Irish Inter-Parliamentary Body since 1993. Member Comhairle Raidio na Gaeltachta 1977-1980. Member National Teachers Organisation since 1965.

THOMAS PRINGLE (NP)

151 Church Road, Killybegs, Co. Donegal;
Constituency Office: Connolly House, Bridge Street, Killybegs; Tel: 074 9741880;
Leinster House: Tel: 01 6183038; Email: thomas.pringle@oireachtas.ie
Website: www.thomaspringle.ie; Twitter: thomaspringleTD; Facebook: votethomaspringle

Born Dublin 30th August 1967. Married with three children. Educated St. Catherine's Vocational School, Killybegs; Letterkenny IT. Former Water Inspector with Donegal County Council. Contested 2002 Dail election as an Independent in Donegal South-West. Contested by-election in Donegal South-West in November 2010. First elected 2011.

Appointed Chairman Committee on Members' Interests December 2011. Member Committee on Communications, Natural Resources and Agriculture. First elected to Donegal County Council in the Donegal electoral area in 1999 as an Independent. Joined Sinn Fein and retained his seat in 2004. Resigned from Sinn Fein and retained his seat as an Independent in 2009.

DONEGAL SOUTH-WEST 2011 FIRST PREFERENCE VOTES							
	Seats	3			10,816		
	Candidate	Party	1st	%	Quota	Count	Status
1	**Doherty, Pearse***	**SF**	**14,262**	**32.97%**	**1.32**	**1**	**Made Quota**
2	**McGinley, Dinny***	**FG**	**8,589**	**19.85%**	**0.79**	**5**	**Made Quota**
3	**Pringle, Thomas**	**NP**	**5,845**	**13.51%**	**0.54**	**5**	**Elected**
4	Ó Domhnaill, Brían	FF	4,789	11.07%	0.44	5	Not Elected
5	Coughlan, Mary*	FF	4,956	11.46%	0.46	4	Eliminated
6	McBrearty, Frank	LB	2,209	5.11%	0.20	3	Eliminated
7	McCahill, Stephen	NP	1,831	4.23%	0.17	3	No Expenses
8	Duffy, John	GP	527	1.22%	0.05	2	No Expenses
9	Sweeney, Ann	NV	255	0.59%	0.02	2	No Expenses
9	***Outgoing**		**43,263**	**100.00%**	**10,816**	**2,705**	**No Expenses**

DONEGAL SOUTH-WEST 2011 PARTY VOTE												
	2011					2007					Change	
Party	Cand	1st	%	Quota	Seats	Cand	1st	%	Quota	Seats	%	Seats
FG	1	8,589	19.85%	0.79	1	1	9,167	23.00%	0.92	1	-3.15%	
LB	1	2,209	5.11%	0.20		1	1,111	2.79%	0.11		+2.32%	
FF	2	9,745	22.53%	0.90		2	20,136	50.53%	2.02	2	-28.00%	-2
SF	1	14,262	32.97%	1.32	1	1	8,462	21.23%	0.85		+11.73%	+1
GP	1	527	1.22%	0.05		1	589	1.48%	0.06		-0.26%	
Others	3	7,931	18.33%	0.73	1	1	388	0.97%	0.04		+17.36%	+1
Total	**9**	**43,263**	**100.0%**	**10,816**	**3**	**7**	**39,853**	**100.0%**	**9,964**	**3**	**0.00%**	**0**
Electorate		**64,568**	**67.00%**				**60,829**	**65.52%**			**+1.49%**	
Spoiled		**332**	**0.76%**				**421**	**1.05%**			**-0.28%**	
Turnout		**43,595**	**67.52%**				**40,274**	**66.21%**			**+1.31%**	

DONEGAL SOUTH-WEST 2011 TRANSFER ANALYSIS							
From	To	FG	LB	FF	GP	Others	Non Trans
LB	3,003	759		516		1,036	692
		25.27%		*17.18%*		*34.50%*	*23.04%*
FF	5,655	782		3,110		1,036	727
		13.83%		*55.00%*		*18.32%*	*12.86%*
SF	3,446	539	673	574	141	1,519	
		15.64%	*19.53%*	*16.66%*	*4.09%*	*44.08%*	
GP	668	101	77	112		278	100
		15.12%	*11.53%*	*16.77%*		*41.62%*	*14.97%*
Others	2,523	599	44	432		898	550
		23.74%	*1.74%*	*17.12%*		*35.59%*	*21.80%*
Total	**15,295**	**2,780**	**794**	**4,744**	**141**	**4,767**	**2,069**
		18.18%	***5.19%***	***31.02%***	***0.92%***	***31.17%***	***13.53%***

DONEGAL SOUTH-WEST 2011 COUNT DETAILS						
Seats	3				Quota	10,816
Candidate	**Party**	**1st**	**2nd** Doherty Surplus	**3rd** Duffy Sweeney	**4th** McBrearty McCahill	**5th** Coughlan Votes
			-3,446			
Doherty, Pearse*	SF	14,262	10,816	10,816	10,816	10,816
			+539	+159	+1,300	+782
McGinley, Dinny*	FG	8,589	9,128	9,287	10,587	11,369
			+1,186	+333	+1,775	+1,036
Pringle, Thomas	NP	5,845	7,031	7,364	9,139	10,175
			+358	+89	+488	+3,110
Ó Domhnaill, Brían	FF	4,789	5,147	5,236	5,724	8,834
			+216	+87	+396	-5,655
Coughlan, Mary*	FF	4,956	5,172	5,259	5,655	Eliminated
			+673	+121	-3,003	
McBrearty, Frank	LB	2,209	2,882	3,003	Eliminated	
			+206	+104	-2,141	
McCahill, Stephen	NP	1,831	2,037	2,141	Eliminated	
			+141	-668		
Duffy, John	GP	527	668	Eliminated		
			+127	-382		
Sweeney, Ann	NV	255	382	Eliminated		
Non-transferable				+157	+1,185	+727
Cumulative			0	157	1,342	2,069
Total		**43,263**	**43,263**	**43,263**	**43,263**	**43,263**

DONEGAL SOUTH-WEST ALL TDs 1937-2011																
	Surname	**Forename**	**Party**	**Elected**												**Total**
1	Breslin	Cormac	FF	37	38	43	44	48	51	54	57	61	65	69	73	12
2	McGinley	Dinny	FG	82	82	87	89	92	97	02	07	11				9
3	Brennan	Joe	FF	51	54	57	61	65	69	73	77					8
4	Gallagher	Pat The Cope	FF	81	82	82	87	89	92	02	07					8
5	O'Donnell	Pa	FG	49*	51	54	57	61	65	69						7
6	Coughlan	Mary	FF	87	89	92	97	02	07							6
7	Brady**	Brian	FF	37	38	43	44	48								5
8	McFadden**	Michael	FG	37	38	43	44	48								5
9	Coughlan	Clem	FF	80*	81	82	82									4
10	White	Jim	FG	73	77	81										3
11	Doherty	Pearse	SF	10*	11											2
12	Delap	Paddy	FF	70*												1
13	Coughlan	Cathal	FF	83*												1
14	Gildea	Tom	NP	97												1
15	Pringle	Thomas	NP	11												1
15	**Total**			***Includes 5 By-Elections & 1977 (Donegal)**											*	**73**
	**** Also elected in another constituency**															
1	McFadden**	Michael	FG	Donegal		27	27	33								3
2	Brady**	Brian	FF	Donegal		32	33									2
2	**Total**															**5**

DONEGAL SOUTH-WEST

MAIN BOUNDARY CHANGES

Dail	Constituency	Seats
9 (1937) - 16 (1957)	Donegal West	3
17 (1961) - 18 (1965)	Donegal South-West	3
19 (1969) - 20 (1973)	Donegal - Leitrim	3
22 (1981) - 31 (2011)	Donegal South-West	3

DONEGAL SOUTH-WEST PARTY VOTE 1937-2011

* No Contest		FG		LB		FF		SF		GP		WP		DL		C na P		C na T		Others	
Dail	Seats	S	% Vote	S	% Vote	S	% Vote	S	% Vote	S	% Vote	S	% Vote	S	% Vote	S	% Vote	S	% Vote	S	% Vote
9 1937	3	1	47.82%			2	52.18%														
10 1938*	3	1				2															
11 1943	3	1	26.39%		17.27%	2	46.36%												9.98%		
12 1944*	3	1				2															
13 1948	3	1	26.66%			2	42.38%										18.62%				12.35%
14 1951	3	1	44.80%			2	55.20%														
15 1954	3	1	47.15%			2	52.85%														
16 1957	3	1	40.05%			2	59.95%														
17 1961	3	1	42.80%			2	49.03%		8.17%												
18 1965	3	1	48.37%			2	51.63%														
19 1969	3	1	29.28%		6.01%	2	50.74%														13.97%
20 1973	3	1	36.30%			2	54.62%		8.65%												0.43%
22 1981	3	1	38.36%			2	45.44%														16.21%
23 1982	3	1	34.05%			2	48.02%						3.19%								14.74%
24 1982	3	1	39.07%			2	54.81%						6.12%								
25 1987	3	1	29.78%			2	58.22%		4.04%				7.96%								
26 1989	3	1	33.44%			2	55.17%						9.59%								1.80%
27 1992	3	1	37.74%			2	48.67%		3.31%						6.12%						4.16%
28 1997	3	1	22.97%		4.20%	1	38.04%				4.21%									1	30.58%
29 2002	3	1	25.42%		3.03%	2	42.09%		10.75%												18.72%
30 2007	3	1	23.00%		2.79%	2	50.53%		21.23%		1.48%										0.97%
31 2011	3	1	19.85%		5.11%		22.53%	1	32.97%		1.22%									1	18.33%
1937-2011	**66**	**22**	**33.70%**		**1.99%**	**41**	**48.06%**	**1**	**5.52%**		**0.41%**		**1.38%**		**0.30%**		**0.81%**		**0.43%**	**2**	**7.39%**
National	**4,618**	**1,453**	**30.77%**	**482**	**11.53%**	**1,985**	**41.86%**	**232**	**1.99%**	**16**	**0.75%**	**17**	**0.78%**	**8**	**0.22%**	**18**	**0.77%**	**43**	**1.08%**	**364**	**10.24%**

DONEGAL REGION		
MAIN BOUNDARY CHANGES		
Dail	**Constituency**	**Seats**
1 (1918)	Donegal North	1
	Donegal South-West	1
	Donegal West	1
2 (1921) - 3 (1922)	Donegal	6
4 (1923) -8 (1933)	Donegal	8
9 (1937) - 16 (1957)	Donegal East	4
	Donegal West	3
17 (1961) - 18 (1965)	Donegal North-East	3
	Donegal South-West	3
19 (1969) - 20 (1973)	Donegal North-East	3
	Donegal - Leitrim	3
21 (1977)	Donegal	5
22 (1981) - 31 (2011)	Donegal North-East	3
	Donegal South-West	3

DONEGAL REGION																			
ALL TDs 1918-2011																			
	Surname	**Forename**	**Party**	**Elected**															**Total**
1	Blaney	Neil T.	IFF	48*	51	54	57	61	65	69	73	77	81	82	82	87	89	92	15
2	Breslin	Cormac	FF	37	38	43	44	48	51	54	57	61	65	69	73				12
3	McMenamin	Daniel	FG	27J	32	33	37	38	43	44	48	51	54	57					11
4	Harte	Paddy	FG	61	65	69	73	77	81	82	82	87	89	92					11
5	McGinley	Dinny	FG	82	82	87	89	92	97	02	07	11							9
6	Blaney	Neil	FF	27	27	32	33	37	43	44	48								8
7	McFadden	Michael	FG	27	27	33	37	38	43	44	48								8
8	Brennan	Joe	FF	51	54	57	61	65	69	73	77								8
9	Gallagher	Pat The Cope	FF	81	82	82	87	89	92	02	07								8
10	Myles	Major James	NP	23	27	27	32	33	37	38									7
11	Brady	Brian	FF	32	33	37	38	43	44	48									7
12	O'Donnell	Pa	FG	49*	51	54	57	61	65	69									7
13	Cunningham	Liam	FF	51	54	57	61	65	69	73									7
14	Coughlan	Mary	FF	87	89	92	97	02	07										6
15	Sheldon	William	NP	43	44	48	51	54	57										6
16	O'Doherty	Joseph	FF	18	21	22	23	33											5
17	Friel	John	FF	37	38	43	44	48											5
18	Conaghan	Hugh	FF	77	81	82	82	87											5
19	McDaid	James	FF	89	92	97	02	07											5
20	Ward	Peter	CG	18	21	22	23												4
21	Doherty	Eugene	CG	23	27	27	32												4
22	White	John	NP	23	27	27	32												4
23	Coughlan	Clem	FF	80*	81	82	82												4
24	Sweeney	Joseph	CT	18	21	22													3
25	McGoldrick	P.J.	CG	21	22	23													3
26	Carney	Frank	FF	27	27	32													3
27	White	Jim	FG	73	77	81													3
28	Keaveney	Cecilia	FF	96*	97	02													3
29	McGinley	Joseph P	CT	21	22														2
30	O'Flaherty	Samuel	CR	21	22														2
31	Law	Hugh	CG	27	27														2
32	Dillon**	James	CP	32	33														2
33	Blaney	Niall	IFF	02	07														2
34	Doherty	Pearse	SF	10*	11														2
35	McHugh	Joe	FG	07	11														2
36	McFadden	Patrick	CG	23															1
37	O'Donnell	Peadar	R	23															1
38	McCullough	Denis	CG	24*															1
39	Cassidy	Archie	LB	27S															1
40	Doherty	Hugh	FF	33															1
41	McDevitt	Henry	FF	38															1
42	Delap	Paddy	FF	70*															1
43	Keaveney	Paddy	IFF	76*															1
44	Coughlan	Cathal	FF	83*															1
45	Blaney	Harry	IFF	97															1
46	Gildea	Tom	NP	97															1
47	MacLochlainn	Pauric	SF	11															1
48	McConalogue	Charlie	FF	11															1
49	Pringle	Thomas	NP	11															1
49	**Total**											***Includes 9 By-Elections**						*	**209**
	**** Also elected in another constituency**																		
	Dillon**	James	FG	Monaghan			37	38	43	44	48	51	54	57	61	65			10

DONEGAL REGION 1918-2011																												
* No Contest			FG		LB		FF		SF		GP		WP		DL		C na P		C na T		Farmers		Nat League		Centre P		Others	
Dail		Seats	S	% Vote	S	% Vote	S	% Vote	S	% Vote	S	% Vote	S	% Vote	S	% Vote	S	% Vote	S	% Vote	S	% Vote	S	% Vote	S	% Vote	S	% Vote
1	1918	3							3																			
2	1921*	6							6																			
3	1922*	6	4				2																					
4	1923	8	4	36.98%		4.66%	2	24.78%													1	14.65%					1	18.93%
5	1927	8	3	29.88%		8.71%	2	25.75%													1	9.74%	1	11.29%			1	14.63%
6	1927	8	3	40.38%	1	6.74%	2	29.56%													1	8.48%					1	14.84%
7	1932	8	3	30.16%		5.00%	3	37.50%																			2	27.34%
8	1933	8	2	25.97%			4	50.88%																	1	7.65%	1	15.50%
9	1937	7	2	35.13%			4	52.07%																			1	12.80%
10	1938	7	2	20.81%		4.38%	4	53.87%																			1	20.94%
11	1943	7	2	21.22%		10.59%	4	46.61%											1	9.87%								11.72%
12	1944	7	2	24.24%			4	55.19%																			1	20.57%
13	1948	7	2	24.01%			4	46.47%										14.65%									1	14.87%
14	1951	7	2	35.07%		1.41%	4	53.72%																			1	9.80%
15	1954	7	2	37.76%			4	51.13%																			1	11.11%
16	1957	7	2	29.86%			4	52.90%																			1	17.24%
17	1961	6	2	40.72%			4	55.19%		4.10%																		
18	1965	6	2	42.32%		2.25%	4	55.43%																				
19	1969	6	2	35.70%		4.80%	4	52.63%																				6.88%
20	1973	6	2	34.85%			3	45.53%		4.30%																	1	15.33%
21	1977	5	2	36.34%			2	36.40%						4.12%													1	23.15%
22	1981	6	2	37.04%		0.70%	3	42.04%																			1	20.22%
23	1982	6	2	36.10%		0.78%	3	41.22%						1.68%													1	20.23%
24	1982	6	2	38.06%		0.90%	3	45.07%						3.16%													1	12.81%
25	1987	6	2	29.74%		0.64%	3	45.73%		5.97%				4.12%													1	13.80%
26	1989	6	2	31.86%			3	47.37%		1.93%				4.89%													1	13.95%
27	1992	6	2	29.84%		5.80%	3	42.57%		2.96%		1.00%				2.99%											1	14.84%
28	1997	6	1	20.83%		4.87%	3	40.01%		4.24%		2.01%															2	28.05%
29	2002	6	1	23.19%		2.92%	4	45.78%		10.34%																	1	17.78%
30	2007	6	2	22.80%		2.31%	4	50.40%		19.38%		1.41%																3.69%
31	2011	6	2	25.35%		7.76%	1	20.15%	2	29.00%		0.90%															1	16.85%
1918-2011		**200**	**63**	**31.09%**	**1**	**2.74%**	**94**	**43.98%**	**11**	**3.60%**		**0.23%**		**0.65%**		**0.11%**		**0.54%**	**1**	**0.36%**	**3**	**1.04%**	**1**	**0.35%**	**1**	**0.32%**	**25**	**14.99%**
National		**4,618**	**1,453**	**30.77%**	**482**	**11.53%**	**1,985**	**41.86%**	**232**	**1.99%**	**16**	**0.75%**	**17**	**0.78%**	**8**	**0.22%**	**18**	**0.77%**	**43**	**1.08%**	**42**	**0.90%**	**10**	**0.24%**	**11**	**0.30%**	**301**	**8.78%**

DUBLIN CENTRAL 2011

"Fianna Fáil don't fare well without Bertie"

There were no boundary changes to this four seat constituency since 2007.

From the death of George Colley in 1983 until he announced on 30th December 2010 that he would not be contesting the 2011 election, Bertie Ahern was the undisputed kingpin here. Running mates came and went, some successful and some not, all left in little doubt that their allotted role was that of subordinate hoping to pick up the crumbs from Bertie's surplus, and that they should not develop any notions of equality. Vote management elsewhere usually means trying to divide a party's votes equally among its candidates, but in Dublin Central it meant trying to direct every available first preference to Bertie and taking it from there.

How would Fianna Fail fare without Bertie? Not well, everyone assumed, and they were right. Mary Fitzpatrick probably benefited from the continued open antagonism of the Drumcondra Mafia and from her appointment to Micheál Martin's front bench, and did well to finish as runner-up. Her time may yet come. The remaining incumbent, Cyprian Brady, may wish he had accompanied his patron into retirement. He increased his 2007 first preference tally by 74 per cent, quite an achievement for a Fianna Fail TD in 2011 – but since he had received only 939 first preferences in 2007, he still ended up amongst the also-rans in 2011. Whether Bertie Ahern himself would have been re-elected had he stood in 2011 will remain forever unknown.

The four seats sorted themselves out without much complication. Paschal Donohue of Fine Gael seemed a certainly based on his performances in 2007 and at the 2009 by-election, and he headed the poll. Labour's Joe Costello, now the veteran of the constituency, took the second seat. The third went to Maureen O'Sullivan, a former member of Tony Gregory's organisation who had won the 2009 by-election brought about by Gregory's death. Mary Lou McDonald's 13 per cent of the vote made some wonder whether she might fall short yet again, but decent transfers, especially from ex-Sinn Fein councillor Christy Burke, ensured that she and Sandra McLellan in Cork East became Sinn Fein's first female TDs since Caitlín Brugha in 1927.

The Technical Group in 31st Dail 2011 with Icelandic MP Lilja Mosesdottir

DUBLIN CENTRAL TDs 2011

PASCHAL DONOHOE (FG)

86 Shandon Park, Phibsborough, Dublin 7; Mobile: 087 2816868
Constituency Office: Phibsborough Plaza; Phibsborough, Dublin 7
Leinster House: 01 6183689; Email: paschal.donohoe@oireachtas.ie
Website: www.paschaldonohoe.ie

Born Dublin, 19th September 1974. Married to Justine Davey, two children. Educated St. Declan's CBS, Cabra; Trinity College, Dublin (Economics and Politics). Former Sales Manager. Contested 2007 general election in Dublin Central. First elected 2011.

Appointed Vice Chair Joint Committee on European Union Affairs June 2011. Member Public Accounts Committee. Elected to Senate on Administration Panel in 2007. Fine Gael Seanad Spokesperson on Transport and Marine, 2007-2011. Member Joint Committee on Transport 2007-2011. Member Dublin City Council 2004-2007.

JOE COSTELLO (LB)

66 Aughrim Street, Dublin 7, Tel: 01 8385358; Mobile: 087 2450777
Constituency Office: 334 North Circular Road, Dublin 7; Tel: 01 8308182
Leinster House: 01 6183896; Email: joe.costello@oireachtas.ie
Website: www.joecostellotd.blogspot.com

Born Sligo 13th July 1945. Married to Emer Malone. Educated Summerhill College, Sligo; St. Patrick's College, Maynooth and UCD. Minister of State. Former Teacher. First elected 1992. Lost his seat in 1997 re-elected 2002, 2007 and 2011.

Appointed Minister of State at the Department of Foreign Affairs and Trade with responsibility for Trade and Development 20th December 2011. Director of Elections for Michael D. Higgins in 2011 Presidency campaign. Chairman Joint Committee on European Union Affairs June -December 2011. Spokesperson on Transport July 2010-2011. Spokesperson on Europe and Human Rights September 2007-July 2010. Member Joint Committee on Transport July 2010-2011. Member Joint Committee on European Affairs 2007-2010. Former Member Joint Committee on European Scrutiny. Spokesperson on Justice 2002-2006. Unsuccessful candidate in Labour Deputy Leadership election in October 2002. Member Joint Committee on Justice, Equality, Defence and Women's Rights 2002-2007. Member Dail Sub-Committee of the Barron Report on the Dublin and Monaghan Bombings in 1974. Senator 1989–1992 and 1997-2002. Party Leader of the Seanad and spokesperson on Education, Science, Trade and Employment, Sport and Finance 1997-2002. Member British-Irish Inter-Parliamentary Body since 1997. Member Dublin City Council 1991-2003. Deputy Lord Mayor 1991/92. Former President of the Association of Secondary Teachers of Ireland. Member Sean McDermott Street Community Association; Save Temple Street Children's Hospital Campaign; Vice-Chair Amnesty International (1984-87). Member of Board of Rotunda Hospital since 1999. Executive member of the Irish Council for Civil Liberties (1976-1990). Founding member of Ireland-Palestine Solidarity Campaign (2002). Chairman Prisoners Rights Organisation 1975-1985. His wife Emer Costello was Lord Mayor of Dublin 2009/2010.

MAUREEN O'SULLIVAN (NP)

39 Fairfield Avenue, East Wall, Dublin 3; Mobile: 087 0550223; Leinster House: 01 6183488; Email: maureen.osullivan@oireachtas.ie; Website: www.maureenosullivan.ie

Born Dublin 10th March 1951. Single. Educated Mount Carmel Secondary, King's Inn Street, Dublin 1; UCD. Former secondary teacher and guidance counsellor. Member of Gregory group and was nominated by them to contest the by-election following his death. Won by-election on 5th June 2009 and retained her seat in 2011.

Member of Technical Group in 31st Dail. Member Committee on Foreign Affairs and Trade. Co-opted onto Dublin City Council as replacement for Mick Rafferty in the North Inner City electoral area in September 2008. Retained her seat in 2009 on the same day as the by-election. Resigned her council seat and was succeeded by Marie Metcalfe. Received the Lord Mayor award in 2007 for her lifetime commitment to voluntary work with young people.

MARY LOU McDONALD (SF)

10 Riverwood Green, Castleknock, Dublin 15;
Constituency Office: 58 Faussagh Avenue, Cabra, Dublin 7; Tel: 01 8683934
Leinster House: 01 6183230; Email: Marylou.mcdonald@oireachtas.ie;
Website: www.maryloumcdonald.ie; Twitter: twitter.com/maryloumcdonald.

Born Dublin 1st May 1969. Married to Martin Lanigan, one son, one daughter. Educated Trinity College (BA Mod), University of Limerick (MA) and Dublin City University. Previously worked as a consultant for the Irish Productivity Centre, a researcher for the Institute of European Affairs and trainer in the trade union sponsored Partnership Unit of the Educational and Training Services Trust. Contested 2002 general election in Dublin West. Contested 2007 election in Dublin Central and the June 2009 by-election. First elected 2011.

Party Deputy Leader and Spokesperson on Public Expenditure and Reform. Member Public Accounts Committee. Member Committee on Finance, Public Expenditure and Reform. Elected to European Parliament in 2004 but lost her seat in 2009. Member of the Sinn Fein Ard Chomhairle. Previously worked for the party in co-ordinating the work of Sinn Fein elected representatives across the island. Headed up the Sinn Fein campaign against the Lisbon Treaty in 2008.

DUBLIN CENTRAL 2011							
FIRST PREFERENCE VOTES							
	Seats	4			6,923		
	Candidate	Party	1st	%	Quota	Count	Status
1	**Donohoe, Paschal**	**FG**	**6,903**	**19.94%**	**1.00**	**2**	**Made Quota**
2	**Costello, Joe***	**LB**	**6,273**	**18.12%**	**0.91**	**5**	**Made Quota**
3	**O'Sullivan, Maureen***	**NP**	**4,139**	**11.96%**	**0.60**	**7**	**Made Quota**
4	**McDonald, Mary Lou**	**SF**	**4,526**	**13.08%**	**0.65**	**8**	**Elected**
5	Fitzpatrick, Mary	FF	3,504	10.12%	0.51	8	Not Elected
6	Clancy, Áine	LB	3,514	10.15%	0.51	6	Eliminated
7	Brady, Cyprian*	FF	1,637	4.73%	0.24	5	Eliminated
8	Perry, Cieran	NP	1,394	4.03%	0.20	4	No Expenses
9	Burke, Christy	NP	1,315	3.80%	0.19	3	No Expenses
10	Kearney, Phil	GP	683	1.97%	0.10	2	No Expenses
11	Steenson, Malachy	WP	274	0.79%	0.04	2	No Expenses
12	O'Loughlin, Paul	CS	235	0.68%	0.03	2	No Expenses
13	Hyland, John Pluto	NP	77	0.22%	0.01	1	No Expenses
14	Hollywood, Thomas	NP	65	0.19%	0.01	1	No Expenses
15	Johnston, Liam	FN	48	0.14%	0.01	1	No Expenses
16	Cooney, Benny	NP	25	0.07%	0.00	1	No Expenses
16	***Outgoing**		**34,612**	**100.00%**	**6,923**	**1,731**	**No Expenses**

DUBLIN CENTRAL 2011												
PARTY VOTE												
	2011					2007					Change	
Party	Cand	1st	%	Quota	Seats	Cand	1st	%	Quota	Seats	%	Seats
FG	1	6,903	19.94%	1.00	1	1	3,302	9.53%	0.48		+10.41%	+1
LB	2	9,787	28.28%	1.41	1	1	4,353	12.57%	0.63	1	+15.71%	
FF	2	5,141	14.85%	0.74		3	15,398	44.45%	2.22	2	-29.60%	-2
SF	1	4,526	13.08%	0.65	1	1	3,182	9.19%	0.46		+3.89%	+1
GP	1	683	1.97%	0.10		1	1,995	5.76%	0.29		-3.79%	
WP	1	274	0.79%	0.04							+0.79%	
CS	1	235	0.68%	0.03							+0.68%	
PD						1	193	0.56%	0.03		-0.56%	
Others	7	7,063	20.41%	1.02	1	5	6,216	17.95%	0.90	1	+2.46%	
Total	**16**	**34,612**	**100.0%**	**6,923**	**4**	**13**	**34,639**	**100.0%**	**6,928**	**4**	**0.00%**	**0**
Electorate		**56,892**	**60.84%**				**63,423**	**54.62%**			**+6.22%**	
Spoiled		**457**	**1.30%**				**510**	**1.45%**			**-0.15%**	
Turnout		**35,069**	**61.64%**				**35,149**	**55.42%**			**+6.22%**	

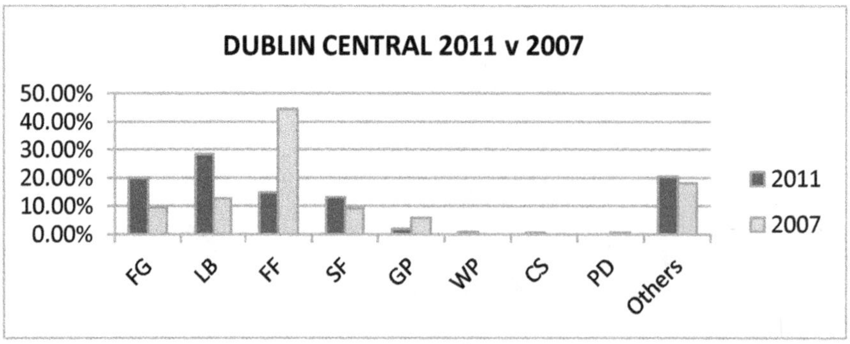

DUBLIN CENTRAL 2011 COUNT DETAILS									
Seats	4							Quota	6,923
Candidate	**Party**	**1st**	**2nd** Hyland Hollywood Johnston Cooney	**3rd** Kearney Steenson O'Loughlin Votes	**4th** Burke Votes	**5th** Perry Votes	**6th** Brady Votes	**7th** Clancy Votes	**8th** O'Sullivan Surplus
			+30						
Donohoe, Paschal	FG	6,903	6,933	6,933	6,933	6,933	6,933	6,933	6,933
			+16	*+139*	*+377*	*+310*			
Costello, Joe*	LB	6,273	6,289	6,428	6,805	7,115	7,115	7,115	7,115
			+32	*+336*	*+323*	*+554*	*+202*	*+2,055*	*-718*
O'Sullivan, Maureen*	NP	4,139	4,171	4,507	4,830	5,384	5,586	7,641	6,923
			+10	*+118*	*+411*	*+357*	*+131*	*+656*	*+378*
McDonald, Mary Lou	SF	4,526	4,536	4,654	5,065	5,422	5,553	6,209	6,587
			+10	*+92*	*+22*	*+88*	*+1,105*	*+582*	*+340*
Fitzpatrick, Mary	FF	3,504	3,514	3,606	3,628	3,716	4,821	5,403	5,743
			+18	*+264*	*+57*	*+125*	*+157*	*-4,135*	
Clancy, Áine	LB	3,514	3,532	3,796	3,853	3,978	4,135	Eliminated	
			+2	*+36*	*+50*	*+28*	*-1,753*		
Brady, Cyprian*	FF	1,637	1,639	1,675	1,725	1,753	Eliminated		
			+32	*+106*	*+83*	*-1,615*			
Perry, Cieran	NP	1,394	1,426	1,532	1,615	Eliminated			
			+8	*+70*	*-1,393*				
Burke, Christy	NP	1,315	1,323	1,393	Eliminated				
			+20	*-703*					
Kearney, Phil	GP	683	703	Eliminated					
			+11	*-285*					
Steenson, Malachy	WP	274	285	Eliminated					
			+16	*-251*					
O'Loughlin, Paul	CS	235	251	Eliminated					
			-77						
Hyland, John Pluto	NP	77	Eliminated						
			-65						
Hollywood, Thomas	NP	65	Eliminated						
			-48						
Johnston, Liam	FN	48	Eliminated						
			-25						
Cooney, Benny	NP	25	Eliminated						
Non-transferable			*+10*	*+78*	*+70*	*+153*	*+158*	*+842*	
Cumulative			10	88	158	311	469	1,311	1,311
Total		**34,612**	**34,612**	**34,612**	**34,612**	**34,612**	**34,612**	**34,612**	**34,612**

DUBLIN CENTRAL 2011 TRANSFER ANALYSIS									
From	**To**	**FG**	**LB**	**FF**	**SF**	**GP**	**WP**	**Others**	**Non Trans**
LB	4,135			582	656			2,055	842
				14.07%	*15.86%*			*49.70%*	*20.36%*
FF	1,753		157	1,105	131			202	158
			8.96%	*63.03%*	*7.47%*			*11.52%*	*9.01%*
GP	703		229	73	67			290	44
			32.57%	*10.38%*	*9.53%*			*41.25%*	*6.26%*
WP	285		93	29	27			118	18
			32.63%	*10.18%*	*9.47%*			*41.40%*	*6.32%*
Others	4,192	30	984	566	1,180	20	11	1,152	249
		0.72%	*23.47%*	*13.50%*	*28.15%*	*0.48%*	*0.26%*	*27.48%*	*5.94%*
Total	**11,068**	**30**	**1,463**	**2,355**	**2,061**	**20**	**11**	**3,817**	**1,311**
		0.27%	***13.22%***	***21.28%***	***18.62%***	***0.18%***	***0.10%***	***34.49%***	***11.84%***

DUBLIN CENTRAL		
MAIN BOUNDARY CHANGES		
Dail	**Constituency**	**Seats**
19 (1969) - 20 (1973)	Dublin Central	4
21 (1977)	Cabra	3
22 (1981) - 26 (1989)	Dublin Central	5
27 (1992) - 31 (2011)	Dublin Central	4

DUBLIN CENTRAL															
ALL TDs 1969-2011															
	Surname	**Forename**	**Party**	**Elected**											**Total**
1	Ahern**	Bertie	FF	81	82	82	87	89	92	97	02	07			9
2	Gregory	Tony	NP	82	82	87	89	92	97	02	07				8
3	Keating**	Michael	FG	81	82	82	87								4
4	Costello	Joe	LB	92	02	07	11								4
5	De Valera**	Vivion	FF	69	73	77									3
6	Colley**	George	FF	81	82	82									3
7	Fitzpatrick	Dermot	FF	87	89	02									3
8	Cluskey**	Frank	LB	69	73										2
9	Dockrell**	Maurice E.	FG	69	73										2
10	Fitzpatrick**	Tom	FF	69	73										2
11	Leonard	Thomas	FF	77	83*										2
12	Glenn	Alice	FG	81	82N										2
13	O'Leary**	Michael	FG	81	82										2
14	Stafford	John	FF	87	89										2
15	Mitchell**	Jim	FG	92	97										2
16	O'Sullivan	Maureen	NP	09*	11										2
17	Byrne**	Hugh	FG	77											1
18	Lee	Pat	FG	89											1
19	McGennis	Marian	FF	97											1
20	Brady	Cyprian	FF	07											1
21	Donohoe	Paschal	FG	11											1
22	McDonald	Mary Lou	SF	11											1
22	**Total**							***Includes 2 By-Elections**						*	**58**
	**** Also elected in another constituency**														
1	Dockrell**	Maurice E.	FG	South/SC			43	44	48	51	54	57	61	65	8
2	De Valera**	Vivion	FF	NW/NC			45*	48	51	54	57	61	65		7
3	Mitchell**	Jim	FG	West			77	81	82	82	87	89			6
4	Colley**	George	FF	NE/NC			61	65	69	73	77				5
5	Cluskey**	Frank	LB	SC			65	77	82	82	87				5
6	O'Leary**	Michael	FG	NC/SW			65	69	73	77	82N				5
7	Fitzpatrick**	Tom	FF	SC			65	77	81	82F					4
8	Byrne**	Hugh	FG	NW			69	73	81						3
9	Ahern**	Bertie	FF	Finglas			77								1
10	Keating**	Michael	FG	NC			77								1
10	**Total**							***Includes 1 By-Election**						*	**45**

DUBLIN CENTRAL 1969-2011																							
* No Contest			FG		LB		FF		SF		GP		WP		CS		PD		DL		Others		
Dail		Seats	S	% Vote	S	% Vote	S	% Vote	S	% Vote	S	% Vote	S	% Vote	S	% Vote	S	% Vote	S	% Vote	S	% Vote	
19	1969	4	1	22.97%	1	**29.27%**	2	37.38%														10.39%	
20	1973	4	1	27.28%	1	23.89%	2	44.42%														4.41%	
21	1977*	3	1	23.75%		23.76%	2	**46.38%**														6.11%	
22	1981	5	2	28.82%	1	17.51%	2	43.03%						3.88%								6.77%	
23	1982	5	1	28.41%	1	11.02%	2	43.10%		3.19%				3.66%							1	10.63%	
24	1982	5	2	**31.88%**		7.50%	2	41.73%						**4.86%**							1	14.02%	
25	1987	5		12.59%		2.95%	3	42.13%		5.27%				3.08%			1	**13.40%**			1	20.58%	
26	1989	5	1	12.81%		6.20%	3	44.85%		6.46%		3.70%		4.42%				3.43%			1	18.13%	
27	1992	4	1	14.08%	1	20.08%	1	39.28%		3.74%		2.55%		1.62%						**1.28%**	1	17.37%	
28	1997	4	1	14.51%		8.49%	2	42.83%		6.65%		3.51%		1.42%							1	**22.59%**	
29	2002	4		11.07%	1	12.15%	2	39.58%		**14.61%**		4.32%				**1.08%**					1	17.19%	
30	2007	4		9.53%	1	12.57%	2	44.45%		9.19%		**5.76%**				0.75%		0.56%			1	17.19%	
31	2011	4	1	19.94%	1	28.28%		14.85%	1	13.08%		1.97%		0.79%		0.68%					1	20.41%	
1969-2011		**56**	**12**	**20.02%**	**8**	**14.71%**	**25**	**40.44%**	**1**	**4.71%**		**1.60%**	**0**	**2.10%**		**0.18%**	**1**	**1.63%**		**0.10%**	**9**	**14.52%**	
National		**4,618**	**1,453**	**30.77%**	**482**	**11.53%**	**1,985**	**41.86%**	**232**	**1.99%**	**16**	**0.75%**	**17**	**0.78%**		**0.04%**	**44**	**1.42%**	**8**	**0.22%**	**381**	**10.63%**	

*** 1977: Cabra**

DUBLIN MID-WEST 2011

"4 in every 10 voters switch from Fianna Fail–PD–Green government to Fine Gael–Labour "

There were no boundary changes in this four seat constituency since 2007.

Here we saw the biggest swing in the entire country, with Fine Gael and Labour increasing their combined vote by a massive 39 per cent while Fianna Fail and the Greens dropped by 29 per cent. The retirement of former PD leader Mary Harney, who had taken 12 per cent of the votes in 2007, meant that four in every ten voters switched from the Fianna Fail –PD– Green government to the Fine Gael –Labour alternative. John Curran of Fianna Fail, government chief whip and seen as a rising star in 2007, lost his seat, while outgoing Green TD Paul Gogarty did not even reach a quarter of the quota, the figure needed to qualify for reimbursement of campaign expenses. Gogarty did at least leave on a high note, becoming the first TD to concede defeat via Twitter.

Fine Gael and Labour vied for supremacy here, with Fine Gael outpolling its future partner by just 76 votes. The 62 per cent of the votes won by the two parties proved enough to take all four seats, making this just one of five constituencies in the country left without an opposition TD. Labour's Joanna Tuffy and Fine Gael Seanad leader Frances Fitzgerald, who had respectively taken the last seat and been the runner-up in 2007, now took the first two seats comfortably. Their fates on 9th March were rather different, Fitzgerald entering cabinet while Tuffy was left on the backbenches.

The second Labour candidate, Clondalkin-based Robert Dowds, attracted transfers from other candidates of the broad left and took the third seat. The fourth seat lay between Fine Gael's Lucan-based Derek Keating, and Eoin Ó Broin of Sinn Fein, who had finished bottom of the poll in Dun Laoghaire in 2007. After the seventh count Ó Broin moved into third position, and the decisive elimination was that of Fianna Fail's John Curran. Sinn Fein's continued inability to attract large-scale transfers was a big factor here: Curran's transfers went heavily to the three candidates of Fine Gael and Labour still in the count, with Ó Broin receiving fewer than 10 per cent of them, so Keating was elected with over 500 votes to spare.

Minister for Children Frances Fitzgerald receives her seal of office from President McAleese

DUBLIN MID-WEST TDs 2011

JOANNA TUFFY (LB)

46A Esker Lawns, Lucan, Co. Dublin; Tel: 01 6280765
Constituency Office: Dispensary Lane, Lucan; Tel: 01 6218400
Leinster House: 01 6183822; Email: joanna.tuffy@oireachtas.ie,
Website: www.joannatuffy.ie Twitter: www.twitter.com/joannatuffytd

Born London 9th March 1965. Partner Philip Long, one daughter. Educated St. Joseph's College, Lucan; Trinity College, Dublin (BA Mod Hons); DIT, Rathmines (Diploma in Legal Studies). Solicitor. Contested 2002 general election in Dublin Mid-West. First elected 2007.

Appointed Chair Committee on the Implementation of the Good Friday Agreement December 2011.Vice Chair Committee on Justice, Defence and Equality June-December 2011. Front Bench spokesperson on Environment and Heritage 2007-2011. Member Joint Committee on the Environment, Heritage and Local Government 2007-2011. Senator 2002-2007. Member Joint Committees on Education and Science; Justice, Equality, Defence and Women's Rights, 2002-2007. Member South Dublin County Council 1999-2003. Daughter of Eamon Tuffy member South Dublin County Council since 2003.

FRANCES FITZGERALD (FG)

116 Georgian Village, Castleknock, Dublin 15; Tel: 01 8211796; Mobile: 087 2579026
Constituency Office: Laurel House, New Road, Clondalkin, Dublin 22; Tel: 01 4577712
Leinster House: 01 6183771; Email: frances.fitzgerald@oireachtas.ie
Website: www. francesfitzgerald.finegael.ie; Twitter: www.twitter.com/joinfrances

Born Croom, Co. Limerick, August 1950. Married to Michael Fitzgerald, three sons. Educated Sion Hill Convent, Blackrock, Co. Dublin; UCD (Social Science) and London School of Economics (BSocSc, MSc). Minister for Children Former Social Worker. TD for Dublin South East 1992-2002. Contested general election in Dublin Mid-West in 2007. Regained her seat in 2011.

Appointed Minister for Children 9th March 2011. Fine Gael Leader in the Seanad 2007-2011. Seanad spokesperson on Health and Children 2007-2011. Member Joint Committee on Health and Children and Member Joint Committee on Constitutional Amendment on Children 2007-2011. Former Member Committee of Selection of Seanad Eireann and former Member Seanad Committee on Procedure and Privileges. Member Committee on Members' Interests of Seanad Eireann. Fine Gael front bench spokesperson on Equality, Opportunity and Family Affairs 2001-2002; on Social, Community and Family Affairs 1999-2001. Member Dublin City Council 1999-2004. Chairperson of the National Women's Council 1989-1992 and a member of the Second Commission on the Status of Women. Former Chairperson Women's Political Association.

ROBERT DOWDS (LB)

43 Castle Park, Clondalkin, Dublin 22; Tel: 01 4594583; Mobile: 087 6520360
Constituency Office: 3 Main Street, Clondalkin, Dublin 22
Leinster House: 01 6183446; Email: robert.dowds@oireachtas.ie; Website: www.robertdowds.ie

Born Dublin 2nd May 1953. Married with two children. Educated Trinity College and St. Patrick's College, Drumcondra. Former special education teacher and school principal. Elected at his first attempt in 2011.

Member Committee on Communications, Natural Resources and Agriculture. Member Committee on Health and Children. Contested 1991 local election in the Clondalkin electoral area of South Dublin County Council. First elected 1999. Retained his seat in 2004 and 2009. Suffers from cerebral palsy.

DEREK KEATING (FG)

66 Beech Park, Lucan, Co. Dublin; Tel: 01 6281053; Mobile: 087 2857435
Leinster House: 01 6184014; Email: derek.keating@oireachtas.ie
Website: www.derekkeating.net; Twitter: twitter.com/derekkeating

Born Ballyfermot, Dublin; 16th May 1955. Married to Anne, two daughters. Educated De La Salle Secondary School, Ballyfermot. Contested 2007 general election in Dublin Mid -West as an independent. Joined Fine Gael in August 2008. First elected 2011.

Member Committee on Health and Children. First elected to South Dublin County Council in the Lucan electoral area in 1999 as Independent. Retained his seat in 2004. Retained his seat as a Fine Gael member in 2009. Former member of PD's.

DUBLIN MID-WEST 2011 FIRST PREFERENCE VOTES							
	Seats	4			8,545		
	Candidate	Party	1st	%	Quota	Count	Status
1	**Tuffy, Joanna***	**LB**	**7,495**	**17.54%**	**0.88**	**7**	**Made Quota**
2	**Fitzgerald, Frances #**	**FG**	**7,281**	**17.04%**	**0.85**	**8**	**Made Quota**
3	**Dowds, Robert**	**LB**	**5,643**	**13.21%**	**0.66**	**9**	**Elected**
4	**Keating, Derek**	**FG**	**5,933**	**13.89%**	**0.69**	**9**	**Elected**
5	Ó Broin Eoin	SF	5,060	11.84%	0.59	9	Not Elected
6	Curran, John*	FF	5,043	11.80%	0.59	7	Eliminated
7	Kenny, Gino	PBPA	2,471	5.78%	0.29	6	Eliminated
8	Gogarty, Paul*	GP	1,484	3.47%	0.17	6	No Expenses
9	Finnegan, Mick	WP	694	1.62%	0.08	5	No Expenses
10	Connolly, Rob	SP	622	1.46%	0.07	5	No Expenses
11	Ryan, Michael	NP	375	0.88%	0.04	4	No Expenses
12	McGrath, Colm	NP	253	0.59%	0.03	3	No Expenses
13	McHale, Jim	NP	255	0.60%	0.03	2	No Expenses
14	Smith, Niall	NP	113	0.26%	0.01	1	No Expenses
14	***Outgoing TD # Former TD**		**42,722**	**100.00%**	**8,545**	**2,137**	**No Expenses**

DUBLIN MID-WEST 2011 PARTY VOTE												
	2011					2007					Change	
Party	Cand	1st	%	Quota	Seats	Cand	1st	%	Quota	Seats	%	Seats
FG	2	13,214	30.93%	1.55	2	1	4,480	12.00%	0.60		+18.93%	+2
LB	2	13,138	30.75%	1.54	2	1	4,075	10.91%	0.55	1	+19.84%	+1
FF	1	5,043	11.80%	0.59		2	12,321	33.00%	1.65	1	-21.19%	-1
SF	1	5,060	11.84%	0.59		1	3,462	9.27%	0.46		+2.57%	
SP	1	622	1.46%	0.07							+1.46%	
PBPA	1	2,471	5.78%	0.29							+5.78%	
GP	1	1,484	3.47%	0.17		1	4,043	10.83%	0.54	1	-7.35%	-1
WP	1	694	1.62%	0.08		1	366	0.98%	0.05		+0.64%	
PD						1	4,663	12.49%	0.62	1	-12.49%	-1
Others	4	996	2.33%	0.12		3	3,929	10.52%	0.53		-8.19%	
Total	**14**	**42,722**	**100.0%**	**8,545**	**4**	**11**	**37,339**	**100.0%**	**7,468**	**4**	**0.00%**	**0**
Electorate		**64,880**	**65.85%**				**61,347**	**60.87%**			**+4.98%**	
Spoiled		**471**	**1.09%**				**319**	**0.85%**			**+0.24%**	
Turnout		**43,193**	**66.57%**				**37,658**	**61.39%**			**+5.19%**	

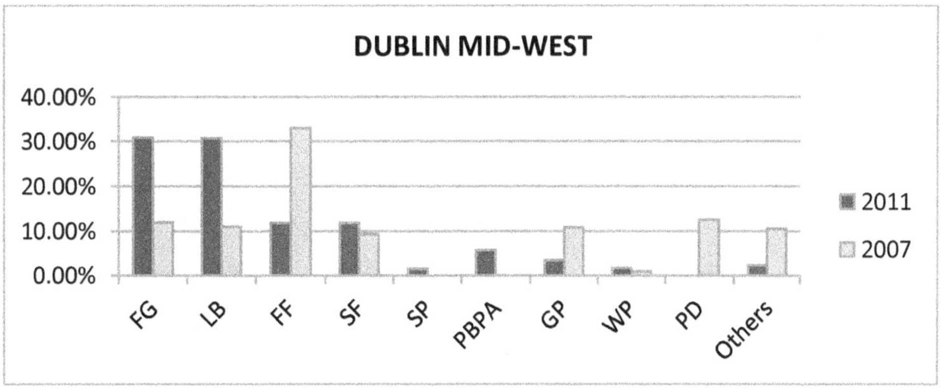

DUBLIN MID-WEST 2011
COUNT DETAILS

Seats 4 | Quota 8,545

Candidate	Party	1st	2nd Smith Votes	3rd McHale Votes	4th McGrath Votes	5th Ryan Votes	6th Finnegan Connolly	7th Kenny Gogarty	8th Curran Votes	9th Fitzgerald Surplus
			+18	+20	+20	+80	+194	+1,121		
Tuffy, Joanna*	LB	7,495	7,513	7,533	7,553	7,633	7,827	8,948	8,948	8,948
			+4	+18	+20	+101	+69	+410	+1,310	-668
Fitzgerald, Frances #	FG	7,281	7,285	7,303	7,323	7,424	7,493	7,903	9,213	8,545
			+2	+16	+34	+39	+136	+649	+1,415	+178
Dowds, Robert	LB	5,643	5,645	5,661	5,695	5,734	5,870	6,519	7,934	8,112
			+5	+7	+19	+28	+80	+431	+741	+459
Keating, Derek	FG	5,933	5,938	5,945	5,964	5,992	6,072	6,503	7,244	7,703
			+6	+22	+29	+47	+235	+1,229	+492	+31
Ó Broin Eoin	SF	5,060	5,066	5,088	5,117	5,164	5,399	6,628	7,120	7,151
			+4	+21	+27	+35	+63	+320	-5,513	
Curran, John*	FF	5,043	5,047	5,068	5,095	5,130	5,193	5,513	Eliminated	
			+10	+32	+23	+61	+462	-3,059		
Kenny, Gino	PBPA	2,471	2,481	2,513	2,536	2,597	3,059	Eliminated		
			+6	+8	+11	+25	+71	-1,605		
Gogarty, Paul*	GP	1,484	1,490	1,498	1,509	1,534	1,605	Eliminated		
			+6	+12	+10	+13	-735			
Finnegan, Mick	WP	694	700	712	722	735	Eliminated			
			+2	+10	+3	+12	-649			
Connolly, Rob	SP	622	624	634	637	649	Eliminated			
			+22	+32	+85	-514				
Ryan, Michael	NP	375	397	429	514	Eliminated				
			+16	+50	-319					
McGrath, Colm	NP	253	269	319	Eliminated					
			+9	-264						
McHale, Jim	NP	255	264	Eliminated						
			-113							
Smith, Niall	NP	113	Eliminated							
Non-transferable			+3	+16	+38	+73	+74	+504	+1,555	
Cumulative			3	19	57	130	204	708	2,263	2,263
Total		**42,722**	**42,722**	**42,722**	**42,722**	**42,722**	**42,722**	**42,722**	**42,722**	**42,722**

DUBLIN MID-WEST 2011
TRANSFER ANALYSIS

From	To	FG	LB	FF	SF	SP	PBPA	GP	WP	Others	Non Trans
FG	668	459	178		31						
		68.71%	*26.65%*		*4.64%*						
FF	5,513	2,051	1,415		492						1,555
		37.20%	*25.67%*		*8.92%*						*28.21%*
SP	649	70	155	29	110		217	33			35
		10.79%	*23.88%*	*4.47%*	*16.95%*		*33.44%*	*5.08%*			*5.39%*
PBPA	3,059	552	1,161	210	806						330
		18.05%	*37.95%*	*6.86%*	*26.35%*						*10.79%*
GP	1,605	289	609	110	423						174
		18.01%	*37.94%*	*6.85%*	*26.36%*						*10.84%*
WP	735	79	175	34	125		245	38			39
		10.75%	*23.81%*	*4.63%*	*17.01%*		*33.33%*	*5.17%*			*5.31%*
Others	1,210	202	229	87	104	27	126	50	41	214	130
		16.69%	*18.93%*	*7.19%*	*8.60%*	*2.23%*	*10.41%*	*4.13%*	*3.39%*	*17.69%*	*10.74%*
Total	**13,439**	**3,702**	**3,922**	**470**	**2,091**	**27**	**588**	**121**	**41**	**214**	**2,263**
		27.55%	***29.18%***	***3.50%***	***15.56%***	***0.20%***	***4.38%***	***0.90%***	***0.31%***	***1.59%***	***16.84%***

DUBLIN MID-WEST		
MAIN BOUNDARY CHANGES		
Dail	**Constituency**	**Seats**
29 (2002)	Dublin Mid-West	3
30 (2007) - 31 (2011)	Dublin Mid-West	4

DUBLIN MID-WEST 2002-2011																							
* No Contest		FG		LB		FF		SF		SP		PBPA		GP		WP		CS		PD		Others	
Dail	**Seats**	**S**	**% Vote**	**S**	**% Vote**	**S**	**% Vote**	**S**	**% Vote**	**S**	**% Vote**	**S**	**% Vote**	**S**	**% Vote**	**S**	**% Vote**	**S**	**% Vote**	**S**	**% Vote**	**S**	**% Vote**
29 2002	3		11.51%		9.01%	1	32.06%		6.52%					1	12.33%		1.38%		0.38%	1	20.05%		6.77%
30 2007	4		12.00%	1	10.91%	1	33.00%		9.27%				2.83%	1	10.83%		0.98%			1	12.49%		7.69%
31 2011	4	2	30.93%	2	30.75%		11.80%		11.84%		1.46%		5.78%		3.47%		1.62%						2.33%
2002-2011	**11**	**2**	**19.32%**	**3**	**18.22%**	**2**	**24.41%**		**9.56%**		**0.57%**		**3.25%**	**2**	**8.33%**		**1.34%**		**0.10%**	**2**	**9.56%**		**5.34%**
National	**4,618**	**1,453**	**30.77%**	**482**	**11.53%**	**1,985**	**41.86%**	**232**	**1.99%**	**4**	**0.16%**	**2**	**0.09%**	**16**	**0.75%**	**17**	**0.78%**		**0.04%**	**44**	**1.42%**	**383**	**10.60%**

DUBLIN MID-WEST													
ALL TDs 2002-2011													
	Surname	**Forename**	**Party**	**Elected**									**Total**
1	Harney**	Mary	PD	02	07								2
2	Curran	John	FF	02	07								2
3	Gogarty	Paul	GP	02	07								2
4	Tuffy	Joanna	LB	07	11								2
5	Fitzgerald**	Frances	FG	11									1
6	Dowds	Robert	LB	11									1
7	Keating	Derek	FG	11									1
7	**Total**												**11**
	** Also elected in another constiteuncy												
1	Harney**	Mary	PD	DSW		81	82	82	87	89	92	97	7
2	Fitzgerald**	Frances	FG	DSE		92	97						2
2	**Total**												**9**

DUBLIN NORTH 2011

"All change as only one outgoing deputy returned."

There were major Constituency Commission changes here since 2007. A population of 12,768 in the Swords-Forrest/Airport area was transferred to Dublin West, and a population of 9,021 in the Portmarnock and Balgriffin areas was transferred to Dublin North-East. However, the constituency did retain its four seats.

This was another good performance by Fine Gael with their vote up 17 points and with 1.6 quotas spread over the party's two candidates they were in contention for two seats. Dr. James Reilly topped the poll and was over the quota on the first count for an impressive performance by the party's deputy leader and health spokesperson. His running mate Alan Farrell failed to live up to his senior colleague's performance but his 5,310 first preferences put him in the frame and over 1,100 votes ahead of his nearest rivals. Farrell's first count lead proved to be sufficient as he went on to beat O'Brien for the final seat by 1,092 votes.

The Labour party's vote was up 17 points on 2007 and with 1.3 quotas spread over the party's two candidates they were well placed to take back the seat that they had lost in 2007. Outgoing Senator Brendan Ryan, whose brother Sean had previously held the Labour seat in this constituency, was just short of the quota on the first count and went on to take the second seat on the third count. Cllr Tom Kelleher polled just 6.5% and was never in contention.

This was another disastrous performance by Fianna Fáil with their vote down 27 points but with 0.8 quotas they should still have been in contention for a seat. But the party failed to recognise their precarious position which demanded a single candidate strategy and with both outgoing deputies contesting, their reduced vote was split between them and both lost out. Darragh O'Brien got 4,115 first preferences to leave him outside the frame with just 0.4 of a quota on the first count. Michael Kennedy had a similar performance winning just 3,519 first preferences. This left both of them too far off the pace and another double loss and another blank constituency for Fianna Fáil.

Clare Daly of the Socialist Party has been knocking on the door here for the last few elections. She was tipped to win a seat in 2007 but came up short. She made no mistake at this election as she was in 3rd place on the first count and she went on to take the third seat comfortably and became one of five TD's returned for the new United Left Alliance.

This was another poor performance by the Green Party with former leader Trevor Sargent losing his seat. Sargent was outside the frame in fifth place on the first count and was too far off the pace. He was eliminated on the fifth count with Farrell and Daly the main beneficiaries of his transfers.

DUBLIN NORTH TDs 2011

DR. JAMES REILLY (FG)

Seafoam, South Shore Road, Rush, Co. Dublin, Tel: 01 8075547;
Constituency Office: 19 Bridge Street, Balbriggan, Co. Dublin, Tel: 01 8437014
Leinster House: Tel: 01 6183749; Email: james.reilly@oireachtas.ie
Website: www.reilly.ie; Twitter: twitter.com/drjamesreilly

Born Lusk, Co. Dublin, 16th August 1955. Married to Dorothy McEvoy, one daughter, four sons. Educated Gormanstown College, Co. Meath; Royal College of Surgeons (LRCPSI, MB, BAO, BCL). Minister for Health. Medical Doctor. First elected 2007. Retained his seat in 2011.

Appointed Minister for Health 9th March 2011. Appointed Deputy Leader and front bench spokesperson on Health 1st July 2010. Supported Enda Kenny during Richard Bruton's failed leadership challenge in June 2010. Party Spokesperson on Health September 2007-July 2010. Member Joint Committee on Health and Children 2007-2011. Former President Irish Medical Organisation (IMO). Former Chairman and President of GP Committee of IMO and is currently Chairman GP Development Team and IMO representative at World Medical Association. Former member Eastern Health Board; Eastern Regional Health Authority and Northern Health Board.

BRENDAN RYAN (LB)

Baltrasna, Skerries, Co. Dublin, Tel: 01 8490265; Leinster House: 01 6183421
Email: brendan.ryan@oireachtas.ie; Website; www.brendan-ryan.ie

Born Portrane, Co. Dublin, 15th February 1953. Married to Margie Monks, three daughters. Educated DIT; UCD and DCU. Operations Manager. Contested 2007 general election in Dublin North. First elected 2011.

Member Committee on Jobs, Social Protection and Education. Senator 2007-2011. Labour Party Spokesperson on Consumer Affairs and Seanad Spokesperson on Education and Science, Transport and Defence, 2007-2011. Member Joint Committee on Education and Science and Member Joint Committee on Enterprise, Trade and Employment 2007-2011. Representative on Fingal Community Forum. Member and Treasurer Skerries Community Association. Secretary of the Hills and District Residents Association. Member Skerries Community Centre Board of Management. Brother of Sean Ryan TD for Dublin North 1989-1997, 1998-2007. Senator 1997-1998.

CLARE DALY (SP)

21 Elmwood Drive, Swords, Co. Dublin; Tel: 01 8408059; Mobile: 087 2415576
Leinster House: 01 6183390; Email: clare.daly@oireachtas.ie
Website: www.claredaly.ie

Born 11th April 1968. Married. Educated Dublin City University, Accounting and Finance graduate. Airport Worker. Contested 1997, 2002 and 2007 general elections in Dublin North. Contested Dail by-election in Dublin North 11th March 1998. First elected 2011.

Member Committee on Environment, Transport, Culture and the Gaeltacht. Member Committee on the Implementation of the Good Friday Agreement. First elected to Fingal County Council in the Swords electoral area in 1999. Retained her seat in 2004 and 2009. Former President of the Student's Union in NIHE Dublin and later at DCU.

ALAN FARRELL (FG)

4 Drynam Drive, Drynam Hall, Kinsealy, Co. Dublin; Tel: 01 8456500; Mobile: 086 8203320
Leinster House: 01 6184008; Email: alan.farrell@oireachtas.ie; Website: www.alanfarrell.ie
Twitter: twitter.com/alanfarrell

Born Dublin 29th December 1977. Married. Educated Chanel College, Coolock; Waterford IT.

Member Committee on the Implementation of the Good Friday Agreement. Member Committee on Investigations, Oversight and Petitions. First elected to Fingal County Council in the Malahide electoral area in 2004. Elected in new Howth-Malahide EA in 2009.

United Left Alliance TDs

	Candidate	Party	1st	%	Quota	Count	Status
	DUBLIN NORTH 2011						
	FIRST PREFERENCE VOTES						
	Seats	**4**			**9,870**		
	Candidate	**Party**	**1st**	**%**	**Quota**	**Count**	**Status**
1	**Reilly, Dr. James***	**FG**	**10,178**	**20.63%**	**1.03**	**1**	**Made Quota**
2	**Ryan, Brendan**	**LB**	**9,809**	**19.88%**	**0.99**	**3**	**Made Quota**
3	**Daly, Clare**	**SP**	**7,513**	**15.22%**	**0.76**	**6**	**Made Quota**
4	**Farrell, Alan**	**FG**	**5,310**	**10.76%**	**0.54**	**7**	**Elected**
5	O'Brien, Darragh*	FF	4,115	8.34%	0.42	7	Not Elected
6	Sargent, Trevor*	GP	4,186	8.48%	0.42	5	Eliminated
7	Kennedy, Michael*	FF	3,519	7.13%	0.36	4	Eliminated
8	Kelleher, Tom	LB	3,205	6.49%	0.32	3	Eliminated
9	Harrold, Mark	NP	1,512	3.06%	0.15	2	No Expenses
9	***Outgoing**		**49,347**	**100.00%**	**9,870**	**2,468**	**No Expenses**

DUBLIN NORTH 2011												
PARTY VOTE												
	2011					**2007**					**Change**	
Party	**Cand**	**1st**	**%**	**Quota**	**Seats**	**Cand**	**1st**	**%**	**Quota**	**Seats**	**%**	**Seats**
FG	2	15,488	31.39%	1.57	2	1	7,667	14.03%	0.70	1	+17.35%	+1
LB	2	13,014	26.37%	1.32	1	1	5,256	9.62%	0.48		+16.75%	+1
FF	2	7,634	15.47%	0.77		3	22,998	42.09%	2.10	2	-26.62%	-2
SF						1	1,454	2.66%	0.13		-2.66%	
SP	1	7,513	15.22%	0.76	1	1	4,872	8.92%	0.45		+6.31%	+1
GP	1	4,186	8.48%	0.42		2	9,107	16.67%	0.83	1	-8.18%	-1
PD						1	1,395	2.55%	0.13		-2.55%	
Others	1	1,512	3.06%	0.15		3	1,892	3.46%	0.17		-0.40%	
Total	**9**	**49,347**	**100.0%**	**9,870**	**4**	**13**	**54,641**	**100.0%**	**10,929**	**4**	**0.00%**	**0**
Electorate		**70,413**	**70.08%**				**80,221**	**68.11%**			**+1.97%**	
Spoiled		**452**	**0.91%**				**411**	**0.75%**			**+0.16%**	
Turnout		**49,799**	**70.72%**				**55,052**	**68.63%**			**+2.10%**	

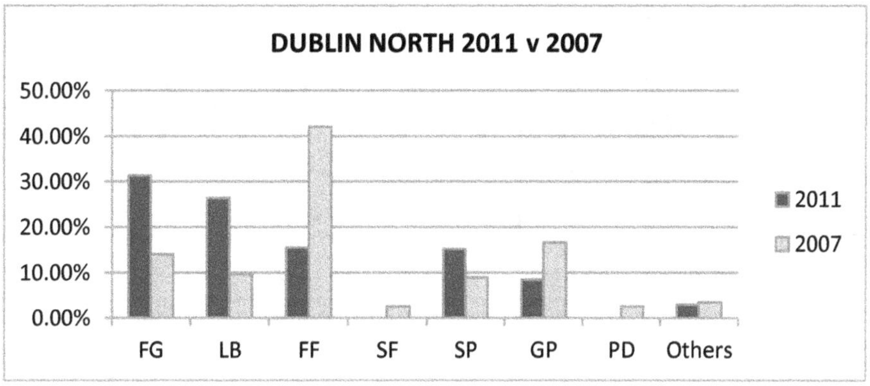

DUBLIN NORTH 2011 COUNT DETAILS								
Seats	4						Quota	9,870
Candidate	Party	1st	2nd Reilly Surplus	3rd Harrold Votes	4th Kelleher Votes	5th Kennedy Votes	6th Sargent Votes	7th Daly Surplus
			-308					
Reilly, Dr. James*	FG	10,178	9,870	9,870	9,870	9,870	9,870	9,870
			+59	+190				
Ryan, Brendan	LB	9,809	9,868	10,058	10,058	10,058	10,058	10,058
			+20	+342	+1,221	+369	+1,707	-1,302
Daly, Clare	SP	7,513	7,533	7,875	9,096	9,465	11,172	9,870
			+165	+248	+683	+263	+1,781	+709
Farrell, Alan	FG	5,310	5,475	5,723	6,406	6,669	8,450	9,159
			+9	+125	+158	+2,479	+935	+246
O'Brien, Darragh*	FF	4,115	4,124	4,249	4,407	6,886	7,821	8,067
			+27	+270	+686	+441	-5,610	
Sargent, Trevor*	GP	4,186	4,213	4,483	5,169	5,610	Eliminated	
			+12	+73	+201	-3,805		
Kennedy, Michael*	FF	3,519	3,531	3,604	3,805	Eliminated		
			+10	+152	-3,367			
Kelleher, Tom	LB	3,205	3,215	3,367	Eliminated			
			+6	-1,518				
Harrold, Mark	NP	1,512	1,518	Eliminated				
Non-transferable				+118	+418	+253	+1,187	+347
Cumulative			0	118	536	789	1,976	2,323
Total		**49,347**	**49,347**	**49,347**	**49,347**	**49,347**	**49,347**	**49,347**

DUBLIN NORTH 2011 TRANSFER ANALYSIS								
From	To	FG	LB	FF	SP	GP	Others	Non Trans
FG	308	165	69	21	20	27	6	
		53.57%	*22.40%*	*6.82%*	*6.49%*	*8.77%*	*1.95%*	
LB	3,367	683		359	1,221	686		418
		20.29%		*10.66%*	*36.26%*	*20.37%*		*12.41%*
FF	3,805	263		2,479	369	441		253
		6.91%		*65.15%*	*9.70%*	*11.59%*		*6.65%*
SP	1,302	709		246				347
		54.45%		*18.89%*				*26.65%*
GP	5,610	1,781		935	1,707			1,187
		31.75%		*16.67%*	*30.43%*			*21.16%*
Others	1,518	248	342	198	342	270		118
		16.34%	*22.53%*	*13.04%*	*22.53%*	*17.79%*		*7.77%*
Total	**15,910**	**3,849**	**411**	**4,238**	**3,659**	**1,424**	**6**	**2,323**
		24.19%	***2.58%***	***26.64%***	***23.00%***	***8.95%***	***0.04%***	***14.60%***

DUBLIN NORTH		
MAIN BOUNDARY CHANGES		
Dail	**Constituency**	**Seats**
19 (1969) - 20 (1973)	Dublin North County	4
21 (1977)	North County	3
22 (1981) - 26 (1989)	Dublin North	3
27 (1992) - 31 (2011)	Dublin North	4

DUBLIN NORTH															
ALL TDs 1969-2011															
	Surname	**Forename**	**Party**	**Elected**											**Total**
1	Burke	Ray	FF	73	77	81	82	82	87	89	92	97			9
2	Owen	Nora	FG	81	82	82	89	92	97						6
3	Boland	John	FG	77	81	82	82	87							5
4	Ryan	Sean	LB	89	92	98*	02								4
5	Sargent	Trevor	GP	92	97	02	07								4
6	Wright	G.V.	FF	87	97	02									3
7	Clinton**	Mark	FG	69	73										2
8	Keating	Justin	LB	69	73										2
9	Reilly	Dr. James	FG	07	11										2
10	Burke**	Patrick J.	FF	69											1
11	Foley**	Des	FF	69											1
12	Walsh**	Sean	FF	73											1
13	Fox	Christopher	FF	77											1
14	Glennon	Jim	FF	02											1
15	Kennedy	Michael	FF	07											1
16	O'Brien	Darragh	FF	07											1
17	Ryan	Brendan	LB	11											1
18	Daly	Clare	SP	11											1
19	Farrell	Alan	FG	11											1
19	**Total**							***Includes 1 By-Election**						*	**47**
	**** Also elected in another constituency**														
1	Burke**	Patrick J.	FF	Dublin County				44	48	51	54	57	61	65	7
2	Walsh**	Sean	FF	Dublin Co Mid/SW				77/	81	82	82	87			5
3	Clinton**	Mark	FG	Dublin County				61	65	77					3
4	Foley**	Des	FF	Dublin County				65							1
4	**Total**							***Includes 1 By-Election**						*	**16**

DUBLIN NORTH 1969-2011																					
* No Contest			FG		LB		FF		SF		SP		GP		CS		PD		Others		
Dail		Seats	S	% Vote	S	% Vote	S	% Vote	S	% Vote	S	% Vote	S	% Vote	S	% Vote	S	% Vote	S	% Vote	
19	1969	4	1	24.88%	1	30.18%	2	44.94%													
20	1973	4	1	27.67%	1	24.88%	2	39.81%												7.65%	
21	1977*	3	1	25.59%		12.97%	2	55.31%												6.13%	
22	1981	3	2	37.65%		15.95%	1	46.39%													
23	1982	3	2	39.08%		14.40%	1	46.52%													
24	1982	3	2	42.21%		12.37%	1	45.42%													
25	1987	3	1	26.10%		10.09%	2	48.63%						3.12%				11.78%		0.28%	
26	1989	3	1	23.83%	1	17.97%	1	46.48%						8.73%				2.99%			
27	1992	4	1	16.61%	1	34.03%	1	36.51%		0.95%			1	8.77%						3.12%	
28	1997	4	1	18.98%		13.64%	2	38.65%				7.22%	1	13.64%		1.62%		3.48%		2.77%	
29	2002	4		11.81%	1	14.47%	2	38.24%		3.07%		12.52%	1	16.60%		0.56%				2.73%	
30	2007	4	1	14.03%		9.62%	2	42.09%		2.66%		8.92%	1	16.67%		0.38%		2.55%		3.08%	
31	2011	4	2	31.39%	1	26.37%		15.47%			1	15.22%		8.48%						3.06%	
1969-2011		**46**	**16**	**24.73%**	**6**	**18.62%**	**19**	**40.71%**		**0.64%**	**1**	**4.18%**	**4**	**6.81%**		**0.22%**		**1.57%**		**2.51%**	
National		**4,618**	**1,453**	**30.77%**	**482**	**11.53%**	**1,985**	**41.86%**	**232**	**1.99%**	**4**	**0.16%**	**16**	**0.75%**		**0.04%**	**44**	**1.42%**	**402**	**11.47%**	

* 1977: North County

DUBLIN NORTH-CENTRAL 2011

"The end of the Haughey dynasty as Fianna Fail draw another blank in a Dublin constituency"

The Constituency Commission made a boundary revision here since 2007 with a population of 2,758 in the Edenmore electoral division transferring in from Dublin North East. However, the constituency did retain its three seats.

The Fine Gael vote was up 12 points since 2007 and with 1.5 quotas they were in contention for two seats. Richard Bruton topped the poll and was just 9 votes short of the quota on the first count. His running mate Naoise Ó Muirí was just outside the frame in fourth place with half a quota and failed to make up his first count deficit of over 1,000 votes on outgoing independent TD Finian McGrath.

Labour had won a seat here in 1992 and 1997 but lost it in 2002 and failed again in 2007. The party made no mistake in this election with Aodháin O Riordáin taking second place with 0.9 of a quota on the first count as he increased the Labour vote by 15 points for an impressive performance.

This was another disastrous performance by Fianna Fáil with their vote down 31 points, their seventh largest loss of support in this election. Sean Haughey did poorly and with just 0.5 quotas was in fourth place on the first count, just ahead of O Muiri. He failed to make any headway during the count and was overtaken by the Fine Gael man and was finally eliminated on the sixth count with his transfers ensuring McGrath's election. So this election marked the end of an era in Irish politics with the Haughey name missing from Dáil Eireann for the first time since 1957.

Outgoing Independent deputy Finian McGrath was in third place on the first count and went on to hold off Ó Muírí for the final seat by the very comfortable margin of 4,626 votes.

The turnout was up five points in this constituency and at 73.17% was five points above the Dublin turnout of 68.20%.

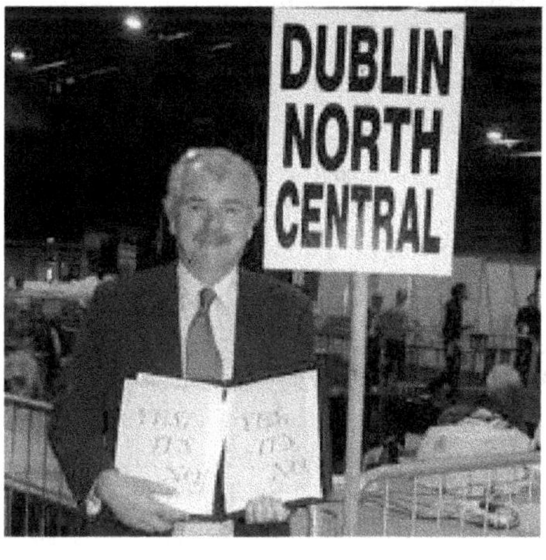

Finian McGrath TD

DUBLIN NORTH-CENTRAL TDs 2011

RICHARD BRUTON (FG)

210 Griffith Avenue, Dublin 9, Tel: 01 8368185
Leinster House: 01 6183103; Email: richard.bruton@oireachtas.ie
Website: www.richardbruton.net

Born Dublin 15th March 1953. Married to Susan Meehan, two sons, two daughters. Educated Belvedere College, Dublin; Clongowes Wood College, Co. Kildare; UCD and Nuffield College, Oxford (BA, MA Mphil (Oxon) Economics). Government Minister. Economist. First elected February 1982 and at each subsequent election.

Appointed Minister for Enterprise, Jobs and Innovation 9th March 2011. Front bench spokesperson on Enterprise, Jobs & Economic Planning July 2010-March 2011. Led failed attempt to oust Enda Kenny as party leader in June 2010. Deputy Leader of Fine Gael and Finance spokesperson, September 2007-July 2010. Member Joint Committee on Finance and the Public Service 2007-2011. Contested Fine Gael Leadership election in June 2002. Director of Policy February 2001- 2002. Front Bench spokesperson on Policy and Press Director 2000-2001. Front Bench spokesperson on Education, Science and Technology, Relations with the Social Partners 1997-2002. Minister for Enterprise and Employment 1994-1997. Fine Gael Front Bench spokesperson on Enterprise and Employment 1987-1994. Minister of State, Department of Industry and Commerce 1986-1987. Senator 1981-1982. Member of Dublin City Council 1991-1994 and 1999-2003. Member of Meath County Council 1979-1982. Author of "Irish Public Debt" (1979). Joint author of "Irish Economy" (1975) and "Drainage Policy in Ireland" (1982). Brother of John Bruton, Taoiseach 1994-1997; Dáil Deputy for Meath 1969-2004; leader of Fine Gael 1990-2001; EU Ambassador to USA 2004-2010.

AODHÁN O RIORDÁIN (LB)

76a Clontarf Park, Dublin 3; Tel: 01 8551016; Mobile: 086 8190336
Constituency Office; 203 Philipsburgh Avenue, Marino, Dublin 3.
Leinster House: 01 6183209; Email: aodhan.oriordain@oireachtas.ie
Website: www.aodhanoriordain.blogspot.com; Twitter: twitter.com/aodhanoriordain
Facebook: facebook/aodhanoriordain

Born Dublin 22nd July 1976. Married to Aine Kerr. Educated Malahide Community School, UCD; Marino Institute of Education. Former Primary School Principal. First elected 2011.

Member Committee on the Implementation of the Good Friday Agreement. Member Committee on Jobs, Social Protection and Education. First elected to Dublin City Council in 2004 in North Inner City. Deputy Lord Mayor 2006-2007. Re-elected in Clontarf in 2009.

FINIAN McGRATH (IND)

342 Charlemont, Griffith Avenue, Dublin 9, Tel: 01 8378028; Mobile: 087 6738041.
Constituency Office; Le Chéile Community Centre, Donnycarney, Dublin 5.
Leinster House: Tel: 6183031; Email: finian.mcgrath@oireachtas.ie
Website: www.finianmcgrath.ie

Born Tuam, Co. Galway 9th April 1953. Widower, two daughters Caoimhe and Cliodhna. Educated CBS Tuam; St. Patrick's Training College, Drumcondra, Dublin. Formerly North Inner City School Principle. Contested 1989, 1992 and 1997 elections. First elected 2002 and at each subsequent election.

Member Committee on Justice, Defence and Equality. One of four independent deputies that pledged their support to the Fianna Fail/GP/PD government during the lifetime of the 30th Dail. Withdrew support for Government 20th October 2008 over Medical Cards for over 70's budgetary issue. Member Joint Committee on Justice, Equality, Defence and Women's Rights and Member Joint Committee on Climate Change and Energy Security 2007-2011. Member Joint Committee on Justice, Equality, Defence and Women's Rights and Member Joint House Services Committee 2002-2007. Member Dublin City Council 1999-2003. Board Member Northside Centre for the Unemployed, Coolock. Former Chairperson Dublin Branch Down's syndrome Ireland. Board Member Orthopaedic Hospital, Clontarf. Member Cumann na mBubscol, GAA. Former full-time voluntary worker with the Simon Community. Founder member and former Chairperson of Charlemont Residents' Association. Member of the INTO.

DUBLIN NORTH-CENTRAL 2011 FIRST PREFERENCE VOTES							
	Seats	3			9,694		
	Candidate	Party	1st	%	Quota	Count	Status
1	**Bruton, Richard***	**FG**	**9,685**	**24.98%**	**1.00**	**2**	**Made Quota**
2	**Ó Ríordáin, Aodhán**	**LB**	**8,731**	**22.52%**	**0.90**	**4**	**Made Quota**
3	**McGrath, Finian***	**NP**	**5,986**	**15.44%**	**0.62**	**7**	**Made Quota**
4	Ó Muirí, Naoise	FG	4,959	12.79%	0.51	7	Not Elected
5	Haughey, Sean*	FF	5,017	12.94%	0.52	6	Eliminated
6	McCormack, Helen	SF	2,140	5.52%	0.22	3	Eliminated
7	Lyons, John	PBPA	1,424	3.67%	0.15	2	No Expenses
8	Cooney, Donna	GP	501	1.29%	0.05	1	No Expenses
9	Clarke, Paul	NP	331	0.85%	0.03	1	No Expenses
9	***Outgoing**		**38,774**	**100.00%**	**9,694**	**2,423**	**No Expenses**

DUBLIN NORTH-CENTRAL 2011 PARTY VOTE												
	2011					2007					Change	
Party	Cand	1st	%	Quota	Seats	Cand	1st	%	Quota	Seats	%	Seats
FG	2	14,644	37.77%	1.51	1	1	9,303	25.55%	1.02	1	+12.22%	
LB	1	8,731	22.52%	0.90	1	1	2,649	7.27%	0.29		+15.24%	+1
FF	1	5,017	12.94%	0.52		2	16,029	44.02%	1.76	1	-31.08%	-1
SF	1	2,140	5.52%	0.22		1	1,375	3.78%	0.15		+1.74%	
PBPA	1	1,424	3.67%	0.15							+3.67%	
GP	1	501	1.29%	0.05		1	1,891	5.19%	0.21		-3.90%	
Others	2	6,317	16.29%	0.65	1	1	5,169	14.19%	0.57	1	+2.10%	
Total	**9**	**38,774**	**100.0%**	**9,694**	**3**	**7**	**36,416**	**100.0%**	**9,105**	**3**	**0.00%**	**0**
Electorate		**52,992**	**73.17%**				**53,443**	**68.14%**			**+5.03%**	
Spoiled		**413**	**1.05%**				**342**	**0.93%**			**+0.12%**	
Turnout		**39,187**	**73.95%**				**36,758**	**68.78%**			**+5.17%**	

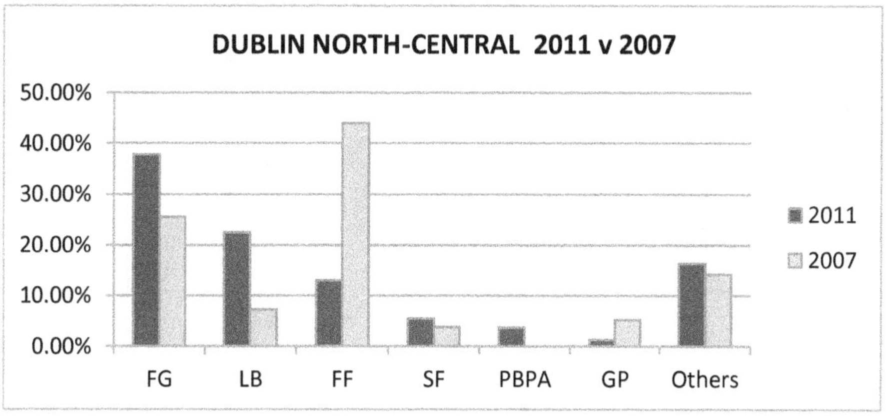

DUBLIN NORTH-CENTRAL 2011 COUNT DETAILS								
Seats	3						Quota	9,694
Candidate	**Party**	**1st**	**2nd** Cooney Clarke	**3rd** Lyons Votes	**4th** McCormack Votes	**5th** Ó Ríordáin Surplus	**6th** Bruton Surplus	**7th** Haughey Votes
			+105				*-96*	
Bruton, Richard*	FG	9,685	9,790	9,790	9,790	9,790	9,694	9,694
			+180	*+418*	*+863*	*-498*		
Ó Ríordáin, Aodhán	LB	8,731	8,911	9,329	10,192	9,694	9,694	9,694
			+170	*+545*	*+1,076*	*+342*	*+31*	*2,875*
McGrath, Finian*	NP	5,986	6,156	6,701	7,777	8,119	8,150	11,025
			+74	*+65*	*+142*	*+113*	*+50*	*+996*
Ó Muirí, Naoise	FG	4,959	5,033	5,098	5,240	5,353	5,403	6,399
			+60	*+51*	*+167*	*+43*	*+10*	*-5,348*
Haughey, Sean*	FF	5,017	5,077	5,128	5,295	5,338	5,348	Eliminated
			+47	*+415*	*-2,602*			
McCormack, Helen	SF	2,140	2,187	2,602	Eliminated			
			+163	*-1,587*				
Lyons, John	PBPA	1,424	1,587	Eliminated				
			-501					
Cooney, Donna	GP	501	Eliminated					
			-331					
Clarke, Paul	NP	331	Eliminated					
Non-transferable			*+33*	*+93*	*+354*		*+5*	*+1,477*
Cumulative			33	126	480	480	485	1,962
Total		**38,774**	**38,774**	**38,774**	**38,774**	**38,774**	**38,774**	**38,774**

DUBLIN NORTH-CENTRAL 2011 TRANSFER ANALYSIS								
From	**To**	**FG**	**LB**	**FF**	**SF**	**PBPA**	**Others**	**Non Trans**
FG	96	50		10			31	5
		52.08%		*10.42%*			*32.29%*	*5.21%*
LB	498	113		43			342	
		22.69%		*8.63%*			*68.67%*	
FF	5,348	996					2,875	1,477
		18.62%					*53.76%*	*27.62%*
SF	2,602	142	863	167			1,076	354
		5.46%	*33.17%*	*6.42%*			*41.35%*	*13.60%*
PBPA	1,587	65	418	51	415		545	93
		4.10%	*26.34%*	*3.21%*	*26.15%*		*34.34%*	*5.86%*
GP	501	108	108	36	28	98	103	20
		21.56%	*21.56%*	*7.19%*	*5.59%*	*19.56%*	*20.56%*	*3.99%*
Others	331	71	72	24	19	65	67	13
		21.45%	*21.75%*	*7.25%*	*5.74%*	*19.64%*	*20.24%*	*3.93%*
Total	**10,963**	**1,545**	**1,461**	**331**	**462**	**163**	**5,039**	**1,962**
		14.09%	***13.33%***	***3.02%***	***4.21%***	***1.49%***	***45.96%***	***17.90%***

DUBLIN NORTH-CENTRAL		
MAIN BOUNDARY CHANGES		
Dail	**Constituency**	**Seats**
13 (1948) - 16 (1957)	Dublin North-Central	3
17 (1961) - 20 (1973)	Dublin North-Central	4
21 (1977)	Artane	3
	Dublin North-Central	3
22 (1981) - 29 (2002)	Dublin North-Central	4
30 (2007) - 31 (2011)	Dublin North-Central	3

DUBLIN NORTH-CENTRAL													
ALL TDs 1948-2011													
	Surname	**Forename**	**Party**	**Elected**									**Total**
1	Bruton	Richard	FG	82	82	87	89	92	97	02	07	11	9
2	De Valera**	Vivion	FF	48	51	54	57	61	65				6
3	Brady	Vincent	FF	77	81	82	82	87	89				6
4	McGilligan**	Patrick	FG	48	51	54	57	61					5
5	Haughey**	Charles J.	FF	81	82	82	87	89					5
6	Lynch**	Celia	FF	61	65	69	73						4
7	O'Leary**	Michael	FG	65	69	73	77						4
8	Birmingham	George	FG	81	82	82	87						4
9	Callely	Ivor	FF	89	92	97	02						4
10	Haughey	Sean	FF	92	97	02	07						4
11	Belton**	Luke	FG	65	69	73							3
12	McGrath	Finian	NP	02	07	11							3
13	Gallagher	Colm	FF	51	57								2
14	Sherwin	Frank	NP	*57	61								2
15	Colley**	George	FF	69	73								2
16	McDowell	Derek	LB	92	97								2
17	O'Sullivan**	Martin	LB	48									1
18	O'Carroll	Maureen	LB	54									1
19	Keating**	Michael	FG	77									1
20	Browne**	Noel	SLP	81									1
21	O Riordain	Aodhan	LB	11									1
21	**Total**					***Includes 1 By-election**						*	**70**
	**** Also elected in another constituency**												
1	Browne**	Noel	SLP	Dublin SE			48	51	57	61	69	77	6
2	Haughey**	Charles J.	FF	Dublin NE			57	61	65	69	73	77	6
3	Colley**	George	FF	Dublin NE/C			61	65	77/	81	82	82	6
4	McGilligan**	Patrick	FG	Dublin NW			37	38	43	44			4
5	De Valera**	Vivion	FF	Dublin NW/C			45*/	69	73	77			4
6	Keating**	Michael	FG	Dublin Central			81	82	82	87			4
7	O'Leary**	Michael	FG	Dublin C/SW			81	82/	82				3
8	O'Sullivan**	Martin	LB	Dublin NW			43	44					2
9	Lynch**	Celia	FF	Dublin SC			54	57					2
10	Belton**	Luke	FG	Finglas			77						1
10	**Total**					***Includes 1 By-election**						*	**38**

DUBLIN NORTH-CENTRAL 1948-2011																											
		FG		LB		FF		SF		PBPA		GP		WP		PD		DL		DSP		Soc Lab		C na P		Others	
Dail	Seats	S	% Vote	S	% Vote	S	% Vote	S	% Vote	S	% Vote	S	% Vote	S	% Vote	S	% Vote	S	% Vote	S	% Vote	S	% Vote	S	% Vote	S	% Vote
13 1948	3	1	18.29%	1	16.30%	1	46.16%																		18.11%		1.14%
14 1951	3	1	21.84%		15.54%	2	51.57%																		4.74%		6.32%
15 1954	3	1	34.75%	1	13.04%	1	40.34%																		11.87%		
16 1957	3	1	22.26%		6.77%	2	48.20%																		3.54%		19.24%
17 1961	4	1	20.88%		7.42%	2	40.73%																			1	30.97%
18 1965	4	1	24.20%	1	22.46%	2	42.72%																		4.00%		6.63%
19 1969	4	1	28.25%	1	28.64%	2	43.10%																				
20 1973	4	1	28.83%	1	21.01%	2	42.23%		4.83%																		3.09%
21 1977	6	1	18.30%	1	16.54%	3	45.55%								2.13%											1	17.49%
22 1981	4	1	25.48%		4.49%	2	50.92%															1	12.40%				6.71%
23 1982	4	2	32.66%		5.32%	2	51.16%																				10.86%
24 1982	4	2	36.63%		7.62%	2	48.74%								3.65%						0.55%						2.81%
25 1987	4	2	24.22%		6.93%	2	49.73%		1.81%						3.83%		8.34%				1.59%						3.55%
26 1989	4	1	26.01%		8.69%	3	51.64%								6.78%		1.80%										5.08%
27 1992	4	1	22.40%	1	23.12%	2	38.96%		1.40%										3.00%								11.11%
28 1997	4	1	26.03%	1	6.60%	2	46.44%				1.62%		3.82%				3.30%		2.77%								9.43%
29 2002	4	1	17.00%		10.49%	2	50.05%		5.74%		1.59%		5.68%													1	9.44%
30 2007	3	1	25.55%		7.27%	1	44.02%		3.78%				5.19%													1	14.19%
31 2011	3	1	37.77%	1	22.52%		12.94%		5.52%		3.67%		1.29%													1	16.29%
1918-2011	**72**	**22**	**25.93%**	**9**	**13.20%**	**35**	**44.46%**		**1.34%**		**0.41%**		**0.95%**		**1.03%**		**0.85%**		**0.39%**		**0.14%**	**1**	**0.76%**		**1.42%**	**5**	**9.13%**
National	**4,618**	**1,453**	**30.77%**	**482**	**11.53%**	**1,985**	**41.86%**	**232**	**1.99%**	**2**	**0.09%**	**16**	**0.75%**	**17**	**0.78%**	**44**	**1.42%**	**8**	**0.22%**	**2**	**0.06%**	**1**	**0.02%**	**18**	**0.77%**	**358**	**9.73%**

DUBLIN NORTH-EAST 2011

"Another Dublin three-seater, another blank for Fianna Fáil"

There were major Constituency Commission changes here since 2007. A population of 9,021 in the Portmarnock and Balgriffin areas was transferred into Dublin North-East from Dublin North, and a population of 2,758 in the Edenmore electoral division was transferred to Dublin North-Central. However, the constituency did retain its three seats.

Fine Gael's single candidate, outgoing deputy Terence Flanagan put in an impressive performance and topped the poll and was well over the quota on the first count with the Fine Gael vote up 7 points on 2007.

Tommy Broughan was just short of the quota on the first count and went on take the second seat on the second count. This was one of only two constituencies in the 'Spring Tide' election of 1992 to deliver two seats for Labour. Remarkably the same two candidates that won in 1992, pulled off the same feat in 2011. With the party vote up 19 points in this election, Labour was well placed to repeat the 1992 performance. Sean Kenny trailed both Larry O'Toole and Averil Power on the first count but managed to do better on transfers and passed out the Sinn Fein and Fianna Fáil candidates. He comfortably took the final seat ahead of Sinn Fein in an impressive performance. Labour did well to convert 1.4 quotas into two seats with Kenny coming from outside the frame on the first count and with just 0.4 of a quota. This was another example of Labour's strong transfer performance in this election.

This result was another disappointment for Sinn Féin and for veteran candidate Larry O'Toole. He looked well placed on the first count but the party's old failing of not gaining transfers once again came into play and O'Toole was well beaten in the battle for the final seat.

This was another disastrous performance for Fianna Fáil with its vote down 28 points and with just under half a quota they were struggling. Newcomer Averil Power had been selected to replace the long-serving TD and former Cabinet Minister Michael Woods who had retired. Power was never really in contention and her first count vote of 4,794 left her in fourth place. Power was just too far off the pace and she was the final candidate eliminated. Her transfers went nearly 4:1 to Kenny over O'Toole to decide the battle for the final seat.

Eamon Blaney son of the former long serving Donegal deputy Neil Blaney, contested this constituency for "New Vision" but got just 4% and was never in contention. Five candidates lost the right to reclaim their expenses including Jimmy Guerin, brother of the late Veronica Guerin.

DUBLIN NORTH-EAST TDs 2011

TERENCE FLANAGAN (FG)

74 Old Malahide Road, Dublin 5, Mobile: 087 9952031
Leinster House: 01 6183634; Email: terence.flanagan@oireachtas.ie
Website: www.terenceflanagan.finegael.ie Twitter: twitter.com/tflanaganTD

Born Dublin, January 1975. Single. Educated Chanel College, Malahide Road, Dublin 5; Dublin Business School, Aungier Street, Dublin 2 (Accountancy Qualification). Accountant. First Elected 2007. Retained his seat in 2011.

Member Committee on Environment, Transport, Culture and the Gaeltacht. Deputy Spokesperson on the Environment with Special Responsibility for Housing, October 2007-2011. Member Joint Committee on Finance and the Public Service 2007-2011. Member Dublin City Council 2003-2007. Member of Artane Senior Band.

TOMMY BROUGHAN (LB)

18 Thormanby Lawns, Howth, Dublin 13, Tel: 8477634; Leinster House: 01 6183557;
E-mail: thomas.broughan@oireachtas.ie; Website: www.tommybroughan.com
Twitter: @TommyBroughanTD

Born Clondalkin, Dublin August 1947. Married to Carmel Healy. Educated Moyle Park College, Clondalkin, Dublin; UCD (BA HDipED) and London University, (BSc, MSc [Econ]). Former Teacher. Contested 1989 general election. First elected 1992 and at each subsequent election.

Lost Labour whip after voting against the government over renewal of the bank guarantee scheme 1st December 2011. Member Committee on Finance, Public Expenditure and Reform. Lost Labour Whip 29th June 2010 following abstention on Wildlife Bill. Front Bench Spokesperson on Transport 2007-2011. Member Public Accounts Committee and Member Joint Committee on Transport and Member Dail Committee on Procedure and Privileges 2007-2011. Former Front Bench Spokesperson on Communications, Marine and Natural Resources and Assistant Whip. Member Joint Committee on Communications, Marine and Natural Resources 2002-2007. Spokesperson on Enterprise, Trade and Employment 1997-2002. Member Dublin City Council 1991-2003. Founding Secretary Community Enterprise Donaghmede and Artane; Founding Chairman Coolock Development Council. Director Northside Centre for the Unemployed. Member of several Dublin northside GAA and Soccer clubs.

SEAN KENNY (LB)

44 Woodbine Road, Raheny, Dublin 5; Tel: 01 8481806; Mobile: 086 8126340
Email: info@seankenny.ie; Website: www.seankenny.ie

Born Ballinasloe, Co. Galway, 1st October 1942. Married to Mairéad Armstrong, one son, one daughter. Educated Garbally College, Ballinasloe. TCD. Contested Dail elections in Dublin North-East in 1981, 1982, 1987 and 1989. First elected 1992 in Dublin North East. Lost his seat in 1997. Re-elected 2011.

Member Committee on Environment, Transport, Culture and the Gaeltacht. Member Committee on Justice, defence and Equality. First elected to Dublin City Council in 1979. Retained his seat in 1985, 1991, 1999, 2004 and 2009. Dublin Lord mayor 1991/1992.

DUBLIN NORTH-EAST 2011							
FIRST PREFERENCE VOTES							
	Seats	**3**			**10,460**		
	Candidate	**Party**	**1st**	**%**	**Quota**	**Count**	**Status**
1	**Flanagan, Terence***	**FG**	**12,332**	**29.47%**	**1.18**	**1**	**Made Quota**
2	**Broughan, Tommy***	**LB**	**10,006**	**23.92%**	**0.96**	**2**	**Made Quota**
3	**Kenny, Seán #**	**LB**	**4,365**	**10.43%**	**0.42**	**9**	**Elected**
4	O'Toole, Larry	SF	5,032	12.03%	0.48	9	Not Elected
5	Power, Averil	FF	4,794	11.46%	0.46	8	Eliminated
6	Blaney, Eamonn	NV	1,773	4.24%	0.17	7	Eliminated
7	Guerin, Jimmy	NP	1,283	3.07%	0.12	6	No Expenses
8	Healy, David	GP	792	1.89%	0.08	5	No Expenses
9	Greene, Brian	SP	869	2.08%	0.08	4	No Expenses
10	Sexton, Raymond	NP	351	0.84%	0.03	3	No Expenses
11	Eastwood, Robert	NP	242	0.58%	0.02	3	No Expenses
11	***Outgoing TD # Former TD**		**41,839**	**100.00%**	**10,460**	**2,616**	**No Expenses**

DUBLIN NORTH-EAST 2011												
PARTY VOTE												
	2011					**2007**					**Change**	
Party	**Cand**	**1st**	**%**	**Quota**	**Seats**	**Cand**	**1st**	**%**	**Quota**	**Seats**	**%**	**Seats**
FG	1	12,332	29.47%	1.18	1	2	8,012	22.94%	0.92	1	+6.54%	
LB	2	14,371	34.35%	1.37	2	1	5,294	15.16%	0.61	1	+19.19%	+1
FF	1	4,794	11.46%	0.46		2	13,864	39.69%	1.59	1	-28.23%	-1
SF	1	5,032	12.03%	0.48		1	4,661	13.34%	0.53		-1.32%	
SP	1	869	2.08%	0.08							+2.08%	
GP	1	792	1.89%	0.08		1	2,349	6.73%	0.27		-4.83%	
PD						1	749	2.14%	0.09		-2.14%	
Others	4	3,649	8.72%	0.35							+8.72%	
Total	**11**	**41,839**	**100.0%**	**10,460**	**3**	**8**	**34,929**	**100.0%**	**8,733**	**3**	**0.00%**	**0**
Electorate		**58,542**	**71.47%**				**53,778**	**64.95%**			**+6.52%**	
Spoiled		**448**	**1.06%**				**323**	**0.92%**			**+0.14%**	
Turnout		**42,287**	**72.23%**				**35,252**	**65.55%**			**+6.68%**	

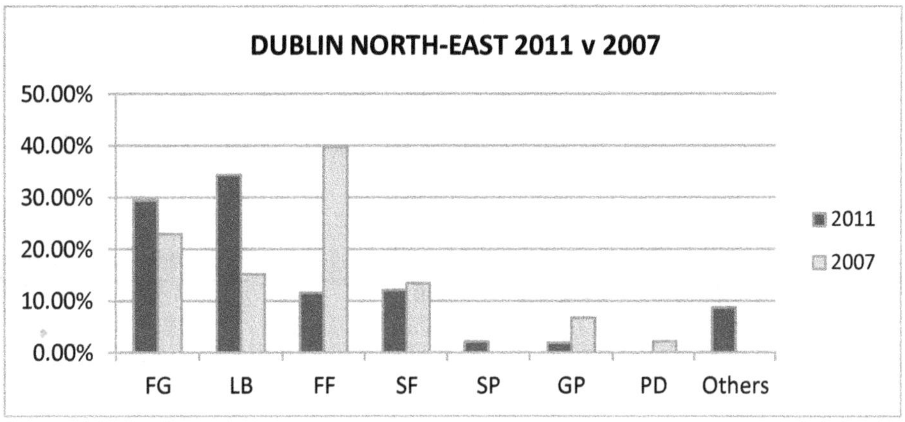

DUBLIN NORTH-EAST 2011 COUNT DETAILS											
Seats	3								Quota	10,460
Candidate	Party	1st	2nd Flanagan Surplus	3rd Broughan Surplus	4th Sexton Eastwood	5th Greene Votes	6th Healy Votes	7th Guerin Votes	8th Blaney Votes	9th Power Votes
			-1,872							
Flanagan, Terence*	FG	12,332	10,460	10,460	10,460	10,460	10,460	10,460	10,460	10,460
			+732	-278						
Broughan, Tommy*	LB	10,006	10,738	10,460	10,460	10,460	10,460	10,460	10,460	10,460
			+363	+157	+100	+231	+364	+420	+1,013	+2,356
Kenny, Seán #	LB	4,365	4,728	4,885	4,985	5,216	5,580	6,000	7,013	9,369
			+88	+23	+36	+298	+77	+200	+508	+661
O'Toole, Larry	SF	5,032	5,120	5,143	5,179	5,477	5,554	5,754	6,262	6,923
			+219	+23	+73	+25	+180	+265	+462	-6,041
Power, Averil	FF	4,794	5,013	5,036	5,109	5,134	5,314	5,579	6,041	Eliminated
			+121	+19	+186	+134	+168	+554	-2,955	
Blaney, Eamonn	NV	1,773	1,894	1,913	2,099	2,233	2,401	2,955	Eliminated	
			+136	+28	+125	+113	+114	-1,799		
Guerin, Jimmy	NP	1,283	1,419	1,447	1,572	1,685	1,799	Eliminated		
			+127	+15	+53	+62	-1,049			
Healy, David	GP	792	919	934	987	1,049	Eliminated			
			+24	+4	+38	-935				
Greene, Brian	SP	869	893	897	935	Eliminated				
			+40	+6	-397					
Sexton, Raymond	NP	351	391	397	Eliminated					
			+22	+3	-267					
Eastwood, Robert	NP	242	264	267	Eliminated					
Non-transferable					+53	+72	+146	+360	+972	+3,024
Cumulative			0	0	53	125	271	631	1,603	4,627
Total		**41,839**	**41,839**	**41,839**	**41,839**	**41,839**	**41,839**	**41,839**	**41,839**	**41,839**

DUBLIN NORTH EAST 2011 TRANSFER ANALYSIS								
From	To	LB	FF	SF	SP	GP	Others	Non Trans
FG	1,872	1,095	219	88	24	127	319	
		58.49%	*11.70%*	*4.70%*	*1.28%*	*6.78%*	*17.04%*	
LB	278	157	23	23	4	15	56	
		56.47%	*8.27%*	*8.27%*	*1.44%*	*5.40%*	*20.14%*	
FF	6,041	2,356		661				3,024
		39.00%		*10.94%*				*50.06%*
SP	935	231	25	298		62	247	72
		24.71%	*2.67%*	*31.87%*		*6.63%*	*26.42%*	*7.70%*
GP	1,049	364	180	77			282	146
		34.70%	*17.16%*	*7.34%*			*26.88%*	*13.92%*
Others	5,418	1,533	800	744	38	53	865	1,385
		28.29%	*14.77%*	*13.73%*	*0.70%*	*0.98%*	*15.97%*	*25.56%*
Total	**15,593**	**5,736**	**1,247**	**1,891**	**66**	**257**	**1,769**	**4,627**
		36.79%	***8.00%***	***12.13%***	***0.42%***	***1.65%***	***11.34%***	***29.67%***

DUBLIN NORTH-EAST		
MAIN BOUNDARY CHANGES		
Dail	**Constituency**	**Seats**
9 (1937) - 12 (1944)	Dublin North-East	3
13 (1948) - 18 (1965)	Dublin North-East	5
19 (1969) - 20 (1973)	Dublin North-East	4
21 (1977)	Clontarf	3
22 (1981) - 28 (1997)	Dublin North-East	4
29 (2002) - 31 (2011)	Dublin North-East	3

DUBLIN NORTH-EAST																
ALL TDs 1937-2011																
	Surname	**Forename**	**Party**	**Elected**												**Total**
1	Woods	Michael	FF	77	81	82	82	87	89	92	97	02	07			10
2	Traynor**	Oscar	FF	37	38	43	44	48	51	54	57					8
3	Byrne**	Alfred	NP	37	38	43	44	48	51	54						7
4	Cosgrave	Michael Joe	FG	77	81	82	82	87	89	97						7
5	Belton	Jack	FG	48	51	54	57	61								5
6	Haughey**	Charles J.	FF	57	61	65	69	73								5
7	Fitzgerald	Liam	FF	81	82N	87	89	92								5
8	Broughan	Tommy	LB	92	97	02	07	11								5
9	Colley	Harry	FF	44	48	51	54									4
10	Byrne	Patrick	FG	56*	57	61	65									4
11	Belton	Patrick	FG	63*	65	69	73									4
12	Larkin	Denis	LB	54	57	65										3
13	Colley**	George	FF	61	65	77										3
14	Timmons	Eugene	FF	61	69	73										3
15	Larkin(sen)**	James	LB	37	43											2
16	Cowan	Peadar	NP	48	51											2
17	Cruise O'Brien	Conor	LB	69	73											2
18	Manning	Maurice	FG	82	82											2
19	McCartan	Pat	WP	87	89											2
20	Brady	Martin	FF	97	02											2
21	Kenny	Sean	LB	92	11											2
22	Flanagan	Terence	FG	07	11											2
23	Mulcahy**	Gen. Richard	FG	38												1
24	Loftus	Sean D.	NP	81												1
25	Brennan	Ned	FF	82F												1
25	**Total**								***Includes 2 By-Elections**						*	**92**
	**** Also elected in another constituency**															
1	Mulcahy**	Gen. Richard	FG	Dublin North				18	21	22	23	27	27	32	33	8
2	Byrne**	Alfred	NP	Dublin Mid/North				22/	23	27	27	32	33			6
3	Haughey**	Charles J.	FF	Artane/Dublin NC				77/	81	82	82	87	89			6
4	Colley**	George	FF	Dublin NC/Central				69	73/	81	82	82				5
5	Traynor**	Oscar	FF	Dublin North				25*	27J	32	33					4
6	Larkin(sen)**	James	LB	Dublin North				27S								1
6	**Total**															**30**

DUBLIN NORTH-EAST 1937-2011																									
* No Contest		FG		LB		FF		SF		SP		GP		WP		PD		DL		C na P		Nat Lab		Others	
Dail	Seats	S	% Vote	S	% Vote	S	% Vote	S	% Vote	S	% Vote	S	% Vote	S	% Vote	S	% Vote	S	% Vote	S	% Vote	S	% Vote	S	% Vote
9 1937	3		14.34%			1	35.85%																	2	49.81%
10 1938	3	1	24.74%			1	41.88%																	1	33.39%
11 1943	3		14.70%	1	15.11%	1	39.75%																	1	30.44%
12 1944	3		12.97%		12.09%	2	48.52%																3.26%	1	23.15%
13 1948	5	1	13.05%		5.16%	2	34.88%													1	15.54%		2.06%	1	29.32%
14 1951	5	1	19.46%		7.94%	2	42.78%																	2	29.82%
15 1954	5	1	23.09%	1	10.71%	2	32.08%														3.23%			1	30.90%
16 1957	5	2	24.62%	1	9.30%	2	41.53%		8.28%												1.45%				14.81%
17 1961	5	2	34.36%		8.33%	3	46.57%		3.67%																7.08%
18 1965	5	2	32.49%	1	16.11%	2	49.21%																		2.19%
19 1969	4	1	20.98%	1	31.23%	2	42.74%																		5.05%
20 1973	4	1	24.62%	1	28.75%	2	43.54%																		3.09%
21 1977	3	1	23.77%		14.55%	2	43.44%																		18.23%
22 1981	4	1	28.16%		8.80%	2	43.49%								3.38%									1	16.18%
23 1982	4	2	31.91%		6.70%	2	49.15%								5.72%										6.51%
24 1982	4	2	33.02%		9.50%	2	42.80%								9.40%										5.28%
25 1987	4	1	18.92%		5.82%	2	51.37%		1.71%					1	8.61%		12.16%								1.41%
26 1989	4	1	19.05%		8.14%	2	47.21%						3.78%	1	16.95%		2.32%								2.55%
27 1992	4		13.73%	2	30.08%	2	33.83%		2.72%				4.31%		0.60%		5.08%		9.36%						0.29%
28 1997	4	1	18.90%	1	17.25%	2	40.61%		5.93%				3.57%				7.80%		3.70%						2.24%
29 2002	3		15.36%	1	16.23%	2	40.12%		10.24%				5.65%				4.16%								8.24%
30 2007	3	1	22.94%	1	15.16%	1	39.69%		13.34%				6.73%				2.14%								
31 2011	3	1	29.47%	2	34.35%		11.46%		12.03%		2.08%		1.89%												8.72%
1937-2011	**90**	**23**	**22.45%**	**13**	**13.71%**	**41**	**40.78%**		**2.43%**		**0.10%**		**1.03%**	**2**	**1.74%**		**1.40%**		**0.58%**	**1**	**1.02%**		**0.24%**	**10**	**14.52%**
National	**4,618**	**1,453**	**30.77%**	**482**	**11.53%**	**1,985**	**41.86%**	**232**	**1.99%**	**4**	**0.16%**	**16**	**0.75%**	**17**	**0.78%**	**44**	**1.42%**	**8**	**0.22%**	**18**	**0.77%**	**9**	**0.16%**	**350**	**9.58%**

DUBLIN NORTH-WEST 2011

"Three 'left' seats for the first time and the first constituency not to return either a Fine Gael or a Fianna Fáil TD"

There were no Constituency Commission boundary changes since 2007 and it remained a three-seat constituency.

This was one of Labour's best performances in this election with the party's vote up 23 points, its largest increase in support in this election and it managed to convert 1.7 quotas into two seats. Róisín Shortall put in one of the best performances of this election as she topped the poll with 1.1 quotas to take the first seat and she also managed to bring in a running mate. John Lyons was in the frame in third place on the first count with 0.6 quotas and was over 1,000 votes ahead of outgoing Minister Pat Carey and he increased his lead throughout the count and comfortably held off Fine Gael for the final seat.

Sinn Féin finally made the breakthrough in this constituency with Dessie Ellis delivering a seat. He had gone close in the past and was particularly disappointed in 2007 but he made no mistake in this election and was in second place with 0.9 of a quota on the first count and he comfortably took the second seat.

Fine Gael decided to run two candidates and with just 0.7 of a quota between them Gerry Breen and Dr Bill Tormey were both outside the frame on the first count and both had less than half a quota and they duly failed to win a seat. Fine Gael has now failed to win a seat here since Mary Flaherty in 1992 and this constituency was the only one in the country not to return a Fine Gael deputy in 2011.

Noel Ahern retired at this election and fellow outgoing Fianna Fáil TD Pat Carey did poorly with the Fianna Fáil vote down a massive 37 points, the largest drop in support for Fianna Fáil in the country and the largest drop in the party's history. Carey was outside the frame on the first count with just 3,869 votes. He was the final candidate eliminated and his transfers favoured Lyons and ensured his election.

The turnout was up seven points, one of the largest increases in this election.

Minister of State at the Department of Health Róisín Shortall

DUBLIN NORTH-WEST TDs 2011

RÓISÍN SHORTALL (LB)

12 Iveragh Road, Gaeltacht Park, Whitehall, Dublin 9, Tel: 01 8370563
Leinster House: Tel: 01 6183593; Email: roisin.shortall@oireachtas.ie
Website: www.labour.ie/roisinshortall

Born Dublin 25th April 1954. Married to Séamus O'Byrne, three daughters. Educated Dominican College, Eccles Street, Dublin and UCD; St. Mary's College of Education, Marino (BA, Dip Teacher of the Deaf). Minister of State. Former teacher of the deaf.
First elected 1992 and at each subsequent election.

Appointed Minister of State at the Department of Health with Special Responsibility for Primary Care 10th March 2011. Front bench spokesperson on Social and Family Affairs 2007-2011. Member Public Accounts Committee and Member Joint Committee on Social and Family Affairs 2007-2011. Unsuccessful candidate in Labour Leadership election in October 2002. Spokesperson on Transport 2002-2007. Member Joint Committee on Transport 2003-2007. Spokesperson on Health and Children 1997-2002. Member Dublin City Council 1991-2003. Member Eastern Health Board 1991-2003 (Chair 1996-1998).

DESSIE ELLIS (SF)

19 Dunsink Road, Finglas West, Dublin 11; Tel: 01 8343390; Mobile: 086 8541941
Constituency Office: Unit 1, 50 Main Street, Finglas Village, Dublin 11; Tel: 01 8343390
Leinster House: 01 6183006; Email: dessie.ellis@oireachtas.ie
Website: www.sinnfein.ie Twitter: twitter.com/cllrdessieellis

Born Finglas Dublin October 1953. Married to Ann. Educated Coláiste Eoin, Finglas; Kevin Street College of Technology. Technician. Contested Dail election in Dublin North-West in 2002 and 2007.
First elected 2011.

Appointed Sinn Fein Spokesperson on Transport and Housing 22nd March 2011. Member Committee on Environment, Transport, Culture and the Gaeltacht. Member Joint Administration Committee. First elected to Dublin City Council in 1999 in the Finglas electoral area. Retained his seat in 2004. Re-elected 2009 in Ballymun-Finglas. Former IRA prisoner.

JOHN LYONS (LB)

15 Cromlech Court, Poppintree, Dublin 11; Mobile: 087 2113154;
Leinster House: 01 6183280; Email: john.lyons@oireachtas.ie;
Website; www.Labour.ie/johnlyons; Twitter: twitter.com/johnlyonsTD

Born Dublin June 1977. Single. Educated Trinity Comprehensive, Ballymun; NUI Maynooth (BA and HDip); Trinity College (Special Education). Formerly Secondary Teacher.
First elected 2011.

Member Committee on Procedure and Privileges. Member Joint Administration Committee. Member Committee on Jobs, Social Protection and Education. Co-opted onto Dublin City Council as replacement for Mary Murphy 4th February 2008. Retained his seat in 2009 in the Ballymun-Finglas electoral area. .

DUBLIN NORTH-WEST 2011							
FIRST PREFERENCE VOTES							
	Seats	3			8,203		
	Candidate	Party	1st	%	Quota	Count	Status
1	**Shortall, Róisín***	**LB**	**9,359**	**28.52%**	**1.14**	**1**	**Made Quota**
2	**Ellis, Dessie**	**SF**	**7,115**	**21.68%**	**0.87**	**7**	**Made Quota**
3	**Lyons, John**	**LB**	**4,799**	**14.63%**	**0.59**	**7**	**Elected**
4	Breen, Gerry	FG	2,988	9.11%	0.36	7	Not Elected
5	Carey, Pat*	FF	3,869	11.79%	0.47	6	Eliminated
6	Tormey, Dr. Bill	FG	2,508	7.64%	0.31	5	Eliminated
7	Keegan, Andrew	PBPA	677	2.06%	0.08	4	No Expenses
8	Mooney, Sean	NP	433	1.32%	0.05	4	No Expenses
9	Dunne, John	WP	345	1.05%	0.04	4	No Expenses
10	Holohan, Ruairí	GP	328	1.00%	0.04	4	No Expenses
11	Loftus, Michael J.	NV	217	0.66%	0.03	3	No Expenses
12	Larkin, Michael	CS	173	0.53%	0.02	2	No Expenses
12	***Outgoing**		**32,811**	**100.00%**	**8,203**	**2,051**	**No Expenses**

DUBLIN NORTH-WEST 2011												
PARTY VOTE												
	2011					2007					Change	
Party	Cand	1st	%	Quota	Seats	Cand	1st	%	Quota	Seats	%	Seats
FG	2	5,496	16.75%	0.67		1	3,083	9.96%	0.40		+6.79%	
LB	2	14,158	43.15%	1.73	2	1	6,286	20.30%	0.81	1	+22.85%	+1
FF	1	3,869	11.79%	0.47		2	15,124	48.84%	1.95	2	-37.05%	-2
SF	1	7,115	21.68%	0.87	1	1	4,873	15.74%	0.63		+5.95%	+1
PBPA	1	677	2.06%	0.08							+2.06%	
GP	1	328	1.00%	0.04		1	853	2.75%	0.11		-1.76%	
WP	1	345	1.05%	0.04		1	240	0.78%	0.03		+0.28%	
CS	1	173	0.53%	0.02							+0.53%	
Others	2	650	1.98%	0.08		1	505	1.63%	0.07		+0.35%	
Total	**12**	**32,811**	**100.0%**	**8,203**	**3**	**8**	**30,964**	**100.0%**	**7,742**	**3**	**0.00%**	**0**
Electorate		**49,269**	**66.60%**				**51,951**	**59.60%**			**+6.99%**	
Spoiled		**451**	**1.36%**				**423**	**1.35%**			**+0.01%**	
Turnout		**33,262**	**67.51%**				**31,387**	**60.42%**			**+7.09%**	

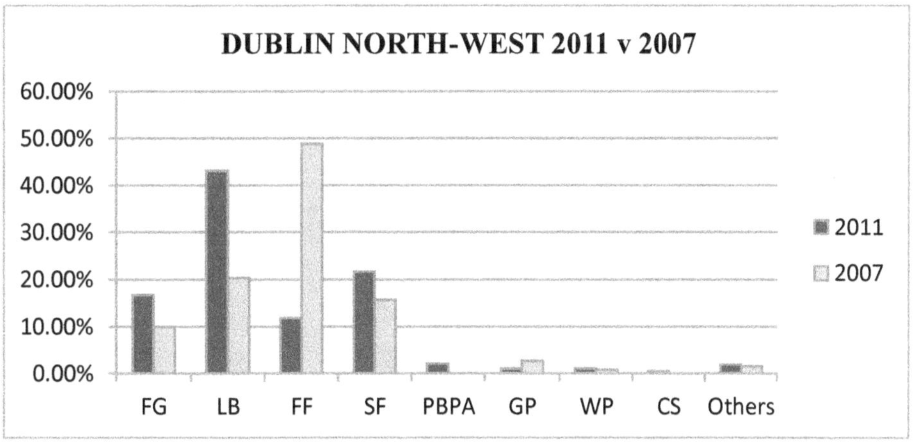

DUBLIN NORTH-WEST 2011
COUNT DETAILS

Seats 3							Quota	8,203
Candidate	**Party**	**1st**	**2nd**	**3rd**	**4th**	**5th**	**6th**	**7th**
			Shortall Surplus	Larkin Votes	Loftus Votes	Keegan Mooney Dunne Holohan	Tormey Votes	Carey Votes
			-1,156					
Shortall, Róisín*	LB	9,359	8,203	8,203	8,203	8,203	8,203	8,203
			+101	+13	+14	+628	+248	+854
Ellis, Dessie	SF	7,115	7,216	7,229	7,243	7,871	8,119	8,973
			+715	+11	+37	+632	+474	+1,169
Lyons, John	LB	4,799	5,514	5,525	5,562	6,194	6,668	7,837
			+95	+35	+14	+115	+1,663	+892
Breen, Gerry	FG	2,988	3,083	3,118	3,132	3,247	4,910	5,802
			+65	+21	+11	+158	+226	-4,350
Carey, Pat*	FF	3,869	3,934	3,955	3,966	4,124	4,350	Eliminated
			+115	+13	+12	+132	-2,780	
Tormey, Dr. Bill	FG	2,508	2,623	2,636	2,648	2,780	Eliminated	
			+20	+19	+33	-749		
Keegan, Andrew	PBPA	677	697	716	749	Eliminated		
			+11	+11	+84	-539		
Mooney, Sean	NP	433	444	455	539	Eliminated		
			+10	+7	+9	-371		
Dunne, John	WP	345	355	362	371	Eliminated		
			+14	+6	+10	-358		
Holohan, Ruairí	GP	328	342	348	358	Eliminated		
			+8	+20	-245			
Loftus, Michael J.	NV	217	225	245	Eliminated			
			+2	-175				
Larkin, Michael	CS	173	175	Eliminated				
Non-transferable				+19	+21	+352	+169	+1,435
Cumulative			0	19	40	392	561	1,996
Total		**32,811**	**32,811**	**32,811**	**32,811**	**32,811**	**32,811**	**32,811**

DUBLIN NORTH-WEST 2011
TRANSFER ANALYSIS

From	To	FG	LB	FF	SF	PBPA	GP	WP	Others	Non Trans
FG	2,780	1,663	474	226	248					169
		59.82%	*17.05%*	*8.13%*	*8.92%*					*6.08%*
LB	1,156	210	715	65	101	20	14	10	21	
		18.17%	*61.85%*	*5.62%*	*8.74%*	*1.73%*	*1.21%*	*0.87%*	*1.82%*	
FF	4,350	892	1,169		854					1,435
		20.51%	*26.87%*		*19.63%*					*32.99%*
PBPA	749	92	235	59	233					130
		12.28%	*31.38%*	*7.88%*	*31.11%*					*17.36%*
GP	358	44	112	28	111					63
		12.29%	*31.28%*	*7.82%*	*31.01%*					*17.60%*
WP	371	45	116	29	116					65
		12.13%	*31.27%*	*7.82%*	*31.27%*					*17.52%*
Others	959	140	217	74	195	52	16	16	115	134
		14.60%	*22.63%*	*7.72%*	*20.33%*	*5.42%*	*1.67%*	*1.67%*	*11.99%*	*13.97%*
Total	**10,723**	**3,086**	**3,038**	**481**	**1,858**	**72**	**30**	**26**	**136**	**1,996**
		28.78%	***28.33%***	***4.49%***	***17.33%***	***0.67%***	***0.28%***	***0.24%***	***1.27%***	***18.61%***

DUBLIN NORTH-WEST MAIN BOUNDARY CHANGES		
Dail	**Constituency**	**Seats**
9 (1937) - 12 (1944)	Dublin North-West	5
13 (1948) - 18 (1965)	Dublin North-West	3
19 (1969) - 20 (1973)	Dublin North-West	4
21 (1977)	Finglas	3
22 (1981) - 28 (1997)	Dublin North-West	4
29 (2002) - 31 (2011)	Dublin North-West	3

DUBLIN NORTH-WEST ALL TDs 1937-2011																		
	Surname	**Forename**	**Party**	**Elected**														**Total**
1	Tunney	Jim	FF	69	73	77	81	82	82	87	89							8
2	Breathnach**	Cormac	FF	37	38	43	44	48	51									6
3	Gogan	Dick	FF	54	57	61	65	69	73									6
4	Flaherty	Mary	FG	81	82	82	87	89	92									6
5	De Rossa	Proinsias	DL	82	82	87	89	92	97									6
6	Byrne	Alfred P.	NP	37	38	43	48	51										5
7	Costello**	Declan	FG	51	54	57	61	65										5
8	Barrett	Michael	FF	81	82	82	87	89										5
9	Shortall	Roisin	LB	92	97	02	07	11										5
10	McGilligan**	Patrick	FG	37	38	43	44											4
11	O'Kelly**	Sean T.	FF	37	38	43	44											4
12	Ahern	Noel	FF	92	97	02	07											4
13	Byrne	Hugh	FG	69	73	81												3
14	Byrne	Thomas	NP	52*	54	57												3
15	Carey	Pat	FF	97	02	07												3
16	O'Sullivan	Martin	LB	43	44													2
17	Mullen	Michael	LB	61	65													2
18	Thornley	David	LB	69	73													2
19	Heron	Archibald	LB	37														1
20	Cooney**	Eamonn	FF	38														1
21	O'Connor	John	FF	44														1
22	De Valera**	Vivion	FF	45*														1
23	Fitzpatrick	Michael	CnaP	48														1
24	Ahern**	Bertie	FF	77														1
25	Belton**	Luke	FG	77														1
26	Ellis	Dessie	SF	11														1
27	Lyons	John	LB	11														1
27	**Total**										***Includes 2 By-Elections**						*	**88**
	**** Also elected in another constituency**																	
1	De Valera**	Vivion	FF	Dublin NC/C			48	51	54	57	61	65/	69	73	77			9
2	O'Kelly**	Sean T.	FF	Dublin Mid/N			18	21/	22	23	27	27	32	33				8
3	Ahern**	Bertie	FF	Dublin Central			81	82	82	87	89	92	97	02				8
4	McGilligan**	Patrick	FG	NUI/Dublin NC			23	27	27	32	33/	48	48	51	54	57	61	5
5	Cooney**	Eamonn	FF	Dublin North			27S	32	33									3
6	Belton**	Luke	FG	Dublin NC			65	69	73									3
7	Breathnach**	Cormac	FF	Dublin North			32	33										2
8	Costello**	Declan	FG	Dublin SW			73											1
8	**Total**																	**39**

DUBLIN NORTH-WEST 1937-2011

		FG		LB		FF		SF		PBPA		GP		WP		CS		DL		C na P		Others	
Dail	**Seats**	**S**	**% Vote**	**S**	**% Vote**	**S**	**% Vote**	**S**	**% Vote**	**S**	**% Vote**	**S**	**% Vote**	**S**	**% Vote**	**S**	**% Vote**	**S**	**% Vote**	**S**	**% Vote**	**S**	**% Vote**
9 1937	5	1	20.73%	1	13.34%	2	43.39%															1	22.54%
10 1938	5	1	22.22%		12.30%	3	51.96%															1	13.52%
11 1943	5	1	16.16%	1	21.46%	2	42.23%															1	20.15%
12 1944	5	1	16.44%	1	17.99%	3	51.52%																14.04%
13 1948	3		14.40%		9.92%	1	40.99%													1	14.56%	1	20.13%
14 1951	3	1	22.17%		11.21%	1	45.82%														1.93%	1	18.88%
15 1954	3	1	32.84%		12.89%	1	36.06%															1	18.21%
16 1957	3	1	20.70%		11.88%	1	45.19%														5.49%	1	16.73%
17 1961	3	1	26.01%	1	17.99%	1	42.58%																13.42%
18 1965	3	1	28.61%	1	23.58%	1	45.95%																1.86%
19 1969	4	1	23.27%	1	37.57%	2	39.15%																
20 1973	4	1	28.66%	1	24.65%	2	44.46%																2.23%
21 1977	3	1	22.92%		15.27%	2	51.60%								4.76%								5.46%
22 1981	4	2	32.80%		12.41%	2	44.68%								7.28%								2.83%
23 1982	4	1	30.99%		7.64%	2	48.05%							1	12.37%								0.95%
24 1982	4	1	30.33%		6.45%	2	40.17%							1	19.78%								3.27%
25 1987	4	1	18.75%		3.96%	2	48.34%		3.08%				1.46%	1	21.61%								2.81%
26 1989	4	1	14.82%		8.23%	2	35.39%		4.19%				4.43%	1	29.50%								3.43%
27 1992	4	1	12.33%	1	23.06%	1	33.38%		3.21%				2.40%		3.29%			1	12.19%				10.15%
28 1997	4		15.60%	1	11.13%	2	47.04%						4.16%		1.33%			1	10.08%				10.66%
29 2002	3		7.96%	1	16.79%	2	47.54%		18.28%				2.32%		2.32%		0.59%						4.21%
30 2007	3		9.96%	1	20.30%	2	48.84%		15.74%				2.75%		0.78%								1.63%
31 2011	3		16.75%	2	43.15%		11.79%	1	21.68%		2.06%		1.00%		1.05%		0.53%						1.98%
1937-2011	**86**	**19**	**20.79%**	**13**	**16.81%**	**39**	**43.07%**	**1**	**2.75%**		**0.09%**		**0.82%**	**4**	**4.48%**		**0.04%**	**2**	**1.12%**	**1**	**0.67%**	**7**	**9.36%**
National	**4,618**	**1,453**	**30.77%**	**482**	**11.53%**	**1,985**	**41.86%**	**232**	**1.99%**	**2**	**0.09%**	**16**	**0.75%**	**17**	**0.78%**		**0.04%**	**8**	**0.22%**	**18**	**0.77%**	**405**	**11.19%**

DUBLIN SOUTH 2011

"Fine Gael take three out of five as Independent Shane Ross tops the poll with one of the biggest votes in this election"

There were major Constituency Commission changes here since 2007. A population of 11,673 in the Cabinteely-Loughlinstown, Foxrock-Carrickmines, Foxrock-Torquay and Stillorgan-Leopardstown areas were transferred into this constituency from Dún Laoghaire. However, the constituency retained its five seats.

Seamus Brennan was elected here in 2007 but died in July 2008. Fine Gael's George Lee won the subsequent by-election in June 2009 but resigned his seat in February 2010. Outgoing Fianna Fáil TD Tom Kitt retired ahead of this election.

Fine Gael increased its vote by 9 points on 2007 and managed to convert 2.2 quotas into three seats with an excellent vote management performance. Olivia Mitchell was the party's leading vote getter and took the third seat with 9,635 first preferences and was followed home by newcomer Peter Mathews who took the fourth seat with 9,053. Alan Shatter had a tougher fight on his hands winning just 7,716 first preferences to leave him in fifth place, 872 ahead of Corrigan. Shatter got the better of the transfer battle and extended his advantage to 1,448 by the final count.

The Labour vote was up 8 points and Alex White delivered on his strong June 2009 by-election performance, which he had been favoured to win prior to the arrival of George Lee. White got 8,524 on the first count and went on to take the second seat. His running mate Aidan Culhane got just 4,535 to leave him in eighth place and out of contention.

The big winner in this constituency was independent candidate and long-serving Senator Shane Ross, who topped the poll with an impressive 17,075 first preferences or 1.41 quotas. He had the second best first preference vote in the country behind Enda Kenny.

It was all change for Fianna Fail as they contested this election without the names of Brennan or Kitt which had been on the ballot paper since 1981. The party selected outgoing Senator Maria Corrigan but its vote collapsed and was down 32 points to just 9.42%, their lowest in this election. Corrigan was outside the frame on the first count and never recovered. She failed to make any inroads into her first count deficit of nearly 900 votes on Alan Shatter and was well beaten in the end.

The Green vote was down four points and with just 7% Eamonn Ryan was in seventh place on the first count and virtually out of contention. Eight candidates failed to get enough votes to reclaim their expenses and this was a feature of this historic election.

DUBLIN SOUTH TD's 2011

SHANE ROSS (IND)

Glenbrook, Enniskerry, Co. Wicklow, Tel: 01 2116692
Leinster House: 01 6183014; Email: shane.ross@oireachtas.ie
Website: www.shane-ross.ie; Facebook: www.facebook.com/voteshaneross.ie

Born Dublin 11th July 1949. Married to Ruth Buchanan, one son, one daughter. Educated Rugby School, England; University of Geneva; TCD (BA [Mod]). Business Editor Sunday Independent, former Stockbroker. Joined Fine Gael prior to 1991 Local Elections. Unsuccessful candidate in 1992 General Election in Wicklow. Resigned from Fine Gael in 1996.
First elected 2011.

Member Committee of Public Accounts. Senator 1981-2011. Member Joint Committee on Transport and Member Joint Committee on Economic and Regulatory Affairs 2007-2011. Member Joint Committee on Enterprise and Small Business 2002-2007. Member British-Irish Parliamentary Body. Contested 1984 European election in Dublin. Member Wicklow County Council 1991-1999. Member Board of Royal City of Dublin Hospital since 1982. Director of Barings New Russia Fund 1997. Director Banque Worms Haussmann International Fund Plc 1997. Honorary President of the Irish Institute of Industrial Engineers 1994-1996. Executive Chairman ABMS Stockbrokers 1988-1990. Son of Senator John N. Ross (University of Dublin Panel).

ALEX WHITE (LB)

30 Fortfield Road, Terenure, Dublin 6W; Mobile: 087 2208533;
Constituency Office: 1 Main Street, Rathfarnham, Dublin 14; Tel: 01 4903889;
Leinster House: 01 6183972; Email: alex.white@oireachtas.ie
Website: www.alexwhite.ie Twitter: twitter.com/alexwhiteTD

Born Dublin 3rd December 1958. Married to Mary Corcoran, one daughter, one son. Educated Chanel College, Coolock; Trinity College, Dublin and Kings Inns. Barrister and former RTE producer. Contested 2007 General Election in Dublin South. Contested by-election 5th June 2009.
First elected 2011.

Chairman Committee on Finance, Public Expenditure and Reform. Senator 2007-2011. Labour Party Spokesperson on Children 2007-2011. Seanad Group Leader and Spokesperson on Children; Foreign Affairs; Northern Ireland; Enterprise, Trade and Employment; Equality and Immigration. Member Joint Committee on the Constitution. Member Joint Committee on Constitutional Amendment on Children. Member Committee of Selection of Seanad Eireann. Member Seanad Committee on Procedure and Privileges. Member Committee on Members' Interests of Seanad Eireann. Member South Dublin County Council 2004-2007 (Leas Cathaoirleach 2006-2007). Producer, The Late Late Show 1990-1994. Member International Commission for Trade Union Rights, Irish Society for Labour Law.

OLIVIA MITCHELL (FG)

18 Balally Court, Dundrum, Dublin 16, Tel: 01 2953033
Leinster House: 01 6183088; Email: olivia.mitchell@oireachtas.ie
Website: www.oliviamitchell.finegael.ie Twitter: @omitchellTD

Born Birr, Co. Offaly 31st July 1947. Married to James Mitchell, two sons, one daughter. Educated Dominican College, Eccles Street; Trinity College, Dublin (BA Economics and Politics, HDip Ed). Former teacher of Economics. Contested 1989 and 1992 general elections in Dublin South. First elected 1997 and at each subsequent election.

Member Committee on Members Interest. Member Committee on Finance, Public Expenditure and Reform. Supported Richard Bruton in his failed attempt to oust Enda Kenny as party leader in June 2010. Fine Gael front bench spokesperson on Arts, Sport and Tourism, September 2007-June 2010. Member Joint Committee on Arts, Sport, Tourism, Community, Rural and Gaeltacht Affairs. Front bench spokesperson on Transport 2004-2007. Front bench spokesperson on Health and Children 2002-2004. Former Member Joint Committee on Health and Children. Front bench spokesperson on Housing & Local Government 2001-2002. Junior spokesperson on Traffic 2000- 2001. Junior spokesperson on Local Development, National Drugs Strategy 1997– 2000. Member Dublin County Council 1985-1991. Member Dun Laoghaire Rathdown County Council 1992-2003 (Cathoirleach 1995-1996). Former Member Dublin Regional Authority; Eastern Health Board; DTO Advisory Committee; Dublin Healthy Cities Project and Dublin representative on World Health Organisation multi city action plan.

PETER MATHEWS (FG)

64 The Rise, Mount Merrion, Co. Dublin; Mobile; 086 1091500; Leinster House: 01 6184443; Email: peter.mathews@oireachtas.ie; Website; www.petermathewsfg.ie

Born Dublin August 1951. Married to Susan with four adult children. Educated Gonzaga College, Dublin and UCD (B.Comm, MBA). Chartered Accountant and Consultant (Banking and Finance). First elected 2011.

Member Committee on Finance, Public Expenditure and Reform. Member Committee on Investigations, Oversight and Petitions. Came to prominence during banking crisis and regular contributor to Vincent Browne Show. Joined Fine Gael in 2010 and election 2011 was his electoral debut.

ALAN SHATTER (FG)

57 Delbrook Manor, Ballinteer, Dublin 16, Tel: 01 2983045
Department of Justice, 94 St. Stephen's Green, Dublin 2,
Leinster House: 01 6133911; Email: alan.shatter@oireachtas.ie,
Website: www.alanshatter.ie Twitter: twitter.com/alanshatterTD

Born Dublin, February 1951. Married to Carol Danker, one son Dylan, one daughter Kelly. Educated The High School, Dublin; TCD; University of Amsterdam and Law School of the Incorporated Law Society of Ireland (MA, DipEL); Fellow of the International Academy of Matrimonial Lawyers. Solicitor. Minister for Justice. First elected 1981. Retained his seat until 2002 and regained his seat in 2007. Retained his seat in 2011.

Appointed Minister for Justice and Defence 9th March 2011. Fine Gael front bench spokesperson on Justice & Law Reform 1st July 2010-2011. Fine Gael front bench spokesperson on Children, September 2007-June 2010. Member Joint Committee on Foreign Affairs and Member Joint Committee on Constitutional Amendment on Children 2007-2011. Spokesperson on Health and Children 1997-2002; Equality and Law reform 1993-1194; Justice 1992-1993; Labour 1991; Environment 1989-1991; Law reform 1982, 1987-1988. Member Committee on Foreign Affairs; Health and Children 1997-2002. Member Dail Committee on the Solicitors (Amendment) Bill 1991; Dail Select Committee on Crime; on the Childcare Act 1990 and on Women's Rights 1988-1989. Achieved the rare feat of getting a private member's bill enacted into law through his Bills on Judicial Separation and Family Law Reform (1989) and Adoption (1991) and Landlord and Tenant (Amendment) Bill (1993). Member Dublin County Council 1979-1993 and South Dublin County Council 1994-1999. Former Chairman of Free legal Advice Centres (FLAC) and of CARE (Campaign for deprived Children). Former President of Irish Council against Blood Sports. Author of "Family Law in the Republic of Ireland" and "Family Planning Irish Style" and the novel "Laura".

DUBLIN SOUTH 2011							
FIRST PREFERENCE VOTES							
	Seats	5			12,108		
	Candidate	Party	1st	%	Quota	Count	Status
1	**Ross, Shane**	**NP**	**17,075**	**23.50%**	**1.41**	**1**	**Made Quota**
2	**White, Alex**	**LB**	**8,524**	**11.73%**	**0.70**	**6**	**Made Quota**
3	**Mitchell, Olivia***	**FG**	**9,635**	**13.26%**	**0.80**	**8**	**Made Quota**
4	**Mathews, Peter**	**FG**	**9,053**	**12.46%**	**0.75**	**8**	**Elected**
5	**Shatter, Alan***	**FG**	**7,716**	**10.62%**	**0.64**	**8**	**Elected**
6	Corrigan, Maria	FF	6,844	9.42%	0.57	8	Not Elected
7	Ryan, Eamonn*	GP	4,929	6.78%	0.41	7	Eliminated
8	Culhane, Aidan	LB	4,535	6.24%	0.37	5	Eliminated
9	Nic Cormaic, Sorcha	SF	1,915	2.64%	0.16	4	No Expenses
10	Curry, Nicola	PBPA	1,277	1.76%	0.11	3	No Expenses
11	Murphy, Jane	CS	277	0.38%	0.02	2	No Expenses
12	Hussein Hamed, Buhidma	NP	273	0.38%	0.02	2	No Expenses
13	Doyle, John	NP	246	0.34%	0.02	2	No Expenses
14	Dolan, Gerard	NP	156	0.21%	0.01	2	No Expenses
15	Whitehead, Raymond	NP	120	0.17%	0.01	2	No Expenses
16	Zaidan, Eamonn	NP	71	0.10%	0.01	2	No Expenses
16	***Outgoing**		**72,646**	**96.67%**	**12,108**	**3,027**	**No Expenses**

DUBLIN SOUTH 2011												
PARTY VOTE												
	2011					2007					Change	
Party	Cand	1st	%	Quota	Seats	Cand	1st	%	Quota	Seats	%	Seats
FG	3	26,404	36.35%	2.18	3	3	16,686	27.26%	1.64	2	+9.08%	+1
LB	2	13,059	17.98%	1.08	1	2	6,384	10.43%	0.63		+7.55%	+1
FF	1	6,844	9.42%	0.57		3	25,298	41.33%	2.48	2	-31.91%	-2
SF	1	1,915	2.64%	0.16		2	1,843	3.01%	0.18		-0.38%	
PBPA	1	1,277	1.76%	0.11							+1.76%	
GP	1	4,929	6.78%	0.41		1	6,768	11.06%	0.66	1	-4.27%	-1
CS	1	277	0.38%	0.02							+0.38%	
PD						1	4,045	6.61%	0.40		-6.61%	
Others	6	17,941	24.70%	1.48	1	1	180	0.29%	0.02		+24.40%	+1
Total	**16**	**72,646**	**100.0%**	**12,108**	**5**	**13**	**61,204**	**100.0%**	**10,201**	**5**	**0.00%**	**0**
Electorate		**102,387**	**70.95%**				**89,464**	**68.41%**			**+2.54%**	
Spoiled		**459**	**0.63%**				**418**	**0.68%**			**-0.05%**	
Turnout		**73,105**	**71.40%**				**61,622**	**68.88%**			**+2.52%**	

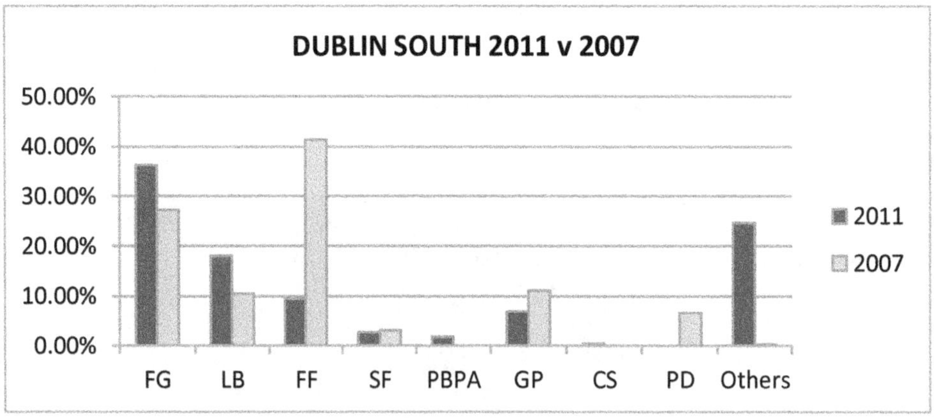

DUBLIN SOUTH 2011 COUNT DETAILS									
Seats	5							Quota	12,108
Candidate	**Party**	**1st**	**2nd** Ross Surplus	**3rd** Murphy Hussein Doyle Dolan Whitehed Zaidan	**4th** Curry Votes	**5th** Nic Cormaic Votes	**6th** Culhane Votes	**7th** White Surplus	**8th** Ryan Votes
			-4,967						
Ross, Shane	NP	17,075	12,108	12,108	12,108	12,108	12,108	12,108	12,108
			+795	*+148*	*+280*	*+660*	*+3,796*	*-2,095*	
White, Alex	LB	8,524	9,319	9,467	9,747	10,407	14,203	12,108	12,108
			+819	*+123*	*+84*	*+102*	*+396*	*+468*	*1,752*
Mitchell, Olivia*	FG	9,635	10,454	10,577	10,661	10,763	11,159	11,627	13,379
			+752	*+182*	*+60*	*+126*	*+321*	*+326*	*+1,250*
Mathews, Peter	FG	9,053	9,805	9,987	10,047	10,173	10,494	10,820	12,070
			+783	*+81*	*+46*	*+112*	*+228*	*+335*	*+1,310*
Shatter, Alan*	FG	7,716	8,499	8,580	8,626	8,738	8,966	9,301	10,611
			+324	*+164*	*+68*	*+164*	*+198*	*+170*	*+1,231*
Corrigan, Maria	FF	6,844	7,168	7,332	7,400	7,564	7,762	7,932	9,163
			+560	*+137*	*+172*	*+322*	*+416*	*+796*	*-7,332*
Ryan, Eamonn*	GP	4,929	5,489	5,626	5,798	6,120	6,536	7,332	Eliminated
			+304	*+101*	*+292*	*+459*	*-5,691*		
Culhane, Aidan	LB	4,535	4,839	4,940	5,232	5,691	Eliminated		
			+150	*+121*	*+431*	*-2,617*			
Nic Cormaic, Sorcha	SF	1,915	2,065	2,186	2,617	Eliminated			
			+178	*+209*	*-1,664*				
Curry, Nicola	PBPA	1,277	1,455	1,664	Eliminated				
			+19	*-296*					
Murphy, Jane	CS	277	296	Eliminated					
			+45	*-318*					
Hussein Hamed, Buhidma	NP	273	318	Eliminated					
			+97	*-343*					
Doyle, John	NP	246	343	Eliminated					
			+36	*-192*					
Dolan, Gerard	NP	156	192	Eliminated					
			+91	*-211*					
Whitehead, Raymond	NP	120	211	Eliminated					
			+14	*-85*					
Zaidan, Eamonn	NP	71	85	Eliminated					
Non-transferable				*+179*	*+231*	*+672*	*+336*		*+1,789*
Cumulative			0	179	410	1,082	1,418	1,418	3,207
Total		**72,646**	**72,646**	**72,646**	**72,646**	**72,646**	**72,646**	**72,646**	**72,646**

DUBLIN SOUTH 2011 TRANSFER ANALYSIS									
From	**To**	**FG**	**LB**	**FF**	**SF**	**PBPA**	**GP**	**Others**	**Non Trans**
LB	7,786	2,074	3,796	368			1,212		336
		26.64%	*48.75%*	*4.73%*			*15.57%*		*4.32%*
SF	2,617	340	1,119	164			322		672
		12.99%	*42.76%*	*6.27%*			*12.30%*		*25.68%*
PBPA	1,664	190	572	68	431		172		231
		11.42%	*34.38%*	*4.09%*	*25.90%*		*10.34%*		*13.88%*
GP	7,332	4,312		1,231					1,789
		58.81%		*16.79%*					*24.40%*
Others	6,412	2,740	1,348	488	271	387	697	302	179
		42.73%	*21.02%*	*7.61%*	*4.23%*	*6.04%*	*10.87%*	*4.71%*	*2.79%*
Total	**25,811**	**9,656**	**6,835**	**2,319**	**702**	**387**	**2,403**	**302**	**3,207**
		37.41%	***26.48%***	***8.98%***	***2.72%***	***1.50%***	***9.31%***	***1.17%***	***12.42%***

DUBLIN SOUTH		
MAIN BOUNDARY CHANGES		
Dail	**Constituency**	**Seats**
22 (1981) - 31 (2011)	Dublin South	5

DUBLIN SOUTH													
ALL TDs 1981-2011													
	Surname	**Forename**	**Party**	**Elected**									**Total**
1	Brennan	Seamus	FF	81	82	82	87	89	92	97	02	07	9
2	Shatter	Alan	FG	81	82	82	87	89	92	97	07	11	9
3	Kitt	Tom	FF	87	89	92	97	02	07				6
4	Fennell	Nuala	FG	81	82	82	89						4
5	Kelly*	John	FG	81	82	82	87						4
6	Mitchell	Olivia	FG	97	02	07	11						4
7	Andrews*	Niall	FF	81	82	82							3
8	O'Donnell	Liz	PD	92	97	02							3
9	Ryan	Eamonn	GP	02	07								2
10	Colley	Anne	PD	87									1
11	Garland	Roger	GP	89									1
12	FitzGerald	Eithne	LB	92									1
13	Lee	George	FG	09*									1
14	Ross	Shane	NP	11									1
15	White	Alex	LB	11									1
16	Mathews	Peter	FG	11									1
16	**Total**						***Includes 1 By-Election**					*	**51**
	**** Also elected in another constituency**												
1	Kelly*	John	FG	Dublin SC				73	77				2
2	Andrews*	Niall	FF	Dublin Co. South				77					1
2	**Total**												**3**

Minister Shatter during visit of Queen Elizabeth

DUBLIN SOUTH 1981-2011

		FG		LB		FF		SF		SP		PBPA		GP		WP		CS		PD		DL		DSP		Others	
Dail	**Seats**	**S**	**% Vote**	**S**	**% Vote**	**S**	**% Vote**	**S**	**% Vote**	**S**	**% Vote**	**S**	**% Vote**	**S**	**% Vote**	**S**	**% Vote**	**S**	**% Vote**	**S**	**% Vote**	**S**	**% Vote**	**S**	**% Vote**	**S**	**% Vote**
22 1981	5	3	46.00%		9.79%	2	42.34%																				1.87%
23 1982	5	3	50.33%		8.92%	2	40.75%																				0.00%
24 1982	5	3	52.47%		8.20%	2	36.60%																		0.91%		1.81%
25 1987	5	2	30.88%		4.68%	2	35.75%								2.40%		2.28%			1	20.86%						3.15%
26 1989	5	2	29.06%		7.63%	2	43.34%							1	8.81%		2.66%				8.51%						
27 1992	5	1	20.25%	1	28.94%	2	32.64%		0.81%						3.79%					1	8.66%		1.07%				3.85%
28 1997	5	2	29.09%		10.60%	2	38.62%				1.08%				6.10%					1	9.39%						5.12%
29 2002	5	1	19.78%		9.49%	2	36.64%		3.93%		1.92%			1	9.45%					1	15.00%						3.78%
30 2007	5	2	27.26%		10.43%	2	41.33%		3.01%					1	11.06%						6.61%						0.29%
31 2011	5	3	36.35%	1	17.98%		9.42%		2.64%				1.76%		6.78%				0.38%							1	24.70%
1981-2011	**50**	**22**	**33.72%**	**2**	**12.00%**	**18**	**34.89%**		**1.12%**		**0.29%**		**0.22%**	**3**	**5.04%**		**0.48%**		**0.05%**	**4**	**6.90%**		**0.11%**		**0.08%**	**1**	**5.09%**
National	**4,618**	**1,453**	**30.77%**	**482**	**11.53%**	**1,985**	**41.86%**	**232**	**1.99%**	**4**	**0.16%**	**2**	**0.09%**	**16**	**0.75%**	**17**	**0.78%**		**0.04%**	**44**	**1.42%**	**8**	**0.22%**	**2**	**0.06%**	**373**	**10.32%**

DUBLIN SOUTH-CENTRAL 2011

"The left sweep the board to take 4 out of 5 seats"

There were no constituency boundary changes here since 2007.

In the People's Republic of Dublin South-Central the left virtually swept the board, taking four of the five seats. Labour took pole position with 35 per cent of the votes, its second best performance in the country, and two of its three candidates were elected. The main surprise was that Henry Upton, nephew and son of the two previous Labour incumbents, was the one to lose out, being outpolled by former TD Eric Byrne and by the new TD, though veteran councillor, Michael Conaghan. Byrne, who had missed out on a seat by 5 votes in 1992 and by 69 votes in 2007, headed the poll this time.

Sinn Fein's Aengus Ó Snodaigh was comfortably re-elected to a third term, and the other left-wing seat was taken by Joan Collins of People before Profit, part of the United Left Alliance. She virtually trebled her 2007 vote, and while her TV cameo berating Bertie Ahern outside Leinster House no doubt helped her profile, she was probably on course for a seat anyway.

The Fine Gael vote rose by 9 per cent, but this was enough only to retain the seat it already held through Catherine Byrne (the only former professional footballer in the Dáil), with neither of her running mates coming close.

Most striking, perhaps, was the failure of Fianna Fail, represented now just by Michael Mulcahy following the retirement of Seán Ardagh, to win a seat in this former stronghold. With Seán Lemass leading its team, the party won 55 per cent of the votes here in 1951; now, it could not win even 10 per cent.

Joan Collins United Left Alliance TD

DUBLIN SOUTH CENTRAL TDs 2011

ERIC BYRNE (LB)

32 Ashdale Road, Terenure, Dublin 6W; Tel: 01 4901305; Mobile: 087 2548429 Leinster House: 01 6183223; Email: eric.byrne@oireachtas.ie; Website: www.ericbyrne.ie Twitter: @EricByrneTD.

Born Dublin 21st April 1947. Married to Prof. Ellen Hazelkorn, two daughters. Educated Synge Street, Dublin; Bolton Street College of Technology. Former Buildings Officer. Contested 1977 Dail election in Dublin Rathmines for SF. Contested 1981 and February 1982 Dail elections in Dublin South Central for SF. Contested November 1982 and 1989 Dail elections in Dublin South Central for WP. First elected 1989 Dail election for WP in Dublin South-Central. Lost his seat in 1992 but regained it at by-election in 1994 for DL. Contested 1997 Dail election for DL in Dublin South Central. Contested 2002 and 2007 Dail elections for LB. Re-elected 2011.

Member Joint Administration Committee. Member Committee on Foreign Affairs and Trade. Contested 2007 Senate election. First elected to Dublin City Council in 1985 in the Crumlin electoral area. Re-elected 1991. Retained his seat in Crumlin-Kimmage in 1999 and re-elected 2004 and 2009.

CATHERINE BYRNE (FG)

30 Bulfin Road, Inchicore, Dublin 8, Mobile 086 8543276
Constituency Office: 5A Tyrconnell Road, Inchicore, Dublin 8; Tel: 01 4735080
Leinster House: Tel: 01 6183083; Email: catherine.byrne@oireachtas.ie
Website: www.catherinebyrne@finegael.ie

Born Bluebell, Dublin 26th February 1956. Married to Joe Byrne, four daughters, one son. Educated Holy Faith, The Coombe, Dublin 8; Cathal Brugha Catering College, Dublin 1. Completed a Lay Ministry Course in All Hallows College. Unsuccessful candidate in By-election in Dublin South-Central in 1999 and again in 2002. First elected 2007. Retained her seat in 2011.

Member Committee on Health and Children. Front bench spokesperson on Older Citizens July 2010-2011. Deputy Spokesperson on Community, Rural and Gaeltacht Affairs with special responsibility for National Drugs Strategy, October 2007-June 2010. Member Joint Committee on Social and Family Affairs 2007-2011. Member Dublin City Council 1999-2007. Lord Mayor 2005-2006. Former Member Dublin Regional Authority; Inichore/Bluebell Garda Police Forum; St. Michael's Estate and Fatima Mansions Regeneration Boards. Former Chairperson St. Michael's Community Centre and former member Board of Management Mercy Convent Secondary School, Goldenbridge. Leader of St. Michael's Folk/Gospel Group for 15 years.

MICHAEL CONAGHAN (LB)

33 Lally Road, Ballyfermot, Dublin 10; Tel: 01 6269892; Mobile: 086 1753747
Leinster House: 01 6184033; E-mail: michael.conaghan@oireachtas.ie
Website: www.labour.ie/michaelconaghan

Born Donegal September 1945. Married to Marian, two daughters. Educated Four Masters, Donegal Town; Manchester University; UCD. Former Teacher in Inchicore College of Further Education. Contested Dail By-election in Dublin West in 1982 for DSP. Contested Dail elections in November 1982, 1987, 1989 and 1997 as an Independent. First elected 2011.

Member Committee on Investigations, Oversight and Petitions. Member Committee on Jobs, Social Protection and Education. Contested 1985 local election for DSP. First elected 1991 for Labour in Ballyfermot. Retained his seat in 1999 and 2004. Re-elected in Ballyfermot-Drimnagh in 2009.

JOAN COLLINS (PBPA)

30 Ring Street, Inchicore, Dublin 8; Mobile: 086 3888151; Leinster House: 01 6183215;
Email: joan.collins@peoplebeforeprofit.ie; Website: www.joan-collins.org
Twitter: CllrJoanCollins.

Born Dublin 17th June 1961. Partner Dermot Connolly. Educated St. John of God Secondary School, Coolock. Former Post Office Clerk. Contested 2007 Dail election in Dublin South-Central. First elected 2011.

Member Committee on Investigations, Oversight and Petitions. Member Committee on Jobs, Social Protection and Education. First elected to Dublin City Council in 2004 as an Independent in the Crumlin-Kimmage electoral area. Re-elected for PBPA in 2009.

AENGUS Ó SNODAIGH (SF)

12 Bothar na Deise, Ballyfermot, Dublin 10,
Constituency Office: 347 Ballyfermot Road, Dublin 10; Tel: 01 6259320,
Leinster House: 01 6184084, Email: aosnodaigh@oireachtas.ie
Website: www.aengusosnodaigh.ie; Twitter: twitter.com/aosnodaigh

Born Dublin 31st July 1964. Married to Aisling O Dalaigh, two sons, one daughter. Educated Coláiste Eoin, Booterstown, Co. Dublin; UCD (BA, HdipEd). Former employee of Bord na Gaeilge and SIPTU shop steward. Contested 1987 general election in Dublin South-East. Contested 1999 by-election in Dublin South-Central. First elected 2002 and at each subsequent election.

Appointed Sinn Fein Spokesperson on Social Protection and Party Whip March 2011.Member Committee on Procedure and Privileges. Member Committee on Investigations, Oversight and Petitions. Member Committee on Jobs, Social Protection and Education. Party Whip and spokesperson on Justice and Equality 2007-2011. Also responsible for Culture and the Gaeltacht, International Affairs and Defence. Member Joint Administration Committee and Member Dail Committee on Procedure and Privileges 2007-2011. Member Select Committee on European Affairs and member of Committee on Procedure and Privileges 2002-2007. Member Sinn Fein Ard Comhairle since 1999.

	DUBLIN SOUTH-CENTRAL 2011 FIRST PREFERENCE VOTES						
	Seats	5			8,488		
	Candidate	**Party**	**1st**	**%**	**Quota**	**Count**	**Status**
1	**Byrne, Eric #**	**LB**	**8,357**	**16.41%**	**0.98**	**8**	**Made Quota**
2	**Byrne, Catherine***	**FG**	**5,604**	**11.00%**	**0.66**	**12**	**Made Quota**
3	**Conaghan, Michael**	**LB**	**5,492**	**10.78%**	**0.65**	**13**	**Made Quota**
4	**Collins, Joan**	**PBPA**	**6,574**	**12.91%**	**0.77**	**13**	**Elected**
5	**Ó Snodaigh, Aengus***	**SF**	**6,804**	**13.36%**	**0.80**	**13**	**Elected**
6	Mulcahy, Michael*	FF	4,837	9.50%	0.57	13	Not Elected
7	Brophy, Colm	FG	3,376	6.63%	0.40	11	Eliminated
8	Upton, Henry	LB	4,183	8.21%	0.49	10	Eliminated
9	McGinley, Ruairí	FG	2,976	5.84%	0.35	8	Eliminated
10	Ó hAlmhain, Oisín	GP	1,015	1.99%	0.12	7	No Expenses
11	O'Neill, Peter	NP	456	0.90%	0.05	7	No Expenses
12	Bradley, Neville	NP	323	0.63%	0.04	7	No Expenses
13	Callanan, Colm	CS	239	0.47%	0.03	6	No Expenses
14	Connolly Farrell, Seán	NP	178	0.35%	0.02	5	No Expenses
15	King, Paul	NP	146	0.29%	0.02	4	No Expenses
16	Kelly, Gerry	NP	137	0.27%	0.02	3	No Expenses
17	Bennett, Noel	NP	128	0.25%	0.02	2	No Expenses
18	Mooney, Dominic	NP	102	0.20%	0.01	1	No Expenses
18	***Outgoing TD # Former TD**		**50,927**	**100.00%**	**8,488**	**2,122**	**No Expenses**

DUBLIN SOUTH-CENTRAL 2011 PARTY VOTE												
	2011					2007					Change	
Party	**Cand**	**1st**	**%**	**Quota**	**Seats**	**Cand**	**1st**	**%**	**Quota**	**Seats**	**%**	**Seats**
FG	3	11,956	23.48%	1.41	1	2	6,838	14.39%	0.86	1	+9.09%	
LB	3	18,032	35.41%	2.12	2	2	10,041	21.13%	1.27	1	+14.28%	+1
FF	1	4,837	9.50%	0.57		2	15,725	33.08%	1.99	2	-23.59%	-2
SF	1	6,804	13.36%	0.80	1	1	4,825	10.15%	0.61	1	+3.21%	
PBPA	1	6,574	12.91%	0.77	1						+12.91%	+1
GP	1	1,015	1.99%	0.12		1	2,756	5.80%	0.35		-3.81%	
WP						1	256	0.54%	0.03		-0.54%	
CS	1	239	0.47%	0.03							+0.47%	
PD						2	912	1.92%	0.12		-1.92%	
Others	7	1,470	2.89%	0.17		5	6,178	13.00%	0.78		-10.11%	
Total	**18**	**50,927**	**100.0%**	**8,488**	**5**	**16**	**47,531**	**100.0%**	**7,922**	**5**	**0.00%**	**0**
Electorate		**80,268**	**63.45%**				**86,710**	**54.82%**			**+8.63%**	
Spoiled		**817**	**1.58%**				**789**	**1.63%**			**-0.05%**	
Turnout		**51,744**	**64.46%**				**48,320**	**55.73%**			**+8.74%**	

DUBLIN SOUTH-CENTRAL 2011
COUNT DETAILS

Seats 5 — Quota 8,488

Candidate	Party	1st	2nd	3rd	4th	5th	6th	7th	8th	9th	10th	11th	12th	13th
			Mooney Votes	Bennett Votes	Kelly Votes	King Votes	Connolly Votes	Callanan Votes	O hAlmhain O'Neill Bradley	McGinley Votes	Byrne, E Surplus	Upton Votes	Brophy Votes	Byrne, C. Surplus
			+10	*+13*	*+11*	*+10*	*+10*	*+5*	*+305*		*-233*			
Byrne, Eric #	LB	8,357	8,367	8,380	8,391	8,401	8,411	8,416	8,721	8,721	8,488	8,488	8,488	8,488
			+6	*+4*	*+4*	*+8*	*+4*	*+33*	*+252*	*+1,205*	*+22*	*+638*	*+4,087*	*-3,379*
Byrne, Catherine*	FG	5,604	5,610	5,614	5,618	5,626	5,630	5,663	5,915	7,120	7,142	7,780	11,867	8,488
			+5	*+4*	*+4*	*+4*	*+28*	*+7*	*+182*	*+93*	*+85*	*+2,290*	*+269*	*+1,395*
Conaghan, Michael	LB	5,492	5,497	5,501	5,505	5,509	5,537	5,544	5,726	5,819	5,904	8,194	8,463	9,858
			+11	*+21*	*+24*	*+23*	*+38*	*+37*	*+344*	*+94*	*+28*	*+579*	*+205*	*+481*
Collins, Joan	PBPA	6,574	6,585	6,606	6,630	6,653	6,691	6,728	7,072	7,166	7,194	7,773	7,978	8,459
			+15	*+6*	*+13*	*+11*	*+25*	*+11*	*+156*	*+70*	*+12*	*+332*	*+114*	*+150*
Ó Snodaigh, Aengus*	SF	6,804	6,819	6,825	6,838	6,849	6,874	6,885	7,041	7,111	7,123	7,455	7,569	7,719
			+7	*+1*	*+5*	*+15*	*+4*	*+63*	*+127*	*+127*	*+9*	*+270*	*+233*	*+463*
Mulcahy, Michael*	FF	4,837	4,844	4,845	4,850	4,865	4,869	4,932	5,059	5,186	5,195	5,465	5,698	6,161
			+1	*+7*	*+3*	*+6*	*+3*	*+22*	*+119*	*+1,305*	*+5*	*+352*	*-5,199*	
Brophy, Colm	FG	3,376	3,377	3,384	3,387	3,393	3,396	3,418	3,537	4,842	4,847	5,199	Eliminated	
			+4	*+5*	*+16*	*+10*	*+8*	*+5*	*+228*	*+216*	*+72*	*-4,747*		
Upton, Henry	LB	4,183	4,187	4,192	4,208	4,218	4,226	4,231	4,459	4,675	4,747	Eliminated		
			+4	*+3*		*+8*	*+5*	*+14*	*+118*	*-3,128*				
McGinley, Ruairí	FG	2,976	2,980	2,983	2,983	2,991	2,996	3,010	3,128	Eliminated				
				+4	*+12*	*+7*	*+4*	*+9*	*-1,051*					
Ó hAlmhain, Oisín	GP	1,015	1,015	1,019	1,031	1,038	1,042	1,051	Eliminated					
			+9	*+4*	*+10*	*+22*	*+38*	*+10*	*-549*					
O'Neill, Peter	NP	456	465	469	479	501	539	549	Eliminated					
			+5	*+36*	*+4*	*+23*	*+19*	*+15*	*-425*					
Bradley, Neville	NP	323	328	364	368	391	410	425	Eliminated					
				+2	*+5*	*+1*	*+4*	*-251*						
Callanan, Colm	CS	239	239	241	246	247	251	Eliminated						
			+4	*+8*	*+8*	*+19*	*-217*							
Connolly Farrell, Seán	NP	178	182	190	198	217	Eliminated							
			+10	*+2*	*+18*	*-176*								
King, Paul	NP	146	156	158	176	Eliminated								
			+2	*+4*	*-143*									
Kelly, Gerry	NP	137	139	143	Eliminated									
				-128										
Bennett, Noel	NP	128	128	Eliminated										
			-102											
Mooney, Dominic	NP	102	Eliminated											
Non-transferable			*+9*	*+4*	*+6*	*+9*	*+27*	*+20*	*+194*	*+18*		*+286*	*+291*	*+890*
Cumulative			9	13	19	28	55	75	269	287	287	573	864	1,754
Total		50,927	50,927	50,927	50,927	50,927	50,927	50,927	50,927	50,927	50,927	50,927	50,927	50,927

DUBLIN SOUTH-CENTRAL 2011
TRANSFER ANALYSIS

From	To	FG	LB	FF	SF	PBPA	GP	Others	Non Trans
FG	11,706	6,597	1,973	823	334	780			1,199
		56.36%	*16.85%*	*7.03%*	*2.85%*	*6.66%*			*10.24%*
LB	4,980	1,017	2,447	279	344	607			286
		20.42%	*49.14%*	*5.60%*	*6.91%*	*12.19%*			*5.74%*
GP	1,051	254	371	66	81	178			101
		24.17%	*35.30%*	*6.28%*	*7.71%*	*16.94%*			*9.61%*
Others	1,991	370	503	156	156	320	36	282	168
		18.58%	*25.26%*	*7.84%*	*7.84%*	*16.07%*	*1.81%*	*14.16%*	*8.44%*
Total	**19,728**	**8,238**	**5,294**	**1,324**	**915**	**1,885**	**36**	**282**	**1,754**
		41.76%	***26.83%***	***6.71%***	***4.64%***	***9.55%***	***0.18%***	***1.43%***	***8.89%***

DUBLIN SOUTH-CENTRAL		
MAIN BOUNDARY CHANGES		
Dail	**Constituency**	**Seats**
13 (1948) - 18 (1965)	Dublin South-Central	5
19 (1969) - 20 (1973)	Dublin South-Central	4
21 (1977)	Dublin South-Central	3
22 (1981) - 26 (1989)	Dublin South-Central	5
27 (1992) - 28 (1997)	Dublin South-Central	4
29 (2002) - 31 (2011)	Dublin South-Central	5

DUBLIN SOUTH-CENTRAL																			
ALL TDs 1948-2011																			
	Surname	**Forename**	**Party**	**Elected**															**Total**
1	Briscoe*	Ben	FF	69	73	81	82	82	87	89	92	97							9
2	Mitchell	Gay	FG	81	82	82	87	89	92	97	02								8
3	Dockrell*	Maurice E.	FG	48	51	54	57	61	65										6
4	Lemass*	Sean F.	FF	48	51	54	57	61	65										6
5	Brady	Philip	FF	51	57	61	65	69	73										6
6	Cluskey*	Frank	LB	65	77	82	82	87											5
7	O'Brien*	Fergus	FG	77	81	82N	87	89											5
8	O'Connell*	John	FF	81	82	82	89	92											5
9	Fitzpatrick*	Tom	FF	65	77	81	82F												4
10	Larkin(jun)*	James	LB	48	51	54													3
11	Ardagh	Sean	FF	97	02	07													3
12	Byrne	Eric	DL	89	94*	11													3
13	O Snodaigh	Aengus	SF	02	07	11													3
14	McCann*	John	FF	48	51														2
15	Lynch*	Celia	FF	54	57														2
16	Cummins	Patrick	FF	58*	61														2
17	Ryan*	Richie	FG	69	73														2
18	Upton	Pat	LB	92	97														2
19	Mulcahy	Michael	FF	02	07														2
20	Upton	Mary	LB	02	07														2
21	Byrne	Catherine	FG	07	11														2
22	Lehane	Con	CnaP	48															1
23	Finlay jun	Thomas	FG	54															1
24	Murphy	John	IndUW	57															1
25	Barron	Joseph	CnaP	61															1
26	O'Donovan*	John	LB	69															1
27	Kelly*	John	FG	73															1
28	Mooney	Mary	FF	87															1
29	Conaghan	Michael	LB	11															1
30	Collins	Joan	11																1
30	**Total**										***Includes 2 By-Elections**							*	**91**
	**** Also elected in another constituency**																		
1	Lemass*	Sean F.	FF	Dublin S						24*	27	27	32	33	37	38	43	44	9
2	Ryan*	Richie	FG	Dublin SW/Rathmines W/SE						59*	61	65	77	81					5
3	Kelly*	John	FG	Dublin S						77	81	82	82	87					5
4	Dockrell*	Maurice E.	FG	Dublin S/C						43	44/	69	73						4
5	Lynch*	Celia	FF	Dublin NC						61	65	69	73						4
6	O'Connell*	John	FF	Dublin SW/Ballyfermot						65	69	73	77						4
7	McCann*	John	FF	Dublin S						39*	43	44							3
8	Larkin(jun)*	James	LB	Dublin S						43	44								2
9	Briscoe*	Ben	FF	Dublin SW/Rathmines W						65	77								2
10	Cluskey*	Frank	LB	Dublin C						69	73								2
11	Fitzpatrick*	Tom	FF	Dublin C						69	73								2
12	O'Donovan*	John	FG	Dublin SE						54									1
13	O'Brien*	Fergus	FG	Dublin SE						73									1
13	**Total**										***Includes 3 By-Elections**							*	**44**

DUBLIN SOUTH-CENTRAL 1948-2011																											
		FG		LB		FF		SF		SP		PBPA		GP		WP		CS		PD		DL		C na P		Others	
Dail	**Seats**	**S**	**% Vote**	**S**	**% Vote**	**S**	**% Vote**	**S**	**% Vote**	**S**	**% Vote**	**S**	**% Vote**	**S**	**% Vote**	**S**	**% Vote**	**S**	**% Vote**	**S**	**% Vote**	**S**	**% Vote**	**S**	**% Vote**	**S**	**% Vote**
13 1948	5	1	21.47%	1	13.62%	2	43.52%																	1	18.81%		2.57%
14 1951	5	1	23.59%	1	13.64%	3	55.13%																		7.64%		
15 1954	5	2	33.08%	1	15.27%	2	41.43%																		8.46%		1.76%
16 1957	5	1	23.43%		6.05%	3	49.17%		5.43%																6.42%	1	9.51%
17 1961	5	1	29.37%		10.29%	3	47.86%		1.94%															1	9.68%		0.86%
18 1965	5	1	24.66%	1	19.89%	3	48.72%																		6.22%		0.51%
19 1969	4	1	31.54%	1	22.97%	2	37.56%																				7.93%
20 1973	4	2	38.00%		16.89%	2	38.56%		4.34%																		2.21%
21 1977	3	1	40.42%	1	16.94%	1	37.06%										5.58%										
22 1981	5	2	29.18%		12.02%	2	34.35%										4.91%									1	19.54%
23 1982	5	1	36.55%	1	14.02%	2	41.77%										6.72%									1	0.94%
24 1982	5	2	39.56%	1	14.01%	1	37.11%										8.23%									1	1.09%
25 1987	5	2	27.60%	1	9.09%	2	40.91%		2.45%								7.63%				10.08%						2.23%
26 1989	5	2	26.64%		7.68%	2	39.53%		2.75%						5.02%	1	15.19%				2.91%						0.27%
27 1992	4	1	19.05%	1	29.63%	2	29.56%		1.68%						3.22%		1.78%				4.69%		7.43%				2.97%
28 1997	4	1	24.95%	1	10.41%	2	34.43%		4.77%		0.81%		0.54%		3.95%		0.73%				5.01%		11.30%				3.11%
29 2002	5	1	16.94%	1	19.72%	2	34.32%	1	12.70%				1.40%		5.22%		1.87%				3.13%						4.70%
30 2007	5	1	14.39%	1	21.13%	2	33.08%	1	10.15%				4.39%		5.80%		0.54%		0.33%		1.92%						8.28%
31 2011	5	1	23.48%	2	35.41%		9.50%	1	13.36%			1	12.91%		1.99%				0.47%								2.89%
1948-2011	**89**	**25**	**27.14%**	**15**	**16.40%**	**38**	**37.96%**	**3**	**3.36%**		**0.04%**	**1**	**1.22%**		**1.44%**	**1**	**3.02%**		**0.05%**		**1.63%**		**0.97%**	**2**	**2.84%**	**4**	**3.92%**
National	**4,618**	**1,453**	**30.77%**	**482**	**11.53%**	**1,985**	**41.86%**	**232**	**1.99%**	**4**	**0.16%**	**2**	**0.09%**	**16**	**0.75%**	**17**	**0.78%**		**0.04%**	**44**	**1.42%**	**8**	**0.22%**	**18**	**0.77%**	**357**	**9.61%**

DUBLIN SOUTH-EAST 2011

"Fine Gael and Labour share the four seats"

There were no Constituency Commission boundary changes here since 2007 and it remained a four-seat constituency.

This was another good performance by Fine Gael as its vote was up 17 points and with 1.8 quotas the party comfortably took two seats. Outgoing deputy Lucinda Creighton topped the poll with 6,619 first preferences and was close to the quota on the first count. She went on to take the second seat on the sixth count. She was followed home by Eoghan Murphy who was in second place with 5,783 on the first count and he went on to take the third seat.

The Labour vote was up nine points and the party managed to convert just 1.3 quotas into two seats at the expense of Fianna Fáil. Ruairi Quinn took the first seat with 5,407 first preferences. Kevin Humphreys had a much tougher battle as he was outside the frame on the first count with half a quota and trailed Chris Andrews by 472 votes. But he won the transfer battle, in particular from independent Sommerville and went on to extend his lead over the Fianna Fáil candidate, taking the final seat by over 1,200 votes.

This constituency was another disappointment for Fianna Fáil with its vote down 17.5 points to just 11%, one of the party's lowest in this election. Outgoing deputy Chris Andrews was in the frame in fourth place on the first count, ahead of Humphreys but was beaten by the Labour man on every count except one and Andrews duly lost his seat on the tenth and final count.

This was another poor performance by the Greens with John Gormley's vote down 7 points to just 7%. His vote halved to leave him in seventh place on the first count and he was never in contention.

Eight independents contested this area with Paul Sommerville and Dylan Haskins the only ones to get enough votes to reclaim their expenses. The business candidate Sommerville had a good media profile going into this election but it was not enough to put him in contention for a seat. One of the independents Peadar Ó Ceallaigh got just 18 first preferences, the lowest by any of the 566 candidates that contested this election and the second lowest on record, behind Maria McCool who got 13 first preferences in Dublin North West in 1997.

The turnout was up seven points to 60.54% in this constituency but it still had the lowest turnout in this election as it had in 2007.

DUBLIN SOUTH EAST TDs 2011

RUAIRÍ QUINN (LB)

23 Strand Road, Sandymount, Dublin 4, Tel: 01 2602852; Mobile: 087 2621946.
Leinster House: 01 6183434; Email: ruairi_quinn@education.gov.ie
Website: www.ruairiquinn.ie

Born Dublin 2nd April 1946. Divorced from his first wife, one son Malachi, one daughter Sine. Married to Liz Allman, one son Conan. Educated Blackrock College, Dublin and UCD (BArch); Athens Centre of Ekistics, Greece (HCE). Lecturer in Architecture, UCD 1971-1982. Government Minister. Former Architect. First elected 1977. Lost his seat in June 1981 but regained it in February 1982 and elected at each subsequent election.

Appointed Minister for Education and Skills 9th March 2011. Spokesperson on Education and Science October 2007-2011. Vice-chairman Joint Committee on Education and Science 2007-2011. Member Joint Committee on the Implementation of the Good Friday Agreement 2007-2011. Spokesperson on European Affairs 2002-2007. Member Joint Committee on Foreign Affairs 2002-2007. Leader of the Labour Party 1997- 2002. Deputy Leader 1989–1997. Minister for Finance 1994-1997. Minister for Enterprise and Employment 1993-1994. Spokesman on Finance 1989-1993, Environment 1987-1989. Minister for the Public Service 1986-1987. Minister for Labour 1983-1986. Minister of State for Housing and Urban Affairs 1982-1983. Senator 1981-1982, 1976-1977. Member Dublin City Council 1974-1977, 1991-1993. Vice-President and Treasurer, Party of European Socialists since 1998. Chairman of Campaign Committee and Director of Elections for Mary Robinson's Presidential campaign 1990. Member Royal Institute of Architects of Ireland. Member Amnesty International.

LUCINDA CREIGHTON (FG)

75 Wilfield Road, Sandymount, Dublin 4, Tel: 01 2195841; Mobile: 086 6009296
Constituency Office: 55 Shelbourne Road, Dublin 4; Website: www.lucindacreighton.ie
Leinster House: 01 6183527; Email: lucinda.creighton@taoiseach.gov.ie

Born Mayo 20th January 1980. Married to Senator Paul Bradford. Educated Convent of Mercy, Claremorris, Co. Mayo; Trinity College, Dublin (LLB). Qualified as an Attorney at Law for State of New York 2003. Worked as political advisor in Dáil Eireann; as campaign co-ordinator for Democratic Party in New York and in public relations for a State Agency in Dublin. Minister for State. Solicitor. First elected 2007.

Appointed Minister of State at the Department of the Taoiseach and at the Department of Foreign Affairs and Trade with special responsibility for European Affairs March 2011. Deputy Spokesperson on Foreign Affairs with Special Responsibility for European Affairs, October 2007-2011. Member Joint Committee on European Affairs and Member Joint Committee on European Scrutiny 2007-2011. Member Dublin City Council 2004-2007. Former Member Fine Gael National Executive. Board member YEPP (the Young European Christian Democrats) and was selected by the Government to represent Ireland at the Youth Convention on the Future of Europe in Brussels. In 2004 served on advisory committee to the Department of Education for the Irish Presidency of the EU.

EOGHAN MURPHY (FG)

Apt 15, Block 2, Gallery Quay, Dublin 2; Mobile: 086 0863832,
Leinster House: 01 6183324; Email: eoghan.murphy@oireachtas.ie;
Website: www.eoghanmurphy.ie

Born Dublin 23rd April 1982. Single. Educated at St. Michael's College, Ballsbridge, Dublin 4; UCD (BA) and King's College, London (MA International Relations). Worked in international arms control, mostly in the area of nuclear weapon disarmament.
First elected 2011.

Member Public Accounts Committee. First elected to Dublin City Council in the Pembroke-Rathmines electoral area in 2009.

KEVIN HUMPHREYS (LB)

14 O'Connell Gardens, Bath Avenue, Dublin 4; Tel: 01 6686854; Mobile: 087 2989103
Leinster House: 01 6183224; Email: kevin.humphreys@oireachtas.ie
Born Dublin 4th February 1958. Married to Catherine, two children. Educated Ringsend Technical School. Process Technician. First elected 2011.

Member Committee on the Environment, Transport, Culture and the Gaeltacht. Member Committee on Finance, Public Expenditure and Reform. First elected to Dublin City Council in the South East Inner City electoral area in 1999. Retained his seat in 2004 and 2009.

DUBLIN SOUTH-EAST 2011							
FIRST PREFERENCE VOTES							
	Seats	4			6,984		
	Candidate	**Party**	**1st**	**%**	**Quota**	**Count**	**Status**
1	**Quinn, Ruairí***	**LB**	**5,407**	**15.48%**	**0.77**	**6**	**Made Quota**
2	**Creighton, Lucinda***	**FG**	**6,619**	**18.96%**	**0.95**	**6**	**Made Quota**
3	**Murphy, Eoghan**	**FG**	**5,783**	**16.56%**	**0.83**	**9**	**Made Quota**
4	**Humphreys, Kevin**	**LB**	**3,450**	**9.88%**	**0.49**	**10**	**Elected**
5	Andrews, Chris*	FF	3,922	11.23%	0.56	10	Not Elected
6	Sommerville, Paul	NP	2,343	6.71%	0.34	8	Eliminated
7	Gormley, John*	GP	2,370	6.79%	0.34	5	Eliminated
8	Haskins, Dylan	NP	1,383	3.96%	0.20	4	Eliminated
9	MacAodháin, Ruadhán	SF	1,272	3.64%	0.18	3	No Expenses
10	Flynn, Mannix	NP	1,248	3.57%	0.18	2	No Expenses
11	Mooney, Annette	PBPA	629	1.80%	0.09	1	No Expenses
12	Sheehy, Hugh	NP	195	0.56%	0.03	1	No Expenses
13	Coyle, James	NP	164	0.47%	0.02	1	No Expenses
14	Watson, Noel	NP	89	0.25%	0.01	1	No Expenses
15	Keigher, John	NP	27	0.08%	0.00	1	No Expenses
16	Ó Ceallaigh, Peadar	FN	18	0.05%	0.00	1	No Expenses
16	***Outgoing**		**34,919**	**100.00%**	**6,984**	**1,747**	**No Expenses**

DUBLIN SOUTH-EAST 2011												
PARTY VOTE												
	2011					2007					Change	
Party	**Cand**	**1st**	**%**	**Quota**	**Seats**	**Cand**	**1st**	**%**	**Quota**	**Seats**	**%**	**Seats**
FG	2	12,402	35.52%	1.78	2	1	6,311	18.65%	0.93	1	+16.87%	+1
LB	2	8,857	25.36%	1.27	2	1	5,636	16.65%	0.83	1	+8.71%	+1
FF	1	3,922	11.23%	0.56		2	9,720	28.72%	1.44	1	-17.49%	-1
SF	1	1,272	3.64%	0.18		1	1,599	4.72%	0.24		-1.08%	
PBPA	1	629	1.80%	0.09							+1.80%	
GP	1	2,370	6.79%	0.34		1	4,685	13.84%	0.69	1	-7.06%	-1
PD						1	4,450	13.15%	0.66		-13.15%	
Others	8	5,467	15.66%	0.78		6	1,441	4.26%	0.21		+11.40%	
Total	**16**	**34,919**	**100.0%**	**6,984**	**4**	**13**	**33,842**	**100.0%**	**6,769**	**4**	**0.00%**	**0**
Electorate		**58,217**	**59.98%**				**63,468**	**53.32%**			**+6.66%**	
Spoiled		**327**	**0.93%**				**292**	**0.86%**			**+0.07%**	
Turnout		**35,246**	**60.54%**				**34,134**	**53.78%**			**+6.76%**	

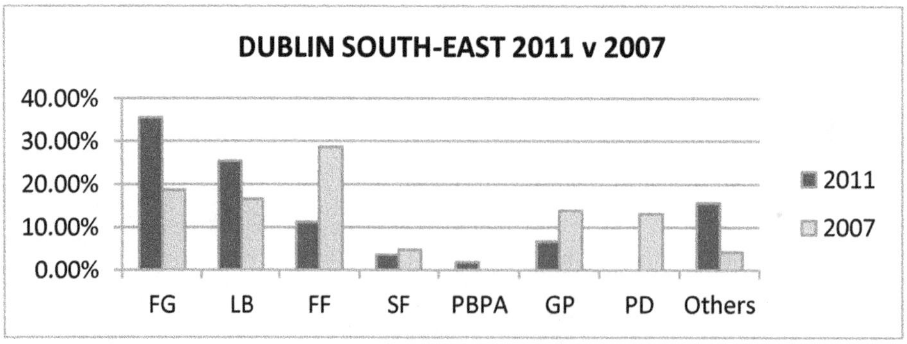

DUBLIN SOUTH-EAST 2011 COUNT DETAILS											
Seats	4									Quota	6,984
Candidate	Party	1st	2nd Mooney Sheehy Coyle Watson Keigher O Ceallaigh	3rd Flynn Votes	4th MacAodhain Votes	5th Haskins Votes	6th Gormley Votes	7th Quinn Surplus	8th Creighton Surplus	9th Sommerville Votes	10th Murphy Surplus
Quinn, Ruairí*	LB	5,407	+155 5,562	+238 5,800	+347 6,147	+453 6,600	+955 7,555	-571 6,984	6,984	6,984	6,984
Creighton, Lucinda*	FG	6,619	+75 6,694	+107 6,801	+54 6,855	+114 6,969	+459 7,428	7,428	-444 6,984	6,984	6,984
Murphy, Eoghan	FG	5,783	+60 5,843	+48 5,891	+47 5,938	+198 6,136	+398 6,534	+102 6,636	+279 6,915	+1,441 8,356	-1,372 6,984
Humphreys, Kevin	LB	3,450	+118 3,568	+196 3,764	+295 4,059	+235 4,294	+380 4,674	+345 5,019	+38 5,057	+837 5,894	+527 6,421
Andrews, Chris*	FF	3,922	+59 3,981	+78 4,059	+101 4,160	+88 4,248	+250 4,498	+47 4,545	+49 4,594	+356 4,950	+243 5,193
Sommerville, Paul	NP	2,343	+150 2,493	+128 2,621	+194 2,815	+381 3,196	+261 3,457	+77 3,534	+32 3,566	-3,566 Eliminated	
Gormley, John*	GP	2,370	+65 2,435	+112 2,547	+112 2,659	+249 2,908	-2,908 Eliminated				
Haskins, Dylan	NP	1,383	+109 1,492	+262 1,754	+174 1,928	-1,928 Eliminated					
MacAodháin, Ruadhán	SF	1,272	+133 1,405	+144 1,549	-1,549 Eliminated						
Flynn, Mannix	NP	1,248	+155 1,403	-1,403 Eliminated							
Mooney, Annette	PBPA	629	-629 Eliminated								
Sheehy, Hugh	NP	195	-195 Eliminated								
Coyle, James	NP	164	-164 Eliminated								
Watson, Noel	NP	89	-89 Eliminated								
Keigher, John	NP	27	-27 Eliminated								
Ó Ceallaigh, Peadar	FN	18	-18 Eliminated								
Non-transferable			+43	+90	+225	+210	+205		+46	+932	+602
Cumulative			43	133	358	568	773	773	819	1,751	2,353
Total		**34,919**	**34,919**	**34,919**	**34,919**	**34,919**	**34,919**	**34,919**	**34,919**	**34,919**	**34,919**

DUBLIN SOUTH-EAST 2011 TRANSFER ANALYSIS								
From	To	FG	LB	FF	SF	GP	Others	Non Trans
FG	1,816	279 *15.36%*	565 *31.11%*	292 *16.08%*			32 *1.76%*	648 *35.68%*
LB	571	102 *17.86%*	345 *60.42%*	47 *8.23%*			77 *13.49%*	
SF	1,549	101 *6.52%*	642 *41.45%*	101 *6.52%*		112 *7.23%*	368 *23.76%*	225 *14.53%*
PBPA	629	76 *12.08%*	153 *24.32%*	33 *5.25%*	75 *11.92%*	36 *5.72%*	232 *36.88%*	24 *3.82%*
GP	2,908	857 *29.47%*	1,335 *45.91%*	250 *8.60%*			261 *8.98%*	205 *7.05%*
Others	7,390	1,967 *26.62%*	2,079 *28.13%*	548 *7.42%*	202 *2.73%*	390 *5.28%*	953 *12.90%*	1,251 *16.93%*
Total	**14,863**	**3,382** ***22.75%***	**5,119** ***34.44%***	**1,271** ***8.55%***	**277** ***1.86%***	**538** ***3.62%***	**1,923** ***12.94%***	**2,353** ***15.83%***

DUBLIN SOUTH-EAST		
MAIN BOUNDARY CHANGES		
Dail	**Constituency**	**Seats**
9 (1937) - 12 (1944)	Dublin Townships	3
13 (1948) - 20 (1973)	Dublin South-East	3
21 (1977)	Rathmines West	3
	Dublin South-East	3
22 (1981) - 31 (2011)	Dublin South-East	4

DUBLIN SOUTH-EAST														
ALL TDs 1937-2011														
	Surname	**Forename**	**Party**	**Elected**										**Total**
1	MacEntee**	Sean	FF	37	38	43	44	48	51	54	57	61	65	10
2	Quinn	Ruairi	LB	77	82	82	87	89	92	97	02	07	11	10
3	Costello**	John A.	FG	37	38	44	48	51	54	57	61	65		9
4	FitzGerald	Garret	FG	69	73	77	81	82	82	87	89			8
5	Browne**	Noel	SLP	48	51	57	61	69						5
6	Moore	Sean	FF	65	69	73	77	81						5
7	Brady**	Gerard	FF	81	82	82	87	89						5
8	Benson	Ernest	FG	37	38	43								3
9	McDowell	Michael	PD	87	92	02								3
10	Ryan	Eoin	FF	92	97	02								3
11	Gormley	John	GP	97	02	07								3
12	Butler**	Bernard	FF	43	44									2
13	Doyle	Joe	FG	82N	89									2
14	Fitzgerald	Frances	FG	92	97									2
15	Creighton	Lucinda	FG	07	11									2
16	O'Donovan**	John	LB	54										1
17	O'Brien**	Fergus	FG	73										1
18	Ryan**	Richie	FG	81										1
19	Fitzgerald	Alexis	FG	82F										1
20	Andrews	Chris	FF	07										1
21	Murphy	Eoghan	FG	11										1
22	Humphreys	Kevin	LB	11										1
22	**Total**													**79**
	**** Also elected in another constituency**													
1	MacEntee**	Sean	FF	Monaghan/Dublin				18	21	27	27	32	33	6
2	Ryan**	Richie	FG	SW/SC				59*	61	65	69	73	77	6
3	O'Brien**	Fergus	FG	South Central				77	81	82N	87	89		5
4	Butler**	Bernard	FF	South West				48	51	54	57			4
5	Browne**	Noel	SLP	Artane/NC				77	81					2
6	Costello**	John A.	FG	County				33						1
7	O'Donovan**	John	FG	South Central				69						1
8	Brady**	Gerard	FF	Rathmines West				77						1
9	Fitzgerald	Frances	FG	Dublin Mid-West				11						1
9	**Total**							***Includes 1 By-Election**						**21**

DUBLIN SOUTH-EAST 1937-2011																											
			FG		LB		FF		SF		PBPA		GP		WP		PD		DL		C na P		NPD		Others	
Dail		Seats	S	% Vote	S	% Vote	S	% Vote	S	% Vote	S	% Vote	S	% Vote	S	% Vote	S	% Vote	S	% Vote	S	% Vote	S	% Vote	S	% Vote
9	1937	3	2	45.25%			1	37.08%																		17.67%
10	1938	3	2	52.29%			1	47.71%																		
11	1943	3	1	42.65%		11.14%	2	46.21%																		
12	1944	3	1	45.29%		5.75%	2	48.96%																		
13	1948	3	1	38.66%		8.10%	1	34.76%													1	18.48%				
14	1951	3	1	33.85%			1	35.34%														1.94%			1	28.88%
15	1954	3	2	51.84%		5.43%	1	42.73%																		
16	1957	3	1	33.87%			1	34.44%														1.63%			1	30.07%
17	1961	3	1	36.69%			1	44.24%															1	19.07%		
18	1965	3	1	32.65%		18.56%	2	48.79%																		
19	1969	3	1	35.23%	1	23.82%	1	39.19%																		1.76%
20	1973	3	2	43.89%		11.45%	1	40.07%		4.23%																0.35%
21	1977	6	2	36.28%	1	17.23%	3	44.35%								2.14%										
22	1981	4	2	42.98%		12.23%	2	38.47%								4.82%										1.49%
23	1982	4	2	46.18%	1	13.45%	1	33.51%								4.72%										2.13%
24	1982	4	2	47.40%	1	14.78%	1	31.15%								4.57%										2.09%
25	1987	4	1	32.01%	1	9.09%	1	32.72%		2.12%				2.86%		4.99%	1	15.58%								0.63%
26	1989	4	2	27.66%	1	12.20%	1	34.81%						10.12%		5.52%		8.67%								1.02%
27	1992	4	1	21.79%	1	25.79%	1	27.15%		2.11%				6.15%		1.42%	1	11.19%		2.17%						2.23%
28	1997	4	1	27.38%	1	16.67%	1	25.79%				1.12%	1	11.71%		1.89%		10.97%								4.47%
29	2002	4		16.06%	1	12.43%	1	27.03%		7.39%		0.88%	1	16.23%		0.88%	1	18.79%								0.31%
30	2007	4	1	18.65%	1	16.65%	1	28.72%		4.72%		1.75%	1	13.84%				13.15%								2.51%
31	2011	4	2	35.52%	2	25.36%		11.23%		3.64%		1.80%		6.79%												15.66%
1937-2011		**82**	**32**	**36.77%**	**12**	**11.80%**	**28**	**36.17%**		**1.02%**		**0.24%**	**3**	**2.99%**		**1.54%**	**3**	**3.54%**		**0.11%**	**1**	**0.82%**	**1**	**0.60%**	**2**	**4.41%**
National		**4,618**	**1,453**	**30.77%**	**482**	**11.53%**	**1,985**	**41.86%**	**232**	**1.99%**	**2**	**0.09%**	**16**	**0.75%**	**17**	**0.78%**	**44**	**1.42%**	**8**	**0.22%**	**18**	**0.77%**	**2**	**0.03%**	**359**	**9.78%**

DUBLIN SOUTH-WEST 2011

"Labour gets its biggest vote share since 1969"

There were no boundary changes to this four seat constituency since 2007.

With Fianna Fail on the ropes nationally, this always looked like a constituency in which the party could lose both its seats, and so it proved. Even so, the scale of the slump was astonishing. Its two TDs had each won about 8,000 first preferences in 2007; now, neither even won as many as 3,000. The rivalry between them was intense. Conor Lenihan ended up nearly 400 votes behind Charlie O'Connor, whose 2,718 first preferences was probably less than the number of times he managed to work the word 'Tallaght' into media interviews.

Three of the four seats here were nailed down from the start. Former Labour leader Pat Rabbitte received nearly 13,000 first preferences, more than any other Labour candidate in the country. For Fine Gael, Brian Hayes easily retained the seat he had regained in 2007. In 2007 the defeat of Seán Crowe of Sinn Fein had been one of the most surprising results; he had lost his seat despite having been 1–20 with the bookies on polling day to retain it. In 2011, he comfortably took the third seat.

The only uncertainty was whether the fourth and final seat would go to Fine Gael or to Labour. The first preference distribution answered this: Labour took 4,000 votes more than Fine Gael, with Dublin South-West becoming its strongest constituency in the country. Labour took 36 per cent of the votes, the most it has won in any constituency since 1969. Its second candidate, Eamonn Maloney, finished over 3,000 votes ahead of the Fine Gael runner-up Cáit Keane. Labour may not have won a seat in Donegal since 1927 but, in Maloney and Michael Conaghan (Dublin South-Central), it does have two Donegal men in the Dáil.

Pat Rabbitte attacks Minister Pat Carey on RTE's Prime Time

DUBLIN SOUTH WEST TDs 2011

PAT RABBITTE (LB)

56 Monastery Drive, Clondalkin, Dublin 22; Tel: 01 4593191
Constituency Office: 29-31 Adelaide Road, Dublin 2; Tel: 01 6782011;
Leinster House: 01 6183772; Email: minister.rabbitte@dcenr.gov.ie
Website: www.patrabbitte.ie

Born Claremorris, Co. Mayo, 18th May 1949. Married to Derry McDermott, three daughters. Educated St. Colman's College, Claremorris and UCG (BA, HdipEd, LLB). Government Minister. Former Trade Union official. Contested 1987 general election for the Workers Party. First elected 1989 as a WP deputy. Elected 1992 as a DL deputy and again in 1997. Following merger between Labour and DL retained seat as a Labour deputy in 2002, 2007 and 2009.

Appointed Minister for Communications, Energy and Natural Resources 9th March 2011. Front bench spokesperson on Justice 2007-2011. Member Committee of Public Accounts 2010-2011. Member Houses of the Oireachtas Commission and Member Joint Committee on Justice, Equality, Defence and Women's Rights 2007-2011. Leader of the Labour Party 2002-2007. Former Spokesperson on Northern Ireland. Former Member Committee of Public Accounts and Committee on Procedure and Privileges. Member of the Public Accounts Committee that carried out the DIRT enquiry during the 29th Dail. When the Rainbow Government was formed in 1994, he became Minister to the Government, which allowed him to attend Cabinet Meetings without the right to vote. Minister of State at the Department of Enterprise and Employment with responsibility for Commerce Science and Technology 1994-1997. Member Dublin County Council 1985-1995. Member South Dublin County Council 1999-2003. Member of the Labour Party until 1976. Former National Secretary of the Irish Transport and General Workers Union (now SIPTU). President of UCG Students Union 1970-1971 and President of the Union of Students in Ireland 1972-1974.

BRIAN HAYES (FG)

48 Dunmore Park, Kingswood Heights, Tallaght, Dublin 24; Tel: 01 4626545.
Leinster House: Tel: 01 6183567; Email: brian.hayes@oireachtas.ie
Website: www. Brianhayes.ie

Born Dublin 23rd August 1969. Married, to Genevieve Deering, one daughter two sons. Educated Garbally Park, Ballinasloe; Maynooth (BA) and Trinity College, Dublin (HDipEd). Minister of State. Former secondary school teacher and Fine Gael National Youth Officer. Contested Dublin South Central by-election in 1994. First elected 1997. Lost his seat in 2002. Re-elected 2007 and 2011.

Appointed Minister of State at the Department of Public Expenditure and Reform and at the Department of Finance with special responsibility for Public Sector Reform and OPW 10th March 2011. Supported Richard Bruton in his failed attempt to oust Enda Kenny as party leader in June 2010. Fine Gael spokesperson on Education and Science September 2007-June 2010. Member Joint Committee on Education and Science 2007-2011. Front Bench spokesperson on Social & Community Affairs 2001-2002. Spokesperson on Northern Ireland 2000-2001. Fine Gael Junior spokesperson on Housing, House Prices, Urban Renewal 1997–2001. Senator 1995-1997 and 2002-2007. Leader Fine Gael in the Seanad 2002-2007 and Front Bench spokesperson on Dublin and Northern Ireland. Former Secretary to Fine Gael Group at the Forum for Peace and Reconciliation. Member of South Dublin County Council 1995-2003.

SEAN CROWE (SF)

16 Raheen Green, Tallaght, Dublin 24; Tel: 01 4524950; Mobile: 086 3864303
Leinster House: 01 6183719; Email: sean.crowe@oireachtas.ie Website: www.seancrowe.ie

Born Dublin 7th March 1957. Married to Pamela. Educated Dundrum Technical School. Formerly party officer. Contested 1989, 1992 and 1997 general elections in Dublin South-West. First elected 2002. Lost his seat in 2007 but regained it in 2011.

Sinn Fein spokesperson on Education and Skills. Member Committee on the Implementation of the Good Friday Agreement. Member Committee on Jobs, Social Protection and Education. Member Joint Committee on Education and Science 2002-2007. Contested European elections in Dublin in 1999. Member South Dublin County Council 1999-2003. Co-opted as replacement for Mark Daly in 2008 and retained his seat in 2009. Member South Dublin URBAN Initiative; Member Tallaght Drugs Task Force; Member South Dublin Inter-Agency Working Group to Combat "Joy-riding". Member Forum for Peace and Reconciliation. Member of Sinn Fein team in the multi-party negotiations that led to the Good Friday Agreement.

EAMONN MALONEY (LB)

84 St. Maelruans Park, Old Bawn, Tallaght, Dublin 24; Tel: 01 4525298
Leinster House: 01 6183588; Email: eamonn.maloney@oireachtas.ie
Website: www.labour.ie/eamonnmaloney

Born Letterkenny, Co. Donegal May 1953. Married to Vivienne, two daughters, one son. Educated Letterkenny Vocational School. Worked with a recycling company until 2009 when he was made redundant after 23 years. Contested Dail election in Dublin South-West in 1987 for DSP. First elected 2011.

Member Committee on Health and Children. Contested 1991 local election in Tallaght-Oldbawn. First elected 1999 in Tallaght Central. Retained his seat in 2004. Moved to Tallaght South in 2009 and re-elected. Mayor 2010/2011. Former member Democratic Socialist Party led by Jim Kemmy. Brother of Sean Maloney, Senator 1993-1997.

DUBLIN SOUTH-WEST 2011 FIRST PREFERENCE VOTES							
	Seats	4			9,393		
	Candidate	Party	1st	%	Quota	Count	Status
1	**Rabbitte, Pat***	**LB**	**12,867**	**27.40%**	**1.37**	**1**	**Made Quota**
2	**Hayes, Brian***	**FG**	**9,366**	**19.94%**	**1.00**	**2**	**Made Quota**
3	**Crowe, Sean #**	**SF**	**8,064**	**17.17%**	**0.86**	**6**	**Made Quota**
4	**Maloney, Eamonn**	**LB**	**4,165**	**8.87%**	**0.44**	**8**	**Made Quota**
5	Keane, Cait	FG	3,678	7.83%	0.39	8	Not Elected
6	O'Connor, Charlie*	FF	2,718	5.79%	0.29	7	Eliminated
7	Murphy, Mick	SP	2,462	5.24%	0.26	5	Eliminated
8	Lenihan, Conor*	FF	2,341	4.98%	0.25	4	Eliminated
9	Kelly, Ray	NP	823	1.75%	0.09	3	No Expenses
10	Duffy, Francis	GP	480	1.02%	0.05	3	No Expenses
10	***Outgoing # Former TD**		**46,964**	**100.00%**	**9,393**	**2,349**	**No Expenses**

DUBLIN SOUTH-WEST 2011 PARTY VOTE													
	2011					2007					Change	
Party	Cand	1st	%	Quota	Seats	Cand	1st	%	Quota	Seats	%	Seats
FG	2	13,044	27.77%	1.39	1	1	8,346	20.04%	1.00	1	+7.74%	
LB	2	17,032	36.27%	1.81	2	1	8,325	19.99%	1.00	1	+16.28%	+1
FF	2	5,059	10.77%	0.54		2	16,355	39.27%	1.96	2	-28.49%	-2
SF	1	8,064	17.17%	0.86	1	1	5,066	12.16%	0.61		+5.01%	+1
SP	1	2,462	5.24%	0.26		1	1,580	3.79%	0.19		+1.45%	
GP	1	480	1.02%	0.05		1	1,546	3.71%	0.19		-2.69%	
Others	1	823	1.75%	0.09		1	434	1.04%	0.05		+0.71%	
Total	**10**	**46,964**	**100.0%**	**9,393**	**4**	**8**	**41,652**	**100.0%**	**8,331**	**4**	**0.00%**	**0**
Electorate		**70,613**	**66.51%**				**67,148**	**62.03%**			**+4.48%**	
Spoiled		**511**	**1.08%**				**370**	**0.88%**			**+0.20%**	
Turnout		**47,475**	**67.23%**				**42,022**	**62.58%**			**+4.65%**	

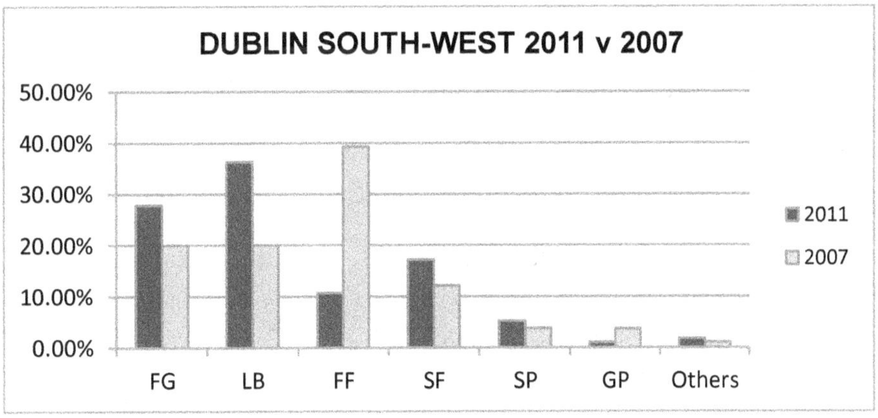

DUBLIN SOUTH-WEST 2011
COUNT DETAILS

Seats	4							Quota	9,393
Candidate	**Party**	**1st**	**2nd** Rabitte Surplus	**3rd** Hayes Surplus	**4th** Kelly Duffy	**5th** Lenihan Votes	**6th** Murphy Votes	**7th** Crowe Surplus	**8th** O'Connor Votes
			-3,474						
Rabbitte, Pat*	LB	12,867	9,393	9,393	9,393	9,393	9,393	9,393	9,393
			+514	*-487*					
Hayes, Brian*	FG	9,366	9,880	9,393	9,393	9,393	9,393	9,393	9,393
			+365	*+86*	*+257*	*+139*	*+1,278*	*-796*	
Crowe, Sean #	SF	8,064	8,429	8,515	8,772	8,911	10,189	9,393	9,393
			+2,043	*+155*	*+340*	*+166*	*+914*	*+543*	*+1,331*
Maloney, Eamonn	LB	4,165	6,208	6,363	6,703	6,869	7,783	8,326	9,657
			+145	*+122*	*+210*	*+560*	*+187*	*+149*	*+1,082*
Keane, Cait	FG	3,678	3,823	3,945	4,155	4,715	4,902	5,051	6,133
			+115	*+31*	*+84*	*+1,415*	*+160*	*+77*	*-4,600*
O'Connor, Charlie*	FF	2,718	2,833	2,864	2,948	4,363	4,523	4,600	Eliminated
			+162	*+38*	*+258*	*+55*	*-2,975*		
Murphy, Mick	SP	2,462	2,624	2,662	2,920	2,975	Eliminated		
			+52	*+21*	*+74*	*-2,488*			
Lenihan, Conor*	FF	2,341	2,393	2,414	2,488	Eliminated			
			+47	*+13*	*-883*				
Kelly, Ray	NP	823	870	883	Eliminated				
			+31	*+10*	*-521*				
Duffy, Francis	GP	480	511	521	Eliminated				
Non-transferable				*+11*	*+181*	*+153*	*+436*	*+27*	+2,187
Cumulative			0	11	192	345	781	808	2,995
Total		**46,964**	**46,964**	**46,964**	**46,964**	**46,964**	**46,964**	**46,964**	**46,964**

DUBLIN SOUTH-WEST 2011
TRANSFER ANALYSIS

From	To	FG	LB	FF	SF	SP	GP	Others	Non Trans
FG	487	122	155	52	86	38	10	13	11
		25.05%	*31.83%*	*10.68%*	*17.66%*	*7.80%*	*2.05%*	*2.67%*	*2.26%*
LB	3,474	659	2,043	167	365	162	31	47	
		18.97%	*58.81%*	*4.81%*	*10.51%*	*4.66%*	*0.89%*	*1.35%*	
FF	7,088	1,642	1,497	1,415	139	55			2,340
		23.17%	*21.12%*	*19.96%*	*1.96%*	*0.78%*			*33.01%*
SF	796	149	543	77					27
		18.72%	*68.22%*	*9.67%*					*3.39%*
SP	2,975	187	914	160	1,278				436
		6.29%	*30.72%*	*5.38%*	*42.96%*				*14.66%*
GP	521	78	126	59	95	96			67
		14.97%	*24.18%*	*11.32%*	*18.23%*	*18.43%*			*12.86%*
Others	883	132	214	99	162	162			114
		14.95%	*24.24%*	*11.21%*	*18.35%*	*18.35%*			*12.91%*
Total	**16,224**	**2,969**	**5,492**	**2,029**	**2,125**	**513**	**41**	**60**	**2,995**
		18.30%	***33.85%***	***12.51%***	***13.10%***	***3.16%***	***0.25%***	***0.37%***	***18.46%***

DUBLIN SOUTH-WEST		
MAIN BOUNDARY CHANGES		
Dail	**Constituency**	**Seats**
13 (1948) - 18 (1965)	Dublin South-West	5
19 (1969) - 20 (1973)	Dublin South-West	4
21 (1977)	Mid-County	3
22 (1981) - 26 (1989)	Dublin South-West	4
27 (1992) - 28 (1997)	Dublin South-West	5
29 (2002) - 31 (2011)	Dublin South-West	4

	DUBLIN SOUTH-WEST																
	ALL TDs 1948-2011																
	Surname	**Forename**	**Party**	**Elected**													**Total**
1	Harney**	Mary	PD	81	82	82	87	89	92	97							7
2	Lemass	Noel	FF	56*	57	61	65	69	73								6
3	Taylor	Mervyn	LB	81	82	82	87	89	92								6
4	Rabbitte	Pat	LB	89	92	97	02	07	11								6
5	Briscoe**	Robert	FF	48	51	54	57	61									5
6	Walsh**	Sean	FF	77	81	82	82	87									5
7	Butler**	Bernard	FF	48	51	54	57										4
8	Flood	Chris	FF	87	89	92	97										4
9	Doyle**	Peadar	FG	48	51	54											3
10	MacBride**	Sean	CnaP	48	51	54											3
11	O'Higgins**	Michael	FG	48	54	57											3
12	Ryan**	Richie	FG	59*	61	65											3
13	Dowling	Joseph	FF	65	69	73											3
14	O'Connell**	John	FF	65	69	73											3
15	McMahon**	Larry	FG	77	81	82F											3
16	Lenihan	Conor	FF	97	02	07											3
17	Hayes	Brian	FG	97	07	11											3
18	Carroll	James	NP	57	61												2
19	O'Connor	Charlie	FF	02	07												2
20	Crowe	Sean	SF	02	11												2
21	Ffrench-O'Carroll	Michael	NP	51													1
22	O'Keeffe	James	FG	61													1
23	Briscoe**	Ben	FF	65													1
24	Dunne**	Sean	LB	69													1
25	Sherwin	Sean	FF	70*													1
26	Costello**	Declan	FG	73													1
27	De Valera**	Sile	FF	77													1
28	O'Leary**	Michael	FG	82													1
29	Walsh	Eamonn	LB	92													1
30	Maloney	Eamonn	LB	11													1
30	**Total**									***Includes 3 By-Elections**						*	**86**
	**** Also elected in another constituency**																
1	Briscoe**	Ben	FF	Dublin SC			69	73	77	81	82	82	87	89	92	97	10
2	Doyle**	Peadar	FG	Dublin South				23	27	27	32	33	37	38	43	44	9
3	Briscoe**	Robert	FF	Dublin South				27	32	33	37	38	43	44			7
4	O'Leary**	Michael	FG	Dublin NC/C				65	69	73	77/	81	82				6
5	O'Connell**	John	FF	Dublin SC				77	81	82	82	89	92				6
6	Dunne**	Sean	LB	Dublin County				48	51	54	61	65					5
7	Costello**	Declan	FG	Dublin NW				51	54	57	61	65					5
8	De Valera**	Sile	FF	Clare				87	89	92	97	02					5
9	Ryan**	Richie	FG	Dublin SC/SE				69	73	77/	81						4
10	Butler**	Bernard	FF	Dublin Townships				43	44								2
11	O'Higgins**	Michael	FG	Wicklow				61	65								2
12	McMahon**	Larry	FG	Dublin Co. South				70*	73								2
13	Harney**	Mary	PD	Dublin Mid-West				02	07								2
14	MacBride**	Sean	CnaP	Dublin County				47*									1
15	Walsh**	Sean	FF	Dublin Co. North				73									1
15	**Total**										***Includes 2 By-Elections**						**67**

DUBLIN SOUTH-WEST 1948-2011																										
* No Contest			FG		LB		FF		SF		SP		GP		WP		CS		PD		DL		C na P		Others	
Dail		Seats	S	% Vote	S	% Vote	S	% Vote	S	% Vote	S	% Vote	S	% Vote	S	% Vote	S	% Vote	S	% Vote	S	% Vote	S	% Vote	S	% Vote
13	1948	5	2	28.16%		7.05%	2	38.41%															1	26.38%		
14	1951	5	1	23.31%		5.56%	2	48.10%															1	8.42%	1	14.61%
15	1954	5	2	29.50%		9.56%	2	40.25%															1	14.09%		6.60%
16	1957	5	1	20.43%		5.16%	3	45.42%		6.16%														6.76%	1	16.07%
17	1961	5	2	27.78%		5.02%	2	44.06%		1.32%														6.36%	1	15.47%
18	1965	5	1	26.39%	1	19.52%	3	45.53%																		8.56%
19	1969	4		14.21%	2	44.34%	2	33.84%																		7.60%
20	1973	4	1	19.32%	1	35.72%	2	37.29%		3.22%																4.44%
21	1977	3	1	26.07%		19.61%	2	54.31%																		
22	1981	4	1	38.18%	1	17.75%	2	39.87%																		4.20%
23	1982	4	1	33.31%	1	19.79%	2	46.91%																		
24	1982	4	1	33.47%	1	20.75%	2	36.53%								6.28%										2.97%
25	1987	4		12.66%	1	12.22%	2	38.61%		3.33%						12.27%			1	19.71%						1.21%
26	1989	4		8.58%	1	22.39%	1	33.53%		2.61%				3.23%	1	18.37%			1	11.08%						0.22%
27	1992	5		6.13%	2	33.92%	1	29.12%		1.98%				2.04%		0.69%			1	11.64%	1	8.78%				5.71%
28	1997	5	1	15.50%		9.72%	2	29.94%		8.90%		4.84%		3.14%					1	13.64%	1	12.17%				2.15%
29	2002	4		12.65%	1	19.80%	2	38.68%	1	20.29%		2.59%		3.14%				2.07%								0.79%
30	2007	4	1	20.04%	1	19.99%	2	39.27%		12.16%		3.79%		3.71%												1.04%
31	2011	4	1	27.77%	2	36.27%		10.77%	1	17.17%		5.24%		1.02%												1.75%
1948-2011		**83**	**17**	**22.27%**	**15**	**18.80%**	**36**	**38.17%**	**2**	**4.25%**		**0.95%**		**0.90%**	**1**	**2.02%**		**0.10%**	**4**	**3.14%**	**2**	**1.20%**	**3**	**3.38%**	**3**	**4.83%**
National		**4,618**	**1,453**	**30.77%**	**482**	**11.53%**	**1,985**	**41.86%**	**232**	**1.99%**	**4**	**0.16%**	**16**	**0.75%**	**17**	**0.78%**		**0.04%**	**44**	**1.42%**	**8**	**0.22%**	**18**	**0.77%**	**359**	**9.69%**

DUBLIN WEST 2011

'Three outgoing TDs and Joe Higgins win seats in most predictable constituency in this most volatile election'

There were Constituency Commission boundary changes here and the constituency increased from three to four seats for the 2011 election. The constituency gained a seat following a major boundary change with a population of 12,768 in the Swords-Forrest areas transferred in from Dublin North.

This was the most predictable constituency in this election with the three outgoing deputies joined by Joe Higgins following the addition of an extra seat. It was practically all over after the announcement of the first count with the four leading candidates well clear of the rest of the field.

The Fine Gael vote was up 12 points and with 1.4 quotas the party could have been in contention for two seats but its vote was badly divided with Leo Varadkar just short of the quota and Kieran Dennison outside the frame in fifth place with a mere 0.4 quotas. Varadkar duly took the second seat on the second count and Dennison ended up in sixth place.

The Labour vote was up 12 points and with 1.5 quotas they also could have been in contention for two seats. Joan Burton topped the poll and was well over the quota on the first count and was the first deputy declared elected in the 2011 general election. Her running mate Patrick Nulty did poorly and with just 2,686 first preferences, was too far off the pace.

Socialist Party leader Joe Higgins lost his seat here in 2007. He went on to win a European parliament seat in 2009 and continued his winning ways in 2011. Higgins was just short of the quota on the first count and went on to comfortably take the third seat on the third count.

This was another poor Dublin performance by Fianna Fáil as its vote was down 21 points but at least the party held its seat here unlike the rest of the Dublin constituencies. Brian Lenihan was in fourth place after the first count on 6,421 first preference votes. But he was well clear of the rest of the field and there was never any doubt that he would hold his seat. He thus become Fianna Fáil's only Dublin-based deputy. His running mate David McGuinness got just 623 first preferences and lost his expenses as did two others.

Dublin West By-election winner Patrick Nulty with Eamon Gilmore and Joan Burton

DUBLIN WEST TDs 2011

JOAN BURTON (LB)

81 Old Cabra Road, Dublin 7; Tel: 01 8388711; Email: joan.burton@oireachtas.ie
Leinster House: 01 6184006; Website: www.joanburton.ie

Born Dublin 1st February 1949. Married to Pat Carroll, one daughter Aoife. Educated Sisters of Charity, Stanhope St. Dublin; UCD (BComm); Fellow of the Institute of Chartered Accountants. Deputy Leader of the Labour Party, Government Minister and former Lecturer. First elected 1992. Lost her seat in 1997 but regained it again in 2002 and retained it in 2007 and 2011.

Appointed Minister for Social Protection 9th March 2011. Front Bench Spokesperson on Finance, 2007-2011. Elected Deputy Leader of the Labour Party October 2007. Member Joint Committee on Finance and the Public Service 2007-2011. Unsuccessful candidate in Labour Deputy Leadership election in October 2002. Front bench spokesperson on Finance 2002-2007. Member Joint Committees on Finance and the Public Service and Public Accounts 2002-2007. Minister for Overseas Development 1995-1997. Minister of State for Social Welfare 1992-1994. Member Dublin/ Fingal County Council 1991-2003. Chair of Steering Committee of Blanchardstown Women's Refuge. Board member of Centre for Independent Living Campaign for Transport rights of wheelchair users. Member DIT Strategy Working Party. Hon Secretary Irish Anti-Apartheid Movement 1979-1983. Former lecturer at University of Dar Es Salaam, Tanzania.

LEO VARADKAR (FG)

30 Rosehaven, Carpenterstown Road, Castleknock, Dublin 15; Tel: 01 8103717
Constituency Office: 37A Main Street, Ongar, Dublin 15; Tel: 01 6403133
Leinster House: 01 6183819; Email: leo.varadkar@oireachtas.ie

Born Dublin 18th January 1979. Single. Educated The King's Hospital and Trinity College, Dublin. Government Minister. Medical Doctor. First elected 2007.

Appointed Minister for Transport, Tourism and Sport 11th March 2011. Front bench spokesperson on Communications & Natural Resources 1st July 2010-2011. Supported Richard Bruton in his failed attempt to oust Enda Kenny as party leader in June 2010. Front Bench Spokesperson on Enterprise, Trade and Employment September 2007-June 2010. Member Joint Committee on Enterprise, Trade and Employment and Member Joint Committee on Economic and Regulatory Affairs 2007-2011. Member Fingal County Council 2003-2007. Leas Cathaoirleach 2004. Got highest first preference vote in the country in the local elections in 2004. National Executive member of Young Fine Gael 1998-2001. Vice-President of the Youth of European People's Party (YEPP) 2001-2003. US Congressional Intern 2000.

JOE HIGGINS (SP)

155 Briarwood Close, Mulhuddart, Dublin 15; Tel: 8201753; Leinster House: 01 6183370; Email: joe.higgins@oireachtas.ie Website: www.joehiggins.eu

Born in Dingle, Co. Kerry 20th May 1949. Single. Educated at Dingle CBS and University College, Dublin (BA, HdipEd). Former Teacher. Contested 1992 general election and 1996 by-election in Dublin West. First elected 1997. Retained his seat in 2002 but was a surprise loser in 2007. Regained his seat in 2011.

Member Committee on Finance, Public Expenditure and Reform. Founded Socialist Party in 1997 and became its first T.D.in 1997. Contested 1999 and 2004 Euro election in Dublin. First elected a MEP in 2009. Resigned his euro seat following his election to Dáil Eireann in February 2011 and replaced by Ruth Coppinger. Member Dublin/Fingal County Council 1991 -2002. Re-elected 2009. Resigned his council seat following his election to the European Parliament in 2009 and replaced by Matthew Waine. Former member of Labour Party.

BRIAN LENIHAN (FF)

"Longwood", Somerton Road, Strawberry Beds, Dublin 20; Tel: 8214058.
Constituency Office: Laurel Lodge Shopping Centre, Castleknock, Dublin 15;
Tel: 01 8220970.

Born Dublin 21st May 1959. Died 10th June 2011. Married to Patricia Ryan, one son, one daughter. Educated Belvedere College, Dublin; Trinity College, Dublin (Foundation Scholar, First Class Honours BA (Moderatorship) in Legal Science); Cambridge University, (First Class Honours LLB); Kings Inns. Former Lecturer in Law. First elected at By-Election in 1996 (caused by death of his father) and at each subsequent election.

Fianna Fail Deputy Leader and spokesperson on Finance 2011. Minister for Finance 7th May 2008-March 2011. Minister for Justice, Equality and Law Reform June 2007-May 2008. Minister for Children and attended Cabinet meetings 2005-2007. Minister of State at Departments of Health and Children, Justice, Equality and Law Reform, Education and Science (with special responsibility for children) 2002-2005. Chairman, All Party Oireachtas Committee on the Constitution 1997-2002. Member Incorporated Council of Law Reporting. Member Criminal Injuries Compensation Board 1992–1995; Garda Complaints Appeal Board 1992-1995. Son of the late Brian Lenihan, former Tánaiste and Minister and TD 1961-1973 and 1977-1995 and brother of Conor Lenihan, TD for Dublin South West 1997-2011. Nephew of former Minister Mary O'Rourke and TD for Longford-Westmeath.

PATRICK NULTY (LB)

5 Greenridge Court, Corduff, Blanchardstown, Dublin 15; Mobile: 087 9688259
Leinster House: 01 6183111; Email: patrick.nulty@oireachtas.ie
Website: www.patricknulty.wordpress.com

Born Dublin, 18th November 1982. When two weeks old, he was injured in a house fire, leaving him with burn scars on his face and arms. Educated Riversdale Community College; TCD (BA in Social Policy); UCD (Masters in Social Science). Previously worked in the community and voluntary sector for a leading homeless charity as a Social Policy Analyst. Contested 2011 general election in Dublin West. First elected at a by-election on 27th October 2011 which was caused by the death of Brian Lenihan.

Voted against the government in the budget debate 13th December 2011 and lost the Labour whip. First elected to Fingal County Council in the Mulhuddart electoral area in 2009.Member Blanchardstown Local drugs Taskforce. Ireland-Palestine Solidarity Campaign.

DUBLIN WEST 2011							
FIRST PREFERENCE VOTES							
	Seats	**4**			**8,495**		
	Candidate	**Party**	**1st**	**%**	**Quota**	**Count**	**Status**
1	**Burton, Joan***	**LB**	**9,627**	**22.67%**	**1.13**	**1**	**Made Quota**
2	**Varadkar, Leo***	**FG**	**8,359**	**19.68%**	**0.98**	**2**	**Made Quota**
3	**Higgins, Joe #**	**SP**	**8,084**	**19.03%**	**0.95**	**3**	**Made Quota**
4	**Lenihan, Brian***	**FF**	**6,421**	**15.12%**	**0.76**	**5**	**Elected**
5	Nulty, Patrick	LB	2,686	6.32%	0.32	5	Not Elected
6	Dennison, Kieran	FG	3,190	7.51%	0.38	4	Eliminated
7	Donnelly, Paul	SF	2,597	6.11%	0.31	3	Eliminated
8	McGuinness, David	FF	623	1.47%	0.07	2	No Expenses
9	O'Gorman, Roderic	GP	605	1.42%	0.07	2	No Expenses
10	Esebamen, Clement	NP	280	0.66%	0.03	2	No Expenses
10	***Outgoing # Former TD**		**42,472**	**100.00%**	**8,495**	**2,124**	**No Expenses**

DUBLIN WEST 2011												
PARTY VOTE												
	2011					**2007**					**Change**	
Party	**Cand**	**1st**	**%**	**Quota**	**Seats**	**Cand**	**1st**	**%**	**Quota**	**Seats**	**%**	**Seats**
FG	2	11,549	27.19%	1.36	1	1	6,928	20.39%	0.82	1	+6.80%	
LB	2	12,313	28.99%	1.45	1	1	5,799	17.06%	0.68	1	+11.93%	
FF	2	7,044	16.59%	0.83	1	2	12,726	37.45%	1.50	1	-20.86%	
SF	1	2,597	6.11%	0.31		1	1,624	4.78%	0.19		+1.34%	
SP	1	8,084	19.03%	0.95	1	1	5,066	14.91%	0.60		+4.13%	+1
GP	1	605	1.42%	0.07		1	1,286	3.78%	0.15		-2.36%	
PD						1	553	1.63%	0.07		-1.63%	
Others	1	280	0.66%	0.03							+0.66%	
Total	**10**	**42,472**	**100.0%**	**8,495**	**4**	**8**	**33,982**	**100.0%**	**8,496**	**3**	**0.00%**	**+1**
Electorate		**62,348**	**68.12%**				**52,193**	**65.11%**			**+3.01%**	
Spoiled		**327**	**0.76%**				**206**	**0.60%**			**+0.16%**	
Turnout		**42,799**	**68.65%**				**34,188**	**65.50%**			**+3.14%**	

DUBLIN WEST 2011									
TRANSFER ANALYSIS									
From	**To**	**FG**	**LB**	**FF**	**SF**	**SP**	**GP**	**Others**	**Non Trans**
FG	3,693		1,628	966					1,099
			44.08%	*26.16%*					*29.76%*
LB	1,132	254	500	81	49	220	20	8	
		22.44%	*44.17%*	*7.16%*	*4.33%*	*19.43%*	*1.77%*	*0.71%*	
FF	631	79	108	227	42	122			53
		12.52%	*17.12%*	*35.97%*	*6.66%*	*19.33%*			*8.40%*
SF	2,749	253	1,251	273					972
		9.20%	*45.51%*	*9.93%*					*35.36%*
GP	625	77	107	225	42	121			53
		12.32%	*17.12%*	*36.00%*	*6.72%*	*19.36%*			*8.48%*
Others	288	36	49	104	19	56			24
		12.50%	*17.01%*	*36.11%*	*6.60%*	*19.44%*			*8.33%*
Total	**9,118**	**699**	**3,643**	**1,876**	**152**	**519**	**20**	**8**	**2,201**
		7.67%	***39.95%***	***20.57%***	***1.67%***	***5.69%***	***0.22%***	***0.09%***	***24.14%***

DUBLIN WEST 2011
COUNT DETAILS

Seats 4 — **Quota** 8,495

Candidate	Party	1st	2nd	3rd	4th	5th
			Burton Surplus	McGuinness O'Gorman Esebamen	Donnelly Votes	Dennison Votes
			-1,132			
Burton, Joan*	LB	9,627	8,495	8,495	8,495	8,495
			+196			
Varadkar, Leo*	FG	8,359	8,555	8,555	8,555	8,555
			+220	+299		
Higgins, Joe #	SP	8,084	8,304	8,603	8,603	8,603
			+73	+556	+273	+966
Lenihan, Brian*	FF	6,421	6,494	7,050	7,323	8,289
			+500	+264	+1,251	+1,628
Nulty, Patrick	LB	2,686	3,186	3,450	4,701	6,329
			+58	+192	+253	-3,693
Dennison, Kieran	FG	3,190	3,248	3,440	3,693	Eliminated
			+49	+103	-2,749	
Donnelly, Paul	SF	2,597	2,646	2,749	Eliminated	
			+8	-631		
McGuinness, David	FF	623	631	Eliminated		
			+20	-625		
O'Gorman, Roderic	GP	605	625	Eliminated		
			+8	-288		
Esebamen, Clement	NP	280	288	Eliminated		
Non-transferable				+130	+972	+1,099
Cumulative			0	130	1,102	2,201
Total		**42,472**	**42,472**	**42,472**	**42,472**	**42,472**

DUBLIN WEST
ALL TDs 1981-2011

	Surname	Forename	Party	Elected							Total
1	Lenihan*	Brian Snr.	FF	81	82	82	87	89	92		6
2	Mitchell*	Jim	FG	81	82	82	87	89			5
3	Lawlor*	Liam	FF	82F	87	89	92	97			5
4	Lenihan	Brian	FF	96*	97	02	07	11			5
5	Burton	Joan	LB	92	02	07	11				4
6	MacGiolla	Tomas	WP	82N	87	89					3
7	Currie	Austin	FG	89	92	97					3
8	Higgins	Joe	SP	97	02	11					3
9	Burke*	Dick	FG	81	82F						2
10	Fleming	Brian	FG	81	82F						2
11	Lemass*	Eileen	FF	81	82N						2
12	Skelly	Liam	FG	82*	82N						2
13	Varadkar	Leo	FG	07	11						2
14	O'Malley	Pat	PD	87							1
15	Nulty	Patrick	LB	11*							1
15	**Total**			***Includes 3 By-Elections**						*	**46**
	**** Also elected in another constituency**										
1	Mitchell*	Jim	FG	Ballyfermot/Central				77/	92	97	3
2	Burke*	Dick	FG	Dublin Co. South				69	73		2
3	Lawlor*	Liam	FF	Dublin Co. West				77			1
4	Lemass*	Eileen	FF	Ballyfermot				77			1
5	Lenihan*	Brian	FF	Dublin Co. West				77			1
5	**Total**										**8**

DUBLIN WEST		
MAIN BOUNDARY CHANGES		
Dail	**Constituency**	**Seats**
21 (1977)	Ballyfermot	3
	West County	3
22 (1981) - 26 (1989)	Dublin West	5
27 (1992) - 28 (1997)	Dublin West	4
29 (2002) - 30 (2007)	Dublin West	3
31 (2011) -	Dublin West	4

DUBLIN WEST 1977-2011

		FG		LB		FF		SF		SP		GP		WP		CS		PD		DSP		Soc Lab		Others	
Dail	**Seats**	**S**	**% Vote**	**S**	**% Vote**	**S**	**% Vote**	**S**	**% Vote**	**S**	**% Vote**	**S**	**% Vote**	**S**	**% Vote**	**S**	**% Vote**	**S**	**% Vote**	**S**	**% Vote**	**S**	**% Vote**	**S**	**% Vote**
21 1977	6	2	22.44%	1	24.32%	3	50.35%								2.24%										0.64%
22 1981	5	3	42.09%		7.90%	2	38.66%		6.49%						4.30%								0.13%		0.43%
23 1982	5	3	42.47%		5.79%	2	41.69%								7.26%										2.79%
24 1982	5	2	43.18%		3.94%	2	36.61%							1	14.70%						1.02%				0.56%
25 1987	5	1	22.15%		2.29%	2	40.45%		2.01%				1.14%	1	12.86%			1	11.63%		1.16%				6.30%
26 1989	5	2	24.58%		4.30%	2	39.93%		2.91%				3.99%	1	17.11%				5.36%		1.39%				0.44%
27 1992	4	1	14.37%	1	22.60%	2	31.31%		2.78%				2.44%		7.34%				4.03%						15.13%
28 1997	4	1	16.94%		12.11%	2	33.19%		5.00%	1	16.21%		4.32%		2.83%				7.61%						1.79%
29 2002	3		12.32%	1	12.71%	1	34.63%		8.02%	1	21.48%		2.49%				0.45%		7.90%						
30 2007	3	1	20.39%	1	17.06%	1	37.45%		4.78%		14.91%		3.78%						1.63%						
31 2011	4	1	27.19%	1	28.99%	1	16.59%		6.11%	1	19.03%		1.42%												0.66%
1981-2011	**49**	**17**	**26.96%**	**5**	**12.73%**	**20**	**37.26%**		**3.13%**	**3**	**5.39%**		**1.61%**	**3**	**6.67%**		**0.03%**	**1**	**3.32%**		**0.36%**		**0.01%**		**2.52%**
1918-2011	**4,618**	**1,453**	**30.77%**	**482**	**11.53%**	**1,985**	**41.86%**	**232**	**1.99%**	**4**	**0.16%**	**16**	**0.75%**	**17**	**0.78%**		**0.04%**	**44**	**1.42%**	**2**	**0.06%**	**1**	**0.02%**	**382**	**10.61%**

DÚN LAOGHAIRE 2011

"Good vote management wins Fine Gael two seats"

Dún Laoghaire lost territory containing around 12,000 people, mainly in Cabinteely and Foxrock, to Dublin South, and was reduced from a five-seater to a four-seater, making it more competitive than ever, especially as all five incumbents stood for re-election. Only two of them made it back to Leinster House. The smiles were on the faces of Fine Gael and the ULA, while Fianna Fail and, surprisingly, Labour were not so happy.

For Fine Gael Dún Laoghaire was traditionally a happy hunting ground. The party took three seats out of five here in November 1982, but by 2002 it had lost them all. The rebuilding was spectacularly successful; Seán Barrett returned to the Dáil in 2007, and in 2011 he was joined by new TD Mary Mitchell-O'Connor. The party won a less than overwhelming 35 per cent of the votes, but good vote management turned this comfortably into two seats.

Labour was also hoping for two seats, and party leader Éamon Gilmore was joined on the ticket by Senator Ivana Bacik, who had done well in two previous electoral outings without being successful in either. With good vote management Labour would have been sure of two seats. Instead, Gilmore got almost twice as many first preferences as Bacik; the margin between the two, over 5,000 votes, proved costly when Bacik was eliminated on the tenth count, because if just 148 of Gilmore's first preferences had been switched to Bacik, she would have taken a seat.

Instead, her elimination carried Richard Boyd Barrett of People before Profit into a seat. Boyd Barrett had come close in 2007 when Dún Laoghaire had been a five-seater, and now overcame the tougher challenge of getting elected in a four-seater.

The game of chicken played in the months before the election by the two Fianna Fail candidates, Barry Andrews and Mary Hanafin, both of them ministers, had fascinated the nation and appalled party headquarters. Despite hints and entreaties, neither would move to the emptier territory of Dublin South, and, inevitably, both lost their seats. To complete the rout of the outgoing government, Green TD and junior minister Ciarán Cuffe barely reached 2,000 votes and did not even qualify for reimbursement of his expenses.

Eamon Gilmore on campaign trail

DÚN LAOGHAIRE TDs 2011

EAMON GILMORE (LB)

1 Corbawn Close, Shankill, Co. Dublin, Tel: 01 2821363; Mobile: 087 2200495.
Leinster House: 01 6182112; Email: eamon.gilmore@oireachtas.ie

Born Caltra, Co. Galway 24th April 1955. Married to Carol Hanney, two sons, one daughter. Educated Garbally College, Ballinasloe, Co. Galway and UCG (BA). Tánaiste and Leader of the Labour Party and former Trade Union official. Contested November 1982 and 1987 general elections in Dun Laoghaire. First elected 1989 as a Workers Party Deputy. Elected for DL in 1992 and 1997. Following merger between DL and Labour elected as a Labour deputy in 2002 and retained his seat in 2007 and 2011.

Appointed Tánaiste and Minister for Foreign Affairs and Trade 9th March 2011. Leader of the Labour Party since September 2007. Unsuccessful candidate in Labour leadership election in October 2002. Spokesperson on Environment and Local Government 2002-2007. Member Joint Committee on Environment and Local Government 2002-2007. Spokesperson on Environment, Marine, Agriculture and Public Enterprise 1997-2002. Minister of State at the Department of the Marine 1994-1997. Member Dublin County Council 1985-1994. Member Dun Laoghaire Rathdown County Council 1997-2003. President of the Union of Students in Ireland 1976-1978. Worked for the Irish Transport and General Workers Union (now SIPTU) where he was responsible for organising professional and managerial staff. One of the first organisers of the Peace Train in 1989. Chaired the Commission reorganising the Worker's Party, which ultimately led to the formation of Democratic Left.

SEAN BARRETT (FG)

"Avondale", Ballinclea Road, Killiney, Co. Dublin. Tel: 01 2852077; Mobile: 087 2855848
Constituency Office: 6 Rogan's Court, Patrick Street, Dun Laoghaire; Tel: 01 2845333; Leinster House: 01 6183343; Email: ceann.comhairle@oireachtas.ie
Website: www.ceanncomhairle.oireachtas.ie

Born Dublin 9th August 1944. Married to Sheila Hyde, three daughters, two sons. Educated CBC, Monkstown; Presentation College, Glasthule; College of Commerce, Rathmines. Ceann Comhairle. Formerly company director and insurance broker.
First elected 1981. Retired in 2002 but re-elected 2007. Retained his seat in 2011.

Elected Ceann Comhairle of the 31st Dáil on 9th March 2011. Appointed Chairman Committee on Procedure and Privileges June 2011. Fine Gael front bench spokesperson on Foreign Affairs 2010-2011. Chairman Joint Committee on Climate Change and Energy Security 2007-2011. Member Joint Committee on Finance and the Public Service and Member Dail Committee on Procedure and Privileges 2007-2011. Minister for Defence and the Marine 1995-1997. President of the EU Council of Ministers during Ireland's Presidency 1996. Government Whip and Minister for State at the Department of the Taoiseach and Department of Defence 1994-1995. Minister for Sport and Leader of the House 1986-1987. Government Chief Whip 1982-1987. Minister of State at the Department of the Taoiseach and Department of Defence 1981-1982. Member Dublin County Council 1974-1982 (Chairman 1981-1982). Member Dun Laoghaire Rathdown County Council 1991-1999. President Bective Rangers Rugby Club 2005-2006. Honorary president Ballybrack Boy's Football Club and Rathmichael Shankill Football Club. Member Killiney Golf Club. Member Killiney Lions Club.

MARY MITCHELL O'CONNOR (FG)

31 Maple Manor, Cabinteely, Co. Dublin; Tel: 01 2986975; Mobile: 086 8186725; Leinster House: 01 6183302; Email: mary.mitchelloconnor@oireachtas.ie

Born Milltown, Co. Galway 10th June 1959. Divorced with two sons. Educated Presentation Convent, Tuam, Co. Galway; Carysfort College, Blackrock, Co. Dublin; NUI Maynooth. Former School Principal. First elected 2011.

Member Committee on Jobs, Social Protection and Education. First elected to Dun Laoghaire County Council in 2004 for Progressive Democrats. Joined Fine Gael on 11th December 2007. Retained her seat in the Dun Laoghaire electoral area in 2009.

RICHARD BOYD BARRETT (PBPA)

Brigadoon, Station Road, Glenageary, Co. Dublin; Mobile: 086 7814520
Leinster House: 01 6183449; Email: richard.boydbarrett@oireachtas.ie
Website: www.richardboydbarrett.ie

Born London 15th November 1967. Partner, one son, one stepson. Educated St. Michael's College, Ballsbridge, Dublin 4; UCD (BA and MA in English Lit). Contested 2002 and 2007 Dail elections in Dun Laoghaire. First elected 2011.

Member Committee on Finance, Public Expenditure and Reform. Contested 2004 local elections in Dun Laoghaire for SWP. First elected in the Dun Laoghaire electoral area in 2009 for PBPA. Founding member of People Before Profit Alliance and United Left Alliance. Chairperson of Irish Anti-War Movement.

	DÚN LAOGHAIRE 2011 FIRST PREFERENCE VOTES						
	Seats	4			11,336		
	Candidate	Party	1st	%	Quota	Count	Status
1	**Gilmore, Eamon***	**LB**	**11,468**	**20.23%**	**1.01**	**1**	**Made Quota**
2	**Barrett, Sean***	**FG**	**10,504**	**18.53%**	**0.93**	**8**	**Made Quota**
3	**Mitchell O'Connor, Mary**	**FG**	**9,087**	**16.03%**	**0.80**	**10**	**Made Quota**
4	**Boyd Barrett, Richard**	**PBPA**	**6,206**	**10.95%**	**0.55**	**11**	**Elected**
5	Hanafin, Mary*	FF	5,090	8.98%	0.45	11	Not Elected
6	Bacik, Ivana	LB	5,749	10.14%	0.51	9	Eliminated
7	Andrews, Barry*	FF	3,542	6.25%	0.31	7	Eliminated
8	Cuffe, Ciaran*	GP	2,156	3.80%	0.19	6	No Expenses
9	Boyhan, Victor	NP	834	1.47%	0.07	5	No Expenses
10	Haughton, Carl	NP	456	0.80%	0.04	5	No Expenses
11	Patton, Trevor	NP	445	0.79%	0.04	5	No Expenses
12	Fitzgerald, Daire	CS	434	0.77%	0.04	4	No Expenses
13	Crawford, Nick	NV	394	0.70%	0.03	3	No Expenses
14	Deegan, Mick	NP	311	0.55%	0.03	2	No Expenses
14	***Outgoing**		**56,676**	**100.00%**	**11,336**	**2,835**	**No Expenses**

DÚN LAOGHAIRE 2011 PARTY VOTE												
	2011					2007					Change	
Party	Cand	1st	%	Quota	Seats	Cand	1st	%	Quota	Seats	%	Seats
FG	2	19,591	34.57%	1.73	2	3	13,832	23.56%	1.41	1	+11.01%	+1
LB	2	17,217	30.38%	1.52	1	2	9,392	16.00%	0.96	1	+14.38%	
FF	2	8,632	15.23%	0.76		2	20,471	34.87%	2.09	2	-19.64%	-2
SF						1	1,292	2.20%	0.13		-2.20%	
PBPA	1	6,206	10.95%	0.55	1	1	5,233	8.91%	0.53		+2.04%	+1
GP	1	2,156	3.80%	0.19		1	4,534	7.72%	0.46	1	-3.92%	
CS	1	434	0.77%	0.04							+0.77%	
PD						1	3,959	6.74%	0.40		-6.74%	
Others	5	2,440	4.31%	0.22							+4.31%	
Total	**14**	**56,676**	**100.0%**	**11,336**	**4**	**11**	**58,713**	**100.0%**	**9,786**	**5**	**0.00%**	**0**
Electorate		**80,115**	**70.74%**				**89,035**	**65.94%**			**+4.80%**	
Spoiled		**481**	**0.84%**				**397**	**0.67%**			**+0.17%**	
Turnout		**57,157**	**71.34%**				**59,110**	**66.39%**			**+4.95%**	

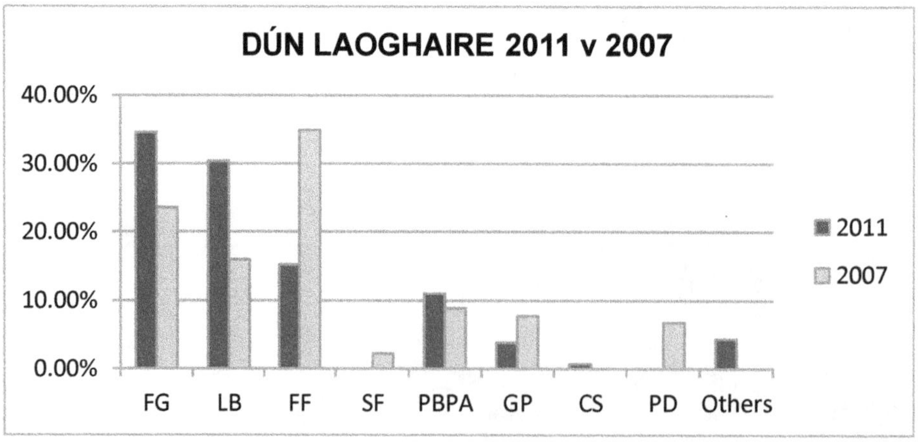

DÚN LAOGHAIRE 2011 COUNT DETAILS												
Seats	4										Quota	11,336
Candidate	Party	1st	2nd	3rd	4th	5th	6th	7th	8th	9th	10th	11th
			Gilmore Surplus	Deegan Votes	Crawford Votes	Fitzgerald Votes	Boyhan Haughton Patton	Cuffe Votes	Andrews Votes	Barrett Surplus	Bacik Votes	Mitchell Surplus
			-132									
Gilmore, Eamon*	LB	11,468	11,336	11,336	11,336	11,336	11,336	11,336	11,336	11,336	11,336	11,336
			+12	+22	+35	+93	+247	+361	+449	-387		
Barrett, Sean*	FG	10,504	10,516	10,538	10,573	10,666	10,913	11,274	11,723	11,336	11,336	11,336
			+7	+26	+43	+76	+329	+430	+311	+142	+2,554	-1,669
Mitchell O'Connor, Mary	FG	9,087	9,094	9,120	9,163	9,239	9,568	9,998	10,309	10,451	13,005	11,336
			+22	+43	+61	+52	+411	+337	+281	+40	+2,461	+880
Boyd Barrett, Richard	PBPA	6,206	6,228	6,271	6,332	6,384	6,795	7,132	7,413	7,453	9,914	10,794
			+6	+11	+23	+87	+175	+214	+2,268	+139	+876	+531
Hanafin, Mary*	FF	5,090	5,096	5,107	5,130	5,217	5,392	5,606	7,874	8,013	8,889	9,420
			+77	+31	+47	+12	+284	+753	+307	+46	-7,306	
Bacik, Ivana	LB	5,749	5,826	5,857	5,904	5,916	6,200	6,953	7,260	7,306	Eliminated	
			+3	+9	+15	+25	+119	+173	-3,886			
Andrews, Barry*	FF	3,542	3,545	3,554	3,569	3,594	3,713	3,886	Eliminated			
			+2	+29	+35	+12	+195	-2,429				
Cuffe, Ciaran*	GP	2,156	2,158	2,187	2,222	2,234	2,429	Eliminated				
			+1	+16	+61	+29	-941					
Boyhan, Victor	NP	834	835	851	912	941	Eliminated					
			+1	+43	+63	+31	-594					
Haughton, Carl	NP	456	457	500	563	594	Eliminated					
			+1	+21	+33	+15	-515					
Patton, Trevor	NP	445	446	467	500	515	Eliminated					
				+7	+9	-450						
Fitzgerald, Daire	CS	434	434	441	450	Eliminated						
				+44	-438							
Crawford, Nick	NV	394	394	438	Eliminated							
				-311								
Deegan, Mick	NP	311	311	Eliminated								
Non-transferable				+9	+13	+18	+290	+161	+270	+20	+1,415	+258
Cumulative			0	9	22	40	330	491	761	781	2,196	2,454
Total		**56,676**	**56,676**	**56,676**	**56,676**	**56,676**	**56,676**	**56,676**	**56,676**	**56,676**	**56,676**	**56,676**

DUN LAOGHAIRE 2011 TRANSFER ANALYSIS								
From	**To**	**FG**	**LB**	**FF**	**PBPA**	**GP**	**Others**	**Non Trans**
FG	2,056	142	46	670	920			278
		6.91%	*2.24%*	*32.59%*	*44.75%*			*13.52%*
LB	7,438	2,573	77	885	2,483	2	3	1,415
		34.59%	*1.04%*	*11.90%*	*33.38%*	*0.03%*	*0.04%*	*19.02%*
FF	3,886	760	307	2,268	281			270
		19.56%	*7.90%*	*58.36%*	*7.23%*			*6.95%*
GP	2,429	791	753	387	337			161
		32.56%	*31.00%*	*15.93%*	*13.87%*			*6.63%*
Others	3,249	871	374	464	567	271	372	330
		26.81%	*11.51%*	*14.28%*	*17.45%*	*8.34%*	*11.45%*	*10.16%*
Total	**19,058**	**5,137**	**1,557**	**4,674**	**4,588**	**273**	**375**	**2,454**
		26.95%	***8.17%***	***24.53%***	***24.07%***	***1.43%***	***1.97%***	***12.88%***

DÚN LAOGHAIRE		
MAIN BOUNDARY CHANGES		
Dail	**Constituency**	**Seats**
13 (1948) - 16 (1957)	Dún Laoghaire & Rathdown	3
17 (1961) - 20 (1973)	Dún Laoghaire & Rathdown	4
21 (1977)	Dún Laoghaire	4
22 (1981) - 30 (2007)	Dún Laoghaire	5
31 (2011) -	Dún Laoghaire	4

DÚN LAOGHAIRE															
All TDs 1948-2011															
	Surname	**Forename**	**Party**	**Elected**											**Total**
1	Andrews	David	FF	65	69	73	77	81	82	82	87	89	92	97	11
2	Cosgrave*	Liam	FG	48	51	54	57	61	65	69	73	77			9
3	Barrett	Sean	FG	81	82	82	87	89	92	97	07	11			9
4	Desmond	Barry	LB	69	73	77	81	82	82	87					7
5	Dockrell	Henry P.	FG	51	54	61	65	69	73						6
6	Gilmore	Eamon	WP	89	92	97	02	07	11						6
7	Brady*	Sean	FF	48	51	54	57	61							5
8	Barnes	Monica	FG	82N	87	89	97								4
9	Booth	Lionel	FF	57	61	65									3
10	O'Donoghue	Martin	FF	77	81	82F									3
11	Cosgrave	Liam T.	FG	81	82	82									3
12	Hanafin	Mary	FF	97	02	07									3
13	Andrews	Barry	FF	02	07										2
14	Cuffe	Ciaran	GP	02	07										2
15	Brennan	Joseph P.	CP	48											1
16	Kennedy	Geraldine	PD	87											1
17	Hillery	Brian	FF	89											1
18	Bhreathnach	Niamh	LB	92											1
19	Keogh	Helen	PD	92											1
20	O'Malley	Fiona	PD	02											1
21	Mitchell O'Connor	Mary	FG	11											1
22	Boyd Barrett	Richard	PBPA	11											1
22	**Total**														**81**
	***Also elected in another constituency**														
1	Brady*	Sean	FF	Dublin Co.			27	32	33	37	38	43	44		7
2	Cosgrave*	Liam	FG	Dublin Co.			43	44							2
2	**Total**														**9**

DÚN LAOGHAIRE 1948-2011																								
		FG		LB		FF		SF		PBPA		GP		WP		CS		PD		DL		C na P		Others	
Dail	Seats	S	% Vote	S	% Vote	S	% Vote	S	% Vote	S	% Vote	S	% Vote	S	% Vote	S	% Vote	S	% Vote	S	% Vote	S	% Vote	S	% Vote
13 1948	3	1	40.79%		4.84%	1	31.51%															1	22.86%		
14 1951	3	2	44.50%		12.56%	1	42.94%																		
15 1954	3	2	47.72%		13.50%	1	38.79%																		
16 1957	3	1	38.92%		10.87%	2	45.27%																4.94%		
17 1961	4	2	44.78%		9.64%	2	38.97%																		6.61%
18 1965	4	2	37.87%		12.76%	2	47.50%																		1.87%
19 1969	4	2	40.30%	1	18.19%	1	36.08%																		5.43%
20 1973	4	2	42.37%	1	18.66%	1	37.56%																		1.41%
21 1977	4	1	37.54%	1	14.56%	2	38.99%																		8.91%
22 1981	5	2	43.42%	1	16.03%	2	37.43%																		3.12%
23 1982	5	2	48.20%	1	16.03%	2	32.61%																		3.16%
24 1982	5	3	52.53%	1	12.22%	1	30.06%								2.73%										2.47%
25 1987	5	2	30.66%	1	11.64%	1	26.17%		2.16%				1.67%		7.28%			1	19.79%						0.64%
26 1989	5	2	32.75%		5.70%	2	32.62%		1.79%				5.12%	1	12.83%				8.98%						0.21%
27 1992	5	1	21.55%	1	16.97%	1	31.18%		1.35%				3.00%		0.19%			1	10.94%	1	11.87%				2.95%
28 1997	5	2	30.96%		8.66%	2	25.83%						5.09%				3.69%		8.55%	1	13.89%				3.34%
29 2002	5		15.04%	1	22.68%	2	30.29%		4.03%		1.63%	1	9.33%				0.49%	1	13.36%						3.15%
30 2007	5	1	23.56%	1	16.00%	2	34.87%		2.20%		8.91%	1	7.72%						6.74%						
31 2011	4	2	34.57%	1	30.38%		15.23%			1	10.95%		3.80%				0.77%								4.31%
1948-2011	**81**	**32**	**36.04%**	**11**	**14.78%**	**28**	**33.36%**		**0.74%**	**1**	**1.43%**	**2**	**2.31%**	**1**	**1.42%**		**0.31%**	**3**	**4.42%**	**2**	**1.69%**	**1**	**1.03%**		**2.46%**
National	**4,618**	**1,453**	**30.77%**	**482**	**11.53%**	**1,985**	**41.86%**	**232**	**1.99%**	**2**	**0.09%**	**16**	**0.75%**	**17**	**0.78%**		**0.04%**	**44**	**1.42%**	**8**	**0.22%**	**18**	**0.77%**	**361**	**9.77%**

DUBLIN REGION					
MAIN BOUNDARY CHANGES					
Dail	**Constituency**	**Seats**	**Dail**	**Constituency**	**Seats**
1 (1918)	Dublin (Clontarf)	1	22 (1981) - 26 (1989)	Dublin Central	5
	Dublin (College Green)	1		Dublin North	3
	Dublin Harbour	1		Dublin North-Central	4
	Dublin (Pembroke)	1		Dublin North-East	4
	Dublin (St. James's)	1		Dublin North-West	4
	Dublin (St. Michan's)	1		Dublin South	5
	Dublin (St. Patrick's)	1		Dublin South-Central	5
	Dublin (St. Stephens Green)	1		Dublin South-East	4
	Dublin Co. North	1		Dublin South-West	4
	Dublin Co. South	1		Dublin West	5
	10	10		Dun Laoghaire	5
2 (1921) - 3 (1922)	Dublin Mid	4		11	48
	Dublin North-West	4	27 (1992) - 28 (1997)	Dublin Central	4
	Dublin South	4		Dublin North	4
	Dublin County	6		Dublin North-Central	4
	4	18		Dublin North-East	4
4 (1923) - 8 (1933)	Dublin North	8		Dublin North-West	4
	Dublin South	7		Dublin South	5
	Dublin County	8		Dublin South-Central	4
	3	23		Dublin South-East	4
9 (1937) - 12 (1944)	Dublin North-East	3		Dublin South-West	5
	Dublin North-West	5		Dublin West	4
	Dublin South	7		Dun Laoghaire	5
	Dublin Townships	3		11	47
	Dublin County	5	29 (2002)	Dublin Central	4
	5	23		Dublin Mid-West	3
13 (1948) - 16 (1957)	Dublin North-Central	3		Dublin North	4
	Dublin North-East	5		Dublin North-Central	4
	Dublin North-West	3		Dublin North-East	3
	Dublin South-Central	5		Dublin North-West	3
	Dublin South-East	3		Dublin South	5
	Dublin South-West	5		Dublin South-Central	5
	Dun Laoghaire & Rathdown	3		Dublin South-East	4
	Dublin County	3		Dublin South-West	4
	8	30		Dublin West	3
17 (1961) - 18 (1965)	Dublin North-Central	4		Dun Laoghaire	5
	Dublin North-East	5		12	47
	Dublin North-West	3	30 (2007)	Dublin Central	4
	Dublin South-Central	5		Dublin Mid-West	4
	Dublin South-East	3		Dublin North	4
	Dublin South-West	5		Dublin North-Central	3
	Dun Laoghaire & Rathdown	4		Dublin North-East	3
	Dublin County	5		Dublin North-West	3
	8	34		Dublin South	5
19 (1969) - 20 (1973)	Dublin Central	4		Dublin South-Central	5
	Dublin North-Central	4		Dublin South-East	4
	Dublin North-East	4		Dublin South-West	4
	Dublin North-West	4		Dublin West	3
	Dublin South-Central	4		Dun Laoghaire	5
	Dublin South-East	3		12	47
	Dublin South-West	4	31 (2011)	Dublin Central	4
	Dun Laoghaire & Rathdown	4		Dublin Mid-West	4
	Dublin North County	4		Dublin North	4
	Dublin South County	3		Dublin North-Central	3
	10	38		Dublin North-East	3
21 (1977)	Artane	3		Dublin North-West	3
	Ballyfermot	3		Dublin South	5
	Cabra	3		Dublin South-Central	5
	Clontarf	3		Dublin South-East	4
	Finglas	3		Dublin South-West	4
	Rathmines West	3		Dublin West	4
	Dublin North-Central	3		Dun Laoghaire	4
	Dublin South-Central	3		12	47
	Dublin South-East	3			
	Dun Laoghaire	4			
	Mid-County	3			
	North County	3			
	South County	3			
	West County	3			
	14	15			

	DUBLIN REGION																		
	ALL TDs 1918-2011																		
	Surname	Forename	Party	Elected															Total
1	Lemass	Sean F.	FF	24*	27	27	32	33	37	38	43	44	48	51	54	57	61	65	15
2	MacEntee**	Sean	FF	27	27	32	33	37	38	43	44	48	51	54	57	61	65		14
3	Byrne	Alfred	NP	22	23	27	27	32	33	37	38	43	44	48	51	54			13
4	O'Kelly	Sean T.	FF	18	21	22	23	27	27	32	33	37	38	43	44				12
5	Doyle	Peadar	FG	23	27	27	32	33	37	38	43	44	48	51	54				12
6	Traynor	Oscar	FF	25*	27J	32	33	37	38	43	44	48	51	54	57				12
7	Brady	Sean	FF	27	32	33	37	38	43	44	48	51	54	57	61				12
8	Briscoe	Robert	FF	27	32	33	37	38	43	44	48	51	54	57	61				12
9	Cosgrave	Liam	FG	43	44	48	51	54	57	61	65	69	73	77					11
10	Haughey	Charles J.	FF	57	61	65	69	73	77	81	82	82	87	89					11
11	Andrews	David	FF	65	69	73	77	81	82	82	87	89	92	97					11
12	Briscoe	Ben	FF	65	69	73	77	81	82	82	87	89	92	97					11
13	Costello	John A.	FG	33	37	38	44	48	51	54	57	61	65						10
14	Dockrell	Maurice E.	FG	43	44	48	51	54	57	61	65	69	73						10
15	De Valera	Vivion	FF	45*	48	51	54	57	61	65	69	73	77						10
16	Ahern	Bertie	FF	77	81	82	82	87	89	92	97	02	07						10
17	Woods	Michael	FF	77	81	82	82	87	89	92	97	02	07						10
18	Quinn	Ruairi	LB	77	82	82	87	89	92	97	02	07	11						10
19	Mulcahy**	Gen. Richard	FG	18	21	22	23	27	27	32	33	38							9
20	McGilligan**	Patrick	FG	37	38	43	44	48	51	54	57	61							9
21	O'Connell	John	FF	65	69	73	77	81	82	82	89	92							9
22	Burke	Ray	FF	73	77	81	82	82	87	89	92	97							9
23	Brennan	Seamus	FF	81	82	82	87	89	92	97	02	07							9
24	Harney	Mary	PD	81	82	82	87	89	92	97	02	07							9
25	Barrett	Sean	FG	81	82	82	87	89	92	97	07	11							9
26	Shatter	Alan	FG	81	82	82	87	89	92	97	07	11							9
27	Bruton	Richard	FG	82	82	87	89	92	97	02	07	11							9
28	Breathnach	Cormac	FF	32	33	37	38	43	44	48	51								8
29	Burke	Patrick J.	FF	44	48	51	54	57	61	65	69								8
30	Colley	George	FF	61	65	69	73	77	81	82	82								8
31	FitzGerald	Garret	FG	69	73	77	81	82	82	87	89								8
32	Tunney	Jim	FF	69	73	77	81	82	82	87	89								8
33	Mitchell	Jim	FG	77	81	82	82	87	89	92	97								8
34	Mitchell	Gay	FG	81	82	82	87	89	92	97	02								8
35	Gregory	Tony	NP	82	82	87	89	92	97	02	07								8
36	Browne	Noel	SLP	48	51	57	61	69	77	81									7
37	Ryan	Richie	FG	59*	61	65	69	73	77	81									7
38	Cluskey	Frank	LB	65	69	73	77	82	82	87									7
39	O'Leary	Michael	FG	65	69	73	77	81	82	82									7
40	Desmond	Barry	LB	69	73	77	81	82	82	87									7
41	Cosgrave	Michael Joe	FG	77	81	82	82	87	89	97									7
42	Lenihan**	Brian Senior	FF	77	81	82	82	87	89	92									7
43	Fitzgerald**	Desmond	CG	18	21	22	23	27	27										6
44	Kelly	Thomas	FF	18	21	22	33	37	38										6
45	Keogh	Myles	FG	22	23	27	27	32	37										6
46	Dockrell	Henry M.	FG	32	33	37	38	43	44										6
47	Butler	Bernard	FF	43	44	48	51	54	57										6
48	Dunne	Sean	LB	48	51	54	61	65	69										6
49	Brady	Philip	FF	51	57	61	65	69	73										6
50	Costello	Declan	FG	51	54	57	61	65	73										6
51	Dockrell	Henry	FG	51	54	61	65	69	73										6
52	Gogan	Dick	FF	54	57	61	65	69	73										6
53	Lynch	Celia	FF	54	57	61	65	69	73										6
54	Lemass	Noel	FF	56*	57	61	65	69	73										6
55	Fitzpatrick	Tom	FF	65	69	73	77	81	82F										6
56	Kelly	John	FG	73	77	81	82	82	87										6
57	O'Brien	Fergus	FG	73	77	81	82N	87	89										6
58	Walsh	Sean	FF	73	77	81	82	82	87										6
59	Brady	Gerard	FF	77	81	82	82	87	89										6
60	Brady	Vincent	FF	77	81	82	82	87	89										6
61	Lawlor	Liam	FF	77	82F	87	89	92	97										6
62	Flaherty	Mary	FG	81	82	82	87	89	92										6
63	Owen	Nora	FG	81	82	82	89	92	97										6
64	Taylor	Mervyn	LB	81	82	82	87	89	92										6
65	De Rossa	Proinsias	DL	82	82	87	89	92	97										6
66	Kitt	Tom	FF	87	89	92	97	02	07										6
67	Gilmore	Eamon	LB	89	92	97	02	07	11										6

	Surname	Forename	Party	Elected						Total
68	Rabbitte	Pat	LB	89	92	97	02	07	11	6
69	Good	John	NP	23	27	27	32	33		5
70	O'Connor	Batt	CG	24*	27	27	32	33		5
71	Beckett	James	FG	27	27	32	33	38		5
72	Lynch	James	FF	32	33	38	43	44		5
73	Byrne	Alfred P.	NP	37	38	43	48	51		5
74	McCann	John	FF	39*	43	44	48	51		5
75	Larkin(jun)	James	LB	43	44	48	51	54		5
76	Belton	Jack	FG	48	51	54	57	61		5
77	Rooney	Eamonn	FG	48	51	54	57	61		5
78	Clinton	Mark	FG	61	65	69	73	77		5
79	Moore	Sean	FF	65	69	73	77	81		5
80	McMahon	Larry	FG	70*	73	77	81	82F		5
81	Boland	John	FG	77	81	82	82	87		5
82	Keating	Michael	FG	77	81	82	82	87		5
83	Barrett	Michael	FF	81	82	82	87	89		5
84	Fitzgerald	Liam	FF	81	82N	87	89	92		5
85	Broughan	Tommy	LB	92	97	02	07	11		5
86	Shortall	Roisin	LB	92	97	02	07	11		5
87	Lenihan	Brian	FF	96*	97	02	07	11		5
88	De Markievicz	Constance	FF	18	21	23	27J			4
89	Collins-O'Driscoll	Margaret	CG	23	27	27	32			4
90	Hennessy	Thomas	CG	25*	27*	27S	32			4
91	O'Sullivan**	Gearoid	CG	27*	27S	32	33			4
92	Cooney	Eamonn	FF	27S	32	33	38			4
93	Fogarty	Patrick	FF	37	38	43	44			4
94	Colley	Harry	FF	44	48	51	54			4
95	MacBride	Sean	CnaP	47*	48	51	54			4
96	Byrne	Patrick	FG	56*	57	61	65			4
97	Boland	Kevin	FF	57	61	65	69			4
98	Belton	Patrick	FG	63*	65	69	73			4
99	Belton	Luke	FG	65	69	73	77			4
100	Burke	Dick	FG	69	73	81	82F			4
101	Byrne	Hugh	FG	69	73	77	81			4
102	Andrews	Niall	FF	77	81	82	82			4
103	Birmingham	George	FG	81	82	82	87			4
104	Fennell	Nuala	FG	81	82	82	89			4
105	Barnes	Monica	FG	82N	87	89	97			4
106	Flood	Chris	FF	87	89	92	97			4
107	Callely	Ivor	FF	89	92	97	02			4
108	Ryan	Sean	LB	89	92	98*	02			4
109	Ahern	Noel	FF	92	97	02	07			4
110	Haughey	Sean	FF	92	97	02	07			4
111	Sargent	Trevor	GP	92	97	02	07			4
112	Burton	Joan	LB	92	02	07	11			4
113	Costello	Joe	LB	92	02	07	11			4
114	Mitchell	Olivia	FG	97	02	07	11			4
115	Duffy	George Gavan	CT	18	21	22				3
116	McGrath**	Joseph	CT	18	21	22				3
117	Staines	Michael	CT	18	21	22				3
118	Cosgrave	Philip	CG	21	22	23				3
119	Derham	Michael	CG	21	22	23				3
120	McCarthy	Daniel	CG	21	22	23				3
121	McGarry	Sean	CG	21	22	23				3
122	Johnson	Thomas	LB	22	23	27J				3
123	Cooper	Maj. Bryan	CG	23	27	27				3
124	Byrne	John J.	CG	27	27	32				3
125	Belton	Patrick	FF	27J	33	38				3
126	Rice	Vincent	CG	27J	28*	33				3
127	Larkin(sen)	James	LB	27S	37	43				3
128	Benson	Ernest	FG	37	38	43				3
129	O'Sullivan	Martin	LB	43	44	48				3
130	O'Higgins**	Michael	FG	48	54	57				3
131	Byrne	Thomas	NP	52*	54	57				3
132	Larkin	Denis	LB	54	57	65				3
133	Booth	Lionel	FF	57	61	65				3
134	Timmons	Eugene	FF	61	69	73				3
135	Dowling	Joseph	FF	65	69	73				3
136	Lemass	Eileen	FF	77	81	82N				3

	Surname	Forename	Party	Elected															Total
137	O'Donoghue	Martin	FF	77	81	82F													3
138	Cosgrave	Liam T.	FG	81	82	82													3
139	MacGiolla	Tomas	WP	82N	87	89													3
140	Fitzpatrick	Dermot	FF	87	89	02													3
141	McDowell	Michael	PD	87	92	02													3
142	Wright	G.V.	FF	87	97	02													3
143	Currie	Austin	FG	89	92	97													3
144	O'Donnell	Liz	PD	92	97	02													3
145	Ryan	Eoin	FF	92	97	02													3
146	Ardagh	Sean	FF	97	02	07													3
147	Carey	Pat	FF	97	02	07													3
148	Gormley	John	GP	97	02	07													3
149	Hanafin	Mary	FF	97	02	07													3
150	Lenihan	Conor	FF	97	02	07													3
151	Upton	Mary	LB	00*	02	07													3
152	Byrne	Eric	DL	89	94*	11													3
153	Fitzgerald	Frances	FG	92	97	11													3
154	Hayes	Brian	FG	97	07	11													3
155	Higgins	Joe	SP	97	02	11													3
156	McGrath	Finian	NP	02	07	11													3
157	O Snodaigh	Aengus	SF	02	07	11													3
158	Lawless	Frank	SF	18	21														2
159	Shanahan	Philip	SF	18	21														2
160	Clarke	Kathleen	R	21	27J														2
161	Murphy	Charles	R	21	23														2
162	Figgis	Darrell	NP	22	23														2
163	O'Higgins**	Kevin	CG	23	27J														2
164	Leonard	Patrick	CG	25*	27S														2
165	Lawlor	Thomas	LB	27	37														2
166	Finlay	Thomas	CG	30*	32														2
167	Lavery	Cecil	FG	35*	37														2
168	Hannigan	Joseph	NP	37	38														2
169	Cowan	Peadar	NP	48	51														2
170	Gallagher	Colm	FF	51	57														2
171	O'Donovan	John	LB	54	69														2
172	Carroll	James	NP	57	61														2
173	Sherwin	Frank	NP	57*	61														2
174	Cummins	Patrick	FF	58*	61														2
175	Mullen	Michael	LB	61	65														2
176	Foley	Des	FF	65	69														2
177	Cruise O'Brien	Conor	LB	69	73														2
178	Keating	Justin	LB	69	73														2
179	Thornley	David	LB	69	73														2
180	Leonard	Thomas	FF	77	83*														2
181	Fleming	Brian	FG	81	82F														2
182	Glenn	Alice	FG	81	82N														2
183	Manning	Maurice	FG	82	82														2
184	Skelly	Liam	FG	82*	82N														2
185	Doyle	Joe	FG	82N	89														2
186	McCartan	Pat	WP	87	89														2
187	Stafford	John	FF	87	89														2
188	McDowell	Derek	LB	92	97														2
189	Upton	Pat	LB	92	97														2
190	Brady	Martin	FF	97	02														2
191	Andrews	Barry	FF	02	07														2
192	Cuffe	Ciaran	GP	02	07														2
193	Curran	John	FF	02	07														2
194	Gogarty	Paul	GP	02	07														2
195	Mulcahy	Michael	FF	02	07														2
196	O'Connor	Charlie	FF	02	07														2
197	Ryan	Eamonn	GP	02	07														2
198	Kenny	Sean	LB	92	11														2
199	Crowe	Sean	SF	02	11														2
200	Byrne	Catherine	FG	07	11														2
201	Creighton	Lucinda	FG	07	11														2
202	Flanagan	Terence	FG	07	11														2
203	Reilly	Dr. James	FF	07	11														2
204	Tuffy	Joanne	LB	07	11														2
205	Varadkar	Leo	FG	07	11														2

	Surname	Forename	Party	Elected															Total
206	O'Sullivan	Maureen	NP	09*	11														2
207	Dwyer	James J.	SF	21															1
208	Pearse	Margaret	SF	21															1
209	O'Brien**	William	LB	22															1
210	O'Neill	Laurence	NP	22															1
211	Rooney	John	F	22															1
212	Cahill	Francis	CG	23															1
213	Hayes**	Michael	CG	23															1
214	Hewat	William	BP	23															1
215	Lynn	Kathleen	R	23															1
216	O'Malley	Ernest	R	23															1
217	Kennedy	Hugh	CG	23*															1
218	O'Meara	James	CG	24*															1
219	Norton**	William	LB	26*															1
220	Cullen	Denis	LB	27J															1
221	Kerlin	Frank	FF	27S															1
222	Murphy	Joseph	NP	27S															1
223	O'Higgins(sen.)**	Thomas F.	CG	29*															1
224	Curran	Patrick	LB	32															1
225	McGuire	James	CG	33															1
226	Pearse	Margaret M.	FF	33															1
227	Heron	Archibald	LB	37															1
228	McGowan	Gerard	LB	37															1
229	Mullen	Thomas	FF	38															1
230	Tunney	James	LB	43															1
231	O'Connor	John	FF	44															1
232	Brennan	Joseph	CnaP	48															1
233	Fitzpatrick	Michael	CnaP	48															1
234	Lehane	Con	CnaP	48															1
235	Ffrench-O'Carroll	Michael	NP	51															1
236	Finlay jun	Thomas	FG	54															1
237	O'Carroll	Maureen	LB	54															1
238	Murphy	John	IndUW	57															1
239	Barron	Joseph	CnaP	61															1
240	O'Keeffe	James	FG	61															1
241	O'Higgins(jun)**	Thomas F.	FG	69															1
242	Sherwin	Sean	FF	70*															1
243	Brugha	Ruairi	FF	73															1
244	Halligan	Brendan	LB	76*															1
245	De Valera**	Sile	FF	77															1
246	Fox	Christopher	FF	77															1
247	Horgan	John	LB	77															1
248	Killeen	Timothy	FF	77															1
249	Loftus	Sean D.	NP	81															1
250	Brennan	Ned	FF	82F															1
251	Fitzgerald	Alexis	FG	82F															1
252	Colley	Anne	PD	87															1
253	Kennedy	Geraldine	PD	87															1
254	Mooney	Mary	FF	87															1
255	O'Malley	Pat	PD	87															1
256	Garland	Roger	GP	89															1
257	Hillery	Brian	FF	89															1
258	Lee	Pat	FG	89															1
259	Bhreathnach	Niamh	LB	92															1
260	FitzGerald	Eithne	LB	92															1
261	Keogh	Helen	PD	92															1
262	Walsh	Eamonn	LB	92															1
263	McGennis	Marian	FF	97															1
264	Glennon	Jim	FF	02															1
265	O'Malley	Fiona	PD	02															1
266	Andrews	Chris	FF	07															1
267	Brady	Cyprian	FF	07															1
268	Kennedy	Michael	FF	07															1
269	O'Brien	Darragh	FF	07															1
270	Lee	George	FG	09*															1
271	Donohoe	Paschal	FG	11															1
272	McDonald	Mary Lou	SF	11															1
273	Dowds	Robert	LB	11															1
274	Keating	Derek	FG	11															1

	Surname	Forename	Party	Elected															Total
275	Ryan	Brendan	LB	11															1
276	Daly	Clare	SP	11															1
277	Farrell	Alan	FG	11															1
278	O Riordáin	Aodhán	LB	11															1
279	Ellis	Dessie	SF	11															1
280	Lyons	John	LB	11															1
281	Ross	Shane	NP	11															1
282	White	Alex	LB	11															1
283	Mathews	Peter	FG	11															1
284	Conaghan	Michael	LB	11															1
285	Collins	Joan	PBPA	11															1
286	Murphy	Eoghan	FG	11															1
287	Humphreys	Kevin	LB	11															1
288	Maloney	Eamonn	LB	11															1
289	Mitchell O'Connor	Mary	FG	11															1
290	Boyd Barrett	Richard	PBPA	11															1
291	Nulty	Patrick	LB	11*															1
291	**Total**											***Includes 36 By-Elections**						*	**1071**
**** Also elected in another constituency**																			
	Norton**	William	LB	Kildare							32-61								11
	O'Higgins(sen.)**	Thomas F.	CG	Laois-Offaly							32	33	37	38	43	44			6
	O'Higgins(sen.)**	Thomas F.	CG	Cork							48	51							2
	O'Higgins(jun)**	Thomas F.	FG	Laois-Offaly							48	51	54	57	61	65			6
	Hayes**	Michael	CG	NUI							21	22	23	27	27	32			6
	De Valera**	Sile	FF	Clare							87	89	92	97	02				5
D	McGilligan**	Patrick	FG	NUI							23	27	27	32	33				5
D	Mulcahy**	Gen. Richard	FG	Tipperary							44	48	51	54	57				5
	O'Higgins**	Kevin	CG	Leix-Offaly							18	21	22						3
D	Lenihan**	Brian	FF	Roscommon							61	65	69						3
D	Fitzgerald**	Desmond	CG	Carlow-Kilkenny							32	33							2
D	O'Sullivan**	Gearoid	CG	Carlow-Kilkenny							21	22							2
D	MacEntee**	Sean	FF	Monaghan							18	21							2
	O'Brien**	William	LB	Tipperary							27J	37							2
D	O'Higgins**	Michael	FG	Wicklow							61	65							2
D	McGrath**	Joseph	CT	Mayo							23								1
D	**Counted in Dublin Total**																		63

UNIVERSITIES											
All TDs 1918-1933											
	Surname	**Forename**	**Party**	**Elected**							**Total**
1	Alton	Prof. Ernest	NP	21	22	23	27	27	32	33	7
2	Craig	Prof. Sir James	NP	21	22	23	27	27	32	33	7
3	Thrift	Prof. William	NP	21	22	23	27	27	32	33	7
4	Hayes**	Michael	CG	21	22	23	27	27	32		6
5	McGilligan**	Patrick	CG	23*	27	27	32	33			5
6	MacNeill**	Prof. Eoin	CG	18	21	22	23				4
7	Fitzgibbon	Gerald	NP	21	22						2
8	Stockley	Prof. William	CR	21	22						2
9	Magennis	Prof. William	CG	22	23						2
10	Maguire	Conor	FF	32	33						2
11	English	Dr. Ada	SF	21							1
12	Clery	Prof. Arthur	NP	27							1
13	Tierney**	Prof. Michael	CG	27S							1
14	Concannon	Helena	FF	33							1
15	Rowlette	Robert	NP	33*							1
15	**Total**			***Includes 2 By-Elections**						*	**49**
	** Also elected in another constituency										
	McGilligan**	Patrick	CG	Dublin			37-61				9
N	MacNeill**	Prof. Eoin	CG	Derry/Clare			18/	23			2
N	Hayes**	Michael	CG	Dublin			23				1
N	Tierney**	Prof. Michael	CG	Mayo			*25				1

DUBLIN REGION 1918-2011																																
* No Contest			FG		LB		FF		SF		SP		PBPA		GP		WP		CS		PD		DL		C na P		Farmers		Nat League		Others	
Dail		Seats	S	% Vote	S	% Vote	S	% Vote	S	% Vote	S	% Vote	S	% Vote	S	% Vote	S	% Vote	S	% Vote	S	% Vote	S	% Vote	S	% Vote	S	% Vote	S	% Vote	S	% Vote
1	1918	10							10																							
2	1921*	18							18																							
3	1922	18	10	40.86%	2	13.43%	1	11.66%																			1	2.74%			4	31.31%
4	1923	23	11	50.28%	1	4.60%	5	17.21%																				1.39%			6	26.53%
5	1927	23	8	30.76%	3	10.31%	6	24.31%	1	4.55%																			1	7.03%	4	23.04%
6	1927	23	12	47.78%		5.21%	7	26.58%																						0.24%	4	20.20%
7	1932	23	11	38.87%	1	6.26%	9	34.11%																							2	20.76%
8	1933	23	10	40.39%		3.57%	11	43.43%																							2	12.61%
9	1937	23	7	30.04%	3	7.69%	9	41.31%																							4	20.96%
10	1938	23	8	33.87%		6.72%	12	49.29%																							3	10.12%
11	1943	23	6	26.04%	4	16.18%	11	45.09%																							2	12.69%
12	1944	23	6	26.35%	2	11.61%	14	51.81%																							1	10.23%
13	1948	30	8	24.57%	3	9.65%	11	38.85%																	6	19.26%					2	7.67%
14	1951	30	9	26.22%	2	10.79%	13	46.39%																	1	3.77%					5	12.83%
15	1954	30	12	34.59%	4	13.21%	11	39.27%																	1	4.82%					2	8.12%
16	1957	30	9	26.48%	1	8.12%	16	46.82%		3.04%																3.71%					4	11.83%
17	1961	34	12	31.70%	1	8.42%	16	44.61%		1.07%															1	2.14%					4	12.05%
18	1965	34	10	29.48%	6	18.54%	18	48.24%																		1.11%						2.63%
19	1969	38	11	28.40%	10	28.26%	17	39.47%																								3.87%
20	1973	38	14	32.19%	7	22.30%	17	40.38%		1.49%																						3.63%
21	1977	43	13	27.55%	6	17.54%	23	46.75%										1.48%													1	6.68%
22	1981	48	21	36.24%	3	12.17%	21	41.35%		0.67%								2.58%													3	6.98%
23	1982	48	20	38.86%	5	11.17%	20	42.57%		0.33%							1	3.54%													2	3.54%
24	1982	48	22	41.09%	4	10.54%	18	38.28%									2	6.48%													2	3.60%
25	1987	48	13	23.71%	4	7.09%	21	40.52%		2.17%						1.13%	3	7.47%			6	13.57%									1	4.36%
26	1989	48	15	23.02%	3	9.48%	21	40.73%		1.89%					1	5.19%	6	11.43%			1	5.40%									1	2.86%
27	1992	47	9	16.99%	13	26.08%	16	32.94%		1.95%					1	3.51%		1.34%			4	5.50%	3	5.28%							1	6.40%
28	1997	47	12	22.37%	5	11.20%	21	36.38%		2.63%	1	2.67%		0.28%	2	5.72%		0.67%		0.57%	2	6.59%	3	5.05%							1	5.87%
29	2002	47	3	14.46%	9	14.89%	21	37.13%	2	8.91%	1	3.07%		0.53%	5	8.04%		0.46%		0.45%	4	7.10%									2	4.96%
30	2007	47	10	18.74%	9	14.53%	19	38.75%	1	6.97%		2.28%		1.77%	5	8.27%		0.17%		0.12%	1	4.14%									2	4.27%
31	2011	47	17	29.93%	18	29.32%	1	12.45%	4	8.17%	2	3.59%	2	3.54%		3.59%		0.24%		0.25%											3	8.92%
1918-2011		**1,035**	**329**	**29.14%**	**129**	**13.87%**	**406**	**38.09%**	**36**	**1.99%**	**4**	**0.61%**	**2**	**0.34%**	**14**	**1.79%**	**12**	**1.74%**		**0.07%**	**18**	**2.12%**	**6**	**0.52%**	**9**	**0.96%**	**1**	**0.06%**	**1**	**0.14%**	**68**	**8.55%**
National		**4,618**	**1,453**	**30.77%**	**482**	**11.53%**	**1,985**	**41.86%**	**232**	**1.99%**	**4**	**0.16%**	**2**	**0.09%**	**16**	**0.75%**	**17**	**0.78%**		**0.04%**	**44**	**1.42%**	**8**	**0.22%**	**18**	**0.77%**	**42**	**0.90%**	**10**	**0.24%**	**305**	**8.46%**

DUBLIN v NATIONAL 1918-2011

* No Contest		FG		LB		FF		SF		SP		PBPA		GP		WP		CS		PD		DL		Others	
Dail		Dublin	National	Dublin	National	Dublin	National	Dublin	National	Dublin	National	Dublin	National	Dublin	National	Dublin	National	Dublin	National	Dublin	National	Dublin	National	Dublin	National
1	1918																								
2	1921*																								
3	1922	40.86%	38.48%	13.43%	21.33%	11.66%	21.26%																	34.05%	18.93%
4	1923	50.28%	38.97%	4.60%	10.62%	17.21%	27.40%																	27.92%	23.01%
5	1927	30.76%	27.45%	10.31%	12.55%	24.31%	26.12%	4.55%	3.61%															30.07%	30.27%
6	1927	47.78%	38.69%	5.21%	9.07%	26.58%	35.17%																	20.43%	17.07%
7	1932	38.87%	35.28%	6.26%	7.71%	34.11%	44.47%																	20.76%	12.54%
8	1933	40.39%	30.47%	3.57%	5.71%	43.43%	49.70%																	12.61%	14.12%
9	1937	30.04%	34.82%	7.69%	10.25%	41.31%	45.23%																	20.96%	9.70%
10	1938	33.87%	33.32%	6.72%	10.02%	49.29%	51.93%																	10.12%	4.72%
11	1943	26.04%	23.09%	16.18%	15.68%	45.09%	41.87%																	12.69%	19.36%
12	1944	26.35%	20.48%	11.61%	8.77%	51.81%	48.90%																	10.23%	21.85%
13	1948	24.57%	19.83%	9.65%	8.69%	38.85%	41.85%																	26.93%	29.62%
14	1951	26.22%	25.75%	10.79%	11.40%	46.39%	46.28%																	16.60%	16.57%
15	1954	34.59%	31.98%	13.21%	12.06%	39.27%	43.36%		0.15%															12.93%	12.45%
16	1957	26.48%	26.63%	8.12%	9.11%	46.82%	48.33%	3.04%	5.35%															15.54%	10.59%
17	1961	31.70%	32.02%	8.42%	11.65%	44.61%	43.83%	1.07%	3.12%															14.20%	9.39%
18	1965	29.48%	34.08%	18.54%	15.38%	48.24%	47.67%																	3.74%	2.86%
19	1969	28.40%	34.10%	28.26%	17.02%	39.47%	45.66%																	3.87%	3.22%
20	1973	32.19%	35.08%	22.30%	13.71%	40.38%	46.24%	1.49%	4.37%															3.63%	3.83%
21	1977	27.55%	30.49%	17.54%	11.63%	46.75%	50.63%									1.48%	1.70%							6.68%	5.55%
22	1981	36.24%	36.46%	12.17%	9.89%	41.35%	45.26%	0.67%	2.49%							2.58%	1.72%							6.98%	4.18%
23	1982	38.86%	37.30%	11.17%	9.12%	42.57%	47.26%	0.33%	1.01%							3.54%	2.29%							3.54%	3.02%
24	1982	41.09%	39.22%	10.54%	9.36%	38.28%	45.20%		0.00%							6.48%	3.25%							3.60%	2.97%
25	1987	23.71%	27.07%	7.09%	6.45%	40.52%	44.15%	2.17%	1.85%					1.13%	0.40%	7.47%	3.79%			13.57%	11.85%			4.36%	4.44%
26	1989	23.02%	29.29%	9.48%	9.48%	40.73%	44.15%	1.89%	1.21%					5.19%	1.50%	11.43%	4.97%			5.40%	5.49%			2.86%	3.92%
27	1992	16.99%	24.47%	26.08%	19.31%	32.94%	39.11%	1.95%	1.61%					3.51%	1.40%	1.34%	0.67%			5.50%	4.68%	5.28%	2.78%	6.40%	5.97%
28	1997	22.37%	27.95%	11.20%	10.40%	36.38%	39.33%	2.63%	2.55%	2.67%	0.70%	0.28%	0.11%	5.72%	2.76%	0.67%	0.44%	0.57%	0.47%	6.59%	4.68%	5.05%	2.51%	5.87%	8.11%
29	2002	14.46%	22.48%	14.89%	10.77%	37.13%	41.48%	8.91%	6.51%	3.07%	0.80%	0.53%	0.18%	8.04%	3.85%	0.46%	0.22%	0.45%	0.26%	7.10%	3.96%			4.96%	9.49%
30	2007	18.74%	27.32%	14.53%	10.13%	38.75%	41.56%	6.97%	6.94%	2.28%	0.64%	1.77%	0.45%	8.27%	4.69%	0.17%	0.15%	0.12%	0.08%	4.14%	2.73%			4.27%	5.31%
31	2011	29.93%	36.10%	29.32%	19.45%	12.45%	17.45%	8.17%	9.94%	3.59%	1.21%	3.54%	0.97%	3.59%	1.85%	0.24%	0.14%	0.25%	0.09%					8.92%	12.81%
1918-2011		**29.14%**	**30.77%**	**13.87%**	**11.53%**	**38.09%**	**41.86%**	**1.99%**	**1.99%**	**0.61%**	**0.16%**	**0.34%**	**0.09%**	**1.79%**	**0.75%**	**1.74%**	**0.78%**	**0.07%**	**0.04%**	**2.12%**	**1.42%**	**0.52%**	**0.22%**	**9.72%**	**10.38%**

GALWAY EAST 2011

"Labour wins its first seat in this constituency as Fine Gael in contention for three out of four seats"

There were no Constituency Commission boundary changes here since 2007 and it remained a four-seat constituency.

The long-serving outgoing Fine Gael deputies Paul Connaughton and Ulick Burke retired so Fine Gael had to field a new team. They managed to convert their 2.1 quotas into two seats and were even in contention for a remarkable three out of four. Paul Connaughton, son of the former deputy, topped the poll with 7,255 first preferences. He was just ahead of former Progressive Democrats leader and outgoing Senator Ciaran Cannon and they were both elected on the penultimate count. Tom McHugh was in the frame in fourth place on the first count with half a quota and in contention for the final seat. Fine Gael's fourth candidate Jimmy McClearn was in sixth place on the first count.

The big battle in this constituency was for the final seat with five candidates in contention. The Labour vote was up ten points and with 0.7 quotas they were well placed for a seat but their vote was spread over two candidates which made their task more difficult. Colm Keaveney was well outside the frame in eighth place on the first count and with just 0.4 quotas, but he did well on transfers and went on to beat McHugh for the final seat. This was the biggest move throughout a count achieved in this election and Keaveney was helped in no small way by a 53% transfer from his running mate Lorraine Higgins, which resulted in him leap-frogging McHugh and he retained his advantage with a final winning margin of 1,278 votes.

Fianna Fáil had another poor performance in this constituency with its vote down by 22 points and the party lost one of its outgoing seats. Long-serving TD Noel Treacy retired ahead of the election. Their other outgoing deputy Micheal Kitt was in third place on the first count. He was helped by 64% of Dolan's transfers and this moved him up to first place and he retained this lead and got elected on the eight count. His running mate Michael Dolan was well off the pace with just 4,109 first preferences and was never in contention.

The Independents did well in this constituency winning nearly a quota between the three of them. Sean Canney was in fifth place on the first count with 5,567 and Tim Broderick was in seventh with 5,137 first preferences. Broderick moved into fourth place with the help of 28% of fellow Ballinasloe based Dermot Connolly's (Sinn Fein) transfers on the third count and he maintained this position until the seventh count. The Tuam factor then came into play with Canney's transfers favouring McHugh and Keaveney and Broderick was eliminated by a mere five votes.

GALWAY EAST TDs 2011

MICHAEL P. KITT (FF)

Castleblakeney, Ballinasloe, Co. Galway, Tel: 090 9678147; Mobile: 087 2544345;
Leinster House: 01 6183473; Email: michael.kitt@oireachtas.ie

Born Tuam, Co. Galway 17th May 1950. Married to Catherine Mannion, three sons, one daughter. Educated St. Jarlath's College, Tuam, St. Patrick's Teacher Training College, Drumcondra, Dublin; UCD (BA, HDipEd) and UCG. Former Teacher. First elected to the Dail in 1975 in a by-election caused by the death of his father Michael F. Kitt. Lost his seat in 1977. Re-elected 1981 and at each subsequent election until 2002. Re-elected 2007 and 2009.

Appointed Leas Ceann Comhairle March 2011. Party spokesperson on Housing, Planning and Gaeltacht Affairs. Member Committee on the Implementation of the Good Friday Agreement. Minister of State at the Department of Environment, Heritage and Local Government with special responsibility for Local Services May 2008-April 2009. Minister of State at the Department of Foreign Affairs with special responsibility for Overseas Development June 2007-May 2008. Member Joint Committee on Foreign Affairs; Agriculture, Food and the Marine; Education and Science 2002-2007. Fianna Fail spokesperson on Emigration and the Third World 1995-1997. Minister of State at the Department of An Taoiseach 1991-1992. Senator 1977-1981, 2002-2007. Member Galway County Council 1975-1991 (Chairman 1985-1986). Member of Observer Committee to the Western European Union. Son of Michael F. Kitt, Dáil Deputy 1948-1951, 1957-1975. Brother of former Minister of State Tom Kitt, Dáil Deputy for Dublin South 1987-2011 and Aine Brady Minister of State and TD for Kildare North 2007-2011.

PAUL CONNAUGHTON (FG)

Ballinlass, Mountbellew, Ballinasloe, Co. Galway; Tel: 090 9679249; Mobile: 087 2354682
Leinster House: 01 6184373; Email: paul.connaughton@oireachtas.ie
Website; www.paulconnaughton.finegael.ie

Born Mountbellew, Co. Galway 18th January 1982. Married to Edel Burke. Educated Holy Rosary College, Mountbellew; Mountbellew Agricultural College; GMIT (Business degree). NUI Galway (HDip in Marketing). Former Youth Worker with Foróige.
First elected 2011.

Member Committee of Public Accounts. First elected to Galway County Council in the Ballinasloe electoral area in 2009. Son of Paul Connaughton TD for Galway East 1981-2011.

CIARAN CANNON (FG)

Carrabane, Athenry, Co. Galway; Tel: 091 847668; Mobile: 087 2283377
Constituency Office: King Street, Loughrea, Co. Galway; Tel: 091 880790
Leinster House: 01 6183185; Email: ciaran.cannon@oireachtas.ie
Website: www.ciarancannon.ie

Born Kiltulla, Co. Galway 19th September 1965. Married to Niamh Lawless, one son. Educated Presentation College, Athenry, Co. Galway and Trinity College Dublin (Computer Science). Minister of State and former Chief Executive The Irish Pilgrimage Trust, national charity caring for children and young people with disabilities. Contested 2007 general election in Galway East for PD's.
First elected 2011.

Appointed Minister of State at the Department of Education and Skills with special responsibility for Training and Skills March 2011. Leader of the Progressive Democrats 17th April 2008-8th November 2008. Joined Fine Gael 2009. Taoiseach's nominee to Seanad Eireann 2007-2011. Member Joint Committee on the Environment, Heritage and Local Government 2007-2011. Member Galway County Council 2004-2007. Former Chairman Carrabane Community Council.

.

COLM KEAVENEY (LB)

Kilcreevanty, Tuam, Co. Galway; Tel: 093 60586; Mobile: 087 6776812
Leinster House: 01 6183821; Email: colm.keaveney@oireachtas.ie.
Website: www.colmkeaveney.ie

Born Dunmore, Co. Galway 11th January 1971. Married to Deirdre, 3 sons. Educated St. Jarlath's College, Tuam; Letterkenny IT; Smurfit Business School, UCD. Former Trade Union Official. Contested 1997 and 2007 Dail elections in Galway East. First elected 2011.

Member Committee on Communications, Natural Resources and Agriculture. Member Select Committee on European Union Affairs. Resigned from Labour Party in August 2007 but rejoined on 30th June 2008.Contested 1999 local elections. First elected to Galway County Council in 2004 in the Tuam electoral area. Retained his seat in 2009. Elected to Tuam Town Council in 1999. Did not contest in 2004. President of Union of Students' in Ireland in 1995-1996.

GALWAY EAST 2011							
FIRST PREFERENCE VOTES							
	Seats	4			11,856		
	Candidate	Party	1st	%	Quota	Count	Status
1	**Kitt, Michael P.***	**FF**	**6,585**	**11.11%**	**0.56**	**8**	**Made Quota**
2	**Connaughton, Paul**	**FG**	**7,255**	**12.24%**	**0.61**	**8**	**Made Quota**
3	**Cannon, Ciaran**	**FG**	**6,927**	**11.69%**	**0.58**	**8**	**Made Quota**
4	**Keaveney, Colm**	**LB**	**4,254**	**7.18%**	**0.36**	**9**	**Elected**
5	McHugh, Tom	FG	5,832	9.84%	0.49	9	Not Elected
6	Broderick, Tim	NP	5,137	8.67%	0.43	7	Eliminated
7	Canney, Seán	NP	5,567	9.39%	0.47	6	Eliminated
8	McClearn, Jimmy	FG	5,395	9.10%	0.46	5	Eliminated
9	Higgins, Lorrainne	LB	3,577	6.03%	0.30	4	Eliminated
10	Dolan, Michael F.	FF	4,109	6.93%	0.35	3	Eliminated
11	Connolly, Dermot	SF	3,635	6.13%	0.31	2	Eliminated
12	O'Donnell, Emer	NP	601	1.01%	0.05	1	No Expenses
13	Kennedy, Ciaran	GP	402	0.68%	0.03	1	No Expenses
13	***Outgoing**		**59,276**	**100.00%**	**11,856**	**2,965**	**No Expenses**

GALWAY EAST 2011												
PARTY VOTE												
	2011					2007					Change	
Party	Cand	1st	%	Quota	Seats	Cand	1st	%	Quota	Seats	%	Seats
FG	4	25,409	42.87%	2.14	2	4	21,832	39.13%	1.96	2	+3.74%	+0
LB	2	7,831	13.21%	0.66	1	1	1,747	3.13%	0.16		+10.08%	+1
FF	2	10,694	18.04%	0.90	1	3	22,137	39.68%	1.98	2	-21.64%	-1
SF	1	3,635	6.13%	0.31		1	1,789	3.21%	0.16		+2.93%	
GP	1	402	0.68%	0.03		1	1,057	1.89%	0.09		-1.22%	
PD						1	3,321	5.95%	0.30		-5.95%	
Others	3	11,305	19.07%	0.95		3	3,911	7.01%	0.35		+12.06%	
Total	**13**	**59,276**	**100.0%**	**11,856**	**4**	**14**	**55,794**	**100.0%**	**11,159**	**4**	**0.00%**	**0**
Electorate		**83,651**	**70.86%**				**81,684**	**68.30%**			**+2.56%**	
Spoiled		**560**	**0.94%**				**480**	**0.85%**			**+0.08%**	
Turnout		**59,836**	**71.53%**				**56,274**	**68.89%**			**+2.64%**	

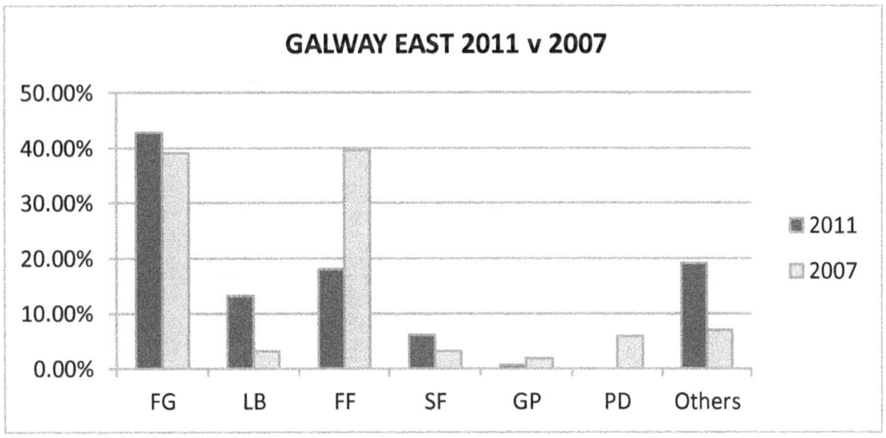

GALWAY EAST 2011 COUNT DETAILS										
Seats	4								Quota	11,856
Candidate	**Party**	**1st**	**2nd** O'Donnell Kennedy	**3rd** Connolly Votes	**4th** Dolan Votes	**5th** Higgins Votes	**6th** McClearn Votes	**7th** Canney Votes	**8th** Broderick Votes	**9th** Kitt Surplus
			+47	+228	+2,666	+267	+430	+892	+1,735	-994
Kitt, Michael P.*	FF	6,585	6,632	6,860	9,526	9,793	10,223	11,115	12,850	11,856
			+55	+247	+245	+289	+1,733	+1,053	+1,733	
Connaughton, Paul	FG	7,255	7,310	7,557	7,802	8,091	9,824	10,877	12,610	12,610
			+134	+207	+297	+560	+1,837	+317	+1,582	
Cannon, Ciaran	FG	6,927	7,061	7,268	7,565	8,125	9,962	10,279	11,861	11,861
			+90	+349	+92	+2,451	+233	+1,167	+1,170	+320
Keaveney, Colm	LB	4,254	4,344	4,693	4,785	7,236	7,469	8,636	9,806	10,126
			+36	+82	+84	+91	+611	+1,635	+294	+183
McHugh, Tom	FG	5,832	5,868	5,950	6,034	6,125	6,736	8,371	8,665	8,848
			+105	+1,036	+238	+330	+795	+724	-8,365	
Broderick, Tim	NP	5,137	5,242	6,278	6,516	6,846	7,641	8,365	Eliminated	
			+78	+295	+187	+214	+90	-6,431		
Canney, Seán	NP	5,567	5,645	5,940	6,127	6,341	6,431	Eliminated		
			+45	+194	+144	+209	-5,987			
McClearn, Jimmy	FG	5,395	5,440	5,634	5,778	5,987	Eliminated			
			+236	+610	+228	-4,651				
Higgins, Lorrainne	LB	3,577	3,813	4,423	4,651	Eliminated				
			+46	+135	-4,290					
Dolan, Michael F.	FF	4,109	4,155	4,290	Eliminated					
			+88	-3,723						
Connolly, Dermot	SF	3,635	3,723	Eliminated						
			-601							
O'Donnell, Emer	NP	601	Eliminated							
			-402							
Kennedy, Ciaran	GP	402	Eliminated							
Non-transferable			+43	+340	+109	+240	+258	+643	+1,851	+491
Cumulative			43	383	492	732	990	1,633	3,484	3,975
Total		**59,276**	**59,276**	**59,276**	**59,276**	**59,276**	**59,276**	**59,276**	**59,276**	**59,276**

GALWAY EAST 2011 TRANSFER ANALYSIS							
From	**To**	**FG**	**LB**	**FF**	**SF**	**Others**	**Non Trans**
FG	5,987	4,181	233	430		885	258
		69.83%	3.89%	7.18%		14.78%	4.31%
LB	4,651	1,149	2,451	267		544	240
		24.70%	52.70%	5.74%		11.70%	5.16%
FF	5,284	953	640	2,666		425	600
		18.04%	12.11%	50.45%		8.04%	11.36%
SF	3,723	730	959	363		1,331	340
		19.61%	25.76%	9.75%		35.75%	9.13%
GP	402	108	131	37	36	73	17
		26.87%	32.59%	9.20%	8.96%	18.16%	4.23%
Others	15,397	6,776	2,532	2,683	52	834	2,520
		44.01%	16.44%	17.43%	0.34%	5.42%	16.37%
Total	**35,444**	**13,897**	**6,946**	**6,446**	**88**	**4,092**	**3,975**
		39.21%	**19.60%**	**18.19%**	**0.25%**	**11.54%**	**11.21%**

GALWAY EAST		
MAIN BOUNDARY CHANGES		
Dail	**Constituency**	**Seats**
9 (1937) - 12 (1944)	Galway East	4
17 (1961) - 18 (1965)	Galway East	5
19 (1969) - 20 (1973)	Galway North-East	3
21 (1977)	Galway East	4
22 (1981) - 27 (1992)	Galway East	3
28 (1997) - 31 (2011)	Galway East	4

GALWAY EAST All TDs 1937-2011																		
	Surname	**Forename**	**Party**	**Elected**														**Total**
1	Kitt	Michael P.	FF	75*	81	82	82	87	89	92	97	07	11					10
2	Connaughton	Paul	FG	81	82	82	87	89	92	97	02	07						9
3	Treacy	Noel	FF	82*	82	87	89	92	97	02	07							8
4	Donnellan**	John	FG	64*	65	69	73	77										5
5	Beegan**	Patrick	FF	37	38	43	44											4
6	Fahy**	Frank	FF	37	38	43	44											4
7	Killilea(sen)**	Mark	FF	37	38	43	44											4
8	Kitt**	Michael F.	FF	61	65	69	73											4
9	Donnellan**	Michael	CnaT	43	44	61												3
10	Hussey	Thomas	FF	69	73	77												3
11	Callanan**	John	FF	77	81	82F												3
12	Broderick**	Sean	FG	37	38													2
13	Carty**	Michael	FF	61	65													2
14	Hogan-O'Higgins**	Brigid	FG	61	65													2
15	Millar**	Anthony	FF	61	65													2
16	Burke	Ulick	FG	97	07													2
17	Killilea**	Mark	FF	77														1
18	Callanan	Joe	FF	02														1
19	McHugh	Paddy	NP	02														1
20	Connaughton	Paul	FG	11														1
21	Cannon	Ciaran	FG	11														1
22	Keaveney	Colm	LB	11														1
22	**Total**										***Includes 3 By-Elections**						*	**73**
	****Also elected in another constituency**																	
1	Fahy**	Frank	FF	Galway/South				18	21	22	23	27	27	32	33	48	51	10
2	Killilea(sen)**	Mark	FF	Galway/North				27	27	33	48	51	54	57				7
3	Beegan**	Patrick	FF	Galway/South				32	33	48	51	54	57					6
4	Broderick**	Sean	FG	Galway				23	27	27	32	33						5
5	Donnellan**	Michael	CnaT	Galway North				48	51	54	57							4
6	Donnellan**	John	FG	Galway West				81	82	82	87							4
7	Hogan-O'Higgins**	Brigid	FG	Galway South				57	69	73								3
8	Kitt**	Michael F.	FF	Galway North				48	57									2
9	Carty**	Michael	FF	Galway South				57	69									2
10	Millar**	Anthony	FF	Galway South				58*										1
11	Callanan**	John	FF	Galway South				73										1
12	Killilea**	Mark	FF	Galway West				81										1
12	**Total**										***Includes 1 By-Election**						*	**46**

GALWAY EAST 1937-2011																				
		FG		LB		FF		SF		GP		CS		PD		C na T		Others	
Dail	**Seats**	**S**	**% Vote**	**S**	**% Vote**	**S**	**% Vote**	**S**	**% Vote**	**S**	**% Vote**	**S**	**% Vote**	**S**	**% Vote**	**S**	**% Vote**	**S**	**% Vote**
9 1937	4	1	29.92%		10.83%	3	59.24%												
10 1938	4	1	29.91%		7.86%	3	62.23%												
11 1943	4		7.93%		13.96%	3	49.44%									1	28.67%		
12 1944	4					3	61.04%									1	38.96%		
17 1961	5	1	21.80%			3	54.74%		8.70%							1	14.76%		
18 1965	5	2	41.84%			3	54.31%												3.85%
19 1969	3	1	42.71%		6.60%	2	50.69%												
20 1973	3	1	42.03%			2	57.97%												
21 1977	4	1	34.19%		1.96%	3	58.86%												4.99%
22 1981	3	1	47.09%			2	52.91%												
23 1982	3	1	41.92%		2.95%	2	55.14%												
24 1982	3	1	45.17%		2.82%	2	51.51%												0.50%
25 1987	3	1	31.63%			2	51.78%								16.59%				
26 1989	3	1	39.11%			2	59.47%												1.41%
27 1992	3	1	31.66%		5.46%	2	48.48%		1.05%						13.35%				
28 1997	4	2	31.17%		7.92%	2	48.60%								7.41%				4.90%
29 2002	4	1	31.52%			2	46.77%		3.70%		2.07%		0.19%					1	15.75%
30 2007	4	2	39.13%		3.13%	2	39.68%		3.21%		1.89%		0.52%		5.95%				6.49%
31 2011	4	2	42.87%	1	13.21%	1	18.04%		6.13%		0.68%								19.07%
1937-2011	**70**	**21**	**33.41%**	**1**	**4.28%**	**44**	**49.98%**		**1.55%**		**0.35%**		**0.05%**		**2.22%**	**3**	**4.06%**	**1**	**4.10%**
National	**4,618**	**1,453**	**30.77%**	**482**	**11.53%**	**1,985**	**41.86%**	**232**	**1.99%**	**16**	**0.75%**		**0.04%**	**44**	**1.42%**	**43**	**1.08%**	**363**	**10.55%**

GALWAY WEST 2011

"Fine Gael hold off independents for the final seat"

There were no Constituency Commission boundary changes here since 2007 and it remained a five-seat constituency.

Veteran Fine Gael TD Pádraic McCormack retired prior to the 2007 general election but was persuaded to run again and went on to retain his seat. He had decided to run again in 2011 but was beaten at the convention and finally retired. The Fine Gael vote was up ten points and with 1.8 quotas they should have been well placed for two seats but their vote was divided over four candidates and this led to them struggling for the final seat. Brian Walsh was in fourth place on the first count with 5,425 votes and he went on to take the third seat on the penultimate count. Their second candidate Sean Kyne had a much tougher battle. He was outside the frame in seventh place on the first count behind independent candidate Catherine Connolly and running mate Fidelma Healy-Eames. He battled with both of them throughout the count and was just 54 votes ahead of his running mate when she was eliminated at the end of the 11th count. He then fell behind Connolly on the 12th count and had to rely on a better share of Walsh's small surplus to finally see off Connolly by a mere 17 votes. This was the closest winning margin of this election.

The long-serving Labour TD and former Minister Michael D Higgins retired at this election as he intends to seek the Labour nomination for the Presidential election. In his absence, the Labour party turned to councillor Derek Nolan and he put in an impressive performance and topped the poll with 7,489 first preferences and went on to take the second seat on the tenth count.

The Fianna Fáil vote was down 16 points and with just 1.3 quotas spread over their three candidates, one seat was as much as they could hope for. Outgoing Minister Eamon Ó Cuív was in second place on the first count with 7,441 and he went on to comfortably retain his seat on the eight count. Long serving TD Frank Fahey did poorly, winning just 6% and he was eliminated on the 7th count. Fianna Fáil's third candidate, Michael Crowe got just 3% and was never in contention.

Noel Grealish was elected for the Progressive Democrats in 2007 but he became an independent on the dissolution of the party in 2009. He was in third place on the first count and went on to take the fourth seat on the final count. Former Labour councillor Catherine Connolly was outside the frame in sixth place on the first count with just half a quota and she was just ahead of Kyne of Fine Gael. She battled with Fine Gael for the final seat but eventually lost out following a couple of recounts.

Sinn Fein's Trevor Ó Clochartaigh doubled the party's vote but with just 6%, was too far off the pace in eighth place.

GALWAY WEST TDs 2011

EAMON Ó CUÍV (FF)

Corr na Móna, Conamara, Co. na Gaillimhe; Tel: 094 9548021
Constituency Office: 3 Plás Victoria, Gailimh, Tel: 091 562846
Leinster House: 01 6184231; Email: eamon.ocuiv@oireachtas.ie

Born Dublin 1st June 1950. Married to Áine Ni Choincheannain, three sons, one daughter. Educated Oatlands College, Mount Merrion, Dublin; UCD (BSc). Formerly Co-op Manager. First elected 1992 and at each subsequent election.

Appointed Deputy Leader Fianna Fail 4th August 2011. But resigned 29th February 2012 due to the party's position on the European Fiscal Compact Treaty. Party spokesperson on Communications, Energy and Natural Resources 2011-29th February 2012. Member Committee on Communications, Natural Resources and Agriculture. Minister for Social Protection 23rd March 2010-March 2011. Minister for Community, Rural and Gaeltacht Affairs 7th May 2008-March 2010. Minister for Community, Rural and Gaeltacht Affairs June 2007-May 2008. Minister for Community, Rural and Family Affairs 2002-2007. Minister of State at the Department of Agriculture, Food and Rural Development 2001-2002. Minister of State at the Department of Arts, Heritage, Gaeltacht and Islands with special responsibility for the Gaeltacht areas and Irish Language and for Island Development 1997-2001. Senator 1989-1992. Member Galway County Council 1991-1997. Former Manager of a Gaeltacht Co-operative involved in agricultural services including agriculture, timber milling, tourism and cultural and social development. He is a cousin of Sile de Valera TD for Dublin Mid-County 1977-1981 and Clare 1987-2007; MEP 1979-1984. Grandson of Eamon de Valera, President of Ireland 1959-1973; Taoiseach 1937-1948, 1951-1954, 1957-1959; President of the Executive Council of the Irish Free State 1932-1937; President, first Dáil 1919-1921; President, second Dáil 1921-1922.

DEREK NOLAN (LB)

3 Crescent View, Riverside, Galway; Tel: 091 561006; Mobile: 086 3777624
Leinster House: 01 6183287; Email: derek.nolan@oireachtas.ie
Website: www.dereknolan.com

Born Galway October 1982. Single. Educated St. Mary's College, Galway; NUI Galway. Trainee Solicitor. Elected at his first attempt in 2011.

Youngest Labour TD in 31st Dáil. Member Public Accounts Committee. Member Committee on Investigations, Oversight and Petitions. First elected to Galway City Council in 2009.

BRIAN WALSH (FG)

5 Drum East, Bushypark, Galway; Mobile: 086 8333054; Leinster House: 01 6184236; Email: brian.walsh@oireachtas.ie; Website: www.brianwalshcampaign.ie

Born Galway, 28th September 1972. Married to Fiona Flatley, one daughter. Educated St. Joseph's College, Nun's Island ("The Bish"), Galway; GMIT. Financial Consultant. Elected at his first attempt in 2011.

Member Committee on Environment, Transport, Culture and the Gaeltacht. First elected to Galway City Council in 2004 in Galway East. Retained his seat in 2009 in Galway City East.

NOEL GREALISH (NP)

Carnmore, Oranmore, Co. Galway, Tel: 091 794991; Mobile: 086 8509466
Constituency Office: Unit 14, Briarhill Business Park, Briarhill, Galway; Tel: 091 764807
Leinster House: 01 6184280; Email: noel.grealish@oireachtas.ie

Born Galway 16th December 1965. Single. Educated St. Mary's College, Galway. Businessman. First elected 2002 for PD's. Retained his seat in 2007. Changed to Independent following dissolution of PD's in April 2009 and retained his seat as an independent in 2011.

Member Joint Committee on European Scrutiny and Member Committee on Members' Interests Dail Eireann 2007-2011. Member Dail Committee on Procedure and Privileges 2007-2011. Member Joint Committee on Environment and Local Government; Joint House Services Committee; Agriculture Committee and Roads Special Policy Committee 2002-2007. Chairman PD Parliamentary Party 2004-2009. Member Galway County Council 1999-2003. Member Carnmore Hurling Club.

SEAN KYNE (FG)

Clydagh, Moycullen, Co. Galway; Tel: 091 555174; Mobile: 087 6137372
Leinster House: 01 6184426; Email: sean.kyne@oireachtas.ie; Website: www.seankyne.ie

Born Galway 16th May 1975. Single. Educated St. Mary's College, Galway; NUI Galway; UCD (Masters in Agricultural Science). Agricultural Consultant. Contested 2007 Dail election in Galway West. First elected 2011.

Member Committee on European Union Affairs. Member Committee on Jobs, Social Protection and Education. Contested 2007 Seanad election on Agricultural Panel. First elected to Galway County Council in Conamara electoral area in 2004. Retained his seat in 2009.

GALWAY WEST 2011							
FIRST PREFERENCE VOTES							
	Seats	**5**			**10,105**		
	Candidate	**Party**	**1st**	**%**	**Quota**	**Count**	**Status**
1	**Cuív, Éamon Ó***	**FF**	**7,441**	**12.27%**	**0.74**	**8**	**Made Quota**
2	**Nolan, Derek**	**LB**	**7,489**	**12.35%**	**0.74**	**10**	**Made Quota**
3	**Walsh, Brian**	**FG**	**5,425**	**8.95%**	**0.54**	**12**	**Made Quota**
4	**Grealish, Noel***	**NP**	**6,229**	**10.27%**	**0.62**	**13**	**Elected**
5	**Kyne, Seán**	**FG**	**4,550**	**7.51%**	**0.45**	**13**	**Elected**
6	Connolly, Catherine	NP	4,766	7.86%	0.47	13	Not Elected
7	Healy Eames, Fidelma	FG	5,046	8.32%	0.50	11	Eliminated
8	Ó Clochartaigh, Trevor	SF	3,808	6.28%	0.38	9	Eliminated
9	Fahey, Frank*	FF	3,448	5.69%	0.34	7	Eliminated
10	Naughten, Hildegarde	FG	3,606	5.95%	0.36	6	Eliminated
11	Welby, Thomas	NP	3,298	5.44%	0.33	5	Eliminated
12	Crowe, Michael	FF	1,814	2.99%	0.18	4	No Expenses
13	Walsh, Eamon	NP	1,481	2.44%	0.15	3	No Expenses
14	Brolcháin, Niall Ó	GP	1,120	1.85%	0.11	2	No Expenses
15	Cubbard, Mike	NP	853	1.41%	0.08	1	No Expenses
16	Holmes, Uinseann Eoin	NP	186	0.31%	0.02	1	No Expenses
17	King, Thomas	NP	65	0.11%	0.01	1	No Expenses
17	***Outgoing**		**60,625**	**100.00%**	**10,105**	**2,527**	**No Expenses**

GALWAY WEST 2011												
PARTY VOTE												
	2011					**2007**					**Change**	
Party	**Cand**	**1st**	**%**	**Quota**	**Seats**	**Cand**	**1st**	**%**	**Quota**	**Seats**	**%**	**Seats**
FG	4	18,627	30.72%	1.84	2	3	11,235	20.39%	1.22	1	+10.33%	+1
LB	1	7,489	12.35%	0.74	1	1	6,086	11.05%	0.66	1	+1.31%	
FF	3	12,703	20.95%	1.26	1	3	20,468	37.15%	2.23	2	-16.20%	-1
SF	1	3,808	6.28%	0.38		1	1,629	2.96%	0.18		+3.32%	
GP	1	1,120	1.85%	0.11		1	3,026	5.49%	0.33		-3.64%	
PD						3	8,868	16.10%	0.97	1	-16.10%	-1
Others	7	16,878	27.84%	1.67	1	3	3,784	6.87%	0.41		+20.97%	+1
Total	**17**	**60,625**	**100.0%**	**10,105**	**5**	**15**	**55,096**	**100.0%**	**9,183**	**5**	**0.00%**	**0**
Electorate		**88,840**	**68.24%**				**86,602**	**63.62%**			**+4.62%**	
Spoiled		**643**	**1.05%**				**533**	**0.96%**			**+0.09%**	
Turnout		**61,268**	**68.96%**				**55,629**	**64.24%**			**+4.73%**	

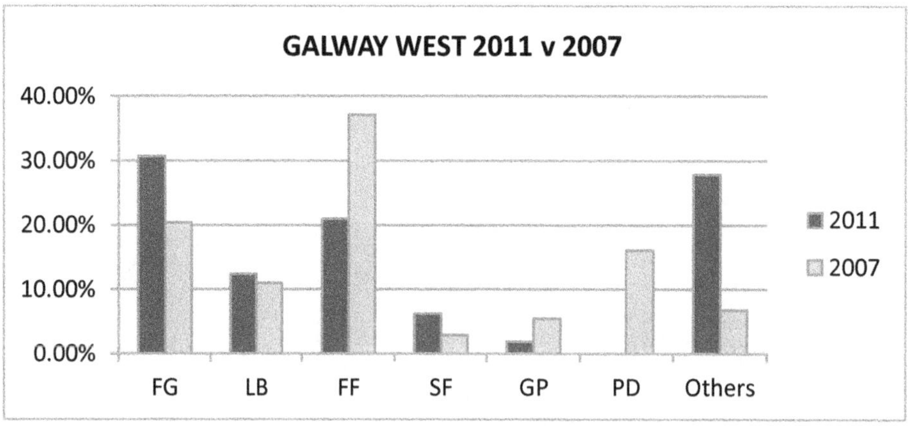

GALWAY WEST 2011
COUNT DETAILS

Seats 5 | Quota 10,105

Candidate	Party	1st	2nd Cubbard Holmes King	3rd O Brolchain Votes	4th Walsh, E Votes	5th Crowe Votes	6th Welby Votes	7th Naughton Votes	8th Fahey Votes	9th Cuiv Surplus	10th O Clochartaigh Votes	11th Nolan Surplus	12th Healy-E Votes	13th Walsh, B Surplus
			+45	+61	+102	+549	+729	+108	+2,103	-1,033				
Cuiv, Éamon Ó*	FF	7,441	7,486	7,547	7,649	8,198	8,927	9,035	11,138	10,105	10,105	10,105	10,105	10,105
			+183	+334	+260	+197	+240	+416	+189	+107	+1,016	-326		
Nolan, Derek	LB	7,489	7,672	8,006	8,266	8,463	8,703	9,119	9,308	9,415	10,431	10,105	10,105	10,105
			+48	+42	+129	+225	+95	+1,044	+234	+101	+148	+29	+2,707	-122
Walsh, Brian	FG	5,425	5,473	5,515	5,644	5,869	5,964	7,008	7,242	7,343	7,491	7,520	10,227	10,105
			+117	+50	+193	+221	+306	+208	+592	+396	+370	+54	+1,075	+18
Grealish, Noel*	NP	6,229	6,346	6,396	6,589	6,810	7,116	7,324	7,916	8,312	8,682	8,736	9,811	9,829
			+31	+49	+74	+25	+1,012	+729	+151	+84	+324	+45	+1,946	+92
Kyne, Seán	FG	4,550	4,581	4,630	4,704	4,729	5,741	6,470	6,621	6,705	7,029	7,074	9,020	9,112
			+207	+241	+285	+104	+285	+260	+242	+161	+1,656	+168	+708	+12
Connolly, Catherine	NP	4,766	4,973	5,214	5,499	5,603	5,888	6,148	6,390	6,551	8,207	8,375	9,083	9,095
			+34	+93	+117	+57	+140	+1,055	+170	+89	+189	+30	-7,020	
Healy Eames, Fidelma	FG	5,046	5,080	5,173	5,290	5,347	5,487	6,542	6,712	6,801	6,990	7,020	Eliminated	
			+119	+72	+97	+45	+266	+40	+141	+95	-4,683			
Ó Clochartaigh, Trevor	SF	3,808	3,927	3,999	4,096	4,141	4,407	4,447	4,588	4,683	Eliminated			
			+26	+15	+37	+307	+184	+45	-4,062					
Fahey, Frank*	FF	3,448	3,474	3,489	3,526	3,833	4,017	4,062	Eliminated					
			+49	+90	+113	+50	+85	-3,993						
Naughten, Hildegarde	FG	3,606	3,655	3,745	3,858	3,908	3,993	Eliminated						
			+27	+20	+139	+20	-3,504							
Welby, Thomas	NP	3,298	3,325	3,345	3,484	3,504	Eliminated							
			+41	+15	+25	-1,895								
Crowe, Michael	FF	1,814	1,855	1,870	1,895	Eliminated								
			+100	+43	-1,624									
Walsh, Eamon	NP	1,481	1,581	1,624	Eliminated									
			+33	-1,153										
Brolcháin, Niall Ó	GP	1,120	1,153	Eliminated										
			-853											
Cubbard, Mike	NP	853	Eliminated											
			-186											
Holmes, Uinseann Eoin	NP	186	Eliminated											
			-65											
King, Thomas	NP	65	Eliminated											
Non-transferable			+44	+28	+53	+95	+162	+88	+240		+980		+584	
Cumulative			44	72	125	220	382	470	710	710	1,690	1,690	2,274	2,274
Total		**60,625**	**60,625**	**60,625**	**60,625**	**60,625**	**60,625**	**60,625**	**60,625**	**60,625**	**60,625**	**60,625**	**60,625**	**60,625**

GALWAY WEST 2011
TRANSFER ANALYSIS

From	To	FG	LB	FF	SF	GP	Others	Non Trans
FG	11,135	7,573	416	153	40		2,281	672
		68.01%	*3.74%*	*1.37%*	*0.36%*		*20.48%*	*6.04%*
LB	326	104					222	
		31.90%					*68.10%*	
FF	6,990	1,186	493	2,959	281		1,736	335
		16.97%	*7.05%*	*42.33%*	*4.02%*		*24.84%*	*4.79%*
SF	4,683	661	1,016				2,026	980
		14.11%	*21.70%*				*43.26%*	*20.93%*
GP	1,153	274	334	91	72		354	28
		23.76%	*28.97%*	*7.89%*	*6.24%*		*30.70%*	*2.43%*
Others	6,232	1,927	683	1,189	482	33	1,659	259
		30.92%	*10.96%*	*19.08%*	*7.73%*	*0.53%*	*26.62%*	*4.16%*
Total	**30,519**	**11,725**	**2,942**	**4,392**	**875**	**33**	**8,278**	**2,274**
		38.42%	***9.64%***	***14.39%***	***2.87%***	***0.11%***	***27.12%***	***7.45%***

GALWAY WEST		
MAIN BOUNDARY CHANGES		
Dail	**Constituency**	**Seats**
9 (1937) - 20 (1973)	Galway West	3
21 (1977)	Galway West	4
22 (1981) - 31 (2011)	Galway West	5

GALWAY WEST															
All TDs 1937-2011															
	Surname	**Forename**	**Party**	**Elected**											**Total**
1	Molloy	Bobby	PD	65	69	73	77	81	82	82	87	89	92	97	11
2	Bartley	Gerald	FF	37	38	43	44	48	51	54	57	61			9
3	Geoghegan-Quinn	Maire	FF	75*	77	81	82	82	87	89	92				8
4	Higgins	Michael D.	LB	81	82F	87	89	92	97	02	07				8
5	Fahey	Frank	FF	82	82	87	89	97	02	07					7
6	Coogan	Fintan	FG	54	57	61	65	69	73						6
7	Geoghegan	John	FF	54	57	61	65	69	73						6
8	Mongan	Joseph	FG	37	38	43	44	48							5
9	McCormack	Padraic	FG	89	92	97	02	07							5
10	Ó Cuív	Eamon	FF	92	97	02	07	11							5
11	Donnellan	John	FG	81	82	82	87								4
12	Grealish	Noel	PD	02	07	11									3
13	Tubridy	Seán	FF	37	38										2
14	Lydon	Michael	FF	44	48										2
15	Keane	John	FF	40*											1
16	Corbett	Eamonn	FF	43											1
17	Duignan	Peadar	FF	51											1
18	Mannion	John	FG	51											1
19	Loughnane**	Bill	FF	77											1
20	Mannion	John M.	FG	77											1
21	Killilea	Mark	FF	81											1
22	Coogan	Fintan	FG	82N											1
23	Nolan	Derek	LB	11											1
24	Walsh	Brian	FG	11											1
25	Kyne	Seán	FG	11											1
25	**Total**							***Includes 2 By-Elections**						*	**92**
	**** Also elected in another constituency**														
	Loughnane**	Bill	FF	Clare-Galway South					69	73					2

GALWAY WEST 1937-2011																										
			FG		LB		FF		SF		GP		WP		PD		DL		C na P		C na T		Nat Lab		Others	
Dail		Seats	S	% Vote	S	% Vote	S	% Vote	S	% Vote	S	% Vote	S	% Vote	S	% Vote	S	% Vote	S	% Vote	S	% Vote	S	% Vote	S	% Vote
9	1937	3	1	28.08%			2	71.92%																		
10	1938	3	1	24.38%		7.15%	2	68.47%																		
11	1943	3	1	22.23%		9.86%	2	46.47%														13.55%				7.90%
12	1944	3	1	27.60%			2	60.24%																		12.16%
13	1948	3	1	21.86%			2	49.67%												13.36%				15.11%		
14	1951	3	1	31.15%		8.84%	2	53.18%												6.83%						
15	1954	3	1	34.76%		3.11%	2	53.46%												8.67%						
16	1957	3	1	40.84%			2	59.16%																		
17	1961	3	1	32.92%		8.19%	2	45.85%												7.94%						5.10%
18	1965	3	1	39.44%		7.31%	2	53.25%																		
19	1969	3	1	28.17%		11.36%	2	54.05%																		6.42%
20	1973	3	1	26.45%		13.48%	2	53.91%																		6.16%
21	1977	4	1	27.03%		11.69%	3	59.09%						2.19%												
22	1981	5	1	30.00%	1	12.25%	3	55.07%						2.13%												0.56%
23	1982	5	1	28.42%	1	11.77%	3	57.32%						2.49%												
24	1982	5	2	34.06%		9.02%	3	53.30%						3.62%												
25	1987	5	1	18.19%	1	7.35%	2	37.87%						2.97%	1	21.53%										12.09%
26	1989	5	1	22.87%	1	15.66%	2	39.82%						3.15%	1	18.07%										0.43%
27	1992	5	1	16.92%	1	17.68%	2	43.77%		0.69%					1	13.39%		0.78%								6.76%
28	1997	5	1	22.21%	1	10.07%	2	45.94%		2.51%		3.44%			1	12.27%										3.55%
29	2002	5	1	16.90%	1	10.54%	2	41.33%		5.62%		4.43%			1	12.52%										8.67%
30	2007	5	1	20.39%	1	11.05%	2	37.15%		2.96%		5.49%			1	16.10%										6.87%
31	2011	5	2	30.72%	1	12.35%	1	20.95%		6.28%		1.85%													1	27.84%
1937-2011		**90**	**25**	**26.04%**	**9**	**9.79%**	**49**	**48.05%**		**1.16%**		**0.95%**		**0.97%**	**6**	**5.72%**		**0.05%**		**0.92%**		**0.45%**		**0.38%**	**1**	**5.51%**
National		**4,618**	**1,453**	**30.77%**	**482**	**11.53%**	**1,985**	**41.86%**	**232**	**1.99%**	**16**	**0.75%**	**17**	**0.78%**	**44**	**1.42%**	**8**	**0.22%**	**18**	**0.77%**	**43**	**1.08%**	**9**	**0.16%**	**311**	**8.65%**

GALWAY REGION		
MAIN BOUNDARY CHANGES		
Dail	**Constituency**	**Seats**
1 (1918)	Galway Connemara	1
	Galway East	1
	Galway North	1
	Galway South	1
2 (1921) - 3 (1922)	Galway	7
4 (1923) -8 (1933)	Galway	9
9 (1937) - 12 (1944)	Galway East	4
	Galway West	3
13 (1948) - 16 (1957)	Galway North	3
	Galway South	3
	Galway West	3
17 (1961) - 18 (1965)	Galway East	5
	Galway West	3
19 (1969) - 20 (1973)	Galway North-East	3
	Galway West	3
	Clare - South Galway	3
21 (1977)	Galway East	4
	Galway West	4
22 (1981) - 27 (1992)	Galway East	3
	Galway West	5
28 (1997) - 31 (2017)	Galway East	4
	Galway West	5

GALWAY REGION																		
All TDs 1918-2011																		
	Surname	**Forename**	**Party**	**Elected**														**Total**
1	Fahy	Frank	FF	18	21	22	23	27	27	32	33	37	38	43	44	48	51	14
2	Killilea(sen)	Mark	FF	27	27	33	37	38	43	44	48	51	54	57				11
3	Bartley	Gerald	FF	32	33	37	38	43	44	48	51	54	57	61				11
4	Molloy	Bobby	PD	65	69	73	77	81	82	82	87	89	92	97				11
5	Beegan	Patrick	FF	32	33	37	38	43	44	48	51	54	57					10
6	Kitt	Michael P.	FF	75*	81	82	82	87	89	92	97	07	11					10
7	Donnellan	John	FG	64*	65	69	73	77	81	82	82	87						9
8	Connaughton	Paul	FG	81	82	82	87	89	92	97	02	07						9
9	Geoghegan-Quinn	Maire	FF	75*	77	81	82	82	87	89	92							8
10	Higgins	Michael D.	LB	81	82F	87	89	92	97	02	07							8
11	Treacy	Noel	FF	82*	82	87	89	92	97	02	07							8
12	Hogan	Patrick J.	CG	21	22	23	27	27	32	33								7
13	Broderick	Sean	FG	23	27	27	32	33	37	38								7
14	Mongan	Joseph	FG	27	32	37	38	43	44	48								7
15	Donnellan	Michael	CnaT	43	44	48	51	54	57	61								7
16	Fahey	Frank	FF	82	82	87	89	97	02	07								7
17	Kitt	Michael F.	FF	48	57	61	65	69	73									6
18	Coogan	Fintan	FG	54	57	61	65	69	73									6
19	Geoghegan	John	FF	54	57	61	65	69	73									6
20	Hogan-O'Higgins	Brigid	FG	57	61	65	69	73										5
21	McCormack	Padraic	FG	89	92	97	02	07										5
22	Ó Cuív	Eamon	FF	92	97	02	07	11										5
23	O Maille	Padraic	CG	18	21	22	23											4

	Surname	Forename	Party	Elected														Total
24	McDonagh	Martin	CG	27	27	32	33											4
25	Tubridy	Sean	FF	27	27	37	38											4
26	Carty	Michael	FF	57	61	65	69											4
27	Callanan	John	FF	73	77	81F	82F											4
28	Cusack	Bryan	CR	18	21	22												3
29	Nicolls	George	CG	21	22	23												3
30	Jordan	Stephen	FF	27	32	33												3
31	Powell	Thomas	FF	27	27	32												3
32	Lahiffe	Robert	FF	48	53*	54												3
33	Millar	Anthony	FF	58*	61	65												3
34	Hussey	Thomas	FF	69	73	77												3
35	Loughnane**	Bill	FF	69	73	77												3
36	Grealish	Noel	PD	02	07	11												3
37	Mellows**	Liam	SF	18	21													2
38	Whelehan	Joseph	CT	21	22													2
39	O'Connell**	Thomas	LB	22	23													2
40	Corbett	Eamonn	FF	35*	43													2
41	Lydon	Michael	FF	44	48													2
42	Hession	James	FG	51	54													2
43	Killilea	Mark	FF	77	81													2
44	Burke	Ulick	FG	97	07													2
45	Cosgrave	James	NP	23														1
46	Mellows	Herbert	R	23														1
47	O'Dea	Louis	R	23														1
48	Duffy	William	NL	27J														1
49	Lynch	Gilbert	LB	27J														1
50	Keely	Seamus	FF	33														1
51	Neilan	Martin	FF	36*														1
52	Keane	John	FF	40*														1
53	Cawley	Patrick	FG	51														1
54	Duignan	Peadar	FF	51														1
55	Mannion	John	FG	51														1
56	Glynn	Brendan	FG	54														1
57	Mannion	John M.	FG	77														1
58	Coogan	Fintan	FG	82N														1
59	Callanan	Joe	FF	02														1
60	McHugh	Paddy	NP	02														1
61	Connaughton	Paul	FG	11														1
62	Cannon	Ciaran	FG	11														1
63	Keaveney	Colm	LB	11														1
64	Nolan	Derek	LB	11														1
65	Walsh	Brian	FG	11														1
66	Kyne	Seán	FG	11														1
66	**Total**										***Includes 9 By-Elections**						*	**262**
	**** Also elected in another constituency**																	
G	Loughnane**	Bill	FF	Clare				81	82									2
	O'Connell**	Thomas	LB	Mayo				27	27									2
G	Mellows**	Liam	SF	Meath				18										1
G	**Included in Galway Total**																	**5**

GALWAY REGION 1918-2011																										
* No Contest			FG		LB		FF		SF		GP		WP		PD		C na P		C na T		Farmers		Nat League		Others	
Dail		Seats	S	% Vote	S	% Vote	S	% Vote	S	% Vote	S	% Vote	S	% Vote	S	% Vote	S	% Vote	S	% Vote	S	% Vote	S	% Vote	S	% Vote
1	1918	4							4																	
2	1921*	7							7																	
3	1922	7	4	54.51%	1	13.21%	2	32.28%																		
4	1923	9	4	43.67%	1	5.97%	3	33.54%														8.66%			1	8.16%
5	1927	9	3	35.02%	1	4.60%	4	33.55%		4.41%												6.35%	1	10.83%		5.24%
6	1927	9	4	45.48%		4.88%	5	42.71%																		6.92%
7	1932	9	4	39.58%		3.88%	5	55.04%																		1.49%
8	1933	9	3	33.36%		4.22%	6	62.42%																		
9	1937	7	2	29.13%		6.15%	5	64.72%																		
10	1938	7	2	27.42%		7.54%	5	65.04%																		
11	1943	7	1	14.14%		12.18%	5	48.15%											1	22.10%						3.43%
12	1944	7	1	12.01%			5	60.69%											1	22.02%						5.29%
13	1948	9	1	15.50%		3.37%	7	54.05%										14.24%	1	8.09%						4.75%
14	1951	9	3	24.18%		2.77%	5	52.38%										9.04%	1	11.63%						
15	1954	9	3	29.11%		0.95%	5	52.88%										5.46%	1	11.59%						
16	1957	9	2	25.61%			6	55.82%		7.16%									1	11.42%						
17	1961	8	2	25.59%		2.79%	5	51.71%		5.73%								2.70%	1	9.73%						1.74%
18	1965	8	3	40.99%		2.57%	5	53.94%																		2.50%
19	1969	9	3	36.59%		7.41%	6	54.03%																		1.97%
20	1973	9	3	35.63%		4.33%	6	56.40%																		3.64%
21	1977	8	2	30.71%		6.70%	6	58.97%						1.06%												2.56%
22	1981	8	2	36.73%	1	7.42%	5	54.22%						1.29%												0.34%
23	1982	8	2	33.79%	1	8.26%	5	56.45%						1.50%												
24	1982	8	3	38.50%		6.54%	5	52.58%						2.18%												0.20%
25	1987	8	2	23.36%	1	4.53%	4	43.21%						1.83%	1	19.63%										7.44%
26	1989	8	2	28.90%	1	9.85%	4	47.11%						1.98%	1	11.36%										0.79%
27	1992	8	2	22.31%	1	13.21%	4	45.50%		0.82%					1	13.38%										4.78%
28	1997	9	3	26.43%	1	9.06%	4	47.20%		1.33%		1.82%			1	9.98%										4.18%
29	2002	9	2	24.20%	1	5.27%	4	44.05%		4.66%		3.25%			1	6.26%									1	12.30%
30	2007	9	3	29.82%	1	7.06%	4	38.42%		3.08%		3.68%			1	10.99%										6.94%
31	2011	9	4	36.73%	2	12.78%	2	19.51%		6.21%		1.27%													1	23.51%
1918-2011		**253**	**75**	**30.61%**	**13**	**6.34%**	**137**	**48.98%**	**11**	**1.31%**		**0.49%**		**0.38%**	**6**	**2.99%**		**0.99%**	**7**	**2.88%**		**0.37%**	**1**	**0.29%**	**3**	**4.36%**
National		**4,618**	**1,453**	**30.77%**	**482**	**11.53%**	**1,985**	**41.86%**	**232**	**1.99%**	**16**	**0.75%**	**17**	**0.78%**	**44**	**1.42%**	**18**	**0.77%**	**43**	**1.08%**	**42**	**0.90%**	**10**	**0.24%**	**276**	**7.88%**

KERRY NORTH-WEST LIMERICK 2011

"Dynasty change sees Spring in as McEllistrim loses out"

A significantly redrawn constituency, with about 4,000 voters around Castleisland being moved into Kerry South and around 10,000 voters from west Limerick finding themselves part of this constituency.

Only one of the candidates was from the Limerick part of the constituency, John Sheahan from Glin, and he was the surprise of the election, polling a very strong fourth. In a three-seater that's not quite good enough, though, and this was one of the most predictable constituencies in the country.

The collapse of Fianna Fail support nationally meant that Tom McEllistrim really had no chance of retaining his seat. The third of the dynasty to hold a seat here, like his father and grandfather – both also called Tom – he tended to concentrate on the grassroots rather than hold forth in the Dáil chamber or to the media.

The other two incumbents were comfortably re-elected. Jimmy Deenihan, now a cabinet minister, has firmly established himself as the dominant figure in the constituency, and has led Fine Gael to heights (41 per cent of the votes) that it has never before reached in Kerry. Martin Ferris of Sinn Fein, having been first elected in 2002, has been reasonably secure at subsequent elections.

The newcomer was Labour's Arthur Spring who, with a little help from his uncle Dick, nearly doubled the party vote from its 2007 base, and he took Tom McEllistrim's seat. Extraordinarily, there has been both a Spring and a McEllistrim on the ballot paper at all but one (2007) of the last twenty-one elections. The Spring dynasty dates only to 1943, twenty years after the first Tom McEllistrim was elected, but for the moment the Springs are in and the McEllistrims are out.

Arthur Spring with his uncle Dick Spring

KERRY NORTH-WEST LIMERICK TDs 2011

JIMMY DEENIHAN (FG)

Finuge, Lixnaw, Co. Kerry; Tel: 068 40235; Mobile: 087 8113661
Constituency Office: 18A The Square, Listowel, Co. Kerry; Tel: 068 57446
Leinster House: 01 6313806; Email: jimmy.deenihan@oireachtas.ie
Website: www.jimmydeenihan.com

Born Listowel, Co. Kerry 11th September 1952. Married to Mary Dowling. Educated St. Michael's College, Listowel, Co. Kerry; St. Mary's College, Twickenham, London; National College of Physical Education, Limerick (BEd). Government Minister. Former Teacher.
First elected 1987 and at each subsequent election.

Appointed Minister for Arts, Heritage and Gaeltacht Affairs 9th March 2011. Front bench spokesperson on Tourism, Culture & Sport July 2010-February 2011. Front Bench Spokesperson on Defence September 2007-June 2010. Member Joint Committee on Justice, Equality, Defence and Women's Rights 2007-2011. Spokesperson on Arts, Sports and Tourism, 2002-2007. Member Joint Committee on Arts, Sport, Tourism, Community Rural and Gaeltacht Affairs 2002-2007. Adviser to party leader on Northern Ireland Policy and party spokesperson on Sport 2001-2002. Junior spokesperson on Environmental Information and Protection 2000-2002. Fine Gael Junior spokesperson for the Office of Public Works 1997–2000. Member British-Irish Inter-parliamentary Body since 1997. Minister of State at the Department of Agriculture, Food and Forestry with special responsibility for Rural Development, the LEADER programme and monitoring the activities of An Bord Bia and the food industry 1994-1997. Fine Gael spokesperson on Tourism and Trade 1993-1994; on Youth and Sports 1988-1993. Senator 1982-1987. Member Kerry County Council 1985–1994 and 1999-2003. Member GAA. Won All Ireland football medals with Kerry 1975, 1978, 1979, 1980 and 1981 (Captain). Also won four National League medals and five Railway Cup medals. Received a GAA All-Star Award in 1981.

ARTHUR SPRING (LB)

1 Brook Lodge, Oakview Village, Tralee, Co. Kerry; Tel: 066 7125337; Mobile: 087 0977260
Leinster House: 01 6313471; Email: arthur.spring@oireachtas.ie;
Website: www.labour.ie/arthurspring

Born Tralee, Co. Kerry, 5th July 1976. Married to Fiona. Educated Tralee CBS; Cistercian College, Roscrea; Dublin Institute of Technology; Jonkoping International Business School, Sweden (BSc in Management). Owns a juice bar in Tralee. First elected 2011.

Member Committee on Finance, Public Expenditure and Reform. First elected to Kerry County Council in 2009 in Tralee electoral area. Elected to Tralee Town Council in 2009. Nephew of Dick Spring former Tánaiste and Labour Party Leader. Grandson of Dan Spring TD for North Kerry 1943-1981.

MARTIN FERRIS (SF)

"Glenrowan", The Village, Ardfert, Kerry, Tel: 066 7134814
Constituency Office: 2 Moyderwell, Tralee. Tel: 066 7129545;
Leinster House: Tel: 01 6184248, E-mail: martin.ferris@oireachtas.ie

Born Tralee, Co. Kerry, 28th March 1952. Married to Maire Hoare, three sons, three daughters. Educated Tralee CBS. Formerly fisherman. Contested 1997 general election.
First elected 2002 and at each subsequent election.

Appointed Sinn Fein spokesperson on Communications, Energy and Natural Resources March 2011. Member Committee on Communications, Natural Resources and Agriculture. Member Committee on the Implementation of the Good Friday Agreement. Sinn Fein spokesperson on Agriculture and Rural Development 2007-2011. He also had responsibility for Marine and Natural Resources and Tourism and Sport. Member Joint Committee on Agriculture, Fisheries and Food and Member Joint Committee on Climate Change and Energy Security 2007-2011. Member Joint Committee on Agriculture and Food 2002-2007. Contested 1999 European elections in Munster. Member Kerry County Council 1999-2003. Member Tralee UDC 1999-2003. Member Sinn Fein's Ard Chomhairle (National Executive) and part of Sinn Fein negotiating team. He was jailed for ten years in 1984 when he was captured on board the Marita Anne gunrunning ship. Has been an active republican since 1970.

KERRY NORTH-WEST LIMERICK 2011							
FIRST PREFERENCE VOTES							
	Seats	3			11,404		
	Candidate	Party	1st	%	Quota	Count	Status
1	**Deenihan, Jimmy***	**FG**	**12,304**	**26.97%**	**1.08**	**1**	**Made Quota**
2	**Spring, Arthur**	**LB**	**9,159**	**20.08%**	**0.80**	**7**	**Made Quota**
3	**Ferris, Martin***	**SF**	**9,282**	**20.35%**	**0.81**	**7**	**Made Quota**
4	Sheahan, John	FG	6,295	13.80%	0.55	7	Not Elected
5	McEllistrim, Tom*	FF	5,230	11.47%	0.46	6	Eliminated
6	O'Brien, Bridget	NP	1,455	3.19%	0.13	5	No Expenses
7	Fitzgibon, Mary	NP	706	1.55%	0.06	4	No Expenses
8	Locke, Sam	NP	486	1.07%	0.04	4	No Expenses
9	Reidy, Michael	NV	357	0.78%	0.03	3	No Expenses
10	Donovan, Tom	GP	239	0.52%	0.02	2	No Expenses
11	McKenna, John	NP	101	0.22%	0.01	2	No Expenses
11	***Outgoing**		**45,614**	**100.00%**	**11,404**	**2,851**	**No Expenses**

KERRY NORTH-WEST LIMERICK 2011													
PARTY VOTE													
	2011					2007					Change	
Party	Cand	1st	%	Quota	Seats	Cand	1st	%	Quota	Seats	%	Seats
FG	2	18,599	40.77%	1.63	1	1	12,697	32.30%	1.29	1	+8.48%	
LB	1	9,159	20.08%	0.80	1	1	4,287	10.90%	0.44		+9.17%	+1
FF	1	5,230	11.47%	0.46		2	12,304	31.30%	1.25	1	-19.83%	-1
SF	1	9,282	20.35%	0.81	1	1	8,030	20.43%	0.82	1	-0.08%	
GP	1	239	0.52%	0.02		1	747	1.90%	0.08		-1.38%	
Others	5	3,105	6.81%	0.27		4	1,248	3.17%	0.13		+3.63%	
Total	**11**	**45,614**	**100.0%**	**11,404**	**3**	**10**	**39,313**	**100.0%**	**9,829**	**3**	**0.00%**	**0**
Electorate		**63,614**	**71.70%**				**56,216**	**69.93%**			**+1.77%**	
Spoiled		**413**	**0.90%**				**334**	**0.84%**			**+0.05%**	
Turnout		**46,027**	**72.35%**				**39,647**	**70.53%**			**+1.83%**	

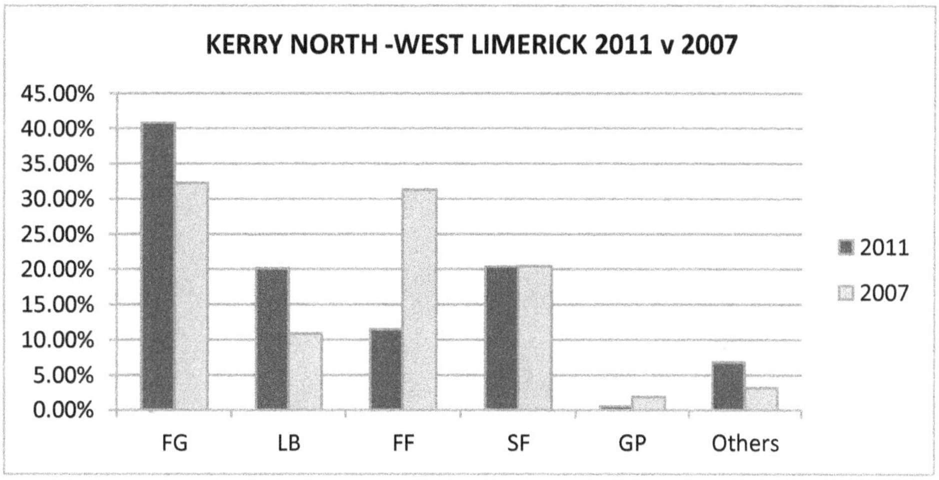

KERRY NORTH-WEST LIMERICK 2011
COUNT DETAILS

Seats 3 **Quota** 11,404

Candidate	Party	1st	2nd Deenihan Surplus	3rd Donovan McKenna	4th Reidy Votes	5th Fitzgibon Locke	6th O'Brien Votes	7th McEllistrim Votes
			-900					
Deenihan, Jimmy*	FG	12,304	11,404	11,404	11,404	11,404	11,404	11,404
			+256	*+99*	*+57*	*+376*	*+738*	*+1,560*
Spring, Arthur	LB	9,159	9,415	9,514	9,571	9,947	10,685	12,245
			+158	*+49*	*+51*	*+244*	*+380*	*+1,252*
Ferris, Martin*	SF	9,282	9,440	9,489	9,540	9,784	10,164	11,416
			+382	*+49*	*+55*	*+111*	*+250*	*+902*
Sheahan, John	FG	6,295	6,677	6,726	6,781	6,892	7,142	8,044
			+45	*+31*	*+23*	*+122*	*+227*	*-5,678*
McEllistrim, Tom*	FF	5,230	5,275	5,306	5,329	5,451	5,678	Eliminated
			+22	*+44*	*+56*	*+373*	*-1,950*	
O'Brien, Bridget	NP	1,455	1,477	1,521	1,577	1,950	Eliminated	
			+16	*+43*	*+84*	*-849*		
Fitzgibon, Mary	NP	706	722	765	849	Eliminated		
			+6	*+6*	*+21*	*-519*		
Locke, Sam	NP	486	492	498	519	Eliminated		
			+5	*+11*	*-373*			
Reidy, Michael	NV	357	362	373	Eliminated			
			+8	*-247*				
Donovan, Tom	GP	239	247	Eliminated				
			+2	*-103*				
McKenna, John	NP	101	103	Eliminated				
Non-transferable				*+18*	*+26*	*+142*	*+355*	*+1,964*
Cumulative			0	18	44	186	541	2,505
Total		**45,614**	**45,614**	**45,614**	**45,614**	**45,614**	**45,614**	**45,614**

KERRY NORTH-WEST LIMERICK 2011
TRANSFER ANALYSIS

From	To	FG	LB	FF	SF	GP	Others	Non Trans
FG	900	382	256	45	158	8	51	
		42.44%	*28.44%*	*5.00%*	*17.56%*	*0.89%*	*5.67%*	
FF	5,678	902	1,560		1,252			1,964
		15.89%	*27.47%*		*22.05%*			*34.59%*
GP	247	34	70	22	35		73	13
		13.77%	*28.34%*	*8.91%*	*14.17%*		*29.55%*	*5.26%*
Others	3,794	431	1,200	381	689		565	528
		11.36%	*31.63%*	*10.04%*	*18.16%*		*14.89%*	*13.92%*
Total	**10,619**	**1,749**	**3,086**	**448**	**2,134**	**8**	**689**	**2,505**
		16.47%	***29.06%***	***4.22%***	***20.10%***	***0.08%***	***6.49%***	***23.59%***

KERRY NORTH		
MAIN BOUNDARY CHANGES		
Dail	**Constituency**	**Seats**
9 (1937) - 16 (1957)	Kerry North	4
17 (1961) - 30 (2007)	Kerry North	3
31 (2011) -	Kerry North-West Limerick	3

KERRY NORTH															
All TDs 1937-2011															
	Surname	**Forename**	**Party**	**Elected**											**Total**
1	Spring	Dan	LB	43	44	48	51	54	57	61	65	69	73	77	11
2	McEllistrim**	Thomas	FF	37	38	43	44	48	51	54	57	61	65		10
3	Finucane	Patrick	IndF	43	44	48	51	54	57	61	65				8
4	McEllistrim(jun.)	Thomas	FF	69	73	77	81	82	82	89					7
5	Spring	Dick	LB	81	82	82	87	89	92	97					7
6	Deenihan	Jimmy	FG	87	89	92	97	02	07	11					7
7	Foley	Denis	FF	81	82	82	87	92	97						6
8	Kissane**	Eamon	FF	37	38	43	44	48							5
9	Ferris	Martin	SF	02	07	11									3
10	Fuller	Stephen	FF	37	38										2
11	O'Sullivan**	John M.	FG	37	38										2
12	Lynch	Gerard	FG	69	73										2
13	McEllistrim	Tom	FF	02	07										2
14	Lynch	John	FG	51											1
15	Connor	John	CnaP	54											1
16	O'Connor	Kathleen	CnaP	56*											1
17	Moloney	Daniel	FF	57											1
18	Ahern	Kit	FF	77											1
19	Spring	Arthur	LB												1
19	**Total**							***Includes 1 By-Election**						*	**78**
	**** Also elected in another constituency**														
1	McEllistrim**	Thomas	FF	Kerry			23	27	27	32	33				5
2	O'Sullivan**	John M.	FG	Kerry			23	27	27	32	33				5
3	Kissane**	Eamon	FF	Kerry			32	33							2
3	**Total**														**12**

KERRY NORTH 1937-2011																						
			FG		LB		FF		SF		GP		Aont Eir		C na P		C na T		Nat Lab		Others	
Dail		**Seats**	**S**	**% Vote**	**S**	**% Vote**	**S**	**% Vote**	**S**	**% Vote**	**S**	**% Vote**	**S**	**% Vote**	**S**	**% Vote**	**S**	**% Vote**	**S**	**% Vote**	**S**	**% Vote**
9	1937	4	1	29.52%		13.65%	3	56.83%														
10	1938	4	1	23.82%		9.27%	3	**66.91%**														
11	1943	4		11.63%	1	19.75%	2	42.30%									1	**26.32%**				
12	1944	4					2	49.53%									1	25.76%	1	**24.72%**		
13	1948	4		5.84%			2	48.69%								**16.51%**	1	12.67%	1	16.29%		
14	1951	4	1	15.30%	1	19.94%	1	38.80%								12.60%					1	13.36%
15	1954	4		13.64%	1	16.31%	1	41.31%							1	13.92%	1	14.82%				
16	1957	4		10.15%	1	18.26%	2	38.32%		9.20%											1	24.08%
17	1961	3		6.94%	1	20.44%	1	40.50%		5.24%											1	**26.88%**
18	1965	3		13.48%	1	25.09%	1	42.00%													1	19.43%
19	1969	3	1	24.84%	1	17.53%	1	48.97%														8.65%
20	1973	3	1	23.40%	1	20.99%	1	46.77%						**2.49%**								6.35%
21	1977	3		24.47%	1	18.21%	2	57.32%														
22	1981	3		21.19%	1	16.58%	2	50.97%		11.26%												
23	1982	3		17.04%	1	25.83%	2	53.45%														3.68%
24	1982	3		19.87%	1	28.91%	2	51.22%														
25	1987	3	1	29.02%	1	19.38%	1	48.07%		3.53%												
26	1989	3	1	25.50%	1	29.68%	1	44.82%														
27	1992	3	1	23.93%	1	**33.93%**	1	36.47%		2.36%												3.31%
28	1997	3	1	24.29%	1	29.90%	1	26.31%		15.91%												3.60%
29	2002	3	1	22.09%		22.40%	1	30.15%	1	**24.24%**												1.13%
30	2007	3	1	32.30%		10.90%	1	31.30%	1	20.43%		**1.90%**										3.17%
31	2011	3	1	**40.77%**	1	20.08%		11.47%	1	20.35%		0.52%										6.81%
1937-2011		**77**	**12**	**20.38%**	**17**	**18.85%**	**34**	**42.90%**	**3**	**5.44%**		**0.12%**		**0.09%**	**1**	**1.95%**	**4**	**3.62%**	**2**	**1.81%**	**4**	**4.85%**
National		**4,618**	**1,453**	**30.77%**	**482**	**11.53%**	**1,985**	**41.86%**	**232**	**1.99%**	**16**	**0.75%**		**0.03%**	**18**	**0.77%**	**43**	**1.08%**	**9**	**0.16%**	**380**	**11.05%**

KERRY SOUTH 2011

"First constituency for sixty years to return two independents"

There was a major boundary change here with a population of 5,098 around Castleisland and Cordal transferred from the old Kerry North constituency. It remains a three seat constituency.

Everything changed in Kerry South, as one incumbent retired and the other two were defeated. Jackie Healy-Rae hung up his tartan cap after 14 years and handed over the mantle to his son Michael, who proved equally adept at enunciating the well-rehearsed 'I am not a gombeen politician and it is disrespectful to the people of Kerry for the Dublin media to say so' line. It worked for his father and it worked for him – though, to establish that he is his own man, his cap of choice is usually black.

The sole Fianna Fail candidate was John O'Donoghue, who had fought the 2007 campaign as a senior government minister. Much had changed since; he had first been shuffled off against his will to the post of Ceann Comhairle and had then become the first occupant of that office to have to stand down after the disclosure of his remarkable expenses claims. These were shaky credentials in an election where Fianna Fail itself was on the ropes, and O'Donoghue did not last beyond the fourth count. His departure speech, claiming credit for obtaining the funding for the building in which the votes were counted, was eloquent indeed.

Fine Gael, often seatless in this constituency, won more votes than Fianna Fail and Labour combined, but not quite enough for two seats. Tom Sheahan, who had won a seat for Fine Gael in 2007 after the party had been unrepresented here since 1987, was surprisingly unseated by his youthful running mate Brendan Griffin, who gained national publicity by promising to take only half of a TD's salary if elected, a pledge he found himself unexpectedly called upon to live up to.

In contrast, the Labour vote actually dropped, the only constituency in the country where this happened, and a marked contrast to the Labour surge in North Kerry.

With Fianna Fail and Labour struggling, Independents won 42 per cent of the votes, and Kerry South became the first constituency for sixty years to return two independents. Joining Michael Healy-Rae in the 31st Dáil was Tom Fleming, who, as a Fianna Fail candidate, had finished a close runner-up in both 2002 and 2007 and who was now aided by the transfer of a sizeable pocket of votes around Castleisland, close to his own base of Scartaglin, into Kerry South. Fianna Fail may regret not selecting Fleming as its sole candidate; as it was, Kerry became yet another county left without a Fianna Fail TD.

KERRY SOUTH TDs 2011

BRENDAN GRIFFIN (FG)

Keel, Castlemaine, Co. Kerry; Mobile: 087 6528841;
Leinster House: 01 6184480; Email: brendan.griffin@oireachtas.ie;
Website: www.brendangriffin.ie

Born Cork 9th March 1982. Married to Róisín. Educated Intermediate School, Killorglin, NUI Galway (BA Hons history, sociology and politics). Formerly Publican.
Elected at first attempt in 2011.

Member Committee on Jobs, Social Protection and Education. Promised to accept only half of TD's salary if elected. Contested 2004 local election. First elected in Dingle electoral area in 2009.

TOM FLEMING (IND)

Scartaglen Village, Killarney, Co. Kerry; Tel: 066 7147384; Mobile: 087 7814781
Leinster House: Tel: 01 6183354; Email: tom.fleming@oireachtas.ie
Website: www.tomflemimgelection.com

Born Kerry February 1951. Married to Lena, three daughters. Educated St. Patrick's College, Castleisland, Co. Kerry. Publican. Contested 2002 and 2007 Dáil elections for Fianna Fail. First elected 2011.

Member Joint Administration Committee. Member Committee on Jobs, Social Protection and Education. Contested 2007 Seanad election on Administrative Panel. First elected to Kerry County Council in 1985 in Killarney electoral area. Retained his seat in 1991, 1999, 2004 and 2009.

MICHAEL HEALY-RAE (IND)

Sandymount, Kilgarvan, Co. Kerry; Tel: 064 6632467; Mobile: 087 2461678
Constituency Office: Main Street, Kilgarvan, Co. Kerry; Tel: 064 37376.
Leinster House: 01 6184319; Email: michael.healy-rae@oireachtas.ie

Born Kilgarvan, Co. Kerry, 9th January 1967. Married to Eileen, five children. Educated Kenmare Vocational School; Salesian Brothers Pallaskenry, Co. Limerick. Shopkeeper and owner of Plant Hire Business. First elected 2011.

Member Committee on Investigations, Oversight and Petitions. First elected to Kerry County Council in 1999 in the Killorglin electoral area. Retained his seat in 2004 and 2009. Son of Jackie Healy-Rae, TD for Kerry South 1997-2009.

KERRY SOUTH 2011							
FIRST PREFERENCE VOTES							
	Seats	3			11,096		
	Candidate	Party	1st	%	Quota	Count	Status
1	**Griffin, Brendan**	**FG**	**8,808**	**19.85%**	**0.79**	**5**	**Made Quota**
2	**Fleming, Tom**	**NP**	**6,416**	**14.46%**	**0.58**	**6**	**Elected**
3	**Healy-Rae, Michael**	**NP**	**6,670**	**15.03%**	**0.60**	**6**	**Elected**
4	Sheahan, Tom*	FG	5,674	12.79%	0.51	6	Not Elected
5	Gleeson, Michael	SKIA	4,939	11.13%	0.45	4	Eliminated
6	O'Donoghue, John*	FF	5,917	13.33%	0.53	3	Eliminated
7	Moloney, Marie	LB	4,926	11.10%	0.44	2	Eliminated
8	Comerford, Oonagh	GP	401	0.90%	0.04	1	No Expenses
9	Behal, Richard	NP	348	0.78%	0.03	1	No Expenses
10	Finn, Dermot	NP	281	0.63%	0.03	1	No Expenses
10	***Outgoing**		**44,380**	**100.00%**	**11,096**	**2,775**	**No Expenses**

KERRY SOUTH 2011												
PARTY VOTE												
	2011					2007					Change	
Party	Cand	1st	%	Quota	Seats	Cand	1st	%	Quota	Seats	%	Seats
FG	2	14,482	32.63%	1.31	1	2	9,795	25.09%	1.00	1	+7.54%	
LB	1	4,926	11.10%	0.44		1	5,263	13.48%	0.54		-2.38%	
FF	1	5,917	13.33%	0.53		2	15,868	40.65%	1.63	1	-27.32%	-1
SF						1	1,375	3.52%	0.14		-3.52%	
GP	1	401	0.90%	0.04		1	738	1.89%	0.08		-0.99%	
Others	5	18,654	42.03%	1.68	2	1	5,993	15.35%	0.61	1	+26.68%	+1
Total	**10**	**44,380**	**100.0%**	**11,096**	**3**	**8**	**39,032**	**100.0%**	**9,759**	**3**	**0.00%**	**0**
Electorate		**59,629**	**74.43%**				**53,660**	**72.74%**			**+1.69%**	
Spoiled		**299**	**0.67%**				**293**	**0.75%**			**-0.08%**	
Turnout		**44,679**	**74.93%**				**39,325**	**73.29%**			**+1.64%**	

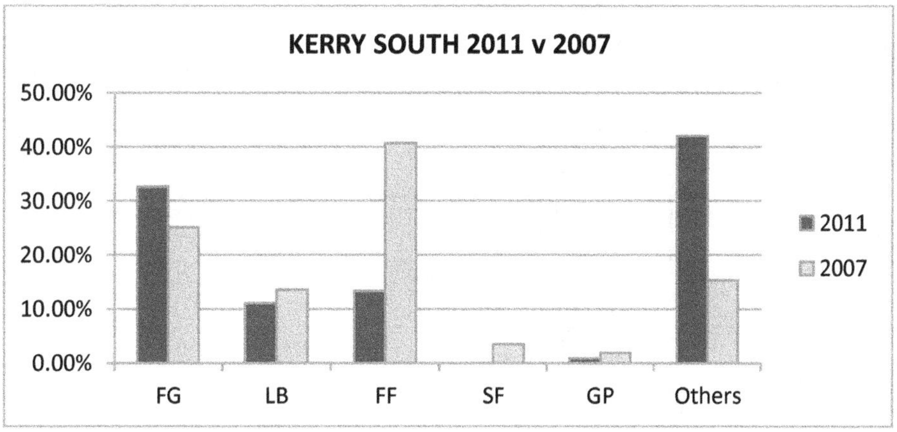

KERRY SOUTH 2011 COUNT DETAILS							
Seats	3					Quota	11,096
Candidate	**Party**	**1st**	**2nd** Comerford Behal Finn	**3rd** Moloney Votes	**4th** O'Donoghue Votes	**5th** Gleeson Votes	**6th** Griffin Surplus
Griffin, Brendan	FG	8,808	+135 8,943	+1,071 10,014	+851 10,865	+1,771 12,636	-1,540 11,096
Fleming, Tom	NP	6,416	+132 6,548	+809 7,357	+1,389 8,746	+1,643 10,389	+308 10,697
Healy-Rae, Michael	NP	6,670	+119 6,789	+623 7,412	+1,734 9,146	+983 10,129	+197 10,326
Sheahan, Tom*	FG	5,674	+62 5,736	+841 6,577	+749 7,326	+1,342 8,668	+741 9,409
Gleeson, Michael	SKIA	4,939	+283 5,222	+1,156 6,378	+659 7,037	-7,037 Eliminated	
O'Donoghue, John*	FF	5,917	+43 5,960	+240 6,200	-6,200 Eliminated		
Moloney, Marie	LB	4,926	+206 5,132	-5,132 Eliminated			
Comerford, Oonagh	GP	401	-401 Eliminated				
Behal, Richard	NP	348	-348 Eliminated				
Finn, Dermot	NP	281	-281 Eliminated				
Non-transferable Cumulative			+50 50	+392 442	+818 1,260	+1,298 2,558	+294 2,852
Total		**44,380**	**44,380**	**44,380**	**44,380**	**44,380**	**44,380**

KERRY SOUTH 2011 TRANSFER ANALYSIS						
From	**To**	**FG**	**LB**	**FF**	**Others**	**Non Trans**
FG	1,540	741 *48.12%*			505 *32.79%*	294 *19.09%*
LB	5,132	1,912 *37.26%*		240 *4.68%*	2,588 *50.43%*	392 *7.64%*
FF	6,200	1,600 *25.81%*			3,782 *61.00%*	818 *13.19%*
GP	401	77 *19.20%*	80 *19.95%*	17 *4.24%*	208 *51.87%*	19 *4.74%*
Others	7,666	3,233 *42.17%*	126 *1.64%*	26 *0.34%*	2,952 *38.51%*	1,329 *17.34%*
Total	**20,939**	**7,563** ***36.12%***	**206** ***0.98%***	**283** ***1.35%***	**10,035** ***47.92%***	**2,852** ***13.62%***

KERRY SOUTH		
MAIN BOUNDARY CHANGES		
Dail	Constituency	Seats
9 (1937) - 31 (2011)	Kerry South	3

KERRY SOUTH 1937-2011																							
* No Contest			FG		LB		FF		SF		GP		WP		PD		C na P		C na T		Others		
Dail		Seats	S	% Vote	S	% Vote	S	% Vote	S	% Vote	S	% Vote	S	% Vote	S	% Vote	S	% Vote	S	% Vote	S	% Vote
9	1937	3	1	31.62%			2	54.64%														13.74%
10	1938*	3	1				2															
11	1943	3	1	17.97%		16.52%	2	42.41%												23.10%		
12	1944	3	1	24.05%			2	52.49%												23.46%		
13	1948	3	1	18.85%			1	39.67%										20.29%			1	21.18%
14	1951	3	1	29.53%			1	35.38%										13.90%			1	21.19%
15	1954	3	1	25.56%		10.78%	2	46.36%										7.43%		9.87%		
16	1957	3	1	26.56%			1	48.32%	1	25.13%												
17	1961	3	1	29.86%		14.34%	2	43.00%		12.80%												
18	1965	3	1	32.95%		17.74%	2	44.14%														5.16%
19	1969	3	1	37.09%		9.37%	2	53.54%														
20	1973	3	1	30.78%		13.92%	2	51.59%		3.71%												
21	1977	3	1	30.31%		17.74%	2	48.69%						3.26%								
22	1981	3	1	23.54%	1	24.47%	1	47.23%														4.76%
23	1982	3	1	28.72%	1	21.63%	1	49.21%														0.43%
24	1982	3	1	25.54%	1	23.10%	1	45.84%						2.06%								3.45%
25	1987	3	1	17.90%		13.73%	2	53.98%				2.13%		2.21%		9.68%						0.37%
26	1989	3		20.68%	1	20.46%	2	53.56%								4.66%						0.64%
27	1992	3		19.89%	1	24.05%	2	45.87%		1.06%												9.13%
28	1997	3		13.77%	1	14.05%	1	31.79%													1	40.39%
29	2002	3		17.66%	1	14.48%	1	44.64%													1	23.22%
30	2007	3	1	25.09%		13.48%	1	40.65%		3.52%		1.89%									1	15.35%
31	2011	3	1	32.63%		11.10%		13.33%				0.90%									2	42.03%
1937-2011		**69**	**19**	**25.31%**	**7**	**13.43%**	**35**	**44.01%**	**1**	**1.73%**		**0.28%**		**0.37%**		**0.70%**		**1.60%**		**2.18%**	**7**	**10.40%**
National		**4,618**	**1,453**	**30.77%**	**482**	**11.53%**	**1,985**	**41.86%**	**232**	**1.99%**	**16**	**0.75%**	**17**	**0.78%**	**44**	**1.42%**	**18**	**0.77%**	**43**	**1.08%**	**328**	**9.03%**

KERRY SOUTH														
All TDs 1937-2011														
	Surname	**Forename**	**Party**	**Elected**										**Total**
1	O'Leary	John	FF	66*	69	73	77	81	82	82	87	89	92	10
2	Crowley	Honor	FF	45*	48	51	54	57	61	65				7
3	Begley	Michael	FG	69	73	77	81	82	82	87				7
4	O'Donoghue	John	FF	87	89	92	97	02	07					6
5	Flynn**	John	FF	37	38	48	51	54						5
6	O'Connor	Timothy	FF	61	65	69	73	77						5
7	Crowley**	Frederick	FF	37	38	43	44							4
8	Lynch**	Fionan	FG	37	38	43	44							4
9	Palmer	Patrick	FG	48	51	54	57							4
10	Moynihan	Michael	LB	81	82	82	89							4
11	Moynihan-Cronin	Breeda	LB	92	97	02								3
12	Healy-Rae	Jackie	NP	97	02	07								3
13	Healy	John	FF	43	44									2
14	Connor	Patrick	FG	61	65									2
15	O'Donoghue	Donal	FF	44*										1
16	Rice	John	SF	57										1
17	Sheahan	Tom	FG	07										1
18	Griffin	Brendan	FG	11										1
19	Fleming	Tom	NP	11										1
20	Healy-Rae	Michael	NP	11										1
20	**Total**						***Includes 3 By-Elections**						*	**72**
	**** Also elected in another constituency**													
1	Lynch**	Fionan	FG	Kerry		18	21	22	23	27	27	32	33	8
2	Crowley**	Frederick	FF	Kerry		27S	32	33						3
3	Flynn**	John	FF	Kerry		32	33							2
3	**Total**													**13**

KERRY REGION		
MAIN BOUNDARY CHANGES		
Dail	**Constituency**	**Seats**
1 (1918)	Kerry East	1
	Kerry North	1
	Kerry South	1
	Kerry West	1
2 (1921) - 3 (1922)	Kerry-Limerick West	8
4 (1923) - 8 (1933)	Kerry	7
9 (1937) - 16 (1957)	Kerry North	4
	Kerry South	3
17 (1961) - 30 (2007)	Kerry North	3
	Kerry South	3
30 (2011) -	Kerry North-West Limerick	3
	Kerry South	3

KERRY																			
All TDs 1918-2011																			
	Surname	**Forename**	**Party**	**Elected**															**Total**
1	McEllistrim	Thomas	FF	23	27	27	32	33	37	38	43	44	48	51	54	57	61	65	15
2	Lynch	Fionan	FG	18	21	22	23	27	27	32	33	37	38	43	44				12
3	Spring	Dan	LB	43	44	48	51	54	57	61	65	69	73	77					11
4	O'Leary	John	FF	66*	69	73	77	81	82	82	87	89	92						10
5	Finucane	Patrick	IndF	43	44	48	51	54	57	61	65								8
6	O'Sullivan	John M.	FG	23	27	27	32	33	37	38									7
7	Crowley	Frederick	FF	27S	32	33	37	38	43	44									7
8	Kissane	Eamon	FF	32	33	37	38	43	44	48									7
9	Flynn	John	FF	32	33	37	38	48	51	54									7
10	Crowley	Honor	FF	45*	48	51	54	57	61	65									7
11	Begley	Michael	FG	69	73	77	81	82	82	87									7
12	McEllistrim(jun.)	Thomas	FF	69	73	77	81	82	82	89									7
13	Spring	Dick	LB	81	82	82	87	89	92	97									7
14	Deenihan	Jimmy	FG	87	89	92	97	02	07	11									7
15	Crowley	James	CG	18	21	22	23	27	27										6
16	Foley	Denis	FF	81	82	82	87	92	97										6
17	O'Donoghue	John	FF	87	89	92	97	02	07										6
18	Stack	Austin	SF	18	21	22	23	27J											5
19	O'Connor	Timothy	FF	61	65	69	73	77											5
20	Palmer	Patrick	FG	48	51	54	57												4
21	Moynihan	Michael	LB	81	82	82	89												4
22	Beaslai	Piaras	CT	18	21	22													3
23	Cahill	Patrick	R	21	22	23													3
24	O'Donoghue	Thomas	R	21	22	23													3
25	O'Reilly	Thomas	FF	27	27	32													3
26	Moynihan-Cronin	Breeda	LB	92	97	02													3
27	Healy-Rae	Jackie	NP	97	02	07													3
28	Ferris	Martin	SF	02	07	11													3
29	Collins**	Conor	CR	21	22														2
30	Roche	Edmond	CR	21	22														2
31	O'Leary	William	FF	27	27														2
32	Fuller	Stephen	FF	37	38														2
33	Healy	John	FF	43	44														2
34	Connor	Patrick	FG	61	65														2
35	Lynch	Gerard	FG	69	73														2
36	McEllistrim	Tom	FF	02	07														2
37	Daly	Denis	FF	33															1
38	O'Donoghue	Donal	FF	44*															1
39	Lynch	John	FG	51															1
40	Connor	John	CnaP	54															1
41	O'Connor	Kathleen	CnaP	56*															1
42	Moloney	Daniel	FF	57															1
43	Rice	John	SF	57															1
44	Ahern	Kit	FF	77															1
45	Sheahan	Tom	FG	07															1
46	Spring	Arthur	LB	11															1
47	Griffin	Brendan	FG	11															1
48	Fleming	Tom	NP	11															1
49	Healy-Rae	Michael	NP	11															1
49	**Total**											***Includes 4 By-Elections**						*	**205**
	**** Also elected in another constituency**																		
K	Collins**	Conor	CR	Limerick West				18											1
K	**Included in Kerry total**																		

KERRY REGION 1918-2011																										
* No Contest			FG		LB		FF		SF		GP		WP		PD		C na P		C na T		Nat Lab		Farmers		Others	
Dail		Seats	S	% Vote	S	% Vote	S	% Vote	S	% Vote	S	% Vote	S	% Vote	S	% Vote	S	% Vote	S	% Vote	S	% Vote	S	% Vote	S	% Vote
1	1918	4							4																	
2	1921*	8							8																	
3	1922*	8	3				5																			
4	1923	7	3	32.47%		7.85%	4	45.09%																8.85%		5.74%
5	1927	7	3	33.61%		5.93%	3	33.21%	1	9.54%														8.48%		9.23%
6	1927	7	3	39.87%			4	51.91%																8.22%		
7	1932	7	2	33.17%			5	59.29%																7.54%		
8	1933	7	2	27.72%			5	67.63%																		4.65%
9	1937	7	2	30.41%		7.88%	5	55.90%																		5.82%
10	1938	7	2	23.82%		9.27%	5	66.91%																		
11	1943	7	1	14.24%	1	18.42%	4	42.34%											1	24.99%						
12	1944	7	1	10.22%			4	50.79%											1	24.78%	1	14.22%				
13	1948	7	1	11.31%			3	44.90%										18.10%	1	7.35%	1	9.45%			1	8.89%
14	1951	7	2	21.23%	1	11.64%	2	37.37%										13.14%							2	16.62%
15	1954	7	1	18.53%	1	14.04%	3	43.38%									1	11.26%	1	12.79%						
16	1957	7	1	16.58%	1	11.10%	3	42.24%	1	15.44%															1	14.64%
17	1961	6	1	17.77%	1	17.56%	3	41.68%		8.81%															1	14.19%
18	1965	6	1	23.23%	1	21.41%	3	43.07%																	1	12.29%
19	1969	6	2	30.99%	1	13.43%	3	51.26%																		4.31%
20	1973	6	2	27.05%	1	17.49%	3	49.15%		1.84%																4.47%
21	1977	6	1	27.37%	1	17.98%	4	53.04%						1.62%												
22	1981	6	1	22.35%	2	20.49%	3	49.12%		5.69%																2.36%
23	1982	6	1	22.83%	2	23.75%	3	51.35%																		2.07%
24	1982	6	1	22.68%	2	26.03%	3	48.56%						1.02%												1.71%
25	1987	6	2	23.59%	1	16.62%	3	50.96%		1.81%		1.04%		1.08%		4.73%										0.18%
26	1989	6	1	23.19%	2	25.27%	3	49.00%								2.23%										0.31%
27	1992	6	1	21.99%	2	29.19%	3	40.98%		1.74%																6.10%
28	1997	6	1	19.05%	2	22.01%	2	29.04%		7.98%															1	21.92%
29	2002	6	1	19.95%	1	18.57%	2	37.15%	1	12.52%															1	11.80%
30	2007	6	2	28.71%		12.19%	2	35.96%	1	12.00%		1.90%													1	9.24%
31	2011	6	2	36.76%	1	15.65%		12.39%	1	10.31%		0.71%													2	24.18%
1918-2011		**201**	**47**	**24.39%**	**24**	**14.07%**	**95**	**44.90%**	**17**	**3.41%**		**0.16%**		**0.14%**		**0.27%**	**1**	**1.49%**	**4**	**2.47%**	**2**	**0.82%**		**1.06%**	**11**	**6.84%**
National		**4,618**	**1,453**	**30.77%**	**482**	**11.53%**	**1,985**	**41.86%**	**232**	**1.99%**	**16**	**0.75%**	**17**	**0.78%**	**44**	**1.42%**	**18**	**0.77%**	**43**	**1.08%**	**9**	**0.16%**	**42**	**0.90%**	**277**	**7.97%**

KILDARE NORTH 2011

"Another gain for Fine Gael as Fianna Fáil lose both of their outgoing seats"

There was a minor Constituency Commission boundary revision here with a population of 1,314 in the Kilpatrick and Newtown areas transferred into this constituency from the Kildare South constituency. However, it remained a four seat constituency.

This was another good performance by Fine Gael as its vote was up 12 points and with 1.7 quotas the party was well placed to win two seats. The long serving Bernard Durkan topped the poll and was just short of the quota on the first count. His running mate Anthony Lawlor had a more modest level of support, with 6,882 first preferences to leave him in the frame on the first count with 0.7 quotas and he went on to comfortably hold off Áine Brady for the final seat.

The Labour vote was up 12 points and with 1.5 quotas the party should have been in contention for two seats. Emmet Stagg was short of the quota on the first count and went on to comfortably take the second seat on the third count. His running mate John McGinley was outside the frame in fifth place on the first count but the gap between the Labour man and Lawlor was just too big and he was eventually eliminated at the end of the fourth count with his transfers favouring Murphy (45%) and Lawlor (22%).

This was another poor Fianna Fáil performance with their vote down 25 points and they lost both of their outgoing seats. Both outgoing deputies – Áine Brady and Michael Fitzpatrick - decided to contest and between them they got just 0.7 quotas. The division of the party vote left both candidates outside the frame on the first count and too far off the pace. Brady was in sixth place on the first count but 63% of her running mate's transfers moved her up to fifth place but that was as good as it got and the Minister of State was well beaten in the end.

Catherine Murphy won the by-election in 2004 which was caused by the appointment of Charlie McCreevy as EU Commissioner. Murphy was a surprise loser in 2007 but made no mistake in 2011 as she was in third place on the first count with 6,911 votes and she went on to take the third seat on the final count.

The Sinn Fein vote was up three points but with just 6% Martin Kelly was in seventh place and out of contention.

Catherine Murphy TD

KILDARE NORTH TDs 2011

BERNARD DURKAN (FG)

Timard, Maynooth, Co. Kildare, Tel: 01 6286063; Mobile: 086 2553370
Leinster House: Tel: 01 6183191; Email: bernard.durkan@oireachtas.ie
Website: www. bernarddurkan.finegael.ie

Born Killasser, Swinford, Co. Mayo 26th March 1945. Married to Hilary Spence, two sons. Educated St. John's NS, Corramore, Co. Mayo. Former Agricultural Contractor. First elected 1981. Lost his seat February 1982 but regained it November 1982 and elected at each subsequent election.

Appointed Vice-Chair Committee on Foreign Affairs and Trade June 2011. Member Committee on European Union Affairs. Chairman Joint Committee on European Affairs 2007-2011. Chief Whip 2002-2007. Member Committee on Procedure and Privileges 2002-2007. Junior spokesperson on Overseas Development Assistance and Human Rights 1997-2002. Member Public Accounts Committee that carried out the DIRT enquiry during the 28th Dail. Minister of State at the Department of Social Welfare with responsibility for Customer Information Services and the Integration of the Tax and Social Welfare Codes 1994-1997. Senator April-November 1982. Fine Gael spokesperson on Health 1994; on the Office of Tánaiste and on National Development Plan 1993-1994; on Insurance Industry 1991-1992; on Trade and Marketing 1989-1991; on the Food Industry 1987-1989. Assistant Whip 1986-1987. Fine Gael spokesperson on Industry and Commerce 1981-1982. Member Kildare County Council 1976-1994.

EMMET STAGG (LB)

736 Lodge Park, Straffan, Co. Kildare, Tel: 01 6272149; Mobile: 087 6728555
Leinster House: Tel: 01 6183013; Email: emmet.stagg@oireachtas.ie
Website: www.labour.ie/emmetstagg

Born Hollymount, Co. Mayo October 1944. Married to Mary Morris, one son, one daughter. Educated CBS, Ballinrobe, Co. Mayo and College of Technology, Kevin Street, Dublin. Former Medical Laboratory Technologist. First elected 1987 and at each subsequent election.

Chief Whip since 2002. Member Committee on Procedures and Privileges. Member Joint Administration Committee and Member Dail Committee on Procedure and Privileges 2007-2011. Spokesperson on Nuclear Safety 2002-2007. Member Committee on Procedure and Privileges 2002-2007. Chief Whip and Front Bench spokesperson on Public Enterprise 1997-2002. Minister of State at the Department of Transport, Energy and Communications with special responsibility for Nuclear Safety, Renewable Energy, Gas and Oil Industry, Air Safety, Road Haulage and Bus Regulation 1994-1997. Minister of State at the Department of the Environment with special responsibility for Housing and Urban Renewal 1993-1994. Labour Party spokesperson on Social Welfare 1989-1992; on Agriculture 1987-1989. Vice Chairman of Labour Party 1987-1989. Member Kildare County Council 1978-1993 (Chairperson 1981/1982) and 1999-2003. Member Kildare County Vocational Education Committee 1985-1993; Eastern Health Board 1978-1985; President Celbridge and Maynooth Soccer Clubs.

CATHERINE MURPHY (NP)

46 Leixlip Park, Leixlip, Co. Kildare; Tel: 01 6244903; Mobile: 087 2696450
Constituency Office: Unit 4, The Post House, Leixlip Shopping Mall, Leixlip, Co. Kildare;
Leinster House: 01 6183099; Email: catherine.murphy@oireachtas.ie
Website: www.catherinemurphy.ie

Born Dublin, 1st September 1953. Married to Derek Murphy, one son, one daughter. Educated Dominican Convent, Ballyfermot; College of Commerce, Rathmines; IPA/NCC (Higher diploma in computer studies). Contested 1989 Dail election for Workers Party in Kildare. Contested 1992 and 1997 Dail elections for DL in Kildare North. Won By-election in Kildare North as an Independent on 11th March 2005. Lost her seat in 2007 but regained it in 2011.

Member Committee on Procedures and Privileges. Member Committee on Environment, Transport, Culture and the Gaeltacht. First elected to Kildare County Council in 1991 in Celbridge. Retained her seat in Leixlip in 1999 and 2004. Resigned her seat on becoming a TD in 2005 and was replaced by Gerry McDonagh. Following the loss of her Dail seat in 2007 she returned to the council with McDonagh stepping down. Retained her seat in Celbridge in 2009. Elected to Leixlip TC when it was first set up in 1992. Retained her seat in 1994, 1999, 2004 and 2009.

ANTHONY LAWLOR (FG)

14 River Lawns, Kill, Co. Kildare; Tel: 045 877660; Mobile: 087 2753942
Constituency Office: 56 South Main Street, Naas, Co. Kildare; Tel: 045 888488
Leinster House: 01 6183007; Email: anthony.lawlor@oireachtas.ie

Born Dublin 13th June 1959. Married to Margaret. Educated Dominican College Newbridge; Multyfarnham Agricultural College; UCD (BAgSc); NUI Maynooth (HDipEd). Farmer.
First elected 2011.

Member Committee on Jobs, Social Protection and Education. Co-opted onto Kildare County Council in January 1999 following the death of his mother Patsy Lawlor. Topped the poll in 1999 local election as an Independent. Resigned from the council before 2004 election and shortly afterwards joined Fine Gael. Re-elected in 2009 for Fine Gael.

	KILDARE NORTH 2011						
	FIRST PREFERENCE VOTES						
	Seats	4			10,245		
	Candidate	Party	1st	%	Quota	Count	Status
1	**Durkan, Bernard***	**FG**	**10,168**	**19.85%**	**0.99**	**2**	**Made Quota**
2	**Stagg, Emmet***	**LB**	**9,718**	**18.97%**	**0.95**	**3**	**Made Quota**
3	**Murphy, Catherine #**	**NP**	**6,911**	**13.49%**	**0.67**	**5**	**Made Quota**
4	**Lawlor, Anthony**	**FG**	**6,882**	**13.44%**	**0.67**	**5**	**Elected**
5	Brady, Áine*	FF	4,777	9.33%	0.47	5	Not Elected
6	McGinley, John	LB	5,261	10.27%	0.51	4	Eliminated
7	Kelly, Martin	SF	2,896	5.65%	0.28	3	Eliminated
8	Fitzpatrick, Michael*	FF	2,659	5.19%	0.26	2	Eliminated
9	Fitzgerald, Shane	GP	905	1.77%	0.09	1	No Expenses
10	Doyle-Higgins, Eric	NP	423	0.83%	0.04	1	No Expenses
11	Beirne, Michael	NP	422	0.82%	0.04	1	No Expenses
12	Murphy, Bart	NP	200	0.39%	0.02	1	No Expenses
12	***Outgoing # Former TD**		**51,222**	**100.00%**	**10,245**	**2,562**	**No Expenses**

KILDARE NORTH 2011													
PARTY VOTE													
	2011					2007					Change	
Party	Cand	1st	%	Quota	Seats	Cand	1st	%	Quota	Seats	%	Seats
FG	2	17,050	33.29%	1.66	2	2	9,590	21.22%	1.06	1	+12.07%	+1
LB	2	14,979	29.24%	1.46	1	1	7,882	17.44%	0.87	1	+11.80%	
FF	2	7,436	14.52%	0.73		2	17,851	39.50%	1.97	2	-24.98%	-2
SF	1	2,896	5.65%	0.28		1	1,103	2.44%	0.12		+3.21%	
GP	1	905	1.77%	0.09		1	2,215	4.90%	0.25		-3.13%	
PD						1	983	2.18%	0.11		-2.18%	
Others	4	7,956	15.53%	0.78	1	3	5,567	12.32%	0.62		+3.21%	+1
Total	**12**	**51,222**	**100.0%**	**10,245**	**4**	**11**	**45,191**	**100.0%**	**9,039**	**4**	**0.00%**	**0**
Electorate		**77,959**	**65.70%**				**71,311**	**63.37%**			**+2.33%**	
Spoiled		**388**	**0.75%**				**232**	**0.51%**			**+0.24%**	
Turnout		**51,610**	**66.20%**				**45,423**	**63.70%**			**+2.50%**	

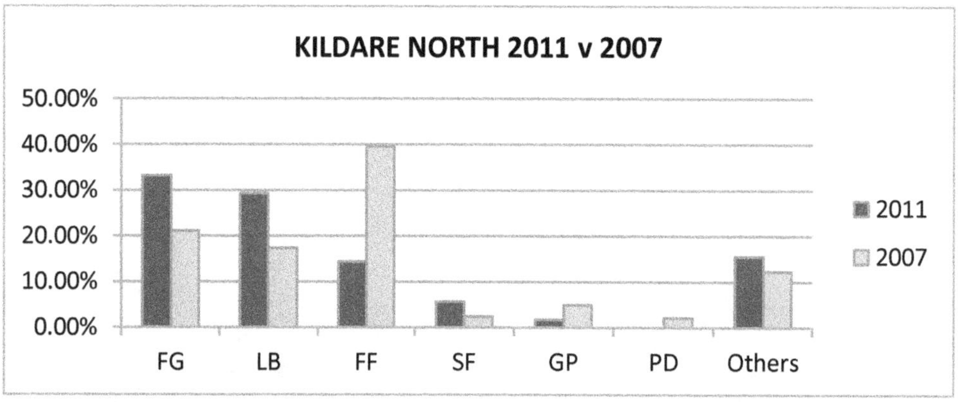

KILDARE NORTH 2011 COUNT DETAILS							
Seats	4					Quota	10,245
Candidate	**Party**	**1st**	**2nd** Fitzgerald Doyle Beirne Murphy	**3rd** Fitzpatrick Votes	**4th** Kelly Votes	**5th** McGinley Votes	
Durkan, Bernard*	FG	10,168	*+252* 10,420	10,420	10,420	10,420	
Stagg, Emmet*	LB	9,718	*+258* 9,976	*+288* 10,264	10,264	10,264	
Murphy, Catherine #	NP	6,911	*+563* 7,474	*+222* 7,696	*+1,020* 8,716	*+2,923* 11,639	
Lawlor, Anthony	FG	6,882	*+192* 7,074	*+209* 7,283	*+384* 7,667	*+1,421* 9,088	
Brady, Áine*	FF	4,777	*+133* 4,910	*+1,717* 6,627	*+194* 6,821	*+467* 7,288	
McGinley, John	LB	5,261	*+228* 5,489	*+101* 5,590	*+859* 6,449	*-6,449* Eliminated	
Kelly, Martin	SF	2,896	*+147* 3,043	*+68* 3,111	*-3,111* Eliminated		
Fitzpatrick, Michael*	FF	2,659	*+55* 2,714	*-2,714* Eliminated			
Fitzgerald, Shane	GP	905	*-905* Eliminated				
Doyle-Higgins, Eric	NP	423	*-423* Eliminated				
Beirne, Michael	NP	422	*-422* Eliminated				
Murphy, Bart	NP	200	*-200* Eliminated				
Non-transferable Cumulative			*+122* 122	*+109* 231	*+654* 885	*+1,638* 2,523	
Total		**51,222**	**51,222**	**51,222**	**51,222**	**51,222**	

KILDARE NORTH 2011 TRANSFER ANALYSIS							
From	**To**	**FG**	**LB**	**FF**	**SF**	**Others**	**Non Trans**
LB	6,449	1,421 *22.03%*		467 *7.24%*		2,923 *45.32%*	1,638 *25.40%*
FF	2,714	209 *7.70%*	389 *14.33%*	1,717 *63.26%*	68 *2.51%*	222 *8.18%*	109 *4.02%*
SF	3,111	384 *12.34%*	859 *27.61%*	194 *6.24%*		1,020 *32.79%*	654 *21.02%*
GP	905	206 *22.76%*	226 *24.97%*	87 *9.61%*	68 *7.51%*	261 *28.84%*	57 *6.30%*
NP	1,045	238 *22.78%*	260 *24.88%*	101 *9.67%*	79 *7.56%*	302 *28.90%*	65 *6.22%*
Total	**14,224**	**2,458** ***17.28%***	**1,734** ***12.19%***	**2,566** ***18.04%***	**215** ***1.51%***	**4,728** ***33.24%***	**2,523** ***17.74%***

KILDARE SOUTH 2011

"Fine Gael reclaim seat in former leader's constituency"

There was a minor boundary revision here with a population of 1, 314 from the Kilpatrick and Newtown areas transferred to Kildare North.

This was a very predictable constituency in the context of 2011. Labour's Jack Wall would be re-elected, Martin Heydon would reclaim a seat for Fine Gael after nine years, and one of the two Fianna Fail incumbents would survive the deluge.

So it proved. Martin Heydon took a third of the votes in the constituency, the highest share of any candidate in the country, and achieved Fine Gael's second largest vote gain outside Dublin. This achieved of course in the constituency of the party's former leader, Alan Dukes, who lost his seat in 2002.

Jack Wall, who unusually for a Labour TD has a strong GAA background, was elected on the first count for the first time in his career.

Fianna Fail duly took its one seat, the loser being Seán Power, a five-term veteran, and the victor Seán Ó Fearghaíl. Remarkably, Ó Fearghaíl had started out on the road before Power, having first stood in 1987 and losing on three further occasions before finally being elected in 2002.

There was almost a sting in the tail on this occasion, as independent councillor Paddy Kennedy from Newbridge nearly deprived Fianna Fail of any representation. Aided by over 1,000 votes from Heydon's surplus, and by nearly 1,700 votes upon the elimination of fellow Newbridge candidate Jason Turner of Sinn Fein, he finished fewer than 1,000 votes behind Ó Fearghaíl on the seventh count.

Martin Heydon newly elected Fine Gael TD for Kildare South

KILDARE SOUTH TDs 2011

MARTIN HEYDON (FG)

Blackrath, Colbinstown, Co. Kildare; Tel: 045 487624; Mobile: 087 6262546
Leinster House: Tel: 01 6183017; Email: martin.heydon@oireachtas.ie
Website: www.martinheydon.com

Born Dublin 9th August 1978. Single. Educated Cross and Passage College, Kilcullen; Kildalton Agricultural College, Kilkenny. Farmer. Elected at his first attempt in 2011.

Member Committee on Procedure and Privileges. Member Committee on Communications, Natural Resources and Agriculture. First elected to Kildare County Council in the Athy electoral area in 2009.

JACK WALL (LB)

Castlemitchell, Athy, Co. Kildare; Tel: 059 8631495; Mobile: 087 2570275.
Constituency Office: 15 Leinster Street, Athy, Co. Kildare; Tel: 059 8632874
Leinster House: 01 6183571; Email: jack.wall@oireachtas.ie
Website: www.jackwall.ie

Born Castledermot, Co. Kildare 1st July 1945. Married to Ann Byrne, two sons, two daughters. Educated Castledermot Vocational School, Kevin Street College of Technology. Formerly Electrician. First elected 1997 and at each subsequent election.

Member Committee on Members' Interests. Member Joint Administration Committee. Spokesperson on Community and Rural Affairs 2007-2011. Vice-Chairman Joint Administration Committee 2007-2011. Member Joint Committee on Arts, Sport, Tourism, Community, Rural and Gaeltacht Affairs and Member Committee on Members' Interests 2007-2011. Elected Chairman of Parliamentary Party 2007. Spokesperson on Arts, Sport and Tourism 2002-2007. Convenor Select Committee on European Affairs 2002-2007. Member Joint Committee on Arts, Sport, Tourism, Community Rural and Gaeltacht Affairs 2002-2007. Front Bench spokesperson on Marine and National Resources 1997-2002. Taoiseach's nominee to the Seanad 1993-1997. Member Kildare County Council 1999-2003. Member, Athy UDC 1993-2003 (Chairman 1994/1995). Former Chairman Kildare GAA County Board.

SEAN O FEARGHAIL (FF)

Fennor House, Kildare, Co. Kildare; Tel: 045 522966; Mobile: 087 2367155
Constituency Office: 4 Offaly Street, Athy, Co. Kildare; Tel: 059 8634805
Leinster House: 01 6183948; Email: sean.ofearghail@oireachtas.ie
Website: www.seanofearghail.ie

Born Dublin 17th April 1960. Married to Mary Clare Meaney, one son Eoghan, three daughters Aoife, Caoimhe and Nessa. Educated St. Joseph's Academy, Kildare. Farmer. Contested 1987, 1989, 1992 and 1997 general elections. First elected 2002 and at each subsequent election.

Appointed Fianna Fail Whip and spokesperson on Foreign Affairs and Trade March 2011. Member Committee on Procedure and Privileges. Member Committee on Finance, Public Expenditure and Reform. Member Committee on Foreign Affairs and Trade. Vice-Chairman British-Irish Inter-Parliamentary Body 2007-2011. Member Joint Committee on Education and Science and Member Joint Committee on Constitutional Amendment on Children 2007-2011. Member Joint Administration Committee and Member Dail Committee on Procedure and Privileges 2007-2011. Member Joint Committee on Agriculture and Food and Committee on Justice, Equality and Law Reform 2002-2007. Won Seanad by-election in 2000. Member Kildare County Council 1985-2003 and former leader of Fianna Fail group on the council.

	KILDARE SOUTH 2011						
	FIRST PREFERENCE VOTES						
	Seats	3			9,568		
	Candidate	Party	1st	%	Quota	Count	Status
1	**Heydon, Martin**	**FG**	**12,755**	**33.33%**	**1.33**	**1**	**Made Quota**
2	**Wall, Jack***	**LB**	**10,645**	**27.82%**	**1.11**	**1**	**Made Quota**
3	**Ó Fearghaíl, Seán***	**FF**	**4,514**	**11.80%**	**0.47**	**7**	**Elected**
4	Kennedy, Paddy	NP	2,806	7.33%	0.29	7	Not Elected
5	Power, Seán*	FF	3,793	9.91%	0.40	6	Eliminated
6	Turner, Jason	SF	2,308	6.03%	0.24	5	Eliminated
7	Reid, Clifford T.	NP	926	2.42%	0.10	4	No Expenses
8	Cummins, Vivian	GP	523	1.37%	0.05	3	No Expenses
8	***Outgoing**		**38,270**	**100.00%**	**9,568**	**2,392**	**No Expenses**

KILDARE SOUTH 2011												
PARTY VOTE												
	2011					2007					Change	
Party	**Cand**	**1st**	**%**	**Quota**	**Seats**	**Cand**	**1st**	**%**	**Quota**	**Seats**	**%**	**Seats**
FG	1	12,755	33.33%	1.33	1	2	5,939	17.17%	0.69		+16.16%	
LB	1	10,645	27.82%	1.11	1	1	7,154	20.68%	0.83	1	+7.13%	
FF	2	8,307	21.71%	0.87	1	2	17,425	50.37%	2.01	2	-28.67%	
SF	1	2,308	6.03%	0.24							+6.03%	
GP	1	523	1.37%	0.05		1	2,136	6.18%	0.25		-4.81%	
PD						1	1,513	4.37%	0.17		-4.37%	
Others	2	3,732	9.75%	0.39		1	424	1.23%	0.05		+8.53%	
Total	**8**	**38,270**	**100.0%**	**9,568**	**3**	**8**	**34,591**	**100.0%**	**8,648**	**3**	**0.00%**	**0**
Electorate		**58,867**	**65.01%**				**56,670**	**61.04%**			**+3.97%**	
Spoiled		**353**	**0.91%**				**347**	**0.99%**			**-0.08%**	
Turnout		**38,623**	**65.61%**				**34,938**	**61.65%**			**+3.96%**	

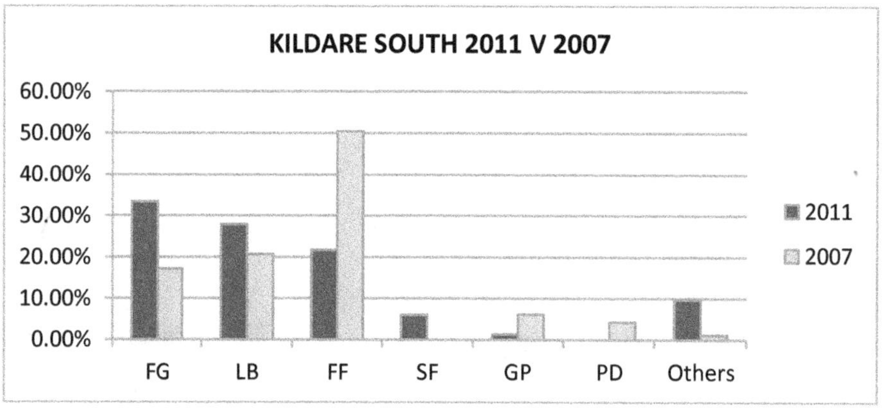

KILDARE SOUTH 2011 COUNT DETAILS								
Seats	3						Quota	9,568
Candidate	**Party**	**1st**	**2nd** Heydon Surplus	**3rd** Wall Surplus	**4th** Cummins Votes	**5th** Reid Votes	**6th** Turner Votes	**7th** Power Votes
			-3,187					
Heydon, Martin	FG	12,755	9,568	9,568	9,568	9,568	9,568	9,568
				-1,077				
Wall, Jack*	LB	10,645	10,645	9,568	9,568	9,568	9,568	9,568
			+447	*+136*	*+80*	*+138*	*+237*	*+3,155*
Ó Fearghaíl, Seán*	FF	4,514	4,961	5,097	5,177	5,315	5,552	8,707
			+1,019	*+256*	*+306*	*+769*	*+1,685*	*+869*
Kennedy, Paddy	NP	2,806	3,825	4,081	4,387	5,156	6,841	7,710
			+514	*+138*	*+97*	*+108*	*+238*	*-4,888*
Power, Seán*	FF	3,793	4,307	4,445	4,542	4,650	4,888	Eliminated
			+302	*+212*	*+82*	*+349*	*-3,253*	
Turner, Jason	SF	2,308	2,610	2,822	2,904	3,253	Eliminated	
			+484	*+234*	*+229*	*-1,873*		
Reid, Clifford T.	NP	926	1,410	1,644	1,873	Eliminated		
			+421	*+101*	*-1,045*			
Cummins, Vivian	GP	523	944	1,045	Eliminated			
Non-transferable					*+251*	*+509*	*+1,093*	*+864*
Cumulative			0	0	251	760	1,853	2,717
Total		**38,270**	**38,270**	**38,270**	**38,270**	**38,270**	**38,270**	**38,270**

KILDARE SOUTH 2011 TRANSFER ANALYSIS						
From	**To**	**FF**	**SF**	**GP**	**Others**	**Non Trans**
FG	3,187	961	302	421	1,503	
		30.15%	*9.48%*	*13.21%*	*47.16%*	
LB	1,077	274	212	101	490	
		25.44%	*19.68%*	*9.38%*	*45.50%*	
FF	4,888	3,155			869	864
		64.55%			*17.78%*	*17.68%*
SF	3,253	475			1,685	1,093
		14.60%			*51.80%*	*33.60%*
GP	1,045	177	82		535	251
		16.94%	*7.85%*		*51.20%*	*24.02%*
NP	1,873	246	349		769	509
		13.13%	*18.63%*		*41.06%*	*27.18%*
Total	**15,323**	**5,288**	**945**	**522**	**5,851**	**2,717**
		34.51%	***6.17%***	***3.41%***	***38.18%***	***17.73%***

KILDARE REGION		
MAIN BOUNDARY CHANGES		
Dail	Constituency	Seats
1 (1918)	Kildare North	1
	Kildare South	1
4 (1923) - 8 (1933)	Kildare	3
9 (1937) - 12 (1944)	Carlow-Kildare	4
13 (1948) - 16 (1957)	Kildare	3
17 (1961) - 18 (1965)	Kildare	4
19 (1969) - 21 (1977)	Kildare	3
22 (1981) - 27 (1992)	Kildare	5
28 (1997) - 29 (2002)	Kildare North	3
	Kildare South	3
30 (2007) - 31 (2011)	Kildare North	4
	Kildare South	3

KILDARE														
All TDs 1918-2011														
	Surname	Forename	Party	Elected										Total
1	Norton**	William	LB	32	33	37	38	43	44	48	51	54	57	61	11
2	Harris	Thomas	FF	31*	32	33	37	38	43	44	48	51	54		10
3	McCreevy	Charlie	FF	77	81	82	82	87	89	92	97	02			9
4	Durkan	Bernard	FG	81	82N	87	89	92	97	02	07	11			9
5	Sweetman	Gerard	FG	48	51	54	57	61	65	69					7
6	Power	Patrick	FF	69	73	77	81	82	82	87					7
7	Dukes	Alan	FG	81	82	82	87	89	92	97					7
8	Stagg	Emmet	LB	87	89	92	97	02	07	11					7
9	Bermingham	Joseph	LB	73	77	81	82	82							5
10	Power	Sean	FF	89	92	97	02	07							5
11	Wall	Jack	LB	97	02	07	11								4
12	Humphreys**	Francis	FF	37	38	43	44								4
13	O Fearghail	Sean	FF	02	07	11									3
14	Buckley**	Donal	FF	18	27	27									3
15	Colohan**	Hugh	LB	23	27	27									3
16	Wolfe	George	CG	23	27	27									3
17	Minch	Capt. Sydney	FG	32	33	37									3
18	Hughes	James	FG	38	43	44									3
19	Boylan	Terence	FF	64*	65	69									3
20	Murphy	Catherine	NP	05*	11										2
21	Dooley	Patrick	FF	57	61										2
22	Crinion**	Brendan	FF	61	65										2
23	Malone	Patrick	FG	70*	73										2
24	O'Connor**	Art	SF	18											1
25	Conlan	John	F	23											1
26	Norton	Patrick	LB	65											1
27	Brady	Gerry	FF	82F											1
28	Brady	Aine	FF	07											1
29	Fitzpatrick	Michael	FF	07											1
30	Lawlor	Anthony	FG	11											1
31	Heydon	Martin	FG	11											1
31	Total							*Includes 4 By-Elections					*	122
	** Also elected in another constituency													
K	Humphreys**	Francis	FF	Carlow-Kilkenny							32	51	57	3
	Crinion**	Brendan	FF	Meath							73	77	81	3
K	Buckley**	Donal	FF	Wicklow							21			1
	O'Connor**	Art	SF	Wicklow							21			1
K	Colohan**	Hugh	LB	Wicklow							22			1
K	Norton**	William	LB	Dublin County							26*			1
6	Total							*Includes 1 By-Election					*	10
K	Included in Kildare Total													

KILDARE REGION 1918-2011																												
			FG		LB		FF		SF		GP		WP		PD		DL		C na P		Farmers		Nat League		Centre P		Others	
Dail		Seats	S	% Vote	S	% Vote	S	% Vote	S	% Vote	S	% Vote	S	% Vote	S	% Vote	S	% Vote	S	% Vote	S	% Vote	S	% Vote	S	% Vote	S	% Vote
1	1918	2							2																			
4	1923	3	1	27.05%	1	32.16%		21.26%													1	19.53%						
5	1927	3	1	18.03%	1	26.97%	1	23.57%		5.11%												10.42%		6.38%				9.51%
6	1927	3	1	29.56%	1	19.28%	1	36.21%														14.95%						
7	1932	3	1	34.67%	1	22.71%	1	42.62%																				
8	1933	3	1	23.84%	1	20.02%	1	39.47%																		16.67%		
9	1937	4	1	33.35%	1	26.04%	2	40.61%																				
10	1938	4	1	33.08%	1	20.84%	2	46.07%																				
11	1943	4	1	24.33%	1	32.13%	2	35.43%																				8.10%
12	1944	4	1	27.57%	1	27.57%	2	44.86%																				
13	1948	3	1	21.14%	1	26.33%	1	38.87%												13.66%								
14	1951	3	1	24.58%	1	30.11%	1	44.87%																				0.44%
15	1954	3	1	28.74%	1	30.42%	1	40.84%																				
16	1957	3	1	23.88%	1	26.51%	1	49.61%																				
17	1961	4	1	34.10%	1	25.37%	2	40.53%																				
18	1965	4	1	30.29%	1	20.90%	2	48.81%																				
19	1969	3	1	35.11%		16.04%	2	43.45%																				5.40%
20	1973	3	1	27.36%	1	22.40%	1	50.24%																				
21	1977	3		19.87%	1	21.35%	2	58.79%																				
22	1981	5	2	31.54%	1	18.35%	2	48.63%																				1.48%
23	1982	5	1	32.05%	1	16.12%	3	51.82%																				
24	1982	5	2	36.50%	1	15.23%	2	47.82%																				0.45%
25	1987	5	2	26.30%	1	14.09%	2	42.66%		2.64%				2.31%		11.77%												0.23%
26	1989	5	2	31.14%	1	17.22%	2	36.33%				2.87%		2.99%		4.18%												5.28%
27	1992	5	2	22.44%	1	26.82%	2	33.48%		1.43%		2.11%				7.00%		3.20%										3.52%
28	1997	6	2	26.33%	2	19.60%	2	36.17%				2.33%				9.96%		4.59%										1.03%
29	2002	6	1	17.65%	2	19.96%	3	44.81%				4.85%				11.90%												0.83%
30	2007	7	1	19.46%	2	18.85%	4	44.22%		1.38%		5.45%				3.13%												7.51%
31	2011	7	3	33.30%	2	28.63%	1	17.59%		5.82%		1.60%															1	13.06%
1918-2011		**118**	**35**	**27.51%**	**31**	**22.29%**	**48**	**40.53%**	**2**	**0.86%**		**1.16%**		**0.25%**		**2.54%**		**0.39%**		**0.32%**	**1**	**0.83%**		**0.13%**		**0.40%**	**1**	**2.79%**
National		**4,618**	**1,453**	**30.77%**	**482**	**11.53%**	**1,985**	**41.86%**	**232**	**1.99%**	**16**	**0.75%**	**17**	**0.78%**	**44**	**1.42%**	**8**	**0.22%**	**18**	**0.77%**	**42**	**0.90%**	**10**	**0.24%**	**11**	**0.30%**	**300**	**8.44%**

LAOIS-OFFALY 2011

"Only one seat changed hands as FF vote fell by 30%"

A revision of the constituency boundary here saw a population of 4,276 in the former Roscrea No.2 Rural District transferred to Tipperary North. It retained its five seats.

When Brian Cowen, who took over 19,000 first preferences in 2007, announced on 31 January that he would not be contesting the 2011 election, other parties immediately fixed covetous eyes on one if not two of the 3 seats that FF had won at every election since 1977.

In the event only one seat changed hands in Laois–Offaly. Although the Fianna Fail vote dropped by virtually 30 per cent, the party held two of its seats, making this the only constituency in the country, other than the new leader's Cork South Central, where it won more than one seat. The party literature here looked like it used to in better days, featuring all the candidates and asking people to 'Vote 1, 2, 3 in order of your choice', rather than the now more common format of candidate advertisements asking people to 'Vote No 1 for Me' with the names of any running mate(s) in tiny print at the bottom. The Taoiseach was replaced on the ticket by his brother Barry, who polled more than 8,000 first preferences and retained the family seat quite comfortably. Seán Fleming had been given no advancement by either Bertie Ahern or Brian Cowen, and this may now have stood to his advantage as he stayed ahead of junior minister John Moloney, his fellow Laois Fianna Fail TD, to return to the Dáil for a fourth term in which he finally has a front-bench position.

Fine Gael had hoped to win three seats here for the first time since 1973, but its vote rose by less than the national average and it was never in the running for the last seat. It retained its existing two seats without difficulty, the retiring Olwyn Enright being succeeded by Marcella Corcoran Kennedy, based in Birr like Enright herself. Charlie Flanagan headed the poll as his father used to do for many years, but, just as in 1994, he had made the mistake of expressing no confidence in his party leader nine months before that leader became Taoiseach, and despite his years of service on the opposition front bench he found himself on the back-benches when the party entered government.

The only seat lost by Fianna Fail was taken by Sinn Fein's Brian Stanley, who almost trebled his 2007 vote to win the party's first seat here since independence. He owed this partly to his ability, not shared by all Sinn Fein candidates, to attract transfers, picking up over 3,700 from first count to last and thus widening his lead over the only serious challenger, John Whelan of Labour. Whelan polled respectably given the fallout over his selection as the Labour candidate, but the dispute cannot have helped.

Other candidates polled nearly 20 per cent of the votes between them, but this was spread among 12 candidates. Dissident Fianna Failer John Foley and county councillor John Leahy both topped 4,000 first preferences, but in the end most of their votes transferred back to the major party candidates.

LAOIS–OFFALY TDs 2011

CHARLIE FLANAGAN (FG)

Glenlahan, Stradbally Road, Portlaoise, Co. Laois; Tel: 057 8660707; Mobile: 087 2578450
Constituency Office: Lismard Court, Portlaoise, Co. Laois; Tel: 057 8620232;
Leinster House: 01 6183625; Email: charles.flanagan@oireachtas.ie
Website: www.charlieflanaganfinegael.ie

Born Mountmellick, Co. Laois November 1956. Married to Mary McCormack, two daughters. Educated Knockbeg College, Carlow; UCD (BA); Incorporated Law Society. Solicitor.
First elected 1987-2002. Lost his seat in 2002. Re-elected 2007 and 2011.

Elected Chairman Parliamentary Party June 2011. Director of Elections for Gay Mitchell for Presidency election 2011. Member Select Committee on Investigations, Oversight and Petitions. Front bench spokesperson on Children 2010-2011. Supported Richard Bruton in his failed attempt to oust Enda Kenny as party leader in June 2010. Spokesperson on Justice and Law Reform September 2007-June 2010. Member Joint Committee on Justice, Equality, Defence and Women's Rights 2007-2011. Junior Spokesperson on Criminal Law Reform, Northern Ireland 1997-2002. Former front bench spokesperson on Health 1993-1994; on Transport and Tourism 1992-1993. Fine Gael Chief Whip 1990-1992. Spokesperson on Law Reform 1988-1990. Former Vice-Chairman British-Irish Inter-Parliamentary Body. Member Laois County Council 1987-2002. Son of the late Oliver J. Flanagan, TD for Laois-Offaly 1943-1987 and Minister for Defence 1976-1977.

MARCELLA CORCORAN KENNEDY (FG)

Oakley Park, Clareen, Birr, Co. Offaly; Tel: 057 9131208; Mobile: 087 6330039;
Constituency Office: 5 The Courtyard, Emmet St., Birr, Co. Offaly; Tel: 057 9125825
Leinster House: 01 6184075; Email: marcella.corcorankennedy@oireachtas.ie
Website: www.corcorankennedy.ie

Born London, 7th January 1963. Married to Seamus Kennedy, one son, one daughter. Educated: St. Joseph's of Cluny and St. Saran's Ferbane; Roscrea Community College, Co. Tipperary; Boston College (Effective Politics Programme). Former ESB employee. Elected at her first attempt in 2011.

Member Committee on Environment, Transport, Culture and the Gaeltacht. Elected to Offaly County Council in 1999 and 2004 but lost her seat in 2009. Chair and company director of Birr Theatre and Arts Centre; Company director of Filmbase and a member of Film Offaly.

BARRY COWEN (FF)

Kilnacarra, Lahinch, Clara, Co. Offaly; Tel: 057 9323277; Mobile: 086 8224928
Constituency Office: Grand Canal House, William Street, Tullamore, Co. Offaly,
Tel: 057 9321976; Leinster House: 01 6183662; Email: barry.cowen@oireachtas.ie

Born Dublin August 1967. Married to Mary; two sons, two daughters. Educated Cistercian College, Roscrea, Co. Tipperary. Auctioneer & Valuer. Elected at first attempt in 2011.

Appointed Spokesperson on Social Protection 12th April 2011. Member Committee on Jobs, Social Protection and Education. Co-opted onto Offaly County Council as replacement for his brother Brian Cowen TD in 1992. Retained his seat in1999, 2004 and 2009. Brother of Brian Cowen, Taoiseach 2008-2011. Son of the late Bernard Cowen, Dáil Deputy 1969-1973, 1977-1984 and Senator 1973-1977; Minister of State 1982.

BRIAN STANLEY (SF)

40 Clonrooske Abbey, Portlaoise, Co. Laois; Tel: 057 8662851;
Leinster House: 01 6183987; Email: brian.stanley@oireachtas.ie

Born 14th January 1958. Married to Caroline, one son, one daughter. Educated Mountrath Vocational School; Waterford Institute of Technology. Former Care Assistant. Contested 2002 and 2007 Dail elections in Laois-Offaly. First elected 2011.

Appointed Spokesperson on Environment, Community and Local Government 22nd March 2011. Member Joint Administration Committee. Member Committee on Environment, Transport, Culture and the Gaeltacht. Contested 1999 local election in Portlaoise. First elected 2004. Retained his seat in 2009. Contested 1994 Portlaoise TC election. First elected 1994. Retained his seat in 1999, 2004 and 2009.

SEAN FLEMING (FF)

Silveracre, Castletown, Portlaoise, Co. Laois; Tel: 057 8732692; Mobile: 087 2943294;
Leinster House: 01 6183472; Email: sean.fleming@oireachtas.ie

Born The Swan, Co. Laois 27th February 1958. Married to Mary O'Gorman, one son Peter. Educated Salesian College, Ballinakill; UCD (BComm); Fellow of the Institute of Chartered Accountants in Ireland. Accountant. First elected 1997 and at each subsequent election.

Appointed Spokesperson on Public Expenditure and Financial Sector Reform 4th August 2011. Spokesperson on Public Sector Reform April–August 2011. Member Committee of Public Accounts. Chairman Joint Committee on the Environment, Heritage and Local Government 2007-2011. Member Public Accounts Committee and Member Joint Committee on Climate Change and Energy Security 2007-2011. Chairman Joint Committee on Finance and the Public Service 2002-2007. Member Committee of Public Accounts 2002-2007. Member Laois County Council 1999-2003. Former Financial Director of the Fianna Fail Party at National Level.

	LAOIS-OFFALY 2011 FIRST PREFERENCE VOTES						
	Seats	5			12,360		
	Candidate	Party	1st	%	Quota	Count	Status
1	**Flanagan, Charles***	**FG**	**10,427**	**14.06%**	**0.84**	**8**	**Made Quota**
2	**Corcoran Kennedy, Marcella**	**FG**	**5,817**	**7.84%**	**0.47**	**13**	**Made Quota**
3	**Cowen, Barry**	**FF**	**8,257**	**11.13%**	**0.67**	**13**	**Elected**
4	**Stanley, Brian**	**SF**	**8,032**	**10.83%**	**0.65**	**13**	**Elected**
5	**Fleming, Sean***	**FF**	**6,024**	**8.12%**	**0.49**	**13**	**Elected**
6	Whelan, John	LB	5,802	7.82%	0.47	13	Not Elected
7	Foley, John	NP	4,465	6.02%	0.36	12	Eliminated
8	Moloney, John*	FF	5,579	7.52%	0.45	11	Eliminated
9	Quinn, Liam	FG	4,482	6.04%	0.36	10	Eliminated
10	Leahy, John	NP	4,882	6.58%	0.39	9	Eliminated
11	Moran, John	FG	4,306	5.81%	0.35	7	Eliminated
12	Fitzpatrick, Eddie	NP	2,544	3.43%	0.21	6	No Expenses
13	Adebari, Rotimi	NP	628	0.85%	0.05	5	No Expenses
14	Bracken, John	NP	625	0.84%	0.05	5	No Expenses
15	Fitzpatrick, Ray	SP	561	0.76%	0.05	5	No Expenses
16	McDonnell, Fergus	NP	525	0.71%	0.04	5	No Expenses
17	Dumpleton, Liam	NP	382	0.52%	0.03	4	No Expenses
18	Fanning, James	NP	335	0.45%	0.03	3	No Expenses
19	Fettes, Christopher	GP	306	0.41%	0.02	2	No Expenses
20	Boland, John	NP	119	0.16%	0.01	1	No Expenses
21	Cox, Michael	NP	60	0.08%	0.00	1	No Expenses
21	***Outgoing**		**74,158**	**100.00%**	**12,360**	**3,091**	**No Expenses**

LAOIS-OFFALY 2011 PARTY VOTE												
	2011					2007					Change	
Party	Cand	1st	%	Quota	Seats	Cand	1st	%	Quota	Seats	%	Seats
FG	4	25,032	33.75%	2.03	2	3	19,560	27.36%	1.64	2	+6.39%	
LB	1	5,802	7.82%	0.47		2	1,703	2.38%	0.14		+5.44%	
FF	3	19,860	26.78%	1.61	2	4	40,307	56.38%	3.38	3	-29.60%	-1
SF	1	8,032	10.83%	0.65	1	1	3,656	5.11%	0.31		+5.72%	+1
SP	1	561	0.76%	0.05							+0.76%	
GP	1	306	0.41%	0.02		1	812	1.14%	0.07		-0.72%	
PD						1	4,233	5.92%	0.36		-5.92%	
Others	10	14,565	19.64%	1.18		4	1,220	1.71%	0.10		+17.93%	
Total	**21**	**74,158**	**100.0%**	**12,360**	**5**	**16**	**71,491**	**100.0%**	**11,916**	**5**	**0.00%**	**0**
Electorate		**108,142**	**68.57%**				**103,673**	**68.96%**			**-0.38%**	
Spoiled		**1,055**	**1.40%**				**662**	**0.92%**			**+0.49%**	
Turnout		**75,213**	**69.55%**				**72,153**	**69.60%**			**-0.05%**	

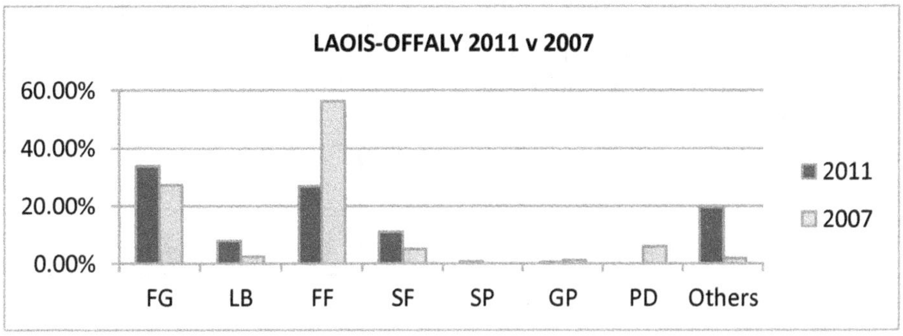

LAOIS-OFFALY 2011 COUNT DETAILS														
Seats	5												Quota	12,360
Candidate	Party	1st	2nd	3rd	4th	5th	6th	7th	8th	9th	10th	11th	12th	13th
			Boland Cox	Fettes Votes	Fanning Votes	Dumpleton Votes	Adebari Bracken Fitzpatrick McDonnell	Fitzpatrick Votes	Moran Votes	Flanagan Surplus	Leahy Votes	Quinn Votes	Moloney Votes	Foley Votes
			+5	+16	+21	+22	+169	+347	+2,508	-1,155				
Flanagan, Charles*	FG	10,427	10,432	10,448	10,469	10,491	10,660	11,007	13,515	12,360	12,360	12,360	12,360	12,360
			+21	+33	+48	+59	+185	+126	+306	+394	+1,302	+3,546	+269	+1,022
Corcoran Kennedy, M.	FG	5,817	5,838	5,871	5,919	5,978	6,163	6,289	6,595	6,989	8,291	11,837	12,106	13,128
			+24	+4	+17	+30	+165	+139	+11	+4	+763	+242	+998	+1,206
Cowen, Barry	FF	8,257	8,281	8,285	8,302	8,332	8,497	8,636	8,647	8,651	9,414	9,656	10,654	11,860
			+10	+16	+21	+53	+461	+326	+193	+58	+623	+269	+645	+1,068
Stanley, Brian	SF	8,032	8,042	8,058	8,079	8,132	8,593	8,919	9,112	9,170	9,793	10,062	10,707	11,775
			+2	+10	+7	+7	+51	+105	+363	+116	+153	+129	+3,226	+658
Fleming, Sean*	FF	6,024	6,026	6,036	6,043	6,050	6,101	6,206	6,569	6,685	6,838	6,967	10,193	10,851
			+3	+85	+22	+39	+304	+234	+275	+101	+423	+526	+394	+818
Whelan, John	LB	5,802	5,805	5,890	5,912	5,951	6,255	6,489	6,764	6,865	7,288	7,814	8,208	9,026
			+4	+9	+22	+24	+406	+560	+16	+7	+817	+901	+290	-7,521
Foley, John	NP	4,465	4,469	4,478	4,500	4,524	4,930	5,490	5,506	5,513	6,330	7,231	7,521	Eliminated
			+9	+9	+10	+9	+54	+319	+104	+23	+177	+106	-6,399	
Moloney, John*	FF	5,579	5,588	5,597	5,607	5,616	5,670	5,989	6,093	6,116	6,293	6,399	Eliminated	
			+4	+13	+17	+10	+93	+165	+564	+449	+478	-6,275		
Quinn, Liam	FG	4,482	4,486	4,499	4,516	4,526	4,619	4,784	5,348	5,797	6,275	Eliminated		
			+17	+9	+52	+72	+227	+179	+11	+3	-5,452			
Leahy, John	NP	4,882	4,899	4,908	4,960	5,032	5,259	5,438	5,449	5,452	Eliminated			
			+1	+11	+8	+2	+45	+64	-4,437					
Moran, John	FG	4,306	4,307	4,318	4,326	4,328	4,373	4,437	Eliminated					
			+9	+12	+21	+33	+157	-2,776						
Fitzpatrick, Eddie	NP	2,544	2,553	2,565	2,586	2,619	2,776	Eliminated						
			+6	+28	+13	+16	-691							
Adebari, Rotimi	NP	628	634	662	675	691	Eliminated							
			+31	+9	+9	+21	-695							
Bracken, John	NP	625	656	665	674	695	Eliminated							
			+1	+22	+10	+10	-604							
Fitzpatrick, Ray	SP	561	562	584	594	604	Eliminated							
			+1	+1	+6	+9	-542							
McDonnell, Fergus	NP	525	526	527	533	542	Eliminated							
			+11	+6	+37	-436								
Dumpleton, Liam	NP	382	393	399	436	Eliminated								
			+8	+9	-352									
Fanning, James	NP	335	343	352	Eliminated									
			+2	-308										
Fettes, Christopher	GP	306	308	Eliminated										
			-119											
Boland, John	NP	119	Eliminated											
			-60											
Cox, Michael	NP	60	Eliminated											
Non-transferable			+10	+6	+11	+20	+215	+212	+86		+716	+556	+577	+2,749
Cumulative			10	16	27	47	262	474	560	560	1,276	1,832	2,409	5,158
Total		**74,158**	**74,158**	**74,158**	**74,158**	**74,158**	**74,158**	**74,158**	**74,158**	**74,158**	**74,158**	**74,158**	**74,158**	**74,158**

LAOIS-OFFALY 2011 TRANSFER ANALYSIS									
From	**To**	**FG**	**LB**	**FF**	**SF**	**SP**	**GP**	**Others**	**Non Trans**
FG	11,867	7,767	902	1,098	520			938	642
		65.45%	*7.60%*	*9.25%*	*4.38%*			*7.90%*	*5.41%*
FF	6,399	269	394	4,224	645			290	577
		4.20%	*6.16%*	*66.01%*	*10.08%*			*4.53%*	*9.02%*
SP	604	117	73	64	110			189	51
		19.37%	*12.09%*	*10.60%*	*18.21%*			*31.29%*	*8.44%*
GP	308	73	85	23	16	22		83	6
		23.70%	*27.60%*	*7.47%*	*5.19%*	*7.14%*		*26.95%*	*1.95%*
NP	18,644	4,097	1,770	3,841	2,452	21	2	2,579	3,882
		21.97%	*9.49%*	*20.60%*	*13.15%*	*0.11%*	*0.01%*	*13.83%*	*20.82%*
Total	**37,822**	**12,323**	**3,224**	**9,250**	**3,743**	**43**	**2**	**4,079**	**5,158**
		32.58%	***8.52%***	***24.46%***	***9.90%***	***0.11%***	***0.01%***	***10.78%***	***13.64%***

LAOIS-OFFALY		
MAIN BOUNDARY CHANGES		
Dail	**Constituency**	**Seats**
1 (1918)	King's County	1
	Queen's County	1
2 (1921) - 3 (1922)	Leix-Offaly	4
4 (1923) - 16 (1957)	Leix-Offaly	5
17 (1961) - 31 (2011)	Laois-Offaly	5

LAOIS-OFFALY																		
All TDs 1918-2011																		
	Surname	**Forename**	**Party**	**Elected**														**Total**
1	Flanagan	Oliver J.	FG	43	44	48	51	54	57	61	65	69	73	77	81	82	82	14
2	Davin	William	LB	22	23	27	27	32	33	37	38	43	44	48	51	54		13
3	Boland	Patrick	FF	27	27	32	33	37	38	43	44	48	51					10
4	Connolly	Ger	FF	69	73	77	81	82	82	87	89	92						9
5	Enright	Tom	FG	69	73	77	81	82	82	87	89	97						9
6	Gorry	Patrick	FF	27S	32	37	38	43	44	48								7
7	Cowen	Brian	FF	84*	87	89	92	97	02	07								7
8	O'Higgins(sen)**	Thomas F.	FG	32	33	37	38	43	44									6
9	O'Higgins(jun)**	Thomas F.	FG	48	51	54	57	61	65									6
10	Hyland	Liam	FF	81	82	82	87	89	92									6
11	Flanagan	Charles	FG	87	89	92	97	07	11									6
12	Lalor	Patrick	FF	61	65	69	73	77										5
13	Cowen	Bernard	FF	69	77	81	82	82										5
14	Egan	Nicholas	FF	54	57	61	65											4
15	Fleming	Sean	FF	97	02	07	11											4
16	O'Higgins**	Kevin	CT	18	21	22												3
17	Bulfin	Francis	CG	21	22	23												3
18	Dwyer	James	CG	26*	27	27												3
19	Maher	Peadar	FF	51	54	57												3
20	Egan	Kieran	FF	56*	57	61												3
21	Moloney	John	FF	97	02	07												3
22	McCartan	Patrick	SF	18	21													2
23	Lynch	Joseph P	CT	21	22													2
24	Finlay	John	FG	33	37													2
25	Enright	Olwyn	FG	02	07													2
26	Brady	Laurence	R	23														1
27	Egan	Patrick	CG	23														1
28	McGuinness	John	R	23														1
29	Gill	John	LB	27J														1
30	Tynan	Thomas	FF	27J														1
31	Aird	William	CG	27S														1
32	O'Brien	Eugene	CG	32														1
33	Donnelly	Eamon	FF	33														1
34	Hogan	Daniel	FF	38														1
35	Byrne	Henry	LB	65														1
36	McDonald	Charles	FG	73														1
37	Gallagher	Pat	LB	92														1
38	Parlon	Tom	PD	02														1
39	Corcoran Kennedy	Marcella	FG	11														1
40	Cowen	Barry	FF	11														1
41	Stanley	Brian	SF	11														1
41	**Total**										***Includes 3 By-Elections**						*	**153**
	**** Also elected in another constituency**																	
L	O'Higgins(sen)**	Thomas F.	FG	Dublin N/Cork				29*	48	51								3
L	O'Higgins**	Kevin	CT	Dublin County				23	27J									2
L	O'Higgins(jun)**	Thomas F.	FG	Dublin Co. South				69										1
3	**Total**										***Includes 1 By-Election**						*	**6**
L	**Included in Laois-Offaly Total**																	

LAOIS-OFFALY 1918-2011

* No Contest

Dail		Seats	FG S	FG % Vote	LB S	LB % Vote	FF S	FF % Vote	SF S	SF % Vote	SP S	SP % Vote	GP S	GP % Vote	CS S	CS % Vote	PD S	PD % Vote	C na P S	C na P % Vote	C na T S	C na T % Vote	Farmers S	Farmers % Vote	Centre P S	Centre P % Vote	Others S	Others % Vote
1	1918	2							2																			
2	1921*	4							4																			
3	1922	4	3	53.46%	1	46.54%																						
4	1923	5	2	26.63%	1	22.42%	2	27.33%																13.57%				10.05%
5	1927	5	1	22.57%	2	31.77%	2	28.97%																7.55%				9.13%
6	1927	5	2	44.87%	1	21.87%	2	33.26%																				
7	1932	5	2	32.14%	1	19.06%	2	45.49%																3.32%				
8	1933	5	1	26.17%	1	14.13%	2	48.22%																	1	11.48%		
9	1937	5	2	31.99%	1	22.77%	2	45.24%																				
10	1938	5	1	29.13%	1	17.20%	3	53.67%																				
11	1943	5	1	18.35%	1	19.97%	2	44.10%														8.40%					1	9.19%
12	1944	5	1	14.83%	1	9.86%	2	40.76%														9.53%					1	25.02%
13	1948	5	1	13.45%	1	7.01%	2	37.52%												4.58%							1	37.44%
14	1951	5	1	20.68%	1	8.30%	2	44.80%																			1	26.22%
15	1954	5	2	45.70%	1	11.31%	2	42.99%																				
16	1957	5	2	38.83%		5.72%	3	48.87%		6.58%																		
17	1961	5	2	43.52%		12.77%	3	40.33%		3.38%																		
18	1965	5	2	45.25%	1	11.33%	2	43.42%																				
19	1969	5	2	43.69%		9.65%	3	45.20%																				1.47%
20	1973	5	3	47.66%		4.91%	2	45.41%																				2.02%
21	1977	5	2	34.32%		5.00%	3	51.01%																				9.67%
22	1981	5	2	45.15%		4.27%	3	49.87%																				0.70%
23	1982	5	2	44.49%		4.85%	3	50.44%																				0.23%
24	1982	5	2	45.65%		3.73%	3	50.27%																				0.36%
25	1987	5	2	31.14%		1.46%	3	53.82%		2.50%								9.54%										1.54%
26	1989	5	2	30.72%		5.79%	3	54.32%										8.42%										0.75%
27	1992	5	1	23.82%	1	12.98%	3	51.82%		1.24%								6.63%										3.51%
28	1997	5	2	28.38%		11.61%	3	49.85%										6.51%										3.66%
29	2002	5	1	23.02%		2.53%	3	51.30%		4.11%				0.82%		0.22%	1	14.38%										3.61%
30	2007	5	2	27.36%		2.38%	3	56.38%		5.11%				1.14%		0.22%		5.92%										1.49%
31	2011	5	2	33.75%		7.82%	2	26.78%	1	10.83%		0.76%		0.41%														19.64%
1918-2011		**150**	**51**	**32.94%**	**16**	**11.35%**	**70**	**44.41%**	**7**	**1.43%**		**0.04%**		**0.11%**		**0.02%**	**1**	**2.09%**		**0.15%**		**0.57%**		**0.71%**	**1**	**0.40%**	**4**	**5.79%**
National		**4,618**	**1,453**	**30.77%**	**482**	**11.53%**	**1,985**	**41.86%**	**232**	**1.99%**	**4**	**0.16%**	**16**	**0.75%**		**0.04%**	**44**	**1.42%**	**18**	**0.77%**	**43**	**1.08%**	**42**	**0.90%**	**11**	**0.30%**	**288**	**8.41%**

LIMERICK 2011

"Fine Gael gain but the Collins' dynasty survives"

More or less the old Limerick West, having gained some territory in the east from Limerick East and lost some in the west to Kerry North. It made the constituency representative of most of rural county Limerick, excluding the western parts.

Since its creation as a 3-seater in 1948, it had been one of the most stable constituencies in the country, returning 2 Fianna Fail TDs at every election bar 1997.

Fianna Fail's decision to run just one candidate, following the last-minute retirement of John Cregan, therefore showed how much things had changed. However, some things remain the same: the Collins family has won a seat here at every election since grandfather James was first elected in 1948, and incumbent Niall maintained this family tradition. Moreover, he headed the poll, the only Fianna Fail candidate apart from party leader Micheál Martin to do this.

Fine Gael was assured of two seats. Incumbent Dan Neville was re-elected, and Fine Gael's second seat was taken by the youthful Patrick O'Donovan, a former President of Young Fine Gael, from Newcastle West, who won more than twice as many votes as Bill O'Donnell, nephew of former minister Tom. O'Donnell and O'Donovan had publicly clashed with each other on Limerick County Council prior to the election over cuts to the minimum wage. O'Donnell had refused to back a motion calling for a reversal of the reduction to the pay rate saying the cut could save businesses and jobs.

Labour's James Heffernan trebled the party's vote share, but despite his impressive performance he was 700 votes behind Niall Collins on the last count. There were three other constituencies where the party won a seat with less than the 17.6 per cent that Heffernan garnered. Former IFA president John Dillon polled respectably but was never in contention for a seat.

LIMERICK TDs 2011

DAN NEVILLE (FG)

Kiltannan, Croagh, Rathkeale, Co. Limerick; Tel: 061 396351; Mobile 086 2435536
Constituency Office: Main Street, Rathkeale, Co. Limerick;
Leinster House: 01 6183356; Email: dan.neville@oireachtas.ie;
Website; www.danneville.ie

Born Croagh, Co. Limerick, 12th December 1946. Widowed, two sons, two daughters. Educated Adare CBS, Co. Limerick; University of Limerick and UCC (Industrial Engineering, Personnel Management, Social Science). Former Personnel Manager. Contested 1987 and 1992 general elections. First elected 1997 and at each subsequent election.

Member Select Committee on Foreign Affairs and Trade. Fine Gael deputy spokesperson on Health with special responsibility for Mental Health 2007-2011. Member Houses of the Oireachtas Commission and Member Joint Committee on Constitutional Amendment on Children 2007-2011. Member Joint Administration Committee and Member Dail Committee on Procedure and Privileges 2007-2011. Deputy spokesperson on Health and Children 2002-2007. Member Joint Committee on Health and Children 2002-2007. Deputy spokesperson on Health, Children and Mental Health Issues 2000-2001. Spokesperson on Children 1997-2000. Senator 1989-1997. Fine Gael deputy Senate Leader and spokesperson on Justice and Law Reform 1993-1997. Member Limerick County Council 1985-2003. Member Mid-Western Health Board 1992-1999, the Association of Health Boards and the General Council of County Councils 1991-1999. Co-founder and National President of Irish Association of Suicidology.

PATRICK O'DONOVAN (FG)

Churchtown Road, Newcastlewest, Co. Limerick; Tel: 069 78660; Mobile: 087 9076267;
Constituency Office: 24 Maiden Street, Newcastle West, Co. Limerick; Tel: 069 77998
Leinster House: 01 6183610; Email: patrick.odonovan@oireachtas.ie
Website: www.patrickodonovan.ie

Born Limerick 21st March 1977. Single. Educated Scoil Mhuire agus Íde, Newcastlewest; UCC (BSc); Mary Immaculate College, Limerick. Primary Teacher, formerly industrial chemist, environmental health and safety officer. Elected at first attempt in 2011.

Member Committee on Environment, Transport, Culture and the Gaeltacht. Co-opted onto Limerick County Council as replacement for Michael Finucane TD in 2003. First elected 2004 in Newcastle electoral area. Retained his seat in 2009. Contested 2007 Seanad election on Labour Panel. Former President Young Fine Gael.

NIALL COLLINS (FF)

Red House Hill, Patrickswell, Co. Limerick; Tel: 061 355219; Mobile: 086 8355219
Leinster House: Tel: 01 6183577; Email: niall.collins@oireachtas.ie
Website: www.niallcollinstd.ie

Born Limerick, 30th March 1973. Married to Dr. Eimear O'Connor, one son, one daughter. Educated St. Munchin's College, Limerick. Limerick Institute of Technology. Accountant, Lecturer and former Deputy CEO with Shannon Regional Fisheries Board.
First elected 2007. Retained his seat in 2011.

Party spokesperson on Environment, Community and Local Government. Member Committee on Environment, Transport, Culture and the Gaeltacht. Convenor Public Accounts Committee 2007-2011. Member Joint Committee on Justice, Equality, Defence and Women's Rights 2007-2011. Member Limerick County Council 2004-2007. Nephew of Gerard Collins M.E.P. for Munster 1994-2004, Dáil Deputy for Limerick West 1967-1997 and former Government Minister. Nephew of Michael Collins TD for Limerick West 1997-2007. Grandson of James J. Collins, Dáil Deputy for Limerick West 1948-1967.

	LIMERICK 2011 FIRST PREFERENCE VOTES						
	Seats	3			11,261		
	Candidate	Party	1st	%	Quota	Count	Status
1	**Neville, Dan***	**FG**	**9,176**	**20.37%**	**0.81**	**4**	**Made Quota**
2	**O'Donovan, Patrick**	**FG**	**8,597**	**19.09%**	**0.76**	**4**	**Made Quota**
3	**Collins, Niall***	**FF**	**9,361**	**20.78%**	**0.83**	**4**	**Elected**
4	Heffernan, James	LB	7,910	17.56%	0.70	4	Not Elected
5	Dillon, John	NP	4,395	9.76%	0.39	3	Eliminated
6	O'Donnell, William	FG	4,152	9.22%	0.37	2	Eliminated
7	Cremin, Con	NP	430	0.95%	0.04	1	No Expenses
8	Sherlock, Seamus	NP	419	0.93%	0.04	1	No Expenses
9	Wall, Stephen	GP	354	0.79%	0.03	1	No Expenses
10	O'Doherty, Patrick	NP	247	0.55%	0.02	1	No Expenses
10	***Outgoing**		**45,041**	**100.00%**	**11,261**	**2,816**	**No Expenses**

LIMERICK 2011 PARTY VOTE												
	2011					2007					Change	
Party	Cand	1st	%	Quota	Seats	Cand	1st	%	Quota	Seats	%	Seats
FG	3	21,925	48.68%	1.95	2	2	16,153	39.95%	1.60	1	+8.73%	+1
LB	1	7,910	17.56%	0.70		1	2,277	5.63%	0.23		+11.93%	
FF	1	9,361	20.78%	0.83	1	2	19,097	47.23%	1.89	2	-26.45%	-1
GP	1	354	0.79%	0.03		1	969	2.40%	0.10		-1.61%	
PD						1	1,935	4.79%	0.19		-4.79%	
Others	4	5,491	12.19%	0.49							+12.19%	
Total	**10**	**45,041**	**100.0%**	**11,261**	**3**	**7**	**40,431**	**100.0%**	**10,108**	**3**	**0.00%**	**0**
Electorate		**65,083**	**69.21%**				**58,712**	**68.86%**			**+0.34%**	
Spoiled		**471**	**1.03%**				**381**	**0.93%**			**+0.10%**	
Turnout		**45,512**	**69.93%**				**40,812**	**69.51%**			**+0.42%**	

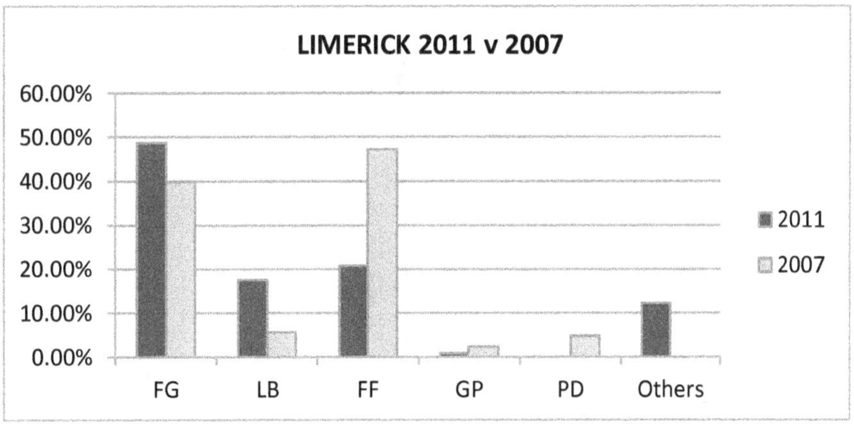

LIMERICK 2011
COUNT DETAILS

Seats **3** **Quota** **11,261**

Candidate	Party	1st	2nd	3rd	4th
			Cremin Sherlock Wall O'Doherty	O'Donnell Votes	Dillon Votes
			+171	*+1,344*	*+1,037*
Neville, Dan*	FG	9,176	9,347	10,691	11,728
			+196	*+1,558*	*+965*
O'Donovan, Patrick	FG	8,597	8,793	10,351	11,316
			+127	*+265*	*+1,056*
Collins, Niall*	FF	9,361	9,488	9,753	10,809
			+326	*+657*	*+1,211*
Heffernan, James	LB	7,910	8,236	8,893	10,104
			+372	*+308*	*-5,075*
Dillon, John	NP	4,395	4,767	5,075	Eliminated
			+70	*-4,222*	
O'Donnell, William	FG	4,152	4,222	Eliminated	
			-430		
Cremin, Con	NP	430	Eliminated		
			-419		
Sherlock, Seamus	NP	419	Eliminated		
			-354		
Wall, Stephen	GP	354	Eliminated		
			-247		
O'Doherty, Patrick	NP	247	Eliminated		
Non-transferable			*+188*	*+90*	*+806*
Cumulative			188	278	1,084
Total		**45,041**	**45,041**	**45,041**	**45,041**

LIMERICK 2011
TRANSFER ANALYSIS

From	To	FG	LB	FF	Others	Non Trans
FG	4,222	2,902	657	265	308	90
		68.74%	*15.56%*	*6.28%*	*7.30%*	*2.13%*
GP	354	107	79	31	91	46
		30.23%	*22.32%*	*8.76%*	*25.71%*	*12.99%*
Others	6,171	2,332	1,458	1,152	281	948
		37.79%	*23.63%*	*18.67%*	*4.55%*	*15.36%*
Total	**10,747**	**5,341**	**2,194**	**1,448**	**680**	**1,084**
		49.70%	***20.41%***	***13.47%***	***6.33%***	***10.09%***

LIMERICK WEST		
MAIN BOUNDARY CHANGES		
Dail	**Constituency**	**Seats**
13 (1948) - 30 (2007)	Limerick West	3
31 (2011) -	Limerick	3

	LIMERICK WEST														
	All TDs 1948-2011														
	Surname	**Forename**	**Party**	**Elected**											**Total**
1	Collins	Gerard	FF	67*	69	73	77	81	82	82	87	89	92		10
2	Noonan	Michael J.	FF	69	73	77	81	82	82	87	89	92			9
3	Collins	James	FF	48	51	54	57	61	65						6
4	O Briain**	Donnchadh	FF	48	51	54	57	61	65						6
5	Jones	Denis	FG	57	61	65	69	73							5
6	O'Brien	William	FG	77	81	82	82								4
7	Neville	Daniel	FG	97	02	07	11								4
8	Madden	David	FG	48	51	54									3
9	Finucane	Michael	FG	89	92	97									3
10	Collins	Michael	FF	97	02										2
11	Cregan	John	FF	02	07										2
12	Collins	Niall	FF	07	11										2
13	Colbert**	Michael	FF	55*											1
14	McCoy	John	PD	87											1
15	O'Donovan	Patrick	FG	11											1
15	**Total**						***Includes 2 By-Elections**						*		**59**
	****Also elected in another constituency**														
1	O Briain**	Donnchadh	FF	Limerick		33	37	38	43	44					5
2	Colbert**	Michael	FF	Limerick		37	44								2
2	**Total**														**7**

Niall Collins TD with his uncles Michael and Gerard and his father Sean

LIMERICK WEST 1948-2011																				
		FG		LB		FF		SF		GP		CS		PD		C na P		Others		
Dail		Seats	S	% Vote	S	% Vote	S	% Vote	S	% Vote	S	% Vote	S	% Vote	S	% Vote	S	% Vote	S	% Vote
13	1948	3	1	23.24%		6.17%	2	55.01%										8.15%		7.44%
14	1951	3	1	39.61%			2	60.39%												
15	1954	3	1	34.12%		11.77%	2	54.11%												
16	1957	3	1	30.79%			2	67.22%												1.99%
17	1961	3	1	40.87%			2	59.13%												
18	1965	3	1	36.41%		9.09%	2	54.50%												
19	1969	3	1	40.40%		6.19%	2	52.60%												0.80%
20	1973	3	1	47.14%			2	52.86%												
21	1977	3	1	36.33%		4.32%	2	59.35%												
22	1981	3	1	35.66%			2	64.34%												
23	1982	3	1	36.19%			2	63.81%												
24	1982	3	1	37.79%			2	62.21%												
25	1987	3		27.83%		1.53%	2	51.29%							1	19.35%				
26	1989	3	1	27.01%			2	60.38%								12.61%				
27	1992	3	1	30.87%		10.83%	2	47.41%		1.09%						7.36%				2.43%
28	1997	3	2	37.19%		4.22%	1	32.44%								4.18%				21.96%
29	2002	3	1	41.65%			2	53.43%				2.66%		0.40%						1.86%
30	2007	3	1	39.95%		5.63%	2	47.23%				2.40%				4.79%				
31	2011	3	2	48.68%		17.56%	1	20.78%				0.79%								12.19%
1948-2011		**57**	**20**	**36.75%**		**4.35%**	**36**	**52.49%**		**0.06%**		**0.38%**		**0.02%**	**1**	**2.71%**		**0.37%**		**2.86%**
National		**4,618**	**1,453**	**30.77%**	**482**	**11.53%**	**1,985**	**41.86%**	**232**	**1.99%**	**16**	**0.75%**		**0.04%**	**44**	**1.42%**	**18**	**0.77%**	**388**	**10.86%**

LIMERICK CITY 2011

"Noonan tops the poll in one of the country's least marginal constituencies"

This constituency was affected by boundary redrawing, losing an area with over 17,000 people to the new Limerick County and consequently changing from a mainly urban 5-seater to an overwhelmingly urban 4-seater.

As a 4-seater, it was one of the most predictable constituencies in the country. Fine Gael's Michael Noonan, restored to front-bench prominence as an unforeseen but fortuitous side-effect of the heave against Enda Kenny the previous summer, headed the poll with his largest vote ever, and the party vote advanced by nearly 18 per cent, its second biggest gain in the country. Nearly 3,000 votes from Noonan's surplus helped Kieran O'Donnell into the second seat.

Willie O'Dea had headed the poll here with a sizeable surplus at every election going back to 1989, but now he lost over 12,000 of his huge 2007 vote, the national swing against Fianna Fail being compounded by the local difficulties that had seen him leave the government a year earlier. This was still enough to secure him the third seat, but his running mate Peter Power, a junior minister seemingly on the way up, found himself down among the also-rans and was eliminated on the sixth count.

The Labour vote was up, and Jan O'Sullivan was comfortably re-elected, but hopes that the party could take a second seat through her running mate Joe Leddin came nowhere near materialising. Sinn Fein's Maurice Quinlivan gained publicity through his role in the events that brought about O'Dea's downfall in 2010 and achieved runner-up status, but on this showing Limerick City is one of the least marginal constituencies in the country.

Taoiseach Enda Kenny with Minister for Finance Michael Noonan

LIMERICK CITY TDs 2011

MICHAEL NOONAN (FG)

18 Gouldavoher Estate, Father Russell Road, Limerick; Tel: 061 229350
Leinster House: 01 6767571; Email: michael.noonan@oireachtas.ie

Born Limerick 22nd May 1943. Married to Florence Knightly, three sons, two daughters. Educated St. Patrick's Secondary School, Glin, Co. Limerick; St. Patrick's Teacher Training College, Drumcondra, Dublin and UCD (BA, HDipEd). Former Teacher.
First elected 1981 and at each subsequent election.

Appointed Minister for Finance 9th March 2011. Front bench spokesperson on Finance July 2010 –February 2011. Vice-Chairman Joint Committee on Constitutional Amendment on Children 2007-2011. Member Joint Committee on Foreign Affairs 2007-2011. Chairman Public Accounts Committee 2002-2007. Leader of Fine Gael February 2001-May 2002 and Spokesperson on Northern Ireland. Fine Gael Front Bench spokesperson on Finance 1997–2001. Minister for Health 1994-1997. Front Bench spokesperson on Transport, Communications and Energy 1993-1994; on Finance 1987-1993. Minister for Energy January-February 1987. Minister for Industry, Commerce and Trade 1986–1987. Minister for Justice 1982-1986. Member Limerick County Council 1974-1982, 1991-1994.

KIERAN O'DONNELL (FG)

8 Milltown Manor, Monaleen, Castletroy, Limerick; Tel: 061 330652; Mobile: 086 8430202
Constituency Office: 27 William Street, Limerick; Tel: 061 204040
Leinster House: 01 6183808; Email: kieran.odonnell@oireachtas.ie,
Website: www. kieranodonnell.ie

Born Limerick City 8th May 1963. Married to Phil Fitzgerald, 2 sons, 2 daughters. Educated Ard Scoil Mhuire, Bruff, Co. Limerick; UL (Business Studies). Chartered Accountant.
First elected 2007. Retained his seat in 2011.

Appointed Vice-Chair of Public Accounts Committee June 2011. Member Committee on Finance, Public Expenditure and Reform. Supported Richard Bruton in his failed attempt to oust Enda Kenny as party leader in June 2010. Deputy Spokesperson on Finance, with special responsibility for Freedom of Information, Procurement Reform and the Office of Public Works, 2007-2010. Member Joint Committee on Finance and the Public Service and Member Joint Committee on Economic and Regulatory Affairs 2007-2011. Member Limerick County Council 2004-2007. Member Mid-West Regional Authority and Limerick Market Trustees. Nephew of former Minister Tom O'Donnell, TD for Limerick East 1961-1987; Minister for the Gaeltacht 1973-1977; MEP 1979-1989.

WILLIE O'DEA (FF)

Milltown, Kilteely, Co. Limerick, Tel: 061 454488; Mobile: 087 9193666
Constituency Office: 2 Glenview Gardens, Farranshore, Limerick; Tel: 061 454488,
Leinster House: 01 6184259; Email: willie.odea@oceanfree.net
Website: www.willieodea.ie

Born Limerick November 1952. Married to Geraldine Kennedy. Educated Patrician Brothers College, Ballyfin, Co. Laois; UCD; Kings Inns and the Institute of Certified Accountants (BCL, LLM, BL, Certified Accountant). Formerly a Barrister and Accountant and has lectured at UCD and the University of Limerick. Contested 1981 general election. First elected February 1982 and at each subsequent election.

Party spokesperson on Enterprise, Jobs and Innovation. Member Committee on Jobs, Social Protection and Education. Resigned as Minister for Defence 18th February 2010. Minister for Defence 2004-2007 and 2007-2010. Minister of State at the Department of Justice, Equality and Law Reform (with special responsibility for Equality Issues including Disability Issues) 2002-2004. Minister of State at the Department of Education (with responsibility for Youth Affairs, Adult Education and School Transport) 1997-2002. Minister of State at the Department of Justice and Health 1993-1994. Minister of State at the Department of Justice 1992-1993. A regular contributor to the Sunday Independent.

JAN O'SULLIVAN (LB)

7 Lanahrone Avenue, Corbally, Limerick; Tel: 061 346522; Mobile: 087 2430299
Constituency Office: Mechanic's Institute, Hartstonge Street, Limerick; Tel: 061 312316,
Leinster House: 01 6182316; Email: jan.osullivan@oireachtas.ie
Website: www.labour.ie/janosullivan

Born Limerick 6th December 1950. Married to Dr. Paul O'Sullivan, one son Paddy, one daughter Emily. Educated Villiers School, Limerick; Trinity College, Dublin. Minister of State. Formerly Pre-School Teacher. Contested 1997 general election. First elected at by-election in March 1998 caused by death of Jim Kemmy and at each subsequent election.

Appointed 20th December 2011 Minister of State at the Department of the Environment, Community and Local Government with special responsibility for Housing and Planning and she has the right to attend Government meetings. Minister of State at the Department of Foreign Affairs and Trade with special responsibility for Trade and Development March-December 2011. Labour Party Spokesperson on Health 2007-2011. Beaten by Joan Burton in election for Party Deputy Leader, September 2007. Vice-Chairperson Committee on Health and Children 2007-2011. Spokesperson on Education and Science 2002-2007. Vice-Chair Joint Committee on Education and Science 2002-2007. Senator 1993-1997 (Leader Labour Group). Member Limerick City Council 1985-2003. Mayor of Limerick 1993-1994. Became first woman Alderman in 1999. Member Mid-Western Health Board 1991-2003. Member Democratic Socialist Party until its merger with Labour in 1990.

LIMERICK CITY 2011							
FIRST PREFERENCE VOTES							
	Seats	**4**			**8,638**		
	Candidate	**Party**	**1st**	**%**	**Quota**	**Count**	**Status**
1	**Noonan, Michael***	**FG**	**13,291**	**30.77%**	**1.54**	**1**	**Made Quota**
2	**O'Donnell, Kieran***	**FG**	**5,405**	**12.52%**	**0.63**	**5**	**Made Quota**
3	**O'Dea, Willie***	**FF**	**6,956**	**16.11%**	**0.81**	**6**	**Made Quota**
4	**O'Sullivan, Jan***	**LB**	**6,353**	**14.71%**	**0.74**	**7**	**Elected**
5	Quinlivan, Maurice	SF	3,711	8.59%	0.43	7	Not Elected
6	Leddin, Joe	LB	2,411	5.58%	0.28	7	Not Elected
7	Power, Peter*	FF	2,303	5.33%	0.27	5	Eliminated
8	Kiely, Kevin	NP	1,129	2.61%	0.13	4	No Expenses
9	Prendiville, Cian	SP	721	1.67%	0.08	4	No Expenses
10	Cahill, Sheila	GP	490	1.13%	0.06	3	No Expenses
11	O'Donoghue, Conor	CS	186	0.43%	0.02	2	No Expenses
12	Riordan, Denis	NP	173	0.40%	0.02	2	No Expenses
13	Larkin, Matt	NP	59	0.14%	0.01	2	No Expenses
13	***Outgoing**		**43,188**	**100.00%**	**8,638**	**2,160**	**No Expenses**

LIMERICK CITY 2011												
PARTY VOTE												
	2011					**2007**					**Change**	
Party	**Cand**	**1st**	**%**	**Quota**	**Seats**	**Cand**	**1st**	**%**	**Quota**	**Seats**	**%**	**Seats**
FG	2	18,696	43.29%	2.16	2	2	12,601	25.52%	1.53	2	+17.77%	
LB	2	8,764	20.29%	1.01	1	1	5,098	10.33%	0.62	1	+9.97%	
FF	2	9,259	21.44%	1.07	1	3	24,042	48.69%	2.92	2	-27.25%	-1
SF	1	3,711	8.59%	0.43		1	2,081	4.21%	0.25		+4.38%	
SP	1	721	1.67%	0.08							+1.67%	
GP	1	490	1.13%	0.06		1	1,296	2.62%	0.16		-1.49%	
CS	1	186	0.43%	0.02							+0.43%	
PD						1	3,354	6.79%	0.41		-6.79%	
Others	3	1,361	3.15%	0.16		5	903	1.83%	0.11		+1.32%	
Total	**13**	**43,188**	**100.0%**	**8,638**	**4**	**14**	**49,375**	**100.0%**	**8,230**	**5**	**0.00%**	-1
Electorate		**64,909**	**66.54%**				**76,874**	**64.23%**			**+2.31%**	
Spoiled		**429**	**0.98%**				**431**	**0.87%**			**+0.12%**	
Turnout		**43,617**	**67.20%**				**49,806**	**64.79%**			**+2.41%**	

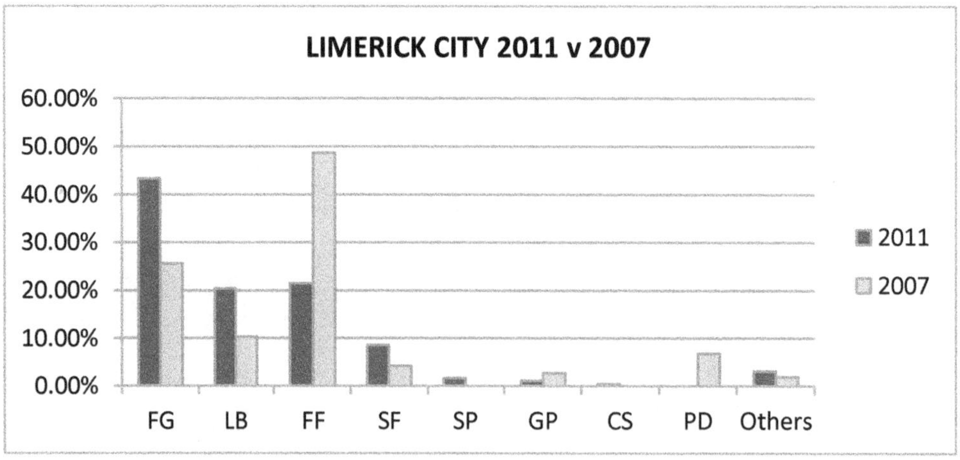

LIMERICK CITY 2011 COUNT DETAILS								
Seats	4					Quota	8,638	
Candidate	**Party**	**1st**	**2nd** Noonan Surplus	**3rd** O'Donoghue Riordan Larkin	**4th** Cahill Votes	**5th** Kiely Prendiville Votes	**6th** Power Votes	**7th** O'Dea Surplus
			-4,653					
Noonan, Michael*	FG	13,291	8,638	8,638	8,638	8,638	8,638	8,638
			+2,901	*+108*	*+131*	*+229*		
O'Donnell, Kieran*	FG	5,405	8,306	8,414	8,545	8,774	8,774	8,774
			+413	*+34*	*+29*	*+336*	*+1,656*	*-786*
O'Dea, Willie*	FF	6,956	7,369	7,403	7,432	7,768	9,424	8,638
			+769	*+39*	*+153*	*+414*	*+351*	*+441*
O'Sullivan, Jan*	LB	6,353	7,122	7,161	7,314	7,728	8,079	8,520
			+118	*+48*	*+17*	*+624*	*+116*	*+124*
Quinlivan, Maurice	SF	3,711	3,829	3,877	3,894	4,518	4,634	4,758
			+217	*+17*	*+67*	*+214*	*+158*	*+207*
Leddin, Joe	LB	2,411	2,628	2,645	2,712	2,926	3,084	3,291
			+96	*+30*	*+37*	*+67*	*-2,533*	
Power, Peter*	FF	2,303	2,399	2,429	2,466	2,533	Eliminated	
			+71	*+70*	*+36*	*-1,306*		
Kiely, Kevin	NP	1,129	1,200	1,270	1,306	Eliminated		
			+19	*+29*	*+30*	*-799*		
Prendiville, Cian	SP	721	740	769	799	Eliminated		
			+30	*+22*	*-542*			
Cahill, Sheila	GP	490	520	542	Eliminated			
			+11	*-197*				
O'Donoghue, Conor	CS	186	197	Eliminated				
			+5	*-178*				
Riordan, Denis	NP	173	178	Eliminated				
			+3	*-62*				
Larkin, Matt	NP	59	62	Eliminated				
Non-transferable				*+40*	*+42*	*+221*	*+252*	*+14*
Cumulative			0	40	82	303	555	569
Total		**43,188**	**43,188**	**43,188**	**43,188**	**43,188**	**43,188**	**43,188**

LIMERICK CITY 2011 TRANSFER ANALYSIS									
From	**To**	**FG**	**LB**	**FF**	**SF**	**SP**	**GP**	**Others**	**Non Trans**
FG	4,653	2,901	986	509	118	19	30	90	
		62.35%	*21.19%*	*10.94%*	*2.54%*	*0.41%*	*0.64%*	*1.93%*	
FF	3,319		1,157	1,656	240				266
			34.86%	*49.89%*	*7.23%*				*8.01%*
SP	799	87	238	153	237				84
		10.89%	*29.79%*	*19.15%*	*29.66%*				*10.51%*
GP	542	131	220	66	17	30		36	42
		24.17%	*40.59%*	*12.18%*	*3.14%*	*5.54%*		*6.64%*	*7.75%*
Others	1,743	250	446	314	435	29	22	70	177
		14.34%	*25.59%*	*18.01%*	*24.96%*	*1.66%*	*1.26%*	*4.02%*	*10.15%*
Total	**11,056**	**3,369**	**3,047**	**2,698**	**1,047**	**78**	**52**	**196**	**569**
		30.47%	***27.56%***	***24.40%***	***9.47%***	***0.71%***	***0.47%***	***1.77%***	***5.15%***

LIMERICK EAST/CITY		
MAIN BOUNDARY CHANGES		
Dail	**Constituency**	**Seats**
13 (1948) - 21 (1977)	Limerick East	4
22 (1981) - 30 (2007)	Limerick East	5
31 (2011) -	Limerick City	4

LIMERICK EAST/CITY 1948-2011

			FG		LB		FF		SF		SP		GP		WP		CS		PD		DL		DSP		Cn na P		C na T		Others	
Dail		**Seats**	**S**	**% Vote**	**S**	**% Vote**	**S**	**% Vote**	**S**	**% Vote**	**S**	**% Vote**	**S**	**% Vote**	**S**	**% Vote**	**S**	**% Vote**	**S**	**% Vote**	**S**	**% Vote**	**S**	**% Vote**	**S**	**% Vote**	**S**	**% Vote**	**S**	**% Vote**
13	1948	4	1	21.21%	1	15.61%	2	42.67%																		14.74%		5.78%		
14	1951	4	1	22.30%	1	16.97%	2	47.21%																		13.52%				
15	1954	4	1	28.98%	1	13.31%	2	42.77%																		14.94%				
16	1957	4	1	16.24%		5.79%	2	44.55%		8.52%																9.37%			1	15.53%
17	1961	4	1	23.10%	1	21.13%	2	45.01%																						10.76%
18	1965	4	1	30.53%	1	15.93%	2	53.54%																						
19	1969	4	1	24.56%	1	27.71%	2	38.38%																						9.36%
20	1973	4	1	34.47%	1	23.63%	2	41.90%																						
21	1977	4	1	24.26%		7.91%	2	45.75%								0.58%													1	21.49%
22	1981	5	2	33.77%		11.82%	2	42.26%																					1	12.14%
23	1982	5	2	31.64%		5.67%	2	45.25%																					1	17.43%
24	1982	5	2	33.88%	1	10.15%	2	46.56%																8.74%						0.68%
25	1987	5	1	17.90%		4.44%	1	25.46%		1.14%				0.49%		0.50%			2	37.14%			1	11.93%						1.01%
26	1989	5	1	18.39%		2.17%	1	32.43%											2	27.23%			1	19.78%						
27	1992	5	1	15.61%	1	23.48%	1	30.25%		0.83%									2	26.14%		1.73%								1.97%
28	1997	5	1	26.51%	1	9.19%	2	39.72%						1.61%					1	12.42%		6.85%								3.69%
29	2002	5	1	27.84%	1	9.26%	2	39.95%						1.83%				0.17%	1	9.77%										11.18%
30	2007	5	2	25.52%	1	10.33%	2	48.69%		4.21%				2.62%				0.35%		6.79%										1.48%
31	2011	4	2	43.29%	1	20.29%	1	21.44%		8.59%		1.67%		1.13%				0.43%												3.15%
1948-2011		**85**	**24**	**26.36%**	**13**	**12.89%**	**34**	**40.35%**		**1.21%**		**0.09%**		**0.46%**		**0.06%**		**0.05%**	**8**	**7.14%**		**0.52%**	**2**	**2.36%**		**2.40%**		**0.26%**	**4**	**5.85%**
National		**4,618**	**1,453**	**30.77%**	**482**	**11.53%**	**1,985**	**41.86%**	**232**	**1.99%**	**4**	**0.16%**	**16**	**0.75%**	**17**	**0.78%**		**0.04%**	**44**	**1.42%**	**8**	**0.22%**	**2**	**0.06%**	**18**	**0.77%**	**43**	**1.08%**	**314**	**8.55%**

LIMERICK CITY															
All TDs 1948-2011															
	Surname	**Forename**	**Party**	**Elected**											**Total**
1	O'Malley	Desmond	PD	68*	69	73	77	81	82	82	87	89	92	97	11
2	Noonan	Michael	FG	81	82	82	87	89	92	97	02	07	11		10
3	O'Dea	Willie	FF	82	82	87	89	92	97	02	07	11			9
4	O'Donnell	Tom	FG	61	65	69	73	77	81	82	82				8
5	Kemmy	Jim	LB	81	82F	87	89	92	97						6
6	O'Malley	Donogh	FF	54	57	61	65								4
7	Coughlan	Stephen	LB	61	65	69	73								4
8	Clohessy	Peadar	PD	81	87	89	92								4
9	O'Sullivan	Jan	LB	98*	02	07	11								4
10	Keyes**	Michael	LB	48	51	54									3
11	Carew	John	FG	52*	54	57									3
12	Clohessy	Patrick	FF	57	61	65									3
13	Herbert	Michael	FF	69	73	77									3
14	Bourke**	Daniel	FF	48	51										2
15	Reidy**	James	FG	48	51										2
16	Crowley**	Tadhg	FF	51	54										2
17	Power	Peter	FF	02	07										2
18	O'Donnell	Kieran	FG	07	11										2
19	Ryan**	Robert	FF	48											1
20	Russell	George	NP	57											1
21	Lipper	Michael	NP	77											1
22	Wade	Eddie	FF	97											1
23	Prendergast	Frank	LB	82N											1
24	O'Malley	Tim	PD	02											1
24	**Total**							***Includes 3 By-Elections**						*	**88**
1	Bourke**	Daniel	FF	Limerick	27S	32	33	37	38	43	44				7
2	Crowley**	Tadhg	FF	Limerick	27	27	32	33	38	43					6
3	Keyes**	Michael	LB	Limerick	27J	33	37	38	43	44					6
4	Ryan**	Robert	FF	Limerick	32	33	37	38	43	44					6
5	Reidy**	James	FG	Limerick	32	33	38	43	44						5
5	**Total**														**30**

LIMERICK REGION		
MAIN BOUNDARY CHANGES		
Dail	**Constituency**	**Seats**
1 (1918)	Limerick City	1
	Limerick East	1
	Limerick West	1
2 (1921) - 3 (1922)	Limerick City-Limerick East	4
4 (1923) - 12 (1944)	Limerick	7
13 (1948) - 21 (1977)	Limerick East	4
	Limerick West	3
22 (1981) - 30 (2007)	Limerick East	5
	Limerick West	3
31 (2011) -	Limerick City	4
	Limerick	3

							LIMERICK REGION								
							All TDs 1918-2011								
	Surname	**Forename**	**Party**					**Elected**							**Total**
1	O Briain	Donnchadh	FF	33	37	38	43	44	48	51	54	57	61	65	11
2	O'Malley	Desmond	PD	68*	69	73	77	81	82	82	87	89	92	97	11
3	Collins	Gerard	FF	67*	69	73	77	81	82	82	87	89	92		10
4	Noonan	Michael	FG	81	82	82	87	89	92	97	02	07	11		10
5	Bourke	Daniel	FF	27S	32	33	37	38	43	44	48	51			9
6	Keyes	Michael	LB	27J	33	37	38	43	44	48	51	54			9
7	Noonan	Michael J.	FF	69	73	77	81	82	82	87	89	92			9
8	O'Dea	Willie	FF	82	82	87	89	92	97	02	07	11			9
9	Bennett	George	FG	27	27	32	33	37	38	43	44				8
10	Crowley	Tadhg	FF	27	27	32	33	38	43	51	54				8
11	O'Donnell	Tom	FG	61	65	69	73	77	81	82	82				8
12	Ryan	Robert	FF	32	33	37	38	43	44	48					7
13	Reidy	James	FG	32	33	38	43	44	48	51					7
14	Collins	James	FF	48	51	54	57	61	65						6
15	Kemmy	Jim	LB	81	82F	87	89	92	97						6
16	Jones	Denis	FG	57	61	65	69	73							5
17	Hayes	Richard	CG	18	21	22	23								4
18	Colbert	James	FF	23	27	27	32								4
19	O'Malley	Donogh	FF	54	57	61	65								4
20	Coughlan	Stephen	LB	61	65	69	73								4
21	O'Brien	William	FG	77	81	82	82								4
22	Clohessy	Peadar	PD	81	87	89	92								4
23	Neville	Daniel	FG	97	02	07	11								4
24	O'Sullivan	Jan	LB	98*	02	07	11								4
25	Colivet	Michael	CR	18	21	22									3
26	Clancy	Patrick	LB	23	27	27									3
27	O'Connell	Richard	CG	24*	27	27									3
28	Madden	David	FG	48	51	54									3
29	Colbert	Michael	FF	37	44	55*									3
30	Carew	John	FG	52*	54	57									3
31	Clohessy	Patrick	FF	57	61	65									3
32	Herbert	Michael	FF	69	73	77									3
33	Finucane	Michael	FG	89	92	97									3
34	Hayes	William	CT	21	22										2
35	O'Callaghan	Katherine	CR	21	22										2
36	Nolan	John	CG	23	27S										2
37	O'Shaughnessy	John	FG	32	37										2
38	Collins	Michael	FF	97	02										2
39	Cregan	John	FF	02	07										2
40	Power	Peter	FF	02	07										2
41	Collins	Niall	FF	07	11										2
42	O'Donnell	Kieran	FG	07	11										2
43	Collins**	Conor	SF	18											1
44	Carroll	Sean	R	23											1
45	Hogan	Patrick K.	F	23											1
46	Ledden	James	CG	23											1
47	Hewson	Gilbert	NP	27J											1
48	Russell	George	NP	57											1
49	Lipper	Michael	NP	77											1
50	Prendergast	Frank	LB	82N											1
51	McCoy	John	PD	87											1
52	Wade	Eddie	FF	97											1
53	O'Malley	Tim	PD	02											1
54	O'Donovan	Patrick	GH	11											1
54	**Total**							***Includes 6 By-Elections**						*	**222**
	****Also elected in another constituency**														
	Collins**	Conor	SF	Kerry				21	22						2

LIMERICK REGION 1918-2011																														
* No Contest			FG		LB		FF		SF		SP		GP		WP		PD		DL		DSP		C na P		C na T		Farmers		Others	
Dail		Seats	S	% Vote	S	% Vote	S	% Vote	S	% Vote	S	% Vote	S	% Vote	S	% Vote	S	% Vote	S	% Vote	S	% Vote	S	% Vote	S	% Vote	S	% Vote	S	% Vote
1	1918	3							3																					
2	1921*	4							4																					
3	1922*	4	2				2																							
4	1923	7	3	41.54%	1	17.44%	2	26.38%																			1	11.72%		2.93%
5	1927	7	2	26.71%	2	13.95%	2	30.17%																				7.64%	1	21.52%
6	1927	7	3	38.00%	1	15.35%	3	34.73%																				6.03%		5.89%
7	1932	7	2	32.27%		7.42%	4	46.47%																			1	7.91%		5.93%
8	1933	7	2	28.92%	1	8.80%	4	52.58%																						9.71%
9	1937	7	2	35.41%	1	16.81%	4	45.73%																						2.05%
10	1938	7	2	34.14%	1	11.93%	4	53.93%																						
11	1943	7	2	28.25%	1	17.50%	4	46.85%																		7.40%				
12	1944	7	2	24.80%	1	13.66%	4	53.25%																		8.29%				
13	1948	7	2	22.08%	1	11.58%	4	47.94%																11.92%		3.31%				3.18%
14	1951	7	2	29.60%	1	9.81%	4	52.77%																7.82%						
15	1954	7	2	31.15%	1	12.66%	4	47.55%																8.64%						
16	1957	7	2	22.30%		3.38%	4	53.99%		4.97%														5.47%					1	9.89%
17	1961	7	2	30.83%	1	11.93%	4	51.16%																						6.08%
18	1965	7	2	32.99%	1	13.07%	4	53.94%																						
19	1969	7	2	31.61%	1	18.13%	4	44.71%																						5.55%
20	1973	7	2	39.97%	1	13.37%	4	46.65%																						
21	1977	7	2	29.41%		6.38%	4	51.55%								0.33%													1	12.32%
22	1981	8	3	34.54%		7.03%	4	51.22%																					1	7.21%
23	1982	8	3	33.47%		3.40%	4	52.70%																					1	10.44%
24	1982	8	3	35.45%	1	6.07%	4	52.86%														5.22%								0.41%
25	1987	8	1	21.94%		3.25%	3	35.97%		0.68%				0.29%		0.29%	3	29.91%			1	7.08%								0.60%
26	1989	8	2	21.87%		1.29%	3	43.72%									2	21.32%			1	11.79%								
27	1992	8	2	21.66%	1	18.46%	3	37.06%		0.93%							2	18.69%		1.04%										2.15%
28	1997	8	3	30.82%	1	7.18%	3	36.78%						0.96%			1	9.10%		4.08%										11.06%
29	2002	8	2	33.59%	1	5.40%	4	45.56%						2.18%			1	5.70%												7.57%
30	2007	8	3	32.02%	1	8.21%	4	48.04%		2.32%				2.52%				5.89%												1.01%
31	2011	7	4	46.04%	1	18.90%	2	21.10%		4.21%		0.82%		0.96%																7.98%
1918-2011		**216**	**66**	**31.13%**	**22**	**10.46%**	**103**	**45.11%**	**7**	**0.52%**		**0.04%**		**0.31%**		**0.03%**	**9**	**3.79%**		**0.22%**	**2**	**0.98%**		**1.11%**		**0.61%**	**2**	**0.94%**	**5**	**4.75%**
National		**4,618**	**1,453**	**30.77%**	**482**	**11.53%**	**1,985**	**41.86%**	**232**	**1.99%**	**4**	**0.16%**	**16**	**0.75%**	**17**	**0.78%**	**44**	**1.42%**	**8**	**0.22%**	**2**	**0.06%**	**18**	**0.77%**	**43**	**1.08%**	**42**	**0.90%**	**272**	**7.69%**

LONGFORD-WESTMEATH 2011

'Fine Gael go close to winning a remarkable three out of four as Fianna Fáil hang on to a single seat'

There were no Constituency Commission boundary changes here since 2007 and it remained a four-seat constituency.

Fine Gael's vote was up 7 points and with 1.9 quotas they were well in line for two seats and remarkably were even in contention for a third. James Bannon led the way with 9,129 first preferences and he went on to take the second seat on the sixth count. Outgoing senator Nicky McFadden and Councillor Peter Burke were within 500 votes of one another on the first count and were in a battle with Robert Troy of Fianna Fáil for the final two seats. In the end McFadden took the Athlone seat and Burke lost out to Troy.

Willie Penrose once again topped the poll as the Labour vote was up 9 points but with just 1.3 quotas on the first count the party was unlikely to improve on its single seat. Former Progressive Democrats' deputy Mae Sexton did poorly, winning just 3,960 first preferences to leave her too far off the pace in seventh place. A more even division of the Labour vote would have given the party a better chance but Penrose's poll topping performance put an end to that.

The Fianna Fáil vote was down 22 points and with just one quota, one seat was as much as the party could hope for. Its vote was divided among three candidates - the two outgoing deputies Mary O'Rourke and Peter Kelly, along with newcomer Robert Troy. They were not helped by the presence of former party colleague Kevin 'Boxer' Moran on the ticket as he was just behind Kelly and outpolled O'Rourke with 3,707 first preferences. Troy was in sixth place ahead of his party colleagues on the first count and he retained his advantage throughout the count and went on to beat Fine Gael for the final seat. He was one of only three new deputies elected for Fianna Fail in this disastrous election.

The Sinn Fein vote doubled in this election and Paul Hogan was just outside the frame in fifth place on the first count with 0.4 quotas. He survived the various counts and was the last candidate eliminated with his transfers favouring fellow Athlone based McFadden.

Willie Penrose TD who resigned his Minister of State position on 15th November 2011

LONGFORD-WESTMEATH TDs 2011

WILLIE PENROSE (LB)

Ballintue, Ballynacargy, Co. Westmeath; Tel: 044 9373264; Mobile: 087 8241933
Constituency Office: Convent Lane, Bishopgate Street, Mullingar; Tel: 044 9343966
Leinster House: 01 6183734; Email: willie.penrose@oireachtas.ie
Website: www.penrose.ie

Born Mullingar, Co. Westmeath August 1956. Married to Anne Fitzsimmons, three daughters. Educated St. Mary's CBS, Mullingar; Multyfarnham Agricultural College, Co. Westmeath; UCD (BAgrSc, MAgrSc [Economics]) and Kings Inns. Barrister. First elected 1992 and at each subsequent election.

Appointed Minister of State at the Department of the Environment, Community and Local Government with special responsibility for Housing and Planning March 2011. Resigned 15th November 2011 over closure of Columb barracks in Mullingar. Chairman Joint Committee on Enterprise, Trade and Employment 2007-2011. Spokesperson on Enterprise, Trade and Employment 2007-2011. Unsuccessful candidate in Labour Deputy Leadership election in October 2002. Front Bench spokesperson on Social and Family Affairs 2002-2007. Chairman Joint Committee on Social and Family Affairs 2002-2007. Spokesperson on Agriculture and Food 1997-2002. Spokesperson on Agriculture and Rural Development 1992-1997. Member Westmeath County Council 1984-2003. Member Ballynacargy GAA Club and Cullion Hurling Club. Member Royal Canal Amenity Group.

JAMES BANNON (FG)

Newtown, Legan, Co. Longford; Tel: 044 9357575; Mobile: 087 2031816
Constituency Office: Richmond Street, Longford; Tel: 043 3336185
Leinster House: 01 6184226; Email: james.bannon@oireachtas.ie
Website; www.jamesbannon.finegael.ie

Born Legan, Co. Longford 26th March 1958. Single. Educated Convent of Mercy, Ballymahon, Co. Longford. Auctioneer and Farmer. First elected 2007. Retained his seat in 2011.

Member Committee on Environment, Transport, Culture and the Gaeltacht. Deputy spokesperson on Environment, with special responsibility for Heritage, 2007-2011. Member Joint Committee on the Environment, Heritage and Local Government 2007-2011. Senator 2002-2007. Party spokesperson on Environment, Local Government and Heritage 2002-2007. Member Joint Committee on Environment and Local Government 2002-2007. Member Longford County Council 1985-2003. Former General Secretary of the Local Authority Members Association. Member Midland Health Board. Member National Rural Development Forum. Vice-chairman Midland Regional Authority's Infrastructural and Economic Committee. Member County Longford Strategy Group. Director Ardagh Heritage Trust. Director Longford Leisure Ltd. Member GAA. Member County Committee Group Water Schemes.

NICKY McFADDEN (FG)

9 Arcadia Crescent, Athlone, Co. Westmeath; Tel: 090 6478004; Mobile: 087 6771267
Constituency Office: Irishtown, Athlone; Leinster House: 01 6183938;
Email: nicky.mcfadden@oireachtas.ie; Website: www.nickymcfadden.finegael.ie

Born Athlone, 6th December 1962. Divorced, two children, Caren and Eoin. Educated St. Joseph's College Summerhill, Athlone; Athlone IT (Legal Studies Diploma). Former Medical Secretary. Contested general election in Westmeath in 2002 and in Longford-Westmeath in 2007. First elected 2011.

Member Committee on Procedure and Privileges. Member Committee on Jobs, Social Protection and Education. Elected to the Senate in 2007 on Administration Panel. Fine Gael Seanad spokesperson on Social and Family Affairs 2007-2011. Member Joint Committee on Social and Family Affairs 2007-2011. Member Westmeath County Council 2003-2007. Member Athlone TC 1999-2007. Member Westmeath VEC. Member Governing Body Athlone IT. Chairperson Board of Management Athlone Community College. President Athlone Guide Dogs Association.

ROBERT TROY (FF)

Ballynacargy, Co. Westmeath; Tel: 044 9373101; Mobile: 087 7979890
Constituency Office: Dominic Street, Mullingar; Tel: 044 9330769;
Leinster House: 01 6183059; Email: robert.troy@oireachtas.ie Website: www.roberttroy.ie

Born Ballynacargy, Co. Westmeath, January 1982. Single. Educated St. Finian's College, Mullingar. Currently studying for a BES at Trinity College, Dublin. Former Postmaster. Elected at his first attempt in 2011.

Appointed Party Spokesperson on Arts and Heritage April 2011. Member Committee on Environment, Transport, Culture and the Gaeltacht. First elected to Westmeath County Council in 2004 in Mullingar West electoral area. . Retained his seat in 2009. Involved with voluntary groups including North Westmeath Suicide Outreach Group, North Westmeath Hospice, Mullingar St. Patrick's Day Parade Committee, Mullingar Arts Centre.

LONGFORD-WESTMEATH 2011							
FIRST PREFERENCE VOTES							
	Seats	**4**			**11,506**		
	Candidate	**Party**	**1st**	**%**	**Quota**	**Count**	**Status**
1	**Penrose, Willie***	**LB**	**11,406**	**19.83%**	**0.99**	**2**	**Made Quota**
2	**Bannon, James***	**FG**	**9,129**	**15.87%**	**0.79**	**6**	**Made Quota**
3	**McFadden, Nicky**	**FG**	**6,129**	**10.65%**	**0.53**	**8**	**Elected**
4	**Troy, Robert**	**FF**	**4,275**	**7.43%**	**0.37**	**8**	**Elected**
5	Burke, Peter	FG	6,629	11.52%	0.58	8	Not Elected
6	Hogan, Paul	SF	4,339	7.54%	0.38	7	Eliminated
7	Kelly, Peter*	FF	3,876	6.74%	0.34	5	Eliminated
8	Moran, Kevin "Boxer"	NP	3,707	6.44%	0.32	4	Eliminated
9	Sexton, Mae #	LB	3,960	6.88%	0.34	3	Eliminated
10	O'Rourke, Mary*	FF	3,046	5.30%	0.26	2	Eliminated
11	Boland, John	NP	330	0.57%	0.03	1	No Expenses
12	Kinahan, Siobhán	GP	309	0.54%	0.03	1	No Expenses
13	D'Arcy, David	NV	159	0.28%	0.01	1	No Expenses
14	Cooney, Benny	NP	130	0.23%	0.01	1	No Expenses
15	Jackson, Donal	NP	101	0.18%	0.01	1	No Expenses
15	***Outgoing # Former TD**		**57,525**	**100.00%**	**11,506**	**2,877**	**No Expenses**

LONGFORD-WESTMEATH 2011												
PARTY VOTE												
	2011					**2007**					**Change**	
Party	**Cand**	**1st**	**%**	**Quota**	**Seats**	**Cand**	**1st**	**%**	**Quota**	**Seats**	**%**	**Seats**
FG	3	21,887	38.05%	1.90	2	3	16,999	30.95%	1.55	1	+7.09%	+1
LB	2	15,366	26.71%	1.34	1	1	9,692	17.65%	0.88	1	+9.06%	
FF	3	11,197	19.46%	0.97	1	3	22,599	41.15%	2.06	2	-21.69%	-1
SF	1	4,339	7.54%	0.38		1	2,136	3.89%	0.19		+3.65%	
GP	1	309	0.54%	0.03		1	960	1.75%	0.09		-1.21%	
PD						1	2,298	4.18%	0.21		-4.18%	
Others	5	4,427	7.70%	0.38		3	232	0.42%	0.02		+7.27%	
Total	**15**	**57,525**	**100.0%**	**11,506**	**4**	**13**	**54,916**	**100.0%**	**10,984**	**4**	**0.00%**	**0**
Electorate		**85,918**	**66.95%**				**83,980**	**65.39%**			**+1.56%**	
Spoiled		**661**	**1.14%**				**613**	**1.10%**			**+0.03%**	
Turnout		**58,186**	**67.72%**				**55,529**	**66.12%**			**+1.60%**	

LONGFORD-WESTMEATH 2011							
TRANSFER ANALYSIS							
From	**To**	**FG**	**LB**	**FF**	**SF**	**Others**	**Non Trans**
FG	934	284		267	147		236
		30.41%		*28.59%*	*15.74%*		*25.27%*
LB	4,175	2,128		762	519	226	540
		50.97%		*18.25%*	*12.43%*	*5.41%*	*12.93%*
FF	8,262	2238	129	4148	460	434	853
		27.09%	*1.56%*	*50.21%*	*5.57%*	*5.25%*	*10.32%*
SF	6,487	2,199		644			3,644
		33.90%		*9.93%*			*56.17%*
GP	309	74	72	39	38	58	28
		23.95%	*23.30%*	*12.62%*	*12.30%*	*18.77%*	*9.06%*
NP	5,279	2,391	168	606	984	134	996
		45.29%	*3.18%*	*11.48%*	*18.64%*	*2.54%*	*18.87%*
Total	**25,446**	**9,314**	**369**	**6,466**	**2,148**	**852**	**6,297**
		36.60%	***1.45%***	***25.41%***	***8.44%***	***3.35%***	***24.75%***

LONGFORD-WESTMEATH 2011
COUNT DETAILS

Seats 4 | Quota 11,506

Candidate	Party	1st	2nd Boland Kinahan D'Arcy Cooney Jackson	3rd O'Rourke Votes	4th Sexton Votes	5th Moran Votes	6th Kelly Votes	7th Bannon Surplus	8th Hogan Votes
Penrose, Willie*	LB	11,406	*+154* 11,560	11,560	11,560	11,560	11,560	11,560	11,560
Bannon, James*	FG	9,129	*+49* 9,178	*+114* 9,292	*+1,596* 10,888	*+129* 11,017	*+1,423* 12,440	*-934* 11,506	11,506
McFadden, Nicky	FG	6,129	*+111* 6,240	*+386* 6,626	*+363* 6,989	*+1,917* 8,906	*+165* 9,071	*+174* 9,245	*1,419* 10,664
Troy, Robert	FF	4,275	*+48* 4,323	*+1,130* 5,453	*+171* 5,624	*+329* 5,953	*+2,537* 8,490	*+267* 8,757	*+644* 9,401
Burke, Peter	FG	6,629	*+88* 6,717	*+90* 6,807	*+169* 6,976	*+171* 7,147	*+60* 7,207	*+110* 7,317	*+780* 8,097
Hogan, Paul	SF	4,339	*+125* 4,464	*+183* 4,647	*+519* 5,166	*+897* 6,063	*+277* 6,340	*+147* 6,487	*-6,487* Eliminated
Kelly, Peter*	FF	3,876	*+28* 3,904	*+481* 4,385	*+591* 4,976	*+185* 5,161	*-5,161* Eliminated		
Moran, Kevin "Boxer"	NP	3,707	*+192* 3,899	*+434* 4,333	*+226* 4,559	*-4,559* Eliminated			
Sexton, Mae #	LB	3,960	*+86* 4,046	*+129* 4,175	*-4,175* Eliminated				
O'Rourke, Mary*	FF	3,046	*+55* 3,101	*-3,101* Eliminated					
Boland, John	NP	330	*-330* Eliminated						
Kinahan, Siobhán	GP	309	*-309* Eliminated						
D'Arcy, David	NV	159	*-159* Eliminated						
Cooney, Benny	NP	130	*-130* Eliminated						
Jackson, Donal	NP	101	*-101* Eliminated						
Non-transferable Cumulative			*+93* 93	*+154* 247	*+540* 787	*+931* 1,718	*+699* 2,417	*+236* 2,653	*+3,644* 6,297
Total		**57,525**	**57,525**	**57,525**	**57,525**	**57,525**	**57,525**	**57,525**	**57,525**

LONGFORD-WESTMEATH		
MAIN BOUNDARY CHANGES		
Dail	**Constituency**	**Seats**
1 (1918)	Longford	1
	Westmeath	1
2 (1921) - 3 (1922)	Longford - Westmeath	4
4 (1923) - 8 (1933)	Longford - Westmeath	5
9 (1937) - 12 (1944)	Athlone - Longford	3
13 (1948) - 16 (1957)	Longford - Westmeath	5
17 (1961) - 26 (1989)	Longford - Westmeath	4
27 (1992) - 29 (2002)	Westmeath	3
30 (2007) - 31 (2011)	Longford - Westmeath	4

LONGFORD-WESTMEATH																	
ALL TDs 1918-2011																	
	Surname	**Forename**	**Party**	**Elected**													**Total**
1	MacEoin**	Gen. Sean	FG	21	22	32	33	37	38	43	44	48	51	54	57	61	13
2	Kennedy**	Michael	FF	27	27	32	33	48	51	54	57	61					9
3	Childers**	Erskine	FF	38	43	44	48	51	54	57							7
4	L'Estrange	Gerald	FG	65	69	73	77	81	82	82							7
5	Carter	Frank	FF	51	54	61	65	69	73								6
6	Cooney	Patrick	FG	70*	73	81	82	82	87								6
7	Reynolds**	Albert	FF	77	81	82	82	87	89								6
8	O'Rourke	Mary	FF	82N	87	89	92	97	07								6
9	Fagan**	Charles	FG	33	48	51	54	57									5
10	Sheridan	Joseph	NP	61	65	69	73	77									5
11	Penrose	Willie	LB	92	97	02	07	11									5
12	Shaw	Patrick	CG	23	27	27	32										4
13	Victory	James	FF	27J	33	37	38										4
14	McGrath	Paul	FG	89	92	97	02										4
15	Ginnell	Laurence	CR	18	21	22											3
16	Geoghegan	James	FF	30*	32	33											3
17	Carter**	Thomas	FF	43	44	48											3
18	Keegan	Sean	FF	77	81	82F											3
19	McGuinness	Joseph	SF	18	21												2
20	Lyons	John	LB	22	23												2
21	Killane	James	FF	23	27S												2
22	Broderick	Henry	LB	27	27												2
23	Lenihan	Patrick	FF	65	69												2
24	Bannon	James	FG	07	11												2
25	Robbins	Laurence	SF	21													1
26	McGuinness	Francis	CT	22													1
27	Byrne	Conor	R	23													1
28	McKenna	Patrick	F	23													1
29	Garahan	Hugh	F	27J													1
30	Connolly	Michael	CG	27S													1
31	Gormley	Francis	FF	32													1
32	Davis	Matthew	FF	37													1
33	Brady	Rory	SF	57													1
34	Abbott	Henry	FF	87													1
35	Belton**	Louis	FG	89													1
36	Cassidy	Donie	FF	02													1
37	Kelly**	Peter	FF	07													1
38	McFadden	Nicky	FG	11													1
39	Troy	Robert	FF	11													1
39	**Total**									***Includes 2 By-Elections**						*	**126**
	****Also elected in another constituency**																
LW	Fagan**	Charles	FG	Meath					37	38	43	44					4
LW	Kennedy**	Michael	FF	Meath					37	38	43	44					4
LW	Childers**	Erskine	FF	Monaghan					61	65	69	73					4
LW	Carter**	Thomas	FF	Roscommon/Leitrim					21	22/	23						3
LW	Reynolds**	Albert	FF	Longford-Roscommon					92	97							2
LW	MacEoin**	Gen. Sean	FG	Leitrim-Sligo					29*								1
LW	Belton**	Louis	FG	Longford-Roscommon					97								1
LW	Kelly**	Peter	FF	Longford-Roscommon					02								1
LW	**Included in Longford-Westmeath total**									***Includes 1 By-Election**						*	**20**

LONGFORD-WESTMEATH 1918-2011																												
* No Contest			FG		LB		FF		SF		GP		CS		PD		C na P		C na T		Farmers		Nat League		Centre P		Others	
Dail		Seats	S	% Vote	S	% Vote	S	% Vote	S	% Vote	S	% Vote	S	% Vote	S	% Vote	S	% Vote	S	% Vote	S	% Vote	S	% Vote	S	% Vote	S	% Vote
1	1918	2							2																			
2	1921*	4							4																			
3	1922	4	2	50.13%	1	24.58%	1	17.45%																				7.85%
4	1923	5	1	26.71%		8.25%	2	31.11%													1	20.76%					1	13.17%
5	1927	5	1	26.25%	1	11.33%	2	25.46%		4.67%											1	15.68%		6.34%				10.26%
6	1927	5	2	33.21%	1	10.74%	2	37.60%														10.19%						8.27%
7	1932	5	2	38.58%		9.17%	3	52.25%																				
8	1933	5	1	16.44%		10.00%	3	52.50%																	1	21.06%		
9	1937	3	1	37.84%		10.25%	2	35.67%																				16.24%
10	1938	3	1	38.21%		8.83%	2	52.96%																				
11	1943	3	1	34.92%		18.08%	2	42.75%																				4.25%
12	1944	3	1	33.55%		12.34%	2	54.12%																				
13	1948	5	1	19.21%		6.94%	3	44.05%										11.57%		3.07%							1	15.17%
14	1951	5	1	25.19%		4.27%	3	44.67%										7.49%									1	18.38%
15	1954	5	2	42.24%		7.83%	3	45.94%										4.00%										
16	1957	5	2	35.60%		3.40%	2	45.49%	1	14.10%																		1.41%
17	1961	4	1	35.49%		4.58%	2	38.96%		7.61%																	1	13.36%
18	1965	4	1	36.76%		8.16%	2	39.04%																			1	16.04%
19	1969	4	1	35.18%		10.56%	2	34.77%																			1	19.49%
20	1973	4	2	36.97%		5.84%	1	38.39%																			1	18.79%
21	1977	4	1	31.97%		5.85%	2	45.95%																			1	16.24%
22	1981	4	2	36.07%		7.10%	2	46.76%		10.08%																		
23	1982	4	2	40.57%		2.22%	2	52.29%		4.92%																		
24	1982	4	2	43.26%		3.77%	2	52.98%																				
25	1987	4	1	27.50%		2.30%	3	57.62%								11.96%												0.62%
26	1989	4	2	36.06%			2	54.24%								1.73%												7.96%
27	1992	3	1	26.69%	1	20.13%	1	45.58%		1.05%																		6.54%
28	1997	3	1	25.88%	1	24.51%	1	45.67%																				3.94%
29	2002	3	1	27.20%	1	26.05%	1	41.65%		3.44%				0.37%														1.29%
30	2007	4	1	30.95%	1	17.65%	2	41.15%		3.89%		1.75%		0.23%		4.18%												0.20%
31	2011	4	2	38.05%	1	26.71%	1	19.46%		7.54%		0.54%																7.70%
1918-2011		**124**	**40**	**33.19%**	**8**	**10.53%**	**58**	**42.71%**	**7**	**2.19%**		**0.11%**		**0.02%**		**0.75%**		**0.86%**		**0.11%**	**2**	**1.53%**		**0.21%**	**1**	**0.84%**	**8**	**6.95%**
National		**4,618**	**1,453**	**30.77%**	**482**	**11.53%**	**1,985**	**41.86%**	**232**	**1.99%**	**16**	**0.75%**		**0.04%**	**44**	**1.42%**	**18**	**0.77%**	**43**	**1.08%**	**42**	**0.90%**	**10**	**0.24%**	**11**	**0.30%**	**282**	**8.33%**

LOUTH 2011

"Gerry Adams tops the poll and Fianna Fáil draw another blank"

There were major Constituency Commission changes here since the 2007 election. The number of seats was increased from four to five, and the boundaries of the constituency was expanded to include a population of 17,333 transferring in from the areas of St Mary's and Julianstown, previously in Meath East.

Seamus Kirk was automatically returned as the outgoing Ceann Comhairle, meaning only four of the five seats were contested in the election.

Fine Gael came close to winning a second seat here in 2007 but Mairead McGuinness failed to deliver. The party's vote was up just two points in one of its poorer performances of this election but with 1.6 quotas they were in contention for two seats. Fergus O'Dowd was Fine Gael's leading vote getter and was over the quota on the first count. His running mate, Louth Gaelic football manager Peter Fitzpatrick was in fourth place on the first count with a more modest 7,845 first preferences and he battled with Fianna Fáil for the final seat. Fitzpatrick's first count lead was sufficient to withstand Carroll's challenge.

The Labour vote was up 14 points and with one quota the party was well placed to regain the seat previously held by Michael Bell. Labour surprisingly ran two candidates and Gerald Nash was in third place on the first count with 8,718 and he went on to take the fourth seat on the penultimate count. Mary Moran was a late addition to the ticket and her 4,546 first preferences left her in seventh place on the first count but she was too far off the pace and was never in contention. Her transfers (57%) put Nash over the quota.

Outgoing TD Dermot Ahern was among the Fianna Fáil Ministers to retire ahead of this election. The Fianna Fáil vote was down a huge 26 points and with just 0.8 quotas spread over its two candidates the party struggled to retain even one seat. Outgoing Senator James Carroll was its leading candidate with 5,681 first preferences but this left him outside the frame on the first count with just 0.4 of a quota. Likewise his running mate Declan Breathnach with 5,177 and 0.4 of a quota was also outside the frame and out of contention. This was another case of Fianna Fáil running too many candidates, dividing their depressed vote and failing to win a seat.

There was much media attention on this constituency following the arrival of Sinn Fein President Gerry Adams. Outgoing Sinn Fein deputy Arthur Morgan retired and Adams decided to enter southern politics. Adams topped the poll with the third largest number of first preferences (15,072) in this election, behind Enda Kenny (17,472) and Shane Ross (17,075). He was over the quota in the first count for an impressive performance with the Sinn Fein vote up 7 points on 2007.

LOUTH TDs 2011

SEAMUS KIRK (FF)

Rathiddy, Knockbridge, Dundalk, Co. Louth; Tel: 042 9331032;
Leinster House: 01 6183362; Email: seamus.kirk@oireachtas.ie

Born Drumkeith, Co. Louth 26th April 1945. Married to Mary McGeough, three sons, one daughter. Educated CBS, Dundalk, Co. Louth. Farmer. First elected November 1982 and at each subsequent election. Automatically returned 2011 as outgoing Ceann Comhairle.

Party Spokesperson on Horticulture and Rural affairs. Member Joint Administration Committee. Elected Ceann Comhairle 15th October 2009 following resignation of John O'Donoghue. Vice-chairman Joint Committee on European Affairs 2002-2007. Chairperson Fianna Fail Parliamentary Party June 2002- Oct 2009. Co-vice-chairman British-Irish Inter-Parliamentary Body 2002-2007. Minister of State at the Department of Agriculture and Food with special responsibility for Horticulture 1987-1992. Front bench spokesperson on Horticulture 1983-1987. Member Louth County Council 1974-1985. Member of East Border Region Committee; Co. Louth Health Committee; Co. Louth Archaeological and Historical Society. Member of the GAA and former Louth County footballer.

GERRY ADAMS (SF)

Ballymakellett, Ravensdale, Co. Louth.
Constituency Office: 7 Williamsons Place, Dundalk; Tel: 042 9328859
Leinster House: 01 6184442; Email: gerry.adams@oireachtas.ie

Born Belfast 6th October 1948. Married to Colette McArdle, three children. Educated St. Mary's Grammar School, Falls Road, Belfast. Elected at his first attempt in 2011.

Party Leader shadowing Taoiseach. President Sinn Fein since 1983. MP for West Belfast 1983-1992 and 1997-2011. Member of Northern Ireland Assembly 1998-2010.

FERGUS O'DOWD (FG)

24 St. Mary's Villas, Drogheda, Co. Louth; Tel: 041 9833392; Mobile: 087 2352920
Constituency Office: 10 Boyne Shopping Centre, Drogheda, Co. Louth; Tel: 041 9842275
Leinster House: 01 6183078; Email: fergus.odowd@oireachtas.ie
Website: www.fergusodowd@finegael.ie

Born Thurles, Co. Tipperary September 1948. Married to Agnes Thornton, three sons. Educated Drogheda CBS. Crawford Technical Institute, Cork. Diploma in General and Rural Science. Minister of State. Former Teacher. Contested 1997 General Election. First elected 2002 and at each subsequent election.

Appointed March 2011 Minister of State at Department of Communications, Energy and Natural resources and at Department of Environment, Community and Local Government with responsibility for New Era Project. Front bench spokesperson on Education & Skills 2010-2011. Supported Richard Bruton in his failed attempt to oust Enda Kenny as party leader in June 2010. Front bench spokesperson on Transport and Marine September 2007-June 2010. Member Joint Committee on Transport and Member Joint Committee on the Implementation of the Good Friday Agreement and Member Joint Committee on Economic and Regulatory Affairs 2007-2011. Spokesperson on Environment, Heritage and Local Government 2004-2007. Spokesperson on Community, Rural and Gaeltacht Affairs, 2002-2004. Senator (Administrative Panel) 1997-2002. Member Louth County Council 1979-2003. Member Drogheda Corporation 1974-2003 (Mayor 1977-1978, 1981-1982, 1994-1995). Founding Chairman, Droichead Arts Centre, Drogheda.

GERALD NASH (LB)

115 Newfield Estate, Drogheda, Co. Louth; Tel: 041 9834442; Mobile: 087 2716816
Leinster House: 01 6183576; Website: www.geraldnash.com

Born Drogheda, Co. Louth, 20th December 1975. Single. Educated St. Joseph's CBS, Drogheda; UCD. Public Relations Consultant. Formerly assistant to Nessa Childers MEP. Contested 2007 Dail election in Louth. First elected 2011.

Member Committee on Environment, Transport, Culture and the Gaeltacht. Contested 1999 local election in Louth County Council. Co-opted as replacement for Patsy Kirwan in 2000. First elected 2004 in Drogheda West. Moved to Drogheda East in 2009 and retained his seat. Elected to Drogheda Borough Council in Drogheda No. 2 in 1999, 2004 and 2009.

PETER FITZPATRICK (FG)

18 Belfry Gardens, Dundalk, Co. Louth; Mobile: 086 2512577
Constituency Office: 2 The Courthouse Square, Co. Louth. Tel: 042 9330100;
Leinster House: 01 6183563; Email: peter.fitzpatrick@oireachtas.ie
Website: www. Peterfitzpatrick.finegael.ie

Born Dundalk, May 1962. Married, one son, two daughters. Educated O'Fiaich College, Dundalk. Public Relations Consultant. Elected at his first attempt in 2011.

Member Committee on Health and Children. Manager Louth Gaelic football team.

Sinn Fein TDs in 31st Dail

LOUTH 2011							
FIRST PREFERENCE VOTES							
	Seats	4			13,864		
	Candidate	Party	1st	%	Quota	Count	Status
1	**Kirk, Seamus***	**FF**	**Returned Automatically**				**Ceann Comhairle**
2	**Adams, Gerry**	**SF**	**15,072**	**21.74%**	**1.09**	**1**	**Made Quota**
3	**O'Dowd, Fergus***	**FG**	**13,980**	**20.17%**	**1.01**	**1**	**Made Quota**
4	**Nash, Gerald**	**LB**	**8,718**	**12.58%**	**0.63**	**12**	**Made Quota**
5	**Fitzpatrick, Peter**	**FG**	**7,845**	**11.32%**	**0.57**	**13**	**Elected**
6	Carroll, James	FF	5,681	8.20%	0.41	13	Not Elected
7	Moran, Mary	LB	4,546	6.56%	0.33	11	Eliminated
8	Breathnach, Declan	FF	5,177	7.47%	0.37	10	Eliminated
9	Dearey, Mark	GP	3,244	4.68%	0.23	9	Eliminated
10	Clare, Thomas	NV	2,233	3.22%	0.16	8	No Expenses
11	Matthews, Fred	NP	957	1.38%	0.07	7	No Expenses
12	Godfrey, Frank	NP	649	0.94%	0.05	7	No Expenses
13	Wilson, Robin	NP	536	0.77%	0.04	6	No Expenses
14	Martin, Luke	NP	224	0.32%	0.02	5	No Expenses
15	Crilly, Gerry	NP	222	0.32%	0.02	5	No Expenses
16	Bradley, David	NP	174	0.25%	0.01	4	No Expenses
17	Glynn, Robert	NP	61	0.09%	0.00	2	No Expenses
17	***Outgoing**		**69,319**	**100.00%**	**13,864**	**3,467**	**No Expenses**

LOUTH 2011													
PARTY VOTE													
	2011					2007					Change	
Party	Cand	1st	%	Quota	Seats	Cand	1st	%	Quota	Seats	%	Seats
FG	2	21,825	31.48%	1.57	2	3	16,159	29.37%	1.47	1	+2.11%	+1
LB	2	13,264	19.13%	0.96	1	1	2,739	4.98%	0.25		+14.16%	+1
FF	2	10,858	15.66%	0.78	1	3	23,181	42.14%	2.11	2	-26.47%	-1
SF	1	15,072	21.74%	1.09	1	1	8,274	15.04%	0.75	1	+6.70%	
GP	1	3,244	4.68%	0.23		1	4,172	7.58%	0.38		-2.90%	
WP						1	193	0.35%	0.02		-0.35%	
Others	8	5,056	7.29%	0.36		2	296	0.54%	0.03		+6.76%	
Total	**16**	**69,319**	**100.0%**	**13,864**	**5**	**12**	**55,014**	**100.0%**	**11,003**	**4**	**0.00%**	+1
Electorate		**99,530**	**69.65%**				**86,007**	**63.96%**			**+5.68%**	
Spoiled		**871**	**1.24%**				**592**	**1.06%**			**+0.18%**	
Turnout		**70,190**	**70.52%**				**55,606**	**64.65%**			**+5.87%**	

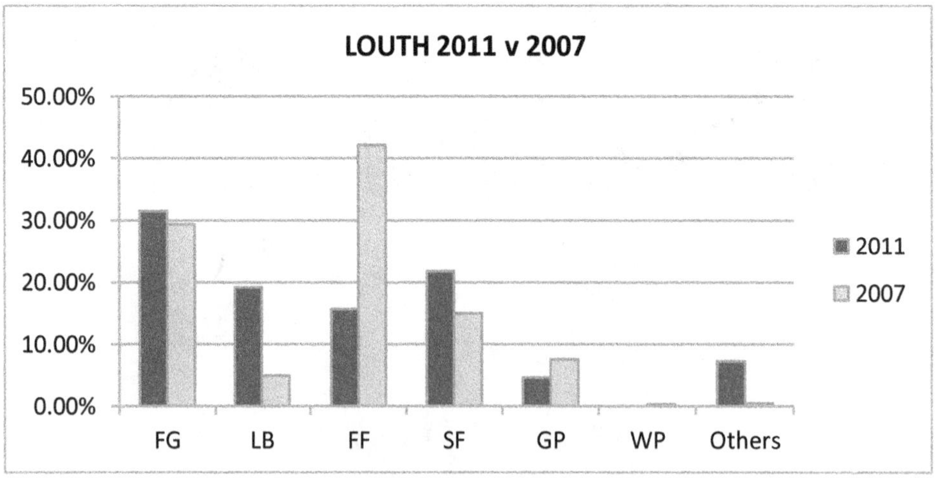

LOUTH 2011 COUNT DETAILS														
Seats	4												Quota	13,864
Candidate	Party	1st	2nd Adams Surplus	3rd Glynn Votes	4th O'Dowd Surplus	5th Bradley Votes	6th Martin Crilly	7th Wilson Votes	8th Matthews Godfrey	9th Clare Votes	10th Dearey Votes	11th Breathnach Votes	12th Moran Votes	13th Nash Surplus
			-1,208											
Adams, Gerry	SF	15,072	13,864	13,864	13,864	13,864	13,864	13,864	13,864	13,864	13,864	13,864	13,864	13,864
					-116									
O'Dowd, Fergus*	FG	13,980	13,980	13,980	13,864	13,864	13,864	13,864	13,864	13,864	13,864	13,864	13,864	13,864
			+224	+6	+36	+14	+39	+61	+306	+417	+659	+178	+3,962	-756
Nash, Gerald	LB	8,718	8,942	8,948	8,984	8,998	9,037	9,098	9,404	9,821	10,480	10,658	14,620	13,864
			+153	+4	+50	+17	+61	+47	+298	+507	+948	+696	+1,144	+553
Fitzpatrick, Peter	FG	7,845	7,998	8,002	8,052	8,069	8,130	8,177	8,475	8,982	9,930	10,626	11,770	12,323
			+68	+2	+8	+15	+18	+11	+184	+494	+288	+3,942	+474	+203
Carroll, James	FF	5,681	5,749	5,751	5,759	5,774	5,792	5,803	5,987	6,481	6,769	10,711	11,185	11,388
			+192	+4	+5	+1	+60	+100	+216	+312	+994	+544	-6,974	
Moran, Mary	LB	4,546	4,738	4,742	4,747	4,748	4,808	4,908	5,124	5,436	6,430	6,974	Eliminated	
			+68		+2	+16	+22	+12	+76	+230	+398	-6,001		
Breathnach, Declan	FF	5,177	5,245	5,245	5,247	5,263	5,285	5,297	5,373	5,603	6,001	Eliminated		
			+114	+4	+4	+8	+47	+85	+166	+267	-3,939			
Dearey, Mark	GP	3,244	3,358	3,362	3,366	3,374	3,421	3,506	3,672	3,939	Eliminated			
			+85	+6	+4	+62	+66	+113	+455	-3,024				
Clare, Thomas	NV	2,233	2,318	2,324	2,328	2,390	2,456	2,569	3,024	Eliminated				
			+47	+9	+2	+9	+65	+118	-1,207					
Matthews, Fred	NP	957	1,004	1,013	1,015	1,024	1,089	1,207	Eliminated					
			+65	+13	+4	+23	+27	+48	-829					
Godfrey, Frank	NP	649	714	727	731	754	781	829	Eliminated					
			+56	+5	+1	+12	+82	-692						
Wilson, Robin	NP	536	592	597	598	610	692	Eliminated						
			+65	+4		+7	-300							
Martin, Luke	NP	224	289	293	293	300	Eliminated							
			+30	+2		+13	-267							
Crilly, Gerry	NP	222	252	254	254	267	Eliminated							
			+37	+4		-215								
Bradley, David	NP	174	211	215	215	Eliminated								
			+4	-65										
Glynn, Robert	NP	61	65	Eliminated										
Non-transferable				+2		+18	+80	+97	+335	+797	+652	+641	+1,394	
Cumulative			0	2	2	20	100	197	532	1,329	1,981	2,622	4,016	4,016
Total		**69,319**	**69,319**	**69,319**	**69,319**	**69,319**	**69,319**	**69,319**	**69,319**	**69,319**	**69,319**	**69,319**	**69,319**	**69,319**

LOUTH 2011 TRANSFER ANALYSIS							
From	**To**	**FG**	**LB**	**FF**	**GP**	**Others**	**Non Trans**
FG	116	50	41	10	4	11	
		43.10%	*35.34%*	*8.62%*	*3.45%*	*9.48%*	
LB	7,730	1,697	3,962	677			1,394
		21.95%	*51.25%*	*8.76%*			*18.03%*
FF	6,001	696	722	3942			641
		11.60%	*12.03%*	*65.69%*			*10.68%*
SF	1,208	153	416	136	114	389	
		12.67%	*34.44%*	*11.26%*	*9.44%*	*32.20%*	
GP	3,939	948	1,653	686			652
		24.07%	*41.96%*	*17.42%*			*16.55%*
NP	6,599	934	1,536	1,080	577	1,143	1,329
		14.15%	*23.28%*	*16.37%*	*8.74%*	*17.32%*	*20.14%*
Total	**25,593**	**4,478**	**8,330**	**6,531**	**695**	**1,543**	**4,016**
		17.50%	***32.55%***	***25.52%***	***2.72%***	***6.03%***	***15.69%***

LOUTH		
MAIN BOUNDARY CHANGES		
Dail	**Constituency**	**Seats**
1 (1918)	Louth	1
2 (1921) - 3 (1922)	Louth-Meath	5
4 (1923) -20 (1973)	Louth	3
21 (1977) - 30 (2007)	Louth	4
31 (2011) -	Louth	5

LOUTH																				
ALL TDs 1918-2011																				
	Surname	**Forename**	**Party**	**Elected**																**Total**
1	Aiken	Frank	FF	23	27	27	32	33	37	38	43	44	48	51	54	57	61	65	69	16
2	Coburn	James	FG	27	27	32	33	37	38	43	44	48	51							10
3	Faulkner	Padraig	FF	57	61	65	69	73	77	81	82	82								9
4	Kirk	Seamus	FF	82N	87	89	92	97	02	07	11									8
5	Murphy	James	CG	21	22	23	27	27	32	33										7
6	Donegan	Patrick	FG	54	61	65	69	73	77											6
7	Ahern	Dermot	FF	87	89	92	97	02	07											6
8	Bell	Michael	LB	82N	87	89	92	97												5
9	McGahon	Brendan	FG	82N	87	89	92	97												5
10	Walsh	Laurence	FF	37	38	44	51													4
11	O'Kelly	John	CR	18	21	22														3
12	Hughes	Peter	CG	21	22	23														3
13	Coburn	George	FG	54*	54	57														3
14	Filgate	Edward	FF	77	81	82F														3
15	O'Dowd	Fergus	FG	02	07	11														3
16	Duggan**	Edmund	CT	21	22															2
17	Connolly	Roderick	LB	43	48															2
18	Farrell	Joseph	FF	73	77															2
19	Markey	Bernard	FG	81	82F															2
20	Morgan	Arthur	SF	02	07															2
21	McKenna	Justin	SF	21																1
22	O'Shannon	Cathal	LB	22																1
23	Agnew	Paddy	Hblk	81																1
24	Bellew	Thomas	FF	82F																1
25	Adams	Gerry	SF	11																1
26	Nash	Gerald	LB	11																1
27	Fitzpatrick	Peter	FG	11																1
27	**Total**												***Includes 1 By-Election**						*	**108**
	**** Also elected in another constituency**																			
	Duggan**	Edmund	CT	Meath								18	23	27	27	32				5

LOUTH 1918-2011																									
* No Contest		FG		LB		FF		SF		GP		WP		PD		C na P		C na T		Farmers		Nat League		Others	
Dail	Seats	S	% Vote	S	% Vote	S	% Vote	S	% Vote	S	% Vote	S	% Vote	S	% Vote	S	% Vote	S	% Vote	S	% Vote	S	% Vote	S	% Vote
1 1918	1							1																	
2 1921*	5							5																	
3 1922	5	3	45.95%	1	38.34%	1	15.71%																		
4 1923	3	2	46.77%		10.27%	1	27.14%														15.82%				
5 1927	3	1	28.52%		10.40%	1	28.25%															1	26.37%		6.46%
6 1927	3	1	46.30%			1	32.39%															1	21.31%		
7 1932	3	1	38.32%		7.92%	1	33.55%																	1	20.21%
8 1933	3	1	26.03%			1	49.14%																	1	24.83%
9 1937	3	1	46.16%			2	53.84%																		
10 1938	3	1	41.32%		6.79%	2	51.90%																		
11 1943	3	1	31.39%	1	15.79%	1	38.96%												11.96%						1.89%
12 1944	3	1	22.82%		11.24%	2	46.13%												17.10%						2.72%
13 1948	3	1	36.14%	1	12.26%	1	44.57%										7.04%								
14 1951	3	1	35.42%		15.24%	2	49.34%																		
15 1954	3	2	45.77%		7.63%	1	43.60%		3.00%																
16 1957	3	1	39.80%		4.50%	2	46.26%		9.45%																
17 1961	3	1	41.17%			2	43.66%		4.42%																10.76%
18 1965	3	1	40.70%		12.25%	2	47.05%																		
19 1969	3	1	40.31%		12.81%	2	46.89%																		
20 1973	3	1	32.95%		8.23%	2	51.17%		4.63%																3.02%
21 1977	4	1	32.06%		5.15%	3	50.67%						4.44%												7.68%
22 1981	4	1	29.89%		6.25%	2	41.21%	1	18.29%				1.72%												2.64%
23 1982	4	1	30.43%		7.98%	3	47.11%		8.54%				1.71%												4.24%
24 1982	4	1	33.77%	1	14.73%	2	43.10%						1.54%												6.86%
25 1987	4	1	23.12%	1	13.26%	2	39.46%		5.55%				1.22%		11.15%										6.25%
26 1989	4	1	26.99%	1	19.20%	2	43.26%		5.25%						4.92%										0.36%
27 1992	4	1	24.92%	1	22.10%	2	41.77%		3.92%				0.57%												6.71%
28 1997	4	1	27.90%	1	10.50%	2	40.02%		8.11%		3.12%				5.32%										5.04%
29 2002	4	1	20.23%		6.69%	2	43.57%	1	14.95%		4.16%		0.37%												10.03%
30 2007	4	1	29.37%		4.98%	2	42.14%	1	15.04%		7.58%		0.35%												0.54%
31 2011	5	2	31.48%	1	19.13%	1	15.66%	1	21.74%		4.68%														7.29%
1918-2011	**107**	**34**	**33.26%**	**9**	**11.05%**	**50**	**40.61%**	**10**	**5.59%**		**1.02%**		**0.50%**		**0.92%**		**0.20%**		**0.82%**		**0.37%**	**2**	**1.20%**	**2**	**4.46%**
National	**4,618**	**1,453**	**30.77%**	**482**	**11.53%**	**1,985**	**41.86%**	**232**	**1.99%**	**16**	**0.75%**	**17**	**0.78%**	**44**	**1.42%**	**18**	**0.77%**	**43**	**1.08%**	**42**	**0.90%**	**10**	**0.24%**	**276**	**7.88%**

MAYO 2011

"A record breaking four out of five for Enda Kenny and Fine Gael"

There were no Constituency Commission boundary changes here since 2007 and it remained a five-seat constituency.

This constituency was over as a contest following the first count as the leading five contenders were well clear of the rest of the field.

The Fine Gael vote was up 11 points to a remarkable 65% of the first preference vote and with 3.9 quotas they were on track to succeed in their aim of winning four seats. Enda Kenny topped the poll with 17,472 first preferences, the highest in this election and with 1.4 quotas he took the first seat on the first count. He was joined by Michael Ring who was also elected on the first count. Michelle Mulherin, who lost out in 2007 made no mistake in this election and she was in third place on the first count and went on to take the third seat. John O'Mahony was a surprise winner in 2007 and the former Galway All-Ireland winning manager was in fourth place on the first count and went on take the final seat.

Beverley Flynn contested the 2007 election as an independent candidate and she rejoined Fianna Fáil in April 2008. She announced in December 2010 that she would not be contesting the general election. The Fianna Fáil vote was down 8 points and with just one quota spread over two candidates, one seat was as much as they could hope for. Dara Calleary had won a seat here in 2007 at his first attempt and had performed well in the 30th Dáil. He was in fifth place on the first count and went on to take the fourth seat comfortably and Fianna Fáil's only seat in Mayo. A late addition to the ticket, Lisa Chambers got 3,343 first preferences to leave her well off the pace in eight place and out of contention.

This was a disappointing performance by Labour with former independent deputy Dr. Jerry Cowley winning just 5% to leave him outside the frame on the first count with 0.3 quotas and out of contention.

Sinn Féin surprisingly ran two female candidates – Rose Conway-Walsh and Thérese Ruane - and between them they got just 6.5% and both were too far off the pace to contest for a seat.

Independent local councillor Michael Kilcoyne had been fancied for a seat in the run up to this election but with just under 4,000 first preferences was outside the frame on the first count with just 0.3 quotas and out of contention.

MAYO TDs 2011

ENDA KENNY (FG)

Hawthorn Avenue, Lightfort, Castlebar, Co. Mayo;
Constituency Office: Tucker Street, Castlebar, Co. Mayo; Tel: 094 9025600;
Email: taoiseach@taoiseach.ie; Website: www.endakenny.finegael.ie

Born Castlebar, Co. Mayo 24th April 1951. Married to Fionnuala O'Kelly, two sons, and one daughter. Educated St. Gerald's College, Castlebar; St. Patrick's Teacher Training College, Drumcondra, Dublin and UCG. Taoiseach and Leader of Fine Gael. Former Teacher. First elected 1975 at by-election caused by the death of his father Henry Kenny and at each subsequent election.

Elected Taoiseach 9th March 2011. Defeated leadership challenge by Richard Bruton in June 2010. Elected Leader of Fine Gael, June 2002 following resignation of Michael Noonan. Contested Fine Gael leadership in February 2001 and subsequently dropped from front bench by new leader Michael Noonan. Front bench spokesperson on Arts, Heritage, Gaeltacht and the Islands 1997-2001. Minister for Tourism and Trade 1994-1997. Negotiated Programme for Government with Labour and DL in 1994. Fine Gael Chief Whip 1992-1994. Minister of State at the Department of Education and at the Department of Labour with special responsibility for Youth Affairs 1986-1987. Front bench spokesperson on the Gaeltacht 1987-1988; on Western Development 1982; on Youth Affairs and Sport 1977-1980. Member, British-Irish Inter-Parliamentary Body 1991-1992. Member Mayo County Council 1975-1995. Son of the late Henry Kenny, Dáil Deputy for Mayo South 1954-1969, Mayo West 1969-1975 and Parliamentary Secretary to the Minister for Finance 1973-1975.

MICHAEL RING (FG)

The Paddock, Westport, Co. Mayo, Tel: 098 25734;
Constituency Office: Quay Street, Westport; Tel: 098 27012;
Leinster House: 01 6183838; Email: michael.ring@oireachtas.ie
Website: www.michaelringtd.com

Born Westport, Co. Mayo 24th December 1953. Married to Ann Fitzgerald, one son, two daughters Educated Westport Vocational School. Minister of State and Former Auctioneer. Contested 1992 General Election in Mayo West. First elected at by-election in Mayo West in 1994 and at each subsequent election.

Appointed Minister of State at the Department of Transport, Tourism and Sport with special responsibility for Tourism and Sport March 2010. Fine Gael front bench spokesperson on Social Protection 2010-2011. Fine Gael Front Bench Spokesperson on Community, Rural and Gaeltacht Affairs September 2007-June 2010. Member Joint Committee on Arts, Sport, Tourism, Community, Rural and Gaeltacht Affairs 2007-2011. Spokesperson on Social and Family Affairs, 2002-2004. Member Joint Committee on Social and Family Affairs 2002-2007. Junior spokesperson on Agriculture, Livestock Breeding and Horticulture 1997-2002. Member British-Irish Inter-Parliamentary Body. Member Mayo County Council 1991-2003. Member Westport UDC 1979-2003. Winner, All Ireland Medal with Mayo Vocational School 1971. Former Westport United player.

MICHELLE MULHERIN (FG)

47 Moy Heights, Ballina, Co. Mayo; Tel: 096 71935; Mobile: 087 9317406
Leinster House: 01 6183065; Email:michelle.mulherin@oireachtas.ie

Born Castlebar 20th January 1972. Single. Educated St. Mary's Convent of Mercy, Ballina; UCD; Law Society of Ireland. Solicitor. Contested 2007 Dail election in Mayo.
First elected 2011.

Member Committee on Investigations, Oversight and Petitions. Elected to Mayo County Council in 2004 in Ballina electoral area. Retained her seat in 2009. Elected to Ballina TC in 1999, 2004 and 2009. Contested 2007 Seanad election on Administrative Panel.

DARA CALLEARY (FF)

8 Quignalecka, Sligo Road, Ballina, Co. Mayo; Mobile: 086 2238810
Constituency Office: 19 Pearse Street, Ballina, Co. Mayo; Tel: 096 777613;
Leinster House: 01 6183331; Email: dara.calleary@oireachtas.ie
Website: www.daracalleary.ie

Born Mayo General Hospital, 10th May 1973. Single. Educated St. Muredach's College, Ballina; Trinity College, Dublin (BA). Formerly Manager Chamber Development and BMW Regional Co-Ordinator Chambers Ireland. First elected 2007. Retained his seat in 2011.

Appointed Party Spokesperson on Justice, Defence and Equality April 2011. Member Committee on Investigations, Oversight and Petitions. Member Committee on Justice, Defence and Equality. Minister of State at the Department of Enterprise, Trade and Employment with special responsibility for Labour Affairs 2009-2011. Vice-Chairman Joint Committee on Climate Change and Energy Security October 2007-April 2009. Member Fianna Fail National Executive 1997-2007. Chairman Ballina Chamber Infrastructural Committee 2005-2007. Member Irish European Movement, Ballina Rugby Club, Ballina Stephanites GAA Club and Ballina Salmon Festival Committee. Son of former Minister of State Sean Calleary TD for East Mayo 1973-1992. Grandson of PA Calleary TD for North Mayo 1952-1969.

JOHN O'MAHONY (FG)

"Tower House", Charlestown Road, Ballaghadereen, Co. Mayo; Mobile: 086 8338017
Constituency Office: D'Alton Street, Claremorris, Co. Mayo, Tel: 094 9373560;
Leinster House: 01 6183706, Email: john.omahony@oireachtas.ie
Website: www.johnomahony.ie

Born Kilmovee, Co. Mayo, 8th June 1953. Married to Geraldine Towey, five daughters. Educated St. Nathy's College, Ballaghadereen; St. Patrick's College, Maynooth, (BA); UCG (H Dip Ed). Teacher in St. Nathy's 1974-2006. First elected 2007. Retained his seat in 2011.

Appointed vice-chair Committee on Environment, Transport, Culture and the Gaeltacht June 2011. Deputy spokesperson on Arts, Sport and Tourism with special responsibility for Sport 2007-2011. Member Joint Committee on Arts, Sport, Tourism, Community, Rural and Gaeltacht Affairs and Member Joint Committee on Education and Science 2007-2011. Managed Galway to All Ireland success in 1998 and 2001. Manager of the Mayo senior team 2006-2010.

	MAYO 2011 FIRST PREFERENCE VOTES						
	Seats	5			12,360		
	Candidate	Party	1st	%	Quota	Count	Status
1	**Kenny, Enda***	**FG**	**17,472**	**23.56%**	**1.41**	**1**	**Made Quota**
2	**Ring, Michael***	**FG**	**13,180**	**17.77%**	**1.07**	**1**	**Made Quota**
3	**Mulherin, Michelle**	**FG**	**8,851**	**11.94%**	**0.72**	**8**	**Made Quota**
4	**Calleary, Dara***	**FF**	**8,577**	**11.57%**	**0.69**	**8**	**Made Quota**
5	**O'Mahony, John***	**FG**	**8,667**	**11.69%**	**0.70**	**8**	**Elected**
6	Kilcoyne, Michael	NP	3,996	5.39%	0.32	8	Not Elected
7	Cowley, Dr. Jerry #	LB	3,644	4.91%	0.29	7	Eliminated
8	Conway-Walsh, Rose	SF	2,660	3.59%	0.22	6	Eliminated
9	Chambers, Lisa	FF	3,343	4.51%	0.27	5	Eliminated
10	Ruane, Thérése	SF	2,142	2.89%	0.17	4	No Expenses
11	Daly, Martin	NV	893	1.20%	0.07	3	No Expenses
12	Carey, John	GP	266	0.36%	0.02	3	No Expenses
13	Clarke, Loretta	NP	218	0.29%	0.02	3	No Expenses
14	McDonnell, Dermot	NP	216	0.29%	0.02	3	No Expenses
15	Forkin, Sean	NP	29	0.04%	0.00	3	No Expenses
15	***Outgoing # Former TD**		**74,154**	**100.00%**	**12,360**	**3,090**	**No Expenses**

MAYO 2011 PARTY VOTE												
	2011					2007					Change	
Party	Cand	1st	%	Quota	Seats	Cand	1st	%	Quota	Seats	%	Seats
FG	4	48,170	64.96%	3.90	4	4	38,426	53.83%	3.23	3	+11.13%	+1
LB	1	3,644	4.91%	0.29		1	831	1.16%	0.07		+3.75%	
FF	2	11,920	16.07%	0.96	1	3	17,459	24.46%	1.47	1	-8.38%	
SF	2	4,802	6.48%	0.39		1	3,608	5.05%	0.30		+1.42%	
GP	1	266	0.36%	0.02		1	580	0.81%	0.05		-0.45%	
PD						1	296	0.41%	0.02		-0.41%	
Others	5	5,352	7.22%	0.43		2	10,186	14.27%	0.86	1	-7.05%	-1
Total	**15**	**74,154**	**100.0%**	**12,360**	**5**	**13**	**71,386**	**100.0%**	**11,898**	**5**	**0.00%**	**0**
Electorate		**101,160**	**73.30%**				**98,696**	**72.33%**			**+0.97%**	
Spoiled		**641**	**0.86%**				**700**	**0.97%**			-0.11%	
Turnout		**74,795**	**73.94%**				**72,086**	**73.04%**			**+0.90%**	

MAYO 2011 TRANSFER ANALYSIS								
From	To	FG	LB	FF	SF	GP	Others	Non Trans
FG	5,932	4,103	393	346	288	16	786	
		69.17%	*6.63%*	*5.83%*	*4.86%*	*0.27%*	*13.25%*	
LB	5,899	1,912		775			1,242	1,970
		32.41%		*13.14%*			*21.05%*	*33.40%*
FF	3,619	235	185	2,539	160		334	166
		6.49%	*5.11%*	*70.16%*	*4.42%*		*9.23%*	*4.59%*
SF	6,965	1,145	1,420	781	1,428		856	1,335
		16.44%	*20.39%*	*11.21%*	*20.50%*		*12.29%*	*19.17%*
GP	282	83	43	42	47		38	29
		29.43%	*15.25%*	*14.89%*	*16.67%*		*13.48%*	*10.28%*
Others	1,423	418	214	213	240		194	144
		29.37%	*15.04%*	*14.97%*	*16.87%*		*13.63%*	*10.12%*
Total	**24,120**	**7,896**	**2,255**	**4,696**	**2,163**	**16**	**3,450**	**3,644**
		32.74%	***9.35%***	***19.47%***	***8.97%***	***0.07%***	***14.30%***	***15.11%***

MAYO 2011
COUNT DETAILS

Seats 5 | **Quota 12,360**

Candidate	Party	1st	2nd	3rd	4th	5th	6th	7th	8th
			Kenny Surplus	Ring Surplus	Daly Carey Clarke McDonnell Forkin	Ruane Votes	Chambers Votes	Conway Votes	Cowley Votes
			-5,112						
Kenny, Enda*	FG	17,472	12,360	12,360	12,360	12,360	12,360	12,360	12,360
				-820					
Ring, Michael*	FG	13,180	13,180	12,360	12,360	12,360	12,360	12,360	12,360
			+1,963	*+296*	*+324*	*+143*	*+95*	*+490*	*1,141*
Mulherin, Michelle	FG	8,851	10,814	11,110	11,434	11,577	11,672	12,162	13,303
			+168	*+30*	*+194*	*+94*	*+2,539*	*+620*	*+775*
Calleary, Dara*	FF	8,577	8,745	8,775	8,969	9,063	11,602	12,222	12,997
			+1,623	*+221*	*+177*	*+176*	*+140*	*+336*	*+771*
O'Mahony, John*	FG	8,667	10,290	10,511	10,688	10,864	11,004	11,340	12,111
			+645	*+74*	*+232*	*+181*	*+334*	*+675*	*+1,242*
Kilcoyne, Michael	NP	3,996	4,641	4,715	4,947	5,128	5,462	6,137	7,379
			+311	*+82*	*+257*	*+235*	*+185*	*+1,185*	*-5,899*
Cowley,Dr. Jerry #	LB	3,644	3,955	4,037	4,294	4,529	4,714	5,899	Eliminated
			+92	*+61*	*+126*	*+1,428*	*+160*	*-4,527*	
Conway-Walsh, Rose	SF	2,660	2,752	2,813	2,939	4,367	4,527	Eliminated	
			+121	*+27*	*+61*	*+67*	*-3,619*		
Chambers, Lisa	FF	3,343	3,464	3,491	3,552	3,619	Eliminated		
			+118	*+17*	*+161*	*-2,438*			
Ruane, Thérése	SF	2,142	2,260	2,277	2,438	Eliminated			
			+26	*+7*	*-926*				
Daly, Martin	NV	893	919	926	Eliminated				
			+14	*+2*	*-282*				
Carey, John	GP	266	280	282	Eliminated				
			+8	*+2*	*-228*				
Clarke, Loretta	NP	218	226	228	Eliminated				
			+21	*+1*	*-238*				
McDonnell, Dermot	NP	216	237	238	Eliminated				
			+2		*-31*				
Forkin, Sean	NP	29	31	31	Eliminated				
Non-transferable					*+173*	*+114*	*+166*	*+1,221*	*+1,970*
Cumulative			0	0	173	287	453	1,674	3,644
Total		**74,154**	**74,154**	**74,154**	**74,154**	**74,154**	**74,154**	**74,154**	**74,154**

MAYO

MAIN BOUNDARY CHANGES

Dail	Constituency	Seats
1 (1918)	Mayo East	1
	Mayo North	1
	Mayo South	1
	Mayo West	1
2 (1921) - 3 (1922)	Mayo North and West	4
	Mayo South-Roscommon South	4
4 (1923) - 8 (1933)	Mayo North	4
	Mayo South	5
9 (1937) - 12 (1944)	Mayo North	3
	Mayo South	5
13 (1948) - 18 (1965)	Mayo North	3
	Mayo South	4
19 (1969) - 27 (1992)	Mayo East	3
	Mayo West	3
28 (1997) - 31 (2011)	Mayo	5

								MAYO									
								ALL TDs 1918-2007									
	Surname	**Forename**	**Party**						**Elected**								**Total**
1	Ruttledge	Patrick	FF	21	22	23	27	27	32	33	37	38	43	44	48	51	13
2	Kenny	Enda	FG	75*	77	81	82	82	87	89	92	97	02	07	11		12
3	Moran	Michael	FF	38	43	44	48	51	54	57	61	65	69				10
4	Nally	Martin	FG	23	27	27	32	33	37	38							7
5	Fitzgerald-Kenney	James	FG	27	27	32	33	37	38	43							7
6	Clery	Michael	FF	27S	32	33	37	38	43	44							7
7	Walsh	Richard	FF	27S	32	33	37	38	44	48							7
8	Blowick	Joseph	CnaT	43	44	48	51	54	57	61							7
9	Flanagan	Sean	FF	51	54	57	61	65	69	73							7
10	Calleary	Sean	FF	73	77	81	82	82	87	89							7
11	Flynn	Padraig	FF	77	81	82	82	87	89	92							7
12	Morley	P.J.	FF	77	81	82	82	87	89	92							7
13	Browne	Patrick	FG	37	38	43	44	48	51								6
14	Kenny	Henry	FG	54	57	61	65	69	73								6
15	Gallagher	Denis	FF	73	77	81	82	82	87								6
16	Kilroy	Michael	FF	23	27	27	32	33									5
17	Calleary	Phelim	FF	52*	54	57	61	65									5
18	Ring	Michael	FG	94*	97	02	07	11									5
19	Crowley	John	R	18	21	22	23										4
20	McBride	Joseph	CG	18	21	22	23										4
21	Sears	William	CG	18	21	22	23										4
22	Davis	Michael	CG	27	27	32	33										4
23	O'Hara	Thomas	FG	51	54	65	69										4
24	O'Toole	Patrick	FG	77	81	82	82										4
25	Higgins	Jim	FG	87	89	92	97										4
26	Maguire	Thomas	R	21	22	23											3
27	Moane	Edward	FF	32	33	37											3
28	Cafferky	Dominick	CnaT	43	44	51											3
29	Kilroy	James	FF	43	44	48											3
30	Lindsay	Patrick	FG	54	57	65											3
31	Flynn	Beverley	NP	97	02	07											3
32	Boland**	Harry	CR	21	22												2
33	Derrig**	Thomas	CR	21	22												2
34	O'Rourke**	Daniel	CR	21	22												2
35	Madden	John	FF	24*	27J												2
36	Henry	Mark	CG	27	27												2
37	O'Connell**	Thomas	LB	27	27												2
38	Munnelly	John	FF	37	38												2
39	Commons	Bernard	CnaT	45*	48												2
40	Leneghan	Joseph	FF	61	69												2
41	Finn	Martin	FG	69	73												2
42	Moffatt	Tom	FF	92	97												2
43	Calleary	Dara	FF	07	11												2
44	O'Mahony	John	FG	07	11												2
45	De Valera**	Eamon	SF	18													1
46	Coyle	Henry	CG	23													1
47	McGrath**	Joseph	CG	23													1
48	Tierney**	Prof. Michael	CG	25*													1
49	Mullen	Eugene	FF	27J													1
50	O'Hara	Patrick	CG	32													1
51	Morrisroe	James	CG	33													1
52	Doherty	Sean	FF	57													1
53	Browne	Michael	FG	61													1
54	Lyons	Michael	FG	65													1
55	Staunton	Myles	FG	73													1
56	O'Toole	Martin J.	FF	89													1
57	Hughes	Seamus	FF	92													1
58	Carty	John	FF	02													1
59	Cowley	Jerry	NP	02													1
60	Mulherin	Michelle	FG	11													1
	Total									***Includes 6 By-Elections**						*	**219**
	**** Also elected in another constituency**																
	De Valera**	Eamon	SF	Clare				1918-1957									16
	Derrig**	Thomas	CR	Carlow-Kilkenny				1927-1954									11
	O'Rourke**	Daniel	CR	Roscommon				32	37	38	44	48					5
	McGrath**	Joseph	CG	Dublin				18	21	22							3
M	O'Connell**	Thomas	LB	Galway				22	23								2
M	Boland**	Harry	CR	Roscommon				18									1
	Tierney**	Prof. Michael	CG	NUI				27S									1
M	**Included in Mayo total**																**39**

MAYO 1918-2011																								
* No Contest			FG		LB		FF		SF		GP		PD		C na P		C na T		Farmers		Nat League		Others	
Dail		Seats	S	% Vote	S	% Vote	S	% Vote	S	% Vote	S	% Vote	S	% Vote	S	% Vote	S	% Vote	S	% Vote	S	% Vote	S	% Vote
1	1918	4							4															
2	1921*	8							8															
3	1922	8	3				5																	
4	1923	9	5	53.83%		3.34%	4	37.43%												3.21%				2.19%
5	1927	9	4	38.96%	1	7.64%	3	35.64%	1	5.62%										3.43%		8.71%		
6	1927	9	4	47.54%	1	5.89%	4	46.56%																
7	1932	9	4	38.95%		4.40%	5	54.09%																2.56%
8	1933	9	4	40.39%			5	59.61%																
9	1937	8	3	40.78%			5	56.35%																2.87%
10	1938	8	3	36.53%		1.33%	5	62.13%																
11	1943	8	2	18.79%		2.79%	4	44.19%									2	28.88%						5.35%
12	1944	8	1	19.37%			5	52.78%									2	27.85%						
13	1948	7	1	15.52%			4	41.66%								16.21%	2	25.84%						0.78%
14	1951	7	1	19.07%			3	43.95%								4.95%	3	32.03%						
15	1954	7	2	24.22%			3	42.53%								4.86%	2	25.55%						2.84%
16	1957	7	2	23.64%			4	47.75%								2.02%	1	26.59%						
17	1961	7	2	33.03%		1.03%	3	41.62%									1	14.73%					1	9.58%
18	1965	7	4	50.25%		0.54%	3	46.07%								3.14%								
19	1969	6	3	47.04%		2.56%	3	50.41%																
20	1973	6	3	46.31%		2.81%	3	50.88%																
21	1977	6	2	46.82%			4	51.30%																1.88%
22	1981	6	2	46.01%			4	53.99%																
23	1982	6	2	43.69%		1.00%	4	55.09%																0.22%
24	1982	6	2	44.13%		2.09%	4	53.06%																0.73%
25	1987	6	2	42.67%			4	56.23%		1.09%														
26	1989	6	2	39.31%			4	51.49%																9.19%
27	1992	6	2	41.91%			4	50.34%																7.75%
28	1997	5	3	48.75%			2	42.95%				1.52%												6.78%
29	2002	5	2	37.59%			2	39.98%		3.28%		1.05%		1.45%									1	16.64%
30	2007	5	3	53.83%		1.16%	1	24.46%		5.05%		0.81%		0.41%									1	14.27%
31	2011	5	4	64.96%		4.91%	1	16.07%		6.48%		0.36%												7.22%
1918-2011		**213**	**77**	**39.49%**	**2**	**1.51%**	**105**	**46.60%**	**13**	**0.84%**		**0.14%**		**0.07%**		**1.10%**	**13**	**6.42%**		**0.23%**		**0.31%**	**3**	**3.29%**
National		**4,618**	**1,453**	**30.77%**	**482**	**11.53%**	**1,985**	**41.86%**	**232**	**1.99%**	**16**	**0.75%**	**44**	**1.42%**	**18**	**0.77%**	**43**	**1.08%**	**42**	**0.90%**	**10**	**0.24%**	**293**	**8.67%**

MEATH EAST 2011

"Another blank for Fianna Fáil as Fine Gael and Labour both gain seats"

This constituency was created before the 2007 general election and it formed the eastern part of the old five-seat Meath constituency. There have been major Constituency Commission changes here since 2007. A population of 17,333 in the areas of St Mary's and Julianstown was transferred to Louth. A population of 6,776 in the Kells area was transferred in from Meath West. The number of seats remained the same with three TDs returned.

This constituency was virtually over as a contest following the first count as the leading three contenders were well clear of the rest of the field.

The Fine Gael vote was up 15 points and with 1.6 quotas equally divided between its two candidates they were well placed to take two seats. Outgoing deputy Shane McEntee was in second place on the first count, just ahead of his running mate Regina Doherty. The two Fine Gael candidates were well clear of the rest of the field and were within 117 votes of one another and they were duly elected on the fourth and final count.

The Labour vote was up nine points and Dominic Hannigan who had been widely tipped for a win here duly delivered. He topped the poll with just under 9,000 first preferences and went on to take the first seat on the final count.

This was another disaster for Fianna Fáil as the party's vote was down 24 points and they lost both of their seats. Mary Wallace retired but Fianna Fáil decided to replace her. Thomas Byrne was the party's leading candidate but with just 5,715 first preferences was well outside the frame on the first count and struggling. He trailed Doherty by nearly 3,000 votes and this was a bridge too far. The second Fianna Fáil candidate Nick Killian got just 2,669 first preferences and was never in contention. He was eliminated early and 54% of his transfers went to his running mate.

The Sinn Fein vote was up five points to leave Michael Gallagher in fifth place but with just 3,795 first preferences he was too far off the pace and out of contention.

Minister of State at the Dept. of Agriculture Shane McEntee with his senior Minister Simon Coveney

MEATH EAST TDs 2011

DOMINIC HANNIGAN (LB)

68 Lagavooran Manor, Drogheda, Co. Meath; Tel: 041 9801801; Mobile: 087 6418960
Constituency Office: 01 8353871; Leinster House: 01 6184007;
Email: dominic.hannigan@oireachtas.ie; Website: www.dominichannigan.com

Born Drogheda, 1st July 1965. Single. Educated St. Mary's CBS, Drogheda; UCD (BE); City University, London (MSc). Engineer and Planner. Contested Meath by-election in 2005 and general election in Meath East in 2007. First elected 2011.

Appointed Chairman Committee on European Union Affairs December 2011. Chairman Committee on the Implementation of Good Friday Agreement June-December 2011. Elected to Seanad on the Industrial and Commercial Panel in 2007. Front Bench Spokesperson on Commuter Issues and Party Whip and Seanad Spokesperson on Crime and Policing, Environment and Climate Change, Community and Rural Affairs 2007-2011. Member Joint Committee on the Environment, Heritage and Local Government and Member Joint Committee on Foreign Affairs 2007-2011. Member Meath County Council 2004-2007. Board member Meath Leader.

REGINA DOHERTY (FG)

2 Glebe Park, Ratoath, Co. Meath; Tel: 01 8257204; Mobile: 087 2680182
Leinster House: Tel: 01 6183573; Email: regina.doherty@oireachtas.ie
Website: www.reginadoherty.com

Born Dublin 26th January 1971. Married to Declan Doherty, 2 sons, 2 daughters. Educated St. Mary's Holy Faith, Glasnevin; College of Marketing and Design, Dublin. Businesswoman. Contested 2007 Dail election in Meath East. First elected 2011.

Member Committee on Health and Children. Member Committee on the Implementation of Good Friday Agreement. First elected to Meath County Council in Dunshaughlin electoral area in 2009.

SHANE McENTEE (FG)

Castletown, Kilpatrick, Navan, Co. Meath;
Constituency Office: 3 Copper Beach, Duleek, Co. Meath; Tel: 041 9882727;
Leinster House: 01 6184447; Email: shane.mcentee@oireachtas.ie
Website: www.shanemcentee.finegael.ie

Born Nobber, Co. Meath 19th December 1956. Married to Kathleen Corbally, one son, two daughters. Educated St. Finian's College, Mullingar. Minister of State. Bar and restaurant owner, former farmer and agricultural sales representative. First elected at by-election in 2005 which was caused by the appointment of John Briton as EU Ambassador to the US. Retained his seat in 2007 and 2011.

Appointed Minister of State at the Department of Agriculture, Marine and Food with special responsibility for Food, Horticulture and Food Safety March 2011. Deputy spokesperson on Transport with special responsibility for Road Safety, 2007-2011. Member Joint Committee on Transport 2007-2011. Member GAA. Brother of Gerry McEntee, All Ireland winner with Meath.

	MEATH EAST 2011						
	FIRST PREFERENCE VOTES						
	Seats	3			10,689		
	Candidate	**Party**	**1st**	**%**	**Quota**	**Count**	**Status**
1	**Hannigan, Dominic**	**LB**	**8,994**	**21.04%**	**0.84**	**4**	**Made Quota**
2	**Doherty, Regina**	**FG**	**8,677**	**20.30%**	**0.81**	**4**	**Elected**
3	**McEntee, Shane***	**FG**	**8,794**	**20.57%**	**0.82**	**4**	**Elected**
4	Byrne, Thomas*	FF	5,715	13.37%	0.53	4	Not Elected
5	Gallagher, Michael	SF	3,795	8.88%	0.36	3	Eliminated
6	Bonner, Joe	NP	2,479	5.80%	0.23	3	Eliminated
7	Killian, Nick	FF	2,669	6.24%	0.25	2	Eliminated
8	Keogan, Sharon	NV	1,168	2.73%	0.11	1	No Expenses
9	Ó Buachalla, Seán	GP	461	1.08%	0.04	1	No Expenses
9	***Outgoing**		**42,752**	**100.00%**	**10,689**	**2,673**	**No Expenses**

MEATH EAST 2011												
PARTY VOTE												
	2011					2007					Change	
Party	**Cand**	**1st**	**%**	**Quota**	**Seats**	**Cand**	**1st**	**%**	**Quota**	**Seats**	**%**	**Seats**
FG	2	17,471	40.87%	1.63	2	2	11,129	25.88%	1.04	1	+14.99%	+1
LB	1	8,994	21.04%	0.84	1	1	5,136	11.94%	0.48		+9.10%	+1
FF	2	8,384	19.61%	0.78		2	18,735	43.56%	1.74	2	-23.95%	-2
SF	1	3,795	8.88%	0.36		1	1,695	3.94%	0.16		+4.94%	
GP	1	461	1.08%	0.04		1	1,330	3.09%	0.12		-2.01%	
PD						1	957	2.23%	0.09		-2.23%	
Others	2	3,647	8.53%	0.34		3	4,025	9.36%	0.37		-0.83%	
Total	**9**	**42,752**	**100.0%**	**10,689**	**3**	**11**	**43,007**	**100.0%**	**10,752**	**3**	**0.00%**	**0**
Electorate		**64,873**	**65.90%**				**67,443**	**63.77%**			**+2.13%**	
Spoiled		**346**	**0.80%**				**359**	**0.83%**			**-0.03%**	
Turnout		**43,098**	**66.43%**				**43,366**	**64.30%**			**+2.13%**	

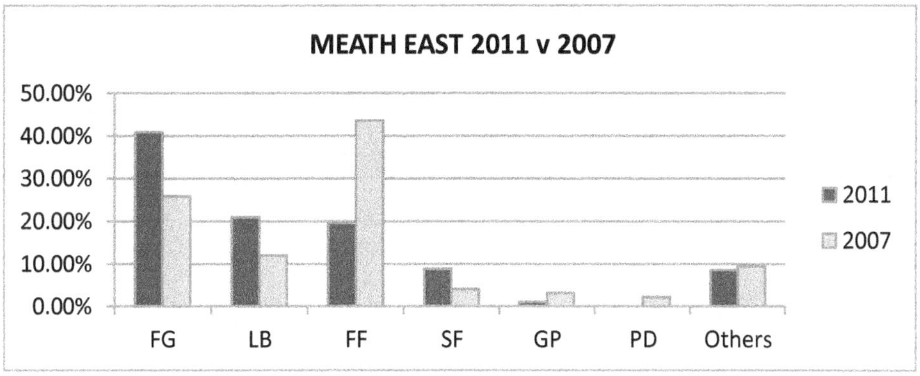

MEATH EAST 2011 COUNT DETAILS					
Seats	3			Quota	10,689
Candidate	**Party**	**1st**	**2nd** Keoghan O Buachalla Votes	**3rd** Killian Votes	**4th** Bonner Gallagher Votes
Hannigan, Dominic	LB	8,994	*+389* 9,383	*+286* 9,669	*+2,713* 12,382
Doherty, Regina	FG	8,677	*+181* 8,858	*+447* 9,305	*+1,142* 10,447
McEntee, Shane*	FG	8,794	*+200* 8,994	*+148* 9,142	*+1,001* 10,143
Byrne, Thomas*	FF	5,715	*+177* 5,892	*+1,462* 7,354	*+819* 8,173
Gallagher, Michael	SF	3,795	*+163* 3,958	*+67* 4,025	*-4,025* Eliminated
Bonner, Joe	NP	2,479	*+387* 2,866	*+208* 3,074	*-3,074* Eliminated
Killian, Nick	FF	2,669	*+50* 2,719	*-2,719* Eliminated	
Keogan, Sharon	NV	1,168	*-1,168* Eliminated		
Ó Buachalla, Seán	GP	461	*-461* Eliminated		
Non-transferable			*+82*	*+101*	*+1,424*
Cumulative			82	183	1,607
Total		**42,752**	**42,752**	**42,752**	**42,752**

MEATH EAST 2011 TRANSFER ANALYSIS							
From	**To**	**FG**	**LB**	**FF**	**SF**	**Others**	**Non Trans**
FF	2,719	595	286	1,462	67	208	101
		21.88%	*10.52%*	*53.77%*	*2.46%*	*7.65%*	*3.71%*
SF	4,025	1,215	1,538	465			807
		30.19%	*38.21%*	*11.55%*			*20.05%*
GP	461	108	110	64	46	110	23
		23.43%	*23.86%*	*13.88%*	*9.98%*	*23.86%*	*4.99%*
NP	4,242	1,201	1,454	517	117	277	676
		28.31%	*34.28%*	*12.19%*	*2.76%*	*6.53%*	*15.94%*
Total	**11,447**	**3,119**	**3,388**	**2,508**	**230**	**595**	**1,607**
		27.25%	***29.60%***	***21.91%***	***2.01%***	***5.20%***	***14.04%***

MEATH WEST 2011

"Another blank for Fianna Fáil as Fine Gael gain and Sinn Fein make a breakthrough"

This constituency was created before the 2007 general election and it formed the western part of the old five-seat Meath constituency. There have also been major Constituency Commission changes here since 2007. A population of 6,776 in the Kells area has been transferred out to Meath East. The number of seats remained the same with three TDs returned.

The Fine Gael vote was up 17 points and with 1.8 quotas it was on track for two seats. Outgoing deputy Damien English comfortably topped the poll, well clear of his nearest rivals and he went on to take the first seat on the third count. Newcomer Ray Butler was outside the frame on the first count, just 170 votes behind Labour's Jenny McHugh but he won the transfer battle, in particular with the help of 55% of running mate Yore's transfers. The third Fine Gael candidate Catherine Yore would be disappointed with her performance as she had been fancied for a seat and had to settle for her transfers electing her running mate.

The Labour vote was up 9 points and with half a quota Jenny McHugh was in the frame in third place on the first count. She was just ahead of Fine Gael's Ray Butler but Fine Gael had too much of an advantage and she was duly overtaken and lost the battle for the final seat by a margin of 1,128 votes.

This was another poor performance by Fianna Fáil with its vote down a massive 33 points, their second largest loss of support in this election and they lost their two outgoing seats. Long-serving TD and senior Minister Noel Dempsey retired and Fianna Fáil decided to replace him with 2005 by-election candidate Shane Cassells. Outgoing deputy Johnny Brady did poorly and was well off the pace on the first count and never recovered. Cassells had a similar performance and this division of a depleted Fianna Fáil vote left them with no chance of a seat. This was another example of Fianna Fáil fielding too many candidates.

This was another breakthrough in this election for Sinn Féin with their vote up 6 points to 0.7 of a quota. Peadar Tóibín was in second place on the first count, well clear of his nearest rivals and he went on to win the second seat on the fifth and final count for an impressive performance. Joe Reilly had done well here for Sinn Féin in 2007 when he was the last candidate standing. His strong performance was a forerunner to Tóibín's success in 2011.

MEATH WEST TDs 2011

DAMIEN ENGLISH (FG)

Castlemartin, Navan, Co. Meath; Mobile: 086 8143495;
Constituency Office: 16 Bridge Street, Navan; Tel: 046 9071667
Leinster House: 01 6184021; Email: damien.english@oireachtas.ie
Website: www.damienenglish.ie

Born Drogheda, Co. Louth 21st Feb 1978. Married to Laura Kenny, one son. Educated Kells Community School; DIT Aungier Street; Chartered Institute of Management Accountants. First elected 2002 and was the youngest TD in the 29th Dail. Retained his seat in 2007 and 2011.

Appointed Chairman Committee on Jobs, Social Protection and Education June 2011. Deputy spokesperson on Enterprise, with special responsibility for Labour Affairs and Small Business in 30th Dail. 2007-2011: Member Joint Committee on Enterprise, Trade and Employment; Member Joint Committee on European Scrutiny; Member Joint Committee on Economic and Regulatory Affairs; Member Joint Administration Committee. Deputy spokesperson on Justice and Community Affairs, with special responsibility for Drugs, Alcohol and Crime Prevention 2004-2007. Deputy spokesperson on Arts, Sports and Tourism, 2002-2004. Member Joint Committee on Arts, Sport, Tourism, Community Rural and Gaeltacht Affairs 2002-2007. Member British-Irish Inter-Parliamentary Body. Member Meath County Council 1999-2003. Member Meath Enterprise Board. Member Navan Shamrock Festival Organisers Board. Member Meath County Development Board.

PEADAR TÓIBÍN (SF)

123 An Coillearnach, An Uaimh, Co. Na Mí; Mobile: 087 2707985
Leinster House: 01 6183518; Email: peadar.toibin@oireachtas.ie
Website: www.peadartoibin.ie

Born Co. Louth June 1974. Married. Educated UCD (BA Economics and Politics and postgrad in enterprise studies, Michael Smurfit School of Business); NUI Maynooth (Certificate in training and further education). Former Management Consultant. Elected at his first attempt in 2011.

Appointed Party Spokesperson on Enterprise, Jobs and Innovation and An Gaeltacht March 2011. Appointed Chairman Committee on Investigations, Oversight and Petitions June 2011. Member Committee on Jobs, Social Protection and Education. Member Navan Town Council 2009-2011.

RAY BUTLER (FG)

7 Swift Court, Trim, Co. Meath; Tel: 046 9437589; Mobile: 087 2596680
Constituency Office: 1 St. Martin's House, Finnegan's Way, Trim; Tel: 046 9486717;
Leinster House: 01 6183378; Email: ray.butler@oireachtas.ie

Born Virginia, Co. Cavan, 30th December 1965. Married to Maire, four children. Educated Kells CBS. Shoe Shop Owner. Elected at his first attempt in 2011.

Member Committee on Jobs, Social Protection and Education. First elected to Meath County Council in Trim electoral area in 2009. Elected to Trim TC 2004 and 2009.

MEATH WEST 2011							
FIRST PREFERENCE VOTES							
	Seats	3			10,045		
	Candidate	Party	1st	%	Quota	Count	Status
1	**English, Damien***	**FG**	**9,290**	**23.12%**	**0.92**	**3**	**Made Quota**
2	**Tóibín, Peadar**	**SF**	**6,989**	**17.40%**	**0.70**	**5**	**Elected**
3	**Butler, Ray**	**FG**	**5,262**	**13.10%**	**0.52**	**5**	**Elected**
4	McHugh, Jenny	LB	5,432	13.52%	0.54	5	Not Elected
5	Brady, Johnny*	FF	3,789	9.43%	0.38	4	Eliminated
6	Yore, Catherine	FG	3,898	9.70%	0.39	3	Eliminated
7	Cassells, Shane	FF	3,496	8.70%	0.35	2	Eliminated
8	Irwin, Fiona	GP	479	1.19%	0.05	1	No Expenses
9	Ball, Stephen	NP	475	1.18%	0.05	1	No Expenses
10	Stevens, Daithi	NP	387	0.96%	0.04	1	No Expenses
11	Carolan, Ronan	NP	258	0.64%	0.03	1	No Expenses
12	MacMeanmain, Manus	CS	234	0.58%	0.02	1	No Expenses
13	McDonagh, Seamus	WP	189	0.47%	0.02	1	No Expenses
13	***Outgoing**		**40,178**	**100.00%**	**10,045**	**2,512**	**No Expenses**

MEATH WEST 2011												
PARTY VOTE												
	2011					2007					Change	
Party	Cand	1st	%	Quota	Seats	Cand	1st	%	Quota	Seats	%	Seats
FG	3	18,450	45.92%	1.84	2	3	11,745	29.03%	1.16	1	+16.89%	+1
LB	1	5,432	13.52%	0.54		1	1,634	4.04%	0.16		+9.48%	
FF	2	7,285	18.13%	0.73		2	20,874	51.59%	2.06	2	-33.45%	-2
SF	1	6,989	17.40%	0.70	1	1	4,567	11.29%	0.45		+6.11%	+1
GP	1	479	1.19%	0.05		1	1,011	2.50%	0.10		-1.31%	
WP	1	189	0.47%	0.02							+0.47%	
CS	1	234	0.58%	0.02							+0.58%	
Others	3	1,120	2.79%	0.11		2	633	1.56%	0.06		+1.22%	
Total	**13**	**40,178**	**100.0%**	**10,045**	**3**	**10**	**40,464**	**100.0%**	**10,116**	**3**	**0.00%**	**0**
Electorate		**62,776**	**64.00%**				**56,267**	**71.91%**			**-7.91%**	
Spoiled		**413**	**1.02%**				**388**	**0.95%**			**+0.07%**	
Turnout		**40,591**	**64.66%**				**40,852**	**72.60%**			**-7.94%**	

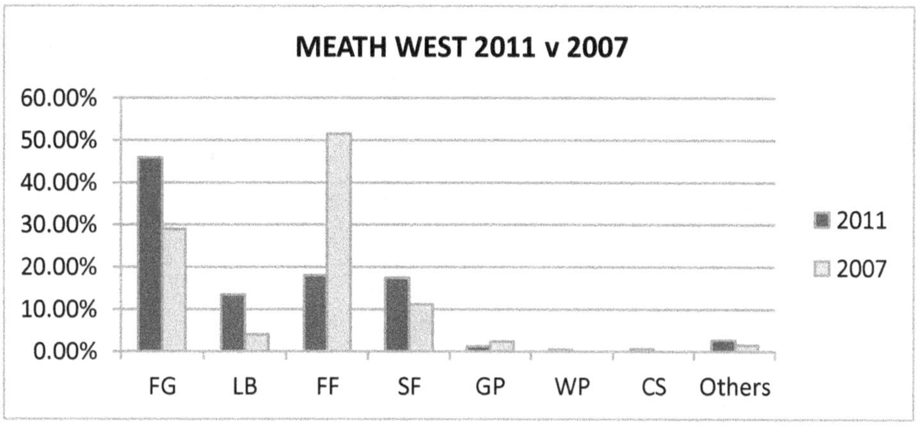

MEATH WEST 2011 COUNT DETAILS						
Seats	3				Quota	10,045
Candidate	Party	1st	2nd Irwin, Ball Stevens Carolan MacMeanmain McDonagh	3rd Cassells Votes	4th Yore Votes	5th Brady Votes
English, Damien*	FG	9,290	+319 9,609	+513 10,122	10,122	10,122
Tóibín, Peadar	SF	6,989	+432 7,421	+290 7,711	+444 8,155	+957 9,112
Butler, Ray	FG	5,262	+152 5,414	+160 5,574	+2,305 7,879	+1,047 8,926
McHugh, Jenny	LB	5,432	+420 5,852	+188 6,040	+754 6,794	+1,004 7,798
Brady, Johnny*	FF	3,789	+85 3,874	+2,191 6,065	+372 6,437	-6,437 Eliminated
Yore, Catherine	FG	3,898	+174 4,072	+136 4,208	-4,208 Eliminated	
Cassells, Shane	FF	3,496	+135 3,631	-3,631 Eliminated		
Irwin, Fiona	GP	479	-479 Eliminated			
Ball, Stephen	NP	475	-475 Eliminated			
Stevens, Daithi	NP	387	-387 Eliminated			
Carolan, Ronan	NP	258	-258 Eliminated			
MacMeanmain, Manus	CS	234	-234 Eliminated			
McDonagh, Seamus	WP	189	-189 Eliminated			
Non-transferable Cumulative			+305 305	+153 458	+333 791	+3,429 4,220
Total		**40,178**	**40,178**	**40,178**	**40,178**	**40,178**

MEATH WEST 2011 TRANSFER ANALYSIS						
From	To	FG	LB	FF	SF	Non Trans
FG	4,208	2,305 *54.78%*	754 *17.92%*	372 *8.84%*	444 *10.55%*	333 *7.91%*
FF	10,068	1,856 *18.43%*	1,192 *11.84%*	2,191 *21.76%*	1,247 *12.39%*	3,582 *35.58%*
GP	479	153 *31.94%*	100 *20.88%*	52 *10.86%*	102 *21.29%*	72 *15.03%*
WP	189	60 *31.75%*	39 *20.63%*	21 *11.11%*	40 *21.16%*	29 *15.34%*
NP	1,354	432 *31.91%*	281 *20.75%*	147 *10.86%*	290 *21.42%*	204 *15.07%*
Total	**16,298**	**4,806** ***29.49%***	**2,366** ***14.52%***	**2,783** ***17.08%***	**2,123** ***13.03%***	**4,220** ***25.89%***

MEATH		
MAIN BOUNDARY CHANGES		
Dail	Constituency	Seats
1 (1918)	Meath North	1
	Meath South	1
4 (1923) - 8 (1933)	Meath	3
9 (1937) - 12 (1944)	Meath - Westmeath	5
13 (1948) - 20 (1973)	Meath	3
21 (1977)	Meath	4
22 (1981) - 29 (2002)	Meath	5
30 (2007) - 31 (2011)	Meath East	3
	Meath West	3

MEATH															
ALL TDs 1918-2011															
	Surname	Forename	Party	Elected											Total
1	Bruton	John	FG	69	73	77	81	82	82	87	89	92	97	02	11
2	O'Reilly	Matthew	FF	27	27	32	33	37	38	43	44	48	51		10
3	Hilliard	Michael	FF	43	44	48	51	54	57	61	65	69			9
4	Giles	Capt. Patrick	FG	37	38	43	44	48	51	54	57				8
5	Tully	James	LB	54	61	65	69	73	77	81					7
6	Farrelly	John V.	FG	81	82	82	87	89	97						6
7	Dempsey	Noel	FF	87	89	92	97	02	07						6
8	Duggan**	Edmund	CG	18	23	27	27	32							5
9	Hilliard	Colm	FF	82	82	87	89	92							5
10	Wallace	Mary	FF	89	92	97	02	07							5
11	Kelly	James	FF	32	33	37	38								4
12	Fagan**	Charles	FG	37	38	43	44								4
13	Kennedy**	Michael	FF	37	38	43	44								4
14	Fitzsimmons	James	FF	77	81	82	82								4
15	Crinion**	Brendan	FF	73	77	81									3
16	Brady	Johnny	FF	97	02	07									3
17	English	Damien	FG	02	07	11									3
18	McEntee	Shane	FG	05*	07	11									3
19	Hall	David	LB	23	27J										2
20	Farrelly	Denis	FG	61	65										2
21	Lynch	Michael	FF	82F	87										2
22	Mellows**	Liam	SF	18											1
23	Mulvany	Patrick	F	23											1
24	Matthews	Arthur	CG	27S											1
25	Davitt	Robert	CG	33											1
26	Griffin	James	FF	57											1
27	Johnston	Henry	FF	59*											1
28	McLoughlin	Frank	LB	82N											1
29	Fitzgerald	Brian	LB	92											1
30	Byrne	Thomas	FF	07											1
31	Hannigan	Dominic	LB	11											1
32	Doherty	Regina	FG	11											1
33	Toibin	Peadar	SF	11											1
34	Butler	Ray	FG	11											1
34	**Total**							***Includes 2 By-Elections**						*	**119**
	**** Also elected in another constituency**														
	Kennedy**	Michael	FF	Westmeat		27	27	32	33	48	51	54	57	61	9
	Fagan**	Charles	FG	Longford-Westmeath				33	48	51	54	57			5
	Mellows**	Liam	SF	Galway				18	21						2
M	Duggan**	Edmund	CG	Louth				21	22						2
M	Crinion**	Brendan	FF	Kildare				61	65						2
M	**Included in Meath total**														**20**

MEATH 1918-2011																											
		FG		LB		FF		SF		GP		WP		CS		PD		DL		C na T		Farmers		Nat League		Others	
Dail	**Seats**	**S**	**% Vote**	**S**	**% Vote**	**S**	**% Vote**	**S**	**% Vote**	**S**	**% Vote**	**S**	**% Vote**	**S**	**% Vote**	**S**	**% Vote**	**S**	**% Vote**	**S**	**% Vote**	**S**	**% Vote**	**S**	**% Vote**	**S**	**% Vote**
1 1918	2							2																			
4 1923	3	1	42.62%	1	22.57%		16.91%															1	17.12%				0.79%
5 1927	3	1	24.92%	1	20.92%	1	27.27%																13.50%		13.38%		
6 1927	3	2	46.38%		10.47%	1	37.19%																		4.37%		1.59%
7 1932	3	1	44.05%			2	55.95%																				
8 1933	3	1	23.35%			2	55.87%																				20.78%
9 1937	5	2	37.22%		7.95%	3	53.82%																				1.01%
10 1938	5	2	36.19%		9.51%	3	54.30%																				
11 1943	5	2	28.62%		14.27%	3	44.70%														9.61%						2.80%
12 1944	5	2	27.35%		10.90%	3	55.42%														6.33%						
13 1948	3	1	21.44%		11.58%	2	51.37%																				15.62%
14 1951	3	1	33.97%		13.63%	2	52.40%																				
15 1954	3	1	30.62%	1	23.05%	1	45.83%																				0.51%
16 1957	3	1	23.44%		16.04%	2	51.56%		8.97%																		
17 1961	3	1	22.65%	1	26.73%	1	44.76%																				5.86%
18 1965	3	1	23.57%	1	28.79%	1	47.64%																				
19 1969	3	1	27.55%	1	23.41%	1	49.04%																				
20 1973	3	1	29.68%	1	19.05%	1	46.61%																				4.67%
21 1977	4	1	23.69%	1	16.92%	2	54.48%																				4.90%
22 1981	5	2	33.87%	1	17.06%	2	44.16%																				4.90%
23 1982	5	2	38.86%		7.22%	3	50.89%																				3.03%
24 1982	5	2	36.26%	1	16.24%	2	47.50%																				
25 1987	5	2	25.68%		6.58%	3	50.17%		1.83%				1.43%				8.75%										5.55%
26 1989	5	2	29.88%		9.15%	3	52.25%		1.98%				1.76%				2.23%										2.74%
27 1992	5	1	26.48%	1	17.55%	3	45.08%		1.25%		1.27%						2.22%		1.58%								4.56%
28 1997	5	2	36.92%		6.52%	3	41.88%		3.53%		1.95%				1.82%		2.37%		1.41%								3.61%
29 2002	5	2	27.23%		4.26%	3	44.92%		9.43%		3.65%				0.28%												10.23%
30 2007	6	2	27.40%		8.11%	4	47.45%		7.50%		2.80%						1.15%										5.58%
31 2011	6	4	43.31%	1	17.40%		18.89%	1	13.00%		1.13%		0.23%		0.28%												5.75%
1918-2011	**117**	**44**	**31.52%**	**12**	**12.80%**	**57**	**45.71%**	**3**	**2.54%**		**0.62%**		**0.16%**		**0.12%**		**0.79%**	**0**	**0.13%**		**0.62%**	**1**	**0.62%**		**0.38%**		**3.99%**
National	**4,618**	**1,453**	**30.77%**	**482**	**11.53%**	**1,985**	**41.86%**	**232**	**1.99%**	**16**	**0.75%**	**17**	**0.78%**		**0.04%**	**44**	**1.42%**	**8**	**0.22%**	**43**	**1.08%**	**42**	**0.90%**	**10**	**0.24%**	**286**	**8.39%**

ROSCOMMON-SOUTH LEITRIM 2011

"Independent Luke 'Ming' Flanagan wins seat at Fianna Fáil's expense"

This constituency was created before the 2007 general election and it was formed from the Roscommon part of the old Longford-Roscommon constituency and the southern portion of County Leitrim. There was also significant Constituency Commission changes here since 2007. A population of 3,376 in the area north of Carrick-on-Shannon was transferred from this constituency to Sligo-North Leitrim. The number of seats remained the same with three TDs returned.

The three leading candidates were well clear of the rest of the field and this constituency was virtually over as a contest following the declaration of the first count.

This was one of the few constituencies in which the Fine Gael vote was down on 2007, albeit by less than 1%. But with 1.5 quotas the party was well-placed to retain its two seats. Denis Naughten topped the poll with 9,320 first preferences and went on to take the third seat on the final count. His fellow outgoing deputy Frank Feighan was in second place on the first count and also went onto retain his seat on the final count.

The big surprise here was the performance of independent candidate Luke 'Ming' Flanagan, who ran on a 'New Vision' ticket. Flanagan was in third place on the first count, just behind the two outgoing Fine Gael deputies and he went on to take the first seat on the fourth count.

The Fianna Fáil vote was down 24 points and the party lost its single outgoing seat. Outgoing Minister of State, Michael Finneran retired and was replaced by Ivan Connaughton and Gerry Kilrane. Between them, they garnered just 0.6 quotas, or just 0.3 of a quota each, to leave the two of them well outside the frame on the first count and out of contention.

Former independent councillor John Kelly joined the Labour party for this election and increased the party vote by 8 points but with just 0.4 of a quota he was in fifth place on the first count and out of contention.

Sinn Fein will be disappointed with its performance here as its vote was up just one point on 2007 and with just 4,637 first preferences Martin Kenny was outside the frame on the first count with just 0.4 quotas and was too far off the pace to contend for a seat.

Newly elected TD Luke Ming Flanagan

ROSCOMMON-SOUTH LEITRIM TDs 2011

LUKE "MING" FLANAGAN (NP)

Priory House, Barrack St. Castlerea, Co. Roscommon; Tel: 094 9622878; Mobile: 086 3685680
Leinster House: 01 6183058; Email: lukeming.flanagan@oireachtas.ie;
Website: www.lukemingflanagan.ie

Born Roscommon, 22nd January 1972. Married, two children. Contested 1997 Dail election in Galway West. Contested 1999 European election in Connaught-Ulster. Contested 2002 Dail election in Longford Roscommon. First elected 2011 as a New Vision candidate.

Member Committee on Environment, Transport, Culture and the Gaeltacht. Member Committee on the Implementation of Good Friday Agreement. First elected to Roscommon County Council in Castlerea electoral area in 2004. Retained his seat in 2009. Mayor of Roscommon 2010-2011.

FRANK FEIGHAN (FG)

Bridge Street, Boyle, Co. Roscommon; Tel: 071 9662608; Mobile: 086 8331234
Leinster House: 01 6183289; Email: frank.feighan@oireachtas.ie
Website: www.frankfeighan.finegael.ie

Born Roscommon 4th July 1962. Educated St. Mary's College, Boyle, Co. Roscommon. Businessman. First elected 2007. Retained his seat in 2011.

Member Committee on the Implementation of Good Friday Agreement. Front bench spokesperson on Community, Equality and Gaeltacht Affairs 2010-2011. Deputy spokesperson on Transport and Education, with special responsibility for Rural and School Transport October 2007-June 2010. Member Joint Committee on Transport and Member Joint Committee on Education and Science 2007-2011. Senator 2002-2007. Party Spokesperson on Arts, Sports and Tourism in the Upper House 2002-2007. Member Joint Committee on Health and Children 2002-2007. Member Roscommon County Council 1999-2003. Chairman Roscommon VEC 2000-2002. Member Roscommon County Enterprise Board. Chairman Roscommon Adult Education Board. Member Irish Kidney Association.

DENIS NAUGHTEN (FG)

Abbey Street, Roscommon; Tel: 090 6627557; Mobile: 086 1708800
Constituency Office: Ardkeenan, Drum, Co. Roscommon; Tel: 090 6437324
Leinster House: 01 6183545; Email: denis.naughten@oireachtas.ie
Website: www.denisnaughten.ie

Born Drum, Roscommon 23rd June 1973. Married to Mary Tiernan, two sons and daughter Ava. Educated St. Aloysius College, Athlone, UCD (B.Sc [Hons] in Industrial Microbiology); UCC (MSc in Food Microbiology). Formerly Research Scientist. First elected 1997 and at each subsequent election.

Lost party whip July 2011after he voted against the government over the closure of the A & E department in Roscommon Hospital. Member Committee on Health and Children. Supported Richard Bruton in his failed attempt to oust Enda Kenny as party leader in June 2010. Front bench spokesperson on Immigration and Integration September 2007-June 2010. Member Joint Committee on the Constitution and Member Joint Committee on Justice, Equality, Defence and Women's Rights 2007-2011. Front bench spokesperson on Agriculture and Food 2004-2007. Spokesperson on Transport 2002-2004. Member Joint Committee on Transport. Spokesperson on Enterprise Trade & Employment 2000-2001. Youngest member of the 28th Dáil. Junior spokesperson on Adult Education, Youth Affairs and School Transport 1997-2000. Elected to Seanad Eireann following the death in a car accident of his father and youngest member of Seanad, January-June 1997. Seanad spokesperson on Sport and Youth Affairs. Member of Roscommon County Council 1997-2003. Member of the Western Health Board 1997-2003. Son of Liam Naughten, Dáil Deputy 1982-1989; Senator 1981-1982 and 1989-1996; Leas-Cathaoirleach of the Seanad 1989-1995 and Cathaoirleach 1995-1996.

ROSCOMMON-SOUTH LEITRIM 2011							
FIRST PREFERENCE VOTES							
	Seats	3			11,877		
	Candidate	Party	1st	%	Quota	Count	Status
1	**Flanagan, Luke "Ming"**	**NV**	**8,925**	**18.79%**	**0.75**	**4**	**Made Quota**
2	**Feighan, Frank***	**FG**	**8,983**	**18.91%**	**0.76**	**6**	**Made Quota**
3	**Naughten, Denis***	**FG**	**9,320**	**19.62%**	**0.78**	**6**	**Made Quota**
4	Connaughton, Ivan	FF	4,070	8.57%	0.34	6	Not Elected
5	Kenny, Martin	SF	4,637	9.76%	0.39	5	Eliminated
6	Kelly, John	LB	4,455	9.38%	0.38	3	Eliminated
7	McDermott, John	NP	3,770	7.94%	0.32	2	Eliminated
8	Kilrane, Gerry	FF	3,033	6.38%	0.26	1	Eliminated
9	McDaid, Garreth	GP	220	0.46%	0.02	1	No Expenses
10	Kearns, Sean	NP	91	0.19%	0.01	1	No Expenses
10	***Outgoing**		**47,504**	**100.00%**	**11,877**	**2,970**	**No Expenses**

ROSCOMMON-SOUTH LEITRIM 2011												
PARTY VOTE												
	2011					2007					Change	
Party	Cand	1st	%	Quota	Seats	Cand	1st	%	Quota	Seats	%	Seats
FG	2	18,303	38.53%	1.54	2	2	18,031	39.13%	1.57	2	-0.60%	
LB	1	4,455	9.38%	0.38		1	832	1.81%	0.07		+7.57%	
FF	2	7,103	14.95%	0.60		2	17,897	38.84%	1.55	1	-23.89%	-1
SF	1	4,637	9.76%	0.39		1	3,876	8.41%	0.34		+1.35%	
GP	1	220	0.46%	0.02		1	836	1.81%	0.07		-1.35%	
Others	3	12,786	26.92%	1.08	1	2	4,605	9.99%	0.40		+16.92%	+1
Total	**10**	**47,504**	**100.0%**	**11,877**	**3**	**9**	**46,077**	**100.0%**	**11,520**	**3**	**0.00%**	**0**
Electorate		**60,998**	**77.88%**				**62,437**	**73.80%**			**+4.08%**	
Spoiled		**531**	**1.11%**				**393**	**0.85%**			**+0.26%**	
Turnout		**48,035**	**78.75%**				**46,470**	**74.43%**			**+4.32%**	

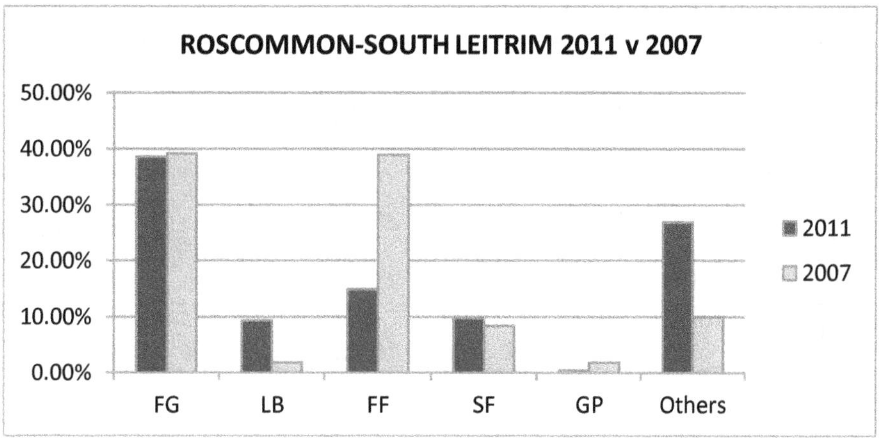

ROSCOMMON-SOUTH LEITRIM 2011 COUNT DETAILS							
Seats	3					Quota	11,877
Candidate	**Party**	**1st**	**2nd** Kilrane McDaid Kearns	**3rd** McDermott Votes	**4th** Kelly Votes	**5th** Flanagan Surplus	**6th** Kenny Votes
Flanagan, Luke "Ming"	NV	8,925	*+326* 9,251	*+1,197* 10,448	*+1,701* 12,149	*-272* 11,877	11,877
Feighan, Frank*	FG	8,983	*+474* 9,457	*+445* 9,902	*+1,228* 11,130	*+109* 11,239	*+2,027* 13,266
Naughten, Denis*	FG	9,320	*+109* 9,429	*+1,189* 10,618	*+731* 11,349	*+66* 11,415	*+707* 12,122
Connaughton, Ivan	FF	4,070	*+1,309* 5,379	*+477* 5,856	*+398* 6,254	*+31* 6,285	*+749* 7,034
Kenny, Martin	SF	4,637	*+732* 5,369	*+157* 5,526	*+516* 6,042	*+66* 6,108	*-6,108* Eliminated
Kelly, John	LB	4,455	*+162* 4,617	*+277* 4,894	*-4,894* Eliminated		
McDermott, John	NP	3,770	*+112* 3,882	*-3,882* Eliminated			
Kilrane, Gerry	FF	3,033	*-3,033* Eliminated				
McDaid, Garreth	GP	220	*-220* Eliminated				
Kearns, Sean	NP	91	*-91* Eliminated				
Non-transferable			*+120*	*+140*	*+320*		*+2,625*
Cumulative			120	260	580	580	3,205
Total		**47,504**	**47,504**	**47,504**	**47,504**	**47,504**	**47,504**

ROSCOMMON-SOUTH LEITRIM 2011 TRANSFER ANALYSIS							
From	**To**	**FG**	**LB**	**FF**	**SF**	**Others**	**Non Trans**
LB	4,894	1,959		398	516	1,701	320
		40.03%		*8.13%*	*10.54%*	*34.76%*	*6.54%*
FF	3,033	529	147	1,187	664	397	109
		17.44%	*4.85%*	*39.14%*	*21.89%*	*13.09%*	*3.59%*
SF	6,108	2,734		749			2,625
		44.76%		*12.26%*			*42.98%*
GP	220	38	11	86	48	29	8
		17.27%	*5.00%*	*39.09%*	*21.82%*	*13.18%*	*3.64%*
Others	4,245	1,825	281	544	243	1,209	143
		42.99%	*6.62%*	*12.82%*	*5.72%*	*28.48%*	*3.37%*
Total	**18,500**	**7,085**	**439**	**2,964**	**1,471**	**3,336**	**3,205**
		38.30%	***2.37%***	***16.02%***	***7.95%***	***18.03%***	***17.32%***

ROSCOMMON-SOUTH LEITRIM		
MAIN BOUNDARY CHANGES		
Dail	**Constituency**	**Seats**
1 (1918)	Roscommon North	1
	Roscommon South	1
2 (1921) - 3 (1922)	Leitrim-Roscommon North	4
4 (1923) - 8 (1933)	Roscommon	4
9 (1937) - 12 (1944)	Roscommon	3
13 (1948) - 18 (1965)	Roscommon	4
19 (1969) - 21 (1977)	Roscommon-Leitrim	3
22 (1981) - 26 (1989)	Roscommon	3
27 (1992) - 29 (2002)	Longford-Roscommon	4
30 (2007) - 31 (2011)	Roscommon-South Leitrim	3

ROSCOMMON																	
ALL TDs 1918-2011																	
	Surname	**Forename**	**Party**	**Elected**													**Total**
1	Boland	Gerald	FF	23	27	27	32	33	37	38	43	44	48	51	54	57	13
2	Doherty	Sean	FF	77	81	82	82	87	92	97							7
3	Leyden	Terry	FF	77	81	82	82	87	89								6
4	Brennan	Michael	FG	27	27	33	37	38									5
5	O'Rourke**	Daniel	FF	32	37	38	44	48									5
6	McQuillan	John	NPD	48	51	54	57	61									5
7	Burke	Joan	FG	64*	65	69	73	77									5
8	Plunkett	George	R	18	21	22	23										4
9	Conlon	Martin	CG	25*	27	27	32										4
10	Beirne(jun.)	John	CnaT	48	51	54	57										4
11	Naughten	Denis	FG	97	02	07	11										4
12	Lavin	Andrew	CG	21	22	23											3
13	O'Dowd	Patrick	FF	27	27	33											3
14	Burke	James J.	FG	54	57	61											3
15	Lenihan**	Brian	FF	61	65	69											3
16	Reynolds	Patrick J.	FG	61	65	73											3
17	Gibbons	Hugh	FF	65	69	73											3
18	Connor	John	FG	81	89	92											3
19	Naughten	Liam	FG	82	82	87											3
20	Carter**	Thomas	CT	21	22												2
21	Dolan**	James	CT	21	22												2
22	MacDermot	Frank	CP	32	33												2
23	Beirne(sen.)	John	CnaT	43	44												2
24	Foxe	Tom	NP	89	92												2
25	Reynolds**	Albert	FF	92	97												2
26	Finneran	Michael	FF	02	07												2
27	Feighan	Frank	FG	07	11												2
28	Boland**	Harry	SF	18													1
29	Finlay	Henry	CG	23													1
30	Meighan	John	CnaT	43													1
31	Finan	John	CnaT	51													1
32	Belton**	Louis	FG	97													1
33	Kelly**	Peter	FF	02													1
34	Sexton	Mae	PD	02													1
35	Flanagan	Luke "Ming"	NP	11													1
35	**Total**									***Includes 2 By-Elections**						*	**110**
	**** Also elected in another constituency**																
	Lenihan**	Brian	FF	Dublin West				77	81	82	82	87	89	92			7
	Reynolds**	Albert	FF	Longford-Wmeath				77	81	82	82	87	89				6
	Dolan**	James	CT	Sligo-Leitrim				18	23	27	27	33					5
	Carter**	Thomas	CT	Leitrim-Sligo/Longfo				23/	43	44	48						4
	Boland**	Harry	SF	Mayo-Roscommon				21	22								2
R	O'Rourke**	Daniel	FF	Mayo				21	22								2
	Belton**	Louis	FG	Longford-Wmeath				89									1
	Kelly**	Peter	FF	Longford-Wmeath				07									1
R	**Included in Roscommon total**																**28**

ROSCOMMON-SOUTH LEITRIM 1918-2011																										
* No Contest			FG		LB		FF		SF		GP		PD		C na P		C na T		NPD		Farmers		Centre P		Others	
Dail		Seats	S	% Vote	S	% Vote	S	% Vote	S	% Vote	S	% Vote	S	% Vote	S	% Vote	S	% Vote	S	% Vote	S	% Vote	S	% Vote	S	% Vote
1	1918	2							2																	
2	1921*	4							4																	
3	1922*	4	3				1																			
4	1923	4	2	41.63%		4.95%	2	36.52%														12.26%				4.64%
5	1927	4	1	29.16%		7.25%	2	31.25%		5.06%															1	27.28%
6	1927	4	1	31.14%			2	42.57%																	1	26.29%
7	1932	4	1	33.06%			2	54.04%																	1	12.90%
8	1933	4	1	21.06%			2	59.51%															1	19.43%		
9	1937	3	1	41.72%			2	46.81%																		11.46%
10	1938	3	1	40.23%			2	59.77%																		
11	1943	3		10.21%		9.81%	1	42.63%									2	37.35%								
12	1944	3		7.82%			2	48.46%									1	39.75%								3.97%
13	1948	4		5.41%			2	45.47%							1	16.10%	1	26.31%								6.71%
14	1951	4		12.45%			1	37.36%								8.08%	2	31.35%							1	10.76%
15	1954	4	1	13.70%		2.69%	1	37.74%								3.73%	1	27.80%							1	14.32%
16	1957	4	1	12.78%		7.64%	1	36.89%		8.95%							1	20.45%							1	13.30%
17	1961	4	2	28.50%			1	30.97%		3.25%						4.58%		9.18%	1	15.11%						8.41%
18	1965	4	2	44.24%		12.65%	2	43.11%																		
19	1969	3	1	45.16%		6.62%	2	48.23%																		
20	1973	3	2	48.28%		1.77%	1	45.45%		2.70%																1.80%
21	1977	3	1	45.80%		1.11%	2	50.68%																		2.41%
22	1981	3	1	39.41%			2	48.30%																		12.29%
23	1982	3	1	45.30%			2	54.70%																		
24	1982	3	1	46.70%			2	53.30%																		
25	1987	3	1	37.37%			2	50.06%																		12.57%
26	1989	3	1	39.68%			1	37.89%																	1	22.43%
27	1992	4	1	29.92%		1.31%	2	52.28%		0.35%		0.23%													1	15.90%
28	1997	4	2	36.91%		1.48%	2	47.02%						4.84%												9.75%
29	2002	4	1	30.69%		1.28%	2	40.76%		3.37%		0.86%	1	9.42%												13.63%
30	2007	3	2	39.13%		1.81%	1	38.84%		8.41%		1.81%														9.99%
31	2011	3	2	38.53%		9.38%		14.95%		9.76%		0.46%													1	26.92%
1918-2011		**108**	**34**	**32.05%**		**2.50%**	**47**	**43.83%**	**6**	**1.67%**		**0.16%**	**1**	**0.70%**	**1**	**1.14%**	**8**	**6.34%**	**1**	**0.53%**		**0.39%**	**1**	**0.78%**	**9**	**9.92%**
National		**4,618**	**1,453**	**30.77%**	**482**	**11.53%**	**1,985**	**41.86%**	**232**	**1.99%**	**16**	**0.75%**	**44**	**1.42%**	**18**	**0.77%**	**43**	**1.08%**	**2**	**0.03%**	**42**	**0.90%**	**11**	**0.30%**	**290**	**8.58%**

SLIGO-NORTH LEITRIM 2011

“Gains for Fine Gael and Sinn Féin at Fianna Fáil’s expense”

This constituency was created just before the 2007 general election. It was formed from the old Sligo-Leitrim constituency which lost part of County Leitrim south of Lough Allen. There were also significant Constituency Commission changes here since 2007. A population of 3,376 in the area north of Carrick-on-Shannon was transferred into the Roscommon-South Leitrim constituency. The number of seats remained the same with three TDs returned.

Fine Gael managed to gain a seat in this constituency despite a two point drop in its vote as it managed to convert 1.5 quotas into two seats. Outgoing deputy John Perry topped the poll with 8,663 first preferences and he went on to take the first seat on the penultimate count. His running mate Tony McLoughlin was in second place in the first count and comfortably took the second seat on the final count.

The big battle here was for the final seat between Sinn Fein, Fianna Fáil and to a lesser extent Labour.

Michael Colreavy narrowly increased the Sinn Féin vote but it was enough to put him in the frame on the first count with 5,911 votes. Colreavy was just under 900 votes ahead of his nearest rival Eamon Scanlon and that was sufficient as he held off the Fianna Fáil challenge and took the final seat by a margin of 646 votes.

The Fianna Fáil vote was down 19 points and with just 0.9 of a quota evenly spread over its two candidates the party fell short of a seat. Outgoing deputy Jimmy Devins decided to retire and Eamon Scanlon was the party’s leading vote getter with 5,075 first preferences. This left him outside the frame in fourth place on the first count, just ahead of his running mate Marc MacSharry. Scanlon failed to bridge the first count gap between himself and Sinn Féin’s Colreavy, despite a 48% vote transfer from his running mate MacSharry.

Labour had high hopes of a seat gain here with former journalist Susan O’Keefe on the ticket. She joined the party prior to the European elections in 2009 and she contested that election in the Ireland North-West constituency. She disappointed once again in this election and with just 4,553 on the fist count was in sixth place and was well beaten in the end. Her transfers were evenly divided among the three winning candidates.

O’Keefe was not helped by the presence of former Labour members Veronica Cawley and Declan Bree. Both unsuccessfully contested as independents and their presence did not help the Labour cause.

SLIGO-NORTH LEITRIM TDs 2011

JOHN PERRY (FG)

Grianán Iuda, Carrownanty, Ballymote, Co. Sligo; Mobile: 087 2459407;
Constituency Office: Teeling Street, Ballymote, Co. Sligo; Tel: 071 9189333
Leinster House: 01 6183765; Email: john.perry@oireachtas.ie
Website: www.johnperry.ie

Born Ballymote, Co. Sligo 15th August 1956. Married to Marie Mulvey, one son Jude. Educated Corran College, Ballymote. Minister of State. Former Businessman. First elected 1997 and at each subsequent election.

Appointed Minister of State at the Department of Enterprise, Jobs and innovation with special responsibility for Small Business March 2010. Fine Gael front bench spokesperson on Small Business 2010-2011. Chairman Joint Committee on European Scrutiny 2007-2011. Party Spokesperson on Marine 2004-2007. Chairman Public Accounts Committee 2002-2004. Assistant Director of Organisation and junior spokesperson with special responsibility for Border Issues 2000-2001. Junior spokesperson on Science, Technology, Small Business and Enterprise, Border Counties 1997-2000. Member Sligo County Council 1999-2003. Chairman of Ballymote Community Enterprise. Chairman of Ballymote Horse and Cattle Show. Winner of the Irish Quality Business Award in 1991 and 1992. Sligo Person of the Year 1993.

TONY McLOUGHLIN (FG)

"Beechlawn", Barnasraghy, Sligo, Co. Sligo; Tel: 071 9160768; Mobile: 087 6633587
Leinster House: 01 6183537; Email: tony.mcloughlin@oireachtas.ie

Born Sligo 21st January 1949. Married to Paula, two sons, one daughter. Educated Mount St. Joseph's College, Roscrea, Co. Tipperary. Former Sales Representative. Contested 1981 Dail election in Sligo Leitrim. First elected 2011.

Member Committee on Environment, Transport, Culture and the Gaeltacht. First elected to Sligo County Council in 1974. Retained his seat in 1979, 1985, 1991, 1999, 2004, and 2009. Elected to Sligo BC in 1985, 1994, 1999, 2004 and 2009.

MICHAEL COLREAVY (SF)

Main Street, Manorhamilton, Co. Leitrim; Tel: 071 9855716; Mobile: 087 2499476
Leinster House: 01 6183745; Email: michael.colreavy@oireachtas.ie

Born Leitrim September 1948. Married to Alice, four sons, four daughters. Educated Summerhill College, Sligo; National Computing centre, England (Diploma in Systems Analysis); Institute of Public Administration (Diploma in Healthcare Management). Former IT project t manager with Health Service Executive. Elected at his first attempt in 2011.

Appointed Front Bench Spokesperson on Agriculture, Food and Marine March 2011. Member Committee on Communications, Natural Resources and Agriculture. Member Committee on Health and Children. First elected to Leitrim County Council in 1999. Retained his seat in 2004 and 2009.

SLIGO-NORTH LEITRIM 2011 FIRST PREFERENCE VOTES							
	Seats	3			11,108		
	Candidate	Party	1st	%	Quota	Count	Status
1	**Perry, John***	**FG**	**8,663**	**19.50%**	**0.78**	**8**	**Made Quota**
2	**McLoughlin, Tony**	**FG**	**7,715**	**17.37%**	**0.69**	**9**	**Made Quota**
3	**Colreavy, Michael**	**SF**	**5,911**	**13.30%**	**0.53**	**9**	**Elected**
4	Scanlon, Eamon*	FF	5,075	11.42%	0.46	9	Not Elected
5	O'Keeffe, Susan	LB	4,553	10.25%	0.41	7	Eliminated
6	MacSharry, Marc	FF	4,633	10.43%	0.42	6	Eliminated
7	Bree, Declan #	ULA	2,284	5.14%	0.21	5	Eliminated
8	Clarke, Michael	NP	2,415	5.44%	0.22	4	No Expenses
9	Cawley, Veronica	NP	1,119	2.52%	0.10	3	No Expenses
10	Love, Alwyn Robert	NV	779	1.75%	0.07	3	No Expenses
11	McSharry, Gabriel	NP	747	1.68%	0.07	2	No Expenses
12	Gogan, Johnny	GP	432	0.97%	0.04	1	No Expenses
13	Cahill, Dick	NP	102	0.23%	0.01	1	No Expenses
13	***Outgoing # Former TD**		**44,428**	**100.00%**	**11,108**	**2,777**	**No Expenses**

SLIGO-NORTH LEITRIM 2011 PARTY VOTE												
	2011					2007					Change	
Party	Cand	1st	%	Quota	Seats	Cand	1st	%	Quota	Seats	%	Seats
FG	2	16,378	36.86%	1.47	2	3	15,684	39.27%	1.57	1	-2.41%	+1
LB	1	4,553	10.25%	0.41		1	1,555	3.89%	0.16		+6.35%	
FF	2	9,708	21.85%	0.87		2	16,360	40.97%	1.64	2	-19.12%	-2
SF	1	5,911	13.30%	0.53	1	1	4,684	11.73%	0.47		+1.58%	+1
GP	1	432	0.97%	0.04		1	1,209	3.03%	0.12		-2.06%	
Others	6	7,446	16.76%	0.67		2	442	1.11%	0.04		+15.65%	
Total	**13**	**44,428**	**100.0%**	**11,108**	**3**	**10**	**39,934**	**100.0%**	**9,985**	**3**	**0.00%**	**0**
Electorate		**63,432**	**70.04%**				**57,517**	**69.43%**			**+0.61%**	
Spoiled		**409**	**0.91%**				**396**	**0.98%**			**-0.07%**	
Turnout		**44,837**	**70.69%**				**40,330**	**70.12%**			**+0.57%**	

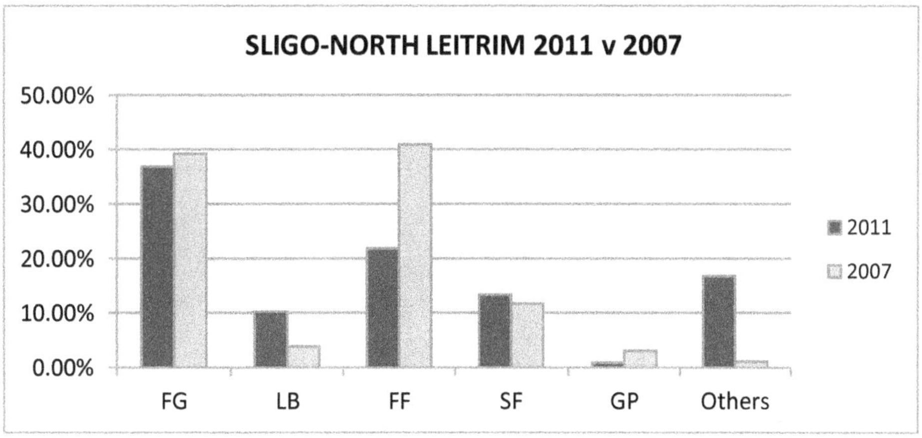

SLIGO-NORTH LEITRIM 2011 COUNT DETAILS										
Seats	3								Quota	11,108
Candidate	Party	1st	2nd	3rd	4th	5th	6th	7th	8th	9th
			Gogan Cahill	McSharry Votes	Cawley Love	Clarke Votes	Bree Votes	MacSharry Votes	O'Keeffe Votes	Perry Surplus
			+40	*+38*	*+227*	*+580*	*+220*	*+651*	*+1,554*	*-865*
Perry, John*	FG	8,663	8,703	8,741	8,968	9,548	9,768	10,419	11,973	11,108
			+63	*+113*	*+236*	*+193*	*+379*	*+794*	*+1,488*	*+527*
McLoughlin, Tony	FG	7,715	7,778	7,891	8,127	8,320	8,699	9,493	10,981	11,508
			+61	*+260*	*+233*	*+381*	*+929*	*+364*	*+1,477*	*+155*
Colreavy, Michael	SF	5,911	5,972	6,232	6,465	6,846	7,775	8,139	9,616	9,771
			+22	*+68*	*+70*	*+390*	*+74*	*+2,690*	*+553*	*+183*
Scanlon, Eamon*	FF	5,075	5,097	5,165	5,235	5,625	5,699	8,389	8,942	9,125
			+156	*+60*	*+444*	*+217*	*+666*	*+550*	*-6,646*	
O'Keeffe, Susan	LB	4,553	4,709	4,769	5,213	5,430	6,096	6,646	Eliminated	
			+14	*+39*	*+179*	*+437*	*+284*	*-5,586*		
MacSharry, Marc	FF	4,633	4,647	4,686	4,865	5,302	5,586	Eliminated		
			+50	*+46*	*+383*	*+183*	*-2,946*			
Bree, Declan #	ULA	2,284	2,334	2,380	2,763	2,946	Eliminated			
			+16	*+32*	*+144*	*-2,607*				
Clarke, Michael	NP	2,415	2,431	2,463	2,607	Eliminated				
			+21	*+31*	*-1,171*					
Cawley, Veronica	NP	1,119	1,140	1,171	Eliminated					
			+57	*+45*	*-881*					
Love, Alwyn Robert	NV	779	836	881	Eliminated					
			+23	*-770*						
McSharry, Gabriel	NP	747	770	Eliminated						
			-432							
Gogan, Johnny	GP	432	Eliminated							
			-102							
Cahill, Dick	NP	102	Eliminated							
Non-transferable			*+11*	*+38*	*+136*	*+226*	*+394*	*+537*	*+1,574*	
Cumulative			11	49	185	411	805	1,342	2,916	2,916
Total		**44,428**	**44,428**	**44,428**	**44,428**	**44,428**	**44,428**	**44,428**	**44,428**	**44,428**

SLIGO-NORTH LEITRIM 2011 TRANSFER ANALYSIS							
From	**To**	**FG**	**LB**	**FF**	**SF**	**Others**	**Non Trans**
FG	865	527		183	155		
		60.92%		*21.16%*	*17.92%*		
LB	6,646	3,042		553	1,477		1,574
		45.77%		*8.32%*	*22.22%*		*23.68%*
FF	5,586	1,445	550	2,690	364		537
		25.87%	*9.85%*	*48.16%*	*6.52%*		*9.61%*
GP	432	84	126	29	49	135	9
		19.44%	*29.17%*	*6.71%*	*11.34%*	*31.25%*	*2.08%*
Others	8,477	2,005	1,417	1,548	1,815	896	796
		23.65%	*16.72%*	*18.26%*	*21.41%*	*10.57%*	*9.39%*
Total	**22,006**	**7,103**	**2,093**	**5,003**	**3,860**	**1,031**	**2,916**
		32.28%	***9.51%***	***22.73%***	***17.54%***	***4.69%***	***13.25%***

SLIGO-NORTH LEITRIM		
MAIN BOUNDARY CHANGES		
Dail	**Constituency**	**Seats**
1 (1918)	Leitrim	1
	Sligo North	1
	Sligo South	1
2 (1921) - 3 (1922)	Sligo - Mayo East	5
4 (1923) - 8 (1933)	Leitrim - Sligo	7
9 (1937) - 12 (1944)	Leitrim	3
	Sligo	3
13 (1948) - 16 (1957)	Sligo - Leitrim	5
17 (1961) - 18 (1965)	Sligo - Leitrim	4
19 (1969) - 21 (1977)	Sligo - Leitrim	3
22 (1981) - 29 (2002)	Sligo - Leitrim	4
30 (2007) - 31 (2011)	Sligo-North Leitrim	3

SLIGO-NORTH LEITRIM														
ALL TDs 1918-2011														
	Surname	**Forename**	**Party**	**Elected**										**Total**
1	Flynn	Stephen	FF	32	33	37	38	43	44	48	51	54	57	10
2	Carty	Frank	FF	21	22	23	27	27	32	33	37	38		9
3	Maguire	Ben	FF	27S	32	33	37	38	43	44	48	54		9
4	Reynolds	Mary	FG	32	37	38	43	44	48	51	54	57		9
5	Roddy	Martin	FG	25*	27	27	32	33	37	43	44			8
6	Rogers	Patrick	FG	33	37	38	43	44	51	57				7
7	McSharry	Ray	FF	69	73	77	81	82	82	87				7
8	Ellis	John	FF	81	82F	87	89	92	97	02				7
9	Gilbride	Eugene	FF	48	51	54	57	61	65					6
10	Nealon	Ted	FG	81	82	82	87	89	92					6
11	Brennan	Matt	FF	82	82	87	89	92	97					6
12	Dolan**	James	CG	18	23	27	27	33						5
13	McLoughlin	Joseph	FG	61*	61	65	69	73						5
14	McCabe	Alexander	CG	18	21	22	23							4
15	Hennigan	John	CG	23	27	27	32							4
16	Gallagher	James	FF	61	65	69	77							4
17	Gilhawley	Eugene	FG	61	65	73	77							4
18	Perry	John	FG	97	02	07	11							4
19	Holt	Samuel	FF	25*	27	27								3
20	Brennan	Martin	FF	38	43	44								3
21	Roddy	Joseph	FG	48	51	54								3
22	Devins	James	CR	21	22									2
23	Ferran	Francis	CR	21	22									2
24	O'Donnell	Thomas	CT	21	22									2
25	Browne	William	FF	32	33									2
26	McCartin	Joe	FG	81	82N									2
27	Reynolds	Gerry	FG	89	97									2
28	Devins	Jimmy	FF	02	07									2
29	Clancy	John	SF	18										1
30	Carter**	Thomas	CG	23										1
31	Farrell	Sean	R	23										1
32	McGowan	Martin	R	23										1
33	Carter	Michael	F	27J										1
34	Jinks	John	NL	27J										1
35	Reynolds	Patrick T.	CG	27S										1
36	MacEoin**	Gen. Sean	CG	29*										1
37	McGirl	John Joe	SF	57										1
38	Bree	Declan	LB	92										1
39	Harkin	Marian	NP	02										1
40	Scanlon	Eamon	FF	07										1
41	McLoughlin	Tony	FG	11										1
42	Colreavy	Michael	SF	11										1
	Total						***Includes 4 By-Elections**						*	**151**
	**** Also elected in another constituency**													
	MacEoin**	Gen. Sean	CG	Longford-Wmeath					21	22	32-61			13
S	Dolan**	James	CG	Roscommon					21	22				2
	Carter**	Thomas	CG	Roscommon/Longford-Westı					21	22/	43	44	48	5
S	**Included in Sligo-Leitrim total**													**20**

SLIGO-NORTH LEITRIM 1918-2011

* No Contest			FG		LB		FF		SF		GP		CS		PD		C na P		Cn na T		Nat Lab		Farmers		Nat League		Centre P		Others	
Dail		Seats	S	% Vote	S	% Vote	S	% Vote	S	% Vote	S	% Vote	S	% Vote	S	% Vote	S	% Vote	S	% Vote	S	% Vote	S	% Vote	S	% Vote	S	% Vote	S	% Vote
1	1918	3							3																					
2	1921*	5							5																					
3	1922	5	2	29.55%			3	56.40%																						14.06%
4	1923	7	4	47.94%		3.22%	3	36.10%																9.50%						3.24%
5	1927	7	3	43.23%		4.36%	2	23.11%		6.94%													1	14.13%	1	4.47%				3.78%
6	1927	7	4	45.46%		4.17%	3	34.76%																12.70%						2.90%
7	1932	7	3	41.81%		3.51%	4	48.92%																3.60%						2.16%
8	1933	7	2	35.77%		1.58%	4	52.16%																			1	10.49%		
9	1937	6	3	43.99%			3	40.02%																						15.99%
10	1938	6	2	44.11%			4	55.89%																						
11	1943	6	3	33.08%		7.69%	2	30.92%												8.24%									1	20.07%
12	1944	6	3	35.31%		6.93%	2	34.61%												9.91%									1	13.24%
13	1948	5	2	28.97%			2	30.29%										8.55%		10.78%		3.56%							1	17.85%
14	1951	5	3	40.09%		6.19%	2	39.62%										6.59%												7.50%
15	1954	5	2	40.55%			2	35.24%										5.72%		1.22%									1	17.27%
16	1957	5	2	38.31%			2	34.79%	1	15.71%																				11.19%
17	1961	4	2	39.37%		7.61%	2	35.48%		7.28%										2.93%										7.35%
18	1965	4	2	41.69%		11.66%	2	44.11%																						2.54%
19	1969	3	1	44.18%		9.09%	2	46.73%																						
20	1973	3	2	41.99%		7.39%	1	50.62%																						
21	1977	3	1	38.64%		3.01%	2	48.03%																						10.33%
22	1981	4	2	35.58%		0.76%	2	49.88%		11.82%																				1.96%
23	1982	4	1	37.47%		0.87%	3	53.32%		6.07%																				2.26%
24	1982	4	2	41.44%		1.21%	2	53.02%																						4.33%
25	1987	4	1	30.98%			3	51.58%		5.75%						5.52%														6.18%
26	1989	4	2	35.94%			2	46.10%		3.46%						2.93%														11.56%
27	1992	4	1	30.35%	1	17.15%	2	45.61%		3.07%																				3.82%
28	1997	4	2	36.63%		10.86%	2	40.41%		7.10%				3.01%		1.65%														0.34%
29	2002	4	1	26.67%		4.96%	2	38.97%		10.21%				0.34%															1	18.85%
30	2007	3	1	39.27%		3.89%	2	40.97%		11.73%		3.03%																		1.11%
31	2011	3	2	36.86%		10.25%		21.85%	1	13.30%		0.97%																		16.76%
1918-2011		**147**	**61**	**38.08%**	**1**	**4.10%**	**67**	**41.76%**	**10**	**3.47%**		**0.12%**		**0.12%**		**0.34%**		**0.78%**		**1.25%**		**0.14%**	**1**	**1.52%**	**1**	**0.17%**	**1**	**0.46%**	**5**	**7.69%**
National		**4,618**	**1,453**	**30.77%**	**482**	**11.53%**	**1,985**	**41.86%**	**232**	**1.99%**	**16**	**0.75%**		**0.04%**	**44**	**1.42%**	**18**	**0.77%**	**43**	**1.08%**	**9**	**0.16%**	**42**	**0.90%**	**10**	**0.24%**	**11**	**0.30%**	**273**	**8.17%**

TIPPERARY NORTH 2011

"Lowry's vote hits record high"

Parts of South West Offaly, with a population of 4,276, was transferred to this three seat constituency since 2007. It included Moneygal, the ancestral Offaly home of the US President Barack Obama.

There was a familiar pattern to the headline result here though. Michael Lowry may not bask in the approval of the Moriarty Tribunal or the national media, but if anything that seems to increase the loyalty of his supporters in Tipperary North. Lowry headed the poll, as he has done at every election since he became an Independent in 1997, and pushed his vote total to a new record high. He won 14,104 first preference votes. This was a 29% share of the vote. Just to rub it in, it was his surplus that took incumbent Fine Gael TD Noel Coonan into the second seat.

Fianna Fail had taken 2 of the 3 seats here as recently as 2002, but the odds were against it holding even one in 2011. Máire Hoctor, seen as one of the dissidents after Brian Cowen dropped her from her junior ministerial post in April 2009, had the advantage of being the party's sole candidate, and she did not do badly; she increased her personal vote, and the swing away from Fianna Fail, at a mere 17.8 per cent, was one of the smallest in the country. However, that was not enough.

For Labour, Kathleen O'Meara had stepped aside after mounting strong challenges in 1997, 2002 and 2007, and the party standard-bearer now was former Senator Alan Kelly. He had left the Seanad in 2009 to run in the European Parliament elections in 2009. He was elected as MEP for the South constituency. Although he vowed in that campaign not to contest the next General Election, a request from the party leader was enough to lure him home. He nearly doubled the party's vote share and took the final seat over 2,000 votes ahead of Hoctor. His European Parliament seat remained within Tipperary, passing on to Clonmel-based Phil Prendergast.

Michael Lowry TD and Richard Quirke with a model of the Tipperary Venue

TIPPERARY NORTH TDs 2011

MICHAEL LOWRY (IND)

Glenreigh, Holycross, Thurles, Co. Tipperary; Mobile: 087 2323828;
Constituency Office: Abbey Road, Thurles, Co. Tipperary; Tel: 0504 22022;
Leinster House: 01 6183504; Email: michael.lowry@oireachtas.ie
Website: www.michaellowry.ie

Born Holycross, Co. Tipperary 13th March 1954. Married to Catherine McGrath, two sons, one daughter. Educated Thurles CBS. Company Director. Fine Gael TD 1987-1997. Independent since 1997.

One of four independent deputies that pledged their support to the Fianna Fail/GP/PD government during the lifetime of the 30th Dail. Member Joint Committee on Transport 2007-2011. Member Joint Committee on Transport 2002-2007. Minister for Transport, Energy and Communications 1994-1996 when he resigned. He resigned from the Fine Gael Parliamentary Party in 1997. Chairman, Fine Gael Parliamentary Party 1993-1994. Member of Front Bench 1993-1994. Fine Gael Leader of the British-Irish Inter-Parliamentary Body 1994. Member Tipperary (North Riding) County Council 1979-1995 and 1999-2003. Member of County Development Team; Mid Western Health Board and Association of Health Boards in Ireland. Chairman Semple Stadium Management Committee; former Chairman County Tipperary GAA Board and Mid Tipperary GAA Board.

NOEL COONAN (FG)

Gortnagoona, Roscrea, Co. Tipperary; Tel: 0504 32816; Mobile: 086 2427733
Constituency Office: Bank Street Templemore, Co. Tipperary; Tel: 0504 32544
Leinster House: 01 6183842; Email: noel.coonan@oireachtas.ie
Website: www.noelcoonan.com

Born Tipperary, 6th Jan 1951. Married to Pauline. Educated CBS, Templemore, Co. Tipperary. Contested 2002 general election in Tipperary North. First elected 2007. Retained his seat in 2011.

Appointed Vice-Chairman Committee on Environment, Transport, Culture and the Gaeltacht June 2011. Deputy spokesperson on Communications, Energy and Natural Resources with special responsibility for Telecommunications 2007-2011. Member Joint Committee on Communications, Energy and Natural Resources 2007-2011. Senator 2002-2007. Fine Gael's Spokesperson on Agriculture and Food in the Upper House. Member Joint Committee on Agriculture and Food 2002-2007. Member Tipperary North Riding County Council 1991-2004. Member Templemore UDC 1994-2004. Member Mid-Western Health Board.

ALAN KELLY (LB)

Loughtea, Ballina, Nenagh, Co. Tipperary; Tel: 067 34190; Mobile: 086 6061101
Constituency Office: 1 Summerhill, Nenagh, Co. Tipperary, Tel: 067 34190;
Email: alan.kelly@oirechtas.ie Website: www.alankelly.ie

Born Limerick, 13th July 1975. Married to Regina O'Connor, one daughter. Educated Nenagh CBS; UCC (BA); Boston College (Certificate in Leadership 1999); UCD (MBS in eCommerce 2002). Minister of State. Former eBusiness Executive/Manager. Elected at his first attempt in 2011.

Appointed March 2011 Minister of State at Department of Transport, Tourism and Sport with special responsibility for Public and Commuter Transport. First elected to European Parliament in 2009. Senator 2007-2009. Brother of Declan Kelly former US Economic Envoy to Northern Ireland.

TIPPERARY NORTH 2011							
FIRST PREFERENCE VOTES							
	Seats	3			12,069		
	Candidate	Party	1st	%	Quota	Count	Status
1	**Lowry, Michael***	**NP**	**14,104**	**29.22%**	**1.17**	**1**	**Made Quota**
2	**Coonan, Noel***	**FG**	**11,425**	**23.67%**	**0.95**	**2**	**Made Quota**
3	**Kelly, Alan**	**LB**	**9,559**	**19.80%**	**0.79**	**3**	**Elected**
4	Hoctor, Máire*	FF	7,978	16.53%	0.66	3	Not Elected
5	Morris, Séamus	SF	3,034	6.29%	0.25	2	Eliminated
6	Clancy, Billy	NV	1,442	2.99%	0.12	2	No Expenses
7	O'Malley, Olwyn	GP	409	0.85%	0.03	2	No Expenses
8	Bopp, Kate	NP	322	0.67%	0.03	2	No Expenses
8	***Outgoing**		**48,273**	**100.00%**	**12,069**	**3,018**	**No Expenses**

TIPPERARY NORTH 2011												
PARTY VOTE												
	2011					2007					Change	
Party	Cand	1st	%	Quota	Seats	Cand	1st	%	Quota	Seats	%	Seats
FG	1	11,425	23.67%	0.95	1	1	7,061	15.89%	0.64	1	+7.78%	
LB	1	9,559	19.80%	0.79	1	1	4,561	10.27%	0.41		+9.54%	+1
FF	1	7,978	16.53%	0.66		2	15,245	34.31%	1.37	1	-17.78%	-1
SF	1	3,034	6.29%	0.25		1	1,672	3.76%	0.15		+2.52%	
GP	1	409	0.85%	0.03		1	495	1.11%	0.04		-0.27%	
PD						1	634	1.43%	0.06		-1.43%	
Others	3	15,868	32.87%	1.31	1	2	14,763	33.23%	1.33	1	-0.36%	
Total	**8**	**48,273**	**100.0%**	**12,069**	**3**	**9**	**44,431**	**100.0%**	**11,108**	**3**	**0.00%**	**0**
Electorate		**63,235**	**76.34%**				**57,084**	**77.83%**			**-1.50%**	
Spoiled		**516**	**1.06%**				**352**	**0.79%**			**+0.27%**	
Turnout		**48,789**	**77.16%**				**44,783**	**78.45%**			**-1.30%**	

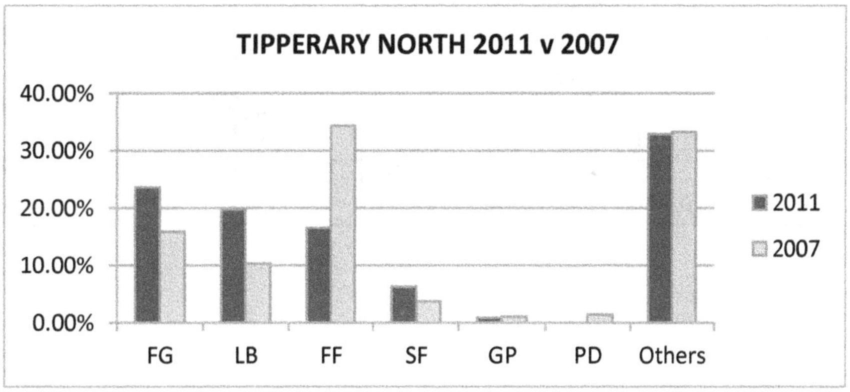

TIPPERARY NORTH 2011 COUNT DETAILS				
	Seats	3	Quota	12,069
Candidate	Party	1st	2nd	3rd
			Lowry Surplus	Morris Clancy O'Malley Bopp
			-2,035	
Lowry, Michael*	NP	14,104	12,069	12,069
			+705	
Coonan, Noel*	FG	11,425	12,130	12,130
			+545	+1,961
Kelly, Alan	LB	9,559	10,104	12,065
			+378	+1,085
Hoctor, Máire*	FF	7,978	8,356	9,441
			+146	-3,180
Morris, Séamus	SF	3,034	3,180	Eliminated
			+211	-1,653
Clancy, Billy	NV	1,442	1,653	Eliminated
			+20	-429
O'Malley, Olwyn	GP	409	429	Eliminated
			+30	-352
Bopp, Kate	NP	322	352	Eliminated
Non-transferable				+2,568
Cumulative			0	2,568
Total		**48,273**	**48,273**	**48,273**

TIPPERARY NORTH 2011 TRANSFER ANALYSIS								
From	To	FG	LB	FF	SF	GP	Others	Non Trans
SF	3,180		1,111	614				1,455
			34.94%	*19.31%*				*45.75%*
GP	429		150	83				196
			34.97%	*19.35%*				*45.69%*
Others	4,040	705	1,245	766	146	20	241	917
		17.45%	*30.82%*	*18.96%*	*3.61%*	*0.50%*	*5.97%*	*22.70%*
Total	**7,649**	**705**	**2,506**	**1,463**	**146**	**20**	**241**	**2,568**
		9.22%	***32.76%***	***19.13%***	***1.91%***	***0.26%***	***3.15%***	***33.57%***

TIPPERARY NORTH		
MAIN BOUNDARY CHANGES		
Dail	**Constituency**	**Seats**
13 (1948) - 31 (2011)	Tipperary North	3

TIPPERARY NORTH														
ALL TDs 1948-2011														
	Surname	**Forename**	**Party**	**Elected**										**Total**
1	O'Kennedy	Michael	FF	69	73	77	82	82	87	89	97			8
2	Smith	Michael	FF	69	77	81	87	89	92	97	02			8
3	Lowry	Michael	NP	87	89	92	97	02	07	11				7
4	Ryan	John	LB	73	77	81	82	82	92					6
5	Fanning	John	FF	51	54	57	61	65						5
6	Ryan**	Mary	FF	48	51	54	57							4
7	Dunne	Thomas	FG	61	65	69	73							4
8	Morrissey**	Daniel	FG	48	51	54								3
9	Tierney	Patrick	LB	57	61	65								3
10	Molony	David	FG	81	82	82								3
11	Hoctor	Maire	FF	02	07									2
12	Coonan	Noel	FG	07	11									2
13	Kinane**	Patrick	CnaP	48										1
14	Kelly	Alan	LB	11										1
14	**Total**													**57**
	**Also elected in Tipperary													
1	Morrissey**	Daniel	FG	22	23	27	27	32	33	37	38	43	44	10
2	Kinane**	Patrick	CnaP	47*										1
3	Ryan**	Mary	FF	44										1
	Total 3						***Includes 1 By-Election**						*	**12**

TIPPERARY NORTH 1948-2011																			
			FG		LB		FF		SF		GP		PD		C na P		Others		
Dail		**Seats**	**S**	**% Vote**	**S**	**% Vote**	**S**	**% Vote**	**S**	**% Vote**	**S**	**% Vote**	**S**	**% Vote**	**S**	**% Vote**	**S**	**% Vote**
13	1948	3	1	22.55%		15.62%	1	39.71%							1	22.11%		
14	1951	3	1	33.23%		13.30%	2	44.33%								9.15%		
15	1954	3	1	28.40%		16.84%	2	44.72%								10.03%		
16	1957	3		22.66%	1	15.79%	2	46.41%		9.44%						5.70%		
17	1961	3	1	27.56%	1	21.93%	1	46.15%		4.37%								
18	1965	3	1	35.41%	1	20.42%	1	44.17%										
19	1969	3	1	34.09%		12.70%	2	53.21%										
20	1973	3	1	30.32%	1	19.14%	1	50.54%										
21	1977	3		22.51%	1	22.63%	2	54.87%										
22	1981	3	1	29.33%	1	23.20%	1	45.66%										1.81%
23	1982	3	1	25.81%	1	24.48%	1	49.15%										0.55%
24	1982	3	1	28.67%	1	22.32%	1	49.01%										
25	1987	3	1	23.61%		13.69%	2	51.36%		2.64%				7.34%				1.36%
26	1989	3	1	26.12%		22.81%	2	50.82%										0.25%
27	1992	3	1	28.07%	1	22.75%	1	47.98%		1.20%								
28	1997	3		11.32%		10.33%	2	42.29%						3.48%			1	32.59%
29	2002	3		14.91%		13.52%	2	42.66%						3.53%			1	25.39%
30	2007	3	1	15.89%		10.27%	1	34.31%		3.76%		1.11%		1.43%			1	33.23%
31	2011	3	1	23.67%	1	19.80%		16.53%		6.29%		0.85%					1	32.87%
1948-2011		**57**	**15**	**24.69%**	**10**	**17.75%**	**27**	**43.93%**		**1.55%**		**0.14%**		**0.95%**	**1**	**2.12%**	**4**	**8.88%**
National		**4,618**	**1,453**	**30.77%**	**482**	**11.53%**	**1,985**	**41.86%**	**232**	**1.99%**	**16**	**0.75%**	**44**	**1.42%**	**18**	**0.77%**	**388**	**10.90%**

TIPPERARY SOUTH 2011

"Former Fianna Fail TD wins seat after shedding party colours"

There were no boundary changes to this three-seat constituency since 2007. Indeed Fianna Fail's achievement that year when it took two of the three seats, ousting left-wing independent Séamus Healy, was one of the surprises of that election. In 2011 Healy, who was now part of the United Left Alliance, was certain to regain his seat, and Fine Gael incumbent Tom Hayes was equally certain to retain his.

That left just one seat between four credible contenders: Fianna Fail junior minister Martin Mansergh, Labour senator Phil Prendergast, Fine Gael's second candidate Michael Murphy, and Mattie McGrath. McGrath had been elected for Fianna Fail in 2007, but had rapidly acquired maverick status, and in June 2010 he lost the party whip, becoming an independent TD, for voting against the government bill banning stag-hunting. At the end of January 2011 he left Fianna Fail itself and announced that he would be standing as an independent.

Martin Mansergh, whose PhD thesis was on the history of 18th century France on the eve of the Revolution, may have sensed the upheaval that was about to happen, though his assertion on RTE radio on election count day that this was 'not a wipe-out' for Fianna Fáil had a ring of the Marie Antoinette about it. Sure enough, as the tumbrils left the counting centre and rolled through the streets of Clonmel, it was Dr Mansergh's Dáil career that they bore away.

Mansergh's elimination on the final count took Mattie McGrath comfortably into the third seat. Michael Murphy did better than predicted and finished runner-up, but Labour's performance was disappointing, its vote up only 2 per cent on 2007 compared with the national swing of 9 per cent. For Phil Prendergast, though, there was significant consolation: the European Parliament seat that Labour won in the South constituency in 2009 came to her, as a result of the election of MEP Alan Kelly in Tipperary North.

Tipperary South TDs with members of the Carers Association

TIPPERARY SOUTH TDs 2011

SEAMUS HEALY (ULA)

Scrouthea, Old Bridge, Clonmel, Co. Tipperary; Tel: 0502 23184; Mobile: 087 2802199
Constituency Office: 56 Queen Street, Clonmel, Co. Tipperary; Tel: 052 6121883;
Email: seamus.healy@oireachtas.ie

Born Clonmel, Co. Tipperary 9th August 1950. Married, four daughters. Educated CBS High School, Clonmel. Former hospital administrator. Contested Dail elections in Tipperary South in 1987, 1989, 1992 and 1997. Elected at by-election 22nd June 2000. Retained his seat in 2002 but lost it in 2007. Regained his seat in 2011 as a member of the United Left Alliance.

Member Committee on Health and Children. First elected to Tipperary South County Council in Clonmel electoral area in 1991. Retained his seat in 1999. Co-opted as replacement for Pat English 2007. Retained his seat in 2009 Elected to Clonmel Borough Council in 1985, 1994, 1999 and 2009. Founder member of Workers and Unemployed Action Group (WUAG) in Clonmel.

TOM HAYES (FG)

Cahirvilhallow, Golden, Co. Tipperary, Tel: 062 62892; Mobile: 087 8105016
Constituency Office: The Green, Cashel, Co. Tipperary; Tel: 052 80731
Leinster House: 01 6183168; Email: tom.hayes@oireachtas.ie
Website; www.tomhayes.ie

Born Golden, Co. Tipperary 16th February 1952. Married to Marian Thornton, three sons. Educated Mount Melleray College, Co. Waterford; Tipperary Vocational School; UCC (Diploma in Social Studies). Farmer. First elected July 2001 at by-election caused by death of Theresa Ahearn. Retained his seat at each subsequent election.

Appointed Chairman Joint Administration Committee June 2011. Member Committee on Justice, Defence and Equality. Member Houses of the Oireachtas Commission and Member Joint Committee on the Constitution and Member Dail Committee on Procedure and Privileges 2007-2011. Chairman of the Fine Gael Parliamentary Party September 2002-March 2010. Deputy spokesperson on Agriculture and Food 2002-2007. Member Joint Committee on Agriculture and Food 2002-2007. Senator 1997-2001. Fine Gael spokesperson on Agriculture in the Senate. Member Tipperary South Riding County Council 1991-2003. Member VEC; County Enterprise Board; Cashel Heritage and Development Trust. Board Member Cashel Community School.

MATTIE McGRATH (NP)

Mullough, Newcastle, Clonmel, Co. Tipperary; Tel: 052 36352; Mobile: 086 8184307;
Constituency Office: 2 Joyce's Lane, The Quay, Clonmel, Co. Tipperary; Tel: 052 6129155;
Leinster House: 01 6184062; Email: mattie.mcgrath@oireachtas.ie,
Website: www.mattiemcgrath.ie

Born Newcastle, Co. Tipperary September 1958. Married to Margaret Sherlock, five daughters, three sons. Educated St. Joseph's College, Cahir; Kildalton Agricultural College, Co. Kilkenny; UCC (Certificate in Communication Skills). Businessman. First elected for Fianna Fail in 2007. Retained his seat as an Independent in 2011.

Member Committee on Communications, Natural Resources and Agriculture. Member Committee on Health and Children. Lost Fianna Fail party whip over Wildlife Bill in July 2010. Appointed Convenor Committee on Communications October 2007. Member Joint Committee on Agriculture, Fisheries and Food and Member Joint Committee on Communications, Energy and Natural Resources and Member Joint Committee on Social and Family Affairs 2007-2011. Member South Tipperary County Council 1999-2007 (Chairman 2004-2005). Member VEC and Chairman Adult Education Board. Board member Tipperary Leader. Director of the Irish Council for Social Housing. Director Muintir Na Tire. All Ireland Set Dancer 1974.

	TIPPERARY SOUTH 2011 FIRST PREFERENCE VOTES						
	Seats	3			10,341		
	Candidate	Party	1st	%	Quota	Count	Status
1	**Healy, Séamus #**	**ULA**	**8,818**	**21.32%**	**0.85**	**3**	**Made Quota**
2	**Hayes, Tom***	**FG**	**8,896**	**21.51%**	**0.86**	**4**	**Made Quota**
3	**McGrath, Mattie***	**NP**	**6,074**	**14.69%**	**0.59**	**5**	**Elected**
4	Murphy, Michael	FG	5,402	13.06%	0.52	5	Not Elected
5	Mansergh, Martin*	FF	5,419	13.10%	0.52	4	Eliminated
6	Prendergast, Phil	LB	4,525	10.94%	0.44	2	Eliminated
7	Browne, Michael	SF	1,860	4.50%	0.18	1	No Expenses
8	McNally, Paul	GP	367	0.89%	0.04	1	No Expenses
8	***Outgoing # Former TD**		**41,361**	**100.00%**	**10,341**	**2,586**	**No Expenses**

TIPPERARY SOUTH 2011 PARTY VOTE												
	2011					2007					Change	
Party	Cand	1st	%	Quota	Seats	Cand	1st	%	Quota	Seats	%	Seats
FG	2	14,298	34.57%	1.38	1	1	8,200	21.14%	0.85	1	+13.42%	
LB	1	4,525	10.94%	0.44		1	3,400	8.77%	0.35		+2.17%	
FF	1	5,419	13.10%	0.52		3	18,004	46.42%	1.86	2	-33.32%	-2
SF	1	1,860	4.50%	0.18		1	1,198	3.09%	0.12		+1.41%	
ULA	1	8,818	21.32%	0.85	1						+21.32%	+1
GP	1	367	0.89%	0.04		1	591	1.52%	0.06		-0.64%	
PD						2	541	1.39%	0.06		-1.39%	
Others	1	6,074	14.69%	0.59	1	2	6,848	17.66%	0.71		-2.97%	+1
Total	**8**	**41,361**	**100.0%**	**10,341**	**3**	**11**	**38,782**	**100.0%**	**9,696**	**3**	**0.00%**	**0**
Electorate		**57,420**	**72.03%**				**54,637**	**70.98%**			**+1.05%**	
Spoiled		**432**	**1.03%**				**330**	**0.84%**			**+0.19%**	
Turnout		**41,793**	**72.78%**				**39,112**	**71.59%**			**+1.20%**	

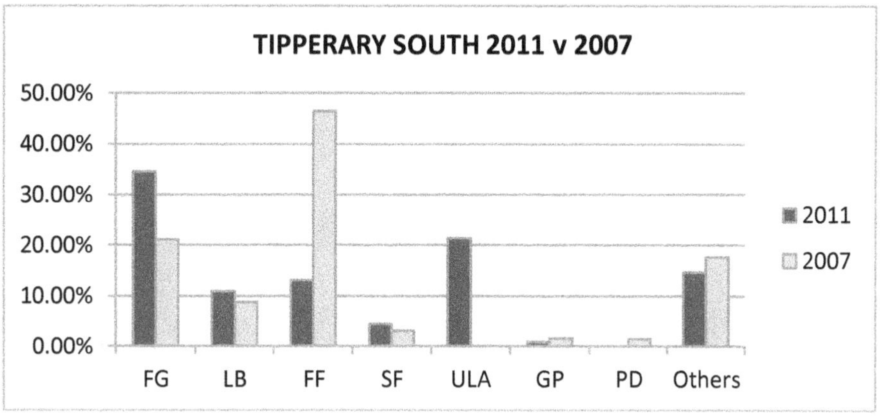

TIPPERARY SOUTH 2011 COUNT DETAILS						
Seats	3				Quota	10,341
Candidate	Party	1st	2nd Browne McNally	3rd Prendergast Votes	4th Healy Surplus	5th Mansergh Votes
Healy, Séamus #	ULA	8,818	+724 9,542	+1,723 11,265	-924 10,341	10,341
Hayes, Tom*	FG	8,896	+318 9,214	+972 10,186	+277 10,463	10,463
McGrath, Mattie*	NP	6,074	+275 6,349	+729 7,078	+335 7,413	+2,565 9,978
Murphy, Michael	FG	5,402	+161 5,563	+841 6,404	+229 6,633	+1,315 7,948
Mansergh, Martin*	FF	5,419	+169 5,588	+277 5,865	+83 5,948	-5,948 Eliminated
Prendergast, Phil	LB	4,525	+441 4,966	-4,966 Eliminated		
Browne, Michael	SF	1,860	-1,860 Eliminated			
McNally, Paul	GP	367	-367 Eliminated			
Non-transferable			+139	+424		+2,068
Cumulative			139	563	563	2,631
Total		**41,361**	**41,361**	**41,361**	**41,361**	**41,361**

TIPPERARY SOUTH 2011 TRANSFER ANALYSIS						
From	To	FG	LB	FF	Others	Non Trans
LB	4,966	1,813 *36.51%*		277 *5.58%*	2,452 *49.38%*	424 *8.54%*
FF	5,948	1,315 *22.11%*			2,565 *43.12%*	2,068 *34.77%*
SF	1,860	400 *21.51%*	368 *19.78%*	141 *7.58%*	835 *44.89%*	116 *6.24%*
GP	367	79 *21.53%*	73 *19.89%*	28 *7.63%*	164 *44.69%*	23 *6.27%*
Others	924	506 *54.76%*		83 *8.98%*	335 *36.26%*	
Total	**14,065**	**4,113** ***29.24%***	**441** ***3.14%***	**529** ***3.76%***	**6,351** ***45.15%***	**2,631** ***18.71%***

TIPPERARY SOUTH		
MAIN BOUNDARY CHANGES		
Dail	Constituency	Seats
13 (1948) - 20 (1973)	Tipperary South	4
21 (1977)	Tipperary South	3
22 (1981) - 27 (1992)	Tipperary South	4
28 (1997) - 31 (2011)	Tipperary South	3

TIPPERARY SOUTH 1948-2011																							
		FG		LB		FF		SF		GP		WP		CS		PD		C na P		C na T		Others	
Dail	Seats	S	% Vote	S	% Vote	S	% Vote	S	% Vote	S	% Vote	S	% Vote	S	% Vote	S	% Vote	S	% Vote	S	% Vote	S	% Vote
13 1948	4	1	23.23%		6.35%	2	49.59%											1	11.86%		8.97%		
14 1951	4	2	28.19%		10.21%	2	50.66%												4.08%				6.86%
15 1954	4	2	37.40%		9.47%	2	53.13%																
16 1957	4	1	32.20%		12.91%	3	54.89%																
17 1961	4	1	35.15%	1	19.46%	2	43.15%		2.24%														
18 1965	4	1	33.54%	1	19.02%	2	47.45%																
19 1969	4	1	29.88%	1	15.44%	2	51.79%																2.89%
20 1973	4	1	30.09%	1	20.59%	2	49.32%																
21 1977	3	1	28.81%	1	16.22%	1	53.84%																1.13%
22 1981	4	1	28.13%	1	21.53%	2	41.41%																8.93%
23 1982	4	1	31.57%	1	19.60%	2	48.43%																0.40%
24 1982	4	1	33.58%	1	19.98%	2	46.44%																
25 1987	4	1	20.43%		9.20%	2	42.56%						0.98%				10.61%					1	16.22%
26 1989	4	1	28.36%	1	18.08%	1	43.04%										2.99%					1	7.54%
27 1992	4	1	27.62%	1	20.94%	1	38.22%		0.52%													1	12.70%
28 1997	3	1	24.09%	1	16.11%	1	37.28%																22.52%
29 2002	3	1	24.54%		9.14%	1	38.51%		3.30%						0.33%							1	24.18%
30 2007	3	1	21.14%		8.77%	2	46.42%		3.09%		1.52%						1.39%						17.66%
31 2011	3	1	34.57%		10.94%		13.10%		4.50%		0.89%											2	36.00%
1948-2011	**71**	**21**	**29.05%**	**11**	**15.00%**	**32**	**44.38%**		**0.74%**		**0.13%**		**0.06%**		**0.02%**		**0.85%**	**1**	**0.81%**		**0.45%**	**6**	**8.50%**
National	**4,618**	**1,453**	**30.77%**	**482**	**11.53%**	**1,985**	**41.86%**	**232**	**1.99%**	**16**	**0.75%**	**17**	**0.78%**		**0.04%**	**44**	**1.42%**	**18**	**0.77%**	**43**	**1.08%**	**328**	**8.99%**

TIPPERARY SOUTH																	
ALL TDs 1948-2011																	
	Surname	Forename	Party	Elected													Total
1	Treacy	Sean	NP	61	65	69	73	77	81	82	82	87	89	92			11
2	Davern	Noel	FF	69	73	77	87	89	92	97	02						8
3	Griffin	Brendan	FG	73	77	81	82	82	87								6
4	Breen**	Dan	FF	48	51	54	57	61									5
5	Davern	Michael	FF	48	51	54	57	61									5
6	Mulcahy**	Gen. Richard	FG	48	51	54	57										4
7	McCarthy	Sean	FF	81	82	82	87										4
8	Hayes	Tom	FG	01*	02	07	11										4
9	Hogan	Patrick	FG	61	65	69											3
10	Fahey**	Jackie	FF	65	69	73											3
11	Ahearn	Theresa	FG	89	92	97											3
12	Ferris	Michael	LB	89	92	97											3
13	Healy	Seamus	NP	00*	02	11											3
14	Crowe	Patrick	FG	51	54												2
15	Byrne	Sean	FF	82	82												2
16	McGrath	Mattie	FF	07	11												2
17	Timoney	John	CnaP	48													1
18	Loughman**	Francis	FF	57													1
19	Davern	Donal	FF	65													1
20	Acheson	Carrie	FF	81													1
21	Mansergh	Martin	FF	07													1
21	**Total**									***Includes 2 By-Elections**						*	**73**
	**** Also elected in another constituency**																
	Mulcahy**	Gen. Richard	FG	Dublin/Tipp			18	21	22	23	27	27	32	33	38	44	10
	Breen**	Dan	FF	Tipperary			23	32	33	37	38	43	44				7
	Fahey**	Jackie	FF	Waterford			77	81	82	82	87	89					6
	Loughman**	Francis	FF	Tipperary			38	44									2
4	**Total**																**25**

TIPPERARY REGION		
MAIN BOUNDARY CHANGES		
Dail	**Constituency**	**Seats**
1 (1918)	Tipperary East	1
	Tipperary Mid	1
	Tipperary North	1
	Tipperary South	1
2 (1921) - 3 (1922)	Tipperary Mid, North & South	4
4 (1923) - 12 (1944)	Tipperary	7
13 (1948) - 20 (1973)	Tipperary North	3
	Tipperary South	4
21 (1977)	Tipperary North	3
	Tipperary South	3
22 (1981) - 27 (1992)	Tipperary North	3
	Tipperary South	4
28 (1997) - 31 (2011)	Tipperary North	3
	Tipperary South	3

	TIPPERARY																
	ALL TDs 1918-2011																
	Surname	**Forename**	**Party**	**Elected**													**Total**
1	Morrissey	Daniel	FG	22	23	27	27	32	33	37	38	43	44	48	51	54	13
2	Breen	Dan	FF	23	32	33	37	38	43	44	48	51	54	57	61		12
3	Treacy	Sean	NP	61	65	69	73	77	81	82	82	87	89	92			11
4	Burke	Seamus	FG	18	21	22	23	27	27	32	33	37					9
5	Fogarty	Andrew	FF	27	27	32	33	37	38	43	44						8
6	O'Kennedy	Michael	FF	69	73	77	82	82	87	89	97						8
7	Davern	Noel	FF	69	73	77	87	89	92	97	02						8
8	Smith	Michael	FF	69	77	81	87	89	92	97	02						8
9	Lowry	Michael	NP	87	89	92	97	02	07	11							7
10	Griffin	Brendan	FG	73	77	81	82	82	87								6
11	Ryan	John	LB	73	77	81	82	82	92								6
12	Mulcahy**	Gen. Richard	FG	44	48	51	54	57									5
13	Ryan	Mary	FF	44	48	51	54	57									5
14	Davern	Michael	FF	48	51	54	57	61									5
15	Fanning	John	FF	51	54	57	61	65									5
16	Hayes	Sean	FF	27	27	32	33										4
17	Ryan	Martin	FF	33	37	38	43										4
18	Dunne	Thomas	FG	61	65	69	73										4
19	McCarthy	Sean	FF	81	82	82	87										4
20	Hayes	Tom	FG	01*	02	07	11										4
21	MacDonagh	Joseph	CR	18	21	22											3
22	Moloney	Patrick	CR	18	21	22											3
23	Heffernan	Michael	F	23	27	27											3
24	Hassett	John	CG	27	27	32											3
25	Ryan	Col. Jeremiah	FG	37	38	43											3
26	Loughman	Francis	FF	38	44	57											3
27	Tierney	Patrick	LB	57	61	65											3
28	Hogan	Patrick	FG	61	65	69											3
29	Fahey**	Jackie	FF	65	69	73											3
30	Molony	David	FG	81	82	82											3
31	Ahearn	Theresa	FG	89	92	97											3
32	Ferris	Michael	LB	89	92	97											3
33	Healy	Seamus	NP	00*	02	11											3
34	Sheehy	Timothy	FF	27S	32												2
35	O'Brien**	William	LB	27J	37												2
36	Curran	Richard	FG	33	38												2
37	O'Donnell	William	CnaT	43	44												2
38	Kinane	Patrick	CnaP	47*	48												2
39	Crowe	Patrick	FG	51	54												2
40	Byrne	Sean	FF	82	82												2
41	Hoctor	Maire	FF	02	07												2
42	Coonan	Noel	FG	07	11												2
43	McGrath	Mattie	FF	07	11												2
44	McCann	Pierce	SF	18													1
45	O'Byrne	Patrick	SF	21													1
46	D'Alton	Louis	CG	23													1
47	MacCurtin	John	CG	23													1
48	Ryan	Patrick	R	23													1
49	Stapleton	Richard	LB	43													1
50	Timoney	John	CnaP	48													1
51	Davern	Donal	FF	65													1
52	Acheson	Carrie	FF	81													1
53	Mansergh	Martin	FF	07													1
54	Kelly	Alan	LB	11													1
	Total 53									***Includes 3 By-Elections**						*	**206**
	**** Also elected in another constituency**																
	Mulcahy**	Gen. Richard	FG	Dublin				18	21	22	23	27	27	32	33	38	9
	Fahey**	Jackie	FF	Waterford				77	81	82	82	87	89				6
T	O'Brien**	William	LB	Dublin				22									1
T	**Included in Tipperary total**																**16**

TIPPERARY 1918-2011																														
* No Contest			FG		LB		FF		SF		GP		WP		CS		PD		C na P		C na T		Farmers		Nat League		Centre P		Others	
Dail		Seats	S	% Vote	S	% Vote	S	% Vote	S	% Vote	S	% Vote	S	% Vote	S	% Vote	S	% Vote	S	% Vote	S	% Vote	S	% Vote	S	% Vote	S	% Vote	S	% Vote
1	1918	4							4																					
2	1921*	4							4																					
3	1922	4	1	32.51%	1	27.30%	2	40.19%																						
4	1923	7	3	39.43%	1	15.61%	2	29.44%															1	12.42%						3.09%
5	1927	7	2	26.61%	2	20.93%	2	28.49%															1	11.25%		5.18%				7.54%
6	1927	7	2	36.90%	1	18.78%	3	34.23%															1	10.09%						
7	1932	7	2	35.29%		4.60%	4	50.28%																					1	9.83%
8	1933	7	2	27.88%		5.93%	4	49.87%																			1	16.33%		
9	1937	7	3	39.94%	1	9.45%	3	44.58%																						6.03%
10	1938	7	3	38.80%		8.85%	4	52.35%																						
11	1943	7	2	25.14%	1	11.30%	3	38.88%													1	10.91%								13.77%
12	1944	7	2	24.70%		10.19%	4	50.86%													1	12.51%								1.75%
13	1948	7	2	22.93%		10.40%	3	45.27%											2	16.34%		5.05%								
14	1951	7	3	30.38%		11.55%	4	47.91%												6.29%										3.87%
15	1954	7	3	33.45%		12.71%	4	49.44%												4.40%										
16	1957	7	1	27.96%	1	14.19%	5	51.12%		4.20%										2.53%										
17	1961	7	2	32.05%	2	20.47%	3	44.37%		3.10%																				
18	1965	7	2	34.32%	2	19.61%	3	46.07%																						
19	1969	7	2	31.72%	1	14.24%	4	52.41%																						1.63%
20	1973	7	2	30.19%	2	19.96%	3	49.85%																						
21	1977	6	1	25.58%	2	19.50%	3	54.37%																						0.55%
22	1981	7	2	28.65%	2	22.26%	3	43.27%																						5.82%
23	1982	7	2	29.01%	2	21.77%	3	48.75%																						0.47%
24	1982	7	2	31.40%	2	21.02%	3	47.58%																						
25	1987	7	2	21.85%		11.20%	4	46.48%		1.17%				0.54%				9.15%											1	9.61%
26	1989	7	2	27.36%	1	20.19%	3	46.51%										1.65%											1	4.28%
27	1992	7	2	27.82%	2	21.74%	2	42.57%		0.82%																			1	7.05%
28	1997	6	1	17.30%	1	13.04%	3	39.94%										1.85%											1	27.87%
29	2002	6	1	19.46%		11.45%	3	40.70%		1.56%						0.15%		1.86%											2	24.82%
30	2007	6	2	18.34%		9.57%	3	39.96%		3.45%		1.31%						1.41%											1	25.97%
31	2011	6	2	28.70%	1	15.71%		14.95%		5.46%		0.87%																	3	34.32%
1918-2011		**203**	**58**	**28.77%**	**28**	**15.02%**	**90**	**43.65%**	**8**	**0.77%**		**0.10%**		**0.02%**		**0.01%**		**0.62%**	**2**	**0.98%**	**2**	**0.93%**	**3**	**1.00%**		**0.16%**	**1**	**0.58%**	**11**	**7.38%**
National		**4,618**	**1,453**	**30.77%**	**482**	**11.53%**	**1,985**	**41.86%**	**232**	**1.99%**	**16**	**0.75%**	**17**	**0.78%**		**0.04%**	**44**	**1.42%**	**18**	**0.77%**	**43**	**1.08%**	**42**	**0.90%**	**10**	**0.24%**	**11**	**0.30%**	**265**	**7.54%**

WATERFORD 2011

"First woman in 59 years elected in Waterford"

There were no changes to the boundaries of this four-seat constituency that compromises almost the entire country of Waterford, excluding only a population of 1,500 north of the Comeragh Mountains.

After Martin Cullen moved from the PDs to Fianna Fail in 1994 this became one of the most predictable constituencies in the country, consistently returning 2 Fianna Fail TDs and 1 each from Fine Gael and Labour.

In 2011 it was clear that Fine Gael would advance to two seats, and it duly did. Maverick John Deasy headed the poll, and an even divide of the Fine Gael vote ensured that running mate Paudie Coffey was not far behind.

Waterford, despite its urban centres, has never been a Labour stronghold. When Tom Kyne won a seat here in 1948 he became the first Labour TD for 25 years, and when he retired in 1977 it took the party 12 years to regain the seat through Brian O'Shea. With O'Shea now retiring himself, there was some concern that the seat could be lost, but the national swing to the party ensured that it was not. Waterford city councillor Séamus Ryan was favourite to take the seat, but he was outpolled by Ciara Conway, who took a seat despite the competition in her Dungarvan base from poll-topper Deasy, being aided by strong Tramore connections. She became the first woman to represent the constituency since the death of Bridget Mary Redmond in 1952.

The main excitement lay in the race for the final seat. With Cullen's retirement due to ill-health in March 2010, Waterford-based Brendan Kenneally – son and grandson of TDs, and not to be confused with the poet of similar name – was the sole Fianna Fail candidate. Even though the party vote share dropped by a massive 32 percentage points, the fifth largest in the country, it seemed that he had a chance, as on first preferences he was over 2,000 votes ahead of his two rivals. However, the main challenger turned out not to be Sinn Fein's David Cullinane, who might have lacked the transfer-friendliness to overhaul Kenneally, but John Halligan, a Waterford city councillor who had run twice with little success for the Workers' Party. Now running as an independent, Halligan trebled his first preference vote, and with the aid of over 2,000 transfers on Cullinane's elimination he sailed past Kenneally to take the final seat with nearly 1,000 votes to spare.

WATERFORD TDs 2011

JOHN DEASY (FG)

Kilrush, Dungarvan, Co. Waterford; Tel: 058 43003; Mobile: 087 2565620
Constituency Office: 1 Coady's Quay, Dungarvan; Tel: 058 43003;
Leinster House: 01 6183596; Email: john.deasy@oireachtas.ie
Website; www.johndeasy.finegael.ie

Born Dungarvan, Co. Waterford, 8th October 1967. Married to Maura Derrane. Educated Coláiste na Rinne, Ring, Dungarvan; St. Augustine's College, Dungarvan; Mercyhurst College, Erie, Pennsylvania, USA (BA History and Communications); UCC (BCL). Former legislative assistant in United States Senate (1990-1992) and in House of Representatives (1993-1995).
First elected 2002 and at each subsequent election.

Member Committee of Public Accounts. Deputy spokesperson on Foreign Affairs, with special responsibility for Overseas Development Aid, 2007-2011. Member Joint Committee on Foreign Affairs 2007-2011. Chairman European Affairs Committee and member Public Accounts Committee 2004-2007. Front bench spokesperson on Justice, Equality and Law Reform, 2002-2004. Member Waterford County Council 1999-2003. Member Dungarvan UDC 1999-2003. Chairman Waterford County Development Board and the strategic policy committee on Housing, Social, Cultural, Heritage and Corporate Affairs. Board member Waterford Regional Airport. Son of Austin Deasy, former Minister for Agriculture 1982-1987, TD for Waterford 1977-2002 and Senator 1973-1977.

PAUDIE COFFEY (FG)

Barr Beithe, Mount Bolton, Portlaw, Co. Waterford, Tel: 051 387295; Mobile; 087 2874015
Constituency Office: 051 835867; Leinster House: 01 6183902;
Email: paudie.coffey@oireachtas.ie; Website: www. paudiecoffey.finegael.ie

Born Waterford, 15th May 1969. Married to Suzanne McAleenan, two daughters, one son. Educated St. Declan's Community College, Kilmacthomas; WRTC (National Craft Certificate); UCD (Cert in Occupational Health and Safety). Former ESB Engineering Officer. Contested 2007 general election in Waterford. First elected 2011.

Member Committee on Environment, Transport, Culture and the Gaeltacht. Elected to Senate in 2007. Seanad spokesperson on Environment, Heritage and Local Government, 2007-2011. Member Joint Committee on the Environment, Heritage and Local Government and Member Joint Committee on Climate Change and Energy Security 2007-2011. Member Waterford County Council 1999-2007. Chairman South East Regional Authority 2006-2007. Member Portlaw Heritage Committee; Tidy Towns Committee, Amateur Musical Society and GAA Club. Member Carrick-on-Suir Golf Club.

CIARA CONWAY (LB)

34 Cluain Garbhan, Abbeyside, Dungarvan, Co. Waterford; Mobile: 086 1022958;
Constituency Office: 058 24514; Leinster House: 01 6184011;
Email: ciara.conway@oireachtas.ie; Website: www. labour.ie/ciaraconway

Born Waterford, 13th August 1980. Single, one daughter. Educated Our Lady of Mercy Secondary School, Waterford; NUI Galway (BA Hons Public and Social Policy); UCC (Masters in Social Work); Waterford IT (Masters in Business Administration); Former Social Worker with Barnados.
Elected at her first attempt in 2011.

Appointed Vice-Chair Committee on Health and Children June 2011. Elected to Dungarvan TC in 2009. Mentor with Abbeyside Ladies Football Club. Member Abbeyside/Ballinacourty GAA Club.

JOHN HALLIGAN (NP)

47 Johns Hill, Waterford; Mobile: 086 2678622; Leinster House: 01 6183498;
Email: john.halligan@oireachtas.ie; Website: www.johnhalligan.net

Born Waterford January 1955. Living with partner, three daughters. Educated Mount Sion Christian Brothers Secondary School. Waterford Technical College. Formerly Radio Operator for Bell Lines and previously a supervisor for Performance Sail Craft. Contested 2002 and 2007 general elections for Workers Party. First elected 2011.

Member Committee on Jobs, Social Protection and Education. First elected to Waterford City Council in 1999 for Workers Party in Waterford No. 3. Retained his seat in 2004. Changed to Independent in 2009 and retained his seat in Waterford City South. Mayor of Waterford 2009/10.

	WATERFORD 2011 FIRST PREFERENCE VOTES						
	Seats	4			10,745		
	Candidate	Party	1st	%	Quota	Count	Status
1	**Deasy, John***	**FG**	**10,718**	**19.95%**	**1.00**	**3**	**Made Quota**
2	**Coffey, Paudie**	**FG**	**9,698**	**18.05%**	**0.90**	**9**	**Made Quota**
3	**Conway, Ciara**	**LB**	**5,554**	**10.34%**	**0.52**	**10**	**Made Quota**
4	**Halligan, John**	**NP**	**5,546**	**10.32%**	**0.52**	**11**	**Elected**
5	Kenneally, Brendan*	FF	7,515	13.99%	0.70	11	Not Elected
6	Cullinane, David	SF	5,342	9.94%	0.50	9	Eliminated
7	Ryan, Seamus	LB	4,638	8.63%	0.43	8	Eliminated
8	Higgins, Tom	NP	1,130	2.10%	0.11	7	No Expenses
9	Collery, Justin	NP	967	1.80%	0.09	7	No Expenses
10	Tobin, Joe	WP	873	1.63%	0.08	6	No Expenses
11	Conway, Joe	NP	725	1.35%	0.07	5	No Expenses
12	Power, Jody	GP	462	0.86%	0.04	4	No Expenses
13	Nutty, Ben	FN	257	0.48%	0.02	3	No Expenses
14	Waters, Declan	NP	222	0.41%	0.02	2	No Expenses
15	Kiersey, Gerard	NP	73	0.14%	0.01	1	No Expenses
15	***Outgoing**		**53,720**	**100.00%**	**10,745**	**2,687**	**No Expenses**

WATERFORD 2011 PARTY VOTE												
	2011					2007					Change	
Party	Cand	1st	%	Quota	Seats	Cand	1st	%	Quota	Seats	%	Seats
FG	2	20,416	38.00%	1.90	2	3	13,552	27.36%	1.37	1	+10.64%	+1
LB	2	10,192	18.97%	0.95	1	1	5,610	11.33%	0.57	1	+7.65%	
FF	1	7,515	13.99%	0.70		3	23,025	46.49%	2.32	2	-32.50%	-2
SF	1	5,342	9.94%	0.50		1	3,327	6.72%	0.34		+3.23%	
GP	1	462	0.86%	0.04		1	1,049	2.12%	0.11		-1.26%	
WP	1	873	1.63%	0.08		1	1,708	3.45%	0.17		-1.82%	
Others	7	8,920	16.60%	0.83	1	3	1,257	2.54%	0.13		+14.07%	+1
Total	**15**	**53,720**	**100.0%**	**10,745**	**4**	**13**	**49,528**	**100.0%**	**9,906**	**4**	**0.00%**	**0**
Electorate		**78,435**	**68.49%**				**73,434**	**67.45%**			**+1.04%**	
Spoiled		**578**	**1.06%**				**430**	**0.86%**			**+0.20%**	
Turnout		**54,298**	**69.23%**				**49,958**	**68.03%**			**+1.20%**	

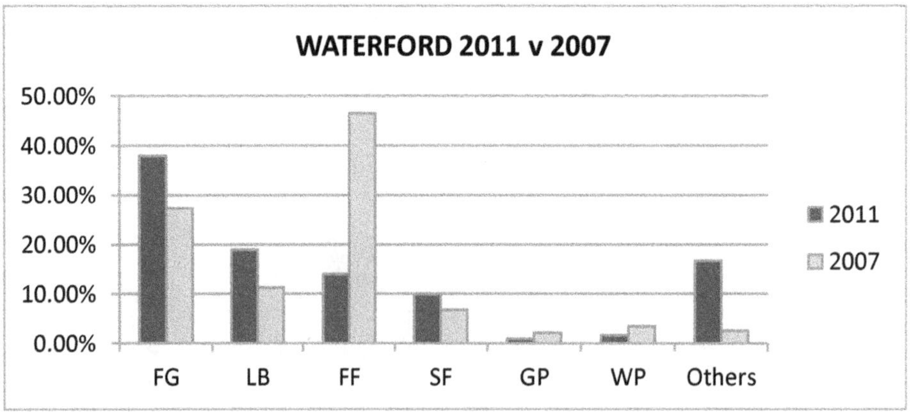

WATERFORD 2011 COUNT DETAILS												
Seats	**4**										**Quota**	**10,745**
Candidate	**Party**	**1st**	**2nd** Kiersey Votes	**3rd** Waters Votes	**4th** Nutty Votes	**5th** Power Votes	**6th** Conway Votes	**7th** Tobin Votes	**8th** Higgins Collery	**9th** Ryan Votes	**10th** Cullinane Votes	**11th** Coffey Surplus
			+13	*+20*								
Deasy, John*	FG	10,718	10,731	10,751	10,751	10,751	10,751	10,751	10,751	10,751	10,751	10,751
			+7	*+32*	*+37*	*+78*	*+147*	*+56*	*+648*	*+533*		*-491*
Coffey, Paudie	FG	9,698	9,705	9,737	9,774	9,852	9,999	10,055	10,703	11,236	11,236	10,745
			+6	*+5*	*+32*	*+111*	*+159*	*+70*	*+487*	*+2,792*	*+1,966*	
Conway, Ciara	LB	5,554	5,560	5,565	5,597	5,708	5,867	5,937	6,424	9,216	11,182	11,182
			+6	*+17*	*+25*	*+45*	*+137*	*+275*	*+397*	*+925*	*+2,229*	*+216*
Halligan, John	NP	5,546	5,552	5,569	5,594	5,639	5,776	6,051	6,448	7,373	9,602	9,818
			+6	*+34*	*+12*	*+33*	*+72*	*+64*	*+232*	*+239*	*+575*	*+63*
Kenneally, Brendan*	FF	7,515	7,521	7,555	7,567	7,600	7,672	7,736	7,968	8,207	8,782	8,845
			+5	*+14*	*+26*	*+27*	*+44*	*+178*	*+232*	*+430*	*-6,298*	
Cullinane, David	SF	5,342	5,347	5,361	5,387	5,414	5,458	5,636	5,868	6,298	Eliminated	
			+6	*+8*	*+12*	*+66*	*+61*	*+180*	*+142*	*-5,113*		
Ryan, Seamus	LB	4,638	4,644	4,652	4,664	4,730	4,791	4,971	5,113	Eliminated		
			+3	*+17*	*+14*	*+37*	*+26*	*+19*	*-1,246*			
Higgins, Tom	NP	1,130	1,133	1,150	1,164	1,201	1,227	1,246	Eliminated			
			+4	*+12*	*+42*	*+50*	*+54*	*+37*	*-1,166*			
Collery, Justin	NP	967	971	983	1,025	1,075	1,129	1,166	Eliminated			
			+5	*+11*	*+17*	*+19*	*+12*	*-937*				
Tobin, Joe	WP	873	878	889	906	925	937	Eliminated				
			+4	*+9*	*+13*	*+11*	*-762*					
Conway, Joe	NP	725	729	738	751	762	Eliminated					
				+3	*+36*	*-501*						
Power, Jody	GP	462	462	465	501	Eliminated						
			+4	*+15*	*-276*							
Nutty, Ben	FN	257	261	276	Eliminated							
			+1	*-223*								
Waters, Declan	NP	222	223	Eliminated								
			-73									
Kiersey, Gerard	NP	73	Eliminated									
			+3	*+26*	*+10*	*+24*	*+50*	*+58*	*+274*	*+194*	*+1,528*	*+212*
Cumulative			3	29	39	63	113	171	445	639	2,167	2,379
Total		**53,720**	**53,720**	**53,720**	**53,720**	**53,720**	**53,720**	**53,720**	**53,720**	**53,720**	**53,720**	**53,720**

WATERFORD 2011									
TRANSFER ANALYSIS									
From	**To**	**FG**	**LB**	**FF**	**SF**	**GP**	**WP**	**Others**	**Non Trans**
FG	491			63				216	212
				12.83%				*43.99%*	*43.18%*
LB	5,113	533	2,792	239	430			925	194
		10.42%	*54.61%*	*4.67%*	*8.41%*			*18.09%*	*3.79%*
SF	6,298		1,966	575				2,229	1,528
			31.22%	*9.13%*				*35.39%*	*24.26%*
GP	501	78	177	33	27		19	143	24
		15.57%	*35.33%*	*6.59%*	*5.39%*		*3.79%*	*28.54%*	*4.79%*
WP	937	56	250	64	178			331	58
		5.98%	*26.68%*	*6.83%*	*19.00%*			*35.33%*	*6.19%*
Others	3,746	904	918	356	321	39	45	800	363
		24.13%	*24.51%*	*9.50%*	*8.57%*	*1.04%*	*1.20%*	*21.36%*	*9.69%*
Total	**17,086**	**1,571**	**6,103**	**1,330**	**956**	**39**	**64**	**4,644**	**2,379**
		9.19%	***35.72%***	***7.78%***	***5.60%***	***0.23%***	***0.37%***	***27.18%***	***13.92%***

WATERFORD		
MAIN BOUNDARY CHANGES		
Dail	**Constituency**	**Seats**
1 (1918)	Waterford County	1
2 (1921) - 3 (1922)	Waterford - Tipperary East	5
4 (1923) - 16 (1957)	Waterford	4
17 (1961) - 20 (1973)	Waterford	3
21 (1977) - 31 (2011)	Waterford	4

WATERFORD														
ALL TDs 1918-2011														
	Surname	**Forename**	**Party**	**Elected**										**Total**
1	Little	Patrick	FF	27	27	32	33	37	38	43	44	48	51	10
2	Deasy	Austin	FG	77	81	82	82	87	89	92	97			8
3	Redmond	Bridget	FG	33	37	38	43	44	48	51				7
4	Kyne	Thomas	LB	48	51	54	57	61	65	73				7
5	Ormonde	John	FF	47*	48	51	54	57	61					6
6	Collins	Edward	FG	69	73	77	81	82	82					6
7	Fahey**	Jackie	FF	77	81	82	82	87	89					6
8	Kenneally	Willie	FF	65	69	73	77	81						5
9	Cullen	Martin	FF	87	92	97	02	07						5
10	O'Shea	Brian	LB	89	92	97	02	07						5
11	White	Vincent	CG	21	22	27	27							4
12	Redmond	Capt. William	CG	23	27	27	32							4
13	Morrissey	Michael	FF	37	38	43	44							4
14	Lynch	Thaddeus	FG	54	57	61	65							4
15	Kenneally	Brendan	FF	89	92	97	07							4
16	Brugha	Cathal	CR	18	21	22								3
17	Wall	Nicholas	FG	23	33	37								3
18	Goulding	Sean	FF	27S	32	33								3
19	Kenneally	William	FF	52*	54	57								3
20	Deasy	John	FG	02	07	11								3
21	Butler	John	LB	22	23									2
22	Brugha	Caitlin	SF	23	27J									2
23	Heskin	Denis	CnaT	43	44									2
24	Browne	Patrick	FF	66*	69									2
25	Dee	Eamon	SF	21										1
26	Drohan	Frank	SF	21										1
27	Robinson	Seamus	SF	21										1
28	Byrne	Daniel J	F	22										1
29	Phelan	Nicholas	LB	22										1
30	Kiersey	John	CG	32										1
31	Broderick**	William	FG	38										1
32	Gallagher	Patrick	WP	82F										1
33	Ormonde	Donal	FF	82N										1
34	Swift	Brian	FF	87										1
35	Wilkinson	Ollie	FF	02										1
36	Coffey	Paudie	FG	11										1
37	Conway	Ciara	LB	11										1
38	Halligan	John	NP	11										1
38	**Total**						***Includes 3 By-Elections**						*	**122**
	**** Also elected in another constituency**													
W	Fahey**	Jackie	FF	Tipperary S			65	69	73					3
	Broderick**	William	FG	Cork East			32	33						2
W	**Included in Waterford total**													**5**

WATERFORD 1918-2011																												
* No Contest			FG		LB		FF		SF		GP		WP		PD		DL		C na P		C na T		Farmers		Nat League		Centre P	Others
Dail		Seats	S	% Vote	S	% Vote	S	% Vote	S	% Vote	S	% Vote	S	% Vote	S	% Vote	S	% Vote	S	% Vote	S	% Vote	S	% Vote	S	% Vote	S	% Vote	S	% Vote
1	1918	1							1																					
2	1921*	5							5																					
3	1922	5	1	19.89%	2	31.28%	1	20.66%															1	17.23%						10.95%
4	1923	4		14.72%	1	18.11%	1	25.38%															1	16.65%					1	25.13%
5	1927	4	1	16.16%		6.63%	1	18.23%	1	11.33%														10.69%	1	24.34%				12.62%
6	1927	4	1	17.43%			2	37.94%																14.28%	1	20.63%				9.71%
7	1932	4	2	46.12%		9.00%	2	44.88%																						
8	1933	4	1	34.11%		2.16%	2	50.21%																			1	13.53%		
9	1937	4	2	42.76%		7.87%	2	47.91%																						1.47%
10	1938	4	2	40.03%		5.60%	2	54.37%																						
11	1943	4	1	25.52%		13.31%	2	46.14%																					1	15.03%
12	1944	4	1	21.61%		9.74%	2	51.62%																					1	17.03%
13	1948	4	1	23.15%	1	17.48%	2	40.83%												7.72%		10.81%								
14	1951	4	1	33.43%	1	19.01%	2	47.56%																						
15	1954	4	1	32.83%	1	20.01%	2	47.17%																						
16	1957	4	1	26.71%	1	18.31%	2	54.98%																						
17	1961	3	1	27.84%	1	29.86%	1	40.04%		2.27%																				
18	1965	3	1	27.25%	1	24.61%	1	48.14%																						
19	1969	3	1	31.84%		21.51%	2	46.66%																						
20	1973	3	1	36.88%	1	16.01%	1	47.12%																						
21	1977	4	2	30.64%		6.29%	2	48.14%						10.56%																4.38%
22	1981	4	2	41.94%		3.73%	2	38.77%		7.63%				7.92%																
23	1982	4	2	37.80%		4.77%	1	39.56%					1	16.05%																1.82%
24	1982	4	2	39.59%		4.11%	2	38.96%						10.68%																6.67%
25	1987	4	1	27.85%		7.53%	2	42.61%		1.70%				7.64%	1	11.99%														0.68%
26	1989	4	1	26.41%	1	18.93%	2	34.77%						11.06%		8.44%														0.38%
27	1992	4	1	22.13%	1	26.14%	1	28.39%		1.19%				6.98%	1	9.34%		2.42%												3.43%
28	1997	4	1	24.55%	1	11.77%	2	35.79%				1.81%		9.24%		6.46%														10.38%
29	2002	4	1	21.48%	1	13.36%	2	46.34%		6.35%		2.92%		2.73%		4.59%														2.24%
30	2007	4	1	27.36%	1	11.33%	2	46.49%		6.72%		2.12%		3.45%																2.54%
31	2011	4	2	38.00%	1	18.97%		13.99%		9.94%		0.86%		1.63%															1	16.60%
1918-2011		**119**	**36**	**29.87%**	**16**	**13.19%**	**48**	**40.51%**	**7**	**1.85%**		**0.33%**	**1**	**3.46%**	**2**	**1.62%**		**0.09%**		**0.24%**		**0.34%**	**2**	**1.74%**	**2**	**1.30%**	**1**	**0.47%**	**4**	**5.00%**
National		**4,618**	**1,453**	**30.77%**	**482**	**11.53%**	**1,985**	**41.86%**	**232**	**1.99%**	**16**	**0.75%**	**17**	**0.78%**	**44**	**1.42%**	**8**	**0.22%**	**18**	**0.77%**	**43**	**1.08%**	**42**	**0.90%**	**10**	**0.24%**	**11**	**0.30%**	**257**	**7.36%**

WEXFORD 2011

"Independent Mick Wallace wins a seat at his first attempt as Fianna Fail lose out"

There were no Constituency Commission boundary changes here since 2007 and it remained a five-seat constituency.

Property developer and independent candidate, Mick Wallace, caused a major surprise in this constituency with his poll-topping performance. He got a remarkable 13,329 first preferences and was well over the quota on the first count. The rest of the results paled into insignificance behind the scale of Wallace's performance.

Fine Gael had targeted three seats in this five-seater but the arrival of Wallace put paid to that ambition. The party vote was up 3 points and with just 2.1 quotas they were unlikely to take more than two seats. Outgoing deputy Michael D'Arcy was the big loser as former deputy Liam Twomey took his seat. Twomey was first elected as an independent TD in 2002. He later joined Fine Gael and was made its health spokesperson but he lost his seat in 2007 to D'Arcy. He made no mistake in this election and he was the leading Fine Gael vote getter with 9,230 first preferences. The final seat was always going to be between himself and D'Arcy and so it proved with Twomey overturning the 2007 result. Chief Whip Paul Kehoe, despite coming third of the three Fine Gael candidates, went on to take the party's first seat when he took the fourth seat on the final count. D'Arcy was in the frame in fourth place on the first count but lost the transfer battle to Twomey. The Gorey man had taken a prominent anti-Kenny position in Fine Gael's attempted leadership coup in June 2010, and ended up on the losing side again in 2011.

The Labour vote was up 7 points but with just 1.2 quotas it was unlikely to improve on its single seat. Brendan Howlin was in second place on the first count with 11,005 first preferences and went on to retain his seat on the fourth count. His running mate Pat Cody had a much more modest performance winning just 4,457 first preferences to leave him well off the pace and out of contention.

The Fianna Fáil vote was down 24 points and with just 1.1 quotas spread over the party's two outgoing deputies, one seat was as much as it could hope for. John Browne was outside the frame in sixth place on the first count and was ahead of running mate Sean Connick. But Browne won the transfer battle and stayed ahead and went on to take the third seat on the final count with the help of 58% of Connick's transfers.

The Sinn Féin vote was down two points on 2007. Anthony Kelly got just 4,353 on the first count and his vote may have been affected by the presence of former party councillor John Dwyer who ran as an independent.

WEXFORD TDs 2011

MICK WALLACE (NP)

Wellingtonbridge, Co. Wexford; Mobile: 087 2454510
Leinster House: 01 6183287; Email: mick.wallace@oireachtas.ie
Website: www.mickwallace.net

Born Wexford November 1955. Divorced three sons, one daughter. Educated St. Augustine's College, Dungarvan Co. Wexford; Good Counsel College, New Ross, Co. Wexford. Builder. Elected at his first attempt in 2011.

Member Select Committee on European Union Affairs. Member Select Committee on Investigations, Oversight and Petitions. Driving force behind Wexford Youths Soccer Club.

BRENDAN HOWLIN (LB)

Whiterock Hill, Wexford,
Constituency Office: Coolcotts, Wexford; Tel: 053 9124036
Department Office: 01 6318102; Email: brendan.howlin@oireachtas.ie
Website: www.brendanhowlin.ie

Born Wexford 9th May 1956. Single. Educated CBS Wexford and St. Patrick's Teacher Training College, Drumcondra, Dublin. Government Minister and former National School Teacher. First elected 1987 and at each subsequent election

Appointed Minister for Public Expenditure and Reform 9th March 2011. Leas-Cheann Comhairle of Dail Eireann 2007-2011. Front bench spokesperson on European Affairs 2010-2011. Front bench spokesperson on Constitutional Matters and Law Reform 2007-2011. Member Joint Committee on European Affairs and the Committee on European Scrutiny 2007-2011. Member Joint Committee on the Constitution and Member Joint Committee on Constitutional Amendment on Children 2007-2011. Spokesperson on Justice 2006-2007. Spokesperson on Enterprise, Trade and Employment 2002-2006. Member Joint Committee on Enterprise and Small Business 2002-2007. Unsuccessful candidate in Labour leadership election in October 2002, following resignation of Ruairi Quinn. Previously beaten by Quinn in leadership contest following resignation of Dick Spring in November 1997. Deputy Leader and spokesperson on the Environment and Local Government 1997-2002. Minister for Health 1993-1994. Minister for the Environment 1994-1997. Chief Whip, Labour Party 1987-1993. Party spokesperson on Health and Youth Affairs 1989-1993; on Health and Women's Rights 1987-1989. Senator 1983-1987. Member Wexford County Council 1985-1993; Wexford Borough Council 1981-1993 (Alderman 1985/1993, Mayor 1986/1987).

JOHN BROWNE (FF)

34 Beechpark, Enniscorthy, Co. Wexford; Tel: 053 8935089; Mobile: 087 2469234
Constituency Office: 6 Court Street, Enniscorthy, Co. Wexford; Tel 053 9235046,
Leinster House: 01 6183094; Email: john.browne@oireachtas.ie
Website: johnbrownetd.ie

Born Marshallstown, Enniscorthy, 1st August 1948. Married to Judy Doyle, one son, three daughters. Educated St. Mary's CBS, Enniscorthy, Co. Wexford. Former Salesman.
First elected November 1982 and at each subsequent election.

Appointed Party spokesperson on Marine and Fisheries April 2011. Chairman Fianna Fail Parliamentary since October 2009. Member Committee on Member's Interests. Member Joint Administration Committee. Minister of State at Department of Agriculture, Fisheries and Food with special responsibility for Fisheries, June 2007-May 2008. Minister of State at Department of Communications, Marine and Natural Resources 2006-2007. Minister of State at Department of Agriculture, Food and Forestry 2004-2006. Minister of State at Department of Communications, Marine and Natural Resources 2002-2004. Minister of State at the Department of the Environment (with special responsibility for Environmental Protection) 1993-1994. Minister of State at the Department of Agriculture and Food (with special responsibility for the Food Industry) 1992-1993. Assistant Chief Whip 1982-1987. Member of Wexford County Council 1979-1992 and 1996-2002. Member of Enniscorthy UDC 1979-1992 and 1996-2002. Member of Wexford Tourism Committee 1979-1992. Member of Gaelic Athletic Association and former Chairman of Shamrocks/Raparees GAA Club, Enniscorthy. Former Wexford inter-county hurler. Nephew of Sean Browne, Fianna Fail TD for Wexford 1957-1961, 1969-1981 and Feb-Nov 1982, Leas Cheann Comhairle 1977-1981, Senator 1961-1969.

LIAM TWOMEY (FG)

Anne Street, Wexford, Co. Wexford; Tel: 053 9146682; Mobile: 087 8267940
Constituency Office: Rosslare Medical Centre, Rosslare Strand, Co. Wexford; Tel: 053 32800
Leinster House: 01 6184299; Email: liam.twomey@oireachtas.ie
Website: www.liamtwomey.org

Born Cork, 3rd April 1967. Married to Dr. Elizabeth O'Sullivan, two sons, one daughter. Educated St. Finbarr's Seminary, Cork; Trinity College, Dublin (MB, BCH, BAO, BA) MICGP; Diploma Geriatric Medicine. General Practitioner. First elected 2002. Lost his seat in 2007. Regained his seat in 2011.

Appointed Vice-Chairman Committee on Finance, Public Expenditure and Reform June 2011. Senator 2007-2011. Fine Gael's Deputy Leader in the Seanad and Spokesperson on Finance 2007-2011. Member Joint Committee on Finance and the Public Service 2007-2011. Elected as an Independent Deputy for Wexford in 2002. Joined Fine Gael in 2004. Fine Gael front bench spokesperson on Health 2004-2007. Member Joint Committee on Finance and the Public Service 2002-2007. PRO Irish College of GP's in Wexford. Branch Chairman IMO in Wexford.

PAUL KEHOE (FG)

Coolteigue, Bree, Enniscorthy, Co. Wexford; Mobile: 087 2021383
Constituency Office: 7 Weafer Street, Enniscorthy; Tel: 053 9243558;
Leinster House: 01 6184473; Email: paul.kehoe@taoiseach.gov.ie
Website: www.paulkehoe.com

Born Wexford 11th January 1973. Married to Brigid O'Connor. Educated St. Mary's CBS, Enniscorthy; Kildalton Agricultural College. Minister of State. Farmer.
First elected 2002 and at each subsequent election.

Appointed Government Chief Whip and Minister of State at the Departments of the Taoiseach and Defence on 9th March 2011. Fine Gael Chief Whip since 2004. Member Committee on Procedure and Privileges. Member Joint Administration Committee. Member Joint Administration Committee and Member Dail Committee on Procedure and Privileges 2007-2011. Deputy spokesperson on Communications, Marine and Natural Resources and Assistant Whip, 2002-2004. Member Joint Committee on Communications, Marine and Natural Resources 2002-2007. Former chairman Macra na Feirme (holder of Macra's National Leadership Award). Member Fleadh Cheoil na hEireann Inish Cortaidh. Former Youth Officer with Wexford GAA. Member Wexford GAA supporters club and the Irish Handicapped Children's Pilgrimage Trust.

	WEXFORD 2011 FIRST PREFERENCE VOTES						
	Seats	**5**			**12,590**		
	Candidate	**Party**	**1st**	**%**	**Quota**	**Count**	**Status**
1	**Wallace, Mick**	**NP**	**13,329**	**17.65%**	**1.06**	**1**	**Made Quota**
2	**Howlin, Brendan***	**LB**	**11,005**	**14.57%**	**0.87**	**4**	**Made Quota**
3	**Browne, John***	**FF**	**7,352**	**9.73%**	**0.58**	**7**	**Made Quota**
4	**Twomey, Dr. Liam #**	**FG**	**9,230**	**12.22%**	**0.73**	**7**	**Elected**
5	**Kehoe, Paul***	**FG**	**8,386**	**11.10%**	**0.67**	**7**	**Elected**
6	D'Arcy, Michael*	FG	8,418	11.14%	0.67	7	Not Elected
7	Connick, Sean*	FF	6,675	8.84%	0.53	6	Eliminated
8	Kelly, Anthony	SF	4,353	5.76%	0.35	4	Eliminated
9	Cody, Pat	LB	4,457	5.90%	0.35	3	Eliminated
10	Dwyer, John	NP	908	1.20%	0.07	2	No Expenses
11	O'Brien, Séamus	PBPA	741	0.98%	0.06	2	No Expenses
12	Forde, Danny	GP	391	0.52%	0.03	2	No Expenses
13	Roseingrave, Siobhán	NP	175	0.23%	0.01	2	No Expenses
14	De Valera, Ruairí	NP	119	0.16%	0.01	2	No Expenses
14	***Outgoing # Former TD**		**75,539**	**100.00%**	**12,590**	**3,147**	**No Expenses**

WEXFORD 2011 PARTY VOTE												
	2011					2007					Change	
Party	Cand	1st	%	Quota	Seats	Cand	1st	%	Quota	Seats	%	Seats
FG	3	26,034	34.46%	2.07	2	3	21,658	31.56%	1.89	2	+2.90%	
LB	2	15,462	20.47%	1.23	1	1	9,445	13.77%	0.83	1	+6.70%	
FF	2	14,027	18.57%	1.11	1	3	28,949	42.19%	2.53	2	-23.62%	-1
SF	1	4,353	5.76%	0.35		1	5,068	7.39%	0.44		-1.62%	
PBPA	1	741	0.98%	0.06							+0.98%	
GP	1	391	0.52%	0.03		1	802	1.17%	0.07		-0.65%	
PD						1	2,162	3.15%	0.19		-3.15%	
Others	4	14,531	19.24%	1.15	1	1	532	0.78%	0.05		+18.46%	+1
Total	**14**	**75,539**	**100.0%**	**12,590**	**5**	**11**	**68,616**	**100.0%**	**11,437**	**5**	**0.00%**	**0**
Electorate		**111,063**	**68.01%**				**103,562**	**66.26%**			**+1.76%**	
Spoiled		**812**	**1.06%**				**827**	**1.19%**			**-0.13%**	
Turnout		**76,351**	**68.75%**				**69,443**	**67.05%**			**+1.69%**	

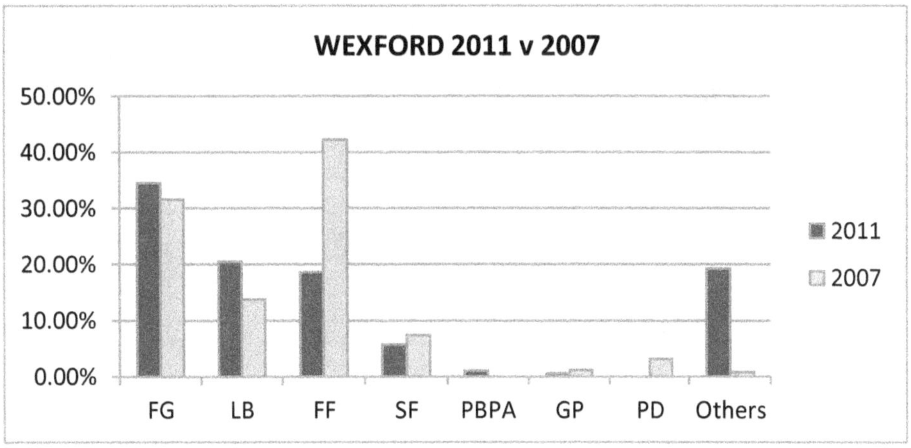

WEXFORD 2011 COUNT DETAILS								
Seats	5						Quota	12,590
Candidate	**Party**	**1st**	**2nd**	**3rd**	**4th**	**5th**	**6th**	**7th**
			Wallace Surplus	Dwyer O'Brien Forde Roseingrave De Valera	Cody Votes	Kelly Votes	Howlin Surplus	Connick Votes
			-739					
Wallace, Mick	NP	13,329	12,590	12,590	12,590	12,590	12,590	12,590
			+161	*+496*	*+2,852*		*-1,924*	
Howlin, Brendan*	LB	11,005	11,166	11,662	14,514	14,514	12,590	12,590
			+42	*+76*	*+279*	*+426*	*+225*	*+4,357*
Browne, John*	FF	7,352	7,394	7,470	7,749	8,175	8,400	12,757
			+119	*+176*	*+168*	*+760*	*+421*	*+722*
Twomey, Dr. Liam #	FG	9,230	9,349	9,525	9,693	10,453	10,874	11,596
			+73	*+168*	*+498*	*+549*	*+582*	*+790*
Kehoe, Paul*	FG	8,386	8,459	8,627	9,125	9,674	10,256	11,046
			+48	*+129*	*+365*	*+532*	*+494*	*+424*
D'Arcy, Michael*	FG	8,418	8,466	8,595	8,960	9,492	9,986	10,410
			+69	*+270*	*+130*	*+252*	*+119*	*-7,515*
Connick, Sean*	FF	6,675	6,744	7,014	7,144	7,396	7,515	Eliminated
			+69	*+479*	*+280*	*-5,181*		
Kelly, Anthony	SF	4,353	4,422	4,901	5,181	Eliminated		
			+48	*+247*	*-4,752*			
Cody, Pat	LB	4,457	4,505	4,752	Eliminated			
			+35	*-943*				
Dwyer, John	NP	908	943	Eliminated				
			+37	*-778*				
O'Brien, Séamus	PBPA	741	778	Eliminated				
			+8	*-399*				
Forde, Danny	GP	391	399	Eliminated				
			+20	*-195*				
Roseingrave, Siobhán	NP	175	195	Eliminated				
			+10	*-129*				
De Valera, Ruairí	NP	119	129	Eliminated				
Non-transferable				*+403*	*+180*	*+2,662*	*+83*	*+1,222*
Cumulative			0	403	583	3,245	3,328	4,550
Total		**75,539**	**75,539**	**75,539**	**75,539**	**75,539**	**75,539**	**75,539**

WEXFORD 2011 TRANSFER ANALYSIS									
From	**To**	**FG**	**LB**	**FF**	**SF**	**PBPA**	**GP**	**Others**	**Non Trans**
LB	6,676	2,528	2,852	753	280				263
		37.87%	*42.72%*	*11.28%*	*4.19%*				*3.94%*
FF	7,515	1,936		4,357					1,222
		25.76%		*57.98%*					*16.26%*
SF	5,181	1,841		678					2,662
		35.53%		*13.09%*					*51.38%*
PBPA	778	151	237	110	152				128
		19.41%	*30.46%*	*14.14%*	*19.54%*				*16.45%*
GP	399	77	121	57	78				66
		19.30%	*30.33%*	*14.29%*	*19.55%*				*16.54%*
NP	2,006	485	594	290	318	37	8	65	209
		24.18%	*29.61%*	*14.46%*	*15.85%*	*1.84%*	*0.40%*	*3.24%*	*10.42%*
Total	**22,555**	**7,018**	**3,804**	**6,245**	**828**	**37**	**8**	**65**	**4,550**
		31.12%	***16.87%***	***27.69%***	***3.67%***	***0.16%***	***0.04%***	***0.29%***	***20.17%***

WEXFORD		
MAIN BOUNDARY CHANGES		
Dail	**Constituency**	**Seats**
1 (1918)	Wexford North	1
	Wexford South	1
2 (1921) - 3 (1922)	Wexford	4
4 (1923) - 16 (1957)	Wexford	5
17 (1961) - 21 (1977)	Wexford	4
22 (1981) - 31 (2011)	Wexford	5

	WEXFORD																			
	ALL TDs 1918-2011																			
	Surname	**Forename**	**Party**	**Elected**																**Total**
1	Ryan	James	FF	18	21	23	27	27	32	33	37	38	43	44	48	51	54	57	61	16
2	Corish	Richard	LB	21	22	23	27	27	32	33	37	38	43	44						11
3	Allen	Denis	FF	27S	32	36*	37	38	43	44	48	51	54	57						11
4	Corish	Brendan	LB	45*	48	51	54	57	61	65	69	73	77	81						11
5	Browne	John	FF	82N	87	89	92	97	02	07	11									8
6	Allen	Lorcan	FF	61	65	69	73	77	81	82F										7
7	Yates	Ivan	FG	81	82	82	87	89	92	97										7
8	Howlin	Brendan	LB	87	89	92	97	02	07	11										7
9	Keating	John	FG	27J	32	33	37	38	44											6
10	Esmonde	Sir Anthony	FG	51	54	57	61	65	69											6
11	D'Arcy	Michael	FG	77	81	82	82	89	97											6
12	Byrne	Hugh	FF	81	82	82	87	92	97											6
13	O'Leary	John	LB	43	44	48	51	54												5
14	Browne	Sean	FF	57	69	73	77	82F												5
15	Esmonde	Osmond	CG	23	27S	32	33													4
16	Esmonde	Sir John	FG	37	38	43	48													4
17	Doyle	Michael	F	22	23	27J														3
18	Doyle	Avril	FG	82N	87	92														3
19	Kehoe	Paul	FG	02	07	11														3
20	Doyle	Seamus	CR	21	22															2
21	Twomey	Liam	NP	02	11															2
22	Sweetman	Roger M	SF	18																1
23	Etchingham**	Sean	SF	21																1
24	O'Callaghan	Daniel	LB	22																1
25	Lambert	Robert	R	23																1
26	Shannon	James	LB	27J																1
27	Jordan	Michael	F	27S																1
28	Kehoe	Patrick	FF	33																1
29	Kennedy	James	FF	65																1
30	Esmonde	John	FG	73																1
31	Cullimore	Seamus	FF	89																1
32	Dempsey	Tony	FF	02																1
33	Connick	Sean	FF	07																1
34	D'Arcy	Michael Jnr.	FG	07																1
35	Wallace	Mick	NP	11																1
35	**Total**													***Includes 2 By-Elections**					*	**147**
	**** Also elected in another constituency**																			
W	Etchingham**	Sean	SF	Wicklow East				18												1
W	**Included in Wexford total**																			

WEXFORD 1918-2011																											
* No Contest		FG		LB		FF		SF		GP		WP		PD		DL		C na P		Nat Lab		Farmers		Nat League		Others	
Dail	Seats	S	% Vote	S	% Vote	S	% Vote	S	% Vote	S	% Vote	S	% Vote	S	% Vote	S	% Vote	S	% Vote	S	% Vote	S	% Vote	S	% Vote	S	% Vote
1 1918	2							2																			
2 1921*	4							4																			
3 1922	4		7.19%	2	42.23%	1	26.95%															1	23.62%				
4 1923	5	1	17.61%	1	27.45%	2	27.07%															1	24.04%				3.82%
5 1927	5		12.03%	2	25.98%	1	27.95%															1	18.87%	1	15.16%		
6 1927	5	1	16.25%	1	24.35%	2	33.85%															1	18.77%		6.78%		
7 1932	5	2	27.39%	1	21.06%	2	43.85%																				7.70%
8 1933	5	2	33.80%	1	17.33%	2	41.27%																				7.61%
9 1937	5	2	35.29%	1	17.99%	2	46.72%																				
10 1938	5	2	32.80%	1	19.61%	2	47.59%																				
11 1943	5	1	30.21%	2	29.72%	2	40.07%																				
12 1944	5	1	26.12%	1	13.10%	2	42.15%													1	18.62%						
13 1948	5	1	19.61%	1	17.19%	2	37.82%												8.24%	1	13.05%						4.10%
14 1951	5	1	23.67%	2	32.46%	2	41.88%												1.99%								
15 1954	5	1	27.04%	2	31.59%	2	41.37%																				
16 1957	5	1	18.17%	1	29.80%	3	50.03%																				2.00%
17 1961	4	1	24.89%	1	28.84%	2	39.94%		3.82%																		2.51%
18 1965	4	1	26.73%	1	32.26%	2	41.01%																				
19 1969	4	1	27.22%	1	28.98%	2	39.23%																				4.57%
20 1973	4	1	30.25%	1	28.12%	2	41.63%																				
21 1977	4	1	25.67%	1	25.59%	2	48.74%																				
22 1981	5	2	36.17%	1	13.63%	2	48.23%																				1.97%
23 1982	5	2	37.66%		9.62%	3	48.59%		3.32%																		0.81%
24 1982	5	3	41.42%		9.85%	2	46.17%						1.83%														0.72%
25 1987	5	2	31.71%	1	9.61%	2	43.90%						2.36%		8.90%												3.52%
26 1989	5	2	32.97%	1	18.03%	2	45.78%						2.04%		1.17%												
27 1992	5	2	34.47%	1	19.82%	2	42.44%		0.79%								1.53%										0.96%
28 1997	5	2	38.58%	1	17.08%	2	38.95%				1.68%						2.61%										1.11%
29 2002	5	1	25.74%	1	13.23%	2	40.09%		8.22%																	1	12.72%
30 2007	5	2	31.56%	1	13.77%	2	42.19%		7.39%		1.17%				3.15%												0.78%
31 2011	5	2	34.46%	1	20.47%	1	18.57%		5.76%		0.52%															1	20.22%
1918-2011	**145**	**41**	**28.77%**	**32**	**20.98%**	**57**	**40.35%**	**6**	**1.32%**		**0.16%**		**0.24%**		**0.56%**		**0.17%**		**0.32%**	**2**	**1.01%**	**4**	**2.37%**	**1**	**0.65%**	**2**	**3.10%**
National	**4,618**	**1,453**	**30.77%**	**482**	**11.53%**	**1,985**	**41.86%**	**232**	**1.99%**	**16**	**0.75%**	**17**	**0.78%**	**44**	**1.42%**	**8**	**0.22%**	**18**	**0.77%**	**9**	**0.16%**	**42**	**0.90%**	**10**	**0.24%**	**302**	**8.59%**

WICKLOW 2011

"Fine Gael emerges as the dominant party to take three seats."

There were no boundary change here since 2007 but with 24 candidates, the most in the country, this was always likely to be a long count. So it was, with demands for recounts protracting matters further. As well as the five candidates elected, the constituency can claim a sixth TD, as Pat Deering, the Fine Gael TD for Carlow–Kilkenny, lives in the area of east Carlow that, to the resentment of its inhabitants, makes up part of the Wicklow constituency.

Fine Gael emerged as the dominant party, winning close to 40 per cent of the votes and three of the five seats. In 2002 it had been down to 16 per cent and one seat, so this represented very impressive growth. Andrew Doyle, first elected in 2007, headed the poll, Billy Timmins was second home, and yet another case of good Fine Gael vote management meant that the youthful newcomer Simon Harris came in third.

Labour suffered from the retirement of former deputy leader Liz McManus. The party's vote scarcely rose compared with 2007, and its three candidates made heavy weather of holding the seat in a constituency where in 2002, when the national conditions were much less favourable, it had come within 20 votes of taking two seats. Despite receiving fewer than half of running mate Tom Fortune's transfers on the sixteenth count, Anne Ferris took the fourth seat quite securely.

Fianna Fail had won 2 seats in 2007, but one of these disappeared quite quickly when Joe Behan left the party in October 2008. He stood now as an independent but was never in the race. Fianna Fail ran two candidates, outgoing TD and junior minister Dick Roche being joined on the ticket by Councillor Pat Fitzgerald from Arklow. Although Roche led on first preferences, Fitzgerald overhauled him. The elimination on the fourteenth count of Roche, whose combative style as a politician was not to everyone's liking, produced wild applause among supporters of other parties in the counting centre.

With only 11 per cent of the votes Fianna Fail was well short of a seat, and the fifth seat lay between Sinn Fein's John Brady and independent Stephen Donnelly. Brady led on first preferences, but Donnelly, who used his media appearances impressively during the campaign, fared better on transfers and took the last seat by just over 100 votes.

WICKLOW TDs 2011

ANDREW DOYLE (FG)

Lickeen, Roundwood, Co. Wicklow; Tel: 0404 45404; Mobile: 086 837009
Constituency Office: 2A The Lower Mall, Wicklow; Tel: 0404 66622;
Leinster House: 01 6183611; Email: andrew.doyle@oireachtas.ie,
Website: www. andrewdoyle.ie

Born Dublin, 2nd July 1960. Married to Ann Smith, three sons, one daughter. Educated De La Salle, Wicklow Town; Rockwell Agriculture College Farm Apprenticeship Scheme, Farm Management Diploma. Farmer. First elected 2007. Retained his seat in 2011.

Appointed Chairman Committee on Communications, Natural Resources and Agriculture June 2011. Member Joint Administration Committee. Front bench spokesperson on Agriculture, Fisheries & Food 2010-2011. Deputy spokesperson on Agriculture with special responsibility for Food and Horticulture, 2007- 2010. Member Joint Committee on Agriculture, Fisheries and Food and Member Joint Committee on Climate Change and Energy Security 2007-2011. Member Wicklow County Council 1999-2007 (Chairman 2005-2006). Member Wicklow's Uplands Council; Wicklow Working Together; Rathdrum Community Resource Committee (Acorn) and the Health Board Authority.

BILLY TIMMINS (FG)

Sruhaun, Baltinglass, Co. Wicklow; Tel: 059 6481655; Mobile: 087 8159090
Constituency Office: Weaver Square, Baltinglass; Tel: 059 6481016;
Leinster House: Tel: 01 6183384; E-mail: billy.timmins@oireachtas.ie
Website: www.billytimmins.com

Born Baltinglass, 1st October 1959. Married to Madeleine Hyland, two sons, three daughters. Educated Patrician College, Ballyfin, Co. Laois; UCG (BA Diploma in Public Relations and Marketing). Former Army Officer. First elected 1997 and at each subsequent election.

Member Committee on Finance, Public Expenditure and Reform. Member Committee on Justice, Defence and Equality. Supported Richard Bruton in his failed attempt to oust Enda Kenny as party leader in June 2010. Fine Gael spokesperson on Foreign Affairs September 2007-June 2010. Member Joint Committee on Foreign Affairs and Member Joint Committee on European Affairs 2007-2011. Front bench spokesperson on Defence 2004-2007. Front bench spokesperson on Agriculture and Food, 2002-2004. Member Joint Committee on Agriculture and Food 2002-2007. Deputy spokesperson on Justice and Defence 2001-2002. Spokesperson on Housing 2000-2001. Junior spokesperson on Defence, Peacekeeping and Humanitarian Relief 1997-2000. Member National Economic and Social Forum. Former Army Officer and has served overseas with the United Nations in Lebanon and Cyprus. Holds ten Senior Football Championship Medals and one Leinster and All Ireland Club Medals. Son of Godfrey Timmins, Dáil Deputy for Wicklow 1968-1987, 1989-1997.

SIMON HARRIS (FG)

79 Redford Park, Greystones, Co. Wicklow; Tel:01 2764619; Mobile: 086 0759984
Leinster House: 01 6183805; Email: simon.harris@oireachtas.ie
Website: www.simonharris.ie

Born Dublin 17th October 1986. Single. Educated St. David's Secondary School, Greystones, Co. Wicklow; DIT Aungier Street (Journalism). Formerly Parliamentary Assistant to Frances Fitzgerald. Elected at his first attempt in 2011.

Member Public Accounts Committee. First elected to Wicklow County Council in Greystones electoral area in 2009. Elected to Greystones TC in 2004 and 2009. Established an Autism support and lobby group, the Wicklow Triple A Alliance, to provide support to families living with autism. Awarded a Greystones Person of the Year award in 2002 in recognition of his work as a disability advocate.

ANNE FERRIS (LB)

10 Seapoint Court, Bray, Co. Wicklow; Tel:01 2865144; Mobile: 086 2364780
Constituency Office: 115 Main Street, Bray, Co. Wicklow; Tel: 01 2764699
Leinster House: 01 6183539; Email: anne.ferris@oireachtas.ie
Website: www.labour.ie/anneferris

Born Dublin 24th September 1954. Divorced; in long-term relationship, three daughters. Educated Goldenbridge Secondary School, Inchicore; Maynooth College (Diploma in Women's Studies). Worked in Liz McManus's Bray office for 18 years. Elected at her first attempt in 2011.

Appointed Vice-Chair Committee on Justice, Defence and Equality December 2011. Member Public Accounts Committee. Co-opted onto Wicklow County Council as replacement for Liz McManus TD in 2003. Retained her seat in 2004. Chairperson Wicklow County Council 2007. Co-opted onto Bray TC in 1995 and retained her seat in 1999 and 2004. Former member Wicklow VEC. Director Mermaid Arts Centre and Bray Tourism. Formerly Director of Bray Chamber of Commerce. SIPTU member.

STEPHEN DONNELLY (NP)

Greystones, Co. Wicklow; Mobile: 086 0513493
Leinster House: 01 6184293; Email: stephen.donnelly@oireachtas.ie
Website: www.stephendonnelly.ie

Born Dublin 19th February 1975. Married to Susan Leavy, two sons. Educated St. David's Secondary School, Greystones, Co. Wicklow; UCD (BE Mechanical Engineering); MIT in Boston (Engineering); Harvard (Master in Public Administration in International Development). Formerly Managing Consultant with McKinsey & Company and the London-based consulting firm Eden McCallum. Elected at his first attempt in 2011.

Member Committee on Finance, Public Expenditure and Reform.

WICKLOW 2011							
FIRST PREFERENCE VOTES							
	Seats	5			11,751		
	Candidate	Party	1st	%	Quota	Count	Status
1	**Doyle, Andrew***	**FG**	**10,035**	**14.23%**	**0.85**	**16**	**Made Quota**
2	**Timmins, Billy***	**FG**	**9,165**	**13.00%**	**0.78**	**17**	**Made Quota**
3	**Harris, Simon**	**FG**	**8,726**	**12.38%**	**0.74**	**19**	**Elected**
4	**Ferris, Anne**	**LB**	**5,436**	**7.71%**	**0.46**	**19**	**Elected**
5	**Donnelly, Stephen**	**NP**	**6,530**	**9.26%**	**0.56**	**19**	**Elected**
6	Brady, John	SF	7,089	10.06%	0.60	19	Not Elected
7	Fitzgerald, Pat	FF	3,576	5.07%	0.30	16	Eliminated
8	Fortune, Tom	LB	3,420	4.85%	0.29	15	Eliminated
9	Behan, Joe*	NP	4,197	5.95%	0.36	14	Eliminated
10	Roche, Dick*	FF	3,891	5.52%	0.33	13	Eliminated
11	Kavanagh, Conal	LB	3,231	4.58%	0.27	12	Eliminated
12	Dempsey, Peter	NP	1,409	2.00%	0.12	11	No Expenses
13	Byrne, Niall	GP	1,026	1.46%	0.09	11	No Expenses
14	Kelly, Nicky	NP	518	0.73%	0.04	10	No Expenses
15	Kiernan, Donal	NP	403	0.57%	0.03	10	No Expenses
16	Kinsella, Gerry	FN	324	0.46%	0.03	9	No Expenses
17	Kavanagh, Pat	FN	291	0.41%	0.02	8	No Expenses
18	Finnegan, Eugene	NP	286	0.41%	0.02	7	No Expenses
19	Keddy, Charlie	NP	233	0.33%	0.02	6	No Expenses
20	Mulvihill, Michael	NP	187	0.27%	0.02	5	No Expenses
21	Fitzgerald, Anthony	NP	184	0.26%	0.02	4	No Expenses
22	Tallon, Jim	NP	166	0.24%	0.01	3	No Expenses
23	Clarke, Thomas	NP	103	0.15%	0.01	2	No Expenses
24	Carroll, Kevin	NP	74	0.10%	0.01	1	No Expenses
24	***Outgoing**		**70,500**	**100.00%**	**11,751**	**2,938**	**No Expenses**

WICKLOW 2011								
TRANSFER ANALYSIS								
From	To	FG	LB	FF	SF	GP	Others	Non Trans
FG	356	120	122		57		57	
		33.71%	*34.27%*		*16.01%*		*16.01%*	
LB	8,785	2,140	4,606	258	622		603	556
		24.36%	*52.43%*	*2.94%*	*7.08%*		*6.86%*	*6.33%*
FF	11,133	2,453	940	2,296	900		1,377	3,167
		22.03%	*8.44%*	*20.62%*	*8.08%*		*12.37%*	*28.45%*
GP	1,113	257	233	174	109		245	95
		23.09%	*20.93%*	*15.63%*	*9.79%*		*22.01%*	*8.54%*
NP	9,693	2,474	1,867	938	1,077	87	2,472	778
		25.52%	*19.26%*	*9.68%*	*11.11%*	*0.90%*	*25.50%*	*8.03%*
Total	**31,080**	**7,444**	**7,768**	**3,666**	**2,765**	**87**	**4,754**	**4,596**
		23.95%	***24.99%***	***11.80%***	***8.90%***	***0.28%***	***15.30%***	***14.79%***

WICKLOW 2011												
PARTY VOTE												
	2011					2007					Change	
Party	Cand	1st	%	Quota	Seats	Cand	1st	%	Quota	Seats	%	Seats
FG	3	27,926	39.61%	2.38	3	2	15,033	23.15%	1.39	2	+16.46%	+1
LB	3	12,087	17.14%	1.03	1	2	10,608	16.34%	0.98	1	+0.81%	
FF	2	7,467	10.59%	0.64		3	24,706	38.05%	2.28	2	-27.46%	-2
SF	1	7,089	10.06%	0.60		1	3,234	4.98%	0.30		+5.07%	
GP	1	1,026	1.46%	0.09		1	4,790	7.38%	0.44		-5.92%	
PD						1	903	1.39%	0.08		-1.39%	
Others	14	14,905	21.14%	1.27	1	5	5,651	8.70%	0.52		+12.44%	+1
Total	**24**	**70,500**	**100.0%**	**11,751**	**5**	**15**	**64,925**	**100.0%**	**10,821**	**5**	**0.00%**	**0**
Electorate		**95,341**	**73.95%**				**91,492**	**70.96%**			**+2.98%**	
Spoiled		**811**	**1.14%**				**554**	**0.85%**			**+0.29%**	
Turnout		**71,311**	**74.80%**				**65,479**	**71.57%**			**+3.23%**	

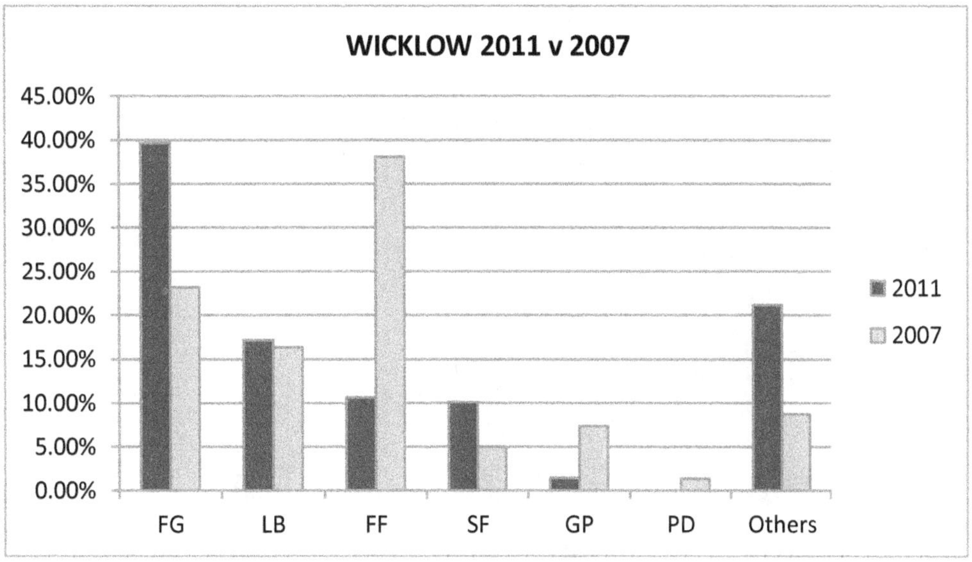

WICKLOW 2011
COUNT DETAILS

Seats 5 | Quota 11,751

Candidate	Party	1st	2nd Carroll Votes	3rd Clarke Votes	4th Tallon Votes	5th Fitzgerald Votes	6th Mulvihill Votes	7th Keddy Votes	8th Finnegan Votes	9th Kavanagh Votes	10th Kinsella Votes	11th Kelly Kiernan	12th Dempsey Byrne	13th Kavanagh Votes	14th Roche Votes	15th Behan Votes	16th Fortune Votes	17th Fitzgerald Votes	18th Doyle Surplus	19th Timmins Surplus
			+3	+2	+16	+14	+36	+11	+16	+18	+56	+57	+302	+316	+205	+535	+369		-240	
Doyle, Andrew*	FG	10,035	10,038	10,040	10,056	10,070	10,106	10,117	10,133	10,151	10,207	10,264	10,566	10,882	11,087	11,622	11,991	11,991	11,751	11,751
			+2	+4	+10	+13	+8	+11	+11	+17	+12	+67	+147	+289	+428	+266	+279	+1,138		-116
Timmins, Billy*	FG	9,165	9,167	9,171	9,181	9,194	9,202	9,213	9,224	9,241	9,253	9,320	9,467	9,756	10,184	10,450	10,729	11,867	11,867	11,751
			+3	+6	+6	+11	+3	+37	+46	+9	+25	+66	+195	+120	+191	+690	+767	+491	+67	+53
Harris, Simon	FG	8,726	8,729	8,735	8,741	8,752	8,755	8,792	8,838	8,847	8,872	8,938	9,133	9,253	9,444	10,134	10,901	11,392	11,459	11,512
			+3	+13	+4	+13	+7	+5	+33	+45	+18	+80	+340	+928	+111	+677	+2,530	+705	+94	+28
Ferris, Anne	LB	5,436	5,439	5,452	5,456	5,469	5,476	5,481	5,514	5,559	5,577	5,657	5,997	6,925	7,036	7,713	10,243	10,948	11,042	11,070
			+6	+21	+14	+33	+20	+23	+45	+40	+60	+127	+470	+119	+162	+906	+404	+929	+37	+20
Donnelly, Stephen	NP	6,530	6,536	6,557	6,571	6,604	6,624	6,647	6,692	6,732	6,792	6,919	7,389	7,508	7,670	8,576	8,980	9,909	9,946	9,966
			+1	+9	+16	+5	+24	+19	+24	+33	+49	+135	+272	+211	+140	+599	+411	+760	+42	+15
Brady, John	SF	7,089	7,090	7,099	7,115	7,120	7,144	7,163	7,187	7,220	7,269	7,404	7,676	7,887	8,027	8,626	9,037	9,797	9,839	9,854
					+16	+6	+6	+7	+2	+3	+2	+54	+388	+80	+2,296	+462	+106	-7,004		
Fitzgerald, Pat	FF	3,576	3,576	3,576	3,592	3,598	3,604	3,611	3,613	3,616	3,618	3,672	4,060	4,140	6,436	6,898	7,004	Eliminated		
			+1	+2		+4	+8	+33	+14	+13	+12	+44	+108	+1,148	+124	+351	-5,282			
Fortune, Tom	LB	3,420	3,421	3,423	3,423	3,427	3,435	3,468	3,482	3,495	3,507	3,551	3,659	4,807	4,931	5,282	Eliminated			
			+3	+7	+3	+13	+8	+14	+32	+13	+22	+95	+144	+80	+286	-4,917				
Behan, Joe*	NP	4,197	4,200	4,207	4,210	4,223	4,231	4,245	4,277	4,290	4,312	4,407	4,551	4,631	4,917	Eliminated				
				+4	+3	+23	+5	+18	+20	+3	+10	+33	+47	+72	-4,129					
Roche, Dick*	FF	3,891	3,891	3,895	3,898	3,921	3,926	3,944	3,964	3,967	3,977	4,010	4,057	4,129	Eliminated					
			+3	+3	+6	+6	+11	+12	+8	+16	+21	+52	+134	-3,503						
Kavanagh, Conal	LB	3,231	3,234	3,237	3,243	3,249	3,260	3,272	3,280	3,296	3,317	3,369	3,503	Eliminated						
			+6	+19	+20	+6	+8	+10	+8	+11	+19	+157	-1,673							
Dempsey, Peter	NP	1,409	1,415	1,434	1,454	1,460	1,468	1,478	1,486	1,497	1,516	1,673	Eliminated							
			+1	+4	+2	+5	+4	+3	+9	+19	+19	+21	-1,113							
Byrne, Niall	GP	1,026	1,027	1,031	1,033	1,038	1,042	1,045	1,054	1,073	1,092	1,113	Eliminated							
			+4	+1	+11	+2	+6	+7	+7	+15	+14	-585								
Kelly, Nicky	NP	518	522	523	534	536	542	549	556	571	585	Eliminated								
			+2		+1	+9	+4	+14	+11	+12	+16	-472								
Kiernan, Donal	NP	403	405	405	406	415	419	433	444	456	472	Eliminated								
			+1	+2	+4	+4	+11	+13	+3	+32	-394									
Kinsella, Gerry	FN	324	325	327	331	335	346	359	362	394	Eliminated									
			+2	+5	+2	+2	+11	+9	+5	-327										
Kavanagh, Pat	FN	291	293	298	300	302	313	322	327	Eliminated										
			+2	+5	+2	+8	+2	+4	-309											
Finnegan, Eugene	NP	286	288	293	295	303	305	309	Eliminated											
			+3	+5	+20	+1	+4	-266												
Keddy, Charlie	NP	233	236	241	261	262	266	Eliminated												
			+1	+3	+4	+1	-196													
Mulvihill, Michael	NP	187	188	191	195	196	Eliminated													
				+1	+1	-186														
Fitzgerald, Anthony	NP	184	184	185	186	Eliminated														
				+3	-169															
Tallon, Jim	NP	166	166	169	Eliminated															
			+22	-125																
Clarke, Thomas	NP	103	125	Eliminated																
			-74																	
Carroll, Kevin	NP	74	Eliminated																	
Non-transferable			+5	+6	+8	+7	+10	+16	+15	+28	+39	+69	+239	+140	+186	+431	+416	+2,981		
Cumulative			5	11	19	26	36	52	67	95	134	203	442	582	768	1,199	1,615	4,596	4,596	4,596
Total		70,500	70,500	70,500	70,500	70,500	70,500	70,500	70,500	70,500	70,500	70,500	70,500	70,500	70,500	70,500	70,500	70,500	70,500	70,500

WICKLOW		
MAIN BOUNDARY CHANGES		
Dail	**Constituency**	**Seats**
1 (1918)	Wicklow East	1
	Wicklow West	1
2 (1921) - 3 (1922)	Kildare - Wicklow	5
4 (1923) - 21 (1977)	Wicklow	3
22 (1981) - 26 (1989)	Wicklow	4
27 (1992) - 31 (2011)	Wicklow	5

WICKLOW																				
ALL TDs 1918-2011																				
	Surname	**Forename**	**Party**	**Elected**																**Total**
1	Everett	James	LB	22	23	27	27	32	33	37	38	43	44	48	51	54	57	61	65	16
2	Timmins	Godfrey	FG	68*	69	73	77	81	82	82	89	92								9
3	Kavanagh	Liam	LB	69	73	77	81	82	82	87	89	92								9
4	Brennan	Paudge	FF	54	57	61	65	69	81	82N										7
5	Moore	Seamus	FF	27	27	32	33	37	38											6
6	O'Mahony	Dermot	FG	27	27	32	33	37												5
7	Cogan	Patrick	NP	38	43	44	48	51												5
8	Jacob	Joe	FF	87	89	92	97	02												5
9	Roche	Dick	FF	87	89	97	02	07												5
10	Byrne	Christopher	FF	21	22	23	43													4
11	Murphy	Ciaran	FF	73	77	81	82F													4
12	McManus	Liz	LB	92	97	02	07													4
13	Timmins	Billy	FG	97	02	07	11													4
14	Barton	Robert C	CR	18	21	22														3
15	Brennan	Thomas	FF	44	48	51														3
16	Hussey	Gemma	FG	82	82	87														3
17	Fox	Mildred	NP	95*	97	02														3
18	Wilson	Richard	F	22	23															2
19	Deering	Mark	FG	53*	54															2
20	O'Higgins**	Michael	FG	61	65															2
21	Doyle	Andrew	FG	07	11															2
22	Etchingham**	Sean	SF	18																1
23	Buckley**	Donal	SF	21																1
24	Childers	Erskine R	SF	21																1
25	O'Connor**	Art	SF	21																1
26	Colohan**	Hugh	LB	22																1
27	O'Toole	Seamus	FF	57																1
28	Fox	Johnny	NP	92																1
29	Behan	Joe	FF	07																1
30	Harris	Simon	FG	11																1
31	Ferris	Anne	LB	11																1
32	Donnelly	Stephen	NP	11																1
32	**Total**													***Includes 3 By-Elections**					*	**114**
	**** Also elected in another constituency**																			
	Buckley**	Donal	SF	Kildare			18	27	27											3
	Colohan**	Hugh	LB	Kildare			23	27	27											3
	O'Higgins**	Michael	FG	Dublin SW			48	54	57											3
	Etchingham**	Sean	SF	Wexford			21													1
W	O'Connor**	Art	SF	Kildare			18													1
W	**Included in Wicklow total**																			**11**

WICKLOW 1918-2011

* No Contest			FG		LB		FF		SF		GP		WP		PD		DL		C na P		C na T		Nat Lab		Farmers		Nat League		Centre P		Others	
Dail		Seats	S	% Vote	S	% Vote	S	% Vote	S	% Vote	S	% Vote	S	% Vote	S	% Vote	S	% Vote	S	% Vote	S	% Vote	S	% Vote	S	% Vote	S	% Vote	S	% Vote	S	% Vote
1	1918	2							2																							
2	1921*	5							5																							
3	1922	5	1	26.57%	2	36.26%	1	19.03%																	1	18.14%						
4	1923	3	1	34.64%	1	23.06%		18.42%																	1	18.70%						5.19%
5	1927	3	1	16.47%	1	28.85%	1	21.73%																		12.62%		9.11%				11.22%
6	1927	3	1	27.82%	1	22.05%	1	23.23%																		11.64%						15.25%
7	1932	3	1	33.83%	1	23.48%	1	26.20%																								16.49%
8	1933	3	1	26.74%	1	23.63%	1	31.80%																						17.83%		
9	1937	3	1	23.03%	1	29.35%	1	32.04%																								15.58%
10	1938	3		20.20%	1	28.30%	1	33.08%																							1	18.41%
11	1943	3		21.50%	1	30.86%	1	29.27%													1	18.37%										
12	1944	3		13.65%		5.80%	1	36.43%													1	17.38%	1	19.20%								7.54%
13	1948	3		14.90%		7.83%	1	35.22%												10.09%			1	18.28%							1	13.68%
14	1951	3		14.34%	1	24.21%	1	45.33%																							1	16.11%
15	1954	3	1	33.65%	1	26.29%	1	40.05%																								
16	1957	3		23.10%	1	22.94%	2	53.96%																								
17	1961	3	1	29.43%	1	23.83%	1	43.86%																								2.88%
18	1965	3	1	28.93%	1	23.04%	1	48.03%																								
19	1969	3	1	33.74%	1	23.18%	1	43.08%																								
20	1973	3	1	33.26%	1	14.65%	1	36.96%		6.66%																						8.47%
21	1977	3	1	27.95%	1	19.81%	1	45.62%						3.73%																		2.89%
22	1981	4	1	34.95%	1	14.36%	2	41.50%						7.24%																		1.95%
23	1982	4	2	36.23%	1	20.04%	1	36.49%						6.84%																		0.41%
24	1982	4	2	36.76%	1	18.29%	1	35.68%						8.17%																		1.10%
25	1987	4	1	26.49%	1	16.86%	2	32.58%				1.43%		7.63%		11.85%																3.17%
26	1989	4	1	28.26%	1	20.13%	2	38.08%						4.83%		4.97%																3.73%
27	1992	5	1	17.71%	1	22.82%	1	25.25%		0.92%		2.59%		0.27%		2.63%	1	10.62%													1	17.18%
28	1997	5	1	19.71%		13.80%	2	29.87%				2.48%				3.30%	1	9.99%													1	20.84%
29	2002	5	1	15.95%	1	29.61%	2	31.25%		2.80%		5.88%																			1	14.51%
30	2007	5	2	23.15%	1	16.34%	2	38.05%		4.98%		7.38%				1.39%																8.70%
31	2011	5	3	39.61%	1	17.14%		10.59%		10.06%		1.46%																			1	21.14%
1918-2011		**111**	**28**	**26.54%**	**27**	**21.10%**	**34**	**32.83%**	**7**	**1.40%**		**1.21%**		**1.57%**		**1.13%**	**2**	**1.05%**		**0.26%**	**2**	**0.94%**	**2**	**0.96%**	**2**	**1.61%**		**0.22%**		**0.49%**	**7**	**8.68%**
National		**4,618**	**1,453**	**30.77%**	**482**	**11.53%**	**1,985**	**41.86%**	**232**	**1.99%**	**16**	**0.75%**	**17**	**0.78%**	**44**	**1.42%**	**8**	**0.22%**	**18**	**0.77%**	**43**	**1.08%**	**9**	**0.16%**	**42**	**0.90%**	**10**	**0.24%**	**11**	**0.30%**	**248**	**7.20%**

PART 2

GENERAL ELECTION

FOR

31st DAIL

POLLING DATE: Thursday 25th February, 2007

SUMMARIES

DAIL CONSTITUENCY COMMISSION REPORT 2007

The commission recommended that the total membership of Dail Eireann should remain at 166 and that the seats should be arranged in 43 constituencies (43 at present).

There should be an increase of one seat in Dáil representation in both the Louth (4 to 5 seats) and Dublin West (3 to 4) constituencies, together with changes in the areas covered by the constituencies.

There should be a reduction of one seat in Dáil representation in both the Dún Laoghaire (5 to 4 seats) and Limerick East (5 to 4) constituencies, with the latter to be renamed as Limerick City; changes in the areas covered by the constituencies are also recommended.

Revisions should be made to 20 other constituencies – Cork East, Cork North-Central, Cork North-West, Donegal North-East, Donegal South-West, Dublin North, Dublin North-Central, Dublin North-East, Dublin South, Kerry North, Kerry South, Kildare North, Kildare South, Laois-Offaly, Limerick West, Meath East, Meath West, Roscommon-South Leitrim, Sligo-North Leitrim and Tipperary North.

The revisions proposed above involve changes in the area of the constituencies concerned. In addition, it is recommended that the names of the Kerry North and Limerick West constituencies should be amended to Kerry North-West Limerick and Limerick respectively.

There were no changes in 19 constituencies (Carlow-Kilkenny, Cavan-Monaghan, Clare, Cork South-Central, Cork South-West, Dublin Central, Dublin Mid-West, Dublin North-West, Dublin South-Central, Dublin South-East, Dublin South-West, Galway East, Galway West, Longford-Westmeath, Mayo, Tipperary South, Waterford, Wexford and Wicklow).

The following points about the Commission's recommendations are relevant:

National average representation based on the 2006 population and the recommended 166 seats is 25,541 population per TD. The highest number of persons per TD in the recommended constituencies is 26,749 in the (unchanged) Carlow-Kilkenny constituency (i.e. a variance of +4.73% from national average representation). The lowest number of persons per member is 24,000 in the (unchanged) Cavan-Monaghan constituency (i.e. a variance of -6.03% from national average representation).

Three new breaches of county boundaries are involved in the revised constituencies: in Kerry/Limerick, Louth/Meath and Offaly/Tipperary.

Eleven 5-seat constituencies are proposed (12 at present): Carlow-Kilkenny, Cavan-Monaghan, Cork South-Central, Dublin South, Dublin South-Central, Galway West, Laois-Offaly, Louth, Mayo, Wexford and Wicklow.

Fifteen 4-seaters are proposed (13 at present): Clare, Cork East, Cork North-Central, Dublin Central, Dublin Mid-West, Dublin North, Dublin South-East, Dublin South-West, Dublin West, Dun Laoghaire, Galway East, Kildare North, Limerick City, Longford-Westmeath and Waterford.

Seventeen 3-seaters are proposed (18 at present): Cork North-West, Cork South-West, Donegal North-East, Donegal South-West, Dublin North-Central, Dublin North-East, Dublin North-West, Kerry North-West Limerick, Kerry South, Kildare South, Limerick, Meath East, Meath West, Roscommon-South Leitrim, Sligo-North Leitrim, Tipperary North and Tipperary South.

The following county boundaries are breached:

(a) part of County Carlow is included in the Wicklow constituency.
(b) part of County Clare is included in the constituency of Limerick East.
(c) part of the administrative county of Tipperary South Riding is included in the constituency of Tipperary North.
(d) part of County Waterford is included in the constituency of Tipperary South.
(e) part of County Limerick is included in the constituency of Kerry North-West Limerick.
(f) part of County Meath is included in the constituency of Louth.
(g) part of County Tipperary is included in the constituency of Laois-Offaly.

The 2011 census showed a population increase of 341,421 since 2006. The Dail constituency of Laois-Offaly experienced the largest increase in population with an extra 19,173 resident within its boundaries which left it with a population per TD of 30,565 or 10.75% above the average of 27,598. Dublin North had the highest percentage increase 16.07%. At the other end of the scale Dublin North-Central actually experienced a drop in population of -910 to give them a population per TD of just 24,789 or -10.18% deviation from the average representation.

In the 2011 general election the five-seat constituency of Wexford had the highest electorate, 111,063 just ahead of Laois-Offaly on 108,142 and Carlow-Kilkenny with 105,449. Dublin North-West had the smallest, 49,269. The average electorate per population is 70%, down from 73% in 2006. Donegal South-West is well above the average at 83% which would indicate an aging population and or higher then average level of voter registration. Dublin Central has the smallest electorate per population, 50%. This would indicate a young population with a higher than average number below the voting age of 18. It could also indicate a below average voter registration with a large immigrant population.

On average each TD represents an electorate of 19,333, (18,755 in 2007) with Wexford having the lowest representation, one member per 22,213 voters. Dublin Central has the best representation with an electorate per seat of just 14,223.

CENSUS 2011

			2006			2011			2011-2006		2011		
	Constituency	Seats	Population	per TD	% Dev	Population	per TD	% Dev	Change		Electorate	E/P %	E/S
1	Carlow-Kilkenny	5	133,745	26,749	+4.73%	145,533	29,107	+5.47%	+11,788	+8.81%	105,449	72.46%	21,090
2	Cavan-Monaghan	5	120,000	24,000	-6.03%	133,369	26,674	-3.35%	+13,369	+11.14%	99,178	74.36%	19,836
3	Clare	4	105,571	26,393	+3.33%	111,177	27,794	+0.71%	+5,606	+5.31%	82,745	74.43%	20,686
4	Cork East	4	100,168	25,042	-1.95%	113,954	28,489	+3.23%	+13,786	+13.76%	83,651	73.41%	20,913
5	Cork North Central	4	100,180	25,045	-1.94%	104,846	26,212	-5.02%	+4,666	+4.66%	75,302	71.82%	18,826
6	Cork North West	3	74,619	24,873	-2.62%	81,521	27,174	-1.54%	+6,902	+9.25%	62,870	77.12%	20,957
7	Cork South Central	5	129,379	25,876	+1.31%	134,992	26,998	-2.17%	+5,613	+4.34%	91,619	67.87%	18,324
8	Cork South West	3	76,949	25,650	+0.42%	82,815	27,605	+0.03%	+5,866	+7.62%	62,967	76.03%	20,989
9	Donegal North East	3	73,874	24,625	-3.59%	82,779	27,593	-0.02%	+8,905	+12.05%	59,084	71.38%	19,695
10	Donegal South West	3	73,390	24,463	-4.22%	78,148	26,049	-5.61%	+4,758	+6.48%	64,568	82.62%	21,523
11	Dublin Central	4	104,674	26,169	+2.46%	113,028	28,257	+2.39%	+8,354	+7.98%	56,892	50.33%	14,223
12	Dublin Mid West	4	100,399	25,100	-1.73%	110,464	27,616	+0.07%	+10,065	+10.03%	64,880	58.73%	16,220
13	Dublin North	4	98,340	24,585	-3.74%	114,143	28,536	+3.40%	+15,803	+16.07%	70,413	61.69%	17,603
14	Dublin North Central	3	75,276	25,092	-1.76%	74,366	24,789	-10.18%	-910	-1.21%	52,992	71.26%	17,664
15	Dublin North East	3	76,160	25,387	-0.61%	81,022	27,007	-2.14%	+4,862	+6.38%	58,542	72.25%	19,514
16	Dublin North West	3	73,327	24,442	-4.30%	78,692	26,231	-4.95%	+5,365	+7.32%	49,269	62.61%	16,423
17	Dublin South	5	130,377	26,075	+2.09%	141,333	28,267	+2.42%	+10,956	+8.40%	102,387	72.44%	20,477
18	Dublin South Central	5	122,168	24,434	-4.34%	126,777	25,355	-8.13%	+4,609	+3.77%	80,268	63.31%	16,054
19	Dublin South East	4	100,305	25,076	-1.82%	103,163	25,791	-6.55%	+2,858	+2.85%	58,217	56.43%	14,554
20	Dublin South West	4	97,989	24,497	-4.09%	105,614	26,404	-4.33%	+7,625	+7.78%	70,613	66.86%	17,653
21	Dublin West	4	105,668	26,417	+3.43%	117,126	29,282	+6.10%	+11,458	+10.84%	62,348	53.23%	15,587
22	Dun Laoghaire	4	102,493	25,623	+0.32%	104,875	26,219	-5.00%	+2,382	+2.32%	80,115	76.39%	20,029
23	Galway East	4	100,629	25,157	-1.50%	110,075	27,519	-0.29%	+9,446	+9.39%	83,651	75.99%	20,913
24	Galway West	5	131,041	26,208	+2.61%	140,466	28,093	+1.79%	+9,425	+7.19%	88,840	63.25%	17,768
25	Kerry North-West Limerick	3	77,492	25,831	+1.13%	80,650	26,883	-2.59%	+3,158	+4.08%	63,614	78.88%	21,205
26	Kerry South	3	75,489	25,163	-1.48%	77,756	25,919	-6.09%	+2,267	+3.00%	59,629	76.69%	19,876
27	Kildare North	4	106,500	26,625	+4.24%	119,680	29,920	+8.41%	+13,180	+12.38%	77,959	65.14%	19,490
28	Kildare South	3	79,835	26,612	+4.19%	90,275	30,092	+9.04%	+10,440	+13.08%	58,867	65.21%	19,622
29	Laois Offaly	5	133,651	26,730	+4.66%	152,824	30,565	+10.75%	+19,173	+14.35%	108,142	70.76%	21,628
30	Limerick City	4	100,993	25,248	-1.15%	102,121	25,530	-7.49%	+1,128	+1.12%	65,083	63.73%	16,271
31	Limerick	3	75,295	25,098	-1.73%	81,535	27,178	-1.52%	+6,240	+8.29%	64,909	79.61%	21,636
32	Longford-Westmeath	4	106,211	26,553	+3.96%	116,592	29,148	+5.62%	+10,381	+9.77%	85,918	73.69%	21,480
33	Louth	5	128,600	25,720	+0.70%	143,168	28,634	+3.75%	+14,568	+11.33%	99,530	69.52%	19,906
34	Mayo	5	123,839	24,768	-3.03%	130,552	26,110	-5.39%	+6,713	+5.42%	101,160	77.49%	20,232
35	Meath East	3	76,631	25,544	+0.01%	86,531	28,844	+4.51%	+9,900	+12.92%	64,873	74.97%	21,624
36	Meath West	3	76,393	25,464	-0.30%	85,482	28,494	+3.25%	+9,089	+11.90%	62,776	73.44%	20,925
37	Roscommon-South -Leitrim	3	74,384	24,795	-2.92%	80,794	26,931	-2.42%	+6,410	+8.62%	60,998	75.50%	20,333
38	Sligo-North Leitrim	3	74,228	24,743	-3.13%	80,152	26,717	-3.19%	+5,924	+7.98%	63,432	79.14%	21,144
39	Tipperary North	3	80,203	26,734	+4.67%	84,938	28,313	+2.59%	+4,735	+5.90%	63,235	74.45%	21,078
40	Tipperary South	3	74,748	24,916	-2.45%	79,770	26,590	-3.65%	+5,022	+6.72%	57,420	71.98%	19,140
41	Waterford	4	106,530	26,633	+4.27%	112,091	28,023	+1.54%	+5,561	+5.22%	78,435	69.97%	19,609
42	Wexford	5	131,749	26,350	+3.17%	145,273	29,055	+5.28%	+13,524	+10.26%	111,063	76.45%	22,213
43	Wicklow	5	130,356	26,071	+2.07%	140,807	28,161	+2.04%	+10,451	+8.02%	95,341	67.71%	19,068
	Total 43	**166**	**4,239,848**	**25,541**	**0.00%**	**4,581,269**	**27,598**	**0.00%**	**341,421**	**+8.05%**	**3,209,244**	**70.05%**	**19,333**
	Dublin	47	1,187,176	25,259	-1.10%	1,270,603	25,259	-8.48%	83,427	+7.03%	806,936	63.51%	17,169
	Leinster	42	1,103,671	26,278	+2.88%	1,226,165	27,023	-2.08%	122,494	+11.10%	869,918	70.95%	20,712
	Munster	46	1,177,616	25,600	+0.23%	1,248,166	24,965	-9.54%	70,550	+5.99%	911,479	73.03%	19,815
	Connaught/Ulster	31	771,385	24,883	-2.58%	836,335	24,883	-9.84%	64,950	+8.42%	620,911	74.24%	20,029

MEMBERS OF THE CABINET (Appointed 9th March 2011)

Taoiseach: Enda Kenny

Tánaiste and Minister for Foreign Affairs and Trade: Eamon Gilmore

Minister for Finance: Michael Noonan

Minister for Education and Skills: Ruairí Quinn

Minister for Public Expenditure and Reform: Brendan Howlin

Minister for Enterprise, Jobs and Innovation: Richard Bruton

Minister for Social Protection: Joan Burton

Minister for Arts, Heritage & Gaeltacht Affairs: Jimmy Deenihan

Minister for Communications, Energy and Natural Resources: Pat Rabbitte

Minister for the Environment, Community and Local Government: Phil Hogan

Minister for Justice, Equality and Defence: Alan Shatter

Minister for Agriculture, Marine and Food: Simon Coveney

Minister for Children: Frances Fitzgerald

Minister for Health: Dr. James Reilly

Minister for Transport, Tourism and Sport: Leo Varadkar

Attorney General: Márie Whelan S.C.

MINISTERS OF STATE (Appointed 11th March 2011)

Paul Kehoe
Minister of State at the Department of the Taoiseach and Defence with special responsibility as Government Chief Whip.

Jan O'Sullivan (Appointed 20/12/2011)
Minister of State at the Department of Environment, Community and Local Government with special responsibility for Housing and Planning. Entitled to attend meetings of the Cabinet.

Dinny McGinley
Department of Arts, Heritage and Gaeltacht Affairs with special responsibility for Gaeltacht Affairs

Róisín Shortall
Minister of State at the Department of Health with special responsibility for Primary Care

John Perry
Minister of State at the Department of Enterprise, Jobs and Innovation with special responsibility for Small Business

Michael Ring
Minister of State at the Department of Transport, Tourism and Sport with special responsibility for Tourism and Sport

Minister of State at the Department of Foreign Affairs and Trade with special responsibility for Trade and Development

Kathleen Lynch
Minister of State at the Department of Health and at the Department of Justice, Equality and Defence with special responsibility for Disability, Equality and Mental Health

Willie Penrose (resigned 15/11/2011)
Minister of State at the Department of Environment, Community and Local Government with special responsibility for Housing and Planning. Entitled to attend meetings of the Cabinet.

Fergus O'Dowd
Minister of State at the Department of Communications, Energy and Natural Resources and at the Department of Environment, Community and Local Government with special responsibility for New Era Project

Brian Hayes
Minister of State at the Department of Public Expenditure and Reform and at the Department of Finance with special responsibility for Public Sector Reform and OPW

Shane McEntee
Minister of State at the Department of Agriculture, Marine and Food with special responsibility for Food, Horticulture and Food Safety

Lucinda Creighton
Minister of State at the Department of the Taoiseach and at the Department of Foreign Affairs and Trade with special responsibility for European Affairs

Sean Sherlock
Minister of State at the Department of Enterprise, Jobs and Innovation and at the Department of Education and Skills with special responsibility for Research and Innovation

Ciaran Cannon
Minister of State at the Department of Education & Skills with special responsibility for Training and Skills

Alan Kelly
Minister of State at the Department of Transport, Tourism and Sport with special responsibility for Public and Commuter Transport

Joe Costello (Appointed 20/12/2011)
Minister of State at the Department of Foreign Affairs and Trade with special responsibility for Trade and Development

FIANNA FAIL FRONT BENCH
(Appointed 12th April 2011)

Party Leader & Northern Ireland	Micheál Martin
Deputy Leader and Communications, Energy and Natural Resources	Eamon Ó Cuiv
Finance	Michael McGrath
Fianna Fail Whip and Foreign Affairs and Trade	Seán Ó Fearghail
Public Expenditure & Financial Sector Reform	Sean Fleming
Public Sector Reform	Sean Fleming
Education and Skills	Brendan Smith
Enterprise, Jobs and Innovation	Willie O'Dea
Social Protection	Barry Cowen
Environment, Community and Local Government	Niall Collins
Children	Charlie McConalogue
Justice, Equality and Defence	Dara Calleary
Health	Billy Kelleher
Transport, Tourism and Sport	Timmy Dooley
Agriculture and Food	Michael Moynihan
Arts and Heritage	Robert Troy
Marine and Fisheries	John Browne
Horticulture and Rural Affairs	Seamus Kirk
Small Business Regulatory Framework	John McGuinness

SINN FEIN FRONT BENCH
(Appointed 22nd March 2011)

Party Leader	Gerry Adams
Deputy Leader and Public Expenditure and Reform	Mary Lou McDonald
Finance	Pearse Doherty
Foreign Affairs and Trade	Padraig MacLochlainn
Enterprise, Jobs and Innovation and An Gaeltacht	Peadar Tóibín
Communications, Energy and Natural Resources	Martin Ferris
Transport and Housing	Dessie Ellis
Justice, Equality and Defence	Jonathan O'Brien
Education and Skills	Sean Crowe
Agriculture, Food and Marine	Michael Colreavy
Environment, Community and Local Government	Brian Stanley
Party Whip and Social Protection	Aengus Ó Snodaigh
Arts, Heritage, Tourism and Sport	Sandra McLellan
Health and Children	Caoimhghín Ó Caoláin

PARLIAMENTARY COMMITTEES

Each House of the Oireachtas has power under its Standing Orders (Rules) to form Committees for specific purposes. There are four types of Committees – Standing, Select, Joint and Special.

Standing Committees – Standing Orders provide for the automatic creation of such Committees in a new Dail or Seanad e.g. Committee of Public Accounts, Joint Committee on Consolidation Bills.

Select Committees – Comprise membership of one House only, whether Dail or Seanad.

Joint Committees – Comprise Select Committees from both Houses sitting and voting together under common Orders of reference.

Special Committees – Established for the sole purpose of considering a specific Bill.

Each House decides the terms of reference, membership and powers of a Committee. It is practice for Committee membership to be proportionally representative of the House which sets it up. Committee Reports are published but it is for the House(s) to decide on any follow up action. With the exception of the month of August, Committees meet throughout the year.

All Committees have a secretariat and, where necessary, some have an annual budget to engage consultants to assist them. Some Committee Chairpersons are members of the Opposition and it is not practice for Ministers or Ministers of State to be Chairpersons.

As required, Ministers are ex officio members of Dail select Committees when they are considering Bills or Estimates for Public Services. In the case of the Joint Committee on Foreign Affairs and the Joint Committee on European Affairs, Irish M.E.P's (including Northern Ireland M.E.P's) and members of the Irish delegation to the Parliamentary Assembly of the Council of Europe can attend and participate at their meetings but without voting rights. These Committees can also invite M.E.P's of other Member States to attend under similar conditions. The terms of reference of some Committees also allow for the appointment of substitute members or indeed the attendance of members of the Houses who are not formal members.

COMMITTEES OF THE 31st DAIL					
	JOINT COMMITTEES				
	Title of Committee	**TD's**	**Senators**	**Chairperson**	**Vice-Chairperson**
1	Joint Committee on Communications, Natural Resources & Agriculture	15	6	Andrew Doyle	John O'Mahony
2	Joint Committee on the Environment, Transport, Culture and the Gaeltacht	21	6	Ciaran Lynch	Noel Coonan
3	Joint Committee on European Union Affairs	9	5	Dominic Hannigan	Paschal Donohoe
4	Joint Committee on Finance, Public Expenditure and Reform	21	6	Alex White	Liam Twomey
5	Joint Committee on Foreign Affairs and Trade	9	6	Pat Breen	Bernard Durkan
6	Joint Committee on Health and Children	15	7	Jerry Buttimer	Ciara Conway
7	Joint Committee on Implementation of the Good Friday Agreement	15	5	Joanna Tuffy	Joe O'Reilly
8	Joint Committee on Investigations, Oversight and Petitions	15	5	Peadar Tóibín	Michael McCarthy
9	Joint Committee on Jobs, Social Protection and Education	21	6	Damien English	Aodhan Ó Riordáin
10	Joint Committee on Justice, Defence and Equality	9	5	David Stanton	Anne Ferris
11	Joint Administration Committee	16	4	Tom Hayes	Jerry Buttimer
	STANDING COMMITTEES				
1	Committee of Public Accounts	13		John McGuinness	Kieran O'Donnell
2	Committee on Procedure and Privileges	10	4	Sean Barrett	
3	Committee on Members' Interests of Dail Eireann	5		Thomas Pringle	
	OTHER COMMITTEES				
1	Houses of the Oireachtas Commission				
2	British-Irish Inter-Parliamentary Body				

TURNOUT, SPOILED VOTES, VALID POLL, QUOTA, CANDIDATES, COUNTS

ELECTORATE

3,209,244 people were registered to vote in the 2011 general election, an increase of 98,330 on 2007. Munster had the largest electorate 911,479 with Leinster next at 869,918. Dublin had an electorate of 806,936 with Connaught/Ulster the smallest region with 620,911. But these figures come with a health warning as the register of electors has been proven in the past to be substantially inaccurate despite the efforts to update it for the 2007 election.

TURNOUT

2,243,176 voters actually turned out or 69.90%, up from 67.03% in 2007. Munster had the largest regional turnout, 71.34% marginally ahead of Connaught-Ulster at 71.32% with Roscommon–South Leitrim having the best constituency turnout at 78.75%. Dublin had the lowest regional turnout, 68.20%. Dublin South-East had the lowest constituency turnout, 53.78% in 2007 and held the same position in 2011 with 60.54%.

SPOILED VOTES

There were 22,817 spoiled votes or 1.02%, up marginally on 2007 (0.93%). Dublin South-Central had the highest percentage of spoiled votes 1.58% as it had in 2007 (1.63%). Kildare North had the lowest at 0.75% as it had in 2007 (0.51%).

VALID POLL

The overall valid poll was 69.19% up three points from 2007 (66.41%) and the highest since 1987 (72.67%). Roscommon-South Leitrim had the largest valid poll, 77.88% with Tipperary North next at 76.34% a reversal of their 2007 positions. With the lowest turnout it was inevitable that Dublin South-East would have the lowest valid poll, 59.98% and was the only constituency below 60%.

QUOTA

The quota is calculated by dividing the valid poll by the number of seats plus one and adding one, ignoring any decimal points,

e.g. Carlow-Kilkenny: $\text{Quota} = \frac{(73{,}743)}{(5+1)} + 1 = 12{,}290.5+1 = 12{,}291$

Because of the automatic return of the Ceann Comhairle Seamus Kirk, Louth was reduced to four seats and thus had by far the highest quota 13,864. Wexford was next at 12,590. Laois-Offaly and Mayo had the same quota 12,360. Dublin Central had the lowest quota 6,923 and was one of only two below 7,000 with Dublin South-East on 6,984.

CANDIDATES

There was a record 566 candidates for the 165 seats in this election, 96 more than 2007. Fine Gael ran 104, up 13 on last time and Labour increased their number from 50 in 2007 to 68 in 2011. Fianna Fail recognised their changed political position and reduced their candidates from 106 in 2007 to just 75. Sinn Fein ran 41, the same as 2007 and the Greens ran 43, one less than last time but lost all their seats. The number of small party and independent candidates was up from just 138 in 2007 to a record 235. Wicklow had the largest number of candidates, 24 with Laois-Offaly next at 21. Kildare South and the two Tipperarys had the smallest number 8.

COUNTS

It took 361 counts to fill the 165 seats in this election. This was up from 290 in 2007, 304 in 2002, 320 in 1997 and down from 377 in 1992. Wicklow had the most counts, 19 and in contrast it took only three counts to complete Tipperary North.

CONSTITUENCY DETAILS 2011												
			Total	%	Invalid	%	Total	%		Candidates		No. of
Constituency	**Seats**	**Electorate**	**Votes Cast**	**Turnout**	**Votes**	**Invalid**	**Valid Poll**	**Valid**	**Quota**	**2007**	**2011**	**Counts**
Carlow-Kilkenny	5	105,449	74,564	70.71%	821	1.10%	73,743	69.93%	12,291	11	19	13
Cavan-Monaghan	5	99,178	72,142	72.74%	867	1.20%	71,275	71.87%	11,880	9	14	9
Clare	4	82,745	58,495	70.69%	579	0.99%	57,916	69.99%	11,584	12	16	12
Cork East	4	83,651	57,459	68.69%	526	0.92%	56,933	68.06%	11,387	10	13	7
Cork North Central	4	75,302	52,709	70.00%	572	1.09%	52,137	69.24%	10,428	13	15	11
Cork North West	3	62,870	46,194	73.48%	454	0.98%	45,740	72.75%	11,436	7	9	6
Cork South Central	5	91,619	64,664	70.58%	624	0.96%	64,040	69.90%	10,674	14	17	12
Cork South West	3	62,967	46,048	73.13%	390	0.85%	45,658	72.51%	11,415	7	13	6
Donegal North East	3	59,084	38,324	64.86%	406	1.06%	37,918	64.18%	9,480	11	11	9
Donegal South West	3	64,568	43,595	67.52%	332	0.76%	43,263	67.00%	10,816	7	9	5
Dublin Central	4	56,892	35,069	61.64%	457	1.30%	34,612	60.84%	6,923	13	16	8
Dublin Mid West	4	64,880	**43,193**	66.57%	471	1.09%	42,722	65.85%	8,545	11	14	9
Dublin North	4	70,413	49,799	70.72%	452	0.91%	49,347	70.08%	9,870	13	9	7
Dublin North Central	3	52,992	39,187	73.95%	413	1.05%	38,774	73.17%	9,694	7	9	7
Dublin North East	3	58,542	42,287	72.23%	448	1.06%	41,839	71.47%	10,460	8	11	9
Dublin North West	3	49,269	33,262	67.51%	451	1.36%	32,811	66.60%	8,203	8	12	7
Dublin South	5	102,387	73,105	71.40%	459	0.63%	72,646	70.95%	12,108	13	16	8
Dublin South Central	5	80,268	51,744	64.46%	817	1.58%	50,927	63.45%	8,488	16	18	13
Dublin South East	4	58,217	35,246	60.54%	327	0.93%	34,919	59.98%	6,984	13	16	10
Dublin South West	4	70,613	47,475	67.23%	511	1.08%	46,964	66.51%	9,393	8	10	8
Dublin West	4	62,348	42,799	68.65%	327	0.76%	42,472	68.12%	8,495	8	10	5
Dun Laoghaire	4	80,115	57,157	71.34%	481	0.84%	56,676	70.74%	11,336	11	14	11
Galway East	4	83,651	59,836	71.53%	560	0.94%	59,276	70.86%	11,856	14	13	9
Galway West	5	88,840	61,268	68.96%	643	1.05%	60,625	68.24%	10,105	15	17	13
Kerry North-West Limerick	3	63,614	46,027	72.35%	413	0.90%	45,614	71.70%	11,404	10	11	7
Kerry South	3	59,629	44,679	74.93%	299	0.67%	44,380	74.43%	11,096	8	10	6
Kildare North	4	77,959	51,610	66.20%	388	0.75%	51,222	65.70%	10,245	11	12	5
Kildare South	3	58,867	38,623	65.61%	353	0.91%	38,270	65.01%	9,568	8	8	7
Laoighis Offaly	5	108,142	75,213	69.55%	1,055	1.40%	74,158	68.57%	12,360	16	21	13
Limerick	3	65,083	45,512	69.93%	471	1.03%	45,041	69.21%	11,261	14	10	4
Limerick City	4	64,909	43,617	67.20%	429	0.98%	43,188	66.54%	8,638	7	13	7
Longford-Westmeath	4	85,918	58,186	67.72%	661	1.14%	57,525	66.95%	11,506	13	15	8
Louth	5	99,530	70,190	70.52%	871	1.24%	69,319	69.65%	13,864	12	16	13
Mayo	5	101,160	74,795	73.94%	641	0.86%	74,154	73.30%	12,360	13	15	8
Meath East	3	64,873	43,098	66.43%	346	0.80%	42,752	65.90%	10,689	11	9	4
Meath West	3	62,776	40,591	64.66%	413	1.02%	40,178	64.00%	10,045	10	13	5
Roscommon-South -Leitrim	3	60,998	48,035	78.75%	531	1.11%	47,504	77.88%	11,877	9	10	6
Sligo-North Leitrim	3	63,432	44,837	70.69%	409	0.91%	44,428	70.04%	11,108	10	13	9
Tipperary North	3	63,235	48,789	77.16%	516	1.06%	48,273	76.34%	12,069	9	8	3
Tipperary South	3	57,420	41,793	72.78%	432	1.03%	41,361	72.03%	10,341	11	8	5
Waterford	4	78,435	54,298	69.23%	578	1.06%	53,720	68.49%	10,745	13	15	11
Wexford	5	111,063	76,351	68.75%	**812**	1.06%	75,539	68.01%	12,590	11	14	7
Wicklow	5	95,341	71,311	74.80%	811	1.14%	70,500	73.95%	11,751	15	24	19
2011 43	**166**	**3,209,244**	**2,243,176**	**69.90%**	**22,817**	**1.02%**	**2,220,359**	**69.19%**	**10,636**	**470**	**566**	**361**
2007 43	**166**	**3,110,914**	**2,085,245**	**67.03%**	**19,435**	**0.93%**	**2,065,810**	**66.41%**			**470**	**290**
2011-2007		**+98,330**	**+157,931**	**+2.87%**	**+3,382**	**+0.09%**	**+154,549**	**+2.78%**			**+96**	**+71**
Dublin	47	806,936	550,323	68.20%	5,614	1.02%	544,709	67.50%		129	155	102
Leinster	42	869,918	599,737	68.94%	6,531	1.09%	593,206	68.19%		118	151	94
Munster	46	911,479	650,284	71.34%	6,283	0.97%	644,001	70.65%		135	158	97
Connaught/Ulster	31	620,911	442,832	71.32%	4,389	0.99%	438,443	70.61%		88	102	68

DUBLIN SUMMARY 2011												
PARTY VOTE												
	2011					2007					Change	
Party	Cand	1st	%	Quota	Seats	Cand	1st	%	Quota	Seats	%	Seats
FG	24	163,023	29.93%	14.36	17	18	94,788	18.74%	8.99	10	+11.19%	+7
LB	24	159,709	29.32%	14.07	18	15	73,490	14.53%	6.97	9	+14.79%	+9
FF	17	67,836	12.45%	5.98	1	27	196,029	38.75%	18.60	19	-26.30%	-18
SF	10	44,525	8.17%	3.92	4	13	35,256	6.97%	3.35	1	+1.20%	+3
SP	5	19,550	3.59%	1.72	2	3	11,518	2.28%	1.09		+1.31%	+2
PBPA	7	19,258	3.54%	1.70	2						+3.54%	+2
GP	12	19,529	3.59%	1.72		13	41,813	8.27%	3.97	5	-4.68%	-5
WP	3	1,313	0.24%	0.12		3	862	0.17%	0.08		+0.07%	
CS	5	1,358	0.25%	0.12		3	625	0.12%	0.06		+0.13%	
PD						10	20,919	4.14%	1.98	1	-4.14%	-1
Others	48	48,608	8.92%	4.28	3	24	30,552	6.04%	2.90	2	+2.88%	+1
Total	**155**	**544,709**	**100.0%**	**11,349**	**47**	**129**	**505,852**	**100.0%**	**10,540**	**47**	**0.00%**	**0**
Electorate		**806,936**	**67.50%**				**812,181**	**62.28%**			+5.22%	
Spoiled		**5,614**	**1.02%**				**4,800**	**0.94%**			+0.08%	
Turnout		**550,323**	**68.20%**				**510,652**	**62.87%**			+5.32%	

LEINSTER SUMMARY 2011												
PARTY VOTE												
	2011					2007					Change	
Party	Cand	1st	%	Quota	Seats	Cand	1st	%	Quota	Seats	%	Seats
FG	26	217,354	36.64%	15.75	21	26	147,843	27.08%	11.37	12	+9.56%	+9
LB	17	114,011	19.22%	8.26	8	13	62,317	11.42%	4.79	5	+7.80%	+3
FF	23	115,542	19.48%	8.37	7	27	246,899	45.23%	19.00	22	-25.75%	-15
SF	11	61,906	10.44%	4.49	3	9	32,301	5.92%	2.49	1	+4.52%	+2
SP	2	1,696	0.29%	0.12							+0.29%	
PBPA	1	741	0.12%	0.05							+0.12%	
GP	10	9,716	1.64%	0.70		10	23,614	4.33%	1.82	1	-2.69%	-1
WP	1	189	0.03%	0.01		1	193	0.04%	0.01		-0.00%	
CS	1	234	0.04%	0.02		2	280	0.05%	0.02		-0.01%	
PD						8	14,122	2.59%	1.09		-2.59%	
Others	59	71,817	12.11%	5.21	3	22	18,300	3.35%	1.41		+8.75%	+3
Total	**151**	**593,206**	**100.0%**	**13,796**	**42**	**118**	**545,869**	**100.0%**	**12,998**	**41**	**0.00%**	**1**
Electorate		**869,916**	**68.19%**				**822,421**	**66.37%**			+1.82%	
Spoiled		**6,531**	**1.09%**				**5,279**	**0.96%**			+0.13%	
Turnout		**599,737**	**68.94%**				**551,148**	**67.02%**			+1.93%	

MUNSTER SUMMARY 2011												
PARTY VOTE												
	2011					2007					Change	
Party	Cand	1st	%	Quota	Seats	Cand	1st	%	Quota	Seats	%	Seats
FG	31	245,589	38.13%	17.92	21	27	178,183	29.62%	14.22	17	+8.52%	+4
LB	18	119,794	18.60%	8.74	9	14	59,707	9.92%	4.76	5	+8.68%	+4
FF	19	121,134	18.81%	8.84	7	32	256,955	42.71%	20.50	22	-23.90%	-15
SF	10	49,445	7.68%	3.61	3	11	31,910	5.30%	2.55	1	+2.37%	+2
SP	2	5,524	0.86%	0.40		1	1,700	0.28%	0.14		+0.58%	
PBPA	1	1,552	0.24%	0.11							+0.24%	
GP	13	8,091	1.26%	0.59		13	21,310	3.54%	1.70		-2.29%	+0
WP	2	1,554	0.24%	0.11		2	1,971	0.33%	0.16		-0.09%	
CS	2	510	0.08%	0.04		1	171	0.03%	0.01		+0.05%	
PD						7	8,870	1.47%	0.71		-1.47%	
Others	60	90,808	14.10%	6.63	6	27	40,840	6.79%	3.26	2	+7.31%	+4
Total	**158**	**644,001**	**100.0%**	**13,703**	**46**	**135**	**601,617**	**100.0%**	**12,535**	**47**	**0.00%**	**-1**
Electorate		**911,486**	**70.65%**				**879,055**	**68.44%**			+2.21%	
Spoiled		**6,283**	**0.97%**				**5,287**	**0.87%**			+0.10%	
Turnout		**650,284**	**71.34%**				**606,904**	**69.04%**			+2.30%	

CONNAUGHT-ULSTER SUMMARY 2011												
PARTY VOTE												
	2011					2007					Change	
Party	**Cand**	**1st**	**%**	**Quota**	**Seats**	**Cand**	**1st**	**%**	**Quota**	**Seats**	**%**	**Seats**
FG	23	175,662	40.06%	12.82	17	20	143,614	34.82%	11.14	12	+5.25%	+5
LB	9	38,282	8.73%	2.79	2	8	13,661	3.31%	1.06	1	+5.42%	+1
FF	16	82,846	18.90%	6.05	5	20	158,682	38.47%	12.31	15	-19.58%	-10
SF	10	64,785	14.78%	4.73	4	8	43,943	10.65%	3.41	1	+4.12%	+3
SP											+0.00%	+0
PBPA											+0.00%	+0
GP	8	3,703	0.84%	0.27		8	10,199	2.47%	0.79		-1.63%	+0
WP											+0.00%	+0
CS						2	629	0.15%	0.05		-0.15%	+0
PD						5	12,485	3.03%	0.97	1	-3.03%	-1
Others	36	73,165	16.69%	5.34	3	17	29,259	7.09%	2.27	1	+9.59%	+2
Total	**102**	**438,443**	**100.0%**	**13,702**	**31**	**88**	**412,472**	**100.0%**	**12,891**	**31**	**0.00%**	**0**
Electorate		**620,911**	**70.61%**				**597,257**	**69.06%**			+1.55%	
Spoiled		**4,389**	**0.99%**				**4,069**	**0.98%**			+0.01%	
Turnout		**442,832**	**71.32%**				**416,541**	**69.74%**			+1.58%	

NATIONAL SUMMARY 2011												
PARTY VOTE												
	2011					2007					Change	
Party	**Cand**	**1st**	**%**	**Quota**	**Seats**	**Cand**	**1st**	**%**	**Quota**	**Seats**	**%**	**Seats**
FG	104	801,628	36.10%	60.29	76	91	564,428	27.32%	45.62	51	+8.78%	+25
LB	68	431,796	19.45%	32.47	37	50	209,175	10.13%	16.91	20	+9.32%	+17
FF	75	387,358	17.45%	29.13	20	106	858,565	41.56%	69.40	78	-24.11%	-58
SF	41	220,661	9.94%	16.60	14	41	143,410	6.94%	11.59	4	+3.00%	+10
SP	9	26,770	1.21%	2.01	2	4	13,218	0.64%	1.07		+0.57%	+2
PBPA	9	21,551	0.97%	1.62	2						+0.97%	+2
GP	43	41,039	1.85%	3.09		44	96,936	4.69%	7.84	6	-2.84%	-6
WP	6	3,056	0.14%	0.23		6	3,026	0.15%	0.24		-0.01%	+0
CS	8	2,102	0.09%	0.16		8	1,705	0.08%	0.14		+0.01%	+0
PD						30	56,396	2.73%	4.56	2	-2.73%	-2
Others	203	284,398	12.81%	21.39	15	90	118,951	5.76%	9.62	5	+7.05%	+10
Total	**566**	**2,220,359**	**100.0%**	**13,297**	**166**	**470**	**2,065,810**	**100.0%**	**12,371**	**166**	**0.00%**	**0**
Electorate		**3,209,249**	**69.19%**				**3,110,914**	**66.41%**			+2.78%	
Spoiled		**22,817**	**1.02%**				**19,435**	**0.93%**			+0.09%	
Turnout		**2,243,176**	**69.90%**				**2,085,245**	**67.03%**			+2.87%	

FF seats include outgoing Ceann Comhairle Seamus Kirk

PARTY VOTE PER CONSTITUENCY 2011

	Fine Gael		Labour		Fianna Fail		Sinn Fein		Socialist Pty		PBPA		Greens		WP		CS		Non Party		Total	ULA	
Constituency	**Votes**	**%**	**Votes**	**%**	**Votes**	**%**	**Votes**	**%**	**Votes**	**%**	**Votes**	**%**	**Votes**	**%**	**Votes**	**%**	**Votes**	**%**	**Votes**	**%**	**Votes**	**Votes**	**%**
Carlow-Kilkenny	28,924	39.22	11,980	16.25	20,721	28.10	7,033	9.54	1,135	1.54			2,072	2.81					1,878		73,743	1,135	1.54
Cavan-Monaghan	28,199	39.56	4,011	5.63	14,360	20.15	18,452	25.89					530	0.74					5,723	8.03	71,275		
Clare	24,524	42.34	8,572	14.80	12,804	22.11							1,154	1.99					10,862	18.75	57,916		
Cork East	20,847	36.62	17,563	30.85	9,642	16.94	6,292	11.05					635	1.12					1,954	3.43	56,933		
Cork North Central	13,669	26.22	13,801	26.47	7,896	15.14	7,923	15.20	4,803	9.21			524	1.01	681	1.31	324	0.62	2,516	4.83	52,137	4,803	9.21
Cork North West	22,321	48.80	6,421	14.04	11,390	24.90	3,405	7.44			1,552	3.39	651	1.42							45,740	1,552	3.39
Cork South Central	22,225	34.70	11,869	18.53	17,936	28.01	5,250	8.20					1,640	2.56					5,120	8.00	64,040		
Cork South West	22,162	48.54	6,533	14.31	10,787	23.63	3,346	7.33					765	1.68					2,065	4.52	45,658		
Donegal North East	11,987	31.61	4,090	10.79	6,613	17.44	9,278	24.47					206	0.54					5,744	15.15	37,918		
Donegal South West	8,589	19.85	2,209	5.11	9,745	22.53	14,262	32.97					527	1.22					7,931	18.33	43,263		
Dublin Central	6,903	19.94	9,787	28.28	5,141	14.85	4,526	13.08					683	1.97	274	0.79	235	0.68	7,063	20.41	34,612		
Dublin Mid West	13,214	30.93	13,138	30.75	5,043	11.80	5,060	11.84	622	1.46	2,471	5.78	1,484	3.47	694	1.62			996	2.33	42,722	3,093	7.24
Dublin North	15,488	31.39	13,014	26.37	7,634	15.47			7,513	15.22			4,186	8.48					1,512	3.06	49,347	7,513	15.22
Dublin North Central	14,644	37.77	8,731	22.52	5,017	12.94	2,140	5.52			1,424	3.67	501	1.29					6,317	16.29	38,774	1,424	3.67
Dublin North East	12,332	29.47	14,371	34.35	4,794	11.46	5,032	12.03	869	2.08			792	1.89					3,649	8.72	41,839	869	2.08
Dublin North West	5,496	16.75	14,158	43.15	3,869	11.79	7,115	21.68			677	2.06	328	1.00	345	1.05	173	0.53	650	1.98	32,811	677	2.06
Dublin South	26,404	36.35	13,059	17.98	6,844	9.42	1,915	2.64			1,277	1.76	4,929	6.78			277	0.38	17,941	24.70	72,646	1,277	1.76
Dublin South Central	11,956	23.48	18,032	35.41	4,837	9.50	6,804	13.36			6,574	12.91	1,015	1.99			239	0.47	1,470	2.89	50,927	6,574	12.91
Dublin South East	12,402	35.52	8,857	25.36	3,922	11.23	1,272	3.64			629	1.80	2,370	6.79					5,467	15.66	34,919	629	1.80
Dublin South West	13,044	27.77	17,032	36.27	5,059	10.77	8,064	17.17	2,462	5.24			480	1.02					823	1.75	46,964	2,462	5.24
Dublin West	11,549	27.19	12,313	28.99	7,044	16.59	2,597	6.11	8,084	19.03			605	1.42					280	0.66	42,472	8,084	19.03
Dun Laoghaire	19,591	34.57	17,217	30.38	8,632	15.23					6,206	10.95	2,156	3.80			434	0.77	2,440	4.31	56,676	6,206	10.95
Galway East	25,409	42.87	7,831	13.21	10,694	18.04	3,635	6.13					402	0.68					11,305	19.07	59,276		
Galway West	18,627	30.72	7,489	12.35	12,703	20.95	3,808	6.28					1,120	1.85					16,878	27.84	60,625		
Kerry North	18,599	40.77	9,159	20.08	5,230	11.47	9,282	20.35					239	0.52					3,105	6.81	45,614		
Kerry South	14,482	32.63	4,926	11.10	5,917	13.33							401	0.90					18,654	42.03	44,380		
Kildare North	17,050	33.29	14,979	29.24	7,436	14.52	2,896	5.65					905	1.77					7,956	15.53	51,222		
Kildare South	12,755	33.33	10,645	27.82	8,307	21.71	2,308						523	1.37					3,732	9.75	38,270		
Laois Offaly	25,032	33.75	5,802	7.82	19,860	26.78	8,032	10.83	561	0.76			306	0.41					14,565	19.64	74,158	561	0.76
Limerick	21,925	48.68	7,910	17.56	9,361	20.78							354	0.79					5,491	12.19	45,041		
Limerick City	18,696	43.29	8,764	20.29	9,259	21.44	3,711	8.59	721	1.67			490	1.13			186	0.43	1,361	3.15	43,188	721	1.67
Longford-Westmeath	21,887	38.05	15,366	26.71	11,197	19.46	4,339	7.54					309	0.54					4,427	7.70	57,525		
Louth	21,825	31.48	13,264	19.13	10,858	15.66	15,072	21.74					3,244	4.68					5,056	7.29	69,319		
Mayo	48,170	64.96	3,644	4.91	11,920	**16.07**	4,802	6.48					266	0.36					5,352	7.22	74,154		
Meath East	17,471	40.87	8,994	21.04	8,384	19.61	3,795	8.88					461	1.08					3,647	8.53	42,752		
Meath West	18,450	45.92	5,432	13.52	7,285	18.13	6,989	17.40					479	1.19	189	0.47	234	0.58	1,120	2.79	40,178		
Roscommon-South Leitrim	18,303	38.53	4,455	9.38	7,103	14.95	4,637	9.76					220	0.46					12,786	26.92	47,504		
Sligo-North Leitrim	16,378	36.86	4,553	10.25	9,708	21.85	5,911	13.30					432	0.97					7,446	16.76	44,428	2,284	5.14
Tipperary North	11,425	23.67	9,559	19.80	7,978	16.53	3,034	6.29					409	0.85					15,868	**32.87**	48,273		
Tipperary South	14,298	34.57	4,525	10.94	5,419	13.10	1,860	4.50					367	0.89					14,892	36.00	41,361	8,818	21.32
Waterford	20,416	38.00	10,192	18.97	7,515	13.99	5,342	9.94					462	0.86	873	1.63			8,920	16.60	53,720		
Wexford	26,034	34.46	15,462	20.47	14,027	18.57	4,353	5.76			741		391	0.52					14,531	19.24	75,539	741	0.98
Wicklow	27,926	39.61	12,087	17.14	7,467	10.59	7,089	10.06					1,026	1.46					14,905	21.14	70,500		
Total 43	**801,628**	**36.10**	**431,796**	**19.45**	**387,358**	**17.45**	**220,661**	**9.94**	**26,770**	**1.21**	**21,551**	**0.97**	**41,039**	**1.85**	**3,056**	**0.14**	**2,102**	**0.09**	**284,398**	**12.81**	**2,220,359**	**59,423**	**2.68**
Dublin	163,023	29.93	159,709	29.32	67,836	12.45	44,525	8.17	19,550	3.59	19,258	3.54	19,529	3.59	1,313	0.24	1,358	0.25	48,608	8.92	544,709	38,808	7.12
Leinster	217,354	36.64	114,011	19.22	115,542	19.48	61,906	10.44	1,696	0.29	741	0.12	9,716	1.64	189	0.03	234	0.04	71,817	12.11	593,206	2,437	0.41
Munster	245,589	38.13	119,794	18.60	121,134	18.81	49,445	7.68	5,524	0.86	1,552	0.24	8,091	1.26	1,554	0.24	510	0.08	90,808	14.10	644,001	15,894	2.47
Connaught/Ulster	175,662	40.06	38,282	8.73	82,846	18.90	64,785	14.78					3,703	0.84					73,165	16.69	438,443	2,284	0.52
Ulster	48,775	31.99	10,310	6.76	30,718	20.15	41,992	27.54					1,263	0.83					19,398	12.72	152,456		

CHANGE IN PARTY VOTE PER CONSTITUENCY 2011-2007						
Constituency	**FG**	**LB**	**FF**	**SF**	**GP**	**Others**
Carlow-Kilkenny	+9.61	+6.90	-19.60	+5.74	-5.15	+2.50
Cavan-Monaghan	+8.36	+4.42	-17.63	+5.88	-2.88	+1.85
Clare	+7.13	+13.22	-21.92	-3.42	-3.08	+8.06
Cork East	+5.76	+9.94	-21.03	+4.23	-1.81	+2.91
Cork North Central	-1.35	+14.14	-20.60	+7.04	-2.54	+3.32
Cork North West	+10.38	+9.13	-28.15	+7.44	-2.20	+3.39
Cork South Central	+6.29	+9.28	-16.27	+3.09	-5.81	+3.42
Cork South West	+12.54	+4.67	-18.95	+2.27	-5.05	+4.52
Donegal North East	+9.01	+8.96	-32.82	+7.00	-0.81	+8.65
Donegal South West	-3.15	+2.32	-28.00	+11.73	-0.26	+17.36
Dublin Central	+10.41	+15.71	-29.60	+3.89	-3.79	+3.37
Dublin Mid West	+18.93	+19.84	-21.19	+2.57	-7.35	-12.80
Dublin North	+17.35	+16.75	-26.62	-2.66	-8.18	+3.36
Dublin North Central	+12.22	+15.24	-31.08	+1.74	-3.90	+5.77
Dublin North East	+6.54	+19.19	-28.23	-1.32	-4.83	+8.65
Dublin North West	+6.79	+22.85	-37.05	+5.95	-1.76	+3.22
Dublin South	+9.08	+7.55	-31.91	-0.38	-4.27	+19.93
Dublin South Central	+9.09	+14.28	-23.59	+3.21	-3.81	+0.81
Dublin South East	+16.87	+8.71	-17.49	-1.08	-7.06	+0.05
Dublin South West	+7.74	+16.28	-28.49	+5.01	-2.69	+2.16
Dublin West	+6.80	+11.93	-20.86	+1.34	-2.36	+3.16
Dun Laoghaire	+11.01	+14.38	-19.64	-2.20	-3.92	+0.37
Galway East	+3.74	+10.08	-21.64	+2.93	-1.22	+6.11
Galway West	+10.33	+1.31	-16.20	+3.32	-3.64	+4.88
Kerry North	+8.48	+9.17	-19.83	-0.08	-1.38	+3.63
Kerry South	+7.54	-2.38	-27.32	-3.52	-0.99	+26.68
Kildare North	+12.07	+11.80	-24.98	+3.21	-3.13	+1.04
Kildare South	+16.16	+7.13	-28.67	+6.03	-4.81	+4.15
Laoighis Offaly	+6.39	+5.44	-29.60	+5.72	-0.72	+12.77
Limerick	+8.73	+11.93	-26.45	+0.00	-1.61	+7.41
Limerick City	+17.77	+9.97	-27.25	+4.38	-1.49	-3.37
Longford-Westmeath	+7.09	+9.06	-21.69	+3.65	-1.21	+3.09
Louth	+2.11	+14.16	-26.47	+6.70	-2.90	+6.40
Mayo	+11.13	+3.75	-8.38	+1.42	-0.45	-7.47
Meath East	+14.99	+9.10	-23.95	+4.94	-2.01	-3.05
Meath West	+16.89	+9.48	-33.45	+6.11	-1.31	+2.28
Roscommon-South Leitrim	-0.60	+7.57	-23.89	+1.35	-1.35	+16.92
Sligo-North Leitrim	-2.41	+6.35	-19.12	+1.58	-2.06	+15.65
Tipperary North	+7.78	+9.54	-17.78	+2.52	-0.27	-1.78
Tipperary South	+13.42	+2.17	-33.32	+1.41	-0.64	+16.95
Waterford	+10.64	+7.65	-32.50	+3.23	-1.26	+12.24
Wexford	+2.90	+6.70	-23.62	-1.62	-0.65	+16.29
Wicklow	+16.46	+0.81	-27.46	+5.07	-5.92	+11.05
Total 43	+8.78	+9.32	-24.11	+3.00	-2.84	+5.86
Dublin	+11.19	+14.79	-26.30	+1.20	-4.68	+3.79
Leinster	+9.56	+7.80	-25.75	+4.52	-2.69	+6.56
Munster	+8.52	+8.68	-23.90	+2.37	-2.29	+6.62
Connaught/Ulster	+5.25	+5.42	-19.58	+4.12	-1.63	+6.41
Ulster	+5.36	+4.95	-24.49	+7.88	-1.59	+7.90

SEATS SUMMARY 2011

	Constituency	Seats	FG	LB	FF	SF	ULA	GP	Others
1	Carlow-Kilkenny	5	3	1	1				
2	Cavan-Monaghan	5	3		1	1			
3	Clare	4	2	1	1				
4	Cork East	4	2	1		1			
5	Cork North Central	4	1	1	1	1			
6	Cork North West	3	2		1				
7	Cork South Central	5	2	1	2				
8	Cork South West	3	2	1					
9	Donegal North East	3	1		1	1			
10	Donegal South West	3	1			1			1
11	Dublin Central	4	1	1		1			1
12	Dublin Mid West	4	2	2					
13	Dublin North	4	2	1			1		
14	Dublin North Central	3	1	1					1
15	Dublin North East	3	1	2					
16	Dublin North West	3		2		1			
17	Dublin South	5	3	1					1
18	Dublin South Central	5	1	2		1	1		
19	Dublin South East	4	2	2					
20	Dublin South West	4	1	2		1			
21	Dublin West	4	1	1	1		1		
22	Dun Laoghaire	4	2	1			1		
23	Galway East	4	2	1	1				
24	Galway West	5	2	1	1				1
25	Kerry North-West Limerick	3	1	1		1			
26	Kerry South	3	1						2
27	Kildare North	4	2	1					1
28	Kildare South	3	1	1	1				
29	Laois-Offaly	5	2		2	1			
30	Limerick	3	2		1				
31	Limerick City	4	2	1	1				
32	Longford-Westmeath	4	2	1	1				
33	Louth	5	2	1	1	1			
34	Mayo	5	4		1				
35	Meath East	3	2	1					
36	Meath West	3	2			1			
37	Roscommon-Sth Leitrim	3	2						1
38	Sligo-North Leitrim	3	2			1			
39	Tipperary North	3	1	1					1
40	Tipperary South	3	1				1		1
41	Waterford	4	2	1					1
42	Wexford	5	2	1	1				1
43	Wicklow	5	3	1					1
	2011	166	76	37	20	14	5	0	14
	2007	166	51	20	78	4	0	6	7
	Change 2011-2007	**+/-**	**+25**	**+17**	**-58**	**+10**	**+5**	**-6**	**+7**
12	Dublin	47	17	18	1	4	4		3
10	Leinster	42	21	8	7	3			3
13	Munster	46	21	9	7	3	1		5
8	Connaught-Ulster	31	17	2	5	4	0		3

CANDIDATES 2011-1989												
	2011		2007		2002		1997		1992		1989	
Party	**Cands**	**% Total**	**Cands**	**% Total**	**Cands**	**% Total**	**Cands**	**% Total**	**Cands**	**% Total**	**Cands**	**% Total**
FG	104	18.34%	91	19.32%	85	18.36%	90	18.60%	91	18.88%	86	23.18%
LB	68	11.99%	50	10.62%	46	9.94%	44	9.09%	42	8.71%	33	8.89%
FF	76	13.40%	107	22.72%	106	22.89%	112	23.14%	122	25.31%	115	31.00%
SF	41	7.23%	41	8.70%	37	7.99%	15	3.10%	41	8.51%	14	3.77%
ULA	20	3.53%										
SP			4	0.85%	5	1.08%	5	1.03%				
GP	43	7.58%	44	9.34%	31	6.70%	26	5.37%	19	3.94%	11	2.96%
WP	6	1.06%	6	1.27%	8	1.73%	7	1.45%	18	3.73%	23	6.20%
CS	8	1.41%	8	1.70%	23	4.97%	8	1.65%				
PD			30	6.37%	20	4.32%	30	6.20%	20	4.15%	35	9.43%
SW					7	1.51%	4	0.83%				
DL							13	2.69%	20	4.15%		
Others	201	35.45%	90	19.11%	95	20.52%	130	26.86%	109	22.61%	54	14.56%
Total	**567**	**100.00%**	**471**	**100.00%**	**463**	**100.00%**	**484**	**100.00%**	**482**	**100.00%**	**371**	**100.00%**

Candidates include outgoing Ceann Comhairle when returned automatically

2011 GENERAL ELECTION NUMBER OF SEATS WON PER PARTY PER CONSTITUENCY							
Party	**4 Seats**	**3 Seats**	**2 Seats**	**1 Seat**	**0 Seats**	**Total**	**Seats**
FG	1	4	23	14	1	43	76
LB			6	25	12	43	37
FF			2	16	25	43	20
SF				14	29	43	14
Others			2	15	26	43	19
Total	**1**	**4**	**33**	**84**	**93**		**166**

PARTIES HIGHEST & LOWEST % VOTE 2011				
Party	**Highest**	**Constituency**	**Lowest**	**Constituency**
FG	64.96%	Mayo	16.75%	Dublin North West
LB	43.15%	Dublin North West	4.91%	Mayo
FF	28.01%	Cork South Central	9.42%	Dublin South
SF	32.97%	Donegal South West	3.64%	Dublin South East
ULA	21.32%	Tipperary South	0.76%	Laois-Offaly
GP	8.48%	Dublin North	0.36%	Mayo
Others	42.03%	Kerry South	0.66%	Dublin West

LARGEST CHANGE IN % VOTE 2011				
Party	**Gain**	**Constituency**	**Loss**	**Constituency**
FG	+18.93%	Dublin Mid-West	-3.15%	Donegal South West
LB	+22.85%	Dublin North West	-2.38%	Kerry South
FF			-37.10%	Dublin North West
SF	+11.73%	Donegal South West	-3.52%	Kerry South*
GP			-8.18%	Dublin North
Others	+26.68%	Kerry South	-10.11%	Dublin South Central

*Did not contest in 2011

FINE GAEL'S TOP CONSTITUENCIES						
	Constituency	Seats	1st Prefs	%	Quotas	FG Seats
1	Mayo	5	48,170	64.96%	3.90	4
2	Wicklow	5	27,926	39.61%	2.38	3
3	Cavan-Monaghan	5	28,199	39.56%	2.37	3
4	Carlow-Kilkenny	5	28,924	39.22%	2.35	3
5	Dublin South	5	26,404	36.35%	2.18	3
6	Limerick City	4	18,696	43.29%	2.16	2
7	Galway East	4	25,409	42.87%	2.14	2
8	Clare	4	24,524	42.34%	2.12	2
9	Cork South Central	5	22,225	34.70%	2.08	2
10	Wexford	5	26,034	34.46%	2.07	2
11	Laois-Offaly	5	25,032	33.75%	2.03	2
12	Cork North West	3	22,321	48.80%	1.95	2
13	Limerick	3	21,925	48.68%	1.95	2
14	Cork South West	3	22,162	48.54%	1.94	2
15	Longford-Westmeath	4	21,887	38.05%	1.90	2
16	Waterford	4	20,416	38.00%	1.90	2
17	Meath West	3	18,450	45.92%	1.84	2
18	Galway West	5	18,627	30.72%	1.84	2
19	Cork East	4	20,847	36.62%	1.83	2
20	Dublin South East	4	12,402	35.52%	1.78	2

FINE GAEL'S TOP TEN INCREASED SUPPORT						
	Constituency	Seats	2011	2007	Gain	FG Seats
1	Dublin Mid-West	4	30.93%	12.00%	+18.93%	2
2	Limerick City	4	43.29%	25.52%	+17.77%	2
3	Dublin North	4	31.39%	14.03%	+17.36%	2
4	Meath West	3	45.92%	29.03%	+16.89%	2
5	Dublin South East	4	35.52%	18.65%	+16.87%	1
6	Wicklow	5	39.61%	23.15%	+16.46%	2
7	Kildare South	3	33.33%	17.17%	+16.16%	1
8	Meath East	3	40.87%	25.88%	+14.99%	2
9	Tipperary South	3	34.57%	21.14%	+13.43%	1
10	Cork South West	3	48.54%	36.00%	+12.54%	2

LABOUR'S TOP CONSTITUENCIES						
	Constituency	Seats	1st Prefs	%	Quotas	LB Seats
1	Dublin South Central	5	18,032	35.41%	2.12	2
2	Dublin South West	4	17,032	36.27%	1.81	2
3	Dublin North West	3	14,158	43.15%	1.73	2
4	Dublin Mid-West	4	13,138	30.75%	1.54	2
5	Cork East	4	17,563	30.85%	1.54	1
6	Dun Laoghaire	4	17,217	30.38%	1.52	1
7	Kildare North	4	14,979	29.24%	1.46	1
8	Dublin West	4	12,313	28.99%	1.45	1
9	Dublin Central	4	9,787	28.28%	1.41	1
10	Dublin North East	3	14,371	34.35%	1.37	2
11	Longford-Westmeath	4	15,366	26.71%	1.34	1
12	Cork North Central	4	13,801	26.47%	1.32	1
13	Dublin North	4	13,014	26.37%	1.32	1
14	Dublin South East	4	8,857	25.36%	1.27	2
15	Wexford	5	15,462	20.47%	1.23	1
16	Kildare South	3	10,645	27.82%	1.11	1
17	Cork South Central	5	11,869	18.53%	1.11	1
18	Dublin South	5	13,059	17.98%	1.08	1
19	Wicklow	5	12,087	17.14%	1.03	1
20	Limerick City	4	8,764	20.29%	1.01	1

LABOUR'S TOP TEN INCREASED SUPPORT						
	Constituency	Seats	2011	2007	Gain	LB Seats
1	Dublin North West	3	43.15%	20.30%	+22.85%	2
2	Dublin Mid-West	4	30.75%	10.91%	+19.84%	2
3	Dublin North East	3	34.35%	15.16%	+19.19%	2
4	Dublin North	4	26.37%	9.62%	+16.75%	1
5	Dublin South West	4	36.27%	19.99%	+16.28%	2
6	Dublin Central	4	28.28%	12.57%	+15.71%	1
7	Dublin North Central	3	22.52%	7.27%	+15.25%	1
8	Dun Laoghaire	4	30.38%	16.00%	+14.38%	1
9	Dublin South Central	5	35.41%	21.13%	+14.28%	2
10	Louth	4	19.13%	4.98%	+14.15%	1

	FIANNA FAIL'S TOP CONSTITUENCIES					
	Constituency	Seats	1st Prefs	%	Quotas	FF Seats
1	Carlow-Kilkenny	5	20,721	28.10%	1.69	1
2	Cork South Central	5	17,936	28.01%	1.68	2
3	Laois-Offaly	5	19,860	26.78%	1.61	2
4	Galway West	5	12,703	20.95%	1.26	1
5	Cavan-Monaghan	5	14,360	20.15%	1.21	1
6	Clare	4	12,804	22.11%	1.11	1
7	Wexford	5	14,027	18.57%	1.11	1
8	Limerick City	4	9,259	21.44%	1.07	1
9	Cork North West	3	11,390	24.90%	1.00	1
10	Longford-Westmeath	4	11,197	19.46%	0.97	1

	FIANNA FAIL'S TOP TEN LOST SUPPORT					
	Constituency	Seats	2011	2007	Loss	FF Seats
1	Dublin North West	3	11.79%	48.84%	-37.05%	0
2	Meath West	3	18.13%	51.59%	-33.46%	0
3	Tipperary South	3	13.10%	46.42%	-33.32%	0
4	Donegal North East	3	17.44%	50.26%	-32.82%	1
5	Waterford	4	13.99%	46.49%	-32.50%	0
6	Dublin South	5	9.42%	41.33%	-31.91%	0
7	Dublin North Central	3	12.94%	44.02%	-31.08%	0
8	Laois-Offaly	5	26.78%	56.38%	-29.60%	2
9	Dublin Central	4	14.85%	44.45%	-29.60%	0
10	Kildare South	3	21.71%	50.37%	-28.66%	1

	SINN FEIN'S TOP CONSTITUENCIES					
	Constituency	Seats	1st Prefs	%	Quotas	SF Seats
1	Cavan-Monaghan	5	18,452	25.89%	1.55	1
2	Donegal South West	3	14,262	32.97%	1.32	1
3	Louth	4	15,072	21.74%	1.09	1
4	Donegal North East	3	9,278	24.47%	0.98	1
5	Dublin North West	3	7,115	21.68%	0.87	1
6	Dublin South West	4	8,064	17.17%	0.86	1
7	Kerry North-West Limerick	3	9,282	20.35%	0.81	1
8	Dublin South Central	5	6,804	13.36%	0.80	1
9	Cork North Central	4	7,923	15.20%	0.76	1
10	Meath West	3	6,989	17.40%	0.70	1

	SINN FEIN'S TOP TEN INCREASED SUPPORT					
	Constituency	Seats	2011	2007	Gain	SF Seats
1	Donegal South West	3	32.97%	21.23%	+11.74%	1
2	Cork North West	3	7.44%		+7.44%	1
3	Cork North Central	4	15.20%	8.16%	+7.04%	1
4	Donegal North East	3	24.47%	17.47%	+7.00%	1
5	Louth	4	21.74%	15.04%	+6.70%	1
6	Meath West	3	17.40%	11.29%	+6.11%	1
7	Dublin North West	3	21.68%	15.74%	+5.94%	1
8	Cavan-Monaghan	5	25.89%	20.01%	+5.88%	1
9	Carlow-Kilkenny	5	9.54%	3.80%	+5.74%	1
10	Laois-Offaly	5	10.83%	5.11%	+5.72%	1

TURNOVER OF SEATS 2011

This election delivered the biggest number of retirements to date 39 which was well above the previous highest, 29 in June 1927. This number included the three deputies that had retired earlier but for whom the by-elections had not been held, George Lee, Fine Gael Dublin South, Martin Cullen, Fianna Fail Waterford and Dr. James McDaid, Fianna Fail Donegal North-East. The large majority of these retirements were from Fianna Fail, 23 with nine from Fine Gael, four from Labour, one from Sinn Fein and two independents.

There was a high rate of attrition in this election with 45 outgoing deputies losing their seats, up 15 on 2007. Thus there were 84 new TD's (49 in 2007), 8 of whom were former deputies. Fine Gael had the highest number of new members, 34 with two former deputies also returned. The Labour Party gained 19 new faces, along with two former deputies. Fianna Fail despite their sharp decline returned three new faces. Sinn Fein returned nine new TD's and one former deputy. The ULA got three new deputies elected along with two former members. There were eight new independent deputies returned along with former independent Catherine Murphy.

Galway East was destined to be one of the most changed constituencies with three of its four sitting deputies retiring and it duly returned three new TD's. It was all change in Cork South-West and Kerry South as all three returned in both three seaters were new members. There were also three new deputies in Carlow-Kilkenny, Cavan-Monaghan, Dublin Mid-West, Dublin North, Dublin South, Dublin South-Central, Galway West, Laois-Offaly, Louth, Waterford and Wicklow. With all this change it came as no surprise that not a single constituency returned the same deputies as 2007.

TURNOVER OF SEATS 2011

	Constituency	Seats	Outgoing TD's who did not run	Party	Outgoing TD's who lost	Party	New TD's	Party
1	Carlow-Kilkenny	5	M.J. Nolan	FF	Bobby Aylward	FF	Ann Phelan	LB
					Mary White	GP	John Paul Phelan	FG
							Pat Deering	FG
2	Cavan-Monaghan	5	Rory O'Hanlon	FF	Margaret Conlon	FF	Joe O'Reilly	FG
			Seymour Crawford	FG			Sean Conlan	FG
							Heather Humphreys	FG
3	Clare	4	Tony Killeen	FF			Michael McNamara	LB
4	Cork East	4	Ned O'Keeffe	FF	Michael Ahern	FF	Tom Barry	FG
							Sandra McLellan	SF
5	Cork North Central	4	Bernard Allen	FG			Jonathan O'Brien	SF
			Noel O'Flynn	FF			Dara Murphy	FG
6	Cork North West	3	Batt O'Keeffe	FF			Aine Collins	FG
7	Cork South Central	5			Deidre Clune	FG	Jerry Buttimer	FG
8	Cork South West	3	Jim O'Keeffe	FG	Christy O'Sullivan	FF	Jim Daly	FG
			P.J. Sheehan	FG			Noel Harrington	FG
							Michael McCarthy	LB
9	Donegal North East	3	James McDaid	FF			Padraig MacLochlainn	SF
			Niall Blaney	FF			Charlie McConalogue	FF
10	Donegal South West	3			Mary Coughlan	FF	Thomas Pringle	NP
11	Dublin Central	4	Bertie Ahern	FF	Cyprian Brady	FF	Paschal Donohoe	FG
							Mary Lou McDonald	SF
12	Dublin Mid West	4	Mary Harney	NP	John Curran	FF	Frances Fitzgerald	FG
					Paul Gogarty	GP	Derek Keating	FG
							Robert Dowds	LB
13	Dublin North	4			Trevor Sargent	GP	Brendan Ryan	LB
					Darragh O'Brien	FF	Clare Daly	SP
					Michael Kennedy	FF	Alan Farrell	FG
14	Dublin North Central	3			Sean Haughey	FF	Aodhan O Riordain	LB
15	Dublin North East	3	Michael Woods	FF			Sean Kenny	LB

TURNOVER OF SEATS 2011

	Constituency	Seats	Outgoing TD's who did not run	Party	Outgoing TD's who lost	Party	New TD's	Party
16	Dublin North West	3	Noel Ahern	FF	Pat Carey	FF	Dessie Ellis	SF
							John Lyons	LB
17	Dublin South	5	Tom Kitt	FF	Eamon Ryan	GP	Shane Ross	NP
			George Lee	FG			Alex White	LB
							Peter Mathews	FG
18	Dublin South Central	5	Mary Upton	LB	Michael Mulcahy	FF	Eric Byrne	LB
			Sean Ardagh	FF			Michael Conaghan	LB
							Joan Collins	PBPA
19	Dublin South East	4			Chris Andrews	FF	Eoghan Murphy	FG
					John Gormley	GP	Kevin Humphreys	LB
20	Dublin South West	4			Charlie O'Connor	FF	Sean Crowe	SF
					Conor Lenihan	FF	Eamonn Maloney	LB
21	Dublin West*	4					Joe Higgins	SP
22	Dun Laoghaire*	4			Mary Hanafin	FF	Mary Mitchell O'Connor	FG
					Barry Andrews	FF	Richard Boyd Barrett	PBPA
					Ciaran Cuffe	GP		
23	Galway East	4	Paul Connaughton	FG			Paul Connaughton	FG
			Ulick Burke	FG			Ciaran Cannon	FG
			Noel Treacy	FF			Colm Keaveney	LB
24	Galway West	5	Michael D. Higgins	LB	Frank Fahey	FF	Derek Nolan	LB
			Pauric McCormack	FG			Brian Walsh	FG
							Sean Kyne	FG
25	Kerry North-West Limerick	3			Thomas McEllistrim	FF	Arthur Spring	LB
26	Kerry South	3	Jackie Healy-Rae	NP	John O'Donoghue	FF	Michael Healy Rae	NP
					John Sheahan	FG	Brendan Griffin	FG
							Tom Fleming	NP
27	Kildare North	4			Aine Brady	FF	Anthony Lawlor	FG
					Michael Fitzpatrick	FF	Catherine Murphy	NP
28	Kildare South	3			Sean Power	FF	Martin Heydon	FG
29	Laoighis-Offaly	5	Olwyn Enright	FG	John Moloney	FF	Barry Cowen	FF
			Brian Cowen	FF			Brian Stanley	SF
							Marcella Corcoran-Kennedy	FG
30	Limerick	3	John Cregan	FF			Patrick O'Donovan	FG
31	Limerick City*	4			Peter Power	FF		
32	Longford-Westmeath	4			Mary O'Rourke	FF	Nicky McFadden	FG
					Peter Kelly	FF	Robert Troy	FF
33	Louth*	5	Arthur Morgan	SF			Gerry Adams	SF
			Dermot Ahern	FF			Gerald Nash	LB
							Peter Fitzpatrick	FG
34	Mayo	5	Beverley Flynn	FF			Michelle Mulherin	FG
35	Meath East	3	Mary Wallace	FF	Thomas Byrne	FF	Regina Doherty	FG
							Dominic Hannigan	LB
36	Meath West	3	Noel Dempsey	FF	Johnny Brady	FF	Peadar Toibin	SF
							Ray Butler	FG
37	Roscommon-South Leitrim	3	Michael Finneran	FF			Luke "Ming" Flanagan	NP
38	Sligo-North Leitrim	3	Jimmy Devins	FF	Eamon Scanlon	FF	Tony McLoughlin	FG
							Michael Colreavy	SF
39	Tipperary North	3			Maire Hoctor	FF	Alan Kelly	LB
40	Tipperary South	3			Martin Mansergh	FF	Seamus Healy	ULA
41	Waterford	4	Martin Cullen	FF	Brendan Keneally	FF	Paudie Coffey	FG
			Brian O'Shea	LB			Ciara Conway	LB
							John Halligan	NP
42	Wexford	5			Sean Connick	FF	Mick Wallace	NP
					Michael D'Arcy	FG	Liam Twomey	FG
43	Wicklow	5	Liz McManus	LB	Dick Roche	FF	Simon Harris	FG
					Joe Behan	NP	Anne Ferris	LB
43	Total	166					Stephen Donnelly	NP
	* Change in number of seats since 2007						**Former TD**	8
	2011	**166**	**39**		**45**		**76**	8
	2007	**166**	**19**		**30**		**38**	11
	2002	**166**	**22**		**33**		**48**	7
	1997	**166**	**17**		**28**		**32**	13
	1992	**166**	**11**		**32**		**33**	10
	1989	**166**	**13**		**27**		**32**	9

TRANSFERS 2011

Fine Gael got the largest share of transfers in 2011 at 28.99%, down slightly on 2007 (31.29%). Labour were next with 17.73% (14.24%) of all transfers, just ahead of Fianna Fail on 17.13% which was down nine points on 2007 (25.78%). Sinn Fein were in fourth place with 6.95% of all transfers (3.46%). The Fine Gael internal transfer rate of 56.44% was up on 2007 (54.92%) and above 2002 (46.33%), 1997 (52.45%) and 1992 (54.42%). After internal transfers, Labour were the main recipient of Fine Gael transfers winning 12.77% with Fianna Fail gaining 10.26%. The majority of Labour transfers 28.57% went to Fine Gael with an internal rate of 24.71%. Fianna Fail's internal transfer rate was 37.78% with 18.19% going to Fine Gael up slightly on 2007 (16.30%). The majority of Sinn Fein's transfers were non-transferrable at 26.54% (16.91%) with Labour the main beneficiary with 23.71%.

In the 2011 general election 812,424 votes (665,516 in 2007, 589,948 in 2002 and 590,816 in 1997) were transferred or 36.59% of all votes cast in this election and 15% of them were non-transferable (11% in 2007, 12% in 2002 and 1997). This level of transfers was up four points on 2007 and was a reflection of the large increase in the number of independent candidates contesting this election, most of whom polled poorly and were eliminated. The net total of transfers was 688,214 or just 31% of the valid vote which was up two points on previous elections.

Parties normally get a similar share of the transfers as of the first preferences. Fine Gael got 36.10% of the first preferences (27.32% in 2007) and got 28.99% (31.29%) of all transfers and won 45.78% (30.72%) of the seats. Labour got 17.73% (14.24% in 2007) of the transfers and converted their 19.45% (10.13% in 2007) share of the first preference vote into 22.29% (12.05%) of the seats. Fianna Fail got 17.45% (41.56% in 2007) of the first preferences and 17.13% (25.78%) of the transfers and just 12% (47%) of the seats. Sinn Fein got 9.94% of the first preference vote and 6.95% of the transfers and ended up with 8.43% of the seats.

Fine Gael did well on transfers and increased their vote by 4.59% (3.89% in 2007) to 40.69% (31.21%). All other parties and independents ended up with fewer votes at the conclusion of the counts with independents the biggest losers with a net loss of 4.21%.

DUBLIN 2011

TRANSFER ANALYSIS

From	To	FG	LB	FF	SF	SP	PBPA	GP	WP	Others	Non Trans
FG	25,482	9,477	6,183	3,279	787	82	1,700	164		401	3,409
		37.19%	*24.26%*	*12.87%*	*3.09%*	*0.32%*	*6.67%*	*0.64%*		*1.57%*	*13.38%*
LB	34,815	7,685	10,080	2,899	1,538	1,607	3,110	1,980	10	2,609	3,297
		22.07%	*28.95%*	*8.33%*	*4.42%*	*4.62%*	*8.93%*	*5.69%*	*0.03%*	*7.49%*	*9.47%*
FF	38,415	6,683	7,009	7,494	2,319	546	281	441		3,077	10,565
		17.40%	*18.25%*	*19.51%*	*6.04%*	*1.42%*	*0.73%*	*1.15%*		*8.01%*	*27.50%*
SF	10,313	985	4,418	782				434		1,444	2,250
		9.55%	*42.84%*	*7.58%*				*4.21%*		*14.00%*	*21.82%*
SP	5,861	966	1,300	460	1,686		217	95		247	890
		16.48%	*22.18%*	*7.85%*	*28.77%*		*3.70%*	*1.62%*		*4.21%*	*15.19%*
PBPA	7,688	975	2,539	421	1,960			208		777	808
		12.68%	*33.03%*	*5.48%*	*25.49%*			*2.71%*		*10.11%*	*10.51%*
GP	24,692	8,591	4,114	3,580	924	1,924	613			936	4,010
		34.79%	*16.66%*	*14.50%*	*3.74%*	*7.79%*	*2.48%*			*3.79%*	*16.24%*
WP	1,391	124	384	92	268		245	38		118	122
		8.91%	*27.61%*	*6.61%*	*19.27%*		*17.61%*	*2.73%*		*8.48%*	*8.77%*
Others	33,841	6,807	7,944	3,608	3,052	625	1,517	1,803	68	4,322	4,095
		20.11%	*23.47%*	*10.66%*	*9.02%*	*1.85%*	*4.48%*	*5.33%*	*0.20%*	*12.77%*	*12.10%*
Total	**182,498**	**42,293**	**43,971**	**22,615**	**12,534**	**4,784**	**7,683**	**5,163**	**78**	**13,931**	**29,446**
		23.17%	***24.09%***	***12.39%***	***6.87%***	***2.62%***	***4.21%***	***2.83%***	***0.04%***	***7.63%***	***16.13%***

LEINSTER 2011

TRANSFER ANALYSIS

From	To	FG	LB	FF	SF	SP	PBPA	GP	Others	Non Trans
FG	20,668	10,526	1,819	2,708	1,470			425	2,509	1,211
		50.93%	*8.80%*	*13.10%*	*7.11%*			*2.06%*	*12.14%*	*5.86%*
LB	41,444	11,583	13,867	4,056	1,934			101	4,242	5,661
		27.95%	*33.46%*	*9.79%*	*4.67%*			*0.24%*	*10.24%*	*13.66%*
FF	65,335	11,530	4,485	30,252	3,719				3,400	11,949
		17.65%	*6.86%*	*46.30%*	*5.69%*			*0.00%*	*5.20%*	*18.29%*
SF	29,645	6,373	3,878	3,753	1,885			114	3,094	10,548
		21.50%	*13.08%*	*12.66%*	*6.36%*			*0.38%*	*10.44%*	*35.58%*
SP	1,821	361	353	222	398			85	189	213
		19.82%	*19.38%*	*12.19%*	*21.86%*			*4.67%*	*10.38%*	*11.70%*
PBPA	778	151	237	110	152					128
		19.41%	*30.46%*	*14.14%*	*19.54%*					*16.45%*
GP	11,236	2,601	3,343	1,817	748	22			1,292	1,413
		23.15%	*29.75%*	*16.17%*	*6.66%*	*0.20%*			*11.50%*	*12.58%*
WP	189	60	39	21	40					29
		31.75%	*20.63%*	*11.11%*	*21.16%*					*15.34%*
Others	57,069	13,908	9,825	8,519	6,023	103	37	795	8,172	9,687
		24.37%	*17.22%*	*14.93%*	*10.55%*	*0.18%*	*0.06%*	*1.39%*	*14.32%*	*16.97%*
Total	**228,185**	**57,093**	**37,846**	**51,458**	**16,369**	**125**	**37**	**1,520**	**22,898**	**40,839**
		25.02%	***16.59%***	***22.55%***	***7.17%***	***0.05%***	***0.02%***	***0.67%***	***10.03%***	***17.90%***

MUNSTER 2011										
TRANSFER ANALYSIS										
From	**To**	**FG**	**LB**	**FF**	**SF**	**SP**	**GP**	**WP**	**Others**	**Non Trans**
FG	51,744	32,841	6,255	4,620	1,578	19	38		1,958	4,435
		63.47%	*12.09%*	*8.93%*	*3.05%*	*0.04%*	*0.07%*		*3.78%*	*8.57%*
LB	39,754	11,589	9,781	2,975	3,487		5		5,978	5,939
		29.15%	*24.60%*	*7.48%*	*8.77%*		*0.01%*		*15.04%*	*14.94%*
FF	40,300	7,611	4,382	12,537	1,955		1		7,402	6,412
		18.89%	*10.87%*	*31.11%*	*4.85%*		*0.00%*		*18.37%*	*15.91%*
SF	19,836	2,635	7,142	2,301					3,064	4,694
		13.28%	*36.01%*	*11.60%*					*15.45%*	*23.66%*
SP	6,118	513	2,003	311	2,801					490
		8.39%	*32.74%*	*5.08%*	*45.78%*					*8.01%*
PBPA	1,552	448	454	178	360					112
		28.87%	*29.25%*	*11.47%*	*23.20%*					*7.22%*
GP	8,594	2,405	2,736	848	607	67		36	1,049	846
		27.98%	*31.84%*	*9.87%*	*7.06%*	*0.78%*		*0.42%*	*12.21%*	*9.84%*
WP	1,678	120	414	98	379	191			382	94
		7.15%	*24.67%*	*5.84%*	*22.59%*	*11.38%*			*22.77%*	*5.60%*
Others	46,781	12,840	9,454	5,058	3,798	317	459	88	8,379	6,388
		27.45%	*20.21%*	*10.81%*	*8.12%*	*0.68%*	*0.98%*	*0.19%*	*17.91%*	*13.66%*
Total	**216,357**	**71,002**	**42,621**	**28,926**	**14,965**	**594**	**503**	**124**	**28,212**	**29,410**
		32.82%	***19.70%***	***13.37%***	***6.92%***	***0.27%***	***0.23%***	***0.06%***	***13.04%***	***13.59%***

CONNAUGHT-ULSTER 2011								
TRANSFER ANALYSIS								
From	**To**	**FG**	**LB**	**FF**	**SF**	**GP**	**Others**	**Non Trans**
FG	35,815	22,628	2,820	3,116	921	16	3,952	2,362
		63.18%	*7.87%*	*8.70%*	*2.57%*	*0.04%*	*11.03%*	*6.60%*
LB	30,417	10,979	2,451	3,185	3,296		4,745	5,761
		36.09%	*8.06%*	*10.47%*	*10.84%*		*15.60%*	*18.94%*
FF	38,233	7,330	2,015	18,581	2,182		3,928	4,197
		19.17%	*5.27%*	*48.60%*	*5.71%*		*10.27%*	*10.98%*
SF	25,030	5,833	4,086	2,488	1,428	141	5,774	5,280
		23.30%	*16.32%*	*9.94%*		*0.56%*	*23.07%*	*21.09%*
GP	3,893	869	865	483	356		1,094	226
		22.32%	*22.22%*	*12.41%*	*9.14%*		*28.10%*	*5.81%*
Others	51,996	17,510	7,348	8,341	4,382	33	7,693	6,689
		33.68%	*14.13%*	*16.04%*	*8.43%*	*0.06%*	*14.80%*	*12.86%*
Total	**185,384**	**65,149**	**19,585**	**36,194**	**12,565**	**190**	**27,186**	**24,515**
		35.14%	***10.56%***	***19.52%***	***6.78%***	***0.10%***	***14.66%***	***13.22%***

NATIONAL 2011											
TRANSFER ANALYSIS											
From	To	FG	LB	FF	SF	SP	PBPA	GP	WP	Others	Non Trans
FG	133,709	75,472	17,077	13,723	4,756	101	1,700	643		8,820	11,417
		56.44%	12.77%	10.26%	3.56%	0.08%	1.27%	0.48%		6.60%	8.54%
LB	146,430	41,836	36,179	13,115	10,255	1,607	3,110	2,086	10	17,574	20,658
		28.57%	24.71%	8.96%	7.00%	1.10%	2.12%	1.42%	0.01%	12.00%	14.11%
FF	182,283	33,154	17,891	68,864	10,175	546	281	442		17,807	33,123
		18.19%	9.81%	37.78%	5.58%	0.30%	0.15%	0.24%		9.77%	18.17%
SF	88,849	17,041	21,062	9,789	3,313			689		13,376	23,579
		19.18%	23.71%	11.02%	3.73%			0.78%		15.05%	26.54%
SP	13,800	1,840	3,656	993	4,885		217	180		436	1,593
		13.33%	26.49%	7.20%	35.40%		1.57%	1.30%		3.16%	11.54%
PBPA	10,018	1,574	3,230	709	2,472			208		777	1,048
		15.71%	32.24%	7.08%	24.68%			2.08%		7.76%	10.46%
GP	48,415	14,466	11,058	6,728	2,635	2,013	613		36	4,371	6,495
		29.88%	22.84%	13.90%	5.44%	4.16%	1.27%		0.07%	9.03%	13.42%
WP	3,258	304	837	211	687	191	245	38		500	245
		9.33%	25.69%	6.48%	21.09%	5.86%	7.52%	1.17%		15.35%	7.52%
Others	185,662	49,850	33,033	25,061	17,255	1,045	1,554	3,090	156	28,566	26,052
		26.85%	17.79%	13.50%	9.29%	0.56%	0.84%	1.66%	0.08%	15.39%	14.03%
Total	**812,424**	**235,537**	**144,023**	**139,193**	**56,433**	**5,503**	**7,720**	**7,376**	**202**	**92,227**	**124,210**
		28.99%	***17.73%***	***17.13%***	***6.95%***	***0.68%***	***0.95%***	***0.91%***	***0.02%***	***11.35%***	***15.29%***

SHARE OF TRANSFERS 1992-2011														
Election	FG	LB	FF	SF	SP	PBPA	GP	WP	PD	Others	Non Trans	Total	Net Trans	Valid
2011	235,537	144,023	139,193	56,433	5,503	7,720	7,376	202		92,227	124,210	812,424	688,214	2,220,359
	28.99%	17.73%	17.13%	6.95%	0.68%	0.95%	0.91%	0.02%		11.35%	15.29%	36.59%	31.00%	
2007	208,239	94,742	171,575	23,059	3,791		39,044	402	14,288	38,736	71,640	665,516	593,876	2,065,810
	31.29%	14.24%	25.78%	3.46%	0.57%		5.87%	0.06%	2.15%	5.82%	10.76%	32.22%	28.75%	
2002	162,991	78,244	154,380	19,329	3,673		29,201	383	20,037	51,298	70,412	589,948	519,536	1,857,902
	27.63%	13.26%	26.17%	3.28%	0.62%		4.95%	0.06%	3.40%	8.70%	11.94%	31.75%	27.96%	
1997	148,776	77,619	188,531	7,175	2,270		16,306	1,979	23,661	52,874	71,625	590,816	519,191	1,788,985
	25.18%	13.14%	31.91%	1.21%	0.38%		2.76%	0.33%	4.00%	8.95%	12.12%	33.03%	29.02%	
1992	166,618	32,881	168,496	3,190			15,598	32,891	31,496	31,319	82,538	565,027	482,489	1,724,853
	29.49%	5.82%	29.82%	0.56%			2.76%	5.82%	5.57%	5.54%	14.61%	32.76%	27.97%	

SHARE OF TRANSFERS V SHARE OF VOTES & SEATS 2011												
	First Preferences		Transfers				Votes			Seats		
Party	1st	%	Gained	%	Lost	Net	Total	%	Change	Seats	% Seats	S/V
FG	801,628	36.10%	235,537	28.99%	133,709	+101,828	903,456	40.69%	+4.59%	76	45.78%	126.81%
LB	431,796	19.45%	144,023	17.73%	146,430	-2,407	429,389	19.34%	-0.11%	37	22.29%	114.61%
FF	387,358	17.45%	139,193	17.13%	182,283	-43,090	344,268	15.51%	-1.94%	20	12.05%	69.06%
SF	220,661	9.94%	56,433	6.95%	88,849	-32,416	188,245	8.48%	-1.46%	14	8.43%	84.86%
SP	26,770	1.21%	5,503	0.68%	13,800	-8,297	18,473	0.83%	-0.37%	2	1.20%	99.93%
PBPA	21,551	0.97%	7,720	0.95%	10,018	-2,298	19,253	0.87%	-0.10%	2	1.20%	124.13%
GP	41,039	1.85%	7,376	0.91%	48,415	-41,039			-1.85%			
WP	3,056	0.14%	202	0.02%	3,258	-3,056			-0.14%			
Others	286,500	12.90%	92,227	11.35%	185,662	-93,435	193,065	8.70%	-4.21%	15	9.04%	70.03%
Non-trans			124,210	15.29%		+124,210	124,210	5.59%	+5.59%			
Total	**2,220,359**	**100.0%**	**812,424**	**100.0%**	**812,424**	**0**	**2,220,359**	**100.0%**	**0.0%**	**166**	**100.0%**	

Sean Donnelly's Election Rules

1. Candidates have to be in the frame on the first count

For a candidate to have a good chance of getting elected they have to be in the frame on the first count. This means that as a general rule in a five-seat constituency the candidate has to come in the first five on the first count. In a three-seat constituency the candidate has to be in the first three places and in the first four in a four-seat constituency. In the 2011 general election there were only 11 candidates who came from outside the frame to get elected. In other words 93% of those elected were within the frame on the first count.

An example of one of those 11 occurred in the four-seat Clare constituency in 2011 where Fine Gael's Tony Mulcahy was in fourth place on the first count. Fianna Fail's Timmy Dooley was in fifth place but managed to overtake Mulcahy and went on to take the fourth and final seat. Thus Dooley came from just outside the frame to claim a seat. The idea of a "Lazarus" type recovery rarely happens and when this rule is broken it is usually from a position just outside the frame as in Dooley's case. Transfers are important but they don't always have the influence that we often think they do.

2. Candidates must have at least half a quota on the first count

A candidate must have at least half a quota on the first count to have any chance of getting elected. Only four of those elected in 2011 got below half a quota on the first count with only two in 2007 and three in 1997. In other words 98% of those elected had at least half a quota on the first count. It is important to note that half a quota will not guarantee a seat but less than that level will leave a candidate with very little chance of getting elected.

These two election rules are usually broken by political parties running too many candidates. A good example of this in 2011 was in the constituency of Donegal South West where Fianna Fáil ran two candidates, Mary Coughlan and Brían Ó Domhnaill. Both candidates were outside the frame on the first count and both were below the half quota level and Independent Thomas Pringle slipped through for the final seat. Thus Fianna Fail with 0.9 of a quota on the first count were beaten by Pringle who had just 0.5 of a quota. The Fianna Fail Donegal South-West performance contrasted sharply with its neighbouring constituency of Donegal North-East where they won just 17.44% of the first preference vote as against 22.53% in South West but won a seat by running just a single candidate. It is not so much the number of votes you have but rather how you manage these votes.

The Donnelly Rules and Election 2011: Seats Changed By Transfers

Our voting system is based on proportional representation using the single transferable vote (PR-STV). The general view is that the distribution of transfers substantially affects the final outcome in most constituencies. But on closer examination, this is not quite the case. Of the 165 seats filled in the 2011 election, in only 11 cases (14 in 2007) was the first count result changed after the transfers were completed. In other words, if the election had been declared after the first count, it would have differed by only 11 seats from the eventual result or by just 7% of the total seats. This figure was 8% in 2007, 11% in 2002 and 1997 and 10% in both 1992 and 1987 and only 8% in 1989. In 2011 two of these were battles between two candidates of the same party, thus the transfers only changed the overall party seats by 9 or just 5% of the total.

Of course, if we were operating a first past the post system, parties would run less candidates and the result would be different, but the point remains that the transfers do not significantly change the first count result. Thus, the first count is extremely important and what the figures clearly indicate is that if a candidate is not "in the frame" on the first count, he or she has less than a 10% chance of eventually winning a seat. This illustrates the advantage of running the minimum number of candidates as once the vote is divided the chances are that the candidates end up outside the frame on the first count.

Furthermore, as can be seen from the table of first count bases from which candidates were elected, it is obvious that to have a reasonable chance of a seat, a candidate must attain at least half a quota on the first count as all but four of the candidates elected in 2011 (two in 2007 & 2002 and three in 1997 and 1987) had at least that level of support. Only two of the members elected in 1992 had less than 0.5 quotas. Cyprian Brady really pushed the boat out in 2007 as he went on to win a seat from a first count of 939, just 0.1 of a quota or a mere 2.71% of the first preference vote.

GENERAL ELECTION 2011								
SEATS CHANGED BY TRANSFERS								
					1st Count			1st Count
	Constituency	Seats	Winner	Party	Position	Loser	Party	Position
1	Clare	4	Dooley, Timmy	FF	5	Mulcahy, Tony	FG	4
2	Cork North Central	4	Murphy, Dara	FG	5	Burton, Pat	FG	4
3	Dublin North East	3	Kenny, Sean	LB	5	O'Toole, Larry	SF	3
4	Dublin South East	4	Humphreys, Kevin	LB	5	Andrews, Chris	FF	4
5	Galway East	4	Keaveney, Colm	LB	8	McHugh, Tom	FG	4
6	Galway West	5	Kyne, Sean	FG	7	Healy-Eames, Fidelma	FG	5
7	Longford-Westmeath	4	Troy, Robert	FF	6	Burke, Peter	FG	3
8	Meath West	3	Butler, Ray	FG	4	McHugh, Jenny	LB	3
9	Waterford	4	Halligan, John	NP	5	Kenneally, Brendan	FF	3
10	Wexford	5	Browne, John	FF	6	D'Arcy, Michael	FG	3
11	Wicklow	5	Ferris, Anne	LB	6	Brady, John	SF	4

SUMMARY SEATS CHANGED BY TRANSFERS								
GENERAL ELECTIONS								
	2011	2007	2002	1997	1992	1989	1987	2011-1987
Total Seats	166	166	166	166	166	166	166	166
Seats Changed by Transfers	11	14	18	18	16	14	16	15
% Seats Changed by Transfers	7%	8%	11%	11%	10%	8%	10%	9%

LOCAL ELECTIONS								
	2009		2004		1999		1991	2009-1987
Total Seats	883		883		883		883	883
Seats Changed by Transfers	66		86		70		79	75
% Seats Changed by Transfers	7%		10%		8%		9%	9%

FIRST COUNT BASE FROM WHICH CANDIDATES WERE ELECTED												
	2011		2007		2002		1997		1992		1989	
Quotas	Elected	%	Elected	%	Elected	%	Elected	%	Elected	%	Elected	%
2.3			1	0.60%								
2.0											1	0.60%
1.8			1	0.60%								
1.7							1	0.60%	2	1.20%		
1.6			1	0.60%	3	1.81%			1	0.60%	1	0.60%
1.5	1	0.60%					2	1.20%	3	1.81%	1	0.60%
1.4	3	1.81%					1	0.60%	5	3.01%	1	0.60%
1.3	2	1.20%	3	1.81%	0	0.00%	2	1.20%	5	3.01%	2	1.20%
1.2	2	1.20%	8	4.82%	4	2.41%	5	3.01%	5	3.01%	6	3.61%
1.1	7	4.22%	5	3.01%	8	4.82%	7	4.22%	12	7.23%	25	15.06%
1.0	19	11.45%	22	13.25%	20	12.05%	16	9.64%	16	9.64%	24	14.46%
>1.0	34	20.48%	41	24.70%	35	21.08%	34	20.48%	49	29.52%	61	36.75%
0.9	22	13.25%	23	13.86%	26	15.66%	27	16.27%	19	11.45%	28	16.87%
0.8	35	21.08%	25	15.06%	39	23.49%	34	20.48%	35	21.08%	35	21.08%
0.7	31	18.67%	33	19.88%	31	18.67%	29	17.47%	23	13.86%	19	11.45%
0.6	24	14.46%	34	20.48%	24	14.46%	30	18.07%	21	12.65%	13	7.83%
0.5	16	9.64%	8	4.82%	9	5.42%	9	5.42%	17	10.24%	7	4.22%
0.4	4	2.41%	1	0.60%	1	0.60%	1	0.60%	2	1.20%	3	1.81%
0.3					1	0.60%	2	1.20%				
0.1			1	0.60%								
Total	166	100.00%	166	100.00%	166	100.00%	166	100.00%	166	100.00%	166	100.00%

SUMMARY GENERAL ELECTIONS												
Quotas	2011		2007		2002		1997		1992		1989	
> 1.0	34	20.48%	41	24.70%	35	21.08%	34	20.48%	49	29.52%	61	36.75%
0.5-0.9	128	77.11%	123	74.10%	129	77.71%	129	77.71%	115	69.28%	102	61.45%
< 0.5	4	2.41%	2	1.20%	2	1.20%	3	1.81%	2	1.20%	3	1.81%
Total	166	100.00%	166	100.00%	166	100.00%	166	100.00%	166	100.00%	166	100.00%

VOTE MANAGEMENT 2011

Fine Gael had a disastrous election in 2002 and got their poorest seats to votes ratio since the Dail was increased to 166 seats in 1981. They managed to convert their 22.48% of the first preference vote into only 18.7% of the seats and got less seats share than votes share for the first time. Their ratio of 83% was bettered by all of the main parties except Sinn Fein. They improved considerably in 2007 and increased their seats to votes ratio to a more normal 112.5%. They went on to beat this in 2011 with their best performance to date of 127% or a seats bonus of 16, the highest ever achieved by a party since PR was first used in 1922. Fine Gaels' best performance in 2011 was in Mayo where Enda Kenny managed to bring home three running mates for a remarkable four out of five and a feat never achieved previously. Fine Gael won three seats from 2.4 quotas in the five seaters of Carlow-Kilkenny, Cavan-Monaghan, and Wicklow and managed three from just 2.2 quotas in Dublin South. They were also in contention for a remarkable three out of four seats in Galway East and Longford-Westmeath.

Labour may not have had a great election in 2007 but they got their best seats to votes ratio to date of 119%, which was well above their average of 104%, since the Dail was increased to 166 seats in 1981. They dropped below this high point in 2011 with a seats to votes ratio of 115% or a seats bonus of five.

Fianna Fail took vote management seriously for the first time in 1997 and with practically the same vote as 1992, the party managed an extra nine seats. By running the minimum number of candidates and with better distribution of their votes, they got one of their best returns of seats for votes with a ratio of 118% compared to 105% in 1992. They repeated this performance in 2002 and again achieved a seats to vote ratio of 118%, which was well above their average since 1981 of 108%. They fell below this level in 2007 as they won three fewer seats than 2002 with the same vote, to give them a ratio of 113%. Fianna Fail had last won 78 seats in 1981 but it required 45.26% of the first preference vote. In 2007 they did it with four points less. But it was all change for Fianna Fail in 2011 with the collapse in their vote dropping them into a negative seats bonus for the first time as they got a seats to votes ratio of just 69% or ten seats less than their 17.45% first preference vote merited.

Smaller parties do not normally get a seats bonus and Sinn Fein are no exception to that rule. They managed a seats to votes ratio of 85% in this latest election, their best return since this latest version of Sinn Fein won its first seat in 1997. Despite this it was two seats less than their 9.94% of the first preference vote warranted.

GENERAL ELECTION 26/2/2011						
		Seats				
Party	**% First Pref**	**Per 1st Pref**	**Actual**	**Bonus**	**% Seats**	**% S/V**
FG	36.10%	60	76	+16	46.06%	127.59%
LB	19.45%	32	37	+5	22.42%	115.29%
FF	17.45%	29	19	-10	11.52%	65.99%
SF	9.94%	16	14	-2	8.48%	85.36%
ULA	2.68%	4	5	+1	3.03%	113.07%
GP	1.85%	3	0	-3	0.00%	0.00%
Others	12.53%	21	14	-7	8.48%	67.72%
Total	**100.00%**	**165**	**165**	**0**	100.00%	

UNUSED VOTES 2011

Most of the votes cast under our Proportional Representation system end up electing a candidate but there are a significant number of votes that are not used i.e. those of the surviving last candidate, as these votes usually are not transferred.

There were 476,643 or 21.5% (20.0% in 2007, 20.7% in 2002 and 20.1% in 1997) of the total votes cast, including 124,210 non transferrable votes, unused in this election. Fine Gael had 10 candidates (12 in 2007, 19 in 2002 and only 7 in 1997) left in the race at the end with the equivalent of 7.5 quotas between them. Labour had just 6 candidates as against just 4 in 2007 in the running for the last seat with a total of 5 quotas unused. Fianna Fail had 17 candidates beaten for the last seat (15 in 2007, 12 in 2002 and 13 in 1997) and their aggregate votes were equivalent to 13 quotas. Sinn Fein had 6 candidates left standing with 5 quotas.

James Carroll of Fianna Fail had the largest number of votes for a runner up, accumulating 11,238 votes in Louth. This is exaggerated somewhat due to the fact that only four of the five seats were contested as the outgoing Ceann Comhairle was automatically returned. Independent Catherine Connolly in Galway West and James Heffernan of Labour in Limerick got closest to the quota as they ended up with 0.9 quotas each. Maurice Quinlivan, Sinn Fein in Limerick City was at the other end of the scale reaching just 0.55 quotas. The smallest losing margin was 17 votes by Catherine Connolly in Galway West with John Brady, Sinn Fein beaten by 112 votes in Wicklow.

Fine Gael took the final seat in 15 constituencies, with Labour and Fianna Fail doing likewise in 8. Sinn Fein won the final seat in 5 constituencies with Independents taking the last seat in 7. Fianna Fail were beaten for the final seat in 17 constituencies with Fine Gael in the running in 10. Labour and Sinn Fein were the last party standing in 6 constituencies with Independents losing out in 4.

UNUSED VOTES PER CONSTITUENCY 2011

					Final			Final	Losers		% Swing	Valid	Non	Unused Votes	
	Constituency	Quota	Winner	Party	Votes	Loser	Party	Votes	Quotas	Margin	Required	Votes	Trans	Total	%
1	Carlow-Kilkenny	12,291	Pat Deering	FG	10,486	Bobby Aylward	FF	8,610	0.70	1,876	2.54%	73,743	5,155	13,765	18.67%
2	Cavan-Monaghan	11,880	Heather Humphreys	FG	10,861	Kathryn Reilly	SF	10,340	0.87	521	0.73%	71,275	3,669	14,009	19.65%
3	Clare	11,584	Timmy Dooley	FF	11,021	James Breen	NP	9,520	0.82	1,501	2.59%	57,916	1,419	10,939	18.89%
4	Cork East	11,387	Sandra McLellan	SF	9,785	Kevin O'Keeffe	FF	9,136	0.80	649	1.14%	56,933	3,788	12,924	22.70%
5	Cork North Central	10,428	Dara Murphy	FG	9,515	Pat Burton	FG	9,233	0.89	282	0.54%	52,137	2,938	12,171	23.34%
6	Cork North West	11,436	Aine Collins	FG	11,242	Martin Coughlan	LB	10,128	0.89	1,114	2.44%	45,740	1,511	11,639	25.45%
7	Cork South Central	10,674	Michael McGrath	FF	10,023	Chris O'Leary	SF	8,187	0.77	1,836	2.87%	64,040	2,936	11,123	17.37%
8	Cork South West	11,415	Michael McCarthy	LB	10,754	Denis O'Donovan	FF	10,155	0.89	599	1.31%	45,658	2,230	12,385	27.13%
9	Donegal North East	9,480	Charlie McConalogue	FF	8,976	Jimmy Harte	LB	7,219	0.76	1,757	4.63%	37,918	2,763	9,982	26.33%
10	Donegal South West	10,816	Thomas Pringle	NP	10,175	Brian O Domhnaill	FF	8,834	0.82	1,341	3.10%	43,263	2,069	10,903	25.20%
11	Dublin Central	6,923	Mary Lou McDonald	SF	6,587	Mary Fitzpatrick	FF	4,556	0.66	2,031	5.87%	34,612	1,311	5,867	16.95%
12	Dublin Mid West	8,545	Derek Keating	FG	7,703	Eoin O Broin	SF	7,151	0.84	552	1.29%	42,722	2,263	9,414	22.04%
13	Dublin North	9,870	Alan Farrell	FG	9,159	Darragh O'Brien	FF	8,067	0.82	1,092	2.21%	49,347	2,323	10,390	21.05%
14	Dublin North Central	9,694	Finian McGrath	NP	11,025	Naoise O Muiri	FG	6,399	0.66	4,626	11.93%	38,774	1,962	8,361	21.56%
15	Dublin North East	10,460	Sean Kenny	LB	9,369	Larry O'Toole	SF	6,923	0.66	2,446	5.85%	41,839	4,627	11,550	27.61%
16	Dublin North West	8,203	John Lyons	LB	7,837	Gerry Breen	FG	5,802	0.71	2,035	6.20%	32,811	1,996	7,798	23.77%
17	Dublin South	12,108	Alan Shatter	FG	10,611	Maria Corrigan	FF	9,163	0.76	1,448	1.99%	72,646	3,207	12,370	17.03%
18	Dublin South Central	8,488	A. O Snodaigh	SF	7,719	Michael Mulcahy	FF	6,161	0.73	1,558	3.06%	50,927	1,754	7,915	15.54%
19	Dublin South East	6,984	Kevin Humphreys	LB	6,421	Chris Andrews	FF	5,193	0.74	1,228	3.52%	34,919	2,353	7,546	21.61%
20	Dublin South West	9,393	Eamonn Maloney	LB	9,657	Cait Keane	FG	6,133	0.65	3,524	7.50%	46,964	2,995	9,128	19.44%
21	Dublin West	8,495	Brian Lenihan	FF	8,289	Patrick Nulty	LB	6,329	0.75	1,960	4.61%	42,472	2,201	8,530	20.08%
22	Dun Laoghaire	11,336	R.Boyd-Barrett	ULA	10,794	Mary Hanafin	FF	9,420	0.83	1,374	2.42%	56,676	2,454	11,874	20.95%
23	Galway East	11,856	Colm Keaveney	LB	10,126	Tom McHugh	FG	8,848	0.75	1,278	2.16%	59,276	3,975	12,823	21.63%
24	Galway West	10,105	Sean Kyne	FG	9,112	Catherine Connolly	NP	9,095	0.90	17	0.03%	60,625	2,274	11,369	18.75%
25	Kerry North	11,404	Martin Ferris	SF	11,416	John Sheahan	FG	8,044	0.71	3,372	7.39%	45,614	2,505	10,549	23.13%
26	Kerry South	11,096	Michael Healy-Rae	NP	10,326	Tom Sheahan	FG	9,409	0.85	917	2.07%	44,380	2,852	12,261	27.63%
27	Kildare North	10,245	Anthony Lawlor	FG	9,088	Aine Brady	FF	7,288	0.71	1,800	3.51%	51,222	2,523	9,811	19.15%
28	Kildare South	9,568	Sean O Fearghail	FF	8,707	Paddy Kennedy	NP	7,710	0.81	997	2.61%	38,270	2,717	10,427	27.25%
29	Laoighis Offaly	12,360	Sean Fleming	FF	10,851	John Whelan	LB	9,026	0.73	1,825	2.46%	74,158	5,158	14,184	19.13%
30	Limerick	11,261	Niall Collins	FF	10,809	James Heffernan	LB	10,104	0.90	705	1.57%	45,041	1,084	11,188	24.84%
31	Limerick City	8,638	Jan O'Sullivan	LB	8,520	Maurice Quinlivan	SF	4,758	0.55	3,762	8.71%	43,188	569	8,618	19.95%
32	Longford-Westmeath	11,506	Robert Troy	FF	9,401	Peter Burke	FG	8,097	0.70	1,304	2.27%	57,525	6,297	14,394	25.02%
33	Louth	13,864	Peter Fitzpatrick	FG	12,323	James Carroll	FF	11,388	0.82	935	1.35%	69,319	4,016	15,404	22.22%
34	Mayo	12,360	John O'Mahony	FG	12,111	Michael Kilcoyne	NP	7,379	0.60	4,732	6.38%	74,154	3,644	11,023	14.87%
35	Meath East	10,689	Shane McEntee	FG	10,143	Thomas Byrne	FF	8,173	0.76	1,970	4.61%	42,752	1,607	9,780	22.88%
36	Meath West	10,045	Ray Butler	FG	8,926	Jenny McHugh	LB	7,798	0.78	1,128	2.81%	40,178	4,220	12,018	29.91%
37	Roscommon-Sth Leitrim	11,877	Denis Naughten	FG	12,122	Ivan Connaughton	FF	7,034	0.59	5,088	10.71%	47,504	3,205	10,239	21.55%
38	Sligo-North Leitrim	11,108	Michael Colreavy	SF	9,711	Eamon Scanlon	FF	9,125	0.82	586	1.32%	44,428	2,916	12,041	27.10%
39	Tipperary North	12,069	Alan Kelly	LB	12,065	Maire Hoctor	FF	9,441	0.78	2,624	5.44%	48,273	2,568	12,009	24.88%
40	Tipperary South	10,341	Mattie McGrath	NP	9,978	Michael Murphy	FG	7,948	0.77	2,030	4.91%	41,361	2,631	10,579	25.58%
41	Waterford	10,745	John Halligan	NP	9,818	Brendan Kenneally	FF	8,845	0.82	973	1.81%	53,720	2,379	11,224	20.89%
42	Wexford	12,590	Liam Twomey	FG	11,596	Michael D'Arcy	FG	10,410	0.83	1,186	1.57%	75,539	4,550	14,960	19.80%
43	Wicklow	11,751	Stephen Donnelly	NP	9,966	John Brady	SF	9,854	0.84	112	0.16%	70,500	4,596	14,450	20.50%
	2011	**10,636**			**425,124**			**352,433**	**33.01**	**72,691**		**2,220,359**	**124,210**	**476,643**	**21.47%**
	2007				420,512			341,998	34.42	78,514		2,065,810	71,640	413,638	20.02%
	2002				366,705			313,346	34.98	53,359		1,857,902	70,412	383,758	20.66%
	1997				342,305			287,366	33.36	54,939		1,788,985	71,625	358,991	20.07%
			15	FG	154,998	10	FG	80,323	7.5	20,554	4.16%	494,381			
			8	LB	74,749	6	LB	50,604	5	8,489	2.97%	285,507			
			8	FF	78,077	17	FF	140,589	13	27,172	3.10%	875,942			
			5	SF	45,218	6	SF	47,213	5	9,229	2.77%	333,564			
			7	NP	72,082	4	NP	33,704	3	7,247	3.14%	230,965			
			43		**425,124**	**43**		**352,433**	**33.01**	**72,691**		**2,220,359**			

WOMEN ELECTED 2011

Twenty five women deputies were returned to the 31st Dail, up one on the outgoing Dail, as Maureen O'Sullivan had been elected in a by-election in Dublin Central in 2009. This is the most women elected in a general election to date with the previous record at 23 which was achieved in 1992, 2002 and 2007. Eight (Six in 2007) outgoing women TDs lost their seats 6FF, 1FG & 1GP with Deidre Clune the only non government female deputy to lose her seat. A further six women deputies retired. Fourteen women were elected for the first time and two former deputies, Frances Fitzgerald and Catherine Murphy regained their seats.

In all elections to date, women have won 260 out of the 4,744 seats filled or just 5.5%. Out of 1,235 TD's in Dail Eireann to date, only 92 of them are women or just 7.5%. The PDs have had the best female representation with 17 of their 44 (39%) seats won between 1987 and 2007 held by women. The Fianna Fail female representation is just 4%, with Fine Gael on 6% and Labour on 8%. The Greens got their first female deputy with the election of Mary White in 2007. Mildred Fox became the first Independent female deputy when she was elected at a by-election in 1995 which was caused by the death of her father. She was joined by Marian Harkin in 2002 but both retired in 2007. There are two female independents in the 31st Dail, Maureen O'Sullivan and Catherine Murphy.

Mary Harney is now the longest serving woman T.D., with 30 years unbroken service from 1981 to 2011. Mary Reynolds is in second place having won nine general elections, the same as Mary Harney and having served for 25 years in Sligo-Leitrim from 1932-1933 and from 1937 to 1961. Sile De Valera is in third place having served for 24 years and Mary Coughlan is in fourth place with 24 years service from 1987-2011, just ahead of Mary O'Rourke on 23 years service. Róisín Shortall is the longest serving female in the present Dail with 18 years service since 1992.

WOMEN ELECTED TO THE 31st DAIL

	Candidate	Party	Constituency	1st	%	Quotas	Seat
1	Shortall, Roisin*	LB	Dublin North West	9,359	28.52%	1.14	1
2	Burton, Joan*	LB	Dublin West	9,627	22.67%	1.13	1
3	Creighton, Lucinda*	FG	Dublin South East	6,619	18.96%	0.95	2
4	Tuffy, Joanna*	LB	Dublin Mid-West	7,495	17.54%	0.88	1
5	Fitzgerald, Frances**	FG	Dublin Mid-West	7,281	17.04%	0.85	2
6	Doherty, Regina	FG	Meath East	8,677	20.30%	0.81	2
7	Mitchell O'Connor, Mary	FG	Dun Laoghaire	9,087	16.03%	0.80	3
8	Mitchell, Olivia*	FG	Dublin South	9,635	13.26%	0.80	3
9	Collins, Joan	PBPA	Dublin South Central	6,574	13.07%	0.77	4
10	Daly, Clare	SP	Dublin North	7,513	15.22%	0.76	3
11	Lynch, Kathleen*	LB	Cork North Central	7,676	14.72%	0.74	2
12	O'Sullivan, Jan*	LB	Limerick East	6,353	14.71%	0.74	4
13	Mulherin, Michelle	FG	Mayo	8,851	11.94%	0.72	3
14	Collins, Aine	FG	Cork North West	7,884	17.24%	0.69	3
15	Humphreys, Heather	FG	Cavan-Monaghan	8,144	11.43%	0.69	5
16	Murphy, Catherine**	NP	Kildare North	6,911	13.49%	0.67	3
17	Byrne, Catherine*	FG	Dublin South Central	5,604	11.14%	0.66	2
18	Phelan, Ann	LB	Carlow-Kilkenny	8,072	10.95%	0.66	1
19	McDonald, Mary Lou	SF	Dublin Central	4,526	13.08%	0.65	4
20	O'Sullivan, Maureen*	NP	Dublin Central	4,139	11.96%	0.60	3
21	McLellan, Sandra	SF	Cork East	6,292	11.05%	0.55	4
22	McFadden, Nicky	FG	Longford-Westmeath	6,129	10.65%	0.53	3
23	Conway, Ciara	LB	Waterford	5,554	10.34%	0.52	3
24	Corcoran Kennedy, Marcella	FG	Laois Offaly	5,817	7.84%	0.47	2
25	Ferris, Anne	LB	Wicklow	5,436	7.71%	0.46	4
	*Outgoing TD	9	**Former TD	2		New TD	14

LEADING VOTEGETTERS BY QUOTA 2011									
	Candidate	Party	Constituency	1st Prefs	%	Quota	M/F	Count	Status
1	Noonan, Michael*	FG	Limerick City	13,291	30.77%	1.54	M	1	Made Quota
2	Kenny, Enda*	FG	Mayo	17,472	23.56%	1.41	M	1	Made Quota
3	Ross, Shane	NP	Dublin South	17,075	23.50%	1.41	M	1	Made Quota
4	Rabbitte, Pat*	LB	Dublin South West	12,867	27.40%	1.37	M	1	Made Quota
5	Heydon, Martin	FG	Kildare South	12,755	33.33%	1.33	M	1	Made Quota
6	Doherty, Pearse*	SF	Donegal South West	14,262	32.97%	1.32	M	1	Made Quota
7	Flanagan, Terence*	FG	Dublin North East	12,332	29.47%	1.18	M	1	Made Quota
8	Lowry, Michael*	NP	Tipperary North	14,104	29.22%	1.17	M	1	Made Quota
9	Shortall, Roisin*	LB	Dublin North West	9,359	28.52%	1.14	F	1	Made Quota
10	Burton, Joan*	LB	Dublin West	9,627	22.67%	1.13	F	1	Made Quota
11	Wall, Jack*	LB	Kildare South	10,645	27.82%	1.11	M	1	Made Quota
12	Adams, Gerry	SF	Louth	15,072	21.74%	1.09	M	1	Made Quota
13	Deenihan, Jimmy*	FG	Kerry North-West Limerick	12,304	26.97%	1.08	M	1	Made Quota
14	Ring, Michael*	FG	Mayo	13,180	17.77%	1.07	M	1	Made Quota
15	Wallace, Mick	NP	Wexford	13,329	17.65%	1.06	M	1	Made Quota
16	Sherlock, Sean*	LB	Cork East	11,862	20.84%	1.04	M	1	Made Quota
17	Reilly, Dr. James*	FG	Dublin North	10,178	20.63%	1.03	M	1	Made Quota
18	Gilmore, Eamon*	LB	Dun Laoghaire	11,468	20.23%	1.01	M	1	Made Quota
19	O'Dowd, Fergus*	FG	Louth	13,980	20.17%	1.01	M	1	Made Quota
20	Martin, Micheal*	FF	Cork South Central	10,715	16.73%	1.00	M	1	Made Quota
21	O Caolain, Caoimhghin*	SF	Cavan-Monaghan	11,913	16.71%	1.00	M	1	Made Quota
22	Bruton, Richard*	FG	Dublin North Central	9,685	24.98%	1.00	M	2	Made Quota
23	Deasy, John*	FG	Waterford	10,718	19.95%	1.00	M	3	Made Quota
24	Donohoe, Paschal	FG	Dublin Central	6,903	19.94%	1.00	M	2	Made Quota
25	Hayes, Brian*	FG	Dublin South West	9,366	19.94%	1.00	M	2	Made Quota
26	Ryan, Brendan	LB	Dublin North	9,809	19.88%	0.99	M	3	Made Quota
27	Durkan, Bernard*	FG	Kildare North	10,168	19.85%	0.99	M	2	Made Quota
28	Penrose, Willie*	LB	Longford-Westmeath	11,406	19.83%	0.99	M	2	Made Quota
29	Byrne, Eric	LB	Dublin South Central	8,357	16.41%	0.98	M	8	Made Quota
30	Varadkar, Leo*	FG	Dublin West	8,359	19.68%	0.98	M	2	Made Quota
31	MacLochlainn, Padraig	SF	Donegal North East	9,278	24.47%	0.98	M	3	Made Quota
32	Broughan, Tommy*	LB	Dublin North East	10,006	23.92%	0.96	M	2	Made Quota
33	Higgins, Joe #	SP	Dublin West	8,084	19.03%	0.95	M	3	Made Quota
34	Stagg, Emmet*	LB	Kildare North	9,718	18.97%	0.95	M	3	Made Quota
35	Creighton, Lucinda*	FG	Dublin South East	6,619	18.96%	0.95	F	6	Made Quota
36	Coonan, Noel*	FG	Tipperary North	11,425	23.67%	0.95	M	2	Made Quota
37	Barrett, Sean*	FG	Dun Laoghaire	10,504	18.53%	0.93	M	8	Made Quota
38	English, Damien*	FG	Meath West	9,290	23.12%	0.92	M	3	Made Quota
39	Costello, Joe*	LB	Dublin Central	6,273	18.12%	0.91	M	5	Made Quota
40	Coffey, Paudie	FG	Waterford	9,698	18.05%	0.90	M	9	Made Quota
41	O Riordain, Aodhan	LB	Dublin North Central	8,731	22.52%	0.90	M	4	Made Quota
42	Phelan, John Paul	FG	Carlow-Kilkenny	10,929	14.82%	0.89	M	12	Made Quota
43	Coveney, Simon*	FG	Cork South Central	9,447	14.75%	0.89	M	10	Made Quota
44	Creed, Michael*	FG	Cork North West	10,112	22.11%	0.88	M	5	Made Quota
45	Stanton, David*	FG	Cork East	10,019	17.60%	0.88	M	5	Made Quota
46	Tuffy, Joanna*	LB	Dublin Mid-West	7,495	17.54%	0.88	F	7	Made Quota
47	Howlin, Brendan*	LB	Wexford	11,005	14.57%	0.87	M	4	Made Quota
48	Ellis, Dessie	SF	Dublin North West	7,115	21.68%	0.87	M	7	Made Quota
49	Hayes, Tom*	FG	Tipperary South	8,896	21.51%	0.86	M	4	Made Quota
50	Crowe, Sean #	SF	Dublin South West	8,064	17.17%	0.86	M	6	Made Quota
51	Hogan, Phil*	FG	Carlow-Kilkenny	10,525	14.27%	0.86	M	13	Elected
52	Doyle, Andrew*	FG	Wicklow	10,035	14.23%	0.85	M	16	Made Quota
53	Healy, Seamus #	ULA	Tipperary South	8,818	21.32%	0.85	M	3	Made Quota
54	Fitzgerald, Frances	FG	Dublin Mid-West	7,281	17.04%	0.85	F	8	Made Quota
55	Breen, Pat*	FG	Clare	9,855	17.02%	0.85	M	11	Made Quota
56	Flanagan, Charles*	FG	Laois-Offaly	10,427	14.06%	0.84	M	8	Made Quota
57	Hannigan, Dominic	LB	Meath East	8,994	21.04%	0.84	M	4	Made Quota
58	Collins, Niall*	FF	Limerick	9,361	20.78%	0.83	M	4	Elected
59	Murphy, Eoghan	FG	Dublin South East	5,783	16.56%	0.83	M	9	Made Quota
60	McEntee, Shane*	FG	Meath East	8,794	20.57%	0.82	M	4	Elected

LONGEST SERVING TD's IN 31st DAIL							
					First	Elections	19/03/2012
	Surname	First Name	Party	Constituency	Elected	Won	Service
1	Kenny	Enda	FG	Mayo	*12/11/1975*	12	36.35
2	Quinn	Ruairi	LB	Dublin South East	16/06/1977	10	34.07
3	Noonan	Michael	FG	Limerick City	11/06/1981	10	30.77
4	Bruton	Richard	FG	Dublin North Central	18/02/1982	9	30.08
5	McGinley	Dinny	FG	Donegal South West	18/02/1982	9	30.08
6	O'Dea	Willie	FF	Limerick City	18/02/1982	9	30.08
7	Durkan	Bernard	FG	Kildare North	11/06/1981	9	30.01
8	Browne	John	FF	Wexford	24/11/1982	8	29.32
9	Kirk	Seamus	FF	Louth	24/11/1982	8	29.32
10	Kitt	Michael	FF	Galway East	*04/03/1975*	10	28.03
11	Barrett	Sean	FG	Dun Laoghaire	11/06/1981	9	25.75
12	Shatter	Alan	FG	Dublin South	11/06/1981	9	25.75
13	Deenihan	Jimmy	FG	Kerry North	17/02/1987	7	25.08
14	Howlin	Brendan	LB	Wexford	17/02/1987	7	25.08
15	Lowry	Michael	NP	Tipperary North	17/02/1987	7	25.08
16	Stagg	Emmet	LB	Kildare North	17/02/1987	7	25.08
17	Gilmore	Eamon	LB	Dun Laoghaire	15/06/1989	6	22.76
18	Hogan	Phil	FG	Carlow-Kilkenny	15/06/1989	6	22.76
19	Martin	Micheal	FF	Cork South Central	15/06/1989	6	22.76
20	Rabbitte	Pat	LB	Dublin South West	15/06/1989	6	22.76
21	Flanagan	Charlie	FG	Laoighis Offaly	17/02/1987	6	20.06
22	Broughan	Tommy	LB	Dublin North East	25/11/1992	5	19.31
23	O Cuiv	Eamon	FF	Galway West	25/11/1992	5	19.31
24	Penrose	Willie	LB	Longford-Westmeath	25/11/1992	5	19.31
25	Shortall	Roisin	LB	Dublin North West	25/11/1992	5	19.31
26	Smith	Brendan	FF	Cavan-Monaghan	25/11/1992	5	19.31
27	Ring	Michael	FG	Mayo	*09/06/1994*	5	17.78
28	Creed	Michael	FG	Cork North West	15/06/1989	5	17.74
29	Lenihan	Brian	FF	Dublin West	*02/04/1996*	5	15.96
30	Fleming	Sean	FF	Laoighis Offaly	06/06/1997	4	14.78
31	Kelleher	Billy	FF	Cork North Central	06/06/1997	4	14.78
32	McGuinness	John	FF	Carlow-Kilkenny	06/06/1997	4	14.78
33	Mitchell	Olivia	FG	Dublin South	06/06/1997	4	14.78
34	Moynihan	Michael	FF	Cork North West	06/06/1997	4	14.78
35	Naughten	Denis	FG	Roscommon-Sth Leitrim	06/06/1997	4	14.78
36	Neville	Dan	FG	Limerick	06/06/1997	4	14.78
37	O Caolain	Caoimhghin	SF	Cavan-Monaghan	06/06/1997	4	14.78
38	Perry	John	FG	Sligo-North Leitrim	06/06/1997	4	14.78
39	Stanton	David	FG	Cork East	06/06/1997	4	14.78
40	Timmins	Billy	FG	Wicklow	06/06/1997	4	14.78
41	Wall	Jack	LB	Kildare South	06/06/1997	4	14.78
42	Burton	Joan	LB	Dublin West	25/11/1992	4	14.37
43	Costello	Joe	LB	Dublin Central	25/11/1992	4	14.37
44	O'Sullivan	Jan	LB	Limerick City	*11/03/1998*	4	14.02
45	Coveney	Simon	FG	Cork South Central	*23/10/1998*	4	13.40
46	Lynch	Kathleen	LB	Cork North Central	*10/11/1994*	4	12.42
47	Higgins*	Joe	SP	Dublin West	06/06/1997	3	11.02
48	Hayes	Tom	FG	Tipperary South	*30/06/2001*	4	10.72
49	Fitzgerald*	Frances	FG	Dublin Mid West	25/11/1992	3	10.53
	Former TD*			Broken Service	*By-Election*	**Service to:**	**19/03/2012**

					Final			Final	
	CLOSE FINISHES 2011								
	Constituency	Quota	Winner	Party	Votes	Loser	Party	Votes	Margin
1	Galway West	10,105	Sean Kyne	FG	9,112	Catherine Connolly	NP	9,095	17
2	Wicklow	11,751	Stephen Donnelly	NP	9,966	John Brady	SF	9,854	112
3	Cork North Central	10,428	Dara Murphy	FG	9,515	Pat Burton	FG	9,233	282
4	Cavan-Monaghan	11,880	Heather Humphreys	FG	10,861	Kathryn Reilly	SF	10,340	521
5	Dublin Mid West	8,545	Derek Keating	FG	7,703	Eoin O Broin	SF	7,151	552
6	Sligo-North Leitrim	11,108	Michael Colreavy	SF	9,711	Eamon Scanlon	FF	9,125	586
7	Cork South West	11,415	Michael McCarthy	LB	10,754	Denis O'Donovan	FF	10,155	599
8	Cork East	11,387	Sandra McLellan	SF	9,785	Kevin O'Keeffe	FF	9,136	649
9	Limerick	11,261	Niall Collins	FF	10,809	James Heffernan	LB	10,104	705
10	Waterford	10,745	John Halligan	NP	9,818	Brendan Kenneally	FF	8,945	873
11	Kerry South	11,096	Michael Healy-Rae	NP	10,326	Tom Sheahan	FG	9,409	917
12	Louth	13,864	Peter Fitzpatrick	FG	12,323	James Carroll	FF	11,388	935
13	Kildare South	9,568	Sean O Fearghail	FF	8,707	Paddy Kennedy	NP	7,710	997
14	Dublin North	9,870	Alan Farrell	FG	9,159	Darragh O'Brien	FF	8,067	1,092

	LOWEST VOTE-GETTERS 2011				
	Candidate	Party	Constituency	1st Prefs	%
1	O Ceallaigh, Peadar	FN	Dublin South East	18	0.05%
2	Cooney, Benny	NP	Dublin Central	25	0.07%
3	Keigher, John	NP	Dublin South East	27	0.08%
4	Forkin, Sean	NP	Mayo	29	0.04%
5	Johnston, Liam	FN	Dublin Central	48	0.14%
6	Larkin, Matt	NP	Limerick City	59	0.14%
7	Cox, Michael	NP	Laois-Offaly	60	0.08%
8	Glynn, Robert	NP	Louth	61	0.09%
9	Hollywood, Thomas	NP	Dublin Central	65	0.19%
10	King, Thomas	NP	Galway West	65	0.11%
11	Dalton, John	NP	Carlow-Kilkenny	70	0.09%
12	Zaidan, Eamonn	NP	Dublin South	71	0.10%
13	Kiersey, Gerard	NP	Waterford	73	0.14%
14	Carroll, Kevin	NP	Wicklow	74	0.10%
15	Hyland, John Pluto	NP	Dublin Central	77	0.22%
16	Watson, Noel	NP	Dublin South East	89	0.25%
17	Linehan, Gerard	NP	Cork South Central	90	0.14%
18	Kearns, Sean	NP	Roscommon-South Leitrim	91	0.19%
19	O'Driscoll, Finbar	NP	Cork South Central	92	0.14%
20	O'Rourke, Fergus	NP	Cork North Central	95	0.18%

LOST EXPENSES 2011							
	2011			2007	2002	1997	1992
Party	Candidates	Lost Expenses	%	Lost Expenses	Lost Expenses	Lost Deposit	Lost Deposit
FG	104		0.00%	4	9	8	7
LB	68		0.00%	12	8	10	14
FF	75	3	4.00%	0	0	1	6
SF	41	4	9.76%	17	12	3	39
ULA	20	11	55.00%	2	3	2	
GP	43	39	90.70%	26	17	15	15
WP	6	6	100.00%	6	8	6	16
CS	8	8	100.00%	7	23	8	
PD				21	6	9	2
Others	201	167	83.08%	71	77	117	92
Total	566	238	42.05%	166	163	179	191
Candidates		566		470	463	484	482
Lost Expenses %		**42.05%**		**35.32%**	**35.21%**	**36.98%**	**39.63%**

A candidate loses the right to reclaim their election expenses if they fail to reach at least 25% of the quota by the time they are eliminated

GENERAL ELECTION 2011: SPENDING						
			Candidate		Total	
Party	1st Prefs	Candidates	Spending	Cost per Vote	Spending	Cost per Vote
FG	801,628	104	1,926,874.79	2.40	3,120,237.95	3.89
LB	431,796	68	1,167,480.71	2.70	1,956,812.93	4.53
FF	387,358	75	1,456,344.82	3.76	2,138,792.58	5.52
SF	220,661	41	436,713.58	1.98	496,928.28	2.25
SP	26,770	9	81,449.62	3.04	85,124.45	3.18
PBPA	21,551	9	46,341.41	2.15	47,756.93	2.22
GP	41,039	43	214,402.01	5.22	241,788.62	5.89
WP	3,056	6	11,986.57	3.92	11,986.57	3.92
CS	2,102	8	20,113.69	9.57	20,113.69	9.57
Others	284,398	203	1,158,095.59	4.07	1,158,095.59	4.07
2011	**2,220,359**	**566**	**6,519,802.79**	**2.94**	**9,277,637.59**	**4.18**
2007	**2,065,810**	**470**	**7,857,291.94**	**3.80**	**11,082,313.10**	**5.36**

GENERAL ELECTION 2011: TOP SPENDERS										
	Candidate	Party	Constituency	1st Prefs	%	Quota	Count	Status	Spending	Cost /Vote
1	Grealish, Noel*	NP	Galway West	6,229	10.27%	0.62	13	Elected	39,164.98	6.29
2	Ross, Shane	NP	Dublin South	17,075	23.50%	1.41	1	Made Quota	38,394.32	2.25
3	Corrigan, Maria	FF	Dublin South	6,844	9.42%	0.57	8	Not Elected	33,545.11	4.90
4	Fitzpatrick, Peter	FG	Louth	7,845	11.32%	0.57	13	Elected	33,428.34	4.26
5	Ryan, Eamonn*	GP	Dublin South	4,929	6.78%	0.41	7	Eliminated	32,525.00	6.60
6	Mitchell-O'Connor, Mary	FG	Dun Laoghaire	9,087	16.03%	0.80	10	Made Quota	31,716.43	3.49
7	Mulcahy, Tony	FG	Clare	6,829	11.79%	0.59	10	Eliminated	31,068.81	4.55
8	Donnelly, Stephen	NP	Wicklow	6,530	9.26%	0.56	19	Elected	31,050.48	4.76
9	Breathnach, Declan	FF	Louth	5,177	7.47%	0.37	10	Eliminated	30,982.66	5.98
10	Murphy, Dara	FG	Cork North Central	6,597	12.65%	0.63	11	Elected	30,152.47	4.57
11	Lowry, Michael*	NP	Tipperary North	14,104	29.22%	1.17	1	Made Quota	29,593.23	2.10
12	Mulcahy, Michael*	FF	Dublin South Central	4,837	9.50%	0.57	13	Not Elected	29,509.69	6.10
13	McGuinness, John*	FF	Carlow-Kilkenny	9,531	12.92%	0.78	12	Made Quota	28,999.45	3.04
14	Harris, Simon	FG	Wicklow	8,726	12.38%	0.74	19	Elected	28,490.83	3.27
15	Yore, Catherine	FG	Meath West	3,898	9.70%	0.39	3	Eliminated	28,257.87	7.25
16	Smith, Brendan*	FF	Cavan-Monaghan	9,702	13.61%	0.82	8	Made Quota	28,181.44	2.90
17	Nolan, Derek	LB	Galway West	7,489	12.35%	0.74	10	Made Quota	28,081.08	3.75
18	MacSharry, Marc	FF	Sligo-North Leitrim	4,633	10.43%	0.42	6	Eliminated	28,025.66	6.05
19	Crowe, Michael	FF	Galway West	1,814	2.99%	0.18	4	No Expenses	27,321.05	15.06
20	Murphy, Eoghan	FG	Dublin South East	5,783	16.56%	0.83	9	Made Quota	27,039.87	4.68
21	Cuffe, Ciaran*	GP	Dun Laoghaire	2,156	3.80%	0.19	6	No Expenses	27,038.49	12.54
22	Kelleher, Tom	LB	Dublin North	3,205	6.49%	0.32	3	Eliminated	26,900.56	8.39
23	Martin, Micheal*	FF	Cork South Central	10,715	16.73%	1.00	1	Made Quota	26,660.97	2.49
24	Coonan, Noel*	FG	Tipperary North	11,425	23.67%	0.95	2	Made Quota	26,406.67	2.31
25	O'Sullivan, Christy*	FF	Cork South West	4,803	10.52%	0.42	3	Eliminated	26,333.52	5.48
26	Gormley, John*	GP	Dublin South East	2,370	6.79%	0.34	5	Eliminated	26,204.38	11.06
27	Twomey, Liam #	FG	Wexford	9,230	12.22%	0.73	7	Elected	26,136.88	2.83
28	Mathews, Peter	FG	Dublin South	9,053	12.46%	0.75	8	Elected	26,100.37	2.88
29	Hogan, Phil*	FG	Carlow-Kilkenny	10,525	14.27%	0.86	13	Elected	25,930.64	2.46
30	Connick, Sean*	FF	Wexford	6,675	8.84%	0.53	6	Eliminated	25,600.59	3.84
31	Kiely, Kevin	NP	Limerick City	1,129	2.61%	0.13	4	No Expenses	25,559.48	22.64
32	Keating, Derek	FG	Dublin Mid-West	5,933	13.89%	0.69	9	Elected	25,536.32	4.30
33	Heydon, Martin	FG	Kildare South	12,755	33.33%	1.33	1	Made Quota	25,518.57	2.00
34	O'Donoghue, John*	FF	Kerry South	5,917	13.33%	0.53	3	Eliminated	25,502.67	4.31
35	Kelly, Alan	LB	Tipperary North	9,559	19.80%	0.79	3	Elected	25,319.58	2.65
36	Calleary, Dara*	FF	Mayo	8,577	11.57%	0.69	8	Made Quota	25,282.77	2.95
37	Creighton, Lucinda*	FG	Dublin South East	6,619	18.96%	0.95	6	Made Quota	25,272.73	3.82
38	McGrath, Finian*	NP	Dublin North Central	5,986	15.44%	0.62	7	Made Quota	24,938.42	4.17
39	McConalogue, Charlie	FF	Donegal North East	6,613	17.44%	0.70	9	Elected	24,677.35	3.73
40	McGrath, Mattie*	NP	Tipperary South	6,074	14.69%	0.59	5	Elected	24,629.45	4.05
	Spending Limits:		**3 seater: €30,150**		**4 seater: €37,650**			**5 seater: €45,200**		

GENERAL ELECTION 2011: TOP SPENDERS COST/VOTE

	Candidate	Party	Constituency	1st Prefs	%	Quota	Count	Status	Spending	Cost /Vote
1	Kinsella, Gerry	FN	Wicklow	324	0.46%	0.03	9	No Expenses	21,579.33	66.60
2	Walsh, Noel G.	NP	Carlow-Kilkenny	119	0.16%	0.01	1	No Expenses	6,735.79	56.60
3	Coyle, James	NP	Dublin South East	164	0.47%	0.02	1	No Expenses	7,284.20	44.42
4	Hollywood, Thomas	NP	Dublin Central	65	0.19%	0.01	1	No Expenses	2,842.04	43.72
5	Fanning, James	NP	Laois-Offaly	335	0.45%	0.03	3	No Expenses	11,636.75	34.74
6	O Ceallaigh, Peadar	FN	Dublin South East	18	0.05%	0.00	1	No Expenses	610.00	33.89
7	Fitzgerald, Anthony	NP	Wicklow	184	0.26%	0.02	4	No Expenses	6,115.85	33.24
8	Boland, John	NP	Laois-Offaly	119	0.16%	0.01	1	No Expenses	3,353.49	28.18
9	Sexton, Raymond	NP	Dublin North East	351	0.84%	0.03	3	No Expenses	9,108.24	25.95
10	MacMeanmain, Manus	CS	Meath West	234	0.58%	0.02	1	No Expenses	5,883.09	25.14
11	Daly, Martin	NV	Mayo	893	1.20%	0.07	3	No Expenses	20,769.09	23.26
12	Kiely, Kevin	NP	Limerick City	1,129	2.61%	0.13	4	No Expenses	25,559.48	22.64
13	McCabe, J.J.	NP	Clare	248	0.43%	0.02	2	No Expenses	5,607.20	22.61
14	McDonnell, Fergus	NP	Laois-Offaly	525	0.71%	0.04	5	No Expenses	11,720.60	22.32
15	Kiernan, Donal	NP	Wicklow	403	0.57%	0.03	10	No Expenses	8,541.39	21.19
16	Haughton, Carl	NP	Dun Laoghaire	456	0.80%	0.04	5	No Expenses	8,674.03	19.02
17	Sheehy, Hugh	NP	Dublin South East	195	0.56%	0.03	1	No Expenses	3,679.83	18.87
18	McGrath, Colm	NP	Dublin Mid-West	253	0.59%	0.03	3	No Expenses	4,764.16	18.83
19	McGuinness, David	FF	Dublin West	623	1.47%	0.07	2	No Expenses	11,686.63	18.76
20	Crawford, Nick	NV	Dun Laoghaire	394	0.70%	0.03	3	No Expenses	7,163.84	18.18
21	McHale, Jim	NP	Dublin Mid-West	255	0.60%	0.03	2	No Expenses	4,454.16	17.47
22	Keigher, John	NP	Dublin South East	27	0.08%	0.00	1	No Expenses	441.92	16.37
23	Linehan, Gerard	NP	Cork South Central	90	0.14%	0.01	2	No Expenses	1,452.00	16.13
24	Hussein Hamed, Buhidma	NP	Dublin South	273	0.38%	0.02	2	No Expenses	4,385.35	16.06
25	Nutty, Ben	FN	Waterford	257	0.48%	0.02	3	No Expenses	4,073.09	15.85
26	O'Rourke, Fergus	NP	Cork North Central	95	0.18%	0.01	1	No Expenses	1,481.00	15.59
27	Crowe, Michael	FF	Galway West	1,814	2.99%	0.18	4	No Expenses	27,321.05	15.06
28	Jackson, Donal	NP	Longford-Westmeath	101	0.18%	0.01	1	No Expenses	1,517.50	15.02
29	Matthews, Fred	NP	Louth	957	1.38%	0.07	7	No Expenses	14,371.97	15.02
30	Behal, Richard	NP	Kerry South	348	0.78%	0.03	1	No Expenses	5,199.67	14.94

GENERAL ELECTION 2011: BEST VALUE PER VOTE

	Candidate	Party	Constituency	1st Prefs	%	Quota	Count	Status	Spending	Cost /Vote
1	Wallace, Mick	NP	Wexford	13,329	17.65%	1.06	1	Made Quota	9,328.18	0.70
2	Kenny, Enda*	FG	Mayo	17,472	23.56%	1.41	1	Made Quota	12,771.98	0.73
3	Rabbitte, Pat*	LB	Dublin South West	12,867	27.40%	1.37	1	Made Quota	11,646.09	0.91
4	Doherty, Pearse*	SF	Donegal South West	14,262	32.97%	1.32	1	Made Quota	13,848.16	0.97
5	Flanagan, Terence*	FG	Dublin North East	12,332	29.47%	1.18	1	Made Quota	12,303.91	1.00
6	Ó Caoláin, Caoimhghín*	SF	Cavan-Monaghan	11,913	16.71%	1.00	1	Made Quota	12,147.55	1.02
7	Ring, Michael*	FG	Mayo	13,180	17.77%	1.07	1	Made Quota	14,261.37	1.08
8	Penrose, Willie*	LB	Longford-Westmeath	11,406	19.83%	0.99	2	Made Quota	12,396.48	1.09
9	O'Dowd, Fergus*	FG	Louth	13,980	20.17%	1.01	1	Made Quota	15,867.15	1.13
10	Pringle, Thomas	NP	Donegal South West	5,845	13.51%	0.54	5	Elected	6,793.05	1.16
11	Deenihan, Jimmy*	FG	Kerry North-West Limerick	12,304	26.97%	1.08	1	Made Quota	15,508.54	1.26
12	Sherlock, Sean*	LB	Cork East	11,862	20.84%	1.04	1	Made Quota	15,417.83	1.30
13	Creed, Michael*	FG	Cork North West	10,112	22.11%	0.88	5	Made Quota	13,155.94	1.30
14	Neville, Dan*	FG	Limerick	9,176	20.37%	0.81	4	Made Quota	11,995.07	1.31
15	O'Reilly, Joe	FG	Cavan-Monaghan	8,333	11.69%	0.70	9	Elected	10,982.97	1.32
16	O'Brien, Jonathan	SF	Cork North Central	7,923	15.20%	0.76	8	Made Quota	10,825.25	1.37
17	Higgins, Joe #	SP	Dublin West	8,084	19.03%	0.95	3	Made Quota	11,073.65	1.37
18	Adams, Gerry	SF	Louth	15,072	21.74%	1.09	1	Made Quota	20,895.98	1.39
19	English, Damien*	FG	Meath West	9,290	23.12%	0.92	3	Made Quota	12,890.25	1.39
20	Coffey, Paudie	FG	Waterford	9,698	18.05%	0.90	9	Made Quota	13,516.08	1.39
21	Noonan, Michael*	FG	Limerick City	13,291	30.77%	1.54	1	Made Quota	18,623.96	1.40
22	Broughan, Tommy*	LB	Dublin North East	10,006	23.92%	0.96	2	Made Quota	14,100.05	1.41
23	Healy, Seamus #	ULA	Tipperary South	8,818	21.32%	0.85	3	Made Quota	12,739.26	1.44
24	Hayes, Tom*	FG	Tipperary South	8,896	21.51%	0.86	4	Made Quota	12,978.30	1.46
25	Flanagan, Charles*	FG	Laois-Offaly	10,427	14.06%	0.84	8	Made Quota	15,445.34	1.48
26	Bruton, Richard*	FG	Dublin North Central	9,685	24.98%	1.00	2	Made Quota	14,354.15	1.48
27	Bannon, James*	FG	Longford-Westmeath	9,129	15.87%	0.79	6	Made Quota	13,619.54	1.49
28	Ferris, Martin*	SF	Kerry North-West Limerick	9,282	20.35%	0.81	7	Made Quota	13,927.13	1.50
29	Shortall, Roisin*	LB	Dublin North West	9,359	28.52%	1.14	1	Made Quota	14,048.22	1.50
30	Humphreys, Heather	FG	Cavan-Monaghan	8,144	11.43%	0.69	9	Elected	12,330.03	1.51

POLLS 2007-2009

	25/05/2007	23/09/2007	28/10/2007	02/11/2007	25/11/2007	25/01/2008	27/01/2008	02/03/2008	30/03/2008	06/04/2008	27/04/2008	16/05/2008	25/05/2008
	General	Red C	Red C	MRBI	Red C	MRBI	Red C	Red C	Red C	Red C	Red C	MRBI	Red C
Party	Election	Bus. Post	Bus. Post	Irish Times	Bus. Post	Irish Times	Bus. Post	Bus. Post	Bus. Post	Bus. Post	Bus. Post	Irish Times	Bus. Post
FF	41.56%	40.00%	39.00%	33.00%	32.00%	34.00%	36.00%	37.00%	35.00%	40.00%	38.00%	42.00%	40.00%
FG	27.32%	27.00%	27.00%	31.00%	31.00%	31.00%	32.00%	31.00%	30.00%	28.00%	29.00%	26.00%	28.00%
LB	10.13%	11.00%	10.00%	15.00%	13.00%	12.00%	10.00%	10.00%	11.00%	11.00%	10.00%	15.00%	10.00%
GP	4.69%	7.00%	7.00%	5.00%	9.00%	6.00%	7.00%	7.00%	8.00%	9.00%	8.00%	4.00%	5.00%
SF	6.94%	6.00%	8.00%	7.00%	7.00%	8.00%	9.00%	8.00%	9.00%	6.00%	7.00%	6.00%	9.00%
PD	2.73%	3.00%	2.00%	2.00%	2.00%	3.00%	2.00%	2.00%	1.00%	1.00%	2.00%	1.00%	2.00%
Others	6.63%	6.00%	7.00%	7.00%	7.00%	6.00%	4.00%	6.00%	7.00%	5.00%	6.00%	6.00%	6.00%
Total	**100.00%**	**100.00%**	**100.00%**	**100.00%**	**101.00%**	**100.00%**	**100.00%**	**101.00%**	**101.00%**	**100.00%**	**100.00%**	**100.00%**	**100.00%**

	25/05/2007	22/06/2008	21/09/2008	26/10/2008	27/10/2008	23/11/2008	01/02/2009	13/02/2009	27/02/2009	01/03/2009	29/03/2009	26/04/2009	15/05/2009
	General	Red C	Red C	Red C	MRBI	Red C	Red C	MRBI	IMS	Red C	Red C	Red C	MRBI
Party	Election	Bus. Post	Bus. Post	Bus. Post	Irish Times	Bus. Post	Bus. Post	Irish Times	Indo	Bus. Post	Bus. Post	Bus. Post	Irish Times
FF	41.56%	40.00%	36.00%	26.00%	27.00%	30.00%	28.00%	22.00%	25.00%	23.00%	28.00%	23.00%	21.00%
FG	27.32%	25.00%	28.00%	33.00%	34.00%	35.00%	33.00%	32.00%	30.00%	30.00%	31.00%	33.00%	38.00%
LB	10.13%	10.00%	9.00%	15.00%	14.00%	14.00%	14.00%	24.00%	22.00%	22.00%	17.00%	19.00%	20.00%
GP	4.69%	7.00%	7.00%	6.00%	4.00%	5.00%	8.00%	4.00%	5.00%	6.00%	7.00%	7.00%	3.00%
SF	6.94%	10.00%	9.00%	10.00%	8.00%	8.00%	9.00%	8.00%	7.00%	11.00%	7.00%	8.00%	9.00%
PD	2.73%	2.00%	3.00%	2.00%									
Others	6.63%	6.00%	8.00%	8.00%	13.00%	8.00%	8.00%	9.00%	11.00%	8.00%	10.00%	10.00%	9.00%
Total	**100.00%**	**100.00%**	**100.00%**	**100.00%**	**100.00%**	**100.00%**	**100.00%**	**99.00%**	**100.00%**	**100.00%**	**100.00%**	**100.00%**	**100.00%**

	25/05/2007	17/05/2009	29/05/2009	31/05/2009	06/06/2009	05/06/2009	03/09/2009	13/09/2009	25/09/2009	27/09/2009	25/10/2009	22/11/2009	22/01/2010
	General	Red C	MRBI	Red C	Exit Poll	Local	MRBI	Red C	MRBI	Red C	Red C	Red C	MRBI
Party	Election	Bus. Post	Irish Times	Bus. Post	RTE	Election	Irish Times	Bus. Post	Irish Times	Bus. Post	Bus. Post	Bus. Post	Irish Times
FF	41.56%	24.00%	20.00%	21.00%	24.00%	25.38%	17.00%	24.00%	20.00%	24.00%	25.00%	23.00%	22.00%
FG	27.32%	34.00%	36.00%	34.00%	34.00%	32.19%	34.00%	33.00%	31.00%	35.00%	35.00%	36.00%	32.00%
LB	10.13%	18.00%	23.00%	18.00%	17.00%	14.71%	24.00%	19.00%	25.00%	18.00%	19.00%	17.00%	24.00%
GP	4.69%	5.00%	3.00%	4.00%	3.00%	2.35%	3.00%	5.00%	4.00%	4.00%	3.00%	5.00%	3.00%
SF	6.94%	7.00%	8.00%	10.00%	9.00%	7.36%	10.00%	8.00%	9.00%	8.00%	9.00%	10.00%	8.00%
Others	9.36%	12.00%	10.00%	13.00%	13.00%	18.01%	12.00%	11.00%	11.00%	11.00%	9.00%	9.00%	11.00%
Total	**100.00%**	**100.00%**	**100.00%**	**100.00%**	**100.00%**	**100.00%**	**100.00%**	**100.00%**	**100.00%**	**100.00%**	**100.00%**	**100.00%**	**100.00%**

POLLS 2010

	25/05/2007	22/01/2010	31/01/2010	13/02/2010	28/02/2010	28/03/2010	02/05/2010	30/05/2010	11/06/2010	27/06/2010	24/09/2010	26/09/2010	30/09/2010
	General	MRBI	Red C	Milward B	Red C	Red C	Red C	Red C	MRBI	Red C	Milward B	Red C	MRBI
Party	Election	Irish Times	Bus. Post	Indo	Bus. Post	Bus. Post	Bus. Post	Bus. Post	Irish Times	Bus. Post	TV3	Bus. Post	Irish Times
FF	41.56%	22.00%	27.00%	27.00%	27.00%	24.00%	23.00%	24.00%	17.00%	24.00%	22.00%	24.00%	24.00%
FG	27.32%	32.00%	34.00%	34.00%	34.00%	35.00%	33.00%	30.00%	28.00%	33.00%	30.00%	31.00%	24.00%
LB	10.13%	24.00%	17.00%	19.00%	17.00%	17.00%	24.00%	22.00%	32.00%	27.00%	35.00%	23.00%	33.00%
GP	4.69%	3.00%	5.00%	2.00%	5.00%	5.00%	6.00%	5.00%	3.00%	2.00%	2.00%	3.00%	2.00%
SF	6.94%	8.00%	8.00%	8.00%	9.00%	10.00%	6.00%	10.00%	9.00%	8.00%	4.00%	10.00%	8.00%
Others	9.36%	11.00%	9.00%	10.00%	8.00%	9.00%	8.00%	9.00%	11.00%	6.00%	8.00%	9.00%	9.00%
Total	**100.00%**	**100.00%**	**100.00%**	**100.00%**	**100.00%**	**100.00%**	**100.00%**	**100.00%**	**100.00%**	**100.00%**	**101.00%**	**100.00%**	**100.00%**

POLLS 2010/2011

	25/05/2007	24/10/2010	21/11/2010	03/12/2010	16/12/2010	18/12/2010	07/01/2011	30/01/2011	30/01/2011	02/02/2011	02/02/2011	03/02/2011	06/02/2011
	General	Red C	Red C	Red C	MRBI	Red C	Red C	Red C	Milward B	Milward B	Red C	MRBI	Red C
Party	Election	Bus. Post	Bus. Post	Sun	Irish Times	Bus. Post	P. Power	Bus. Post	Sun Ind	Indo	P. Power	Irish Times	Bus. Post
FF	41.56%	18.00%	17.00%	13.00%	17.00%	17.00%	14.00%	16.00%	16.00%	16.00%	18.00%	15.00%	17.00%
FG	27.32%	32.00%	33.00%	32.00%	30.00%	34.00%	35.00%	33.00%	34.00%	30.00%	37.00%	33.00%	35.00%
LB	10.13%	27.00%	27.00%	24.00%	25.00%	23.00%	21.00%	21.00%	24.00%	24.00%	19.00%	24.00%	22.00%
GP	4.69%	4.00%	3.00%	3.00%	2.00%	2.00%	4.00%	2.00%	1.00%	1.00%	3.00%	1.00%	2.00%
SF	6.94%	9.00%	11.00%	16.00%	15.00%	14.00%	14.00%	13.00%	10.00%	13.00%	12.00%	12.00%	13.00%
Others	9.36%	10.00%	9.00%	12.00%	11.00%	10.00%	12.00%	15.00%	15.00%	16.00%	11.00%	15.00%	11.00%
Total	**100.00%**	**100.00%**	**100.00%**	**100.00%**	**100.00%**	**100.00%**	**100.00%**	**100.00%**	**100.00%**	**100.00%**	**100.00%**	**100.00%**	**100.00%**

POLLS 2011

	25/05/2007	13/02/2011	16/02/2011	17/02/2011	20/02/2011	20/02/2011	21/02/2011	22/02/2011	23/02/2011	23/02/2011	26/02/2011	27/02/2011
	General	Red C	Milward B	OI Research	Red C	Milward B	MRBI	Milward B	Red C	Average	Milward B	General
Party	Election	Bus. Post	Indo	Star	Bus. Post	Sun Ind	Irish Times	Indo	P. Power	20-23/02/11	Exit Poll	Election
FF	41.56%	15.00%	12.00%	17.00%	16.00%	16.00%	16.00%	14.00%	15.00%	15.40%	15.10%	17.45%
FG	27.32%	38.00%	38.00%	39.00%	39.00%	37.00%	37.00%	38.00%	40.00%	38.20%	36.10%	36.10%
LB	10.13%	20.00%	23.00%	18.00%	17.00%	20.00%	19.00%	20.00%	18.00%	18.80%	20.50%	19.45%
GP	4.69%	3.00%	1.00%	2.00%	2.00%	1.00%	2.00%	1.00%	3.00%	1.80%	2.70%	1.85%
SF	6.94%	10.00%	10.00%	10.00%	12.00%	12.00%	11.00%	11.00%	10.00%	11.20%	10.10%	9.94%
Others	9.36%	14.00%	16.00%	14.00%	14.00%	14.00%	15.00%	16.00%	14.00%	14.60%	15.50%	15.21%
Total	**100.00%**	**100.00%**	**100.00%**	**100.00%**	**100.00%**	**100.00%**	**100.00%**	**100.00%**	**100.00%**	**100.00%**	**100.00%**	**100.00%**

AGE & YEARS OF SERVICE OF TD's IN 31st DAIL									
							19/03/2012	**First**	**Years**
	Constituency	**Seats**	**Surname**	**First Name**	**Party**	**Born**	**Age**	**Elected**	**Service**
1	Carlow-Kilkenny	5	Phelan	Ann	LB	Sep-61	50.5	25/02/2011	1.1
1	Carlow-Kilkenny	5	Hogan	Phil	FG	Jul-60	51.7	15/06/1989	22.8
1	Carlow-Kilkenny	5	McGuinness	John	FF	Mar-55	57.0	06/06/1997	14.8
1	Carlow-Kilkenny	5	Phelan	John Paul	FG	Sep-78	33.5	25/02/2011	1.1
1	Carlow-Kilkenny	5	Deering	Pat	FG	Feb-67	45.1	25/02/2011	1.1
2	Cavan-Monaghan	5	O'Reilly	Joe	FG	Apr-55	56.9	25/02/2011	1.1
2	Cavan-Monaghan	5	Conlan	Sean	FG	Jan-75	37.2	25/02/2011	1.1
2	Cavan-Monaghan	5	O Caolain	Caoimhghin	SF	Sep-53	58.5	06/06/1997	14.8
2	Cavan-Monaghan	5	Humphreys	Heather	FG			25/02/2011	1.1
2	Cavan-Monaghan	5	Smith	Brendan	FF	Jun-56	55.8	25/11/1992	19.3
3	Clare	4	Breen	Pat	FG	Mar-57	55.0	17/05/2002	9.8
3	Clare	4	Carey	Joe	FG	Jun-75	36.7	24/05/2007	4.8
3	Clare	4	Dooley	Timmy	FF	Feb-69	43.1	24/05/2007	4.8
3	Clare	4	McNamara	Michael	LB	Mar-74	38.1	25/02/2011	1.1
4	Cork East	4	Barry	Tom	FG	Oct-68	43.4	25/02/2011	1.1
4	Cork East	4	McLellan	Sandra	SF	May-61	50.9	25/02/2011	1.1
4	Cork East	4	Sherlock	Sean	LB	Dec-72	39.3	24/05/2007	4.8
4	Cork East	4	Stanton	David	FG	Feb-57	55.1	06/06/1997	14.8
5	Cork North-Central	4	O'Brien	Jonathan	SF	Dec-71	40.3	25/02/2011	1.1
5	Cork North-Central	4	Kelleher	Billy	FF	Jan-68	44.2	06/06/1997	14.8
5	Cork North-Central	4	Lynch	Kathleen	LB	Jun-53	58.8	*10/11/1994*	12.4
5	Cork North-Central	4	Murphy	Dara	FG	Dec-69	42.3	25/02/2011	1.1
6	Cork North-West	3	Creed	Michael	FG	Jun-63	48.7	15/06/1989	17.7
6	Cork North-West	3	Moynihan	Michael	FF	Jan-68	44.2	06/06/1997	14.8
6	Cork North-West	3	Collins	Aine	FG	Sep-69	42.5	25/02/2011	1.1
7	Cork South Central	5	Buttimer	Jerry	FG	Mar-67	45.0	25/02/2011	1.1
7	Cork South Central	5	Coveney	Simon	FG	Jun-72	39.8	*23/10/1998*	13.4
7	Cork South Central	5	Lynch	Ciaran	LB	Jun-64	47.8	24/05/2007	4.8
7	Cork South Central	5	Martin	Micheal	FF	Aug-60	51.6	15/06/1989	22.8
7	Cork South Central	5	McGrath	Michael	FF	Aug-76	35.6	24/05/2007	4.8
8	Cork South West	3	Daly	Jim	FG	Dec-72	39.2	25/02/2011	1.1
8	Cork South West	3	Harrington	Noel	FG	Dec-70	41.2	25/02/2011	1.1
8	Cork South West	3	McCarthy	Michael	LB	Nov-76	35.3	25/02/2011	1.1
9	Donegal North East	3	MacLochlainn	Padraig	SF	Jun-73	38.8	25/02/2011	1.1
9	Donegal North East	3	McHugh	Joe	FG	Jul-71	40.7	24/05/2007	4.8
9	Donegal North East	3	McConalogue	Charlie	FF	Oct-77	34.4	25/02/2011	1.1
10	Donegal South West	3	Pringle	Thomas	NP	Aug-67	44.6	25/02/2011	1.1
10	Donegal South West	3	Doherty	Pearse	SF	Jul-77	34.7	*26/11/2010*	1.3
10	Donegal South West	3	McGinley	Dinny	FG	Apr-45	66.9	18/02/1982	30.1
11	Dublin Central	4	Donohoe	Paschal	FG	Sep-74	37.5	25/02/2011	1.1
11	Dublin Central	4	McDonald	Mary Lou	SF	May-69	42.9	25/02/2011	1.1
11	Dublin Central	4	Costello	Joe	LB	Jul-45	66.7	25/11/1992	14.4
11	Dublin Central	4	O'Sullivan	Maureen	NP	Mar-51	61.0	*05/06/2009*	2.8
12	Dublin Mid West	4	Fitzgerald*	Frances	FG	Aug-50	61.6	25/11/1992	10.5
12	Dublin Mid West	4	Keating	Derek	FG	May-55	56.8	25/02/2011	1.1
12	Dublin Mid West	4	Dowds	Robert	LB	May-53	58.9	25/02/2011	1.1
12	Dublin Mid West	4	Tuffy	Joanna	LB	Mar-65	47.0	24/05/2007	4.8
13	Dublin North	4	Ryan	Brendan	LB	Feb-53	59.1	25/02/2011	1.1
13	Dublin North	4	Daly	Clare	SP	Apr-68	43.9	25/02/2011	1.1
13	Dublin North	4	Reilly	James	FG	Aug-55	56.6	24/05/2007	4.8
13	Dublin North	4	Farrell	Alan	FG	Dec-77	34.2	25/02/2011	1.1
14	Dublin North Central	3	Bruton	Richard	FG	Mar-53	59.0	18/02/1982	30.1
14	Dublin North Central	3	Ó Ríordáin	Aodhán	LB	Jul-76	35.7	25/02/2011	1.1
14	Dublin North Central	3	McGrath	Finian	NP	Apr-53	58.9	17/05/2002	9.8

AGE & YEARS OF SERVICE OF TD's IN 31st DAIL										
							19/03/2012	First	Years
	Constituency	Seats	Surname	First Name	Party	Born	Age	Elected	Service
15	Dublin North East	3	Broughan	Tommy	LB	Aug-47	64.6	25/11/1992	19.3
15	Dublin North East	3	Flanagan	Terence	FG	Jan-75	37.2	24/05/2007	4.8
15	Dublin North East	3	Kenny*	Sean	LB	Oct-42	69.5	25/11/1992	5.6
16	Dublin North West	3	Ellis	Dessie	SF	Oct-53	58.4	25/02/2011	1.1
16	Dublin North West	3	Lyons	John	LB	Jun-77	34.8	25/02/2011	1.1
16	Dublin North West	3	Shortall	Roisin	LB	Apr-54	57.9	25/11/1992	19.3
17	Dublin South	5	Ross	Shane	NP	Jul-49	62.7	25/02/2011	1.1
17	Dublin South	5	Mitchell	Olivia	FG	Jul-47	64.6	06/06/1997	14.8
17	Dublin South	5	White	Alex	LB	Dec-58	53.3	25/02/2011	1.1
17	Dublin South	5	Mathews	Peter	FG	Aug-51	60.6	25/02/2011	1.1
17	Dublin South	5	Shatter	Alan	FG	Feb-51	61.1	11/06/1981	25.8
18	Dublin South Central	5	Conaghan	Michael	LB	Sep-45	66.5	25/02/2011	1.1
18	Dublin South Central	5	Byrne	Catherine	FG	Feb-56	56.1	24/05/2007	4.8
18	Dublin South Central	5	Collins	Joan	PBPA	Jun-61	50.8	25/02/2011	1.1
18	Dublin South Central	5	O Snodaigh	Aengus	SF	Jul-64	47.6	17/05/2002	9.8
18	Dublin South Central	5	Byrne*	Eric	LB	Apr-47	64.9	15/06/1989	7.5
19	Dublin South East	4	Murphy	Eoghan	FG	Apr-82	29.9	25/02/2011	1.1
19	Dublin South East	4	Creighton	Lucinda	FG	Jan-80	32.2	24/05/2007	4.8
19	Dublin South East	4	Humphreys	Kevin	LB	Feb-58	54.1	25/02/2011	1.1
19	Dublin South East	4	Quinn	Ruairi	LB	Apr-46	66.0	16/06/1977	34.1
20	Dublin South West	4	Hayes	Brian	FG	Aug-69	42.6	06/06/1997	9.8
20	Dublin South West	4	Crowe*	Sean	SF	Mar-57	55.0	17/05/2002	6.1
20	Dublin South West	4	Maloney	Eamonn	LB	May-53	58.9	25/02/2011	1.1
20	Dublin South West	4	Rabbitte	Pat	LB	May-49	62.8	15/06/1989	22.8
21	Dublin West	4	Burton	Joan	LB	Feb-49	63.1	25/11/1992	14.4
21	Dublin West	4	Nulty	Patrick	LB	Nov-82	29.3	*27/10/2011*	0.4
21	Dublin West	4	Varadkar	Leo	FG	Jan-79	33.2	24/05/2007	4.8
21	Dublin West	4	Higgins*	Joe	SP	May-49	62.8	06/06/1997	11.0
22	Dun Laoghaire	4	Mitchell O'Connor	Mary	FG	Jun-59	52.8	25/02/2011	1.1
22	Dun Laoghaire	4	Barrett	Sean	FG	Aug-44	67.6	11/06/1981	25.8
22	Dun Laoghaire	4	Boyd Barrett	Richard	PBPA	Nov-67	44.3	25/02/2011	1.1
22	Dun Laoghaire	4	Gilmore	Eamon	LB	Apr-55	56.9	15/06/1989	22.8
23	Galway East	4	Cannon	Ciaran	FG	Sep-65	46.5	25/02/2011	1.1
23	Galway East	4	Connaughton	Paul	FG	Jan-82	30.2	25/02/2011	1.1
23	Galway East	4	Kitt	Michael	FF	May-50	61.8	*04/03/1975*	28.0
23	Galway East	4	Keaveney	Colm	LB	Jan-71	41.2	25/02/2011	1.1
24	Galway West	5	Nolan	Derek	LB	Oct-82	29.5	25/02/2011	1.1
24	Galway West	5	Grealish	Noel	NP	Dec-65	46.3	17/05/2002	9.8
24	Galway West	5	Walsh	Brian	FG	Sep-72	39.5	25/02/2011	1.1
24	Galway West	5	Kyne	Sean	FG	May-75	36.8	25/02/2011	1.1
24	Galway West	5	O Cuiv	Eamon	FF	Jun-50	61.8	25/11/1992	19.3
25	Kerry North	3	Deenihan	Jimmy	FG	Sep-52	59.5	17/02/1987	25.1
25	Kerry North	3	Ferris	Martin	SF	Mar-52	60.0	17/05/2002	9.8
25	Kerry North	3	Spring	Arthur	LB	Jul-76	35.7	25/02/2011	1.1
26	Kerry South	3	Healy-Rae	Michael	NP	Jan-67	45.2	25/02/2011	1.1
26	Kerry South	3	Fleming	Tom	NP	Feb-51	61.1	25/02/2011	1.1
26	Kerry South	3	Griffin	Brendan	FG	Mar-82	30.0	25/02/2011	1.1
27	Kildare North	4	Lawlor	Anthony	FG	Jun-59	52.8	25/02/2011	1.1
27	Kildare North	4	Durkan	Bernard	FG	Mar-45	67.0	11/06/1981	30.0
27	Kildare North	4	Murphy*	Catherine	NP	Sep-53	58.5	*11/03/2005*	3.3
27	Kildare North	4	Stagg	Emmet	LB	Oct-44	67.5	17/02/1987	25.1
28	Kildare South	3	O Fearghail	Sean	FF	Apr-60	51.9	17/05/2002	9.8
28	Kildare South	3	Heydon	Martin	FG	Aug-78	33.6	25/02/2011	1.1
28	Kildare South	3	Wall	Jack	LB	Jul-45	66.7	06/06/1997	14.8
29	Laoighis Offaly	5	Cowen	Barry	FF	Aug-67	44.6	25/02/2011	1.1
29	Laoighis Offaly	5	Corcoran-Kennedy	Marcella	FG	Jan-63	49.2	25/02/2011	1.1
29	Laoighis Offaly	5	Flanagan	Charlie	FG	Nov-56	55.4	17/02/1987	20.1
29	Laoighis Offaly	5	Fleming	Sean	FF	Feb-58	54.1	06/06/1997	14.8
29	Laoighis Offaly	5	Stanley	Brian	SF	Jan-58	54.2	25/02/2011	1.1

AGE & YEARS OF SERVICE OF TD's IN 31st DAIL										
							19/03/2012	First	Years
	Constituency	Seats	Surname	First Name	Party	Born	Age	Elected	Service
31	Limerick	3	Collins	Niall	FF	Mar-73	39.0	24/05/2007	4.8
31	Limerick	3	Neville	Dan	FG	Dec-46	65.3	06/06/1997	14.8
31	Limerick	3	O'Donovan	Patrick	FG	Mar-77	35.0	25/02/2011	1.1
30	Limerick City	5	Noonan	Michael	FG	May-43	68.8	11/06/1981	30.8
30	Limerick City	5	O'Dea	Willie	FF	Nov-52	59.4	18/02/1982	30.1
30	Limerick City	5	O'Donnell	Kieran	FG	May-63	48.9	24/05/2007	4.8
30	Limerick City	5	O'Sullivan	Jan	LB	Dec-50	61.3	*11/03/1998*	14.0
32	Longford-Westmeath	4	Bannon	James	FG	Mar-58	54.0	24/05/2007	4.8
32	Longford-Westmeath	4	McFadden	Nicky	FG	Dec-62	49.3	25/02/2011	1.1
32	Longford-Westmeath	4	Troy	Robert	FF	Jan-82	30.2	25/02/2011	1.1
32	Longford-Westmeath	4	Penrose	Willie	LB	Aug-56	55.6	25/11/1992	19.3
33	Louth	5	Nash	Gerald	LB	Dec-75	36.2	25/02/2011	1.1
33	Louth	5	Kirk	Seamus	FF	Apr-45	66.9	24/11/1982	29.3
33	Louth	5	Adams	Gerry	SF	Oct-48	63.5	25/02/2011	1.1
33	Louth	5	O'Dowd	Fergus	FG	Sep-48	63.5	17/05/2002	9.8
33	Louth	5	Fitzpatrick	Peter	FG	May-62	49.9	25/02/2011	1.1
34	Mayo	5	Calleary	Dara	FF	May-73	38.9	24/05/2007	4.8
34	Mayo	5	Mulherin	Michelle	FG	Jan-72	40.2	25/02/2011	1.1
34	Mayo	5	Kenny	Enda	FG	Apr-51	60.9	*12/11/1975*	36.4
34	Mayo	5	O'Mahony	John	FG	Jun-53	58.8	24/05/2007	4.8
34	Mayo	5	Ring	Michael	FG	Dec-53	58.2	*09/06/1994*	17.8
35	Meath East	3	Doherty	Regina	FG	Jan-71	41.1	25/02/2011	1.1
35	Meath East	3	McEntee	Shane	FG	Dec-56	55.2	*11/03/2005*	7.0
35	Meath East	3	Hannigan	Dominic	LB	Jul-65	46.7	25/02/2011	1.1
36	Meath West	3	Tóibín	Peadar	SF	Jun-74	37.8	25/02/2011	1.1
36	Meath West	3	Butler	Ray	FG	Dec-65	46.2	25/02/2011	1.1
36	Meath West	3	English	Damien	FG	Feb-78	34.1	17/05/2002	9.8
37	Roscommon-Sth Leitrim	3	Feighan	Frank	FG	Jul-62	49.7	24/05/2007	4.8
37	Roscommon-Sth Leitrim	3	Flanagan	Luke "Ming"	NP	Jan-72	40.2	25/02/2011	1.1
37	Roscommon-Sth Leitrim	3	Naughten	Denis	FG	Jun-73	38.7	06/06/1997	14.8
38	Sligo-North Leitrim	3	McLoughlin	Tony	FG	Jan-49	63.2	25/02/2011	1.1
38	Sligo-North Leitrim	3	Perry	John	FG	Aug-56	55.6	06/06/1997	14.8
38	Sligo-North Leitrim	3	Colreavy	Michael	SF	Sep-48	63.5	25/02/2011	1.1
39	Tipperary North	3	Coonan	Noel	FG	Jan-51	61.2	24/05/2007	4.8
39	Tipperary North	3	Kelly	Alan	LB	Jul-75	36.7	25/02/2011	1.1
39	Tipperary North	3	Lowry	Michael	NP	Mar-54	58.0	17/02/1987	25.1
40	Tipperary South	3	Hayes	Tom	FG	Feb-52	60.1	*30/06/2001*	10.7
40	Tipperary South	3	Healy*	Seamus	NP	Aug-50	61.6	*22/06/2000*	8.0
40	Tipperary South	3	McGrath	Mattie	NP	Sep-58	53.5	24/05/2007	4.8
41	Waterford	4	Deasy	John	FG	Oct-67	44.4	17/05/2002	9.8
41	Waterford	4	Coffey	Paudie	FG	May-69	42.8	25/02/2011	1.1
41	Waterford	4	Conway	Ciara	LB	Aug-80	31.6	25/02/2011	1.1
41	Waterford	4	Halligan	John	NP	Jan-55	57.2	25/02/2011	1.1
42	Wexford	5	Browne	John	FF	Aug-48	63.6	24/11/1982	29.3
42	Wexford	5	Wallace	Mick	NP	Nov-55	56.4	25/02/2011	1.1
42	Wexford	5	Twomey*	Liam	FG	Apr-67	45.0	17/05/2002	6.1
42	Wexford	5	Howlin	Brendan	LB	May-56	55.9	17/02/1987	25.1
42	Wexford	5	Kehoe	Paul	FG	Jan-73	39.2	17/05/2002	9.8
43	Wicklow	5	Harris	Simon	FG	Oct-86	25.4	25/02/2011	1.1
43	Wicklow	5	Doyle	Andrew	FG	Jul-60	51.7	24/05/2007	4.8
43	Wicklow	5	Ferris	Anne	LB	Sep-54	57.5	25/02/2011	1.1
43	Wicklow	5	Donnelly	Stephen	NP	Feb-75	37.1	25/02/2011	1.1
43	Wicklow	5	Timmins	Billy	FG	Oct-59	52.5	06/06/1997	14.8
43	**Average**	**166**				**Sep-62**	**49.9**	**15/08/2003**	**7.9**
	Former TD*	**8***				Broken Service		*By-Election*	***13***

PART 3

GENERAL ELECTIONS 1918-2011

First Dáil 1919

ELECTIONS 1918-2011

The 1918 General Election was the last all-Ireland general election to the United Kingdom parliament at Westminster. The Sinn Fein members of the House of Commons became members of the first Dáil Eireann, which met in Dublin on 21st January 1919. The new assembly elected a cabinet. The second Dáil met for the first time on August 26th, 1921 and again elected a cabinet. The cabinet was superseded by the Provisional Government in January 1922, which was in turn superseded by the Executive Council in December 1922.

The first and second Dála lacked official status, being private meetings of Sinn Fein MP's returned at general elections held under the authority of the British Government in 1918 and 1921, though the second Dáil subsequently received effective official recognition as the legitimate parliament of Southern Ireland under the terms of the Anglo Irish Treaty of 1921. The general election to the third Dáil was initiated by the Irish Free State (Agreement) Act, passed by the UK parliament in March 1922 and was sanctioned by the second Dáil in May. Elections to subsequent Dála were held under the authority of a sovereign Irish government.

Elections were operated under a system of proportional representation using the single transferable vote from 1921 onwards; however, as all the seats in the general election of 1921 were uncontested the system was not brought into use until 1922.

BOUNDARY COMMISSIONS									
			Number of members in constituencies						
Year	**Constituencies**	**Seats**	**3**	**4**	**5**	**6**	**7**	**8**	**9**
1918	72	73							
1921	28	128	3	16	4	2	1	2	
1923	30	153	8	4	9		5	3	1
1935	34	138	15	8	8		3		
1947	40	147	22	9	9				
1959*	39	144	21	9	9				
1961	38	144	17	12	9				
1969	42	144	26	14	2				
1974	42	148	26	10	6				
1980	41	166	13	13	15				
1983	41	166	13	13	15				
1990	41	166	12	15	14				
1995	41	166	12	15	14				
1998	42	166	16	12	14				
2004	43	166	18	13	12				
2007	43	166	17	15	11				
* This revision was found to be unconstitutional by the High Court									

DÁIL DETAILS 1918-2011								
* Uncontested					Valid			
Dail	Seats	Population	Electorate	E/P	Votes	%	Pop/Seat	E/Seat
1 1918	73	3,139,688					43,009	
2 1921*	128	3,139,688					24,529	
3 1922	128	3,139,688	1,430,024	**45.55%**	**621,587**	60.27%	24,529	11,172
4 1923	153	3,139,688	1,784,918	56.85%	1,053,955	**59.05%**	20,521	11,666
5 1927	153	2,971,992	1,730,177	58.22%	1,146,460	66.26%	**19,425**	11,308
6 1927	153	2,971,992	1,728,093	58.15%	1,170,869	67.75%	**19,425**	11,295
7 1932	153	2,971,992	1,691,993	56.93%	1,274,026	75.30%	**19,425**	**11,059**
8 1933	153	2,971,992	1,724,420	58.02%	1,386,558	***80.41%***	**19,425**	11,271
9 1937	138	2,968,420	1,775,055	59.80%	1,324,449	74.61%	21,510	12,863
10 1938	138	2,968,420	1,697,323	57.18%	1,286,259	75.78%	21,510	12,299
11 1943	138	2,968,420	1,816,142	61.18%	1,331,709	73.33%	21,510	13,160
12 1944	138	2,968,420	1,776,950	59.86%	1,217,349	68.51%	21,510	12,876
13 1948	147	**2,955,107**	1,800,210	60.92%	1,323,443	73.52%	20,103	12,246
14 1951	147	2,960,593	1,785,144	60.30%	1,331,573	74.59%	20,140	12,144
15 1954	147	2,960,593	1,763,209	59.56%	1,335,202	75.73%	20,140	11,995
16 1957	147	2,898,264	1,738,278	59.98%	1,227,019	70.59%	19,716	11,825
17 1961	144	2,818,341	**1,670,860**	59.29%	1,168,404	69.93%	19,572	11,603
18 1965	144	2,818,341	1,683,019	59.72%	1,253,122	74.46%	19,572	11,688
19 1969	144	2,884,002	1,735,388	60.17%	1,318,953	76.00%	20,028	12,051
20 1973	144	2,978,248	1,783,604	59.89%	1,350,537	75.72%	20,682	12,386
21 1977	148	2,978,248	2,118,606	71.14%	1,603,027	75.66%	20,123	14,315
22 1981	166	3,368,217	2,275,450	67.56%	1,718,211	75.51%	20,290	13,708
23 1982	166	3,368,217	2,275,450	67.56%	1,665,133	73.18%	20,290	13,708
24 1982	166	3,368,217	2,335,153	69.33%	1,688,720	72.32%	20,290	14,067
25 1987	166	3,540,643	2,445,515	69.07%	1,777,165	72.67%	21,329	14,732
26 1989	166	3,540,643	2,448,810	69.16%	1,656,813	67.66%	21,329	14,752
27 1992	166	3,525,719	2,557,036	72.53%	1,724,853	67.46%	21,239	15,404
28 1997	166	3,626,087	2,741,262	75.60%	1,788,985	65.26%	21,844	16,514
29 2002	166	3,917,203	3,002,173	***76.64%***	1,857,902	61.89%	23,598	18,085
30 2007	166	***4,239,848***	3,110,914	73.37%	2,065,810	66.41%	***25,541***	18,740
31 2011	166	***4,239,848***	***3,209,244***	75.69%	***2,220,359***	69.19%	***25,541***	***19,333***
Total	**4,618**	**99,306,779**	**59,634,420**	**60.05%**	**41,888,452**	**70.24%**	**21,504**	**12,913**
						High	**Low**	

POPULATION 1841-2011					
Census Year	Population	Average Size of Household	Census Year	Population	Average Size of Household
1841	6,528,799	5.60	1956	2,898,264	
1851	5,111,557		1961	2,818,341	3.97
1861	4,402,111		1966	2,884,002	4.01
1871	4,053,187		1971	2,978,248	3.93
1881	3,870,020		1979	3,368,217	3.72
1891	3,468,694		1981	3,443,405	3.66
1901	3,221,823		1986	3,540,643	3.53
1911	3,139,688		1991	3,525,719	3.34
1926	2,971,992	4.48	1996	3,626,087	3.14
1936	2,968,420	4.31	2002	3,917,203	2.94
1946	2,955,107	4.16	2006	4,239,848	2.81
1951	2,960,593		2011	4,581,269	2.68

GOVERNMENTS

The government elected in 2011 was the fourth Fine Gael/Labour coalition. The 1994-1997 "Rainbow Coalition" was the first between Fine Gael, Labour and Democratic Left and the only one to be formed without a general election. The first Fianna Fail/Green/Progressive Democrat Government elected in 2007 was the fifth Coalition Government involving Fianna Fail. There have been three Fianna Fail/PD and one Fianna Fail/Labour coalitions. There have also been two Inter-Party governments, in 1948 and 1954. Fianna Fail have been part of 19 of the 29 governments since the foundation of the state in 1922 and in power on their own on 14 occasions.

The 2011 Fine Gael/Labour coalition has by far the largest majority 60, in the history of the state. Only four previous governments had majorities in double figures: 1938 (16), 1944 (14) and 1977 (20) - all Fianna Fail governments along with the 36 seat majority of the Fianna Fail/Labour Party government in the 27th Dail in 1992. The Fianna Fail/Green/PD Coalition elected in 2007 had a combined total of 86 seats and also had the support of four of the five Independents to give it a comfortable majority. Minority governments are not unusual, as of the 29 governments to date, 15 had no majority with 3 having a majority of just one.

Enda Kenny is the twelfth Taoiseach and the fifth from Fine Gael. Eamon de Valera is by far the longest serving Taoiseach having served eight terms. W.T. Cosgrave and C.J. Haughey each served four terms and Sean Lemass, Jack Lynch and Bertie Ahern served three terms. J.A. Costello, Garrett Fitzgerald and Albert Reynolds each served on 2 occasions. Liam Cosgrave served only one term as Taoiseach from 1973-1977 and Brian Cowen also did just one term and served for the second shortest period behind Albert Reynolds. John Bruton had the shortest period in office, December 1994 to June 1997.

Micheal Martin became the eighth leader of Fianna Fail when he won the leadership election on 26th January 2011. Brian Cowen had been elected leader designate of Fianna Fail on 8th April 2008 but did not officially take over the leadership until 8th May when he was elected Taoiseach. He thus became the seventh leader of Fianna Fail, all of whom went on to serve as Taoiseach. Eamon de Valera was by far the longest serving leader of the party having served 33 years from 1926 until he was elected President of Ireland in 1959. Bertie Ahern was the next longest serving leader having served for 14 years from 1994 until 6th May 2008. Jack Lynch and Charles Haughey served as leaders for 13 years with Sean Lemass serving for seven and Albert Reynolds leader for just two years from 1992-1994. Bertie Ahern was unique in that he did not inherit the position of Taoiseach as he was in opposition for the first two years of his leadership of Fianna Fail unlike the rest of De Valera's successors who became Taoiseach following their elevation to party leader as did their recent leader Brian Cowen. Micheal Martin, like Bertie Ahern also did not inherit the position of Taoiseach.

There have been ten leaders of Fine Gael/Cumann na nGaedheal and unlike Fianna Fail, only five of them have gone on to become Taoiseach with one of them John Bruton doing so without a general election.

There have been ten leaders of the Labour party with none of them reaching the office of Taoiseach.

GOVERNMENTS 1919-2011					
Dail	Election Date	Seats	Government	Taoiseach (from 1937)	Ceann Comhairle
1	14th Dec 1918	73	Sinn Fein	C. Brugha 22/1/1919-1/4/1919	Sean T. O'Kelly
			Sinn Fein	E. de Valera 1/4/1919-26/8/1921	
2	24th May 1921	128	Sinn Fein	E. de Valera 26/8/1921-9/1/1922	Eoin MacNeill
			Sinn Fein	A. Griffith 10/1/1922-12/8/1922*	
			Sinn Fein	W.T. Cosgrave 12/8/1922-9/9/1922	
			Provisional Government	M. Collins 16/1/1922-22/8/1922	
			Provisional Government	W.T. Cosgrave 25/8/1922-6/12/1922	
3	16th June 1922	128	Pro Treaty	W.T. Cosgrave	Michael Hayes
4	27th Aug 1923	153	Cumann na nGael	W.T. Cosgrave	Michael Hayes
5	9th June 1927	153	Cumann na nGael	W.T. Cosgrave	Michael Hayes
6	15th Sept 1927	153	Cumann na nGael	W.T. Cosgrave	Michael Hayes
7	16th Feb 1932	153	Fianna Fail	E. de Valera	Frank Fahy
8	24th Jan 1933	153	Fianna Fail	E. de Valera	Frank Fahy
9	1st July 1937	138	Fianna Fail	E. de Valera	Frank Fahy
10	17th June 1938	138	Fianna Fail	E. de Valera	Frank Fahy
11	23rd June 1943	138	Fianna Fail	E. de Valera	Frank Fahy
12	30th May 1944	138	Fianna Fail	E. de Valera	Frank Fahy
13	4th Feb 1948	147	Inter Party	J.A. Costello	Frank Fahy
14	30th May 1951	147	Fianna Fail	E. de Valera	Frank Fahy
15	18th May 1954	147	Inter Party	J.A. Costello	Patrick Hogan
16	5th Mar 1957	147	Fianna Fail	E. de Valera to 23/6/1959	Patrick Hogan
				S. Lemass from 23/6/1959	Patrick Hogan
17	4th Oct 1961	144	Fianna Fail	S. Lemass	Patrick Hogan
18	7th Apr 1965	144	Fianna Fail	S. Lemass to 10/11/1966	Patrick Hogan to 1968
				J. Lynch from 10/11/1966	Cormac Breslin from 1968
19	18th June 1969	144	Fianna Fail	J .Lynch	Cormac Breslin
20	28th Feb 1973	144	Fine Gael/Labour	L. Cosgrave	Sean Treacy
21	16th June 1977	148	Fianna Fail	J. Lynch to 11/12/1979	Joe Brennan died 13/7/1980
				C.J. Haughey from 11/12/1979	Padraig Faulkner from 16/10/80
22	11th June 1981	166	Fine Gael/Labour	G. Fitzgerald	John O'Connell
23	18th Feb 1982	166	Fianna Fail	C.J. Haughey	John O'Connell
24	24th Nov 1982	166	Fine Gael/Labour	G. Fitzgerald	Thomas J. Fitzpatrick
25	17th Feb 1987	166	Fianna Fail	C.J. Haughey	Sean Treacy
26	15th June 1989	166	Fianna Fail/PD	C.J. Haughey to 11/2/1992	Sean Treacy
				A. Reynolds from 11/2/1992	Sean Treacy
27	25th Nov 1992	166	Fianna Fail /Labour	A. Reynolds to 15th Dec 1994	Sean Treacy
			FG/Lab/DL	J. Bruton from 5th Dec 1994	Sean Treacy
28	6th June 1997	166	Fianna Fail/PD	B. Ahern	Seamus Pattison
29	17th May 2002	166	Fianna Fail/PD	B. Ahern	Dr. Rory O'Hanlon
30	24th May 2007	166	Fianna Fail/GP/PD	B. Ahern to 7/5/08	John O'Donoghue to 14/10/09
				B. Cowen from 7/5/08	Seamus Kirk from 14/10/09
31	25th Feb 2011	166	Fine Gael/Labour	Enda Kenny	Sean Barrett
Total	**31**	**4,618**	**29**	**16**	**16**

1 Cathal Brugha was acting President of the First Dáil, 22 January - 1 April 1919.
2 Upon his release from prison, Éamon de Valera became President of the first Dáil, 1 April 1919 - 26th August 1921 and President of the second Dáil from 26th August 1921 - 9th January 1922.
De Valera and others who opposed the Anglo-Irish Treaty withdrew from the Dáil in January 1922.
3 Michael Collins was Chairman of the Provisional Government which came into being after the Dail ratified the Anglo-Irish Treaty in January 1922.
4 W. T. Cosgrave became Chairman of the Provisional Government following the assassination of Michael Collins on 22nd August 1922.
5 From December 1922 until December 1937, the office of Prime Minister was known as President of the Executive Council. Following the adoption of the 1937 Constitution the title was changed to "An Taoiseach".

PRESIDENT OF THE EXECUTIVE COUNCIL/TAOISEACH: DAYS IN OFFICE					
	Head of Government	**Terms**	**From**	**To**	**Days**
1	Eamon de Valera	10	*01/04/1919*	*23/06/1959*	8748
2	Bertie Ahern	3	26/06/1997	07/05/2008	3968
3	W.T. Cosgrave	5	*12/08/1922*	*16/02/1932*	3512
4	Jack Lynch	3	*10/11/1966*	*11/12/1979*	3205
5	Sean Lemass	3	23/06/1959	10/11/1966	2697
6	Charles Haughey	4	*11/12/1979*	*11/02/1992*	2646
7	John A. Costello	2	*04/02/1948*	*05/03/1957*	2233
8	Garret Fitzgerald	2	*30/06/1981*	*10/03/1987*	1799
9	Liam Cosgrave	1	14/03/1973	05/07/1977	1574
10	Albert Reynolds	2	11/02/1992	15/12/1994	1038
11	Brian Cowen	1	07/05/2008	09/03/2011	1036
12	John Bruton	1	15/12/1994	26/06/1997	924
13	Enda Kenny	1	09/03/2011	20/03/2012	377
14	Michael Collins	1	16/01/1922	22/08/1922	218
15	Arthur Griffith	1	10/01/1922	12/08/1922	214
16	Cathal Brugha	1	22/01/1919	01/04/1911	69

Broken Service

MAIN PARTY LEADERS				
	Fianna Fail	**From**	**To**	**Years**
1	Eamon de Valera	1926	1959	33
2	Sean Lemass	1959	1966	7
3	Jack Lynch	1966	1979	13
4	Charles Haughey	1979	1992	13
5	Albert Reynolds	1992	1994	2
6	Bertie Ahern	1994	2008	14
7	Brian Cowen	2008	2010	2
8	Michael Martin	26/01/2011		

	Fine Gael*	**From**	**To**	**Years**
1	General Eoin O'Duffy	1933	1934	1
2	W.T. Cosgrave	1934	1944	10
3	General Richard Mulcahy	1944	1959	15
4	James Dillon	1959	1965	6
5	Liam Cosgrave	1965	1977	12
6	Garret Fitzgerald	1977	1987	10
7	Alan Dukes	1987	1990	3
8	John Bruton	1990	2001	11
9	Michael Noonan	2001	2002	1
10	Enda Kenny	Jun-02		
	*Cumann na nGaedheal merged with the Blueshirts and the			
	Centre Party to form Fine Gael in September 1933			

	Labour Party	**From**	**To**	**Years**
1	Tom Johnson	1922	1927	5
2	T.J. O'Connell	1927	1932	5
3	William Norton	1932	1960	28
4	Brendan Corish	1960	1977	17
5	Frank Cluskey	1977	1981	4
6	Michael O'Leary	1981	1982	1
7	Dick Spring	1982	1997	15
8	Ruairi Quinn	1997	2002	5
9	Pat Rabbitte	2002	2007	5
10	Eamon Gilmore	Sep-07		

OVERALL RESULTS 1918-2011

Turnout

The valid poll has averaged 70.71% from 1922 to 2011. The Turnout in 2011 was up three points on 2007 but still below the average. The turnout has shown a steady decline since 1969 and the 2007 election was the first occasion on which this decline was arrested and there was further improvement in 2011. But the present figures are well below the largest turnout in 1933 (80.41%). Question marks remain over the state of the electoral register and so these figures come with a serious health warning and until an electoral commission is set up and the register of electors is reformed it is extremely difficult to assess an accurate level of turnout.

Fine Gael

Fine Gael have won 1,453 of the 4,618 seats contested from 30.77% of the first preference vote. They have done better since 1981, winning 561 of the 1,660 seats from a first preference vote of 30.73%. Fine Gael achieved their highest share of the vote in the second election of 1982 when they got 39.22% but they have failed to reach those heights since and were down to just 31 seats and 22.48% in 2002, their lowest since 1948. They recovered most of their losses in 2007 with their vote up to 27.32% and they won 51 seats. They improved considerably on that performance in 2011 winning 36.10% of the vote and a record 76 seats.

Fine Gael got their largest share of seats 45.78% in 2011. Their previous best performance was in 1922 when they won 45.31% of the seats. They have now won 40% or more of the seats at five elections.

Fine Gael have a seats to votes ratio of 102% since 1922. They have performed much better since the Dail was increased to 166 seats in 1981, achieving a seats to votes ratio of 110%. They have managed to win a larger share of seats than votes on all but four occasions with their poorest performance in 2002 when they got just 83%. They improved their ratio considerably in 2007 winning 112% and improved it considerably more in 2011 managing 127%, the largest ratio by any party to date.

Labour

Labour have won 11.53% of the vote since 1922, winning 482 of the 4,618 seats contested. They have done somewhat better since 1981 winning 201 out of 1,660 seats from a first preference vote of 11.63%. They achieved their highest share of the vote in 1922 when they got 21.33% with their next best coming in 1992 when Dick Spring won 19.31% and a record 33 seats. But they failed to reach those heights subsequently and dropped to just 17 seats and 10.40% at the next election in 1997 and won 10.13% and 20 seats in 2007. But like their government partners Fine Gael they had a very good result in 2011 and beat the "Spring Tide" election result of 1992, winning 19.45% and a record 37 seats.

Labour got their largest share of seats 22.29% in 2011 beating their previous best of 19.88% in 1992. Their next best performance was in 1965 when they won 15.28% of the seats.

Labour have achieved a seats to votes ratio of just 91% since 1922. They have done much better since 1981 with their seats to votes ratio up to 104%. But overall Labour have performed poorly in their conversion of votes into seats and have only got over 100% on nine occasions. They improved their ratio considerably at the last three elections, winning 115% in 2011, 117% in 2002 and gaining their best to date 119% in 2007.

Fianna Fail

Fianna Fail have won 1,985 seats from 41.86% of the first preference vote since 1922. They have not done so well since the Dail was increased to its present level of 166 seats in 1981, winning 716 seats from a first preference vote of 39.85%. Fianna Fail achieved their highest share of the vote in 1938 when they got 51.93%. They are the only party to achieve more than 50% of the vote in any one election and they repeated this in 1977 with 50.63%. Fianna Fail dropped below 40% for the first time since 1927 when they got just 39.11% in 1992, with little improvement in 1997 when they won 39.33%. They got back above the 40% level in 2002 winning 41.48% and got practically the same in 2007 (41.56%). But it was all change in 2011 with the party vote collapsing to just 17.45% and a mere twenty seats.

Fianna Fail got their largest share of seats in 1977 when they won an overall majority with 84 of the 148 seats on offer or 56.76% of the seats. Their next best performance was in 1938 when they won 55.80% of the seats. The nation's largest party prior to this latest election has won 50% or more of the seats at seven elections to date, the last being in 1977.

Fianna Fail have achieved a seats to votes ratio of 103% since 1922. They have performed much better since the Dail was increased to 166 seats in 1981, winning a seats to votes ratio of 108%. They have managed to win a larger share of seats than votes on all but two occasions, the second election of 1982 and the latest election in 2011 when they managed only a 69% seats to votes ratio. They had considerably improved their ratio in the previous three elections managing 118% in both 1997 and 2002 and 113% in 2007 to offset the drop in their first preference vote.

TURNOUTS 1922-2011					
* No Contest					
Dail		Seats	Electorate	Valid	%
1	1918	73			
2	1921*	128			
3	1922	128	1,031,342	621,587	60.27%
4	1923	153	1,784,918	1,053,955	59.05%
5	1927	153	1,730,177	1,146,460	66.26%
6	1927	153	1,728,093	1,170,869	67.75%
7	1932	153	1,691,993	1,274,026	75.30%
8	1933	153	1,724,420	1,386,558	80.41%
9	1937	138	1,775,055	1,324,449	74.61%
10	1938	138	1,697,323	1,286,259	75.78%
11	1943	138	1,816,142	1,331,709	73.33%
12	1944	138	1,776,950	1,217,349	68.51%
13	1948	147	1,800,210	1,323,443	73.52%
14	1951	147	1,785,144	1,331,573	74.59%
15	1954	147	1,763,209	1,335,202	75.73%
16	1957	147	1,738,278	1,227,019	70.59%
17	1961	144	1,670,860	1,168,404	69.93%
18	1965	144	1,683,019	1,253,122	74.46%
19	1969	144	1,735,388	1,318,953	76.00%
20	1973	144	1,783,604	1,350,537	75.72%
21	1977	148	2,118,606	1,603,027	75.66%
22	1981	166	2,275,450	1,718,211	75.51%
23	1982	166	2,275,450	1,665,133	73.18%
24	1982	166	2,335,153	1,688,720	72.32%
25	1987	166	2,445,515	1,777,165	72.67%
26	1989	166	2,448,810	1,656,813	67.66%
27	1992	166	2,557,036	1,724,853	67.46%
28	1997	166	2,741,262	1,788,985	65.26%
29	2002	166	3,002,173	1,857,902	61.89%
30	2007	166	3,110,914	2,065,810	66.41%
31	2011	166	3,209,244	2,220,359	69.19%
Total		**4,618**	**59,235,738**	**41,888,452**	**70.71%**

Note: Total electorate in 1922 was 1,430,024 as eight constituencies were uncontested

DISTRIBUTION OF SEATS & SHARE OF THE FIRST PREFERENCE VOTE 1918-2011

* No Contest			FG		LB		FF		SF		SP		PBPA		GP		WP		PD		DL		C na P		C na T		Farmers		Others	
Dail		Seats	S	Votes	S	Votes	S	Votes	S	Votes	S	Votes	S	Votes	S	Votes	S	Votes	S	Votes	S	Votes	S	Votes	S	Votes	S	Votes	S	Votes
1	1918	73							73																					
2	1921*	128							124																				4	
3	1922	128	58	239,195	17	132,565	36	132,163																			7	48,719	10	68,945
4	1923	153	63	410,695	14	111,939	44	288,794																			15	127,184	17	115,343
5	1927	153	47	314,703	22	143,849	44	299,486	5	41,401																	11	101,955	24	245,066
6	1927	153	62	453,028	13	106,184	57	411,777																			6	74,626	15	125,254
7	1932	153	57	449,506	7	98,286	72	566,498																			3	26,436	14	133,300
8	1933	153	48	422,495	8	79,221	77	689,054																					20	195,788
9	1937	138	48	461,171	13	135,758	69	599,040																					8	128,480
10	1938	138	45	428,633	9	128,945	77	667,996																					7	60,685
11	1943	138	32	307,490	17	208,812	67	557,525																	11	130,452			11	127,430
12	1944	138	30	249,329	8	106,767	76	595,259																	9	122,745			15	143,249
13	1948	147	31	262,393	14	115,073	68	553,914															10	174,823	7	73,813			17	143,427
14	1951	147	40	342,922	16	151,828	69	616,212															2	54,210	6	38,872			14	127,529
15	1954	147	50	427,031	19	161,034	65	578,960		1,990													3	51,069	5	41,249			5	73,869
16	1957	147	40	326,699	12	111,747	78	592,994	4	65,640													1	20,632	3	28,905			9	80,402
17	1961	144	47	374,099	16	136,111	70	512,073		36,396													1	13,170	2	17,693			8	78,862
18	1965	144	47	427,081	22	192,740	72	597,414															1	9,427					2	26,460
19	1969	144	50	449,749	18	224,498	75	602,234																					1	42,472
20	1973	144	54	473,781	19	185,117	69	624,528		15,366																			2	51,745
21	1977	148	43	488,767	17	186,410	84	811,615										27,209											4	89,026
22	1981	166	65	626,376	15	169,990	78	777,616	2	42,803							1	29,561											5	71,865
23	1982	166	63	621,088	15	151,875	81	786,951		16,894							3	38,088											4	50,237
24	1982	166	70	662,284	16	158,115	75	763,313									2	54,888											3	50,120
25	1987	166	51	481,127	12	114,551	81	784,547		32,933						7,159	4	67,273	14	210,583									4	78,992
26	1989	166	55	485,307	15	156,989	77	731,472		20,003					1	24,827	7	82,263	6	91,013									5	64,939
27	1992	166	45	422,106	33	333,013	68	674,650		27,809					1	24,110		11,533	10	80,787	4	47,945							5	102,900
28	1997	166	54	499,936	17	186,044	77	703,682	1	45,614	1	12,445		2,028	2	49,323		7,808	4	83,765	4	44,901							6	153,439
29	2002	166	31	417,619	21	200,130	81	770,748	5	121,020	1	14,896		3,333	6	71,470		4,012	8	73,628									13	181,046
30	2007	166	51	564,428	20	209,175	78	858,565	4	143,410		13,218		9,333	6	96,936		3,026	2	56,396									5	111,323
31	2011	166	76	801,628	37	431,796	20	387,358	14	220,661	2	26,770	2	21,551		41,039		3,056											15	286,500
1918-2011		**4,618**	**1,453**	**12,890,666**	**482**	**4,828,562**	**1,985**	**17,536,438**	**232**	**831,940**	**4**	**67,329**	**2**	**36,245**	**16**	**314,864**	**17**	**328,717**	**44**	**596,172**	**8**	**92,846**	**18**	**323,331**	**43**	**453,729**	**42**	**378,920**	**272**	**3,208,693**
1981-2011		**1,660**	**561**	**5,581,899**	**201**	**2,111,678**	**716**	**7,238,902**	**26**	**671,147**	**4**	**67,329**	**2**	**36,245**	**16**	**314,864**	**17**	**301,508**	**44**	**596,172**	**8**	**92,846**							**65**	**1,151,361**

DISTRIBUTION OF SEATS & SHARE OF THE FIRST PREFERENCE VOTE PER REGIONS 1918-2011

		FG		LB		FF		SF		SP		PBPA		GP		WP		CS		PD		DL	
Constituency	Seats	S	Votes	S	Votes	S	Votes	S	Votes	S		S		S	Votes	S		S		S	Votes	S	Votes
Carlow-Kilkenny	143	49	448,831	23	210,331	54	594,615	7	11,679		1,135			1	15,535		10,308			1	15,388		
Cavan-Monaghan	186	55	521,818		30,189	87	734,474	16	92,375						4,012		1,976		2,383		1,131		
Clare	128	34	324,737	15	92,779	65	631,593	6	11,306						8,597				675		16,519		
Cork Region	544	183	1,670,237	73	705,053	209	1,983,456	27	80,377		7,439		1,769	1	33,616	4	61,718		1,886	6	70,772		17,453
Donegal Region	200	63	517,348	1	45,616	94	731,977	11	59,959						3,819		10,813		339				1,825
Dublin Region	1,035	329	2,767,989	129	1,317,308	406	3,617,991	36	189,479	4	57,473	2	31,969	14	170,309	12	165,005		6,682	18	201,597	6	48,930
Universities	47	13	8,327			4	5,027	5															
Galway Region	253	75	652,604	13	135,185	137	1,044,386	11	27,993						10,480		8,127		383	6	63,848		392
Kerry Region	201	47	426,936	24	246,271	95	786,059	17	59,724						2,833		2,479				4,673		
Kildare Region	118	35	306,223	31	248,127	48	451,112	2	9,579						12,890		2,758				28,273		4,375
Laois-Offaly	150	51	478,735	16	164,919	70	645,416	7	20,720		561				1,638				298	1	30,423		
Limerick Region	216	66	609,780	22	204,938	103	883,492	7	10,188		721				6,017		508		587	9	74,321		4,238
Longford-Westmeath	124	40	371,997	8	118,049	58	478,721	7	24,547						1,269				250		8,432		
Louth	107	34	353,177	9	117,364	50	431,317	10	59,377						10,798		5,280		79		9,760		
Mayo	213	77	691,571	2	26,380	105	815,926	13	14,713						2,453						1,215		
Meath	117	44	376,811	12	152,987	57	546,342	3	30,401						7,371		1,869		1,445		9,395		1,607
Roscommon	108	34	317,528	0	24,737	47	434,199	6	16,570						1,585				80	1	6,968		
Sligo	147	61	500,301	1	53,902	67	548,605	10	45,584						1,641				1,525		4,521		
Tipperary Region	203	58	558,387	28	291,533	90	847,120	8	14,944						1,862		407		120		12,028		
Waterford	119	36	329,991	16	145,743	48	447,555	7	20,410				1,002		3,681	1	38,178		0	2	17,884		1,039
Wexford	145	41	386,117	32	281,509	57	541,545	6	17,721				741		2,131		3,219		173		7,469		2,251
Wicklow	111	28	271,221	27	215,642	34	335,510	7	14,294				764		12,327		16,072				11,555	2	10,736
Others 1918	3							3															
1918-2011	**4,618**	**1,453**	**12,890,666**	**482**	**4,828,562**	**1,985**	**17,536,438**	**232**	**831,940**	**4**	**67,329**	**2**	**36,245**	**16**	**314,864**	**17**	**328,717**	**0**	**16,905**	**44**	**596,172**	**8**	**92,846**

		DSP		Soc Lab		Aontacht E		C na P		C na T		NPD		Nat Lab		Farmers		Nat League		Centre P		Others		Total
Constituency	Seats	S	Votes	S	Votes	S	Votes	S	Votes	S	Votes	S	Votes	S	Votes	S	Votes	S	Votes	S	Votes	S	Votes	Votes
Carlow-Kilkenny	143								7,213				1,484	2	11,473	4	23,224		2,096	1	6,482	1	30,968	1,390,762
Cavan-Monaghan	186						2,068	5	37,326		7,970					2	23,905		4,338	1	8,663	20	277,379	1,750,007
Clare	128								5,572		10,245					2	12,404		2,830		4,041	6	73,890	1,195,188
Cork Region	544		369				1,500		13,937	6	62,780			1	9,414	12	88,540	1	7,629	2	25,697	19	279,129	5,122,771
Donegal Region	200								8,910	1	5,972					3	17,385	1	5,828	1	5,319	25	249,122	1,664,232
Dublin Region	1,035		4,690	1	6,660		6,001	9	91,608		1,563	1	4,717		3,188	1	5,903	1	13,569		2,833	66	782,310	9,497,774
Universities	47																					25	3,348	16,702
Galway Region	253						416		21,117	7	61,370				3,205		7,856	1	6,253			3	88,470	2,132,085
Kerry Region	201						695	1	26,056	4	43,180			2	14,306		18,569				3,141	11	115,831	1,750,753
Kildare Region	118								3,600							1	9,244		1,415		4,408	1	31,078	1,113,082
Laois-Offaly	150						906		2,172		8,281						10,281			1	5,784	4	83,215	1,453,349
Limerick Region	216	2	19,213						21,737		11,877					2	18,376		2,853		6,398	5	83,273	1,958,517
Longford-Westmeath	124								9,618		1,277					2	17,116		2,396	1	9,383	8	77,886	1,120,941
Louth	107						735		2,162		8,698						3,877	2	12,759			2	46,596	1,061,979
Mayo	213								19,320	13	112,359						4,041		5,497			3	57,584	1,751,059
Meath	117								2,784		7,437					1	7,426		4,562		5,873	0	39,041	1,195,351
Roscommon	108							1	11,279	8	62,778	1	5,289				3,824			1	7,703	9	98,178	990,718
Sligo	147								10,226		16,486		0		1,785	1	19,943	1	2,224	1	6,001	5	101,030	1,313,774
Tipperary Region	203							2	19,027	2	18,057		0			3	19,441		3,100	1	11,301	11	143,226	1,940,553
Waterford	119								2,680		3,750		0			2	19,252	2	14,310	1	5,228	4	54,208	1,104,911
Wexford	145				447				4,319				0	2	13,550	4	31,846	1	8,723		3,606	2	36,686	1,342,053
Wicklow	111								2,668	2	9,649		0	2	9,826	2	16,467		2,206		5,045	7	87,909	1,021,891
Others 1918	3																							
1918-2011	**4,618**	**2**	**24,272**	**1**	**7,107**		**12,321**	**18**	**323,331**	**43**	**453,729**	**2**	**11,490**	**9**	**66,747**	**42**	**378,920**	**10**	**102,588**	**11**	**126,906**	**237**	**2,840,357**	**41,888,452**

DISTRIBUTION OF SEATS & % SHARE OF THE FIRST PREFERENCE VOTE 1918-2011																														
* No Contest			FG		LB		FF		SF		SP		PBPA		GP		WP		PD		DL		C na P		C na T		Farmers		Others	
Dail		Seats	S	%	S	%	S	%	S	%	S	%	S	%	S	%	S	%	S	%	S	%	S	%	S	%	S	%	S	%
1	1918	73							73																					
2	1921*	128							124																				4	
3	1922	128	58	38.48%	17	21.33%	36	21.26%																			7	7.84%	10	11.09%
4	1923	153	63	38.97%	14	10.62%	44	27.40%																			15	12.07%	17	10.94%
5	1927	153	47	27.45%	22	12.55%	44	26.12%	5	3.61%																	11	8.89%	24	21.38%
6	1927	153	62	38.69%	13	9.07%	57	35.17%																			6	6.37%	15	10.70%
7	1932	153	57	35.28%	7	7.71%	72	44.47%																			3	2.07%	14	10.46%
8	1933	153	48	30.47%	8	5.71%	77	49.70%																					20	14.12%
9	1937	138	48	34.82%	13	10.25%	69	45.23%																					8	9.70%
10	1938	138	45	33.32%	9	10.02%	77	51.93%																					7	4.72%
11	1943	138	32	23.09%	17	15.68%	67	41.87%																	11	9.80%			11	9.57%
12	1944	138	30	20.48%	8	8.77%	76	48.90%																	9	10.08%			15	11.77%
13	1948	147	31	19.83%	14	8.69%	68	41.85%															10	13.21%	7	5.58%			17	10.84%
14	1951	147	40	25.75%	16	11.40%	69	46.28%															2	4.07%	6	2.92%			14	9.58%
15	1954	147	50	31.98%	19	12.06%	65	43.36%		0.15%													3	3.82%	5	3.09%			5	5.53%
16	1957	147	40	26.63%	12	9.11%	78	48.33%	4	5.35%													1	1.68%	3	2.36%			9	6.55%
17	1961	144	47	32.02%	16	11.65%	70	43.83%		3.12%													1	1.13%	2	1.51%			8	6.75%
18	1965	144	47	34.08%	22	15.38%	72	47.67%															1	0.75%					2	2.11%
19	1969	144	50	34.10%	18	17.02%	75	45.66%																					1	3.22%
20	1973	144	54	35.08%	19	13.71%	69	46.24%		1.14%																			2	3.83%
21	1977	148	43	30.49%	17	11.63%	84	50.63%										1.70%											4	5.55%
22	1981	166	65	36.46%	15	9.89%	78	45.26%	2	2.49%							1	1.72%											5	4.18%
23	1982	166	63	37.30%	15	9.12%	81	47.26%		1.01%							3	2.29%											4	3.02%
24	1982	166	70	39.22%	16	9.36%	75	45.20%									2	3.25%											3	2.97%
25	1987	166	51	27.07%	12	6.45%	81	44.15%		1.85%						0.40%	4	3.79%	14	11.85%									4	4.44%
26	1989	166	55	29.29%	15	9.48%	77	44.15%		1.21%					1	1.50%	7	4.97%	6	5.49%									5	3.92%
27	1992	166	45	24.47%	33	19.31%	68	39.11%		1.61%					1	1.40%		0.67%	10	4.68%	4	2.78%							5	5.97%
28	1997	166	54	27.95%	17	10.40%	77	39.33%	1	2.55%	1	0.70%		0.11%	2	2.76%		0.44%	4	4.68%	4	2.51%							6	8.58%
29	2002	166	31	22.48%	21	10.77%	81	41.48%	5	6.51%	1	0.80%		0.18%	6	3.85%		0.22%	8	3.96%									13	9.74%
30	2007	166	51	27.32%	20	10.13%	78	41.56%	4	6.94%		0.64%		0.45%	6	4.69%		0.15%	2	2.73%									5	5.39%
31	2011	166	76	36.10%	37	19.45%	20	17.45%	14	9.94%	2	1.21%	2	0.97%		1.85%		0.14%											15	12.90%
1918-2011		**4,618**	**1,453**	**30.77%**	**482**	**11.53%**	**1,985**	**41.86%**	**232**	**1.99%**	**4**	**0.16%**	**2**	**0.09%**	**16**	**0.75%**	**17**	**0.78%**	**44**	**1.42%**	**8**	**0.22%**	**18**	**0.77%**	**43**	**1.08%**	**42**	**0.90%**	**272**	**7.66%**
1981-2011		**1,660**	**561**	**30.73%**	**201**	**11.63%**	**716**	**39.85%**	**26**	**3.69%**	**4**	**0.37%**	**2**	**0.20%**	**16**	**1.73%**	**17**	**1.66%**	**44**	**3.28%**	**8**	**0.51%**							**65**	**6.34%**

PARTY % VOTE SHARE PER CONSTITUENCY 1922-2011									
Constituency	**Dail**	**FG**	**LB**	**FF**	**SF**	**SP**	**PBPA**	**GP**	**Others**
Carlow - Kilkenny	1922-2011	32.27%	15.12%	42.75%	0.84%	0.08%		1.12%	7.81%
Cavan - Monaghan	1922-2011	29.82%	1.73%	41.97%	5.28%			0.23%	20.98%
Clare	1923-2011	27.17%	7.76%	52.84%	0.95%			0.72%	10.57%
Cork East	1922-2011	33.44%	10.60%	39.03%	2.30%			0.30%	14.33%
Cork North Central	1981-2011	28.44%	14.84%	34.60%	4.67%	1.68%		1.20%	14.59%
Cork North West	1981-2011	44.51%	7.65%	44.11%	0.93%		0.42%	0.64%	1.73%
Cork South Central	1981-2011	29.80%	12.17%	39.55%	2.01%			3.00%	13.48%
Cork South West	1923-2011	35.65%	15.93%	34.74%	0.92%			0.61%	12.16%
Donegal North East	1937-2011	27.95%	2.79%	44.97%	3.77%			0.19%	20.34%
Donegal South West	1937-2011	33.70%	1.99%	48.06%	5.52%			0.41%	10.31%
Dublin Central	1969-2011	20.02%	14.71%	40.44%	4.71%			1.60%	18.53%
Dublin Mid-West	2002-2011	19.32%	18.22%	24.41%	9.56%	0.57%	3.25%	8.33%	16.34%
Dublin North	1969-2011	24.73%	18.62%	40.71%	0.64%	4.18%		6.81%	4.30%
Dublin North Central	1948-2011	25.93%	13.20%	44.46%	1.34%		0.41%	0.95%	13.72%
Dublin North East	1937-2011	22.45%	13.71%	40.78%	2.43%	0.10%		1.03%	19.50%
Dublin North West	1937-2011	20.79%	16.81%	43.07%	2.75%		0.09%	0.82%	15.67%
Dublin South	1981-2011	33.72%	12.00%	34.89%	1.12%	0.29%	0.22%	5.04%	12.71%
Dublin South Central	1948-2011	27.14%	16.40%	37.96%	3.36%	0.04%	1.22%	1.44%	12.43%
Dublin South East	1937-2011	36.77%	11.80%	36.17%	1.02%		0.24%	2.99%	11.02%
Dublin South West	1948-2011	22.27%	18.80%	38.17%	4.25%	0.95%		0.90%	14.67%
Dublin West	1981-2011	26.96%	12.73%	37.26%	3.13%	5.39%		1.61%	12.91%
Dun Laoghaire	1948-2011	36.04%	14.78%	33.36%	0.74%		1.43%	2.31%	11.33%
Galway East	1937-2011	33.41%	4.28%	49.98%	1.55%			0.35%	10.43%
Galway West	1937-2011	26.04%	9.79%	48.05%	1.16%			0.95%	14.00%
Kerry North-West Limerick	1937-2011	20.38%	18.85%	42.90%	5.44%			0.12%	12.32%
Kerry South	1937-2011	25.31%	13.43%	44.01%	1.73%			0.28%	15.25%
Kildare	1923-2011	27.51%	22.29%	40.53%	0.86%			1.16%	7.65%
Laois - Offaly	1922-2011	32.94%	11.35%	44.41%	1.43%	0.04%		0.11%	9.73%
Limerick	1948-2011	36.75%	4.35%	52.49%	0.06%			0.38%	5.96%
Limerick City	1948-2011	26.36%	12.89%	40.35%	1.21%	0.09%		0.46%	18.64%
Longford-Westmeath	1922-2011	33.19%	10.53%	42.71%	2.19%			0.11%	11.27%
Louth	1922-2011	33.26%	11.05%	40.61%	5.59%			1.02%	8.47%
Mayo	1923-2011	39.49%	1.51%	46.60%	0.84%			0.14%	11.42%
Meath	1923-2011	31.52%	12.80%	45.71%	2.54%			0.62%	6.81%
Roscommon-South Leitrim	1923-2011	32.05%	2.50%	43.83%	1.67%			0.16%	19.80%
Sligo-North Leitrim	1922-2011	38.08%	4.10%	41.76%	3.47%			0.12%	12.47%
Tipperary North	1948-2011	24.69%	17.75%	43.93%	1.55%			0.14%	11.95%
Tipperary South	1948-2011	29.05%	15.00%	44.38%	0.74%			0.13%	10.69%
Waterford	1922-2011	29.87%	13.19%	40.51%	1.85%			0.33%	14.26%
Wexford	1922-2011	28.77%	20.98%	40.35%	1.32%			0.16%	8.42%
Wicklow	1922-2011	26.54%	21.10%	32.83%	1.40%			1.21%	16.91%
National	**1922-2011**	**30.77%**	**11.53%**	**41.86%**	**1.99%**	**0.16%**	**0.09%**	**0.75%**	**12.83%**
National	**1981-2011**	**30.73%**	**11.63%**	**39.85%**	**3.69%**	**0.37%**	**0.20%**	**1.73%**	**11.79%**

NATIONAL SEATS & % VOTES SHARE MAIN PARTIES 1918-2011

* No Contest			Fine Gael				Labour				Fianna Fail			
Dail		Seats	% Vote	Seats	% Seat	% S/V	% Vote	Seats	% Seat	% S/V	% Vote	Seats	% Seat	% S/V
1	1918	73												
2	1921*	128												
3	1922	128	38.48%	58	45.31%	117.76%	21.33%	17	13.28%	62.27%	21.26%	36	28.13%	132.29%
4	1923	153	38.97%	63	41.18%	105.66%	10.62%	14	9.15%	86.16%	27.40%	44	28.76%	104.96%
5	1927	153	27.45%	47	30.72%	111.91%	12.55%	22	14.38%	114.57%	26.12%	44	28.76%	110.10%
6	1927	153	38.69%	62	40.52%	104.74%	9.07%	13	8.50%	93.68%	35.17%	57	37.25%	105.93%
7	1932	153	35.28%	57	37.25%	105.60%	7.71%	7	4.58%	59.34%	44.47%	72	47.06%	105.82%
8	1933	153	30.47%	48	31.37%	102.96%	5.71%	8	5.23%	91.57%	49.70%	77	50.33%	101.26%
9	1937	138	34.82%	48	34.78%	99.89%	10.25%	13	9.42%	91.91%	45.23%	69	50.00%	110.55%
10	1938	138	33.32%	45	32.61%	97.87%	10.02%	9	6.52%	65.09%	51.93%	77	55.80%	107.45%
11	1943	138	23.09%	32	23.19%	100.43%	15.68%	17	12.32%	78.56%	41.87%	67	48.55%	115.96%
12	1944	138	20.48%	30	21.74%	106.15%	8.77%	8	5.80%	66.10%	48.90%	76	55.07%	112.62%
13	1948	147	19.83%	31	21.09%	106.35%	8.69%	14	9.52%	109.60%	41.85%	68	46.26%	110.53%
14	1951	147	25.75%	40	27.21%	105.67%	11.40%	16	10.88%	95.48%	46.28%	69	46.94%	101.42%
15	1954	147	31.98%	50	34.01%	106.36%	12.06%	19	12.93%	107.17%	43.36%	65	44.22%	101.98%
16	1957	147	26.63%	40	27.21%	102.18%	9.11%	12	8.16%	89.61%	48.33%	78	53.06%	109.79%
17	1961	144	32.02%	47	32.64%	101.93%	11.65%	16	11.11%	95.37%	43.83%	70	48.61%	110.91%
18	1965	144	34.08%	47	32.64%	95.77%	15.38%	22	15.28%	99.34%	47.67%	72	50.00%	104.89%
19	1969	144	34.10%	50	34.72%	101.82%	17.02%	18	12.50%	73.44%	45.79%	75	52.08%	113.74%
20	1973	144	35.08%	54	37.50%	106.90%	13.71%	19	13.19%	96.24%	46.24%	69	47.92%	103.63%
21	1977	148	30.49%	43	29.05%	95.29%	11.63%	17	11.49%	98.77%	50.63%	84	56.76%	112.10%
22	1981	166	36.46%	65	39.16%	107.40%	9.89%	15	9.04%	91.37%	45.26%	78	46.99%	103.82%
23	1982	166	37.30%	63	37.95%	101.75%	9.12%	15	9.04%	99.08%	47.26%	81	48.80%	103.25%
24	1982	166	39.22%	70	42.17%	107.52%	9.36%	16	9.64%	102.98%	45.20%	75	45.18%	99.96%
25	1987	166	27.07%	51	30.72%	113.49%	6.45%	12	7.23%	112.08%	44.15%	81	48.80%	110.52%
26	1989	166	29.29%	55	33.13%	113.12%	9.48%	15	9.04%	95.32%	44.15%	77	46.39%	105.06%
27	1992	166	24.47%	45	27.11%	110.78%	19.31%	33	19.88%	102.95%	39.11%	68	40.96%	104.74%
28	1997	166	27.95%	54	32.53%	116.39%	10.40%	17	10.24%	98.47%	39.33%	77	46.39%	117.94%
29	2002	166	22.48%	31	18.67%	83.07%	10.77%	21	12.65%	117.46%	41.48%	81	48.80%	117.64%
30	2007	166	27.32%	51	30.72%	112.46%	10.13%	20	12.05%	118.94%	41.56%	78	46.99%	113.06%
31	2011	166	36.10%	76	45.78%	126.82%	19.45%	37	22.29%	114.60%	17.45%	20	12.05%	69.04%
1918-2011		**4,618**	**30.77%**	**1,453**	**31.46%**	**102.25%**	**11.53%**	**482**	**10.44%**	**90.52%**	**41.86%**	**1,985**	**42.98%**	**102.69%**
1981-2011		**1,660**	**30.73%**	**561**	**33.80%**	**109.97%**	**11.63%**	**201**	**12.11%**	**104.11%**	**39.85%**	**716**	**43.13%**	**108.24%**

CANDIDATES 1922-2011

* No Contest																Nat		Nat	Centre		
Dail		Seats	Cands	FG	LB	FF	SF	SP	PBPA	GP	WP	PD	DL	CnaP	CnaT	Lab	Farm	Lge	Party	Others	Total
1	1918	73	73				73														73
2	1921*	128	128				128														128
3	1922	128	176	65	18	58											13			22	176
4	1923	153	376	107	44	85											64			76	376
5	1927	153	377	97	44	87	15										39	30		65	377
6	1927	153	265	89	28	88											20	6		34	265
7	1932	153	279	101	33	104											7			34	279
8	1933	153	246	85	19	103													26	13	246
9	1937	138	255	95	23	101														36	255
10	1938	138	214	76	30	97														11	214
11	1943	138	354	87	70	106									40					51	354
12	1944	138	252	55	31	100									27	9				30	252
13	1948	147	407	82	43	119								93	25	14				31	407
14	1951	147	297	77	37	119								26	7					31	297
15	1954	147	303	89	41	112								20	10					31	303
16	1957	147	289	82	31	112	19							12	7					26	289
17	1961	144	301	96	35	107	21							5	6					31	301
18	1965	144	281	102	44	111								4						20	281
19	1969	144	373	125	99	122														27	373
20	1973	144	335	111	56	119	10													39	335
21	1977	148	376	116	57	132					16									55	376
22	1981	166	404	126	60	139	9				15									55	404
23	1982	166	366	113	41	131	7				15									59	366
24	1982	166	365	115	40	132					20									58	365
25	1987	166	466	97	37	122	27			9	29	51								94	466
26	1989	166	371	86	33	115	14			11	23	35								54	371
27	1992	166	482	91	42	122	41			19	18	20	20							109	482
28	1997	166	484	90	44	112	15	5		26		30	13							149	484
29	2002	166	463	85	46	106	37	5		31		20								133	463
30	2007	166	471	91	50	107	41	4		44		30								104	471
31	2011	166	567	104	68	76	41	9	9	43	6									211	567
Total		**4,618**	**10,396**	**2,735**	**1,244**	**3,144**	**498**	**23**	**9**	**183**	**142**	**186**	**33**	**160**	**122**	**23**	**143**	**36**	**26**	**1,689**	**10,396**

SEATS WON BY INDEPENDENTS & FORMER PARTIES

The largest of the former parties were the Farmers and Clann na Talmhan, who won a total of 42 and 43 seats respectively. The Farmers Party was also known as the Farmer's Union and it was an organisation of the larger farmers and won 15 seats at its peak in 1923. Clann na Talmhan was founded by John Donnellan in 1938 to represent small farmers and it won 11 seats in 1943 but had declined to 2 by 1961.

The Centre Party was founded in 1932 by 3 independent TD's who were later joined by James Dillon. It won 11 seats in 1933 and merged with Blueshirts and Cumann na nGaedheal in September 1933 to form Fine Gael.

Clann na Poblachta was founded in July 1946 by Sean MacBride and other ex-members of the IRA. It won 10 seats in 1948 and was part of the inter party government. It declined after this and was reduced to a single seat by 1965 when it was dissolved.

National League was founded by Captain William Redmond, son of John Redmond ex Home Rule Party MP, in September 1926. It won 8 seats in June 1927 but declined after that and was dissolved in 1931.

National Labour Party was formed when the ITGWU disaffiliated from the Labour Party with five of its eight TD's forming the new party. It was part of the first Inter-Party Government in 1948 and it rejoined the mother party in 1950.

Neil Blaney split from Fianna Fail following the 1970 "Arms Crisis" and set up Independent Fianna Fail in Donegal. The seat stayed within the Blaney family with the exception of a short period between April 1996 (when the bye-election caused by Neil Blaney's death was lost to Cecilia Keaveney of Fianna Fail) and the general election in June 1997. The party rejoined Fianna Fail in 2006 and Niall Blaney nephew of Neil won a seat for Fianna Fail in Donegal North East in 2007. He retired prior to the 2011 election to bring to an end the Blaney dynasty in Dáil Eireann.

Democratic Left split from the Workers Party in 1992 with all of their TD's moving to the new party, leaving former TD Tomas MacGiolla as the main personality with the Workers Party. DL amalgamated with the Labour Party in 1999 with two of their members going on to lead their new party, Pat Rabbitte and present Tánaiste Eamonn Gilmore.

The Progressive Democrats were formed in 1985 and won 14 seats at their first general election in 1987. They experienced a major reversal at their next election in 1989 and were reduced to just six seats but the Dail arithmetic was in their favour to allow Des O'Malley form a coalition government with his former cabinet colleague Charles Haughey. The party increased their seats to ten in 1992 but dropped to just four in 1997 but were back in government and remained there until they were dissolved in 2009.

SEATS WON BY INDEPENDENTS & FORMER POLITICAL PARTIES 1918-2011

			Clann na	Clann na	National	Ind		Ind	National	Centre	
*No Contest	Total	Ind	Poblacta	Talmhan	Labour	Labour	Farmers	Farmers	League	Party	Others
Dail	Seats	Seats	Seats	Seats	Seats	Seats	Seats	Seats	Seats	Seats	Seats
1 1918	0										
2 1921*	4	4									
3 1922	17	10					7				
4 1923	32	11				2	15				2BP, 2PA
5 1927	35	12				1	11	1	8		2 Ind R
6 1927	21	12					6		2		1 IWL
7 1932	17	12				2	3				
8 1933	20	8				1				11	
9 1937	8	5				2		1			
10 1938	7	6						1			
11 1943	22	6		11				4			1 MR
12 1944	24	6		9	4			4			1 MR
13 1948	34	11	10	7	5			1			
14 1951	22	14	2	6							
15 1954	13	5	3	5							
16 1957	13	5	1	3				2			1 Ind R,Ind UW
17 1961	11	4	1	2		1		1			2 NPD
18 1965	3	1	1					1			
19 1969	1	1									
20 1973	2	1									1 IFF
21 1977	4	1				2					1 IFF
22 1981	7	2				1					1 IFF,1SLP,2HBlk
23 1982	4	2				1					1 IFF
24 1982	3	2									1 IFF
25 1987	4	2									1 IFF, 1 DSP
26 1989	5	3									1 IFF, 1 DSP
27 1992	5	4									1 IFF
28 1997	6	5									1 IFF
29 2002	13	12									1 IFF
30 2007	5	5									
31 2011	14	14									
Total 31	**376**	**186**	**18**	**43**	**9**	**13**	**42**	**16**	**10**	**11**	**28**

INDEPENDENT & FORMER PARTIES SEATS & SHARE OF THE FIRST PREFERENCE VOTE 1918-2011

* No Contest			PD		DL		DSP		Soc Lab		Aont Eir		CnaP		CnaT		NPD		Nat Lab		Farmers		Nat Lge		Centre P		Others	
Dail		Seats	S	%	S	%	S	%	S	%	S	%	S	%	S	%	S	%	S	%	S	%	S	%	S	%	S	%
1	1918	73																										
2	1921*	128																									4	
3	1922	128																			7	7.84%					10	11.09%
4	1923	153																			15	12.07%					17	10.94%
5	1927	153																			11	8.89%	8	7.29%			16	14.08%
6	1927	153																			6	6.37%	2	1.62%			13	9.08%
7	1932	153																			3	2.07%					14	10.46%
8	1933	153																							11	9.15%	9	4.97%
9	1937	138																									8	9.70%
10	1938	138																									7	4.72%
11	1943	138													11	9.80%											11	9.57%
12	1944	138													9	10.08%			4	2.69%							11	9.08%
13	1948	147											10	13.21%	7	5.58%			5	2.55%							12	8.26%
14	1951	147											2	4.07%	6	3.58%											14	8.92%
15	1954	147											3	3.82%	5	3.83%											5	4.79%
16	1957	147											1	1.68%	3	2.36%											9	6.55%
17	1961	144											1	1.13%	2	1.51%	2	0.98%									6	6.75%
18	1965	144											1	0.75%													2	2.11%
19	1969	144																									1	3.09%
20	1973	144										0.91%															2	3.77%
21	1977	148																									4	5.55%
22	1981	166							1	0.41%																	4	4.26%
23	1982	166																									4	3.02%
24	1982	166						0.42%																			3	2.97%
25	1987	166	14	11.85%			1	0.42%																			3	4.44%
26	1989	166	6	5.49%			1	0.59%																			4	3.88%
27	1992	166	10	4.68%	4	2.78%																					5	5.97%
28	1997	166	4	4.68%	4	2.51%																					6	8.11%
29	2002	166	8	3.96%																							13	9.49%
30	2007	166	2	2.73%																							5	5.76%
31	2011	166																									15	12.81%
1918-2011		**4,618**	**44**	**1.42%**	**8**	**0.22%**	**2**	**0.06%**	**1**	**0.02%**		**0.03%**	**18**	**0.77%**	**43**	**1.08%**	**2**	**0.03%**	**9**	**0.16%**	**42**	**0.90%**	**10**	**0.24%**	**11**	**0.30%**	**237**	**6.78%**

TDs 1918-2011

In the 31 Dálai to date, 4,618 seats have been filled. Another 127 have been elected through by-elections to give a total of 4,745 seats. These seats have been won by 1,285 TDs. Some of these TDs were elected in more than one constituency at various times. Five TD's were elected for two constituencies in the same election: Eamon de Valera elected for Clare and Mayo in 1918, Arthur Griffith for Cavan East and Tyrone North-West in 1918, Liam Mellows for Galway East and Meath North in 1918, W.T. Cosgrave elected for Carlow-Kilkenny and Cork Borough in September 1927 (he chose to sit for Cork); Michael Hayes decided to sit for NUI despite being also elected for Dublin South in 1923. Prof. Eoin MacNeill was unique in that he was elected for two constituencies in two elections, Londonderry City and NUI in 1918 and Clare and NUI in 1923 (he sat for Clare).

To date 1,236 different TD's have been elected to Dáil Eireann including the latest, Patrick Nulty following the recent by-election in Dublin West. On average each TD has won 4 elections with Donegal having the highest average 4.3 with Kerry and Wexford next on 4.2 respectively. Roscommon has the shortest serving members (3.1 terms). 31% of TDs were elected just once, 16% were elected twice and 14% won 3 elections.

Patrick Smith (FF Cavan) and Eamon de Valera (16 in Clare and 1 in Mayo East) were the only TDs to win 17 elections. Four TDs won 16 elections: Frank Aiken (FF Louth), Sean MacEntee (14 in Dublin South East and 2 in Monaghan), James Everett (LB Wicklow) and James Ryan (FF Wexford). Patrick Smith was also the longest serving TD with 54 years unbroken service between 1923 and 1977. Frank Aiken was the only other TD to reach 50 years service. To date 62 TD's have served for 30 years or more including Enda Kenny, Ruairi Quinn and Michael Noonan of the 31st Dáil. Mary Harney is the longest serving female member with 30 continuous years of service from 1981 to 2011.

Richard Mulcahy, Cumann na nGaedheal, won the largest first preference vote ever when he obtained 22,005 in Dublin North in 1923. Four other candidates obtained over 20,000 votes with Jack Lynch the most recent, winning 20,079 in 1977. Brian Cowen moved up to sixth place following his 19,102 first preferences in 2007 and was just ahead of Willie O'Dea on 19,082. Enda Kenny was the leading vote-getter in 2011 with 17,472 first preferences with Shane Ross a close second on 17,075.

Most TD's are reluctant to give up their seats with on average 87% of them contesting each constituency from 1918 to 2011. This historical average is reflected in the recent elections with between 77% and 93% of outgoing deputies contesting the last four general elections. Kerry South, Kildare and Limerick City has the largest average of TD's contesting at 93% with 79% of outgoing TDs contesting in Dublin Central. The number of deputies retiring has increased in recent elections, from 11 in 1992 to 22 in 2002, but dropped slightly in 2007 to 19. The latest election showed a sharp rise in retirements to 39.

Outgoing deputies have a very good chance of being re-elected with only 18% of those that decide to run, losing their seats. The latest election has indicated less stability with 35% losing in 2011 up from 20% in 2007. Limerick West has the best record for outgoing deputies with only 4% of them losing their seats. Dublin North is the least TD friendly with a failure rate of 26%. Thus outgoing deputies dominate each new Dail with historically 71% of the total number being outgoing TD's. Three of the last five elections reflected this level with Fine Gael's meltdown in 2002 responsible for a below average 67% with Fianna Fails collapse in 2011 resulting in a record low of just 49%. Donegal South West is again the most consistent constituency with 86% of their members being outgoing deputies. Dublin North has the lowest return at 61%, ignoring the new constituency of Dublin Mid-West.

A slight majority of the new members elected, do so at the first attempt with on average 13% of them tasting success in their first Dáil election. The last two general elections have returned above this average with 16% winning at the first attempt in 2002 and 17% in 2007. This increased to 24% in 2011. Cork East, Dublin North and Longford-Westmeath have the highest number of first timers 20% (ignoring the new constituency of Dublin Mid-West) with Galway East a tough nut to crack with only 3% winning at the first time of asking. The number of candidates that persevere and eventually take a seat is only 9% but the 2011 election broke all records with 22% new members. Dublin North East is the most receptive to rewarding a trier (16%) with only 4% eventually succeeding in Donegal North East. Overall each Dail has 22% new members with 2007 reflecting that average with 23%. Fine Gael's failure in 2002 resulted in an above average number of new members at 28% but this was easily beaten by Fianna Fail's failure in 2011 leading to 46% new members. Only 7% of the Dail are former members with 2011 down to 5%. Dublin South-Central has the best record for former TD's with that constituency's members made up of 15% former deputies. Limerick West is not impressed by those that went before and has never returned a former deputy.

We can see from the above that there is a strong consistency in the makeup of our Dálai with over 70% outgoing members, 22% new members and 7% former members. This consistency also extends to the individual constituencies. So if you want to get elected your best chance is at your first attempt and once you get inside Leinster House, you have a very good chance of staying there. Finally if you are a former member hoping to make a comeback don't attempt it in Limerick West.

SEATS CONTESTED AND NUMBER OF TDS PER REGION 1918-2011							
	Seats		Total	TDs			Ave. Term
Constituency	General E	By-E	A	B	Adj.	Net	A/B
Carlow - Kilkenny	143	4	147	41	-4	37	3.6
Cavan - Monaghan	186	2	188	49	-2	47	3.8
Clare	128	3	131	33	-2	31	4.0
Cork	544	17	561	167	-1	166	3.4
Donegal	200	9	209	49	-1	48	4.3
Dublin	1035	36	1071	291	-7	284	3.7
Galway	253	9	262	66	-1	65	4.0
Kerry	201	4	205	49	0	49	4.2
Kildare	118	4	122	31	-2	29	3.9
Laois-Offaly	150	3	153	41	0	41	3.7
Limerick	216	6	222	54	-1	53	4.1
Longford - Westmeath	124	2	126	39	0	39	3.2
Louth	107	1	108	27	-1	26	4.0
Mayo	213	6	219	60	-5	55	3.7
Meath	117	2	119	34	-3	31	3.5
Roscommon	108	2	110	35	-7	28	3.1
Sligo - Leitrim	147	4	151	42	-2	40	3.6
Tipperary	203	3	206	54	-2	52	3.8
Waterford	119	3	122	38	-1	37	3.2
Wexford	145	2	147	35	0	35	4.2
Wicklow	111	3	114	32	-4	28	3.6
Universities	47	2	49	15	-1	14	3.3
Others*	3		3	3	-2	1	
Total	**4,618**	**127**	**4,745**	**1,285**	**-49**	**1,236**	**3.7**

*1918: Fermanagh South, Londonderry City, Tyrone North-West TD's Average Service: 11.1

NUMBER OF ELECTIONS WON PER TD PER REGION 1918-2011

Constituency	Seats	TDs	1	2	3	4	5	6	7	8	9	10	11	12	13	14	15	16	17
Carlow - Kilkenny	147	41	16	3	7	2	1	5	4		1		1		1				
Cavan - Monaghan	188	49	16	5	7	5	5	1	5	1		3							1
Clare	131	33	7	8	4	3	3	3	2	1					1			1	
Cork	561	167	55	28	18	20	14	12	4	7	5	2	1			1			
Donegal	209	49	14	7	5	4	4	2	4	4	1		2	1			1		
Dublin	1071	291	85	49	43	27	19	26	7	8	9	6	4	5	1	1	1		
Galway	262	66	22	8	9	5	3	3	5	3	2	2	3			1			
Kerry	205	49	13	8	7	2	2	3	9	1		1	1	1			1		
Kildare	122	31	8	4	7	2	2		4		2	1	1						
Laois - Offaly	153	41	16	4	6	2	2	4	2		2	1			1	1			
Limerick	222	54	12	9	9	8	1	2	2	3	4	2	2						
Longford-Westmeath	126	39	15	6	4	3	3	4	2		1				1				
Louth	108	27	7	5	5	1	2	2	1	1	1	1						1	
Mayo	219	60	16	13	6	7	3	3	9			1		1	1				
Meath	119	34	13	3	4	4	3	2	1	1	1	1	1						
Roscommon	110	35	8	8	8	4	4	1	1						1				
Sligo - Leitrim	151	42	14	7	3	5	2	3	3	1	3	1							
Tipperary	206	54	11	10	13	5	4	2	1	4	1		1	1	1				
Waterford	122	38	14	4	5	5	3	3	2	1		1							
Wexford	147	35	14	2	3	2	2	4	3	1			3					1	
Wicklow	114	32	11	4	4	4	4	1	1		2							1	
Universities	49	15	5	4		1	1	1	3										
Others	3	3	3																
Total	**4,745**	**1,285**	**395**	**199**	**177**	**121**	**87**	**87**	**75**	**37**	**35**	**23**	**20**	**9**	**8**	**4**	**3**	**4**	**1**
%			**30.7%**	**15.5%**	**13.8%**	**9.4%**	**6.8%**	**6.8%**	**5.8%**	**2.9%**	**2.7%**	**1.8%**	**1.6%**	**0.7%**	**0.6%**	**0.3%**	**0.2%**	**0.3%**	**0.1%**

TDs STATUS 1918-2011								
			Outgoing TD		Elected TD			
Constituency	Dail	Seats	Contested	Lost	Outgoing	1st Attempt	New	Former
Carlow - Kilkenny	1918-2011	143	88%	21%	67%	18%	7%	8%
Cavan - Monaghan	1918-2011	186	89%	18%	71%	18%	6%	5%
Clare	1918-2011	128	90%	17%	72%	18%	5%	5%
Cork East	1918-2011	119	85%	22%	64%	20%	11%	5%
Cork North Central	1981-2011	48	84%	12%	75%	8%	13%	4%
Cork North West	1981-2011	30	90%	23%	67%	17%	7%	10%
Cork South Central	1981-2011	50	88%	23%	68%	12%	10%	10%
Cork South West	1923-2011	102	86%	21%	66%	18%	9%	8%
Donegal North East	1937-2011	74	91%	9%	84%	11%	4%	1%
Donegal South West	1937-2011	66	91%	5%	86%	8%	5%	2%
Dublin Central	1969-2011	56	79%	16%	66%	7%	13%	14%
Dublin Mid-West	2002-2011	11	80%	38%	45%	27%	18%	9%
Dublin North	1969-2011	46	83%	26%	61%	20%	15%	4%
Dublin North Central	1948-2011	69	87%	15%	74%	10%	9%	7%
Dublin North East	1937-2011	90	89%	23%	68%	8%	16%	9%
Dublin North West	1937-2011	86	80%	11%	72%	13%	9%	6%
Dublin South	1981-2011	50	86%	19%	70%	12%	14%	4%
Dublin South Central	1948-2011	89	82%	22%	64%	10%	11%	15%
Dublin South East	1937-2011	79	90%	24%	67%	10%	11%	11%
Dublin South West	1948-2011	83	83%	19%	69%	8%	14%	8%
Dublin West	1981-2011	43	89%	23%	70%	9%	7%	14%
Dun Laoghaire	1948-2011	81	92%	21%	72%	15%	10%	4%
Galway East	1937-2011	70	89%	11%	80%	3%	11%	6%
Galway West	1937-2011	90	86%	13%	73%	9%	9%	9%
Kerry North	1937-2011	77	92%	15%	79%	9%	9%	3%
Kerry South	1937-2011	69	93%	17%	77%	14%	6%	3%
Kildare	1918-2011	118	93%	16%	75%	13%	8%	4%
Laois - Offaly	1918-2011	150	88%	12%	73%	17%	7%	3%
Limerick	1948-2011	57	86%	4%	82%	11%	7%	0%
Limerick City	1948-2011	85	93%	16%	78%	7%	11%	5%
Longford - Westmeath	1918-2011	124	83%	21%	64%	20%	8%	8%
Louth	1918-2011	107	87%	13%	72%	15%	8%	5%
Mayo	1918-2011	213	90%	17%	74%	12%	10%	3%
Meath	1918-2011	117	87%	15%	70%	16%	9%	5%
Roscommon	1918-2011	108	87%	25%	63%	19%	7%	10%
Sligo - Leitrim	1918-2011	147	84%	20%	66%	19%	6%	9%
Tipperary North	1948-2011	57	88%	18%	72%	7%	12%	9%
Tipperary South	1948-2011	71	88%	14%	73%	13%	10%	4%
Waterford	1918-2011	119	89%	23%	66%	17%	10%	7%
Wexford	1918-2011	145	91%	21%	69%	14%	9%	8%
Wicklow	1918-2011	111	92%	21%	69%	19%	5%	7%
Average	**1918-2011**	**3,764**	**87%**	**18%**	**71%**	**13%**	**9%**	**7%**
National	2011	166	77%	35%	49%	24%	22%	5%
National	2007	166	89%	20%	70%	17%	6%	7%
National	2002	166	87%	23%	67%	16%	12%	5%
National	1997	166	90%	19%	73%	9%	10%	8%
National	1992	166	93%	21%	74%	10%	10%	6%

TD's							
Election	Retired	Contested	Lost	Re-elected	1st Attempt	New	Former
2011	39	127	45	82	40	36	8
2007	19	147	30	117	28	10	11
2002	22	144	33	111	27	20	8
1997	17	149	28	121	15	17	13
1992	11	155	32	123	17	16	10

WOMEN IN THE DAIL 1918-2011														
Dail	Election	General	By-E	Total	FG	LB	FF	SF	ULA	GP	PD	Others	Total	TD's
1	1918	73		73				1					1	
2	1921	128		128				6					6	
3	1922	128		128			2						2	
4	1923	153	21	174	1		4						5	
5	1927	153	2	155	1		2	1					4	
6	1927	153	7	160	1								1	
7	1932	153		153	2								2	
8	1933	153	5	158	1		2						3	
9	1937	138		138	2								2	
10	1938	138	2	140	2		1						3	
11	1943	138		138	2		1						3	
12	1944	138	10	148	2		**3**						5	
13	1948	147	3	150	2		3						5	
14	1951	147	9	156	2		3						5	
15	1954	147	7	154	1	1	3					1	6	
16	1957	147	8	155	2		3						5	
17	1961	144	6	150	2	1	**3**						6	
18	1965	144	7	151	2	1	2						5	
19	1969	144	6	150	2		1						3	
20	1973	144	7	151	2	1	**2**						5	
21	1977	148	3	151	2	1	4						7	
22	1981	166		166	6	1	4						11	
23	1982	166	2	168	5	1	2						8	
24	1982	166	3	169	9	1	4						14	
25	1987	166		166	5		5				4		14	
26	1989	166		166	6		5				2		13	
27	1992	166	7	173	5	5	6				4	3	23	
28	1997	166	6	172	6	4	8				2	2	22	
29	2002	166	2	168	2	7	7				4	**3**	23	
30	2007	166	3	169	5	7	7			1	1	2	23	
31	2011	166	1	167	11	8		2	2			2	25	
	Women*				**91**	**39**	**87**	**10**	**2**	**1**	**17**	**13**	**260**	**92**
	Total**	**4,618**	**127**	**4,745**	**1,503**	**491**	**2,037**	**233**	**5**	**16**	**44**	**416**	**4,745**	**1,236**
	% Women				**6.05%**	**7.94%**	**4.27%**	**4.29%**	**40.00%**	**6.25%**	**38.64%**	**3.13%**	**5.48%**	**7.44%**

***Includes 14 By-Elections** ****Includes 127 By-Elections**

WOMEN ELECTED 1918-2011 IN ORDER OF SERVICE																		
	Surname	Forename	Constituency	Party	Elected									Terms	From	To	Service
1	Harney	Mary	Dublin South West	PD	81	82	82	87	89	92	97	02	07	9	11/06/1981	25/02/2011	29.71
2	Reynolds	Mary	Sligo-Leitrim	FG	32	37	38	43	44	48	51	54	57	9	16/02/1932	04/10/1961	25.20
3	De Valera	Sile*	Dublin Co.Mid/Clare	FF	77/	87	89	92	97	02				6	16/06/1977	24/05/2007	24.26
4	Coughlan	Mary	Donegal South West	FF	87	89	92	97	02	07				6	17/02/1987	25/02/2011	24.02
5	O'Rourke	Mary	Longford-Westmeath	FF	82N	87	89	92	97	07				6	24/11/1982	25/02/2011	23.24
6	Lynch	Celia	Dublin North Central	FF	54	57	61	65	69	73				6	18/05/1954	16/06/1977	23.08
7	Geoghegan-Quinn	Maire	Galway West	FF	75*	77	81	82	82	87	89	92		8	*04/03/1975*	06/06/1997	22.26
8	Wallace	Mary	Meath East	FF	89	92	97	02	07					5	15/06/1989	25/02/2011	21.70
9	Crowley	Honor	Kerry South	FF	45*	48	51	54	57	61	65			7	*04/12/1945*	18/10/1966	20.87
10	Hogan-O'Higgins	Brigid	Galway South	FG	57	61	65	69	73					5	05/03/1957	16/06/1977	20.28
11	Shortall	Roisin	Dublin North West	LB	92	97	02	07	11					5	25/11/1992		19.32
12	Redmond	Bridget	Waterford	FG	33	37	38	43	44	48	51			7	24/01/1933	03/05/1952	19.27
13	Owen	Nora	Dublin North	FG	81	82	82	89	92	97				6	11/06/1981	17/05/2002	18.61
14	McManus	Liz	Wicklow	LB	92	97	02	07						4	25/11/1992	25/02/2011	18.25
15	Desmond	Eileen	Cork South Central	LB	65*	65	73	77	81	82	82			7	*10/03/1965*	17/02/1987	18.24
16	Ryan	Mary	Tipperary North	FF	44	48	51	54	57					5	30/05/1944	04/10/1961	17.35
17	Burke	Joan	Roscommon	FG	64*	65	69	73	77					5	*08/07/1964*	11/06/1981	16.93
18	Flaherty	Mary	Dublin North West	FG	81	82	82	87	89	92				6	11/06/1981	06/06/1997	15.99
19	Rice	Bridget Mary	Monaghan	FF	38	43	44	48	51					5	17/06/1938	18/05/1954	15.92
20	Barnes	Monica	Dun Laoghaire	FG	82N	87	89	97						4	24/11/1982	17/05/2002	14.95
21	Mitchell	Olivia	Dublin South	FG	97	02	07	11						4	06/06/1997		14.79
22	Moynihan-Cronin	Breeda	Kerry South	LB	92	97	02							3	25/11/1992	24/05/2007	14.49
23	O'Donnell	Liz	Dublin South	PD	92	97	02							3	25/11/1992	24/05/2007	14.49
24	Burton	Joan	Dublin West	LB	92	02	07	11						4	25/11/1992		14.38
25	O'Sullivan	Jan	Limerick East	LB	98*	02	07	11						4	*11/03/1998*		14.03

WOMEN ELECTED 1918-2011 IN ORDER OF SERVICE

	Surname	Forename	Constituency	Party	Elected				Terms	From	To	Service
26	Flynn	Beverley	Mayo	FF	97	02	07		3	06/06/1997	25/02/2011	13.72
27	Hanafin	Mary	Dun Laoghaire	FF	97	02	07		3	06/06/1997	25/02/2011	13.72
28	Lynch	Kathleen	Cork North Central	LB	94*	02	07	11	4	10/11/1994		12.42
29	Fox	Mildred	Wicklow	NP	95*	97	02		3	29/06/1995	24/05/2007	11.90
30	Upton	Mary	Dublin South Central	LB	99*	02	07		3	27/10/1999	25/02/2011	11.33
31	Ahearn	Theresa	Tipperary South	FG	89	92	97		3	15/06/1989	20/09/2000	11.27
32	Keaveney	Cecilia	Donegal North East	FF	96*	97	02		3	02/04/1996	24/05/2007	11.14
33	Doyle	Avril	Wexford	FG	82N	87	92		3	24/11/1982	06/06/1997	11.08
34	Taylor-Quinn	Madeleine	Clare	FG	81	82N	87	89	4	11/06/1981	25/11/1992	10.70
35	Fitzgerald	Frances	Dublin South East	FG	92	97	11		3	25/11/1992		10.54
36	Quill	Mairin	Cork North Central	PD	87	89	92		3	17/02/1987	06/06/1997	10.30
37	Collins-O'Driscoll	Margaret	Dublin North	CG	23	27	27	32	4	27/08/1923	24/01/1933	9.41
38	Fennell	Nuala	Dublin South	FG	81	82	82	89	4	11/06/1981	25/11/1992	9.14
39	Lemass	Eileen	Dublin West	FF	77	81	82N		3	16/06/1977	17/02/1987	8.91
40	Enright	Olwyn	Laoighis-Offaly	FG	02	07			2	17/05/2002	25/02/2011	8.78
41	Hoctor	Maire	Tipperary North	FF	02	07			2	17/05/2002	25/02/2011	8.78
42	Clune	Deirdre	Cork South Central	FG	97	07			2	06/06/1997	25/02/2011	8.70
43	Hussey	Gemma	Wicklow	FG	82	82	87		3	18/02/1982	15/06/1989	7.32
44	Barry	Myra	Cork East	FG	79*	81	82	82	4	07/11/1979	17/02/1987	7.28
45	De Markievicz	Constance	Dublin South	FF	18	21	23	27J	4	21/01/1919	15/07/1927	7.28
46	MacSwiney	Mary	Cork Borough	R	21	22	23		3	24/05/1921	09/06/1927	6.04
47	Harkin	Marian	Sligo-Leitrim	NP	02				1	17/05/2002	24/05/2007	5.02
48	O'Malley	Fiona	Dun Laoghaire	PD	02				1	17/05/2002	24/05/2007	5.02
49	Sexton	Mae	Longford-Roscommon	PD	02				1	17/05/2002	24/05/2007	5.02
50	McGennis	Marian	Dublin Central	FF	97				1	06/06/1997	17/05/2002	4.94
51	Glenn	Alice	Dublin Central	FG	81	82N			2	11/06/1981	17/02/1987	4.93
52	Byrne	Catherine	Dublin South Central	FG	07	11			2	24/05/2007		4.82
53	Creighton	Lucinda	Dublin South East	FG	07	11			2	24/05/2007		4.82
54	Tuffy	Joanna	Dublin Mid-West	LB	07	11			2	24/05/2007		4.82
55	Bhreathnach	Niamh	Dun Laoghaire	LB	92				1	25/11/1992	06/06/1997	4.53
56	FitzGerald	Eithne	Dublin South	LB	92				1	25/11/1992	06/06/1997	4.53
57	Keogh	Helen	Dun Laoghaire	PD	92				1	25/11/1992	06/06/1997	4.53
58	Concannon	Helena	N.U.I.	FF	33				1	24/01/1933	01/07/1937	4.43
59	Pearse	Margaret M.	Dublin County	FF	33				1	24/01/1933	01/07/1937	4.43
60	Brugha	Caitlin	Waterford	SF	23	27J			2	27/08/1923	15/09/1927	4.05
61	Ahern	Kit	Kerry North	FF	77				1	16/06/1977	11/06/1981	3.99
62	Lynn	Kathleen	Dublin County	R	23				1	27/08/1923	09/06/1927	3.78
63	Brady	Aine	Kildare North	FF	07				1	24/05/2007	25/02/2011	3.76
64	Conlon	Margaret	Cavan-Monaghan	FF	07				1	24/05/2007	25/02/2011	3.76
65	White	Mary	Carlow-Kilkenny	GP	07				1	24/05/2007	25/02/2011	3.76
66	Murphy	Catherine	Kildare North	NP	05*	11			2	11/03/2005		3.27
67	O'Carroll	Maureen	Dublin North Central	LB	54				1	18/05/1954	05/03/1957	2.80
68	O'Sullivan	Maureen	Dublin Central	NP	09*	11			2	06/06/2009		2.79
69	Colley	Anne	Dublin South	PD	87				1	17/02/1987	15/06/1989	2.32
70	Kennedy	Geraldine	Dun Laoghaire	PD	87				1	17/02/1987	15/06/1989	2.32
71	Mooney	Mary	Dublin South Central	FF	87				1	17/02/1987	15/06/1989	2.32
72	O'Callaghan	Kathleen	Limerick East	CR	21	22			2	24/05/1921	27/08/1923	2.26
73	Clarke	Kathleen	Dublin North	R	21	27J			2	24/05/1921	15/09/1927	1.33
74	Galvin	Sheila	Cork Borough	FF	64*				1	19/02/1964	07/04/1965	1.13
75	Collins	Joan	Dublin South Central	PBPA	11				1	25/02/2011		1.07
76	Collins	Aine	Cork North West	FG	11				1	25/02/2011		1.07
77	Conway	Ciara	Waterford	LB	11				1	25/02/2011		1.07
78	Corcoran Kennedy	Marcella	Laoighis-Offaly	FG	11				1	25/02/2011		1.07
79	Daly	Clare	Dublin North	SP	11				1	25/02/2011		1.07
80	Doherty	Regina	Meath East	FG	11				1	25/02/2011		1.07
81	Ferris	Anne	Wicklow	LB	11				1	25/02/2011		1.07
82	Humphreys	Heather	Cavan-Monaghan	FG	11				1	25/02/2011		1.07
83	McDonald	Mary Lou	Dublin Central	SF	11				1	25/02/2011		1.07
84	McFadden	Nicky	Longford-Westmeath	FG	11				1	25/02/2011		1.07
85	McLellan	Sandra	Cork East	SF	11				1	25/02/2011		1.07
86	Mitchell O'Connor	Mary	Dun Laoghaire	FG	11				1	25/02/2011		1.07
87	Mulherin	Michelle	Mayo	FG	11				1	25/02/2011		1.07
88	Phelan	Ann	Carlow-Kilkenny	LB	11				1	25/02/2011		1.07
89	English	Dr. Ada	N.U.I.	SF	21				1	24/05/1921	16/06/1922	1.06
90	Pearse	Margaret	Dublin County	SF	21				1	24/05/1921	16/06/1922	1.06
91	O'Connor	Kathleen	Kerry North	CnaP	56*				1	29/02/1956	05/03/1957	1.01
92	Acheson	Carrie	Tipperary South	FF	81				1	11/06/1981	18/02/1982	0.69
92	**Total**	* Elected in more than one constituency							260	*By-election		8.87

Service: Members 31st Dail to 20/03/2012 Interupted Service

TOP 50 VOTEGETTERS 1918-2011					
	Name	Party	Votes	Constituency	Election
1	Richard Mulcahy	CG	22,005	Dublin North	1923
2	Kevin O'Higgins	CG	20,821	Dublin County	1923
3	James Walsh	SF	20,801	Cork City	1918
4	Liam de Roiste	SF	20,506	Cork City	1918
5	Jack Lynch	FF	20,079	Cork City	1977
6	Brian Cowen	FF	19,102	Laois-Offaly	2007
7	Willie O'Dea	FF	19,082	Limerick East	2007
8	Eamon de Valera	FF	18,574	Clare	1933
9	Alfie Byrne	NP	18,170	Dublin North	1932
10	Wiliam T. Cosgrave	CG	18,125	Cork Borough	1932
11	Alfie Byrne	NP	17,780	Dublin North	1927(J)
12	Eamon de Valera	R	17,762	Clare	1923
13	James Dolan	SF	17,711	Leitrim	1918
14	Wiliam T. Cosgrave	CG	17,709	Carlow-Kilkenny	1923
15	Charles J. Haughey	FF	17,637	Dublin North-Central	1981
16	Enda Kenny	FG	17,472	Mayo	**2011**
17	Wiliam T. Cosgrave	CG	17,395	Cork Borough	1927(S)
18	Eithne Fitzgerald	LB	17,256	Dublin South	1992
19	James Walsh	CG	17,151	Cork Borough	1923
20	Michael Collins	CT	17,106	Cork Mid-North	1922
21	Shane Ross	NP	17,075	Dublin South	**2011**
22	Sean T. O'Kelly	FF	17,053	Dublin North	1933
23	Sean Lemass	FF	16,399	Dublin South	1943
24	Stephen Barrett	FG	16,393	Cork Borough	1954
25	Eamon de Valera	FF	16,159	Clare	1957
26	Charles J. Haughey	FF	16,143	Dublin North-Central	1982(F)
27	Philip Cosgrave	CG	16,011	Dublin South	1923
28	Sean Lemass	FF	15,969	Dublin South	1937
29	Kevin O'Higgins	CG	15,918	Dublin County	1927(J)
30	Sean MacEntee	FF	15,644	Dublin County	1933
31	Brendan Smith	FF	15,548	Cavan-Monaghan	2007
32	Bryan Cooper	CG	15,462	Dublin County	1927(S)
33	Sean Lemass	FF	15,385	Dublin South	1944
34	Sean Brady	FF	15,299	Dublin County	1943
35	William Davin	LB	15,167	Leix-Offaly	1922
36	Darrell Figgis	NP	15,087	Dublin County	1922
37	Gerry Adams	SF	15,072	Louth	**2011**
38	Eamon de Valera	FF	14,961	Clare	1943
39	William T. Cosgrave	CG	14,863	Cork Borough	1933
40	Gerard Collins	FF	14,776	Limerick West	1981
41	Micheal Martin	FF	14,742	Cork South-Central	2002
42	Eamon de Valera	FF	14,723	Clare	1938
43	Enda Kenny	FG	14,717	Mayo	2007
44	Sean Lemass	FF	14,716	Dublin South	1933
45	Sean Ryan	LB	14,693	Dublin North	1992
46	Richard Mulcahy	CG	14,597	Dublin North	1927(S)
47	Charles J. Haughey	FF	14,516	Dublin North-Central	1982(N)
48	Sean Brady	FF	14,493	Dublin County	1944
49	Alfie Byrne	NP	14,472	Dublin North	1933
50	Patrick Hillery	FF	14,372	Clare	1965

TOP VOTEGETTERS PER REGION 1918-2011				
Constituency	Top Votegetter	Party	Votes	Election
Carlow-Kilkenny	William T.Cosgrave	CG	17,709	1923
Cavan-Monaghan	Brendan Smith	FF	15,548	2007
Clare	Eamon de Valera	FF	18,574	1933
Cork	James Walsh	SF	20,801	1918
Donegal	Pearse Doherty	SF	14,262	**2011**
Dublin	Richard Mulcahy	CG	22,005	1923
Universities	Eoin MacNeill	SF	1,644	1918
Galway	Padraic O Maille	SF	11,754	1918
Kerry	Jimmy Deenihan	FG	12,697	2007
Kildare	Martin Heydon	FG	12,755	**2011**
Laoighis-Offaly	Brian Cowen	FF	19,102	2007
Limerick	Willie O'Dea	FF	19,082	2007
Longford-Westmeath	Laurence Ginnell	SF	12,433	1918
Louth	Gerry Adams	SF	15,072	**2011**
Mayo	Enda Kenny	FG	17,472	**2011**
Meath	John Bruton	FG	13,037	1997
Roscommon	Gerard Boland	FF	10,719	1938
Sligo-Leitrim	James Dolan	SF	17,711	1918
Tipperary	Michael Lowry	NP	14,104	**2011**
Waterford	Cathal Brugha	SF	12,890	1918
Wexford	Mick Wallace	NP	13,329	**2011**
Wicklow	Liam Kavanagh	LB	11,843	1992

LOWEST VOTEGETTERS 1918 -2011					
	Candidate	Party	Constituency	1st Prefs	Election
1	Maria McCool	NP	Dublin North-West	13	1997
2	Peadar O Ceallaigh	NP	Dublin South-East	18	**2011**
3	Aidan Ryan	NP	Limerick East	19	2002
4	Hugh O'Brien	NP	Clare	21	1981
5	David Henry	NP	Dublin South-Central	23	1997
6	Jim Tallon	NP	Meath	24	1997
7	Seamus Cunningham	NP	Longford-Westmeath	24	2007
8	John Olahan	NP	Dublin North-West	25	1992
9	Benny Cooney	NP	Dublin Central	25	**2011**
10	Noel O'Gara	NP	Dublin South-East	27	2007
11	John Keigher	NP	Dublin South-East	27	**2011**
12	Patrick Moore	NP	Limerick East	28	2007
13	John Harpur	NP	Dublin South-East	29	1997
14	Sean Forkin	NP	Mayo	29	**2011**
15	Patrick Clarke	NP	Dublin South-East	29	1987
16	Maurice Fitzgerald	NP	Cork South-Central	30	2007
17	Michael Murphy	NP	Cork South Central	31	1987
18	Barbara Hyland	NP	Dublin North-West	33	1987
19	James Tallon	NP	Wexford	33	1987
20	Peter O'Sullivan	NP	Dublin South-East	34	2007
21	Ciara Malone	NP	Dublin West	36	1997
22	Norman Hunt	NP	Dublin North-Central	36	1997
23	Sean Gormley	NP	Meath	36	1987
24	Patrick Shelley	NP	Dublin Central	39	1997
25	Lar Fraser	NP	Dublin North-East	39	1997
26	John Malone	NP	Dublin (Clontarf)	40	1977
27	Rory Stokes	NP	Dun Laoghaire	41	1997
28	Dermot Shanley	NP	Galway West	41	1987
29	Paul Coyle	NP	Dublin North	42	1997
30	Aidan Walsh	NP	Dublin Central	43	1997
31	Barbara Hyland	NP	Dublin West	43	1987
32	Noel O'Gara	NP	Laois-Offaly	45	2007
33	Sean O'Flaherty	SF	Donegal East	46	1918
34	Martin McAneny	NP	Dun Laoghaire	48	1992
35	Liam Johnston	NP	Dublin Central	48	**2011**

LONGEST SERVING TDs 1918-2012

	Surname	Forename	Constituency	Party	Terms	From	To	Service	Born	Died	Age
1	Smith	Patrick	Cavan	FF	17	27/08/1923	16/06/1977	53.81	17/07/1901	18/03/1982	80
2	Aiken	Frank	Louth	FF	16	27/08/1923	28/02/1973	49.51	13/02/1898	18/05/1983	85
3	Blaney	Neil T.	Donegal North East	IFF	15	07/12/1948	08/11/1995	46.92	30/10/1922	08/11/1995	73
4	McEllistrim	Thomas	Kerry North	FF	15	27/08/1923	18/06/1969	45.81	14/10/1894	04/12/1973	79
5	Pattison	Seamus	Carlow-Kilkenny	LB	13	04/10/1961	24/05/2007	45.64	19/04/1936		76
6	Everett	James	Wicklow	LB	16	16/06/1922	18/12/1967	45.51	1/5/1894	18/12/1967	73
7	MacEntee	Sean*	Monaghan/Dublin SE	FF	16	21/01/1919	18/06/1969	45.43	1889	10/01/1984	95
8	Ryan	James	Wexford	FF	16	21/01/1919	07/04/1965	45.01	6/12/1891	25/09/1970	78
9	Lemass	Sean F.	Dublin South Central	FF	15	18/11/1924	18/06/1969	44.58	15/7/1899	11/05/1971	71
10	Flanagan	Oliver J.	Laoighis-Offaly	FG	14	23/06/1943	17/02/1987	43.66	22/05/1920	26/04/1987	66
11	Corry	Martin J.	Cork North East	FF	14	09/06/1927	18/06/1969	42.03	12/12/1890	14/02/1979	88
12	McGilligan	Patrick*	N.U.I. / Dublin N.C.	FG	14	03/11/1923	07/04/1965	41.43	12/4/1889	15/11/1979	90
13	Mulcahy	Gen. Richard*	Dublin / Tipperary S	FG	14	21/01/1919	04/10/1961	40.80	10/5/1886	16/12/1971	85
14	De Valera	Eamon*	Mayo East/Clare	FF	17	21/01/1919	23/06/1959	40.42	14/10/1882	29/08/1975	92
15	Breslin	Cormac	Donegal-Leitrim	FF	12	01/07/1937	16/06/1977	39.96	25/04/1902	23/01/1978	75
16	Boland	Gerald	Roscommon	FF	13	27/08/1923	04/10/1961	38.11	25/05/1885	05/01/1973	87
17	MacEoin	Gen. Sean*	Longford-Westmeath/Sligo	FG	14	24/05/1921	07/04/1965	38.09	1893	07/07/1973	80
18	Cosgrave	Liam	Dun Laoghaire	FG	11	23/06/1943	11/06/1981	37.97	13/04/1920		92
19	Spring	Dan	Kerry North	LB	11	23/06/1943	11/06/1981	37.97	01/07/1910	01/01/1998	87
20	Kennedy	Michael*	Lngfrd-Westmeath/Meath	FF	13	09/06/1927	14/02/1965	37.69		14/02/1965	
21	Brady	Sean	Dun Laoghaire	FF	12	15/09/1927	07/04/1965	37.56	28/5/1890	24/02/1969	78
22	Briscoe	Robert	Dublin South West	FF	12	15/09/1927	07/04/1965	37.56	25/9/1894	30/05/1969	74
23	Dillon	James*	Donegal/Monaghan	FG	12	16/02/1932	18/06/1969	37.34	26/09/1902	10/02/1986	83
24	Andrews	David	Dun Laoghaire	FF	11	07/04/1965	17/05/2002	37.11	15/03/1935		77
25	Briscoe	Ben	Dublin South Central	FF	11	07/04/1965	17/05/2002	37.11	11/03/1934		78
26	Molloy	Bobby	Galway West	PD	11	07/04/1965	17/05/2002	37.11	06/07/1936		76
27	Breen	Dan	Tipperary South	FF	12	27/08/1923	07/04/1965	36.92	11/8/1894	27/12/1969	75
28	Hogan	Patrick	Clare	LB	13	27/08/1923	24/01/1969	36.71	1886	24/01/1969	83
29	O Briain	Donnchadh	Limerick West	FF	11	24/01/1933	18/06/1969	36.40	17/11/1897	22/09/1981	83
30	Kenny	Enda	Mayo	FG	12	12/11/1975		36.35	24/04/1951		61
31	Corish	Brendan	Wexford	LB	11	04/12/1945	18/02/1982	36.21	19/11/1918	17/02/1990	71
32	Haughey	Charles J.	Dublin North Central	FF	11	05/03/1957	25/11/1992	35.73	16/09/1925	13/06/2006	80
33	Harte	Paddy	Donegal North East	FG	11	04/10/1961	06/06/1997	35.67	26/07/1931		81
34	Treacy	Sean	Tipperary South	NP	11	04/10/1961	06/06/1997	35.67	23/09/1923		88
35	De Valera	Vivion	Dublin Central	FF	10	04/12/1945	11/06/1981	35.52	13/12/1910	16/02/1982	71
36	Costello	John A.	Dublin South East	FG	10	24/01/1933	18/06/1969	35.46	20/6/1891	05/01/1976	84
37	Bruton	John	Meath	FG	11	18/06/1969	01/11/2004	35.37	18/05/1947		65
38	Childers	Erskine*	Lgford-Wmeath/Monaghan	FF	11	17/06/1938	01/06/1973	34.96	11/12/1905	17/11/1974	68
39	Morrissey	Daniel	Tipperary North	FG	13	16/06/1922	05/03/1957	34.72		1981	
40	Moran	Michael	Mayo West	FF	10	17/06/1938	28/02/1973	34.70	25/12/1912	06/05/1983	70
41	Fahy	Frank	Galway South	FF	14	21/01/1919	14/07/1953	34.48	12/1/1880	14/07/1953	73
42	Quinn	Ruairi	Dublin South East	LB	10	16/06/1977		34.07	22/04/1946		66
43	O'Malley	Desmond	Limerick East	PD	11	22/05/1968	17/05/2002	33.99	01/02/1939		73
44	Dockrell	Maurice E.	Dublin Central	FG	10	23/06/1943	16/06/1977	33.98	06/10/1908	09/12/1986	78
45	Davin	William	Laoighis-Offaly	LB	13	16/06/1922	01/03/1956	33.71	1890	01/03/1956	66
46	Ahern	Bertie	Dublin Central	FF	10	16/06/1977	25/02/2011	33.70	12/09/1951		61
47	O'Hanlon	Rory	Cavan-Monaghan	FF	10	16/06/1977	25/02/2011	33.70	07/02/1934		78
48	O'Keeffe	Jim	Cork South West	FG	10	16/06/1977	25/02/2011	33.70	31/03/1941		71
49	Woods	Michael	Dublin North East	FF	10	16/06/1977	25/02/2011	33.70	08/12/1935		76
50	Killilea(sen)	Mark	Galway North	FF	11	09/06/1927	04/10/1961	33.38	1896	29/09/1970	74
51	Lynch	Jack	Cork Borough	FF	9	04/02/1948	11/06/1981	33.35	15/08/1917	20/10/1999	82
52	Bartley	Gerald	Galway West	FF	11	16/02/1932	07/04/1965	33.14	12/06/1898	10/05/1974	75
53	Norton	William*	Dublin Co. / Kildare	LB	12	18/02/1926	04/12/1963	33.10	1900	04/12/1963	63
54	Doyle	Peadar	Dublin South West	FG	12	27/08/1923	04/08/1956	32.94		04/08/1956	
55	Davern	Noel	Tipperary South	FF	8	18/06/1969	24/05/2007	32.25	24/12/1945		66
56	Traynor	Oscar	Dublin North East	FF	12	11/03/1925	04/10/1961	32.15	21/3/1886	21/12/1963	77
57	Derrig	Thomas*	Mayo/Carlow-Kilkenny	FF	13	24/05/1921	19/11/1956	31.71		19/11/1956	
58	Ruttledge	Patrick	Mayo North	FF	13	24/05/1921	08/05/1952	30.96	1892	08/05/1952	60
59	Noonan	Michael	Limerick East	FG	10	11/06/1981		30.77	21/05/1943		69
60	Byrne	Alfred	Dublin North East	NP	13	16/06/1922	13/03/1956	30.75	17/3/1882	13/03/1956	73
61	O'Leary	John	Kerry South	FF	10	07/12/1966	06/06/1997	30.50	03/05/1933		79
62	Bruton	Richard	Dublin North Central	FG	9	18/02/1982		30.08	15/03/1953		59
63	McGinley	Dinny	Donegal South West	FG	9	18/02/1982		30.08	27/04/1945		67
64	O'Dea	Willie	Limerick East	FF	9	18/02/1982		30.08	01/11/1952		59
65	Murphy	Michael Pat	Cork South West	LB	8	30/05/1951	11/06/1981	30.03	12/03/1919	28/10/2000	81
	* Elected in more than one constituency						Service: Members 31st Dail to			20/03/2012	76
	Member 31st Dail		Broken Service				Age: Living Members to			20/03/2012	

SHORTEST SERVING TDs 1918-2012

	Surname	Forename	Constituency	Party	Terms	From	To	Years Service	Born	Died	Age
1	McCann	Pierce	Tipperary East	SF	1	21/01/1919	06/03/1919	0.12	2/8/1882	06/03/1919	36
2	Doherty	Kieran	Cavan-Monaghan	HBlk	1	11/06/1981	02/08/1981	0.14	16/10/1955	02/08/1981	25
3	Carter	Michael	Leitrim-Sligo	F	1	09/06/1927	15/09/1927	0.27			
4	Clery	Prof. Arthur	N.U.I.	NP	1	09/06/1927	15/09/1927	0.27			
5	Cullen	Denis	Dublin North	LB	1	09/06/1927	15/09/1927	0.27	23/9/1878	26/11/1971	93
6	Duffy	William	Galway	NL	1	09/06/1927	15/09/1927	0.27	7/4/1865	1945	80
7	Falvey	Thomas	Clare	R	1	09/06/1927	15/09/1927	0.27		17/02/1941	
8	Garahan	Hugh	Longford-Westmeath	F	1	09/06/1927	15/09/1927	0.27		07/06/1940	
9	Gill	John	Laoighis-Offaly	LB	1	09/06/1927	15/09/1927	0.27	27/12/1898	10/06/1971	72
10	Hewson	Gilbert	Limerick	NP	1	09/06/1927	15/09/1927	0.27		1951	
11	Horgan	John	Cork Borough	NL	1	09/06/1927	15/09/1927	0.27			
12	Jinks	John	Leitrim-Sligo	NL	1	09/06/1927	15/09/1927	0.27	1872	11/09/1934	62
13	Lynch	Gilbert	Galway	LB	1	09/06/1927	15/09/1927	0.27		01/11/1969	
14	Mullen	Eugene	Mayo South	FF	1	09/06/1927	15/09/1927	0.27			
15	O'Gorman	David	Cork East	F	1	09/06/1927	15/09/1927	0.27		1945	
16	Quill	Timothy	Cork North	LB	1	09/06/1927	15/09/1927	0.27	09/05/1901	10/06/1960	59
17	Shannon	James	Wexford	LB	1	09/06/1927	15/09/1927	0.27			
18	Tynan	Thomas	Laoighis-Offaly	FF	1	09/06/1927	15/09/1927	0.27	1859	24/09/1953	94
19	Kennedy	Hugh	Dublin South	CG	1	25/10/1923	05/06/1924	0.61	11/7/1879	01/12/1936	57
20	Drohan	Frank	Waterford	SF	1	24/05/1921	05/01/1922	0.62	13/8/1879	05/03/1953	73
21	Lee	George	Dublin South	FG	1	05/06/2009	08/02/2010	0.68	27/09/1962		49
22	Acheson	Carrie	Tipperary South	FF	1	11/06/1981	18/02/1982	0.69	11/09/1934		73
23	Agnew	Paddy	Louth	Hblk	1	11/06/1981	18/02/1982	0.69	09/03/1955		53
24	Joyce	Carey	Cork East	FF	1	11/06/1981	18/02/1982	0.69	01/08/1922		85
25	Loftus	Sean D.	Dublin North-East	NP	1	11/06/1981	18/02/1982	0.69	01/11/1927	10/07/2010	82
26	Coyle	Henry	Mayo North	CG	1	27/08/1923	09/05/1924	0.70		29/05/1979	
27	Bellew	Thomas	Louth	FF	1	18/02/1982	24/11/1982	0.76	11/04/1944	29/10/1995	51
28	Brady	Gerry	Kildare	FF	1	18/02/1982	24/11/1982	0.76	19/08/1948		59
29	Brennan	Ned	Dublin North-East	FF	1	18/02/1982	24/11/1982	0.76	01/08/1920	21/09/1988	68
30	Corr	James	Cork South-Central	FG	1	18/02/1982	24/11/1982	0.76	25/01/1934		74
31	Fitzgerald	Alexis	Dublin South-East	FG	1	18/02/1982	24/11/1982	0.76	07/05/1945		62
32	Gallagher	Patrick	Waterford	WP	1	18/02/1982	24/11/1982	0.76	01/12/1946		61
							Age: Living Members to			**20/03/2012**	

GOVERNMENTS 1919 TO 2011

General Notes:

1. Following the dissolution of a Dail the Government remain in office, even if it loses the General Election, until the new Dail meets and nominates a new Government.
2. Ministers can be assigned more then one Department.
3. Under the Ministers and Secretaries Act, the Government can create new Departments and assign Ministers to them. It can also amalgamate existing Departments or separate the functions of a particular Department into new or separate Departments.
4. The Government can change the name of a Department.
5. The list below does not contain details of short term appointments e.g. where Ministers deputise for colleagues.
6. The Parliamentary Secretary to the Taoiseach is also the Government Chief Whip.
7. The post of Parliamentary Secretary was abolished with effect from 1/1/78 and replaced by a new post of Minister of State. More than one Minister of State can be assigned to a particular Department.

First Dail: 21st January 1919 to 24th May 1921

Post	First Ministry (Temporary) 21st January to 1st April 1919	Second Ministry 1st April 1919 to 26th August 1921
Priomh Aire (President)	Cathal Brugha	Eamon de Valera
Home Affairs	Michael Collins	Arthur Griffith
Defence	Richard Mulcahy	Cathal Brugha
External Affairs	George Noble Count Plunkett	George Noble Count Plunkett
Finance	Eoin McNeill	Michael Collins
Industries		Eoin McNeill
Labour		Countess Markievicz
Local Government		William T. Cosgrave
Trade & Commerce		Ernest Blythe
Irish		Sean T. O'Kelly (from 29/6/20)
		Non-Cabinet Members (Title: Director)
Propaganda		Laurence Ginnell
Agriculture		Robert C. Barton
Fisheries		Sean Etchingham

Notes:

1. Single-party Sinn Fein Government.
2. Cathal Brugha was acting President of the First Dail and resigned with his Ministry on 1st April 1919.
3. Upon his release from prison Eamon de Valera took over as President of the First Dail.
4. On 17th June 1919 Arthur Griffith was appointed Deputy President during the absence of the President.
5. Michael Collins acted as Deputy President from 1st December 1920 during the imprisonment of Arthur Griffith, who was arrested on 26th November 1920.
6. In all there were 11 Departments of which at first, 8 were Cabinet and 3 non-Cabinet, and later, 9 were Cabinet and 2 non-Cabinet, the Minister for Trade & Commerce being included in the Cabinet from 17th June 1919.
7. Sean Etchingham was appointed by Cabinet on 28/11/19 but could not be ratified by the Dail until 29/6/20.
8. Sean T. O'Kelly was appointed to new Ministry of Irish from 29/6/20.

Second Dail: 24th May 1921 to 9th Sept 1922

Ministers (Secretaries of State)	First Ministry (Pre-Treaty) 26th Aug 1921 to 9th Jan 1922	Second Ministry (Post Treaty) 10th Jan to 9th Sept 1922
President	Eamon De Valera	Arthur Griffith (died 12/8/22)
External Affairs	Arthur Griffith	George Gavan Duffy (resigned 25/7/22)
External Affairs		Arthur Griffith (26/7/22 to 12/8/22)
External Affairs		Michael Hayes (from 21/8/22)
Home Affairs	Austin Stack	Edmund Duggan
Defence	Cathal Brugha	Richard Mulcahy (to 1/7/22)
Defence		Michael Collins (1/7/22 to 22/8/22)
Finance	Michael Collins	Michael Collins (killed 22/8/22)
Local Government	William T. Cosgrave	William T. Cosgrave
Economic Affairs	Robert C. Barton	Kevin O'Higgins
Non-Cabinet Members (Secretaries)		
Local Government (Asst.)	Kevin O'Higgins	
Fine Arts	George Noble Count Plunkett	
Publicity	Desmond Fitzgerald	Desmond Fitzgerald
Education	John J. O'Kelly (Sceilig)	Michael Hayes
Labour	Countess Markievicz	Joseph McGrath
Trade & Commerce	Ernest Blythe	Ernest Blythe
Agriculture	Art O'Connor	Patrick Hogan
Fisheries	Sean Etchingham	
Director of Belfast Boycott		Michael Staines (to 28th Feb 1922)
Law Officer		Hugh Kennedy

Notes:

1. First Ministry (Pre Treaty): Single-party Sinn Fein Government.
2. President De Valera resigned with his Ministers on 9th January 1922, following the ratification by Dail Eireann on 7/1/22 of the Treaty with Great Britain dated 6th December 1921, leading to the formation of The Second Ministry.
3. Sinn Fein split into Pro and Anti Treaty Sinn Fein when the Anglo-Irish Treaty was debated.

Second Dail: 24th May 1921 to 9th Sept 1922

	Provisional Government 16th Jan to 9th Sept 1922	Ministerial Substitute
Chairman	Michael Collins (killed 22/8/22)	William T. Cosgrave
Finance	Michael Collins	William T. Cosgrave
Home Affairs	Edmund Duggan	
Economic Affairs	Kevin O'Higgins	Ernest Blythe
Labour	Joseph McGrath	Patrick Hogan
Agriculture	Patrick Hogan	
Education	Finian Lynch	Michael Hayes
Local Government	William T. Cosgrave	
Postmaster General	James J. Walsh	

Notes:

1. From 16/1/22 until 9/9/22 there was a dual system of Government:
   (a) The Second Dail Cabinet responsible to Dail Eireann.
   (b) The Provisional Government, set up after the Dail ratified the Treaty, apparently responsible to no Parliament.
   The dual system terminated with the fusion of the two systems under the Third Dail on 9th September, 1922.
2. The Civil War commenced on 29th June, 1922 and certain members of the Provisional Government were seconded for Military service. Substitutes were appointed to carry on their duties in their absence.
3. Ernest Blyth and Michael Hayes were co-opted as permanent members of the Provisional Government on 27/7/22.
4. Michael Collins was killed in action on 22nd August, 1922 and W. T. Cosgrave was appointed as his successor as Chairman of the Provisional Government on 25th August.

Third Dail: 9th Sept 1922 to 9th Aug 1923

	Provisional Government 9th Sept to 6th Dec 1922	First Executive Council 6th Dec 1922 to 21st Sept 1923
President	William T. Cosgrave	William T. Cosgrave
Finance	William T. Cosgrave	William T. Cosgrave
Vice President		Kevin O'Higgins
Home Affairs	Kevin O'Higgins	Kevin O'Higgins
Industry & Commerce	Joseph McGrath	Joseph McGrath
Education	Eoin McNeill	Eoin McNeill
Local Government	Ernest Blythe	Ernest Blythe
External Affairs	Desmond Fitzgerald	Desmond Fitzgerald
Defence	Richard Mulcahy	Richard Mulcahy
Agriculture	Patrick Hogan	Patrick Hogan*
Postmaster General	James J. Walsh	James J. Walsh *
Fisheries		Finian Lynch *
Without Portfolio	Finian Lynch	* Not a member of the Executive Council
Without Portfolio	Edmund Duggan	
Law Officer	Hugh Kennedy	Hugh Kennedy

Notes:

1. Single-party Pro-Treaty Sinn Fein Government (Cumann na nGaedheal from March 1923).
   Cumann na nGaedheal was established in March 1923 by the pro-treaty former members of Sinn Fein.
2. After 9th September 1922, the newly constituted Provisional Government appointed by the Third Dail continued in being as the sole Government, until superseded on 6/12/22, by the formation of the First Executive Council pursuant to the Constitution of Saorstat Eireann which became law on that date.
3. The President as such was not a member of the Provisional Government. He was the head of the Dail or Parliament. This office lapsed with the establishment of the First Executive Council.

Fourth Dail: 19th Sept 1923 to 23rd May 1927

Second Executive Council	21st Sept 1923 to 23rd June 1927
President	William T. Cosgrave
Vice-President	Kevin O'Higgins
Home Affairs	Kevin O'Higgins
Finance	Ernest Blythe
Education	Eoin McNeill (to 24/11/25)
Education	John M. O'Sullivan (from 28/1/26)
Industry & Commerce	Joseph McGrath (to 7/3/24)
Industry & Commerce	Patrick McGilligan (from 4/4/24)
Defence	Richard Mulcahy (to 19/3/24)
Defence	William T. Cosgrave (to 21/11/24)
Defence	Peter Hughes (from 21/11/24)
External Affairs	Desmond Fitzgerald
Agriculture	Patrick Hogan*
Fisheries	Finian Lynch *
Local Government	Seamus Bourke*
Postmaster General	James J. Walsh *
Attorney-General	Hugh Kennedy (Appointed Chief Justice 5/6/24)
Attorney-General	John O'Byrne (Appointed High Court Judge 9/1/26)
Attorney-General	John A. Costello (from 9/1/26)
	* Not a member of the Executive Council

Notes:

1. Single-party Cumann na nGaedheal Government.
2. Department of Home Affairs changed to Department of Justice from 2/6/24.
3. Department of Agriculture changed to Department of Lands & Agriculture from 2/6/24.
4. Department of Local Government changed to Department of Local Government & Public Health from 2/6/24.
5. Department of Postmaster General changed to Department of Posts & Telegraphs from 2/6/24.

Fifth Dail: 23rd June 1927 to 11th Oct 1927

Third Executive Council	23rd June to 12th Oct 1927
President	William T. Cosgrave
Vice-President	Kevin O'Higgins (killed 10/7/27)
Vice-President	Ernest Blythe (from 14/7/27)
Justice & External Affairs	Kevin O'Higgins (killed 10/7/27)
Justice & External Affairs	William T. Cosgrave (from 14/7/27)
Education	John M. O'Sullivan
Defence	Desmond Fitzgerald
Finance	Ernest Blythe
Industry & Commerce	Patrick McGilligan
Lands & Agriculture	Patrick Hogan
Fisheries	Finian Lynch
Posts & Telegraphs	James J. Walsh
Local Government & Public Health	Richard Mulcahy
Attorney-General	John A. Costello

Notes:

1. Single-party Cumann na nGaedheal Government.
2. Fianna Fail, "The Republican Party", was founded by Eamon de Valera in May 1926 from members of the anti-Treaty Sinn Fein and the IRA after Sinn Fein rejected a motion that they should enter the Dail if the Oath of Allegiance was removed. Contested the June 1927 election winning 44 seats and entered the Dail in August 1927.

Sixth Dail: 11th Oct 1927 to 29th Jan 1932

	Fourth Executive Council 12th Oct 1927 to 3rd Apr 1930	Fifth Executive Council 3rd Apr 1930 to 9th March 1932
President	William T. Cosgrave	William T. Cosgrave
Vice-President	Ernest Blythe	Ernest Blythe
Finance	Ernest Blythe	Ernest Blythe
Posts & Telegraphs	Ernest Blythe	Ernest Blythe
Defence	Desmond Fitzgerald	Desmond Fitzgerald
Education	John M. O'Sullivan	John M.O'Sullivan
Industry & Commerce	Patrick McGilligan	Patrick McGilligan
External Affairs	Patrick McGilligan	Patrick McGilligan
Lands & Agriculture	Patrick Hogan	
Agriculture		Patrick Hogan
Fisheries	Finian Lynch	
Lands & Fisheries		Finian Lynch
Local Government & Public Health	Richard Mulcahy	Richard Mulcahy
Justice	James Fitzgerald-Kenney	James Fitzgerald-Kenney
Attorney-General	John A. Costello	John A. Costello

Note: Single-party Cumann na nGaedheal Government.

Seventh Dail: 9th March 1932 to 2nd Jan 1933

Sixth Executive Council	9th March 1932 to 8th Feb 1933
President	Eamon de Valera
External Affairs	Eamon de Valera
Vice-President	Sean T. O'Kelly
Local Government & Public Health	Sean T. O'Kelly
Lands & Fisheries	Patrick Ruttledge
Industry & Commerce	Sean Lemass
Finance	Sean MacEntee
Agriculture	James Ryan
Defence	Frank Aiken
Education	Thomas Derrig
Justice	James Geoghegan
Posts & Telegraphs	Joseph Connolly (Senator)
Attorney-General	Conor A. Maguire

Note: First Single-party Fianna Fail Government.

Eighth Dail: 8th Feb 1933 to 14th June 1937

Seventh Executive Council	**8th Feb 1933 to 21st July 1937**
President	Eamon de Valera
External Affairs	Eamon de Valera
Vice-President	Sean T. O'Kelly
Local Government & Public Health	Sean T. O'Kelly
Justice	Patrick Ruttledge
Industry & Commerce	Sean Lemass
Finance	Sean MacEntee
Agriculture	James Ryan
Defence	Frank Aiken
Lands & Fisheries	Joseph Connolly (to 29/5/36)
Lands & Fisheries	Frank Aiken (to 11/11/36)
Lands & Fisheries	Gerald Boland (from 11/11/36)
Posts & Telegraphs	Gerald Boland (to 11/11/36)
Posts & Telegraphs	Oscar Traynor (from 11/11/36)
Education	Thomas Derrig
Attorney-General	Conor A. Maguire (Appointed High Court Judge 2/11/36)
Attorney-General	James Geoghegan (Appointed Judge of the Supreme Court 22/12/36)
Attorney-General	Patrick Lynch (from 22/12/36)

Notes:

1. Single-party Fianna Fail Government.
2. Fine Gael formed by merger of the Blueshirts, the Centre Party and Cumann na nGaedheal in September 1933.

Ninth Dail: 21st July 1937 to 27th May 1938

Eighth Executive Council & First Government	**21st July 1937 to 30th June 1938**
President/Taoiseach	Eamon de Valera
External Affairs	Eamon de Valera
Vice-President/Tánaiste	Sean T. O'Kelly
Local Government & Public Health	Sean T. O'Kelly
Justice	Patrick Ruttledge
Industry & Commerce	Sean Lemass
Finance	Sean MacEntee
Agriculture	James Ryan
Defence	Frank Aiken
Education	Thomas Derrig
Lands	Gerald Boland
Posts & Telegraphs	Oscar Traynor
Attorney-General	Patrick Lynch

Notes:

1. Single-party Fianna Fail Government.
2. The new Constitution came into operation on 29th December 1937.
3. The Eighth Executive Council become known as the First Government.
4. The title of President of the Executive Council was changed to that of Taoiseach, the Vice-President to Tánaiste.
5. There was no new election and no change in personnel of the Government. The members of the Eighth Executive Council who were in office on the date of the coming into operation of the Constitution, received formal appointments from the President of Ireland on 28/6/38.

Tenth Dail: 30th June 1938 to 26th June 1943

	Second Government 30th June 1938 to 8th Sept 1939	**Reorganised Cabinet-European War 8th Sept 1939 to 2nd July 1943**
Taoiseach	Eamon de Valera	Eamon de Valera
Tánaiste	Sean T. O'Kelly	Sean T. O'Kelly
External Affairs	Eamon de Valera	Eamon de Valera
Local Government & Public Health	Sean T. O'Kelly	Patrick Ruttledge (to 14/8/41)
Local Government & Public Health		Sean MacEntee (from 18/8/41)
Justice	Patrick Ruttledge	Gerald Boland
Industry & Commerce	Sean Lemass	Sean MacEntee (to 18/8/41)
Industry & Commerce		Sean Lemass (from 18/8/41)
Supplies		Sean Lemass
Finance	Sean MacEntee	Sean T. O'Kelly
Agriculture	James Ryan	James Ryan
Defence	Frank Aiken	Oscar Traynor
Co-ordination of Defence Measures		Frank Aiken
Education		Eamon de Valera (to 18/6/40)
Education	Thomas Derrig	Thomas Derrig (from 18/6/40)
Lands	Gerald Boland	Thomas Derrig
Posts & Telegraphs	Oscar Traynor	Patrick Little
Attorney-General	Patrick Lynch	Patrick Lynch (resigned 1/3/40)
Attorney-General		Kevin Haugh (Appointed High Court Judge)
Attorney-General		Kevin Dixon (from 10/10/42)

Note: Single-party Fianna Fail Government

Eleventh Dail: 1st July 1943 to 7th June 1944

Third Government	**2nd July 1943 to 9th June 1944**
Taoiseach	Eamon de Valera
Tánaiste	Sean T. O'Kelly
External Affairs	Eamon de Valera
Finance	Sean T. O'Kelly
Industry & Commerce	Sean Lemass
Supplies	Sean Lemass
Local Government & Public Health	Sean MacEntee
Agriculture	James Ryan
Education	Thomas Derrig
Justice	Gerald Boland
Defence	Oscar Traynor
Posts & Telegraphs	Patrick J. Little
Lands	Sean Moylan
Co-ordination of Defensive Measures	Frank Aiken
Attorney-General	Kevin Dixon

Note: Single-party Fianna Fail Government.

Twelfth Dail: 9th June 1944 to 12th Jan 1948

Fourth Government	**9th June 1944 to 18th Feb 1948**
Taoiseach	Eamon de Valera
Tánaiste	Sean T. O'Kelly (to 14/6/45)
Tánaiste	Sean Lemass (from 19/6/45)
External Affairs	Eamon de Valera
Finance	Sean T. O'Kelly (to 14/6/45)
Finance	Frank Aiken (from 19/6/45)
Industry & Commerce	Sean Lemass
Supplies	Sean Lemass (to 31/7/45)
Co-ordination of Defensive Measures	Frank Aiken (to 19/6/45)
Local Government & Public Health	Sean MacEntee
Agriculture	James Ryan (to 21/1/47)
Agriculture	Patrick Smith (from 22/1/47)
Education	Thomas Derrig
Justice	Gerald Boland
Defence	Oscar Traynor
Posts & Telegraphs	Patrick J. Little
Lands	Sean Moylan
Health & Social Welfare	James Ryan (22/1/47 to 18/2/47)
Attorney-General	Kevin Dixon (Appointed High Court Judge)
Attorney-General	Cearbhail O Dalaigh (from 30/4/46)

Notes:

1. Single-party Fianna Fail Government.
2. Sean T. O'Kelly elected President of Ireland 14/6/45.
3. Department of Supplies terminated 31/7/45 and functions transferred to Industry & Commerce.
4. Department of Co-ordination of Defensive Measures terminated 31/7/45.
5. Department of Local Government & Public Health changed to Department of Local Government from 22/1/47.

Thirteenth Dail: 18th February 1948 to 7th May 1951

Fifth Government	**18th Feb 1948 to 13th June 1951**
Taoiseach	John A. Costello (FG)
Tánaiste	William Norton (LB)
Social Welfare	William Norton (LB)
External Affairs	Sean MacBride (CnaP)
Finance	Patrick McGilligan (FG)
Industry & Commerce	Daniel Morrissey (FG) (to 7/3/51)
Industry & Commerce	Thomas F. O'Higgins (FG) (from 7/3/51)
Local Government	Timothy J. Murphy (LB) (died 29/4/49)
Local Government	Michael Keyes (LB) (from 11/5/49)
Health	Noel Browne (NP) (resigned 11/4/51)
Health	John A. Costello (FG) (from 12/4/51)
Agriculture	James Dillon (NP)
Education	Richard Mulcahy (FG)
Justice	Sean MacEoin (FG) (to 7/3/51)
Justice	Daniel Morrissey (FG) (from 7/3/51)
Defence	Thomas F. O'Higgins (FG) (to 7/3/51)
Posts & Telegraphs	James Everett (LB)
Lands	Joseph Blowick (CnaT)
Chief Whip	Liam Cosgrave
Attorney-General	C. Lavery

Note:

First Inter-party Government comprising of Fine Gael, Labour, Clann na Talmhan & Clann na Poblachta.

Fourteenth Dail: 13th June 1951 to 24th May 1954

Sixth Government	**13th June 1951 to 2nd June 1954**
Taoiseach	Eamon de Valera
Tánaiste	Sean Lemass
Industry & Commerce	Sean Lemass
Finance	Sean MacEntee
Health & Social Welfare	James Ryan
External Affairs	Frank Aiken
Lands	Thomas Derrig
Justice	Gerald Boland
Defence	Oscar Traynor
Education	Sean Moylan
Local Government	Patrick Smith
Posts & Telegraphs	Erskine Childers
Agriculture	Thomas Walsh
Chief Whip	Jack Lynch
Attorney-General	Cearbhail O Dalaigh

Note: Single-party Fianna Fail Government.

Fifteenth Dail: 2nd June1954 to 12th February 1957

Seventh Government	**2nd June 1954 to 20th Mar 1957**
Taoiseach	John A. Costello (FG)
Tánaiste	William Norton (LB)
Industry & Commerce	William Norton (LB)
Education	Richard Mulcahy (FG)
Gaeltacht	Richard Mulcahy (from 2/7/56 to 24/10/56)
Gaeltacht	James Lindsay (FG) (from 24/10/56)
Lands	Joseph Blowick (CnaT)
Justice	James Everett (LB)
Agriculture	James Dillon (FG)
Defence	Sean MacEoin (FG)
Posts & Telegraphs	Michael J. Keyes (LB)
External Affairs	Liam Cosgrave (FG)
Social Welfare	Brendan Corish (LB)
Finance	Gerald Sweetman (FG)
Local Government	Patrick O'Donnell (FG)
Health	Thomas F. O'Higgins (FG)
Chief Whip	John O'Donovan
Attorney-General	P. McGilligan

Notes:

1. Second Inter-party Government comprising of Fine Gael, Labour, Clann na Talmhan & Clann na Poblachta.
2. New Department of the Gaeltacht created 2/7/56.

Sixteenth Dail: 20th March 1957 to 15th September 1961

	Eighth Government 20th Mar 1957 to 23rd June 1959	Ninth Government 23rd June 1959 to 11th Oct 1961
Taoiseach	Eamon de Valera	Sean Lemass (appointed 23/6/59)
Tánaiste	Sean Lemass	Sean MacEntee
Industry & Commerce	Sean Lemass	Jack Lynch
Health	Sean MacEntee	Sean MacEntee
Finance	James Ryan	James Ryan
External Affairs	Frank Aiken	Frank Aiken
Justice	Oscar Traynor	Oscar Traynor
Agriculture	Frank Aiken (to 16/5/57)	
Agriculture	Sean Moylan (died 16/11/57)	
Agriculture	Patrick Smith (from 27/11/57)	Patrick Smith (FF)
Local Government	Patrick Smith (to 27/11/57)	
Local Government	Neil Blaney (from 27/11/57)	Neil Blaney
Social Welfare	Patrick Smith (to 27/11/57)	
Social Welfare	Sean MacEntee (from 27/11/57)	Sean MacEntee
Lands	Erskine Childers	Erskine Childers (to 23/7/59)
Lands		Michael Moran (from 23/7/59)
Education	Jack Lynch	Patrick J. Hillery
Posts & Telegraphs	Neil Blaney (to 4/12/57)	
Posts & Telegraphs	John Ormonde (from 4/12/57)	Michael Hilliard
Defence	Kevin Boland	Kevin Boland
Gaeltacht	Jack Lynch (to 26/6/57)	Michael Moran (to 23/7/59)
Gaeltacht	Michael Moran (from 26/6/57)	Gerald Bartley (from 23/7/59)
Transport & Power		Erskine Childers (from 27/7/59)
Chief Whip	Donnchadh O Briain	Donnchadh O Briain
Attorney-General	A. O Caoimh	A. O Caoimh

Notes:

1. Single-party Fianna Fail Government.
2. Eamon de Valera elected President of Ireland 23/6/59 and was succeeded by Sean Lemass. Fianna Fail continued in Government as there was no need for a General Election.
3. A new Department of Transport and Power was created on 27/7/59.

Seventeenth Dail: 11th October 1961 to 18th March 1965

Tenth Government	11th Oct 1961 to 21st Apr 1965
Taoiseach	Sean Lemass
Tánaiste	Sean MacEntee
Health	Sean MacEntee
Finance	James Ryan
External Affairs	Frank Aiken
Agriculture	Patrick Smith (resigned 8/10/64)
Agriculture	Charles J. Haughey (from 8/10/64)
Transport & Power	Erskine Childers
Industry & Commerce	Jack Lynch
Local Government	Neil Blaney
Social Welfare	Kevin Boland
Lands & the Gaeltacht	Michael Moran
Posts & Telegraphs	Michael Hilliard
Education	Patrick Hillery
Defence	Gerald Bartley
Justice	Charles J. Haughey (to 8/10/64)
Justice	Brian Lenihan (from 3/11/64)
Chief Whip	Joseph Brennan
Attorney-General	A. O Caoimh

Note: Single-party Fianna Fail Government

Eighteenth Dail: 21st April 1965 to 22nd May 1969

	Eleventh Government 21st April 1965 to 10th Nov 1966	**Twelfth Government 10th Nov 1966 to 2nd July 1969**
Taoiseach	Sean Lemass (resigned 10/11/66)	Jack Lynch
Tánaiste	Frank Aiken	Frank Aiken
External Affairs	Frank Aiken	Frank Aiken
Transport & Power	Erskine Childers	Erskine Childers
Finance	Jack Lynch	Charles J. Haughey
Local Government	Neil Blaney	Kevin Boland
Social Welfare	Kevin Boland	Joseph Brennan
Lands & the Gaeltacht	Michael Moran	Michael Moran (to 26/3/68)
Lands & the Gaeltacht		Padraig Faulkner (from 27/3/68)
Defence	Michael Hilliard	Michael Hilliard
Industry & Commerce	Patrick Hillery (to 13/7/66)	
Industry & Commerce	George Colley (from 13/7/66)	George Colley
Labour	Patrick Hillery (from 13/7/66)	Patrick Hillery
Agriculture & Fisheries	Charles J. Haughey	Neil Blaney
Justice	Brian Lenihan	Brian Lenihan (to 26/3/68)
Justice		Michael Moran (from 27/3/68)
Posts & Telegraphs	Joseph Brennan	Erskine Childers
Health	Donogh O'Malley (to 13/7/66)	
Health	Sean Flanagan (from 13/7/66)	Sean Flanagan
Education	George Colley (to 13/7/66)	Donogh O'Malley (died 10/3/68)
Education	Donogh O'Malley (from 13/7/66)	Brian Lenihan (from 26/3/68)
Chief Whip	Michael Carty	Michael Carty
Attorney-General	Colm Condon	Colm Condon

Notes:
1. Single-party Fianna Fail Government.
2. Sean Lemass retired from politics on 10/11/66 and was succeeded by Jack Lynch and Fianna Fail continued in office as there was no need for a General Election.
3. Department of Labour established 13/7/66.
4. Department of Agriculture changed to Agriculture & Fisheries from 6/7/65.

Nineteenth Dail: 18th June 1969 to 5th February 1973

Thirteenth Government	**2nd July 1969 to 14th Mar 1973**
Taoiseach	Jack Lynch
Tánaiste	Erskine Childers
Health	Erskine Childers
Agriculture & Fisheries	Neil Blaney (dismissed 7/5/70)
Agriculture & Fisheries	James Gibbons (from 9/5/70)
Defence	James Gibbons (to 9/5/70)
Defence	Jerry Cronin (from 9/5/70)
Local Government & Social Welfare	Kevin Boland (resigned 7/5/70)
Local Government	Bobby Molloy (from 9/5/70)
Justice	Michael Moran (resigned 5/5/70)
Justice	Desmond O'Malley (from 7/5/70)
External Affairs	Patrick Hillery (resigned 3/1/73)
External Affairs	Brian Lenihan (from 3/1/73)
Transport & Power	Brian Lenihan (to 3/1/73)
Transport & Power	Michael O'Kennedy (from 3/1/73)
Finance	Charles J. Haughey (dismissed 7/5/70)
Finance	George Colley (from 9/5/70)
Industry & Commerce	George Colley (to 9/5/70)
Industry & Commerce	Patrick J. Lalor (from 9/5/70)
Labour	Joseph Brennan
Social Welfare	Joseph Brennan (from 9/5/70)
Gaeltacht	George Colley
Posts & Telegraphs	Patrick J. Lalor (to 9/5/70)
Posts & Telegraphs	Gerry Collins (from 9/5/70)

Lands	Sean Flanagan
Education	Padraig Faulkner
Without Portfolio	Michael O'Kennedy (8/12/72- 3/1/73)
Chief Whip	Desmond O'Malley (to 7/5/70)
Chief Whip	David Andrews (from 7/5/70)
Attorney-General	Colm Condon

Notes:
1. Single-party Fianna Fail Government.
2. Patrick Hillery was appointed as Ireland's EC Commissioner on 3/1/73.
3. Department of External Affairs changed to Foreign Affairs from 3/3/71.
4. C.J. Haughey and Neil Blaney dismissed and Kevin Boland and Michael Moran resigned May 1970 over what later became known as the arms crisis. There followed a major Cabinet re-shuffle.

Twentieth Dail: 14th March 1973 to 25th May 1977

Fourteenth Government	**14th Mar 1973 to 5th July 1977**
Taoiseach	Liam Cosgrave (FG)
Tánaiste	Brendan Corish (LB)
Health & Social Welfare	Brendan Corish (LB)
Defence	Patrick Donegan (FG) (to 2/12/76)
Defence	Oliver J. Flanagan (FG) (from 16/12/76)
Local Government	James Tully (LB)
Finance	Richie Ryan (FG)
Public Service	Richie Ryan (FG) (from 1/11/73)
Agriculture & Fisheries	Mark Clinton (FG)
Labour	Michael O'Leary (LB)
Gaeltacht	Tom O'Donnell (FG)
Lands	Tom Fitzpatrick (FG) (to 2/12/76)
Lands	Patrick Donegan (FG) (from 2/12/76)
Foreign Affairs	Garret Fitzgerald (FG)
Posts & Telegraphs	Conor Cruise O'Brien (LB)
Transport & Power	Peter Barry (FG) (to 2/12/76)
Transport & Power	Tom Fitzpatrick (FG) (from 2/12/76)
Industry & Commerce	Justin Keating (LB)
Education	Dick Burke (FG) (resigned 2/12/76)
Education	Peter Barry (FG) (from 2/12/76)
Justice	Patrick Cooney (FG)
Chief Whip	John Kelly (FG)
Attorney-General	Declan Costello

Notes:
1. First Fine Gael / Labour Coalition Government.
2. The Department of the Public Service was established on 1/11/73.
3. Dick Burke was appointed as Ireland's EC Commissioner on 2/12/76.
4. Department of Agriculture & Fisheries became Department of Agriculture from 9/2/77.
5. Department of Lands became Department of Fisheries from 9/2/77.

Twenty First Dail: 5th July 1977 to 21st May 1981

	Fifteenth Government 5th July 1977 to 11th Dec 1979	Sixteenth Government 11th Dec 1979 to 30th June 1981
Taoiseach	Jack Lynch (resigned 11/12/79)	Charles J. Haughey
Tánaiste	George Colley	George Colley
Finance	George Colley	Michael O'Kennedy (resigned 16/12/80)
Finance		Gene Fitzgerald (from 16/12/80)
Public Service	George Colley	Michael O'Kennedy (to 24/3/80)
Public Service		Gene Fitzgerald (from 24/3/80)
Health & Social Welfare	Charles J. Haughey	Michael Woods
Fisheries & Forestry	Brian Lenihan	Patrick Power
Posts & Telegraphs	Padraig Faulkner	Albert Reynolds
Tourism & Transport	Padraig Faulkner	George Colley (to 25/1/80)
Transport		Albert Reynolds (from 25/1/80)
Agriculture	James Gibbons	Ray McSharry
Industry Commerce & Energy	Desmond O'Malley	Desmond O'Malley (to 23/1/80)
Industry Commerce & Tourism		Desmond O'Malley (from 23/1/80)
Defence	Bobby Molloy	Padraig Faulkner (resigned 15/10/80)
Defence		Sylvester Barrett (from 15/10/80)
Justice	Gerry Collins	Gerry Collins
Foreign Affairs	Michael O'Kennedy	Brian Lenihan
Environment	Sylvester Barrett	Sylvester Barrett (to 15/10/80)
Environment	Sylvester Barrett	Ray Burke (from 15/10/80)
Labour	Gene Fitzgerald	Gene Fitzgerald (to 16/12/80)
Labour		Tom Nolan (from 16/12/80)
Gaeltacht	Denis Gallagher	Maire Geoghegan-Quinn
Education	John Wilson	John Wilson
Economic Planning & Development	Martin O'Donoghue	Michael O'Kennedy (to 21/1/80)
Energy		George Colley (from 21/1/80)
Chief Whip	Patrick J. Lalor (to 1/7/79)	
Chief Whip	Michael Woods (from 1/7/79)	Sean Moore
Attorney-General	A. J. Hederman	A. J. Hederman

Notes:

1. Single-party Fianna Fail Government.
2. Jack Lynch retired from politics on 11/12/79 and was succeeded by Charles J. Haughey and Fianna Fail continued in office as there was no need for a General Election.
3. New Department of Economic Planning & Development established on 13/7/77.
4. Department of Local Government became Department of Environment on 16/8/77.
5. Department of Transport & Power became Department of Tourism & Transport on 23/9/77.
6. Department of Industry & Commerce became Department of Industry Commerce & Energy on 23/9/77.
7. Michael O'Kennedy was appointed as Ireland's EC Commissioner on 16/12/80.
8. Department of Industry Commerce & Energy became Department of Industry Commerce & Tourism on 23/1/80.
9. Department of Economic Planning & Development functions transferred to Energy on 21/1/80.
10. Department of Tourism & Transport became Department of Transport on 25/1/80.

Twenty Second Dail: 30th June 1981 to 27th January 1982

Seventeenth Government	**30th June 1981 to 9th Mar 1982**
Taoiseach	Garret Fitzgerald (FG)
Tánaiste	Michael O'Leary (LB)
Energy	Michael O'Leary (LB)
Environment	Peter Barry (FG)
Defence	James Tully (LB)
Fisheries & Forestry	Tom Fitzpatrick (FG)
Health & Social Welfare	Eileen Desmond (LB)
Finance	John Bruton (FG)
Labour & Public Service	Liam Kavanagh (LB)
Transport & Posts & Telegraphs	Patrick Cooney (FG)
Industry Commerce & Tourism	John Kelly (FG)
Foreign Affairs	John Kelly (FG) (to 21/10/81)
Foreign Affairs	Senator James Dooge (FG) (from 21/10/81)
Education	John Boland (FG)
Gaeltacht	Paddy O'Toole (FG)
Justice	Jim Mitchell (FG)
Agriculture	Alan Dukes (FG)
Chief Whip	Gerry L'Estrange (FG)
Attorney-General	A. J. Hederman

Notes:

1. Fine Gael / Labour Coalition Government.
2. Senator James Doodge was not appointed Minister for Foreign Affairs until after the Seanad Elections, which do not take place until after the new Dail has met and a Government has been appointed. John Kelly held the post of Minister for Foreign Affairs pending Mr. Dooge's appointment.
3. Department of Energy became Department of Industry & Energy on 21/8/81.
4. Department of Industry, Commerce & Tourism became Department of Trade, Commerce & Tourism on 21/8/81.

Twenty Third Dail: 9th March 1982 to 14th December 1982

Eighteenth Government	**9th Mar 1982 to 14th Dec 1982**
Taoiseach	Charles J. Haughey
Tánaiste	Ray McSharry
Finance	Ray McSharry
Agriculture	Brian Lenihan
Trade Commerce & Tourism	Desmond O'Malley (resigned 6/10/82)
Trade Commerce & Tourism	Padraig Flynn (from 27/10/82)
Foreign Affairs	Gerry Collins
Labour & Public Service	Gene Fitzgerald
Transport & Posts & Telegraphs	John Wilson
Education	M. O'Donoghue (resigned 6/10/82)
Education	Gerard Brady (from 27/10/82)
Health & Social Welfare	Michael Woods
Defence	Patrick Power
Industry & Energy	Albert Reynolds
Environment	Ray Burke
Fisheries & Forestry	Brendan Daly
Justice	Sean Doherty
Gaeltacht	Padraig Flynn (to 27/10/82)
Gaeltacht	Denis Gallagher (from 27/10/82)
Chief Whip	Bertie Ahern
Attorney-General	Patrick Connolly

Notes:

1. Single-party Fianna Fail Government.
2. Charles J. Haughey and Albert Reynolds acted as Ministers for Education and Trade Commerce & Tourism respectively, from 6th to 27th Oct 1982, following the resignations of Desmond O'Malley and Martin O'Donoghue, until new appointments were made.

Twenty Fourth Dail: 14th December 1982 to 21st January 1987

Nineteenth Government	**14th Dec 1982 to 10th Mar 1987**
Taoiseach	Garret Fitzgerald (FG)
Tánaiste	Dick Spring (LB) (resigned 20/1/87)
Environment	Dick Spring (LB) (to 13/12/83)
Environment	Liam Kavanagh (LB) (to 14/2/86)
Environment	John Boland (FG) (from 14/2/86)
Foreign Affairs	Peter Barry (FG)
Industry & Energy	John Bruton (FG) (to 13/12/83)
Energy	Dick Spring (LB) (from 13/12/83)
Labour	Liam Kavanagh (LB) (to 13/12/83)
Labour	Ruairi Quinn (LB) (from 13/12/83)
Defence	Patrick Cooney (FG) (to 14/2/86)
Defence	Paddy O'Toole (FG) (from 14/2/86)
Public Service	John Boland (FG) (to 14/2/86)
Public Service	Ruairi Quinn (LB) (from 14/2/86)
Fisheries & Forestry	Paddy O'Toole (FG) (to 14/2/86)
Tourism Fisheries & Forestry	Liam Kavanagh (LB) (from 14/2/86)
Gaeltacht	Paddy O'Toole (FG)
Transport & Posts & Telegraphs	Jim Mitchell (FG)
Communications	Jim Mitchell (FG) (from 2/1/84)
Finance	Alan Dukes (FG) (to 14/2/86)
Finance	John Bruton (FG) (from 14/2/86)
Trade Commerce & Tourism	Frank Cluskey (LB) (resigned 8/12/83)
Industry Trade Commerce & Tourism	John Bruton (FG) (to 14/2/86)
Industry & Commerce	Michael Noonan (FG) (from 14/2/86)
Health	Barry Desmond (LB) (to 20/1/87)
Social Welfare	Barry Desmond (LB) (to 14/2/86)
Social Welfare	Gemma Hussey (FG) (from 14/2/86)
Agriculture	Austin Deasy (FG)
Justice	Michael Noonan (FG) (to 14/2/86)
Justice	Alan Dukes (FG) (from 14/2/86)
Education	Gemma Hussey (FG) (to 14/2/86)
Education	Patrick Cooney (FG) (from 14/2/86)
Chief Whip	Sean Barrett (FG) (to 13/2/86)
Chief Whip	Fergus O'Brien (FG) (from 13/2/86)
Attorney-General	Peter Sutherland (to 1986)
Attorney-General	John Rogers

Notes:
1. Fine Gael / Labour Coalition Government.
2. Frank Cluskey's resignation of 13/12/83 resulted in Government re-shuffle.
3. A second re-shuffle took place on 14/2/86.
4. The Labour members resigned from the Government on 20/1/87 and their portfolios were re-assigned to serving Fine Gael Ministers.
5. Department of Industry & Energy became Department of Energy on 17/12/83.
6. Department of Trade, Commerce & Tourism became Dept. of Industry, Trade, Commerce & Tourism on 17/12/83.
7. New Department of Communications established on 2/1/84 to replace Transport & Power.
8. Department of Fisheries & Forestry became Department of Tourism Fisheries & Forestry on 19/2/86.
9. Department of Industry, Trade, Commerce & Tourism became Department of Industry & Commerce on 19/2/86.

Twenty Fifth Dail: 10th March 1987 to 25th May 1989

Twentieth Government	**10th Mar 1987 to 12th July 1989**
Taoiseach	Charles J. Haughey
Gaeltacht	Charles J. Haughey
Tánaiste	Brian Lenihan
Foreign Affairs	Brian Lenihan
Finance	Ray McSharry (to 24/11/88)
Finance	Albert Reynolds (from 24/11/88)
Justice	Gerry Collins
Communications	John Wilson (to 31/3/87)
Communications	Ray Burke (from 31/3/87)
Public Service	Ray McSharry (to 20/3/87)
Tourism & Transport	Ray McSharry (20/3/87 to 31/3/87)
Tourism & Transport	John Wilson (from 31/3/87)
Agriculture & Food	Michael O'Kennedy
Social Welfare	Michael Woods
Industry & Commerce	Albert Reynolds (to 24/11/88)
Industry & Commerce	Ray Burke (from 24/11/88)
Energy	Ray Burke (to 24/11/88)
Energy	Michael Smith (from 24/11/88)
Marine	Brendan Daly
Environment	Padraig Flynn
Labour	Bertie Ahern
Health	Rory O'Hanlon
Defence	Michael J. Noonan
Education	Mary O'Rourke
Energy & Communications	Ray Burke (FF)
Chief Whip	Vincent Brady (FF)
Attorney-General	John Murray

Notes:

1. Single-party Fianna Fail Government.
2. Department of Public Service became Department of Tourism & Transport on 20/3/87.
3. Department of Tourism Fisheries & Forestry became Department of Marine on 20/3/87.
4. Department of Agriculture became Department of Agriculture & Food on 31/3/87.
5. Ray McSharry was appointed as Ireland's EC Commissioner on 24/11/88.

Twenty Sixth Dail: 12th July 1989 to 5th November 1992

	Twenty First Government 12th July 1989 to 11th Feb 1992	Twenty Second Government 11th Feb 1992 to 12th Jan 1993
Taoiseach	Charles J. Haughey	Albert Reynolds
Tánaiste	Brian Lenihan (dismissed 31/10/90)	
Tánaiste	John Wilson (from 13/11/90)	John Wilson
Gaeltacht	Charles J. Haughey	John Wilson
Defence	Brian Lenihan (dismissed 31/10/90)	John Wilson
Defence	Brendan Daly (5/2/91 to 14/11/91)	
Defence	Vincent Brady (from 14/11/91)	
Marine	John Wilson	Michael Woods
Finance	Albert Reynolds (dismissed 7/11/91)	Bertie Ahern
Finance	Bertie Ahern (from 14/11/91)	
Labour	Bertie Ahern (to 14/11/91)	Brian Cowen
Labour	Michael O'Kennedy (from 14/11/91)	
Foreign Affairs	Gerry Collins	David Andrews
Agriculture & Food	Michael O'Kennedy (to 14/11/91)	
Agriculture & Food	Michael Woods (from 14/11/91)	Joe Walsh
Social Welfare	Michael Woods (to 14/11/91)	
Social Welfare	Brendan Daly (from 14/11/91)	Charlie McCreevy
Industry & Commerce	Desmond O'Malley (PD)	Desmond O'Malley (PD) (resigned 4/11/92)
Industry & Commerce		Padraig Flynn (5/11/92 to 4/1/93)
Energy	Bobby Molloy (PD)	Bobby Molloy (PD) (resigned 4/11/92)
Energy		Albert Reynolds (from 4/11/92)
Justice	Ray Burke	Padraig Flynn (resigned 4/1/93)
Communications	Ray Burke (to 6/2/91)	
Environment	Padraig Flynn (dismissed 8/11/91)	
Environment	Rory O'Hanlon (from 14/11/91)	Michael Smith
Health	Rory O'Hanlon (to 14/11/91)	
Health	Mary O'Rourke (from 14/11/91)	John O'Connell
Education	Mary O'Rourke (to 14/11/91)	
Education	Noel Davern (from 14/11/91)	Seamus Brennan
Tourism & Transport	Seamus Brennan (to 6/2/91)	
Tourism Transport & Communications	Seamus Brennan (from 6/2/91)	Maire Geoghegan Quinn
Chief Whip	Vincent Brady (to 14/11/91)	
Chief Whip	Dermot Ahern (from 14/11/91)	Noel Dempsey
Attorney-General	John Murray	Harry Whelehan

Notes:

1. First Fianna Fail / Progressive Democrats Coalition Government.
2. Charles J. Haughey retired from politics on 11/2/92 and was succeeded by Albert Reynolds and the Fianna Fail/Progressive Democrats Coalition continued in Government.
3. Department of Tourism & Transport amalgamated with Department of Communications to became Department of Tourism, Transport & Communications from 6/2/91.
4. PD Ministers resigned on 17/11/94 and portfolios re-assigned to serving Ministers and the Government continued until it lost a "confidence" vote in the Dail and a General Election ensued.
5. Padraig Flynn was appointed as Ireland's EC Commissioner on 6/1/93.

Twenty Seventh Dail: 14th December 1992 to 15th May 1997

	Twenty Third Government 12th Jan 1993 to 15th Dec 1994	Twenty Fourth Government 15th Dec 1994 to 26th June 1997
Taoiseach	Albert Reynolds (FF)	John Bruton (FG)
Tánaiste	Dick Spring (LB) (to 17/11/94)	Dick Spring (LB)
Tánaiste	Bertie Ahern (from 19/11/94)	
Foreign Affairs	Dick Spring (LB) (to 17/11/94)	
Foreign Affairs	Albert Reynolds (from 18/11/94)	Dick Spring (LB)
Finance	Bertie Ahern (FF)	Ruairi Quinn (LB)
Justice	Maire Geoghegan Quinn (FF)	Nora Owen (FG)
Enterprise & Employment	Ruairi Quinn (LB) (to 17/11/94)	
Enterprise & Employment	Charlie McCreevy (from 18/11/94)	Richard Bruton (FG)
Environment	Michael Smith (FF)	Brendan Howlin (LB)
Defence & The Marine	David Andrews (FF)	Hugh Coveney (FG) (to 23/5/95)
Defence & The Marine		Sean Barrett (FG) (from 23/5/95)
Agriculture Food & Forestry	Joe Walsh (FF)	Ivan Yates (FG)
Tourism Transport & Communications	Charlie McCreevy (FF) (to 22/1/93)	
Tourism & Trade	Charlie McCreevy (from 22/1/93)	Enda Kenny (FG)
Energy	Brian Cowen (FF) (to 22/1/93)	
Transport Energy & Communications	Brian Cowen (FF) (from 22/1/93)	Michael Lowry (FG) (to 30/11/96)
Transport Energy & Communications		Alan Dukes (FG) (from 30/11/96)
Equality & Law Reform	Mervyn Taylor (LB) (to 17/11/94)	Mervyn Taylor (LB)
Equality & Law Reform	Maire Geoghegan Quinn (from 18/11/94)	
Arts Culture & The Gaeltacht	Michael D. Higgins (LB) (to 17/11/94)	Michael D. Higgins (LB)
Arts Culture & The Gaeltacht	Bertie Ahern (from 18/11/94)	
Health	Brendan Howlin (LB) (to 17/11/94)	Michael Noonan (FG)
Health	Michael Woods (from 18/11/94)	
Social Welfare	Michael Woods (FF)	Proinsias De Rossa (DL)
Education	Niamh Bhreathnach (LB) (to 17/11/94)	Niamh Bhreathnach (LB)
Education	Michael Smith (from 18/11/94)	
Minister of State to the Government		Pat Rabbitte (DL)
Chief Whip	Noel Dempsey (FF)	Sean Barrett (FG) (to 23/5/95)
Chief Whip		Jim Higgins (FG) (from 23/5/95)
Attorney-General	Harry Whelehan	Dermot Gleeson

Notes:

1. First Fianna Fail / Labour Coalition Government.
2. Labour Ministers resigned on 17/11/94 and portfolios re-assigned to serving Ministers.
3. Change of Government on 15/12/94 without dissolution of Dail and "Rainbow Coalition" of Fine Gael, Labour and Democratic Left formed.
4. Department of Agriculture & Food changed to Department of Agriculture, Food & Forestry from 21/1/93.
5. Department of Energy changed to Department of Tourism & Trade from 22/1/93.
6. Department of Industry & Commerce changed to Department of Enterprise & Employment from 21/1/93.
7. Department of Labour changed to Department of Equality & Law Reform from 21/1/93.
8. Department of the Gaeltacht changed to Department of Arts, Culture & the Gaeltacht from 21/1/93.
9. Michael Lowry resigned 30/11/96 and was replaced by Alan Dukes.
10. Hugh Coveney resigned 23/5/95 and was replaced by Sean Barrett.
11. Minister of State Rabbitte while not a member of Cabinet was allowed to attend Cabinet meetings (referred to as a "Super Junior").

Twenty Eighth Dail: 26th June 1997 to 25th April 2002

Twenty Fifth Government	**26th June 1997 to 6th June 2002**
Taoiseach	Bertie Ahern (FF)
Tánaiste	Mary Harney (PD)
Enterprise Trade & Employment	Mary Harney (PD)
Finance	Charlie McCreevy (FF)
Foreign Affairs	Ray Burke (FF) (to 7/10/97)
Foreign Affairs	David Andrews (FF) (to 27/1/00)
Foreign Affairs	Brian Cowen (FF) (from 26/1/00)
Justice Equality & Law Reform	John O'Donoghue (FF)
Public Enterprise	Mary O'Rourke (FF)
Health & Children	Brian Cowen (FF) (to 26/1/00)
Health & Children	Michael Martin (FF) (from 27/1/00)
Environment	Noel Dempsey (FF)
Education	Michael Martin (FF) (to 27/1/00)
Education	Michael Woods (FF) (from 27/1/00)
Agriculture & Food	Joe Walsh (FF)
Social Community & Family Affairs	Dermot Ahern (FF)
Defence	David Andrews (FF) (to 8/10/97)
Defence	Michael Smith (FF) (from 8/10/97)
Arts Heritage Gaeltacht & The Islands	Sile de Valera (FF)
The Marine & Natural Resources	Michael Woods (FF) (to 27/1/00)
The Marine & Natural Resources	Frank Fahey (FF) (from 27/1/00)
Tourism Sport & Recreation	James McDaid (FF)
Minister of State to the Government	Bobby Molloy (PD) (To April 2002)
	Liz O'Donnell (PD) (Since April 2002)
Chief Whip	Seamus Brennan (FF)
Attorney-General	David Byrne (To July 1999)
Attorney-General	Michael McDowell (From July 1999)

Notes:

1. Second Fianna Fail / Progressive Democrats Coalition Government.
2. Ray Burke resigned 7/10/97 and was replaced as Minister for Foreign Affairs by David Andrews, with Michael Smith replacing Andrews at Defence.
3. David Andrews resigned 27/1/00 leading to Cabinet Reshuffle.
4. Minister of State Molloy while not a member of Cabinet was allowed to attend Cabinet meetings. Resigned April 2002.
5. Department of Enterprise & Employment changed to Department of Enterprise, Trade & Employment from 12/7/97.
6. Department of Marine changed to Department of Marine & Natural Resources from 12/7/97.
7. Department of Transport, Energy & Communications changed to Department of Public Enterprise from 12/7/97.
8. Department of Agriculture, Food & Forestry changed to Department of Agriculture & Food from 12/7/97.
9. Department of Agriculture & Food changed to Department of Agriculture, Food & Rural Development from 27/9/99.
10. Department of Health changed to Department of Health & Children from 12/7/97.
11. Department of Environment changed to Department of Environment & Local Government from 12/7/97.
12. Department of Social Welfare changed to Department of Social, Community & Family Affairs from 12/7/97.
13. Department of Arts, Culture & the Gaeltacht changed to Department of Arts, Heritage, Gaeltacht & the Islands.
14. Dept. of Justice & Dept. of Equality & Law Reform changed to Department of Justice, Equality & Law Reform.
15. Department of Tourism & Trade changed to Department of Tourism, Sport & Recreation from 12/7/97.
16. Department of Education changed to Department of Education & Science from 30/9/97.

Twenty Ninth Dail: 6th June 2002 to 5th June 2007

Twenty Sixth Government	**6th June 2002 to 14th June 2007**
Taoiseach	Bertie Ahern (FF)
Tánaiste	Mary Harney (PD) (to 13/9/06)
Tánaiste	Michael McDowell (PD) (from 13/9/06)
Finance	Charlie McCreevy (FF) (to 29/9/04)
Finance	Brian Cowen (FF) (from 29/9/04)
Justice Equality & Law Reform	Michael McDowell (PD)
Health & Children	Micheal Martin (FF) (to 29/9/04)
Health & Children	Mary Harney (PD) (from 29/9/04)
Enterprise Trade & Employment	Mary Harney (PD) (to 29/9/04)
Enterprise Trade & Employment	Micheal Martin (FF) (from 29/9/04)
Foreign Affairs	Brian Cowen (FF) (to 29/9/04)
Foreign Affairs	Dermot Ahern (FF) (from 29/9/04)
Environment & Local Government	Martin Cullen (FF) (to 29/9/04)
Environment & Local Government	Dick Roche (FF) (from 29/9/04)
Transport	Seamus Brennan (FF) (to 29/9/04)
Transport	Martin Cullen (FF) (from 29/9/04)
Communications, Marine & Natural Resources	Dermot Ahern (FF) (to 29/9/04)
Communications, Marine & Natural Resources	Noel Dempsey (FF) (from 29/9/04)
Education & Science	Noel Dempsey (FF) (to 29/9/04)
Education & Science	Mary Hanafin (FF) (from 29/9/04)
Agriculture & Food	Joe Walsh (FF) (to 29/9/04)
Agriculture & Food	Mary Coughlan (FF) (from 29/9/04)
Social & Family Affairs	Mary Coughlan (FF) (to 29/9/04)
Social & Family Affairs	Seamus Brennan (FF) (from 29/9/04)
Defence	Michael Smith (FF) (to 29/9/04)
Defence	Willie O'Dea (FF) (from 29/9/04)
Arts, Sport & Tourism	John O'Donoghue (FF)
Community, Rural & Family Affairs	Eamon O Cuiv (FF)
Chief Whip	Mary Hanafin (FF) (to 29/9/04)
Chief Whip	Tom Kitt (FF) (from 29/9/04)
Attorney-General	Rory Brady SC

Notes:

1. Third Fianna Fail / Progressive Democrats Coalition Government.
2. Department of Agriculture, Food & Rural Development changed to Department of Agriculture & Food.
3. Department of Marine & Natural Resources changed to Department of Communications, Marine & Natural Resources.
4. Department of Tourism, Sport & Recreation changed to Department of Arts, Sport & Tourism.
5. Department of Public Enterprise changed to Department of Transport.
6. Department of Arts, Heritage, Gaeltacht & the Islands changed to Department of Community, Rural and Family Affairs.
7. Department of Social, Community & Family Affairs changed to Department of Social & Family Affairs.

Thirtieth Dail: 6th June 2007 to 8th March 2011

	Twenty Seventh Government 14th June 2007-7th May 2008	Twenty Eighth Government 7th May 2008 - 23rd March 2010
Taoiseach	Bertie Ahern (FF)	Brian Cowen (FF)
Tánaiste	Brian Cowen (FF)	Mary Coughlan (FF)
Finance	Brian Cowen (FF)	Brian Lenihan (FF)
Justice Equality & Law Reform	Brian Lenihan (FF)	Dermot Ahern (FF)
Health & Children	Mary Harney (PD)	Mary Harney (PD)
Enterprise Trade & Employment	Micheal Martin (FF)	Mary Coughlan (FF)
Foreign Affairs	Dermot Ahern (FF)	Micheal Martin (FF)
Environment, Heritage & Local Government	John Gormley (GP)	John Gormley (GP)
Transport	Noel Dempsey (FF)	Noel Dempsey (FF)
Communications, Energy & Natural Resources	Eamon Ryan (GP)	Eamon Ryan (GP)
Education & Science	Mary Hanafin (FF)	Batt O'Keeffe (FF)
Agriculture, Fisheries & Food	Mary Coughlan (FF)	Brendan Smith (FF)
Social & Family Affairs	Martin Cullen (FF)	Mary Hanafin (FF)
Defence	Willie O'Dea (FF)	Willie O'Dea (FF)
Arts, Sport & Tourism	Seamus Brennan (FF)	Martin Cullen (FF)
Community, Rural & Family Affairs	Eamon O Cuiv (FF)	Eamon O Cuiv (FF)
Chief Whip	Tom Kitt (FF)	Pat Carey (FF)
Attorney-General	Paul Gallagher	Paul Gallagher

Notes:

1. First Fianna Fail /Green Party / Progressive Democrats Coalition Government.
2. Department of Agriculture & Food changed to Department of Agriculture, Fisheries & Food.
3. Department of Communications, Marine & Natural Resources changed to Department of Communications, Energy & Natural Resources.
4. Department of Transport changed to Department of Transport & Marine.
5. Bertie Ahern resigned as Taoiseach 6th May 2008
6. Brian Cowen elected Taoiseach 7th May 2008.

Thirtieth Dail: 6th June 2007 to 8th March 2011

	Twenty Eighth Government 23rd March 2010-23rd Jan. 2011	Twenty Eighth Government 24th January 2011-8th March 2011
Taoiseach	Brian Cowen (FF)	Brian Cowen (FF)
Tánaiste	Mary Coughlan (FF)	Mary Coughlan (FF)
Finance	Brian Lenihan (FF)	Brian Lenihan (FF)
Justice & Law Reform	Dermot Ahern (FF) (to 20/1/2011)	Brendan Smith (FF)
Health & Children	Mary Harney (NP) (to 20/1/2011)	Mary Coughlan (FF)
Enterprise Trade & Innovation	Batt O'Keeffe (FF) (to 20/1/2011)	Mary Coughlan (FF)
Foreign Affairs	Micheal Martin (FF) (to 19/1/2011)	Brian Cowen (FF)
Environment, Heritage & Local Government	John Gormley (GP) (to 23/1/2011)	Eamon O Cuiv (FF)
Transport	Noel Dempsey (FF) (to 20/1/2011)	Pat Carey (FF)
Communications, Energy & Natural Resources	Eamon Ryan (GP) (to 23/1/2011)	Pat Carey (FF)
Education & Skills	Mary Coughlan (FF)	Mary Coughlan (FF)
Agriculture, Fisheries & Food	Brendan Smith (FF)	Brendan Smith (FF)
Social Protection	Eamon O Cuiv (FF)	Eamon O Cuiv (FF)
Defence	Tony Killeen (FF) (to 20/1/2011)	Eamon O Cuiv (FF)
Tourism , Culture & Sport	Mary Hanafin (FF)	Mary Hanafin (FF)
Community, Equality & Gaeltacht Affairs	Pat Carey (FF)	Pat Carey (FF)
Chief Whip	John Curran (FF)	John Curran (FF)
Attorney-General	Paul Gallagher	Paul Gallagher

Notes:

1. Fianna Fail /Green Party / Independent Coalition Government.
2. Willie O'Dea resigned 18th February 2010
3. Martin Cullen resigned 9th March 2010
4. Department of Justice, Equality & Law Reform changed to Department of Justice & Law Reform
5. Department of Enterprise, Trade & Employment changed to Department of Enterprise, Trade & Innovation
6. Department of Transport & Marine changed to Department of Transport
7. Department of Education & Science changed to Department of Education & Skills
8. Department of Social & Family Affairs changed to Department of Social Protection
9. Department of Arts, Sport & Tourism changed to Department of Tourism, Culture & Sport
10. Department of Community, Rural & Family Affairs changed to Department of Community, Equality & Gaeltacht Affairs

Thirty First Dail: 9th March 2011-
Twenty Ninth Government
9th March 2011-

Taoiseach	Enda Kenny (FG)
Tánaiste	Eamon Gilmore (LB)
Finance	Michael Noonan (FG)
Justice, Equality and Defence	Alan Shatter (FG)
Health	James Reilly (FG)
Enterprise Jobs & Innovation	Richard Bruton (FG)
Foreign Affairs and Trade	Eamon Gilmore (LB)
Public Expenditure and Reform	Brendan Howlin (LB)
Environment, Community & Local Government	Phil Hogan (FG)
Transport, Tourism and Sport	Leo Varadkar (FG)
Communications, Energy & Natural Resources	Pat Rabbitte (LB)
Education & Skills	Ruairí Quinn (LB)
Agriculture, Marine & Food	Simon Coveney (FG)
Social Protection	Joan Burton (LB)
Arts, Heritage and Gaeltacht Affairs	Jimmy Deenihan (FG)
Children	Frances Fitzgerald (FG)
Chief Whip	Paul Kehoe (FG)
Attorney-General	Marie Whelan

Notes:

1. Fianna Fail /Labour Coalition Government.
2. New Department of Public Expenditure and Reform
3. Department of Foreign Affairs changed to Department of Foreign Affairs and Trade
4. Department of Justice & Law Reform changed to Department of Justice, Equality and Defence
5. Department of Enterprise, Trade & Innovation changed to Department of Enterprise, Jobs & Innovation
6. Department of Transport changed to Department of Transport, Tourism and Sport
7. Department of Agriculture, Fisheries and Food changed to Department of Agriculture, Marine and Food
8. Department of Tourism, Culture & Sport changed to Department of Arts, Heritage & Gaeltacht Affairs
9. Department of Community, Equality & Gaeltacht Affairs changed to Department of Children
10. Department of Health & Children changed to Department of Health
11. Department of Environment, Heritage & Local Government changed to Department of Environment, Community and Local Government

DID YOU KNOW

1. The 2011 election had the biggest number of retirements to date, 39 which was well above the previous highest 29 in June 1927. This number included the three deputies that had retired earlier but for whom the by-elections had not been held, George Lee (FG Dublin South), Martin Cullen (FF Waterford) and Dr. James McDaid (FF Donegal North East).

2. There was a high rate of attrition in election 2011 with 45 outgoing deputies losing their seats, up 15 on 2007. There were 84 new TD's (49 in 2007) in the 31st Dail, 8 of whom were former deputies.

3. It was all change in Cork South West and Kerry South as all three TDs returned in both three seaters were new members. There were also three new deputies in twelve other constituencies which contrasts sharply with 2007 when only two constituencies Cork South-Central and Dublin North elected three new deputies. With all this change it came as no surprise that not a single constituency returned the same deputies as 2007.

4. A record 566 candidates contested the 2011 general election which was well ahead of the previous high of 484 in 1997.

5. Two constituencies Laois-Offaly and Mayo had the same quota 12,360 in 2011. They also happen to be the home constituencies of the previous and present Taoiseach.

6. The Fianna Fail vote dropped the same amount 29.60 percentage points in two constituencies Dublin Central and Laois Offaly. They also happen to be the home constituencies of the previous two Taoisí.

7. The People Before Profit Alliance won their first two Dáil seats in election 2011 and were joined by two Socialist Party deputies and WUAG leader Seamus Healy to give the United Left Alliance five TD's in the 31st Dáil.

8. Election 2011 promised to be the election of the new parties but some of them never even got to the starting line. In the end New Vision fielded 20 candidates and their only success was Luke "Ming" Flanagan in Roscommon-South Leitrim with most of the others failing to save their expenses. Another New Vision called Fis Nua ran five candidates but all did poorly as did the four who ran for CPPC (An Chaothdhail Phobail/ The People's Convention) in the Cork area.

9. The most predictable constituency: Dublin West.

10. The most surprising constituency: Take your pick.

11. Highest first preference vote per Party:
    Fine Gael: Mayo 64.96% — Labour: Dublin North West 43.15%
    Fianna Fail: Carlow-Kilkenny 28.10% — Sinn Fein: Donegal South West 32.97%

12. Fine Gael got the largest increase in their vote in Dublin Mid-West where their vote was up 19 percentage points. Labour got their best increase of 23 percentage points in Dublin North-West. In contrast Fianna Fail suffered their greatest loss in support in Dublin North-West where their vote was down by 37 percentage points.

13. Fine Gael won a record four out of five seats in Mayo and won three seats in four constituencies. Labour won two seats in six constituencies, all in Dublin. Fianna Fail won two seats in only two constituencies, Cork South-Central, the home of their present leader and Laois-Offaly the home constituency of their previous leader.

13. Fine Gael won a record 76 seats in election 2011, beating their previous best of 70 in November 1982. They gained two seats in three constituencies, Carlow-Kilkenny, Cavan-Monaghan and Dublin Mid-West.

14. Michael Noonan was the leading vote-getter in election 2011 with 1.54 quotas (13,291first preferences) in Limerick City and was followed by Enda Kenny with 1.41(17,472) in Mayo and Shane Ross with 1.41 (17,075) in Dublin South. Kenny's and Ross's first preference vote moved them up to 16th and 21st place on the top vote-getters list to date which is headed by Richard Mulcahy who got 22,005 in 1923.

15. Fine Gael got the best ever seats bonus in election 2011 as they managed to win 45.78% of the seats from just 36.10% of the first preference vote and gained a seat bonus of 16. Labour managed a seat bonus of five but Fianna Fail were again the big losers as they won ten seats less than their first preference vote warranted.

16. A record 25 women were elected in 2011which was up two on the previous best which was achieved in 1992, 2002 and 2007. Six women deputies retired at this election and eight lost their seats. Fourteen women were elected for the first time with two former deputies regaining their seats. Róisín Shortall is the longest serving woman in the 31st Dail with over 19 years service since 1992. Mary Harney is the longest serving woman deputy with 30 years continuous service, having won nine elections from 1981 to 2007. Fourteen of the 92 women elected to Dail Eireann were called Mary.

17. The Government formed in 2011is the fourth Fine Gael/Labour coalition. The 1994-1997 "Rainbow Coalition" was the first between Fine Gael, Labour and Democratic Left and the only one to be formed without a general election. Fianna Fail have been part of 19 of the 29 governments since the foundation of the state and in power on their own on 14 occasions.

18. Enda Kenny is the twelfth Taoiseach and the fifth from Fine Gael. John Bruton was the shortest serving Taoiseach from December 1994 to June 1997.

19. The turnout has been in decline since 1969 but the 2007 election reversed that trend with the turnout up 4.5 points on the previous election in 2002. The 2011 election showed further improvement with the turnout up another three percentage points.

20. Fianna Fail have won a total of 17,536,438 first preference votes or 41.86% since the first PR election in 1922. Fine Gael have aggregated 12,890,666 or 30.77% and Labour's total is 4,828,562 or 11.53%.

21. The 4,618 general election and 127 by-election seats have been held by 1,236 individual TD's with each deputy serving an average four terms.

22. On average the Dail is made up of 72% outgoing TD's, 22% new and 6% former deputies. Limerick West has never returned a former member.

23. Patrick Smith is the longest serving member of Dail Eireann having won 17 elections between 1923 and 1973. Enda Kenny is the longest serving member in the 31st Dail having been first elected at a by-election in 1975 which was caused by the death of his father and his 12 election victories and over 36 years of continuous service to date leaves him in 31st place on the list of longest serving members in Dáil Eireann. Most of the longest serving members in the present Dáil are members of the government, Enda Kenny, Ruairi Quinn (34 years service), Michael Noonan (30), Richard Bruton (30) and Dinny McGinley (30), with Fianna Fail's Willie O'Dea (30) the only exception.

24. Fine Gael got the largest share 29% of all transfers in 2011, down from 31% in 2007. Labour got 18% with Fianna Fail down from 26% in 2007 to 17% and Sinn Fein doubled their 2007 share to 7%.

25. Patrick McCartan TD for Leix-Offaly 1918-1923, contested the Presidential election in 1945. His daughter the late Deirdre Drew was married to Ronnie Drew of the Dubliners. The comedian Brendan O'Carroll's mother Maureen O'Carroll was a Labour Party TD for Dublin North Central from 1954-1957. The actor Don Wycherley's father Florence Wycherley was an Independent Farmer's TD for Cork West from 1957 to 1961.

HOW THE DÁIL IS ELECTED (LOWER HOUSE OF PARLIAMENT)

1. STRUCTURE OF THE DÁIL

The Dáil (Lower House of Parliament) is composed at present of 166 members representing 43 constituencies. The Constitution requires the total membership of the Dáil to be so set that the national average population per member will be between 20,000 and 30,000. The Constitution also requires that the ratio of population to member must, as far as is practicable, be equal in each constituency. No constituency may have less than 3 members. The constituencies must be revised at least once in every twelve years. In practice, constituencies are revised on the publication of the results of each census of population: a census is normally taken every fifth year. An independent Commission draws up a revised scheme of constituencies which is given effect by an Act of the Oireachtas (National Parliament).

2. DURATION OF DÁIL

The maximum life of the Dáil is limited by the Constitution to 7 years but a limit of 5 years has been set by law. The Dáil may be dissolved by the President on the advice of the Taoiseach (Prime Minister) at any time.

3. WHO CAN BE ELECTED?

Every citizen of Ireland over 21 years of age who is not disqualified by the Constitution or by law is eligible to be elected to the Dáil. A member of the Dáil is referred to as Teachta Dála (TD). Persons undergoing a prison sentence in excess of six months, undischarged bankrupts and persons of unsound mind are disqualified for election. Certain occupations are incompatible with membership of the Dáil, for example, members of the judiciary, senior officials of the institutions of the European Union, civil servants, wholetime members of the Defence Forces and Gardaí (police).

4. THE ELECTORAL SYSTEM

Voting at a Dáil election is by secret ballot on the system of proportional representation by means of the single transferable vote. The system enables the elector to indicate his/her first and subsequent choices for the candidates on the ballot paper. The form of ballot paper is prescribed by law.

5. WHO CAN VOTE AT A DÁIL ELECTION?

There are approximately 3.2 million registered electors entitled to vote at Dáil elections.

Every citizen of Ireland and British citizen, over 18 years, whose name appears on the register of electors, is entitled to vote. A register of electors is compiled each year by the county or city council. A draft register is published on 1st November and is displayed for public inspection in public libraries, post offices and other public buildings. Claims for correction to the draft may be made up to 25th November. Claims are adjudicated on by the county registrar who is a legally qualified court officer. An appeal may be made to the Circuit Court against a county registrar's decision. The register of electors comes into force on 15th February. Eligible persons not included in the published register may apply for inclusion in a supplement to the register.

Members of the Garda Síochána (police force), Defence Forces and civil servants (and their spouses) attached to Irish missions abroad and electors living at home who are unable to go in person to vote at a polling station due to a physical illness or physical disability may vote by post. Electors who because the circumstances of their occupation render it unlikely that they will be able to go to their designated polling station on polling day may also apply to have their names entered on the postal voters list. This category includes students who are attending an educational institution in the State on a full time basis, who are registered as electors and are living away from their address of registration for study purposes.

Electors living in a hospital, nursing home or similar institution who are unable to go in person to vote at a polling station due to a physical illness or physical disability may apply to be included on the Special Voters List. A ballot paper is delivered to them at their hospital, nursing home etc. by a special presiding officer, accompanied by a member of the Garda Síochána. Electors with physical disabilities, who have difficulty in gaining access to their local polling station, may be authorised to vote at a more accessible station in the constituency. Otherwise, electors vote in person at their local polling station.

6. GENERAL ELECTIONS

A general election must be held within thirty days after the dissolution of the Dáil. The Clerk of the Dáil issues a writ to the returning officer in each constituency instructing him/her to hold an election of the prescribed number of members. The returning officer is the county registrar or, in Dublin and Cork, the city or county sheriff. The Ceann Comhairle (chairman of the Dáil) is automatically returned without an election unless he/she signifies that he/she does not wish to continue as a member. The latest time for nominating a person as a candidate is 12 noon on the ninth day after the issue of the writs.

The Minister for the Environment appoints the polling day which must be between the 17th and 25th day (excluding Sundays and public holidays) after the issue of the writ. He also appoints the polling period which must consist of at least 12 hours between 8.00 a.m. and 10.30 p.m.

7. THE COUNT

Counting arrangements:

All ballot boxes are taken to a central counting place for each constituency. Agents of the candidates are permitted to attend at the counting place to oversee the counting process. Before the counting of votes begins, the envelopes containing the postal and special voters' ballot papers are opened in the presence of the agents of the candidates and the ballot papers are associated with the other ballot papers for the constituency.

The count commences at 9 a.m. on the day after polling day. Each ballot box is opened and the number of ballot papers checked against a return furnished by each presiding officer. They are then thoroughly mixed and sorted according to the first preferences recorded for each candidate, invalid papers being rejected.

Quota: The quota is the minimum number of votes necessary to guarantee the election of a candidate. It is ascertained by dividing the total number of valid ballot papers by one more than the number of seats to be filled and adding one to the result. Thus, if there were 40,000 valid papers and 4 seats to be filled, the quota would be 8,001, i.e.

40,000/ (4 + 1) +1.

It will be seen that in this example only four candidates (the number to be elected) could possibly reach the quota.

Transfer of Surplus: At the end of the first count any candidate who has received a number of votes equal to or greater than the quota is deemed to be elected. If a candidate receives more than the quota, the surplus votes are transferred proportionately to the remaining candidates in the following way. If the candidate's votes are all first preference votes, all his/her ballot papers are sorted into separate parcels according to the next preference shown on them. A separate parcel is made of the non-transferable papers (papers on which an effective subsequent preference is not shown). If the surplus is equal to or greater than the number of transferable votes, each remaining candidate will receive all the votes from the appropriate parcel of transferable papers. If the surplus is less than the number of transferable papers each remaining candidate will receive from the appropriate parcel of transferable papers a number of votes calculated as follows:-

$$\frac{\text{surplus x number of papers in parcel}}{\text{(Total number of transferable papers)}}$$

If the surplus arises out of transferred papers, only the papers in the parcel last transferred to that candidate are examined and this parcel is then treated in the same way as a surplus consisting of first preference votes. If two or more candidates exceed the quota, the larger surplus is distributed first.

Elimination of Candidate: If no candidate has a surplus or the surplus is insufficient to elect one of the remaining candidates or materially affect the progress of the count, the lowest of the remaining candidates is eliminated and his/her papers are transferred to remaining candidates accordingly to the next preference indicated on them. If a ballot paper is to be transferred and the second preference shown on it is for a candidate already elected or eliminated, the vote passes to the third choice and so on.

Completion of Counting: Counting continues until all the seats have been filled. If the position is reached where the number of seats left to be filled is equal to the number of candidates still in the running, these candidates are declared elected without having obtained the quota.

Recount: A returning officer may recount all or any of the papers at any stage of a count. A candidate or the election agent of a candidate is entitled to ask for a recount of the papers dealt with at a particular count or to ask for one complete recount of all the parcels of ballot papers. When recounting, the order of the papers must not be disturbed. When a significant error is discovered, the papers must be counted afresh from the point at which the error occurred.

Results: When the count is completed, the returning officer declares the results of the election, endorses the names of the elected members on the writ issued to him/her by the Clerk of the Dáil and returns the writ.

8. BYE-ELECTIONS

Casual vacancies in the membership of the Dáil are filled by bye-elections. On the instruction of the Dáil, the Clerk issues a writ to the returning officer for the constituency concerned directing the holding of a bye-election to fill the vacancy. Procedure at a bye-election is the same as at a general election.

9. ELECTORAL LAW

The law relating to the election of members to the Dáil is contained in Article 16 of the Constitution of Ireland, the Electoral Act, 1992, the Electoral (Amendment) Act, 1995, the Electoral (Amendment) Act, 1996 and the Electoral Act, 1997. These publications are available from the Government Publications Sale Office, Sun Alliance House, Molesworth Street, Dublin 2.

PART 4

BY-ELECTIONS 1923-2011

BY-ELECTIONS 1923-2011

There have been 127 by-elections to date with three of them taking place during the lifetime of the 30th Dail.

Of the 127 TD's elected in by-elections, 22 of them (17%) were never subsequently re-elected. This trend was reversed in the 2002 general election with all six by-election winners retaining their seats. George Lee won a by-election in Dublin South during the lifetime of the 30th Dail but resigned a few months later and the by-election was not held. By-elections were also not held in Donegal North-East (James McDaid) and Waterford (Martin Cullen). 14 members of the 31st Dail were elected in by-elections from Enda Kenny in 1975 to Patrick Nulty in 2011.

Most by-elections were caused by the death of a sitting member but some have been due to the resignation or disqualification of a member. The by-elections in 1925 were due to the resignation of 9 Cumann Na nGaedheal TD's over the government's handling of the army mutiny.

Sixty one (48%) of the by-elections have seen the failure of the outgoing party to retain its seat. This trend was repeated during the last Dail when Fianna Fail failed to retain Seamus Brennan's seat in Dublin South or Pat the Cope Gallagher's in Donegal South-West. They also lost their only seat in Dublin in the recent by-election in Dublin West.

Patrick McGilligan achieved the largest first preference vote in a by-election when taking 76.49% of the vote in 1923. Three other winning candidates have taken over 70% of the first preference vote with the most recent being Patrick Shanahan in 1945. Catherine Murphy's share of the first preference vote of 23.64% in Kildare North in 2005 was the third lowest ever by a winning candidate in a by-election. The lowest winning vote at a single seat by-election, was by Patrick Kinane who won 21.44%, in Tipperary in 1947 (Samuel Holt got just 20.25% in Leitrim-Sligo in 1925 but there were two seats on offer at that by-election).

Samuel Holt won a by-election in Leitrim-Sligo in 1925 but his death gave rise to a by-election in 1926 (won by General Sean MacEoin). Similarly William Norton of Labour won a by-election in Dublin County in 1926 and his death subsequently gave rise to a by-election in 1964 in Kildare. T. F. O'Higgins (senior) was also elected at a by-election in 1929 and his death gave rise to a by-election in 1954. Hugh Coveney won a by-election in 1994 but his death gave rise to another one in 1998. Brian Lenihan jnr. was first elected at a by-election in 1996 and his death caused the most recent by-election in Dublin West. Thomas Hennessy is the only candidate to win two by-elections - Dublin South in 1925 and 1927.

The turnout for the 1999 by-election in Dublin South-Central was the lowest ever with the valid poll of 27.88% eclipsing the previous lowest of 28.29% in 1945 in Dublin North-West. But low turnouts at by-elections are not unusual as Wm. Norton was elected in Dublin County in 1926 with a valid poll of just 34.25% of which he got a higher percentage, 35.69%. The average turnout for by-elections is about 10 points below the general election figure with the average valid poll at 60.39% compared to 70.71% for General Elections.

BY-ELECTIONS 1923 - 2011								
No.	Constituency	Date	Outgoing	Party	Winner	Party	% Vote	Valid %
1	Dublin South	25-Oct-23	Michael Hayes	CG	Hugh Kennedy**	CG	67.30%	45.09%
2	NUI	3-Nov-23	Prof. Eoin MacNeill	CG	Patrick McGilligan	CG	76.49%	70.84%
3	Dublin South	12-Mar-24	Philip Cosgrave*	CG	James O'Meara**	CG	48.95%	42.21%
4	Dublin County	19-Mar-24	James Derham*	CG	Batt O'Connor	CG	39.03%	42.94%
5	Limerick	28-May-24	Richard Hayes	CG	Richard O'Connell	CG	54.33%	65.80%
6	Cork East	18-Nov-24	Thomas O'Mahony*	CG	Michael Noonan**	CG	58.83%	56.03%
7	Dublin South	18-Nov-24	Hugh Kennedy	CG	Sean Lemass	R	51.42%	42.75%
8	Mayo North	18-Nov-24	Henry Coyle	CG	John Madden	R	51.53%	61.53%
9	Cork Borough	19-Nov-24	Alfred O'Rahilly	CG	Michael Egan	CG	64.76%	64.26%
10	Donegal	20-Nov-24	Peter Ward	CG	Denis McCullough**	CG	57.56%	44.73%
11	Carlow-Kilkenny	11-Mar-25	Sean Gibbons	CG	Thomas Bolger**	CG	58.92%	64.92%
12	Cavan	11-Mar-25	Sean Milroy	CG	John O'Reilly	CG	38.51%	59.94%
13	Dublin North	11-Mar-25	Frank Cahill	CG	Patrick Leonard	CG	34.78%	55.20%
14	Dublin North	11-Mar-25	Sean McGarry	CG	Oscar Traynor	R	31.30%	55.20%
15	Dublin South	11-Mar-25	Daniel McCarthy	CG	Thomas Hennessy	CG	57.03%	53.87%
16	Leitrim-Sligo	11-Mar-25	Thomas Carter	CG	Samuel Holt	R	20.25%	62.70%
17	Leitrim-Sligo	11-Mar-25	Alex McCabe	CG	Martin Roddy	CG	32.87%	62.70%
18	Mayo North	11-Mar-25	Joseph McGrath	CG	Michael Tierney	CG	57.74%	69.02%
19	Roscommon	11-Mar-25	Henry Finlay	CG	Martin Conlon	CG	61.16%	65.23%
20	Dublin County	18-Feb-26	Darrell Figgis*	NP	William Norton	LB	35.69%	33.66%
21	Laois-Offaly	18-Feb-26	John McGuinness	R	James Dwyer	CG	40.33%	64.18%
22	Dublin South	24-Aug-27	Constance Markievicz*	FF	Thomas Hennessy	CG	54.99%	54.11%
23	Dublin County	24-Aug-27	Kevin O'Higgins*	CG	Gearoid O'Sullivan	CG	69.60%	51.81%
24	Carlow-Kilkenny	3-Nov-27	W. T. Cosgrave	CG	Denis Gorey	CG	50.30%	74.11%
25	Dublin North	3-Apr-28	James Larkin	IWL	Vincent Rice	CG	50.20%	45.86%
26	Dublin North	14-Mar-29	Alfie Byrne	NP	Thomas F. O'Higgins	CG	50.13%	58.65%
27	Leitrim-Sligo	7-Jun-29	Samuel Holt*	FF	Gen. Sean MacEoin	CG	53.74%	73.33%
28	Longford-Westmeath	13-Jun-30	James Killane*	FF	James Geoghegan	FF	53.57%	72.86%
29	Dublin County	9-Dec-30	Bryan Cooper*	CG	Thomas Finlay	CG	70.18%	44.49%
30	Kildare	29-Jun-31	Hugh Colohan*	LB	Thomas Harris	FF	40.03%	64.62%
31	Dublin University	13-Oct-33	Sir James Craig*	NP	Dr. Robert Rowlette**	NP	No Contest	
32	Dublin County	17-Jun-35	Batt O'Connor*	FG	Cecil Lavery	FG	57.22%	59.52%
33	Galway	19-Jun-35	Martin McDonagh*	FG	Eamon Corbett	FF	60.83%	62.98%
34	Galway	13-Aug-36	Patrick Hogan*	FG	Martin Neilan**	FF	60.63%	67.47%
35	Wexford	17-Aug-36	Osmond Esmonde*	FG	Denis Allen	FF	51.04%	79.00%
36	Dublin South	6-Jun-39	James Beckett*	FG	John McCann	FF	55.82%	44.39%
37	Galway West	30-May-40	Sean Turbridy	FF	John J. Keane**	FF	72.12%	47.74%
38	Kerry South	10-Nov-44	Fionan Lynch	FG	Donal O'Donoghue**	FF	48.60%	62.88%
39	Clare	4-Dec-45	Patrick Burke*	FG	Patrick Shanahan**	FF	72.17%	48.90%
40	Dublin North West	4-Dec-45	Sean T. O'Kelly	FF	Vivion de Valera	FF	67.85%	28.29%
41	Kerry South	4-Dec-45	Frederick Crowley*	FF	Honor Mary Crowley	FF	56.66%	51.47%
42	Mayo South	4-Dec-45	Michael Clery	FF	Bernard Commons	CT	53.32%	53.96%
43	Wexford	4-Dec-45	Richard Corish*	LB	Brendan Corish	LB	50.23%	54.27%
44	Cork Borough	14-Jun-46	William Dwyer	NP	Pa McGrath	FF	47.92%	55.38%
45	Dublin County	29-Oct-47	Patrick Fogarty*	FF	Sean MacBride	CnaP	28.43%	53.67%
46	Tipperary	29-Oct-47	William O'Donnell*	CT	Patrick Kinane	CnaP	21.44%	65.97%
47	Waterford	29-Oct-47	Michael Morrissey*	FF	John Ormonde	FF	36.75%	63.17%
48	Donegal East	7-Dec-48	Neil Blaney*	FF	Neil T. Blaney	FF	55.53%	73.15%
49	Cork West	15-Jun-49	Timothy Murphy*	LB	William Murphy**	LB	63.33%	81.56%
50	Donegal West	16-Nov-49	Brian Brady*	FF	Patrick O'Donnell	FG	42.05%	71.30%
51	Limerick East	26-Jun-52	Daniel Bourke*	FF	John Carew	FG	34.24%	78.69%
52	Mayo North	26-Jun-52	Patrick Ruttledge*	FF	Phelim Calleary	FF	48.29%	67.47%
53	Waterford	26-Jun-52	Bridget Redmond*	FG	William Kenneally	FF	45.15%	76.79%
54	Dublin North West	12-Nov-52	Alfred Byrne*	NP	Thomas Byrne	NP	61.11%	62.06%
55	Cork East	18-Jun-53	Sean Keane*	LB	Richard Barry	FG	42.77%	78.86%
56	Wicklow	18-Jun-53	Thomas Brennan*	FF	Mark Deering	FG	23.06%	74.45%
57	Galway South	21-Aug-53	Frank Fahy*	FF	Robert Lahiffe	FF	54.50%	83.29%
58	Cork Borough	3-Mar-54	T. F. O'Higgins (Sen.)*	FG	Stephan Barrett	FG	44.31%	61.76%
59	Louth	3-Mar-54	James Coburn*	FG	George Coburn	FG	43.34%	73.35%
60	Limerick West	13-Dec-55	David Madden*	FG	Michael Colbert	FF	56.21%	80.69%
61	Kerry North	29-Feb-56	John Connor*	CnaP	Kathleen O'Connor**	CnaP	53.45%	74.18%
62	Dublin North East	30-Apr-56	Alfred Byrne*	NP	Patrick Byrne	NP	56.51%	49.43%
63	Leix - Offaly	30-Apr-56	William Davin*	LB	Kieran Egan	FF	55.54%	71.82%
64	Cork Borough	2-Aug-56	Patrick McGrath*	FF	John Galvin	FF	52.59%	56.02%

No.	Constituency	Date	Outgoing	Party	Winner	Party	% Vote	Valid %
			BY-ELECTIONS 1923 - 2011					
65	Carlow-Kilkenny	14-Nov-56	Thomas Walsh*	FF	Martin Medlar	FF	57.79%	70.69%
66	Dublin South West	14-Nov-56	Peadar Doyle*	FG	Noel Lemass	FF	59.82%	38.08%
67	Dublin North Central	14-Nov-57	Colm Gallagher*	FF	Frank Sherwin	NP	33.37%	45.42%
68	Galway South	30-May-58	Patrick Beegan*	FF	Anthony Millar	FF	53.54%	75.59%
69	Dublin South Central	25-Jun-58	John Murphy	NP	Patrick Cummins	FF	34.20%	34.10%
70	Clare	22-Jul-59	Eamon de Valera	FF	Sean O Ceallaigh	FF	56.05%	68.58%
71	Dublin South West	22-Jul-59	Bernard Butler*	FF	Richie Ryan	FG	26.12%	40.03%
72	Meath	22-Jul-59	James Griffin*	FF	Henry Johnston**	FF	43.18%	67.99%
73	Carlow-Kilkenny	23-Jun-60	Joseph Hughes*	FG	Patrick Teehan**	FF	40.74%	68.19%
74	Sligo - Leitrim	1-Mar-61	Stephen Flynn*	FF	Joseph McLoughlin	FG	52.00%	58.09%
75	Dublin North East	30-May-63	Jack Belton*	FG	Patrick Belton	FG	41.64%	57.29%
76	Cork Borough	19-Feb-64	John Galvin*	FF	Sheila Galvin**	FF	53.29%	69.08%
77	Kildare	19-Feb-64	William Norton*	LB	Terence Boylan	FF	43.53%	72.97%
78	Roscommon	8-Jul-64	James Burke*	FG	Joan Burke	FG	49.70%	78.02%
79	Galway East	3-Dec-64	Michael Donnellan*	CT	John Donnellan	FG	49.78%	78.09%
80	Cork Mid	10-Mar-65	Daniel Desmond*	LB	Eileen Desmond	LB	33.49%	75.82%
81	Kerry South	7-Dec-66	Honor Mary Crowley*	FF	John O'Leary	FF	45.91%	75.97%
82	Waterford	7-Dec-66	Thaddeus Lynch*	FG	Patrick Browne	FF	42.62%	77.28%
83	Cork Borough	9-Nov-67	Sean Casey*	LB	Sean French	FF	47.07%	66.29%
84	Limerick West	9-Nov-67	James Collins*	FF	Gerard Collins	FF	53.94%	80.92%
85	Clare	14-Mar-68	William Murphy*	FG	Sylvester Barrett	FF	58.72%	67.39%
86	Wicklow	14-Mar-68	James Everett*	LB	Godfrey Timmins	FG	30.78%	71.20%
87	Limerick East	22-May-68	Donogh O'Malley*	FF	Desmond O'Malley	FF	43.74%	81.28%
88	Dublin South West	4-Mar-70	Sean Dunne*	LB	Sean Sherwin**	FF	32.97%	57.23%
89	Kildare	14-Apr-70	Gerard Sweetman*	FG	Patrick Malone	FG	35.89%	71.69%
90	Longford-Westmeath	14-Apr-70	Patrick Lenihan*	FF	Patrick Cooney	FG	46.73%	75.19%
91	Donegal - Leitrim	2-Dec-70	Patrick O'Donnell*	FG	Patrick Delap**	FF	53.00%	75.68%
92	Dublin County South	2-Dec-70	Kevin Boland	FF	Lawrence McMahon	FG	38.32%	61.97%
93	Cork Mid	2-Aug-72	Patrick Forde*	FF	Gene Fitzgerald	FF	49.94%	80.89%
94	Monaghan	27-Nov-73	Erskine Childers	FF	Brendan Toal**	FG	47.32%	77.48%
95	Cork North East	13-Nov-74	Liam Ahern*	FF	Sean Brosnan	FF	49.36%	42.89%
96	Galway North East	4-Mar-75	Michael Kitt*	FF	Michael Kitt	FF	52.80%	73.76%
97	Galway West	4-Mar-75	John Geoghegan*	FF	M. Geoghegan Quinn	FF	45.29%	62.87%
98	Mayo West	12-Nov-75	Henry Kenny*	FG	Enda Kenny	FG	52.80%	77.16%
99	Donegal North East	10-Jun-76	Liam Cunningham*	FF	Patrick Keaveney**	IFF	31.12%	75.71%
100	Dublin South West	10-Jun-76	Noel Lemass*	FF	Brendan Halligan**	LB	27.49%	53.65%
101	Cork City	7-Nov-79	Patrick Kerrigan*	LB	Liam Burke	FG	33.19%	55.10%
102	Cork North East	7-Nov-79	Sean Brosnan*	FF	Myra Barry	FG	38.68%	68.59%
103	Donegal	6-Nov-80	Joseph Brennan*	FF	Clement Coughlan	FF	39.04%	73.86%
104	Dublin West	25-May-82	Dick Burke	FG	Liam Skelly	FG	38.96%	61.34%
105	Galway East	20-Jul-82	John Callanan*	FF	Noel Treacy	FF	50.21%	77.06%
106	Donegal South West	13-May-83	Clement Coughlan*	FF	Cathal Coughlan**	FF	56.55%	69.31%
107	Dublin Central	23-Nov-83	George Colley*	FF	Thomas Leonard	FF	46.59%	46.45%
108	Laoighis - Offaly	14-Jun-84	Bernard Cowen*	FF	Brian Cowen	FF	54.69%	64.22%
109	Dublin South Central	9-Jun-94	John O'Connell	FF	Eric Byrne**	DL	27.81%	42.98%
110	Mayo West	9-Jun-94	Padraig Flynn	FF	Michael Ring	FG	35.68%	63.40%
111	Cork North Central	10-Nov-94	Gerry O'Sullivan*	LB	Kathleen Lynch	DL	26.35%	53.25%
112	Cork South Central	10-Nov-94	Pat Cox	PD	Hugh Coveney	FG	31.16%	53.73%
113	Wicklow	29-Jun-95	Johnny Fox*	NP	Mildred Fox	NP	26.90%	53.47%
114	Donegal North East	2-Apr-96	Neil Blaney*	IFF	Cecilia Keaveney	FF	32.24%	60.71%
115	Dublin West	2-Apr-96	Brian Lenihan*	FF	Brian Lenihan	FF	24.62%	45.43%
116	Dublin North	11-Mar-98	Ray Burke	FF	Sean Ryan	LB	33.32%	49.98%
117	Limerick East	11-Mar-98	Jim Kemmy*	LB	Jan O'Sullivan	LB	24.87%	54.43%
118	Cork South Central	23-Oct-98	Hugh Coveney*	FG	Simon Coveney	FG	37.70%	49.09%
119	Dublin South Central	27-Oct-99	Pat Upton*	LB	Mary Upton	LB	28.02%	27.88%
120	Tipperary South	22-Jun-00	Michael Ferris*	LB	Seamus Healy	NP	30.81%	56.90%
121	Tipperary South	30-Jun-01	Theresa Ahearn*	FG	Tom Hayes	FG	26.52%	58.45%
122	Kildare North	11-Mar-05	Charlie McCreevy	FF	Catherine Murphy	NP	23.64%	38.90%
123	Meath	11-Mar-05	John Bruton	FG	Shane McEntee	FG	34.13%	41.07%
124	Dublin Central	5-Jun-09	Tony Gregory*	NP	Maureen O'Sullivan	NP	26.89%	45.72%
125	Dublin South	5-Jun-09	Seamus Brennan*	FF	George Lee**	FG	53.36%	57.31%
126	Donegal South West	25-Nov-10	Pat the Cope Gallagher	FF	Pearse Doherty	SF	39.85%	55.26%
127	Dublin West	27-Oct-11	Brian Lenihan*	FF	Patrick Nulty	LB	24.27%	57.22%
127	**Average**						**45.24%**	**60.39%**
	***By-Election caused by death of TD: 90 (71%)**				****Never subsequently re-elected: 22 (17%)**			

DUBLIN CENTRAL BY-ELECTION 5TH JUNE 2009							
FIRST PREFERENCE VOTES							
	Seats	1			14,207		
	Candidate	Party	1st	%	Quota	Count	Status
1	**O'Sullivan, Maureen**	**NP**	**7,639**	**26.89%**	**0.54**	**8**	**Elected**
2	Donohoe, Paschal	FG	6,439	22.66%	0.45	8	Not Elected
3	Bacik, Ivana	LB	4,926	17.34%	0.35	7	Eliminated
4	Burke, Christy	SF	3,770	13.27%	0.27	6	Eliminated
5	Ahern, Maurice	FF	3,483	12.26%	0.25	5	Eliminated
6	Geary, David	GP	819	2.88%	0.06	4	No Expenses
7	Talbot, Patrick	ICP	614	2.16%	0.04	3	No Expenses
8	Steenson, Malachy	WP	519	1.83%	0.04	2	No Expenses
9	O'Loughlin, Paul	CS	203	0.71%	0.01	1	No Expenses
	Total		**28,412**	**100.00%**	**14,207**	**3,552**	No Expenses

DUBLIN CENTRAL BY-ELECTION 2009													
PARTY VOTE													
	2009					2007					Change	
Party	Cand	1st	%	Quota	Seats	Cand	1st	%	Quota	Seats	%	Seats
FF	1	3,483	12.26%	0.25		3	15,398	44.45%	2.22	2	-32.19%	
FG	1	6,439	22.66%	0.45		1	3,302	9.53%	0.48		+13.13%	
LB	1	4,926	17.34%	0.35		1	4,353	12.57%	0.63	1	+4.77%	
GP	1	819	2.88%	0.06		1	1,995	5.76%	0.29		-2.88%	
SF	1	3,770	13.27%	0.27		1	3,182	9.19%	0.46		+4.08%	
WP	1	519	1.83%	0.04							+1.83%	
CS	1	203	0.71%	0.01		1	260	0.75%	0.04		-0.04%	
ICP	1	614	2.16%	0.04							+2.16%	
PD						1	193	0.56%	0.03		-0.56%	
Others	1	7,639	26.89%	0.54	1	4	5,956	17.19%	0.86	1	+9.69%	
Total	**9**	**28,412**	**100.0%**	**14,207**	**1**	**13**	**34,639**	**100.0%**	**6,928**	**4**	**0.00%**	**0**
Electorate		**62,141**	**45.72%**				**63,423**	**54.62%**			**-8.89%**	
Spoiled		**391**	**1.36%**				**510**	**1.45%**			**-0.09%**	
Turnout		**28,803**	**46.35%**				**35,149**	**55.42%**			**-9.07%**	

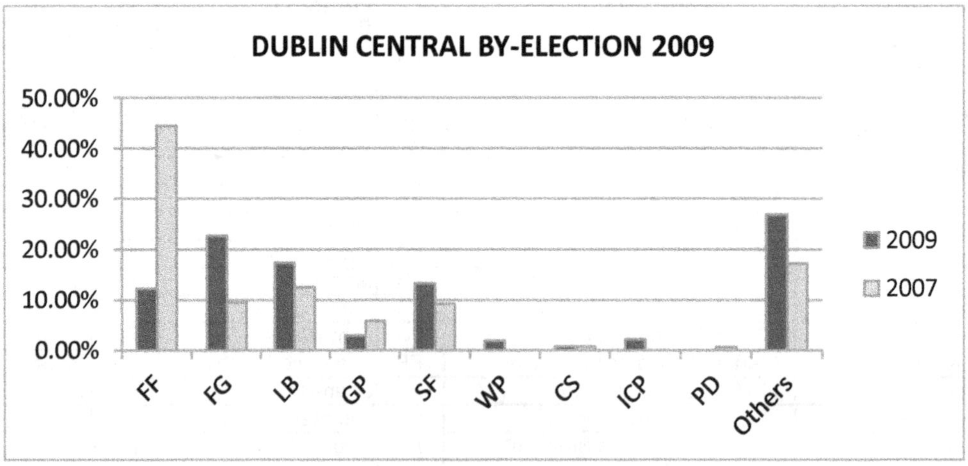

DUBLIN CENTRAL BY-ELECTION 2009 COUNT DETAILS									
Seats	1							Quota	14,207
Candidate	Party	1st	2nd O'Loughlin Votes	3rd Steenson Votes	4th Talbot Votes	5th Geary Votes	6th Ahern Votes	7th Burke Votes	8th Bacik Votes
			+72	*151*	*243*	*236*	*1,011*	*1,710*	*2,677*
O'Sullivan, Maureen	NP	7,639	7,711	7,862	8,105	8,341	9,352	11,062	13,739
			+22	*+27*	*+90*	*+159*	*+675*	*+468*	*+2318*
Donohoe, Paschal	FG	6,439	6,461	6,488	6,578	6,737	7,412	7,880	10,198
			+5	*+77*	*+65*	*+265*	*+436*	*+763*	*-6,537*
Bacik, Ivana	LB	4,926	4,931	5,008	5,073	5,338	5,774	6,537	Eliminated
			+10	*+122*	*+88*	*+52*	*+378*	*-4,420*	
Burke, Christy	SF	3,770	3,780	3,902	3,990	4,042	4,420	Eliminated	
			+29	*+14*	*38*	*+57*	*-3,621*		
Ahern, Maurice	FF	3,483	3,512	3,526	3,564	3,621	Eliminated		
			+10	*+20*	*+44*	*-893*			
Geary, David	GP	819	829	849	893	Eliminated			
			+22	*+40*	*-676*				
Talbot, Pat	ICP	614	636	676	Eliminated				
			+9	*-528*					
Steenson, Malachy	WP	519	528	Eliminated					
			-203						
O'Loughlin, Paul	CS	203	Eliminated						
Non-transferable			*+24*	*+77*	*+108*	*+124*	*+1121*	*+1479*	*+1542*
Cumulative			24	101	209	333	1,454	2,933	4,475
Total		**28,412**	**28,412**	**28,412**	**28,412**	**28,412**	**28,412**	**28,412**	**28,412**

DUBLIN CENTRAL BY-ELECTION 2009 TRANSFER ANALYSIS										
From	To	FF	FG	LB	GP	SF	WP	ICP	NP	Non Trans
FF	3,621		675	436		378			1,011	1,121
			18.64%	*12.04%*		*10.44%*			*27.92%*	*30.96%*
LB	6,537		2,328						3,489	720
			35.61%						*53.37%*	*11.01%*
GP	893	57	159	265		52			236	124
		6.38%	*17.81%*	*29.68%*		*5.82%*			*26.43%*	*13.89%*
SF	4,420		468	763					1,710	1,479
			10.59%	*17.26%*					*38.69%*	*33.46%*
WP	528	14	27	77	20	122		40	151	77
		2.65%	*5.11%*	*14.58%*	*3.79%*	*23.11%*		*7.58%*	*28.60%*	*14.58%*
CS	203	29	22	5	10	10	9	22	72	24
		14.29%	*10.84%*	*2.46%*	*4.93%*	*4.93%*	*4.43%*	*10.84%*	*35.47%*	*11.82%*
ICP	676	38	90	65	44	88			243	108
		5.62%	*13.31%*	*9.62%*	*6.51%*	*13.02%*			*35.95%*	*15.98%*
Total	**16,878**	**138**	**3,769**	**1,611**	**74**	**650**	**9**	**62**	**6,912**	**3,653**
		0.82%	***22.33%***	***9.54%***	***0.44%***	***3.85%***	***0.05%***	***0.37%***	***40.95%***	***21.64%***

DUBLIN SOUTH BY-ELECTION 5TH JUNE 2009							
FIRST PREFERENCE VOTES							
	Seats	1			26,019		
	Candidate	Party	1st	%	Quota	Count	Status
1	Lee, George	FG	27,768	53.36%	1.07	1	Made Quota
2	White, Alex	LB	10,294	19.78%	0.40	1	Not Elected
3	Brennan, Shay	FF	9,250	17.78%	0.36	1	Not Elected
4	Davidson, Elizabeth	GP	1,846	3.55%	0.07	1	No Expenses
5	Tracey, Shaun	SF	1,705	3.28%	0.07	1	No Expenses
6	O'Mullane, Ross	NP	650	1.25%	0.02	1	No Expenses
7	O'Gorman, Frank	NP	351	0.67%	0.01	1	No Expenses
8	O'Gara, Noel	NP	172	0.33%	0.01	1	No Expenses
8	**Total**		**52,036**	**100.00%**	**26,019**	**6,505**	**No Expenses**

DUBLIN SOUTH BY-ELECTION 2009												
PARTY VOTE												
	2009					2007					Change	
Party	Cand	1st	%	Quota	Seats	Cand	1st	%	Quota	Seats	%	Seats
FF	1	9,250	17.78%	0.36		3	25,298	41.33%	2.48	2	-23.56%	-1
FG	1	27,768	53.36%	1.07	1	3	16,686	27.26%	1.64	2	+26.10%	+1
LB	1	10,294	19.78%	0.40		2	6,384	10.43%	0.63		+9.35%	
GP	1	1,846	3.55%	0.07		1	6,768	11.06%	0.66	1	-7.51%	
SF	1	1,705	3.28%	0.07		2	1,843	3.01%	0.18		+0.27%	
PD						1	4,045	6.61%	0.40		-6.61%	
Others	3	1,173	2.25%	0.05		1	180	0.29%	0.02		+1.96%	
Total	**8**	**52,036**	**100.0%**	**26,018**	**1**	**13**	**61,204**	**100.0%**	**10,201**	**5**	**0.00%**	**0**
Electorate		**90,802**	**57.31%**				**89,464**	**68.41%**			**-11.10%**	
Spoiled		**443**	**0.84%**				**418**	**0.68%**			**+0.17%**	
Turnout		**52,479**	**57.79%**				**61,622**	**68.88%**			**-11.08%**	

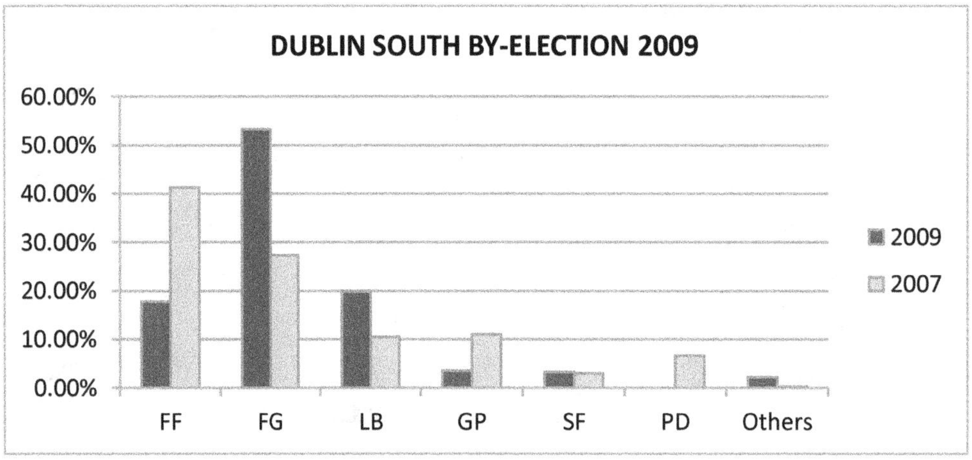

DONEGAL SOUTH-WEST BY-ELECTION 25TH NOVEMBER 2010							
FIRST PREFERENCE VOTES							
	Seats	1			17,213		
	Candidate	Party	1st	%	Quota	Count	Status
1	**Doherty, Pearse**	**SF**	**13,719**	**39.85%**	**0.80**	**4**	**Elected**
2	O Domhnaill, Brian	FF	7,344	21.33%	0.43	4	Not Elected
3	O'Neill, Barry	FG	6,424	18.66%	0.37	4	Not Elected
4	Pringle, Thomas	NP	3,438	9.99%	0.20	3	Eliminated
5	McBrearty, Frank	LB	3,366	9.78%	0.20	2	Eliminated
6	Sweeney, Ann	NP	133	0.39%	0.01	1	No Expenses
6	**Total**		**34,424**	**100.00%**	**17,213**	**2,152**	**No Expenses**

DONEGAL SOUTH-WEST BY-ELECTION 2010												
PARTY VOTE												
	2010					2007					Change	
Party	Cand	1st	%	Quota	Seats	Cand	1st	%	Quota	Seats	%	Seats
FF	1	7,344	21.33%	0.43		2	20,136	50.53%	2.02	2	-29.19%	-1
FG	1	6,424	18.66%	0.37		1	9,167	23.00%	0.92	1	-4.34%	
LB	1	3,366	9.78%	0.20		1	1,111	2.79%	0.11		+6.99%	
SF	1	13,719	39.85%	0.80	1	1	8,462	21.23%	0.85		+18.62%	+1
GP						1	589	1.48%	0.06		-1.48%	
Others	2	3,571	10.37%	0.21		1	388	0.97%	0.04		+9.40%	
Total	**6**	**34,424**	**100.0%**	**17,213**	**1**	**7**	**39,853**	**100.0%**	**9,964**	**3**	**0.00%**	**0**
Electorate		**62,299**	**55.26%**				**60,829**	**65.52%**			**-10.26%**	
Spoiled		**484**	**1.39%**				**421**	**1.05%**			**+0.34%**	
Turnout		**34,908**	**56.03%**				**40,274**	**66.21%**			**-10.18%**	

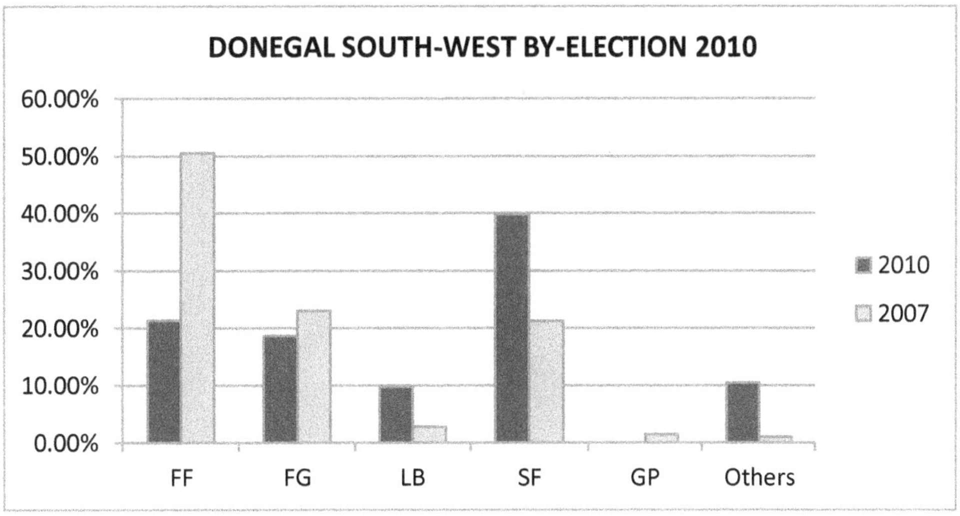

DONEGAL SOUTH-WEST BY-ELECTION 2010 COUNT DETAILS					
Seats	1			Quota	17,213
Candidate	**Party**	**1st**	**2nd** Sweeney Votes	**3rd** McBrearty Votes	**4th** Pringle Votes
			17	*1,452*	*1,709*
Doherty, Pearse	SF	13,719	13,736	15,188	16,897
			+18	*+871*	*+869*
O'Neill, Barry	FG	6,424	6,442	7,313	8,182
			+14	*+278*	*433*
O Domhnaill, Brian	FF	7,344	7,358	7,636	8,069
			+53	*+272*	*-3,763*
Pringle, Thomas	NP	3,438	3,491	3,763	Eliminated
			+9	*-3,375*	
McBrearty, Frank	LB	3,366	3,375	Eliminated	
			-133		
Sweeney, Ann	NP	133	Eliminated		
Non-transferable			+22	+502	+752
Cumulative			22	524	1,276
Total		**34,424**	**34,424**	**34,424**	**34,424**

DONEGAL SOUTH-WEST BY-ELECTION 2010 TRANSFER ANALYSIS							
From	**To**	**FF**	**FG**	**LB**	**SF**	**NP**	**Non Trans**
LB	3,375	278	871		1,452	272	502
		8.24%	*25.81%*		*43.02%*	*8.06%*	*14.87%*
NP	3,896	447	887	9	1,726	53	774
		11.47%	*22.77%*	*0.23%*	*44.30%*	*1.36%*	*19.87%*
Total	**7,271**	**725**	**1,758**	**9**	**3,178**	**325**	**1,276**
		9.97%	***24.18%***	***0.12%***	***43.71%***	***4.47%***	***17.55%***

DUBLIN WEST BY-ELECTION 27th OCTOBER 2011							
FIRST PREFERENCE VOTES							
	Seats	1			17,852		
	Candidate	Party	1st	%	Quota	Count	Status
1	**Nulty, Patrick**	**LB**	**8,665**	**24.27%**	**0.49**	**5**	**Elected**
2	McGuinness, David	FF	7,742	21.69%	0.43	5	Not Elected
3	Copinger, Ruth	SP	7,542	21.12%	0.42	4	Eliminated
4	Loftus, Eithne	FG	5,263	14.74%	0.29	3	Eliminated
5	Donnelly, Paul	SF	3,173	8.89%	0.18	2	Eliminated
6	O'Gorman, Roderic	GP	1,787	5.01%	0.10	2	Eliminated
7	Hunt, Barry Caesar	NP	775	2.17%	0.04	1	No Expenses
8	Kidd, John Frank	NP	311	0.87%	0.02	1	No Expenses
9	Bermingham, Gary	NP	185	0.52%	0.01	1	No Expenses
10	Doris, Brendan	NP	95	0.27%	0.01	1	No Expenses
11	Tallon, Jim	NP	73	0.20%	0.00	1	No Expenses
12	Cooney, Benny	NP	51	0.14%	0.00	1	No Expenses
13	Ó Ceallaigh, Peadar	NP	40	0.11%	0.00	1	No Expenses
13	**Total**		**35,702**	**100.00%**	**17,852**	**4,464**	**No Expenses**

DUBLIN WEST BY-ELECTION 2011												
PARTY VOTE												
	2011 By-Election					2011 General Election					Change	
Party	Cand	1st	%	Quota	Seats	Cand	1st	%	Quota	Seats	%	Seats
FG	1	5,263	14.74%	0.29		2	11,549	27.19%	1.36	1	-12.45%	
LB	1	8,665	24.27%	0.49	1	2	12,313	28.99%	1.45	1	-4.72%	+1
FF	1	7,742	21.69%	0.43		2	7,044	16.59%	0.83	1	+5.10%	-1
SF	1	3,173	8.89%	0.18		1	2,597	6.11%	0.31		+2.77%	
SP	1	7,542	21.12%	0.42		1	8,084	19.03%	0.95	1	+2.09%	
GP	1	1,787	5.01%	0.10		1	605	1.42%	0.07		+3.58%	
Others	7	1,530	4.29%	0.09		1	280	0.66%	0.03		+3.63%	
Total	**13**	**35,702**	**100.0%**	**17,852**	**1**	**10**	**42,472**	**100.0%**	**8,495**	**4**	**0.00%**	
Electorate		**62,396**	**57.22%**				**62,348**	**68.12%**			**-10.90%**	
Spoiled		**689**	**1.89%**				**327**	**0.76%**			**+1.13%**	
Turnout		**36,391**	**58.32%**				**42,799**	**68.65%**			**-10.32%**	

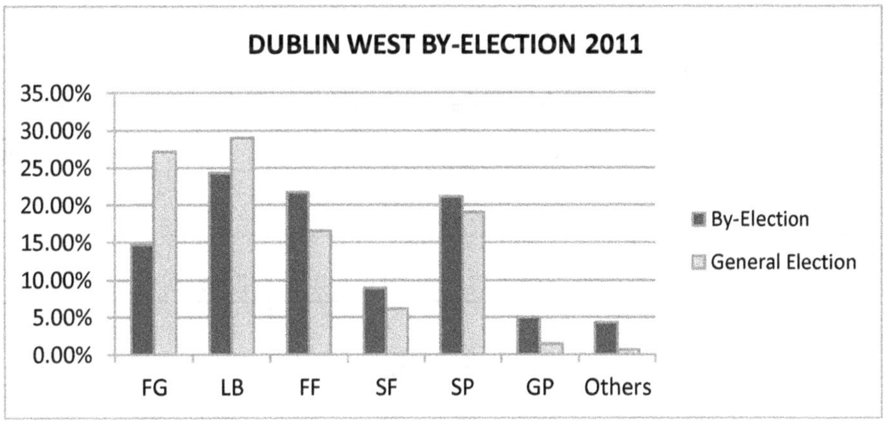

DUBLIN WEST BY-ELECTION 2011 COUNT DETAILS						
Seats	1				Quota	17,852
Candidate	**Party**	**1st**	**2nd** Hunt, Kidd Bermingham Doris, Tallon Cooney Ó Ceallaigh	**3rd** Donnelly O'Gorman	**4th** Loftus Votes	**5th** Coppinger Votes
			+220	*+1,301*	*+2,841*	*+4,609*
Nulty, Patrick	LB	8,665	8,885	10,186	13,027	17,636
			+193	*+785*	*+1,153*	*+1,717*
McGuinness, David	FF	7,742	7,935	8,720	9,873	11,590
			+292	*+1,534*	*+505*	*-9,873*
Coppinger, Ruth	SP	7,542	7,834	9,368	9,873	Eliminated
			+147	*+532*	*-5,942*	
Loftus, Eithne	FG	5,263	5,410	5,942	Eliminated	
			+136	*-3,309*		
Donnelly, Paul	SF	3,173	3,309	Eliminated		
			+138	*-1,925*		
O'Gorman, Roderic	GP	1,787	1,925	Eliminated		
			-775			
Hunt, Barry Caesar	NP	775	Eliminated			
			-311			
Kidd, John Frank	NP	311	Eliminated			
			-185			
Bermingham, Gary	NP	185	Eliminated			
			-95			
Doris, Brendan	NP	95	Eliminated			
			-73			
Tallon, Jim	NP	73	Eliminated			
			-51			
Cooney, Benny	NP	51	Eliminated			
			-40			
Ó Ceallaigh, Peadar	NP	40	Eliminated			
Non-transferable			*+404*	*+1,082*	*+1,443*	*+3,547*
Cumulative			404	1,486	2,929	6,476
Total		**35,702**	**35,702**	**35,702**	**35,702**	**35,702**

DUBLIN WEST BY-ELECTION 2011 TRANSFER ANALYSIS								
From	**To**	**FG**	**LB**	**FF**	**SF**	**SP**	**GP**	**Non Trans**
FG	5,942		2,841	1,153		505		1,443
			47.81%	*19.40%*		*8.50%*		*24.28%*
SF	3,309	336	823	496		970		684
		10.16%	*24.86%*	*15.00%*		*29.31%*		*20.67%*
SP	9,873		4,609	1,717				3,547
			46.68%	*17.39%*				*35.93%*
GP	1,925	196	478	289		564		398
		10.16%	*24.86%*	*15.00%*		*29.31%*		*20.67%*
Others	1,530	147	220	193	136	292	138	404
		9.61%	*14.38%*	*12.61%*	*8.89%*	*19.08%*	*9.02%*	*26.41%*
Total	**22,579**	**679**	**8,971**	**3,848**	**136**	**2,331**	**138**	**6,476**
		3.01%	***39.73%***	***17.04%***	***0.60%***	***10.32%***	***0.61%***	***28.68%***

PART 5

SEANAD ELECTION

APRIL 2011

ADMINISTRATIVE PANEL 2011

MARK DALY (FF)

34 Henry Street, Kenmare, Co. Kerry; Mobile: 086 8032612
Leinster House: 01 6183830, Email: mark.daly@oireactas.ie; Website: www.senatormarkdaly.com

Born Cork, 12th March 1973. Single. Educated Holy Cross College, Kenmare; DIT Bolton Street (Diploma in Valuations); Greenwich University, London (BSc in Management). Harvard Kennedy School. Auctioneer, Journalist and Radio/TV Presenter. Former assistant to MEP Brian Crowley. Senator since 2007.

Member Committee on Foreign Affairs and Trade. Spokesperson for Overseas Development. National Forum on Europe, Co-ordinator Munster Region and Member Joint Committee on Foreign Affairs 2007-2011. Member of Brian Crowley MEP election team. Finished third in Reality TV programme "Treasure Island". President Great Famine Memorial Committee 2005-2007. Founder of the Wall of Ireland 2002-2007.Chairman Kenmare GAA Club 1999-2005.

JOHN KELLY (LB)

The Avenue, Castlemore, Ballaghadereen, Co. Roscommon; Tel: 094 9861027;
Mobile: 086 8094698; Leinster House: 01 6183049; Email: john.kelly@oireactas.ie;

Born in Rath, Ballintubber, Co Roscommon 21st February 1960. Married to Brid who is currently teaching at the Community school in Castlerea and hails originally from Donegal. Three children, Amy, Darragh and Ronan. Educated at St Bride's National School Ballintubber and CBS Roscommon, John commenced work at the Health Service Executive in the Western Region in 1980.He has been the Community Welfare Officer for the Ballaghadereen area for over 24 years. Contested 2007 Dail election in Roscommon South-Leitrim as an Independent. Joined Labour Party on 15th February 2010. Contested 2011 Dail election in Roscommon South-Leitrim for Labour. New Senator.

Member Committee on Jobs, Social Protection and Education. Elected to Roscommon County Council in 2004 in Ballaghadereen electoral area. Retained his seat in 2009.

DIARMUID WILSON (FF)

46 Carrickfern, Keadue Lane, Cavan, Co. Cavan; Tel: 049 4362256; Mobile; 087 2323959
Leinster House: 01 6183561; Email: diarmuid.wilson@oireachtas.ie

Born Cavan 20th November 1965. Married to Marian Kelly, four children. Educated Cavan Vocational School; St. Patrick's, Maynooth; Brunel University, London (Extern Graduate). Youth Worker. Senator since 2002.

Fianna Fail Whip in the Seanad since 2007. Member Joint Administration Committee. Spokesperson for Labour Affairs, Trade and Commerce 2007-2011. Member Joint Committee on Economic and Regulatory Affairs and Member Joint Administration Committee 2007-2011. Former Member Committee of Selection of Seanad Eireann and Seanad Committee on Procedure and Privileges. Member Joint Committee on Social and Family Affairs 2002-2007. Member Cavan County Council 1999-2003.

MICHAEL D'ARCY (FG)

Annagh, Gorey, Co. Wexford, Tel: 053 9428177; Mobile: 087 9901055
Constituency Office: Waygood, Dublin Road, Gorey, Co. Wexford; Tel: 053 9483966,
Leinster House: 01 6183059; Email: michael.darcy@oireachtas.ie,
Website: www.michaeldarcy.finegael.ie

Born Wexford 26th February 1970. Married to Shelly Vaughan, two children. Educated Gorey CBS; University of London (Diploma in Law). Farmer. First elected to Dáil 2007. Lost his seat in 2011. New Senator.

Member Committee on Finance, Public Expenditure and Reform. Supported move against party leader Enda Kenny in June 2010. Deputy spokesperson on Justice with special responsibility for Equality October 2007-2010. Member Joint Committee on Communications, Energy and Natural Resources and Member Joint Committee on the Constitution 2007-2011. Member Wexford County Council 2004-2007 (Vice-Chairman 2004-2005). Chairman VEC. Member Boards of Management Gorey Community School and Kilmuckridge Vocational College. Director Wexford County Enterprise Board (CEB); Wexford Organisation for Rural Development (WORD) and Courtown Water World Ltd. Former inter-county footballer. Member Amnesty International; IFA; ICMSA. Son of former Minister of State Michael D'Arcy, TD for Wexford 1977-1987, 1989-1992, 1997-2002; Senator 1992-1997.

MARTIN CONWAY (FG)

Woodmount, Ennistymon, Co. Clare; Tel: 065 7071157; Mobile: 087 2612977
Constituency Office: 065 7072222;
Leinster House: 01 6183035; Email: martin.conway@oireachtas.ie

Born Ennistymon, 8th April 1974. Married to Breege Hannify. Educated Ennistymon CBS; UCD (BA in Economics and Politics). Businessman. New Senator.

Member Committee on Justice, Defence and Equality. Contested 1999 local election in the Ennistymon electoral area of Clare County Council. First elected 2004. Retained his seat in 2009. Founder member of AHEAD, which aims to improve third-level access for people with disabilities.

TOM SHEAHAN (FG)

Rathbeg, Rathmore, Co. Kerry, Tel: 064 61971; Mobile: 087 2021661
Constituency Office: 31 College Street, Killarney, Co. Kerry; Tel: 064 7758102
Leinster House: 01 6183812; Email: tom.sheahan@oireachtas.ie
Website: www.tomsheahan.finegael.ie

Born Killarney, Co. Kerry 5th September 1968. Married to Mary Lenihan, two daughters, one son. Educated De La Salle Brothers; Coláiste Iosagain, Ballyvourney, Co. Cork. Company Director. First elected to Dáil Eireann 2007. Lost his seat in 2011. New Senator.

Member Committee on Finance, Public Expenditure and Reform. Deputy Spokesperson on Agriculture with special responsibility for Fisheries, 2007-2011. Member Joint Committee on Agriculture, Fisheries and Food 2007-2011. Member Kerry County Council 2004-2007. Member Kerry Mental Health Association; Rathmore Community Council and Rathmore GAA Club.

DENIS LANDY (LB)

Mainstown, Carrick-on-Suir, Co. Tipperary; Tel: 051 641641; Mobile: 087 2326138
Leinster House: 01 6183351; Email: denis.landy@oireachtas.ie

Born Carrick-on-Suir, 28th February 1962. Married to Nancy, one son. Educated CBS, Carrick-on-Suir; UCC (Diploma in Rural Development; IPA (Certificate in Local Government). Former Community Worker. Contested by-election in Tipperary South 30th June 2001. Contested 2002 Dail election. New Senator.

Member Committee on Environment, Transport, Culture and Gaeltacht. First elected to Tipperary South Riding County Council in Fethard electoral area in 1991. Retained his seat in 1999, 2004 and 2009. Elected to Carrick-on-Suir TC in 1994, 1999, 2004 and 2009.

ADMINISTRATIVE PANEL 2011																	
Candidate *Oireachtas Sub-Panel*	**Party**	**1st**	**2nd** Brady	**3rd** Bugler	**4th** Lyons	**5th** O'Grady	**6th** Dennison	**7th** Buckley	**8th** Ward	**9th** Boland	**10th** Daly	**11th** Hourigan	**12th** Moran	**13th** Kelly	**14th** Wilson	**15th** McGloin	**16th** Fitzpatrick
			+2,000		+2,000	+2,000				+7,000	-999						
Daly, Mark*	FF	121,000	123,000	123,000	125,000	127,000	127,000	127,000	127,000	134,000	133,001	133,001	133,001	133,001	133,001	133,001	133,001
						+12,000		+1,000		+8,000			+50,000	-10,999			
Kelly, John	LB	73,000	73,000	73,000	73,000	85,000	85,000	86,000	86,000	94,000	94,000	94,000	144,000	133,001	133,001	133,001	133,001
			+6,000		+2,000	+1,000		+1,000	+1,000	+6,000		+2,000	+4,000	+229	-228		
*Wilson, Diarmuid**	FF	110,000	116,000	116,000	118,000	119,000	119,000	120,000	121,000	127,000	127,000	129,000	133,000	133,229	133,001	133,001	133,001
				+2,000			+11,000	+2,000	+9,000	+3,000		+15,000				+26,000	
D'Arcy, Michael	FG	89,000	89,000	91,000	91,000	91,000	102,000	104,000	113,000	116,000	116,000	131,000	131,000	131,000	131,000	157,000	157,000
				+2,000			+4,000	+3,000	+6,000	+2,000		+14,000	+1,000		+228	+21,000	
Conway, Martin	FG	86,000	86,000	88,000	88,000	88,000	92,000	95,000	101,000	103,000	103,000	117,000	118,000	118,000	118,228	139,228	139,228
				+2,000	+1,000		+1,000	+3,000	+13,000	+1,000		+12,000				+39,000	
Sheahan, Tom	FG	62,000	62,000	64,000	65,000	65,000	66,000	69,000	82,000	83,000	83,000	95,000	95,000	95,000	95,000	134,000	134,000
					+1,000	+4,000				+3,000		+2,000	+13,000	+10,763			+33,000
Landy, Denis	LB	75,000	75,000	75,000	76,000	80,000	80,000	80,000	80,000	83,000	83,000	85,000	98,000	108,763	108,763	108,763	141,763
			+1,000					+2,000		+3,000	+999	+1,000	+2,000			+3,000	-117,999
Fitzpatrick, Mary	FF	105,000	106,000	106,000	106,000	106,000	106,000	108,000	108,000	111,000	111,999	112,999	114,999	114,999	114,999	117,999	Eliminated
				+1,000			+3,000	+4,000	+6,000	+1,000		+6,000				-91,000	
McGloin, Enda	FG	70,000	70,000	71,000	71,000	71,000	74,000	78,000	84,000	85,000	85,000	91,000	91,000	91,000	91,000	Eliminated	
					+1,000	+2,000				+4,000			-70,000				
Moran, Mary	LB	63,000	63,000	63,000	64,000	66,000	66,000	66,000	66,000	70,000	70,000	70,000	Eliminated				
				+3,000			+2,000	+10,000	+4,000	+1,000		-52,000					
Hourigan, Mary	FG	32,000	32,000	35,000	35,000	35,000	37,000	47,000	51,000	52,000	52,000	Eliminated					
					+12,000			+1,000		-43,000							
Boland, Seamus	NP	30,000	30,000	30,000	42,000	42,000	42,000	43,000	43,000	Eliminated							
				+3,000		+1,000	+4,000	+4,000	-39,000								
Ward, Barry	FG	27,000	27,000	30,000	30,000	31,000	35,000	39,000	Eliminated								
			+1,000	+5,000			+2,000	-31,000									
Buckley, Molly	FG	23,000	24,000	29,000	29,000	29,000	31,000	Eliminated									
			+1,000	+1,000			-28,000										
Dennison, Kieran	FG	26,000	27,000	28,000	28,000	28,000	Eliminated										
					+1,000	-23,000											
O'Grady, Sean	LB	22,000	22,000	22,000	23,000	Eliminated											
			+1,000		-20,000												
Lyons, Sean	NP	19,000	20,000	20,000	Eliminated												
				-19,000													
Bugler, Phyll	FG	19,000	19,000	Eliminated													
			-12,000														
*Brady, Martin**	FF	12,000	Eliminated														
Non-transferable						+1,000	+1,000			+4,000				+7		+2,000	+84,999
Cumulative			0	0	0	1,000	2,000	2,000	2,000	6,000	6,000	6,000	6,000	6,007	6,007	8,007	93,006
*** Outgoing**		**1,064,000**	**1,064,000**	**1,064,000**	**1,064,000**	**1,064,000**	**1,064,000**	**1,064,000**	**1,064,000**	**1,064,000**	**1,064,000**	**1,064,000**	**1,064,000**	**1,064,000**	**1,064,000**	**1,064,000**	**1,064,000**
Electorate:		**1,092**	**Valid:**	**1,064**	**Value:**	**1,064,000**	**Seats:**	**7**	**Quota:**	**133,001**	**Candidates**	**19**					

AGRICULTURAL PANEL 2011

JAMES HEFFERNAN (LB)

Main Street, Kilfinane, Co. Limerick; Tel:063 91520; Mobile: 087 3243315
Leinster House: 01 6183057; Email: james.heffernan@oireachtas.ie.

Born Limerick 3rd October 1979. Single. Educated University of Limerick with an honours degree in History, Politics & Social Studies. Teacher. Contested 2007 Dail election in Limerick West. Contested 2011 general election in Limerick. New Senator.

Member Committee on European Union Affairs. Elected to Limerick County Council in the Kilmallock electoral area in 2009.

PADDY BURKE (FG)

Knockaphunta, Westport Road, Castlebar, Co. Mayo; Tel: 094 9022568; Mobile: 087 2441802; Leinster House: 01 6183574; Email: paddy.burke@oireachtas.ie

Born Castlebar, Co. Mayo, 15th January 1955. Married to Dolores Barrett, one son. Educated Ballinfad College, Castlebar; Rockwell College of Agriculture, Cashel, Co. Tipperary; Franciscan Brothers Agricultural College, Mount Bellew, Co. Galway. Businessman.
Senator since 1993.

Elected Cathaoirleach of the Seanad 25th May 2011. Leas-Cathaoirleach of Seanad 2007-2011. Seanad Spokesperson on Defence and Emigrant Affairs 2007-2011. Chairman Committee of Selection of Seanad Eireann and Member Joint Committee on European Scrutiny 2007-2011. Member Joint Administration Committee and Member Seanad Committee on Procedure and Privileges 2007-2011. Leas-Cathaoirleach of Seanad 2002-2007. Former Fine Gael Whip and Seanad spokesperson on National Resources. Member Mayo County Council 1979-2003. Member Mayo-Galway Regional Development Organisation.

PAUL BRADFORD (FG)

Ballyphibeen, Mourne Abbey, Mallow, Co. Cork; Tel: 022 29375; Mobile: 087 2596204;
Constituency Office: Church View, Sandfield, Mallow, Co. Cork; Tel: 022 42181
Leinster House: 01 6183760; Email: paul.bradford@oireachtas.ie.
Website: www.paulbradford.ie

Born Mallow, Co. Cork, December 1963. Married to Lucinda Creighton TD for Dunlin South-East. Educated Patrician Academy, Mallow. Farmer. Contested 1987 general election and TD for Cork East 1989-2002. Contested 2002 and 2007 general elections. Senator 1987-1989, he was the youngest ever elected Senator at that time. Re-elected 2002, 2007 and 2011.

Member Committee on Justice, Defence and Equality. Seanad Spokesperson on Agriculture, Fisheries and Food 2007-2011. Member Houses of the Oireachtas Commission and Member Joint Committee on Agriculture, Fisheries and Food 2007-2011. Member Council of Europe. Former Member Joint Committee on Foreign Affairs. Fine Gael Chief Whip and member of Leader's cabinet 2001-2002. Junior spokesperson on Youth Affairs, School Transport, Adult Education and liaison with Young Fine Gael 2000-2001. Fine Gael Junior spokesperson on Health, Food Safety and Older People 1997–2000. Fine Gael Front Bench spokesperson on Defence and Marine 1994. Co-Chairman of British-Irish Interparliamentary Body 1995-1997. Member of Cork County Council 1985-2003.

TREVOR Ó CLOCHARTAIGH (SF)

An Caorán Beag, An Ceathrú Rua, Co. Na Gaillimhe; Mobile: 087 2476624;
Leinster House: 01 6184069; Email: trevor.oclochartaigh@oireachtas.ie

Born Huddersfield, England 14th March 1968. Married to Mali, four children. Educated NUI, Galway (BComm). Media Consultant. Contested 2011 general election in Galway West. New Senator.

Member Committee on Investigations, Oversight and Petitions. Contested 2004 local election in Galway County Council for Labour Party. Joined Sinn Fein and contested 2009 local election in Conamara.

BRIAN O DOMHNAILL (FF)

Killult, Falcarragh, Co. Donegal; Tel: 074 9135292; Mobile: 086 8218084
Constituency Office: Main Street, Gortahork, Co. Donegal; Tel: 074 9165466;
Email: brian.odomhnaill@oireachtas.ie

Born Letterkenny, Co. Donegal 18th October 1977. Single. Educated Pobal Scoil Chloich Cheann Fhaola, Falcarragh; University of Ulster (BSc). Food Technology Manager. Contested Dail By-Election in Donegal South West in November 2010. Contested 2011 general election in Donegal SW. Senator since 2007.

Member Committee on Communications, Natural Resources and Agriculture. Seanad Spokesperson on Lifelong Learning, Youth Work and School Transport 2007-2011. Member Joint Committee on Education and Science 2007-2011. Member Donegal County Council 2004-2007. Member Udaras na Gaeltachta since 1999. Member Donegal County Development Board. Member County Donegal Local Sports Partnership.

PAT O'NEILL (FG)

Ballyreddin, Bennettsbridge, Co. Kilkenny; Tel:056 7727438; Mobile: 087 2771483
Leinster House: 01 6183082; Email:pat.oneill@oireachtas.ie

Born Kilkenny 14th November 1958. Married to Brigid. Farmer. New Senator.

Member Committee on Communications, Natural Resources and Agriculture. Elected to Kilkenny County Council in the Thomastown electoral area in 2004. Retained his seat in 2009.

MICHAEL COMISKEY (FG)

Magurk, Leckaun P.O., Co. Leitrim; Tel: 071 9164245; Mobile: 086 2304525;
Leinster House: 01 6183453; Email: michael.comiskey@oireachtas.ie

Born Manorhamilton, Co. Leitrim, 1st October 1953. Married to Elizabeth McMorrow, five sons. Educated Manorhamilton Vocational School. Farmer. Contested 2007 general election in Sligo North-Leitrim. New Senator.

Member Committee on Communications, Natural Resources and Agriculture.

JIM WALSH (FF)

Mountgarrett Castle, New Ross, Co. Wexford; Tel: 051 421771; Mobile: 086 6008155.
Leinster House: 01 6183763; Email: jim.walsh@oireachtas.ie

Born Wexford, 5th May 1947. Married to Marie Furlong, one son, two daughters. Educated New Ross CBS and Carriglea Park, Dun Laoghaire. Company Director, Farmer. Senator since 1997.

Member Committee on Foreign Affairs and Trade. Spokesperson on Communications, Energy and Natural Resources 2007-2011. Member Houses of the Oireachtas Commission and Member Joint Committee on Communications, Energy and Natural Resources 2007-2011. Member Joint Committee on Justice, Equality, Defence and Women's' Rights 2002-2007. Member Wexford County Council 1979-2004 (Chairman 1992-1993); New Ross UDC 1974-2004 (Chairman 9 times). Chairman, LAMA 1997-2002. Member Chartered Institute of Transport. Former President, Irish Road Hauliers' Association.

PASCHAL MOONEY (FF)

Carrick Road, Drumshambo, Co. Leitrim; Tel: 078 41236;
Leinster House: 01 6183148; Email: paschal.mooney@oireachtas.ie

Born Dublin 14th October 1947. Married to Sheila Baldrey, three sons, two daughters. Educated Presentation Bros., Carrick-on-Shannon, Co. Leitrim; Carrick-on-Shannon Vocational College; Camden Institute London. Journalist, Broadcaster and Businessman. Senator 1987-2007. Lost his seat in 2007. Contested European election in North-West in 2009. Won Seanad by-election 19th January 2010 which was caused by death of Peter Callanan. Retained his seat in 2011.

Member Committee on Communications, Natural Resources and Agriculture. Member Joint Committee on Foreign Affairs 2007-2011. Member National Economic and Social Forum and National Forum on Europe. Member British-Irish Inter Parliamentary Body. Member Leitrim County Council 1991-1999. Member VEC since 1984. Chairman of Leitrim Sports Advisory Body; Chairman of Leitrim County Library Committee; President of Leitrim Community Games. Member of Irish Georgian Society; Irish Committee of the European Movement; GAA; County Secretary An Tostal Drumshambo. Leitrim Man of the Year 1991.

DENIS O'DONOVAN (FF)

Montrose House, Slip, Bantry, Co. Cork; Tel: 027 51541; Mobile: 087 2543806;
Constituency Office: Wolfe Tone Square, Bantry, Co. Cork; Tel: 027 53840;
Leinster House: 01 6184479; Email: denis.odonovan@oireachtas.ie
Website: www. denisodonovan.com

Born Bantry, 23rd July 1955. Separated, three sons, one daughter. Educated Bantry Secondary School; Carrignavar Secondary College; UCC (BCL). Solicitor. Contested 1989, 1992 and 1997 general elections. Senator 1989-1993 and 1997-2002. TD for Cork South West 2002-2007. Contested 2007 and 2011 general elections in Cork SW. Senator since 2007.

Member Committee on Justice, Defence and Equality. Former Seanad spokesperson on Justice, Equality and Law Reform. Former Member Joint Committee on Justice, Equality, Defence and Women's Rights and Member Joint Committee on the Constitution. Member Committee on Members' Interests of Seanad Eireann. Chairman All Party Committee on the Constitution, 2002-2007. Member of the Abbeylara Enquiry. Member Cork County Council 1985-2003 (Chairman 1989-1990).

SUSAN O'KEEFFE (LB)

Kinnagrelly House, Collooney, Co. Sligo; Mobile: 085 1314084;
Email:susan.okeeffe@oireachtas.ie

Born Dublin, 18th September 1960. Married with three children. Educated Convent of Sacred Heart, Mount Anville, Dublin; UCC (BSc, Dairy and Food). Journalist. Contested 2011 general election in Sligo-North Leitrim. New Senator.

Member Committee on Investigations, Oversight and Petitions. Contested 2009 euro election in Ireland North West. Her reporting on beef industry for ITV programme World in Action in 1991 led to Hamilton Tribunal of Inquiry and she was only one prosecuted as a result, for refusing to reveal her sources.

AGRICULTURAL PANEL 2011

Candidate Oireachtas Sub-Panel	Party	1st	2nd Heffernan	3rd Coleman	4th Mansergh	5th Brennan	6th Dillon	7th Bailey	8th McDermott	9th Burke	10th Connick	11th Doocey	12th Hogan
Heffernan, James	LB	97,000	-8,166 88,834	88,834	88,834	88,834	88,834	88,834	88,834	88,834	88,834	88,834	88,834
Burke,Paddy*	FG	82,000	82,000	82,000	82,000	82,000	82,000	+3,000 85,000	+4,000 89,000	-166 88,834	88,834	88,834	88,834
Bradford, Paul*	FG	63,000	63,000	63,000	63,000	+4,000 67,000	+2,000 69,000	+5,000 74,000	+3,000 77,000	77,000	77,000	+4,000 81,000	81,000
Ó Clochartaigh, Trevor	SF	82,000	82,000	82,000	82,000	82,000	+1,000 83,000	83,000	83,000	83,000	83,000	83,000	83,000
Ó Domhnaill, Brian*	FF	53,000	53,000	53,000	+2,000 55,000	55,000	55,000	55,000	55,000	55,000	+5,000 60,000	60,000	+4,000 64,000
O'Neill, Pat	FG	40,000	+170 40,170	40,170	40,170	+1,000 41,170	41,170	41,170	41,170	41,170	41,170	+7,000 48,170	48,170
Comiskey, Michael	FG	40,000	+85 40,085	40,085	40,085	40,085	40,085	+1,000 41,085	+3,000 44,085	44,085	44,085	+1,000 45,085	45,085
Walsh,Jim*	FF	53,000	53,000	+1,000 54,000	+2,000 56,000	56,000	+1,000 57,000	57,000	57,000	57,000	+6,000 63,000	63,000	+11,000 74,000
Mooney, Paschal*	FF	40,000	40,000	40,000	+2,000 42,000	42,000	42,000	42,000	42,000	42,000	+1,000 43,000	43,000	+2,000 45,000
O'Donovan, Denis*	FF	42,000	+85 42,085	+1,000 43,085	+1,000 44,085	44,085	+2,000 46,085	46,085	46,085	46,085	+5,000 51,085	51,085	+3,000 54,085
O'Keeffe, Susan	LB	69,000	+7,140 76,140	76,140	76,140	76,140	76,140	76,140	76,140	76,140	+255 76,395	+1,000 77,395	+85 77,480
Sheahan, John	FG	38,000	38,000	38,000	38,000	38,000	+1,000 39,000	+2,000 41,000	+3,000 44,000	44,000	44,000	+2,000 46,000	46,000
Scanlon, Eamon	FF	47,000	47,000	47,000	47,000	47,000	47,000	47,000	47,000	47,000	+1,000 48,000	48,000	+3,000 51,000
Burton, Pat	FG	25,000	25,000	+1,000 26,000	26,000	+1,000 27,000	27,000	+2,000 29,000	+2,000 31,000	31,000	31,000	+4,000 35,000	35,000
Carroll, James*	FF	34,000	34,000	34,000	34,000	34,000	34,000	34,000	34,000	34,000	+6,000 40,000	40,000	+2,000 42,000
Phelan, Martin	FG	26,000	26,000	26,000	26,000	26,000	26,000	26,000	+4,000 30,000	+166 30,166	30,166	+5,000 35,166	+1,000 36,166
Clarke, Michael	NP	32,000	+85 32,085	32,085	32,085	32,085	+4,085 36,170	+1,000 37,170	37,170	37,170	37,170	+2,000 39,170	+1,000 40,170
Markey, Colm	FG	27,000	27,000	27,000	27,000	+1,000 28,000	28,000	+1,000 29,000	+3,000 32,000	32,000	32,000	32,000	32,000
Feeney, Peter	FG	29,000	+85 29,085	29,085	29,085	29,085	29,085	29,085	+1,000 30,085	30,085	30,085	+1,000 31,085	31,085
Hogan, John	FF	23,000	+85 23,085	23,085	+1,000 24,085	+1,000 25,085	+1,000 26,085	26,085	26,085	26,085	+1,000 27,085	27,085	-27,085 Eliminated
Doocey, Declan	FG	24,000	24,000	24,000	24,000	+2,000 26,000	26,000	26,000	+1,000 27,000	27,000	27,000	-27,000 Eliminated	
Connick, Sean	FF	25,000	+255 25,255	25,255	25,255	25,255	25,255	25,255	25,255	25,255	-25,255 Eliminated		
McDermott, Frank	FG	21,000	21,000	21,000	21,000	+1,000 22,000	22,000	+2,000 24,000	-24,000 Eliminated				
Bailey, John	FG	19,000	19,000	19,000	19,000	19,000	19,000	-19,000 Eliminated					
Dillon, John	NP	12,000	+85 12,085	12,085	12,085	12,085	-12,085 Eliminated						
Brennan, Joseph	FG	11,000	11,000	11,000	11,000	-11,000 Eliminated							
Mansergh, Dr. Martin	FF	9,000	9,000	9,000	-9,000 Eliminated								
Coleman, Alan	FF	3,000	3,000	-3,000 Eliminated									
Non-transferable Cumulative			+91 91	91	+1,000 1,091	1,091	1,091	+2,000 3,091	3,091	3,091	3,091	3,091	3,091
*Outgoing		1,066,000	1,066,000	1,066,000	1,066,000	1,066,000	1,066,000	1,066,000	1,066,000	1,066,000	1,066,000	1,066,000	1,066,000
Electorate		1,092	Valid	1,066	Value	1,066,000	Seats	11	Quota	88,834	Candidates	28	

Candidate	13th Feeney	14th Markey	15th Bradford	16th Clarke	17th Ó Clochartaigh	18th Phelan	19th Carroll	20th Ó Domhnaill	21st Burton	22nd O'Neill	23rd Comiskey	24th Scanlon	25th Walsh
Heffernan, James	88,834	88,834	88,834	88,834	88,834	88,834	88,834	88,834	88,834	88,834	88,834	88,834	88,834
Burke,Paddy*	88,834	88,834	88,834	88,834	88,834	88,834	88,834	88,834	88,834	88,834	88,834	88,834	88,834
Bradford, Paul*	+5,000 86,000	+9,000 95,000	-6,166 88,834	88,834	88,834	88,834	88,834	88,834	88,834	88,834	88,834	88,834	88,834
Ó Clochartaigh, Trevor	+85 83,085	83,085	83,085	+6,000 89,085	-251 88,834	88,834	88,834	88,834	88,834	88,834	88,834	88,834	88,834
Ó Domhnaill, Brian*	+1,000 65,000	65,000	65,000	+2,000 67,000	67,000	67,000	+24,000 91,000	-2,166 88,834	88,834	88,834	88,834	88,834	88,834
O'Neill, Pat	+1,000 49,170	+4,000 53,170	+2,740 55,910	+4,000 59,910	59,910	+17,000 76,910	76,910	76,910	+13,685 90,595	-1,761 88,834	88,834	88,834	88,834
Comiskey, Michael	+9,000 54,085	+10,000 64,085	+1,370 65,455	65,455	65,455	+12,000 77,455	77,455	77,455	+13,000 90,455	90,455	-1,621 88,834	88,834	88,834
Walsh,Jim*	+1,000 75,000	75,000	75,000	+5,000 80,000	80,000	+1,000 81,000	+7,000 88,000	+722 88,722	88,722	88,722	88,722	+13,000 101,722	-12,888 88,834
Mooney, Paschal*	+1,000 46,000	46,000	46,000	+6,000 52,000	52,000	+3,000 55,000	+6,000 61,000	61,000	61,000	61,000	61,000	+25,000 86,000	+5,000 91,000
O'Donovan, Denis*	54,085	54,085	54,085	+4,170 58,255	+251 58,506	58,506	+6,000 64,506	+722 65,228	+1,000 66,228	66,228	66,228	+17,722 83,950	+5,000 88,950
O'Keeffe, Susan	77,480	77,480	77,480	+4,000 81,480	81,480	+1,000 82,480	82,480	82,480	+1,000 83,480	83,480	83,480	+1,000 84,480	+1,000 85,480
Sheahan, John	+3,000 49,000	+4,000 53,000	53,000	+1,000 54,000	54,000	+5,166 59,166	59,166	59,166	+18,370 77,536	+1,760 79,296	+1,000 80,296	80,296	80,296
Scanlon, Eamon	+1,000 52,000	52,000	52,000	+2,000 54,000	54,000	54,000	+2,000 56,000	+722 56,722	56,722	56,722	56,722	-56,722 Eliminated	
Burton, Pat	+3,000 38,000	+5,000 43,000	+2,055 45,055	+1,000 46,055	46,055	+4,000 50,055	50,055	50,055	-50,055 Eliminated				
Carroll, James*	42,000	+1,000 43,000	43,000	+2,000 45,000	45,000	45,000	-45,000 Eliminated						
Phelan, Martin	+4,000 40,166	+1,000 41,166	41,166	+3,000 44,166	44,166	-44,166 Eliminated							
Clarke, Michael	40,170	40,170	40,170	-40,170 Eliminated									
Markey, Colm	+2,000 34,000	-34,000 Eliminated											
Feeney, Peter	-31,085 Eliminated												
Hogan, John													
Doocey, Declan													
Connick, Sean													
McDermott, Frank													
Bailey, John													
Dillon, John													
Brennan, Joseph													
Mansergh, Dr. Martin													
Coleman, Alan													
Non-transferable Cumulative	3,091	3,091	+1 3,092	3,092	3,092	+1,000 4,092	4,092	4,092	+3,000 7,092	+1 7,093	+621 7,714	7,714	+1,888 9,602
*Outgoing	1,066,000	1,066,000	1,066,000	1,066,000	1,066,000	1,066,000	1,066,000	1,066,000	1,066,000	1,066,000	1,066,000	1,066,000	1,066,000

CULTURAL AND EDUCATIONAL PANEL 2011

DEIRDRE CLUNE (FG)

144 Blackrock Road, Cork; Tel: 021 4364934; Mobile: 087 2387539;
Constituency Office: Morris House, Douglas Village, Cork; Tel 021 4890000
Leinster House: 01 6183365; Email: deirdre.clune@oireachtas.ie
Website: www.deirdreclune.com

Born Cork, June 1959. Married to Conor Clune, four sons. Educated Ursuline Convent, Blackrock, Cork; UCC (B.Eng. Civil, HDip Env Eng). Civil Engineer. First elected to Dail 1997. Lost her seat in 2002 but regained it in 2007. Lost again in 2011. Contested 2002 Seanad election. New Senator.

Member Committee on Jobs, Social Protection and Education. Member Committee on Foreign Affairs and Trade Front bench spokesperson on Innovation & Research 2010-2011. Deputy spokesperson on Enterprise with special responsibility for Innovation, 2007-2010. Member Public Accounts Committee and Member Joint Committee on Enterprise, Trade and Employment 2007-2011. Junior spokesperson on Environmental Information and Protection 1997-2002. Member Joint Committees on Environment and Local Government; Health and Children 1997-2002. Member Cork City Council 1999-2007. Lord Mayor of Cork 2005-2006. Succeeded her father Peter Barry as TD for Cork South Central in 1997. Peter Barry was TD 1969-1997 and Tánaiste 1987, Minister for Foreign Affairs 1982-1987, Minister for the Environment 1981-1982, Minister for Transport and Power 1973-1976, Minister for Education 1976-1977 and Deputy Leader Fine Gael 1979-1987 and 1989-1993. Grand-daughter of Anthony Barry, TD Cork Borough 1954-1957 and 1961-1965, Senator 1957-1961.

LABHRÁS Ó MURCHÚ (FF)

An Bóithrin Glas, Caiseal, Co. Thiobraid Árann; Tel: 062 61122; Mobile: 087 2528747
Leinster House: 01 6184018; Email: labhras.omurchu@oireachtas.ie

Born Cashel, Co. Tipperary 14th August 1939. Married to Úna Ronan. Educated Cashel CBS. Director-General, Comhaltas Ceoltóiri Éireann. Contested 1993 Senate election. Senator since 1997.

Member Committee on Environment, Transport, Culture and Gaeltacht. Spokesperson for Community, Rural and Gaeltacht Affairs 2007-2011. Member Joint Committee on Arts, Sport, Tourism, Community, Rural and Gaeltacht Affairs and Member Seanad Committee on Procedure and Privileges 2007-2011. Member Joint Committee on Arts, Sport, Tourism, Community, Rural and Gaeltacht Affairs 2002-2007. Member Cashel UDC 1979-1999 (previous Chairman). Director General Comhaltas Ceoltoiri Eireann. National Chairman Irish Family History Foundation.

THOMAS BYRNE (FF)

42 The Boulevard, Grange Rath, Colpe, Co. Meath; Tel: 041 9818435; Mobile: 087 6943942
Constituency Office: Donnycarney, Co. Meath; Leinster House: 01 6183310;
Email: thomas.byrne@oireachtas.ie; Website: www. thomasbyrne.blogspot.com

Born Drogheda 1st June 1977. Married to Ann Hunt, one son, two daughters. Educated St. Mary's Diocesan School, Drogheda; Trinity College, Dublin (LLB); Law Society of Ireland. Solicitor. Qualified as Attorney-at-law, in New York State, USA. First elected to the Dail in 2007. Lost his seat in 2011. Contested 2009 euro elections in Ireland East. First time Senator.

Fianna Fail Seanad spokesperson on Public Expenditure and Financial Sector Reform. Member Committee on Finance, Public Expenditure and Reform. Convenor Joint Committee on Social and Family Affairs 2007-2011. Member Joint Committee on the Constitution and Member Joint Committee on Justice, Equality, Defence and Women's Rights and Member Joint Committee on Constitutional Amendment on Children 2007-2011. Cousin of former Minister Michael Hilliard TD for Meath 1943-1973 and Colm Hilliard TD 1982-1997.

JOHN GILROY (LB)

9 Hazelwood Court, Glanmire, Co. Cork; Tel: 021 4866670; Mobile: 087 2799608
Leinster House: 01 6183089; Email: john.gilroy01@oireachtas.ie

Born Athboy, Co. Meath, 20th July 1967. Married to Marion, one son, one daughter. Educated Our Lady's Hospital, Cork (Certificate in Psychiatric Nursing). Psychiatric nurse. Contested Dail election in Cork North-Central in 2011. First time Senator.

Member Committee on Health and Children. Elected to Cork County Council in Blarney electoral area in 2004. Retained his seat in 2009. Chairman of Glanmire Business Network - a business support network with over 200 local businesses. He is also chairman of Riverstown Football Club (juvenile soccer club), Director of Glanmire Area Community Association and member of SAFE in Glanmire and head of league development with Cork Women's and Schoolgirls League (soccer).

MICHAEL MULLINS (FG)

Cleaghmore, Ballinasloe, Co. Galway; Tel: 090 9642728; Mobile: 087 2607405
Leinster House: 01 6183095; Email: michael.mullins@oireachtas.ie

Born Galway 22nd February 1953. Married to Mary Lyne. Educated St. Joseph's College, Garbally Park, Ballinasloe. Irish Management Institute. Institute of Personnel and Development. Former Human Resources Manager. Contested 1992 Dail election in Galway East. First time Senator.

Member Committee on Foreign Affairs and Trade. Member Committee on Jobs, Social Protection and Education. Elected to Galway County Council in the Ballinasloe electoral area in 1985. Retained his seat in 1991, 1999, 2004 and 2009.

CULTURAL & EDUCATIONAL PANEL 2011

Candidate	Party	1st	2nd	3rd	4th	5th	6th	7th	8th	9th	10th	11th	12th	13th	14th
Oireachtas Sub-Panel			O'Dea	Delaney	Quinn	Hogan	Kennedy	Irish	Boyhan	Quinlan	Tormey	Clune	Ormonde	Walsh	Ó Murchú
Clune, Deidre	FG	103,000	*+4,000* 107,000	*+4,000* 111,000	*+5,000* 116,000	*+8,000* 124,000	*+8,000* 132,000	*+14,000* 146,000	*+3,000* 149,000	*+21,000* 170,000	*+20,000* 190,000	*-12,499* 177,501	177,501	177,501	177,501
Ó Murchú, Labhrás*	FF	104,000	104,000	104,000	104,000	*+1,000* 105,000	*+2,000* 107,000	*+1,000* 108,000	*+11,000* 119,000	*+1,000* 120,000	*+5,000* 125,000	125,000	*+41,000* 166,000	*+45,000* 211,000	*-33,499* 177,501
Byrne, Thomas	FF	129,000	129,000	129,000	129,000	129,000	129,000	129,000	*+9,000* 138,000	138,000	*+4,000* 142,000	142,000	*+14,000* 156,000	*+33,000* 189,000	189,000
Gilroy, John	LB	157,000	157,000	157,000	157,000	157,000	*+1,000* 158,000	158,000	*+4,000* 162,000	*+4,000* 166,000	*+4,000* 170,000	170,000	*+4,000* 174,000	*+3,000* 177,000	*+3,000* 180,000
Mullins, Michael	FG	78,000	78,000	*+3,000* 81,000	*+5,000* 86,000	*+4,000* 90,000	*+5,000* 95,000	*+2,000* 97,000	*+5,000* 102,000	*+18,000* 120,000	*+20,000* 140,000	*+3,744* 143,744	*+2,000* 145,744	*+6,000* 151,744	*+10,000* 161,744
McCartin, John	FG	68,000	*+2,000* 70,000	70,000	*+5,000* 75,000	*+5,000* 80,000	*+4,000* 84,000	*+8,000* 92,000	*+6,000* 98,000	*+7,000* 105,000	*+14,000* 119,000	*+8,112* 127,112	*+1,624* 128,736	*+5,000* 133,736	*+5,000* 138,736
Walsh, Seamus	FF	86,000	86,000	86,000	86,000	86,000	86,000	86,000	*+3,000* 89,000	*+5,000* 94,000	94,000	94,000	*+17,000* 111,000	*-111,000* Eliminated	
Ormonde, Ann*	FF	66,000	66,000	66,000	66,000	66,000	66,000	66,000	*+10,000* 76,000	*+3,000* 79,000	*+2,000* 81,000	*+624* 81,624	*-81,624* Eliminated		
Tormey, Bill	FG	49,000	*+1,000* 50,000	*+1,000* 51,000	*+2,000* 53,000	*+2,000* 55,000	*+4,000* 59,000	*+4,000* 63,000	*+2,000* 65,000	*+4,000* 69,000	*-69,000* Eliminated				
Quinlan, Hilary	FG	47,000	47,000	*+1,000* 48,000	*+2,000* 50,000	*+2,000* 52,000	*+1,000* 53,000	*+10,000* 63,000	*+1,000* 64,000	*-64,000* Eliminated					
Boyhan, Victor	NP	44,000	*+2,000* 46,000	46,000	46,000	*+1,000* 47,000	*+5,000* 52,000	*+3,000* 55,000	*-55,000* Eliminated						
Irish, Anne-Maria	FG	25,000	*+1,000* 26,000	*+4,000* 30,000	*+2,000* 32,000	*+5,000* 37,000	*+6,000* 43,000	*-43,000* Eliminated							
Kennedy, Pat	FG	32,000	32,000	*+2,000* 34,000	34,000	*+2,000* 36,000	*-36,000* Eliminated								
Hogan, Nichola	FG	27,000	27,000	*+1,000* 28,000	*+3,000* 31,000	*-31,000* Eliminated									
Quinn, Liam	FG	23,000	*+1,000* 24,000	24,000	*-24,000* Eliminated										
Delaney, Conor	FG	16,000	16,000	*-16,000* Eliminated											
O'Dea, Jim	FG	11,000	*-11,000* Eliminated												
Non-transferable Cumulative			0	0	0	*+1,000* 1,000	1,000	*+1,000* 2,000	*+1,000* 3,000	*+1,000* 4,000	4,000	*+19* 4,019	*+2,000* 6,019	*+19,000* 25,019	*+15,499* 40,518
***Outgoing**		**1,065,000**	**1,065,000**	**1,065,000**	**1,065,000**	**1,065,000**	**1,065,000**	**1,065,000**	**1,065,000**	**1,065,000**	**1,065,000**	**1,065,000**	**1,065,000**	**1,065,000**	**1,065,000**
	Electorate	**1,092**	**Valid**	**1,065**	**Value**	**1,065,000**	**Seats**	**5**	**Quota**	**177,501**	**Candidates**	**17**			

INDUSTRIAL AND COMMERCIAL PANEL 2011

JIMMY HARTE (LB)

3 Sylvan Park, Letterkenny, Co. Donegal; Tel: 074 9126231; Mobile: 087 2511037; Constituency Office: 074 9111005; Email: jimmy.harte@oireachtas.ie

Born Lifford, Co. Donegal, 27th February 1958. Married to Mary Galligan, two daughters, two sons. Educated St. Eunan's College, Letterkenny; UCD (BA in Psychology). Insurance Broker. Having failed to get a nomination for 2007 Dail election he left Fine Gael and ran as an independent. Joined Labour 6th May 2010 and contested 2011 general election in Donegal North-East as a Labour Party candidate. New Senator.

Member Committee on Investigations, Oversight and Petitions. First elected to Donegal County Council in the Letterkenny electoral area in 1999 for Fine Gael. Retained his seat in 2004. Re-elected 2009 as an Independent. Elected to Letterkenny TC in 1999, 2004 and 2009. Son of Paddy Harte, FG TD for Donegal North-East 1961-1997.

AVERIL POWER (FF)

27 Bayside Square East, Bayside, Dublin 13; Mobile: 086 727770; Leinster House: 01 6183156; Email: averil.powerff@oireachtas.ie; Website: www.averilpower.ie

Born Dublin 26th July 1978. Married to Fionnan Sheehan. Educated TCD (BA in Business, Economics and Social Science). Policy Advisor. Contested 2011 Dail election in Dublin North-East. New Senator.

Fianna Fail spokesperson on Education in the Seanad. Member Committee on Jobs, Social Protection and Education. Contested 2009 local elections in the Howth-Malahide electoral area of Fingal County Council. Former President TCD Students' Union.

MARY M. WHITE (FF)

6 Wyckham Park Road, Dundrum, Dublin 16; Tel: 01 8740365; Mobile: 086 2560533 Leinster House: 01 6183820; Email: mary.white@oireachtas.ie Website: www. senatormarywhite.ie

Born Dundalk, Co. Louth, 7th October 1944. Married to Padraic White (MD IDA 1980-1990), one daughter. Educated Holy Family Convent, Newbridge, Co. Kildare; College of Technology, Bolton Street (Dip Arch Tech); UCD (BA). Co-founder Lir Chocolates. Senator since 2002.

Member Committee on the Implementation of Good Friday Agreement. Spokesperson for Older People and Children 2007-2011. Member Joint Committee on Health and Children 2007-2011. Member Joint Committee on Finance and the Public Service 2002-2007. Member Irish Exporter's Association. Council member International Trade of Ireland. Member Marketing Institute of Ireland. Chairperson Presidents Awards (Gaisce) 1999-2001. Council Member Dublin Chamber of Commerce. Board member Bord Bia. Member Fianna Fail National Executive 1993-1998 and since 2006.

MARC MacSHARRY (FF)

Fatima, Pearse Road, Sligo, Co. Sligo; Tel: 071 9140049; Mobile 086 2674764.
Leinster House: 01 6184221; Email: marc.macsharry@oireachtas.ie

Born Dublin 12th July 1973. Married to Marie Murphy, one son Marc Jnr. and daughter Julie Rose. Educated Castleknock College, Dublin; El Colegio De Espana, Alicante, Spain (Certificate in Advanced Spanish). Former Chief Executive Officer Sligo Chamber Commerce. Contested 2011 general election in Sligo-North Leitrim. Senator since 2002.

Member Committee on Health and Children. Fianna Fail spokesperson on Health in the Seanad. Seanad Spokesperson on Finance 2007-2011. Member Joint Committee on Finance and the Public Service 2007-2011. Spokesperson on Marine and Natural Resources and Member Joint Committee on Communications, Marine and Natural Resources, 2002-2007. Member Board Sligo Leader Partnership. Member Board Sligo Social Economy Programme. Member Board of Marketing Sligo Forum. Member Chambers of Commerce Ireland and a representative on their Border Regional Authority. All Ireland Amateur One Act Drama Champion in 1997. Son of Ray MacSharry, TD for Sligo-Leitrim 1969-1989, Former Minister and EU Commissioner.

IMELDA HENRY (FG)

"Orient", Pearse Road, Sligo, Co. Sligo; Tel: 071 9143313; Mobile: 087 8177777
Leinster House: 01 6183123; Email:imelda.henry@oireachtas.ie

Born Sligo, 5th March 1967. Married to Aiden, one son, one daughter. Educated Ursuline College, Sligo; Secretarial and Business College, Dublin. Self Employed. Contested 2007 Dail election in Sligo North Leitrim. Contested 2007 Seanad election. New Senator.

Member Committee on Health and Children. Elected to Sligo County Council in Sligo Strandhill electoral area in 2004. Retained her seat in 2009.

PAUL COGHLAN (FG)

Ballydowney, Killarney, Co. Kerry; Tel: 064 31733; Mobile: 087 2217400
Constituency Office: 95 New Street, Killarney; Tel: 064 6631892;
Leinster House: 01 6183762; Email: paul.coghlan@oireachtas.ie

Born Killarney, Co. Kerry, June 1944. Married to Peggy O'Shea, two sons, three daughters. Educated St. Brendan's College, Killarney; De La Salle, Waterford. Property Consultant, Insurance Broker and Company Director. Senator since 1997.

Member Joint Administration Committee. Fine Gael Seanad spokesperson on Arts, Sports and Tourism 2007-2011. Member Joint Committee on Economic and Regulatory Affairs and Member Joint Administration Committee 2007-2011. Spokesperson on Enterprise, Trade and Employment 1997-2007. Member Joint Committee on Enterprise and Small Business 2002-2007. Member of Kerry County Council 1991-2003. Member of Killarney UDC 1985-1999. Member of Kerry VEC since 1991. Member of Dingle Harbour Board since 1991. Vice Chairman, Kerry Fisheries and Coastal Management Committee since 1991. Member of the Institute of Bankers in Ireland. Member and past President of Killarney Chamber of Commerce. Founding Director/Member Radio Kerry. Trustee and former Chairman of Muckross House. Member of Institute of Bankers in Ireland, the Life Insurance Association and the Institute of Professional Auctioneers and Valuers.

COLM BURKE (FG)

Gleann Rua, 36 Farranlea Grove, Model Farm Road, Cork; Tel: 021 4271531;
Constituency Office: 021 4348140; Mobile: 087 2592839;
Leinster House: 01 6183115; Email: colm.burke@oireachtas.ie

Born Dripsey, Co. Cork 17th January 1957. Married to Mary McCaffrey. Educated De La Salle College, Macroom and University College Cork where he obtained a BCL Degree. Solicitor. Contested November 1982 general election in Cork North-Central. Contested 1994 by-election in Cork North-Central. New Senator.

Member Committee on Health and Children. Member Committee on European Union Affairs. Member European Parliament 2007-2009, where he replaced Simon Coveney following his re-election to the Dail in 2007. Contested 2009 euro election in Ireland South. Member Cork City Council May 1995 to June 2007, having been re-elected in 1999 and 2004. Lord Mayor of Cork from July 2003 until June 2004. He comes from a farming family and is a former Member of Macra na Feirme.

KATHRYN REILLY (SF)

Farragh, Ballyjamesduff, Co. Cavan; Tel: 049 3510;
Leinster House: 01 6183171; Email:kathryn.reilly@oireachtas.ie

Born Ballyjamesduff, Co Cavan 17th September 1988. Single. Educated Virginia Vocational School; DCU (BA Hons in Economics, Politics and Law). UCD (MEconSc in European Economics and Public Affairs). Economic Advisor. New Senator.

Member Committee on European Union Affairs. Previously worked as a policy advisor on economics and enterprise in Leinster House to Sinn Féin Spokesperson on Finance Arthur Morgan TD.

CATHERINE NOONE (FG)

2 Eglington Court, Donnybrook, Dublin 4; Mobile: 087 2327433;
Leinster House: 01 6183127; Email: catherine.noone@oireachtas.ie

Born Claremorris, Co. Mayo, 24th June 1976. Single. Educated NUI Galway (BA in Law and Italian); Law Society of Ireland. Solicitor. New Senator.

Member Committee on Environment, Transport, Culture and Gaeltacht. First elected to Dublin City Council in South-East Inner City electoral area in 2009. Member of the Housing Strategic Policy Committee on Dublin City Council and a board member of the Hugh Lane Gallery and the Temple Bar Cultural Trust. Committee member of the Council's women's group who work to create awareness and to celebrate International Women's Day.

INDUSTRIAL & COMMERCIAL PANEL 2011

Candidate Oireachtas Sub-Panel	Party	1st	2nd Malone	3rd Keogh	4th Casserly	5th Crotty	6th Kinsella	7th Sheehan	8th Fortune	9th Fitzgerald	10th Byrne	11th Nolan
Harte, Jimmy	LB	70,000	70,000	70,000	+1,000 71,000	71,000	71,000	71,000	+1,000 72,000	72,000	+1,000 73,000	73,000
Power, Averil	FF	75,000	75,000	75,000	75,000	75,000	75,000	+6,000 81,000	+2,000 83,000	83,000	83,000	83,000
White, Mary*	FF	78,000	78,000	78,000	+1,000 79,000	79,000	79,000	+3,000 82,000	82,000	82,000	82,000	+2,000 84,000
MacSharry, Mark*	FF	69,000	69,000	69,000	69,000	69,000	69,000	+1,000 70,000	70,000	70,000	+1,000 71,000	71,000
Henry, Imelda	FG	41,000	41,000	41,000	41,000	41,000	41,000	41,000	41,000	+1,000 42,000	+3,000 45,000	+1,000 46,000
Coghlan, Paul*	FG	45,000	45,000	45,000	45,000	+1,000 46,000	46,000	46,000	46,000	+1,000 47,000	+1,000 48,000	+7,000 55,000
Burke, Colm	FG	40,000	40,000	40,000	40,000	40,000	+3,000 43,000	43,000	43,000	+1,000 44,000	44,000	+2,000 46,000
Reilly, Kathryn	SF	73,000	73,000	73,000	73,000	73,000	73,000	73,000	73,000	73,000	73,000	73,000
Noone, Catherine	FG	33,000	33,000	33,000	33,000	33,000	33,000	+1,000 34,000	34,000	+4,000 38,000	+3,000 41,000	+1,000 42,000
Crowe, John	FG	36,000	36,000	36,000	36,000	+1,000 37,000	37,000	37,000	37,000	+1,000 38,000	38,000	+1,000 39,000
Leddin, Joe	LB	40,000	40,000	40,000	40,000	40,000	40,000	40,000	+4,000 44,000	44,000	44,000	44,000
McVitty, Peter	FG	40,000	40,000	40,000	40,000	40,000	40,000	40,000	40,000	40,000	+2,000 42,000	+1,000 43,000
Conlon, Margaret	FF	47,000	47,000	47,000	47,000	47,000	47,000	+1,000 48,000	48,000	48,000	48,000	48,000
Brophy, Colm	FG	36,000	36,000	36,000	36,000	36,000	+1,000 37,000	37,000	37,000	+4,000 41,000	41,000	41,000
Higgins, Lorraine	LB	36,000	36,000	36,000	36,000	36,000	36,000	36,000	+1,000 37,000	37,000	37,000	37,000
McHugh, Tom	FG	29,000	29,000	29,000	29,000	29,000	29,000	29,000	29,000	29,000	29,000	29,000
Hayden, Aideen	LB	27,000	27,000	27,000	27,000	27,000	27,000	27,000	+1,000 28,000	28,000	28,000	28,000
Burke, Peter	FG	21,000	21,000	21,000	21,000	21,000	+1,000 22,000	22,000	22,000	+2,000 24,000	+1,000 25,000	+1,000 26,000
Hynes, Pat	NP	22,000	22,000	22,000	22,000	22,000	22,000	22,000	+1,000 23,000	23,000	+1,000 24,000	24,000
Breen, Gerry	FG	21,000	21,000	21,000	21,000	21,000	21,000	21,000	21,000	21,000	+1,000 22,000	+2,000 24,000
O'Flynn, Kenneth	FF	24,000	24,000	24,000	24,000	24,000	24,000	24,000	24,000	24,000	24,000	24,000
Butler, Richard	FG	21,000	21,000	21,000	21,000	21,000	21,000	21,000	+2,000 23,000	23,000	23,000	23,000
McGonigle, Laura	FG	21,000	21,000	21,000	21,000	21,000	21,000	21,000	21,000	21,000	+1,000 22,000	+1,000 23,000
Clendennen, John	FG	19,000	19,000	19,000	19,000	19,000	19,000	19,000	19,000	19,000	+1,000 20,000	+1,000 21,000
Boyle, Dan*	GP	19,000	19,000	19,000	19,000	19,000	19,000	19,000	+1,000 20,000	20,000	20,000	20,000
Nolan, Michael	FG	18,000	18,000	18,000	18,000	18,000	18,000	18,000	18,000	+1,000 19,000	+1,000 20,000	-20,000 Eliminated
Byrne, Danny	FG	15,000	15,000	+1,000 16,000	16,000	16,000	16,000	16,000	+1,000 17,000	17,000	-17,000 Eliminated	
Fitzgerald, David	FG	8,000	8,000	8,000	8,000	+4,000 12,000	+3,000 15,000	15,000	15,000	-15,000 Eliminated		
Fortune, Tom	LB	13,000	13,000	13,000	13,000	13,000	+1,000 14,000	14,000	-14,000 Eliminated			
Sheehan, Michael	FF	12,000	12,000	12,000	12,000	12,000	12,000	-12,000 Eliminated				
Kinsella, Michael	FG	9,000	9,000	9,000	9,000	9,000	-9,000 Eliminated					
Crotty, Pat	FG	6,000	6,000	6,000	6,000	-6,000 Eliminated						
Casserly, Mel	NP	2,000	2,000	2,000	-2,000 Eliminated							
Keogh, Paul	NP	1,000	1,000	-1,000 Eliminated								
Malone, Patrick	FG	0	0 Eliminated									
Non-transferable												
Cumulative * Outgoing		1,067,000	+0 1,067,000	+0 1,067,000	+0 1,067,000	+0 1,067,000	+0 1,067,000	+0 1,067,000	+0 1,067,000	+0 1,067,000	+0 1,067,000	+0 1,067,000
Electorate:		1,092	Valid:	1,067	Value:	1,067,000	Seats:	9	Quota:	106,701	Candidates	35

Candidate	12th Boyle	13th Clendennen	14th McGonigle	15th Butler	16th O'Flynn	17th Breen	18th Hynes	19th Burke, P	20th Hayden	21st McHugh	22nd Higgins
Harte, Jimmy	+1,000 74,000	74,000	74,000	74,000	74,000	74,000	+1,000 75,000	75,000	+12,000 87,000	87,000	+28,000 115,000
Power, Averil	+3,000 86,000	86,000	86,000	86,000	+11,000 97,000	97,000	+1,000 98,000	+1,000 99,000	+1,000 100,000	100,000	100,000
White, Mary*	84,000	84,000	84,000	84,000	+2,000 86,000	86,000	+1,000 87,000	87,000	+2,000 89,000	89,000	89,000
MacSharry, Mark*	+1,000 72,000	72,000	72,000	+1,000 73,000	+5,000 78,000	78,000	+1,000 79,000	79,000	+1,000 80,000	+1,000 81,000	+3,000 84,000
Henry, Imelda	46,000	+2,000 48,000	48,000	+1,000 49,000	49,000	+3,000 52,000	52,000	+3,000 55,000	+1,000 56,000	+10,000 66,000	66,000
Coghlan, Paul*	+3,000 58,000	+2,000 60,000	+2,000 62,000	+1,000 63,000	63,000	+5,000 68,000	+4,000 72,000	+4,000 76,000	+1,000 77,000	+2,000 79,000	+1,000 80,000
Burke, Colm	46,000	+3,000 49,000	+9,000 58,000	+3,000 61,000	+1,000 62,000	+4,000 66,000	+1,000 67,000	+4,000 71,000	71,000	71,000	71,000
Reilly, Kathryn	73,000	73,000	73,000	73,000	73,000	73,000	+4,000 77,000	77,000	+1,000 78,000	+1,000 79,000	+6,000 85,000
Noone, Catherine	42,000	+1,000 43,000	+2,000 45,000	+4,000 49,000	49,000	+4,000 53,000	+1,000 54,000	+6,000 60,000	60,000	+4,000 64,000	+3,000 67,000
Crowe, John	39,000	+4,000 43,000	+1,000 44,000	+8,000 52,000	52,000	+1,000 53,000	53,000	+3,000 56,000	56,000	+5,000 61,000	61,000
Leddin, Joe	44,000	44,000	44,000	+1,000 45,000	45,000	45,000	+1,000 46,000	46,000	+8,000 54,000	54,000	+10,000 64,000
McVitty, Peter	+1,000 44,000	+2,000 46,000	+1,000 47,000	47,000	47,000	+1,000 48,000	48,000	+5,000 53,000	53,000	+7,000 60,000	60,000
Conlon, Margaret	+3,000 51,000	+1,000 52,000	52,000	+2,000 54,000	+4,000 58,000	58,000	+3,000 61,000	61,000	61,000	61,000	+1,000 62,000
Brophy, Colm	41,000	+1,000 42,000	+2,000 44,000	+1,000 45,000	45,000	+5,000 50,000	50,000	+5,000 55,000	55,000	+2,000 57,000	57,000
Higgins, Lorraine	+5,000 42,000	+1,000 43,000	43,000	43,000	43,000	+1,000 44,000	+2,000 46,000	46,000	+4,000 50,000	+3,000 53,000	-53,000 Eliminated
McHugh, Tom	29,000	+1,000 30,000	30,000	30,000	+1,000 31,000	+1,000 32,000	+2,000 34,000	+2,000 36,000	36,000	-36,000 Eliminated	
Hayden, Aideen	+1,000 29,000	29,000	+1,000 30,000	30,000	30,000	30,000	+3,000 33,000	33,000	-33,000 Eliminated		
Burke, Peter	26,000	+3,000 29,000	+3,000 32,000	32,000	32,000	+1,000 33,000	33,000	-33,000 Eliminated			
Hynes, Pat	+2,000 26,000	26,000	26,000	26,000	26,000	26,000	-26,000 Eliminated				
Breen, Gerry	24,000	24,000	+2,000 26,000	26,000	26,000	-26,000 Eliminated					
O'Flynn, Kenneth	24,000	24,000	24,000	+1,000 25,000	-25,000 Eliminated						
Butler, Richard	23,000	23,000	23,000	-23,000 Eliminated							
McGonigle, Laura	23,000	23,000	-23,000 Eliminated								
Clendennen, John	21,000	-21,000 Eliminated									
Boyle, Dan*	-20,000 Eliminated										
Nolan, Michael											
Byrne, Danny											
Fitzgerald, David											
Fortune, Tom											
Sheehan, Michael											
Kinsella, Michael											
Crotty, Pat											
Casserly, Mel											
Keogh, Paul											
Malone, Patrick											
Non-transferable					1,000		1,000		2,000	1,000	1,000
Cumulative * Outgoing	+0 1,067,000	+0 1,067,000	+0 1,067,000	+0 1,067,000	+1,000 1,067,000	+1,000 1,067,000	+2,000 1,067,000	+2,000 1,067,000	+4,000 1,067,000	+5,000 1,067,000	+6,000 1,067,000

Candidate	23rd Harte	24th Brophy	25th Conlon	26th Power	27th White	28th MacSharry	29th McVitty	30th Henry	31st Leddin	32nd Coghlan	33rd Crowe
Harte, Jimmy	-8,299 106,701	106,701	106,701	106,701	106,701	106,701	106,701	106,701	106,701	106,701	106,701
Power, Averil	100,000	100,000	+15,000 115,000	-8,299 106,701	106,701	106,701	106,701	106,701	106,701	106,701	106,701
White, Mary*	+307 89,307	89,307	+19,000 108,307	108,307	-1,606 106,701	106,701	106,701	106,701	106,701	106,701	106,701
MacSharry, Mark*	+307 84,307	84,307	+24,000 108,307	108,307	108,307	-1,606 106,701	106,701	106,701	106,701	106,701	106,701
Henry, Imelda	66,000	+6,000 72,000	+1,000 73,000	+2,000 75,000	75,000	75,000	+32,000 107,000	-299 106,701	106,701	106,701	106,701
Coghlan, Paul*	80,000	+4,000 84,000	+1,000 85,000	85,000	+803 85,803	85,803	+17,000 102,803	102,803	+9,000 111,803	-5,102 106,701	106,701
Burke, Colm	71,000	+15,000 86,000	+1,000 87,000	87,000	87,000	87,000	+5,000 92,000	92,000	+11,614 103,614	+1,700 105,314	+21,000 126,314
Reilly, Kathryn	+307 85,307	85,307	85,307	+2,000 87,307	+803 88,110	+803 88,913	+1,000 89,913	89,913	+11,456 101,369	+1,700 103,069	+4,000 107,069
Noone, Catherine	67,000	+17,000 84,000	84,000	+2,000 86,000	86,000	86,000	+7,000 93,000	93,000	+5,921 98,921	+850 99,771	+7,000 106,771
Crowe, John	61,000	+8,000 69,000	69,000	69,000	69,000	69,000	+4,000 73,000	+299 73,299	+8,000 81,299	+850 82,149	-82,149 Eliminated
Leddin, Joe	+7,368 71,368	71,368	71,368	+1,000 72,368	72,368	72,368	72,368	72,368	-72,368 Eliminated		
McVitty, Peter	60,000	+7,000 67,000	67,000	67,000	67,000	+803 67,803	-67,803 Eliminated				
Conlon, Margaret	62,000	62,000	-62,000 Eliminated								
Brophy, Colm	57,000	-57,000 Eliminated									
Higgins, Lorraine											
McHugh, Tom											
Hayden, Aideen											
Burke, Peter											
Hynes, Pat											
Breen, Gerry											
O'Flynn, Kenneth											
Butler, Richard											
McGonigle, Laura											
Clendennen, John											
Boyle, Dan*											
Nolan, Michael											
Byrne, Danny											
Fitzgerald, David											
Fortune, Tom											
Sheehan, Michael											
Kinsella, Michael											
Crotty, Pat											
Casserly, Mel											
Keogh, Paul											
Malone, Patrick											
Non-transferable	10		1,000	1,299			1,803		26,377	2	50,149
Cumulative * Outgoing	+6,010 1,067,000	+6,010 1,067,000	+7,010 1,067,000	+8,309 1,067,000	+8,309 1,067,000	+8,309 1,067,000	+10,112 1,067,000	+10,112 1,067,000	+36,489 1,067,000	+36,491 1,067,000	+86,640 1,067,000

LABOUR PANEL 2011

MAURICE CUMMINS (FG)

34 Ursuline Court, Waterford; Tel: 051 855486; Mobile: 087 6827737;
Leinster House: 01 6184206; Email: maurice.cummins@oireachtas.ie

Born Waterford 25th February 1954. Married to Anne O'Shea, one son, one daughter. Educated De La Salle College, Newtown, Waterford. Formerly Claims Manager. Contested 2002 general election in Waterford. Senator since 2002.

Leader of the Seanad. Member Committee on the Implementation of Good Friday Agreement. Fine Gael Whip in the Seanad and Spokesperson on Foreign Affairs October 2007-2011. Member Joint Committee on Foreign Affairs and Member Joint Committee on European Affairs 2007-2011. Former Member Committee of Selection of Seanad Eireann. Former Member Seanad Committee on Procedure and Privileges. Member Waterford City Council 1991-2003. Mayor of Waterford 1995-1996. Former Chairman Waterford City Development Board. Former Member European Committee of the Regions. Former Member Regional Authority and Assembly. Former Director Waterford Port Company. Former Chairman Waterford International Festival of Light Opera. Former President FAI Schoolboys and Youth Committees.

FIDELMA HEALY-EAMES (FG)

Maree, Oranmore, Co. Galway; Tel: 091 792017; Mobile: 087 6776937;
Leinster House: 01 6183742; Email: fidelma.healy.eames@oireachtas.ie;
Website: www.fidelmahealyeames.finegael.ie

Born Moylough, Co. Galway, 14th July 1962. Married to Michael Eames, one son, one daughter. Educated Carysfort College, Blackrock, Dublin (B.Ed.); Western Connecticut State University, USA (M.Sc); UCG (Ph.D). Former Primary Teacher, College Lecturer and has her own business. Contested 2007 and 2011general elections in Galway West. Senator since 2007.

Member Committee on European Union Affairs. Seanad spokesperson on Education and Science 2007-2011. Member Joint Committee on Education and Science 2007-2011. Member Galway County Council 2004-2007. Former Chairperson VEC. Member GMIT Governing Body; Western Rail Committee; Galway Arts Centre Board; Corrib Lions Club. Director Galway Airport.

MARIE MOLONEY (LB)

Coolick, Kilcummin, Killarney, Co. Kerry; Tel: 066 9764563; Mobile: 086 3049422
Constituency Office: 064 6632034; E-mail: marie.moloney@oireachtas.ie

Born Kerry, 26th August 1958; Married. Educated Killarney Technical College. SIPTU employee. Contested 2011 Dail election in Kerry South. New Senator.

Member Joint Administration Committee. First elected to Kerry County Council in Killarney electoral area in 2009. Administrative Assistant with SIPTU in Killarney. Former assistant to Breeda Moynihan-Cronin TD for Kerry South 1992-2007. Member of Boards of Management in a number of schools. Volunteer with Meals on Wheels service for nearly 25 years. Former Secretary of Killarney Bridge Club and South of Ireland Bridge Congress. Former Cub Scout Leader with Killarney Boy Scouts.

DAVID CULLINANE (SF)

1 Maple Terrace, Lisduggan, Waterford; Tel: 051 854801; Mobile: 086 3725152;
Leinster House: 01 6183176; Email: david.cullinane@oireachtas.ie

Born Waterford City 4th July 1974. Married to Kathleen Funchion, two children. Diploma in Marketing and Business Management. Former Storeman. Contested 2002, 2007 and 2011 Dail elections in Waterford. Contested 2004 Euro election in South constituency. New Senator.

Member Committee on Health and Children. First elected to Waterford County Council in 2004 in Waterford No. 3. Retained his seat in 2009.

TONY MULCAHY (FG)

6 Tullyvarragha Crescent, Shannon, Co. Clare; Tel: 061 360309; Mobile: 086 2436345; Leinster House: 01 6183205; Email: tony.mulcahy@oireachtas.ie

Born Newcastle West, Co. Limerick, 12th April 1959. Married to Carmel, four children. Catering Company Owner. Contested Dail election in Clare in 2007 and 2011. New Senator.

Member Committee on Investigations, Oversight and Petitions. First elected to Clare County Council in Shannon electoral area in 1999. Re-elected 2004 and 2009. Elected to Shannon TC in 1994. Re-elected 1999, 2004 and 2009.

CAIT KEANE (FG)

26 Rushbrook Court, Templeogue, Dublin 6W; Tel: 01 4149064; Mobile: 087 8117824
Leinster House: 01 6183179; Email: cait.keane@soireachtas.ie

Born Galway 24th September 1949; Married to Sean, one son, two daughters; BA, MA; Diploma in Montessori Education. Diploma in Community Development. Former Teacher. Contested Dail elections in Dublin South Central for PDs in 1992 and 1997. Contested By-election 9th June 1994. Joined Fine Gael 7th October 2008. Contested 2011 general election in Dublin South West. New Senator.

Member Committee on Environment, Transport, Culture and Gaeltacht. First elected to South Dublin County Council for PDs in 1991 in Terenure. Retained her seat in Terenure-Rathfarnham in 1999 and 2004. Re-elected in new electoral area of Rathfarnham in 2009.

TERRY BRENNAN (FG)

Ghan Road, Carlingford, Co. Louth; Tel: 042 9373348; Mobile: 087 2942956
Leinster House: 01 6183872; Email: terry.brennan@oireachtas.ie

Born Carlingford, Co. Louth, 24th May 1942. Married. Contested 1997 and 2002 Dail elections in Louth. New Senator.

Member Joint Administration Committee. First elected to Louth County Council in 1985 in Carlingford. Retained his seat in 1991. Re-elected in Dundalk Carlingford in 1999, 2004 and 2009.

DARRAGH O'BRIEN (FF)

49 Galtrim Grange, Malahide, Co. Dublin; Mobile: 086 2519893
Constituency Office: Suite 7 Manor House, Church Road, Malahide; Tel: 01 8450710,
Leinster House: 01 6183802, Email: darragh.obrien@oireachtas.ie
Website: www.darraghobrien.ie

Born Malahide 8th July 1974. Married to Susan Maxwell. Educated Pobail Scoil Iosa, Malahide. Previously worked in Friends Provident. First elected to Dail in 2007. Lost his seat in 2011. Appointed to Senate 4th March 2011 as replacement for Ciaran Cannon who had been elected to the Dail. New Senator.

Member Committee on Investigations, Oversight and Petitions. Convenor Joint Committee on Foreign Affairs 2007-2011. Vice-chair Public Accounts Committee and Member Joint Committee on Justice, Equality, Defence and Women's Rights 2007-2011. Member Fingal County Council 2004-2007. Member Malahide Cricket Club, St. Sylvester's GAA Club and Malahide United.

TERRY LEYDEN (FF)

Castlecoote, Co. Roscommon; Tel: 0903 26422; Mobile: 087 7978922
Leinster House: 01 6183853; Email: terry.leyden@oireachtas.ie
Website: www.terrryleyden.com

Born Roscommon, 1st Oct 1945. Married to Mary Margaret O'Connor, one son (Conor), three daughters (Orla, Mairead and Sinead). Educated Roscommon Vocational School; UCG. Trade and Marketing Consultant, former Architectural Designer. Dail Deputy 1977-1992. Senator November 1992-March 1993 and since 2002.

Member Committee on European Union Affairs. Spokesperson on European Affairs and Integration Policy 2007-2011. Member Joint Committee on European Affairs and Member Joint Committee on European Scrutiny 2007-2011. Spokesperson on Enterprise, Trade and Employment 2002-2007. Member Joint Committee on Enterprise and Small Business 2002-2007. Minister of State Department Industry and Commerce 1989-1992. Minister of State at Department Health 1987-1989. Front bench spokesperson on Posts and Telegraphs 1983-1987. Minister of State at Department Posts and Telegraphs 1982. Member Roscommon County Council 1974-1982, 1985-1987 and 1999-2003.

NED O'SULLIVAN (FF)

Cahirdown, Listowel, Co. Kerry; Tel: 068 21386; Mobile: 087 2459290
Constituency Office: 068 21831; Email: ned.osullivan@oireachtas.ie

Born Listowel, Co. Kerry, 25th November 1950. Married to Madeleine Murphy, three sons. Educated St. Michael's College, Listowel; UCD (BA, HDip Ed); St. Patrick's, Drumcondra. Former Teacher, proprietor of menswear business. Senator since 2007.

Member Committee on Environment, Transport, Culture and Gaeltacht. Seanad Spokesperson on Food and Horticulture, Health Promotion and Food Safety 2007-2011. Member Joint Committee on Climate Change and Energy Security and Member Joint Committee on Economic and Regulatory Affairs 2007-2011. Member Kerry Council 1991-2007. Mayor of Kerry 2004. Member Listowel Town Council 1985-2007. Chairman Shannon Basin Advisory Board. Director Shannon Foynes Harbour Board. Cousin of Kit Ahern TD for Kerry North 1977-1981.

JOHN WHELAN (LB)

Cremorgan, Timahoe, Portlaoise, Co. Laois; Tel:057 8634047; Mobile: 087 2509663
Leinster House: 01 6183244; Email: john.whelan@oireachtas.ie

Born Portlaoise, 24th March 1961; Married to Grazyna Rekosiewicz; two daughters, one son, Faith (26), Ricky (23) and Martyna (22). Educated St. Paul's Secondary School, Monasterevin, Co. Kildare; St. Ignatius Rice College, Dun Laoghaire; Journalist. Contested 2011 Dail election in Laois-Offaly. New Senator.

Member Committee on Communications, Natural Resources and Agriculture. John is a journalist of 30 years based in Laois-Offaly and has worked as Editor of the Leinster Express in Portlaoise, the Offaly Express in Tullamore, Leinster Leader in Naas and as Group Managing Editor of the now defunct Voice group of newspapers. A member of the NUJ since he joined the workforce at 17 years of age he went on to serve as Chairman of the Midlands Branch of the National Union of Journalists and was a member of the NUJ National Council. He is a keen supporter of the GAA and has actively involved over the years in local soccer and basketball clubs as well as a founding member of the Laois Surf Club. He is also a founder of the Portlaoise Jazz Festival, the Mountmellick Mardi Gras and the Laois Arts Festival. He has recently published his first novel, 'The Buddha of Ballyhuppahaun', a satire strongly influenced by George Orwell's Animal Farm and Jonathon Swift's, Gulliver's Travels.

LABOUR PANEL 2011

Candidate	Party	1st	2nd	3rd	4th	5th	6th	7th	8th	9th	10th	11th	12th	13th	14th	15th	16th	17th
Oireachtas Sub-Panel			Cummins	O'Reilly	O'Callaghan	Healy Eames	Nevin	Moloney	Murnane	Donnelly	Cullinane	Campbell	Hanafin	Richmond	Mulcahy	Keane	Brennan	Feeney
Cummins, Maurice*	FG	100,000	-11,166 88,834	88,834	88,834	88,834	88,834	88,834	88,834	88,834	88,834	88,834	88,834	88,834	88,834	88,834	88,834	88,834
Healy Eames, Fidelma*	FG	83,000	+2,553 85,553	85,553	+5,000 90,553	-1,719 88,834	88,834	88,834	88,834	88,834	88,834	88,834	88,834	88,834	88,834	88,834	88,834	88,834
Moloney, Marie	LB	63,000	63,000	+5,000 68,000	+1,000 69,000	69,000	+23,000 92,000	-3,166 88,834	88,834	88,834	88,834	88,834	88,834	88,834	88,834	88,834	88,834	88,834
Cullinane, David	SF	84,000	+444 84,444	+1,000 85,444	85,444	85,444	+2,000 87,444	+137 87,581	87,581	+3,000 90,581	-1,747 88,834	88,834	88,834	88,834	88,834	88,834	88,834	88,834
Mulcahy, Tony	FG	64,000	+2,442 66,442	66,442	+7,000 73,442	+343 73,785	73,785	73,785	73,785	+2,000 75,785	75,785	+9,565 85,350	+1,000 86,350	+16,000 102,350	-13,516 88,834	88,834	88,834	88,834
Keane, Cáit	FG	44,000	+1,332 45,332	45,332	+2,222 47,554	+686 48,240	+1,000 49,240	49,240	49,240	+3,000 52,240	52,240	+17,222 69,462	+1,000 70,462	+20,000 90,462	90,462	-1,628 88,834	88,834	88,834
Brennan, Terry	FG	54,000	+1,554 55,554	+1,000 56,554	+1,222 57,776	57,776	57,776	57,776	57,776	+1,000 58,776	58,776	+9,222 67,998	67,998	+10,342 78,340	+12,660 91,000	91,000	-2,166 88,834	88,834
O'Brien, Darragh*	FF	51,000	51,000	51,000	51,000	51,000	51,000	+274 51,274	+16,000 67,274	+2,000 69,274	69,274	69,274	+7,000 76,274	76,274	76,274	+108 76,382	76,382	+18,000 94,382
Leyden, Terry*	FF	51,000	+111 51,111	+1,000 52,111	+1,000 53,111	53,111	+1,000 54,111	54,111	+6,000 60,111	+10,111 70,222	70,222	70,222	+10,000 80,222	+222 80,444	+844 81,288	+432 81,720	+432 82,152	+8,000 90,152
O'Sullivan, Ned*	FF	55,000	55,000	55,000	+1,000 56,000	56,000	56,000	+274 56,274	+3,000 59,274	+3,000 62,274	+1,746 64,020	+1,000 65,020	+10,000 75,020	75,020	75,020	+108 75,128	+216 75,344	+14,111 89,455
Whelan, John	LB	66,000	66,000	+1,000 67,000	67,000	67,000	+9,000 76,000	+2,329 78,329	+137 78,466	+2,000 80,466	80,466	+1,000 81,466	+2,000 83,466	+1,000 84,466	84,466	+648 85,114	+1,296 86,410	+1,000 87,410
Cassidy, Donie*	FF	42,000	42,000	42,000	42,000	42,000	+1,000 43,000	43,000	+5,000 48,000	+7,000 55,000	55,000	55,000	+9,000 64,000	64,000	64,000	+324 64,324	+216 64,540	+12,000 76,540
Feeney, Geraldine*	FF	44,000	+111 44,111	44,111	44,111	44,111	44,111	44,111	+3,000 47,111	47,111	47,111	47,111	+6,000 53,111	53,111	53,111	53,111	53,111	-53,111 Eliminated
Richmond, Neale	FG	39,000	+888 39,888	39,888	+3,222 43,110	+343 43,453	43,453	43,453	43,453	+1,000 44,453	44,453	+4,111 48,564	48,564	-48,564 Eliminated				
Hanafin, John G.*	FF	39,000	39,000	39,000	39,000	39,000	39,000	39,000	+5,000 44,000	+3,000 47,000	47,000	47,000	-47,000 Eliminated					
Campbell, Sirena	FG	33,000	+666 33,666	33,666	+7,111 40,777	+343 41,120	41,120	41,120	41,120	+1,000 42,120	42,120	-42,120 Eliminated						
Donnelly, Francis	NP	37,000	+111 37,111	+3,000 40,111	40,111	40,111	40,111	40,111	40,111	-40,111 Eliminated								
Murnane O'Connor, Jennifer	FF	38,000	38,000	38,000	38,000	38,000	38,000	+137 38,137	-38,137 Eliminated									
Nevin, Barry	LB	37,000	37,000	37,000	37,000	37,000	-37,000 Eliminated											
O'Callaghan, Joe	FG	28,000	+777 28,777	28,777	-28,777 Eliminated													
O'Reilly, Michael	NP	14,000	+111 14,111	-14,111 Eliminated														
Non-transferable Cumulative			+66 66	+2,111 2,177	2,177	+4 2,181	2,181	+15 2,196	2,196	+2,000 4,196	+1 4,197	4,197	+1,000 5,197	+1,000 6,197	+12 6,209	+8 6,217	+6 6,223	6,223
*Outgoing		1,066,000	1,066,000	1,066,000	1,066,000	1,066,000	1,066,000	1,066,000	1,066,000	1,066,000	1,066,000	1,066,000	1,066,000	1,066,000	1,066,000	1,066,000	1,066,000	1,066,000
	Electorate:	1,092	Valid:	1,066	Value:	1,066,000	Seats:	11	Quota:	88,834	Candidates	21						

NATIONAL UNIVERSITY OF IRELAND 2011

RÓNÁN MULLEN (IND)

Ahascragh, Ballinasloe, Co. Galway; Tel: 01 6769807; Mobile: 087 2446911; Leinster House: 01 6183930; Email: ronan.mullen@oireachtas.ie

Born Ahascragh, Ballinasloe, Co. Galway 13th October 1970. Single. Educated Holy Rosary College, Mountbellew, Co. Galway; UCG (BA); King's Inns (Barrister at Law). Columnist, Lecturer and Barrister. Senator since 2007.

Member Committee on Justice, Defence and Equality. Member Joint Committee on Social and Family Affairs 2007-2011. Member Board of Directors CEIST Ltd. Member Corporate Board of Management, St. Vincent's Trust. Press Officer Dublin Diocese 1996-2001. Academic and Student Affairs Officer Dundalk RTC 1994-1996. President Students Union, UCG 1991-1992.

FEARGAL QUINN (IND)

Sutton Cross, Dublin 13; Tel: 01 8167163; Mobile: 087 6865215
Leinster House: 01 6183222; Email: himself@feargalquinn.ie.
Website: www.feargalquinn.ie

Born Dublin 27th November 1936. Married to Denise Prendergast, three sons, two daughters. Educated Newbridge College, Co. Kildare; UCD (BComm). Former Managing Director, Superquinn. First contested Senate election in 1973. Senator since 1993.

Member Committee on Jobs, Social Protection and Education. Member Joint Committee on Finance and the Public Service and Member Joint Committee on European Affairs 2007-2011. Appointed Adjunct Professor in Marketing at UCG in 2006. Board member of a number of international retailing organisations and has received two honorary doctorates. President of the EU-wide lobbying group Eurocommerce. International Board Member US Food Marketing Institute. Former President of the global Food Business Forum. First chairman of An Post. Author of "Crowning the Customer". Received the papal knighthood, Knight of St. Gregory 1994.

JOHN CROWN (IND)

270 Merrion Road, Dublin 4; Mobile: 087 2647767;
Leinster House: 01 6183260; Email: john.crown@oireachtas.ie
Website: www.JohnCrown.ie

Born 1st March 1957 in New York to Irish emigrants (Leitrim and Kildare). Returned to Ireland in 1967. Divorced, two daughters, one son. Educated: Patrician Brothers NS, Newbridge; Synge Street; Terenure College; UCD. A graduate of UCD and the State University of New York, and holds degrees in medicine, science and business administration. His postdoctoral training took place at Guy's Hospital in London and St. James's Hospital in Dublin. He completed his training in oncology in New York at Mount Sinai Medical Centre and the Memorial Sloan-Kettering Cancer Centre He held the post of assistant professor at Weill Cornell Medical College of Cornell University until 1993 when he returned to Ireland, becoming a consultant at two Dublin hospitals: St. Vincent's and St. Luke's. He holds professorships in cancer research from Dublin City University and University College Dublin. Founded Ireland's first national cancer treatment research group – ICORG in 1997. New Senator.

Member Committee on Health and Children.

NATIONAL UNIVERSITY OF IRELAND 2011																								
Candidate	**1st**	**2nd** Cowley Votes	**3rd** Langan Votes	**4th** O'Donoghue Votes	**5th** Ó Cadhla Votes	**6th** Sullivan Votes	**7th** O'Donnell Votes	**8th** McCurtain Votes	**9th** Kennedy Votes	**10th** Coyle Votes	**11th** Canning Votes	**12th** Ó Broin Votes	**13th** Molloy Votes	**14th** Lynam Votes	**15th** Mooney Votes	**16th** Doorley Votes	**17th** Ó Brolchain Votes	**18th** Price Votes	**19th** Healy Votes	**20th** O'Shea Votes	**21st** O'Connor Votes	**22nd** O'Connell Votes	**23rd** Keogh Votes	**24th** O'Sullivan Votes
***Outgoing**																								
		+8	+15	+16	+17	+10	+16	+21	+22	+18	+42	+60	+40	+65	+37	+65	+148	+84	+125	+131	+253	+443	+280	+653
Mullen, Ronan*	6,459	6,467	6,482	6,498	6,515	6,525	6,541	6,562	6,584	6,602	6,644	6,704	6,744	6,809	6,846	6,911	7,059	7,143	7,268	7,399	7,652	8,095	8,375	9,028
			+20	+17	+19	+27	+29	+34	+36	+85	+78	+43	+110	+105	+76	+102	+141	+202	+131	+281	+372	+415	+784	+784
Quinn, Fergal*	4,591	4,591	4,611	4,628	4,647	4,674	4,703	4,737	4,773	4,858	4,936	4,979	5,089	5,194	5,270	5,372	5,513	5,715	5,846	6,127	6,499	6,914	7,698	8,482
		+4	+8	+4	+8	+29	+18	+17	+32	+56	+74	+37	+210	+85	+85	+100	+136	+173	+171	+188	+198	+476	+486	+649
Crown, John	4,703	4,707	4,715	4,719	4,727	4,756	4,774	4,791	4,823	4,879	4,953	4,990	5,200	5,285	5,370	5,470	5,606	5,779	5,950	6,138	6,336	6,812	7,298	7,947
		+3		+6	+3	+5	+1	+45	+4	+5	+7	+22	+11	+25	+24	+55	+35	+45	+122	+61	+86	+200	+190	+684
Kelleher, Declan	3,771	3,774	3,774	3,780	3,783	3,788	3,789	3,834	3,838	3,843	3,850	3,872	3,883	3,908	3,932	3,987	4,022	4,067	4,189	4,250	4,336	4,536	4,726	5,410
		+3	+6	+7	+5	+4	+9	+25	+6	+9	+13	+36	+8	+25	+27	+33	+42	+70	+288	+178	+244	+190	+566	-3,822
O'Sullivan, Bernadine	2,028	2,031	2,037	2,044	2,049	2,053	2,062	2,087	2,093	2,102	2,115	2,151	2,159	2,184	2,211	2,244	2,286	2,356	2,644	2,822	3,066	3,256	3,822	Eliminated
		+4	+6	+5	+6	+10	+9	+15	+100	+21	+20	+4	+16	+43	+52	+106	+61	+91	+50	+282	+324	+224	-2,811	
Keogh, Helen	1,362	1,366	1,372	1,377	1,383	1,393	1,402	1,417	1,517	1,538	1,558	1,562	1,578	1,621	1,673	1,779	1,840	1,931	1,981	2,263	2,587	2,811	Eliminated	
		+6	+3	+8	+5	+12	+15	+2	+4	+11	+13	+39	+9	+16	+57	+111	+103	+56	+80	+74	+101	-2,354		
O'Connell, Donncha	1,629	1,635	1,638	1,646	1,651	1,663	1,678	1,680	1,684	1,695	1,708	1,747	1,756	1,772	1,829	1,940	2,043	2,099	2,179	2,253	2,354	Eliminated		
		+4	+7	+14	+17	+11	+32	+50	+22	+29	+31	+21	+20	+43	+29	+51	+38	+60	+50	+198	-1,828			
O'Connor, Regina	1,101	1,105	1,112	1,126	1,143	1,154	1,186	1,236	1,258	1,287	1,318	1,339	1,359	1,402	1,431	1,482	1,520	1,580	1,630	1,828	Eliminated			
			+6	+8	+4	+7	+11	+7	+17	+14	+17	+15	+15	+30	+41	+50	+58	+55	+63	-1,501				
O'Shea Farren, Linda	1,083	1,083	1,089	1,097	1,101	1,108	1,119	1,126	1,143	1,157	1,174	1,189	1,204	1,234	1,275	1,325	1,383	1,438	1,501	Eliminated				
		+5	+1	+1	+6	+4	+7	+12	+6	+6	+8	+57	+4	+10	+35	+38	+32	+44	-1,223					
Healy, Paddy	947	952	953	954	960	964	971	983	989	995	1,003	1,060	1,064	1,074	1,109	1,147	1,179	1,223	Eliminated					
		+2	+4	+9	+18	+15	+16	+10	+9	+8	+13	+36	+20	+17	+47	+53	+81	-1,029						
Price, Brendan	671	673	677	686	704	719	735	745	754	762	775	811	831	848	895	948	1,029	Eliminated						
		+4	+2	+5	+10	+2	+4	+7	+7	+10	+11	+39	+10	+20	+38	+35	-922							
Ó Brollcháin, Niall	718	722	724	729	739	741	745	752	759	769	780	819	829	849	887	922	Eliminated							
		+1	+4	+4	+6	+8	+5	+5	+8	+18	+12	+25	+11	+21	+70	-853								
Doorley, James	655	656	660	664	670	678	683	688	696	714	726	751	762	783	853	Eliminated								
		+1	+6	+1	+3	+7	+9	+7	+8	+7	+8	+19	+10	+14	-647									
Mooney, Peter	547	548	554	555	558	565	574	581	589	596	604	623	633	647	Eliminated									
		+1	+4	+5	+3	+3	+2	+6	+10	+8	+10	+16	+9	-553										
Lynam, Paul	476	477	481	486	489	492	494	500	510	518	528	544	553	Eliminated										
			+9		+2	+4	+5	+2	+3	+6	+14	+5	-534											
Molloy, Michael	484	484	493	493	495	499	504	506	509	515	529	534	Eliminated											
		+2	+2	+1	+9	+2	+3	+1	+1	+7	+1	-519												
Ó Broin, Eoin	490	492	494	495	504	506	509	510	511	518	519	Eliminated												
		+4	+5	+4	+2	+4	+2	+3	+8	+11	-397													
Canning, Thomas	354	358	363	367	369	373	375	378	386	397	Eliminated													
		+2	+6	+4	+7	+5	+10	+2	+7	-350														
Coyle, James	307	309	315	319	326	331	341	343	350	Eliminated														
			+4	+4	+4	+22	+3	+4	-320															
Kennedy, John	279	279	283	287	291	313	316	320	Eliminated															
		+2	+1	+4	+18	+5	+2	-294																
McCurtain, David	262	264	265	269	287	292	294	Eliminated																
			+3	+10		+3	-215																	
O'Donnell, Francis	199	199	202	212	212	215	Eliminated																	
			+4	+10	+3	-210																		
Sullivan, Daniel	193	193	197	207	210	Eliminated																		
				+2	-184																			
Ó Cadhla, Diarmaid	182	182	182	184	Eliminated																			
			+1	-155																				
O'Donoghue, James	154	154	155	Eliminated																				
		+1	-130																					
Langan, Mick	129	130	Eliminated																					
		-57																						
Cowley, Matthias	57	Eliminated																						
Non-transferable			+3	+6	+9	+11	+7	+19	+10	+21	+25	+45	+31	+34	+29	+54	+47	+149	+143	+108	+250	+406	+505	+1,052
Cumulative		0	3	9	18	29	36	55	65	86	111	156	187	221	250	304	351	500	643	751	1,001	1,407	1,912	2,964
Total	**33,831**	**33,831**	**33,831**	**33,831**	**33,831**	**33,831**	**33,831**	**33,831**	**33,831**	**33,831**	**33,831**	**33,831**	**33,831**	**33,831**	**33,831**	**33,831**	**33,831**	**33,831**	**33,831**	**33,831**	**33,831**	**33,831**	**33,831**	**33,831**
Electorate:	**102,000**		**Valid:**	**33,831**		**Seats:**	**3**		**Quota:**	**8,458**		**Candidates:**		**27**										

UNIVERSITY OF DUBLIN 2011

DAVID NORRIS (IND)

18 North Great George's Street, Dublin 1; Tel: 01 8724614
Leinster House: 01 6183104; Email: david.norris@oireachtas.ie
Website: www.senatordavidnorris.ie

Born Leopoldville, Belgian Congo July 1944. Educated St. Andrews College and High School, Dublin; Reade Pianoforte School; TCD (BA [Mod], MA). Former University Lecturer. Senator since 1987.

Candidate for the Presidency in 2011. Member Committee on Foreign Affairs and Trade. Member Joint Committee on Foreign Affairs and Member Joint Committee on Transport 2007-2011. Chairman, Campaign for Homosexual Law Reform. Member Royal Zoological Society of Ireland; Royal Dublin Society; An Taisce; Irish Federation of University Teachers; Amnesty International; Irish Georgian Society; Dublin Crisis Conference Steering Committee. Chairman of James Joyce Cultural Centre, Dublin; North Great George's Street Preservation Society and Friends of the Library TCD.

IVANA BACIK (IND)

Portobello, Dublin 8; Tel: 01 8172932; Mobile: 086 8133751;
Leinster House: 01 6183136; Email: ivana.bacik@oireachtas.ie,
Website: www.ivanabacik.com

Born London, 25th May 1968. Partner Alan Saul, two children. Educated Alexandra College, Milltown, Dublin 6; Trinity College; London School of Economics (LLM). Reid Professor of Criminal Law, Criminology and Penology at Trinity College, Dublin. Lecturer and Barrister. Contested By-election in Dublin Central June 2009. Contested 2011 general election in Dun Laoghaire. Contested 2004 and 2009 European elections in Dublin. Contested 1997 and 2002 Senate elections.
Senator since 2007.

Member Committee on Justice, Defence and Equality. Leader of the Labour Party in the Seanad. Member Joint Committee on Justice, Equality, Defence and Women's Rights and Member Joint Committee on the Implementation of the Good Friday Agreement 2007-2011. Honory Secretary of TCD Law Alumni Association 1996-2004. Editor Irish Criminal Law Journal until 2003. Board member Friends of the Earth and Corn Exchange Theatre Company. Board member Irish Family Planning Association until 2004; Irish Penal Reform Trust until 2003. President TCD Students Union 1989-1990. Co-author "Abortion and the Law, Towards a Culture of Human Rights in Ireland and Crime and Poverty in Ireland".

SEAN BARRETT (IND)

Maynooth, Co. Kildare; TCD Office: 01 8961523;
Leinster House: 01 6183264; Email: seand.barrett@oireachtas.ie

Born Cork 1944. Married to Dr. Maeve O'Brien, one daughter. Educated UCD (BA; PhD); McMasters University, Canada (MA). Senior Lecturer in the Department of Economics, Trinity College, specialising in transport, especially aviation and tourism. Contested 1997 and 2002 Senate elections. New Senator.

Member Committee on Finance, Public Expenditure and Reform. Former Director Bord Failte. Member National Economic and Social Council since 2005.

UNIVERSITY OF DUBLIN 2011																		
Candidate * **Outgoing**	**1st**	**2nd** Norris Surplus	**3rd** Donnelly Votes	**4th** Sheehan Votes	**5th** Connolly Votes	**6th** Quinn Votes	**7th** Frost Votes	**8th** Cox Votes	**9th** Martin Votes	**10th** Dudgeon Votes	**11th** Bacik Surplus	**12th** Priestley Votes	**13th** Hanan Votes	**14th** McGovern Votes	**15th** O'Malley Votes	**16th** McDonagh Votes	**17th** Coleman Votes	**18th** Gueret Votes
Norris, David*	5,623	-1,733 3,890	3,890	3,890	3,890	3,890	3,890	3,890	3,890	3,890	3,890	3,890	3,890	3,890	3,890	3,890	3,890	3,890
Bacik, Ivana*	2,982	+703 3,685	3,685	+8 3,693	+8 3,701	+27 3,728	+53 3,781	+52 3,833	+56 3,889	+51 3,940	-50 3,890	3,890	3,890	3,890	3,890	3,890	3,890	3,890
Barrett, Sean	1,051	+197 1,248	+8 1,256	+7 1,263	+10 1,273	+20 1,293	+21 1,314	+26 1,340	+16 1,356	+27 1,383	+8 1,391	+53 1,444	+49 1,493	+129 1,622	+201 1,823	+129 1,952	+498 2,450	+615 3,065
Williams, Tony	1,336	+157 1,493	+1 1,494	+7 1,501	+3 1,504	+18 1,522	+5 1,527	+12 1,539	+19 1,558	+43 1,601	+4 1,605	+37 1,642	+35 1,677	+53 1,730	+75 1,805	+64 1,869	+229 2,098	+382 2,480
Gueret, Maurice	822	+114 936	+2 938	+8 946	+4 950	+8 958	+11 969	+15 984	+21 1,005	+19 1,024	+6 1,030	+47 1,077	+72 1,149	+81 1,230	+103 1,333	+201 1,534	+269 1,803	-1,803 Eliminated
Coleman, Marc	772	+114 886	+6 892	+7 899	+12 911	+14 925	+17 942	+23 965	+12 977	+24 1,001	+3 1,004	+47 1,051	+57 1,108	+72 1,180	+122 1,302	+140 1,442	-1,442 Eliminated	
McDonagh, Rosaleen	446	+65 511	511	+2 513	+9 522	522	+6 528	+16 544	+15 559	+17 576	+8 584	+38 622	+140 762	+75 837	+72 909	-909 Eliminated		
O'Malley, Fiona	441	+109 550	550	550	+4 554	+8 562	+8 570	+26 596	+23 619	+13 632	+5 637	+23 660	+25 685	+67 752	-752 Eliminated			
McGovern, Iggy	397	+44 441	+2 443	+2 445	+6 451	+6 457	+34 491	+5 496	+9 505	+21 526	+5 531	+35 566	+60 626	-626 Eliminated				
Hanan, Robin	406	+37 443	443	443	+4 447	+3 450	+5 455	+13 468	+12 480	+15 495	+3 498	+31 529	-529 Eliminated					
Priestley, William	258	+44 302	+2 304	+4 308	+2 310	+9 319	+15 334	+14 348	+23 371	+9 380	+2 382	-382 Eliminated						
Dudgeon, Jeffrey	205	+31 236	+1 237	237	+4 241	+1 242	+3 245	+7 252	+6 258	-258 Eliminated								
Martin, David	194	+27 221	221	221	+2 223	+3 226	+7 233	+8 241	-241 Eliminated									
Cox, Maeve	174	+39 213	+1 214	+1 215	+2 217	+8 225	+8 233	-233 Eliminated										
Frost, Dermot	178	+21 199	199	+4 203	+4 207	+1 208	-208 Eliminated											
Quinn, Graham	131	+11 142	+1 143	+4 147	147	-147 Eliminated												
Connolly, Bart	72	+8 80	80	80	-80 Eliminated													
Sheehan, Dermot	49	+5 54	+1 55	-55 Eliminated														
Donnelly, Francis	20	+7 27	-27 Eliminated															
Non-transferable Cumulative		0	+2 2	+1 3	+6 9	+21 30	+15 45	+16 61	+29 90	+19 109	+6 115	+71 186	+91 277	+149 426	+179 605	+375 980	+446 1,426	+806 2,232
Total	**15,557**	**15,557**	**15,557**	**15,557**	**15,557**	**15,557**	**15,557**	**15,557**	**15,557**	**15,557**	**15,557**	**15,557**	**15,557**	**15,557**	**15,557**	**15,557**	**15,557**	**15,557**
Electorate:	**53,583**	**Turnout**	**15,814**	**29.51%**	**Spoiled**	**257**	**1.63%**	**Valid:**	**15,557**	**29.03%**	**Seats:**	**3**	**Quota:**	**3,890**	**Cands:**	**19**	**Counts**	**18**

TAOISEACH'S NOMINEES 2011

EAMONN COGHLAN (FG)

5 Homeleigh, Porterstown, Dublin 15; Leinster House: 01 6183027;
Email: eamonn.coghlan@oireachtas.ie

Born Drimnagh, Dublin 21st November 1952. Married to Yvonne, three sons, one daughter. Educated Vilanove University, USA (BSc in Marketing and Communications). Marketing Consultant. New Senator. Joined Fine Gael 7th February 2012.

Member Committee on Environment, Transport, Culture and Gaeltacht. Director of Crumlin Children's Medical and Research Foundation. Former athlete who specialised in middle distance track events and the 5000 metres. He is a 3-time Olympian and former world champion in the 5000m.

JIM D'ARCY (FG)

12 Sandygrove Close, Blackrock, Dundalk, Co. Louth; Tel: 042 9322653; Mobile: 087 6864582
Leinster House: 01 6183059; Email: jim.darcy@oireachtas.ie

Born Drogheda, Co. Louth, 20th July 1954. Separated. Educated St. Patrick's College, Drumcondra; Open University (BA Hons; Diploma in European Humanities). Primary Teacher. Contested 2007 Dail election in Louth. New Senator.

Member Committee on the Implementation of Good Friday Agreement. First elected to Louth County Council 1999. Retained his seat in 2004 and 2009. Elected to Dundalk TC in 2004 and 2009.

AIDEEN HAYDEN (LB)

Upper Albert Road, Glenageary, Co. Dublin; Mobile: 087 2311921;
Leinster House: 01 6183178; Email: aideen.hayden@oireachtas.ie

Born Carlow 1959. Married to Chris O'Malley, two daughters. Educated UCD (BA); Incorporated Law Society; Solicitor. Contested the 2011 Seanad election on the Industrial and Commercial Panel. New Senator.

Member Committee on Finance, Public Expenditure and Reform. Chairwoman of the national housing charity Threshold since 1998.

LORRAINE HIGGINS (LB)

Prospect, Athenry, Co. Galway; Mobile: 087 9034883;
Leinster House: 01 6183186; Email: lorraine.higgins@oireachtas.ie.

Born Galway, 3rd August 1979. Single. Educated NUI Galway (BA Hons in Political and Social Science and History). King's Inns. Barrister. Contested 2011 general election in Galway East. New Senator.

Labour Party spokesperson in Seanad on Foreign Affairs and Trade and on Reform and Public Expenditure. Member Committee on Foreign Affairs and Trade. Contested 2009 local elections for Galway County Council.

FIACH Mac CONGHAIL (NP)

3 Bothar Emmet, Inse Chóir, BAC 8.
Leinster House: 01 6183261; Email: fiach.macconghail@oireachtas.ie

Born Dublin, 4th August 1964. Married to Brid Ní Neachtain, two daughters. Educated Scoil Lorcháin; Scoil Dhún Chaoin; Coláiste na Rinne; Coláiste Eoin; TCD. Director of the Abbey Theatre in Dublin. New Senator.

Chairman of "We the Citizens" an initiative aimed at encouraging people to engage with the political system. Special advisor to John O'Donoghue, Minister for Arts 2002-2007.

DR. MARTIN McALEESE (NP)

Leinster House: 01 6183277; Email: martin.mcaleese@oireachtas.ie

Born East Belfast, Co. Antrim, 24th March 1951. Married to Mary McAleese, President of Ireland 1997-2011; two daughters, one son. Educated Queen's University, Belfast (BSc Hons Physics); TCD (BA, B. Dent. Sc, MA); Notre Dame University, USA; University of Ulster; HETAC (Hon Doctorates of Laws); DCU; DIT (Hon Doctorates of Philosophy). Accountant and Dentist. New Senator.

Member Committee on the Implementation of Good Friday Agreement. Appointed Chancellor Dublin City University August 2011. Credited with behind-the-scenes role in Northern peace process through contacts with Loyalist groups.

MARY MORAN (LB)

Haynestown Road, Haggardstown, Dundalk, Co. Louth; Mobile: 087 1694835
Leinster House: 01 6183522; Email: mary.moran@oireachtas.ie

Born Drogheda, Co. Louth, 28th June 1960. Married to Damian Moran, three daughters, two sons. Educated St. Vincent's Secondary School, Dundalk; UCD (BA in Music, English and Philosophy); DKIT (MA in Music Technology). Secondary Teacher. Contested 2011 general election in Louth. New Senator.

Member Committee on the Implementation of Good Friday Agreement. Member of parents' council and board of management St. Mary's Special School, Drumcar.

MARY ANN O'BRIEN (NP)

Griesebank House, Ballytore, Co. Kildare; Tel: 045 486800; Mobile: 087 7770011
Email: maobrien@lilyobriens.ie

Born Waterford, 8th September 1960. Married to Jonathan Irwin. Educated Ursuline Convent, Waterford. Managing Director. New Senator.

Member Committee on Communications, Natural Resources and Agriculture. Founded Lily O'Brien chocolates in 1992. Founded Jack and Jill Foundation with her husband after baby Jack died.

MARIE-LOUISE O'DONNELL (NP)

15 The Palms, Roebuck Road, Clonskeagh, Dublin 14; Mobile: 087 8483620;
Leinster House: 01 6183635; Email: marielouise.odonnell@oireachtas.ie

Born Castlebar, Co. Mayo, 5th September 1952. Educated Nottingham University (BA); Maynooth (Med); UCD (MA, Modern Drama); Guildhall, London (LGSMD). Communications lecturer in DCU. New Senator.

Member Committee on Jobs, Social Protection and Education. Former actor and theatre administrator and was involved in setting up the Helix Theatre.

JILLIAN VAN TURNHOUT (NP)

Ísiltír, Slatecabin Lane, Dublin 18; Mobile: 087 2333784;
Leinster House: 01 6183375; Email: jillian.vanturnhout@oireachtas.ie

Born Dublin, 29th March 1968. Married. Marketing Executive. New Senator

Member Committee on Health and Children. Chief Executive of the Children's Rights Alliance since 2005. Vice-Chair European Movement since 2008. Chief Commissioner of the Irish Girls Guides 2001-2007.President National Youth Council of Ireland 1993-1999.

DR. KATHERINE ZAPPONE (NP)

The Shanty, Glenaraneen, Brittas, Co. Dublin; Mobile: 087 2333784
Leinster House: 01 6183583; Email: katherine.zappone@oireachtas.ie

Born Spokane, WA., USA, 25th November 1953. Married to Dr. Ann Louise Gilligan. Educated Catholic University of America (MA). UCD (MBA). Boston College (PhD). Lecturer in ethics at TCD. New Senator.

Member Committee on Finance, Public Expenditure and Reform. Member of the Irish Human Rights Commission. Prominent equal rights campaigner. Along with her partner mounted a high profile legal challenge to compel the state to recognise their Canadian marriage. Co-founder and director of The Centre for Progressive Change, Ltd, established to develop and provide resources for community and social change within Ireland and abroad. She is a Commissioner with the Irish Human Rights Commission, appointed in 2001 and re-appointed in 2006. She and her wife, Dr Ann Louise Gilligan, run An Cosán which supports individuals and communities to actively engage in the process of social change through transformative education. As a former CEO of the National Women's Council of Ireland, she represented its membership in Ireland and internationally, contributed to public policy-making and directed its research programme. She has also taught ethics, practical theology and education in Trinity College Dublin. She led and established the Tallaght West Childhood Development Initiative, Ltd, a 10 year strategy and service implementation programme to improve outcomes for children and families, co-funded by the Irish Government and Atlantic Philanthropies.

SEANAD GENERAL ELECTION APRIL 2011

The Seanad has 60 members made up of the following:
1. 43 are elected from 5 vocational panels
2. Three are elected by The National University of Ireland
3. Three are elected by The University of Dublin
4. Eleven are nominated by the Taoiseach

Vocational Panels are divided into two sub panels:
a) The Nominating Bodies sub panel
b) The Oireachtas sub panel

Panels	Seats	Minimun No. Elected from each sub panel
Cultural and Educational	5	2
Agricultural	11	4
Labour	11	4
Industrial & Commercial	9	3
Administrative	7	3
Total	**43**	

Electorate

The electorate consists of the members of the new Dail, the outgoing Seanad and every council of a county or county borough. The electorate for the 2011 Seanad General Election amounted to 1092. The political party affiliation of the electorate is estimated as follows:

	2007	2009	2009-2011	2011	2011		
Party		**Cllrs**	**Changes**	**Cllrs**	**TDs**	**Senators**	**Total**
Fine Gael	349	340	3	343	76	6	425
Labour	127	132	4	136	37	2	175
Fianna Fail	404	218	-1	217	20	27	264
Sinn Fein	58	54	-3	51	14		65
Socialist Party	4	4		4	2		6
PBPA		5		5	2		7
Green Party	25	3		3		3	6
Workers Party	2	2		2			2
Progressive Democrats	26			0			0
Others	101	125	-5	120	15	7	142
Total	**1,096**	**883**	**-2**	**881**	**166**	**45**	**1,092**

PARTY BREAKDOWN OF SEANAD 2011							
Panel	**FG**	**LB**	**FF**	**SF**	**GP**	**Others**	**Total**
Administrative	3	2	2				7
Agricultural	4	2	4	1			11
Cultural & Educational	2	1	2				5
Industrial & Commercial	4	1	3	1			9
Labour	5	2	3	1			11
Universities						6	6
Taoiseach's Nominees	1	3				7	11
Total	**19**	**11**	**14**	**3**	**0**	**13**	**60**
2007	14	6	28	1	2	9	60
2011-2007	**+5**	**+5**	**-14**	**+2**	**-2**	**+4**	

PARTY FIRST PREFERENCE VOTES							
Panel	**FG**	**LB**	**FF**	**SF**	**GP**	**Others**	**Total**
Administrative	434	233	348			49	1,064
Agricultural	445	166	329	82		44	1,066
Cultural & Educational	479	157	385			44	1,065
Industrial & Commercial	459	186	305	73	19	25	1,067
Labour	445	166	320	84		51	1,066
Available	**425**	**175**	**264**	**65**	**6**	**157**	**1,092**

MAKE UP OF SEANAD 2011							
		Outgoing Senators		**Senator**		**Outgoing TDs**	
Panel	**Seats**	**Candidates**	**Elected**	**Former**	**New**	**Candidates**	**Elected**
Administrative	7	3	2		5	2	2
Agricultural	11	7	6		5	3	
Cultural & Educational	5	2	1		4	2	2
Industrial & Commercial	9	4	3		6	1	
Labour	11	8	5		6	1	1
Universities	6	4	4		2		
Taoiseach's Nominees	11				11		
2011	**60**	**28**	**21**	**0**	**39**	**9**	**5**
2007	**60**	**29**	**24**	**4**	**32**	**10**	**10**
2002	**60**	**33**	**25**	**1**	**34**	**14**	**10**
1997	**60**	**32**	**28**	**4**	**28**	**10**	**8**
1992	**60**	**42**	**25**	**2**	**33**	**20**	**14**

PANELS SUMMARY 2011						
Panel	Administrative	Agricultural	Cultural & Educational	Industrial & Commercial	Labour	Total
Electorate	1,092	1,092	1,092	1,092	1,092	1,092
Valid Votes	1,064	1,066	1,065	1,067	1,066	
Value	1,064,000	1,066,000	1,065,000	1,067,000	1,066,000	
Seats	7	11	5	9	11	36
Quota	133,001	88,834	177,501	106,701	88,834	
Min from each sub panel	3	4	2	3	4	
Candidates	19	28	17	35	21	120
Counts	16	25	14	33	17	105

MEMBERS OUTGOING SEANAD ELECTED TO 31st DAIL			
	Senator	Party	Constituency
1	John Paul Phelan	FG	Carlow-Kilkenny
2	Joe O'Reilly	FG	Cavan-Monaghan
3	Jerry Buttimer	FG	Cork South Central
4	Michael McCarthy	LB	Cork South West
5	Paschal Donoghoe	FG	Dublin Central
6	Frances Fitzgerald	FG	Dublin Mid West
7	Brendan Ryan	LB	Dublin North
8	Alex White	LB	Dublin South
9	Shane Ross	NP	Dublin South
10	Ciaran Cannon	FG	Galway East
11	Nicky McFadden	FG	Longford-Westmeath
12	Dominic Hannigan	LB	Meath East
13	Paudie Coffey	FG	Waterford
14	Liam Twomey	FG	Wexford

Elected 2011	**14**
Elected 2007	**14**
Elected 2002	**10**
Elected 1997	**15**

Outgoing Senators who failed to be elected to 31st Dail			
	Senator	Party	Constituency
1	Dan Boyle	GP	Cork South Central
2	Brian O Domhnaill	FF	Donegal South-West
3	Maria Corrigan	FF	Dublin South
4	Ivana Bacik	LB	Dun Laoghaire
5	Fidelma Healy-Eames	FG	Galway West
6	Niall O Brolchain	GP	Galway West
7	James Carroll	FF	Louth
8	Mark Dearey	GP	Louth
9	Marc MacSharry	FF	Sligo-North Leitrim
10	Phil Prendergast	LB	Tipperary South

Distribution of Seats between Nominating Bodies and Oireachtas Sub-Panels General Elections 1982 - 2011								
	Panel		Administrativ	Agricultural	Cultural & Educational	Industrial & Commercial	Labour	Total
	Number of seats		7 (3at least from each sub-panel)	11 (4at least from each sub-panel)	5 (2 at least from each sub-panel)	9 (3at least from each sub-panel)	11 (4at least from each sub-panel)	
1982	Nominating Bodies sub-panel	Nominated	8	14	15	25	12	66
		Elected	4	6	3	4	4	17
	Oireachtas sub-panel	Nominated	9	12	5	10	9	36
		Elected	3	5	2	5	7	19
1983	Nominating Bodies sub-panel	Nominated	8	14	17	21	13	65
		Elected	4	6	2	5	4	17
	Oireachtas sub-panel	Nominated	8	10	5	11	12	38
		Elected	3	5	3	4	7	19
1987	Nominating Bodies sub-panel	Nominated	8	16	18	23	10	67
		Elected	4	6	3	6	4	19
	Oireachtas sub-panel	Nominated	7	10	5	10	10	35
		Elected	3	5	2	3	7	17
1989	Nominating Bodies sub-panel	Nominated	8	14	16	22	11	63
		Elected	4	7	3	6	4	20
	Oireachtas sub-panel	Nominated	6	9	5	8	11	33
		Elected	3	4	2	3	7	16
1992	Nominating Bodies sub-panel	Nominated	9	17	18	19	14	68
		Elected	3	5	3	4	4	16
	Oireachtas sub-panel	Nominated	8	9	5	8	11	33
		Elected	4	6	2	5	7	20
1997	Nominating Bodies sub-panel	Nominated	9	19	14	24	14	71
		Elected	3	7	3	4	6	20
	Oireachtas sub-panel	Nominated	7	9	5	8	9	31
		Elected	4	4	2	5	5	16
2002	Nominating Bodies sub-panel	Nominated	8	19	14	30	12	75
		Elected	3	8	3	3	4	18
	Oireachtas sub-panel	Nominated	7	9	5	8	10	32
		Elected	4	3	2	6	7	18
2007	Nominating Bodies sub-panel	Nominated	11	19	12	29	14	74
		Elected	3	6	2	5	6	19
	Oireachtas sub-panel	Nominated	5	9	5	8	11	33
		Elected	4	5	3	4	5	17
2011	Nominating Bodies sub-panel	Nominated	10	18	12	26	12	68
		Elected	3	7	2	6	5	20
	Oireachtas sub-panel	Nominated	9	10	5	9	9	33
		Elected	4	4	3	3	6	16

PART 6

EUROPEAN ELECTIONS

5th JUNE 2009

DUBLIN 2009

GAY MITCHELL (FG)
Group of the European People's Party (Christian Democrats) and European Democrats

192 Upper Rathmines Road, Dublin 6; Tel: 01 4961940
Brussels: Tel: +32228 45228; Email: gay.mitchell@europarl.europa.eu
Website: http://www.gaymitchell.ie

Born Dublin 30th December 1951. Married to Norma O'Connor, one son, three daughters. Educated St. Michael's CBS, Inchicore, Dublin; Emmet Road Vocational School, Dublin; College of Commerce, Rathmines, Dublin; Queens University, Belfast (MSc Politics); Associate of Institute of Taxation in Ireland; Fellow, Irish Institute of Secretaries and Administrators. Formerly Accountant.
First elected 2004. Re-elected 2009.

Contested 2011 Irish Presidential election. Member Committee on Development. Substitute member Committee on Economic and Monetary Affairs. Dail Deputy for Dublin South Central 1981-2007. Unsuccessful candidate in Fine Gael Leadership election in June 2002. Fine Gael front bench spokesperson on Foreign Affairs 2002-2004. Chairman Select Committee on European Affairs 2002-2004. Spokesperson on Health, 2000-2002. Spokesperson on Foreign Affairs 1997-2000. Minister of State at the Department of Taoiseach and Foreign Affairs with special responsibility for European Affairs, Local Development and the International Financial Services Centre 1994-1997. Member Dublin City Council 1979-1995 and 1999-2003. Lord Mayor 1992-1993. Brother of the late Jim Mitchell, TD for Dublin Central 1977-2002.

PROINSIAS DE ROSSA (LB)
Group of the Progressive Alliance of Socialists and Democrats in the European Parliament

Room 1410 Liberty Hall, Dublin 1; Tel: 01 8746109
Brussels Office: Tel: +322 2847681
Email: proinsiasderossa@europarl.europa.eu; Website: www.derossa.com

Born Dublin 15th May 1940. Two sons, one daughter. Educated Scoil Colmcille, Marlborough Street, Dublin and College of Technology, Kevin Street, Dublin. First elected February 1989 but resigned in 1992 to concentrate on the Dail and was replaced by Des Geraghty. Re-elected 1999, 2004 and 2009. Retired February 2011. Replaced by Cllr. Emer Costello, wife of Joe Costello TD.

Member Committee on Employment and Social Affairs. Substitute member Committee on Development. Vice President Party of European Socialists (1999-2004).President of the Labour Party following merger of Democratic Left and Labour Party in 1999. First elected to the Dail in February 1982 and at each subsequent election until he retired in 2002 to concentrate on the European Parliament. Minister for Social Welfare 1994-1997. Elected leader of Democratic Left at the founding conference in March 1992. President of the Worker's Party 1988-1992.

PAUL MURPHY (SP)
Confederal Group of the European United Left – Nordic Green Left

150 Pearse Street, Dublin 2; Tel: 01 6795030; Email: paul.murphy@europarl.europa.eu

Born Dublin, 13th April 1983. Single. Educated UCD (BCL). Former European Parliament Assistant to Joe Higgins, whom he replaced on the latter's election to Dáil Eireann in 2011.

Member Committee on Employment and Social Affairs and Committee on Petitions; Relations with Mercosur countries.

EURO CONSTITUENCY: DUBLIN 2009 FIRST PREFERENCE VOTES							
	Seats	3			101,658		
	Candidate	**Party**	**1st**	**%**	**Quota**	**Count**	**Status**
1	**Mitchell, Gay***	**FG**	**96,715**	**23.78%**	**0.95**	**4**	**Made Quota**
2	**De Rossa, Proinsias***	**LB**	**83,471**	**20.53%**	**0.82**	**6**	**Made Quota**
3	**Higgins, Joe**	**SP**	**50,510**	**12.42%**	**0.50**	**7**	**Elected**
4	Ryan, Eoin*	FF	55,346	13.61%	0.54	7	Not Elected
5	McDonald, Mary Lou*	SF	47,928	11.79%	0.47	6	Eliminated
6	McKenna, Patricia #	NP	17,521	4.31%	0.17	5	Eliminated
7	De Burca, Deidre	GP	19,086	4.69%	0.19	3	Lost Expenses
8	Byrne, Eibhlin	FF	18,956	4.66%	0.19	2	Lost Expenses
9	Simons, Caroline	LIB	13,514	3.32%	0.13	1	Lost Expenses
10	Sweeney, Emmanuel	NP	3,583	0.88%	0.04	1	Lost Expenses
10	***Outgoing MEP #Former MEP**		**406,630**	**100.00%**	**101,658**	**25,415**	**Lost Expenses**

EURO CONSTITUENCY : DUBLIN 2009 PARTY VOTE												
	2009					2004					Change	
Party	**Cand**	**1st**	**%**	**Quota**	**Seats**	**Cand**	**1st**	**%**	**Quota**	**Seats**	**%**	**Seats**
FF	2	74,302	18.27%	0.73		2	97,950	23.22%	1.16	1	-4.94%	-1
FG	1	96,715	23.78%	0.95	1	1	90,749	21.51%	1.08	1	+2.27%	
LB	1	83,471	20.53%	0.82	1	2	95,051	22.53%	1.13	1	-2.00%	
GP	1	19,086	4.69%	0.19		1	40,445	9.59%	0.48		-4.89%	
SF	1	47,928	11.79%	0.47		1	60,395	14.32%	0.72	1	-2.53%	-1
SP	1	50,510	12.42%	0.50	1	1	23,218	5.50%	0.28		+6.92%	+1
LIB	1	13,514	3.32%	0.13							+3.32%	
CS						1	5,352	1.27%	0.06		-1.27%	
Others	2	21,104	5.19%	0.21		3	8,737	2.07%	0.10		+3.12%	
Total	**10**	**406,630**	**100.00%**	**101,658**	**3**	**12**	**421,897**	**100.00%**	**84,380**	**4**	**0.00%**	**-1**
Electorate		**812,465**	**50.05%**				**821,723**	**51.34%**			**-1.29%**	
Spoiled		**6,054**	**1.47%**				**13,239**	**3.04%**			**-1.58%**	
Turnout		**412,684**	**50.79%**				**435,136**	**52.95%**			**-2.16%**	

EURO CONSTITUENCY: DUBLIN 2009 TRANSFER ANALYSIS									
From	**To**	**FF**	**FG**	**LB**	**GP**	**SF**	**SP**	**NP**	**Non Trans**
FF	19,448	9,888	1,712	2,057	1,765	883	581	857	1,705
%		50.84%	8.80%	10.58%	9.08%	4.54%	2.99%	4.41%	8.77%
FG	2,755	605		1,330		82	235	423	80
%		21.96%		48.28%		2.98%	8.53%	15.35%	2.90%
GP	21,991	2,312	3,603	7,032		1,467	2,078	2,833	2,666
%		10.51%	16.38%	31.98%		6.67%	9.45%	12.88%	12.12%
SF	55,429	5,426					22,201		27,802
%		9.79%					40.05%		50.16%
Others	42,733	3,871	2,383	9,335	1,140	5,069	6,761	4,002	10,172
%		9.06%	5.58%	21.84%	2.67%	11.86%	15.82%	9.37%	23.80%
Total	**142,356**	**22,102**	**7,698**	**19,754**	**2,905**	**7,501**	**31,856**	**8,115**	**42,425**
		15.53%	**5.41%**	**13.88%**	**2.04%**	**5.27%**	**22.38%**	**5.70%**	**29.80%**

EURO CONSTITUENCY: DUBLIN 2009								
COUNT DETAILS								
Seats	3						Quota	101,658
Candidate	Party	1st	2nd	3rd	4th	5th	6th	7th
			Simons Sweeney	Byrne Votes	De Burca Votes	Mitchell Surplus	McKenna Votes	McDonald Votes
			+2,383	+1,712	+3,603	-2,755		
Mitchell	FG	96,715	99,098	100,810	104,413	101,658	101,658	101,658
			+1,746	+2,057	+7,032	+1,330	+7,589	
De Rossa	LB	83,471	85,217	87,274	94,306	95,636	103,225	103,225
			+1,947	+581	+2,078	+235	+4,814	+22,201
Higgins	SP	50,510	52,457	53,038	55,116	55,351	60,165	82,366
			+971	+9,888	+2,312	+605	+2,408	+5,426
Ryan	FF	55,346	56,317	66,205	68,517	69,122	71,530	76,956
			+2,169	+883	+1,467	+82	+2,900	-55,429
McDonald	SF	47,928	50,097	50,980	52,447	52,529	55,429	Eliminated
			+4,002	+857	+2,833	+423	-25,636	
McKenna	NP	17,521	21,523	22,380	25,213	25,636	Eliminated	
			+1,140	+1,765	-21,991			
De Burca	GP	19,086	20,226	21,991	Eliminated			
			+492	-19,448				
Byrne	FF	18,956	19,448	Eliminated				
			-13,514					
Simons	NP	13,514	Eliminated					
			-3,583					
Sweeney	NP	3,583	Eliminated					
Non-transferable			+2,247	+1,705	+2,666	+80	+7,925	+27,802
Cumulative			2,247	3,952	6,618	6,698	14,623	42,425
Total		**406,630**	**406,630**	**406,630**	**406,630**	**406,630**	**406,630**	**406,630**

EURO CONSTITUENCY: DUBLIN 1979-2009								
Party	**1979**	**1984**	**1989**	**1994**	**1999**	**2004**	**2009**	**2009-2004**
FF	28.44%	33.37%	29.08%	20.85%	24.67%	23.22%	18.27%	-4.95%
FG	30.35%	31.72%	17.23%	23.82%	30.09%	21.51%	23.78%	+2.27%
LB	29.50%	10.04%	12.76%	14.07%	15.90%	22.53%	20.53%	-2.00%
SF		5.17%	2.58%	2.95%	6.64%	14.32%	11.79%	-2.53%
GP		1.85%	8.32%	14.54%	12.70%	9.59%	4.69%	-4.90%
SP					3.78%	5.50%	12.42%	+6.92%
WP	4.03%	6.93%	15.84%	5.70%				
PD			8.12%	2.96%				
DL				8.69%				
Others	7.68%	10.92%	6.07%	6.42%	6.22%	3.33%	8.52%	+5.19%
Total	**100.00%**	**100.00%**	**100.00%**	**100.00%**	**100.00%**	**100.00%**	**100.00%**	**0.00%**

EAST 2009

MAIREAD McGUINNESS (FG)
Group of the European People's Party (Christian Democrats)

Mentrim, Drumconrath, Navan, Co. Meath; Tel: 041 6854633
Brussels: Tel 322 2845214; Email: mairead.mcguinness@europarl.europa.eu
Website: www.maireadmcguinness.ie

Born Ardee, Co. Louth, 13th June 1959. Married to Tom Duff, four children, Orlaith, James, Aine and Cathal. Educated Ardee Community School, UCD B.Agr.Sc. (Econ.), Agricultural Economics (1980). Diploma in Accounting and Finance (1984). Agricultural Journalist.
First elected 2004. Retained her seat in 2009.

Member Committee on Agriculture and Rural Development and Committee on Petitions. Substitute Member Committee on the Environment, Public Health and Food Safety. Former Presenter of "Ear to the Ground" TV Series. Agriculture editor, The Irish Independent (1997). Chairperson of the Guild of Agricultural Journalists (1986).

LIAM AYLWARD (FF)
Group of the Alliance of Liberals and Democrats for Europe

Aghaviller, Hugginstown, Co. Kilkenny; Tel: 056 7768703
Brussels: Tel 322 2845782; Email: liam.aylward@europarl.europa.eu

Born Mullinavat, Co. Kilkenny, 27th September 1952. Married to Kathleen Noonan, two sons, two daughters. Educated St. Kieran's College, Kilkenny. Diploma in Building and Construction (1972). Formerly Laboratory Technician. First elected 2004. Retained his seat in 2009.

Member Committee on Agriculture and Rural Development. Substitute Member Committee on Culture and Education. TD for Carlow-Kilkenny 1977-2007. Minister of State at the Department of Agriculture and Food (with special responsibility for Animal Health and Welfare and Customer Service) 2002-2004. Minister of State at the Department of Education (with special responsibility for Youth and Sport) 1992-1994. Minister of State at Department of Energy 1988-1989. Member Kilkenny County Council 1974-2002. Son of Bob Aylward, Senator 1973-1974. Brother of Bobby Aylward TD for Carlow-Kilkenny 2007-2011.

NESSA CHILDERS (LB)
Group of the Progressive Alliance of Socialists and Democrats in the European Parliament

14 Gledswood Avenue, Clonskeagh, Dublin 14; Tel: 01 2962263; Mobile: 086 8186712;
Email: nessa.childers@europarl.europa.eu; Website: www.nessachilders.ie

Born Dublin 9th October 1956. Arts and Psychology degree from TCD and a postgraduate diploma from NUI UCD. Psychoanalyst. First elected 2009.

Member Committee on the Environment, Public Health and Food Safety. Substitute Member Committee on Culture and Education. Elected as a Green to Dun Laoghaire County Council in 2004. Resigned her seat in August 2008 citing pressure of work as a psychoanalyst as her reason. Changed to Labour in October 2008 and contested 2009 European election as a Labour candidate. Daughter of Erskine Childers, President of Ireland 1973-1974. TD 1938-1973. Granddaughter of Robert Erskine Childers SF TD 1921-1922.

EURO CONSTITUENCY: EAST 2009							
FIRST PREFERENCE VOTES							
	Seats	3			107,313		
	Candidate	Party	1st	%	Quota	Count	Status
1	**McGuinness, Mairead**	**FG**	**110,366**	**25.71%**	**1.03**	**1**	**Made Quota**
2	**Aylward, Liam**	**FF**	**74,666**	**17.39%**	**0.70**	**7**	**Elected**
3	**Childers, Nessa**	**LB**	**78,338**	**18.25%**	**0.73**	**7**	**Elected**
4	Phelan, John Paul	FG	61,851	14.41%	0.58	7	Not Elected
5	Funchion, Kathleen	SF	26,567	6.19%	0.25	6	Eliminated
6	Byrne, Thomas	FF	31,112	7.25%	0.29	5	Eliminated
7	Sharkey, Tomas	SF	20,932	4.88%	0.20	4	Lost Expenses
8	O'Malley, Raymond	LIB	18,557	4.32%	0.17	3	Lost Expenses
9	Garvey, Paddy	NP	2,934	0.68%	0.03	2	Lost Expenses
10	Tallon, Jim	NP	2,412	0.56%	0.02	2	Lost Expenses
11	Grealy, Micheal	NP	1,514	0.35%	0.01	2	Lost Expenses
11	***Outgoing**		**429,249**	**100.00%**	**107,313**	**26,829**	**Lost Expenses**

EURO CONSTITUENCY: EAST 2009												
PARTY VOTE												
	2009					2004					Change	
Party	Cand	1st	%	Quota	Seats	Cand	1st	%	Quota	Seats	%	Seats
FF	2	105,778	24.64%	0.99	1	2	113,660	25.08%	1.00	1	-0.44%	
FG	2	172,217	40.12%	1.60	1	2	183,760	40.55%	1.62	2	-0.43%	-1
LB	1	78,338	18.25%	0.73	1	1	59,158	13.05%	0.52		+5.20%	+1
GP						1	25,576	5.64%	0.23		-5.64%	
SF	2	47,499	11.07%	0.44		1	39,356	8.68%	0.35		+2.38%	
Others	4	25,417	5.92%	0.24		6	31,668	6.99%	0.28		-1.07%	
Total	**11**	**429,249**	**100.00%**	**107,313**	**3**	**13**	**453,178**	**100.00%**	**113,295**	**3**	**0.00%**	
Electorate		**778,502**	**55.14%**				**806,598**	**56.18%**			**-1.05%**	
Spoiled		**13,042**	**2.95%**				**18,717**	**3.97%**			**-1.02%**	
Turnout		**442,291**	**56.81%**				**471,895**	**58.50%**			**-1.69%**	

EURO CONSTITUENCY: EAST 2009								
TRANSFER ANALYSIS								
From	To	FF	FG	LB	SF	LIB	NP	Non Trans
FF	33,383	22,192	1,238	2,701	1,337			5,915
%		66.48%	3.71%	8.09%	4.01%			17.72%
FG	3,053	352	1,739	576	182	171	33	
%		11.53%	56.96%	18.87%	5.96%	5.60%	1.08%	
SF	68,376	6225	7750	15,321	13,780			25,300
%		9.10%	11.33%	22.41%	20.15%			37.00%
LIB	19,396	1,967	3,803	4,053	4,666			4,907
%		10.14%	19.61%	20.90%	24.06%			25.30%
Others	6,893	474	579	1,231	912	668		3,029
%		6.88%	8.40%	17.86%	13.23%	9.69%		43.94%
Total	**131,101**	**31,210**	**15,109**	**23,882**	**20,877**	**839**	**33**	**39,151**
		23.81%	**11.52%**	**18.22%**	**15.92%**	**0.64%**	**0.03%**	**29.86%**

EURO CONSTITUENCY: EAST 2009 COUNT DETAILS								
Seats	3						Quota	107,313
Candidate	**Party**	**1st**	**2nd**	**3rd**	**4th**	**5th**	**6th**	**7th**
			McGuinness Surplus	Garvey Tallon Grealy	O'Malley Votes	Sharkey Votes	Byrne Votes	Funchion Votes
			-3,053					
McGuinness	FG	110,366	107,313	107,313	107,313	107,313	107,313	107,313
			+200	+258	+1,171	+749	+22,192	+4,369
Aylward	FF	74,666	74,866	75,124	76,295	77,044	99,236	103,605
			+576	+1,231	+4,053	+2,456	+2,701	+12,865
Childers	LB	78,338	78,914	80,145	84,198	86,654	89,355	102,220
			+1,739	+579	+3,803	+1,636	+1,238	+6,114
Phelan	FG	61,851	63,590	64,169	67,972	69,608	70,846	76,960
			+80	+485	+2,173	+13,780	+1,337	-44,422
Funchion	SF	26,567	26,647	27,132	29,305	43,085	44,422	Eliminated
			+152	+216	+796	1,107	-33,383	
Byrne	FF	31,112	31,264	31,480	32,276	33,383	Eliminated	
			+102	+427	+2,493	-23,954		
Sharkey	SF	20,932	21,034	21,461	23,954	Eliminated		
			+171	+668	-19,396			
O'Malley	LIB	18,557	18,728	19,396	Eliminated			
			+11	-2,945				
Garvey	NP	2,934	2,945	Eliminated				
			+13	-2,425				
Tallon	NP	2,412	2,425	Eliminated				
			+9	-1,523				
Grealy	NP	1,514	1,523	Eliminated				
Non-transferable				+3,029	+4,907	+4,226	+5,915	+21,074
Cumulative			0	3,029	7,936	12,162	18,077	39,151
Total		**429,249**	**429,249**	**429,249**	**429,249**	**429,249**	**429,249**	**429,249**

EURO CONSTITUENCY: EAST 1979-2009								
Party	**1979**	**1984**	**1989**	**1994**	**1999**	**2004**	**2009**	**2009-2004**
FF	41.49%	43.78%	36.92%	33.46%	34.24%	25.08%	24.64%	-0.44%
FG	40.74%	36.59%	26.90%	27.73%	34.06%	40.55%	40.12%	-0.43%
LB	13.06%	11.87%	13.18%	15.46%	11.13%	13.05%	18.25%	+5.20%
GP			6.28%	11.81%	13.78%	5.64%		-5.64%
SF		4.32%	2.64%	2.49%	5.85%	8.68%	11.07%	+2.39%
WP	4.71%	3.44%	4.38%					
PD			8.37%	4.80%				
Others			1.33%	4.25%	0.94%	7.00%	5.92%	-1.08%
Total	**100.00%**	**100.00%**	**100.00%**	**100.00%**	**100.00%**	**100.00%**	**100.00%**	**0.00%**

NORTH-WEST 2009

MARIAN HARKIN (IND)
Group of the Alliance of Liberals and Democrats for Europe

24 The Park, Strandhill Road, Sligo; Tel: 071 45890/45689.
Constituency Office: 28 Emmet Place, Union Street, Sligo; Tel: 071 9145890
Brussels: Tel: 322 2845797; Email: marian.harkin@europarl.europa.eu
Website: www.marianharkin.ie

Born Ballintogher, Co. Sligo 26th November 1953. Widowed, two sons. Educated Marist College, Tubbercurry; UCD (BSc, HDipEd). Former Secondary School Teacher. Contested 1999 European election in Connaught-Ulster. First elected 2004. Retained her seat in 2009.

Member Committee on Employment and Social Affairs. Substitute member Committee on Agriculture and Rural Development and Committee on Petitions. TD for Sligo-Leitrim 2002-2007. Former Chairperson Council for the West. Former member National Statistics Board. Board member Ulster Community Investment Trust (a cross border community bank). Member core group of the Wheel – the National Community/Voluntary Sector Support Group. Founder member North Leitrim Glens Development Company. Former member of the first North Leitrim Partnership Company. Former member Western Development Partnership Board.

PAT "THE COPE" GALLAGHER (FF)
Group of the Alliance of Liberals and Democrats for Europe

Dungloe, Co. Donegal, Tel: 075 21364; Mobile: 087 2238925
Constituency Office: Main Street, Dungloe; Tel: 074 9521276
E-mail patthecope.gallagher@europarl.europa.eu; Website: www.patthecope.com

Born Burtonport, Co. Donegal 10th March 1948. Married to Ann Gillespie. Educated St. Enda's College, Galway and UCG (BComm). Former Fish processor and exporter. First elected 1994. Re-elected 1999. Did not contest in 2004. But returned to European Parliament in 2009 following outgoing MEP Sean O Neachtain's last minute retirement.

Dáil Deputy 1981-1997 and 2002-2009. Minister of State at Department of Health and Children with special responsibility for Health Promotion and Food Safety June 2007-May 2008. Minister of State at Department of Transport 2006-2007. Minister of State at Department of Communications, Marine and Natural Resources 2004-2006. Minister of State at Department of the Environment, Heritage and Local Government 2002-2004. Minister of State Department of Marine and the Gaeltacht 1987-1994. Member Donegal County Council 1979-1991 (Chairman 1985/1986). Grandson of Paddy The Cope, a pioneer of the Irish Co-operative Movement.

JIM HIGGINS (FG)
Group of the European People's Party (Christian Democrats)

Cloonturk, Kilkelly, Co. Mayo; Tel: 0907 30052; Website: www.jimhiggins.ie
Brussels: Tel: 322 2845843; Email: jim.higgins@europarl.europa.eu

Born Ballyhaunis, Co. Mayo 4th May 1945. Four daughters. Educated St. Jarlath's College, Tuam, Co. Galway and UCG (BA, HDipEd). Former Teacher. Contested 1994 European Elections in Connaught-Ulster. First elected 2004. Re-elected 2009.

Member Committee on Transport and Tourism. Substitute member Committee on Fisheries and Committee on Petitions. Delegation for relations with Japan. Contested 1981, February and November 1982 general elections in Mayo East. Dail Deputy 1987-2002. Senator, Labour Panel 1983-1987 and Taoiseach's Nominee 1981-1982. Re-elected 2002. Front bench spokesperson on Public Enterprise & Tourism 2000-2001. Spokesperson on Justice, Equality and Law Reform 1997-2000. Minister of State and Government Chief Whip 1995-1997. Chairman Fine Gael Parliamentary Party 1994-1995. Fine Gael Front bench spokesperson on Education 1990-1994. Member Mayo County Council 1979-1995.

EURO CONSTITUENCY: NORTH-WEST 2009							
FIRST PREFERENCE VOTES							
	Seats	3			123,827		
	Candidate	**Party**	**1st**	**%**	**Quota**	**Count**	**Status**
1	**Harkin, Marian***	**NP**	**84,813**	**17.12%**	**0.68**	**6**	**Elected**
2	**Gallagher, Pat the Cope**	**FF**	**82,643**	**16.69%**	**0.67**	**6**	**Elected**
3	**Higgins, Jim**	**FG**	**80,093**	**16.17%**	**0.65**	**6**	**Elected**
4	Ganley, Declan	NP	67,638	13.66%	0.55	6	Not Elected
5	MacLochlainn, Padraig	SF	45,515	9.19%	0.37	5	Eliminated
6	Mooney, Paschal	FF	42,985	8.68%	0.35	4	Eliminated
7	O'Reilly, Joe	FG	37,564	7.58%	0.30	3	Eliminated
8	O'Keeffe, Susan	LB	28,708	5.80%	0.23	2	Eliminated
9	McNamara, Michael	NP	12,744	2.57%	0.10	1	Lost Expenses
10	O Luain, Fiachra	NP	6,510	1.31%	0.05	1	Lost Expenses
11	Higgins, John Francis	NP	3,030	0.61%	0.02	1	Lost Expenses
12	McCullagh, Noel	NP	1,940	0.39%	0.02	1	Lost Expenses
13	King, Thomas	NP	1,124	0.23%	0.01	1	Lost Expenses
13	***Outgoing**		**495,307**	**100.00%**	**123,827**	**30,957**	**Lost Expenses**

EURO CONSTITUENCY: NORTH-WEST 2009												
PARTY VOTE												
	2009					2004					Change	
Party	**Cand**	**1st**	**%**	**Quota**	**Seats**	**Cand**	**1st**	**%**	**Quota**	**Seats**	**%**	**Seats**
FF	2	125,628	25.36%	1.01	1	2	114,224	27.10%	1.08	1	-1.74%	
FG	2	117,657	23.75%	0.95	1	2	100,966	23.96%	0.96	1	-0.20%	
LB	1	28,708	5.80%	0.23		1	13,948	3.31%	0.13		+2.49%	
SF	1	45,515	9.19%	0.37		1	65,321	15.50%	0.62		-6.31%	
Others	7	177,799	35.90%	1.44	1	3	126,964	30.13%	1.21	1	+5.77%	
Total	**13**	**495,307**	**100.00%**	**123,827**	**3**	**9**	**421,423**	**100.00%**	**105,356**	**3**	**0.00%**	**0**
Electorate		**805,626**	**61.48%**				**688,804**	**61.18%**			**+0.30%**	
Spoiled		**15,675**	**3.07%**				**14,487**	**3.32%**			**-0.26%**	
Turnout		**510,982**	**63.43%**				**435,910**	**63.29%**			**+0.14%**	

EURO CONSTITUENCY: NORTH-WEST 2009								
TRANSFER ANALYSIS								
From	**To**	**FF**	**FG**	**LB**	**SF**	**LIB**	**NP**	**Non Trans**
FF	47,702	24,908	2,677		2,353	1,711	8,268	7,785
%		52.22%	5.61%		4.93%	3.59%	17.33%	16.32%
FG	42,350	3887	24,536		2,159	1,519	4,381	5,868
%		9.18%	57.94%		5.10%	3.59%	10.34%	13.86%
LB	31,176	2,130	7,636		2,812	2,550	9,623	6,425
%		6.83%	24.49%		9.02%	8.18%	30.87%	20.61%
SF	54,737	8,308	6,375			8,572	9,462	22,020
%		15.18%	11.65%			15.66%	17.29%	40.23%
Others	25,348	3,771	3,654	2,468	1,898	2,287	5,125	6,145
%		14.88%	14.42%	9.74%	7.49%	9.02%	20.22%	24.24%
Total	**201,313**	**43,004**	**44,878**	**2,468**	**9,222**	**16,639**	**36,859**	**48,243**
		21.36%	**22.29%**	**1.23%**	**4.58%**	**8.27%**	**18.31%**	**23.96%**

EURO CONSTITUENCY: NORTH-WEST 2009							
COUNT DETAILS							
Seats	**3**					**Quota**	**123,827**
Candidate	**Party**	**1st**	**2nd**	**3rd**	**4th**	**5th**	**6th**
			McNamara O Luain Higgins, J.F. McCullagh King	O'Keeffe Votes	O'Reilly Votes	Mooney Votes	MacLochlainn Votes
			+5,125	*+9,623*	*+4,381*	*+8,268*	*+9,462*
Harkin	NP	84,813	89,938	99,561	103,942	112,210	121,672
			+2,037	*+1,162*	*+1,872*	*+24,908*	*+8,308*
Gallagher	FF	82,643	84,680	85,842	87,714	112,622	120,930
			+2,364	*+4,140*	*+24,536*	*+2,677*	*+6,375*
Higgins, Jim	FG	80,093	82,457	86,597	111,133	113,810	120,185
			+2,287	*+2,550*	*+1,519*	*+1,711*	*+8,572*
Ganley	NP	67,638	69,925	72,475	73,994	75,705	84,277
			+1,898	*+2,812*	*+2,159*	*+2,353*	*-54,737*
MacLochlainn	SF	45,515	47,413	50,225	52,384	54,737	Eliminated
			+1,734	*+968*	*+2,015*	*-47,702*	
Mooney	FF	42,985	44,719	45,687	47,702	Eliminated	
			+1,290	*+3,496*	*-42,350*		
O'Reilly	FG	37,564	38,854	42,350	Eliminated		
			+2,468	*-31,176*			
O'Keeffe	LB	28,708	31,176	Eliminated			
			-12,744				
McNamara	NP	12,744	Eliminated				
			-6,510				
O Luain	NP	6,510	Eliminated				
			-3,030				
Higgins, J.F.	NP	3,030	Eliminated				
			-1,940				
McCullagh	NP	1,940	Eliminated				
			-1,124				
King	NP	1,124	Eliminated				
Non-transferable			*+6,145*	*+6,425*	*+5,868*	*+7,785*	*+22,020*
Cumulative			6,145	12,570	18,438	26,223	48,243
Total		**495,307**	**495,307**	**495,307**	**495,307**	**495,307**	**495,307**

EURO CONSTITUENCY: NORTH-WEST 1979-2009								
Party	**1979**	**1984**	**1989**	**1994**	**1999**	**2004**	**2009**	**2009-2004**
FF	29.96%	41.41%	32.70%	42.47%	35.60%	27.10%	25.36%	-1.74%
FG	37.02%	33.28%	28.00%	29.65%	19.88%	23.96%	23.75%	-0.21%
LB	4.26%	3.54%	1.59%	8.52%	3.29%	3.31%	5.80%	+2.49%
GP				3.71%				
SF		6.81%	4.99%	5.99%	6.39%	15.50%	9.19%	-6.31%
WP	1.96%	1.10%	2.84%					
PD			12.96%	9.12%				
Others	26.80%	13.86%	16.92%	0.54%	34.84%	30.13%	35.90%	+5.77%
Total	**100.00%**	**100.00%**	**100.00%**	**100.00%**	**100.00%**	**100.00%**	**100.00%**	**0.00%**

SOUTH 2009

BRIAN CROWLEY (FF)
Group of the Alliance of Liberals and Democrats for Europe

Maryborough Lodge, Maryborough Hill, Douglas, Cork; Tel: 021 4896433
Brussels: Tel: 322 2845751; Email: brian.crowley@europarl.europa.eu
Website: www.briancrowleymep.ie

Born Dublin 4th March 1964. Educated Hamilton High School, Bandon, Co. Cork; UCC (BcL). Has been confined to a wheelchair since an accident in 1980. M.E.P. since 1994.

Leader of the Fianna Fail Group in the European Parliament. Member Committee on Industry, Research and Energy. Substitute member Committee on Legal Affairs. Senator 1992-1994. Member of Council of State since 1997. Son of the late Flor Crowley (FF) TD for Cork 1965-1977, 1981-February 1982.

SEAN KELLY (FG)
Group of the European People's Party (Christian Democrats)

Gortroe, Killarney, Co. Kerry;
Constituency Office: 4 Harbour House, Locke Quay, Dublin Road, Limerick
Email: sean.kelly@europarl.europa.eu; Website: www.seankelly.eu

Born Killarney, Co. Kerry, 26th April 1952. Married to Juliette McNeice, 2 boys and 2 girls. Educated Tralee CBS and St. Brendan's College, Killarney. Qualified as a primary school teacher in St. Pat's College of Education and did a B.A. at UCD and HDip.E. First elected 2009.

Member Committee on Regional Development. Substitute member Committee on Culture and Education. President of GAA 2003-2006. Chairman Kerry County Board 1987-1997 and Munster Council 1997-2000. Founding executive chairman, Irish Institute of Sport. Contested 1991 local elections in Killarney.

PHIL PRENDERGAST (LB)
Group of the Progressive Alliance of Socialists and Democrats in the European Parliament

6 Marlfield Road, Clonmel, Co. Tipperary; Tel: 052 24380; Mobile: 086 8555472
Constituency: Central House, Parnell Street, Clonmel, Co. Tipperary; Tel: 052 6124380
Email: phil.prendergast@europarl.europe.eu; Website: www.philprendergast.ie

Born Kilkenny 20th September 1959. Married to Ray, two sons Luke and Alan. Nurse/Midwife. Former member Workers and Unemployed Action Group (WUAG). Appointed to European Parliament in 2011 to replace Alan Kelly TD.

Senator 2007-2011. Labour Spokesperson on Older People. Seanad Spokesperson on Health, Arts and Sports, Social and Family Affairs. Member Joint Committee on Health and Children. Member Joint Committee on European Affairs. Contested 2001 by-election and 2007 general election in Tipperary South. Member South Riding County Council 1999-2007. Member Clonmel Borough Council 1994-2007 (Mayor 2003-2004). Member Irish Nurses Organisation.

EURO CONSTITUENCY: SOUTH 2009							
FIRST PREFERENCE VOTES							
	Seats	3			124,532		
	Candidate	**Party**	**1st**	**%**	**Quota**	**Count**	**Status**
1	**Crowley, Brian***	**FF**	**118,258**	**23.74%**	**0.95**	**1**	**Made Quota**
2	**Kelly, Sean**	**FG**	**92,579**	**18.59%**	**0.74**	**6**	**Made Quota**
3	**Kelly, Alan**	**LB**	**64,152**	**12.88%**	**0.52**	**8**	**Elected**
4	Sinnott, Kathy*	NP	58,485	11.74%	0.47	8	Not Elected
5	Ferris, Toireasa	SF	64,671	12.98%	0.52	7	Eliminated
6	Burke, Colm**	FG	53,721	10.78%	0.43	5	Eliminated
7	O'Keeffe, Ned	FF	16,596	3.33%	0.13	3	Lost Expenses
8	Boyle, Dan	GP	15,499	3.11%	0.12	2	Lost Expenses
9	Stafford, Alexander	NP	11,692	2.35%	0.09	1	Lost Expenses
10	Sexton, Maurice	NP	2,474	0.50%	0.02	1	Lost Expenses
10	***Outgoing **Co-option**		**498,127**	**100.00%**	**124,532**	**31,133**	**Lost Expenses**

EURO CONSTITUENCY : SOUTH 2009												
PARTY VOTE												
	2009					2004					Change	
Party	**Cand**	**1st**	**%**	**Quota**	**Seats**	**Cand**	**1st**	**%**	**Quota**	**Seats**	**%**	**Seats**
FF	2	134,854	27.07%	1.08	1	2	198,670	41.02%	1.64	1	-13.95%	
FG	2	146,300	29.37%	1.17	1	1	118,937	24.56%	0.98	1	+4.81%	
LB	1	64,152	12.88%	0.52	1	1	19,975	4.12%	0.16		+8.75%	+1
GP	1	15,499	3.11%	0.12		1	10,896	2.25%	0.09		+0.86%	
SF	2	64,671	12.98%	0.52		1	32,643	6.74%	0.27		+6.24%	
Others	2	72,651	14.58%	0.58		4	103,149	21.30%	0.85	1	-6.72%	-1
Total	**10**	**498,127**	**100.00%**	**124,532**	**3**	**10**	**484,270**	**100.00%**	**121,068**	**3**	**0.00%**	
Electorate		**802,696**	**62.06%**				**802,359**	**60.36%**			**+1.70%**	
Spoiled		**11,836**	**2.32%**				**14,124**	**2.83%**			**-0.51%**	
Turnout		**509,963**	**63.53%**				**498,394**	**62.12%**			**+1.42%**	

EURO CONSTITUENCY: SOUTH 2009								
TRANSFER ANALYSIS								
From	**To**	**FF**	**FG**	**LB**	**GP**	**SF**	**NP**	**Non Trans**
FF	25,002	10,006	3,705	1,308		1,991	2,625	5,367
%		40.02%	14.82%	5.23%		7.96%	10.50%	21.47%
FG	68,834		36,318	12,930		5,185	8,248	6,153
%			52.76%	18.78%		7.53%	11.98%	8.94%
SF	74,480			21,676			19,966	32,838
%				29.10%			26.81%	44.09%
GP	16,250	3,007	4,296	3,562		1,443	2,238	1,704
%		18.50%	26.44%	21.92%		8.88%	13.77%	10.49%
Others	14,166	1,667	2,747	1,969	751	1,190	3,572	2,270
%		11.77%	19.39%	13.90%	5.30%	8.40%	25.22%	16.02%
Total	**198,732**	**14,680**	**47,066**	**41,445**	**751**	**9,809**	**36,649**	**48,332**
		7.39%	**23.68%**	**20.85%**	**0.38%**	**4.94%**	**18.44%**	**24.32%**

EURO CONSTITUENCY: SOUTH 2009 COUNT DETAILS									
Seats	**3**							**Quota**	**124,532**
Candidate	**Party**	**1st**	**2nd** Stafford Sexton Votes	**3rd** Boyle Votes	**4th** O'Keeffe Votes	**5th** Crowley Surplus	**6th** Burke Votes	**7th** Kelly, S. Surplus	**8th** Ferris Votes
Crowley	FF	118,258	*+1,367* 119,625	*2,779* 122,404	*10,006* 132,410	*-7,878* 124,532	124,532	124,532	124,532
Kelly, S.	FG	92,579	*+1,851* 94,430	*+1,723* 96,153	*+1,329* 97,482	*+912* 98,394	*+36,318* 134,712	*-10,180* 124,532	124,532
Kelly, A	LB	64,152	*+1,969* 66,121	*+3,562* 69,683	*+626* 70,309	*+682* 70,991	*+7,660* 78,651	*+5,270* 83,921	*+21,676* 105,597
Sinnott	NP	58,485	*+3,572* 62,057	*+2,238* 64,295	*+1,223* 65,518	*+1,402* 66,920	*+4,429* 71,349	*+3,819* 75,168	*+19,966* 95,134
Ferris	SF	64,671	*+1,190* 65,861	*+1,443* 67,304	*+992* 68,296	*+999* 69,295	*+4,094* 73,389	*+1,091* 74,480	*-74,480* Eliminated
Burke	FG	53,721	*+896* 54,617	*+2,573* 57,190	*+694* 57,884	*+770* 58,654	*-58,654* Eliminated		
O'Keeffe	FF	16,596	*+300* 16,896	*+228* 17,124	*-17,124* Eliminated				
Boyle	GP	15,499	*+751* 16,250	*-16,250* Eliminated					
Stafford	NP	11,692	*-11,692* Eliminated						
Sexton	NP	2,474	*-2,474* Eliminated						
Non-transferable			*+2,270*	*+1,704*	*+2,254*	*+3,113*	*+6,153*		*+32,838*
Cumulative			2,270	3,974	6,228	9,341	15,494	15,494	48,332
Total		**498,127**	**498,127**	**498,127**	**498,127**	**498,127**	**498,127**	**498,127**	**498,127**

EURO CONSTITUENCY: SOUTH 1979-2009								
Party	**1979**	**1984**	**1989**	**1994**	**1999**	**2004**	**2009**	**2009-2004**
FF	37.48%	38.93%	28.84%	42.11%	52.90%	41.02%	27.07%	-13.95%
FG	26.85%	28.59%	17.57%	18.69%	17.27%	24.56%	29.37%	+4.81%
LB	12.45%	7.63%	8.86%	6.99%	6.30%	4.12%	12.88%	+8.76%
GP				2.75%	2.29%	2.25%	3.11%	+0.86%
SF		3.74%		1.42%	6.48%	6.74%	12.98%	+6.24%
WP	2.68%	5.05%	5.43%	1.72%				
PD			17.30%	8.69%				
Others	20.54%	16.06%	22.00%	17.63%	14.76%	21.31%	14.59%	-6.72%
Total	**100.00%**	**100.00%**	**100.00%**	**100.00%**	**100.00%**	**100.00%**	**100.00%**	**0.00%**

EUROPEAN ELECTIONS SUMMARY 2009					
	Dublin	**East**	**North-West**	**South**	**Ireland**
Electorate	812,465	778,502	805,626	802,696	3,199,289
Turnout	412,684	442,291	510,982	509,963	1,875,920
%	50.79%	56.81%	63.43%	63.53%	58.64%
Spoiled Votes	6,054	13,042	15,675	11,836	46,607
%	1.47%	2.95%	3.07%	2.32%	2.48%
Valid Poll	406,630	429,249	495,307	498,127	1,829,313
%	50.05%	55.14%	61.48%	62.06%	57.18%
Quota	101,658	107,313	123,827	124,532	
Seats	3	3	3	3	12
Candidates	10	11	13	10	44

EUROPEAN ELECTIONS 2009 NATIONAL PARTY VOTE												
	2009					2004					2009-2004	
Party	**Cand**	**1st**	**%**	**Quota**	**Seats**	**Cand**	**1st**	**%**	**Quota**	**Seats**	**%**	**Seats**
FF	8	440,562	24.08%	3.13	3	8	524,504	29.45%	4.12	4	-5.37%	-1
FG	7	532,889	29.13%	3.79	4	6	494,412	27.76%	3.89	5	+1.37%	-1
LB	4	254,669	13.92%	1.81	3	5	188,132	10.56%	1.48	1	+3.36%	+2
GP	2	34,585	1.89%	0.25		3	76,917	4.32%	0.60		-2.43%	
SF	6	205,613	11.24%	1.46		4	197,715	11.10%	1.55	1	+0.14%	-1
SP	1	50,510	2.76%	0.36	1	1	23,218	1.30%	0.18		+1.46%	+1
LIB	3	99,709	5.45%	0.71							+5.45%	
CS						1	5,352	0.30%	0.04		-0.30%	
Others	13	210,776	11.52%	1.50	1	16	270,518	15.19%	2.13	2	-3.67%	-1
Total	**44**	**1,829,313**	**100.00%**	**140,717**	**12**	**44**	**1,780,768**	**100.00%**	**127,199**	**13**	**0.00%**	**-1**
Electorate		**3,199,289**	**57.18%**				**3,119,484**	**57.09%**			**+0.09%**	
Spoiled		**46,607**	**2.48%**				**60,567**	**3.29%**			**-0.80%**	
Turnout		**1,875,920**	**58.64%**				**1,841,335**	**59.03%**			**-0.39%**	

EURO CONSTITUENCY: NATIONAL 2009 TRANSFER ANALYSIS										
From	**To**	**FF**	**FG**	**LB**	**GP**	**SF**	**SP**	**LIB**	**NP**	**Non Trans**
FF	125,535	66,994	9,332	6,066	1,765	6,564	581	1,711	11,750	20,772
%		53.37%	7.43%	4.83%	1.41%	5.23%	0.46%	1.36%	9.36%	16.55%
FG	116,992	4,844	62,593	14,836		7,608	235	1,690	13,085	12,101
%		4.14%	53.50%	12.68%		6.50%	0.20%	1.44%	11.18%	10.34%
LB	31,176	2,130	7,636			2,812		2,550	9,623	6,425
%		6.83%	24.49%			9.02%		8.18%	30.87%	20.61%
GP	38,241	5,319	7,899	10,594		2,910	2,078		5,071	4,370
%		13.91%	20.66%	27.70%		7.61%	5.43%		13.26%	11.43%
SF	253,022	19,959	14,125	36,997		13,780	22,201	8,572	29,428	107,960
%		7.89%	5.58%	14.62%		5.45%	8.77%	3.39%	11.63%	42.67%
LIB	19,396	1,967	3,803	4,053		4,666				4,907
%		10.14%	19.61%	20.90%		24.06%				25.30%
Others	89,140	9,783	9,363	15,003	1,891	9,069	6,761	2,955	12,699	21,616
%		10.97%	10.50%	16.83%	2.12%	10.17%	7.58%	3.32%	14.25%	24.25%
Total	**673,502**	**110,996**	**114,751**	**87,549**	**3,656**	**47,409**	**31,856**	**17,478**	**81,656**	**178,151**
		16.48%	**17.04%**	**13.00%**	**0.54%**	**7.04%**	**4.73%**	**2.60%**	**12.12%**	**26.45%**

NATIONAL EURO RESULTS 1979-2009														
	1979		1984		1989		1994		1999		2004		2009	
Electorate	2,188,798		2,413,404		2,453,451		2,631,575		2,864,361		3,143,025		3,199,289	
Turnout	1,392,285		1,147,745		1,675,119		1,157,296		1,438,287		1,841,335		1,875,920	
Turnout %	63.61%		47.56%		68.28%		43.98%		50.21%		58.58%		58.64%	
Spoiled Votes	53,213		27,329		42,391		19,806		46,547		60,567		46,607	
Spoiled Votes%	3.82%		2.38%		2.53%		1.71%		3.24%		3.29%		2.48%	
Valid Poll	1,339,072		1,120,416		1,632,728		1,137,490		1,391,740		1,780,768		1,829,313	
Valid Poll %	61.18%		46.42%		66.55%		43.22%		48.59%		56.66%		57.18%	
Party	**%**	**Seats**	**%**	**Seats**	**%**	**Seats**	**%**	**Seats**	**%**	**Seats**	**%**	**Seats**	**%**	**Seats**
Fianna Fail	34.68%	5	39.17%	8	31.51%	6	35.00%	7	38.64%	6	29.45%	4	24.08%	3
Fine Gael	33.13%	4	32.21%	6	21.63%	4	24.27%	4	24.59%	4	27.76%	5	29.13%	4
Labour	14.48%	4	8.36%		9.54%	1	10.99%	1	8.73%	1	10.56%	1	13.92%	3
Sinn Fein			4.87%		2.27%		2.97%		6.33%		11.10%	1	11.24%	
Green Party			0.47%		3.74%		7.92%	2	6.69%	2	4.32%		1.89%	
Socialist Party									0.76%		1.30%		2.76%	1
Workers Party	3.28%		4.32%		7.55%	1	1.94%							
Progressive Democrats					11.89%	1	6.48%							
Democratic Left							3.49%							
Others	14.43%	2	10.60%	1	11.87%	2	6.94%	1	14.26%	2	15.51%	2	16.98%	1
Total	**100.00%**	**15**	**100.00%**	**15**	**100.00%**	**15**	**100.00%**	**15**	**100.00%**	**15**	**100.00%**	**13**	**100.00%**	**12**

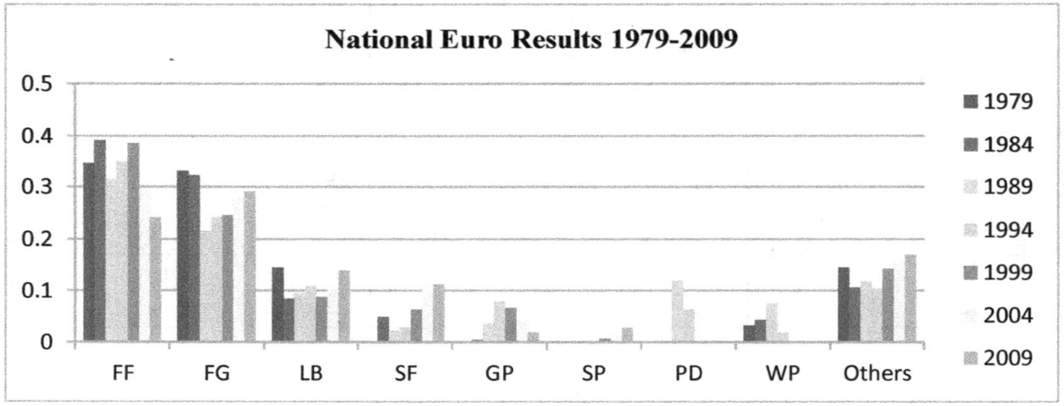

IRISH MEPs 1973-2012					
Date	**Fianna Fail**	**Fine Gael**	**Labour**	**Greens**	**Others**
Jan-73	Michael Herbert	Sir Anthony Esmonde	Justin Keating		
	Michael Hilliard	Charles McDonald	Conor Cruise O'Brien		
	Farrell McElgunn	Richie Ryan			
	Tom Nolan				
	Michael Yeats				
Mar-73	Jim Gibbons	Donal Creed	Liam Kavanagh		
	Michael Herbert	Tom Dunne*			
	Brian Lenihan	Charles McDonald			
	Tom Nolan	* replaced Jan' 77 by			
	Michael Yeats	Gerry L'Estrange			
Dec-77	Sean Brosnan	Gerry L'Estrange	Liam Kavanagh		
	Ruairi Brugha	Charles McDonald			
	Michael Herbert	Richie Ryan			
	Tom Nolan				
	Paddy Power				
	Michael Yeats				
Jun-79	Jerry Cronin	Mark Clinton	Eileen Desmond		Neil Blaney (NP)
	Noel Davern	Joe McCartin	Liam Kavanagh		T.J.Maher (NP)
	Sean Flanagan	Tom O'Donnell	John O'Connell		
	Paddy Lalor	Richie Ryan	Michael O'Leary		
	Sile de Valera		from July-Sept 1981		
			Frank Cluskey		
			John Horgan		
			Seamus Pattison		
			Sean Treacy		
			from March 1983		
			Brendan Halligan		
			Flor O'Mahony		
			Seamus Pattison*		
			Sean Treacy		
			*resigned Dec '83		
			replaced Feb '84 by		
			Justin Keating		
July'84	Niall Andrews	Mary Banotti			T.J.Maher (NP)
	Sylvester Barrett	Mark Clinton			
	Gene Fitzgerald	Joe McCartin			
	Jim Fitzsimons	Tom O'Donnell			
	Sean Flanagan	Tom Raftery			
	Paddy Lalor	Richie Ryan			
	Eileen Lemass				
	Ray McSharry				
Jun-89	Niall Andrews	Mary Banotti	Barry Desmond		Neil Blaney (NP)
	Gene Fitzgerald	Pat Cooney			T.J.Maher (NP)
	Jim Fitzsimons	John Cushanan			Pat Cox (PD)
	Mark Killilea	Joe McCartin			P.de Rossa (WP)
	Paddy Lalor				
	Paddy Lane				
Jun-94	Niall Andrews	Mary Banotti	Bernie Malone	Nuala Ahern	Pat Cox (NP)
	Gerard Collins	John Cushanan		Patricia McKenna	
	Brian Crowley	Alan Gillis			
	Jim Fitzsimons	Joe McCartin			
	Pat the Cope Gallagher				
	Liam Hyland				
	Mark Killilea				
Jun-99	Niall Andrews	Mary Banotti	Proinsias de Rossa	Nuala Ahern	Pat Cox (NP)
	Gerard Collins	John Cushanan		Patricia McKenna	Dana-
	Brian Crowley	Avril Doyle			Rosemary
	Jim Fitzsimons	Joe McCartin			Scallon (NP)
	Pat the Cope Gallagher				
	Liam Hyland				
Jun-04	Liam Aylward	Gay Mitchell	Proinsias de Rossa		Marian Harkin (NP)
	Brian Crowley	Avril Doyle			Kathy Sinnott (NP)
	Eoin Ryan	Jim Higgins			Mary Lou
	Sean O Neachtain	Mairead McGuinness			McDonald (SF)
		Simon Coveney to 2007			
		Colm Burke from 2007			
Jun-09	Liam Aylward	Gay Mitchell	Proinsias de Rossa to 2012		Marian Harkin (NP)
	Brian Crowley	Jim Higgins	Nessa Childers		Joe Higgins (SP)
	Pat the Cope Gallagher	Mairead McGuinness	Alan Kelly to 2011		Paul Murphy (SP)
		Sean Kelly	Phil Prendergast from 2011		from 2011
			Emer Costello from 2012		

EUROPEAN ELECTION TURNOUT PER MEMBER STATE 1979-2009

	Country	Population	Seats	Pop/Seat	1979	1984	1989	1994	1999	2004	2009	Average
1	Germany	82,217,800	99	830,483	65.73%	56.76%	62.28%	60.02%	45.19%	43.00%	43.30%	53.75%
2	France	64,473,140	72	895,460	60.71%	56.72%	48.80%	52.71%	46.76%	42.76%	40.63%	49.87%
3	United Kingdom	60,587,300	72	841,490	32.35%	32.57%	36.37%	36.43%	24.00%	38.52%	34.70%	33.56%
4	Italy	59,619,290	72	828,046	85.65%	82.47%	81.07%	73.60%	69.76%	71.72%	65.05%	75.62%
5	Spain	46,063,000	50	921,260			54.71%	59.14%	63.05%	45.14%	44.90%	53.39%
6	Poland	38,115,967	50	762,319						20.87%	24.53%	22.70%
7	Romania	21,438,000	33	649,636							27.67%	27.67%
8	Netherlands	16,428,071	25	657,123	58.12%	50.88%	47.48%	35.69%	30.02%	39.26%	36.75%	42.60%
9	Greece	11,147,000	22	506,682		80.59%	80.03%	73.18%	70.25%	63.22%	52.61%	69.98%
10	Portugal	10,623,000	22	482,864			51.10%	35.54%	39.93%	38.60%	36.78%	40.39%
11	Belgium	10,584,534	22	481,115	91.36%	92.09%	90.73%	90.66%	91.05%	90.81%	90.39%	91.01%
12	Czech Republic	10,403,136	22	472,870						28.30%	28.20%	28.25%
13	Hungary	10,043,000	22	456,500						38.50%	36.31%	37.41%
14	Sweden	9,201,650	18	511,203					38.84%	37.85%	45.53%	40.74%
15	Austria	8,340,924	17	490,643					49.40%	42.43%	45.97%	45.93%
16	Bulgaria	7,640,238	17	449,426							29.22%	29.22%
17	Denmark	5,482,266	13	421,713	47.82%	52.38%	46.17%	52.92%	50.46%	47.89%	59.54%	51.03%
18	Slovakia	5,402,273	13	415,559						16.97%	19.64%	18.31%
19	Finland	5,313,026	13	408,694					30.14%	39.43%	40.30%	36.62%
20	Ireland	4,239,848	12	353,321	63.61%	47.56%	68.28%	43.98%	50.21%	59.03%	57.57%	55.75%
21	Lithuania	3,361,100	12	280,092						48.38%	20.98%	34.68%
22	Latvia	2,268,000	8	283,500						41.34%	53.70%	47.52%
23	Slovenia	2,028,683	7	289,812						28.35%	28.33%	28.34%
24	Estonia	1,340,600	6	223,433						26.83%	43.90%	35.37%
25	Cyprus	855,000	6	142,500						72.50%	59.40%	65.95%
26	Luxembourg	483,800	6	80,633	88.91%	88.79%	87.39%	88.55%	87.27%	71.35%	90.75%	86.14%
27	Malta	407,000	5	81,400						82.39%	78.79%	80.59%
	Total	**498,107,646**	**736**	**676,777**	**61.99%**	**58.98%**	**58.41%**	**56.67%**	**49.51%**	**45.47%**	**43.00%**	**53.43%**

PART 7

THE PRESIDENCY

POWERS AND FUNCTIONS OF THE PRESIDENT

The Office of President was established by the Constitution. The President is elected directly by the people. To be a candidate a citizen must be over 35 years of age and must be nominated either by:

> not less than 20 members of Dáil or Seanad Éireann, or
> not less than 4 administrative counties (including County Boroughs)

Former or retiring Presidents may become candidates on their own nomination.

The term of office is 7 years and a President may not serve more than 2 terms. The President must reside in or near Dublin. St. Patrick's Hall, Dublin Castle, is the venue for Inauguration ceremonies, at which each President takes an oath as provided in the Constitution.
The President represents all the people when carrying out official engagements at home and abroad. The President is Supreme Commander of the Defence Forces. There have been eight different holders of the office - Mary McAleese is the current President.

Powers and Functions

The formal powers and functions of the President are prescribed in the Constitution. The President, who does not have an executive or policy role, exercises them on the advice of the Government.
There are some specific instances where the President has an absolute discretion, such as in referring a Bill to the Supreme Court for a judgement on its constitutionality or in refusing to dissolve Dáil Éireann (lower house of parliament) on the advice of a Taoiseach (Prime Minister) who has ceased to retain a majority. Additional functions can be conferred on the President by law. A special (Presidential) Commission acts whenever the President is absent.

Appointments

The President appoints the Taoiseach (Prime Minister) on the nomination of Dáil Éireann; and the other members of the Government on the nomination of the Taoiseach after Dáil approval.

Other office holders appointed by the President, on the advice of the Government, include Judges, the Attorney General, the Comptroller and Auditor General, and Commissioned officers of the Defence Forces.

Oireachtas

The Oireachtas is the sole legislative authority of the State and comprises the President, Dáil Éireann and Seanad Éireann. The President summons and dissolves Dáil Éireann on the advice of the Taoiseach.
Bills enacted by Houses of the Oireachtas are signed into law by the President. A Bill must be signed on the 5th, 6th or 7th day after it is presented to the President, but there are some situations when the President may sign a Bill earlier.

The President has an absolute discretion to refer a Bill to the Supreme Court to get a judgement on its constitutionality (but not a Money Bill or a Bill to amend the Constitution). Before making a referral the President must first consult the Council of State. The constitutionality of any Bill signed following a referral may not be subsequently challenged in the courts.

The President, after consultation with the Council of State, may address the Houses of the Oireachtas (parliament) on any matter of national or public importance. The text of any such address must be approved by the Government.

Representing the People

The President represents all the people and does so in many different ways, for example when receiving foreign Heads of State on visits to Ireland or when making State Visits abroad. These and other visits abroad provide valuable opportunities to promote Ireland's interests in the international arena and to strengthen links with the Irish Diaspora around the world. Irish public and private enterprises frequently organise promotional events to coincide with Presidential visits abroad.

At home the President undertakes a wide range of engagements with particular emphasis on valuing the contribution of local community and self-help groups and in promoting peace and reconciliation throughout the island of Ireland. Whether participating in formal ceremonial, addressing international conferences or meeting people in a wide range of informal settings, the President is giving expression to the undertaking in the oath of office to "dedicate my abilities to the service and welfare of the people of Ireland".

HOLDERS OF THE OFFICE OF PRESIDENT

DR DOUGLAS HYDE (DR. DUBHGLAS de hIDE) (1860 - 1949)

Born in Sligo, he was reared in Frenchpark, County Roscommon. Educated Trinity College, Dublin. A renowned Gaelic scholar, he played a leading role in the revival of the Irish language; he was co-founder of the Gaelic League in 1893. He was a distinguished author, playwright and poet, publishing works in English and in Irish, the latter under the name "An Craoibhin Aoibhinn". Professor of Modern Irish at the National University (1909-1932) and Dean of the Faculty of Celtic Studies. Member of the Senate of the National University of Ireland (1909-1919). Chairman of the Irish Folklore Institute (1930-1934). Member of Seanad Éireann (1925-1938). President of Ireland (1938-1945).

SEÁN T. O'KELLY (SEÁN T. Ó CEALLAIGH) (1882 - 1966)

Born in Dublin. Educated O'Connell Schools, Dublin. Joined Gaelic League in 1989. Member Dublin Corporation (1906-1924). Founder member of Sinn Fein and the Irish Volunteers. Staff-Captain in the GPO during the Easter Rising of 1916 and interned. Elected for Dublin to the first Dáil Éireann (1918). Elected Ceann Comhairle (Chairman of the Dáil) on 21st January 1919. Member of the Dáil (1918-1945). Rejected the Anglo Irish Treaty 1921. Founder member of Fianna Fáil. Vice-President of Executive Council (Government) (1932-1938), Minister for Local Government and Public Health (1932-1939), Tánaiste (Deputy Prime Minister) (1937-1945) and Minister for Finance (1939-1945). President of Ireland (1945-1959).

EAMON de VALERA (1882 - 1975)

Born in New York and reared in Bruree, County Limerick. Educated Christian Brothers Schools, Rathluirc, Co. Cork, Blackrock College, Dublin and Royal University of Ireland. Teacher and university lecturer. Joined the Gaelic League in 1908. Commandant of the Irish Volunteers at Bolands Mills during the Easter Rising of 1916. Sentenced to death for his part in insurrection; sentence commuted to penal servitude for life; released June 1917. In 1917 elected MP for East Clare. Represented Clare in Dáil Éireann (1918-1959). Chosen as President of Dáil Éireann 1919. Arrested in 1918, he escaped from Lincoln Jail in 1919. In USA (1919-1921) to seek support, recognition and funds for the Irish Republic. Rejected Articles of Agreement for Anglo - Irish Treaty 1921. Imprisoned in Dublin (1923) and Belfast (1924). Rejected oath of allegiance required for admission to Dáil and pursued abstentionist policy up to 1927. Founded Fianna Fáil (the Republican Party) in 1926; with his colleagues in Fianna Fáil took his Dáil seat after the general election of June 1927. In 1931 founded the "Irish Press" newspaper. Following the general election of 1932, with the support of the Labour Party, he formed his first Government. President of the Council of the League of Nations 1932 and of the Assembly of the League 1938. Introduced new Constitution of Ireland ("Bunreacht na hÉireann") which was approved by plebiscite in 1937. Maintained a policy of neutrality during World War 2. Taoiseach and Minister for External Affairs (1937-1948), Minister for Education (1937-1940) and Taoiseach (1951-1954 and 1957-1959). President of Ireland (1959-1973).

ERSKINE CHILDERS (1905 - 1974)

Born in London; educated at Norfolk and at Trinity College, Cambridge. Worked in Paris (1928-1931); advertising manager of the "Irish Press" (1932-1936). Secretary of the Federation of Irish Manufacturers (1936-1944). Elected to the Dáil 1938 and represented the constituencies of Athlone-Longford (1938-1944), Longford-Westmeath (1948-1957) and Monaghan (1961-1973). Parliamentary Secretary to the Minister for Local Government and Public Health (1944-1947), Parliamentary Secretary to the Minister for Local Government (1947-1948) Minister for Posts and Telegraphs (1951-1954). Minister for Lands (1957-1959), Minister for Transport and Power (1959-1966), Minister for Transport and Power and Minister for Posts and Telegraphs (1966-1969), Tánaiste and Minister for Health (1969-1973). President of Ireland (1973-1974). Died in office on 17th November 1974.

CEARBHALL Ó DÁLAIGH (1911 - 1978)

Born in Bray, County Wicklow. Educated at Scoil na Lèanbh, An Rinn, County Waterford, Synge Street Christian Brothers School, Dublin, University College, Dublin and Kings Inns. Irish language editor of the "Irish Press" (1931-1940). Called to the Bar in 1934 and to the Inner Bar in 1945. Attorney-General (1946-1948 and 1951-1953). Appointed Judge of the Supreme Court in 1953 and Chief Justice (1961-1973). Following Ireland's accession to the European Community, became Judge at the European Court of Justice 1973; appointed President of the First Chamber of the Court in 1974. President of Ireland (1974-1976). Resigned from office in October 1976.

DR. PATRICK HILLERY (PÁDRAIG S. Ó hIRIGHILE) (1923 - 2008)

Born in Miltown Malbay, County Clare 2nd May 1923. Educated Rockwell College and University College, Dublin. Qualified as medical doctor. Member of Dáil for Clare (1951-1973); Minister for Education (1959-1965), Minister for Industry and Commerce (1965-1966), Minister for Labour (1966-1969) and Minister for External Affairs (1969-1972). While Minister for External Affairs he was responsible for the conduct of the negotiations for Ireland's entry into the European Community in 1973. Vice-President of the Commission of the European Communities with special responsibility for Social Affairs (1973-1976). President of Ireland (1976-1990). Died 12th April 2008, aged 84.

MARY ROBINSON (1944 -)

Born (Mary Bourke) in Ballina, County Mayo in 1944. Educated at Trinity College, Dublin, King's Inns,

Dublin and Harvard University. Senior Counsel, member of English Bar, Reid Professor of Constitutional and Criminal Law, Trinity College, Dublin (1969-1975). Lecturer in European Community law, Trinity College (1975-1990). Member of Seanad Éireann for the University of Dublin (1969-1990); member of Dublin Corporation (1979-1983). Member of International Commission of Jurists (1987-1990). Founded Irish Centre for European Law (1988). Published works on aspects of Irish Law and Government and campaigned for family law reform and protection of human rights. President of Ireland (1990-1997). Appointed United Nations Commissioner for Human Rights in September 1997.

MARY McALEESE (1951 -)

Born (Mary Leneghan) in Belfast June 1951. Married to Martin McAleese, one son, two daughters. In 1973, graduated from Queen's University, Belfast with an honours Law Degree after which she studied at the Inn of Court of Northern Ireland. She is qualified Barrister at both the Northern Ireland Bar and the Republic of Ireland Bar and a member of the European Bar Association, the International Bar Association, the Irish Association of Law Teachers and the Society of Public Teachers of Law. She is also fluent in Spanish and a member of the Institute of Linguists. Spent 10 years lecturing in Trinity College's Law school having succeeded Mary Robinson as Reid Professor of Criminal Law, Criminology and Penology. Has extensive knowledge of the Irish Constitution and has written widely on attitudes to crime, punishment, prisons and children in custody. Became the first woman Pro Vice-Chancellor of Queen's University, Belfast in 1994 and was also Director of the Institute of Professional Legal Studies at Queens. Has served on the Council for Social Welfare (Dublin); the Commission for Justice and Peace; the Irish Commission for Prisoners Overseas; Focus Point for Homeless Young People (Dublin) and the BBC Broadcasting Council for Northern Ireland. She was Non Executive Director of Channel 4 Television; Northern Ireland Electricity plc and of the Royal Group of Hospitals Trust. Honorary President of the Northern Ireland Housing Rights Association. Member of the Catholic Church Episcopal Delegation to the New Ireland Forum in 1984. Member of the Catholic Church's five-person delegation, led by Cardinal Daly and Archbishop Brady in December 1996, to the North Commission on Contentious Parades in Northern Ireland. Elected President of Ireland in October 1997. Re-elected unopposed for a second term in October 2004.

MICHAEL D. HIGGINS (1941 -)

Born Limerick 18th April 1941. Married to Sabina Coyne, three sons, one daughter. Educated St. Flannan's College, Ennis, Co. Clare; UCG (BA, BComm); Indiana University (MA) and Manchester University. University Lecturer, Author and Poet. First elected to Dail Eireann 1981. Lost his seat November 1982, regained it in 1987 and held it until he retired at the 2011 election. Labour Party Front Bench spokesperson on Foreign Affairs 2002-2011. President of the Labour Party 2003-2011. Spokesperson on Arts, Heritage, Gaeltacht and the Islands as well as broadcasting 1997-2002. Minister for Arts, Culture and the Gaeltacht 1993-1997. Senator, NUI 1982-1987 and Taoiseach's Nominee 1973-1977. Labour Party spokesperson on Foreign Affairs, Gaeltacht 1989; on Education, the Gaeltacht and Overseas Development 1987-1989. Member Galway City Council 1985-1993, (Mayor 1982-1983, 1991-1992). Member Galway County Council 1974-1985. Member Governing Body, UCG. Chairman of the Labour Party 1977-1987. Member Sociological Association of Ireland and the American Sociological Association. The first recipient of the Sean MacBride Peace Prize of the International Peace Bureau in Helsinki in 1992. Elected President of Ireland in October 2011.

PRESIDENTIAL ELECTIONS 1938 - 2011

PRESIDENTIAL ELECTION 1938

Only one candidate, Dr. Dubhghlas de hÍde of Rath Reidh, Dún Gar, Co. Ros Comáin was nominated at the presidential election of 1938. He was accordingly declared elected and was inaugurated as President on 25th June 1938.

PRESIDENTIAL ELECTION 1945

The presidential election of 1945 was contested by three candidates. The candidates were Patrick McCartan, Mount John, Newtownmountkennedy, County Wicklow, Seán MacEoin, "Cloncoose", Stillorgan Road, Donnybrook, Dublin and Seán T. O'Kelly, 38 Anglesea Road, Dublin.

Voting took place on Thursday 14th June 1945 between the hours of 9.00 am and 9.00 pm. The poll was conducted on the basis of county and county boroughs to facilitate the holding of local elections on the same day. The result of the voting was as follows:-

Electorate	1,803,463
Percentage Poll	63.02
Total Poll	1,136,625

Total Valid Poll	1,086,338	60.24%
Spoiled Votes	50,287	4.42%
Quota	543,170	

FIRST COUNT				*SECOND COUNT*			
Candidate	**Party**	**1st Pref.**	**%**	**Transfer of McCartan's Vote**	**%**	**Result**	**%**
O'Kelly	F.F.	537,965	49.52	+27,200	12.78	565,165	55.49
MacEoin	F.G.	335,539	30.89	+117,886	55.39	453,425	44.50
McCartan	N.P.	212,834	19.59	-212,834			
Non-transferable papers				67,748	31.83		
TOTAL		1,086,338	100		100	1,018,590	

Mr. O'Kelly was declared elected and was inaugurated as President on 25th June 1945.

PRESIDENTIAL ELECTION 1952

Only one candidate, the outgoing President Mr. Seán T. O'Kelly was nominated at the presidential election of 1952. He was accordingly declared elected and was inaugurated as President on 25th June 1952.

PRESIDENTIAL ELECTION 1959

The election was contested by two candidates, Eamon de Valera, Teach Cuilinn, Carraig Dhubh, Contae Átha Cliath, An Taoiseach and Seán MacEoin, "Cloncoose", Stillorgan Road, Donnybrook, Dublin farmer and army officer (retired Lieut-General). Voting took place on Wednesday 17th June 1959 between the hours of 9.00 am and 9.30 pm and the result of the voting was as follows:-

Electorate	1,678,450
Percentage Poll	58.37
Total Poll	979,628

Total Valid Poll	955,539	56.93%
Spoiled Votes	24,089	2.46%
Quota	477,770	

FIRST COUNT			
Candidate	**Party**	**Votes**	**%**
de Valera	F.F.	538,003	56.30
MacEoin	F.G.	417,536	43.70
TOTAL		955,539	

Mr. de Valera was declared elected and was inaugurated as President on 25th June 1959.

PRESIDENTIAL ELECTION 1966

The 1966 presidential election was contested by two candidates, Eamon de Valera, the outgoing President and Thomas F. O'Higgins, "Ulverton", Ulverton Road, Dalkey, County Dublin, Senior Counsel and member of Dáil Éireann. Voting took place on Wednesday 1st June 1966 between the hours of 9.00 am and 10.00 pm and the result of the voting was as follows:-

Electorate	1,709,161
Percentage Poll	65.35
Total Poll	1,116,915

Total Valid Poll	1,107,005	64.77%
Spoiled Votes	9,910	0.89%
Quota	533,503	

FIRST COUNT			
Candidate	**Party**	**Votes**	**%**
de Valera	F.F	558,861	50.48
O'Higgins	F.G	548.144	49.52
TOTAL		1,107.005	

Mr. de Valera was declared elected and was inaugurated as President on 25th June 1966.

PRESIDENTIAL ELECTION 1973

Two candidates contested the presidential election held in 1973. They were Erskine Childers, 68 Highfield Road, Dublin member of Dáil Éireann and former Government Minister and Tom O'Higgins, "Jerpoint", Elton Park, Sandycove, County Dublin, Senior Counsel and former Minister for Health. Mr. O'Higgins had previously contested the 1966 election. Voting took place on Wednesday 30th May 1973 between the hours of 9.00 am and 9.00 pm and the result of the voting was as follows:-

Electorate	1,977,817	Total Valid Poll	1,223,638	61.87%
Percentage Poll	62.22	Spoiled Votes	6,946	0.56%
Total Poll	1,230,584	Quota	611,820	

FIRST COUNT

Candidate	Party	Votes	%
Childers	F.F	635,867	51.97
O'Higgins	F.G	587,771	48.03
TOTAL		1,223,638	

Mr. Childers was declared elected and was inaugurated as President on 25th June 1973.

PRESIDENTIAL ELECTION 1974

Only one candidate, Cearbhall Ó Dálaigh of 33 Route d'Arlon, A/Strassen, Luxembourg was nominated at the presidential election resulting from the death, on 17th November 1974 of Mr. Erskine Childers. Mr. Ó Dálaigh was accordingly declared elected and was inaugurated as President on 19th December 1974.

PRESIDENTIAL ELECTION 1976

President Cearbhall Ó Dálaigh resigned on the 22nd October 1976. The only person nominated at the resulting presidential election was Dr. Patrick Hillery of Spanish Point, Miltown Malbay, County Clare. Dr. Hillery was accordingly declared elected and was inaugurated as President on 3rd December 1976.

PRESIDENTIAL ELECTION 1983

Only one candidate, the outgoing President Dr. Patrick Hillery, was nominated at the presidential election of 1983. He was accordingly declared elected and was inaugurated as President on 3rd December 1983.

PRESIDENTIAL ELECTION 1990

The presidential election of 1990 was contested by three candidates. The candidates were Austin Currie, 37 Esker Lawns, Lucan, County Dublin, member of Dáil Éireann; Brian Lenihan, 24 Park View, Castleknock, Dublin 15, Tánaiste and Minister for Defence; Mary Robinson, 43 Sandford Road, Dublin 6, Senior Counsel. Voting took place on Wednesday 7th November 1990 between the hours of 9.00 am and 9.00 pm. The result of the voting was as follows:-

Electorate	2,471,308
Percentage Poll	64.10
Total Poll	1,584,095

Total Valid Poll	1,574,651	63.72%
Spoiled Votes	9,444	0.60%
Quota	787,326	

FIRST COUNT				*SECOND COUNT*			
Candidate	**Party**	**1st Pref.**	**%**	**Transfer of Currie's Vote**	**%**	**Result**	**%**
Robinson	N.P.	612,265	38.89	+205,565	76.73	817,830	52.79
Lenihan	F.F.	694,484	44.10	+36,789	13.73	731,273	47.21
Currie	F.G.	267,902	17.01	-267,902			
Non-transferable papers				25,548	9.54		
TOTAL		1,574,651	100		100	1,549,103	100

Mary Robinson was declared elected and was inaugurated as President on 3rd December 1990.

The seven candidates for the 2011 Presidential election get ready for another debate

PRESIDENTIAL ELECTION 1997

The presidential election of 1997 was contested by five candidates. The candidates were Mary Banotti, 8 Cambridge Avenue, Ringsend, Dublin 4, Member of the European Parliament; Mary McAleese, 2 Sydenham, 60 Merrion Road, Ballsbridge, Dublin 4, University Professor; Derek Nally, Corrigduff, Bunclody, Enniscorthy, Co. Wexford, company director; Adi Roche, 8 Sidneyville, Bellevue Park, St. Lukes, Cork, charity worker; Dana Rosemary Scallon, 23 Shrewsbury Park, Merrion Road, Dublin 4, entertainer. Voting took place on Thursday 30th October 1997 between the hours of 9.00 am and 9.00 pm. The result of the voting was as follows:-

Electorate	2,688,316
Percentage Poll	64.10
Total Poll	1,279,688

Total Valid Poll	1,269,836	47.24%
Spoiled Votes	9,852	0.77%
Quota	634,919	

FIRST COUNT				*SECOND COUNT*			
Candidate	**Party**	**1st Pref.**	**%**	**Transfer of Nally, Roche & Scallon's Votes**	**%**	**Result**	**%**
McAleese	F.F	574,424	45.24	+131,835	40.76	706,259	58.67
Banotti	F.G	372,002	29.30	+125,514	38.81	497,516	41.35
Scallon	N.P	175,458	13.82	-175,458			
Roche	N.P	88,423	6.96	-88,423			
Nally	N.P	59,529	4.69	-59,529			
Non-transferable papers				66,061	20.43		
TOTAL		1,269,836	100			1,203,775	100

Mary McAleese was declared elected and was inaugurated as President on 11th November 1997.

PRESIDENTIAL ELECTION 2004

Only one candidate, the outgoing President Mary McAleese, was nominated at the presidential election of 2004. She was accordingly declared elected and was inaugurated as President on 11th November 2004.

PRESIDENTIAL ELECTION 2011

The presidential election of 2011 was contested by seven candidates. The candidates were Mary Davis, St. Fintan's, Strand Road, Sutton, Dublin 13, Managing Director, Special Olympics Europe Eurasia; Sean Gallagher, 1 Lios an Uisce, Main Street, Blackrock, Co. Louth, Entrepreneur, Disability Campaigner, Former Youth Worker; Michael D. Higgins, Aimhirgin, Circular Road, Galway, University Lecturer, Poet; Martin McGuinness, 20 Westland Terrace, Derry City, MP, MLA; Gay Mitchell, 192 Rathmines Road Upper, Dublin 6, Member of the European Parliament; David Norris, 18 North Great Georges Street, Dublin 1; Dana Rosemary Scallon, Dromhoney House, Gortatleva, Claregalway, Co. Galway, Businesswoman, Entertainer. Voting took place on Thursday 27th October 2011 between the hours of 7.00 am and 10.00 pm. Michael D. Higgins was declared elected and was inaugurated as President on 11th November 2011.

PRESIDENTIAL ELECTION: 27/10/2011 COUNT DETAILS						
Seats 1					Quota:	885,882
Candidate	**Party**		**1st**	**2nd** Scallon Davis Votes	**3rd** Norris Norris Votes	**4th** McGuinness Mitchell Votes
Higgins, Michael D.	LB	39.57%	701,101	*+29,379* 730,480	*+62,648* 793,128	*+213,976* 1,007,104
Gallagher, Sean	NP	28.50%	504,964	*+24,437* 529,401	*+18,972* 548,373	*+79,741* 628,114
McGuinness, Martin	SF	13.72%	243,030	*+9,581* 252,611	*+12,585* 265,196	*-265,196* Eliminated
Mitchell, Gay	FG	6.40%	113,321	*+14,036* 127,357	*+8,952* **136,309**	*-136,309* Eliminated
Norris, David	NP	6.18%	109,469	*+7,057* **116,526**	*-116,526* Eliminated	
Scallon, Dana Rosemary	NP	2.89%	**51,220**	*-51,220* Eliminated		
Davis, Mary	NP	2.75%	**48,657**	*-48,657* Eliminated		
Non-transferable Cumulative				*+15,387* 15,387	*+13,369* 28,756	*+107,788* 136,544
Total		**100%**	**1,771,762**	**1,771,762**	**1,771,762**	**1,771,762**
Higgins-Gallagher			196,137	201,079	244,755	378,990

Electorate	3,191,157
Turnout	1,790,438
% Turnout	56.11%
Spoiled	18,676
% Spoiled	1.04%
Valid Poll	1,771,762
Quota	885,882
0.25% Q	221,471

TRANSFER ANALYSIS								
From	**Party**	**To**	**Higgins**	**Gallagher**	**McGuinness**	**Mitchell**	**Norris**	**Non Trans**
McGuinness, Martin	SF	265,196	141,332 *53.29%*	52,669 *19.86%*				71,194 *26.85%*
Mitchell, Gay	FG	136,309	72,644 *53.29%*	27,072 *19.86%*				36,594 *26.85%*
Norris	NP	116,526	62,648 *53.76%*	18,972 *16.28%*	12,585 *10.80%*	8,952 *7.68%*		13,369 *11.47%*
Scallon, Dana Rosemary	NP	51,220	15,066 *29.42%*	12,532 *24.47%*	4,913 *9.59%*	7,198 *14.05%*	3,619 *7.07%*	7,891 *15.41%*
Davis, Mary	NP	48,657	14,313 *29.42%*	11,905 *24.47%*	4,668 *9.59%*	6,838 *14.05%*	3,438 *7.07%*	7,496 *15.41%*
Total		**617,908**	**306,003** ***49.52%***	**123,150** ***19.93%***	**22,166** ***3.59%***	**22,988** ***3.72%***	**7,057** ***1.14%***	**136,544** ***22.10%***

PRESIDENTIAL ELECTION 2011: CONSTITUENCY DETAILS								
	Electorate 2011		Turnout		Invalid		Valid Poll	
Constituency	**Dail**	**Presidency**	**Votes**	**%**	**Votes**	**%**	**Votes**	**%**
Carlow-Kilkenny	105,449	106,810	59,328	55.55%	591	1.00%	58,737	55.70%
Cavan-Monaghan	99,178	98,952	58,518	59.14%	554	0.95%	57,964	58.44%
Clare	82,745	81,419	47,417	58.24%	405	0.85%	47,012	56.82%
Cork East	83,651	82,731	45,462	54.95%	509	1.12%	44,953	53.74%
Cork North-Central	75,302	75,622	41,602	55.01%	576	1.38%	41,026	54.48%
Cork North-West	62,870	62,113	37,784	60.83%	371	0.98%	37,413	59.51%
Cork South-Central	91,619	91,716	53,710	58.56%	662	1.23%	53,048	57.90%
Cork South-West	62,967	60,248	35,941	59.66%	370	1.03%	35,571	56.49%
Donegal North-East	59,084	58,579	28,582	48.79%	328	1.15%	28,254	47.82%
Donegal South-West	64,568	64,158	31,068	48.42%	352	1.13%	30,716	47.57%
Dublin Central	56,892	54,500	28,236	51.81%	351	1.24%	27,885	49.01%
Dublin Mid-West	64,880	64,370	34,113	53.00%	396	1.16%	33,717	51.97%
Dublin North	70,413	69,347	39,731	57.29%	401	1.01%	39,330	55.86%
Dublin North-Central	52,992	51,929	33,239	64.01%	381	1.15%	32,858	62.01%
Dublin North-East	58,542	57,627	34,462	59.80%	400	1.16%	34,062	58.18%
Dublin North-West	49,269	50,410	25,361	50.31%	358	1.41%	25,003	50.75%
Dublin South	102,387	104,145	64,492	61.93%	514	0.80%	63,978	62.49%
Dublin South-Central	80,268	77,688	41,604	53.55%	529	1.27%	41,075	51.17%
Dublin South East	58,217	55,533	30,780	55.43%	295	0.96%	30,485	52.36%
Dublin South-West	70,613	69,977	36,669	52.40%	474	1.29%	36,195	51.26%
Dublin West	62,348	61,583	36,319	58.98%	370	1.02%	35,949	57.66%
Dun Laoghaire	80,115	82,033	49,191	59.96%	428	0.87%	48,763	60.87%
Galway East	83,651	81,896	47,092	57.50%	411	0.87%	46,681	55.80%
Galway West	88,840	94,700	50,688	53.52%	414	0.82%	50,274	56.59%
Kerry North-West Limerick	63,614	63,068	34,525	54.74%	391	1.13%	34,134	53.66%
Kerry South	59,629	57,776	31,969	55.33%	356	1.11%	31,613	53.02%
Kildare North	77,959	76,623	43,463	56.72%	329	0.76%	43,134	55.33%
Kildare South	58,867	57,933	31,295	54.02%	333	1.06%	30,962	52.60%
Laoighis Offaly	108,142	107,023	59,365	55.47%	517	0.87%	58,848	54.42%
Limerick	65,083	66,345	36,876	55.58%	359	0.97%	36,517	56.11%
Limerick City	64,909	66,421	34,725	52.28%	363	1.05%	34,362	52.94%
Longford-Westmeath	85,918	85,911	45,543	53.01%	484	1.06%	45,059	52.44%
Louth	99,530	102,941	58,126	56.47%	673	1.16%	57,453	57.72%
Mayo	101,160	97,714	53,627	54.88%	567	1.06%	53,060	52.45%
Meath East	64,873	65,477	35,453	54.15%	309	0.87%	35,144	54.17%
Meath West	62,776	63,111	33,071	52.40%	324	0.98%	32,747	52.16%
Roscommon-South Leitrim	60,998	60,416	36,486	60.39%	394	1.08%	36,092	59.17%
Sligo-North Leitrim	63,432	62,152	34,251	55.11%	361	1.05%	33,890	53.43%
Tipperary North	63,235	62,603	38,381	61.31%	439	1.14%	37,942	60.00%
Tipperary South	57,420	56,295	32,618	57.94%	348	1.07%	32,270	56.20%
Waterford	78,435	78,960	42,731	54.12%	471	1.10%	42,260	53.88%
Wexford	111,063	108,490	58,629	54.04%	**627**	1.07%	58,002	52.22%
Wicklow	95,341	93,812	57,915	61.74%	591	1.02%	57,324	60.13%
2011 43	**3,209,244**	**3,191,157**	**1,790,438**	**56.11%**	**18,676**	**1.04%**	**1,771,762**	**55.52%**
1997 41		**2,688,316**	**1,279,688**	**47.60%**	**9,852**	**0.77%**	**1,269,836**	**47.24%**
2011-1997		**+502,841**	**+510,750**	**+8.50%**	**+8,824**	**+0.27%**	**+501,926**	**+8.29%**
Dublin	806,936	799,142	454,197	56.84%	4,897	1.08%	449,300	55.68%
Leinster	869,918	868,131	482,188	55.54%	4,778	0.99%	477,410	54.88%
Munster	911,479	905,317	513,741	56.75%	5,620	1.09%	508,121	55.75%
Connaught/Ulster	620,911	618,567	340,312	55.02%	3,381	0.99%	336,931	54.26%
2011 Presidency		**3,191,157**	**1,790,438**	**56.11%**	**18,676**	**1.04%**	**1,771,762**	**55.52%**
2011 Dail		**3,209,244**	**2,243,176**	**69.90%**	**22,817**	**1.02%**	**2,220,359**	**69.19%**
2011 Presidency-Dail		-18,087	-452,738	-13.79%	-4,141	**+0.03%**	-448,597	-13.67%

PRESIDENTIAL ELECTION 2011 : FIRST COUNT															
	Higgins		Gallagher		McGuinness		Mitchell		Norris		Scallon		Davis		Total
Constituency	Votes	%	Votes	%	Votes	%	Votes	%	Votes	%	Votes	%	Votes	%	Votes
Carlow-Kilkenny	21,574	36.73%	19,846	33.79%	7,257	12.36%	4,511	7.68%	2,792	4.75%	1,614	2.75%	1,143	1.95%	58,737
Cavan-Monaghan	11,471	19.79%	26,150	45.11%	11,940	20.60%	4,109	7.09%	1,636	2.82%	1,587	2.74%	1,071	1.85%	57,964
Clare	20,828	44.30%	14,779	31.44%	4,950	10.53%	2,545	5.41%	1,707	3.63%	1,313	2.79%	890	1.89%	47,012
Cork East	16,435	36.56%	15,455	34.38%	6,193	13.78%	2,678	5.96%	1,921	4.27%	1,348	3.00%	923	2.05%	44,953
Cork North-Central	15,427	37.60%	11,526	28.09%	8,201	19.99%	1,911	4.66%	2,090	5.09%	1,178	2.87%	693	1.69%	41,026
Cork North-West	12,836	34.31%	14,362	38.39%	4,329	11.57%	2,836	7.58%	1,380	3.69%	1,109	2.96%	561	1.50%	37,413
Cork South-Central	23,861	44.98%	13,224	24.93%	7,496	14.13%	2,488	4.69%	3,423	6.45%	1,476	2.78%	1,080	2.04%	53,048
Cork South-West	12,047	33.87%	12,449	35.00%	4,608	12.95%	3,035	8.53%	1,534	4.31%	1,128	3.17%	770	2.16%	35,571
Donegal North-East	6,516	23.06%	7,978	28.24%	9,085	32.15%	1,384	4.90%	788	2.79%	1,905	6.74%	598	2.12%	28,254
Donegal South-West	7,093	23.09%	9,912	32.27%	8,738	28.45%	1,620	5.27%	916	2.98%	1,777	5.79%	660	2.15%	30,716
Dublin Central	12,267	43.99%	4,577	16.41%	4,485	16.08%	1,392	4.99%	3,588	12.87%	756	2.71%	820	2.94%	27,885
Dublin Mid-West	13,594	40.32%	7,436	22.05%	5,374	15.94%	2,176	6.45%	3,428	10.17%	670	1.99%	1,039	3.08%	33,717
Dublin North	17,630	44.83%	10,014	25.46%	4,097	10.42%	1,742	4.43%	3,868	9.83%	726	1.85%	1,253	3.19%	39,330
Dublin North-Central	15,230	46.35%	6,603	20.10%	3,678	11.19%	1,953	5.94%	3,434	10.45%	812	2.47%	1,148	3.49%	32,858
Dublin North-East	14,956	43.91%	7,138	20.96%	4,484	13.16%	1,727	5.07%	3,512	10.31%	754	2.21%	1,491	4.38%	34,062
Dublin North-West	9,709	38.83%	5,069	20.27%	4,985	19.94%	1,111	4.44%	2,638	10.55%	576	2.30%	915	3.66%	25,003
Dublin South	32,673	51.07%	12,814	20.03%	4,146	6.48%	4,684	7.32%	6,265	9.79%	1,296	2.03%	2,100	3.28%	63,978
Dublin South-Central	16,391	39.91%	6,154	14.98%	6,803	16.56%	4,971	12.10%	4,703	11.45%	937	2.28%	1,116	2.72%	41,075
Dublin South East	16,315	53.52%	4,179	13.71%	2,289	7.51%	2,486	8.15%	3,574	11.72%	667	2.19%	975	3.20%	30,485
Dublin South-West	14,530	40.14%	7,947	21.96%	6,006	16.59%	2,345	6.48%	3,482	9.62%	758	2.09%	1,127	3.11%	36,195
Dublin West	15,539	43.23%	8,677	24.14%	4,278	11.90%	1,916	5.33%	3,632	10.10%	733	2.04%	1,174	3.27%	35,949
Dun Laoghaire	25,616	52.53%	8,626	17.69%	3,355	6.88%	3,424	7.02%	4,973	10.20%	1,058	2.17%	1,711	3.51%	48,763
Galway East	21,554	46.17%	13,473	28.86%	4,849	10.39%	2,905	6.22%	1,177	2.52%	1,670	3.58%	1,053	2.26%	46,681
Galway West	28,970	57.62%	9,281	18.46%	5,392	10.73%	2,326	4.63%	1,660	3.30%	1,745	3.47%	900	1.79%	50,274
Kerry North-West Limerick	12,947	37.93%	9,909	29.03%	5,739	16.81%	2,221	6.51%	1,301	3.81%	1,260	3.69%	757	2.22%	34,134
Kerry South	11,604	36.71%	9,668	30.58%	4,723	14.94%	2,302	7.28%	1,246	3.94%	1,232	3.90%	838	2.65%	31,613
Kildare North	19,775	45.85%	11,615	26.93%	3,796	8.80%	2,364	5.48%	3,490	8.09%	896	2.08%	1,198	2.78%	43,134
Kildare South	12,447	40.20%	9,733	31.44%	3,553	11.48%	1,681	5.43%	1,966	6.35%	645	2.08%	937	3.03%	30,962
Laoighis Offaly	18,686	31.75%	22,115	37.58%	7,663	13.02%	3,891	6.61%	3,547	6.03%	1,765	3.00%	1,181	2.01%	58,848
Limerick	14,134	38.71%	12,238	33.51%	3,854	10.55%	2,864	7.84%	1,369	3.75%	1,239	3.39%	819	2.24%	36,517
Limerick City	16,935	49.28%	7,643	22.24%	4,150	12.08%	1,917	5.58%	2,065	6.01%	1,004	2.92%	648	1.89%	34,362
Longford-Westmeath	15,987	35.48%	15,166	33.66%	5,885	13.06%	3,372	7.48%	2,154	4.78%	1,550	3.44%	945	2.10%	45,059
Louth	20,844	36.28%	17,027	29.64%	11,499	20.01%	2,359	4.11%	3,141	5.47%	1,267	2.21%	1,316	2.29%	57,453
Mayo	20,329	38.31%	13,370	25.20%	6,300	11.87%	4,878	9.19%	1,483	2.79%	1,719	3.24%	4,981	9.39%	53,060
Meath East	13,397	38.12%	11,300	32.15%	4,095	11.65%	2,199	6.26%	2,340	6.66%	818	2.33%	995	2.83%	35,144
Meath West	11,280	34.45%	10,972	33.51%	4,865	14.86%	1,982	6.05%	1,928	5.89%	889	2.71%	831	2.54%	32,747
Roscommon-South Leitrim	11,480	31.81%	13,011	36.05%	5,286	14.65%	2,334	6.47%	1,322	3.66%	1,589	4.40%	1,070	2.96%	36,092
Sligo-North Leitrim	12,363	36.48%	9,943	29.34%	5,464	16.12%	2,360	6.96%	1,349	3.98%	1,299	3.83%	1,112	3.28%	33,890
Tipperary North	13,197	34.78%	13,491	35.56%	4,459	11.75%	3,121	8.23%	1,385	3.65%	1,399	3.69%	890	2.35%	37,942
Tipperary South	11,411	35.36%	11,003	34.10%	4,188	12.98%	2,517	7.80%	1,415	4.38%	975	3.02%	761	2.36%	32,270
Waterford	16,340	38.67%	13,107	31.02%	5,737	13.58%	2,489	5.89%	2,451	5.80%	1,218	2.88%	918	2.17%	42,260
Wexford	21,010	36.22%	19,685	33.94%	8,112	13.99%	3,459	5.96%	2,797	4.82%	1,477	2.55%	1,462	2.52%	58,002
Wicklow	23,873	41.65%	16,299	28.43%	6,644	11.59%	2,736	4.77%	4,599	8.02%	1,386	2.42%	1,787	3.12%	57,324
Total 43	**701,101**	**39.57%**	**504,964**	**28.50%**	**243,030**	**13.72%**	**113,321**	**6.40%**	**109,469**	**6.18%**	**51,220**	**2.89%**	**48,657**	**2.75%**	**1,771,762**
Dublin	204,450	45.50%	89,234	19.86%	53,980	12.01%	29,927	6.66%	47,097	10.48%	9,743	2.17%	14,869	3.31%	449,300
Leinster	178,873	37.47%	153,758	32.21%	63,369	13.27%	28,554	5.98%	28,754	6.02%	12,307	2.58%	11,795	2.47%	477,410
Munster	198,002	38.97%	158,854	31.26%	68,627	13.51%	32,924	6.48%	23,287	4.58%	15,879	3.13%	10,548	2.08%	508,121
Connaught/Ulster	119,776	35.55%	103,118	30.61%	57,054	16.93%	21,916	6.50%	10,331	3.07%	13,291	3.94%	11,445	3.40%	336,931
Ulster	25,080	21.45%	44,040	37.66%	29,763	25.45%	7,113	6.08%	3,340	2.86%	5,269	4.51%	2,329	1.99%	116,934

PRESIDENTIAL ELECTION 2011 : SPENDING							
							Net Cost
Candidate	Election Agent	Donations	Expenses	Refund	Net Cost	1st Prefs	/1st Pref
Mary Davis	Ronan King	120,095.00	414,041.32	0.00	414,041.32	48,657	8.51
Gay Mitchell	Tom Curran	0.00	527,152.01	0.00	527,152.01	113,321	4.65
David Norris	Liam McCabe	17,929.98	331,974.89	0.00	331,974.89	109,469	3.03
Dana Rosemary Scallon	Brendan Kelly	12,017.24	59,591.47	0.00	59,591.47	51,220	1.16
Martin McGuinness	Treasa Quinn	4,348.00	302,563.47	200,000.00	102,563.47	243,030	0.42
Sean Gallagher	Cathal Lee	28,759.00	323,318.45	200,000.00	123,318.45	504,964	0.24
Michael D. Higgins	Kevin O'Driscoll	121,421.53	359,935.48	200,000.00	159,935.48	701,101	0.23
Total		**304,570.75**	**2,318,577.09**	**600,000.00**	**1,718,577.09**	**1,771,762**	**0.97**

PRESIDENTIAL ELECTION 2011 : SECOND COUNT													
	Higgins		Gallagher		McGuinness		Mitchell		Norris		Non-Trans		Total
Constituency	Votes	%	Votes	%	Votes	%	Votes	%	Votes	%	Votes	%	Votes
Carlow-Kilkenny	808	29.31%	685	24.85%	240	8.71%	404	14.65%	183	6.64%	437	15.85%	2,757
Cavan-Monaghan	614	23.10%	822	30.93%	335	12.60%	363	13.66%	164	6.17%	360	13.54%	2,658
Clare	745	33.82%	560	25.42%	202	9.17%	265	12.03%	151	6.85%	280	12.71%	2,203
Cork East	596	26.24%	608	26.77%	200	8.81%	344	15.15%	138	6.08%	385	16.95%	2,271
Cork North-Central	472	25.23%	447	23.89%	206	11.01%	274	14.64%	145	7.75%	327	17.48%	1,871
Cork North-West	441	26.41%	432	25.87%	141	8.44%	266	15.93%	110	6.59%	280	16.77%	1,670
Cork South-Central	740	28.95%	605	23.67%	196	7.67%	394	15.41%	202	7.90%	419	16.39%	2,556
Cork South-West	512	26.98%	481	25.34%	168	8.85%	318	16.75%	100	5.27%	319	16.81%	1,898
Donegal North-East	519	20.74%	661	26.41%	541	21.61%	245	9.79%	123	4.91%	414	16.54%	2,503
Donegal South-West	542	22.24%	683	28.03%	420	17.23%	246	10.09%	119	4.88%	427	17.52%	2,437
Dublin Central	447	28.36%	306	19.42%	146	9.26%	249	15.80%	174	11.04%	254	16.12%	1,576
Dublin Mid-West	502	29.37%	370	21.65%	155	9.07%	239	13.98%	162	9.48%	281	16.44%	1,709
Dublin North	614	31.03%	440	22.23%	160	8.08%	252	12.73%	205	10.36%	308	15.56%	1,979
Dublin North-Central	542	27.65%	423	21.58%	187	9.54%	317	16.17%	163	8.32%	328	16.73%	1,960
Dublin North-East	688	30.65%	526	23.43%	196	8.73%	280	12.47%	218	9.71%	337	15.01%	2,245
Dublin North-West	414	27.77%	339	22.74%	157	10.53%	222	14.89%	127	8.52%	232	15.56%	1,491
Dublin South	1,169	34.42%	723	21.29%	196	5.77%	596	17.55%	295	8.69%	417	12.28%	3,396
Dublin South-Central	524	25.52%	393	19.14%	213	10.38%	412	20.07%	195	9.50%	316	15.39%	2,053
Dublin South East	571	34.77%	318	19.37%	113	6.88%	269	16.38%	164	9.99%	207	12.61%	1,642
Dublin South-West	526	27.90%	423	22.44%	151	8.01%	286	15.17%	171	9.07%	328	17.40%	1,885
Dublin West	543	28.47%	446	23.39%	141	7.39%	260	13.63%	189	9.91%	328	17.20%	1,907
Dun Laoghaire	901	32.54%	599	21.63%	182	6.57%	510	18.42%	265	9.57%	312	11.27%	2,769
Galway East	906	33.27%	665	24.42%	259	9.51%	337	12.38%	139	5.10%	417	15.31%	2,723
Galway West	910	34.40%	558	21.10%	273	10.32%	398	15.05%	148	5.60%	358	13.53%	2,645
Kerry North-West Limerick	574	28.46%	510	25.29%	215	10.66%	254	12.59%	116	5.75%	348	17.25%	2,017
Kerry South	649	31.35%	500	24.15%	199	9.61%	249	12.03%	117	5.65%	356	17.20%	2,070
Kildare North	648	30.95%	522	24.93%	161	7.69%	287	13.71%	169	8.07%	307	14.66%	2,094
Kildare South	492	31.10%	409	25.85%	134	8.47%	195	12.33%	123	7.77%	229	14.48%	1,582
Laoighis Offaly	752	25.53%	810	27.49%	279	9.47%	370	12.56%	236	8.01%	499	16.94%	2,946
Limerick	566	27.50%	515	25.02%	184	8.94%	302	14.67%	125	6.07%	366	17.78%	2,058
Limerick City	504	30.51%	355	21.49%	138	8.35%	253	15.31%	137	8.29%	265	16.04%	1,652
Longford-Westmeath	661	26.49%	646	25.89%	281	11.26%	351	14.07%	153	6.13%	403	16.15%	2,495
Louth	771	29.85%	582	22.53%	302	11.69%	307	11.89%	215	8.32%	406	15.72%	2,583
Mayo	2,503	37.36%	1,755	26.19%	611	9.12%	866	12.93%	228	3.40%	737	11.00%	6,700
Meath East	537	29.62%	439	24.21%	134	7.39%	259	14.29%	146	8.05%	298	16.44%	1,813
Meath West	477	27.73%	430	25.00%	149	8.66%	251	14.59%	141	8.20%	272	15.81%	1,720
Roscommon-South Leitrim	710	26.70%	688	25.87%	303	11.40%	331	12.45%	185	6.96%	442	16.62%	2,659
Sligo-North Leitrim	766	31.77%	654	27.13%	268	11.12%	300	12.44%	106	4.40%	317	13.15%	2,411
Tipperary North	627	27.39%	597	26.08%	180	7.86%	359	15.68%	126	5.50%	400	17.47%	2,289
Tipperary South	523	30.13%	438	25.23%	156	8.99%	230	13.25%	118	6.80%	271	15.61%	1,736
Waterford	629	29.45%	478	22.38%	191	8.94%	278	13.01%	159	7.44%	401	18.77%	2,136
Wexford	759	25.83%	804	27.36%	242	8.23%	402	13.68%	195	6.63%	537	18.27%	2,939
Wicklow	985	31.04%	792	24.96%	276	8.70%	446	14.06%	212	6.68%	462	14.56%	3,173
Total 43	**29,379**	**29.42%**	**24,437**	**24.47%**	**9,581**	**9.59%**	**14,036**	**14.05%**	**7,057**	**7.07%**	**15,387**	**15.41%**	**99,877**
Dublin	7,441	30.23%	5,306	21.56%	1,997	8.11%	3,892	15.81%	2,328	9.46%	3,648	14.82%	24,612
Leinster	6,890	28.59%	6,119	25.39%	2,198	9.12%	3,272	13.58%	1,773	7.36%	3,850	15.97%	24,102
Munster	7,578	28.68%	6,526	24.69%	2,376	8.99%	3,786	14.33%	1,744	6.60%	4,417	16.71%	26,427
Connaught/Ulster	7,470	30.20%	6,486	26.22%	3,010	12.17%	3,086	12.48%	1,212	4.90%	3,472	14.04%	24,736
Ulster	1,675	22.05%	2,166	28.51%	1,296	17.06%	854	11.24%	406	5.34%	1,201	15.81%	7,598

PRESIDENTIAL ELECTION 2011 : THIRD COUNT											
	Higgins		Gallagher		McGuinness		Mitchell		Non-Trans		Total
Constituency	**Votes**	**%**	**Votes**	**%**	**Votes**	**%**	**Votes**	**%**	**Votes**	**%**	**Votes**
Carlow-Kilkenny	1,537	51.66%	558	18.76%	386	12.97%	180	6.05%	314	10.55%	2,975
Cavan-Monaghan	750	41.67%	407	22.61%	234	13.00%	216	12.00%	193	10.72%	1,800
Clare	977	52.58%	364	19.59%	213	11.46%	125	6.73%	179	9.63%	1,858
Cork East	1,097	53.28%	359	17.44%	222	10.78%	124	6.02%	257	12.48%	2,059
Cork North-Central	1,199	53.65%	363	16.24%	298	13.33%	128	5.73%	247	11.05%	2,235
Cork North-West	750	50.34%	335	22.48%	168	11.28%	82	5.50%	155	10.40%	1,490
Cork South-Central	2,010	55.45%	574	15.83%	377	10.40%	243	6.70%	421	11.61%	3,625
Cork South-West	912	55.81%	274	16.77%	167	10.22%	120	7.34%	161	9.85%	1,634
Donegal North-East	401	44.02%	183	20.09%	123	13.50%	73	8.01%	131	14.38%	911
Donegal South-West	467	45.12%	181	17.49%	141	13.62%	93	8.99%	153	14.78%	1,035
Dublin Central	2,269	60.31%	409	10.87%	417	11.08%	237	6.30%	430	11.43%	3,762
Dublin Mid-West	1,810	50.42%	559	15.57%	466	12.98%	313	8.72%	442	12.31%	3,590
Dublin North	2,154	52.88%	729	17.90%	421	10.34%	283	6.95%	486	11.93%	4,073
Dublin North-Central	2,020	56.16%	491	13.65%	373	10.37%	280	7.78%	433	12.04%	3,597
Dublin North-East	1,973	52.90%	589	15.79%	391	10.48%	283	7.59%	494	13.24%	3,730
Dublin North-West	1,363	49.29%	433	15.66%	386	13.96%	204	7.38%	379	13.71%	2,765
Dublin South	3,975	60.59%	940	14.33%	437	6.66%	552	8.41%	656	10.00%	6,560
Dublin South-Central	2,698	55.08%	565	11.54%	578	11.80%	516	10.53%	541	11.05%	4,898
Dublin South East	2,476	66.24%	374	10.01%	264	7.06%	298	7.97%	326	8.72%	3,738
Dublin South-West	1,813	49.63%	588	16.10%	452	12.37%	336	9.20%	464	12.70%	3,653
Dublin West	1,992	52.13%	618	16.17%	407	10.65%	263	6.88%	541	14.16%	3,821
Dun Laoghaire	3,264	62.31%	688	13.13%	317	6.05%	444	8.48%	525	10.02%	5,238
Galway East	678	51.52%	198	15.05%	187	14.21%	100	7.60%	153	11.63%	1,316
Galway West	1,068	59.07%	268	14.82%	210	11.62%	116	6.42%	146	8.08%	1,808
Kerry North-West Limerick	695	49.05%	270	19.05%	194	13.69%	101	7.13%	157	11.08%	1,417
Kerry South	755	55.39%	222	16.29%	155	11.37%	84	6.16%	147	10.79%	1,363
Kildare North	2,016	55.10%	644	17.60%	319	8.72%	268	7.32%	412	11.26%	3,659
Kildare South	1,055	50.50%	400	19.15%	207	9.91%	172	8.23%	255	12.21%	2,089
Laoighis Offaly	1,775	46.92%	804	21.25%	438	11.58%	308	8.14%	458	12.11%	3,783
Limerick	801	53.61%	302	20.21%	153	10.24%	100	6.69%	138	9.24%	1,494
Limerick City	1,270	57.67%	338	15.35%	221	10.04%	143	6.49%	230	10.45%	2,202
Longford-Westmeath	1,180	51.15%	362	15.69%	294	12.74%	183	7.93%	288	12.48%	2,307
Louth	1,784	53.16%	543	16.18%	434	12.93%	225	6.70%	370	11.03%	3,356
Mayo	887	51.84%	269	15.72%	197	11.51%	144	8.42%	214	12.51%	1,711
Meath East	1,292	51.97%	475	19.11%	250	10.06%	196	7.88%	273	10.98%	2,486
Meath West	1,031	49.83%	373	18.03%	227	10.97%	182	8.80%	256	12.37%	2,069
Roscommon-South Leitrim	721	47.84%	291	19.31%	218	14.47%	94	6.24%	183	12.14%	1,507
Sligo-North Leitrim	808	55.53%	229	15.74%	179	12.30%	108	7.42%	131	9.00%	1,455
Tipperary North	768	50.83%	280	18.53%	155	10.26%	130	8.60%	178	11.78%	1,511
Tipperary South	710	46.31%	292	19.05%	185	12.07%	126	8.22%	220	14.35%	1,533
Waterford	1,310	50.19%	473	18.12%	341	13.07%	179	6.86%	307	11.76%	2,610
Wexford	1,474	49.26%	567	18.95%	329	11.00%	240	8.02%	382	12.77%	2,992
Wicklow	2,663	55.35%	791	16.44%	454	9.44%	360	7.48%	543	11.29%	4,811
Total 43	**62,648**	**53.76%**	**18,972**	**16.28%**	**12,585**	**10.80%**	**8,952**	**7.68%**	**13,369**	**11.47%**	**116,526**
Dublin	27,807	56.26%	6,983	14.13%	4,909	9.93%	4,009	8.11%	5,717	11.57%	49,425
Leinster	15,807	51.78%	5,517	18.07%	3,338	10.93%	2,314	7.58%	3,551	11.63%	30,527
Munster	13,254	52.95%	4,446	17.76%	2,849	11.38%	1,685	6.73%	2,797	11.17%	25,031
Connaught/Ulster	5,780	50.07%	2,026	17.55%	1,489	12.90%	944	8.18%	1,304	11.30%	11,543
Ulster	1,618	43.19%	771	20.58%	498	13.29%	382	10.20%	477	12.73%	3,746

PRESIDENTIAL ELECTION 2011 : FOURTH COUNT							
	Higgins		Gallagher		Non-Trans		Total
Constituency	**Votes**	**%**	**Votes**	**%**	**Votes**	**%**	**Votes**
Carlow-Kilkenny	7,217	55.61%	2,616	20.16%	3,145	24.23%	12,978
Cavan-Monaghan	7,474	43.46%	5,041	29.31%	4,682	27.23%	17,197
Clare	5,169	62.28%	1,468	17.69%	1,663	20.04%	8,300
Cork East	5,067	51.91%	2,001	20.50%	2,693	27.59%	9,761
Cork North-Central	5,462	49.57%	2,015	18.29%	3,541	32.14%	11,018
Cork North-West	4,486	57.35%	1,568	20.05%	1,768	22.60%	7,822
Cork South-Central	6,026	53.83%	1,995	17.82%	3,173	28.35%	11,194
Cork South-West	4,553	54.10%	1,844	21.91%	2,019	23.99%	8,416
Donegal North-East	4,159	36.32%	2,644	23.09%	4,648	40.59%	11,451
Donegal South-West	4,256	37.80%	2,619	23.26%	4,383	38.93%	11,258
Dublin Central	3,558	51.37%	1,171	16.91%	2,197	31.72%	6,926
Dublin Mid-West	4,623	53.00%	1,590	18.23%	2,510	28.77%	8,723
Dublin North	3,881	55.80%	1,336	19.21%	1,738	24.99%	6,955
Dublin North-Central	3,864	56.92%	1,157	17.04%	1,767	26.03%	6,788
Dublin North-East	4,006	54.42%	1,341	18.22%	2,014	27.36%	7,361
Dublin North-West	3,397	48.08%	1,370	19.39%	2,298	32.53%	7,065
Dublin South	6,816	64.24%	1,823	17.18%	1,972	18.58%	10,611
Dublin South-Central	7,360	54.55%	2,329	17.26%	3,804	28.19%	13,493
Dublin South East	3,582	62.63%	899	15.72%	1,238	21.65%	5,719
Dublin South-West	4,861	50.76%	1,919	20.04%	2,796	29.20%	9,576
Dublin West	3,839	52.84%	1,390	19.13%	2,036	28.02%	7,265
Dun Laoghaire	5,090	61.83%	1,409	17.12%	1,733	21.05%	8,232
Galway East	5,184	60.02%	1,517	17.56%	1,936	22.42%	8,637
Galway West	5,332	61.18%	1,448	16.62%	1,935	22.20%	8,715
Kerry North-West Limerick	4,489	51.46%	1,525	17.48%	2,710	31.06%	8,724
Kerry South	4,299	55.74%	1,428	18.52%	1,985	25.74%	7,712
Kildare North	4,237	58.89%	1,345	18.69%	1,613	22.42%	7,195
Kildare South	3,153	53.06%	1,243	20.92%	1,546	26.02%	5,942
Laoighis Offaly	6,608	51.03%	2,877	22.22%	3,464	26.75%	12,949
Limerick	4,352	58.36%	1,413	18.95%	1,692	22.69%	7,457
Limerick City	4,011	58.80%	1,090	15.98%	1,721	25.23%	6,822
Longford-Westmeath	5,616	54.18%	2,101	20.27%	2,649	25.55%	10,366
Louth	7,250	47.93%	3,154	20.85%	4,722	31.22%	15,126
Mayo	8,024	61.74%	2,170	16.70%	2,802	21.56%	12,996
Meath East	4,000	56.08%	1,414	19.82%	1,719	24.10%	7,133
Meath West	3,981	52.00%	1,583	20.68%	2,092	27.32%	7,656
Roscommon-South Leitrim	4,372	51.04%	1,947	22.73%	2,247	26.23%	8,566
Sligo-North Leitrim	4,594	52.93%	1,817	20.94%	2,268	26.13%	8,679
Tipperary North	4,672	55.59%	1,778	21.16%	1,954	23.25%	8,404
Tipperary South	4,041	54.59%	1,454	19.64%	1,907	25.76%	7,402
Waterford	4,781	51.88%	1,845	20.02%	2,589	28.10%	9,215
Wexford	6,514	50.95%	2,777	21.72%	3,493	27.32%	12,784
Wicklow	5,720	52.40%	2,270	20.80%	2,926	26.80%	10,916
Total 43	**213,976**	**53.29%**	**79,741**	**19.86%**	**107,788**	**26.85%**	**401,505**
Dublin	54,877	55.59%	17,734	17.97%	26,103	26.44%	98,714
Leinster	54,296	52.69%	21,380	20.75%	27,369	26.56%	103,045
Munster	61,408	54.71%	21,424	19.09%	29,415	26.21%	112,247
Connaught/Ulster	43,395	49.59%	19,203	21.95%	24,901	28.46%	87,499
Ulster	15,889	39.82%	10,304	25.82%	13,713	34.36%	39,906

PRESIDENTIAL ELECTION 2011 : ALL COUNTS																									
	Higgins					Gallagher					McGuinness				Mitchell				Norris			Scallon	Davis
Constituency	1st	2nd	3rd	4th	Total	1st	2nd	3rd	4th	Total	1st	2nd	3rd	Total	1st	2nd	3rd	Total	1st	2nd	Total	1st	1st
Carlow-Kilkenny	36.73%	29.31%	51.66%	55.61%	53.01%	33.79%	24.85%	18.76%	20.16%	40.36%	12.36%	8.71%	12.97%	13.42%	7.68%	14.65%	6.05%	8.67%	4.75%	6.64%	5.07%	2.75%	1.95%
Cavan-Monaghan	19.79%	23.10%	41.67%	43.46%	35.04%	45.11%	30.93%	22.61%	29.31%	55.93%	20.60%	12.60%	13.00%	21.58%	7.09%	13.66%	12.00%	8.09%	2.82%	6.17%	3.11%	2.74%	1.85%
Clare	44.30%	33.82%	52.58%	62.28%	58.96%	31.44%	25.42%	19.59%	17.69%	36.52%	10.53%	9.17%	11.46%	11.41%	5.41%	12.03%	6.73%	6.24%	3.63%	6.85%	3.95%	2.79%	1.89%
Cork East	36.56%	26.24%	53.28%	51.91%	51.60%	34.38%	26.77%	17.44%	20.50%	40.98%	13.78%	8.81%	10.78%	14.72%	5.96%	15.15%	6.02%	7.00%	4.27%	6.08%	4.58%	3.00%	2.05%
Cork North-Central	37.60%	25.23%	53.65%	49.57%	54.99%	28.09%	23.89%	16.24%	18.29%	34.98%	19.99%	11.01%	13.33%	21.22%	4.66%	14.64%	5.73%	5.64%	5.09%	7.75%	5.45%	2.87%	1.69%
Cork North-West	34.31%	26.41%	50.34%	57.35%	49.48%	38.39%	25.87%	22.48%	20.05%	44.63%	11.57%	8.44%	11.28%	12.40%	7.58%	15.93%	5.50%	8.51%	3.69%	6.59%	3.98%	2.96%	1.50%
Cork South-Central	44.98%	28.95%	55.45%	53.83%	61.52%	24.93%	23.67%	15.83%	17.82%	30.91%	14.13%	7.67%	10.40%	15.21%	4.69%	15.41%	6.70%	5.89%	6.45%	7.90%	6.83%	2.78%	2.04%
Cork South-West	33.87%	26.98%	55.81%	54.10%	50.67%	35.00%	25.34%	16.77%	21.91%	42.30%	12.95%	8.85%	10.22%	13.90%	8.53%	16.75%	7.34%	9.76%	4.31%	5.27%	4.59%	3.17%	2.16%
Donegal North-East	23.06%	20.74%	44.02%	36.32%	41.04%	28.24%	26.41%	20.09%	23.09%	40.58%	32.15%	21.61%	13.50%	34.51%	4.90%	9.79%	8.01%	6.02%	2.79%	4.91%	3.22%	6.74%	2.12%
Donegal South-West	23.09%	22.24%	45.12%	37.80%	40.23%	32.27%	28.03%	17.49%	23.26%	43.61%	28.45%	17.23%	13.62%	30.28%	5.27%	10.09%	8.99%	6.38%	2.98%	4.88%	3.37%	5.79%	2.15%
Dublin Central	43.99%	28.36%	60.31%	51.37%	66.49%	16.41%	19.42%	10.87%	16.91%	23.18%	16.08%	9.26%	11.08%	18.10%	4.99%	15.80%	6.30%	6.74%	12.87%	11.04%	13.49%	2.71%	2.94%
Dublin Mid-West	40.32%	29.37%	50.42%	53.00%	60.89%	22.05%	21.65%	15.57%	18.23%	29.53%	15.94%	9.07%	12.98%	17.78%	6.45%	13.98%	8.72%	8.09%	10.17%	9.48%	10.65%	1.99%	3.08%
Dublin North	44.83%	31.03%	52.88%	55.80%	61.73%	25.46%	22.23%	17.90%	19.21%	31.83%	10.42%	8.08%	10.34%	11.89%	4.43%	12.73%	6.95%	5.79%	9.83%	10.36%	10.36%	1.85%	3.19%
Dublin North-Central	46.35%	27.65%	56.16%	56.92%	65.91%	20.10%	21.58%	13.65%	17.04%	26.40%	11.19%	9.54%	10.37%	12.90%	5.94%	16.17%	7.78%	7.76%	10.45%	8.32%	10.95%	2.47%	3.49%
Dublin North-East	43.91%	30.65%	52.90%	54.42%	63.48%	20.96%	23.43%	15.79%	18.22%	28.17%	13.16%	8.73%	10.48%	14.89%	5.07%	12.47%	7.59%	6.72%	10.31%	9.71%	10.95%	2.21%	4.38%
Dublin North-West	38.83%	27.77%	49.29%	48.08%	59.52%	20.27%	22.74%	15.66%	19.39%	28.84%	19.94%	10.53%	13.96%	22.11%	4.44%	14.89%	7.38%	6.15%	10.55%	8.52%	11.06%	2.30%	3.66%
Dublin South	51.07%	34.42%	60.59%	64.24%	69.76%	20.03%	21.29%	14.33%	17.18%	25.48%	6.48%	5.77%	6.66%	7.47%	7.32%	17.55%	8.41%	9.12%	9.79%	8.69%	10.25%	2.03%	3.28%
Dublin South-Central	39.91%	25.52%	55.08%	54.55%	65.67%	14.98%	19.14%	11.54%	17.26%	22.98%	16.56%	10.38%	11.80%	18.49%	12.10%	20.07%	10.53%	14.36%	11.45%	9.50%	11.92%	2.28%	2.72%
Dublin South East	53.52%	34.77%	66.24%	62.63%	75.26%	13.71%	19.37%	10.01%	15.72%	18.93%	7.51%	6.88%	7.06%	8.75%	8.15%	16.38%	7.97%	10.02%	11.72%	9.99%	12.26%	2.19%	3.20%
Dublin South-West	40.14%	27.90%	49.63%	50.76%	60.04%	21.96%	22.44%	16.10%	20.04%	30.05%	16.59%	8.01%	12.37%	18.26%	6.48%	15.17%	9.20%	8.20%	9.62%	9.07%	10.09%	2.09%	3.11%
Dublin West	43.23%	28.47%	52.13%	52.84%	60.96%	24.14%	23.39%	16.17%	19.13%	30.96%	11.90%	7.39%	10.65%	13.43%	5.33%	13.63%	6.88%	6.79%	10.10%	9.91%	10.63%	2.04%	3.27%
Dun Laoghaire	52.53%	32.54%	62.31%	61.83%	71.51%	17.69%	21.63%	13.13%	17.12%	23.22%	6.88%	6.57%	6.05%	7.90%	7.02%	18.42%	8.48%	8.98%	10.20%	9.57%	10.74%	2.17%	3.51%
Galway East	46.17%	33.27%	51.52%	60.02%	60.67%	28.86%	24.42%	15.05%	17.56%	33.96%	10.39%	9.51%	14.21%	11.34%	6.22%	12.38%	7.60%	7.16%	2.52%	5.10%	2.82%	3.58%	2.26%
Galway West	57.62%	34.40%	59.07%	61.18%	72.16%	18.46%	21.10%	14.82%	16.62%	22.98%	10.73%	10.32%	11.62%	11.69%	4.63%	15.05%	6.42%	5.65%	3.30%	5.60%	3.60%	3.47%	1.79%
Kerry North-West Limerick	37.93%	28.46%	49.05%	51.46%	54.80%	29.03%	25.29%	19.05%	17.48%	35.78%	16.81%	10.66%	13.69%	18.01%	6.51%	12.59%	7.13%	7.55%	3.81%	5.75%	4.15%	3.69%	2.22%
Kerry South	36.71%	31.35%	55.39%	55.74%	54.75%	30.58%	24.15%	16.29%	18.52%	37.38%	14.94%	9.61%	11.37%	16.06%	7.28%	12.03%	6.16%	8.34%	3.94%	5.65%	4.31%	3.90%	2.65%
Kildare North	45.85%	30.95%	55.10%	58.89%	61.84%	26.93%	24.93%	17.60%	18.69%	32.75%	8.80%	7.69%	8.72%	9.91%	5.48%	13.71%	7.32%	6.77%	8.09%	8.07%	8.48%	2.08%	2.78%
Kildare South	40.20%	31.10%	50.50%	53.06%	55.38%	31.44%	25.85%	19.15%	20.92%	38.06%	11.48%	8.47%	9.91%	12.58%	5.43%	12.33%	8.23%	6.62%	6.35%	7.77%	6.75%	2.08%	3.03%
Laoighis Offaly	31.75%	25.53%	46.92%	51.03%	47.28%	37.58%	27.49%	21.25%	22.22%	45.21%	13.02%	9.47%	11.58%	14.24%	6.61%	12.56%	8.14%	7.76%	6.03%	8.01%	6.43%	3.00%	2.01%
Limerick	38.71%	27.50%	53.61%	58.36%	54.37%	33.51%	25.02%	20.21%	18.95%	39.62%	10.55%	8.94%	10.24%	11.48%	7.84%	14.67%	6.69%	8.94%	3.75%	6.07%	4.09%	3.39%	2.24%
Limerick City	49.28%	30.51%	57.67%	58.80%	66.12%	22.24%	21.49%	15.35%	15.98%	27.43%	12.08%	8.35%	10.04%	13.12%	5.58%	15.31%	6.49%	6.73%	6.01%	8.29%	6.41%	2.92%	1.89%
Longford-Westmeath	35.48%	26.49%	51.15%	54.18%	52.03%	33.66%	25.89%	15.69%	20.27%	40.56%	13.06%	11.26%	12.74%	14.34%	7.48%	14.07%	7.93%	8.67%	4.78%	6.13%	5.12%	3.44%	2.10%
Louth	36.28%	29.85%	53.16%	47.93%	53.35%	29.64%	22.53%	16.18%	20.85%	37.08%	20.01%	11.69%	12.93%	21.30%	4.11%	11.89%	6.70%	5.03%	5.47%	8.32%	5.84%	2.21%	2.29%
Mayo	38.31%	37.36%	51.84%	61.74%	59.82%	25.20%	26.19%	15.72%	16.70%	33.10%	11.87%	9.12%	11.51%	13.40%	9.19%	12.93%	8.42%	11.10%	2.79%	3.40%	3.22%	3.24%	9.39%
Meath East	38.12%	29.62%	51.97%	56.08%	54.71%	32.15%	24.21%	19.11%	19.82%	38.78%	11.65%	7.39%	10.06%	12.75%	6.26%	14.29%	7.88%	7.55%	6.66%	8.05%	7.07%	2.33%	2.83%
Meath West	34.45%	27.73%	49.83%	52.00%	51.21%	33.51%	25.00%	18.03%	20.68%	40.79%	14.86%	8.66%	10.97%	16.01%	6.05%	14.59%	8.80%	7.38%	5.89%	8.20%	6.32%	2.71%	2.54%
Roscommon-South Leitrim	31.81%	26.70%	47.84%	51.04%	47.89%	36.05%	25.87%	19.31%	22.73%	44.16%	14.65%	11.40%	14.47%	16.09%	6.47%	12.45%	6.24%	7.64%	3.66%	6.96%	4.18%	4.40%	2.96%
Sligo-North Leitrim	36.48%	31.77%	55.53%	52.93%	54.68%	29.34%	27.13%	15.74%	20.94%	37.31%	16.12%	11.12%	12.30%	17.44%	6.96%	12.44%	7.42%	8.17%	3.98%	4.40%	4.29%	3.83%	3.28%
Tipperary North	34.78%	27.39%	50.83%	55.59%	50.77%	35.56%	26.08%	18.53%	21.16%	42.55%	11.75%	7.86%	10.26%	12.64%	8.23%	15.68%	8.60%	9.52%	3.65%	5.50%	3.98%	3.69%	2.35%
Tipperary South	35.36%	30.13%	46.31%	54.59%	51.70%	34.10%	25.23%	19.05%	19.64%	40.86%	12.98%	8.99%	12.07%	14.04%	7.80%	13.25%	8.22%	8.90%	4.38%	6.80%	4.75%	3.02%	2.36%
Waterford	38.67%	29.45%	50.19%	51.88%	54.57%	31.02%	22.38%	18.12%	20.02%	37.63%	13.58%	8.94%	13.07%	14.83%	5.89%	13.01%	6.86%	6.97%	5.80%	7.44%	6.18%	2.88%	2.17%
Wexford	36.22%	25.83%	49.26%	50.95%	51.30%	33.94%	27.36%	18.95%	21.72%	41.09%	13.99%	8.23%	11.00%	14.97%	5.96%	13.68%	8.02%	7.07%	4.82%	6.63%	5.16%	2.55%	2.52%
Wicklow	41.65%	31.04%	55.35%	52.40%	57.99%	28.43%	24.96%	16.44%	20.80%	35.15%	11.59%	8.70%	9.44%	12.86%	4.77%	14.06%	7.48%	6.18%	8.02%	6.68%	8.39%	2.42%	3.12%
Total 43	**39.57%**	**29.42%**	**53.76%**	**53.29%**	**56.84%**	**28.50%**	**24.47%**	**16.28%**	**19.86%**	**35.45%**	**13.72%**	**9.59%**	**10.80%**	**14.97%**	**6.40%**	**14.05%**	**7.68%**	**7.69%**	**6.18%**	**7.07%**	**6.58%**	**2.89%**	**2.75%**
Dublin	45.50%	30.23%	56.26%	55.59%	65.56%	19.86%	21.56%	14.13%	17.97%	26.54%	12.01%	8.11%	9.93%	13.55%	6.66%	15.81%	8.11%	8.42%	10.48%	9.46%	11.00%	2.17%	3.31%
Leinster	37.47%	28.59%	51.78%	52.69%	53.59%	32.21%	25.39%	18.07%	20.75%	39.12%	13.27%	9.12%	10.93%	14.43%	5.98%	13.58%	7.58%	7.15%	6.02%	7.36%	6.39%	2.58%	2.47%
Munster	38.97%	28.68%	52.95%	54.71%	55.15%	31.26%	24.69%	17.76%	19.09%	37.64%	13.51%	8.99%	11.38%	14.53%	6.48%	14.33%	6.73%	7.56%	4.58%	6.60%	4.93%	3.13%	2.08%
Connaught/Ulster	35.55%	30.20%	50.07%	49.59%	52.36%	30.61%	26.22%	17.55%	21.95%	38.83%	16.93%	12.17%	12.90%	18.27%	6.50%	12.48%	8.18%	7.70%	3.07%	4.90%	3.43%	3.94%	3.40%
Ulster	21.45%	22.05%	43.19%	39.82%	37.85%	37.66%	28.51%	20.58%	25.82%	48.99%	25.45%	17.06%	13.29%	26.99%	6.08%	11.24%	10.20%	7.14%	2.86%	5.34%	3.20%	4.51%	1.99%

PRESIDENCY 1938-2011

									FF		FG		LB		Others		
Date	Electorate	Turnout	%	Spoilt	%	Valid	%	Quota	Votes	%	Votes	%	Votes	%	Votes	%	President
1938																	Douglas Hyde
14/06/1945	1,803,463	1,136,625	63.02%	50,287	4.42%	1,086,338	60.24%	543,170	537,965	49.52%	335,539	30.89%			212,834	19.59%	Sean T. O'Kelly
1952																	Sean T. O'Kelly
17/06/1959	1,678,450	979,628	58.37%	24,089	2.46%	955,539	56.93%	477,770	538,003	56.30%	417,536	43.70%					Eamon de Valera
01/06/1966	1,709,161	1,116,915	65.35%	9,910	0.89%	1,107,005	64.77%	553,503	558,861	50.48%	548,144	49.52%					Eamon de Valera
30/05/1973	1,977,817	1,230,584	62.22%	6,946	0.56%	1,223,638	61.87%	611,820	635,867	51.97%	587,771	48.03%					Erskine Childers
1974																	Cearbhall O Dalaigh
1976																	Patrick Hillery
1983																	Patrick Hillery
07/11/1990	2,471,308	1,584,095	64.10%	9,444	0.60%	1,574,651	63.72%	787,326	694,484	44.10%	267,902	17.01%	612,265	38.88%			Mary Robinson
30/10/1997	2,688,316	1,279,688	47.60%	9,852	0.77%	1,269,836	47.24%	634,919	574,424	45.24%	372,002	29.30%	88,423	6.96%	234,987	18.51%	Mary McAleese
2004																	Mary McAleese
27/10/2011	3,191,177	1,790,438	56.11%	18,676	1.04%	1,771,762	55.52%	885,882			113,321	6.40%	701,101	39.57%	957,340	54.03%	Michael D. Higgins

PRESIDENTIAL ELECTION POLLS: 27th October 2011

	Candidate	Party	25/09/2011	06/10/2011	06/10/2011	16/10/2011	23/10/2011	23/10/2011	23/10/2011	24/10/2011	3,191,157	27/10/2011
			Red C	MRBI	Red C	Red C	Quantum R	Behv & Att	Red C	MRBI	1,771,762	
			Bus. Post	Irish Times	Bus. Post	Bus. Post	Sun Ind	Sun Times	Bus. Post	Irish Times	55.52%	Actual
1	Higgins, Michael D.	LB	18%	23%	25%	27%	31%	26%	26%	25%	701,101	39.57%
2	Gallagher, Sean	NP	11%	20%	21%	39%	41%	38%	40%	40%	504,964	28.50%
3	McGuinness, Martin	SF	16%	19%	16%	13%	10%	17%	13%	15%	243,030	13.72%
4	Mitchell, Gay	FG	13%	9%	10%	8%	8%	8%	6%	6%	113,321	6.40%
5	Norris, David	NP	21%	11%	14%	7%	6%	6%	10%	8%	109,469	6.18%
6	Scallon, Dana Rosemary	NP	6%	6%	5%	2%	1%	2%	3%	3%	51,220	2.89%
7	Davis, Mary	NP	13%	12%	9%	4%	3%	3%	2%	3%	48,657	2.75%
7	**Total**		**98%**	**100%**	**100%**	**100%**	**100%**	**100%**	**100%**	**100%**	**1,771,762**	**100.00%**

PART 8

REFERENDA

REFERENDA

The draft Constitution was approved by the people at a plebiscite held on 1st July 1937. The constitution provides for two kinds of referendum: -

> A referendum on a proposal to amend the Constitution (referred to in law as a "constitutional referendum"), and
> A referendum on a proposal other than a proposal to amend the Constitution (referred to in law as an "ordinary referendum").

An ordinary referendum may take place when a proposal contained in a Bill is determined to be of such national importance that the will of the people thereon ought to be ascertained. No ordinary referendum has taken place up to the present.

A constitutional referendum relates to proposals for the amendment of the Constitution. The first two amendments to the Constitution took place during the transitional period within which the Constitution could be amended by ordinary law without a referendum in accordance with Article 51. These amendments were effected by the First Amendment of the Constitution Act, 1939 and the Second Amendment of the Constitution Act, 1941 respectively.

Referenda have taken place on a total of 32 proposals to amend the Constitution. 23 have been approved and 9 have been rejected. The largest majority was for the Adoption Referendum in 1979 when a huge 99% of the voters were in favour. The lowest majority in favour was in the Divorce Referendum in 1995 with 50.28% Yes, followed by Cabinet Confidentiality with only 52.65% in favour. The 1992 Right to Life Referendum was defeated by the largest majority (65.4% against). The largest turnout for a Referendum was in 1972 (70.9%) but this was less than turned out for the Plebiscite on the Draft Constitution in 1937 (75.8%). This Plebiscite also had the largest number of spoilt votes (10%). The 7.65% spoilt votes in the Local Government referendum in 1999 was the highest since 1937. The least turnout was for the Seanad Referendum in 1978 when only 28.6% of the electorate voted. The Nice and Lisbon Treaty Referenda were the only ones to date to be voted on twice as Nice was rejected in 2001 by 54% to 46% but was passed in 2002 by 63% to 37% with Lisbon rejected in 2008 by 53% to 47% and passed in 2009 by 67% to 33%. The electorate passed the three million mark for the first time in 2004 and was up in the latest referendum by 1.5 million from the first Referendum in 1959.

The recent Oireachtas Inquiries Referendum was called the 30th Amendment but this is incorrect as it would have been the 24th Amendment to the Constitution if passed. The error first occurred in 1992 when one of the three amendments up for ratification was defeated. Up to this if an amendment was defeated then that number was carried forward to the next referendum as happened to the third amendment which failed in 1959 and 1968 and was eventually passed at the third attempt in 1971. Thus the Divorce referendum in 1995 should have been the 14th not the 15th. This one and the next seven were passed but number 22 was not used and so going into the first Nice Treaty referendum it should have been the 22nd amendment instead of 24th. As this one failed the next one on Abortion should still have been the 22nd instead of 25th and as it was defeated the next one on the second Nice Treaty should have been 22nd not 26th. Thus the Citizenship referendum which was passed in 2004 was the 23rd amendment not 27th. The first Lisbon Treaty referendum failed and so the second one which was passed became the 24th amendment, making the Judges Pay referendum the 25th not the 29th.

REFERENDUM ON THE TWENTY NINTH AMENDMENT OF THE CONSTITUTION BILL 2011													
REFERENDUM ON JUDGES PAY: 27th October 2011													
		Turnout		Spoiled		Valid		Yes		No		Yes	
Constituency	**Electorate**	**Votes**	**%**	**Votes**	**%**	**Votes**	**%**	**Votes**	**%**	**Votes**	**%**	**Majority**	**%**
Carlow-Kilkenny	106,810	59,274	55.49%	1,488	2.51%	57,786	54.10%	47,454	82.12%	10,332	17.88%	37,122	64.24%
Cavan-Monaghan	98,952	58,425	59.04%	1,743	2.98%	56,682	57.28%	45,487	80.25%	11,195	19.75%	34,292	60.50%
Clare	81,419	47,183	57.95%	1,238	2.62%	45,945	56.43%	37,196	80.96%	8,749	19.04%	28,447	61.92%
Cork East	82,731	45,320	54.78%	1,032	2.28%	44,288	53.53%	35,949	81.17%	8,339	18.83%	27,610	62.34%
Cork North-Central	75,622	41,550	54.94%	850	2.05%	40,700	53.82%	32,629	80.17%	8,071	19.83%	24,558	60.34%
Cork North-West	62,113	37,637	60.59%	841	2.23%	36,796	59.24%	29,601	80.45%	7,195	19.55%	22,406	60.89%
Cork South-Central	91,716	53,572	58.41%	946	1.77%	52,626	57.38%	42,116	80.03%	10,510	19.97%	31,606	60.06%
Cork South-West	60,248	35,794	59.41%	940	2.63%	34,854	57.85%	28,425	81.55%	6,429	18.45%	21,996	63.11%
Donegal North-East	58,579	28,501	48.65%	751	2.63%	27,750	47.37%	20,583	74.17%	7,167	25.83%	13,416	48.35%
Donegal South-West	64,158	30,958	48.25%	965	3.12%	29,993	46.75%	22,849	76.18%	7,144	23.82%	15,705	52.36%
Dublin Central	54,500	28,125	51.61%	426	1.51%	27,699	50.82%	21,191	76.50%	6,508	23.50%	14,683	53.01%
Dublin Mid-West	64,370	34,059	52.91%	422	1.24%	33,637	52.26%	27,242	80.99%	6,395	19.01%	20,847	61.98%
Dublin North	69,347	39,692	57.24%	507	1.28%	39,185	56.51%	31,725	80.96%	7,460	19.04%	24,265	61.92%
Dublin North-Central	51,929	33,172	63.88%	475	1.43%	32,697	62.96%	25,962	79.40%	6,735	20.60%	19,227	58.80%
Dublin North-East	57,627	34,401	59.70%	401	1.17%	34,000	59.00%	27,070	79.62%	6,930	20.38%	20,140	59.24%
Dublin North-West	50,410	25,290	50.17%	389	1.54%	24,901	49.40%	19,736	79.26%	5,165	20.74%	14,571	58.52%
Dublin South	104,145	64,412	61.85%	683	1.06%	63,729	61.19%	50,100	78.61%	13,629	21.39%	36,471	57.23%
Dublin South-Central	77,688	41,396	53.28%	683	1.65%	40,713	52.41%	31,326	76.94%	9,387	23.06%	21,939	53.89%
Dublin South East	55,533	30,619	55.14%	368	1.20%	30,251	54.47%	21,633	71.51%	8,618	28.49%	13,015	43.02%
Dublin South-West	69,977	36,627	52.34%	538	1.47%	36,089	51.57%	29,001	80.36%	7,088	19.64%	21,913	60.72%
Dublin West	61,583	36,267	58.89%	399	1.10%	35,868	58.24%	28,714	80.05%	7,154	19.95%	21,560	60.11%
Dun Laoghaire	82,033	49,087	59.84%	631	1.29%	48,456	59.07%	36,631	75.60%	11,825	24.40%	24,806	51.19%
Galway East	81,896	46,942	57.32%	1,412	3.01%	45,530	55.59%	36,892	81.03%	8,638	18.97%	28,254	62.06%
Galway West	94,700	50,536	53.36%	1,269	2.51%	49,267	52.02%	38,812	78.78%	10,455	21.22%	28,357	57.56%
Kerry North-West Limerick	63,068	34,415	54.57%	966	2.81%	33,449	53.04%	26,728	79.91%	6,721	20.09%	20,007	59.81%
Kerry South	57,776	31,827	55.09%	933	2.93%	30,894	53.47%	24,693	79.93%	6,201	20.07%	18,492	59.86%
Kildare North	76,623	43,426	56.67%	582	1.34%	42,844	55.92%	34,587	80.73%	8,257	19.27%	26,330	61.46%
Kildare South	57,933	31,236	53.92%	584	1.87%	30,652	52.91%	24,779	80.84%	5,873	19.16%	18,906	61.68%
Laoighis Offaly	107,023	59,202	55.32%	1,472	2.49%	57,730	53.94%	46,640	80.79%	11,090	19.21%	35,550	61.58%
Limerick	66,345	36,755	55.40%	997	2.71%	35,758	53.90%	28,783	80.49%	6,975	19.51%	21,808	60.99%
Limerick City	66,421	34,614	52.11%	652	1.88%	33,962	51.13%	27,685	81.52%	6,277	18.48%	21,408	63.04%
Longford-Westmeath	85,911	45,390	52.83%	1,188	2.62%	44,202	51.45%	35,199	79.63%	9,003	20.37%	26,196	59.26%
Louth	102,941	57,993	56.34%	1,102	1.90%	56,891	55.27%	45,117	79.30%	11,774	20.70%	33,343	58.61%
Mayo	97,714	53,553	54.81%	1,503	2.81%	52,050	53.27%	42,678	81.99%	9,372	18.01%	33,306	63.99%
Meath East	65,477	35,367	54.01%	593	1.68%	34,774	53.11%	28,221	81.16%	6,553	18.84%	21,668	62.31%
Meath West	63,111	32,977	52.25%	663	2.01%	32,314	51.20%	25,845	79.98%	6,469	20.02%	19,376	59.96%
Roscommon-South Leitrim	60,416	36,338	60.15%	995	2.74%	35,343	58.50%	27,678	78.31%	7,665	21.69%	20,013	56.63%
Sligo-North Leitrim	62,152	34,168	54.97%	806	2.36%	33,362	53.68%	26,321	78.90%	7,041	21.10%	19,280	57.79%
Tipperary North	62,603	38,234	61.07%	1,130	2.96%	37,104	59.27%	29,975	80.79%	7,129	19.21%	22,846	61.57%
Tipperary South	56,295	32,567	57.85%	922	2.83%	31,645	56.21%	25,498	80.58%	6,147	19.42%	19,351	61.15%
Waterford	78,960	42,706	54.09%	1,004	2.35%	41,702	52.81%	33,453	80.22%	8,249	19.78%	25,204	60.44%
Wexford	108,490	58,442	53.87%	1,271	2.17%	57,171	52.70%	46,783	81.83%	10,388	18.17%	36,395	63.66%
Wicklow	93,812	57,658	61.46%	936	1.62%	56,722	60.46%	44,890	79.14%	11,832	20.86%	33,058	58.28%
Total	**3,191,157**	**1,785,707**	**55.96%**	**37,696**	**2.11%**	**1,748,011**	**54.78%**	**1,393,877**	**79.74%**	**354,134**	**20.26%**	**1,039,743**	**59.48%**
Regions													
Dublin	799,142	453,147	56.70%	5,922	1.31%	447,225	55.96%	350,331	78.33%	96,894	21.67%	253,437	56.67%
Leinster	868,131	480,965	55.40%	9,879	2.05%	471,086	54.26%	379,515	80.56%	91,571	19.44%	287,944	61.12%
Munster	905,317	512,174	56.57%	12,451	2.43%	499,723	55.20%	402,731	80.59%	96,992	19.41%	305,739	61.18%
Connaught/Ulster	618,567	339,421	54.87%	9,444	2.78%	329,977	53.35%	261,300	79.19%	68,677	20.81%	192,623	58.37%

REFERENDUM ON THE THIRTIETH AMENDMENT OF THE CONSTITUTION BILL 2011													
REFERENDUM ON HOUSES OF THE OIREACHTAS INQUIRIES: 27th October 2011													
		Turnout		Spoiled		Valid		Yes		No		No	
Constituency	**Electorate**	**Votes**	**%**	**Votes**	**%**	**Votes**	**%**	**Votes**	**%**	**Votes**	**%**	**Majority**	**%**
Carlow-Kilkenny	106,810	59,264	55.49%	1,812	3.06%	57,452	53.79%	28,339	49.33%	29,113	50.67%	774	1.35%
Cavan-Monaghan	98,952	58,416	59.03%	2,085	3.57%	56,331	56.93%	27,542	48.89%	28,789	51.11%	1,247	2.21%
Clare	81,419	47,153	57.91%	1,458	3.09%	45,695	56.12%	22,273	48.74%	23,422	51.26%	1,149	2.51%
Cork East	82,731	45,324	54.78%	1,217	2.69%	44,107	53.31%	20,966	47.53%	23,141	52.47%	2,175	4.93%
Cork North-Central	75,622	41,532	54.92%	922	2.22%	40,610	53.70%	18,830	46.37%	21,780	53.63%	2,950	7.26%
Cork North-West	62,113	37,620	60.57%	1,101	2.93%	36,519	58.79%	17,232	47.19%	19,287	52.81%	2,055	5.63%
Cork South-Central	91,716	53,551	58.39%	1,064	1.99%	52,487	57.23%	23,459	44.69%	29,028	55.31%	5,569	10.61%
Cork South-West	60,248	35,777	59.38%	1,055	2.95%	34,722	57.63%	16,924	48.74%	17,798	51.26%	874	2.52%
Donegal North-East	58,579	28,477	48.61%	894	3.14%	27,583	47.09%	11,253	40.80%	16,330	59.20%	5,077	18.41%
Donegal South-West	64,158	30,943	48.23%	1,106	3.57%	29,837	46.51%	12,569	42.13%	17,268	57.87%	4,699	15.75%
Dublin Central	54,500	28,124	51.60%	498	1.77%	27,626	50.69%	12,818	46.40%	14,808	53.60%	1,990	7.20%
Dublin Mid-West	64,370	34,057	52.91%	492	1.44%	33,565	52.14%	15,942	47.50%	17,623	52.50%	1,681	5.01%
Dublin North	69,347	39,665	57.20%	583	1.47%	39,082	56.36%	18,294	46.81%	20,788	53.19%	2,494	6.38%
Dublin North-Central	51,929	33,152	63.84%	510	1.54%	32,642	62.86%	14,226	43.58%	18,416	56.42%	4,190	12.84%
Dublin North-East	57,627	34,391	59.68%	552	1.61%	33,839	58.72%	15,404	45.52%	18,435	54.48%	3,031	8.96%
Dublin North-West	50,410	25,280	50.15%	494	1.95%	24,786	49.17%	11,819	47.68%	12,967	52.32%	1,148	4.63%
Dublin South	104,145	64,361	61.80%	859	1.33%	63,502	60.97%	27,758	43.71%	35,744	56.29%	7,986	12.58%
Dublin South-Central	77,688	41,373	53.26%	811	1.96%	40,562	52.21%	18,420	45.41%	22,142	54.59%	3,722	9.18%
Dublin South East	55,533	30,589	55.08%	500	1.63%	30,089	54.18%	11,177	37.15%	18,912	62.85%	7,735	25.71%
Dublin South-West	69,977	36,610	52.32%	637	1.74%	35,973	51.41%	17,432	48.46%	18,541	51.54%	1,109	3.08%
Dublin West	61,583	36,266	58.89%	477	1.32%	35,789	58.12%	16,322	45.61%	19,467	54.39%	3,145	8.79%
Dun Laoghaire	82,033	49,078	59.83%	833	1.70%	48,245	58.81%	20,094	41.65%	28,151	58.35%	8,057	16.70%
Galway East	81,896	46,903	57.27%	1,693	3.61%	45,210	55.20%	22,003	48.67%	23,207	51.33%	1,204	2.66%
Galway West	94,700	50,515	53.34%	1,544	3.06%	48,971	51.71%	22,529	46.00%	26,442	54.00%	3,913	7.99%
Kerry North-West Limerick	63,068	34,403	54.55%	1,173	3.41%	33,230	52.69%	15,892	47.82%	17,338	52.18%	1,446	4.35%
Kerry South	57,776	31,826	55.09%	1,160	3.64%	30,666	53.08%	14,495	47.27%	16,171	52.73%	1,676	5.47%
Kildare North	76,623	43,413	56.66%	740	1.70%	42,673	55.69%	19,389	45.44%	23,284	54.56%	3,895	9.13%
Kildare South	57,933	31,220	53.89%	713	2.28%	30,507	52.66%	14,940	48.97%	15,567	51.03%	627	2.06%
Laoighis Offaly	107,023	59,207	55.32%	1,734	2.93%	57,473	53.70%	27,149	47.24%	30,324	52.76%	3,175	5.52%
Limerick	66,345	34,591	52.14%	829	2.40%	33,762	50.89%	16,820	49.82%	16,942	50.18%	122	0.36%
Limerick City	66,421	36,728	55.30%	1,149	3.13%	35,579	53.57%	17,166	48.25%	18,413	51.75%	1,247	3.50%
Longford-Westmeath	85,911	45,367	52.81%	1,352	2.98%	44,015	51.23%	20,304	46.13%	23,711	53.87%	3,407	7.74%
Louth	102,941	57,967	56.31%	1,295	2.23%	56,672	55.05%	27,089	47.80%	29,583	52.20%	2,494	4.40%
Mayo	97,714	53,531	54.78%	1,782	3.33%	51,749	52.96%	26,091	50.42%	25,658	49.58%	-433	-0.84%
Meath East	65,477	35,360	54.00%	749	2.12%	34,611	52.86%	16,453	47.54%	18,158	52.46%	1,705	4.93%
Meath West	63,111	32,952	52.21%	808	2.45%	32,144	50.93%	15,021	46.73%	17,123	53.27%	2,102	6.54%
Roscommon-South Leitrim	60,416	36,308	60.10%	1,196	3.29%	35,112	58.12%	15,547	44.28%	19,565	55.72%	4,018	11.44%
Sligo-North Leitrim	62,152	34,168	54.97%	997	2.92%	33,171	53.37%	15,353	46.28%	17,818	53.72%	2,465	7.43%
Tipperary North	62,603	38,228	61.06%	1,299	3.40%	36,929	58.99%	17,276	46.78%	19,653	53.22%	2,377	6.44%
Tipperary South	56,295	32,558	57.83%	1,047	3.22%	31,511	55.97%	15,316	48.61%	16,195	51.39%	879	2.79%
Waterford	78,960	42,688	54.06%	1,129	2.64%	41,559	52.63%	20,010	48.15%	21,549	51.85%	1,539	3.70%
Wexford	108,490	58,456	53.88%	1,542	2.64%	56,914	52.46%	28,517	50.11%	28,397	49.89%	-120	-0.21%
Wicklow	93,812	57,816	61.63%	1,134	1.96%	56,682	60.42%	25,555	45.08%	31,127	54.92%	5,572	9.83%
Total	**3,191,157**	**1,785,208**	**55.94%**	**45,025**	**2.52%**	**1,740,183**	**54.53%**	**812,008**	**46.66%**	**928,175**	**53.34%**	**116,167**	**6.68%**
Regions													
Dublin	799,142	452,946	56.68%	7,246	1.60%	445,700	55.77%	199,706	44.81%	245,994	55.19%	46,288	10.39%
Leinster	868,131	481,022	55.41%	11,879	2.47%	469,143	54.04%	222,756	47.48%	246,387	52.52%	23,631	5.04%
Munster	905,317	511,979	56.55%	14,603	2.85%	497,376	54.94%	236,659	47.58%	260,717	52.42%	24,058	4.84%
Connaught/Ulster	618,567	339,261	54.85%	11,297	3.33%	327,964	53.02%	152,887	46.62%	175,077	53.38%	22,190	6.77%

CONSTITUTIONAL REFERENDA 1937-2011

Amendment	Polling Date	Electorate	Turnout Votes	Turnout %	Spoilt Votes	Spoilt %	Valid Votes	Valid %	For Votes	For %	Against Votes	Against %
Plebiscite on Draft Constitution 1937	01/07/1937	1,775,055	1,346,207	*75.84*	134,157	*9.97*	1,212,050	68.28	685,105	56.52	526,945	43.48
3rd Amendment 1958												
Voting System	17/06/1959	1,678,450	979,531	58.36	39,220	4.00	940,311	56.02	453,322	48.21	486,989	51.79
3rd & 4th Amendments 1968												
Formation of Dail Constituency	16/10/1968	1,717,389	1,129,473	65.77	48,485	4.29	1,080,988	62.94	424,185	39.24	656,803	60.76
Voting System	16/10/1968	1,717,389	1,129,606	65.77	48,212	4.27	1,081,394	62.97	423,496	39.16	657,898	60.84
3rd Amendment 1971												
Accesion to European Communities	10/05/1972	1,783,604	1,264,278	70.88	10,497	0.83	1,253,781	*70.29*	1,041,890	83.10	211,891	16.90
4th & 5th Amendments 1972												
Voting Age Reduced to 18	07/12/1972	1,783,604	903,439	50.65	47,089	5.21	856,350	48.01	724,836	84.64	131,514	15.36
Recognition of Specified Religions	07/12/1972	1,783,604	903,659	50.66	49,226	5.45	854,433	47.90	721,003	84.38	133,430	15.62
6th & 7th Amendments 1978												
Adoption	05/07/1979	2,179,464	623,476	28.61	15,517	2.49	607,959	27.89	601,694	*98.97*	6,265	1.03
University Representation in Seanad	05/07/1979	2,179,464	622,646	28.57	24,562	3.94	598,084	27.44	552,600	92.40	45,484	7.60
8th Amendment 1982												
Right to Life of the Unborn	07/09/1983	2,358,651	1,265,994	53.67	8,625	0.68	1,257,369	53.31	841,233	66.90	416,136	33.10
9th Amendment 1984												
Extension of Voting Rights	14/06/1984	2,399,257	1,138,895	47.47	40,162	3.53	1,098,733	45.79	828,483	75.40	270,250	24.60
10th Amendment 1986												
Dissolution of Marriage	26/06/1986	2,436,836	1,482,644	60.84	8,522	0.57	1,474,122	60.49	538,279	36.52	935,843	63.48
10th Amendment 1987												
Single European Act	26/05/1987	2,461,790	1,085,304	44.09	4,904	0.45	1,080,400	43.89	755,423	69.92	324,977	30.08
11th Amendment 1992												
European Union	18/06/1992	2,542,840	1,457,219	57.31	7,488	0.51	1,449,731	57.01	1,001,076	69.05	448,655	30.95
12th, 13th & 14th Amendments '92												
Right to Life	25/11/1992	2,542,841	1,733,309	68.16	81,835	4.72	1,651,474	64.95	572,177	34.65	1,079,297	*65.35*
Travel	25/11/1992	2,542,841	1,733,821	*68.18*	74,454	4.29	1,659,367	65.26	1,035,308	62.39	624,059	37.61
Information	25/11/1992	2,542,841	1,732,433	68.13	74,494	4.30	1,657,939	65.20	992,833	59.88	665,106	40.12
15th Amendment 1995												
Divorce	24/11/1995	2,628,834	1,633,942	62.15	5,372	0.33	1,628,570	61.95	818,842	50.28	809,728	49.72
16th Amendment 1996												
Bail	28/11/1996	2,659,895	777,586	29.23	2,878	0.37	774,708	29.13	579,740	74.83	194,968	25.17
17th Amendment 1997												
Cabinet Confidentiality	30/10/1997	2,688,316	1,268,063	47.17	66,111	5.21	1,201,952	44.71	632,777	52.65	569,175	47.35
18th Amendment 1998												
Amsterdam Treaty	22/05/1998	2,747,088	1,543,930	56.20	33,228	2.15	1,510,702	54.99	932,632	61.74	578,070	38.26
19th Amendment 1998												
Northern Ireland	22/05/1998	2,747,088	1,545,395	56.26	17,064	1.10	1,528,331	55.63	1,442,583	94.39	85,748	5.61
20th Amendment 1998												
Local Government	11/06/1999	2,791,409	1,425,881	51.08	109,066	*7.65*	1,316,815	47.17	1,024,850	77.83	291,965	22.17
21st Amendment 2001												
Death Penalty	07/06/2001	2,867,960	997,885	34.79	14,480	1.45	983,405	34.29	610,455	62.08	372,950	37.92
23rd Amendment 2001												
International Criminal Court	07/06/2001	2,867,960	997,565	34.78	17,819	1.79	979,746	34.16	629,234	64.22	350,512	35.78
24th Amendment 2001												
Nice Treaty	07/06/2001	2,867,960	997,826	34.79	14,887	1.49	982,939	34.27	453,461	46.13	529,478	53.87
25th Amendment 2001												
Abortion	06/03/2002	2,923,918	1,254,175	42.89	6,649	0.53	1,247,526	42.67	618,485	49.58	629,041	50.42
26th Amendment 2002												
Nice Treaty	19/10/2002	2,923,918	1,446,588	49.47	5,384	0.37	1,441,204	49.29	906,317	62.89	534,887	37.11
27th Amendment 2004												
Citizenship	11/06/2004	3,041,688	1,823,434	59.95	20,219	1.11	1,803,215	59.28	1,427,520	79.17	375,695	20.83
28th Amendment 2004												
Lisbon Treaty	12/06/2008	3,051,278	1,621,037	53.13	6,171	0.38	1,614,866	52.92	752,451	46.60	862,415	53.40
28th Amendment 2008												
Lisbon Treaty	02/10/2009	3,078,032	1,816,098	59.00	7,224	0.40	1,808,874	58.77	1,214,268	67.13	594,606	32.87
29th Amendment 2011												
Judges Pay	27/10/2011	3,191,157	1,785,707	55.96	37,696	2.11	1,748,011	54.78	1,393,877	79.74	354,134	20.26
30th Amendment 2011												
Oireachtas Inquiries	27/10/2011	3,191,157	1,785,208	55.94	45,025	2.52	1,740,183	54.53	812,008	46.66	928,175	53.34
Proposed Amendments: 32	*Highest*	Lowest							Yes	23	No	9

CONSTITUTIONAL REFERENDA 1937 - 2011

Plebiscite on the Draft Constitution, 1937 - 1-July-1937

A plebiscite on the draft Constitution was held on 1st July 1937. A general election of members to Dáil Éireann took place on the same day. The total number of votes given at the plebiscite approving of the draft Constitution was 685,105 and the total number of votes not approving was 526,945. As the majority of the votes cast at the plebiscite signified approval, the draft Constitution was deemed to have been approved by the people and came into operation on 1st January 1938.

Referendum on the Voting System (1959)
(Third Amendment of the Constitution Bill, 1958)

Polling at the referendum took place on Wednesday, 17th June 1959, between the hours of 9.00 a.m. and 9.30 p.m. A presidential election took place on the same day.
The following summary of the principal proposals in the THIRD AMENDMENT OF THE CONSTITUTION BILL, 1958, was circulated for the information of voters:
"At present, members of Dáil Éireann are elected on a system of proportional representation for constituencies returning at least three members, each voter having a single transferable vote.
It is proposed in the Bill to abolish the system of proportional representation and to adopt, instead, a system of single-member constituencies, each voter having a single non- transferable vote. It is also proposed in the Bill to set up a Commission for the determination and revision of the constituencies, instead of having this done by the Oireachtas, as at present."
(This statement was prescribed by the Referendum (Amendment) Act, 1959).
The total number of votes recorded in favour of the proposal contained in the Bill was 453,322 and the total number of votes recorded against the proposal was 486,989. The proposal was not, therefore, approved by the people.

Referendum on the Formation of Dáil Constituencies (1968)
(Third Amendment of the Constitution Bill, 1968)

Polling at the referendum took place on Wednesday, 16th October 1968, between the hours of 9 a.m. and 9 p.m. A referendum on the voting system took place on the same day. The subject matter of the referendum was described as follows in the official polling card sent to each elector:
"WHITE BALLOT PAPER
THE THIRD AMENDMENT OF THE CONSTITUTION BILL, 1968, proposes that in forming Dáil constituencies, the population per deputy in any case may not be greater or less than the national average by more than one-sixth and that regard must be had to the extent and accessibility of constituencies, the need for having convenient areas of representation and the desirability of avoiding the over-lapping of county boundaries."
(This statement was prescribed by the Referendum (Amendment) Act, 1968).
The total number of votes recorded in favour of the proposal was 424,185 and the total number of votes recorded against the proposal was 656,803. The proposal was not, therefore, approved by the people.

Referendum on the Voting System (1968)
(Fourth Amendment of the Constitution Bill, 1968)

Polling at the referendum took place on Wednesday, 16th October 1968, between the hours of 9 a.m. and 9 p.m. A referendum on the formation of Dáil constituencies took place on the same day. The subject matter of the referendum was described as follows in the official polling card sent to each elector:
"GREEN BALLOT PAPER
THE FOURTH AMENDMENT OF THE CONSTITUTION BILL, 1968, proposes –(1) To substitute for the present system of voting at Dáil elections the "straight vote "system in single-member constituencies; (2) To establish a Commission to determine constituencies, subject to the right of the Dáil to amend the constituencies as so determined; and (3) To provide that whenever the Dáil is dissolved the outgoing Ceann Comhairle may be returned, without a contest, as a second deputy for a constituency chosen by him which consists of, or includes a part of, the constituency he represented before the dissolution."
(This statement was prescribed by the Referendum (Amendment) Act, 1968).
The total number of votes recorded in favour of the proposal was 423,496 and the total number of votes recorded against the proposal was 657,898. The proposal was not, therefore, approved by the people.

Referendum on Accession to the European Communities (1972)
(Third Amendment of the Constitution Bill, 1971)

Polling at the referendum took place on Thursday, 10th May 1972 between the hours of 9 a.m. and 9 p.m. The subject matter of the referendum was described as follows in the official polling card circulated to each elector:
"THE THIRD AMENDMENT OF THE CONSTITUTION BILL, 1971, proposes to add the subsection here following to Article 29.4 of the Constitution.
3 ° The State may become a member of the European Coal and Steel Community (established by Treaty signed at Paris on the 18th day of April, 1951), the European Economic Community (established by Treaty signed at Rome on the 25th day of March, 1957) and the European Atomic Energy Community (established by Treaty signed at Rome on 25th day of March, 1957). No provision of this Constitution invalidates laws enacted, acts done or measures adopted by the State necessitated by the obligations of membership of the Communities or prevents laws enacted, acts done or measures adopted by the Communities, or institutions thereof, from having the force of law in the State.
The purpose of the proposal is to allow the State to become a member of the Communities commonly known as European Communities."
(This statement was prescribed by the Electoral (Amendment) Act, 1972).
The total number of votes recorded in favour of the proposal was 1,041,890 and the total number of votes recorded against the proposal was 211,891. As the proposal was duly approved by the people, the Bill was signed by the President on 8th June 1972 and promulgated as a law.

Referendum on the Voting Age (1972)
(Fourth Amendment of the Constitution Bill, 1972)

Polling at the referendum took place on Thursday, 7th December 1972, between the hours of 9 a.m. and 9 p.m. A referendum on the recognition of specified religions took place on the same day. The subject matter of the referendum was described as follows in the official polling card sent to each elector:
"GREEN BALLOT PAPER"
THE FOURTH AMENDMENT OF THE CONSTITUTION BILL, 1972, proposes to reduce the minimum voting age at Dáil and Presidential elections and Referendums from 21 years to 18 years."
(This statement was prescribed by the Referendum (Amendment) Act, 1972).
The total number of votes recorded in favour of the proposal was 724,836 and the total number recorded against the proposal was 131,514. As the proposal was duly approved by the people, the Bill was signed by the President on 5th January 1973, and promulgated as a law.

Referendum on Recognition of Specified Religions (1972)
(Fifth Amendment of the Constitution Bill, 1972)

Polling at the referendum took place on Thursday, 7th December 1972, between the hours of 9 a.m. and 9 p.m. A referendum on the voting age took place on the same day.
"WHITE BALLOT PAPER"
THE FIFTH AMENDMENT OF THE CONSTITUTION BILL, 1972, proposes to delete subsection 2 and 3 of Article 44 of the Constitution. If approved Article 44 will provide as follows:
1. The State acknowledges that the homage of public worship is due to Almighty God. It shall hold His Name in reverence, and shall respect and honour religion.
2.1 Freedom of conscience and the free profession and practice of religion are, subject to public order and morality, guaranteed to every citizen.
2 The State guarantees not to endow any religion.
3 The State shall not impose any disabilities or make any discrimination on the ground of religious profession, belief or status.
4 Legislation providing State aid for schools shall not discriminate between schools under the management of different religious denominations, nor be such as to affect prejudicially the right of any child to attend a school receiving public money without attending religious instruction at that school.
5 Every religious denomination shall have the right to manage its own affairs, own, acquire and administer property, movable and immovable, and maintain institutions for religious or charitable purposes.
6 The property of any religious denomination or any educational institution shall not be diverted save for necessary works of public utility and on payment of compensation.
The total number of votes recorded in favour of the proposal was 721,003 and the total number recorded against the proposal was 133,430. As the proposal was duly approved by the people, the Bill was signed by the President on 5th January 1973, and promulgated as a law.

Referendum on Adoption (1979)
(Sixth Amendment of the Constitution (Adoption) Bill, 1978)

Polling at the referendum took place on Thursday, 5th July 1979 between the hours of 9 a.m. and 9 p.m. A referendum on university representation in the Seanad took place on the same day. The following statement for the information of voters on the subject matter of the referendum was prescribed in the Referendum (Amendment) Act, 1979:
"WHITE BALLOT PAPER
THE SIXTH AMENDMENT OF THE CONSTITUTION (ADOPTION) BILL, 1978, proposes that an adoption which is in accordance with laws enacted by the Oireachtas shall not be invalid solely by reason of the fact that the relevant order or authorisation was not made or given by a judge or court but by a person or body designated for the purpose by those laws. The Bill relates to past as well as future adoptions. Its object is to ensure that adoption orders made by an Bord Uchtála (the Adoption Board) will not be in danger of being declared to be invalid because they were not made by a court."
The total number of votes recorded in favour of the proposal was 601,694 and the total number recorded against the proposal was 6,265. As the proposal was duly approved by the people, the Bill was signed by the President on 3rd August 1979 and promulgated as a law.

Referendum on University Representation in Seanad (1979)
(Seventh Amendment of the Constitution (Election of Members of Seanad Éireann by Institutions of Higher Education) Bill, 1979)

Polling at the referendum took place on Thursday, 5th July 1979 between the hours of 9 a.m. and 9 p.m. A referendum on adoption took place on the same day. The following statement for the information of voters on the subject matter of the referendum was prescribed in the Referendum (Amendment) Act, 1979:
"GREEN BALLOT PAPER
THE SEVENTH AMENDMENT OF THE CONSTITUTION (ELECTION OF MEMBERS OF SEANAD ÉIREANN BY INSTITUTIONS OF HIGHER EDUCATION) BILL, 1979, proposes the election by universities and other institutions of higher education specified by law of such number of members of Seanad Éireann, not exceeding 6, as may be specified by law. Those so elected would be in substitution for an equal number of the members elected at present (3 each) by the National University of Ireland and the University of Dublin. The Bill also proposes that nothing in Article 18 of the Constitution shall prohibit the dissolution by law of those Universities."
The total number of votes recorded in favour of the proposal was 552,600 and the total number recorded against the proposal was 45,484. As the proposal was duly approved by the people, the Bill was signed by the President on 3rd August 1979 and promulgated as a law.

Referendum on the Right to Life of the Unborn (1983)
(Eighth Amendment of the Constitution Bill, 1982)

Polling at the referendum took place on Wednesday, 7th September 1983 between the hours of 9 a.m. and 9 p.m.
The subject matter of the referendum was described as follows in the official polling card circulated to each elector:
"THE EIGHTH AMENDMENT OF THE CONSTITUTION BILL, 1982, proposes to add the subsection here following to Article 40.3 of the Constitution
3 ° The State acknowledges the right to life of the unborn and, with due regard to the equal right to life of the mother, guarantees in its laws to respect, and, as far as practicable, by its laws to defend and vindicate that right."
(The statement was prescribed by the Referendum (Amendment) Act, 1983).
The total number of votes recorded in favour of the proposal was 841,233 and the total number of votes recorded against the proposal was 416,136. As the proposal was duly approved by the people, the Bill was signed by the President on 7th October 1983 and promulgated as a law.

Referendum on Extension of Voting Right at Dáil elections (1984)
(Ninth Amendment of the Constitution Bill, 1984)

Polling at the referendum, which was held in conjunction with the European Parliament elections, took place on Thursday 14th June 1984 between the hours of 9 a.m. and 9 p.m.
The subject matter of the referendum was described as follows in the official polling card circulated to each elector:
"THE NINTH AMENDMENT OF THE CONSTITUTION BILL, 1984, proposes to extend the right conferred on citizens to vote at elections for members of Dáil Éireann to such other persons in the State who have reached the age of 18 years as may be specified by legislation enacted by the Oireachtas."
(The statement was prescribed by the Referendum (Amendment) Act, 1984).
The total number of votes recorded in favour of the proposal was 828,483 and the total number of votes recorded against the proposal was 270,250. As the proposal was duly approved by the people, the Bill was signed by the President on 2nd August 1984 and promulgated as law.

Referendum on Dissolution of Marriage (1986)
(Tenth Amendment of the Constitution Bill, 1986)

Polling at the referendum took place on Thursday, 26th June 1986 between the hours of 9 a.m. and 10 p.m.
The subject matter of the referendum was described as follows on the official polling card circulated to each elector:
"THE TENTH AMENDMENT OF THE CONSTITUTION BILL, 1986, proposes to delete subsection 2° of Article 41.3 of the Constitution, which states that no law shall be enacted providing for the grant of a dissolution of marriage, and to substitute the subsection here following:
2° Where, and only where, such court established under this Constitution as may be prescribed by law is satisfied that: -
(i) a marriage has failed,
(ii) the failure has continued for a period of, or periods amounting to, at least five years,
(iii) there is no reasonable possibility of reconciliation between the parties to the marriage, and
(iv) any other condition prescribed by law has been compiled with,
the court may in accordance with law grant a dissolution of the marriage provided that the court is satisfied that adequate and proper provision having regard to the circumstances will be made for any dependent spouse and for any child of or any child who is dependent on either spouse."
(The statement was prescribed by the Electoral (Amendment) Act, 1986).
The total number of votes recorded in favour of the proposal was 538,279 and the total number of votes recorded against the proposal was 935,843. The proposal was not, therefore, approved by the people.

Referendum on Ratification of the Single European Act (1987)
(Tenth Amendment of the Constitution Bill, 1987)

Polling at the referendum took place on Tuesday, 26th May 1987 between the hours of 9 a.m. and 9 p.m.
The subject matter of the referendum was described as follows on the official polling card circulated to each elector:
"THE TENTH AMENDMENT OF THE CONSTITUTIONAL BILL, 1987, proposes to enable the State to ratify the Single European Act by inserting the sentence here following into subsection 3° of section 4 of Article 29 of the Constitution after the first sentence:
The State may ratify the Single European Act (signed on behalf of the Member States of the Communities at Luxembourg on the 17th day of February, 1986, and at The Hague on the 28th day of February, 1986)."
(The statement was prescribed by the Referendum (Amendment) Act, 1987).
The total number of votes recorded in favour of the proposal was 755,423 and the total number of votes recorded against the proposal was 324,977. As the proposal was duly approved by the people, the Bill was signed by the President on 22nd June 1987 and promulgated as law.

Referendum on European Union (1992)
(Eleventh Amendment of the Constitution Bill, 1992)

Polling at the referendum took place on Thursday, 18th June 1992 between the hours of 9 a.m. and 10 p.m. The subject matter of the referendum was described as follows on the official polling card circulated to each elector:
"THE ELEVENTH AMENDMENT OF THE CONSTITUTION BILL, 1992, relating to the amendment of Article 29 of the Constitution proposes to repeal the third sentence in subsection 3° of section 4 thereof and to insert the subsections here following into the said section 4:
4° The State may ratify the Treaty on European Union signed at Maastricht on the 7th day of February 1992, and may become a member of that Union.
5° No provision of this Constitution invalidates laws enacted, acts done or measures adopted by the State which are necessitated by the obligations of membership of the European Union or of the Communities, or prevents laws enacted, acts done or measures adopted by the European Union or by the Communities or by institutions thereof, or by bodies competent under the Treaties establishing the Communities, from having the force of law in the State.
6° The State may ratify the Agreement relating to Community Patents drawn up between the Member States of the Communities and done at Luxembourg on the 15th day of December, 1989."
(The statement was prescribed by the Referendum (Amendment) Act, 1992).
The total number of votes recorded in favour of the proposal was 1,001,076 and the total number of votes recorded against the proposal was 448,655. As the proposal was duly approved by the people, the Bill was signed by the President on 16th July 1992 and promulgated as a law.

Referendum on Right to Life (1992)
(Twelfth Amendment of the Constitution Bill, 1992)

Polling at the referendum took place on Wednesday, 25th November 1992 between the hours of 9 a.m. and 9 p.m. Referendums on travel (Thirteenth Amendment of the Constitution Bill) and Information (Fourteenth Amendment of the Constitution Bill) and a General Election also took place on the same day.
The subject matter of the referendum was described as follows in the official polling card sent to each elector:

'WHITE BALLOT PAPER - RIGHT TO LIFE
THE TWELFTH AMENDMENT OF THE CONSTITUTION BILL, 1992, proposes to amend Article 40 of the Constitution by the addition of the text here following to subsection 3° of section 3 thereof:
"It shall be unlawful to terminate the life of an unborn unless such termination is necessary to save the life, as distinct from the health, of the mother where there is an illness or disorder of the mother giving rise to a real and substantial risk to her life, not being a risk of self-destruction.".'
(This statement was prescribed by the Referendum (Amendment) (No. 2) Act, 1992).
The total number of votes recorded in favour of the proposal was 572,177 and the total number recorded against the proposal was 1,079,297. The proposal was not, therefore, approved by the people.

Referendum on Travel (1992)
(Thirteenth Amendment of the Constitution Bill, 1992)

Polling at the referendum took place on Wednesday, 25th November 1992 between the hours of 9 a.m. and 9 p.m. Referendums on right to life (Twelfth Amendment of the Constitution Bill) and Information (Fourteenth Amendment of the Constitution Bill) and a General Election also took place on the same day.
The subject matter of the referendum was described as follows in the official polling card sent to each elector:
'GREEN BALLOT PAPER - TRAVEL
THE THIRTEENTH AMENDMENT OF THE CONSTITUTION BILL, 1992, proposes to amend Article 40 of the Constitution by the addition of the paragraph here following to subsection 3° of section 3 thereof:
"This subsection shall not limit freedom to travel between the State and another state.".'
(This statement was prescribed by the Referendum (Amendment) (No. 2) Act, 1992).
The total number of votes recorded in favour of the proposal was 1,035,308 and the total number recorded against the proposal was 624,059. As the proposal was duly approved by the people, the Bill was signed by the President on 23rd December 1992 and promulgated as a law.

Referendum on Information (1992)
(Fourteenth Amendment of the Constitution Bill, 1992)

Polling at the referendum took place on Wednesday, 25th November 1992 between the hours of 9 a.m. and 9 p.m. Referendums on right to life (Twelfth Amendment of the Constitution Bill) and Travel (Thirteenth Amendment of the Constitution Bill) and a General Election also took place on the same day.
The subject matter of the referendum was described as follows in the official polling card sent to each elector:
'PINK BALLOT PAPER - INFORMATION
THE FOURTEENTH AMENDMENT OF THE CONSTITUTION BILL, 1992, proposes to amend Article 40 of the Constitution by the addition of the paragraph here following to subsection 3° of section 3 thereof:
"This subsection shall not limit freedom to obtain or make available, in the State, subject to such conditions as may be laid down by law, information relating to services lawfully available in another state".'
(This statement was prescribed by the Referendum (Amendment) (No. 2) Act, 1992).
The total number of votes recorded in favour of the proposal was 992,833 and the total number recorded against the proposal was 665,106. As the proposal was duly approved by the people, the Bill was signed by the President on 23rd December 1992 and promulgated as a law.

Referendum on Dissolution of Marriage (1995)
(Fifteenth Amendment of the Constitution (No. 2) Bill, 1995)

Polling at the referendum took place on Friday, 24th November 1995 between the hours of 9 a.m. and 10 p.m.
The subject matter of the referendum was described as follows in the official polling card sent to each elector:
'THE FIFTEENTH AMENDMENT OF THE CONSTITUTION (NO. 2) BILL, 1995, proposes to substitute the subsection here following for subsection 2° of Article 41.3 of the Constitution:
"2° A Court designated by law may grant a dissolution of marriage where, but only where, it is satisfied that -
i. at the date of the institution of the proceedings, the spouses have lived apart from one another for a period of, or periods amounting to, at least four years during the previous five years,
ii there is no reasonable prospect of reconciliation between the spouses,
iii such provision as the Court considers proper having regard to the circumstances exists or will be made for the spouses, any children of either or both of them and any other person prescribed by law, and
iv any further conditions prescribed by law are compiled with." .'
The total number of votes recorded in favour of the proposal was 818,842 and the total number of votes recorded against the proposal was 809,728. As the proposal was duly approved by the people, the Bill was signed by the President on 17th June 1996 and promulgated as a law.

Referendum on Bail (1996)
(Sixteenth Amendment of the Constitution Bill, 1996)

Polling at the referendum took place on Thursday, 28th November 1996 between the hours of 9 a.m. and 9 p.m.
The subject matter of the referendum was described as follows in the official polling card sent to each elector:
'THE SIXTEENTH AMENDMENT OF THE CONSTITUTION BILL, 1996, proposes to add the following subsection to section 4 of Article 40 of the Constitution:
"7° Provision may be made by law for the refusal of bail by a court to a person charged with a serious offence where it is reasonably considered necessary to prevent the commission of a serious offence by that person." .'
The total number of votes recorded in favour of the proposal was 579,740 and the total number of votes recorded against the proposal was 194,968. As the proposal was duly approved by the people, the Bill was signed by the President on 12th December 1996 and promulgated as a law.

Referendum on Cabinet Confidentiality (1997)
(Seventeenth Amendment of the Constitution (No. 2) Bill, 1997)

Polling at the referendum, which was held in conjunction with a Presidential Election, took place on Thursday 30th October 1997 between the hours of 9 a.m. and 9 p.m.
The subject matter of the referendum was described as follows in the official polling card sent to each elector:
'THE SEVENTEENTH AMENDMENT OF THE CONSTITUTION (NO. 2) BILL, 1997, proposes to insert the following subsection after subsection 2° of section 4 of Article 28 of the Constitution:
"3° The confidentiality of discussions at meetings of the Government shall be respected in all circumstances save only where the High Court determines that disclosure should be made in respect of a particular matter -
i. in the interests of the administration of justice by a Court, or
ii. by virtue of an overriding public interest, pursuant to an application in that behalf by a tribunal appointed by the Government or a Minister of the Government on the authority of the Houses of the Oireachtas to inquire into a matter stated by them to be of public importance.".'
The total number of votes recorded in favour of the proposal was 632,777 and the total number of votes recorded against the proposal was 569,175. As the proposal was duly approved by the people, the Bill was signed by the President on 14th November 1997 and promulgated as a law.

Referendum on Treaty of Amsterdam (1998)
(Eighteenth Amendment of the Constitution Bill, 1998)

Polling at the referendum took place on Friday, 22nd May 1998 between the hours of 8 a.m. and 10 p.m. A referendum on the British-Irish Agreement took place on the same day. The following prescribed statement for the information of voters on the subject matter of the referendum was included in a leaflet sent to each elector:
'GREEN BALLOT PAPER – TREATY OF AMSTERDAM
THE EIGHTEENTH AMENDMENT OF THE CONSTITUTION BILL, 1998, proposes to insert the following subsections after subsection 4° of section 4 of Article 29 of the Constitution:
"5° The State may ratify the Treaty of Amsterdam amending the Treaty on European Union, the Treaties establishing the European Communities and certain related Acts signed at Amsterdam on the 2nd day of October, 1997.
6° The State may exercise the options or discretions provided by or under Articles 1.11, 2.5 and 2.15 of the Treaty referred to in subsection 5° of this section and the second and fourth Protocols set out in the said Treaty but any such exercise shall be subject to the prior approval of both Houses of the Oireachtas.".'
The total number of votes recorded in favour of the proposal was 932,632 and the total number of votes recorded against the proposal was 578,070. As the proposal was duly approved by the people, the Bill was signed by the President on 3rd June 1998 and promulgated as a law.

Referendum on British-Irish Agreement (1998)
(Nineteenth Amendment of the Constitution Bill, 1998)

Polling at the referendum took place on Friday, 22nd May 1998 between the hours of 8 a.m. and 10 p.m. A referendum on the Treaty of Amsterdam took place on the same day. A prescribed statement for the information of voters on the subject matter of the referendum was included in a leaflet sent to each elector.
The total number of votes recorded in favour of the proposal was 1,442,583 and the total number of votes recorded against the proposal was 85,748. As the proposal was duly approved by the people, the Bill was signed by the President on 3rd June 1998 and promulgated as a law.

Referendum on Local Government (1999)
(Twentieth Amendment of the Constitution (No. 2) Bill, 1999)

Polling at the referendum took place on Friday, 11th June 1999 between the hours of 8 a.m. and 9 p.m. Elections to the European Parliament and to local authorities took place on the same day.
The subject matter of the referendum was described as follows in the official polling card sent to each elector: 'THE TWENTIETH AMENDMENT OF THE CONSTITUTION (No. 2) BILL, 1999, proposes to insert the following Article after Article 28 of the Constitution:
"LOCAL GOVERNMENT Article 28A
1. The State recognises the role of local government in providing a forum for the democratic representation of local communities, in exercising and performing at local level powers and functions conferred by law and in promoting by its initiatives the interests of such communities.
2. There shall be such directly elected local authorities as may be determined by law and their powers and functions shall, subject to the provisions of this Constitution, be so determined and shall be exercised and performed in accordance with law.
3. Elections for members of such local authorities shall be held in accordance with law not later than the end of the fifth year after the year in which they were last held.
4. Every citizen who has the right to vote at an election for members of Dáil Éireann and such other persons as may be determined by law shall have the right to vote at an election for members of such of the local authorities referred to in *section 2* of this Article as shall be determined by law.
5. Casual vacancies in the membership of local authorities referred to in *section 2* of this Article shall be filled in accordance with law.".'
The total number of votes recorded in favour of the proposal was 1,024,850 and the total number of votes recorded against the proposal was 291,965. As the proposal was duly approved by the people, the Bill was signed by the President on 23rd June 1999 and promulgated as a law.

Prohibition of Death Penalty (2001)
(The Twenty-first Amendment of the Constitution (No. 2) Bill, 2001) 7th June 2001

The Twenty-first Amendment of the Constitution (No. 2) Bill, 2001, proposes to make the following amendments to the Constitution:
In Article 13.6, to delete ", except in capital cases,";
In Article 15.5, to insert the following subsection:
"2° The Oireachtas shall not enact any law providing for the imposition of the death penalty.";
In Article 28.3.3°, to insert "other than Article 15.5.2°" after "Constitution";
In Article 40.4, to delete subsection 5°.
The total number of votes recorded in favour of the proposal was 610,455 and the total number of votes recorded against the proposal was 372,950. As the proposal was duly approved by the people, the Bill was signed by the President and promulgated as a law.

International Criminal Court (2001)
(The Twenty-third Amendment of the Constitution Bill, 2001) 7th June 2001

The Twenty-third Amendment of the Constitution Bill, 2001, proposes to insert the following section after section 8 of Article 29 of the Constitution:
"9 The State may ratify the Rome Statute of the International Criminal Court done at Rome on the 17th day of July, 1998.".
The total number of votes recorded in favour of the proposal was 629,234 and the total number of votes recorded against the proposal was 350,512. As the proposal was duly approved by the people, the Bill was signed by the President and promulgated as a law.

Treaty of Nice (2001)
(The Twenty-fourth Amendment of the Constitution Bill, 2001) 7th June 2001

The Twenty-fourth Amendment of the Constitution Bill, 2001, proposes to insert the following subsections after subsection 6° of section 4 of Article 29 of the Constitution:
"7° The State may ratify the Treaty of Nice amending the Treaty on European Union, the Treaties establishing the European Communities and certain related Acts signed at Nice on the 26th day of February, 2001.
8° The State may exercise the options or discretions provided by or under Articles 1.6, 1.9, 1.11, 1.12, 1.13 and 2.1 of the Treaty referred to in subsection 7° of this section but any such exercise shall be subject to the prior approval of both Houses of the Oireachtas".
The total number of votes recorded in favour of the proposal was 453,461 and the total number recorded against the proposal was 529,478. The proposal was not, therefore, approved by the people.

Protection of Human life in Pregnancy (2002)
(The 25th Amendment of the Constitution Bill 2002) 6th March 2002

1. The Twenty-fifth Amendment of the Constitution (Protection of Human Life in Pregnancy) Bill, 2001, proposes to insert the following section after section 5 of Article 46 of the Constitution:
"6 1°Notwithstanding the foregoing provisions of this Article, Article 40 of this Constitution shall be amended as follows:
The following subsections shall be added to section 3 of the English text:
'4° In particular, the life of the unborn in the womb shall be protected in accordance with the provisions of the Protection of Human Life in Pregnancy Act, 2002.
5° The provisions of section 2 of Article 46 and sections 1, 3 and 4 of Article 47 of this Constitution shall apply to any Bill passed or deemed to have been passed by both Houses of the Oireachtas containing a proposal to amend the Protection of Human Life in Pregnancy Act, 2002, as they apply to a Bill containing a proposal or proposals for the amendment of this Constitution and any such Bill shall be signed by the President forthwith upon his being satisfied that the Bill has been duly approved by the people in accordance with the provisions of section 1 of Article 47 of this Constitution and shall be duly promulgated by the President as a law.'
2° If a law, containing only the provisions set out in An Dara Sceideal – The Second Schedule to the Twenty-fifth Amendment of the Constitution (Protection of Human Life in Pregnancy) Act, 2001, is enacted by the Oireachtas, this section, other than the amendment of Article 40 of this Constitution effected thereby, shall be omitted from every official text of this Constitution published thereafter, but notwithstanding such omission this section shall continue to have the force of law.
3°
If such a law is not so enacted within 180 days of this section being added to this Constitution, this section shall cease to have effect and shall be omitted from every official text of this Constitution published thereafter.
4°
The provisions of Articles 26 and 27 of this Constitution shall not apply to the Bill for such a law."
The total number of votes recorded in favour of the proposal was 618,485 and the total number recorded against the proposal was 629,478. The proposal was not, therefore, approved by the people.

Treaty of Nice (2001)
(The Twenty-sixth Amendment of the Constitution Bill, 2002) 19th October 2002

1. Twenty-sixth Amendment of the Constitution Bill 2002 (Treaty of Nice) proposes in insert after subsection 6 of section 4 of article 29
   - 7° The State may ratify the Treaty of Nice amending the Treaty on European Union, the Treaties establishing the European Communities and certain related Acts signed at Nice on the 26th day of February 2001.
   - 8° The State may exercise the options or discretions provided by or under articles 1.6, 1.9, 1.11, 1.12, 1.13 and 2.1 of the Treaty referred to in subsection 7° of this section but any such exercise shall be subject to the prior approval of both Houses of the Oireachtas.
   - 9° The State shall not adopt a decision taken by the European Council to establish a common defence pursuant to Article 1.2 of the Treaty referred to in subsection 7° of this section where that common defence would include the State.

The total number of votes recorded in favour of the proposal was 906,317 and the total number of votes recorded against the proposal was 534,887. As the proposal was duly approved by the people, the Bill was signed by the President and promulgated as a law.

Referendum on Citizenship (2004)
(The Twenty-seventh Amendment of the Constitution Bill, 2004) 11th June 2004

1. The twenty-seventh Amendment of the Constitution Bill 2004 proposes to insert after section 2 of article 9
   - 1° Notwithstanding any other provision of this Constitution, a person born in the island of Ireland, which includes its islands and seas, who does not have, at the time of the birth of that person, at least one parent who is an Irish citizen or entitled to be an Irish citizen is not entitled to Irish citizenship or nationality, unless provided by law.
   - 2° This section shall not apply to persons born before the date of the enactment of this section.

The total number of votes recorded in favour of the proposal was 1,427,520 and the total number of votes recorded against the proposal was 375,695. As the proposal was duly approved by the people, the Bill was signed by the President and promulgated as a law.

Treaty of Lisbon (2008)
(The Twenty-eighth Amendment of the Constitution Bill, 2008) 12th June 2008

1. Twenty-eighth Amendment of the Constitution Bill 2008 (Treaty of Lisbon) proposes to amend article 29 as follows
   - 10° The State may ratify the Treaty of Lisbon amending the Treaty on European Union and the Treaties establishing the European Communities, signed at Lisbon on the 13th day of December 2007, and may be a member of the European Union established by virtue of that Treaty.

The total number of votes recorded in favour of the proposal was 752,451 and the total number of votes recorded against the proposal was 862,415. The proposal was not, therefore, approved by the people.

Treaty of Lisbon (2008)
(The Twenty-eighth Amendment of the Constitution Bill, 2008) 2nd October 2009

1. Twenty-eighth Amendment of the Constitution Bill 2008 (Treaty of Lisbon) proposes to amend article 29 as follows
   - 10° The State may ratify the Treaty of Lisbon amending the Treaty on European Union and the Treaties establishing the European Communities, signed at Lisbon on the 13th day of December 2007, and may be a member of the European Union established by virtue of that Treaty.

The total number of votes recorded in favour of the proposal was 1,214,268 and the total number of votes recorded against the proposal was 594,606. As the proposal was duly approved by the people, the Bill was signed by the President and promulgated as a law.

Referendum on Judges' Pay (2011)
(The Twenty-ninth Amendment of the Constitution Bill, 2011) 27th October 2011

1. The twenty-ninth Amendment of the Constitution Bill 2011 proposes to replace article 35.5 with
   - 5.1° The remuneration of judges shall not be reduced during their continuance in office save in accordance with this section.
   - 2° The remuneration of judges is subject to the imposition of taxes, levies or other charges that are imposed by law on persons generally or persons belonging to a particular class.
   - 3° Where, before or after the enactment of this section, reductions have been or are made by law to the remuneration of persons belonging to classes of persons whose remuneration is paid out of public money and such law states that those reductions are in the public interest, provision may also be made by law to make proportionate reductions to the remuneration of judges.

The total number of votes recorded in favour of the proposal was 1,393,877 and the total number of votes recorded against the proposal was 354,134. As the proposal was duly approved by the people, the Bill was signed by the President and promulgated as a law.

Referendum on Oireachtas Inquiries (2011)
(The Thirtieth Amendment of the Constitution Bill, 2011) 27th October 2011

1. The thirtieth Amendment of the Constitution Bill 2011 proposes to renumber article 15.10 as 15.10. 1° and to insert the following subsections
   - 2° Each House shall have the power to conduct an inquiry, or an inquiry with the other house, in a manner provided by law, into any matter stated by the House or Houses concerned to be of general public importance.
   - 3° In the course of any such inquiry the conduct of any person (whether or not a member of either House) may be investigated and the House or Houses concerned may make findings in respect of the conduct of that person concerning the matter to which the inquiry relates.
   - 4° It shall be for the House or Houses concerned to determine, with due regard to the principles of fair procedures, the appropriate balance between the rights of persons and the public interest for the purposes of ensuring an effective inquiry into any matter to which subsection 2° applies.

The total number of votes recorded in favour of the proposal was 812,008 and the total number of votes recorded against the proposal was 928,175. The proposal was not, therefore, approved by the people.

PART 9

INDEXES

INDEX 1: ALL DAIL CANDIDATES 2011

	Candidate	Party	Constituency	1st Prefs	%	Quota	M/F	Count	Status	Spending
2	Adams, Gerry	SF	Louth	15,072	21.74%	1.09	M	1	Made Quota	20,895.98
13	Adams, John	CPPC	Cork North Central	282	0.54%	0.03	M	2	No Expenses	0.00
13	Adebari, Rotimi	NP	Laois-Offaly	628	0.85%	0.05	M	5	No Expenses	5,457.45
8	Ahern, Michael*	FF	Cork East	4,618	8.11%	0.41	M	3	Eliminated	9,711.67
7	Andrews, Barry*	FF	Dun Laoghaire	3,542	6.25%	0.31	M	7	Eliminated	23,345.09
5	Andrews, Chris*	FF	Dublin South East	3,922	11.23%	0.56	M	10	Not Elected	20,291.38
14	Ashu-Arrah, Benjamin	NP	Cork North Central	161	0.31%	0.02	M	1	No Expenses	417.54
6	Aylward, Bobby*	FF	Carlow-Kilkenny	6,762	9.17%	0.55	M	13	Not Elected	12,472.03
6	Bacik, Ivana	LB	Dun Laoghaire	5,749	10.14%	0.51	F	9	Eliminated	24,479.19
9	Ball, Stephen	NP	Meath West	475	1.18%	0.05	M	1	No Expenses	195.00
2	Bannon, James*	FG	Longford-Westmeath	9,129	15.87%	0.79	M	6	Made Quota	13,619.54
2	Barrett, Sean*	FG	Dun Laoghaire	10,504	18.53%	0.93	M	8	Made Quota	19,110.34
7	Barry, Mick	SP	Cork North Central	4,803	9.21%	0.46	M	8	Eliminated	14,735.75
3	Barry, Tom	FG	Cork East	5,798	10.18%	0.51	M	7	Made Quota	21,881.66
9	Behal, Richard	NP	Kerry South	348	0.78%	0.03	M	1	No Expenses	5,199.67
9	Behan, Joe*	NP	Wicklow	4,197	5.95%	0.36	M	14	Eliminated	10,580.52
11	Beirne, Michael	NP	Kildare North	422	0.82%	0.04	M	1	No Expenses	0.00
17	Bennett, Noel	NP	Dublin South Central	128	0.25%	0.02	M	2	No Expenses	0.00
8	Blaney, Dara	NV	Donegal North East	1,228	3.24%	0.13	M	4	No Expenses	4,004.20
6	Blaney, Eamon	NV	Dublin North East	1,773	4.24%	0.17	M	7	Eliminated	8,650.53
20	Boland, John	NP	Laois-Offaly	119	0.16%	0.01	M	1	No Expenses	3,353.49
11	Boland, John	NP	Longford-Westmeath	330	0.57%	0.03	M	1	No Expenses	3,842.74
6	Bonner, Joe	NP	Meath East	2,479	5.80%	0.23	M	3	Eliminated	10,570.80
8	Bopp, Kate	NP	Tipperary North	322	0.67%	0.03	F	2	No Expenses	510.00
4	Boyd Barrett, Richard	PBPA	Dun Laoghaire	6,206	10.95%	0.55	M	11	Elected	12,811.64
9	Boyhan, Victor	NP	Dun Laoghaire	834	1.47%	0.07	M	5	No Expenses	12,168.20
10	Boyle, Dan #	GP	Cork South Central	1,640	2.56%	0.15	M	6	No Expenses	6,300.25
14	Bracken, John	NP	Laois-Offaly	625	0.84%	0.05	M	5	No Expenses	3,719.69
16	Bradley, David	NP	Louth	174	0.25%	0.01	M	4	No Expenses	0.00
12	Bradley, Neville	NP	Dublin South Central	323	0.63%	0.04	M	7	No Expenses	40.00
5	Brady, Aine*	FF	Kildare North	4,777	9.33%	0.47	F	5	Not Elected	20,466.26
7	Brady, Cyprian*	FF	Dublin Central	1,637	4.73%	0.24	M	5	Eliminated	18,972.01
6	Brady, John	SF	Wicklow	7,089	10.06%	0.60	M	19	Not Elected	14,288.21
5	Brady, Johnny*	FF	Meath West	3,789	9.43%	0.38	M	4	Eliminated	10,950.04
16	Brassil, Patrick	NP	Clare	175	0.30%	0.02	M	1	No Expenses	0.00
8	Breathnach, Declan	FF	Louth	5,177	7.47%	0.37	M	10	Eliminated	30,982.66
7	Bree, Declan #	NP	Sligo-North Leitrim	2,284	5.14%	0.21	M	5	Eliminated	9,042.72
4	Breen, Gerry	FG	Dublin North West	2,988	9.11%	0.36	M	7	Not Elected	18,143.66
5	Breen, James #	NP	Clare	6,491	11.21%	0.56	M	12	Not Elected	11,586.99
1	Breen, Pat*	FG	Clare	9,855	17.02%	0.85	M	11	Made Quota	22,245.26
6	Broderick, Tim	NP	Galway East	5,137	8.67%	0.43	M	7	Eliminated	13,608.65
14	Brolchain, Niall O	GP	Galway West	1,120	1.85%	0.11	M	2	No Expenses	8,894.31
7	Brophy, Colm	FG	Dublin South Central	3,376	6.63%	0.40	M	11	Eliminated	22,687.26
2	Broughan, Tommy*	LB	Dublin North East	10,006	23.92%	0.96	M	2	Made Quota	14,100.05
3	Browne, John*	FF	Wexford	7,352	9.73%	0.58	M	7	Made Quota	20,826.81
7	Browne, Michael	SF	Tipperary South	1,860	4.50%	0.18	M	1	No Expenses	6,608.15
1	Bruton, Richard*	FG	Dublin North Central	9,685	24.98%	1.00	M	2	Made Quota	14,354.15
12	Bulman, Patrick	CPPC	Cork East	212	0.37%	0.02	M	2	No Expenses	0.00
9	Burke, Christy	NP	Dublin Central	1,315	3.80%	0.19	M	3	No Expenses	4,622.20
13	Burke, Paul	NP	Cork East	176	0.31%	0.02	M	2	No Expenses	423.49
5	Burke, Peter	FG	Longford-Westmeath	6,629	11.52%	0.58	M	8	Not Elected	15,413.99
1	Burton, Joan*	LB	Dublin West	9,627	22.67%	1.13	F	1	Made Quota	23,402.65
5	Burton, Pat	FG	Cork North Central	7,072	13.56%	0.68	M	11	Not Elected	23,802.31
11	Butler, Edmund	NP	Cork South West	330	0.72%	0.03	M	1	No Expenses	0.00
3	Butler, Ray	FG	Meath West	5,262	13.10%	0.52	M	5	Elected	20,115.58
4	Buttimer, Jerry	FG	Cork South Central	7,128	11.13%	0.67	M	11	Made Quota	18,751.88
2	Byrne, Catherine*	FG	Dublin South Central	5,604	11.00%	0.66	F	12	Made Quota	13,635.70
1	Byrne, Eric	LB	Dublin South Central	8,357	16.41%	0.98	M	8	Made Quota	15,951.00
13	Byrne, Niall	GP	Wicklow	1,026	1.46%	0.09	M	11	No Expenses	4,120.78
4	Byrne, Thomas*	FF	Meath East	5,715	13.37%	0.53	M	4	Not Elected	17,918.57
13	Cahill, Dick	NP	Sligo-North Leitrim	102	0.23%	0.01	M	1	No Expenses	0.00
10	Cahill, Sheila	GP	Limerick City	490	1.13%	0.06	F	3	No Expenses	888.51
13	Callanan, Colm	CS	Dublin South Central	239	0.47%	0.03	M	6	No Expenses	1,401.16
4	Calleary, Dara*	FF	Mayo	8,577	11.57%	0.69	M	8	Made Quota	25,282.77
7	Canney, Sean	NP	Galway East	5,567	9.39%	0.47	M	6	Eliminated	21,131.37
3	Cannon, Ciaran	FG	Galway East	6,927	11.69%	0.58	M	8	Made Quota	17,021.22
5	Canty, Derry	FG	Cork North West	4,325	9.46%	0.38	M	4	Eliminated	12,539.04
3	Carey, Joe*	FG	Clare	7,840	13.54%	0.68	M	12	Made Quota	22,438.26
12	Carey, John	GP	Mayo	266	0.36%	0.02	M	3	No Expenses	1,269.37
5	Carey, Pat*	FF	Dublin North West	3,869	11.79%	0.47	M	6	Eliminated	22,156.35
11	Carolan, Ronan	NP	Meath West	258	0.64%	0.03	M	1	No Expenses	0.00
6	Carroll, James	FF	Louth	5,681	8.20%	0.41	M	13	Not Elected	23,846.94
24	Carroll, Kevin	NP	Wicklow	74	0.10%	0.01	M	1	No Expenses	603.79
7	Cassells, Shane	FF	Meath West	3,496	8.70%	0.35	M	2	Eliminated	17,457.51
10	Cassin, John	SF	Carlow-Kilkenny	2,958	4.01%	0.24	M	8	Eliminated	7,439.26
9	Cawley, Veronica	NP	Sligo-North Leitrim	1,119	2.52%	0.10	F	3	No Expenses	11,162.22
9	Chambers, Lisa	FF	Mayo	3,343	4.51%	0.27	F	5	Eliminated	12,770.11
6	Clancy, Aine	LB	Dublin Central	3,514	10.15%	0.51	F	6	Eliminated	20,489.40
6	Clancy, Billy	NV	Tipperary North	1,442	2.99%	0.12	M	2	No Expenses	6,289.50
10	Clare, Thomas	NV	Louth	2,233	3.22%	0.16	M	8	No Expenses	9,247.00
13	Clarke, Loretta	NP	Mayo	218	0.29%	0.02	F	3	No Expenses	2,110.16

	Candidate	Party	Constituency	1st Prefs	%	Quota	M/F	Count	Status	Spending
8	Clarke, Michael	NP	Sligo-North Leitrim	2,415	5.44%	0.22	M	4	No Expenses	23,919.25
9	Clarke, Paul	NP	Dublin North Central	331	0.85%	0.03	M	1	No Expenses	1,635.75
23	Clarke, Thomas	NP	Wicklow	103	0.15%	0.01	M	2	No Expenses	335.00
7	Clune, Deirdre*	FG	Cork South Central	5,650	8.82%	0.53	F	10	Eliminated	21,552.48
9	Cody, Pat	LB	Wexford	4,457	5.90%	0.35	M	3	Eliminated	14,798.08
2	Coffey, Paudie	FG	Waterford	9,698	18.05%	0.90	M	9	Made Quota	13,516.08
9	Collery, Justin	NP	Waterford	967	1.80%	0.09	M	7	No Expenses	7,291.41
3	Collins, Aine	FG	Cork North West	7,884	17.24%	0.69	F	6	Elected	17,953.40
4	Collins, Joan	PBPA	Dublin South Central	6,574	12.91%	0.77	F	13	Elected	10,789.39
9	Collins, Mark	GP	Cork North West	651	1.42%	0.06	M	1	No Expenses	1,751.68
3	Collins, Niall*	FF	Limerick	9,361	20.78%	0.83	M	4	Elected	18,501.33
3	Colreavy, Michael	SF	Sligo-North Leitrim	5,911	13.30%	0.53	M	9	Elected	15,876.00
8	Comerford, Oonagh	GP	Kerry South	401	0.90%	0.04	F	1	No Expenses	624.18
3	Conaghan, Michael	LB	Dublin South Central	5,492	10.78%	0.65	M	13	Made Quota	21,401.01
4	Conlan, Sean	FG	Cavan-Monaghan	7,864	11.03%	0.66	M	9	Elected	12,036.53
7	Conlon, Margaret*	FF	Cavan-Monaghan	4,658	6.54%	0.39	F	7	Eliminated	18,510.89
4	Connaughton, Ivan	FF	Roscommon-South Leitrim	4,070	8.57%	0.34	M	6	Not Elected	17,443.24
2	Connaughton, Paul	FG	Galway East	7,255	12.24%	0.61	M	8	Made Quota	11,643.05
7	Connick, Sean*	FF	Wexford	6,675	8.84%	0.53	M	6	Eliminated	25,600.59
14	Connolly Farrell, Sean	NP	Dublin South Central	178	0.35%	0.02	M	5	No Expenses	0.00
6	Connolly, Catherine	NP	Galway West	4,766	7.86%	0.47	F	13	Not Elected	15,360.11
11	Connolly, Dermot	SF	Galway East	3,635	6.13%	0.31	M	2	Eliminated	8,801.92
10	Connolly, Jim	NP	Clare	978	1.69%	0.08	M	6	No Expenses	7,075.53
10	Connolly, Rob	SP	Dublin Mid-West	622	1.46%	0.07	M	5	No Expenses	9,215.37
3	Conway, Ciara	LB	Waterford	5,554	10.34%	0.52	F	10	Made Quota	13,894.67
11	Conway, Joe	NP	Waterford	725	1.35%	0.07	M	5	No Expenses	2,086.50
9	Conway, Kevin	NP	Cork North Central	958	1.84%	0.09	M	6	No Expenses	1,277.61
8	Conway-Walsh, Rose	SF	Mayo	2,660	3.59%	0.22	F	6	Eliminated	7,703.59
2	Coonan, Noel*	FG	Tipperary North	11,425	23.67%	0.95	M	2	Made Quota	26,406.67
16	Cooney, Benny	NP	Dublin Central	25	0.07%	0.00	M	1	No Expenses	0.00
14	Cooney, Benny	NP	Longford-Westmeath	130	0.23%	0.01	M	1	No Expenses	1,884.77
8	Cooney, Donna	GP	Dublin North Central	501	1.29%	0.05	F	1	No Expenses	1,295.76
2	Corcoran Kennedy, Marcella	FG	Laois-Offaly	5,817	7.84%	0.47	F	13	Made Quota	16,351.27
6	Corrigan, Maria	FF	Dublin South	6,844	9.42%	0.57	F	8	Not Elected	33,545.11
2	Costello, Joe*	LB	Dublin Central	6,273	18.12%	0.91	M	5	Made Quota	18,987.30
14	Couchman, Johnny	NP	Carlow-Kilkenny	384	0.52%	0.03	M	5	No Expenses	3,129.00
4	Coughlan, Martin	LB	Cork North West	6,421	14.04%	0.56	M	6	Not Elected	11,619.19
5	Coughlan, Mary*	FF	Donegal South West	4,956	11.46%	0.46	F	4	Eliminated	11,607.01
3	Coveney, Simon*	FG	Cork South Central	9,447	14.75%	0.89	M	10	Made Quota	19,107.20
3	Cowen, Barry	FF	Laois-Offaly	8,257	11.13%	0.67	M	13	Elected	18,524.24
7	Cowley,Dr. Jerry #	LB	Mayo	3,644	4.91%	0.29	M	7	Eliminated	18,661.68
21	Cox, Michael	NP	Laois-Offaly	60	0.08%	0.00	M	1	No Expenses	0.00
13	Coyle, James	NP	Dublin South East	164	0.47%	0.02	M	1	No Expenses	7,284.20
13	Crawford, Nick	NV	Dun Laoghaire	394	0.70%	0.03	M	3	No Expenses	7,163.84
1	Creed, Michael*	FG	Cork North West	10,112	22.11%	0.88	M	5	Made Quota	13,155.94
2	Creighton, Lucinda*	FG	Dublin South East	6,619	18.96%	0.95	F	6	Made Quota	25,272.73
7	Cremin, Con	NP	Limerick	430	0.95%	0.04	M	1	No Expenses	780.00
15	Crilly, Gerry	NP	Louth	222	0.32%	0.02	M	5	No Expenses	331.38
12	Cronin, Ann	NP	Clare	419	0.72%	0.04	F	5	No Expenses	0.00
12	Crowe, Michael	FF	Galway West	1,814	2.99%	0.18	M	4	No Expenses	27,321.05
3	Crowe, Sean #	SF	Dublin South West	8,064	17.17%	0.86	M	6	Made Quota	15,498.98
15	Cubbard, Mike	NP	Galway West	853	1.41%	0.08	M	1	No Expenses	380.00
8	Cuffe, Ciaran*	GP	Dun Laoghaire	2,156	3.80%	0.19	M	6	No Expenses	27,038.49
1	Cuiv, Eamon O*	FF	Galway West	7,441	12.27%	0.74	M	8	Made Quota	15,401.10
8	Culhane, Aidan	LB	Dublin South	4,535	6.24%	0.37	M	5	Eliminated	16,955.31
11	Cullinane, Claire	CPPC	Cork East	510	0.90%	0.04	F	2	No Expenses	0.00
6	Cullinane, David	SF	Waterford	5,342	9.94%	0.50	M	9	Eliminated	10,621.83
8	Cummins, Vivian	GP	Kildare South	523	1.37%	0.05	M	3	No Expenses	964.45
6	Curran, John*	FF	Dublin Mid-West	5,043	11.80%	0.59	M	7	Eliminated	12,013.75
10	Curry, Nicola	PBPA	Dublin South	1,277	1.76%	0.11	F	3	No Expenses	1,460.00
19	Dalton, John	NP	Carlow-Kilkenny	70	0.09%	0.01	M	1	No Expenses	0.00
3	Daly, Clare	SP	Dublin North	7,513	15.22%	0.76	F	6	Made Quota	13,208.88
1	Daly, Jim	FG	Cork South West	8,878	19.44%	0.78	M	5	Made Quota	13,576.14
11	Daly, Martin	NV	Mayo	893	1.20%	0.07	M	3	No Expenses	20,769.09
13	D'Arcy, David	NV	Longford-Westmeath	159	0.28%	0.01	M	1	No Expenses	2,073.55
6	D'Arcy, Michael*	FG	Wexford	8,418	11.14%	0.67	M	7	Not Elected	18,050.94
14	De Valera, Ruairi	NP	Wexford	119	0.16%	0.01	M	2	No Expenses	1,460.00
9	Dearey, Mark	GP	Louth	3,244	4.68%	0.23	M	9	Eliminated	19,554.89
1	Deasy, John*	FG	Waterford	10,718	19.95%	1.00	M	3	Made Quota	19,565.22
14	Deegan, Mick	NP	Dun Laoghaire	311	0.55%	0.03	M	2	No Expenses	0.00
1	Deenihan, Jimmy*	FG	Kerry North-West Limerick	12,304	26.97%	1.08	M	1	Made Quota	15,508.54
5	Deering, Pat	FG	Carlow-Kilkenny	7,470	10.13%	0.61	M	13	Elected	24,108.14
12	Dempsey, Peter	NP	Wicklow	1,409	2.00%	0.12	M	11	No Expenses	5,017.20
6	Dennison, Kieran	FG	Dublin West	3,190	7.51%	0.38	M	4	Eliminated	19,644.42
8	Desmond, Paula	LB	Cork South Central	3,388	5.29%	0.32	F	8	Eliminated	14,164.59
5	Dillon, John	NP	Limerick	4,395	9.76%	0.39	M	3	Eliminated	18,025.83
1	Doherty, Pearse*	SF	Donegal South West	14,262	32.97%	1.32	M	1	Made Quota	13,848.16
2	Doherty, Regina	FG	Meath East	8,677	20.30%	0.81	F	4	Elected	17,701.60
14	Dolan, Gerard	NP	Dublin South	156	0.21%	0.01	M	2	No Expenses	1,702.10
10	Dolan, Michael F.	FF	Galway East	4,109	6.93%	0.35	M	3	Eliminated	19,751.41
7	Donnelly, Paul	SF	Dublin West	2,597	6.11%	0.31	M	3	Eliminated	8,372.96

	Candidate	Party	Constituency	1st Prefs	%	Quota	M/F	Count	Status	Spending
5	Donnelly, Stephen	NP	Wicklow	6,530	9.26%	0.56	M	19	Elected	31,050.48
1	Donohoe, Paschal	FG	Dublin Central	6,903	19.94%	1.00	M	2	Made Quota	15,098.41
10	Donovan, Tom	GP	Kerry North-West Limerick	239	0.52%	0.02	M	2	No Expenses	654.38
4	Dooley, Timmy*	FF	Clare	6,789	11.72%	0.59	M	12	Elected	11,637.35
12	Doonan, Paul	NV	Cork South West	239	0.52%	0.02	M	1	No Expenses	2,289.28
3	Dowds, Robert	LB	Dublin Mid-West	5,643	13.21%	0.66	M	9	Elected	24,227.83
1	Doyle, Andrew*	FG	Wicklow	10,035	14.23%	0.85	M	16	Made Quota	19,124.84
13	Doyle, John	NP	Dublin South	246	0.34%	0.02	M	2	No Expenses	200.00
10	Doyle-Higgins, Eric	NP	Kildare North	423	0.83%	0.04	M	1	No Expenses	0.00
10	Duffy, Francis	GP	Dublin South West	480	1.02%	0.05	M	3	No Expenses	1,681.55
8	Duffy, John	GP	Donegal South West	527	1.22%	0.05	M	2	No Expenses	724.86
14	Duffy, Joseph	NP	Cavan-Monaghan	129	0.18%	0.01	M	1	No Expenses	0.00
17	Dumpleton, Liam	NP	Laois-Offaly	382	0.52%	0.03	M	4	No Expenses	0.00
9	Dunne, John	WP	Dublin North West	345	1.05%	0.04	M	4	No Expenses	2,032.80
14	Dunphy, Sean	NP	Cork South Central	448	0.70%	0.04	M	3	No Expenses	741.15
1	Durkan, Bernard*	FG	Kildare North	10,168	19.85%	0.99	M	2	Made Quota	22,346.00
10	Dwyer, John	NP	Wexford	908	1.20%	0.07	M	2	No Expenses	4,496.79
11	Eastwood, Robert	NP	Dublin North East	242	0.58%	0.02	M	3	No Expenses	1,495.75
2	Ellis, Dessie	SF	Dublin North West	7,115	21.68%	0.87	M	7	Made Quota	11,143.63
1	English, Damien*	FG	Meath West	9,290	23.12%	0.92	M	3	Made Quota	12,890.25
10	Esebamen, Clement	NP	Dublin West	280	0.66%	0.03	M	2	No Expenses	1,250.00
9	Fahey, Frank*	FF	Galway West	3,448	5.69%	0.34	M	7	Eliminated	21,540.15
18	Fanning, James	NP	Laois-Offaly	335	0.45%	0.03	M	3	No Expenses	11,636.75
4	Farrell, Alan	FG	Dublin North	5,310	10.76%	0.54	M	7	Elected	21,859.09
2	Feighan, Frank*	FG	Roscommon-South Leitrim	8,983	18.91%	0.76	M	6	Made Quota	13,694.96
14	Ferrigan, Sarah	NP	Clare	252	0.44%	0.02	M	3	No Expenses	0.00
4	Ferris, Anne	LB	Wicklow	5,436	7.71%	0.46	F	19	Elected	14,804.80
3	Ferris, Martin*	SF	Kerry North-West Limerick	9,282	20.35%	0.81	M	7	Made Quota	13,927.13
19	Fettes, Christopher	GP	Laois-Offaly	306	0.41%	0.02	M	2	No Expenses	0.00
10	Finn, Dermot	NP	Kerry South	281	0.63%	0.03	M	1	No Expenses	0.00
9	Finn, Mick	NP	Cork South Central	2,386	3.73%	0.22	M	7	Eliminated	8,445.44
18	Finnegan, Eugene	NP	Wicklow	286	0.41%	0.02	M	7	No Expenses	2,444.38
9	Finnegan, Mick	WP	Dublin Mid-West	694	1.62%	0.08	M	5	No Expenses	3,519.80
21	Fitzgerald, Anthony	NP	Wicklow	184	0.26%	0.02	M	4	No Expenses	6,115.85
12	Fitzgerald, Daire	CS	Dun Laoghaire	434	0.77%	0.04	M	4	No Expenses	2,977.20
2	Fitzgerald, Frances	FG	Dublin Mid-West	7,281	17.04%	0.85	F	8	Made Quota	19,081.88
7	Fitzgerald, Pat	FF	Wicklow	3,576	5.07%	0.30	M	16	Eliminated	17,766.62
9	Fitzgerald, Shane	GP	Kildare North	905	1.77%	0.09	M	1	No Expenses	3,755.40
7	Fitzgibon, Mary	NP	Kerry North-West Limerick	706	1.55%	0.06	F	4	No Expenses	2,734.95
12	Fitzpatrick, Eddie	NP	Laois-Offaly	2,544	3.43%	0.21	M	6	No Expenses	18,665.94
5	Fitzpatrick, Mary	FF	Dublin Central	3,504	10.12%	0.51	F	8	Not Elected	18,534.47
8	Fitzpatrick, Michael*	FF	Kildare North	2,659	5.19%	0.26	M	2	Eliminated	22,976.44
5	Fitzpatrick, Peter	FG	Louth	7,845	11.32%	0.57	M	13	Elected	33,428.34
15	Fitzpatrick, Ray	SP	Laois-Offaly	561	0.76%	0.05	M	5	No Expenses	3,120.00
1	Flanagan, Charles*	FG	Laois-Offaly	10,427	14.06%	0.84	M	8	Made Quota	15,445.34
1	Flanagan, Luke "Ming"	NV	Roscommon-South Leitrim	8,925	18.79%	0.75	M	4	Made Quota	15,818.12
1	Flanagan, Terence*	FG	Dublin North East	12,332	29.47%	1.18	M	1	Made Quota	12,303.91
5	Fleming, Sean*	FF	Laois-Offaly	6,024	8.12%	0.49	M	13	Elected	14,095.45
2	Fleming, Tom	NP	Kerry South	6,416	14.46%	0.58	M	6	Elected	20,677.38
10	Flynn, Mannix	NP	Dublin South East	1,248	3.57%	0.18	M	2	No Expenses	13,694.55
8	Foley, Anne	PBPA	Cork North West	1,552	3.39%	0.14	F	1	No Expenses	1,760.00
7	Foley, John	NP	Laois-Offaly	4,465	6.02%	0.36	M	12	Eliminated	12,026.85
11	Forde, Caroline	NP	Cavan-Monaghan	1,912	2.68%	0.16	F	3	No Expenses	17,642.00
12	Forde, Danny	GP	Wexford	391	0.52%	0.03	M	2	No Expenses	1,264.72
15	Forkin, Sean	NP	Mayo	29	0.04%	0.00	M	3	No Expenses	0.00
8	Fortune, Tom	LB	Wicklow	3,420	4.85%	0.29	M	15	Eliminated	23,282.77
7	Funchion, Kathleen	SF	Carlow-Kilkenny	4,075	5.53%	0.33	F	11	Eliminated	7,270.03
5	Gallagher, Michael	SF	Meath East	3,795	8.88%	0.36	M	3	Eliminated	9,483.80
1	Gilmore, Eamon*	LB	Dun Laoghaire	11,468	20.23%	1.01	M	1	Made Quota	20,358.16
6	Gilroy, John	LB	Cork North Central	6,125	11.75%	0.59	M	9	Eliminated	20,665.42
5	Gleeson, Michael	SKIA	Kerry South	4,939	11.13%	0.45	M	4	Eliminated	15,347.15
17	Glynn, Robert	NP	Louth	61	0.09%	0.00	M	2	No Expenses	0.00
12	Godfrey, Frank	NP	Louth	649	0.94%	0.05	M	7	No Expenses	1,080.00
12	Gogan, Johnny	GP	Sligo-North Leitrim	432	0.97%	0.04	M	1	No Expenses	1,309.59
8	Gogarty, Paul*	GP	Dublin Mid-West	1,484	3.47%	0.17	M	6	No Expenses	11,771.93
7	Gormley, John*	GP	Dublin South East	2,370	6.79%	0.34	M	5	Eliminated	26,204.38
4	Grealish, Noel*	NP	Galway West	6,229	10.27%	0.62	M	13	Elected	39,164.98
9	Greene, Brian	SP	Dublin North East	869	2.08%	0.08	M	4	No Expenses	3,088.33
1	Griffin, Brendan	FG	Kerry South	8,808	19.85%	0.79	M	5	Made Quota	23,240.06
7	Guerin, Jimmy	NP	Dublin North East	1,283	3.07%	0.12	M	6	No Expenses	13,899.24
4	Halligan, John	NP	Waterford	5,546	10.32%	0.52	M	11	Elected	10,762.38
5	Hanafin, Mary*	FF	Dun Laoghaire	5,090	8.98%	0.45	F	11	Not Elected	17,950.46
1	Hannigan, Dominic	LB	Meath East	8,994	21.04%	0.84	M	4	Made Quota	14,780.18
2	Harrington, Noel	FG	Cork South West	6,898	15.11%	0.60	M	6	Elected	13,010.54
3	Harris, Simon	FG	Wicklow	8,726	12.38%	0.74	M	19	Elected	28,490.83
9	Harrold, Mark	NP	Dublin North	1,512	3.06%	0.15	M	2	No Expenses	3,816.95
4	Harte, Jimmy	LB	Donegal North East	4,090	10.79%	0.43	M	9	Not Elected	24,491.37
10	Harty, Malachy	GP	Cork East	635	1.12%	0.06	M	2	No Expenses	327.07
8	Haskins, Dylan	NP	Dublin South East	1,383	3.96%	0.20	M	4	Eliminated	11,632.74
5	Haughey, Sean*	FF	Dublin North Central	5,017	12.94%	0.52	M	6	Eliminated	20,185.84
10	Haughton, Carl	NP	Dun Laoghaire	456	0.80%	0.04	M	5	No Expenses	8,674.03

	Candidate	Party	Constituency	1st Prefs	%	Quota	M/F	Count	Status	Spending
2	Hayes, Brian*	FG	Dublin South West	9,366	19.94%	1.00	M	2	Made Quota	16,545.35
7	Hayes, Paul	SF	Cork South West	3,346	7.33%	0.29	M	2	Eliminated	4,781.17
2	Hayes, Tom*	FG	Tipperary South	8,896	21.51%	0.86	M	4	Made Quota	12,978.30
7	Healy Eames, Fidelma	FG	Galway West	5,046	8.32%	0.50	F	11	Eliminated	16,942.78
3	Healy Rae, Michael	NP	Kerry South	6,670	15.03%	0.60	M	6	Elected	17,940.65
8	Healy, David	GP	Dublin North East	792	1.89%	0.08	M	5	No Expenses	2,360.59
1	Healy, Seamus #	ULA	Tipperary South	8,818	21.32%	0.85	M	3	Made Quota	12,739.26
4	Heffernan, James	LB	Limerick	7,910	17.56%	0.70	M	4	Not Elected	13,699.33
1	Heydon, Martin	FG	Kildare South	12,755	33.33%	1.33	M	1	Made Quota	25,518.57
3	Higgins, Joe #	SP	Dublin West	8,084	19.03%	0.95	M	3	Made Quota	11,073.65
9	Higgins, Lorrainne	LB	Galway East	3,577	6.03%	0.30	F	4	Eliminated	11,272.75
8	Higgins, Tom	NP	Waterford	1,130	2.10%	0.11	M	7	No Expenses	14,491.32
7	Hillery, Dr. John	FF	Clare	6,015	10.39%	0.52	M	9	Eliminated	18,736.16
4	Hoctor, Maire*	FF	Tipperary North	7,978	16.53%	0.66	F	3	Not Elected	21,092.38
8	Hogan, Liam	LB	Cavan-Monaghan	4,011	5.63%	0.34	M	6	Eliminated	16,586.55
6	Hogan, Paul	SF	Longford-Westmeath	4,339	7.54%	0.38	M	7	Eliminated	8,440.23
4	Hogan, Phil*	FG	Carlow-Kilkenny	10,525	14.27%	0.86	M	13	Elected	25,930.64
14	Hollywood, Thomas	NP	Dublin Central	65	0.19%	0.01	M	1	No Expenses	2,842.04
9	Holmes, Betty	NP	Donegal North East	1,150	3.03%	0.12	F	2	No Expenses	2,878.00
16	Holmes, Uinseann Eoin	NP	Galway West	186	0.31%	0.02	M	1	No Expenses	289.00
10	Holohan, Ruairi	GP	Dublin North West	328	1.00%	0.04	M	4	No Expenses	503.37
2	Howlin, Brendan*	LB	Wexford	11,005	14.57%	0.87	M	4	Made Quota	19,699.03
5	Humphreys, Heather	FG	Cavan-Monaghan	8,144	11.43%	0.69	F	9	Elected	12,330.03
4	Humphreys, Kevin	LB	Dublin South East	3,450	9.88%	0.49	M	10	Elected	20,764.58
9	Hurley, Des	LB	Carlow-Kilkenny	3,908	5.30%	0.32	M	9	Eliminated	16,158.80
12	Hussein Hamed, Buhidma	NP	Dublin South	273	0.38%	0.02	M	2	No Expenses	4,385.35
13	Hyland, John Pluto	NP	Dublin Central	77	0.22%	0.01	M	1	No Expenses	0.00
8	Irwin, Fiona	GP	Meath West	479	1.19%	0.05	F	1	No Expenses	684.59
15	Isherwood, Eric	NP	Cork South Central	193	0.30%	0.02	M	2	No Expenses	0.00
15	Jackson, Donal	NP	Longford-Westmeath	101	0.18%	0.01	M	1	No Expenses	1,517.50
15	Johnston, Liam	FN	Dublin Central	48	0.14%	0.01	M	1	No Expenses	0.00
11	Kavanagh, Conal	LB	Wicklow	3,231	4.58%	0.27	M	12	Eliminated	17,515.41
17	Kavanagh, Pat	FN	Wicklow	291	0.41%	0.02	F	8	No Expenses	1,572.00
5	Keane, Cait	FG	Dublin South West	3,678	7.83%	0.39	F	8	Not Elected	17,165.63
8	Kearney, John	NP	Cork South West	772	1.69%	0.07	M	1	No Expenses	1,200.00
10	Kearney, Phil	GP	Dublin Central	683	1.97%	0.10	M	2	No Expenses	706.18
10	Kearns, Sean	NP	Roscommon-South Leitrim	91	0.19%	0.01	M	1	No Expenses	0.00
4	Keating, Derek	FG	Dublin Mid-West	5,933	13.89%	0.69	M	9	Elected	25,536.32
4	Keaveney, Colm	LB	Galway East	4,254	7.18%	0.36	M	9	Elected	19,563.90
19	Keddy, Charlie	NP	Wicklow	233	0.33%	0.02	M	6	No Expenses	3,118.35
7	Keegan, Andrew	PBPA	Dublin North West	677	2.06%	0.08	M	4	No Expenses	1,950.17
4	Kehoe, Paul*	FG	Wexford	8,386	11.10%	0.67	M	7	Elected	16,610.53
15	Keigher, John	NP	Dublin South East	27	0.08%	0.00	M	1	No Expenses	441.92
3	Kelleher, Billy*	FF	Cork North Central	7,896	15.14%	0.76	M	11	Elected	23,349.44
8	Kelleher, Tom	LB	Dublin North	3,205	6.49%	0.32	M	3	Eliminated	26,900.56
3	Kelly, Alan	LB	Tipperary North	9,559	19.80%	0.79	M	3	Elected	25,319.58
8	Kelly, Anthony	SF	Wexford	4,353	5.76%	0.35	M	4	Eliminated	9,421.54
16	Kelly, Gerry	NP	Dublin South Central	137	0.27%	0.02	M	3	No Expenses	1,288.50
6	Kelly, John	LB	Roscommon-South Leitrim	4,455	9.38%	0.38	M	3	Eliminated	16,903.32
7	Kelly, Martin	SF	Kildare North	2,896	5.65%	0.28	M	3	Eliminated	7,975.34
14	Kelly, Nicky	NP	Wicklow	518	0.73%	0.04	M	10	No Expenses	0.00
7	Kelly, Peter*	FF	Longford-Westmeath	3,876	6.74%	0.34	M	5	Eliminated	16,367.40
9	Kelly, Ray	NP	Dublin South West	823	1.75%	0.09	M	3	No Expenses	0.00
13	Kelly, Stephen	NP	Carlow-Kilkenny	601	0.81%	0.05	M	6	No Expenses	0.00
5	Kenneally, Brendan*	FF	Waterford	7,515	13.99%	0.70	M	11	Not Elected	17,604.63
13	Kennedy, Ciaran	GP	Galway East	402	0.68%	0.03	M	1	No Expenses	1,711.46
7	Kennedy, Michael*	FF	Dublin North	3,519	7.13%	0.36	M	4	Eliminated	24,602.30
4	Kennedy, Paddy	NP	Kildare South	2,806	7.33%	0.29	M	7	Not Elected	12,845.92
1	Kenny, Enda*	FG	Mayo	17,472	23.56%	1.41	M	1	Made Quota	12,771.98
7	Kenny, Gino	PBPA	Dublin Mid-West	2,471	5.78%	0.29	M	6	Eliminated	6,996.28
5	Kenny, Martin	SF	Roscommon-South Leitrim	4,637	9.76%	0.39	M	5	Eliminated	12,781.25
3	Kenny, Sean	LB	Dublin North East	4,365	10.43%	0.42	M	9	Elected	9,832.26
8	Keogan, Sharon	NV	Meath East	1,168	2.73%	0.11	F	1	No Expenses	14,728.54
8	Kiely, Kevin	NP	Limerick City	1,129	2.61%	0.13	M	4	No Expenses	25,559.48
15	Kiernan, Donal	NP	Wicklow	403	0.57%	0.03	M	10	No Expenses	8,541.39
15	Kiersey, Gerard	NP	Waterford	73	0.14%	0.01	M	1	No Expenses	0.00
6	Kilcoyne, Michael	NP	Mayo	3,996	5.39%	0.32	M	8	Not Elected	11,219.94
7	Killian, Nick	FF	Meath East	2,669	6.24%	0.25	M	2	Eliminated	18,675.03
8	Kilrane, Gerry	FF	Roscommon-South Leitrim	3,033	6.38%	0.26	M	1	Eliminated	15,693.47
12	Kinahan, Siobhan	GP	Longford-Westmeath	309	0.54%	0.03	F	1	No Expenses	1,145.77
15	King, Paul	NP	Dublin South Central	146	0.29%	0.02	M	4	No Expenses	1,300.00
17	King, Thomas	NP	Galway West	65	0.11%	0.01	M	1	No Expenses	0.00
16	Kinsella, Gerry	FN	Wicklow	324	0.46%	0.03	M	9	No Expenses	21,579.33
1	Kirk, Seamus*	FF	Louth				M		Ceann Com	
1	Kitt, Michael P.*	FF	Galway East	6,585	11.11%	0.56	M	8	Made Quota	12,904.98
5	Kyne, Sean	FG	Galway West	4,550	7.51%	0.45	M	13	Elected	11,766.17
13	Larkin, Matt	NP	Limerick City	59	0.14%	0.01	M	2	No Expenses	0.00
12	Larkin, Michael	CS	Dublin North West	173	0.53%	0.02	M	2	No Expenses	1,672.70
4	Lawlor, Anthony	FG	Kildare North	6,882	13.44%	0.67	M	5	Elected	20,018.06
10	Leahy, John	NP	Laois-Offaly	4,882	6.58%	0.39	M	9	Eliminated	16,032.00
16	Leahy, Ramie	NP	Carlow-Kilkenny	256	0.35%	0.02	M	3	No Expenses	1,550.50

	Candidate	Party	Constituency	1st Prefs	%	Quota	M/F	Count	Status	Spending
6	Leddin, Joe	LB	Limerick City	2,411	5.58%	0.28	M	7	Not Elected	14,994.04
4	Lenihan, Brian*	FF	Dublin West	6,421	15.12%	0.76	M	5	Elected	16,831.94
8	Lenihan, Conor*	FF	Dublin South West	2,341	4.98%	0.25	M	4	Eliminated	22,983.77
17	Linehan, Gerard	NP	Cork South Central	90	0.14%	0.01	M	2	No Expenses	1,452.00
8	Locke, Sam	NP	Kerry North-West Limerick	486	1.07%	0.04	M	4	No Expenses	700.00
11	Loftus, Michael J.	NV	Dublin North West	217	0.66%	0.03	M	3	No Expenses	1,335.72
13	Lonergan, Darcy	GP	Cavan-Monaghan	530	0.74%	0.04	F	1	No Expenses	1,689.16
10	Love Alwyn, Robert	NV	Sligo-North Leitrim	779	1.75%	0.07	M	3	No Expenses	7,102.18
1	Lowry, Michael*	NP	Tipperary North	14,104	29.22%	1.17	M	1	Made Quota	29,593.23
2	Lynch, Ciaran*	LB	Cork South Central	8,481	13.24%	0.79	M	9	Made Quota	16,217.25
2	Lynch, Kathleen*	LB	Cork North Central	7,676	14.72%	0.74	F	10	Made Quota	15,740.55
3	Lyons, John	LB	Dublin North West	4,799	14.63%	0.59	M	7	Elected	10,055.01
7	Lyons, John	PBPA	Dublin North Central	1,424	3.67%	0.15	M	2	No Expenses	4,487.69
9	MacAodhain, Ruadhan	SF	Dublin South East	1,272	3.64%	0.18	M	3	No Expenses	5,906.24
12	MacLiam, Conor	SP	Carlow-Kilkenny	1,135	1.54%	0.09	M	6	No Expenses	8,252.30
1	MacLochlainn, Padraig	SF	Donegal North East	9,278	24.47%	0.98	M	3	Made Quota	15,131.30
12	MacMeanmain, Manus	CS	Meath West	234	0.58%	0.02	M	1	No Expenses	5,883.09
6	MacSharry, Marc	FF	Sligo-North Leitrim	4,633	10.43%	0.42	M	6	Eliminated	28,025.66
4	Maloney, Eamonn	LB	Dublin South West	4,165	8.87%	0.44	M	8	Made Quota	10,422.81
5	Mansergh, Martin*	FF	Tipperary South	5,419	13.10%	0.52	M	4	Eliminated	17,115.25
8	Markham, Brian	NP	Clare	1,543	2.66%	0.13	M	8	No Expenses	1,136.95
14	Martin, Luke	NP	Louth	224	0.32%	0.02	M	5	No Expenses	0.00
1	Martin, Micheal*	FF	Cork South Central	10,715	16.73%	1.00	M	1	Made Quota	26,660.97
4	Mathews, Peter	FG	Dublin South	9,053	12.46%	0.75	M	8	Elected	26,100.37
11	Matthews, Fred	NP	Louth	957	1.38%	0.07	M	7	No Expenses	14,371.97
11	McAleer, Madeline	NP	Clare	428	0.74%	0.04	F	5	No Expenses	1,043.60
6	McBrearty, Frank	LB	Donegal South West	2,209	5.11%	0.20	M	3	Eliminated	8,800.60
15	McCabe, J.J.	NP	Clare	248	0.43%	0.02	M	2	No Expenses	5,607.20
7	McCahill, Stephen	NP	Donegal South West	1,831	4.23%	0.17	M	3	No Expenses	2,445.50
11	McCarthy, David	NV	Cork South Central	880	1.37%	0.08	M	5	No Expenses	7,033.05
3	McCarthy, Michael	LB	Cork South West	6,533	14.31%	0.57	M	6	Elected	15,233.90
9	McCaughey, Kevin	GP	Cork South West	765	1.68%	0.07	M	1	No Expenses	1,150.48
8	McClearn, Jimmy	FG	Galway East	5,395	9.10%	0.46	M	5	Eliminated	12,781.97
3	McConalogue, Charlie	FF	Donegal North East	6,613	17.44%	0.70	M	9	Elected	24,677.35
6	McCormack, Helen	SF	Dublin North Central	2,140	5.52%	0.22	F	3	Eliminated	2,989.35
9	McDaid, Garreth	GP	Roscommon-South Leitrim	220	0.46%	0.02	M	1	No Expenses	160.00
7	McDermott, John	NP	Roscommon-South Leitrim	3,770	7.94%	0.32	M	2	Eliminated	15,405.50
13	McDonagh, Seamus	WP	Meath West	189	0.47%	0.02	M	1	No Expenses	0.00
4	McDonald, Mary Lou	SF	Dublin Central	4,526	13.08%	0.65	F	8	Elected	20,460.99
14	McDonnell, Dermot	NP	Mayo	216	0.29%	0.02	M	3	No Expenses	2,311.10
16	McDonnell, Fergus	NP	Laois-Offaly	525	0.71%	0.04	M	5	No Expenses	11,720.60
5	McEllistrim, Tom*	FF	Kerry North-West Limerick	5,230	11.47%	0.46	M	6	Eliminated	16,769.99
3	McEntee, Shane*	FG	Meath East	8,794	20.57%	0.82	M	4	Elected	15,285.05
3	McFadden, Nicky	FG	Longford-Westmeath	6,129	10.65%	0.53	F	8	Elected	18,517.43
7	McGarvey, Ian	NP	Donegal North East	1,287	3.39%	0.14	M	5	No Expenses	3,899.00
2	McGinley, Dinny*	FG	Donegal South West	8,589	19.85%	0.79	M	5	Made Quota	18,991.06
6	McGinley, John	LB	Kildare North	5,261	10.27%	0.51	M	4	Eliminated	18,402.31
9	McGinley, Ruairi	FG	Dublin South Central	2,976	5.84%	0.35	M	8	Eliminated	24,060.95
12	McGrath, Colm	NP	Dublin Mid-West	253	0.59%	0.03	M	3	No Expenses	4,764.16
3	McGrath, Finian*	NP	Dublin North Central	5,986	15.44%	0.62	M	7	Made Quota	24,938.42
3	McGrath, Mattie*	NP	Tipperary South	6,074	14.69%	0.59	M	5	Elected	24,629.45
5	McGrath, Michael*	FF	Cork South Central	7,221	11.28%	0.68	M	12	Elected	21,249.11
8	McGuinness, David	FF	Dublin West	623	1.47%	0.07	M	2	No Expenses	11,686.63
2	McGuinness, John*	FF	Carlow-Kilkenny	9,531	12.92%	0.78	M	12	Made Quota	28,999.45
12	McGuirk, John	NV	Cavan-Monaghan	1,708	2.40%	0.14	M	2	No Expenses	10,006.68
13	McHale, Jim	NP	Dublin Mid-West	255	0.60%	0.03	M	2	No Expenses	4,454.16
4	McHugh, Jenny	LB	Meath West	5,432	13.52%	0.54	F	5	Not Elected	8,853.76
2	McHugh, Joe*	FG	Donegal North East	7,330	19.33%	0.77	M	8	Made Quota	23,211.88
5	McHugh, Tom	FG	Galway East	5,832	9.84%	0.49	M	9	Not Elected	18,815.68
10	McInerney, Dave	NV	Cork South West	493	1.08%	0.04	M	1	No Expenses	2,722.00
11	McKenna, John	NP	Kerry North-West Limerick	101	0.22%	0.01	M	2	No Expenses	0.00
4	McLellan, Sandra	SF	Cork East	6,292	11.05%	0.55	F	7	Elected	9,938.63
2	McLoughlin, Tony	FG	Sligo-North Leitrim	7,715	17.37%	0.69	M	9	Made Quota	22,834.49
8	McNally, Paul	GP	Tipperary South	367	0.89%	0.04	M	1	No Expenses	1,350.18
2	McNamara, Michael	LB	Clare	8,572	14.80%	0.74	M	11	Made Quota	14,248.42
11	McSharry, Gabriel	NP	Sligo-North Leitrim	747	1.68%	0.07	M	2	No Expenses	5,950.22
9	McVitty, Peter	FG	Cavan-Monaghan	3,858	5.41%	0.32	M	5	Eliminated	8,703.53
9	Meaney, Brian	GP	Clare	1,154	1.99%	0.10	M	7	No Expenses	5,011.20
3	Mitchell, Olivia*	FG	Dublin South	9,635	13.26%	0.80	F	8	Made Quota	19,491.93
3	Mitchell-O'Connor, Mary	FG	Dun Laoghaire	9,087	16.03%	0.80	F	10	Made Quota	31,716.43
8	Moloney, John*	FF	Laois-Offaly	5,579	7.52%	0.45	M	11	Eliminated	17,309.02
7	Moloney, Marie	LB	Kerry South	4,926	11.10%	0.44	F	2	Eliminated	14,711.33
11	Mooney, Annette	PBPA	Dublin South East	629	1.80%	0.09	F	1	No Expenses	2,035.75
18	Mooney, Dominic	NP	Dublin South Central	102	0.20%	0.01	M	1	No Expenses	0.00
8	Mooney, Sean	NP	Dublin North West	433	1.32%	0.05	M	4	No Expenses	0.00
11	Moran, John	FG	Laois-Offaly	4,306	5.81%	0.35	M	7	Eliminated	16,066.90
8	Moran, Kevin "Boxer"	NP	Longford-Westmeath	3,707	6.44%	0.32	M	4	Eliminated	15,154.91
7	Moran, Mary	LB	Louth	4,546	6.56%	0.33	F	11	Eliminated	11,212.54
5	Morris, Seamus	SF	Tipperary North	3,034	6.29%	0.25	M	2	Eliminated	7,401.61
2	Moynihan, Michael*	FF	Cork North West	8,845	19.34%	0.77	M	6	Elected	20,661.66
6	Mulcahy, Michael*	FF	Dublin South Central	4,837	9.50%	0.57	M	13	Not Elected	29,509.69

	Candidate	Party	Constituency	1st Prefs	%	Quota	M/F	Count	Status	Spending
6	Mulcahy, Tony	FG	Clare	6,829	11.79%	0.59	M	10	Eliminated	31,068.81
3	Mulherin, Michelle	FG	Mayo	8,851	11.94%	0.72	F	8	Made Quota	16,083.42
6	Mulvihill, John #	LB	Cork East	5,701	10.01%	0.50	M	6	Eliminated	18,608.50
20	Mulvihill, Michael	NP	Wicklow	187	0.27%	0.02	M	5	No Expenses	1,056.60
8	Murnane O'Connor, Jennifer	FF	Carlow-Kilkenny	4,428	6.00%	0.36	F	10	Eliminated	17,560.38
12	Murphy, Bart	NP	Kildare North	200	0.39%	0.02	M	1	No Expenses	800.00
3	Murphy, Catherine #	NP	Kildare North	6,911	13.49%	0.67	F	5	Made Quota	19,003.84
4	Murphy, Dara	FG	Cork North Central	6,597	12.65%	0.63	M	11	Elected	30,152.47
17	Murphy, David	NP	Carlow-Kilkenny	195	0.26%	0.02	M	2	No Expenses	301.30
3	Murphy, Eoghan	FG	Dublin South East	5,783	16.56%	0.83	M	9	Made Quota	27,039.87
10	Murphy, Humphrey	GP	Donegal North East	206	0.54%	0.02	M	1	No Expenses	624.18
11	Murphy, Jane	CS	Dublin South	277	0.38%	0.02	F	2	No Expenses	1,407.00
5	Murphy, Kevin	FG	Cork South West	6,386	13.99%	0.56	M	4	Eliminated	15,539.43
4	Murphy, Michael	FG	Tipperary South	5,402	13.06%	0.52	M	5	Not Elected	18,325.08
7	Murphy, Mick	SP	Dublin South West	2,462	5.24%	0.26	M	5	Eliminated	11,205.47
4	Nash, Gerald	LB	Louth	8,718	12.58%	0.63	M	12	Made Quota	23,210.36
3	Naughten, Denis*	FG	Roscommon-South Leitrim	9,320	19.62%	0.78	M	6	Made Quota	16,333.10
10	Naughten, Hildegarde	FG	Galway West	3,606	5.95%	0.36	F	6	Eliminated	12,501.87
1	Neville, Dan*	FG	Limerick	9,176	20.37%	0.81	M	4	Made Quota	11,995.07
12	Neville, Ted	NP	Cork South Central	523	0.82%	0.05	M	5	No Expenses	2,670.41
9	Nic Cormaic, Sorcha	SF	Dublin South	1,915	2.64%	0.16	F	4	No Expenses	1,154.00
2	Nolan, Derek	LB	Galway West	7,489	12.35%	0.74	M	10	Made Quota	28,081.08
1	Noonan, Michael*	FG	Limerick City	13,291	30.77%	1.54	M	1	Made Quota	18,623.96
5	Nulty, Patrick	LB	Dublin West	2,686	6.32%	0.32	M	5	Not Elected	14,999.38
13	Nutty, Ben	FN	Waterford	257	0.48%	0.02	M	3	No Expenses	4,073.09
5	O Broin Eoin	SF	Dublin Mid-West	5,060	11.84%	0.59	M	9	Not Elected	8,086.41
9	O Buachalla, Sean	GP	Meath East	461	1.08%	0.04	M	1	No Expenses	809.59
13	O Cadhla, Diarmaid	CPPC	Cork South Central	508	0.79%	0.05	M	4	No Expenses	0.00
1	Ó Caoláin, Caoimhghín*	SF	Cavan-Monaghan	11,913	16.71%	1.00	M	1	Made Quota	12,147.55
16	O Ceallaigh, Peadar	FN	Dublin South East	18	0.05%	0.00	M	1	No Expenses	610.00
8	O Clochartaigh, Trevor	SF	Galway West	3,808	6.28%	0.38	M	9	Eliminated	12,500.55
4	O Domhnaill, Brian	FF	Donegal South West	4,789	11.07%	0.44	M	5	Not Elected	16,791.46
7	O Donnabhain, Daithi	FF	Cork North West	2,545	5.56%	0.22	M	2	No Expenses	13,080.91
3	O Fearghail, Sean*	FF	Kildare South	4,514	11.80%	0.47	M	7	Elected	15,421.99
10	O hAlmhain, Oisin	GP	Dublin South Central	1,015	1.99%	0.12	M	7	No Expenses	4,704.89
4	O Muiri, Naoise	FG	Dublin North Central	4,959	12.79%	0.51	M	7	Not Elected	14,128.37
2	O Riordain, Aodhan	LB	Dublin North Central	8,731	22.52%	0.90	M	4	Made Quota	22,027.41
5	O Snodaigh, Aengus*	SF	Dublin South Central	6,804	13.36%	0.80	M	13	Elected	14,061.99
6	O'Brien, Bridget	NP	Kerry North-West Limerick	1,455	3.19%	0.13	F	5	No Expenses	4,642.10
5	O'Brien, Darragh*	FF	Dublin North	4,115	8.34%	0.42	M	7	Not Elected	23,226.88
1	O'Brien, Jonathan	SF	Cork North Central	7,923	15.20%	0.76	M	8	Made Quota	10,825.25
11	O'Brien, Seamus	PBPA	Wexford	741	0.98%	0.06	M	2	No Expenses	4,050.49
6	O'Connor, Charlie*	FF	Dublin South West	2,718	5.79%	0.29	M	7	Eliminated	12,513.53
3	O'Dea, Willie*	FF	Limerick City	6,956	16.11%	0.81	M	6	Made Quota	20,082.38
10	O'Doherty, Patrick	NP	Limerick	247	0.55%	0.02	M	1	No Expenses	95.00
12	O'Donnell, Emer	NP	Galway East	601	1.01%	0.05	F	1	No Expenses	150.00
2	O'Donnell, Kieran*	FG	Limerick City	5,405	12.52%	0.63	M	5	Made Quota	20,617.15
6	O'Donnell, William	FG	Limerick	4,152	9.22%	0.37	M	2	Eliminated	10,391.13
11	O'Donoghue, Conor	CS	Limerick City	186	0.43%	0.02	M	2	No Expenses	233.21
6	O'Donoghue, John*	FF	Kerry South	5,917	13.33%	0.53	M	3	Eliminated	25,502.67
4	O'Donovan, Denis #	FF	Cork South West	5,984	13.11%	0.52	M	6	Not Elected	16,193.14
2	O'Donovan, Patrick	FG	Limerick	8,597	19.09%	0.76	M	4	Made Quota	17,035.07
3	O'Dowd, Fergus*	FG	Louth	13,980	20.17%	1.01	M	1	Made Quota	15,867.15
16	O'Driscoll, Finbar	NP	Cork South Central	92	0.14%	0.01	M	2	No Expenses	726.60
7	O'Driscoll, Pa	FG	Cork East	5,030	8.83%	0.44	M	4	Eliminated	15,423.29
9	O'Gorman, Roderic	GP	Dublin West	605	1.42%	0.07	M	2	No Expenses	1,305.29
6	O'Grady, Des	SF	Cork North West	3,405	7.44%	0.30	M	3	Eliminated	3,210.08
15	O'Hara, John	NP	Carlow-Kilkenny	253	0.34%	0.02	M	4	No Expenses	0.00
5	O'Keeffe, Kevin	FF	Cork East	5,024	8.82%	0.44	M	7	Not Elected	20,370.90
5	O'Keeffe, Susan	LB	Sligo-North Leitrim	4,553	10.25%	0.41	F	7	Eliminated	16,611.06
6	O'Leary, Chris	SF	Cork South Central	5,250	8.20%	0.49	M	12	Not Elected	12,205.58
12	O'Loughlin, Paul	CS	Dublin Central	235	0.68%	0.03	M	2	No Expenses	1,785.95
5	O'Mahony, John*	FG	Mayo	8,667	11.69%	0.70	M	8	Elected	16,889.10
7	O'Malley, Olwyn	GP	Tipperary North	409	0.85%	0.03	F	2	No Expenses	1,024.59
9	O'Neill, Paul	NV	Cork East	1,056	1.85%	0.09	M	2	No Expenses	4,473.29
11	O'Neill, Peter	NP	Dublin South Central	456	0.90%	0.05	M	7	No Expenses	1,953.35
3	O'Reilly, Joe	FG	Cavan-Monaghan	8,333	11.69%	0.70	M	9	Elected	10,982.97
15	O'Rourke, Fergus	NP	Cork North Central	95	0.18%	0.01	M	1	No Expenses	1,481.00
10	O'Rourke, Mary*	FF	Longford-Westmeath	3,046	5.30%	0.26	F	2	Eliminated	22,763.40
6	O'Sullivan, Christy*	FF	Cork South West	4,803	10.52%	0.42	M	3	Eliminated	26,333.52
4	O'Sullivan, Jan*	LB	Limerick City	6,353	14.71%	0.74	F	7	Elected	16,389.57
3	O'Sullivan, Maureen*	NP	Dublin Central	4,139	11.96%	0.60	F	7	Made Quota	11,233.00
13	O'Sullivan, Michael	NP	Cork South West	231	0.51%	0.02	M	1	No Expenses	1,485.70
8	O'Sullivan, Padraig	NV	Cork North Central	1,020	1.96%	0.10	M	7	No Expenses	7,794.31
4	O'Toole, Larry	SF	Dublin North East	5,032	12.03%	0.48	M	9	Not Elected	8,967.21
11	Patton, Trevor	NP	Dun Laoghaire	445	0.79%	0.04	M	5	No Expenses	0.00
1	Penrose, Willie*	LB	Longford-Westmeath	11,406	19.83%	0.99	M	2	Made Quota	12,396.48
8	Perry, Cieran	NP	Dublin Central	1,394	4.03%	0.20	M	4	No Expenses	5,510.85
1	Perry, John*	FG	Sligo-North Leitrim	8,663	19.50%	0.78	M	8	Made Quota	17,507.60
1	Phelan, Ann	LB	Carlow-Kilkenny	8,072	10.95%	0.66	F	12	Made Quota	20,496.79
3	Phelan, John Paul	FG	Carlow-Kilkenny	10,929	14.82%	0.89	M	12	Made Quota	20,476.09

	Candidate	Party	Constituency	1st Prefs	%	Quota	M/F	Count	Status	Spending
5	Power, Averil	FF	Dublin North East	4,794	11.46%	0.46	F	8	Eliminated	17,761.24
12	Power, Jody	GP	Waterford	462	0.86%	0.04	M	4	No Expenses	2,918.13
7	Power, Peter*	FF	Limerick City	2,303	5.33%	0.27	M	5	Eliminated	21,875.99
5	Power, Sean*	FF	Kildare South	3,793	9.91%	0.40	M	6	Eliminated	9,830.40
6	Prendergast, Phil	LB	Tipperary South	4,525	10.94%	0.44	F	2	Eliminated	16,086.73
9	Prendiville, Cian	SP	Limerick City	721	1.67%	0.08	M	4	No Expenses	7,549.87
3	Pringle, Thomas	NP	Donegal South West	5,845	13.51%	0.54	M	5	Elected	6,793.05
5	Quinlivan, Maurice	SF	Limerick City	3,711	8.59%	0.43	M	7	Not Elected	11,237.05
9	Quinn, Liam	FG	Laois-Offaly	4,482	6.04%	0.36	M	10	Eliminated	16,801.87
1	Quinn, Ruairi*	LB	Dublin South East	5,407	15.48%	0.77	M	6	Made Quota	20,085.39
1	Rabbitte, Pat*	LB	Dublin South West	12,867	27.40%	1.37	M	1	Made Quota	11,646.09
12	Rea, Harry	CS	Cork North Central	324	0.62%	0.03	M	3	No Expenses	4,753.38
7	Reid, Clifford T.	NP	Kildare South	926	2.42%	0.10	M	4	No Expenses	1,011.32
9	Reidy, Michael	NV	Kerry North-West Limerick	357	0.78%	0.03	M	3	No Expenses	786.43
1	Reilly, Dr. James*	FG	Dublin North	10,178	20.63%	1.03	M	1	Made Quota	23,527.73
6	Reilly, Kathryn	SF	Cavan-Monaghan	6,539	9.17%	0.55	F	9	Not Elected	13,539.30
2	Ring, Michael*	FG	Mayo	13,180	17.77%	1.07	M	1	Made Quota	14,261.37
12	Riordan, Denis	NP	Limerick City	173	0.40%	0.02	M	2	No Expenses	140.00
10	Roche, Dick*	FF	Wicklow	3,891	5.52%	0.33	M	13	Eliminated	12,405.66
13	Roseingrave, Siobhan	NP	Wexford	175	0.23%	0.01	F	2	No Expenses	220.00
1	Ross, Shane	NP	Dublin South	17,075	23.50%	1.41	M	1	Made Quota	38,394.32
10	Ruane, Therese	SF	Mayo	2,142	2.89%	0.17	F	4	No Expenses	6,046.16
2	Ryan, Brendan	LB	Dublin North	9,809	19.88%	0.99	M	3	Made Quota	22,064.98
7	Ryan, Eamonn*	GP	Dublin South	4,929	6.78%	0.41	M	7	Eliminated	32,525.00
5	Ryan, John	FG	Donegal North East	4,657	12.28%	0.49	M	7	Eliminated	17,164.15
11	Ryan, Michael	NP	Dublin Mid-West	375	0.88%	0.04	M	4	No Expenses	0.00
7	Ryan, Seamus	LB	Waterford	4,638	8.63%	0.43	M	8	Eliminated	10,296.36
6	Sargent, Trevor*	GP	Dublin North	4,186	8.48%	0.42	M	5	Eliminated	20,493.64
4	Scanlon, Eamon*	FF	Sligo-North Leitrim	5,075	11.42%	0.46	M	9	Not Elected	15,535.27
9	Sexton, Mae #	LB	Longford-Westmeath	3,960	6.88%	0.34	F	3	Eliminated	10,885.32
10	Sexton, Raymond	NP	Dublin North East	351	0.84%	0.03	M	3	No Expenses	9,108.24
5	Shatter, Alan*	FG	Dublin South	7,716	10.62%	0.64	M	8	Elected	17,546.93
4	Sheahan, John	FG	Kerry North-West Limerick	6,295	13.80%	0.55	M	7	Not Elected	16,345.29
4	Sheahan, Tom*	FG	Kerry South	5,674	12.79%	0.51	M	6	Not Elected	22,776.49
12	Sheehy, Hugh	NP	Dublin South East	195	0.56%	0.03	M	1	No Expenses	3,679.83
8	Sherlock, Seamus	NP	Limerick	419	0.93%	0.04	M	1	No Expenses	1,238.34
1	Sherlock, Sean*	LB	Cork East	11,862	20.84%	1.04	M	1	Made Quota	15,417.83
6	Shiels, Dessie	NP	Donegal North East	1,876	4.95%	0.20	M	6	Eliminated	9,221.34
1	Shortall, Roisin*	LB	Dublin North West	9,359	28.52%	1.14	F	1	Made Quota	14,048.22
2	Smith, Brendan*	FF	Cavan-Monaghan	9,702	13.61%	0.82	M	8	Made Quota	28,181.44
14	Smith, Niall	NP	Dublin Mid-West	113	0.26%	0.01	M	1	No Expenses	1,300.00
6	Sommerville, Paul	NP	Dublin South East	2,343	6.71%	0.34	M	8	Eliminated	20,885.24
2	Spring, Arthur	LB	Kerry North-West Limerick	9,159	20.08%	0.80	M	7	Made Quota	16,463.66
2	Stagg, Emmet*	LB	Kildare North	9,718	18.97%	0.95	M	3	Made Quota	20,449.88
4	Stanley, Brian	SF	Laois-Offaly	8,032	10.83%	0.65	M	13	Elected	14,892.54
2	Stanton, David*	FG	Cork East	10,019	17.60%	0.88	M	5	Made Quota	17,211.04
11	Steenson, Malachy	WP	Dublin Central	274	0.79%	0.04	M	2	No Expenses	986.37
10	Stevens, Daithi	NP	Meath West	387	0.96%	0.04	M	1	No Expenses	950.00
11	Stewart, Ryan	NV	Donegal North East	203	0.54%	0.02	M	1	No Expenses	0.00
9	Sweeney, Ann	NV	Donegal South West	255	0.59%	0.02	F	2	No Expenses	1,332.00
22	Tallon, Jim	NP	Wicklow	166	0.24%	0.01	M	3	No Expenses	0.00
2	Timmins, Billy*	FG	Wicklow	9,165	13.00%	0.78	M	17	Made Quota	14,889.13
10	Tobin, Joe	WP	Waterford	873	1.63%	0.08	M	6	No Expenses	3,447.60
2	Toibin, Peadar	SF	Meath West	6,989	17.40%	0.70	M	5	Elected	21,137.59
6	Tormey, Dr. Bill	FG	Dublin North West	2,508	7.64%	0.31	M	5	Eliminated	15,850.93
10	Treanor, Seamus	NP	Cavan-Monaghan	1,974	2.77%	0.17	M	4	No Expenses	6,840.66
4	Troy, Robert	FF	Longford-Westmeath	4,275	7.43%	0.37	M	8	Elected	19,050.68
1	Tuffy, Joanna*	LB	Dublin Mid-West	7,495	17.54%	0.88	F	7	Made Quota	21,678.43
6	Turner, Jason	SF	Kildare South	2,308	6.03%	0.24	M	5	Eliminated	9,695.03
5	Twomey, Liam #	FG	Wexford	9,230	12.22%	0.73	M	7	Elected	26,136.88
10	Tynan, Ted	WP	Cork North Central	681	1.31%	0.07	M	5	No Expenses	2,000.00
8	Upton, Henry	LB	Dublin South Central	4,183	8.21%	0.49	M	10	Eliminated	19,733.98
2	Varadkar, Leo*	FG	Dublin West	8,359	19.68%	0.98	M	2	Made Quota	20,726.04
2	Wall, Jack*	LB	Kildare South	10,645	27.82%	1.11	M	1	Made Quota	19,006.03
9	Wall, Stephen	GP	Limerick	354	0.79%	0.03	M	1	No Expenses	664.45
1	Wallace, Mick	NP	Wexford	13,329	17.65%	1.06	M	1	Made Quota	9,328.18
3	Walsh, Brian	FG	Galway West	5,425	8.95%	0.54	M	12	Made Quota	15,681.39
13	Walsh, Eamon	NP	Galway West	1,481	2.44%	0.15	M	3	No Expenses	16,198.43
11	Walsh, Ken	GP	Cork North Central	524	1.01%	0.05	M	4	No Expenses	805.40
18	Walsh, Noel G.	NP	Carlow-Kilkenny	119	0.16%	0.01	M	1	No Expenses	6,735.79
13	Walshe, Gerry	NP	Clare	328	0.57%	0.03	F	4	No Expenses	3,086.71
14	Waters, Declan	NP	Waterford	222	0.41%	0.02	M	2	No Expenses	3,111.73
14	Watson, Noel	NP	Dublin South East	89	0.25%	0.01	M	1	No Expenses	0.00
11	Welby, Thomas	NP	Galway West	3,298	5.44%	0.33	M	5	Eliminated	8,108.73
6	Whelan, John	LB	Laois-Offaly	5,802	7.82%	0.47	M	13	Not Elected	12,011.43
2	White, Alex	LB	Dublin South	8,524	11.73%	0.70	M	6	Made Quota	20,162.51
11	White, Mary*	GP	Carlow-Kilkenny	2,072	2.81%	0.17	F	7	No Expenses	11,657.33
15	Whitehead, Raymond	NP	Dublin South	120	0.17%	0.01	M	2	No Expenses	0.00
13	Wilson, Robin	NP	Louth	536	0.77%	0.04	M	6	No Expenses	2,300.00
6	Yore, Catherine	FG	Meath West	3,898	9.70%	0.39	F	3	Eliminated	28,257.87
16	Zaidan, Eamonn	NP	Dublin South	71	0.10%	0.01	M	2	No Expenses	103.05
567				**2,220,359**						**6,518,702.79**

INDEX 2: ALL SEANAD CANDIDATES 2011					
	Candidate	**Party**	**1st Prefs**	**Panel**	**Elected**
1	Bacik, Ivana*	NP	2,982	University of Dublin	Elected
2	Bailey, John	FG	19,000	Agricultural	
3	Barrett, Sean	NP	1,051	University of Dublin	Elected
4	Boland, Seamus	NP	30,000	Administrative	
5	Boyhan, Victor	NP	44,000	Cultural & Educational	
6	Boyle, Dan*	GP	19,000	Industrial & Commercial	
7	Bradford, Paul*	FG	63,000	Agricultural	Elected
8	Brady, Martin*	FF	12,000	Administrative	
9	*Breen, Gerry*	FG	21,000	Industrial & Commercial	
10	Brennan, Joseph	FG	11,000	Agricultural	
11	Brennan, Terry	FG	54,000	Labour	Elected
12	Brophy, Colm	FG	36,000	Industrial & Commercial	
13	Buckley, Molly	FG	23,000	Administrative	
14	Bugler, Phyll	FG	19,000	Administrative	
15	Burke, Colm	FG	40,000	Industrial & Commercial	Elected
16	Burke, Peter	FG	21,000	Industrial & Commercial	
17	Burke,Paddy*	FG	82,000	Agricultural	Elected
18	Burton, Pat	FG	25,000	Agricultural	
19	Butler, Richard	FG	21,000	Industrial & Commercial	
20	Byrne, Danny	FG	15,000	Industrial & Commercial	
21	Byrne, Thomas	FF	129,000	Cultural & Educational	Elected
22	Campbell, Sirena	FG	33,000	Labour	
23	Canning, Thomas	NP	354	National University	
24	Carroll, James*	FF	34,000	Agricultural	
25	Casserly, Mel	NP	2,000	Industrial & Commercial	
26	Cassidy, Donie*	FF	42,000	Labour	
27	Clarke, Michael	NP	32,000	Agricultural	
28	Clendennen, John	FG	19,000	Industrial & Commercial	
29	*Clune, Deidre*	FG	103,000	Cultural & Educational	Elected
30	Coghlan, Eamon	NP		Taoiseach's Nominee	Nominated
31	Coghlan,Paul*	FG	45,000	Industrial & Commercial	Elected
32	Coleman, Alan	FF	3,000	Agricultural	
33	Coleman, Marc	NP	772	University of Dublin	
34	Comiskey, Michael	FG	40,000	Agricultural	Elected
35	*Conlon, Margaret*	FF	47,000	Industrial & Commercial	
36	Connick, Sean	FF	25,000	Agricultural	
37	Connolly, Bart	NP	72	University of Dublin	
38	Conway, Martin	FG	86,000	Administrative	Elected
39	Cowley, Matthias Walter	NP	57	National University	
40	Cox, Maeve	NP	174	University of Dublin	
41	Coyle, James	NP	307	National University	
42	Crotty, Pat	FG	6,000	Industrial & Commercial	
43	Crowe, John	FG	36,000	Industrial & Commercial	
44	Crown, John	NP	4,703	National University	Elected
45	*Cullinane, David*	SF	84,000	Labour	Elected
46	Cummins, Maurice*	FG	100,000	Labour	Elected

	Candidate	Party	1st Prefs	Panel	Elected
47	Daly, Mark*	FF	121,000	Administrative	Elected
48	D'Arcy, Jim	FG		Taoiseach's Nominee	Nominated
49	*D'Arcy, Michael*	FG	89,000	Administrative	Elected
50	Delaney, Conor	FG	16,000	Cultural & Educational	
51	*Dennison, Kieran*	FG	26,000	Administrative	
52	Dillon, John	NP	12,000	Agricultural	
53	*Donnelly, Francis*	NP	37,000	Labour	
54	Donnelly, Francis	NP	20	University of Dublin	
55	Doocey, Declan	FG	24,000	Agricultural	
56	Doorley, James	NP	655	National University	
57	Dudgeon, Jeffrey	NP	205	University of Dublin	
58	Feeney, Geraldine*	FF	44,000	Labour	
59	*Feeney, Peter*	FG	29,000	Agricultural	
60	Fitzgerald, David	FG	8,000	Industrial & Commercial	
61	*Fitzpatrick, Mary*	FF	105,000	Administrative	
62	Fortune, Tom	LB	13,000	Industrial & Commercial	
63	Frost, Dermot	NP	178	University of Dublin	
64	Gilroy, John	LB	157,000	Cultural & Educational	Elected
65	Gueret, Maurice	NP	822	University of Dublin	
66	Hanafin, John G.*	FF	39,000	Labour	
67	Hanan, Robin	NP	406	University of Dublin	
68	Harte, Jimmy	LB	70,000	Industrial & Commercial	Elected
69	Hayden, Aideen	LB	27,000	Industrial & Commercial	
70	Hayden, Aideen	LB		Taoiseach's Nominee	Nominated
71	*Healy Eames, Fidelma**	FG	83,000	Labour	Elected
72	Healy, Paddy	NP	947	National University	
73	*Heffernan, James*	LB	97,000	Agricultural	Elected
74	Henry, Imelda	FG	41,000	Industrial & Commercial	Elected
75	Higgins, Lorraine	LB	36,000	Industrial & Commercial	
76	Higgins, Lorraine	LB		Taoiseach's Nominee	Nominated
77	Hogan, John	FF	23,000	Agricultural	
78	Hogan, Nichola	FG	27,000	Cultural & Educational	
79	*Hourigan, Mary*	FG	32,000	Administrative	
80	Hynes, Pat	NP	22,000	Industrial & Commercial	
81	Irish, Anne-Maria	FG	25,000	Cultural & Educational	
82	Keane, Cáit	FG	44,000	Labour	Elected
83	Kelleher, Declan	NP	3,771	National University	
84	Kelly, John	LB	73,000	Administrative	Elected
85	Kennedy, John	NP	279	National University	
86	Kennedy, Pat	FG	32,000	Cultural & Educational	
87	Keogh, Helen	NP	1,362	National University	
88	Keogh, Paul	NP	1,000	Industrial & Commercial	
89	Kinsella, Michael	FG	9,000	Industrial & Commercial	
90	Landy, Denis	LB	75,000	Administrative	Elected
91	Langan, Mick	NP	129	National University	
92	Leddin, Joe	LB	40,000	Industrial & Commercial	
93	Leyden, Terry*	FF	51,000	Labour	Elected

	Candidate	Party	1st Prefs	Panel	Elected
94	Lynam, Paul	NP	476	National University	
95	*Lyons, Sean*	NP	19,000	Administrative	
96	MacConghail, Fiach	NP		Taoiseach's Nominee	Nominated
97	MacSharry, Mark*	FF	69,000	Industrial & Commercial	Elected
98	Malone, Patrick	FG	0	Industrial & Commercial	
99	Mansergh, Dr. Martin	FF	9,000	Agricultural	
100	Markey, Colm	FG	27,000	Agricultural	
101	Martin, David	NP	194	University of Dublin	
102	McAleese, Dr. Martin	NP		Taoiseach's Nominee	Nominated
103	McCartin, John	FG	68,000	Cultural & Educational	
104	McCurtain, David	NP	262	National University	
105	McDermott, Frank	FG	21,000	Agricultural	
106	McDonagh, Rosaleen	NP	446	University of Dublin	
107	McGloin, Enda	FG	70,000	Administrative	
108	McGonigle, Laura	FG	21,000	Industrial & Commercial	
109	McGovern, Iggy	NP	397	University of Dublin	
110	McHugh, Tom	FG	29,000	Industrial & Commercial	
111	McVitty, Peter	FG	40,000	Industrial & Commercial	
112	Molloy, Michael	NP	484	National University	
113	Moloney, Marie	LB	63,000	Labour	Elected
114	Mooney, Paschal*	FF	40,000	Agricultural	Elected
115	Mooney, Peter	NP	547	National University	
116	Moran, Mary	LB	63,000	Administrative	
117	Moran, Mary	LB		Taoiseach's Nominee	Nominated
118	Mulcahy, Tony	FG	64,000	Labour	Elected
119	Mullen, Ronan*	NP	6,459	National University	Elected
120	**Mullins, Michael**	FG	78,000	Cultural & Educational	Elected
121	*Murnane O'Connor, Jennifer*	FF	38,000	Labour	
122	Nevin, Barry	LB	37,000	Labour	
123	Nolan, Michael	FG	18,000	Industrial & Commercial	
124	Noone, Catherine	FG	33,000	Industrial & Commercial	Elected
125	Norris, David*	NP	5,623	University of Dublin	Elected
126	Ó Broin, Eoin	NP	490	National University	
127	Ó Brollcháin, Niall	NP	718	National University	
128	Ó Cadhla, Diarmaid	NP	182	National University	
129	*Ó Clochartaigh, Trevor*	SF	82,000	Agricultural	Elected
130	Ó Domhnaill, Brian*	FF	53,000	Agricultural	Elected
131	Ó Murchú, Labhrás*	FF	104,000	Cultural & Educational	Elected
132	O'Brien, Darragh*	FF	51,000	Labour	Elected
133	O'Brien, Mary Ann	NP		Taoiseach's Nominee	Nominated
134	O'Callaghan, Joe	FG	28,000	Labour	
135	O'Connell, Donncha	NP	1,629	National University	
136	O'Connor, Regina	NP	1,101	National University	
137	O'Dea, Jim	FG	11,000	Cultural & Educational	
138	O'Donnell, Francis	NP	199	National University	
139	O'Donnell, Marie-Louise	NP		Taoiseach's Nominee	Nominated
140	O'Donoghue, James	NP	154	National University	

	Candidate	Party	1st Prefs	Panel	Elected
141	O'Donovan, Denis*	FF	42,000	Agricultural	Elected
142	O'Flynn, Kenneth	FF	24,000	Industrial & Commercial	
143	O'Grady, Sean	LB	22,000	Administrative	
144	O'Keeffe, Susan	LB	69,000	Agricultural	Elected
145	O'Malley, Fiona	NP	441	University of Dublin	
146	O'Neill, Pat	FG	40,000	Agricultural	Elected
147	O'Reilly, Michael	NP	14,000	Labour	
148	Ormonde, Ann*	FF	66,000	Cultural & Educational	
149	O'Shea Farren,Linda	NP	1,083	National University	
150	O'Sullivan, Bernadine	NP	2,028	National University	
151	O'Sullivan, Ned*	FF	55,000	Labour	Elected
152	Phelan, Martin	FG	26,000	Agricultural	
153	*Power, Averil*	FF	75,000	Industrial & Commercial	Elected
154	Price, Brendan	NP	671	National University	
155	Priestley, William	NP	258	University of Dublin	
156	Quinlan, Hilary	FG	47,000	Cultural & Educational	
157	Quinn, Graham	NP	131	University of Dublin	
158	Quinn, Liam	FG	23,000	Cultural & Educational	
159	Quinn,Fergal*	NP	4,591	National University	Elected
160	Reilly, Kathryn	SF	73,000	Industrial & Commercial	Elected
161	*Richmond, Neale*	FG	39,000	Labour	
162	Scanlon, Eamon	FF	47,000	Agricultural	
163	Sheahan, John	FG	38,000	Agricultural	
164	Sheahan, Tom	FG	62,000	Administrative	Elected
165	Sheehan, Dermot	NP	49	University of Dublin	
166	Sheehan, Michael	FF	12,000	Industrial & Commercial	
167	Sullivan, Daniel	NP	193	National University	
168	Tormey, Bill	FG	49,000	Cultural & Educational	
169	Van Turnhout, Jillian	NP		Taoiseach's Nominee	Nominated
170	Walsh, Seamus	FF	86,000	Cultural & Educational	
171	Walsh,Jim*	FF	53,000	Agricultural	Elected
172	Ward, Barry	FG	27,000	Administrative	
173	*Whelan, John*	LB	66,000	Labour	Elected
174	White, Mary*	FF	78,000	Industrial & Commercial	Elected
175	Williams, Tony	NP	1,336	University of Dublin	
176	Wilson, Diarmuid*	FF	110,000	Administrative	Elected
177	Zappone, Dr. Katherine	NP		Taoiseach's Nominee	Nominated
	Oireachtas Sub-Panel				Elected

INDEX ALL TDS 1918-2012

	Surname	Forename	Constituency	Party	Elected																	Terms	From	To	Service	Born	Died	Age
1	Abbott	Henry	Longford-Westmeath	FF	87																	1	17/02/1987	15/06/1989	2.32	18/12/1947		64.3
2	Acheson	Carrie	Tipperary South	FF	81																	1	11/06/1981	18/02/1982	0.69	11/09/1934		77.5
3	Adams	Gerry	Louth	SF	11																	1	25/02/2011		1.07	06/10/1948		63.5
4	Agnew	Paddy	Louth	Hblk	81																	1	11/06/1981	18/02/1982	0.69	09/03/1955		57.0
5	Ahearn	Theresa	Tipperary South	FG	89	92	97															3	15/06/1989	20/09/2000	11.27	01/05/1951	20/09/2000	49
6	Ahern	Bertie	Dublin Central	FF	77	81	82	82	87	89	92	97	02	07								10	16/06/1977	25/02/2011	33.70	12/09/1951		60.5
7	Ahern	Dermot	Louth	FF	87	89	92	97	02	07												6	17/02/1987	25/02/2011	24.02	02/02/1955		57.1
8	Ahern	Kit	Kerry North	FF	77																	1	16/06/1977	11/06/1981	3.99	13/01/1915	27/12/2007	92
9	Ahern	Liam	Cork North East	FF	73																	1	28/02/1973	13/07/1974	1.37	12/01/1916	13/07/1974	58
10	Ahern	Michael	Cork East	FF	82	82	87	89	92	97	02	07										8	18/02/1982	25/02/2011	29.02	20/01/1949		63.2
11	Ahern	Noel	Dublin North West	FF	92	97	02	07														4	25/11/1992	25/02/2011	18.25	28/12/1944		67.2
12	Aiken	Frank	Louth	FF	23	27	27	32	33	37	38	43	44	48	51	54	57	61	65	69		16	27/08/1923	28/02/1973	49.51	13/02/1898	18/05/1983	85
13	Aird	William P.	Laoighis-Offaly	CG	27S																	1	15/09/1927	31/10/1931	4.13		31/10/1931	
14	Allen	Bernard	Cork North Central	FG	81	82	82	87	89	92	97	02	07									9	11/06/1981	25/02/2011	29.71	09/09/1944		67.5
15	Allen	Denis	Wexford	FF	27S	32	36*	37	38	43	44	48	51	54	57							11	15/09/1927	29/03/1961	29.98	02/01/1896	29/03/1961	65
16	Allen	Lorcan	Wexford	FF	61	65	69	73	77	81	82F											7	04/10/1961	24/11/1982	21.14	27/03/1940		72.0
17	Alton	Prof. Ernest	Dublin University	NP	21	22	23	27	27	32	33											7	24/05/1921	01/07/1937	16.10	1873	18/02/1952	79
18	Andrews	Barry	Dun Laoghaire	FF	02	07																2	17/05/2002	25/02/2011	8.78	16/05/1967		44.9
19	Andrews	Chris	Dublin South East	FF	07																	1	24/05/2007	25/02/2011	3.76	25/05/1964		47.8
20	Andrews	David	Dun Laoghaire	FF	65	69	73	77	81	82	82	87	89	92	97							11	07/04/1965	17/05/2002	37.11	15/03/1935		77.0
21	Andrews	Niall	Dublin South	FF	77	81	82	82														4	16/06/1977	17/02/1987	9.67	19/08/1937	16/10/2006	69
22	Anthony	Richard	Cork Borough	LB	27	27	32	33	37	43	44											7	09/06/1927	04/02/1948	15.64	1875	1962	87.0
23	Ardagh	Sean	Dublin South Central	FF	97	02	07															3	06/06/1997	25/02/2011	13.72	25/11/1947		64.3
24	Aylward	Bobby	Carlow-Kilkenny	FF	07																	1	24/05/2007	25/02/2011	3.76	01/04/1955		57.0
25	Aylward	Edward	Carlow-Kilkenny	SF	21																	1	24/05/1921	16/06/1922	1.06	1894	01/02/1976	82
26	Aylward	Liam	Carlow-Kilkenny	FF	77	81	82	82	87	89	92	97	02									9	16/06/1977	24/05/2007	29.94	27/09/1952		59.5
27	Bannon	James	Longford-Westmeath	FG	07	11																2	24/05/2007		4.83	26/03/1958		54.0
28	Barnes	Monica	Dun Laoghaire	FG	82N	87	89	97														4	24/11/1982	17/05/2002	14.95	12/02/1936		76.1
29	Barrett	Michael	Dublin North West	FF	81	82	82	87	89													5	11/06/1981	25/11/1992	11.46	15/01/1927	08/07/2006	79
30	Barrett	Sean	Dun Laoghaire	FG	81	82	82	87	89	92	97	07	11									9	11/06/1981		25.76	09/08/1944		67.6
31	Barrett	Stephen	Cork Borough	FG	54*	54	57	61	65													5	*03/03/1954*	18/06/1969	15.29	26/12/1913	08/09/1976	62
32	Barrett	Sylvester	Clare	FF	68*	69	73	77	81	82	82											7	*14/03/1968*	17/02/1987	18.93	18/05/1926	08/05/2002	75
33	Barron	Joseph	Dublin South Central	CnaP	61																	1	04/10/1961	07/04/1965	3.51		30/07/1968	
34	Barry	Anthony	Cork Borough	FG	54	61																2	18/05/1954	07/04/1965	6.31	07/06/1901	24/10/1983	82
35	Barry	Myra	Cork East	FG	79*	81	82	82														4	*07/11/1979*	17/02/1987	7.28	30/06/1957		54.7
36	Barry	Peter	Cork South Central	FG	69	73	77	81	82	82	87	89	92									9	18/06/1969	06/06/1997	27.97	10/08/1928		83.6
37	Barry	Richard	Cork North East	FG	53*	54	57	61	65	69	73	77										8	*18/06/1953*	11/06/1981	27.98	04/09/1919		92.5
38	Barry	Tom	Cork East	FG	11																	1	25/02/2011		1.07	10/10/1968		43.4
39	Bartley	Gerald	Galway West	FF	32	33	37	38	43	44	48	51	54	57	61							11	16/02/1932	07/04/1965	33.14	12/06/1898	10/05/1974	75
40	Barton	Robert C	Kildare-Wicklow	CR	18	21	22															3	21/01/1919	27/08/1923	4.60	1881	10/08/1975	94
41	Baxter	Patrick	Cavan	F	23	27J																2	27/08/1923	15/09/1927	4.05	01/10/1891	03/04/1959	67
42	Beamish	Richard	Cork Borough	PA	23																	1	27/08/1923	09/06/1927	3.78	16/06/1862	23/02/1938	75
43	Beaslai	Piaras	Kerry-Limerick West	CT	18	21	22															3	21/01/1919	27/08/1923	4.60	15/02/1881	22/06/1965	84
44	Beckett	James	Dublin South	FG	27	27	32	33	38													5	09/06/1927	19/12/1938	10.57	5/7/1875	19/12/1938	63
45	Beegan	Patrick	Galway South	FF	32	33	37	38	43	44	48	51	54	57								10	16/02/1932	02/02/1958	25.96	26/05/1895	02/02/1958	62
46	Begley	Michael	Kerry South	FG	69	73	77	81	82	82	87											7	18/06/1969	15/06/1989	19.99	22/08/1932		79.6
47	Behan	Joe	Wicklow	FF	07																	1	24/05/2007	25/02/2011	3.76	30/07/1959		52.6
48	Beirne(jun.)	John	Roscommon	CnaT	48	51	54	57														4	04/02/1948	04/10/1961	13.66		23/10/1967	
49	Beirne(sen.)	John	Roscommon	CnaT	43	44																2	23/06/1943	04/02/1948	4.62	01/04/1893		
50	Bell	Michael	Louth	LB	82N	87	89	92	97													5	24/11/1982	17/05/2002	19.48	01/10/1936	20/05/2011	74
51	Bellew	Thomas	Louth	FF	82F																	1	18/02/1982	24/11/1982	0.76	11/04/1943	28/10/1995	52
52	Belton	Jack	Dublin North East	FG	48	51	54	57	61													5	04/02/1948	23/02/1963	15.05	30/12/1914	23/02/1963	48

	Surname	Forename	Constituency	Party	Elected																	Terms	From	To	Service	Born	Died	Age
53	Belton	Louis*	Longford-Roscommon	FG	89/	97																2	15/06/1989	17/05/2002	8.39	30/11/1943		68.3
54	Belton	Luke	Dublin North Central	FG	65	69	73	77														4	07/04/1965	11/06/1981	16.18	09/08/1918	18/06/2006	87
55	Belton	Paddy	Dublin North East	FG	63*	65	69	73														4	*30/05/1963*	16/06/1977	14.05	25/10/1926	22/05/1987	60
56	Belton	Patrick	Dublin County	FF	27J	33	38															3	09/06/1927	23/06/1943	9.72	1884	30/01/1945	61
57	Bennett	George	Limerick	FG	27	27	32	33	37	38	43	44										8	09/06/1927	04/02/1948	20.66	1877	20/06/1963	86
58	Benson	Ernest	Dublin Townships	FG	37	38	43															3	01/07/1937	30/05/1944	6.91		17/03/1975	
59	Bermingham	Joseph	Kildare	LB	73	77	81	82	82													5	28/02/1973	17/02/1987	13.97	09/05/1919	11/08/1995	76
60	Bhamjee	Moosajee	Clare	LB	92																	1	25/11/1992	06/06/1997	4.53	11/12/1947		64.3
61	Bhreathnach	Niamh	Dun Laoghaire	LB	92																	1	25/11/1992	06/06/1997	4.53	01/06/1945		66.8
62	Birmingham	George	Dublin North East	FG	81	82	82	87														4	11/06/1981	15/06/1989	8.01	03/08/1954		57.6
63	Blaney	Harry	Donegal North East	IFF	97																	1	06/06/1997	17/05/2002	4.94	01/02/1928		84.1
64	Blaney	Neal	Donegal East	FF	27	27	32	33	37	43	44	48										8	09/06/1927	30/10/1948	16.37	1/11/1893	30/10/1948	54
65	Blaney	Neil T.	Donegal North East	IFF	48*	51	54	57	61	65	69	73	77	81	82	82	87	89	92			15	*07/12/1948*	08/11/1995	46.92	30/10/1922	08/11/1995	73
66	Blaney	Niall	Donegal North East	IFF	02	07																2	17/05/2002	25/02/2011	8.78	29/01/1974		38.1
67	Blowick	Joseph	Mayo South	CnaT	43	44	48	51	54	57	61											7	23/06/1943	07/04/1965	21.79	13/03/1903	12/08/1970	67
68	Blythe	Ernest	Monaghan	CG	18	21	22	23	27	27	32											7	21/01/1919	24/01/1933	14.01	13/4/1889	23/02/1975	85
69	Boland	Gerald	Roscommon	FF	23	27	27	32	33	37	38	43	44	48	51	54	57					13	27/08/1923	04/10/1961	38.11	25/05/1885	05/01/1973	87
70	Boland	Harry*	Roscommon /Mayo	CR	18/	21	22															3	21/01/1919	02/08/1922	3.53	27/4/1887	02/08/1922	35
71	Boland	John	Dublin North	FG	77	81	82	82	87													5	16/06/1977	15/06/1989	12.00	30/11/1944	14/08/2000	55
72	Boland	Kevin	Dublin County South	FF	57	61	65	69														4	05/03/1957	04/11/1970	13.67	15/10/1917	03/10/2001	83
73	Boland	Patrick	Laoighis-Offaly	FF	27	27	32	33	37	38	43	44	48	51								10	09/06/1927	18/05/1954	26.94	1890		
74	Bolger	Thomas	Carlow-Kilkenny	CG	25*																	1	*11/03/1925*	09/06/1927	2.25	29/3/1882	01/05/1938	56
75	Booth	Lionel	Dun Laoghaire	FF	57	61	65															3	05/03/1957	18/06/1969	12.29	12/06/1914	31/05/1997	82
76	Bourke	Daniel	Limerick East	FF	27S	32	33	37	38	43	44	48	51									9	15/09/1927	13/04/1952	24.58	1886	13/04/1952	66
77	Bourke	Seamus	Tipperary	CG	18	21	22	23	27	27	32	33	37									9	21/01/1919	17/06/1938	19.40	14/6/1893	01/01/1967	73
78	Boyd Barrett	Richard	Dun Laoghaire	PBPA	11																	1	25/02/2011		1.07	15/11/1967		44.4
79	Boylan	Andrew	Cavan-Monaghan	FG	87	89	92	97														4	17/02/1987	17/05/2002	15.24	01/01/1939		73.2
80	Boylan	Terence	Kildare	FF	64*	65	69															3	*19/02/1964*	28/02/1973	9.03	10/09/1910	10/01/1991	80
81	Boyle	Dan	Cork South Central	GP	02																	1	17/05/2002	24/05/2007	5.02	14/08/1962		49.6
82	Bradford	Paul	Cork East	FG	89	92	97															3	15/06/1989	17/05/2002	12.92	01/12/1963		48.3
83	Bradley	Michael	Cork Mid	LB	22																	1	16/06/1922	27/08/1923	1.20		23/11/1923	
84	Brady	Aine	Kildare North	FF	07																	1	24/05/2007	25/02/2011	3.76	08/09/1954		57.5
85	Brady	Brian	Donegal West	FF	32	33	37	38	43	44	48											7	16/02/1932	10/09/1949	17.57	01/01/1903	10/09/1949	46
86	Brady	Cyprian	Dublin Central	FF	07																	1	24/05/2007	25/02/2011	3.76	26/06/1962		49.7
87	Brady	Gerard	Dublin South East	FF	77	81	82	82	87	89												6	16/06/1977	25/11/1992	15.44	01/07/1936		75.7
88	Brady	Gerry	Kildare	FF	82F																	1	18/02/1982	24/11/1982	0.76	19/08/1948		63.6
89	Brady	Johnny	Meath West	FF	97	02	07															3	06/06/1997	25/02/2011	13.72	01/01/1948		64.2
90	Brady	Laurence	Laoighis-Offaly	R	23																	1	27/08/1923	09/06/1927	3.78	20/1/1892	14/04/1973	81
91	Brady	Martin	Dublin North East	FF	97	02																2	06/06/1997	24/05/2007	9.96	07/05/1947		64.9
92	Brady	Philip	Dublin South Central	FF	51	57	61	65	69	73												6	30/05/1951	16/06/1977	23.25	10/6/1898	06/01/1995	96
93	Brady	Rory	Longford-Westmeath	SF	57																	1	05/03/1957	04/10/1961	4.58	02/10/1932		79.5
94	Brady	Sean	Dun Laoghaire	FF	27	32	33	37	38	43	44	48	51	54	57	61						12	15/09/1927	07/04/1965	37.56	28/5/1890	24/02/1969	78
95	Brady	Vincent	Dublin North Central	FF	77	81	82	82	87	89												6	16/06/1977	25/11/1992	15.44	14/03/1936		76.0
96	Brasier	Brook	Cork South East	FG	32	37	38															3	16/02/1932	30/08/1940	4.11	1/2/1879	30/08/1940	61
97	Breathnach	Cormac	Dublin North West	FF	32	33	37	38	43	44	48	51										8	16/02/1932	18/05/1954	22.25	01/01/1903	29/05/1956	53
98	Bree	Declan	Sligo-Leitrim	LB	92																	1	25/11/1992	06/06/1997	4.53	01/07/1951		60.7
99	Breen	Dan	Tipperary South	FF	23	32	33	37	38	43	44	48	51	54	57	61						12	27/08/1923	07/04/1965	36.92	11/8/1894	27/12/1969	75
100	Breen	James	Clare	NP	02																	1	17/05/2002	24/05/2007	5.02	23/05/1945		66.8
101	Breen	Pat	Clare	NP	02	07	11															3	17/05/2002		9.85	21/03/1957		55.0
102	Brennan	Joe	Donegal	FF	51	54	57	61	65	69	73	77										8	30/05/1951	13/07/1980	29.12	14/02/1912	13/07/1980	68
103	Brennan	Joseph	Dun Laoghaire	CnaP	48																	1	04/02/1948	30/05/1951	3.32	10/9/1889	04/05/1968	78
104	Brennan	Martin	Sligo	FF	38	43	44															3	17/06/1938	04/02/1948	9.63	01/03/1903	21/06/1956	53
105	Brennan	Matt	Sligo-Leitrim	FF	82	82	87	89	92	97												6	18/02/1982	17/05/2002	20.24	01/10/1936		75.5

	Surname	Forename	Constituency	Party	Elected																	Terms	From	To	Service	Born	Died	Age
106	Brennan	Michael	Roscommon	FG	27	27	33	37	38													5	09/06/1927	23/06/1943	15.10	1884	06/10/1970	86
107	Brennan	Ned	Dublin North East	FF	82F																	1	18/02/1982	24/11/1982	0.76	01/08/1920	21/09/1988	68
108	Brennan	Patrick	Clare	CT	21	22																2	24/05/1921	11/12/1922	1.55			
109	Brennan	Paudge	Wicklow	FF	54	57	61	65	69	81	82N											7	18/05/1954	17/02/1987	23.70	18/02/1922	10/06/1998	76
110	Brennan	Seamus	Dublin South	FF	81	82	82	87	89	92	97	02	07									9	11/06/1981	09/07/2008	27.08	16/02/1948	09/07/2008	60
111	Brennan	Thomas	Wicklow	FF	44	48	51															3	30/05/1944	22/01/1953	8.65	1886	22/01/1953	67
112	Breslin	Cormac	Donegal-Leitrim	FF	37	38	43	44	48	51	54	57	61	65	69	73						12	01/07/1937	16/06/1977	39.96	25/04/1902	23/01/1978	75
113	Briscoe	Ben	Dublin South Central	FF	65	69	73	77	81	82	82	87	89	92	97							11	07/04/1965	17/05/2002	37.11	11/03/1934		78.0
114	Briscoe	Robert	Dublin South West	FF	27	32	33	37	38	43	44	48	51	54	57	61						12	15/09/1927	07/04/1965	37.56	25/9/1894	30/05/1969	74
115	Broderick	Henry	Longford-Westmeath	LB	27	27																2	09/06/1927	16/02/1932	4.69	1870		
116	Broderick	Sean	Galway East	FG	23	27	27	32	33	37	38											7	27/08/1923	23/06/1943	19.82	1/1/1890	20/08/1953	63
117	Broderick	William*	Cork E/Waterford/SE	FG	32	33/	38/	43	44													5	16/02/1932	04/02/1948	15.01	20/5/1877	01/06/1957	80
118	Brosnan	Sean	Cork North East	FF	69	74*	77															3	18/06/1969	18/04/1979	8.12	21/12/1916	18/04/1979	62
119	Broughan	Tommy	Dublin North East	LB	92	97	02	07	11													5	25/11/1992		19.32	01/08/1947		64.6
120	Browne	John	Carlow-Kilkenny	FG	89	92	97															3	15/06/1989	17/05/2002	12.92	01/10/1936		75.5
121	Browne	John	Wexford	FF	82N	87	89	92	97	02	07	11										8	24/11/1982		29.33	01/08/1948		63.6
122	Browne	Michael	Mayo North	FG	61																	1	04/10/1961	07/04/1965	3.51	12/01/1930		82.2
123	Browne	Noel	Dublin North Central	SLP	48	51	57	61	69	77	81											7	04/02/1948	18/02/1982	22.74	12/12/1915	23/05/1997	81
124	Browne	Patrick	Mayo North	FG	37	38	43	44	48	51												6	01/07/1937	18/05/1954	16.88	1888	24/07/1970	82
125	Browne	Patrick (Fad)	Waterford	FF	66*	69																2	07/12/1966	28/02/1973	6.23	12/09/1906	19/02/1991	84
126	Browne	Sean	Wexford	FF	57	69	73	77	82F													5	05/03/1957	24/11/1982	17.32	03/05/1915	27/03/1996	79
127	Browne	William	Leitrim-Sligo	FF	32	33																2	16/02/1932	01/07/1937	5.37			
128	Brugha	Caitlin	Waterford	SF	23	27J																2	27/08/1923	15/09/1927	4.05	11/12/1879	01/12/1959	79
129	Brugha	Cathal	Waterford	CR	18	21	22															3	21/01/1919	07/07/1922	3.46	18/7/1874	07/07/1922	47
130	Brugha	Ruairi	Dublin County South	FF	73																	1	28/02/1973	16/06/1977	4.30	15/10/1917	30/01/2006	88
131	Bruton	John	Meath	FG	69	73	77	81	82	82	87	89	92	97	02							11	18/06/1969	01/11/2004	35.37	18/05/1947		64.8
132	Bruton	Richard	Dublin North Central	FG	82	82	87	89	92	97	02	07	11									9	18/02/1982		30.09	15/03/1953		59.0
133	Buckley	Donal*	Kildare/Wicklow	FF	18/	21/	27	27														4	21/01/1919	16/02/1932	8.09	5/2/1866	30/10/1963	97
134	Buckley	Sean	Cork South	FF	23	38	43	44	48	51												6	27/08/1923	18/05/1954	19.70		01/01/1963	
135	Bulfin	Francis	Laoighis-Offaly	CG	21	22	23															3	24/05/1921	09/06/1927	6.04	12/2/1874	22/03/1951	77
136	Burke**	Dick	Dublin West	FG	69	73	81	82F														4	18/06/1969	30/03/1982	8.26	29/03/1932		80.0
137	Burke	James J.	Roscommon	FG	54	57	61															3	18/05/1954	12/05/1964	9.99		12/05/1964	
138	Burke	James M.	Cork West	CG	33																	1	24/01/1933	10/09/1936	3.63	4/11/1873	10/09/1936	62
139	Burke	Joan	Roscommon	FG	64*	65	69	73	77													5	*08/07/1964*	11/06/1981	16.93	08/02/1928		84.1
140	Burke	Liam	Cork North Central	FG	69	73	79*	81	82	82	87	92	97									9	18/06/1969	17/05/2002	27.07	02/02/1928	21/08/2005	77
141	Burke	Patrick	Clare	FG	32	33	37	38	43	44												6	16/02/1932	07/02/1945	12.98	16/4/1879	07/02/1945	65
142	Burke	Patrick J.	Dublin County North	FF	44	48	51	54	57	61	65	69										8	30/05/1944	28/02/1973	28.75	26/01/1904	09/09/1985	81
143	Burke	Ray	Dublin North	FF	73	77	81	82	82	87	89	92	97									9	28/02/1973	07/10/1997	24.61	30/09/1943		68.5
144	Burke	Thomas	Clare	F	37	38	43	44	48													5	01/07/1937	30/05/1951	13.91	10/06/1908	20/11/1951	43
145	Burke	Ulick	Galway East	FG	97	07																2	06/06/1997	25/02/2011	8.70	19/11/1943		68.3
146	Burton	Joan	Dublin West	LB	92	02	07	11														4	25/11/1992		14.38	01/02/1949		63.1
147	Burton	Philip	Cork Mid	FG	61	65	69															3	04/10/1961	28/02/1973	11.40	26/07/1910	03/01/1995	84
148	Butler	Bernard	Dublin South West	FF	43	44	48	51	54	57												6	23/06/1943	13/03/1959	15.72	1/9/1886	13/03/1959	72
149	Butler	John	Waterford	LB	22	23																2	16/06/1922	09/06/1927	4.98	1891	16/02/1968	77
150	Butler	Ray	Meath West	FG	11																	1	25/02/2011		1.07	30/12/1965		46.2
151	Buttimer	Jerry	Cork South Central	FG	11																	1	25/02/2011		1.07	18/03/1967		45.0
152	Byrne	Alfred	Dublin North East	NP	22	23	27	27	32	33	37	38	43	44	48	51	54					13	16/06/1922	13/03/1956	30.75	17/3/1882	13/03/1956	73
153	Byrne	Alfred P.	Dublin North West	NP	37	38	43	48	51													5	01/07/1937	26/07/1952	11.39	1913	26/07/1952	39
154	Byrne	Catherine	Dublin South Central	FG	07	11																2	24/05/2007		4.83	26/02/1956		56.1
155	Byrne	Christopher	Wicklow	FF	21	22	23	43														4	24/05/1921	30/05/1944	6.98	1886	05/09/1957	71
156	Byrne	Conor	Longford-Westmeath	R	23																	1	27/08/1923	09/06/1927	3.78		19/04/1948	
157	Byrne	Daniel J	Waterford-Tipperary	F	22																	1	16/06/1922	27/08/1923	1.20			
158	Byrne	Eric	Dublin South Central	DL	89	94*	11															3	15/06/1989		7.51	21/04/1947		64.9

	Surname	Forename	Constituency	Party	Elected																	Terms	From	To	Service	Born	Died	Age
159	Byrne	Henry	Laoighis-Offaly	LB	65																	1	07/04/1965	18/06/1969	4.20	06/03/1920	06/04/1976	56
160	Byrne	Hugh	Dublin North West	FG	69	73	77	81														4	18/06/1969	18/02/1982	12.67	05/07/1939		72.7
161	Byrne	Hugh	Wexford	FF	81	82	82	87	92	97												6	11/06/1981	17/05/2002	17.48	03/09/1943		68.6
162	Byrne	John J.	Dublin North	CG	27	27	32															3	09/06/1927	24/01/1933	5.63	23/9/1878	29/07/1942	63
163	Byrne	Patrick	Dublin North East	FG	56*	57	61	65														4	30/04/1956	18/06/1969	13.13	02/04/1925		87.0
164	Byrne	Sean	Tipperary South	FF	82	82																2	18/02/1982	17/02/1987	5.00	16/05/1937		74.9
165	Byrne	Thomas	Dublin North West	NP	52*	54	57															3	*12/11/1952*	04/10/1961	8.89	07/11/1917	16/03/1978	60
166	Byrne	Thomas	Meath East	FF	07																	1	24/05/2007	25/02/2011	3.76	01/06/1977		34.8
167	Cafferky	Dominick	Mayo South	CnaT	43	44	51															3	23/06/1943	18/05/1954	7.58		15/03/1971	
168	Cahill	Francis	Dublin North	CG	23																	1	27/08/1923	30/10/1924	1.18			
169	Cahill	Patrick	Kerry	R	21	22	23															3	24/05/1921	09/06/1927	6.04		01/01/1946	
170	Callanan	Joe	Galway East	FF	02																	1	17/05/2002	24/05/2007	5.02	30/01/1949		63.1
171	Callanan	John	Galway East	FF	73	77	81F	82F														4	28/02/1973	15/06/1982	9.29	20/05/1910	15/06/1982	72
172	Calleary	Dara	Mayo	FF	07	11																2	24/05/2007		4.83	10/05/1973		38.9
173	Calleary	Phelim	Mayo North	FF	52*	54	57	61	65													5	*26/06/1952*	18/06/1969	16.98	3/10/1895	04/01/1974	78
174	Calleary	Sean	Mayo East	FF	73	77	81	82	82	87	89											7	28/02/1973	25/11/1992	19.74	27/10/1931		80.4
175	Callely	Ivor	Dublin North Central	FF	89	92	97	02														4	15/06/1989	24/05/2007	17.94	06/05/1958		53.9
176	Cannon	Ciaran	Galway East	FG	11																	1	25/02/2011		1.07	19/09/1965		46.5
177	Carew	John	Limerick East	FG	52*	54	57															3	*26/06/1952*	04/10/1961	9.27	05/05/1901	12/07/1968	67
178	Carey	Donal	Clare	FG	82	82	87	89	92	97												6	18/02/1982	17/05/2002	20.24	15/10/1937		74.4
179	Carey	Edmond	Cork East	CG	27S																	1	15/09/1927	16/02/1932	4.42	6/3/1883	26/03/1943	60
180	Carey	Joe	Clare	FG	07	11																2	24/05/2007		4.83	24/06/1975		36.7
181	Carey	Pat	Dublin North West	FF	97	02	07															3	06/06/1997	25/02/2011	13.72	09/11/1947		64.4
182	Carney	Frank	Donegal	FF	27	27	32															3	09/06/1927	19/10/1932	5.36	25/4/1896	19/10/1932	36
183	Carroll	James	Dublin South West	NP	57	61																2	05/03/1957	07/04/1965	8.09	29/03/1907	30/07/1973	66
184	Carroll	Sean	Limerick	R	23																	1	27/08/1923	09/06/1927	3.78	20/1/1892	01/02/1954	62
185	Carter	Frank	Longford-Westmeath	FF	51	54	61	65	69	73												6	30/05/1951	16/06/1977	21.47	27/07/1910	17/07/1988	77
186	Carter	Michael	Leitrim-Sligo	F	27J																	1	09/06/1927	15/09/1927	0.27			
187	Carter	Thomas*	Roscommon/Leitrim-Sligo	CG	21	22/	23	43	44	48												6	24/05/1921	30/05/1951	11.37	29/3/1882	11/09/1951	69.0
188	Carty	Frank	Sligo	FF	21	22	23	27	27	32	33	37	38									9	24/05/1921	10/09/1942	21.30	3/4/1897	10/09/1942	45.0
189	Carty	John	Mayo	FF	02																	1	17/05/2002	24/05/2007	5.02	12/08/1950		61.6
190	Carty	Michael	Clare-Galway South	FF	57	61	65	69														4	05/03/1957	28/02/1973	15.99	16/12/1916	23/04/1975	58.0
191	Casey	Sean	Cork Borough	LB	54	57	61	65														4	18/05/1954	29/04/1967	12.95	09/05/1922	29/04/1967	44.0
192	Cassidy	Archie	Donegal	LB	27S																	1	15/09/1927	16/02/1932	4.42			
193	Cassidy	Donie	Westmeath	FF	02																	1	17/05/2002	24/05/2007	5.02	15/09/1945		66.5
194	Cawley	Patrick	Galway South	FG	51																	1	30/05/1951	18/05/1954	2.97	26/12/1904	08/12/1968	63.0
195	Childers	Erskine R.	Kildare-Wicklow	SF	21																	1	24/05/1921	16/06/1922	1.06	25/6/1870	24/11/1922	52.0
196	Childers	Erskine*	Lgford-Wmeath/Monaghan	FF	38	43	44	48	51	54	57/	61	65	69	73							11	17/06/1938	01/06/1973	34.96	11/12/1905	17/11/1974	68.0
197	Clancy	John	Sligo North	SF	18																	1	21/01/1919	24/05/1921	2.34	1891	01/05/1932	41.0
198	Clancy	Patrick	Limerick	LB	23	27	27															3	27/08/1923	16/02/1932	8.47		21/02/1947	
199	Clarke	Kathleen	Dublin North	R	21	27J																2	24/05/1921	15/09/1927	1.33	11/4/1878	29/09/1972	94.0
200	Clery	Michael	Mayo South	FF	27S	32	33	37	38	43	44											7	15/09/1927	04/12/1945	18.22			
201	Clery	Prof. Arthur	N.U.I.	NP	27																	1	09/06/1927	15/09/1927	0.27			
202	Clinton	Mark	Dublin County West	FG	61	65	69	73	77													5	04/10/1961	11/06/1981	19.69	07/02/1915	23/12/2001	86.0
203	Clohessy	Patrick	Limerick East	FF	57	61	65															3	05/03/1957	18/06/1969	12.29	16/04/1908	06/08/1971	63.0
204	Clohessy	Peadar	Limerick East	PD	81	87	89	92														4	11/06/1981	06/06/1997	11.00	01/12/1934		77.3
205	Clune	Deirdre	Cork South Central	FG	97	07																2	06/06/1997	25/02/2011	8.70	01/06/1959		52.8
206	Cluskey	Frank	Dublin South Central	LB	65	69	73	77	82	82	87											7	07/04/1965	07/04/1989	23.31	01/04/1930	07/04/1989	59.0
207	Coburn	George	Louth	FG	54*	54	57															3	*03/03/1954*	04/10/1961	7.59	04/03/1920		92.1
208	Coburn	James	Louth	FG	27	27	32	33	37	38	43	44	48	51								10	09/06/1927	05/12/1953	26.49	13/4/1889	05/12/1953	64.0
209	Coffey	Paudie	Waterford	FG	11																	1	25/02/2011		1.07	15/05/1969		42.9
210	Cogan	Barry	Cork Mid	FF	77																	1	16/06/1977	11/06/1981	3.99	27/09/1936		75.5
211	Cogan	Patrick	Wicklow	NP	38	43	44	48	51													5	17/06/1938	18/05/1954	15.92	23/10/1903	05/01/1977	73.0

	Surname	Forename	Constituency	Party	Elected																	Terms	From	To	Service	Born	Died	Age
212	Colbert	James	Limerick	FF	23	27	27	32														4	27/08/1923	24/01/1933	9.41			
213	Colbert	Michael	Limerick West	FF	37	44	55*															3	01/07/1937	05/03/1957	5.86	1900	01/04/1959	59.0
214	Cole	John J.	Cavan	NP	23	27S	37	38	43													5	27/08/1923	30/05/1944	15.12		25/05/1959	
215	Cole	Walter	Cavan	CT	22																	1	16/06/1922	27/08/1923	1.20		26/04/1943	
216	Colivet	Michael	Limerick City	CR	18	21	22															3	21/01/1919	27/08/1923	4.60	29/3/1882	04/05/1955	73.0
217	Colley	Anne	Dublin South	PD	87																	1	17/02/1987	15/06/1989	2.32	01/07/1951		60.7
218	Colley	George	Dublin Central	FF	61	65	69	73	77	81	82	82										8	04/10/1961	17/09/1983	21.95	18/10/1925	17/09/1983	57.0
219	Colley	Harry	Dublin North East	FF	44	48	51	54														4	30/05/1944	05/03/1957	12.76	21/2/1891	18/01/1972	80.0
220	Collins	Aine	Cork North West	FG	11																	1	25/02/2011		1.07	09/09/1969		42.5
221	Collins	Conor*	Limerick West/Kerry	CR	18/	21	22															3	21/01/1919	27/08/1923	4.60	13/11/1881	23/11/1937	56.0
222	Collins	Edward	Waterford	FG	69	73	77	81	82	82												6	18/06/1969	17/02/1987	17.67	01/02/1941		71.1
223	Collins	Gerard	Limerick West	FF	67*	69	73	77	81	82	82	87	89	92								10	*09/11/1967*	06/06/1997	29.57	16/10/1938		73.4
224	Collins	James	Limerick West	FF	48	51	54	57	61	65												6	04/02/1948	01/09/1967	19.57	31/10/1900	01/09/1967	66.0
225	Collins	Joan	Dublin South Central	PBPA	11																	1	25/02/2011		1.07	17/06/1961		50.8
226	Collins	Michael	Cork Mid	CT	18	21	22															3	21/01/1919	22/08/1922	3.58	16/10/1890	22/08/1922	31.0
227	Collins	Michael	Limerick West	FF	97	02																2	06/06/1997	24/05/2007	9.96	01/11/1940		71.4
228	Collins	Niall	Limerick West	FF	07	11																2	24/05/2007		4.83	30/03/1973		39.0
229	Collins	Sean	Cork South West	FG	48	51	54	61	65													5	04/02/1948	18/06/1969	16.79	10/07/1918	11/04/1975	56.0
230	Collins-O'Driscoll	Margaret	Dublin North	CG	23	27	27	32														4	27/08/1923	24/01/1933	9.41	1878	17/06/1945	67.0
231	Colohan	Hugh*	Wicklow/Kildare	LB	22/	23	27	27														4	16/06/1922	16/04/1931	8.83	30/9/1894	16/04/1931	36.0
232	Colreavy	Michael	Sligo-North Leitrim	SF	11																	1	25/02/2011		1.07	01/09/1948		63.6
233	Commons	Bernard	Mayo South	CnaT	45*	48																2	*04/12/1945*	30/05/1951	5.48	15/05/1913	19/04/1965	51.0
234	Conaghan	Hugh	Donegal North East	FF	77	81	82	82	87													5	16/06/1977	15/06/1989	12.00	06/05/1926		85.9
235	Conaghan	Michael	Dublin South Central	LB	11																	1	25/02/2011		1.07	01/09/1945		66.6
236	Concannon	Helena	N.U.I.	FF	33																	1	24/01/1933	01/07/1937	4.43	1878	27/02/1952	74.0
237	Conlan	John	Kildare	F	23																	1	27/08/1923	09/06/1927	3.78			
238	Conlan	Sean	Cavan-Monaghan	FG	11																	1	25/02/2011		1.07	01/01/1975		37.2
239	Conlon	John F.	Cavan-Monaghan	FG	69	73	77	81	82	82												6	18/06/1969	17/02/1987	17.67	21/05/1928	03/12/2004	76.0
240	Conlon	Margaret	Cavan-Monaghan	FF	07																	1	24/05/2007	25/02/2011	3.76	17/09/1967		44.5
241	Conlon	Martin	Roscommon	CG	25*	27	27	32														4	*11/03/1925*	24/01/1933	7.87	1879	23/01/1966	87.0
242	Connaughton	Paul	Galway East	FG	81	82	82	87	89	92	97	02	07									9	11/06/1981	25/02/2011	29.71	06/06/1944		67.8
243	Connaughton	Paul	Galway East	FG	11																	1	25/02/2011		1.07	18/01/1982		30.2
244	Connick	Sean	Wexford	FF	07																	1	24/05/2007	25/02/2011	3.76	27/08/1963		48.6
245	Connolly	Cornelius	Cork West	CG	23																	1	27/08/1923	09/06/1927	3.78			
246	Connolly	Ger	Laoighis-Offaly	FF	69	73	77	81	82	82	87	89	92									9	18/06/1969	06/06/1997	27.97	16/04/1937		74.9
247	Connolly	Michael	Longford-Westmeath	CG	27S																	1	15/09/1927	16/02/1932	4.42	1860	1945	85.0
248	Connolly	Paudge	Cavan-Monaghan	NP	02																	1	17/05/2002	24/05/2007	5.02	23/09/1953		58.5
249	Connolly	Roderick	Louth	LB	43	48																2	23/06/1943	30/05/1951	4.25	1901	16/12/1980	79.0
250	Connor	John	Kerry North	CnaP	54																	1	18/05/1954	11/12/1955	1.57		11/12/1955	
251	Connor	John	Longford-Roscommon	FG	81	89	92															3	11/06/1981	06/06/1997	8.68	14/02/1944		68.1
252	Connor	Patrick	Kerry South	FG	61	65																2	04/10/1961	18/06/1969	7.70	15/03/1906	26/06/1989	83.0
253	Conway	Ciara	Waterford	LB	11																	1	25/02/2011		1.07	13/08/1980		31.6
254	Coogan	Eamonn	Carlow-Kilkenny	FG	44																	1	30/05/1944	22/01/1948	3.65	1896	22/01/1948	52.0
255	Coogan Jnr	Fintan	Galway West	FG	82N																	1	24/11/1982	17/02/1987	4.23	02/06/1944		67.8
256	Coogan Snr	Fintan	Galway West	FG	54	57	61	65	69	73												6	18/05/1954	16/06/1977	23.08	13/04/1910	01/01/1985	74.0
257	Coonan	Noel	Tipperary North	FG	07	11																2	24/05/2007		4.83	06/01/1951		61.2
258	Cooney	Eamonn	Dublin North West	FF	27S	32	33	38														4	15/09/1927	23/06/1943	14.81		07/02/1975	
259	Cooney	Patrick	Longford-Westmeath	FG	70*	73	81	82	82	87												6	*14/04/1970*	15/06/1989	15.18	02/03/1931		81.1
260	Cooper	Maj. Bryan	Dublin County	CG	23	27	27															3	27/08/1923	05/07/1930	6.86	17/6/1884	05/07/1930	46.0
261	Corbett	Eamonn	Galway West	FF	35*	43																2	*19/06/1935*	30/05/1944	2.97		21/08/1945	
262	Corcoran-Kennedy	Marcella	Laoighis Offaly	FG	11																	1	25/02/2011		1.07	07/01/1963		49.2
263	Corish	Brendan	Wexford	LB	45*	48	51	54	57	61	65	69	73	77	81							11	*04/12/1945*	18/02/1982	36.21	19/11/1918	17/02/1990	71.0
264	Corish	Richard	Wexford	LB	21	22	23	27	27	32	33	37	38	43	44							11	24/05/1921	19/07/1945	24.15	1889	19/07/1945	56.0

	Surname	Forename	Constituency	Party	Elected																	Terms	From	To	Service	Born	Died	Age
265	Corkery	Daniel	Cork North	FF	21	22	23	27	27	33												6	24/05/1921	01/07/1937	15.16	14/2/1878	31/12/1964	86.0
266	Corr	James	Cork South Central	FG	82F																	1	18/02/1982	24/11/1982	0.76	25/01/1934		78.2
267	Corry	Martin J.	Cork North East	FF	27	27	32	33	37	38	43	44	48	51	54	57	61	65				14	09/06/1927	18/06/1969	42.03	12/12/1890	14/02/1979	88.0
268	Cosgrave	James	Galway	NP	23																	1	27/08/1923	09/06/1927	3.78		18/04/1936	
269	Cosgrave	Liam	Dun Laoghaire	FG	43	44	48	51	54	57	61	65	69	73	77							11	23/06/1943	11/06/1981	37.97	13/04/1920		91.9
270	Cosgrave	Liam T.	Dun Laoghaire	FG	81	82	82															3	11/06/1981	17/02/1987	5.69	30/04/1956		55.9
271	Cosgrave	Michael Joe	Dublin North East	FG	77	81	82	82	87	89	97											7	16/06/1977	17/05/2002	20.39	09/03/1938		74.0
272	Cosgrave	Philip	Dublin South	CG	21	22	23															3	24/05/1921	22/10/1923	2.41		22/10/1923	
273	Cosgrave	William T.*	Car-Kil/Cork Borough	FG	18	21	22	23	27	27/	27S	32	33	37	38	43						12	21/01/1919	30/05/1944	25.36	6/6/1880	16/11/1965	85
274	Costello	Declan	Dublin South West	FG	51	54	57	61	65	73												6	30/05/1951	16/06/1977	22.35	01/08/1926	06/06/2011	84
275	Costello	Joe	Dublin Central	LB	92	02	07	11														4	25/11/1992		14.38	13/07/1945		66.7
276	Costello	John A.	Dublin South East	FG	33	37	38	44	48	51	54	57	61	65								10	24/01/1933	18/06/1969	35.46	20/6/1891	05/01/1976	84
277	Cott	Gerard	Cork North East	FG	69																	1	18/06/1969	28/02/1973	3.70	30/04/1940		71.9
278	Cotter	Bill	Cavan-Monaghan	FG	89																	1	15/06/1989	25/11/1992	3.45	10/02/1943		69.1
279	Cotter	Edward	Cork South West	FF	54	57/	61	65														4	18/05/1954	18/06/1969	15.09	27/06/1902	11/12/1972	70
280	Coughlan	Cathal	Donegal South West	FF	83*																	1	*13/05/1983*	21/06/1986	3.11	03/10/1937	21/06/1986	48
281	Coughlan	Clem	Donegal South West	FF	80*	81	82	82														4	*06/11/1980*	01/02/1983	2.24	14/08/1942	01/02/1983	40
282	Coughlan	Mary	Donegal South West	FF	87	89	92	97	02	07												6	17/02/1987	25/02/2011	24.02	01/05/1965		46.9
283	Coughlan	Stephen	Limerick East	LB	61	65	69	73														4	04/10/1961	16/06/1977	15.70	26/12/1910	20/12/1994	83.0
284	Coveney	Hugh	Cork South Central	FG	81	82N	94*	97														4	11/06/1981	14/03/1998	8.27	20/07/1935	14/03/1998	62.0
285	Coveney	Simon	Cork South Central	FG	98*	02	07	11														4	*23/10/1998*		13.41	16/06/1972		39.8
286	Cowan	Peadar	Dublin North East	NP	48	51																2	04/02/1948	18/05/1954	6.28	23/10/1903	09/05/1962	58.0
287	Cowen	Barry	Laoighis Offaly	FF	11																	1	25/02/2011		1.07	01/08/1967		44.6
288	Cowen	Bernard	Laoighis-Offaly	FF	69	77	81	82	82													5	18/06/1969	24/01/1984	10.30	29/01/1932	24/01/1984	51.0
289	Cowen	Brian	Laoighis-Offaly	FF	84*	87	89	92	97	02	07											7	*14/06/1984*	25/02/2011	26.70	10/01/1960		52.2
290	Cowley	Jerry	Mayo	NP	02																	1	17/05/2002	24/05/2007	5.02	11/11/1952		59.4
291	Cox	Pat	Cork South Central	PD	92																	1	25/11/1992	06/06/1997	4.53	28/11/1952		59.3
292	Coyle	Henry	Mayo North	CG	23																	1	27/08/1923	09/05/1924	0.70		29/05/1979	
293	Craig	Prof. Sir James	Dublin University	NP	21	22	23	27	27	32	33											7	24/05/1921	12/07/1933	12.13		12/07/1933	
294	Crawford	Seymour	Cavan-Monaghan	FG	92	97	02	07														4	25/11/1992	25/02/2011	18.25	01/06/1944		67.8
295	Creed	Donal	Cork North West	FG	65	69	73	77/	81	82	82	87										8	07/04/1965	15/06/1989	24.19	07/09/1924		87.5
296	Creed	Michael	Cork North West	FG	89	92	97	07	11													5	15/06/1989		17.75	29/06/1963		48.7
297	Cregan	John	Limerick West	FF	02	07																2	17/05/2002	25/02/2011	8.78	21/05/1961		50.8
298	Creighton	Lucinda	Dublin South East	FG	07	11																2	24/05/2007		4.83	20/01/1980		32.2
299	Crinion	Brendan*	Kildare/Meath	FF	61	65/	73	77	81													5	04/10/1961	18/02/1982	16.68	11/09/1923	02/07/1989	65.0
300	Cronin	Jeremiah	Cork North East	FF	65	69	73	77														4	07/04/1965	11/06/1981	16.18	15/09/1925	19/10/1990	65.0
301	Crotty	Kieran	Carlow-Kilkenny	FG	69	73	77	81	82	82	87											7	18/06/1969	15/06/1989	19.99	30/08/1930		81.6
302	Crotty	Patrick	Carlow-Kilkenny	FG	48	51	54	57	61	65												6	10/02/1948	18/06/1969	21.35	23/11/1902	26/11/1970	68.0
303	Crowe	Patrick	Tipperary South	FG	51	54																2	30/05/1951	05/03/1957	5.77	17/2/1892	08/08/1969	77.0
304	Crowe	Sean	Dublin South West	SF	02	11																2	17/05/2002		6.10	07/03/1957		55.0
305	Crowley	Flor	Cork South West	FF	65	69	73	81														4	07/04/1965	18/02/1982	12.88	27/12/1934	16/05/1997	62.0
306	Crowley	Frank	Cork North West	FG	81	82	82	87	89	92												6	11/06/1981	06/06/1997	15.99	29/05/1939		72.8
307	Crowley	Frederick	Kerry South	FF	27S	32	33	37	38	43	44											7	15/09/1927	05/05/1945	17.64	1880	05/05/1945	65.0
308	Crowley	Honor	Kerry South	FF	45*	48	51	54	57	61	65											7	*04/12/1945*	18/10/1966	20.87	19/10/1903	18/10/1966	62.0
309	Crowley	James	Kerry	CG	18	21	22	23	27	27												6	21/01/1919	16/02/1932	13.07	1880	21/10/1946	66.0
310	Crowley	John	Mayo North	R	18	21	22	23														4	21/01/1919	09/06/1927	8.38		1934	
311	Crowley	Tadhg	Limerick East	FF	27	27	32	33	38	43	51	54										8	09/06/1927	05/03/1957	21.78	1890	12/03/1970	80.0
312	Cruise O'Brien	Conor	Dublin North East	LB	69	73																2	18/06/1969	16/06/1977	7.99	03/11/1917	18/12/2008	91.0
313	Cuffe	Ciaran	Dun Laoghaire	GP	02	07																2	17/05/2002	25/02/2011	8.78	03/04/1963		49.0
314	Cullen	Denis	Dublin North	LB	27J																	1	09/06/1927	15/09/1927	0.27	23/9/1878	26/11/1971	93.0
315	Cullen	Martin	Waterford	FF	87	92	97	02	07													5	17/02/1987	08/03/2010	19.60	02/11/1954		57.4
316	Cullimore	Seamus	Wexford	FF	89																	1	15/06/1989	25/11/1992	3.45	22/07/1954		57.7
317	Cummins	Patrick	Dublin South Central	FF	58*	61																2	*25/06/1958*	07/04/1965	6.78	10/06/1921	07/03/2009	87.0

	Surname	Forename	Constituency	Party	Elected																	Terms	From	To	Service	Born	Died	Age
318	Cunningham	Liam	Donegal North East	FF	51	54	57	61	65	69	73											7	30/05/1951	29/02/1976	24.75	25/01/1915	29/02/1976	61.0
319	Curran	John	Dublin Mid-West	FF	02	07																2	17/05/2002	25/02/2011	8.78	17/06/1960		51.8
320	Curran	Patrick	Dublin County	LB	32																	1	16/02/1932	24/01/1933	0.94			
321	Curran	Richard	Tipperary	FG	33	38																2	24/01/1933	23/06/1943	9.45	18/11/1879	27/01/1961	81.0
322	Currie	Austin	Dublin West	FG	89	92	97															3	15/06/1989	17/05/2002	12.92	11/10/1939		72.4
323	Cusack	Bryan	Galway	CR	18	21	22															3	21/01/1919	27/08/1923	4.60	2/8/1882	24/05/1973	90.0
324	D'Alton	Louis	Tipperary	CG	23																	1	27/08/1923	09/06/1927	3.78	20/9/1862	13/01/1945	82.0
325	Daly	Brendan	Clare	FF	73	77	81	82	82	87	89	97										8	28/02/1973	17/05/2002	24.68	02/02/1940		72.1
326	Daly	Clare	Dublin North	SP	11																	1	25/02/2011		1.07	11/04/1968		43.9
327	Daly	Denis	Kerry	FF	33																	1	24/01/1933	01/07/1937	4.43		1965	
328	Daly	Francis	Cork Borough	FF	43	44																2	23/06/1943	04/02/1948	4.62		18/02/1950	
329	Daly	Jim	Cork South West	FG	11																	1	25/02/2011		1.07	20/12/1972		39.3
330	Daly	John	Cork East	CG	23	27	27	32														4	27/08/1923	23/02/1932	8.49	23/3/1867	23/02/1932	64.0
331	Daly	Patrick	Cork North	FG	33	37	38															3	24/01/1933	23/06/1943	10.41			
332	D'Arcy	Michael	Wexford	FG	77	81	82	82	89	97												6	16/06/1977	17/05/2002	18.07	07/03/1934		78.0
333	D'Arcy	Michael Jnr.	Wexford	FG	07																	1	24/05/2007	25/02/2011	3.76	26/02/1970		42.1
334	Davern	Donal	Tipperary South	FF	65																	1	07/04/1965	02/11/1968	3.57	04/03/1935	02/11/1968	33.0
335	Davern	Michael	Tipperary South	FF	48	51	54	57	61													5	04/02/1948	07/04/1965	17.17	22/07/1900	25/07/1973	73.0
336	Davern	Noel	Tipperary South	FF	69	73	77	87	89	92	97	02										8	18/06/1969	24/05/2007	32.25	24/12/1945		66.2
337	Davin	William	Laoighis-Offaly	LB	22	23	27	27	32	33	37	38	43	44	48	51	54					13	16/06/1922	01/03/1956	33.71	1890	01/03/1956	66.0
338	Davis	Matthew	Longford-Westmeath	FF	37														w			1	01/07/1937	17/06/1938	0.96			
339	Davis	Michael	Mayo North	CG	27	27	32	33														4	09/06/1927	01/07/1937	10.06	1875	03/03/1944	69.0
340	Davitt	Robert	Meath	CG	33																	1	24/01/1933	01/07/1937	4.43	12/12/1899	26/09/1981	81.0
341	Day	Robert	Cork Borough	LB	22																	1	16/06/1922	27/08/1923	1.20	1885	1949	64.0
342	De Loughry	Peter	Carlow-Kilkenny	CG	27S																	1	15/09/1927	23/10/1931	4.10	4/2/1868	23/10/1931	63.0
343	De Markievicz	Constance	Dublin South	FF	18	21	23	27J														4	21/01/1919	15/07/1927	7.28	4/2/1868	15/07/1927	59.0
344	De Roiste	Liam	Cork Borough	CT	18	21	22															3	21/01/1919	27/08/1923	4.60	1882	15/05/1959	77.0
345	De Rossa	Proinsias	Dublin North West	DL	82	82	87	89	92	97												6	18/02/1982	17/05/2002	20.24	15/05/1940		71.9
346	De Valera	Eamon*	Mayo East/Clare	FF	18/	18	21	22	23	27	27	32	33	37	38	43	44	48	51	54	57	17	21/01/1919	23/06/1959	40.42	14/10/1882	29/08/1975	92.0
347	De Valera	Sile*	Dublin Co.Mid/Clare	FF	77/	87	89	92	97	02												6	16/06/1977	24/05/2007	24.26	17/12/1954		57.3
348	De Valera	Vivion	Dublin Central	FF	45*	48	51	54	57	61	65	69	73	77								10	*04/12/1945*	11/06/1981	35.52	13/12/1910	16/02/1982	71.0
349	Deasy	Austin	Waterford	FG	77	81	82	82	87	89	92	97										8	16/06/1977	17/05/2002	24.92	26/08/1936		75.6
350	Deasy	John	Waterford	FG	02	07	11															3	17/05/2002		9.85	08/10/1967		44.5
351	Dee	Eamon	Waterford	SF	21																	1	24/05/1921	16/06/1922	1.06			
352	Deenihan	Jimmy	Kerry North	FG	87	89	92	97	02	07	11											7	17/02/1987		25.09	11/09/1952		59.5
353	Deering	Mark	Wicklow	FG	53*	54																2	*18/06/1953*	05/03/1957	3.71	06/03/1900	26/04/1972	72.0
354	Deering	Pat	Carlow-Kilkenny	FG	11																	1	25/02/2011		1.07	02/02/1967		45.1
355	Delap	Paddy	Donegal-Leitrim	FF	70*																	1	*02/12/1970*	28/02/1973	2.24	17/03/1932	14/05/1987	55.0
356	Dempsey	Noel	Meath West	FF	87	89	92	97	02	07												6	17/02/1987	25/02/2011	24.02	06/01/1953		59.2
357	Dempsey	Tony	Wexford	FF	02																	1	17/05/2002	24/05/2007	5.02	11/05/1944		67.9
358	Dennehy	John	Cork South Central	FF	87	89	97	02														4	17/02/1987	24/05/2007	15.73	22/03/1940		72.0
359	Derham	Michael	Dublin County	CG	21	22	23															3	24/05/1921	20/11/1923	2.49	1889	20/11/1923	34.0
360	Derrig	Thomas*	Mayo/Carlow-Kilkenny	FF	21	22/	27	27	32	33	37	38	43	44	48	51	54					13	24/05/1921	19/11/1956	31.71	26/11/1897	19/11/1956	58.0
361	Desmond	Barry	Dun Laoghaire	LB	69	73	77	81	82	82	87											7	18/06/1969	15/06/1989	19.99	15/05/1935		76.9
362	Desmond	Daniel	Cork Mid	LB	48	51	54	57	61													5	04/02/1948	09/12/1964	16.85	03/10/1913	09/12/1964	51.0
363	Desmond	Eileen	Cork South Central	LB	65*	65	73	77	81	82	82											7	*10/03/1965*	17/02/1987	18.24	29/12/1932	07/01/2005	72.0
364	Desmond	William	Cork Borough	CG	32	33																2	16/02/1932	01/07/1937	5.37		05/09/1941	
365	Devins	James	Sligo-Mayo East	CR	21	22																2	24/05/1921	20/09/1922	1.33	1873	20/09/1922	49.0
366	Devins	Jimmy	Sligo-Leitrim	FF	02	07																2	17/05/2002	25/02/2011	8.78	20/09/1948		63.5
367	Dillon	James*	Donegal/Monaghan	FG	32	33/	37	38	43	44	48	51	54	57	61	65						12	16/02/1932	18/06/1969	37.34	26/09/1902	10/02/1986	83.0
368	Dineen	John	Cork East	F	22	23																2	16/06/1922	09/06/1927	4.98	23/3/1867	01/01/1942	74.0
369	Dockrell	Henry	Dun Laoghaire	FG	51	54	61	65	69	73												6	30/05/1951	16/06/1977	21.47	27/12/1914	22/11/1979	64.0
370	Dockrell	Henry M.	Dun Laoghaire	FG	32	33	37	38	43	44												6	16/02/1932	04/02/1948	15.97	1880	26/10/1955	75.0

	Surname	Forename	Constituency	Party	Elected																	Terms	From	To	Service	Born	Died	Age
371	Dockrell	Maurice E.	Dublin Central	FG	43	44	48	51	54	57	61	65	69	73								10	23/06/1943	16/06/1977	33.98	06/10/1908	09/12/1986	78.0
372	Doherty	Eugene	Donegal	CG	23	27	27	32														4	27/08/1923	24/01/1933	9.41	22/1/1862	01/05/1937	75.0
373	Doherty	Hugh	Donegal	FF	33																	1	24/01/1933	01/07/1937	4.43	01/01/1903	13/10/1972	69.0
374	Doherty	Kieran	Cavan-Monaghan	HBlk	81																	1	11/06/1981	02/08/1981	0.14	16/10/1955	02/08/1981	25.0
375	Doherty	Pearse	Donegal South West	SF	10*	11																2	*26/11/2010*		1.32	06/07/1977		34.7
376	Doherty	Regina	Meath East	FG	11																	1	25/02/2011		1.07	26/01/1971		41.2
377	Doherty	Sean	Mayo North	FF	57																	1	05/03/1957	04/10/1961	4.58		17/03/1985	
378	Doherty	Sean	Roscommon	FF	77	81	82	82	87	92	97											7	16/06/1977	17/05/2002	21.47	29/06/1944	07/06/2005	60.0
379	Dolan	James*	Roscommon/Leitrim-Sligo	CG	18/	21	22/	23	27	27	33											7	21/01/1919	01/07/1937	17.50	29/3/1882	14/07/1955	73.0
380	Dolan	Seamus	Cavan	FF	61																	1	04/10/1961	07/04/1965	3.51	10/12/1914	10/08/2010	95.0
381	Donegan	Batt	Cork North	FF	57																	1	05/03/1957	04/10/1961	4.58	21/12/1910	26/08/1978	67.0
382	Donegan	Patrick	Louth	FG	54	61	65	69	73	77												6	18/05/1954	11/06/1981	22.49	29/10/1923	26/11/2000	77.0
383	Donnellan	John	Galway West	FG	64*	65	69	73	77	81	82	82	87									9	*03/12/1964*	15/06/1989	24.53	27/03/1937		75.0
384	Donnellan	Michael	Galway East	CnaT	43	44	48	51	54	57	61											7	23/06/1943	27/09/1964	21.27	01/01/1900	27/09/1964	64.0
385	Donnelly	Eamon	Laoighis-Offaly	FF	33																	1	24/01/1933	01/07/1937	4.43		28/12/1944	
386	Donnelly	Stephen	Wicklow	NP	11																	1	25/02/2011		1.07	19/02/1975		37.1
387	Donohoe	Paschal	Dublin Central	FG	11																	1	25/02/2011		1.07	19/09/1974		37.5
388	Dooley	Patrick	Kildare	FF	57	61																2	05/03/1957	07/04/1965	8.09	14/01/1910	02/05/1982	72.0
389	Dooley	Timmy	Clare	FF	07	11																2	24/05/2007		4.83	13/02/1969		43.1
390	Dowdall	Thomas P.	Cork Borough	FF	32	33	37	38														4	16/02/1932	07/04/1942	10.14	1870	07/04/1942	72.0
391	Dowds	Robert	Dublin Mid West	LB	11																	1	25/02/2011		1.07	02/05/1953		58.9
392	Dowling	Dick	Carlow-Kilkenny	FG	82N																	1	24/11/1982	17/02/1987	4.23	12/12/1938		73.3
393	Dowling	Joseph	Dublin South West	FF	65	69	73															3	07/04/1965	16/06/1977	12.19	02/02/1922		90.1
394	Doyle	Andrew	Wicklow	FG	07	11																2	24/05/2007		4.83	02/07/1960		51.7
395	Doyle	Avril	Wexford	FG	82N	87	92															3	24/11/1982	06/06/1997	11.08	18/04/1949		62.9
396	Doyle	Edward	Carlow-Kilkenny	LB	23	27	27															3	27/08/1923	16/02/1932	8.47	29/3/1882		
397	Doyle	Joe	Dublin South East	FG	82N	89																2	24/11/1982	25/11/1992	7.68	01/06/1936	08/08/2009	73.0
398	Doyle	Michael	Wexford	F	22	23	27J															3	16/06/1922	15/09/1927	5.25			
399	Doyle	Peadar	Dublin South West	FG	23	27	27	32	33	37	38	43	44	48	51	54						12	27/08/1923	04/08/1956	32.94		04/08/1956	
400	Doyle	Seamus	Wexford	CR	21	22																2	24/05/1921	27/08/1923	2.26		30/04/1971	
401	Drohan	Frank	Waterford	SF	21																	1	24/05/1921	05/01/1922	0.62	13/8/1879	05/03/1953	73.0
402	Duffy	George Gavan	Dublin County	CT	18	21	22															3	21/01/1919	27/08/1923	4.60	21/10/1882	10/06/1951	68.0
403	Duffy	Patrick	Monaghan	CG	23																	1	27/08/1923	09/06/1927	3.78	28/7/1875	21/07/1946	70.0
404	Duffy	William	Galway	NL	27J																	1	09/06/1927	15/09/1927	0.27	7/4/1865	1945	79.0
405	Duggan	Edmund*	Meath/Louth/Meath	CG	18/	21	22/	23	27	27	32											7	21/01/1919	24/01/1933	14.01	1874	06/06/1936	62.0
406	Duignan	Peadar	Galway West	FF	51																	1	30/05/1951	18/05/1954	2.97	26/7/1898	13/04/1955	56.0
407	Dukes	Alan	Kildare	FG	81	82	82	87	89	92	97											7	11/06/1981	17/05/2002	20.93	20/04/1945		66.9
408	Dunne	Sean	Dublin County	LB	48	51	54	61	65	69												6	04/02/1948	25/06/1969	16.81	18/12/1918	25/06/1969	50.0
409	Dunne	Thomas	Tipperary North	FG	61	65	69	73														4	04/10/1961	16/06/1977	15.70	10/03/1926	03/08/1990	64.0
410	Durkan	Bernard	Kildare	FG	81	82N	87	89	92	97	02	07	11									9	11/06/1981		30.02	26/03/1945		67.0
411	Dwyer	James	Leix-Offaly	CG	26*	27	27															3	*18/02/1926*	16/02/1932	5.99	1881	17/12/1932	51.0
412	Dwyer	James J	Dublin County	SF	21																	1	24/05/1921	16/06/1922	1.06			
413	Dwyer	William	Cork Borough	NP	44																	1	30/05/1944	29/03/1946	1.83	1887	10/05/1951	64.0
414	Egan	Barry	Cork Borough	CG	27	27																2	09/06/1927	16/02/1932	4.69		03/03/1954	
415	Egan	Kieran	Laoighis-Offaly	FF	56*	57	61															3	*30/04/1956*	07/04/1965	8.94	26/05/1916	25/03/1976	59.0
416	Egan	Michael	Cork Borough	CG	24*																	1	*19/11/1924*	09/06/1927	2.55	1/2/1866	01/03/1947	81.0
417	Egan	Nicholas	Laoighis-Offaly	FF	54	57	61	65														4	18/05/1954	18/06/1969	15.09	17/07/1903	05/12/1971	68.0
418	Egan	Patrick	Laoighis-Offaly	CG	23																	1	27/08/1923	09/06/1927	3.78		28/04/1960	
419	Ellis	Dessie	Dublin North West	SF	11																	1	25/02/2011		1.07	09/10/1953		58.5
420	Ellis	John	Sligo-Leitrim	FF	81	82F	87	89	92	97	02											7	11/06/1981	24/05/2007	21.72	02/05/1952		59.9
421	English	Damien	Meath West	FG	02	07	11															3	17/05/2002		9.85	21/02/1978		34.1
422	English	Dr. Ada	N.U.I	SF	21																	1	24/05/1921	16/06/1922	1.06	1873	27/01/1944	71.0
423	Enright	Olwyn	Laoighis-Offaly	FG	02	07																2	17/05/2002	25/02/2011	8.78	01/07/1974		37.7

	Surname	Forename	Constituency	Party	Elected																	Terms	From	To	Service	Born	Died	Age
424	Enright	Tom	Laoighis-Offaly	FG	69	73	77	81	82	82	87	89	97									9	18/06/1969	17/05/2002	28.38	26/07/1940		71.7
425	Esmonde	John Grattan	Wexford	FG	73																	1	28/02/1973	16/06/1977	4.30	27/06/1928	16/05/1987	58.0
426	Esmonde	Osmond	Wexford	CG	23	27S	32	33														4	27/08/1923	22/07/1936	12.63	4/4/1896	22/07/1936	40.0
427	Esmonde	Sir Anthony	Wexford	FG	51	54	57	61	65	69												6	30/05/1951	28/02/1973	21.75	18/1/1899	1981	82.0
428	Esmonde	Sir John	Wexford	FG	37	38	43	48														4	01/07/1937	01/05/1951	10.15	15/12/1893	06/07/1958	64.0
429	Etchingham	Sean*	Wicklow E/Wexford	SF	18/	21																2	21/01/1919	16/06/1922	3.40		23/04/1923	
430	Everett	James	Wicklow	LB	22	23	27	27	32	33	37	38	43	44	48	51	54	57	61	65		16	16/06/1922	18/12/1967	45.51	1/5/1894	18/12/1967	73.0
431	Fagan	Charles*	Longford-Wmeath/Meath	FG	33/	37	38	43	44/	48	51	54	57									9	24/01/1933	04/10/1961	28.69	1/10/1881	08/05/1974	92.0
432	Fahey	Frank	Galway West	FF	82	82	87	89	97	02	07											7	18/02/1982	25/02/2011	24.49	06/06/1951		60.8
433	Fahey	Jackie*	Tipperary/Waterford	FF	65	69	73/	77	81	82	82	87	89									9	07/04/1965	25/11/1992	27.64	23/01/1928		84.2
434	Fahy	Frank	Galway South	FF	18	21	22	23	27	27	32	33	37	38	43	44	48	51				14	21/01/1919	14/07/1953	34.48	12/1/1880	14/07/1953	73.0
435	Falvey	Thomas	Clare	R	27J																	1	09/06/1927	15/09/1927	0.27		17/02/1941	
436	Fanning	John	Tipperary North	FF	51	54	57	61	65													5	30/05/1951	18/06/1969	18.05	22/10/1903	1982	78.0
437	Farrell	Alan	Dublin North	FG	11																	1	25/02/2011		1.07	29/12/1977		34.2
438	Farrell	Joseph	Louth	FF	73	77																2	28/02/1973	11/06/1981	8.28	01/07/1905	24/11/1999	94.0
439	Farrell	Sean	Leitrim-Sligo	R	23																	1	27/08/1923	09/06/1927	3.78		01/08/1972	
440	Farrelly	Denis	Meath	FG	61	65																2	04/10/1961	18/06/1969	7.70	18/09/1912	27/12/1974	62.0
441	Farrelly	John V.	Meath	FG	81	82	82	87	89	97												6	11/06/1981	17/05/2002	16.40	04/11/1954		57.4
442	Faulkner	Padraig	Louth	FF	57	61	65	69	73	77	81	82	82									9	05/03/1957	17/02/1987	29.96	12/03/1918		94.0
443	Feighan	Frank	Roscommon-Sth Leitrim	FG	07	11																2	24/05/2007		4.83	04/07/1962		49.7
444	Fennell	Nuala	Dublin South	FG	81	82	82	89														4	11/06/1981	25/11/1992	9.14	25/11/1935	11/08/2009	73.0
445	Ferran	Francis	Sligo-Mayo East	CR	21	22																2	24/05/1921	10/06/1923	2.05		10/06/1923	
446	Ferris	Anne	Wicklow	LB	11																	1	25/02/2011		1.07	24/09/1954		57.5
447	Ferris	Martin	Kerry North	SF	02	07	11															3	17/05/2002		9.85	28/03/1952		60.0
448	Ferris	Michael	Tipperary South	LB	89	92	97															3	15/06/1989	20/03/2000	10.76	21/11/1931	20/03/2000	68.0
449	Ffrench-O'Carroll	Michael	Dublin South West	NP	51																	1	30/05/1951	18/05/1954	2.97	15/09/1919	05/05/2007	87.0
450	Figgis	Darrell	Dublin County	NP	22	23																2	16/06/1922	27/10/1925	3.36	17/9/1882	27/10/1925	43.0
451	Filgate	Edward	Louth	FF	77	81	82F															3	16/06/1977	24/11/1982	5.44	16/09/1915		96.5
452	Finan	John	Roscommon	CnaT	51																	1	30/05/1951	18/05/1954	2.97	10/9/1898	24/05/1984	85.0
453	Finlay	Henry	Roscommon	CG	23																	1	27/08/1923	30/10/1924	1.18		1959	
454	Finlay	John	Laoighis-Offaly	FG	33	37																2	24/01/1933	17/06/1938	5.39		30/09/1942	
455	Finlay	Thomas	Dublin County	CG	30*	32																2	*09/12/1930*	22/11/1932	1.95	11/10/1893	22/11/1932	39.0
456	Finlay(jun)	Thomas	Dublin South Central	FG	54																	1	18/05/1954	05/03/1957	2.80			
457	Finn	Martin	Mayo East	FG	69	73																2	18/06/1969	16/06/1977	7.99	22/08/1917	10/06/1905	71.0
458	Finneran	Michael	Longford-Roscommon	FF	02	07																2	17/05/2002	25/02/2011	8.78	10/09/1947		64.5
459	Finucane	Michael	Limerick West	FG	89	92	97															3	15/06/1989	17/05/2002	12.92	01/02/1943		69.1
460	Finucane	Patrick	Kerry North	IndF	43	44	48	51	54	57	61	65										8	23/06/1943	18/06/1969	25.99	5/12/1890	10/04/1984	93.0
461	Fitzgerald	Alexis	Dublin South East	FG	82F																	1	18/02/1982	24/11/1982	0.76	07/05/1945		66.9
462	Fitzgerald	Brian	Meath	LB	92																	1	25/11/1992	06/06/1997	4.53	01/03/1947		65.1
463	Fitzgerald	Desmond*	Dublin Co/Carlow-Kilkenny	CG	18	21	22	23	27	27/	32	33										8	21/01/1919	01/07/1937	18.44	13/2/1888	09/04/1947	59.0
464	FitzGerald	Eithne	Dublin South	LB	92																	1	25/11/1992	06/06/1997	4.53	01/11/1950		61.4
465	Fitzgerald	Frances	Dublin South East	FG	92	97	11															3	25/11/1992		10.54	01/08/1950		61.6
466	FitzGerald	Garret	Dublin South East	FG	69	73	77	81	82	82	87	89										8	18/06/1969	25/11/1992	23.44	09/02/1926	19/05/2011	85
467	Fitzgerald	Gene	Cork South Central	FF	72*	73	77/	81	82	82												6	*02/08/1972*	17/02/1987	14.54	21/08/1932	14/12/2007	75
468	Fitzgerald	Liam	Dublin North East	FF	81	82N	87	89	92													5	11/06/1981	06/06/1997	15.23	01/09/1949		62.6
469	Fitzgerald	Seamus	Cork Borough	FF	43																	1	23/06/1943	30/05/1944	0.94	21/8/1896	23/07/1972	75
470	Fitzgerald	Seamus	Cork East	SF	21																	1	24/05/1921	16/06/1922	1.06			
471	Fitzgerald-Kenney	James	Mayo South	FG	27	27	32	33	37	38	43											7	09/06/1927	30/05/1944	16.98	1878	21/10/1956	78.0
472	Fitzgibbon	Gerald	Dublin University	NP	21	22																2	24/05/1921	27/08/1923	2.26		06/12/1942	
473	Fitzpatrick	Dermot	Dublin Central	FF	87	89	02															3	17/02/1987	24/05/2007	10.79	12/04/1940		71.9
474	Fitzpatrick	Michael	Dublin North West	CnaP	48																	1	04/02/1948	30/05/1951	3.32		08/10/1968	
475	Fitzpatrick	Michael	Kildare North	FF	07																	1	24/05/2007	25/02/2011	3.76	12/10/1942	14/10/2011	69
476	Fitzpatrick	Peter	Louth	FG	11																	1	25/02/2011		1.07	01/05/1962		49.9

	Surname	Forename	Constituency	Party	Elected																	Terms	From	To	Service	Born	Died	Age
477	Fitzpatrick	Thomas	Cavan-Monaghan	FG	65	69	73	77	81	82	82	87										8	07/04/1965	15/06/1989	24.19	14/02/1918	02/10/2006	88.0
478	Fitzpatrick	Tom	Dublin South Central	FF	65	69	73	77	81	82F												6	07/04/1965	24/11/1982	17.63	29/07/1926		85.6
479	Fitzsimmons	James	Meath	FF	77	81	82	82														4	16/06/1977	17/02/1987	9.67	01/12/1936		75.3
480	Flaherty	Mary	Dublin North West	FG	81	82	82	87	89	92												6	11/06/1981	06/06/1997	15.99	17/05/1953		58.8
481	Flanagan	Charles	Laoighis-Offaly	FG	87	89	92	97	07	11												6	17/02/1987		20.07	01/11/1956		55.4
482	Flanagan	Luke "Ming"	Roscommon-Sth Leitrim	NP	11																	1	25/02/2011		1.07	22/01/1972		40.2
483	Flanagan	Oliver J.	Laoighis-Offaly	FG	43	44	48	51	54	57	61	65	69	73	77	81	82	82				14	23/06/1943	17/02/1987	43.66	22/05/1920	26/04/1987	66.0
484	Flanagan	Sean	Mayo East	FF	51	54	57	61	65	69	73											7	30/05/1951	16/06/1977	26.05	26/01/1922	05/02/1993	71.0
485	Flanagan	Terence	Dublin North East	FG	07	11																2	24/05/2007		4.83	01/01/1975		37.2
486	Fleming	Brian	Dublin West	FG	81	82F																2	11/06/1981	24/11/1982	1.45	20/07/1946		65.7
487	Fleming	Sean	Laoighis-Offaly	FF	97	02	07	11														4	06/06/1997		14.79	27/02/1958		54.1
488	Fleming	Tom	Kerry South	NP	11																	1	25/02/2011		1.07	01/02/1951		61.1
489	Flinn	Hugo	Cork Borough	FF	27	32	33	37	38													5	15/09/1927	28/01/1943	15.37		28/01/1943	
490	Flood	Chris	Dublin South West	FF	87	89	92	97														4	17/02/1987	17/05/2002	15.24	01/05/1947		64.9
491	Flynn	Beverley	Mayo	FF	97	02	07															3	06/06/1997	25/02/2011	13.72	09/06/1966		45.8
492	Flynn	John	Kerry South	FF	32	33	37	38	48	51	54											7	16/02/1932	05/03/1957	20.43		22/08/1968	
493	Flynn**	Padraig	Mayo West	FF	77	81	82	82	87	89	92											7	16/06/1977	04/01/1993	15.55	09/05/1939		72.9
494	Flynn	Stephen	Sligo-Leitrim	FF	32	33	37	38	43	44	48	51	54	57								10	16/02/1932	24/11/1960	28.77		24/11/1960	
495	Fogarty	Andrew	Tipperary	FF	27	27	32	33	37	38	43	44										8	09/06/1927	04/02/1948	20.66	13/4/1879	24/04/1953	74.0
496	Fogarty	Patrick	Dublin County	FF	37	38	43	44														4	01/07/1937	02/05/1947	9.83		02/05/1947	
497	Foley	Denis	Kerry North	FF	81	82	82	87	92	97												6	11/06/1981	17/05/2002	17.48	14/05/1934		77.9
498	Foley	Des	Dublin County	FF	65	69																2	07/04/1965	28/02/1973	7.90	12/09/1940	05/02/1995	54.0
499	Forde	Patrick	Cork Mid	FF	69																	1	18/06/1969	13/05/1972	2.90	22/07/1922	13/05/1972	49.0
500	Fox	Billy	Monaghan	FG	69																	1	18/06/1969	28/02/1973	3.70	03/01/1939	12/03/1974	35.0
501	Fox	Christopher	Dublin Co. North	FF	77																	1	16/06/1977	11/06/1981	3.99	04/04/1931	01/10/1981	50.0
502	Fox	Johnny	Wicklow	NP	92																	1	25/11/1992	17/03/1995	2.31	05/04/1948	17/03/1995	46.0
503	Fox	Mildred	Wicklow	NP	95*	97	02															3	*29/06/1995*	24/05/2007	11.90	17/06/1971		40.8
504	Foxe	Tom	Roscommon	NP	89	92																2	15/06/1989	06/06/1997	7.98	01/06/1937	08/02/2000	62.0
505	French	Sean	Cork Borough	FF	27	27																2	09/06/1927	16/02/1932	4.69	29/5/1890	12/09/1937	47
506	French	Sean	Cork North Central	FF	67*	69	73	77/	81	82F												6	*09/11/1967*	24/11/1982	15.04	08/11/1931	25/12/2011	80
507	Friel	John	Donegal East	FF	37	38	43	44	48													5	01/07/1937	30/05/1951	13.91	1/8/1889	01/10/1963	74
508	Fuller	Stephen	Kerry North	FF	37	38																2	01/07/1937	23/06/1943	5.98		1984	
509	Furlong	Walter	Cork Borough	FF	44																	1	30/05/1944	04/02/1948	3.68	1/9/1893		
510	Gaffney	Patrick	Carlow-Kilkenny	LB	22																	1	16/06/1922	27/08/1923	1.20		1943	
511	Gallagher	Colm	Dublin North Central	FF	51	57																2	30/05/1951	26/06/1957	3.28		26/06/1957	
512	Gallagher	Denis	Mayo West	FF	73	77	81	82	82	87												6	28/02/1973	15/06/1989	16.29	23/11/1923	03/11/2001	77.0
513	Gallagher	James	Sligo-Leitrim	FF	61	65	69	77														4	04/10/1961	11/06/1981	15.39	20/04/1920	11/03/1983	62.0
514	Gallagher	Pat	Laoighis-Offaly	LB	92																	1	25/11/1992	06/06/1997	4.53	29/03/1963		49.0
515	Gallagher	Pat The Cope	Donegal South West	FF	81	82	82	87	89	92	02	07										8	11/06/1981	06/06/2009	23.05	10/03/1948		64.0
516	Gallagher	Patrick	Waterford	WP	82F																	1	18/02/1982	24/11/1982	0.76	01/12/1946		65.3
517	Galligan	Peter	Cavan	SF	18	21																2	21/01/1919	16/06/1922	3.40	20/6/1888	14/12/1966	78.0
518	Galvin	John	Cork Borough	FF	56*	57	61															3	*02/08/1956*	11/10/1963	7.19	15/05/1907	11/10/1963	56.0
519	Galvin	Sheila	Cork Borough	FF	64*																	1	*19/02/1964*	07/04/1965	1.13	23/02/1914	20/03/1983	69.0
520	Garahan	Hugh	Longford-Westmeath	F	27J																	1	09/06/1927	15/09/1927	0.27		07/06/1940	
521	Garland	Roger	Dublin South	GP	89																	1	15/06/1989	25/11/1992	3.45	01/02/1933		79.1
522	Geoghegan	James	Longford-Westmeath	FF	30*	32	33															3	*13/06/1930*	23/12/1936	6.53	8/12/1886	27/03/1951	64.0
523	Geoghegan	John	Galway West	FF	54	57	61	65	69	73												6	18/05/1954	05/01/1975	20.64	05/11/1913	05/01/1975	61.0
524	Geoghegan-Quinn**	Maire	Galway West	FF	75*	77	81	82	82	87	89	92										8	*04/03/1975*	06/06/1997	22.26	05/09/1950		61.5
525	Gibbons	Hugh	Roscommon	FF	65	69	73															3	07/04/1965	16/06/1977	12.19	06/07/1916	15/11/2007	91.0
526	Gibbons	James	Carlow-Kilkenny	FF	57	61	65	69	73	77	82F											7	05/03/1957	24/11/1982	25.03	03/08/1924	20/12/1997	73.0
527	Gibbons	Martin	Carlow-Kilkenny	PD	87																	1	17/02/1987	15/06/1989	2.32	01/03/1953		59.1
528	Gibbons	Sean	Carlow-Kilkenny	FF	23	32	33															3	27/08/1923	01/07/1937	6.55	31/5/1883	19/04/1952	68.0
529	Gilbride	Eugene	Sligo-Leitrim	FF	48	51	54	57	61	65												6	04/02/1948	18/06/1969	21.37	1/10/1892	11/03/1972	79.0

	Surname	Forename	Constituency	Party	Elected																	Terms	From	To	Service	Born	Died	Age
530	Gildea	Tom	Donegal South West	NP	97																	1	06/06/1997	17/05/2002	4.94	01/09/1939		72.6
531	Giles	Capt. Patrick	Meath	FG	37	38	43	44	48	51	54	57										8	01/07/1937	04/10/1961	24.26	1899	13/03/1965	66.0
532	Gilhawley	Eugene	Sligo-Leitrim	FG	61	65	73	77														4	04/10/1961	11/06/1981	15.99	14/04/1910	03/05/1987	77.0
533	Gill	John	Laoighis-Offaly	LB	27J																	1	09/06/1927	15/09/1927	0.27	27/12/1898	10/06/1971	72.0
534	Gilmore	Eamon	Dun Laoghaire	LB	89	92	97	02	07	11												6	15/06/1989		22.77	24/04/1955		56.9
535	Ginnell	Laurence	Longford-Westmeath	CR	18	21	22															3	21/01/1919	17/04/1923	4.24	1854	17/04/1923	69.0
536	Glenn	Alice	Dublin Central	FG	81	82N																2	11/06/1981	17/02/1987	4.93	17/12/1927	16/12/2011	84
537	Glennon	Jim	Dublin North	FF	02																	1	17/05/2002	24/05/2007	5.02	07/07/1953		58.7
538	Glynn	Brendan	Galway South	FG	54																	1	18/05/1954	05/03/1957	2.80	06/01/1910	10/07/1986	76.0
539	Gogan	Dick	Dublin North West	FF	54	57	61	65	69	73												6	18/05/1954	16/06/1977	23.08	29/11/1899	28/04/1982	82.0
540	Gogarty	Paul	Dublin Mid-West	GP	02	07																2	17/05/2002	25/02/2011	8.78	20/12/1968		43.3
541	Good	John	Dublin County	NP	23	27	27	32	33													5	27/08/1923	01/07/1937	13.85		02/04/1941	
542	Gorey	Denis	Carlow-Kilkenny	FG	22	23	27J	27*	32	37	38											7	16/06/1922	20/02/1940	13.12	25/5/1874	20/02/1940	65.0
543	Gormley	Francis	Longford-Westmeath	FF	32																	1	16/02/1932	24/01/1933	0.94			
544	Gormley	John	Dublin South East	GP	97	02	07															3	06/06/1997	25/02/2011	13.72	04/08/1959		52.6
545	Gorry	Patrick	Laoighis-Offaly	FF	27S	32	37	38	43	44	48											7	15/09/1927	30/05/1951	19.27	14/7/1896	23/10/1965	69.0
546	Goulding	Sean	Waterford	FF	27S	32	33															3	15/09/1927	01/07/1937	9.79	1877	15/12/1959	82.0
547	Governey	Desmond	Carlow-Kilkenny	FG	61	65	69	73	81	82F												6	04/10/1961	24/11/1982	17.15	11/09/1920		91.5
548	Grealish	Noel	Galway West	NP	02	07	11															3	17/05/2002		9.85	16/12/1965		46.3
549	Gregory	Tony	Dublin Central	NP	82	82	87	89	92	97	02	07										8	18/02/1982	02/01/2009	26.87	05/12/1947	02/01/2009	61.0
550	Griffin	Brendan	Tipperary South	FG	73	77	81	82	82	87												6	28/02/1973	15/06/1989	16.29	28/08/1935		76.6
551	Griffin	Brendan	Kerry South	FG	11																	1	25/02/2011		1.07	09/03/1982		30.0
552	Griffin	James	Meath	FF	57																	1	05/03/1957	22/03/1959	2.05	17/4/1899	22/03/1959	59.0
553	Griffith	Arthur*	Cavan/Tyrone/Cavan	CT	18/	18/	21	22														4	21/01/1919	12/08/1922	3.56	31/3/1871	12/08/1922	51.0
554	Hales	Sean	Cork Mid	CT	21	22																2	24/05/1921	07/12/1922	1.54		06/12/1922	
555	Hales	Thomas	Cork West	FF	33																	1	24/01/1933	01/07/1937	4.43	5/3/1892	29/04/1966	74.0
556	Hall	David	Meath	LB	23	27J																2	27/08/1923	15/09/1927	4.05	1870		
557	Halliden	Patrick J.	Cork North	CnaT	43	44	48															3	23/06/1943	30/05/1951	7.93			
558	Halligan	Brendan	Dublin South West	LB	76*																	1	*10/06/1976*	16/06/1977	1.02	05/07/1936		75.7
559	Halligan	John	Waterford	NP	11																	1	25/02/2011		1.07	01/01/1955		57.2
560	Hanafin	Mary	Dun Laoghaire	FF	97	02	07															3	06/06/1997	25/02/2011	13.72	01/06/1959		52.8
561	Hannigan	Dominic	Meath East	LB	11																	1	25/02/2011		1.07	01/07/1965		46.7
562	Hannigan	Joseph	Dublin South	NP	37	38																2	01/07/1937	23/06/1943	5.98	1904	1944	40.0
563	Harkin	Marian	Sligo-Leitrim	NP	02																	1	17/05/2002	24/05/2007	5.02	26/11/1953		58.3
564	Harney	Mary	Dublin South West	PD	81	82	82	87	89	92	97	02	07									9	11/06/1981	25/02/2011	29.71	11/03/1953		59.0
565	Harrington	Noel	Cork South West	FG	11																	1	25/02/2011		1.07	24/12/1970		41.2
566	Harris	Simon	Wicklow	FG	11																	1	25/02/2011		1.07	17/10/1986		25.4
567	Harris	Thomas	Kildare	FF	31*	32	33	37	38	43	44	48	51	54								10	*29/06/1931*	05/03/1957	25.68	1895	18/02/1974	79.0
568	Harte	Paddy	Donegal North East	FG	61	65	69	73	77	81	82	82	87	89	92							11	04/10/1961	06/06/1997	35.67	26/07/1931		80.7
569	Haslett	Alexander	Monaghan	NP	27	27	33															3	09/06/1927	01/07/1937	9.12	2/9/1883	17/01/1951	67.0
570	Hassett	John	Tipperary	CG	27	27	32															3	09/06/1927	24/01/1933	5.63		24/11/1955	
571	Haughey	Charles J.	Dublin North Central	FF	57	61	65	69	73	77	81	82	82	87	89							11	05/03/1957	11/02/1992	34.94	16/09/1925	13/06/2006	80.0
572	Haughey	Sean	Dublin North Central	FF	92	97	02	07														4	25/11/1992	25/02/2011	18.25	08/11/1961		50.4
573	Hayes	Brian	Dublin South West	FG	97	07	11															3	06/06/1997		9.77	23/08/1969		42.6
574	Hayes	Michael*	N.U.I./Dublin South/N.U.I.	CG	21	22	23/	23/	27	27	32											7	24/05/1921	24/01/1933	11.67	1/12/1889	11/07/1976	86.0
575	Hayes	Richard	Limerick East	CG	18	21	22	23														4	21/01/1919	10/01/1924	4.97	1878	1958	80.0
576	Hayes	Sean	Cork West	CT	18	21	22															3	21/01/1919	27/08/1923	4.60		1941	
577	Hayes	Sean	Tipperary	FF	27	27	32	33														4	09/06/1927	01/07/1937	10.06	1890	16/02/1968	78.0
578	Hayes	Tom	Tipperary South	FG	*01	02	07	11														4	*30/06/2001*		10.73	16/02/1952		60.1
579	Hayes	William	Limerick	CT	21	22																2	24/05/1921	27/08/1923	2.26			
580	Healy	Gus	Cork Borough	FF	57	65	69	73														4	05/03/1957	16/06/1977	16.77	20/05/1904	10/07/1987	83.0
581	Healy	John	Kerry South	FF	43	44																2	23/06/1943	04/02/1948	4.62		1995	
582	Healy	Seamus	Tipperary South	NP	00*	02	11															3	*22/06/2000*		7.99	09/08/1950		61.6

	Surname	Forename	Constituency	Party	Elected													Terms	From	To	Service	Born	Died	Age
583	Healy-Rae	Jackie	Kerry South	NP	97	02	07											3	06/06/1997	25/02/2011	13.72	09/03/1931		81.0
584	Healy-Rae	Michael	Kerry South	NP	11													1	25/02/2011		1.07	09/01/1967		45.2
585	Heffernan	Michael	Tipperary	F	23	27	27											3	27/08/1923	16/02/1932	8.47	3/4/1885	21/11/1970	85.0
586	Hegarty	Patrick	Cork East	FG	73	77/	81	82	82	87								6	28/02/1973	15/06/1989	16.29	26/12/1926	31/10/2002	75.0
587	Hennessy	Michael	Cork East	CG	22	23	27	27										4	16/06/1922	16/02/1932	9.67			
588	Hennessy	Thomas	Dublin South	CG	25*	27*	27S	32										4	11/03/1925	24/01/1933	7.87			
589	Hennigan	John	Leitrim-Sligo	CG	23	27	27	32										4	27/08/1923	24/01/1933	9.41	1876		
590	Henry	Mark	Mayo North	CG	27	27												2	09/06/1927	16/02/1932	4.69		1952	
591	Herbert	Michael	Limerick East	FF	69	73	77											3	18/06/1969	11/06/1981	11.98	17/05/1925	19/06/2006	81.0
592	Heron	Archibald	Dublin North West	LB	37													1	01/07/1937	17/06/1938	0.96		10/05/1971	
593	Heskin	Denis	Waterford	CnaT	43	44												2	23/06/1943	04/02/1948	4.62	17/2/1899	30/04/1975	76.0
594	Hession	James	Galway North	FG	51	54												2	30/05/1951	05/03/1957	5.77	05/11/1912	12/01/1999	86.0
595	Hewat	William	Dublin North	BP	23													1	27/08/1923	09/06/1927	3.78			
596	Hewson	Gilbert	Limerick	NP	27J													1	09/06/1927	15/09/1927	0.27		1951	
597	Heydon	Martin	Kildare South	FG	11													1	25/02/2011		1.07	09/08/1978		33.6
598	Hickey	James	Cork Borough	LB	38	48	51											3	17/06/1938	18/05/1954	11.30		07/06/1966	
599	Higgins	Jim	Mayo	FG	87	89	92	97										4	17/02/1987	17/05/2002	15.24	04/05/1945		66.9
600	Higgins	Joe	Dublin West	SP	97	02	11											3	06/06/1997		11.03	20/05/1949		62.8
601	Higgins	Michael D.	Galway West	LB	81	82F	87	89	92	97	02	07						8	11/06/1981	25/02/2011	25.48	18/04/1941		70.9
602	Hillery	Brian	Dun Laoghaire	FF	89													1	15/06/1989	25/11/1992	3.45	22/11/1937		74.3
603	Hillery**	Patrick	Clare	FF	51	54	57	61	65	69								6	30/05/1951	03/01/1973	21.60	02/05/1923	12/04/2008	84
604	Hilliard	Colm	Meath	FF	82	82	87	89	92									5	18/02/1982	06/06/1997	15.30	01/05/1936	14/01/2002	65.0
605	Hilliard	Michael	Meath	FF	43	44	48	51	54	57	61	65	69					9	23/06/1943	28/02/1973	29.69	11/03/1903	01/01/1982	78.0
606	Hoctor	Maire	Tipperary North	FF	02	07												2	17/05/2002	25/02/2011	8.78	20/01/1963		49.2
607	Hogan	Conor	Clare	F	23													1	27/08/1923	09/06/1927	3.78	1/4/1892	29/01/1951	58.0
608	Hogan	Daniel	Laoighis-Offaly	FF	38													1	17/06/1938	23/06/1943	5.02	1899	01/08/1980	81.0
609	Hogan	Patrick	Clare	LB	23	27	27	32	33	37	43	48	51	54	57	61	65	13	27/08/1923	24/01/1969	36.71	1886	24/01/1969	83.0
610	Hogan	Patrick	Tipperary South	FG	61	65	69											3	04/10/1961	05/10/1972	11.00	25/03/1907	05/10/1972	65.0
611	Hogan	Patrick J.	Galway	CG	21	22	23	27	27	32	33							7	24/05/1921	14/07/1936	15.14	1891	14/07/1936	45.0
612	Hogan	Patrick K.	Limerick	F	23													1	27/08/1923	09/06/1927	3.78			
613	Hogan	Philip	Carlow-Kilkenny	FG	89	92	97	02	07	11								6	15/06/1989		22.77	04/07/1960		51.7
614	Hogan-O'Higgins	Brigid	Galway South	FG	57	61	65	69	73									5	05/03/1957	16/06/1977	20.28	10/03/1932		80.0
615	Holohan	Richard	Carlow-Kilkenny	F	27	27	33											3	09/06/1927	01/07/1937	9.12	11/1/1882	30/05/1954	72.0
616	Holt	Samuel	Leitrim-Sligo	FF	25*	27	27											3	11/03/1925	18/04/1929	4.10	1887	18/04/1929	42.0
617	Horgan	John	Cork Borough	NL	27J													1	09/06/1927	15/09/1927	0.27			
618	Horgan	John	Dublin Co. South	LB	77													1	16/06/1977	11/06/1981	3.99	26/10/1940		71.4
619	Houlihan	Patrick	Clare	FF	27	27	33											3	09/06/1927	01/07/1937	9.12	25/3/1889	04/05/1963	74.0
620	Howlin	Brendan	Wexford	LB	87	89	92	97	02	07	11							7	17/02/1987		25.09	09/05/1956		55.9
621	Hughes	James	Carlow-Kildare	FG	38	43	44											3	17/06/1938	04/02/1948	9.63		1948	
622	Hughes	Joseph	Carlow-Kilkenny	FG	48	51	54	57										4	10/02/1948	20/01/1960	11.94	18/09/1905	20/01/1960	54.0
623	Hughes	Peter	Louth	CG	21	22	23											3	24/05/1921	09/06/1927	6.04		24/06/1954	
624	Hughes	Seamus	Mayo West	FF	92													1	25/11/1992	06/06/1997	4.53	01/09/1952		59.6
625	Humphreys	Francis*	Carlow-Kilkenny/ Kildare	FF	32/	37	38	43	44/	51	57							7	16/02/1932	19/04/1961	18.62	1891	19/04/1961	70.0
626	Humphreys	Heather	Cavan-Monaghan	FG	11													1	25/02/2011		1.07			
627	Humphreys	Kevin	Dublin South East	LB	11													1	25/02/2011		1.07	04/02/1958		54.1
628	Hunter	Thomas	Cork North East	SF	18	21												2	21/01/1919	16/06/1922	3.40		11/03/1932	
629	Hurley	Jeremiah	Cork South East	LB	37	38												2	01/07/1937	02/02/1943	5.59		02/02/1943	
630	Hussey	Gemma	Wicklow	FG	82	82	87											3	18/02/1982	15/06/1989	7.32	11/11/1938		73.4
631	Hussey	Thomas	Galway East	FF	69	73	77											3	18/06/1969	11/06/1981	11.98	25/01/1936		76.2
632	Hyland	Liam	Laoighis-Offaly	FF	81	82	82	87	89	92								6	11/06/1981	06/06/1997	15.99	24/04/1933		78.9
633	Jacob	Joe	Wicklow	FF	87	89	92	97	02									5	17/02/1987	24/05/2007	20.26	01/04/1939		73.0
634	Jinks	John	Leitrim-Sligo	NL	27J													1	09/06/1927	15/09/1927	0.27	1872	11/09/1934	62.0
635	Johnson	Thomas	Dublin County	LB	22	23	27J											3	16/06/1922	15/09/1927	5.25	17/5/1872	17/01/1963	90.0

	Surname	Forename	Constituency	Party	Elected																	Terms	From	To	Service	Born	Died	Age
636	Johnston	Henry	Meath	FF	59*																	1	*22/07/1959*	04/10/1961	2.20	11/11/1908	09/01/1977	68.0
637	Jones	Denis	Limerick West	FG	57	61	65	69	73													5	05/03/1957	16/06/1977	20.28	12/10/1906	06/05/1987	80.0
638	Jordan	Michael	Wexford	F	27S																	1	15/09/1927	16/02/1932	4.42			
639	Jordan	Stephen	Galway	FF	27	32	33															3	15/09/1927	01/07/1937	9.79	26/12/1886	15/09/1975	88.0
640	Joyce	Carey	Cork East	FF	81																	1	11/06/1981	18/02/1982	0.69	01/08/1922		89.6
641	Kavanagh	Liam	Wicklow	LB	69	73	77	81	82	82	87	89	92									9	18/06/1969	06/06/1997	27.97	09/02/1935		77.1
642	Keane	John	Galway West	FF	40*																	1	*30/05/1940*	23/06/1943	3.06			
643	Keane	Sean	Cork East	LB	48	51																2	04/02/1948	29/03/1953	5.15	14/9/1899	29/03/1953	53.0
644	Keating	Derek	Dublin Mid West	FG	11																	1	25/02/2011		1.07	16/05/1955		56.9
645	Keating	John	Wexford	FG	27J	32	33	37	38	44												6	09/06/1927	04/02/1948	15.30			
646	Keating	Justin	Dublin County North	LB	69	73																2	18/06/1969	16/06/1977	7.99	07/01/1930	31/12/2009	79.0
647	Keating	Michael	Dublin Central	FG	77	81	82	82	87													5	16/06/1977	15/06/1989	12.00	29/09/1946		65.5
648	Keaveney	Cecilia	Donegal North East	FF	96*	97	02															3	*02/04/1996*	24/05/2007	11.14	27/11/1968		43.3
649	Keaveney	Colm	Galway East	LB	11																	1	25/02/2011		1.07	11/01/1971		41.2
650	Keaveney	Paddy	Donegal North East	IFF	76*																	1	*10/06/1976*	16/06/1977	1.02	28/10/1929	19/07/1995	65.0
651	Keegan	Sean	Longford-Westmeath	FF	77	81	82F															3	16/06/1977	24/11/1982	5.44	02/02/1930	09/07/2007	77.0
652	Keely	Seamus	Galway	FF	33																	1	24/01/1933	01/07/1937	4.43	28/12/1889	20/03/1974	84.0
653	Kehoe	Patrick	Wexford	FF	33																	1	24/01/1933	01/07/1937	4.43			
654	Kehoe	Paul	Wexford	FG	02	07	11															3	17/05/2002		9.85	11/01/1973		39.2
655	Kelleher	Billy	Cork North Central	FF	97	02	07	11														4	06/06/1997		14.79	20/01/1968		44.2
656	Kelly	Alan	Tipperary North	LB	11																	1	25/02/2011		1.07	13/07/1975		36.7
657	Kelly	Edward	Monaghan	FF	54																	1	18/05/1954	05/03/1957	2.80	6/10/1883	23/04/1972	88.0
658	Kelly	James	Meath	FF	32	33	37	38														4	16/02/1932	23/06/1943	11.35	1888		
659	Kelly	John	Dublin South	FG	73	77	81	82	82	87												6	28/02/1973	15/06/1989	16.29	31/08/1931	24/01/1991	59.0
660	Kelly	Larry	Cork North West	FF	89																	1	15/06/1989	25/11/1992	3.45	01/12/1946		65.3
661	Kelly	Patrick	Clare	CG	27	27																2	09/06/1927	16/02/1932	4.69	10/8/1875	20/11/1934	59.0
662	Kelly	Peter	Longford-Roscommon	FF	02	07																2	17/05/2002	25/02/2011	8.78	17/08/1944		67.6
663	Kelly	Thomas	Dublin South	FF	18	21	22	33	37	38												6	21/01/1919	20/04/1942	13.83	13/9/1868	20/04/1942	73.0
664	Kemmy	Jim	Limerick East	LB	81	82F	87	89	92	97												6	11/06/1981	25/09/1997	12.06	01/09/1936	25/09/1997	61.0
665	Kenneally	Brendan	Waterford	FF	89	92	97	07														4	15/06/1989	25/02/2011	12.45	28/04/1955		56.9
666	Kenneally Jnr	William (Billy)	Waterford	FF	65	69	73	77	81													5	07/04/1965	18/02/1982	16.87	12/10/1925	27/08/2009	83.0
667	Kenneally Snr	William	Waterford	FF	52*	54	57															3	*26/06/1952*	04/10/1961	9.27		13/09/1964	
668	Kennedy	Geraldine	Dun Laoghaire	PD	87																	1	17/02/1987	15/06/1989	2.32	01/09/1951		60.6
669	Kennedy	Hugh	Dublin South	CG	23*																	1	*25/10/1923*	05/06/1924	0.61	11/7/1879	01/12/1936	57.0
670	Kennedy	James	Wexford	FF	65																	1	07/04/1965	13/09/1968	3.44	10/03/1909	13/09/1968	59.0
671	Kennedy	Michael	Dublin North	FF	07																	1	24/05/2007	25/02/2011	3.76	01/02/1949		63.1
672	Kennedy	Michael*	Lngfrd-Westmeath/Meath	FF	27	27	32	33/	37	38	43	44/	48	51	54	57	61					13	09/06/1927	14/02/1965	37.69		14/02/1965	
673	Kenny	Enda	Mayo	FG	75*	77	81	82	82	87	89	92	97	02	07	11						12	*12/11/1975*		36.36	24/04/1951		60.9
674	Kenny	Henry	Mayo West	FG	54	57	61	65	69	73												6	18/05/1954	25/09/1975	21.36	07/09/1913	25/09/1975	62.0
675	Kenny	Sean	Dublin North East	LB	92	11																2	25/11/1992		5.60	01/10/1942		69.5
676	Kent	David	Cork East	SF	18	21	22	23	27J													5	21/01/1919	15/09/1927	8.65		01/11/1930	
677	Kent	William	Cork East	CP	27S	33																2	15/09/1927	01/07/1937	8.85			
678	Keogh	Helen	Dun Laoghaire	PD	92																	1	25/11/1992	06/06/1997	4.53	03/06/1951		60.8
679	Keogh	Myles	Dublin South	FG	22	23	27	27	32	37												6	16/06/1922	17/06/1938	11.57		30/08/1952	
680	Kerlin	Frank	Dublin South	FF	27S																	1	15/09/1927	16/02/1932	4.42			
681	Kerrigan	Patrick	Cork City	LB	77																	1	16/06/1977	04/07/1979	2.05	21/02/1928	04/07/1979	51.0
682	Keyes	Michael	Limerick East	LB	27J	33	37	38	43	44	48	51	54									9	09/06/1927	05/03/1957	24.38	1886	1957	71.0
683	Keyes	Raphael	Cork West	FF	32																	1	16/02/1932	24/01/1933	0.94			
684	Kiersey	John	Waterford	CG	32																	1	16/02/1932	24/01/1933	0.94	23/10/1895	18/03/1960	64.0
685	Killane	James	Longford-Westmeath	FF	23	27S																2	27/08/1923	26/04/1930	6.39	22/10/1874	26/04/1930	55.0
686	Killeen	Timothy	Dublin (Artane)	FF	77																	1	16/06/1977	11/06/1981	3.99	10/05/1923		88.9
687	Killeen	Tony	Clare	FF	92	97	02	07														4	25/11/1992	25/02/2011	18.25	09/06/1952		59.8
688	Killilea	Mark	Galway West	FF	77	81																2	16/06/1977	18/02/1982	4.68	05/09/1939		72.5

	Surname	Forename	Constituency	Party	Elected																	Terms	From	To	Service	Born	Died	Age
689	Killilea(sen)	Mark	Galway North	FF	27	27	33	37	38	43	44	48	51	54	57							11	09/06/1927	04/10/1961	33.38	1896	29/09/1970	74.0
690	Kilroy	James	Mayo North	FF	43	44	48															3	23/06/1943	30/05/1951	7.93	1890	05/01/1954	64.0
691	Kilroy	Michael	Mayo South	FF	23	27	27	32	33													5	27/08/1923	01/07/1937	13.85	1889		
692	Kinane	Patrick	Tipperary North	CnaP	47*	48																2	*29/10/1947*	30/05/1951	3.58	3/7/1892	15/07/1957	65.0
693	Kirk	Seamus	Louth	FF	82N	87	89	92	97	02	07	11										8	24/11/1982		29.33	26/04/1945		66.9
694	Kissane	Eamon	Kerry North	FF	32	33	37	38	43	44	48											7	16/02/1932	30/05/1951	19.28	1899	21/05/1979	80.0
695	Kitt	Michael F.	Galway East	FF	48	57	61	65	69	73												6	04/02/1948	24/12/1974	21.12	13/09/1914	24/12/1974	60.0
696	Kitt	Michael P.	Galway East	FF	75*	81	82	82	87	89	92	97	07	11								10	*04/03/1975*		28.04	17/05/1950		61.8
697	Kitt	Tom	Dublin South	FF	87	89	92	97	02	07												6	17/02/1987	25/02/2011	24.02	11/07/1952		59.7
698	Kyne	Sean	Galway West	FG	11																	1	25/02/2011		1.07	16/05/1975		36.9
699	Kyne	Thomas	Waterford	LB	48	51	54	57	61	65	73											7	04/02/1948	16/06/1977	25.66	04/02/1905	08/08/1981	76.0
700	Lahiffe	Robert	Galway South	FF	48	53*	54															3	04/02/1948	05/03/1957	6.85		08/03/1975	
701	Lalor	Patrick	Laoighis-Offaly	FF	61	65	69	73	77													5	04/10/1961	11/06/1981	19.69	21/07/1926		85.7
702	Lambert	Robert	Wexford	FF	23																	1	27/08/1923	09/06/1927	3.78			
703	Larkin	Denis	Dublin North East	LB	54	57	65															3	18/05/1954	18/06/1969	11.58	1908	02/07/1987	79.0
704	Larkin (Jnr)	James	Dublin South Central	LB	43	44	48	51	54													5	23/06/1943	05/03/1957	13.70	1904	18/02/1969	65.0
705	Larkin (Snr)	James	Dublin North East	LB	27S	37	43															3	15/09/1927	30/05/1944	1.90	21/1/1876	30/01/1947	71.0
706	Lavery	Cecil	Dublin County	FG	35*	37																2	*17/06/1935*	17/06/1938	3.00	6/10/1894	16/12/1967	73.0
707	Lavin	Andrew	Roscommon	CG	21	22	23															3	24/05/1921	09/06/1927	6.04			
708	Law	Hugh	Donegal	CG	27	27																2	09/06/1927	16/02/1932	4.69	1872	10/04/1943	71.0
709	Lawless	Frank	Dublin County	SF	18	21																2	21/01/1919	16/04/1922	3.23	1871	16/04/1922	51.0
710	Lawlor	Anthony	Kildare North	FG	11																	1	25/02/2011		1.07	13/06/1959		52.8
711	Lawlor	Liam	Dublin West	FF	77	82F	87	89	92	97												6	16/06/1977	17/05/2002	20.00	16/10/1944	22/10/2005	61.0
712	Lawlor	Thomas	Dublin South	LB	27J	37																2	09/06/1927	17/06/1938	1.23			
713	Ledden	James	Limerick	CG	23																	1	27/08/1923	19/01/1927	3.40		19/01/1927	
714	Lee	George	Dublin South	FG	09*																	1	*05/06/2009*	08/02/2010	0.68	27/09/1962		49.5
715	Lee	Pat	Dublin Central	FG	89																	1	15/06/1989	25/11/1992	3.45	26/09/1944		67.5
716	Lehane	Con	Dublin South Central	CnaP	48																	1	04/02/1948	30/05/1951	3.32		18/09/1983	
717	Lehane	Patrick	Cork South	CnaT	48	51																2	04/02/1948	18/05/1954	6.28		01/07/1976	
718	Lemass	Eileen	Dublin West	FF	77	81	82N															3	16/06/1977	17/02/1987	8.91	07/07/1932		79.7
719	Lemass	Noel	Dublin South West	FF	56*	57	61	65	69	73												6	*14/11/1956*	13/04/1976	19.41	14/02/1929	13/04/1976	47
720	Lemass	Sean F.	Dublin South Central	FF	24*	27	27	32	33	37	38	43	44	48	51	54	57	61	65			15	*18/11/1924*	18/06/1969	44.58	15/7/1899	11/05/1971	71
721	Leneghan	Joseph	Mayo West	FF	61	69																2	04/10/1961	28/02/1973	7.20	1916	06/12/1981	65
722	Lenihan	Conor	Dublin South West	FF	97	02	07															3	06/06/1997	25/02/2011	13.72	03/03/1963		49.1
723	Lenihan	Patrick	Longford-Westmeath	FF	65	69																2	07/04/1965	11/03/1970	4.93	04/09/1902	11/03/1970	67
724	Lenihan Jnr	Brian	Dublin West	FF	96*	97	02	07	11													5	*02/04/1996*	10/06/2011	15.97	21/05/1959	10/06/2011	52
725	Lenihan Snr	Brian*	Roscommon/DublinW	FF	61	65	69/	77	81	82	82	87	89	92								10	04/10/1961	01/11/1995	29.78	17/11/1930	01/11/1995	64
726	Lennon	James	Carlow-Kilkenny	SF	18	21																2	21/01/1919	16/06/1922	3.40		13/08/1958	
727	Leonard	James	Cavan-Monaghan	FF	73	77	82	82	87	89	92											7	28/02/1973	06/06/1997	23.58	05/06/1927		84.8
728	Leonard	Patrick	Dublin North	CG	25*	27S																2	*11/03/1925*	16/02/1932	6.67			
729	Leonard	Thomas	Dublin Central	FF	77	83*																2	16/06/1977	17/02/1987	7.23	30/05/1924	05/03/2004	79.0
730	L'Estrange	Gerald	Longford-Westmeath	FG	65	69	73	77	81	82	82											7	07/04/1965	17/02/1987	21.86	07/11/1917	05/04/1996	78.0
731	Leyden	Terry	Roscommon	FF	77	81	82	82	87	89												6	16/06/1977	25/11/1992	15.44	01/10/1945		66.5
732	Liddy	Sean	Clare	CT	21	22																2	24/05/1921	18/12/1922	1.57			
733	Lindsay	Patrick	Mayo North	FG	54	57	65															3	18/05/1954	18/06/1969	11.58	18/01/1914	29/06/1993	79.0
734	Linehan	Timothy	Cork North	FG	37	38	43															3	01/07/1937	30/05/1944	6.91	04/08/1905		
735	Lipper	Michael	Limerick East	NP	77																	1	16/06/1977	11/06/1981	3.99	01/06/1932	18/10/1987	55.0
736	Little	Patrick	Waterford	FF	27	27	32	33	37	38	43	44	48	51								10	09/06/1927	18/05/1954	26.94	17/6/1884	16/05/1963	78.0
737	Loftus	Sean D.	Dublin North East	NP	81																	1	11/06/1981	18/02/1982	0.69	01/11/1927	10/07/2010	82.0
738	Looney	Thomas	Cork South East	LB	43																	1	23/06/1943	30/05/1944	0.94			
739	Loughman	Francis	Tipperary South	FF	38	44	57															3	17/06/1938	04/10/1961	13.27	1892	13/05/1972	80.0
740	Loughnane	Bill*	Galway / Clare	FF	69	73	77/	81	82F													5	18/06/1969	01/10/1982	13.29	05/08/1915	01/10/1982	67.0
741	Lowry	Michael	Tipperary North	NP	87	89	92	97	02	07	11											7	17/02/1987		25.09	13/03/1954		58.0

	Surname	Forename	Constituency	Party	Elected																	Terms	From	To	Service	Born	Died	Age
742	Lydon	Michael	Galway West	FF	44	48																2	30/05/1944	30/05/1951	7.00	10/10/1907		
743	Lynch	Celia	Dublin North Central	FF	54	57	61	65	69	73												6	18/05/1954	16/06/1977	23.08	06/05/1908	16/06/1989	81.0
744	Lynch	Ciaran	Cork South Central	LB	07	11																2	24/05/2007		4.83	13/06/1964		47.8
745	Lynch	Diarmuid	Cork South East	SF	18																	1	21/01/1919	06/08/1920	1.54	10/1/1878	09/11/1950	72.0
746	Lynch	Fionan	Kerry South	FG	18	21	22	23	27	27	32	33	37	38	43	44						12	21/01/1919	03/10/1944	25.70	17/3/1889	03/06/1966	77.0
747	Lynch	Gerard	Kerry North	FG	69	73																2	18/06/1969	16/06/1977	7.99	15/06/1931		80.8
748	Lynch	Gilbert	Galway	LB	27J																	1	09/06/1927	15/09/1927	0.27		01/11/1969	
749	Lynch	Jack	Cork Borough	FF	48	51	54	57	61	65	69	73	77									9	04/02/1948	11/06/1981	33.35	15/08/1917	20/10/1999	82.0
750	Lynch	James	Dublin South	FF	32	33	38	43	44													5	16/02/1932	04/02/1948	15.01		12/03/1954	
751	Lynch	John	Kerry North	FG	51																	1	30/05/1951	18/05/1954	2.97	10/4/1889	10/06/1957	68.0
752	Lynch	Joseph P.	Laoighis-Offaly	CT	21																	1	24/05/1921	16/06/1922	1.06		1954	
753	Lynch	Kathleen	Cork North Central	LB	94*	02	07	11														4	*10/11/1994*		12.42	07/06/1953		58.8
754	Lynch	Michael	Meath	FF	82F	87																2	18/02/1982	15/06/1989	3.09	25/08/1934		77.6
755	Lynch	Thaddeus	Waterford	FG	54	57	61	65														4	18/05/1954	25/10/1966	12.44	1901	25/10/1966	65.0
756	Lynn	Kathleen	Dublin County	R	23																	1	27/08/1923	09/06/1927	3.78	28/1/1874	14/09/1955	81.0
757	Lyons	Denis	Cork North Central	FF	81	82	82	87	89													5	11/06/1981	25/11/1992	11.46	01/08/1935		76.6
758	Lyons	John	Longford-Westmeath	LB	22	23																2	16/06/1922	09/06/1927	4.98			
759	Lyons	John	Dublin North West	LB	11																	1	25/02/2011		1.07	01/06/1977		34.8
760	Lyons	Michael	Mayo South	FG	65																	1	07/04/1965	18/06/1969	4.20	01/11/1910	19/11/1991	81.0
761	MacBride	Sean	Dublin South West	CnaP	47*	48	51	54														4	*29/10/1947*	05/03/1957	9.35	26/01/1904	15/01/1988	83.0
762	MacCarthy	Sean	Cork Mid	FF	44	51	54	57	61													5	30/05/1944	07/04/1965	17.53		14/03/1974	
763	MacDermot	Frank	Roscommon	CP	32	33																2	16/02/1932	01/07/1937	5.37	1886	24/06/1975	89.0
764	MacDonagh	Joseph	Tipperary North	CR	18	21	22															3	21/01/1919	25/12/1922	3.93		25/12/1922	
765	MacEntee	Sean*	Monaghan/Dublin SE	FF	18	21/	27	27	32	33	37	38	43	44	48	51	54	57	61	65		16	21/01/1919	18/06/1969	45.43	22/8/1889	10/01/1984	94.0
766	MacEoin	Gen. Sean*	Longford-Westmeath/Sligo	FG	21	22/	29*/	32	33	37	38	43	44	48	51	54	57	61				14	24/05/1921	07/04/1965	38.09	30/9/1893	07/07/1973	79.0
767	MacGiolla	Tomas	Dublin West	WP	82N	87	89															3	24/11/1982	25/11/1992	10.00	25/01/1924	04/02/2010	86.0
768	MacLochlainn	Padraig	Donegal North East	SF	11																	1	25/02/2011		1.07	12/06/1973		38.8
769	MacNeill	Prof. Eoin*	Derry/ N.U.I / Clare	CG	18/	18	21	22	23/	23												6	21/01/1919	09/06/1927	8.38	15/5/1867	15/10/1945	78.0
770	MacSharry**	Ray	Sligo-Leitrim	FF	69	73	77	81	82	82	87											7	18/06/1969	24/11/1988	19.44	29/04/1938		73.9
771	MacSwiney	Mary	Cork Borough	R	21	22	23															3	24/05/1921	09/06/1927	6.04	27/3/1872	08/03/1942	69.0
772	MacSwiney	Sean	Cork Mid	SF	21																	1	24/05/1921	16/06/1922	1.06			
773	MacSwiney	Terence	Cork Mid	SF	18																	1	21/01/1919	25/10/1920	1.76	20/3/1879	25/10/1920	41.0
774	Madden	David	Limerick West	FG	48	51	54															3	04/02/1948	31/07/1955	7.49	1880	31/07/1955	75.0
775	Madden	John	Mayo North	FF	24*	27J																2	*18/11/1924*	15/09/1927	2.82		1954	
776	Magennis	Prof. William	N.U.I.	CG	22	23																2	16/06/1922	09/06/1927	4.98	18/5/1867	30/03/1946	78.0
777	Maguire	Ben	Sligo-Leitrim	FF	27S	32	33	37	38	43	44	48	54									9	15/09/1927	05/03/1957	26.50			
778	Maguire	Conor	N.U.I.	FF	32	33																2	16/02/1932	03/11/1936	4.71	1889	26/09/1971	82.0
779	Maguire	Patrick J.	Monaghan	FF	48	51																2	04/02/1948	18/05/1954	6.28		04/07/1970	
780	Maguire	Thomas	Mayo South	R	21	22	23															3	24/05/1921	09/06/1927	6.04	28/3/1892	05/07/1993	101.0
781	Maher	Peadar	Laoighis-Offaly	FF	51	54	57															3	30/05/1951	04/10/1961	10.35	01/02/1924		88.1
782	Mahony	Philip	Kilkenny	F	43																	1	23/06/1943	30/05/1944	0.94	1/10/1897	20/04/1972	74.0
783	Malone	Patrick	Kildare	FG	70*	73																2	*14/04/1970*	16/06/1977	7.17	30/05/1916	03/12/1993	77.0
784	Maloney	Eamonn	Dublin South West	LB	11																	1	25/02/2011		1.07	01/05/1953		58.9
785	Manley	Tadhg	Cork South	FG	54	57																2	18/05/1954	04/10/1961	7.38	20/4/1893	24/08/1976	83.0
786	Manning	Maurice	Dublin North East	FG	82	82																2	18/02/1982	17/02/1987	5.00	14/06/1943		68.8
787	Mannion	John	Galway West	FG	51																	1	30/05/1951	18/05/1954	2.97	04/06/1907	10/09/1978	71.0
788	Mannion	John M.	Galway West	FG	77																	1	16/06/1977	11/06/1981	3.99	26/10/1944	02/04/2006	61.0
789	Mansergh	Martin	Tipperary South	FF	07																	1	24/05/2007	25/02/2011	3.76	31/12/1946		65.2
790	Markey	Bernard	Louth	FG	81	82F																2	11/06/1981	24/11/1982	1.45	07/11/1935	23/07/2003	67.0
791	Martin	Micheal	Cork South Central	FF	89	92	97	02	07	11												6	15/06/1989		22.77	01/08/1960		51.6
792	Mathews	Peter	Dublin South	FG	11																	1	25/02/2011		1.07	25/08/1951		60.6
793	Matthews	Arthur	Meath	CG	27S																	1	15/09/1927	16/02/1932	4.42		25/01/1942	
794	McAuliffe	Patrick	Cork North East	LB	44	48	51	54	57	61	65											7	30/05/1944	18/06/1969	25.05	01/08/1914	13/10/1989	75.0

	Surname	Forename	Constituency	Party	Elected																	Terms	From	To	Service	Born	Died	Age
795	McBride	Joseph	Mayo South	CG	18	21	22	23														4	21/01/1919	09/06/1927	8.38		1938	
796	McCabe	Alexander	Leitrim-Sligo	CG	18	21	22	23														4	21/01/1919	30/10/1924	5.77	5/6/1886	31/05/1972	85.0
797	McCann	John	Dublin South Central	FF	39*	43	44	48	51													5	*06/06/1939*	18/05/1954	14.95	17/06/1905	23/02/1980	74.0
798	McCann	Pierce	Tipperary East	SF	18																	1	21/01/1919	06/03/1919	0.12	2/8/1882	06/03/1919	36.0
799	McCartan	Pat	Dublin North East	WP	87	89																2	17/02/1987	25/11/1992	5.77	01/05/1953		58.9
800	McCartan	Patrick	Laoighis-Offaly	SF	18	21	22															3	21/01/1919	27/08/1923	4.60	13/3/1878	28/03/1963	85.0
801	McCarthy	Daniel	Dublin South	CG	21	22	23															3	24/05/1921	30/10/1924	3.44		1957	
802	McCarthy	Michael	Cork South West	LB	11																	1	25/02/2011		1.07	15/11/1976		35.3
803	McCarthy	Sean	Tipperary South	FF	81	82	82	87														4	11/06/1981	15/06/1989	8.01	07/01/1937		75.2
804	McCartin	Joe	Sligo-Leitrim	FG	81	82N																2	11/06/1981	17/02/1987	4.93	24/04/1939		72.9
805	McCarvill	Patrick	Monaghan	FF	22	23	27J															3	16/06/1922	15/09/1927	5.25	23/5/1893	16/03/1955	61.0
806	McConalogue	Charlie	Donegal North East	FF	11																	1	25/02/2011		1.07	29/10/1977		34.4
807	McCormack	Padraic	Galway West	FG	89	92	97	02	07													5	15/06/1989	25/02/2011	21.70	16/05/1942		69.9
808	McCoy	John	Limerick East	PD	87																	1	17/02/1987	15/06/1989	2.32	01/07/1940		71.7
809	McCreevy**	Charlie	Kildare	FF	77	81	82	82	87	89	92	97	02									9	16/06/1977	22/11/2004	27.44	30/09/1949		62.5
810	McCullough	Denis	Donegal	CG	24*																	1	*20/11/1924*	09/06/1927	2.55	24/1/1883	11/09/1968	85.0
811	McCurtin	John	Tipperary	CG	23																	1	27/08/1923	09/06/1927	3.78	24/6/1896	12/11/1982	86.0
812	McDaid	James	Donegal North East	FF	89	92	97	02	07													5	15/06/1989	02/11/2010	21.38	03/10/1949		62.5
813	McDevitt	Henry	Donegal East	FF	38																	1	17/06/1938	23/06/1943	5.02	1904	04/01/1966	62.0
814	McDonald	Charles	Laoighis-Offaly	FG	73																	1	28/02/1973	16/06/1977	4.30	11/06/1935		76.8
815	McDonald	Mary Lou	Dublin Central	SF	11																	1	25/02/2011		1.07	01/05/1969		42.9
816	McDonogh	Martin	Galway	CG	27	27	32	33														4	09/06/1927	24/11/1934	7.46		24/11/1934	
817	McDowell	Derek	Dublin North Central	LB	92	97																2	25/11/1992	17/05/2002	9.47	01/09/1958		53.6
818	McDowell	Michael	Dublin South East	PD	87	92	02															3	17/02/1987	24/05/2007	11.87	01/05/1951		60.9
819	McEllistrim	Thomas	Kerry North	FF	23	27	27	32	33	37	38	43	44	48	51	54	57	61	65			15	27/08/1923	18/06/1969	45.81	14/10/1894	04/12/1973	79.0
820	McEllistrim	Tom	Kerry North	FF	02	07																2	17/05/2002	25/02/2011	8.78	24/10/1968		43.4
821	McEllistrim Jnr	Thomas	Kerry North	FF	69	73	77	81	82	82	89											7	18/06/1969	25/11/1992	21.12	15/01/1926	25/02/2000	74.0
822	McEntee	Shane	Meath East	FG	05*	07	11															3	*11/03/2005*		7.03	19/12/1956		55.3
823	McFadden	Michael	Donegal West	FG	27	27	33	37	38	43	44	48										8	09/06/1927	30/05/1951	23.03	1/1/1885	27/08/1958	73.0
824	McFadden	Nicky	Longford-Westmeath	FG	11																	1	25/02/2011		1.07	06/12/1962		49.3
825	McFadden	Patrick	Donegal	CG	23																	1	27/08/1923	09/06/1927	3.78			
826	McGahon	Brendan	Louth	FG	82N	87	89	92	97													5	24/11/1982	17/05/2002	19.48	22/11/1936		75.3
827	McGarry	Sean	Dublin North	CG	21	22	23															3	24/05/1921	30/10/1924	3.44			
828	McGennis	Marian	Dublin Central	FF	97																	1	06/06/1997	17/05/2002	4.94	01/11/1953		58.4
829	McGilligan	Patrick*	N.U.I. / Dublin N.C.	FG	23*	27	27	32	33/	37	38	43	44	48	51	54	57	61				14	*03/11/1923*	07/04/1965	41.43	12/4/1889	15/11/1979	90.0
830	McGinley	Dinny	Donegal South West	FG	82	82	87	89	92	97	02	07	11									9	18/02/1982		30.09	27/04/1945		66.9
831	McGinley	Joseph P.	Donegal	CT	21	22																2	24/05/1921	27/08/1923	2.26			
832	McGirl	John Joe	Sligo-Leitrim	SF	57																	1	05/03/1957	04/10/1961	4.58	25/03/1921	08/12/1988	67.0
833	McGoldrick	P.J.	Donegal	CG	21	22	23															3	24/05/1921	09/06/1927	6.04	12/8/1865	26/04/1939	73.0
834	McGovern	Patrick	Cavan	FG	33	37	38															3	24/01/1933	23/06/1943	10.41		07/02/1949	
835	McGowan	Gerard	Dublin County	LB	37																	1	01/07/1937	17/06/1938	0.96		17/08/1971	
836	McGowan	Martin	Leitrim-Sligo	R	23																	1	27/08/1923	09/06/1927	3.78		01/01/1958	
837	McGrath	Finian	Dublin North Central	NP	02	07	11															3	17/05/2002		9.85	09/04/1953		59.0
838	McGrath	Joseph*	Dublin N W /Mayo N	CG	18	21	22/	23														4	21/01/1919	29/10/1924	5.77	1887	01/03/1966	79.0
839	McGrath	Mattie	Tipperary South	FF	07	11																2	24/05/2007		4.83	01/09/1958		53.6
840	McGrath	Michael	Cork South Central	FF	07	11																2	24/05/2007		4.83	23/08/1976		35.6
841	McGrath	Pa	Cork Borough	FF	46*	48	51	54														4	*14/06/1946*	20/06/1956	10.02		20/06/1956	
842	McGrath	Paul	Westmeath	FG	89	92	97	02														4	15/06/1989	24/05/2007	17.94	13/02/1948		64.1
843	McGuinness	Francis	Longford-Westmeath	CT	22																	1	16/06/1922	27/08/1923	1.20	1868	30/11/1934	66.0
844	McGuinness	John	Carlow-Kilkenny	FF	97	02	07	11														4	06/06/1997		14.79	15/03/1955		57.0
845	McGuinness	John	Laoighis-Offaly	R	23																	1	27/08/1923	28/11/1925	2.26		28/10/1978	
846	McGuinness	Joseph	Longford-Westmeath	SF	18	21																2	21/01/1919	31/05/1922	3.36	10/4/1875	31/05/1922	47.0
847	McGuire	James	Dublin South	CG	33																	1	24/01/1933	01/07/1937	4.43	24/07/1903	1989	86.0

	Surname	Forename	Constituency	Party	Elected																	Terms	From	To	Service	Born	Died	Age
848	McHugh	Joe	Donegal North East	FG	07	11																2	24/05/2007		4.83	16/07/1971		40.7
849	McHugh	Paddy	Galway East	NP	02																	1	17/05/2002	24/05/2007	5.02	23/01/1953		59.2
850	McKenna	Justin	Louth-Meath	SF	21																	1	24/05/1921	16/06/1922	1.06	9/6/1896	23/03/1950	53.0
851	McKenna	Patrick	Longford-Westmeath	F	23																	1	27/08/1923	09/06/1927	3.78			
852	McLellan	Sandra	Cork East	SF	11																	1	25/02/2011		1.07	01/05/1961		50.9
853	McLoughlin	Frank	Meath	LB	82N																	1	24/11/1982	17/02/1987	4.23	01/08/1946		65.6
854	McLoughlin	Joseph	Sligo-Leitrim	FG	61*	61	65	69	73													5	*01/03/1961*	16/06/1977	16.29	12/08/1916	03/07/1991	74.0
855	McLoughlin	Tony	Sligo-North Leitrim	FG	11																	1	25/02/2011		1.07	21/01/1949		63.2
856	McMahon	Larry	Dublin South West	FG	70*	73	77	81	82F													5	*02/12/1970*	24/11/1982	11.98	09/01/1929	16/02/2006	77.0
857	McManus	Liz	Wicklow	LB	92	97	02	07														4	25/11/1992	25/02/2011	18.25	01/03/1947		65.1
858	McMenamin	Daniel	Donegal East	FG	27J	32	33	37	38	43	44	48	51	54	57							11	09/06/1927	04/10/1961	29.90	1/3/1882		
859	McNamara	Michael	Clare	LB	11																	1	25/02/2011		1.07	01/03/1974		38.1
860	McQuillan	John	Roscommon	NPD	48	51	54	57	61													5	04/02/1948	07/04/1965	17.17	30/08/1920	08/03/1998	77.0
861	Meaney	Con	Cork Mid	FF	37	38	61															3	01/07/1937	07/04/1965	9.49		11/09/1970	
862	Meaney	Thomas	Cork North West	FF	65	69	73	77/	81	82												6	07/04/1965	24/11/1982	17.63	11/08/1931		80.6
863	Medlar	Martin	Carlow-Kilkenny	FF	56*	57	61															3	*14/11/1956*	07/04/1965	8.39	4/12/1899	04/06/1965	65.0
864	Meighan	John	Roscommon	CnaT	43																	1	23/06/1943	30/05/1944	0.94	05/03/1905	04/03/1978	87.0
865	Mellows	Herbert	Galway	R	23																	1	27/08/1923	09/06/1927	3.78		1942	
866	Mellows	Liam*	Meath / Galway	SF	18/	18	21															3	21/01/1919	16/06/1922	3.40	25/5/1895	08/12/1922	27.0
867	Millar	Anthony	Galway East	FF	58*	61	65															3	*30/05/1958*	18/06/1969	11.05	24/09/1934	23/01/1993	58.0
868	Milroy	Sean	Cavan	CG	21	22	23															3	24/05/1921	30/10/1924	3.44	1877	30/11/1946	69.0
869	Minch	Capt. Sydney	Kildare	FG	32	33	37															3	16/02/1932	17/06/1938	6.33	14/6/1893	12/03/1970	76.0
870	Mitchell	Gay	Dublin South Central	FG	81	82	82	87	89	92	97	02										8	11/06/1981	24/05/2007	25.95	01/12/1951		60.3
871	Mitchell	Jim	Dublin Central	FG	77	81	82	82	87	89	92	97										8	16/06/1977	17/05/2002	24.92	19/10/1946	02/12/2002	56.0
872	Mitchell	Olivia	Dublin South	FG	97	02	07	11														4	06/06/1997		14.79	31/07/1947		64.6
873	Mitchell O'Connor	Mary	Dun Laoghaire	FG	11																	1	25/02/2011		1.07	10/06/1959		52.8
874	Moane	Edward	Mayo South	FF	32	33	37															3	16/02/1932	17/06/1938	6.33	2/8/1890	11/07/1973	82.0
875	Moffatt	Tom	Mayo	FF	92	97																2	25/11/1992	17/05/2002	9.47	01/01/1940		72.2
876	Moher	John	Cork North East	FF	54	57	61															3	18/05/1954	07/04/1965	10.89	07/02/1909	10/11/1985	76.0
877	Molloy	Bobby	Galway West	PD	65	69	73	77	81	82	82	87	89	92	97							11	07/04/1965	17/05/2002	37.11	06/07/1936		75.7
878	Moloney	Daniel	Kerry North	FF	57																	1	05/03/1957	04/10/1961	4.58	1909	26/06/1963	54.0
879	Moloney	John	Laoighis-Offaly	FF	97	02	07															3	06/06/1997	25/02/2011	13.72	12/06/1953		58.8
880	Moloney	Patrick	Tipperary South	CR	18	21	22															3	21/01/1919	27/08/1923	4.60	20/3/1869	04/09/1947	78.0
881	Molony	David	Tipperary North	FG	81	82	82															3	11/06/1981	17/02/1987	5.69	23/08/1950	04/09/2002	52.0
882	Mongan	Joseph	Galway West	FG	27	32	37	38	43	44	48											7	15/09/1927	12/03/1951	19.06	11/3/1880	12/03/1951	71.0
883	Mooney	Mary	Dublin South Central	FF	87																	1	17/02/1987	15/06/1989	2.32	01/12/1958		53.3
884	Mooney	Patrick	Monaghan	FF	54	57	61	65														4	18/05/1954	18/06/1969	15.09	12/11/1903	30/10/1989	85.0
885	Moore	Seamus	Wicklow	FF	27	27	32	33	37	38												6	09/06/1927	14/06/1940	13.02		14/06/1940	
886	Moore	Sean	Dublin South East	FF	65	69	73	77	81													5	07/04/1965	18/02/1982	16.87	19/05/1913	01/10/1986	73.0
887	Moran	Michael	Mayo West	FF	38	43	44	48	51	54	57	61	65	69								10	17/06/1938	28/02/1973	34.70	25/12/1912	06/05/1983	70.0
888	Morgan	Arthur	Louth	SF	02	07																2	17/05/2002	25/02/2011	8.78	23/07/1954		57.7
889	Morley	P.J.	Mayo East	FF	77	81	82	82	87	89	92											7	16/06/1977	06/06/1997	19.97	01/03/1931		81.1
890	Morrisroe	James	Mayo North	CG	33																	1	24/01/1933	01/07/1937	4.43		1937	
891	Morrissey	Daniel	Tipperary North	FG	22	23	27	27	32	33	37	38	43	44	48	51	54					13	16/06/1922	05/03/1957	34.72		1981	
892	Morrissey	Michael	Waterford	FF	37	38	43	44														4	01/07/1937	10/05/1947	9.86		10/05/1947	
893	Moylan	Sean	Cork North	FF	21	22	32	33	37	38	43	44	48	51	54							11	24/05/1921	05/03/1957	27.31	19/11/1888	16/11/1957	68.0
894	Moynihan	Donal	Cork North West	FF	82N	87	92	97	02													5	24/11/1982	24/05/2007	21.05	02/10/1941		70.5
895	Moynihan	Michael	Cork North West	FF	97	02	07	11														4	06/06/1997		14.79	12/01/1968		44.2
896	Moynihan	Michael	Kerry South	LB	81	82	82	89														4	11/06/1981	25/11/1992	9.14	17/06/1917	27/06/2001	84.0
897	Moynihan-Cronin	Breeda	Kerry South	LB	92	97	02															3	25/11/1992	24/05/2007	14.49	31/03/1953		59.0
898	Mulcahy	Gen. Richard*	Dublin / Tipperary S	FG	18	21	22	23	27	27	32	33	38/	44	48	51	54	57				14	21/01/1919	04/10/1961	40.80	10/5/1886	16/12/1971	85.0
899	Mulcahy	Michael	Dublin South Central	FF	02	07																2	17/05/2002	25/02/2011	8.78	23/06/1960		51.7
900	Mulherin	Michelle	Mayo	FG	11																	1	25/02/2011		1.07	20/01/1972		40.2

	Surname	Forename	Constituency	Party	Elected												Terms	From	To	Service	Born	Died	Age
901	Mullen	Eugene	Mayo South	FF	27J												1	09/06/1927	15/09/1927	0.27			
902	Mullen	Michael	Dublin North West	LB	61	65											2	04/10/1961	18/06/1969	7.70	01/02/1919	1982	63.0
903	Mullen	Thomas	Dublin County	FF	38												1	17/06/1938	23/06/1943	5.02		1966	
904	Mullins	Thomas	Cork West	FF	27	27											2	09/06/1927	16/02/1932	4.69	1903	02/11/1978	75.0
905	Mulvany	Patrick	Meath	F	23												1	27/08/1923	09/06/1927	3.78	2/7/1871	16/05/1951	79.0
906	Mulvihill	John	Cork East	LB	92												1	25/11/1992	06/06/1997	4.53	01/07/1945		66.7
907	Munnelly	John	Mayo North	FF	37	38											2	01/07/1937	18/10/1941	4.30	1874	18/10/1941	67.0
908	Murphy	Catherine	Kildare North	NP	05*	11											2	*11/03/2005*		3.27	01/09/1953		58.6
909	Murphy	Charles	Dublin South	R	21	23											2	24/05/1921	09/06/1927	4.84	16/2/1880	28/04/1958	78.0
910	Murphy	Ciaran	Wicklow	FF	73	77	81	82F									4	28/02/1973	24/11/1982	9.74	30/05/1940		71.8
911	Murphy	Dara	Cork North Central	FG	11												1	25/02/2011		1.07	02/12/1969		42.3
912	Murphy	Eoghan	Dublin South East	FG	11												1	25/02/2011		1.07	23/04/1982		29.9
913	Murphy	Gerard	Cork North West	FG	02												1	17/05/2002	24/05/2007	5.02	05/03/1951		61.0
914	Murphy	James	Louth	CG	21	22	23	27	27	32	33						7	24/05/1921	01/07/1937	16.10	28/12/1887	07/10/1961	73.0
915	Murphy	John	Dublin South Central	IUW	57												1	05/03/1957	13/05/1958	1.19	1920	1984	64.0
916	Murphy	Joseph	Dublin County	NP	27S												1	15/09/1927	16/02/1932	4.42			
917	Murphy	Michael Pat	Cork South West	LB	51	54	57/	61	65	69	73	77					8	30/05/1951	11/06/1981	30.03	12/03/1919	28/10/2000	81.0
918	Murphy	Patrick	Cork East	FF	32	33											2	16/02/1932	01/07/1937	5.37	13/5/1889	01/05/1968	78.0
919	Murphy	Timothy	Cork West	LB	23	27	27	32	33	37	38	43	44	48			10	27/08/1923	29/04/1949	25.67	1893	29/04/1949	56.0
920	Murphy	William	Clare	FG	51	54	57	61	65								5	30/05/1951	16/11/1967	16.47	12/2/1892	16/11/1967	75.0
921	Murphy	William J.	Cork West	LB	49*												1	*15/06/1949*	30/05/1951	1.95	17/05/1928		83.8
922	Myles	Major James	Donegal East	NP	23	27	27	32	33	37	38						7	27/08/1923	23/06/1943	19.82	1877	13/02/1956	79.0
923	Nagle	Thomas	Cork North	LB	22	23											2	16/06/1922	09/06/1927	4.98			
924	Nally	Martin	Mayo South	FG	23	27	27	32	33	37	38						7	27/08/1923	23/06/1943	19.82	1882	01/08/1966	84.0
925	Nash	Gerald	Louth	LB	11												1	25/02/2011		1.07	20/12/1975		36.3
926	Naughten	Denis	Longford-Roscommon	FG	97	02	07	11									4	06/06/1997		14.79	23/06/1973		38.7
927	Naughten	Liam	Roscommon	FG	82	82	87										3	18/02/1982	15/06/1989	7.32	30/05/1944	16/11/1996	52.0
928	Nealon	Ted	Sligo-Leitrim	FG	81	82	82	87	89	92							6	11/06/1981	06/06/1997	15.99	01/11/1927		84.4
929	Neilan	Martin	Galway	FF	36*												1	*13/08/1936*	01/07/1937	0.88			
930	Neville	Dan	Limerick West	FG	97	02	07	11									4	06/06/1997		14.79	08/12/1946		65.3
931	Nicolls	George	Galway	CG	21	22	23										3	24/05/1921	09/06/1927	6.04		11/05/1942	
932	Nolan	Derek	Galway West	LB	11												1	25/02/2011		1.07	01/10/1982		29.5
933	Nolan	John	Limerick	CG	23	27S											2	27/08/1923	16/02/1932	8.20		01/11/1948	
934	Nolan	M.J.	Carlow-Kilkenny	FF	82N	87	89	92	02	07							6	24/11/1982	25/02/2011	23.32	25/01/1951		61.2
935	Nolan	Sean	Cork Mid	SF	21												1	24/05/1921	16/06/1922	1.06			
936	Nolan	Thomas	Carlow-Kilkenny	FF	65	69	73	77	81								5	07/04/1965	18/02/1982	16.87	27/07/1921	17/08/1992	71.0
937	Noonan	Michael	Limerick East	FG	81	82	82	87	89	92	97	02	07	11			10	11/06/1981		30.78	21/05/1943		68.8
938	Noonan	Michael J.	Limerick West	FF	69	73	77	81	82	82	87	89	92				9	18/06/1969	06/06/1997	27.97	04/08/1935		76.6
939	Noonan	Michael K.	Cork East	FG	24*												1	*18/11/1924*	09/06/1927	2.55			
940	Norton	Patrick	Kildare	LB	65												1	07/04/1965	18/06/1969	4.20	01/08/1928		83.6
941	Norton	William*	Dublin Co. / Kildare	LB	26*/	32	33	37	38	43	44	48	51	54	57	61	12	*18/02/1926*	04/12/1963	33.10	1900	04/12/1963	63.0
942	Nulty	Patrick	Dublin West	LB	11*												1	*27/10/2011*		0.40	18/11/1982		29.3
943	O Briain	Donnchadh	Limerick West	FF	33	37	38	43	44	48	51	54	57	61	65		11	24/01/1933	18/06/1969	36.40	17/11/1897	22/09/1981	83.0
944	O Caolain	Caoimhghin	Cavan-Monaghan	SF	97	02	07	11									4	06/06/1997		14.79	18/09/1953		58.5
945	O Ceallaigh	Sean	Clare	FF	59*	61	65										3	*22/07/1959*	18/06/1969	9.91	17/4/1896	15/06/1994	98.0
946	O Cuiv	Eamon	Galway West	FF	92	97	02	07	11								5	25/11/1992		19.32	01/06/1950		61.8
947	O Fearghail	Sean	Kildare South	FF	02	07	11										3	17/05/2002		9.85	17/04/1960		51.9
948	O hAnnluain	Eineachan	Monaghan	SF	57												1	05/03/1957	04/10/1961	4.58			
949	O Maille	Padraic	Galway	CG	18	21	22	23									4	21/01/1919	09/06/1927	8.38	23/2/1878	19/01/1946	67.0
950	Ó Riordáin	Aodhán	Dublin North Central	LB	11												1	25/02/2011		1.07	22/07/1976		35.7
951	O Snodaigh	Aengus	Dublin South Central	SF	02	07	11										3	17/05/2002		9.85	31/07/1964		47.6
952	O'Brien	Darragh	Dublin North	FF	07												1	24/05/2007	25/02/2011	3.76	08/07/1974		37.7
953	O'Brien	Eugene	Laoighis-Offaly	CG	32												1	16/02/1932	24/01/1933	0.94		1980	

	Surname	Forename	Constituency	Party	Elected										Terms	From	To	Service	Born	Died	Age
954	O'Brien	Fergus	Dublin South Central	FG	73	77	81	82N	87	89					6	28/02/1973	25/11/1992	18.98	30/03/1930		82.0
955	O'Brien	Jonathan	Cork North Central	SF	11										1	25/02/2011		1.07	01/01/1971		41.2
956	O'Brien	William	Limerick	FG	77	81	82	82							4	16/06/1977	17/02/1987	9.67	06/03/1918	05/11/1994	76.0
957	O'Brien	William*	Dublin S / Tipperary	LB	22/	27J	37								3	16/06/1922	17/06/1938	2.43	23/1/1881	31/10/1968	87.0
958	O'Byrne	Patrick	Tipperary	SF	21										1	24/05/1921	16/06/1922	1.06			
959	O'Callaghan	Daniel	Wexford	LB	22										1	16/06/1922	27/08/1923	1.20			
960	O'Callaghan	Donal	Cork Borough	SF	21										1	24/05/1921	16/06/1922	1.06			
961	O'Callaghan	Kathleen (Kate)	Limerick East	CR	21	22									2	24/05/1921	27/08/1923	2.26	1888	16/03/1961	73.0
962	O'Carroll	Maureen	Dublin North Central	LB	54										1	18/05/1954	05/03/1957	2.80	29/03/1913	09/05/1984	71.0
963	O'Connell	John	Dublin South Central	FF	65	69	73	77	81	82	82	89	92		9	07/04/1965	06/06/1997	29.84	30/01/1930		82.1
964	O'Connell	Richard	Limerick	CG	24*	27	27								3	*28/05/1924*	16/02/1932	7.72	13/3/1892	01/10/1964	72.0
965	O'Connell	Thomas*	Galway /Mayo South	LB	22	23/	27	27							4	16/06/1922	16/02/1932	9.67	21/11/1882	21/06/1969	86.0
966	O'Connor	Art*	Kildare / Wicklow	SF	18/	21									2	21/01/1919	16/06/1922	3.40	1888	10/05/1950	62.0
967	O'Connor	Batt	Dublin County	CG	24*	27	27	32	33						5	*19/03/1924*	07/02/1935	10.89		07/02/1935	
968	O'Connor	Charlie	Dublin South West	FF	02	07									2	17/05/2002	25/02/2011	8.78	09/04/1946		66.0
969	O'Connor	John	Dublin North West	FF	44										1	30/05/1944	04/02/1948	3.68	27/12/1896	02/11/1967	70.0
970	O'Connor	Kathleen	Kerry North	CnaP	56*										1	*29/02/1956*	05/03/1957	1.01	30/07/1934		77.6
971	O'Connor	Timothy	Kerry South	FF	61	65	69	73	77						5	04/10/1961	11/06/1981	19.69	01/10/1906	10/07/1986	79.0
972	O'Dea	Louis	Galway	R	23										1	27/08/1923	09/06/1927	3.78		1948	
973	O'Dea	Willie	Limerick East	FF	82	82	87	89	92	97	02	07	11		9	18/02/1982		30.09	01/11/1952		59.4
974	O'Doherty	Joseph	Donegal	FF	18	21	22	23	33						5	21/01/1919	01/07/1937	12.81	1891	10/08/1979	88.0
975	O'Donnell	Kieran	Limerick East	FG	07	11									2	24/05/2007		4.83	08/05/1953		58.9
976	O'Donnell	Liz	Dublin South	PD	92	97	02								3	25/11/1992	24/05/2007	14.49	01/07/1956		55.7
977	O'Donnell	Pa	Donegal South West	FG	49*	51	54	57	61	65	69				7	*16/11/1949*	04/10/1970	20.88	21/08/1907	04/10/1970	63
978	O'Donnell	Peadar	Donegal	R	23										1	27/08/1923	09/06/1927	3.78	22/2/1893	13/05/1986	93.0
979	O'Donnell	Thomas	Sligo-Mayo East	CT	21	22									2	24/05/1921	27/08/1923	2.26		1945	
980	O'Donnell	Tom	Limerick East	FG	61	65	69	73	77	81	82	82			8	04/10/1961	17/02/1987	25.37	30/08/1926		85.6
981	O'Donnell	William	Tipperary	CnaT	43	44									2	23/06/1943	04/02/1947	3.62		04/02/1947	
982	O'Donoghue	Donal	Kerry South	FF	44*										1	*10/11/1944*	04/02/1948	3.23	5/6/1894	26/07/1971	77.0
983	O'Donoghue	John	Kerry South	FF	87	89	92	97	02	07					6	17/02/1987	25/02/2011	24.02	28/05/1956		55.8
984	O'Donoghue	Martin	Dun Laoghaire	FF	77	81	82F								3	16/06/1977	24/11/1982	5.44	13/05/1933		78.9
985	O'Donoghue	Thomas	Kerry	R	21	22	23								3	24/05/1921	09/06/1927	6.04			
986	O'Donovan	Denis	Cork South West	FF	02										1	17/05/2002	24/05/2007	5.02	23/07/1955		56.7
987	O'Donovan	John	Dublin South East/DSC	FG/LB	54	69									2	18/05/1954	28/02/1973	6.49		17/05/1982	
988	O'Donovan	Patrick	Limerick West	FG	11										1	25/02/2011		1.07	21/03/1977		35.0
989	O'Donovan	Timothy	Cork West	FG	23	27	27	32	33	37	38	43			8	27/08/1923	30/05/1944	20.76	4/4/1881	1951	70.0
990	O'Dowd	Fergus	Louth	FG	02	07	11								3	17/05/2002		9.85	01/09/1948		63.6
991	O'Dowd	Patrick	Roscommon	FF	27	27	33								3	09/06/1927	01/07/1937	9.12		19/06/1968	
992	O'Driscoll	Patrick	Cork West	CnaT	43	44									2	23/06/1943	04/02/1948	4.62	14/1/1878	08/08/1949	71.0
993	O'Duffy	Gen Eoin	Monaghan	CT	21	22									2	24/05/1921	11/12/1922	1.55	20/10/1892	30/11/1944	52.0
994	O'Flaherty	Samuel	Donegal	CR	21	22									2	24/05/1921	27/08/1923	2.26		22/05/1930	
995	O'Flynn	Noel	Cork North Central	FF	97	02	07								3	06/06/1997	25/02/2011	13.72	01/12/1951		60.3
996	O'Gorman	David	Cork East	F	27J										1	09/06/1927	15/09/1927	0.27		1945	
997	O'Gorman	Patrick J.	Cork East	FG	48	51									2	04/02/1948	18/05/1954	6.28			
998	O'Grady	Sean	Clare	FF	32	33	37	38	43	44	48				7	16/02/1932	30/05/1951	19.28	1/12/1889	07/04/1966	76.0
999	O'Hanlon	John F.	Cavan	NP	27	27	32								3	09/06/1927	24/01/1933	5.63	4/11/1872	22/12/1956	84.0
1000	O'Hanlon	Rory	Cavan-Monaghan	FF	77	81	82	82	87	89	92	97	02	07	10	16/06/1977	25/02/2011	33.70	07/02/1934		78.1
1001	O'Hara	Patrick	Mayo North	CG	32										1	16/02/1932	24/01/1933	0.94			
1002	O'Hara	Thomas	Mayo East	FG	51	54	65	69							4	30/05/1951	28/02/1973	13.66	20/07/1911	05/04/1984	72.0
1003	O'Higgins	Brian	Clare	R	18	21	22	23							4	21/01/1919	09/06/1927	8.38	1/7/1882	03/03/1963	80.0
1004	O'Higgins	Kevin*	Leix-Offaly/Dublin Co.	CG	18	21	22/	23	27J						5	21/01/1919	10/07/1927	8.47	7/6/1892	10/07/1927	35.0
1005	O'Higgins	Michael*	Dublin SW/ Wicklow	FG	48	54	57/	61	65						5	04/02/1948	18/06/1969	18.40	01/11/1917	29/03/2005	87.0
1006	O'Higgins (jun.)	Thomas F.*	Laoighis-Offaly/Dublin	FG	48	51	54	57	61	65/	69				7	04/02/1948	28/02/1973	25.07	23/07/1916	25/02/2003	86.0

	Surname	Forename	Constituency	Party	Elected																	Terms	From	To	Service	Born	Died	Age
1007	O'Higgins (sen.)	Thomas F.*	Dublin/Laois-Offaly/Cork	FG	29*	/32	33	37	38	43	44/	48	51									9	*14/03/1929*	01/11/1953	24.64	1890	01/11/1953	63.0
1008	O'Keeffe	Batt	Cork South Central/NW	FF	87	92	97	02	07													5	17/02/1987	25/02/2011	<u>20.57</u>	02/04/1945		67.0
1009	O'Keeffe	James	Dublin South West	FG	61																	1	04/10/1961	07/04/1965	3.51			
1010	O'Keeffe	Jim	Cork South West	FG	77	81	82	82	87	89	92	97	02	07								10	16/06/1977	25/02/2011	33.70	31/03/1941		71.0
1011	O'Keeffe	Ned	Cork East	FF	82	87	89	92	97	02	07											7	24/11/1982	25/02/2011	28.26	01/08/1942		69.6
1012	O'Keeffe	Patrick	Cork Mid	SF	18	21																2	21/01/1919	16/06/1922	3.40		20/09/1973	
1013	O'Kelly	John	Louth	CR	18	21	22															3	21/01/1919	27/08/1923	4.60	1873	1957	84.0
1014	O'Kelly	Sean T.	Dublin North West	FF	18	21	22	23	27	27	32	33	37	38	43	44						12	21/01/1919	14/06/1945	26.40	25/8/1882	23/11/1966	84.0
1015	O'Kennedy**	Michael	Tipperary North	FF	69	73	77	82	82	87	89	97										8	18/06/1969	17/05/2002	<u>27.21</u>	21/02/1936		76.1
1016	O'Leary	Daniel	Cork West	FG	27	32	33	37														4	15/09/1927	17/06/1938	10.75	1/9/1877	31/03/1951	73.0
1017	O'Leary	John	Kerry South	FF	66*	69	73	77	81	82	82	87	89	92								10	07/12/1966	06/06/1997	30.50	03/05/1933		78.9
1018	O'Leary	John	Wexford	LB	43	44	48	51	54													5	23/06/1943	05/03/1957	13.70	1/9/1894	21/06/1959	64.0
1019	O'Leary	Michael	Dublin South West	FG	65	69	73	77	81	82	82											7	07/04/1965	17/02/1987	21.86	08/05/1936	11/05/2006	70.0
1020	O'Leary	William	Kerry	FF	27	27																2	09/06/1927	16/02/1932	4.69		1955	
1021	O'Loghlen	Peter	Clare	FF	38	44																2	17/06/1938	04/02/1948	<u>8.69</u>	1883	25/10/1971	88.0
1022	O'Mahony	Dermot	Wicklow	FG	27	27	32	33	37													5	09/06/1927	17/06/1938	11.02	2/4/1881	22/04/1960	79.0
1023	O'Mahony	John	Fermanagh South	SF	18																	1	21/01/1919	24/05/1921	2.34	1864	28/11/1934	70.0
1024	O'Mahony	John	Mayo	FG	07	11																2	24/05/2007		4.83	08/06/1953		58.8
1025	O'Mahony	Thomas	Cork East	CG	23																	1	27/08/1923	20/07/1924	0.90		20/07/1924	
1026	O'Malley	Desmond	Limerick East	PD	68*	69	73	77	81	82	82	87	89	92	97							11	*22/05/1968*	17/05/2002	33.99	01/02/1939		73.1
1027	O'Malley	Donogh	Limerick East	FF	54	57	61	65														4	18/05/1954	10/03/1968	13.81	01/01/1921	10/03/1968	47
1028	O'Malley	Ernest	Dublin North	R	23																	1	27/08/1923	09/06/1927	3.78	26/5/1897	25/03/1957	59.0
1029	O'Malley	Fiona	Dun Laoghaire	PD	02																	1	17/05/2002	24/05/2007	5.02	19/01/1968		44.2
1030	O'Malley	Pat	Dublin West	PD	87																	1	17/02/1987	15/06/1989	2.32	01/07/1943		68.7
1031	O'Malley	Tim	Limerick East	PD	02																	1	17/05/2002	24/05/2007	5.02	03/07/1944		67.7
1032	O'Mara	James	Kilkenny South	SF	18																	1	21/01/1919	24/05/1921	2.34	6/8/1873	21/11/1948	75.0
1033	O'Meara	James	Dublin South	CG	24*																	1	*12/03/1924*	09/06/1927	3.24	6/3/1873	21/11/1948	75.0
1034	O'Neill	Eamonn	Cork West	FG	32	33	37	38	44													5	16/02/1932	04/02/1948	<u>15.03</u>		03/11/1954	
1035	O'Neill	Laurence	Dublin Mid	NP	22																	1	16/06/1922	27/08/1923	1.20	1874	26/07/1943	69.0
1036	O'Rahilly	Alfred	Cork Borough	CG	23																	1	27/08/1923	01/08/1924	0.93	1/10/1884	01/08/1969	84.0
1037	O'Reilly	Joe	Cavan-Monaghan	FG	11																	1	25/02/2011		1.07	14/04/1955		56.9
1038	O'Reilly	John J.	Cavan	CG	25*	27	27	32	33													5	*11/03/1925*	01/07/1937	12.31	21/4/1881	28/12/1967	86.0
1039	O'Reilly	Matthew	Meath	FF	27	27	32	33	37	38	43	44	48	51								10	09/06/1927	18/05/1954	26.94	1/3/1880	13/11/1962	82.0
1040	O'Reilly	Thomas	Kerry	FF	27	27	32															3	09/06/1927	24/01/1933	5.63		1944	
1041	O'Reilly	Thomas P.	Cavan	NP	44																	1	30/05/1944	04/02/1948	3.68	06/08/1915	01/02/1995	79.0
1042	O'Reilly(Castlepoles)	Patrick	Cavan	NP	48																	1	04/02/1948	30/05/1951	3.32	9/1/1893	25/04/1972	79.0
1043	O'Reilly(Murmod)	Patrick	Cavan	FG	43	44	51	54	57	61	69											7	23/06/1943	28/02/1973	<u>22.17</u>	01/04/1927	19/02/1994	66.0
1044	Ormonde	Donal	Waterford	FF	82N																	1	24/11/1982	17/02/1987	4.23	21/01/1943		69.2
1045	Ormonde	John	Waterford	FF	47*	48	51	54	57	61												6	*29/10/1947*	07/04/1965	17.44	15/09/1905	25/06/1981	75.0
1046	O'Rourke	Daniel*	Mayo / Roscommon	FF	21	22/	32	37	38	44	48											7	24/05/1921	30/05/1951	<u>15.43</u>		21/03/1971	
1047	O'Rourke	Mary	Longford-Westmeath	FF	82N	87	89	92	97	07												6	24/11/1982	25/02/2011	<u>23.24</u>	31/05/1937		74.8
1048	O'Shannon	Cathal	Louth-Meath	LB	22																	1	16/06/1922	27/08/1923	1.20	1893	04/10/1969	76.0
1049	O'Shaughnessy	Andrew	Cork Borough	PA	23																	1	27/08/1923	09/06/1927	3.78	28/7/1866	1956	89.0
1050	O'Shaughnessy	John	Limerick	FG	32	37																2	16/02/1932	17/06/1938	<u>1.90</u>			
1051	O'Shea	Brian	Waterford	LB	89	92	97	02	07													5	15/06/1989	25/02/2011	21.70	09/12/1944		67.3
1052	O'Sullivan	Christy	Cork South West	FF	07																	1	24/05/2007	25/02/2011	3.76	27/11/1948		63.3
1053	O'Sullivan	Denis	Cork Mid	FG	51	54	57	61														4	30/05/1951	07/04/1965	13.86	05/03/1918	20/07/1987	69.0
1054	O'Sullivan	Gearoid*	Carlow-Kilkenny/Dublin Co	CG	21	22/	27*	27S	32	33												6	24/05/1921	01/07/1937	<u>12.11</u>	1891	05/08/1944	53.0
1055	O'Sullivan	Gerry	Cork North Central	LB	89	92																2	15/06/1989	05/08/1994	5.14	01/04/1936	05/08/1994	58.0
1056	O'Sullivan	Jan	Limerick East	LB	98*	02	07	11														4	*11/03/1998*		14.03	06/12/1950		61.3
1057	O'Sullivan	John L.	Cork South West	FG	69	73																2	18/06/1969	16/06/1977	7.99	08/06/1901	28/02/1990	88.0
1058	O'Sullivan	John M.	Kerry North	FG	23	27	27	32	33	37	38											7	27/08/1923	23/06/1943	19.82	18/2/1881	09/02/1948	66.0
1059	O'Sullivan	Martin	Dublin North Central	LB	43	44	48															3	23/06/1943	30/05/1951	7.93		20/01/1956	

	Surname	Forename	Constituency	Party	Elected																	Terms	From	To	Service	Born	Died	Age
1060	O'Sullivan	Maureen	Dublin Central	NP	09*	11																2	*06/06/2009*		2.79	10/03/1951		61.0
1061	O'Sullivan	Ted	Cork West	FF	37	38	43	44	48	51												6	01/07/1937	18/05/1954	16.88	26/7/1899	1969	70.0
1062	O'Sullivan	Toddy	Cork South Central	LB	81	82	82	87	89	92												6	11/06/1981	06/06/1997	15.99	01/12/1934		77.3
1063	O'Toole	Martin J.	Mayo West	FF	89																	1	15/06/1989	25/11/1992	3.45	27/06/1925		86.7
1064	O'Toole	Patrick	Mayo East	FG	77	81	82	82														4	16/06/1977	17/02/1987	9.67	15/01/1938		74.2
1065	O'Toole	Seamus	Wicklow	FF	57																	1	05/03/1957	04/10/1961	4.58		24/09/1969	
1066	Owen	Nora	Dublin North	FG	81	82	82	89	92	97												6	11/06/1981	17/05/2002	18.61	01/06/1945		66.8
1067	Palmer	Patrick	Kerry South	FG	48	51	54	57														4	04/02/1948	04/10/1961	13.66		21/03/1971	
1068	Parlon	Tom	Laoighis-Offaly	PD	02																	1	17/05/2002	24/05/2007	5.02	19/08/1953		58.6
1069	Pattison	James	Carlow-Kilkenny	LB	33	37	38	43	44	48	54											7	24/01/1933	05/03/1957	21.14	28/6/1886	31/12/1963	77.0
1070	Pattison	Seamus	Carlow-Kilkenny	LB	61	65	69	73	77	81	82	82	87	89	92	97	02					13	04/10/1961	24/05/2007	45.64	19/04/1936		75.9
1071	Pearse	Margaret	Dublin County	SF	21																	1	24/05/1921	16/06/1922	1.06	1857	01/01/1932	75.0
1072	Pearse	Margaret M.	Dublin County	FF	33																	1	24/01/1933	01/07/1937	4.43	1878	07/11/1968	90.0
1073	Penrose	Willie	Westmeath	LB	92	97	02	07	11													5	25/11/1992		19.32	01/08/1956		55.6
1074	Perry	John	Sligo-Leitrim	FG	97	02	07	11														4	06/06/1997		14.79	15/08/1956		55.6
1075	Phelan	Ann	Carlow-Kilkenny	LB	11																	1	25/02/2011		1.07	16/09/1961		50.5
1076	Phelan	John Paul	Carlow-Kilkenny	FG	11																	1	25/02/2011		1.07	27/09/1978		33.5
1077	Phelan	Nicholas	Waterford-Tipperary E	LB	22																	1	16/06/1922	27/08/1923	1.20	19/9/1893	14/12/1942	49.0
1078	Plunkett	George	Roscommon	R	18	21	22	23														4	21/01/1919	09/06/1927	8.38	1851	1948	97.0
1079	Powell	Thomas	Galway	FF	27	27	32															3	09/06/1927	24/01/1933	5.63	16/4/1892	20/06/1971	79.0
1080	Power	Patrick	Kildare	FF	69	73	77	81	82	82	87											7	18/06/1969	15/06/1989	19.99	19/11/1928		83.3
1081	Power	Peter	Limerick East	FF	02	07																2	17/05/2002	25/02/2011	8.78	26/01/1966		46.2
1082	Power	Sean	Kildare	FF	89	92	97	02	07													5	15/06/1989	25/02/2011	21.70	14/10/1960		51.4
1083	Prendergast	Frank	Limerick East	LB	82N																	1	24/11/1982	17/02/1987	4.23	13/07/1933		78.7
1084	Pringle	Thomas	Donegal South West	NP	11																	1	25/02/2011		1.07	30/08/1967		44.6
1085	Prior	John	Cork West	CG	23																	1	27/08/1923	09/06/1927	3.78			
1086	Quill	Mairin	Cork North Central	PD	87	89	92															3	17/02/1987	06/06/1997	10.30	15/09/1940		71.5
1087	Quill	Timothy	Cork North	LB	27J																	1	09/06/1927	15/09/1927	0.27	09/05/1901	10/06/1960	59.0
1088	Quinn	Ruairi	Dublin South East	LB	77	82	82	87	89	92	97	02	07	11								10	16/06/1977		34.08	02/04/1946		66.0
1089	Rabbitte	Pat	Dublin South West	LB	89	92	97	02	07	11												6	15/06/1989		22.77	18/05/1949		62.8
1090	Redmond	Bridget	Waterford	FG	33	37	38	43	44	48	51											7	24/01/1933	03/05/1952	19.27	1905	03/05/1952	47.0
1091	Redmond	Capt. William	Waterford	CG	23	27	27	32														4	27/08/1923	17/04/1932	8.64	1886	17/04/1932	46.0
1092	Reidy	James	Limerick East	FG	32	33	38	43	44	48	51											7	16/02/1932	18/05/1954	21.29	1890	07/12/1963	73.0
1093	Reilly	James	Dublin North	FG	07	11																2	24/05/2007		4.83	16/08/1955		56.6
1094	Reynolds	Albert*	Longford-Wmeath/Roscomm	FF	77	81	82	82	87	89/	92	97										8	16/06/1977	17/05/2002	24.92	01/11/1932		79.4
1095	Reynolds	Gerry	Sligo-Leitrim	FG	89	97																2	15/06/1989	17/05/2002	8.39	01/04/1961		51.0
1096	Reynolds	Mary	Sligo-Leitrim	FG	32	37	38	43	44	48	51	54	57									9	16/02/1932	04/10/1961	25.20	10/10/1889	29/08/1974	84.0
1097	Reynolds	Patrick J.	Roscommon	FG	61	65	73															3	04/10/1961	16/06/1977	12.00	25/11/1920	27/12/2003	83.0
1098	Reynolds	Patrick T.	Leitrim-Sligo	CG	27S																	1	15/09/1927	16/02/1932	4.42	1/3/1887	14/03/1932	45.0
1099	Rice	Bridget Mary	Monaghan	FF	38	43	44	48	51													5	17/06/1938	18/05/1954	15.92	1885	08/12/1967	82.0
1100	Rice	Eamonn	Monaghan	FF	32	33	37															3	16/02/1932	07/11/1937	5.72	26/4/1873	07/11/1937	64.0
1101	Rice	John	Kerry South	SF	57																	1	05/03/1957	04/10/1961	4.58		01/07/1970	
1102	Rice	Vincent	Dublin North	CG	27J	28*	33															3	09/06/1927	01/07/1937	8.57		01/01/1955	
1103	Ring	Michael	Mayo	FG	94*	97	02	07	11													5	*09/06/1994*		17.79	24/12/1953		58.2
1104	Robbins	Laurence	Longford-Westmeath	SF	21																	1	24/05/1921	16/06/1922	1.06		1939	
1105	Robinson	Seamus	Waterford-Tipperary E	SF	21																	1	24/05/1921	16/06/1922	1.06	6/1/1890	08/12/1961	71.0
1106	Roche	Dick	Wicklow	FF	87	89	97	02	07													5	17/02/1987	25/02/2011	19.49	30/03/1947		65.0
1107	Roche	Edmund	Kerry-Limerick West	CR	21	22																2	24/05/1921	27/08/1923	2.26			
1108	Roddy	Joseph	Sligo-Leitrim	FG	48	51	54															3	04/02/1948	05/03/1957	9.08	1897	03/10/1965	68.0
1109	Roddy	Martin	Leitrim-Sligo	FG	25*	27	27	32	33	37	43	44										8	11/03/1925	08/01/1948	17.81	1887	08/01/1948	61.0
1110	Rogers	Patrick	Sligo-Leitrim	FG	33	37	38	43	44	51	57											7	24/01/1933	04/10/1961	22.57	01/02/1900	22/03/1963	63.0
1111	Rooney	Eamonn	Dublin County	FG	48	51	54	57	61													5	04/02/1948	07/04/1965	17.17		09/11/1993	
1112	Rooney	John	Dublin County	F	22																	1	16/06/1922	27/08/1923	1.20			

	Surname	Forename	Constituency	Party	Elected																	Terms	From	To	Service	Born	Died	Age
1113	Ross	Shane	Dublin South	NP	11																	1	25/02/2011		1.07	11/07/1949		62.7
1114	Rowlette	Robert	Dublin University	NP	33*																	1	13/10/1933	01/07/1937	3.72	1873	13/10/1944	71.0
1115	Russell	George	Limerick East	NP	57																	1	05/03/1957	04/10/1961	4.58	01/04/1912		
1116	Ruttledge	Patrick	Mayo North	FF	21	22	23	27	27	32	33	37	38	43	44	48	51					13	24/05/1921	08/05/1952	30.96	1892	08/05/1952	60.0
1117	Ryan	Brendan	Dublin North	LB	11																	1	25/02/2011		1.07	15/02/1953		59.1
1118	Ryan	Col. Jeremiah	Tipperary	FG	37	38	43															3	01/07/1937	30/05/1944	6.91	30/7/1891		
1119	Ryan	Eamonn	Dublin South	GP	02	07																2	17/05/2002	25/02/2011	8.78	28/07/1963		48.7
1120	Ryan	Eoin	Dublin South East	FF	92	97	02															3	25/11/1992	24/05/2007	14.49	24/02/1953		59.1
1121	Ryan	James	Wexford	FF	18	21	23	27	27	32	33	37	38	43	44	48	51	54	57	61		16	21/01/1919	07/04/1965	45.01	6/12/1891	25/09/1970	78.0
1122	Ryan	John	Tipperary North	LB	73	77	81	82	82	92												6	28/02/1973	06/06/1997	18.49	17/06/1927		84.8
1123	Ryan	Martin	Tipperary	FF	33	37	38	43														4	24/01/1933	22/07/1943	10.49	31/01/1900	22/07/1943	43.0
1124	Ryan	Mary	Tipperary North	FF	44	48	51	54	57													5	30/05/1944	04/10/1961	17.35	31/1/1898	08/02/1981	83.0
1125	Ryan	Patrick	Tipperary	R	23																	1	27/08/1923	09/06/1927	3.78	16/11/1898	21/01/1944	45.0
1126	Ryan	Richie	Dublin South East	FG	59*	61	65	69	73	77	81											7	22/07/1959	18/02/1982	22.58	27/02/1929		83.1
1127	Ryan	Robert	Limerick East	FF	32	33	37	38	43	44	48											7	16/02/1932	30/05/1951	19.28	1882	23/04/1952	70.0
1128	Ryan	Sean	Dublin North	LB	89	92	98*	02														4	15/06/1989	24/05/2007	17.18	27/01/1943		69.2
1129	Sargent	Trevor	Dublin North	GP	92	97	02	07														4	25/11/1992	25/02/2011	18.25	01/07/1960		51.7
1130	Scanlon	Eamon	Sligo-North Leitrim	FF	07																	1	24/05/2007	25/02/2011	3.76	20/09/1954		57.5
1131	Sears	William	Mayo South	CG	18	21	22	23														4	21/01/1919	09/06/1927	8.38		23/03/1929	
1132	Sexton	Mae	Longford-Roscommon	PD	02																	1	17/05/2002	24/05/2007	5.02	28/04/1955		56.9
1133	Sexton	Martin	Clare	FF	27S	32																2	15/09/1927	24/01/1933	5.36		01/02/1966	
1134	Shanahan	Patrick	Clare	FF	45*																	1	04/12/1945	04/02/1948	2.17	10/03/1908	01/02/2000	91.0
1135	Shanahan	Philip	Dublin Mid	SF	18	21																2	21/01/1919	16/06/1922	3.40			
1136	Shannon	James	Wexford	LB	27J																	1	09/06/1927	15/09/1927	0.27			
1137	Shatter	Alan	Dublin South	FG	81	82	82	87	89	92	97	07	11									9	11/06/1981		25.76	01/02/1951		61.1
1138	Shaw	Patrick	Longford-Westmeath	CG	23	27	27	32														4	27/08/1923	24/01/1933	9.41	15/2/1872	14/09/1940	68.0
1139	Sheahan	Tom	Kerry South	FG	07																	1	24/05/2007	25/02/2011	3.76	05/09/1968		43.5
1140	Sheehan	Michael	Cork Borough	NP	48																	1	04/02/1948	30/05/1951	3.32			
1141	Sheehan	P.J.	Cork South West	FG	81	82	82	87	89	92	97	07										8	11/06/1981	25/02/2011	24.69	01/03/1933		79.1
1142	Sheehy	Timothy	Cork West	CG	27	27																2	09/06/1927	16/02/1932	4.69	2/12/1855	05/11/1938	82.0
1143	Sheehy	Timothy	Tipperary	FF	27S	32																2	15/09/1927	24/01/1933	5.36	17/6/1895	15/02/1968	72.0
1144	Sheldon	William	Donegal East	NP	43	44	48	51	54	57												6	23/06/1943	04/10/1961	18.28	18/01/1907	01/11/1999	92.0
1145	Sheridan	Joseph	Longford-Westmeath	NP	61	65	69	73	77													5	04/10/1961	11/06/1981	19.69	27/11/1914	30/09/2000	85.0
1146	Sheridan	Michael	Cavan	FF	32	33	37	38	43	44	48	51	54	57								10	16/02/1932	04/10/1961	29.63	1896	06/04/1970	74.0
1147	Sherlock	Joe	Cork East	LB	81	82F	87	89	02													5	11/06/1981	24/05/2007	12.25	26/09/1935	10/09/2007	71.0
1148	Sherlock	Sean	Cork East	LB	07	11																2	24/05/2007		4.83	06/12/1972		39.3
1149	Sherwin	Frank	Dublin North Central	NP	57*	61																2	14/11/1957	07/04/1965	7.40	1905	1981	76.0
1150	Sherwin	Sean	Dublin South West	FF	70*																	1	04/03/1970	28/02/1973	2.99	12/12/1946		65.3
1151	Shortall	Roisin	Dublin North West	LB	92	97	02	07	11													5	25/11/1992		19.32	25/04/1954		57.9
1152	Skelly	Liam	Dublin West	FG	82*	82N																2	25/05/1982	17/02/1987	4.73	10/10/1941		70.4
1153	Skelly	Michael	Carlow-Kilkenny	R	23																	1	27/08/1923	09/06/1927	3.78			
1154	Skinner	Leo	Cork North	FF	43	44																2	23/06/1943	04/02/1948	4.62	01/08/1901	27/01/1970	68.0
1155	Smith	Brendan	Cavan-Monaghan	FF	92	97	02	07	11													5	25/11/1992		19.32	01/06/1956		55.8
1156	Smith	Michael	Tipperary North	FF	69	77	81	87	89	92	97	02										8	18/06/1969	24/05/2007	28.64	08/11/1940		71.4
1157	Smith	Patrick	Cavan	FF	23	27	27	32	33	37	38	43	44	48	51	54	57	61	65	69	73	17	27/08/1923	16/06/1977	53.81	17/07/1901	18/03/1982	80.0
1158	Spring	Arthur	Kerry North	LB	11																	1	25/02/2011		1.07	05/07/1976		35.7
1159	Spring	Dan	Kerry North	LB	43	44	48	51	54	57	61	65	69	73	77							11	23/06/1943	11/06/1981	37.97	01/07/1910	01/01/1998	87.0
1160	Spring	Dick	Kerry North	LB	81	82	82	87	89	92	97											7	11/06/1981	17/05/2002	20.93	29/08/1950		61.6
1161	Stack	Austin	Kerry	SF	18	21	22	23	27J													5	21/01/1919	15/09/1927	8.65	7/12/1879	27/04/1929	49.0
1162	Stafford	John	Dublin Central	FF	87	89																2	17/02/1987	25/11/1992	5.77	20/05/1944		67.8
1163	Stagg	Emmet	Kildare	LB	87	89	92	97	02	07	11											7	17/02/1987		25.09	01/10/1944		67.5
1164	Staines	Michael	Dublin North West	CT	18	21	22															3	21/01/1919	27/08/1923	4.60	1885	26/10/1955	70.0
1165	Stanley	Brian	Laoighis Offaly	SF	11																	1	25/02/2011		1.07	14/01/1958		54.2

	Surname	Forename	Constituency	Party	Elected																	Terms	From	To	Service	Born	Died	Age
1166	Stanton	David	Cork East	FG	97	02	07	11														4	06/06/1997		14.79	15/02/1957		55.1
1167	Stapleton	Richard	Tipperary	LB	43																	1	23/06/1943	30/05/1944	0.94		31/07/1949	
1168	Staunton	Myles	Mayo West	FG	73																	1	28/02/1973	16/06/1977	4.30	24/09/1935	22/06/2011	75
1169	Stockley	Prof. William	N.U.I	CR	21	22																2	24/05/1921	27/08/1923	2.26		22/07/1943	
1170	Sweeney	Joseph	Donegal	CT	18	21	22															3	21/01/1919	27/08/1923	4.60	1897	25/11/1980	83.0
1171	Sweetman	Gerard	Kildare	FG	48	51	54	57	61	65	69											7	04/02/1948	28/01/1970	21.98	10/06/1908	28/01/1970	61.0
1172	Sweetman	Roger M	Wexford North	SF	18																	1	21/01/1919	24/05/1921	2.34	18/08/1974	20/05/1954	79.0
1173	Swift	Brian	Waterford	FF	87																	1	17/02/1987	15/06/1989	2.32	01/05/1952		59.9
1174	Taylor	Francis	Clare	FG	69	73	77															3	18/06/1969	11/06/1981	11.98	30/05/1914	15/04/1989	74.0
1175	Taylor	Mervyn	Dublin South West	LB	81	82	82	87	89	92												6	11/06/1981	06/06/1997	15.99	01/12/1931		80.3
1176	Taylor-Quinn	Madeleine	Clare	FG	81	82N	87	89														4	11/06/1981	25/11/1992	10.70	26/05/1951		60.8
1177	Teehan	Patrick	Carlow-Kilkenny	FF	60*																	1	23/06/1960	04/10/1961	1.28	14/04/1904	25/12/1985	81.0
1178	Thornley	David	Dublin North West	LB	69	73																2	18/06/1969	16/06/1977	7.99	31/07/1935	18/06/1978	42.0
1179	Thrift	Prof. William	Dublin University	NP	21	22	23	27	27	32	33											7	24/05/1921	01/07/1937	16.10	28/2/1870	23/04/1942	72.0
1180	Tierney	Patrick	Tipperary North	LB	57	61	65															3	05/03/1957	18/06/1969	12.29		29/09/1990	
1181	Tierney	Prof. Michael*	Mayo North / N.U.I.	CG	25*/	27S																2	11/03/1925	16/02/1932	6.67	30/9/1894	10/05/1975	80.0
1182	Timmins	Billy	Wicklow	FG	97	02	07	11														4	06/06/1997		14.79	01/10/1959		52.5
1183	Timmins	Godfrey	Wicklow	FG	68*	69	73	77	81	82	82	89	92									9	14/03/1968	06/06/1997	26.91	06/09/1927	11/04/2001	73.0
1184	Timmons	Eugene	Dublin North East	FF	61	69	73															3	04/10/1961	16/06/1977	11.50		13/05/1999	
1185	Timoney	John	Tipperary South	CnaP	48																	1	04/02/1948	30/05/1951	3.32	23/05/1909	16/05/1961	51.0
1186	Toal	Brendan	Monaghan	FG	73*																	1	27/11/1973	16/06/1977	3.55	01/12/1940		71.3
1187	Tóibín	Peadar	Meath West	SF	11																	1	25/02/2011		1.07	01/06/1974		37.8
1188	Traynor	Oscar	Dublin North East	FF	25*	27J	32	33	37	38	43	44	48	51	54	57						12	11/03/1925	04/10/1961	32.15	21/3/1886	21/12/1963	77.0
1189	Treacy	Noel	Galway East	FF	82*	82	87	89	92	97	02	07										8	20/07/1982	25/02/2011	28.60	18/12/1952		59.3
1190	Treacy	Sean	Tipperary South	NP	61	65	69	73	77	81	82	82	87	89	92							11	04/10/1961	06/06/1997	35.67	23/09/1923		88.5
1191	Troy	Robert	Longford-Westmeath	FF	11																	1	25/02/2011		1.07	01/01/1982		30.2
1192	Tubridy	Sean	Galway West	FF	27	27	37	38														4	09/06/1927	15/07/1939	6.73		15/07/1939	42.0
1193	Tuffy	Joanna	Dublin Mid-West	LB	07	11																2	24/05/2007		4.83	09/03/1965		47.0
1194	Tully	James	Meath	LB	54	61	65	69	73	77	81											7	18/05/1954	18/02/1982	23.18	18/09/1915	20/05/1992	76.0
1195	Tully	John	Cavan	CnaP	48	51	54	57	65													5	04/02/1948	18/06/1969	17.86	15/11/1904	31/10/1977	72.0
1196	Tunney	James	Dublin County	LB	43																	1	23/06/1943	30/05/1944	0.94	1892	12/05/1964	72.0
1197	Tunney	Jim	Dublin North West	FF	69	73	77	81	82	82	87	89										8	18/06/1969	25/11/1992	23.44	25/12/1923	17/01/2002	78.0
1198	Twomey	Liam	Wexford	NP	02	11																2	17/05/2002		6.09	03/04/1967		45.0
1199	Tynan	Thomas	Laoighis-Offaly	FF	27J																	1	09/06/1927	15/09/1927	0.27	1859	24/09/1953	94.0
1200	Upton	Mary	Dublin South Central	LB	99*	02	07															3	27/10/1999	25/02/2011	11.33	30/05/1946		65.8
1201	Upton	Pat	Dublin South Central	LB	92	97																2	25/11/1992	22/02/1999	6.24	01/09/1944	22/02/1999	54.0
1202	Varadkar	Leo	Dublin West	FG	07	11																2	24/05/2007		4.83	18/01/1979		33.2
1203	Vaughan	Daniel	Cork North	F	22	23	27	27	32													5	16/06/1922	24/01/1933	10.61	27/7/1897	23/09/1975	78.0
1204	Victory	James	Longford-Westmeath	FF	27J	33	37	38														4	09/06/1927	23/06/1943	10.68	1880	05/08/1946	66.0
1205	Wade	Eddie	Limerick East	FF	97																	1	06/06/1997	17/05/2002	4.94	01/06/1948		63.8
1206	Wall	Jack	Kildare South	LB	97	02	07	11														4	06/06/1997		14.79	01/07/1945		66.7
1207	Wall	Nicholas	Waterford	FG	23	33	37															3	27/08/1923	17/06/1938	9.18	6/8/1884	03/12/1939	55.0
1208	Wallace	Dan	Cork North Central	FF	82N	87	89	92	97	02												6	24/11/1982	24/05/2007	24.50	14/06/1942		69.8
1209	Wallace	Mary	Meath East	FF	89	92	97	02	07													5	15/06/1989	25/02/2011	21.70	13/06/1959		52.8
1210	Wallace	Mick	Wexford	NP	11																	1	25/02/2011		1.07	01/11/1955		56.4
1211	Walsh	Brian	Galway West	FG	11																	1	25/02/2011		1.07	28/09/1972		39.5
1212	Walsh	Eamonn	Dublin South West	LB	92																	1	25/11/1992	06/06/1997	4.53	20/09/1945		66.5
1213	Walsh	James J.	Cork Borough	CG	18	21	22	23	27J													5	21/01/1919	15/09/1927	8.65	20/2/1880	30/11/1948	68.0
1214	Walsh	Joe	Cork South West	FF	77	82	82	87	89	92	97	02										8	16/06/1977	24/05/2007	29.25	01/05/1943		68.9
1215	Walsh	Laurence	Louth	FF	37	38	44	51														4	01/07/1937	18/05/1954	12.62	1/8/1883	11/08/1962	79.0
1216	Walsh	Richard	Mayo South	FF	27S	32	33	37	38	44	48											7	15/09/1927	30/05/1951	22.76	1889	1955	66.0
1217	Walsh	Sean	Dublin South West	FF	73	77	81	82	82	87												6	28/02/1973	15/06/1989	16.29	03/04/1925	26/12/1989	64.0
1218	Walsh	Thomas	Carlow-Kilkenny	FF	48	51	54															3	10/02/1948	14/07/1956	8.42	18/12/1901	14/07/1956	54.0

	Surname	Forename	Constituency	Party	Elected																	Terms	From	To	Service	Born	Died	Age
1219	Ward	Conn F.	Monaghan	FF	27S	32	33	37	38	43	44											7	15/09/1927	04/02/1948	20.39	12/2/1890	05/12/1966	76.0
1220	Ward	Peter	Donegal	CG	18	21	22	23														4	21/01/1919	01/08/1924	5.53	1/11/1891	06/01/1970	78.0
1221	Whelehan	Joseph	Galway	CT	21	22																2	24/05/1921	27/08/1923	2.26		29/10/1968	
1222	White	Alex	Dublin South	LB	11																	1	25/02/2011		1.07	03/12/1958		53.3
1223	White	Jim	Donegal South West	FG	73	77	81															3	28/02/1973	18/02/1982	8.97	02/01/1938		74.2
1224	White	John	Donegal	NP	23	27	27	32														4	27/08/1923	24/01/1933	9.41			
1225	White	Mary	Carlow-Kilkenny	GP	07																	1	24/05/2007	25/02/2011	3.76	24/11/1948		63.3
1226	White	Vincent	Waterford	CG	21	22	27	27														4	24/05/1921	16/02/1932	6.95	1885	14/12/1958	73.0
1227	Wilkinson	Ollie	Waterford	FF	02																	1	17/05/2002	24/05/2007	5.02	04/10/1944		67.5
1228	Wilson	John	Cavan-Monaghan	FF	73	77	81	82	82	87	89											7	28/02/1973	25/11/1992	19.74	08/07/1923	09/07/2007	84.0
1229	Wilson	Richard	Wicklow	F	22	23																2	16/06/1922	09/06/1927	4.98		20/02/1957	
1230	Wolfe	George	Kildare	CG	23	27	27															3	27/08/1923	16/02/1932	8.47	1860	10/12/1941	81.0
1231	Wolfe	Jasper	Cork West	NP	27	27	32															3	09/06/1927	24/01/1933	5.63	3/8/1872	27/08/1952	80.0
1232	Woods	Michael	Dublin North East	FF	77	81	82	82	87	89	92	97	02	07								10	16/06/1977	25/02/2011	33.70	08/12/1935		76.3
1233	Wright	G.V.	Dublin North	FF	87	97	02															3	17/02/1987	24/05/2007	12.28	03/08/1947		64.6
1234	Wycherley	Florence	Cork West	NP	57																	1	05/03/1957	04/10/1961	4.58	20/02/1908	23/04/1969	61.0
1235	Wyse	Pierse	Cork South Central	PD	65	69	73	77/	81	82	82	87	89									9	07/04/1965	25/11/1992	27.64	02/03/1928	28/04/2009	81.0
1236	Yates	Ivan	Wexford	FG	81	82	82	87	89	92	97											7	11/06/1981	17/05/2002	20.93	01/10/1959		52.5
1236	**Total**	**EU Commissioner													***Includes 127 By-Elections**						*	**4745**			**11.27**			**61.6**
	* Elected in more than one constituency																	*By-Election*				**Broken Service**		**Service: Members 30th Dail to**			**22/03/2012**	
																						Approximate Date		**Age: Living Members to**			**22/03/2012**	

INDEX ALL SENATORS 1922-2012

	Surname	Forename	TD	Panel	Party	Elected													Terms	From	By-E	To	Service	Born	Died	Age
1	Aghas	Padraig		Labour	NP	51													1	01/08/1951		14/07/1954	2.95	1885	22/12/1966	81
2	*Ahern*	Kit	TD	Nominated	FF	61	65	69	73										4	25/11/1964		06/06/1977	12.53	13/01/1915	27/12/2007	92
3	*Ahern*	Liam	TD	Administrative	FF	57	61	65	69										5	09/05/1957		28/02/1973	15.81	12/01/1916	13/07/1974	58
4	Alton	Bryan		NUI	NP	65	69												2	08/06/1965		01/05/1973	7.90	05/06/1919	18/01/1991	71
5	*Alton*	Prof. Ernest	TD	University of Dul	NP	38	38'												2	28/03/1938		25/08/1943	5.41	1873	18/02/1952	79
6	*Anthony*	Richard	TD	Labour	NP	48	54												2	07/04/1948		09/05/1957	6.14	1875	1962	87
7	Aylward	Bob		Agricultural	FF	73													1	01/05/1973		18/07/1974	1.21	1911	18/07/1974	63
8	Bacik	Ivana		University of Dul	NP	07	11												2	23/07/2007			4.67	25/05/1968		43.8
9	Bagwell	John		Nominated	NP	22	25	28	31	34									5	06/12/1922		29/05/1936	13.48	11/08/1874	22/08/1946	72
10	*Bannon*	James	TD	Ind & Comm	FG	02													1	16/07/2002		24/05/2007	4.85	06/03/1958		54.0
11	*Barnes*	Monica	TD	Labour	FG	82													1	21/04/1982		24/11/1982	0.59	12/02/1936		76.1
12	Barniville	Dr. Henry		Elected	NP	22	25	28	31	34	38	38'	43	44	48	51	54	57	13	06/12/1922		23/09/1960	35.97	1887	23/09/1960	73
13	Barrett	Jack		Agricultural	NP	73													1	01/05/1973		17/08/1977	4.30			
14	Barrett	Sean		University of Dul	NP	11													1	25/05/2011			0.83	01/01/1944		68.2
15	Barrington	William		Elected	NP	22	25	28											3	06/12/1922		05/12/1931	9.00			
16	*Barry*	Anthony	TD	Cultural & Educa	FG	57													1	09/05/1957		04/10/1961	4.41	07/06/1901	24/10/1983	82
17	*Baxter*	Patrick F.	TD	Agricultural	F	34	38	38'	43	44	48	51	54	57					9	06/12/1934		03/04/1959	22.49	01/10/1891	03/04/1959	67
18	Bellingham	Sir Edward		Elected	NP	25	28	31	34										4	17/09/1925		29/05/1936	10.70	26/01/1879	19/05/1956	77
19	*Belton*	Louis	TD	Administrative	FG	93													1	01/02/1993		06/06/1997	4.34	30/11/1943		68.3
20	*Belton*	Luke	TD	Administrative	FG	82	83												2	21/04/1982		14/04/1987	4.98	09/08/1918	18/06/2006	87
21	Belton	Richard		Administrative	NP	69													1	12/08/1969		01/05/1973	3.72	08/07/1913	28/05/1974	60
22	*Bennett*	George	TD	Nominated	FG	48													1	07/04/1948		01/08/1951	3.32	1877	20/06/1963	86
23	Bennett	Olga		Nominated	FF	89													1	16/08/1989		01/02/1993	3.46	01/10/1947		64.5
24	Bennett	Thomas		Elected	NP	22	25	28	31	34									5	06/12/1922		29/05/1936	13.48	1867	01/02/1962	95
25	Bergin	Patrick		Nominated	LB	54													1	14/07/1954		09/05/1957	2.82		16/04/1991	
26	Berkery	Tom		Nominated	NP	93													1	13/06/1997	63	06/08/1997	0.15	01/01/1951		61.2
27	*Bhreathnach*	Niamh	TD	Nominated	LB	93													1	13/06/1997	64	06/08/1997	0.15	01/06/1945		66.8
28	Bigger	Joseph		University of Dul	NP	47*	48												2	22/11/1947	25	01/08/1951	3.69	11/09/1891	17/08/1951	59
29	Bigger	Sir Edward		Elected	NP	25	28	31	34										4	17/09/1925		29/05/1936	10.70			
30	*Blaney*	Neal	TD	Agricultural	FF	38'													1	17/08/1938		22/06/1943	4.85	01/11/1893	30/10/1948	54
31	Blennerhasset	John		Labour	FG	73	77	81											3	01/05/1973		21/04/1982	8.97	01/01/1930		82.2
32	*Blythe*	Ernest	TD	Elected	CG	34*	34												2	21/01/1934	20	29/05/1936	2.35	13/04/1889	23/02/1975	85
33	Bohan	Eddie		Ind & Comm	FF	87	89	93	97	02									5	14/04/1987		23/07/2007	20.27	23/11/1932		79.3
34	Bohan	Seamus		Ind & Comm	NP	56*													1	14/05/1956	29	28/03/1957	0.87			
35	*Boland*	Gerald	TD	Ind & Comm	FF	61	65												2	05/12/1961		12/08/1969	7.69	25/05/1885	05/01/1973	87
36	*Boland*	John	TD	Labour	FG	69	73												2	12/08/1969		17/08/1977	8.01	30/11/1944	14/08/2000	55
37	Bolger	Deidre		Ind & Comm	FG	81	82												2	12/08/1981		31/01/1983	1.47	27/07/1938		73.7
38	Bonner	Enda		Nominated	FF	97													1	06/08/1997		16/07/2002	4.94	01/10/1949		62.5
39	*Boyle*	Dan	TD	Nominated	GP	07													1	23/07/2007		25/05/2011	3.84	14/08/1962		49.6
40	Boyle	James Joseph		Elected	NP	34													1	06/12/1934		29/05/1936	1.48			
41	*Bradford*	Paul	TD	Agricultural	FG	87	02	07	11										3	14/04/1987			11.86	01/12/1963		48.3
42	*Brady*	Cyprian	TD	Nominated	FF	02													1	16/07/2002		24/05/2007	4.85	26/06/1962		49.7
43	*Brady*	Martin	TD	Nominated	FF	07													1	23/07/2007		25/05/2011	3.84	07/05/1947		64.9
44	Brady	Patrick W.		Elected	NP	27*													1	26/01/1927	7	05/12/1928	1.86			
45	Brady	Sean		Nominated	FF	57	61												2	09/05/1957		08/06/1965	8.08	1890	29/12/1969	79

	Surname	Forename	TD	Panel	Party	Elected								Terms	From	By-E	To	Service	Born	Died	Age
46	Brennan	John J.		Administrative	NP	60*	61	65	69	73				5	09/02/1960	33	06/08/1977	17.49	1901	06/08/1977	76
47	Brennan	Joseph		Ind & Comm	NP	38'	43	48						3	17/08/1938		01/02/1950	7.78		01/02/1950	
48	Brennan	Michael		Nominated	PD	02								1	16/07/2002		23/07/2007	5.02	24/09/1946		65.5
49	*Brennan*	Paudge	TD	Nominated	FF	82								1	21/04/1982		24/11/1982	0.59	18/02/1922	10/06/1998	76
50	*Brennan*	Seamus	TD	Nominated	FF	77								1	17/08/1977		11/06/1981	3.82	16/02/1948	09/07/2008	60
51	Brennan	Terry		Labour	FG	11								1	25/05/2011			0.83	24/05/1942		69.8
52	Bromell	Tony		Ind & Comm	NP	88*								1	19/12/1988	51	16/08/1989	0.66	01/01/1932		80.2
53	Brosnahan	Sean		Labour	NP	61	65	69	73					4	05/12/1961		17/08/1977	15.70	1911	09/12/1987	76
54	Brown	Samuel		Elected	NP	23*	26*	28	31	34				5	12/12/1923	3,6	29/05/1936	12.06	1858	14/12/1939	81
55	Browne	Edward		Labour	NP	60*								1	01/11/1960	35	05/12/1961	1.09			
56	Browne	Feargal		Labour	FG	02								1	16/07/2002		23/07/2007	5.02	11/09/1973		38.5
57	*Browne*	John	TD	Nominated	FG	83								1	31/01/1983		14/04/1987	4.20	01/10/1936		75.5
58	Browne	Kathleen		Elected	NP	29*	31	34						3	20/06/1929	11	29/05/1936	6.94	1876	1943	67
59	*Browne*	Noel	TD	University of Dul	SLP	73								1	01/05/1973		17/08/1977	4.30	20/12/1915	23/05/1997	81
60	*Browne*	Patrick (Fad)	TD	Ind & Comm	FF	73								1	01/05/1973		17/08/1977	4.30	12/09/1906	19/02/1991	84
61	*Browne*	Sean	TD	Labour	FF	61	65							2	05/12/1961		18/06/1969	7.53	03/05/1915	27/03/1996	80
62	*Brugha*	Ruairi	TD	Ind & Comm	FF	69	77							2	12/08/1969		12/08/1981	7.70	15/10/1917	30/01/2006	88
63	*Bruton*	Richard	TD	Agricultural	FG	81								1	12/08/1981		18/02/1982	0.52	15/03/1953		59.0
64	Budd	Frederick		University of Dul	NP	51								1	01/08/1951		02/10/1951	0.17	11/02/1904	1976	72
65	Bulbulia	Katherine		Administrative	FG	81	82	83	87					4	12/08/1981		16/08/1989	8.01	04/07/1943		68.7
66	Burgess	Henry		Elected	NP	22	25							2	06/12/1922		05/12/1928	6.00	06/04/1859	23/04/1937	78
67	Burke	Colm		Ind & Comm	LB	11								1	25/05/2011			0.83	17/01/1957		55.2
68	Burke	Denis		Ind & Comm	NP	48	51	54	57					4	07/04/1948		05/12/1961	13.66	1904	25/07/1971	67
69	*Burke*	Liam	TD	Administrative	FG	73	77							2	21/06/1977		06/11/1979	2.38	02/02/1928	21/08/2005	77
70	Burke	Paddy		Agricultural	FG	93	97	02	07	11				5	01/02/1993			19.14	15/01/1955		57.2
71	Burke	Robert		Agricultural	NP	48								1	07/04/1948		06/12/1950	2.66		1998	
72	*Burke*	Ulick	TD	Agricultural	FG	81	83	02						3	12/08/1981		24/05/2007	9.74	19/11/1943		68.3
73	*Burton*	Philip	TD	Administrative	FG	73								1	01/05/1973		17/08/1977	4.30	26/07/1910	03/01/1995	84
74	Butler	Eleanor		Nominated	NP	48								1	07/04/1948		01/08/1951	3.32	1915	01/01/1997	82
75	*Butler*	John	TD	Labour	LB	38	38'	43	44	48	51	54	61	8	28/03/1938		08/06/1965	22.62	1891	16/02/1968	77
76	Butler	Larry		Ind & Comm	FF	07								1	23/07/2007		25/04/2011	3.76			
77	Butler	Pierce		Agricultural	NP	69	73	77	81					4	12/08/1969		21/04/1982	12.69	01/09/1922	20/02/1999	76
78	Butler	Richard		Elected	NP	22	29*							2	06/12/1922	13	05/12/1931	4.90			
79	*Buttimer*	Jerry	TD	Labour	FG	07								1	23/07/2007		25/02/2011	3.59	18/03/1967		45.0
80	*Byrne*	Alfred	TD	Elected	NP	28	31							2	06/12/1928	17	10/12/1931	3.01	17/3/1882	13/03/1956	73
81	*Byrne*	Christopher	TD	Administrative	FF	38	38'							2	28/03/1938		22/06/1943	5.23	1886	05/09/1957	71
82	*Byrne*	Hugh	TD	Nominated	FF	89								1	16/08/1989		25/11/1992	3.28	03/09/1943		68.6
83	*Byrne*	Sean	TD	Cultural & Educa	FF	87	89	93						3	14/04/1987		06/08/1997	10.31	16/05/1937		74.9
84	*Byrne*	Thomas	TD	Cultural & Educa	FG	11								1	25/05/2011			0.83	01/06/1977		34.8
85	Byrne	Toddie		Labour	FG	81	82							2	12/08/1981		31/01/1983	1.47	13/04/1934		
86	Caffery	Ernie		Ind & Comm	FG	97								1	06/08/1997		16/07/2002	4.94	01/10/1936		75.5
87	*Caffrey*	William John	TD	Agricultural	NP	38								1	28/03/1938		22/07/1938	0.32			
88	Callanan	Peter		Agricultural	FF	97	02	07						3	06/08/1997		11/10/2009	12.18	29/06/1935	11/10/2009	74
89	*Callely*	Ivor	TD	Nominated	FF	07								1	23/07/2007		25/05/2011	3.84	06/05/1958		53.9
90	Calnan	Michael		Agricultural	LB	93								1	01/02/1993		06/08/1997	4.51			
91	Campbell	Sean		Labour	NP	38'	43	44	48					4	17/08/1938		27/02/1950	11.53	1889	27/02/1950	61

	Surname	Forename	TD	Panel	Party	Elected													Terms	From	By-E	To	Service	Born	Died	Age
92	*Cannon*	Ciaran	TD	Nominated	PD	07													1	23/07/2007		25/02/2011	3.59	19/09/1965		46.5
93	*Carey*	Donal	TD	Labour	FG	81													1	12/08/1981		18/02/1982	0.52	15/10/1937		74.4
94	*Carroll*	James		Administrative	FF	09													1	25/11/2009		25/05/2011	1.49	21/08/1983		28.6
95	Carroll	John		Nominated	LB	81													1	12/08/1981		21/04/1982	0.69			
96	*Carter*	Frank	TD	Labour	FF	57													1	09/05/1957		04/10/1961	4.41	27/07/1910	17/07/1988	77
97	Carton	Victor		Labour	NP	54	57	61	65										4	14/07/1954		12/08/1969	15.08	1902	11/04/1970	68
98	*Carty*	John	TD	Agricultural	FF	07													1	23/07/2007		25/04/2011	3.76	12/08/1950		61.6
99	Cashin	Bill		Nominated	LB	93													1	01/02/1993		06/08/1997	4.51			
100	*Cassidy*	Donie	TD	Labour	FF	82	83	87	89	93	97	02	07						8	21/04/1982		25/04/2011	23.83	15/09/1945		66.5
101	Cassidy	Eileen		Nominated	FF	77													1	17/08/1977		12/08/1981	3.99	22/08/1932	06/10/1995	63
102	Chambers	Frank		Nominated	FF	97													1	06/08/1997		16/07/2002	4.94	03/03/1949		63.1
103	*Clarke*	Kathleen	TD	Elected	FF	28	31	34											3	06/12/1928		29/05/1936	7.48	11/4/1878	29/09/1972	94
104	Clarkin	Andrew		Ind & Comm	NP	44	48	51	54										4	01/08/1944		23/11/1955	11.31		23/11/1955	
105	Clune	Deirdre		Cultural & Educa	FG	11													1	25/05/2011			0.83	01/06/1959		52.8
106	Codd	Patrick		Agricultural	NP	75*													1	23/04/1975	44	17/08/1977	2.32		01/04/2006	
107	*Coffey*	Paudie	TD	Ind & Comm	FG	07													1	23/07/2007		25/02/2011	3.59	15/05/1969		42.9
108	*Cogan*	Barry	TD	Ind & Comm	FF	81													1	12/08/1981		21/04/1982	0.69	27/09/1936		75.5
109	*Cogan*	Patrick	TD	Agricultural	NP	54													1	14/07/1954		09/05/1957	2.82	23/10/1903	05/01/1977	73
110	Coghlan	Eamonn		Nominated	NP	11													1	25/05/2011			0.83	21/11/1952		59.3
111	Coghlan	Paul		Ind & Comm	FG	97	02	07											3	06/08/1997			14.63	01/06/1944		67.8
112	*Colbert*	Michael	TD	Agricultural	FF	38'	43												2	17/08/1938		30/05/1944	5.79	1900	01/04/1959	59.0
113	Cole	John Copeland		Nominated	NP	57	61	65											3	09/05/1957		12/08/1969	12.26		23/04/1987	
114	Colgan	Michael		Labour	NP	43	48	51											3	25/08/1943		22/06/1953	6.14		22/06/1953	
115	*Colley*	Harry	TD	Labour	FF	57													1	09/05/1957		05/12/1961	4.58	21/2/1891	18/01/1972	80
116	Comiskey	Michael		Agricultural	FG	11													1	25/05/2011			0.83	01/10/1953		58.5
117	*Commons*	Bernard	TD	Agricultural	CT	51	54												2	01/08/1951		09/05/1957	5.77	15/05/1913	19/04/1965	51
118	Comyn	Michael		Elected	NP	28	31	34											3	06/12/1928		24/02/1936	7.22		06/10/1952	
119	*Concannon*	Helena	TD	NUI	FF	38	38'	43	44	48	51								6	28/03/1938		27/02/1952	13.92	1878	27/02/1952	74
120	Condon	Thomas		Ind & Comm	NP	38													1	28/03/1938		17/08/1938	0.39		1939	
121	Condon	Thomas			NP	44													1	01/08/1944		07/04/1948	3.68			
122	*Conlon*	John F.	TD	Ind & Comm	FG	65													1	08/06/1965		18/06/1969	4.03	21/05/1928	03/12/2004	75
123	*Conlon*	Martin	TD	Ind & Comm	CG	38'													1	17/08/1938		25/08/1943	5.02	1879	23/01/1966	87
124	*Connaughton*	Paul	TD	Agricultural	FG	77													1	17/08/1977		11/06/1981	3.82	06/06/1944		67.8
125	Connolly	Joseph		Elected	FF	28	31	34											3	06/12/1928		29/05/1936	7.48	19/1/1885	18/01/1961	75
126	*Connolly*	Roderick	TD	Cultural & Educa	LB	75*													1	23/04/1975	45	17/08/1977	2.32	1901	16/12/1980	79
127	Connolly O'Brien	Nora		Nominated	FF	57	61	65											3	09/05/1957		12/08/1969	12.26	1893	17/06/1981	88
128	*Connor*	John	TD	Nominated	FG	83	87	97											3	31/01/1983		16/07/2002	11.31	14/02/1944		68.1
129	*Connor*	Patrick	TD	Administrative	FG	57													1	09/05/1957		04/10/1961	4.41	15/03/1906	26/08/1989	83
130	Conroy	Richard		Cultural & Educa	FF	77	89												2	17/08/1977		01/02/1993	7.45	01/01/1933		79.2
131	Conway	Martin		Administrative	FG	11													1	25/05/2011			0.83	08/04/1974		38.0
132	Conway	Michael		Labour	NP	38													1	28/03/1938		17/08/1938	0.39			
133	Conway	Sean		Administrative	FF	82													1	21/04/1982		31/01/1983	0.78		27/09/1995	
134	Conway	Timothy		Ind & Comm	LB	81	82	83											3	12/08/1981		14/04/1987	5.67	27/10/1942		69.4
135	Coogan	Fintan Jnr.		Administrative	FG	97													1	06/08/1997		16/07/2002	4.94	02/06/1944		67.8
136	*Coonan*	Noel	TD	Cultural & Educa	FG	02													1	16/07/2002		24/05/2007	4.85	06/01/1951		61.2
137	*Cooney*	Patrick	TD	Cultural & Educa	FG	77													1	17/08/1977		11/06/1981	3.82	02/03/1931		81.1

	Surname	Forename	TD	Panel	Party	Elected													Terms	From	By-E	To	Service	Born	Died	Age
138	*Corkery*	Daniel	TD	Ind & Comm	SF	38	38'	43	44	51									5	28/03/1938		14/07/1954	12.98	14/2/1878	31/12/1964	86
139	Corrigan	Maria		Nominated	FF	07													1	23/07/2007		25/05/2011	3.84	09/05/1968		43.9
140	*Cosgrave*	Liam T. Jnr.	TD	Ind & Comm	FG	89	93	97											3	16/08/1989		16/07/2002	12.91	30/04/1956		55.9
141	Cosgrave	Niamh		Nominated	FG	93													1	13/06/1997	65	06/08/1997	0.15	09/10/1964		47.5
142	Costello	Eileen		Elected	NP	22	25	28	31										4	06/12/1922		05/12/1934	12.00		14/03/1962	
143	*Costello*	Joe	TD	Administrative	LB	89	97												2	16/08/1989		17/05/2002	8.05	13/07/1945		66.7
144	Costello	John		Ind & Comm	NP	63*													1	28/11/1963	38	08/06/1965	1.53			
145	*Cotter*	Bill	TD	Labour	FG	93													1	01/02/1993		06/08/1997	4.51	10/02/1943		69.1
146	Counihan	John		Agricultural	NP	22	25	28	31	34	38'	43	44	48					9	06/12/1922		01/08/1951	26.43	1879	30/10/1953	74
147	Countess of Desart			Elected	NP	22	25	28	31										4	06/12/1922	20	29/06/1933	10.56	1/9/1857	29/06/1933	75
148	*Cowen*	Bernard	TD	Agricultural	FF	73													1	01/05/1973		17/08/1977	4.30	29/01/1932	24/01/1984	51
149	Cox	Arthur		Nominated	NP	54													1	14/07/1954		09/05/1957	2.82	1891	12/06/1965	74
150	Cox	Margaret		Ind & Comm	FF	97	02												2	06/08/1997		23/07/2007	9.96	24/09/1963		48.5
151	Cranitch	Micheal		Administrative	NP	69	77	81	82										4	12/08/1969		31/01/1983	9.17	01/12/1912	01/10/1999	86
152	Cregan	Denis		Labour	FG	82	83	87	93	97									5	21/04/1982		16/07/2002	16.77	04/05/1940		71.9
153	*Cregan*	John	TD	Labour	FF	98*													1	23/06/1998	54	17/05/2002	3.90	21/05/1961		50.8
154	*Crinion*	Brendan	TD	Nominated	FF	69													1	12/08/1969		01/05/1973	3.72	11/09/1923	02/07/1989	65
155	Crosbie	George		Elected	NP	31*	32*												2	05/11/1931	16,17	28/11/1934	2.99	1864	28/11/1934	70
156	Crosbie	James		Ind & Comm	NP	38	38'	43	44	48	54								6	28/03/1938		09/05/1957	16.16			
157	*Crowe*	Patrick	TD	Agricultural	FG	57													1	09/05/1957		05/12/1961	4.58	17/2/1892	08/08/1969	77
158	Crowley	Brian		Nominated	FF	93													1	01/02/1993	61	31/08/1994	1.58	04/03/1964		48.1
159	*Crowley*	Flor	TD	Cultural & Educa	FF	77	82												2	17/08/1977		31/01/1983	4.60	27/12/1934	16/05/1997	62
160	Crowley	Patrick		Labour	NP	54	57	61	65										4	14/07/1954		12/08/1969	15.08	14/04/1906	17/12/1993	87
161	*Crowley*	Tadhg	TD	Ind & Comm	FF	44	57												2	01/08/1944		05/12/1961	8.26	1890	12/03/1970	80
162	Crown	John		NUI	NP	11													1	25/05/2011			0.83	01/03/1957		55.1
163	*Cruise O'Brien*	Conor	TD	University of Dul	NP	77													1	17/08/1977	50	13/06/1979	1.82	03/11/1917	18/12/2008	97
164	*Cullen*	Martin	TD	Nominated	PD	89													1	16/08/1989		25/11/1992	3.28	02/11/1954		57.4
165	*Cullimore*	Seamus	TD	Nominated	FF	87													1	14/04/1987		15/06/1989	2.17	22/07/1954		57.7
166	Cullinane	David		Labour	SF	11													1	25/05/2011			0.83	04/07/1974		37.7
167	Cummins	Maurice		Labour	FG	02	07	11											3	16/07/2002			9.69	25/02/1954		58.1
168	Cummins	William		Labour	NP	23*	25	28	31	34	38'								6	21/02/1923	1	14/07/1943	18.17	1874	27/07/1943	69
169	Cunningham	John		NUI	NP	53*													1	25/02/1953	28	14/07/1954	1.38		1954	
170	*Daly*	Brendan	TD	Nominated	FF	89	93	02											3	02/12/1992		23/07/2007	9.53	02/02/1940		72.1
171	Daly	Jack		Ind & Comm	FG	75*	82	83	87										4	23/04/1975	46,51	05/05/1988	8.36	28/05/1915	05/05/1988	72
172	Daly	Mark		Administrative	FF	07	11												2	23/07/2007			4.67	12/03/1973		39.0
173	D'Arcy	Jim		Nominated	FG	11													1	25/05/2011			0.83	20/07/1954		57.7
174	*D'Arcy*	Michael	TD	Agricultural	FG	93													1	01/02/1993		06/06/1997	4.34	07/03/1934		78.0
175	*D'Arcy*	Michael	TD	Administrative	FG	11													1	25/05/2011			0.83	26/02/1970		42.1
176	Dardis	John		Nominated	PD	89	93	97	02										4	16/08/1989		23/07/2007	17.93	25/07/1945		66.7
177	Davidson	Mary		Ind & Comm	LB	50	54	57	61	65									5	16/06/1950	26	24/07/1969	16.15	1902	29/05/1986	84
178	Dawson	Michael		Nominated	NP	87													1	24/06/1989		16/08/1989	0.15			
179	De Brun	Seamus		Nominated	FF	77	82	83											3	17/08/1977		14/04/1987	8.97	01/11/1911	05/03/2003	91
180	De Buitléar	Éamon		Nominated	NP	87													1	14/04/1987		16/08/1989	2.34			
181	De Burca	Deidre		Nominated	GP	07													1	23/07/2007		12/02/2010	2.56	15/10/1963		48.4
182	*De Loughry*	Peter	TD	Elected	NP	22													1	06/12/1922		16/09/1925	2.78	4/2/1868	23/10/1931	63
183	Dearey	Mark		Nominated	GP	10													1	23/02/2010		25/05/2011	1.25	19/03/1963		49.0

	Surname	Forename	TD	Panel	Party	Elected													Terms	From	By-E	To	Service	Born	Died	Age
184	*Deasy*	Austin	TD	Nominated	FG	73													1	01/05/1973		17/08/1977	4.30	26/08/1936		75.6
185	*Deenihan*	Jimmy	TD	Nominated	FG	83													1	31/01/1983		17/02/1987	4.05	11/09/1952		59.5
186	Delany	Thomas		Cultural & Educa	NP	38'													1	17/08/1938		09/07/1939	0.89	1868	09/07/1939	71
187	Desmond	Cornelius		Administrative	NP	61													1	05/12/1961		08/06/1965	3.51		31/10/1974	
188	*Desmond*	Eileen	TD	Ind & Comm	LB	69													1	12/08/1969		01/05/1973	3.72	29/12/1932	06/01/2005	72
189	Dillon	Gerard		Administrative	NP	60*													1	01/11/1960	36	05/12/1961	1.09		03/12/1962	
190	Dillon	James		Elected	NP	25	28	31	34										4	17/09/1925		29/05/1936	10.70		05/11/1955	
191	*Dockrell*	Henry M.	TD	Ind & Comm	FG	48													1	07/04/1948		01/08/1951	3.32	1880	26/10/1955	75
192	Doherty	Michael		Administrative	FF	87													1	14/04/1987		16/08/1989	2.34	29/06/1933		78.7
193	*Doherty*	Pearse	TD	Agricultural	SF	07													1	23/07/2007		24/11/2010	3.34	06/07/1977		34.7
194	*Doherty*	Sean	TD	Administrative	FF	89													1	16/08/1989		25/11/1992	3.28	29/06/1944	07/06/2005	60
195	*Dolan*	Seamus	TD	Labour	FF	65	73	77	81										4	08/06/1965		20/04/1982	13.15	10/12/1914	10/08/2010	95
196	*Donegan*	Bartholomew	TD	Agricultural	FF	63*													1	28/11/1963	39	08/06/1965	1.53	21/12/1910	26/08/1978	67
197	*Donegan*	Patrick	TD	Agricultural	FG	57													1	09/05/1957		04/10/1961	4.41	29/10/1923	26/11/2000	77
198	Donnelly	Michael		Administrative	NP	77*													1	07/12/1977	49	12/08/1981	3.68			
199	*Donohoe*	Paschal	TD	Administrative	FG	07													1	23/07/2007		25/02/2011	3.59	19/09/1974		37.5
200	Dooge	James		NUI	FG	61	65	69	73	81	82	83							7	05/12/1961		14/04/1987	21.37	01/07/1922	20/08/2010	88
201	*Dooley*	Timmy	TD	Administrative	FF	02													1	16/07/2002		24/05/2007	4.85	13/02/1969		43.1
202	Dorgan	Sean		Nominated	FF	02													1	22/06/2007		23/07/2007	0.08	13/03/1968		44.0
203	Douglas	John Harold		Nominated	NP	54													1	01/10/1954		09/05/1957	2.60	29/04/1912	1982	70
204	Douglas	James		Elected	NP	22	25	28	31	34	38	38'	44	48	51	54			11	06/12/1922		16/09/1954	29.01	1887	16/09/1954	67
205	Dowdall	James		Nominated	NP	22	25	28	31	34									5	06/12/1922		29/05/1936	13.48		28/06/1939	
206	Dowdall	Jane		Ind & Comm	FF	51	54	57											3	01/08/1951		05/12/1961	10.35	29/9/1899	10/12/1974	75
207	*Dowling*	Dick	TD	Labour	FG	82													1	21/04/1982		24/11/1982	0.59	12/12/1938		
208	*Dowling*	Joe	TD	Labour	FF	77													1	17/08/1977		12/08/1981	3.99	02/02/1922		90.1
209	*Doyle*	Avril	TD	Agricultural	FG	89	97												2	16/08/1989		16/07/2002	8.22	18/04/1949		62.9
210	*Doyle*	Joe	TD	Administrative	FG	87	93	97											3	14/04/1987		16/07/2002	11.62	01/06/1936	08/08/2009	73
211	Doyle	John		Agricultural	NP	69													1	12/08/1969		01/05/1973	3.72	12/02/1930	29/12/2010	80
212	Doyle	Patrick		Cultural & Educa	NP	38	38'	43	44										4	28/03/1938		07/04/1948	10.03		01/10/1964	
213	Duffy	Luke		Ind & Comm	LB	44	48												2	01/08/1944		22/06/1949	4.89		1949	
214	Duffy	Michael		Elected	LB	22	25	28	31	34									5	06/12/1922		29/05/1936	13.48			
215	*Duggan*	Edmund	TD	Elected	CG	33*	34												2	19/04/1933	18	29/05/1936	3.11	1874	06/06/1936	62
216	Dunne	James		Labour	NP	69													1	12/08/1969		23/02/1972	2.53	1921	23/02/1972	51
217	Dunne	Patrick		Nominated	NP	81													1	12/08/1981		21/04/1982	0.69			
218	Durcan	Patrick		Nominated	FG	83													1	31/01/1983		14/04/1987	4.20			
219	*Durkan*	Bermard	TD	Agricultural	FG	82													1	21/04/1982		24/11/1982	0.59	26/03/1945		67.0
220	Eames	Aidan		Nominated	NP	82													1	13/12/1982		31/01/1983	0.13			
221	Earl of Dunraven			Nominated	NP	22	25												2	06/12/1922	6	27/01/1926	3.14	12/2/1841	14/06/1926	85
222	Earl of Granard			Nominated	NP	22	25	28	31										4	06/12/1922		05/12/1934	12.00	17/9/1874	10/09/1948	73
223	Earl of Kerry			Nominated	NP	22	25	28											3	06/12/1922	12	05/06/1929	6.50	14/1/1872	01/01/1933	61
224	Earl of Mayo			Nominated	NP	22	25												2	06/12/1922	9	31/12/1927	5.07		31/12/1927	
225	Earl of Wicklow			Nominated	NP	22	25												2	06/12/1922		05/12/1928	6.00	24/12/1877	11/10/1946	68
226	*Egan*	Kieran	TD	Administrative	FF	65													1	08/06/1965		12/08/1969	4.18	26/05/1916	25/03/1976	59
227	*Ellis*	John	TD	Agricultural	FF	77	83	07											3	17/08/1977		25/05/2011	11.86	02/05/1952		59.9
228	Enright	Michael		Nominated	NP	93													1	13/06/1997	66	06/08/1997	0.15		15/10/1997	
229	*Enright*	Tom	TD	Administrative	FG	93													1	01/02/1993		06/06/1997	4.34	26/07/1940		71.7

	Surname	Forename	TD	Panel	Party	Elected													Terms	From	By-E	To	Service	Born	Died	Age
230	Eogan	George		Nominated	NP	87													1	14/04/1987		16/08/1989	2.34			
231	Esmonde	Sir Thomas		Nominated	NP	22	25	28	31										4	06/12/1922		05/12/1934	12.00	21/9/1862	15/09/1935	70
232	Everard	Sir Nugent		Nominated	NP	22	25	29*											3	06/12/1922	10,13	12/07/1929	6.26		12/07/1929	
233	Eyre	Edmund		Nominated	NP	22	25												2	06/12/1922		05/12/1928	6.00			
234	*Fahey*	Frank	TD	Labour	FF	93													1	01/02/1993		06/06/1997	4.34	06/06/1951		60.8
235	Fallon	Sean		Ind & Comm	FF	81	82	83	87	89	93								6	12/08/1981	52	04/07/1995	13.89	26/09/1937	04/07/1995	57
236	Fanning	Michael		Elected	NP	25	28	31	34										4	17/09/1925		29/05/1936	10.70			
237	Farnan	Robert		Nominated	NP	38	38'	43	44	51	57								6	28/03/1938		05/12/1961	17.56		07/01/1962	
238	*Farrell*	Joseph	TD	Labour	FF	61	65	69											3	05/12/1961		01/05/1973	11.40	01/07/1905	24/11/1999	94
239	Farrell	Pat		Nominated	FF	89													1	02/12/1992		01/02/1993	0.17			
240	Farrell	Peggy		Nominated	FF	69													1	12/08/1969		01/05/1973	3.72	15/11/1920		
241	Farrell	William		Ind & Comm	FF	82	87	89	93	97									5	21/04/1982		16/07/2002	16.04	28/05/1928	09/04/2010	81
242	*Farrelly*	Denis	TD	Ind & Comm	FG	69	73												2	12/08/1969		17/08/1977	8.01	18/09/1912	27/12/1974	62
243	*Farrelly*	John V.	TD	Agricultural	FG	93													1	01/02/1993		06/06/1997	4.34	04/11/1954		57.4
244	Farren	Thomas		Elected	LB	22	25	28	31	34									5	06/12/1922		29/05/1936	13.48		26/03/1955	
245	Fausset	Robert		Nominated	FG	81													1	12/08/1981		21/04/1982	0.69	08/08/1934		
246	Fearon	William		University of Dul	NP	43	44	48	51	54	57								6	25/08/1943		01/01/1959	15.35		01/01/1959	
247	Feeney	Geraldine		Labour	FF	02	07												2	16/07/2002		25/04/2011	8.77	09/09/1957		54.5
248	*Feighan*	Frank	TD	Administrative	FG	02													1	16/07/2002		24/05/2007	4.85	04/07/1962		49.7
249	*Fennell*	Nuala	TD	Nominated	FG	83	87												2	20/02/1987		15/06/1989	2.32	25/11/1935	11/08/2009	73
250	*Ferris*	Michael	TD	Agricultural	LB	73	81	82	83	87									5	23/04/1975	47	16/08/1989	10.33	21/11/1931	20/03/2000	68
251	*Ffrench-O'Carroll*	Michael	TD	Cultural & Educa	NP	54													1	14/07/1954		09/05/1957	2.82	15/09/1919		
252	*Finan*	John	TD	Administrative	CT	48													1	07/04/1948		30/05/1951	3.14	10/9/1898	24/05/1984	85
253	*Finn*	Martin	TD	Nominated	FG	73													1	21/06/1977		17/08/1977	0.16	22/08/1917	1988	71
254	*Finneran*	Michael	TD	Administrative	FF	89	93	97											3	16/08/1989		17/05/2002	12.75	10/09/1947		64.5
255	*Finucane*	Michael	TD	Labour	FG	02													1	16/07/2002		23/07/2007	5.02	01/02/1943		69.1
256	*Fitzgerald*	Alexis Jnr.	TD	Ind & Comm	FG	81	83												2	12/08/1981		14/04/1987	4.72	07/05/1945		66.9
257	Fitzgerald	Alexis Snr.		Ind & Comm	FG	69	73	77											3	12/08/1969		12/08/1981	12.00	1917	16/06/1985	68
258	*Fitzgerald*	Desmond	TD	Administrative	CG	38'													1	17/08/1938		25/08/1943	5.02	13/2/1888	09/04/1947	59
259	*Fitzgerald*	Frances	TD	Labour	FG	07													1	23/07/2007		25/02/2011	3.59	01/08/1950		61.6
260	*Fitzgerald*	Garret	TD	Ind & Comm	FG	65													1	08/06/1965		18/06/1969	4.03	09/02/1926		86.1
261	Fitzgerald	Jack		Agricultural	NP	61	65	69	73										4	05/12/1961		17/08/1977	15.70	1914	07/10/1994	80
262	*Fitzgerald*	Liam	TD	Labour	FF	97	02												2	06/08/1997		23/07/2007	9.96	01/09/1949		62.6
263	Fitzgerald	Martin		Elected	NP	22	25												2	06/12/1922	8	09/03/1927	4.25		09/03/1927	
264	*Fitzgerald*	Seamus	TD	Elected	FF	34													1	06/12/1934		29/05/1936	1.48	21/8/1896	23/07/1972	75
265	Fitzgerald	Tom		Agricultural	FF	81	82	87	89	93	97								6	12/08/1981	68	04/04/2002	16.44	25/03/1939		73.0
266	*Fitzpatrick*	Dr. Dermot	TD	Nominated	FF	97													1	06/08/1997	69	17/05/2002	4.78	12/04/1940		71.9
267	*Fitzpatrick*	Thomas J.	TD	Administrative	FG	61													1	05/12/1961		08/06/1965	3.51	14/02/1918	02/10/2006	88
268	Fitzsimons	Jack		Ind & Comm	FF	83	87												2	31/01/1983		16/08/1989	6.54	26/04/1930		81.9
269	Fitzsimons	Patrick		Administrative	NP	48	51	57	61	65	69								6	07/04/1948		01/05/1973	22.25			
270	Flanagan	Thomas		Ind & Comm	NP	61	65	69											3	05/12/1961		01/05/1973	11.40		07/10/1980	
271	*Fleming*	Brian	TD	Cultural & Educa	FG	83													1	31/01/1983		14/04/1987	4.20	20/07/1946		65.7
272	*Fogarty*	Andrew	TD	Labour	FF	48													1	07/04/1948		01/08/1951	3.32	13/4/1879	24/04/1953	74
273	*Foley*	Denis	TD	Ind & Comm	FF	89													1	16/08/1989		25/11/1992	3.28	14/05/1934		77.9
274	Foran	Thomas		Elected	NP	23*	25	28	31	34	38'	43	44						8	28/11/1923	2	07/04/1948	22.14		18/03/1951	
275	*Fox*	Billy	TD	Cultural & Educa	FG	73													1	01/05/1973		12/03/1974	0.86	03/01/1939	12/03/1974	35

	Surname	Forename	TD	Panel	Party	Elected													Terms	From	By-E	To	Service	Born	Died	Age
276	Friel	Brian		Nominated	NP	87													1	14/04/1987		16/08/1989	2.34			
277	Gaffney	John		Labour	NP	38													1	28/03/1938		17/08/1938	0.39			
278	Gallagher	Ann		Ind & Comm	LB	93													1	01/02/1993		06/08/1997	4.51	01/03/1967		45.1
279	*Gallagher*	Pat	TD	Ind & Comm	LB	97													1	06/08/1997	55	12/10/1999	2.18	29/03/1963		49.0
280	Gallanagh	Michael		Nominated	NP	69													1	12/08/1969		01/05/1973	3.72		01/12/2001	
281	*Garahan*	Hugh	TD	Elected	F	31	34												2	06/12/1931		29/05/1936	4.48		07/06/1940	
282	Garrett	Jack		Administrative	FF	69	73	77											3	12/08/1969		12/08/1981	12.00	22/05/1914	11/09/1977	63
283	Gibbons	Jim		Nominated	PD	97													1	06/08/1997		16/07/2002	4.94	26/04/1954		57.9
284	*Gibbons*	Sean	TD	Agricultural	NP	38	38'	43	48										4	28/03/1938		01/08/1951	9.66	31/5/1883	19/04/1952	68
285	Gilroy	John		Cultural & Educa	LB	11													1	25/05/2011			0.83	20/07/1967		44.7
286	Glenavy	Lord		Nominated	NP	22	25												2	06/12/1922		05/12/1928	6.00	4/4/1851	22/03/1931	79
287	*Glennon*	Jim	TD	Ind & Comm	FF	00*													1	02/06/2000	55	17/05/2002	1.95	07/07/1953		58.7
288	Glynn	Camillus		Administrative	FF	97	02	07											3	06/08/1997		25/05/2011	13.80	04/10/1941		70.5
289	Gogarty	Oliver St. John		Elected	NP	22	25	28	31	34									5	06/12/1922		29/05/1936	13.48	17/8/1878	22/09/1957	79
290	Goodbody	James		Nominated	NP	22	25												2	06/12/1922		05/12/1928	6.00	22/3/1877	21/03/1952	75
291	*Gorry*	Patrick	TD	Agricultural	FF	51													1	01/08/1951		14/07/1954	2.95	14/7/1896	23/10/1965	69
292	Goulding	Lady Valerie		Nominated	FF	77													1	17/08/1977		12/08/1981	3.99	12/09/1918	28/07/2003	84
293	*Goulding*	Sean	TD	Administrative	FF	38'	43	44	48	51									5	17/08/1938		14/07/1954	15.91	1877	15/12/1959	82
294	*Governey*	Desmond	TD	Ind & Comm	FG	77													1	17/08/1977		11/06/1981	3.82	11/09/1920		
295	Green	Alice		Elected	NP	22	25	28											3	06/12/1922	11	28/05/1929	6.48	31/5/1847	28/05/1929	81
296	Greene	John		Agricultural	NP	38													1	28/03/1938		17/08/1938	0.39			
297	Greer	Capt. Henry		Elected	NP	22	25												2	06/12/1922		05/12/1928	6.00	1/2/1855	25/08/1934	79
298	Griffith	John		Elected	NP	22	25	28	31	34									5	06/12/1922		29/05/1936	13.48			
299	Guinness	Arthur		Nominated	NP	73													1	01/05/1973		17/08/1977	4.30	20/05/1937	1992	55
300	Guinness	Henry		Elected	NP	22	25	28	31										4	06/12/1922		05/12/1934	12.00	24/11/1858	04/04/1945	86
301	Guinness	Henry		Nominated	NP	54													1	14/07/1954		09/05/1957	2.82		1971	
302	*Halligan*	Brendan	TD	Nominated	LB	73													1	01/05/1973		10/06/1976	3.11	05/07/1936		75.7
303	Hanafin	Desmond		Labour	FF	69	73	77	81	82	83	87	89	97					9	12/08/1969		16/07/2002	28.42	09/09/1930		81.5
304	Hanafin	John		Labour	FF	02	07												2	16/07/2002		25/04/2011	8.77	27/09/1960		51.5
305	*Hannigan*	Dominic	TD	Ind & Comm	LB	07													1	23/07/2007		25/02/2011	3.59	01/07/1965		46.7
306	*Hannigan*	Joseph	TD	Administrative	NP	43													1	25/08/1943		01/08/1944	0.94	1904	1944	40
307	Hannon	Camilla		Nominated	FF	82													1	21/04/1982		31/01/1983	0.78	21/07/1936		
308	*Harney*	Mary	TD	Nominated	FF	77													1	17/08/1977		11/06/1981	3.82	11/03/1953		59.0
309	Harris	Eoghan		Nominated	NP	07													1	23/07/2007		25/05/2011	3.84	13/03/1943		69.0
310	Harte	Jack		Labour	LB	73	77	81	82	83	87	89							7	01/05/1973		01/02/1993	19.76	01/12/1920		91.3
311	Harte	Jimmy		Ind & Comm	LB	11													1	25/05/2011			0.83	27/02/1958		54.1
312	Hartnett	Noel		Labour	NP	51													1	01/08/1951		14/07/1954	2.95		1960	
313	Hartney	Sean		Ind & Comm	NP	51	54												2	01/08/1951		09/05/1957	5.77	16/03/1905	11/05/1974	69
314	Haughey	Edward		Nominated	FF	93	97												2	13/12/1994	61	16/07/2002	7.59			
315	*Haughey*	Sean	TD	Administrative	FF	87	89												2	14/04/1987		25/11/1992	5.62	08/11/1961		50.4
316	Haughton	Benjamin		Elected	NP	22	25												2	06/12/1922		05/12/1928	6.00			
317	Hawkins	Frederick		Labour	NP	38	38'	43	46*	48	51	54							7	28/03/1938	24	02/08/1956	16.37		02/08/1956	
318	Hayden	Aideen		Nominated	LB	11													1	25/05/2011			0.83	01/01/1959		53.2
319	Hayden	Thomas		Labour	NP	43	44												2	25/08/1943		07/04/1948	4.62			
320	*Hayes*	Brian	TD	Nominated	FG	93	02												2	20/12/1995	62 67	24/05/2007	6.32	23/08/1969		42.6
321	Hayes	Maurice		Nominated	NP	97	02												2	06/08/1997		23/07/2007	9.96	08/07/1927		84.7

	Surname	Forename	TD	Panel	Party	Elected													Terms	From	By-E	To	Service	Born	Died	Age
322	*Hayes*	Prof. Michael	TD	Cultural & Educa	NP	38	38'	43	44	48	51	54	57	61					9	28/03/1938		08/06/1965	27.20	1/12/1889	11/07/1976	86
323	*Hayes*	Sean	TD	Labour	FF	38	38'	48	51	54	57	61							7	28/03/1938		08/06/1965	22.58	1890	16/02/1968	78
324	*Hayes*	Tom	TD	Agricultural	FG	97													1	06/08/1997	57	30/06/2001	3.90	16/02/1952		60.1
325	*Healy*	Augustine	TD	Nominated	FF	61													1	05/12/1961		08/06/1965	3.51	20/05/1904	10/07/1987	83
326	Healy	Denis		Administrative	NP	34	38'	43	44										3	06/12/1934		07/04/1948	11.12			
327	Healy-Eames	Fidelma		Labour	FG	07	11												2	23/07/2007			4.67	14/07/1962		49.7
328	Hearne	Michael		Administrative	NP	38	43	44	48	51									5	28/03/1938		14/07/1954	11.27		1954	
329	Hederman	Carmencita		University of Dul	NP	89													1	16/08/1989		01/02/1993	3.46	23/10/1939		72.4
330	Hefernan	James		Agricultural	LB	11													1	25/05/2011			0.83	03/10/1979		32.5
331	Henry	Imelda		Ind & Comm	LB	11													1	25/05/2011			0.83	05/03/1967		45.1
332	Henry	Mary		University of Dul	NP	93	97	02											3	01/02/1993		23/07/2007	14.47	11/05/1940		71.9
333	Herbert	Anthony		Labour	FF	77	82												2	17/08/1977		31/01/1983	4.77			
334	*Hickey*	James	TD	Nominated	LB	54													1	14/07/1954		09/05/1957	2.82		07/06/1966	
335	Hickie	Sir William		Elected	NP	25	28	31	34										4	17/09/1925		29/05/1936	10.70	21/5/1865	03/11/1950	85
336	*Higgins*	Jim	TD	Labour	FG	81	83	02											3	12/08/1981		23/07/2007	9.76	04/05/1945		66.9
337	Higgins	Loraine		Nominated	LB	11													1	25/05/2011			0.83	03/08/1979		32.6
338	*Higgins*	Michael D.	TD	NUI	LB	73	83												2	01/05/1973		17/02/1987	8.34	18/04/1941		70.9
339	*Hillery*	Brian	TD	Labour	FF	77	81	83	87	93									5	17/08/1977	60	04/05/1994	12.47	22/11/1937		74.3
340	*Hogan*	Daniel	TD	Agricultural	FF	43	44	57	61										4	25/08/1943		08/06/1965	12.70	1899	01/08/1980	81
341	*Hogan*	Patrick	TD	Labour	LB	38'													1	17/08/1938		22/06/1943	4.85	1886	24/01/1969	83
342	*Hogan*	Phil	TD	Ind & Comm	FG	87													1	14/04/1987		15/06/1989	2.17	04/07/1960		51.7
343	Honan	Cathy		Ind & Comm	PD	93													1	01/02/1993		06/08/1997	4.51	16/09/1951		60.5
344	Honan	Dermot		Ind & Comm	FF	65	69												2	08/06/1965		01/05/1973	7.90	1909	20/07/1986	77
345	Honan	Thomas V.		Nominated	FF	34	38	38'	43	44	48	51							7	06/12/1934		14/07/1954	17.77	1878	21/10/1954	76
346	Honan	Tras		Administrative	FF	77	81	82	83	87	89								6	17/08/1977		01/02/1993	15.46	04/01/1930		82.2
347	Hooper	Patrick J.		Elected	NP	27*	28												2	23/03/1927	8,16	06/09/1931	4.46		06/09/1931	
348	Horan	Edmund		Agricultural	NP	44													1	01/08/1944		07/04/1948	3.68			
349	*Horgan*	John	TD	NUI	LB	69	73												2	12/08/1969		17/08/1977	8.01	26/10/1940		71.4
350	Hourigan	Richard		Agricultural	FG	82	83	89											3	21/04/1982		01/02/1993	8.44	01/04/1939		
351	Howard	Michael		Ind & Comm	FG	77	81	82	83	89	93								6	17/08/1977		06/08/1997	17.63	19/09/1933	17/02/2009	75
352	*Howlin*	Brendan	TD	Nominated	LB	83													1	31/01/1983		17/02/1987	4.05	09/05/1956		55.9
353	Hughes	Gilbert		Labour	NP	38													1	28/03/1938		17/08/1938	0.39			
354	*Hussey*	Gemma	TD	NUI	FG	77	81												2	17/08/1977		18/02/1982	4.51	11/11/1938		73.4
355	*Hussey*	Thomas	TD	Agricultural	FF	81	82	83	87	89									5	12/08/1981		01/02/1993	11.47	25/01/1936		76.2
356	Hyde	Douglas		Elected	NP	25*	38												2	04/02/1925	4,22	04/05/1938	0.94	17/1/1860	12/07/1949	89
357	*Hyland*	Liam	TD	Ind & Comm	FF	77													1	17/08/1977		11/06/1981	3.82	24/04/1933		78.9
358	Ireland	Denis		Nominated	NP	48													1	07/04/1948		01/08/1951	3.32	1894	23/09/1974	80
359	Irwin	Cornelius		Elected	NP	22													1	06/12/1922		16/09/1925	2.78			
360	Jackman	Mary		Labour	FG	89	97												2	16/08/1989		16/07/2002	8.41	30/04/1943		68.9
361	Jackson	Arthur		Nominated	NP	22	25												2	06/12/1922		05/12/1928	6.00			
362	Jago	Valentine		Nominated	FF	77													1	17/08/1977		12/08/1981	3.99	1913	02/11/1983	70
363	Jameson	Rt. Hon. Andrew		Elected	NP	22	25	28	31	34									5	06/12/1922		29/05/1936	13.48			
364	Jessop	William		University of Dul	NP	52*	60*	61	65	69									5	12/03/1952	27,37	01/05/1973	15.30	13/07/1902	11/06/1980	77
365	*Johnson*	Thomas	TD	Elected	LB	28	31	34											3	06/12/1928		29/05/1936	7.48	17/5/1872	17/01/1963	90
366	Johnston	James		Labour	NP	38	38'	43	44										4	28/03/1938		07/04/1948	10.03			
367	Johnston	Joseph		University of Dul	NP	38	38'	44	51										4	28/03/1938		14/07/1954	12.04		1954	

	Surname	Forename	TD	Panel	Party	Elected													Terms	From	By-E	To	Service	Born	Died	Age
368	Kavanagh	Paul		Nominated	FF	87													1	24/06/1989		16/08/1989	0.15			
369	Keane	Cáit		Labour	FG	11													1	25/05/2011			0.83	24/09/1949		62.5
370	Keane	John Thomas		Labour	NP	44													1	01/08/1944		07/04/1948	3.68		22/05/1946	
371	Keane	Sir John		Nominated	NP	22	25	28	31	38	38'	43	44						8	06/12/1922		07/04/1948	22.03	3/6/1872	30/01/1956	83
372	Kearney	Miriam		Nominated	FG	81													1	12/08/1981		21/04/1982	0.69	01/07/1959		52.7
373	*Keating*	Justin	TD	Agricultural	LB	77													1	17/08/1977		12/08/1981	3.99	07/01/1930	31/12/2009	79
374	*Keaveney*	Cecilia	TD	Cultural & Educa	FF	07													1	23/07/2007		25/04/2011	3.76	27/11/1968		43.3
375	*Keegan*	Sean	TD	Administrative	FF	70*	73												2	16/06/1970	41	17/08/1977	7.17	02/02/1930	09/07/2007	77
376	Keery	Neville		Nominated	FF	69													1	12/08/1969		01/05/1973	3.72	01/01/1938		74.2
377	*Kehoe*	Patrick	TD	Agricultural	FF	38	38'	43	44										4	28/03/1938		07/04/1948	10.03			
378	*Kelleher*	Billy	TD	Nominated	FF	93													1	01/02/1993	63	06/06/1997	4.34	20/01/1968		44.2
379	Kelleher	Peter		Labour	FG	83	87												2	31/01/1983		16/08/1989	6.54	25/06/1946		
380	*Kelly*	Alan	TD	Agricultural	LB	07													1	23/07/2007		05/06/2009	1.87	13/07/1975		36.7
381	*Kelly*	John	TD	Cultural & Educa	FG	69													1	12/08/1969		01/05/1973	3.72	31/08/1931	24/01/1991	59
382	Kelly	John		Administrative	LB	11													1	25/05/2011			0.83	21/02/1960		52.1
383	Kelly	Liam		Labour	NP	54													1	14/07/1954		09/05/1957	2.82			
384	Kelly	Mary		Cultural & Educa	LB	93													1	01/02/1993		06/08/1997	4.51	01/05/1952		59.9
385	*Kenneally*	Brendan	TD	Nominated	FF	02													1	16/07/2002		24/05/2007	4.85	01/04/1955		57.0
386	*Kenneally*	William	TD	Administrative	FF	82													1	21/04/1982		31/01/1983	0.78	12/10/1925	27/08/2009	83
387	Kennedy	Cornelius		Elected	NP	25	28	31	34	38									5	17/09/1925		17/08/1938	11.09		04/04/1951	
388	Kennedy	Fintan		Labour	LB	69	73	77											3	12/08/1969		12/08/1981	12.00		24/03/1984	
389	Kennedy	Margaret		Nominated	FF	38	38'	43	44										4	28/03/1938		07/04/1948	10.03	1892		
390	Kennedy	Patrick		Administrative	FG	81	83	87	89										4	12/08/1981		01/02/1993	10.69	23/11/1941		70.3
391	Kennedy	Thomas		Labour	NP	34	43	44											3	06/12/1934		18/09/1947	5.54		18/09/1947	
392	Kenny	Patrick W.		Elected	NP	22	25	28											3	06/12/1922	15	22/04/1931	8.38		22/04/1931	
393	*Keogh*	Helen	TD	Nominated	PD	89	97												2	16/08/1989		16/07/2002	8.10	03/06/1951		60.8
394	Keohane	Patrick		Nominated	NP	38*	38'												2	10/05/1938	22	04/12/1939	1.57	1870	04/12/1939	69
395	*Kerrigan*	Patrick	TD	Nominated	LB	73													1	01/05/1973		16/10/1977	4.46	21/02/1928	04/07/1979	51
396	Kett	Tony		Administrative	FF	97	02	07											3	06/08/1997		18/04/2009	11.70	01/06/1951	18/04/2009	57
397	*Keyes*	Ralph	TD	Elected	FF	34*	34												2	02/01/1934	19	29/05/1936	2.40			
398	Kiely	Dan		Labour	FF	81	87	89	93	97									5	12/08/1981		16/07/2002	15.95	01/05/1940		71.9
399	Kiely	Rory		Agricultural	FF	77	81	83	87	89	93	97	02						8	17/08/1977		23/07/2007	29.15	01/05/1934		77.9
400	Kilbride	Thomas		Administrative	FG	73	77												2	01/05/1973		12/08/1981	8.28	28/04/1911	30/08/1986	75
401	*Killilea*	Mark Jnr.	TD	Labour	FF	69	73	82	83										4	12/08/1969		14/04/1987	13.68	05/09/1939		72.5
402	*Killilea*	Mark Snr.	TD	Labour	FF	61	65												2	05/12/1961		12/08/1969	7.69	1896	29/09/1970	74
403	*Kilroy*	James	TD	Agricultural	FF	51													1	01/08/1951		05/01/1954	2.43	1890	05/01/1954	64
404	King	Frank		Nominated	NP	73													1	22/06/1977		17/08/1977	0.15			
405	Kirwan	Christy		Nominated	LB	83													1	31/01/1983		14/04/1987	4.20			
406	*Kissane*	Eamon	TD	Cultural & Educa	FF	51	54	57	61										4	01/08/1951		08/06/1965	13.85	1899	20/05/1979	80
407	*Kitt*	Michael P.	TD	Administrative	FF	77	02												2	17/08/1977		24/05/2007	8.67	17/05/1950		61.9
408	Kyle	Sam		Labour	NP	43	44												2	25/08/1943		07/04/1948	4.62		1948	
409	*Lahiffe*	Robert	TD	Agricultural	FF	57	61												2	09/05/1957		08/06/1965	8.08	1911	08/03/1975	64
410	Lambert	Gordon		Nominated	NP	77													1	17/08/1977		12/08/1981	3.99	09/04/1919	27/01/2005	85
411	Landy	Denis		Administrative	LB	11													1	25/05/2011			0.83	28/02/1962		50.1
412	Lanigan	Michael		Ind & Comm	FF	77	81	82	83	87	89	93	97						8	17/08/1977		16/07/2002	24.91	30/01/1938		74.1
413	Larkin	James		Nominated	NP	82													1	21/04/1982		31/01/1983	0.78			

	Surname	Forename	TD	Panel	Party	Elected													Terms	From	By-E	To	Service	Born	Died	Age
414	*Lavery*	Cecil	TD	Cultural & Educa	FG	48													1	07/04/1948		21/04/1950	2.04	6/10/1894	16/12/1967	73
415	Lawlor	Patsy		Cultural & Educa	FG	81													1	12/08/1981		21/04/1982	0.69	01/03/1933		
416	Lee	Joe		NUI	NP	93													1	01/02/1993		06/08/1997	4.51	09/07/1942		69.7
417	*Lenehan*	Joseph	TD	Nominated	FF	65													1	08/06/1965		18/06/1969	4.03	1916	06/12/1981	65
418	*Lenihan*	Brian Snr.	TD	Ind & Comm	FF	57	73												2	09/05/1957		17/08/1977	8.87	17/11/1930	01/11/1995	64
419	Lennon	Joseph		Agricultural	FG	82	83												2	21/04/1982		14/04/1987	4.98	22/06/1933	25/01/1990	56
420	Leonard	Ann		Nominated	FF	97													1	06/08/1997		16/07/2002	4.94	02/01/1969		43.2
421	*Leonard*	Jimmy	TD	Administrative	FF	81													1	12/08/1981		18/02/1982	0.52	05/06/1927		84.8
422	*L'Estrange*	Gerald	TD	Administrative	FG	54	57	61											3	14/07/1954		08/06/1965	10.90	07/11/1917	05/04/1996	78
423	*Leyden*	Terry	TD	Labour	FF	89	02	07	11										4	02/12/1992			9.85	01/10/1945		66.5
424	*Lindsay*	Patrick	TD	Ind & Comm	FG	61													1	05/12/1961		08/06/1965	3.51	18/01/1914	29/06/1993	79
425	Linehan	Thomas		Elected	NP	22	25	28	31	34									5	06/12/1922		29/05/1936	13.48			
426	*Loughman*	Francis	TD	Cultural & Educa	FF	48	51												2	07/04/1948		14/07/1954	6.27	1892	13/05/1972	80
427	Loughrey	Joachim		Cultural & Educa	FG	82	83	87											3	21/04/1982		16/08/1989	7.32	01/01/1947		65.2
428	Love	Joseph		Elected	NP	22													1	06/12/1922		16/09/1925	2.78		01/01/1925	
429	Lydon	Don		Labour	FF	87	89	93	97	02									5	14/04/1987		23/07/2007	20.27	07/08/1938		73.6
430	Lynch	Eamonn		Labour	NP	38'													1	17/08/1938		25/08/1943	5.02			
431	*Lynch*	Gerard	TD	Agricultural	FG	77													1	17/08/1977		12/08/1981	3.99	15/06/1931		80.8
432	*Lynch*	James	TD	Cultural & Educa	FF	51													1	01/08/1951		12/03/1954	2.61		12/03/1954	
433	*Lynch*	John	TD	Ind & Comm	FG	54													1	14/07/1954		09/05/1957	2.82	10/4/1889	10/06/1957	68
434	*Lynch*	Michael	TD	Administrative	FF	83													1	31/01/1983		17/02/1987	4.05	25/08/1934		77.6
435	Lynch	Patrick		Elected	NP	34*	34												2	28/09/1934	21	29/05/1936	1.67		09/12/1947	
436	Lynch	Peter		Ind & Comm	NP	38'	43	44	48	51	54	57							7	17/08/1938		05/12/1961	23.30		09/05/1967	
437	*Lyons*	Michael	TD	Labour	FG	69	73	77											3	12/08/1969		12/08/1981	12.00	01/11/1910	19/11/1991	81
438	MacCabe	Dominick		Agricultural	NP	38'	43	44											3	17/08/1938		07/04/1948	9.64			
439	MacConghail	Fiach		Nominated	NP	11													1	25/05/2011			0.83	04/08/1964		47.6
440	MacEllin	Sean E.		Ind & Comm	NP	28	31	34	38'	44									5	06/12/1928		07/04/1948	16.18		01/09/1969	
441	MacEvoy	Edward		Elected	NP	22													1	06/12/1922		16/09/1925	2.78	22/4/1873	01/01/1926	52
442	MacFhionnlach	Peadar		Nominated	NP	38	38'												2	28/03/1938		01/07/1942	4.26		01/07/1942	
443	*MacGuinness*	Francis	TD	Elected	SF	25	28	31											3	17/09/1925		30/11/1934	9.20	1868	30/11/1934	66
444	MacKean	James		Elected	NP	22	25	28	31	34									5	06/12/1922		29/05/1936	13.48			
445	Mackin	Martin		Nominated	FF	97													1	22/05/2002	69	16/07/2002	0.15			
446	MacLoughlin	John		Ind & Comm	NP	22	25	28	31	34	38	38'							7	06/12/1922		14/07/1943	18.77	8/9/1871	11/09/1943	72
447	MacLysaght	Edward		Elected	NP	22													1	06/12/1922		16/09/1925	2.78			
448	MacParland	Daniel		Elected	NP	31	34												2	06/12/1931		29/05/1936	4.48			
449	MacPartlin	Thomas		Elected	LB	22													1	06/12/1922	2	20/10/1923	0.87	1879	20/10/1923	44
450	MacSharry	Marc		Ind & Comm	FF	02	07	11											3	16/07/2002			9.69	12/07/1973		38.7
451	MacWhinney	Linda Kearns		Ind & Comm	FF	38													1	28/03/1938		17/08/1938	0.39	1/7/1888	05/06/1951	62
452	*Madden*	David	TD	Ind & Comm	FG	38	38'	43	44										4	28/03/1938		04/02/1948	9.86	1880	31/07/1955	75
453	*Magennis*	Prof. William	TD	Nominated	NP	38	38'	43	44										4	28/03/1938		30/03/1946	8.01	18/5/1867	30/03/1946	78
454	Magner	Pat		Nominated	LB	81	83	93											3	12/08/1981		06/08/1997	9.40	25/03/1931		81.0
455	Magnier	John		Nominated	NP	87													1	14/04/1987		16/08/1989	2.34	10/02/1948		64.1
456	Maguire	John		Ind & Comm	NP	43													1	25/08/1943		01/08/1944	0.94			
457	Mahon	Sir Bryan		Elected	NP	22	25	28											3	06/12/1922	14	24/09/1930	7.80	2/4/1862	24/09/1930	68
458	Mallon	Seamus		Nominated	NP	82													1	21/04/1982		31/01/1983	0.78	17/08/1936		75.6
459	*Malone*	Patrick	TD	Agricultural	FG	65	69												2	08/06/1965		14/04/1970	4.85	30/05/1916	03/12/1993	77

	Surname	Forename	TD	Panel	Party	Elected													Terms	From	By-E	To	Service	Born	Died	Age
460	Maloney	Sean		Labour	LB	93													1	01/02/1993		06/08/1997	4.51	09/01/1945		67.2
461	*Manning*	Maurice	TD	Cultural & Educa	FG	81	87	89	93	97									5	12/08/1981		16/07/2002	15.78	14/06/1943		68.8
462	*Mannion*	John	TD	Agricultural	FG	69	73	81	82										4	12/08/1969		31/01/1983	9.48	26/10/1944	02/04/2006	61
463	*Mannion*	John Snr.	TD	Agricultural	FG	54	61	65											3	14/07/1954		12/08/1969	10.51	04/06/1907	10/09/1978	71
464	*Mansergh*	Dr. Martin	TD	Agricultural	FF	02													1	16/07/2002		24/05/2007	4.85	31/12/1946		65.2
465	Mansfield	Edward		Elected	LB	22													1	06/12/1922	1	12/12/1922	0.02			
466	Mara	P.J.		Nominated	FF	77	82												2	29/06/1981		31/01/1983	0.90	13/03/1942		70.0
467	*Markey*	Bernard	TD	Labour	FG	73	77												2	01/05/1973		11/06/1981	8.11	07/11/1935	23/07/2003	67
468	Marquess of Headfort			Nominated	NP	22	25												2	06/12/1922		05/12/1928	6.00	12/6/1878	29/01/1943	64
469	Martin	Augustine		NUI	NP	73	77												2	01/05/1973		12/08/1981	8.28		16/10/1995	
470	*Martin*	James	TD	Agricultural	FF	65	69												2	08/06/1965		01/05/1973	7.90	1905	03/10/1969	64
471	McAleese	Martin		Nominated	NP	11													1	25/05/2011			0.83	24/03/1951		61.0
472	McAughtry	Sam		Ind & Comm	NP	96*													1	23/02/1996	52	06/08/1997	1.45			
473	McAuliffe	Timothy		Cultural & Educa	LB	61	65	73	77	81	82								6	05/12/1961		31/01/1983	17.44	01/02/1909	29/09/1985	76
474	McAuliffe-Ennis	Helena		Cultural & Educa	LB	83													1	31/01/1983		14/04/1987	4.20	01/04/1951		61.0
475	*McCartan*	Patrick	TD	Nominated	SF	48													1	07/04/1948		01/08/1951	3.32	13/3/1878	28/03/1963	85
476	*McCarthy*	Dr. Sean	TD	Agricultural	FF	89													1	16/08/1989		17/12/1992	3.34	07/01/1937		75.2
477	*McCarthy*	Michael	TD	Labour	LB	02	07												2	16/07/2002		25/02/2011	8.61	15/11/1976		35.4
478	*McCartin*	Joe	TD	Agricultural	FG	73	77												2	01/05/1973		11/06/1981	8.11	24/04/1939		72.9
479	*McCormack*	Padraig	TD	Agricultural	FG	87													1	14/04/1987		15/06/1989	2.17	16/05/1942		69.9
480	McCrea	James		Agricultural	NP	48	51	54											3	07/04/1948		09/05/1957	9.09		31/01/1969	
481	*McDermott*	Frank	TD	Nominated	CP	38	38'												2	28/03/1938		25/08/1943	5.41	1886	24/06/1975	89
482	McDonagh	Jarlath		Labour	FG	93	97												2	01/02/1993		16/07/2002	9.45	01/06/1945		66.8
483	*McDonald*	Charles	TD	Agricultural	FG	61	65	69	77	81	82	83	87	89					9	05/12/1961		01/02/1993	26.86	11/06/1935		76.8
484	McDonald	Lisa		Nominated	FF	07													1	23/07/2007		25/05/2011	3.84	09/07/1974		37.7
485	McDonell	Frank		Nominated	NP	87													1	24/06/1989		16/08/1989	0.15			
486	*McDowell*	Derek	TD	Ind & Comm	LB	02													1	16/07/2002		23/07/2007	5.02	01/09/1958		53.6
487	*McElgunn*	Farrell	TD	Nominated	FF	65	69												2	21/11/1968		01/05/1973	4.44	05/01/1932		
488	*McEllistrim*	Thomas Jnr.	TD	Nominated	FF	87													1	14/04/1987		15/06/1989	2.17	15/01/1926	25/02/2000	74
489	*McFadden*	Michael Og	TD	Agricultural	FG	51													1	01/08/1951		14/07/1954	2.95	1885	27/08/1958	73
490	*McFadden*	Nicky	TD	Administrative	FG	07													1	23/07/2007		25/02/2011	3.59	06/12/1962		49.3
491	McGee	James		Administrative	NP	38'	43	44	48	51	54								6	17/08/1938		19/01/1956	17.42		19/01/1956	
492	*McGennis*	Marian	TD	Nominated	FF	93													1	01/02/1993	64	06/06/1997	4.34	01/11/1953		58.4
493	McGillicuddy	Ross Kinlough		Agricultural	NP	28	31	34	38	38'									5	06/12/1928		14/07/1943	12.77	26/10/1882	26/04/1950	67
494	McGlinchey	Bernard		Ind & Comm	FF	61	65	69	73	77	82								6	05/12/1961		31/01/1983	20.47	18/10/1932		79.4
495	McGonagle	Stephen		Nominated	NP	83													1	31/01/1983		14/04/1987	4.20	17/09/1914	23/04/2002	87
496	McGowan	Patrick		Agricultural	FF	65	69	73	77	87	89	93	97						8	08/06/1965	56	03/10/1999	28.65	16/07/1926	03/10/1999	73
497	McGrath	Patrick		Nominated	NP	73													1	01/05/1973		17/08/1977	4.30		09/10/2001	
498	McGuinness	Catherine		University of Dul	NP	79*	81	83											3	11/12/1979	50	14/04/1987	6.56	14/11/1934		77.4
499	McGuire	Edward		Ind & Comm	NP	48	51	54	57	61									5	07/04/1948		08/06/1965	17.17	1901	27/10/1992	91
500	*McHugh*	Joe	TD	Administrative	FG	02													1	16/07/2002		24/05/2007	4.85	16/07/1971		40.7
501	McHugh	Roger		NUI	NP	54													1	14/07/1954		09/05/1957	2.82			
502	McHugh	Vincent		Labour	NP	51	65	76*											3	01/08/1951	48	17/08/1977	7.94		1977	
503	McKenna	Tony		Cultural & Educa	FF	87	89												2	14/04/1987		01/02/1993	5.80	22/08/1939		72.6
504	*McMahon*	Larry	TD	Labour	FG	83	87	89											3	31/01/1983		01/02/1993	10.00	09/01/1929	16/02/2006	77
505	McMullen	William		Labour	NP	51													1	01/08/1951		01/09/1953	2.09			

	Surname	Forename	TD	Panel	Party	Elected													Terms	From	By-E	To	Service	Born	Died	Age
506	*McQuillan*	Jack	TD	Administrative	NPD	65													1	08/06/1965		12/08/1969	4.18	30/08/1920	08/03/1998	77
507	*McShea*	Thomas	TD	Labour	NP	38													1	28/03/1938		17/08/1938	0.39			
508	*Meighan*	John Joseph	TD	Labour	CT	44	48	51	54										4	01/08/1944		09/05/1957	12.77	1891	04/03/1978	87
509	*Milroy*	Sean	TD	Labour	FG	28	31	34	38										4	06/12/1928		17/08/1938	7.87	1877	30/11/1946	69
510	Minihan	John		Nominated	PD	02													1	16/07/2002		23/07/2007	5.02	24/11/1957		54.3
511	Molloy	William		Elected	NP	22	25	28											3	06/12/1922		05/12/1931	9.00			
512	*Moloney*	Daniel	TD	Ind & Comm	FF	61													1	05/12/1961		26/06/1963	1.56	1909	26/06/1963	54
513	Moloney	Marie		Labour	LB	11													1	25/05/2011			0.83	26/08/1958		53.6
514	*Molony*	David	TD	Cultural & Educa	FG	77													1	17/08/1977		11/06/1981	3.82	23/08/1950	04/09/2002	52
515	Monahan	Edward		Administrative	NP	43													1	25/08/1943		01/08/1944	0.94		1944	
516	Mooney	Joseph		Nominated	FF	61													1	05/12/1961		08/06/1965	3.51		21/01/1988	
517	Mooney	Paschal		Cultural & Educa	FF	87	89	93	97	02	10*	11							7	14/04/1987			22.45	14/10/1947		64.4
518	Moore	Col. Maurice		Nominated	NP	22	25	28	31	34	38	38'							7	06/12/1922		08/09/1939	14.93	10/8/1854	08/09/1939	85
519	Moore	Theodore		University of Dul	NP	43	44												2	25/08/1943		11/06/1947	3.79	1894	21/01/1979	85
520	Moran	James		Nominated	NP	22	25	28	31										4	06/12/1922		05/12/1934	12.00			
521	Moran	Mary		Nominated	LB	11													1	25/05/2011			0.83	28/06/1960		51.7
522	Morrissey	Tom		Nominated	PD	02													1	16/07/2002		23/07/2007	5.02	16/07/1956		55.7
523	Moylan	Pat		Agricultural	FF	97	02	07											3	06/08/1997		25/04/2011	13.72	12/09/1946		65.5
524	*Moylan*	Sean	TD	Nominated	FF	57													1	09/05/1957		16/11/1957	0.52	1888	16/11/1957	69
525	*Moynihan*	Michael	TD	Ind & Comm	LB	73	77												2	01/05/1973		11/06/1981	8.11	17/06/1917	27/06/2001	84
526	*Mulcahy*	Gen. Richard	TD	Labour	FG	38	43												2	28/03/1938		30/05/1944	1.15	10/5/1886	16/12/1971	85
527	*Mulcahy*	Michael	TD	Nominated	FF	93													1	13/12/1994	60	06/08/1997	2.65	23/06/1960		51.7
528	Mulcahy	Noel		Nominated	FF	77													1	17/08/1977		12/08/1981	3.99			
529	Mulcahy	Tony		Labour	FG	11													1	25/05/2011			0.83	12/04/1959		52.9
530	*Mullen*	Michael	TD	Nominated	LB	73													1	01/05/1973		17/08/1977	4.30	01/02/1919	1982	63
531	Mullen	Ronan		NUI	NP	07	11												2	23/07/2007			4.67	13/10/1970		41.4
532	Mullins	Michael		Cultural & Educa	FG	11													1	25/05/2011			0.83	22/02/1953		59.1
533	*Mullins*	Thomas	TD	Nominated	FF	57	61	65	69										4	09/05/1957		01/05/1973	15.98	1903	02/11/1978	75
534	Mullooly	Brian		Labour	FF	81	82	83	87	89	93	97							7	12/08/1981		16/07/2002	20.93	21/02/1935		77.1
535	Mulroy	Jimmy		Nominated	FF	87													1	14/04/1987		16/08/1989	2.34	01/08/1940		71.6
536	Murphy	Dominick		Labour	NP	54	57	61	65										4	14/07/1954		12/08/1969	15.08			
537	Murphy	John A.		NUI	NP	77	81	82	87	89									5	17/08/1977		01/02/1993	11.26	17/01/1927		85.2
538	Nash	John		Cultural & Educa	NP	61	65	69											3	05/12/1961		01/05/1973	11.40		01/02/1989	
539	*Naughten*	Denis	TD	Agricultural	FG	97*													1	28/01/1997	53	06/06/1997	0.35	23/06/1973		38.7
540	*Naughten*	Liam	TD	Agricultural	FG	81	89	93											3	12/08/1981	53	16/11/1996	7.77	30/05/1944	16/11/1996	52
541	Nesbitt	George		Elected	NP	22													1	06/12/1922		16/09/1925	2.78			
542	*Neville*	Dan	TD	Labour	FG	89	93												2	16/08/1989		06/06/1997	7.81	08/12/1946		65.3
543	Newcome	John Joseph		Administrative	NP	38													1	28/03/1938		17/08/1938	0.39		1938	
544	*Nolan*	M.J.	TD	Agricultural	FF	82	01												2	21/04/1982	57	17/05/2002	1.00	25/01/1951		61.2
545	*Nolan*	Thomas	TD	Nominated	FF	61													1	05/12/1961		08/06/1965	3.51	27/07/1921	17/08/1992	71
546	Noone	Catherine		Ind & Comm	FG	11													1	25/05/2011			0.83	24/06/1976		35.7
547	Norris	David		University of Dul	NP	87	89	93	97	02	07	11							7	14/04/1987			24.94	01/07/1944		67.7
548	*Norton*	Patrick	TD	Administrative	FF	69													1	12/08/1969		01/05/1973	3.72	01/01/1928		
549	Nugent	Sir Walter		Elected	NP	28*	28												2	01/03/1928	9	05/12/1931	3.76	12/12/1865	12/11/1955	89
550	O Brolchain	Niall		Agricultural	GP	09													1	14/12/2009		25/05/2011	1.44	14/04/1965		46.9
551	O Buachalla	Liam		Nominated	NP	38'	43	44	48	51	54	57	61	65					9	07/10/1939		12/08/1969	29.85	1899	15/10/1970	71

	Surname	Forename	TD	Panel	Party	Elected													Terms	From	By-E	To	Service	Born	Died	Age
552	Ó Clochartaigh	Trevor		Agricultural	SF	11													1	25/05/2011			0.83	14/03/1968		44.0
553	O Conallain	Donall		NUI	NP	61	65												2	05/12/1961		12/08/1969	7.69	1907	07/12/1987	80
554	*O Cuiv*	Eamon	TD	Cultural & Educa	FF	89													1	16/08/1989		25/11/1992	3.28	01/06/1950		61.8
555	O Domhnaill	Brian		Nominated	FF	07	11												2	23/07/2007			4.67	18/10/1977		34.4
556	*O Fearghail*	Sean	TD	Agricultural	FF	00*													1	02/06/2000	56	17/05/2002	1.95	17/04/1960		51.9
557	O Foighil	Pol		Labour	FG	89													1	16/08/1989		01/02/1993	3.46	01/06/1928	21/03/2005	76
558	O hEochadha	Seamus		Cultural & Educa	NP	38													1	28/03/1938		01/07/1938	0.26		01/07/1938	
559	*O Maille*	Padraic	TD	Nominated	FF	34	38	38'	43	44									5	06/12/1934		19/01/1946	9.29	23/2/1878	19/01/1946	67
560	Ó Murchú	Labhrás		Cultural & Educa	FF	97	02	07	11										4	06/08/1997			14.63	14/08/1939		72.6
561	O Siochfhradha	Padraig		Nominated	NP	44	51	57	61										4	22/02/1946		19/11/1964	12.61		19/11/1964	
562	O'Beirne	Frank		Ind & Comm	NP	43													1	25/08/1943		01/08/1944	0.94	1898	07/02/1978	80
563	O'Brien	Andy		Labour	FG	69	73	77	81	83									5	12/08/1969		14/04/1987	16.89	21/01/1915	04/12/2006	91
564	O'Brien	Darragh		Labour	FF	11													1	04/03/2011			1.05	08/07/1974		37.7
565	O'Brien	Francis		Agricultural	FF	89	93	97	02	07									5	16/08/1989		25/04/2011	21.69	07/04/1943		69.0
566	O'Brien	George		NUI	NP	48	51	54	57	61									5	07/04/1948		08/06/1965	17.17	1892	31/12/1973	81
567	O'Brien	Mary Ann		Nominated	NP	11													1	25/05/2011			0.83	08/09/1960		51.5
568	*O'Brien*	William	TD	Labour	FG	69	73												2	12/08/1969		17/08/1977	8.01	06/03/1918	05/11/1994	76
569	O'Callaghan	Cornelius		Agricultural	NP	70*	73												2	24/02/1970	40	24/01/1974	3.92	1922	24/01/1974	52
570	O'Callaghan	Vivian		Nominated	FF	87													1	14/04/1987		16/08/1989	2.34	07/08/1944		
571	O'Callaghan	William		Agricultural	NP	38	38'	44	48	51	54	57							7	28/03/1938		05/12/1961	22.75		28/01/1967	
572	*O'Connell*	Dr. John	TD	Nominated	FF	87													1	14/04/1987		15/06/1989	2.17	20/01/1927		85.2
573	O'Connell	Maurice		Labour	FG	81	82												2	12/08/1981		31/01/1983	1.47	01/10/1936		
574	*O'Connell*	Thomas	TD	Nominated	LB	38'	43	48	54										4	22/01/1941		09/05/1957	9.66	21/11/1882	21/06/1969	86
575	O'Connor	Aidan		Nominated	NP	93													1	13/06/1997	67	06/08/1997	0.15			
576	O'Connor	Joseph		Elected	NP	25	28	31	34										4	17/09/1925		29/05/1936	10.70		06/04/1941	
577	O'Connor	Nicholas		Nominated	FF	87													1	14/04/1987		16/08/1989	2.34	20/04/1945		
578	O'Connor	Sean		Nominated	NP	82													1	13/12/1982		31/01/1983	0.13	29/04/1960		51.9
579	*O'Dea*	Louis	TD	Cultural & Educa	SF	44													1	01/08/1944		07/04/1948	3.68		1948	
580	O'Dea	Michael		Elected	NP	22													1	06/12/1922		16/09/1925	2.78			
581	*O'Doherty*	Joseph	TD	Elected	SF	28	31												2	06/12/1928	18	24/11/1933	4.97	1891	10/08/1979	88
582	O'Donnell	Frank		Ind & Comm	NP	43	51	54											3	25/08/1943		09/05/1957	6.71	4/4/1894	04/11/1976	82
583	O'Donnell	Marie-Louise		Nominated	NP	11													1	25/05/2011			0.83	05/09/1952		59.5
584	*O'Donoghue*	Martin	TD	Administrative	FF	83													1	31/01/1983		14/04/1987	4.20	13/05/1933		78.9
585	*O'Donovan*	Denis	TD	Ind & Comm	FF	89	97	07	11										4	16/08/1989			12.91	23/07/1955		56.7
586	*O'Donovan*	John	TD	Cultural & Educa	FG	57													1	09/05/1957		05/12/1961	4.58	1908	17/05/1982	74
587	O'Donovan	Sean		Cultural & Educa	NP	38	38'	43	44	51	57	61	65						8	28/03/1938		12/08/1969	25.24		22/02/1975	
588	*O'Donovan*	Timothy	TD	Agricultural	F	44	48	51											3	01/08/1944		01/01/1951	6.42	4/4/1881	01/01/1951	69
589	*O'Dowd*	Fergus	TD	Administrative	FG	97													1	06/08/1997		17/05/2002	4.78	01/09/1948		63.6
590	O'Dwyer	Martin		Agricultural	NP	38	38'	48	51	60*									4	28/03/1938		15/12/1961	18.14	1886	18/11/1974	88
591	O'Farrell	John		Elected	LB	22	25	28	31	34	48								6	06/12/1922		31/05/1950	15.63		02/01/1971	
592	O'Farrell	Seamus		Nominated	NP	48													1	07/04/1948		01/08/1951	3.32		09/12/1973	
593	O'Gorman	Colm		Nominated	PD	02													1	03/05/2007		23/07/2007	0.22	01/07/1966		45.7
594	*O'Gorman*	Patrick	TD	Nominated	FG	54													1	14/07/1954		09/05/1957	2.82			
595	*O'Grady*	Sean	TD	Nominated	FF	51	57												2	01/08/1951		05/12/1961	7.53	1/12/1889	07/04/1966	76
596	O'Hanlon	Michael F.		Elected	NP	25	28	31	34										4	17/09/1925		29/05/1936	10.70	8/9/1890	27/02/1967	76
597	*O'Higgins*	Michael	TD	Nominated	FG	51	69	73											3	01/08/1951		17/08/1977	10.97	01/11/1917	09/03/2005	87

	Surname	Forename	TD	Panel	Party	Elected													Terms	From	By-E	To	Service	Born	Died	Age
598	*O'Keeffe*	Batt	TD	Labour	FF	89													1	16/08/1989		25/11/1992	3.28	02/04/1945		67.0
599	*O'Keeffe*	James	TD	Ind & Comm	FG	56*	57												2	14/05/1956	30	04/10/1961	5.39			
600	*O'Keeffe*	Ned	TD	Nominated	FF	82													1	21/04/1982		24/11/1982	0.59	01/08/1942		69.6
601	O'Keeffe	Susan		Agricultural	LB	11													1	25/05/2011			0.83	18/09/1960		51.5
602	*O'Kennedy*	Michael	TD	Cultural & Educa	FF	65	93												2	08/06/1965		06/08/1997	8.69	21/02/1936		76.1
603	*O'Leary*	John (Wexford)	TD	Administrative	LB	57													1	09/05/1957		21/06/1959	2.12	1/9/1894	21/06/1959	64
604	O'Leary	Sean A.		Nominated	FG	81	83												2	12/08/1981		14/04/1987	4.89	01/06/1941	22/12/2006	65
605	*O'Loghlen*	Peter	TD	Nominated	FF	43													1	25/08/1943		30/05/1944	0.76	1883	25/10/1971	88
606	O'Mahony	Flor		Administrative	LB	81	82	83											3	12/08/1981		14/04/1987	5.67	23/01/1946		66.2
607	*O'Malley*	Fiona	TD	Nominated	PD	07													1	23/07/2007		25/05/2011	3.84	19/01/1968		44.2
608	O'Mara	Stephen		Elected	NP	25													1	17/09/1925	7	26/07/1926	0.85		26/07/1926	
609	O'Meara	Kathleen		Agricultural	LB	97	02												2	06/08/1997		23/07/2007	9.96	24/01/1960		52.2
610	*O'Neill*	John	TD	Elected	NP	25*													1	05/03/1925	5	16/09/1925	0.53			
611	O'Neill	Joseph		Nominated	NP	77													1	17/08/1977		12/08/1981	3.99			
612	*O'Neill*	Laurence	TD	Elected	NP	29*	31	34	38'										4	20/06/1929	12	26/07/1943	10.50	1874	26/07/1943	69
613	O'Neill	Pat		Agricultural	FG	11													1	25/05/2011			0.83	14/11/1958		53.4
614	O'Quigley	John B.		Labour	NP	57	65												2	09/05/1957		29/05/1969	8.55		29/05/1969	
615	O'Reilly	Joe	TD	Cultural & Educa	FG	89	07												2	16/08/1989		25/02/2011	7.06	14/04/1955		56.9
616	O'Reilly	Patrick (Firmullagh)		Agricultural	NP	44	48	51	54	57	61	65							7	01/08/1944		12/08/1969	25.03			
617	*O'Reilly*	Patrick (Virginia	TD	Administrative	F	65													1	08/06/1965		18/06/1969	4.03	01/04/1927	19/02/1994	66
618	O'Reilly	Patrick F.		Cultural & Educa	NP	51													1	01/08/1951		14/07/1954	2.95			
619	O'Reilly	Patrick John		Cultural & Educa	NP	44													1	01/08/1944		07/04/1948	3.68		16/07/1965	
620	Ormonde	Ann		Cultural & Educa	FF	93	97	02	07										4	01/02/1993		25/04/2011	18.23	20/01/1935		77.2
621	*Ormonde*	Donal	TD	Nominated	FF	89													1	16/08/1989		01/02/1993	3.46	21/01/1943		69.2
622	*Ormonde*	John	TD	Labour	FF	65													1	08/06/1965		12/08/1969	4.18	15/09/1905	25/06/1981	75
623	O'Rourke	Brian		Elected	NP	22	25	28	31	34	38								6	06/12/1922		17/08/1938	13.87	1873		
624	*O'Rourke*	Daniel	TD	Labour	SF	51													1	01/08/1951		14/07/1954	2.95		21/03/1971	
625	*O'Rourke*	Mary	TD	Cultural & Educa	FF	81	82	97	02										4	12/08/1981	68	24/05/2007	6.29	31/05/1937		74.8
626	*O'Shea*	Brian	TD	Ind & Comm	LB	87													1	14/04/1987		15/06/1989	2.17	09/12/1944		67.3
627	*O'Sullivan*	Denis	TD	Ind & Comm	FG	65													1	08/06/1965		12/08/1969	4.18	05/03/1918	20/07/1987	69
628	O'Sullivan	Donal		Cultural & Educa	NP	43													1	25/08/1943		01/08/1944	0.94	1893	1973	80.0
629	*O'Sullivan*	Gearoid	TD	Cultural & Educa	SF	38													1	28/03/1938		17/08/1938	0.39	1891	05/08/1944	53
630	*O'Sullivan*	Jan	TD	Administrative	LB	93													1	01/02/1993		06/06/1997	4.34	06/12/1950		61.3
631	*O'Sullivan*	John L.	TD	Administrative	FG	54	57												2	14/07/1954		01/09/1961	7.13	08/06/1901	28/02/1990	88
632	O'Sullivan	Ned		Labour	FF	07	11												2	23/07/2007			4.67	25/11/1950		61.3
633	O'Sullivan	Terence		Nominated	FF	69													1	12/08/1969		01/05/1973	3.72	1924	14/03/1997	73.0
634	*O'Sullivan*	Timothy	TD	Agricultural	FF	54	57	61	65										4	14/07/1954		12/08/1969	15.08	26/7/1899	1969	70
635	O'Sullivan	William		Elected	NP	22	25	28	31	34									5	06/12/1922		29/05/1936	13.48			
636	O'Toole	Joe		NUI	NP	87	89	93	97	02	07								6	14/04/1987		25/05/2011	24.11	20/07/1947		64.7
637	*O'Toole*	Martin J.	TD	Agricultural	FF	77	81	82	83	87									5	17/08/1977		15/06/1989	11.83	27/06/1925		86.7
638	*O'Toole*	Paddy	TD	Nominated	FG	73	83												2	01/05/1973		14/04/1987	4.27	15/01/1938		74.2
639	Owens	Evelyn		Labour	LB	69	73												2	12/08/1969		17/08/1977	8.01	22/01/1931	27/09/2010	79
640	Pakenham	Edward		Nominated	NP	44													1	07/11/1946		07/04/1948	1.42		1948	
641	Parkinson	James		Cultural & Educa	NP	22	25	28	31	34	38	38'	43	44					9	06/12/1922		31/07/1947	22.82		16/09/1948	
642	*Pearse*	Margaret	TD	Nominated	FF	38	38'	43	44	48	51	54	57	61	65				10	28/03/1938		07/11/1968	30.62	1878	07/11/1968	90
643	*Phelan*	John Paul	TD	Agricultural	FG	02	07												2	16/07/2002		25/02/2011	8.61	27/09/1978		33.5

	Surname	Forename	TD	Panel	Party	Elected													Terms	From	By-E	To	Service	Born	Died	Age
644	Phelan	Kieran		Ind & Comm	FF	02	07												2	16/07/2002		26/05/2010	7.86	19/11/1949	26/05/2010	60
645	Plunkett	Sir Horace		Nominated	NP	22													1	06/12/1922	3	28/11/1923	0.98	24/10/1854	26/03/1932	77
646	Poe	Sir Wm.		Nominated	NP	22													1	06/12/1922	4	09/12/1924	2.01			
647	Power	Averil		Ind & Comm	FF	11													1	25/05/2011			0.83	26/07/1978		33.7
648	Power	Jane		Nominated	NP	22	25	28	31	34									5	06/12/1922		29/05/1936	13.48	1/5/1858	05/01/1941	82
649	Prendergast	Micheal		Agricultural	NP	54	57	61	65	69	75*								6	14/07/1954	43	17/08/1977	21.12		25/03/1998	
650	Prendergast	Phil	MEP	Labour	LB	07													1	23/07/2007		21/04/2011	3.75	01/01/1960		52.2
651	Purcell	Frank		Labour	NP	54	57												2	14/07/1954		02/04/1960	5.72		02/04/1960	
652	Quealy	Michael		Agricultural	FG	83													1	31/01/1983		14/04/1987	4.20			
653	Quigley	Joseph		Ind & Comm	FG	61													1	05/12/1961		08/06/1965	3.51	22/11/1899	25/03/1974	74
654	*Quill*	Mairin	TD	Nominated	PD	97													1	06/08/1997		16/07/2002	4.94	15/09/1940		71.5
655	Quinlan	Patrick		NUI	NP	57	61	65	69	73									5	09/05/1957		17/08/1977	20.27		08/11/2001	
656	Quinn	Feargal		NUI	NP	93	97	02	07	11									5	01/02/1993			19.14	27/11/1936		75.3
657	Quinn	Martin		Agricultural	NP	48													1	07/04/1948		01/08/1951	3.32			
658	*Quinn*	Ruairi	TD	Ind & Comm	LB	73	81												2	01/07/1976		18/02/1982	1.48	02/04/1946		66.0
659	Quirke	William		Agricultural	NP	31	34	38	38'	43	44	48	51	54					9	06/12/1931		05/03/1955	21.42		05/03/1955	
660	Raftery	Tom		Administrative	FG	89													1	16/08/1989		01/02/1993	3.46	15/08/1933		78.6
661	Regan	Eugene		Agricultural	FG	07													1	23/07/2007		25/04/2011	3.76	01/03/1952		60.1
662	*Reidy*	James	TD	Nominated	FG	54													1	14/07/1954		09/05/1957	2.82	1890	07/12/1963	73
663	Reilly	Kathryn		Ind & Comm	SF	11													1	25/05/2011			0.83	17/09/1988		23.5
664	*Reynolds*	Gerry	TD	Ind & Comm	FG	87	93												2	14/04/1987		06/06/1997	6.51	01/04/1961		51.0
665	*Reynolds*	Patrick J.	TD	Ind & Comm	NP	69	77	81	82	83									5	12/08/1969		14/04/1987	13.37	25/11/1920	27/12/2003	83
666	Richards-Orpen	Capt. Edward		Nominated	NP	48													1	07/04/1948		01/08/1951	3.32		01/11/1967	
667	Ridge	Therese		Labour	FG	97													1	06/08/1997		16/07/2002	4.94	01/03/1941		71.1
668	Robb	John		Nominated	NP	82	83	87											3	21/04/1982		16/08/1989	7.32			
669	Robinson	David		Nominated	NP	31	34	38	38'										4	06/12/1931		14/07/1943	9.77		21/08/1943	
670	Robinson	Mary		University of Dul	NP	69	73	77	81	82	83	87							7	12/08/1969		16/08/1989	20.01	21/05/1944		67.8
671	*Robinson*	Seamus	TD	Elected	NP	28	31	34											3	06/12/1928		11/12/1935	7.01	6/1/1890	08/12/1961	71
672	*Roche*	Dick	TD	Nominated	FF	89	93												2	02/12/1992		06/06/1997	4.51	30/03/1947		65.0
673	*Roddy*	Joseph	TD	Ind & Comm	FG	57													1	09/05/1957		05/12/1961	4.58	1897	03/10/1965	68
674	Rodgers	Brid		Nominated	NP	83													1	31/01/1983		14/04/1987	4.20	20/02/1935		77.1
675	*Rooney*	Eamon	TD	Administrative	FG	65													1	08/06/1965		12/08/1969	4.18		09/11/1993	
676	Ross	J.N.		University of Dul	NP	61													1	05/12/1961		08/06/1965	3.51	01/02/1919	24/12/2011	92
677	*Ross*	Shane	TD	University of Dul	NP	81	82	83	87	89	93	97	02	07					9	12/08/1981		25/02/2011	29.54	11/07/1949		62.7
678	*Rowlette*	Robert	TD	University of Dul	NP	38	38'	43											3	28/03/1938		13/10/1944	6.55	1873	13/10/1944	71
679	Ruane	Sean		Labour	NP	43	44	48	51	54									5	25/08/1943		09/05/1957	13.71		24/03/1967	
680	Ruane	Thomas		Administrative	NP	34	38	38'	44	51	54	57	61						8	06/12/1934		08/06/1965	27.74		07/06/1969	
681	*Russell*	George	TD	Ind & Comm	NP	69	73												2	12/08/1969		17/08/1977	8.01	01/04/1912		
682	Ruttle	James		Nominated	NP	77													1	20/06/1980		12/08/1981	1.14			
683	Ryan	Brendan		NUI	LB	82	83	87	89	97	02								6	21/04/1982		23/07/2007	20.75	06/08/1946		65.6
684	*Ryan*	Brendan	TD	Administrative	LB	07													1	23/07/2007		25/02/2011	3.59	15/02/1953		59.1
685	*Ryan*	Col. Jeremiah	TD	Administrative	FG	48													1	07/04/1948		01/08/1951	3.32	30/7/1891		
686	Ryan	Dr. James		Nominated	FF	65													1	08/06/1965		12/08/1969	4.18	6/12/1891		
687	*Ryan*	Eoin	TD	Nominated	FF	89													1	16/08/1989		25/11/1992	3.28	24/02/1953		59.1
688	Ryan	Eoin Snr.		Ind & Comm	FF	57	61	65	69	73	77	81	82	83					9	09/05/1957		14/04/1987	29.93	12/06/1920	14/12/2001	84
689	*Ryan*	John	TD	Ind & Comm	LB	89													1	16/08/1989		25/11/1992	3.28	17/06/1927		84.8

	Surname	Forename	TD	Panel	Party	Elected													Terms	From	By-E	To	Service	Born	Died	Age
690	Ryan	Liam		NUI	NP	81													1	12/08/1981		21/04/1982	0.69			
691	Ryan	Michael J.		NUI	NP	44													1	01/08/1944		07/04/1948	3.68		24/10/1952	
692	Ryan	Patrick		Agricultural	NP	61	65	69											3	05/12/1961		01/05/1973	11.40			
693	Ryan	Seamus		Nominated	NP	31													1	06/12/1931	19	30/06/1933	1.57		30/06/1933	
694	*Ryan*	Sean	TD	Labour	LB	97													1	06/08/1997	54	11/03/1998	0.59	27/01/1943		69.2
695	Ryan	William		Agricultural	FF	61	65	69	73	77	81	82	83	87					9	05/12/1961		16/08/1989	27.70	21/09/1921	02/01/1994	72
696	Sands	Peter		Nominated	FF	02													1	22/06/2007		23/07/2007	0.08	01/05/1924		87.9
697	Sanfey	James		Nominated	NP	73													1	01/05/1973		17/08/1977	4.30		03/04/2000	
698	*Scanlon*	Eamon	TD	Agricultural	FF	02													1	16/07/2002		24/05/2007	4.85	20/09/1954		57.5
699	*Sears*	William	TD	Elected	CG	28													1	06/12/1928	10	23/03/1929	0.29		23/03/1929	
700	*Sheahan*	Tom	TD	Administrative	FG	11													1	25/05/2011			0.83	05/09/1968		43.5
701	Sheehy Skeffingtc	Owen		University of Dul	NP	54	57	65	69										4	14/07/1954		07/06/1970	12.39		07/06/1970	
702	*Sheldon*	William	TD	Nominated	NP	61	65	69											3	05/12/1961		01/05/1973	11.40	18/01/1907	01/11/1999	92
703	Sheridan	John		Agricultural	NP	54	57	61											3	14/07/1954		05/04/1963	8.73		05/04/1963	
704	*Sheridan*	Joseph	TD	Agricultural	NP	56*	57												2	14/05/1956	31	04/10/1961	5.39	27/11/1914	30/09/2000	85
705	*Sherlock*	Joe	TD	Labour	LB	93													1	01/02/1993		06/08/1997	4.51	26/09/1935	09/09/2007	71
706	Sigerson	George		Nominated	NP	22													1	06/12/1922	5	17/02/1925	2.20	11/1/1836	17/02/1925	89
707	Smith	Matthew		Ind & Comm	NP	54													1	14/07/1954		09/05/1957	2.82		03/11/1955	
708	*Smith*	Michael	TD	Agricultural	FF	82	83												2	21/04/1982		17/02/1987	4.83	08/11/1940		71.4
709	Smyth	Michael		Labour	NP	43	44	48											3	25/08/1943		01/08/1951	7.93		21/11/1973	
710	Stafford	Matthew		Nominated	NP	38	38'	43	44										4	28/03/1938		07/04/1948	10.03	1852	12/06/1950	98
711	*Staines*	Michael	TD	Elected	SF	30*	31	34											3	12/12/1930	14	29/05/1936	5.46	1885	26/10/1955	70
712	Stanford	William Bedell		University of Dul	NP	48	51	54	57	61	65								6	07/04/1948		12/08/1969	21.35			
713	*Staunton*	Myles	TD	Administrative	FG	77	81	89											3	17/08/1977		01/02/1993	8.14	24/09/1935	22/06/2011	75
714	Summerfield	Frederick		Ind & Comm	NP	45*	48	51											3	07/03/1945	23	14/07/1954	9.35		22/07/1975	
715	Sweetman	Edmund		Nominated	NP	48													1	07/04/1948		01/08/1951	3.32		16/12/1968	
716	*Sweetman*	Gerard	TD	Agricultural	FG	43	44												2	25/08/1943		04/02/1948	4.45	10/06/1908	28/01/1970	61
717	*Taylor-Quinn*	Madeleine	TD	Cultural & Educa	FG	82	93	97											3	21/04/1982		16/07/2002	10.05	26/05/1951		60.8
718	*Teehan*	Patrick	TD	Administrative	FF	51	54	57	65										4	01/08/1951		12/08/1969	13.07	14/04/1904	25/12/1985	81
719	Terry	Sheila		Ind & Comm	FG	02													1	16/07/2002		23/07/2007	5.02	07/06/1950		61.8
720	*Tierney*	Patrick	TD	Labour	LB	54													1	14/07/1954		05/03/1957	2.64		29/09/1990	
721	*Tierney*	Prof. Michael	TD	NUI	CG	38	38'	43											3	28/03/1938		01/08/1944	6.35	30/9/1894	10/05/1975	80
722	Toal	Thomas		Elected	NP	25	28	31	34										4	17/09/1925		29/05/1936	10.70			
723	Townsend	Jim		Nominated	LB	93													1	01/02/1993		06/08/1997	4.51	20/06/1937		74.8
724	Trainor Kelly	Peter		Ind & Comm	NP	38'	43	44											3	17/08/1938		07/04/1948	9.64		1948	
725	*Tuffy*	Joanne	TD	Administrative	LB	02													1	16/07/2002		24/05/2007	4.85	09/03/1965		47.0
726	*Tunney*	James	TD	Agricultural	LB	38	38'	44	48	51	54	57							7	28/03/1938		05/12/1961	22.75	1892	12/05/1964	72
727	*Twomey*	Liam	TD	Cultural & Educa	FG	07													1	23/07/2007		25/02/2011	3.59	03/04/1967		45.0
728	Twomey	Michael		Agricultural	NP	38													1	28/03/1938		17/08/1938	0.39			
729	*Upton*	Pat	TD	Agricultural	LB	89													1	16/08/1989		25/11/1992	3.28	01/09/1944	22/02/1999	54
730	Van Turnhout	Jillian		Nominated	NP	11													1	25/05/2011			0.83	29/03/1968		44.0
731	Vincent	Arthur A.		Elected	NP	31*	31												2	28/05/1931	15,21	21/02/1934	2.74		01/01/1934	
732	Wall	Chris		Nominated	FF	02													1	22/06/2007		23/07/2007	0.08			
733	Wall	Frank		Nominated	NP	82													1	13/12/1982		31/01/1983	0.13			
734	*Wall*	Jack	TD	Nominated	LB	93													1	01/02/1993	65	06/06/1997	4.34	01/07/1945		66.7
735	*Wallace*	Mary	TD	Administrative	FF	87													1	14/04/1987		15/06/1989	2.17	13/06/1959		52.8

	Surname	Forename	TD	Panel	Party	Elected													Terms	From	By-E	To	Service	Born	Died	Age
736	Walsh	David		Labour	NP	38													1	28/03/1938		17/08/1938	0.39			
737	Walsh	Jim		Agricultural	FF	97	02	07	11										4	06/08/1997			14.63	05/05/1947		64.9
738	*Walsh*	Joe	TD	Cultural & Educa	FF	81													1	12/08/1981		18/02/1982	0.52	01/05/1943		68.9
739	Walsh	Kate		Nominated	PD	02													1	16/07/2002		24/04/2007	4.77	01/03/1947	24/04/2007	60
740	*Walsh*	Laurence	TD	Nominated	FF	57													1	09/05/1957		05/12/1961	4.58	1/8/1883	11/08/1962	79
741	Walsh	Louis		Nominated	NP	54	57												2	14/07/1954		15/11/1961	6.64			
742	Walsh	Mary		Cultural & Educa	FG	73													1	01/05/1973		18/08/1976	3.30	01/10/1929	18/08/1976	46
743	*Walsh*	Richard	TD	Administrative	FF	43													1	25/08/1943		01/08/1944	0.94	1889	1955	66
744	*Walsh*	Sean	TD	Labour	FF	69													1	12/08/1969		01/05/1973	3.72	03/04/1925	26/12/1989	64
745	*Walsh*	Thomas	TD	Agricultural	FF	43													1	25/08/1943		01/08/1944	0.94	18/12/1901	14/07/1956	54
746	West	Timothy		University of Dul	NP	70*	73	77	82										4	19/11/1970		31/01/1983	11.51			
747	Whelan	John		Labour	LB	11													1	25/05/2011			0.83	24/03/1961		51.0
748	Whitaker	Thomas K.		Nominated	NP	77	81												2	17/08/1977		21/04/1982	4.68	01/12/1916		95.3
749	*White*	Alex	TD	Cultural & Educa	LB	07													1	23/07/2007		25/02/2011	3.59	03/12/1958		53.3
750	White	Mary		Ind & Comm	FF	02	07	11											3	16/07/2002			9.69	07/10/1944		67.5
751	Whyte	Liam		Agricultural	NP	73													1	01/05/1973		17/08/1977	4.30			
752	Wilson	Diarmuid		Administrative	FF	02	07	11											3	16/07/2002			9.69	20/11/1965		46.3
753	Wilson	Gordon		Nominated	NP	93													1	01/02/1993	62	27/06/1995	2.40	25/09/1927	27/06/1995	67
754	*Wilson*	Richard	TD	Elected	F	28	31	34											3	06/12/1928		29/05/1936	7.48		20/02/1957	
755	Woods	William		Administrative	NP	56*													1	14/05/1956	32	09/05/1957	0.99		01/10/1966	
756	Woulfe	Patrick		Nominated	NP	48													1	07/04/1948		01/08/1951	3.32			
757	*Wright*	G.V.	TD	Nominated	FF	82	89	93											3	21/04/1982	66	06/06/1997	8.59	03/08/1947		64.6
758	Yeats	Michael		Nominated	FF	51	61	65	69	73	77								6	01/08/1951		12/03/1980	21.22	22/08/1921	03/01/2007	85
759	Yeats	Wm. Butler		Nominated	NP	22	25												2	06/12/1922		05/12/1928	6.00	13/06/1865	28/01/1939	73
760	Zappone	Katherine		Nominated	NP	11													1	25/05/2011			0.83	25/11/1953		58.3
760	**Total**					* By-election				38' : 2nd election in 1938									**2.3**				**6.85**			**68.0**
	TD also	MEP also	*295*	Nominated by the Taoiseach													Broken Service			By-election	TD	Died	Resigned	Approximate		

Service: Members 23rd Senate to 23/03/2012

Age: Living Members to 23/03/2012

HOUSES OF THE OIREACHTAS

The main telephone number for the Houses of the Oireachtas is 01 6183000.

LoCall: Members of the public who are calling Leinster Houses from outside the (01) area can do so for the price of a local call.

T.D's 1890 337889

Senators 1890 732623

Callers who know the extension of the person whom they are calling in Leinster Houses can call the extension directly by placing the digits "(01) 618" in front of the extension number.

Oireachtas email addresses follow the format: firstname.surname@oireachtas.ie

Clerk of the Dail Kieran Coughlan	Tel: 6183314	Email: clerk@oireachtas.ie
Clerk of the Senate Deirdre Lane	Tel: 6183357	Email: clerk.seanad@oireachtas.ie

For further information, please write to:-

Public Relations Officer,
Office of the Houses of the Oireachtas,
Leinster House,
Dublin 2,
Ireland.

Tel: +353 1 6183166
Fax: +353 1 6184118
or Email: info@oireachtas.ie

PARTY PRESS OFFICES

	Tel (01)	Fax (01)	Email
Fine Gael	618 3379	6184144	fgmedia@indigo.ie
Labour	618 3462	6184151	press@labour.ie
Fianna Fail	618 3297	6184164	info@fiannafail.ie
Sinn Fein	6184276	6184210	sinnfeinpress@oireachtas.ie
People Before Profit Alliance			press@peoplebeforeprofit.ie
Green Party	6184088	6184190	Greenparty.press.office@qmail.com

POLITICAL PARTIES HEADQUARTERS

Fine Gael
51 Upper Mount Street,
Dublin 2.
Tel: (01) 6198444
Fax: (01) 6625046
Email: finegael@finegael.com
Website: www.finegael.com
General Secretary: Tom Curran

The Labour Party
17 Ely Place,
Dublin 2.
Tel: (01) 6784700
Fax: (01) 6612640
Email: head_office@labour.ie
Website: www.labour.ie
General Secretary: Ita McAuliffe

Fianna Fail
65-66 Lower Mount Street,
Dublin 2.
Tel: (01) 6761551
Fax: (01) 6785690
Email: info@fiannafail.ie
Website: www.fiannafail.ie
General Secretary: Sean Dorgan

Sinn Féin
44 Parnell Square,
Dublin 1.
Tel: (01) 8726100
Fax: (01) 8733441
Email: sfadmin@eircom.net
Website: www.sinnfein.ie
General Secretary: Dawn Doyle

The Socialist Party
141 Thomas Street,
Dublin 8.
Tel: (01) 6772686
Fax: (01) 6772592
Email: info@socialistparty.net
Website: www.socialistparty.net
General Secretary: Kevin McLoughlin

People Before Profit Alliance
PO Box 11098,
Dublin 1.
Tel: 087 9090166

Email: info@peoplebeforeprofit.ie
Website: www.peoplebeforeprofit.ie

The Green Party/Comhaontas Glas
16/17 Suffolk Street,
Dublin 2.
Tel: (01) 6790012
Fax: (01) 6797168
Email: info@greenparty.ie
Website: www.greenparty.ie
General Secretary:

The Workers' Party
48 North Great George's Street,
Dublin 1.
Tel: (01) 8733916
Fax: (01) 8748702
Email: wpi@indigo.ie
Website: www.workerspartyireland.net
General Secretary: John Lowry

Christian Solidarity Party
14 North Frederick Street
Dublin 1
Tel: (01) 2121037
Fax: 01 2880051
Email: comharcriostai@eircom.net

TDs DIRECTORY 2012

	Surname	First Name	Party	Constituency	Phone	Dail	Email
1	Adams	Gerry	SF	Louth	042 9328859	6184442	gerry.adams@oireachtas.ie
2	Bannon	James	FG	Longford-Westmeath	087 2031816	6184226	james.bannon@oireachtas.ie
3	Barrett	Sean	FG	Dun Laoghaire	087 2855848	6183343	ceann.comhairle@oireachtas.ie
4	Barry	Tom	FG	Cork East	087 7540438	6183328	tom.barry@oireachtas.ie
5	Boyd Barrett	Richard	PBPA	Dun Laoghaire	086 7814520	6183449	richard.boydbarrett@oireachtas.ie
6	Breen	Pat	FG	Clare	087 2422136	6184224	pat.breen@oireachtas.ie
7	Broughan	Tommy	LB	Dublin North East	01 8477634	6183557	thomas.p.broughan@oireachtas.ie
8	Browne	John	FF	Wexford	087 2469234	6183094	john.browne@oireachtas.ie
9	Bruton	Richard	FG	Dublin North Central	01 8368185	6183103	richard.bruton@oireachtas.ie
10	Burton	Joan	LB	Dublin West	01 8388711	6184006	joan.burton@oireachtas.ie
11	Butler	Ray	FG	Meath West	087 2596680	6183378	ray.butler@oireachtas.ie
12	Buttimer	Jerry	FG	Cork South Central	086 2356892	6183380	jerry.buttimer@oireachtas.ie
13	Byrne	Catherine	FG	Dublin South Central	086 8543276	6183083	catherine.byrne@oireachtas.ie
14	Byrne	Eric	LB	Dublin South Central	087 2548429	6183223	eric.byrne@oireachtas.ie
15	Calleary	Dara	FF	Mayo	086 2238810	6183331	dara.colleary@oireachtas.ie
16	Cannon	Ciaran	FG	Galway East	087 2283377	6183185	ciaran.cannon@oireachtas.ie
17	Carey	Joe	FG	Clare	065 6829191	6183337	joe.carey@oireachtas.ie
18	Coffey	Paudie	FG	Waterford	087 2874015	6183902	paudie.coffey@oireachtas.ie
19	Collins	Aine	FG	Cork North West	087 2326945	6183873	aine.collins@oireachtas.ie
20	Collins	Joan	PBPA	Dublin South Central	086 3888151	6183215	joan.collins@peoplebeforeprofit.ie
21	Collins	Niall	FF	Limerick	086 8355219	6183577	niall.collins@oireachtas.ie
22	Colreavy	Michael	SF	Sligo-North Leitrim	087 2499476	6183745	michael.colreavy@oireachtas.ie
23	Conaghan	Michael	LB	Dublin South Central	086 1753747	6184033	michael.conaghan@oireachtas.ie
24	Conlan	Sean	FG	Cavan-Monaghan	087 6679306	6183154	sean.conlan@oireachtas.ie
25	Connaughton	Paul	FG	Galway East	087 2354682	6184373	paul.connaughton@oireachtas.ie
26	Conway	Ciara	LB	Waterford	086 1022958	6184011	ciara.conway@oireachtas.ie
27	Coonan	Noel	FG	Tipperary North	086 2427733	6183842	noel.coonan@oireachtas.ie
28	Corcoran-Kennedy	Marcella	FG	Laoighis Offaly	087 6330039	6184075	marcella.corcorankennedy@oireachtas.ie
29	Costello	Joe	LB	Dublin Central	087 2450777	6183896	joe.costello@oireachtas.ie
30	Coveney	Simon	FG	Cork South Central	087 8321755	6183666	simon.coveney@oireachtas.ie
31	Cowen	Barry	FF	Laoighis Offaly	086 8224928	6183662	barry.cowen@oireachtas.ie
32	Creed	Michael	FG	Cork North West	087 2424631	6183525	michael.creed@oireachtas.ie
33	Creighton	Lucinda	FG	Dublin South East	086 6009296	6183527	lucinda.creighton@oireachtas.ie
34	Crowe	Sean	SF	Dublin South West	086 3864303	6183719	sean.crowe@oireachtas.ie
35	Daly	Jim	FG	Cork South West	087 7465397	6183886	jim.daly@oireachtas.ie
36	Daly	Clare	SP	Dublin North	087 2415576	6183886	clare.daly@oireachtas.ie
37	Deasy	John	FG	Waterford	087 2565620	6183596	john.deasy@oireachtas.ie
38	Deenihan	Jimmy	FG	Kerry North	087 8113661	6313806	jimmy.deenihan@oireachtas.ie
39	Deering	Pat	FG	Carlow-Kilkenny	087 6674024	6184235	pat.deering@oireachtas.ie
40	Doherty	Pearse	SF	Donegal South West	086 3817747	6183960	pearse.doherty@oireachtas.ie
41	Doherty	Regina	FG	Meath East	087 2680182	6183573	regina.doherty@oireachtas.ie
42	Donnelly	Stephen	NP	Wicklow	086 0513493	6184293	stephen.donnelly@oireachtas.ie
43	Donohoe	Paschal	FG	Dublin Central	087 2816868	6183689	paschal.donohoe@oireachtas.ie
44	Dooley	Timmy	FF	Clare	065 6831732	6183514	timmy.dooley@oireachtas.ie
45	Dowds	Robert	LB	Dublin Mid West	087 6520360	6183446	robert.dowds@oireachtas.ie
46	Doyle	Andrew	FG	Wicklow	086 837009	6183611	andrew.doyle@oireachtas.ie
47	Durkan	Bernard	FG	Kildare North	086 2553370	6183191	bernard.durkan@oireachtas.ie
48	Ellis	Dessie	SF	Dublin North West	086 8541941	6183006	dessie.ellis@oireachtas.ie
49	English	Damien	FG	Meath West	086 8143495	6184021	damien.english@oireachtas.ie
50	Farrell	Alan	FG	Dublin North	086 8203320	6184008	alan.farrell@oireachtas.ie
51	Feighan	Frank	FG	Roscommon-Sth Leitrim	086 8331234	6183289	frank.feighan@oireachtas.ie
52	Ferris	Martin	SF	Kerry North	066 7134814	6184248	martin.ferris@oireachtas.ie
53	Ferris	Anne	LB	Wicklow	086 2364780	6183539	anne.ferris@oireachtas.ie
54	Fitzgerald	Frances	FG	Dublin Mid West	087 2579026	6183771	frances.fitzgerald@oireachtas.ie
55	Fitzpatrick	Peter	FG	Louth	086 2512577	6183563	peter.fitzpatrick@oireachtas.ie

TDs DIRECTORY 2012							
	Surname	**First Name**	**Party**	**Constituency**	**Phone**	**Dail**	Email
56	Flanagan	Terence	FG	Dublin North East	087 9952031	6183634	terence.flanagan@oireachtas.ie
57	Flanagan	Charlie	FG	Laoighis Offaly	087 2578450	6183625	charlie.flanagan@oireachtas.ie
58	Flanagan	Luke "Ming"	NP	Roscommon-Sth Leitrim	086 3685680	6183058	luke.flanagan@oireachtas.ie
59	Fleming	Tom	NP	Kerry South	087 7814781	6183354	tom.fleming@oireachtas.ie
60	Fleming	Sean	FF	Laoighis Offaly	087 2943294	6183472	sean.fleming@oireachtas.ie
61	Gilmore	Eamon	LB	Dun Laoghaire	087 2200495	6182112	eamon.gilmore@oireachtas.ie
62	Grealish	Noel	NP	Galway West	086 8509466	6184280	noel.grealish@oireachtas.ie
63	Griffin	Brendan	FG	Kerry South	087 6528841	6184480	brendan.griffin@oireachtas.ie
64	Halligan	John	NP	Waterford	086 2678622	6183498	john.halligan@oireachtas.ie
65	Hannigan	Dominic	LB	Meath East	087 6418960	6184007	dominic.hannigan@oireachtas.ie
66	Harrington	Noel	FG	Cork South West	086 8567178	6183956	noel.harrington@oireachtas.ie
67	Harris	Simon	FG	Wicklow	086 0759984	6183805	simon.harris@oireachtas.ie
68	Hayes	Brian	FG	Dublin South West	01 4626545	6183567	brian.hayes@oireachtas.ie
69	Hayes	Tom	FG	Tipperary South	087 8105016	6183168	tom.hayes@oireachtas.ie
70	Healy	Seamus	NP	Tipperary South	087 2802199		seamus.healy@oireachtas.ie
71	Healy-Rae	Michael	NP	Kerry South	087 2461678	6184319	michael.healy-rae@oireachtas.ie
72	Heydon	Martin	FG	Kildare South	087 6262546	6183017	martin.heydon@oireachtas.ie
73	Higgins	Joe	SP	Dublin West	01 8201753	6183370	joe.higgins@oireachtas.ie
74	Hogan	Phil	FG	Carlow-Kilkenny	056 7771490		phil.hogan@oireachtas.ie
75	Howlin	Brendan	LB	Wexford	053 9124036	6183538	brendan.howlin@oireachtas.ie
76	Humphreys	Heather	FG	Cavan-Monaghan	086 2380765	6183408	heather.humphreys@oireachtas.ie
77	Humphreys	Kevin	LB	Dublin South East	087 2989103	6183224	kevin.humphreys@oireachtas.ie
78	Keating	Derek	FG	Dublin Mid West	087 2857435	6184014	derek.keating@oireachtas.ie
79	Keaveney	Colm	LB	Galway East	087 6776812	6183821	colm.keaveney@oireachtas.ie
80	Kehoe	Paul	FG	Wexford	087 2021383	6184473	paul.kehoe@taoiseach.gov.ie
81	Kelleher	Billy	FF	Cork North Central	087 2580521	6183219	billy.kelleher@oireachtas.ie
82	Kelly	Alan	LB	Tipperary North	086 6061101		alan.kelly@oireachtas.ie
83	Kenny	Sean	LB	Dublin North East	086 8126340		info@seankenny.ie
84	Kenny	Enda	FG	Mayo	094 9025600		taoiseach@taoiseach.ie
85	Kirk	Seamus	FF	Louth	042 9331032	6183362	seamus.kirk@oireachtas.ie
86	Kitt	Michael	FF	Galway East	087 2544345	6183473	michael.kitt@oireachtas.ie
87	Kyne	Sean	FG	Galway West	087 6137372	6184426	sean.kyne@oireachtas.ie
88	Lawlor	Anthony	FG	Kildare North	087 2753942	6183007	anthony.lawlor@oireachtas.ie
89	Lowry	Michael	NP	Tipperary North	087 2323828	6183504	michael.lowry@oireachtas.ie
90	Lynch	Kathleen	LB	Cork North Central	021 4399930		kathleen.lynch@oireachtas.ie
91	Lynch	Ciaran	LB	Cork South Central	086 8562600	6183666	ciaran.lynch@oireachtas.ie
92	Lyons	John	LB	Dublin North West	087 2113154	6183280	john.lyons@oireachtas.ie
93	MacLochlainn	Padraig	SF	Donegal North East	087 2771958	6184061	padraig.maclochlainn@oireachtas.ie
94	Maloney	Eamonn	LB	Dublin South West	01 4525298	6183588	eamonn.maloney@oireachtas.ie
95	Martin	Micheal	FF	Cork South Central	021 4320088	6184350	michael.martin@eircom.net
96	Mathews	Peter	FG	Dublin South	086 1091500	6184443	peter.matthews@oireachtas.ie
97	McCarthy	Michael	LB	Cork South West	087 6481004	6183844	michael.mccarthy@oireachtas.ie
98	McConalogue	Charlie	FF	Donegal North East	086 8161078	6.2E+07	charlie.mcconalogue@oireachtas.ie
99	McDonald	Mary Lou	SF	Dublin Central	01 8683934	6183230	marylou.mcdonald@oireachtas.ie
100	McEntee	Shane	FG	Meath East	041 9882727	6184447	shane.mcentee@oireachtas.ie
101	McFadden	Nicky	FG	Longford-Westmeath	087 6771267	6183938	nicky.mcfadden@oireachtas.ie
102	McGinley	Dinny	FG	Donegal South West	087 2414809	6183452	dinny.mcginley@oireachtas.ie
103	McGrath	Michael	FF	Cork South Central	086 8393304	6183801	michael.mcgrath@oireachtas.ie
104	McGrath	Finian	NP	Dublin North Central	087 6738041	6183031	finian.mcgrath@oireachtas.ie
105	McGrath	Mattie	NP	Tipperary South	086 8184307	6184062	mattie.mcgrath@oireachtas.ie
106	McGuinness	John	FF	Carlow-Kilkenny	087 2855834	6183137	john.mcguinness@oireachtas.ie
107	McHugh	Joe	FG	Donegal North East	087 6241525	6184242	joe.mchugh@oireachtas.ie
108	McLellan	Sandra	SF	Cork East	086 3752944	6183122	sandra.mclellan@oireachtas.ie
109	McLoughlin	Tony	FG	Sligo-North Leitrim	087 6633587	6183537	tony.mcloughlin@oireachtas.ie
110	McNamara	Michael	LB	Clare	087 1384561	6183879	michael.mcnamara@oireachtas.ie

	TDs DIRECTORY 2012						
	Surname	First Name	Party	Constituency	Phone	Dail	Email
111	Mitchell	Olivia	FG	Dublin South	01 2953033	6183088	olivia.mitchell@oireachtas.ie
112	Mitchell O'Connor	Mary	FG	Dun Laoghaire	086 8186725	6183302	mary.mitchelloconnor@oireachtas.ie
113	Moynihan	Michael	FF	Cork North West	087 2745810	6183595	michael.moynihan@oireachtas.ie
114	Mulherin	Michelle	FG	Mayo	087 9317406	6183065	michelle.mulherin@oireachtas.ie
115	Murphy	Dara	FG	Cork North Central	086 2533729	6183862	dara.murphyn@oireachtas.ie
116	Murphy	Eoghan	FG	Dublin South East	086 0863832	6183324	eoghan.murphy@oireachtas.ie
117	Murphy	Catherine	NP	Kildare North	087 2696450	6183099	catherine.murphy@oireachtas.ie
118	Nash	Gerald	LB	Louth	087 2716816	6183576	gernash@montaguecomms.ie
119	Naughten	Denis	FG	Roscommon-Sth Leitrim	086 1708800	6183545	denis.naughten@oireachtas.ie
120	Neville	Dan	FG	Limerick	086 2435536	6183356	dan.neville@oireachtas.ie
121	Nolan	Derek	LB	Galway West	086 3777624	6183287	derek.nolan@oireachtas.ie
122	Noonan	Michael	FG	Limerick City	087 6478111	6767571	michael.noonan@oireachtas.ie
123	Nulty	Patrick	LB	Dublin West		6183111	patrick.nulty@oireachtas.ie
124	O Caolain	Caoimhghin	SF	Cavan-Monaghan	047 82917	6183005	caoimhghin.ocaolain@oireachtas.ie
125	O Cuiv	Eamon	FF	Galway West	094 9548021	6184231	eamon.ocuiv@oireachtas.ie
126	O Fearghail	Sean	FF	Kildare South	087 2367155	6183948	sean.ofearghail@oireachtas.ie
127	O Riordain	Aodhan	LB	Dublin North Central	086 8190336	6183209	aodhan.oriordain@oireachtas.ie
128	O Snodaigh	Aengus	SF	Dublin South Central	01 6259320	6184084	aosnodaigh@oireachtas.ie
129	O'Brien	Jonathan	SF	Cork North Central	085 2133907	6184040	jonathan.obrien@oireachtas.ie
130	O'Dea	Willie	FF	Limerick City	087 9193666	6184259	willie.odea@oceanfree.net
131	O'Donnell	Kieran	FG	Limerick City	086 8430202	6183808	kieran.odonnell@oireachtas.ie
132	O'Donovan	Patrick	FG	Limerick	087 9076267	6183610	patrick.odonovan@oireachtas.ie
133	O'Dowd	Fergus	FG	Louth	087 2352920	6183078	fergus.odowd@oireachtas.ie
134	O'Mahony	John	FG	Mayo	086 8338017	6183706	john.omahony@oireachtas.ie
135	O'Reilly	Joe	FG	Cavan-Monaghan	086 2444321	6183721	joe.oreilly@oireachtas.ie
136	O'Sullivan	Maureen	NP	Dublin Central	087 0550223	6183488	maureen.osullivan@oireachtas.ie
137	O'Sullivan	Jan	LB	Limerick City	087 2430299	6182316	jan.osullivan@oireachtas.ie
138	Penrose	Willie	LB	Longford-Westmeath	087 8241933	6183734	willie.penrose@oireachtas.ie
139	Perry	John	FG	Sligo-North Leitrim	087 2459407	6183765	john.perry@oireachtas.ie
140	Phelan	Ann	LB	Carlow-Kilkenny	086 3294420	6183216	ann.phelan@oireachtas.ie
141	Phelan	John Paul	FG	Carlow-Kilkenny	056 7793210	6184202	johnpaul.phelan@oireachtas.ie
142	Pringle	Thomas	NP	Donegal South West	074 974180	6183038	thomas.pringle@oireachtas.ie
143	Quinn	Ruairi	LB	Dublin South East	087 2621946	6183434	ruairi_quinn@education.gov.ie
144	Rabbitte	Pat	LB	Dublin South West	01 4593191	6183772	minister.rabbitte@dcenr.gov.ie
145	Reilly	James	FG	Dublin North	01 8437014	6183749	james.reilly@oireachtas.ie
146	Ring	Michael	FG	Mayo	098 25734	6183838	michael.ring@oireachtas.ie
147	Ross	Shane	NP	Dublin South	01 2116692	6183014	shane.ross@oireachtas.ie
148	Ryan	Brendan	LB	Dublin North	01 8490265	6183421	brendan.ryan@oireachtas.ie
149	Shatter	Alan	FG	Dublin South	01 2983045	6133911	alan.shater@oireachtas.ie
150	Sherlock	Sean	LB	Cork East	087 7402057	6184049	sean.sherlock@oireachtas.ie
151	Shortall	Roisin	LB	Dublin North West	01 8370563	6183593	roisin.shortall@oireachtas.ie
152	Smith	Brendan	FF	Cavan-Monaghan	049 4362366	6183376	brendan.smith@oireachtas.ie
153	Spring	Arthur	LB	Kerry North	087 0977260	6183471	arthur.spring@oireachtas.ie
154	Stagg	Emmet	LB	Kildare North	087 6728555	6183013	emmet.stagg@oireachtas.ie
155	Stanley	Brian	SF	Laoighis Offaly	057 8662851	6183987	brian.stanley@oireachtas.ie
156	Stanton	David	FG	Cork East	087 2349662	6183181	david.stanton@oireachtas.ie
157	Timmins	Billy	FG	Wicklow	087 8159090	6183384	billy.timmins@oireachtas.ie
158	Toibin	Peadar	SF	Meath West	087 2707985	6183518	peadar.toibin@oireachtas.ie
159	Troy	Robert	FF	Longford-Westmeath	087 7979890	6183059	robert.troy@oireachtas.ie
160	Tuffy	Joanna	LB	Dublin Mid West	01 6280765	6183822	joanna.tuffy@oireachtas.ie
161	Twomey	Liam	FG	Wexford	087 8267940	6184299	liam.twomey@oireachtas.ie
162	Varadkar	Leo	FG	Dublin West	01 9103717	6183819	leo.varadkar@oireachtas.ie
163	Wall	Jack	LB	Kildare South	087 2570275	6183571	jack.wall@oireachtas.ie
164	Wallace	Mick	NP	Wexford	087 2454510	6183287	mick.wallace@oireachtas.ie
165	Walsh	Brian	FG	Galway West	086 8333054	6184236	brian.walsh@oireachtas.ie
166	White	Alex	LB	Dublin South	087 2208533	6183972	alex.white@oireachtas.ie

SENATORS DIRECTORY 2012

	Candidate	Party	Panel	Phone	Senate	Email
1	Bacik, Ivana*	NP	University of Dublin	086 8133751	6183136	ivana.bacik@oireachtas.ie
2	Barrett, Sean	NP	University of Dublin	01 8961523	6183264	seand.barrett@oireachtas.ie
3	Bradford, Paul*	FG	Agricultural	087 2596204	6183760	paul.bradford@oireachtas.ie
4	Brennan, Terry	FG	Labour	087 2942956	6183872	terry.brennan@oireachtas.ie
5	Burke, Colm	FG	Industrial & Commercial	087 2592839	6183115	colm.burke@oireachtas.ie
6	Burke,Paddy*	FG	Agricultural	087 2441802	6183574	paddy.burke@oireachtas.ie
7	Byrne, Thomas	FF	Cultural & Educational	086 6038886	6183310	thomas.byrne@oireachtas.ie
8	Clune, Deidre	FG	Cultural & Educational	087 2387539	6183365	deirdre.clune@oireachtas.ie
9	Coghlan, Eamon	NP	Taoiseach's Nominee		6183027	eamonn.coghlan@oireachtas.ie
10	Coghlan,Paul*	FG	Industrial & Commercial	087 2217400	6183762	paul.coghlan@oireachtas.ie
11	Comiskey, Michael	FG	Agricultural	086 2304525	6183453	michael.comiskey@oireachtas.ie
12	Conway, Martin	FG	Administrative	087 2612977	6183035	martin.conway@oireachtas.ie
13	Crown, John	NP	National University	087 2647767	6183260	john.crown@oireachtas.ie
14	Cullinane, David	SF	Labour	086 3725152	6183176	david.cullinane@oireachtas.ie
15	Cummins, Maurice*	FG	Labour	087 6827737	6184206	maurice.cummins@oireachtas.ie
16	Daly, Mark*	FF	Administrative	086 8032612	6183830	mark.daly@oireachtas.ie
17	D'Arcy, Jim	FG	Taoiseach's Nominee	087 6864582	6183059	jim.darcy@oireachtas.ie
18	D'Arcy, Michael	FG	Administrative	087 9901055	6183542	michael.darcy@oireachtas.ie
19	Gilroy, John	LB	Cultural & Educational	087 2799608	6183089	john.gilroy@oireachtas.ie
20	Harte, Jimmy	LB	Industrial & Commercial	087 2511037		jimmy.harte@oireachtas.ie
21	Hayden, Aideen	LB	Taoiseach's Nominee	087 2311921	6183178	aideen.hayden@oireachtas.ie
22	Healy Eames, Fidelma*	FG	Labour	087 6776937	6183742	fidelma.healyeames@oireachtas.ie
23	Heffernan, James	LB	Agricultural	087 3243315	6183057	james.heffernan@oireachtas.ie
24	Henry, Imelda	FG	Industrial & Commercial	087 8177777	6183123	imelda.henry@oireachtas.ie
25	Higgins, Lorraine	LB	Taoiseach's Nominee	087 9034883	6183186	lorraine.higgins@oireachtas.ie
26	Keane, Cáit	FG	Labour	087 8117824	6183179	cait.keane@oireachtas.ie
27	Kelly, John	LB	Administrative	086 8094698	6183049	john.kelly@oireachtas.ie
28	Landy, Denis	LB	Administrative	087 2326138	6183351	denis.landy@oireachtas.ie
29	Leyden, Terry*	FF	Labour	087 7978922	6183853	terry.leyden@oireachtas.ie
30	MacConghail, Fiach	NP	Taoiseach's Nominee		6183261	fiach.macconghail@oireachtas.ie
31	MacSharry, Mark*	FF	Industrial & Commercial	086 2674764	6184221	marc.macsharry@oireachtas.ie
32	McAleese, Dr. Martin	NP	Taoiseach's Nominee		6183277	martin.mcaleese@oireachtas.ie
33	Moloney, Marie	LB	Labour	086 3049422		marie.maloney@oireachtas.ie
34	Mooney, Paschal*	FF	Agricultural	078 41236	6183148	paschal.money@oireachtas.ie
35	Moran, Mary	LB	Taoiseach's Nominee	087 1694835	6183522	mary.moran@oireachtas.ie
36	Mulcahy, Tony	FG	Labour	086 2436345	6183205	tony.mulcahy@oireachtas.ie
37	Mullen, Ronan*	NP	National University	087 2446911	6183930	ronan.mullen@oireachtas.ie
38	Mullins, Michael	FG	Cultural & Educational	087 2607405	6183095	michael.mullins@oireachtas.ie
39	Noone, Catherine	FG	Industrial & Commercial	087 2327433	6183127	catherine.noone@oireachtas.ie
40	Norris, David*	NP	University of Dublin	01 8724614	6183104	david.norris@oireachtas.ie
41	Ó Clochartaigh, Trevor	SF	Agricultural	087 2476624	6184069	trevor.oclochartaigh@oireachtas.ie
42	Ó Domhnaill, Brian*	FF	Agricultural	086 8218084		brian.odomhnaill@oireachtas.ie
43	Ó Murchú, Labhrás*	FF	Cultural & Educational	087 2528747	6184018	labhras.omurchu@oireachtas.ie
44	O'Brien, Darragh*	FF	Labour	086 2519893	6183802	darragh.obrien@oireachtas.ie
45	O'Brien, Mary Ann	NP	Taoiseach's Nominee	087 7770011		maobrien@lilyobriens.ie
46	O'Donnell, Marie-Louise	NP	Taoiseach's Nominee	087 8483620	6183635	marielouise.odonnell@oireachtas.ie
47	O'Donovan, Denis*	FF	Agricultural	087 2543806	6184479	denis.odonovan@oireachtas.ie
48	O'Keeffe, Susan	LB	Agricultural	085 1314084		susan.okeeffe@oireachtas.ie
49	O'Neill, Pat	FG	Agricultural	087 2771483	6183082	pat.oneill@oireachtas.ie
50	O'Sullivan, Ned*	FF	Labour	087 2459290		ned.osullivan@oireachtas.ie
51	Power, Averil	FF	Industrial & Commercial	086 7277770	6183156	averil.power@oireachtas.ie
52	Quinn,Fergal*	NP	National University	087 6865215	6183222	himself@feargalquinn.ie
53	Reilly, Kathryn	SF	Industrial & Commercial	049 4373510	6183171	kathryn.reilly@oireachtas.ie
54	Sheahan, Tom	FG	Administrative	087 2021661	6183812	tom.sheahan@oireachtas.ie
55	Van Turnhout, Jillian	NP	Taoiseach's Nominee	087 2333784	6183375	jillian.vanturnhout@oireachtas.ie
56	Walsh,Jim*	FF	Agricultural	086 6008155	6183763	jim.walsh@oireachtas.ie
57	Whelan, John	LB	Labour	087 2509663	6183244	john.whelan@oireachtas.ie
58	White, Mary*	FF	Industrial & Commercial	086 2560533	6183820	mary.white@oireachtas.ie
59	Wilson, Diarmuid*	FF	Administrative	087 2323959	6183561	diarmuid.wilson@oireachtas.ie
60	Zappone, Dr. Katherine	NP	Taoiseach's Nominee	087 2333784	6183583	katherine.zappone@oireachtas.ie